The Great Sea

DAVID ABULAFIA

The Great Sea

A Human History of the Mediterranean

ALLEN LANE
an imprint of
PENGUIN BOOKS

ALLEN LANE

Published by the Penguin Group
Penguin Books Ltd, 80 Strand, London WC2R ORL, England
Penguin Group (USA) Inc., 375 Hudson Street, New York, New York 10014, USA
Penguin Group (Canada), 90 Eglinton Avenue East, Suite 700, Toronto, Ontario,
Canada M4P 2Y3 (a division of Pearson Canada Inc.)
Penguin Ireland, 25 St Stephen's Green, Dublin 2, Ireland (a division of Penguin Books Ltd)
Penguin Group (Australia), 250 Camberwell Road, Camberwell,
Victoria 3124, Australia (a division of Pearson Australia Group Pty Ltd)
Penguin Books India Pvt Ltd, 11 Community Centre,
Panchsheel Park, New Dehli – 110 017, India
Penguin Group (NZ), 67 Apollo Drive, Rosedale, Auckland 0632, New Zealand
(a division of Pearson New Zealand Ltd)
Penguin Books (South Africa) (Pty) Ltd, 24 Sturdee Avenue,
Rosebank 2196, South Africa

Penguin Books Ltd, Registered Offices: 80 Strand, London WC2R ORL, England

www.penguin.com

First published 2011
2

Set in 10.2/13.87pt Linotype Sabon
Typeset by Jouve (UK), Milton Keynes
Printed in Great Britain by Clays Ltd, St Ives plc

ISBN: 978-0-713-99934-1

www.greenpenguin.co.uk

MIX
Paper from
responsible sources
FSC
www.fsc.org   FSC™ C018179

Penguin Books is committed to a sustainable
future for our business, our readers and our
planet. This book is made from paper certified
by the Forest Stewardship Council.

a la memoria de mis antecesores

Contents

List of Illustrations	xi
System of Transliteration and Dating	xvi
Preface	xvii
Introduction: A Sea with Many Names	xxiii

PART ONE
The First Mediterranean, 22000 BC–1000 BC

1. Isolation and Insulation, 22000 BC–3000 BC	3
2. Copper and Bronze, 3000 BC–1500 BC	15
3. Merchants and Heroes, 1500 BC–1250 BC	29
4. Sea Peoples and Land Peoples, 1250 BC–1100 BC	42

PART TWO
The Second Mediterranean, 1000 BC–AD 600

1. The Purple Traders, 1000 BC–700 BC	63
2. The Heirs of Odysseus, 800 BC–550 BC	83
3. The Triumph of the Tyrrhenians, 800 BC–400 BC	100
4. Towards the Garden of the Hesperides, 1000 BC–400 BC	119
5. Thalassocracies, 550 BC–400 BC	132
6. The Lighthouse of the Mediterranean, 350 BC–100 BC	149
7. 'Carthage Must Be Destroyed', 400 BC–146 BC	166
8. 'Our Sea', 146 BC–AD 150	191

9. Old and New Faiths, AD 1–450   212

10. Dis-integration, 400–600   226

PART THREE
The Third Mediterranean, 600–1350

1. Mediterranean Troughs, 600–900   241

2. Crossing the Boundaries between Christendom and Islam, 900–1050   258

3. The Great Sea-change, 1000–1100   271

4. 'The Profit That God Shall Give', 1100–1200   287

5. Ways across the Sea, 1160–1185   304

6. The Fall and Rise of Empires, 1130–1260   318

7. Merchants, Mercenaries and Missionaries, 1220–1300   334

8. *Serrata* – Closing, 1291–1350   354

PART FOUR
The Fourth Mediterranean, 1350–1830

1. Would-be Roman Emperors, 1350–1480   373

2. Transformations in the West, 1391–1500   392

3. Holy Leagues and Unholy Alliances, 1500–1550   411

4. *Akdeniz* – the Battle for the White Sea, 1550–1571   428

5. Interlopers in the Mediterranean, 1571–1650   452

6. Diasporas in Despair, 1560–1700   470

7. Encouragement to Others, 1650–1780   488

8. The View through the Russian Prism, 1760–1805   504

9. Deys, Beys and Bashaws, 1800–1830   524

PART FIVE
The Fifth Mediterranean, 1830–2010

1. Ever the Twain Shall Meet, 1830–1900   545

2. The Greek and the unGreek, 1830–1920   562

3. Ottoman Exit, 1900–1918   573

CONTENTS

4. A Tale of Four and a Half Cities, 1900–1950   583

5. *Mare Nostrum* – Again, 1918–1945   601

6. A Fragmented Mediterranean, 1945–1990   613

7. The Last Mediterranean, 1950–2010   628

Conclusion: Crossing the Sea   641

Further Reading   649

Notes   651

Index   728

List of Illustrations

1. Mnajdra, Malta (akg-images/Rainer Hackenberg)
2. The 'Sleeping Lady' (National Archaeological Museum, Valletta, Malta. Photograph: akg-images/Erich Lessing)
3. Cycladic figure, c. 2700 BC, Greek private collection (Heini Schneebeli/The Bridgeman Art Library)
4. Female head, Early Cycladic II Period, c. 2700–2400 BC (Musée du Louvre, Paris. Photograph: Giraudon/The Bridgeman Art Library)
5. Octopus vase from Knossos, c. 1500 BC (Archaeological Museum of Heraklion, Crete, Greece. Photograph: Bernard Cox/The Bridgeman Art Library)
6. Fresco c. 1420 BC from the tomb of Pharaoh's vizier Rekhmire, Upper Egypt (Mary Evans/Interfoto)
7. Akrotiri fresco, Thera, sixteenth century BC (akg-images/Erich Lessing)
8. Gold death mask from Mycenae, c. 1500 BC (National Archaeological Museum, Athens. Photograph: akg-images/Erich Lessing)
9. Early Philistine clay face from a sarcophagus, Beth She'an, northern Israel (Israel Museum (IDAM), Jerusalem. Photograph: akg-images/Erich Lessing)
10. Twelfth-century BC Warrior Vase, Mycenae (National Archaeological Museum, Athens. Photograph: akg-images)
11. Frieze from the temple of Madinat Habu in Upper Egypt (akg-images/Erich Lessing)

12. Phoenician inscription, Nora, Southern Sardinia (Roger-Viollet/ Topfoto)

13. Stele, Carthage, *c.* 400 BC (Roger Wood/Corbis)

14. Model of a Phoenician ship (National Archaeological Museum, Beirut. Photograph: Philippe Maillard/akg-images)

15. Phoenician silver coin (National Archaeological Museum, Beirut. Photograph: akg-images/Erich Lessing)

16. Chigi Vase, found near Veii, *c.* 600 BC (Museo Nazionale di Villa Giulia, Rome. Photograph: akg-images/Nimatallah)

17. Panel from the bronze gates of the Assyrian royal palace, Balawat, *c.* ninth century BC (Musée du Louvre, Paris. Photograph: akg-images/Erich Lessing)

18. Dionysos *krater*, late sixth century BC (Staatliche Antikensammlung & Glypothek, Munich. Photograph: akg-images)

19. Fresco from Tarquinia, late sixth century BC (akg-images/ Nimatallah)

20. Marsiliana *abecedarium*, Etruria, seventh century BC (Florence Archaeological Museum. Photograph: akg-images/ Album/Oronoz)

21. Gold tablet, Pyrgoi, late sixth century BC (Museo Nazionale di Villa Giulia, Rome. Photograph: akg-images/Nimatallah)

22. Etruscan pot helmet (The Trustees of the British Museum)

23. Tower of Orolo, Sardinia (akg-images/Rainer Hackenberg)

24. Sard bronze boat, *c.* 600 BC (Museo Archeologico Nazionale, Cagliari. Photo: akg-images/Electra)

25. Bust of Periandros (Vatican Museum)

26. Bust of Alexander the Great (Print Collector/Heritage-Images/ Imagestate)

27. The 'Dama de Elche' (ullstein bild – United Archives)

28. Bust of Sarapis (akg-images/ullstein bild)

29. Carthaginian Melqart coin (The Trustees of the British Museum)

30. Bronze Nero coin (The Trustees of the British Museum)

31. Cleopatra coin (The Trustees of the British Museum. Photograph: akg-images/Erich Lessing)

32. Nero coin marking the completion of the harbour at Ostia (The Trustees of the British Museum)

33. Relief of Roman quinquireme, Praeneste, now Palestrina (akg-images/Peter Connolly)

34. Fresco of a harbour near Naples, possibly Puteoli (Museo Nazionale Archeologico, Naples. Photograph: akg images/ Erich Lessing)

35. Sixth-century mosaic of the Byzantine fleet at Classis, from the basilica of Sant'Apollinare, Ravenna (akg-images/ Cameraphoto)

36. Cornice from the synagogue at Ostia, second century (Photograph: Setreset/Wikimedia Commons)

37. Inscription from the synagogue at Ostia (akg-images)

38. Panel from the Pala d'Oro, St Mark's Basilica, Venice (akg-images/ Cameraphoto)

39. View of Amalfi, 1885 (Archiv für Kunst und Geschichte, Berlin. Photograph: akg images)

40. Majorcan *bacino* (Museo Nazionale di San Matteo, Pisa)

41. Khan al-'Umdan, Acre, Israel (Photograph: Ariel Palmon/ Wikimedia Commons)

42. The Venice quadriga (Mimmo Jodice/CORBIS)

43. Late-medieval map, after Idrisi (Wikimedia Commons)

44. Majorcan portolan chart, early fourteenth century (British Library)

45. Wall-painting showing the capture of the City of Majorca in 1229 (Museo de Catalunya, Barcelona. Photograph: akg images/ Bildarchiv Steffens)

46. Aigues-Mortes, Carmargue, France (Photo: Bertrand Rieger/ Hemis/Corbis)

47. Genoa, as depicted in Hartmann-Schedel's 1493 *Nuremberg Chronicle* (by permission of the Master and Fellows of Gonville and Caius College, Cambridge)

48. Dubrovnik (Photograph: Jonathan Blair/Corbis)

49. Manises bowl (Victoria and Albert Museum, London)

50. Votive model of a cargo ship, *c.* 1420 (Maritime Museum, Rotterdam)

51. The Exchange in Valencia (Photograph: Felivet/Wikimedia Commons)

52. Early manuscript copy of the *Consulate of the Sea* (Album/Oronoz/akg-images)

53. Portrait of Mehmet II by Giovanni Bellini (akg-images/Erich Lessing)

54. French miniature of the siege of Rhodes (detail) (The Granger Collection, New York)

55. Portrait of Admiral Khair-ed-din, 1540, by Nakkep Reis Haydar (Topkapi Palace Museum, Istanbul, Turkey/The Bridgeman Art Library)

56. Portrait of Andrea Doria (Palazzo Bianco, Genoa. Photograph: akg-images/Electra)

57. Cartoon showing the Spanish capture of Goleta (akg-images/Erich Lessing)

58. The expulsion of Moriscos, 1613, by Pere Oromig and Francisco Peralta (ullstein bild – Aisa)

59. Venetian naval victory over Turkey in 1661 by an anonymous artist of the Venetian School (Museo Correr, Venice. Photograph: akg-images/Erich Lessing)

60. The assault on Mahón, 1756, by an anonymous French artist (Musée de la Marine, Paris. Photograph: akg-images/Erich Lessing)

61. The execution of Admiral Byng, *c.* 1760, British school (National Maritime Museum, Greenwich, London)

62. Portrait of Admiral Fyodor Ushakov by an anonymous nineteenth-century artist (Central Naval Museum, St Petersburg. Photograph: akg-images/RIA Novosti)

63. Portrait of Admiral Samuel Hood, 1784, by James Northcote (National Maritime Museum, London/The Bridgeman Art Library)

64. Portrait of Ferdinand von Hompesch by Antonio Xuereb (attrib.), Presidential Palace, Valletta (Malta) (Photograph by and courtesy of Heritage Malta)

65. Portrait of Stephen Decatur, *c.* 1814, by Thomas Sully (Atwater Kent Museum of Philadelphia/courtesy of the Historical Society of Pennsylvania Collection/The Bridgeman Art Library)

66. Port Said, 1880 (Wikimedia Commons)

67. Lloyd's quay, Trieste, *c.* 1890 (adoc-photos)

68. The Grand Square, or Place Mehmet Ali, Alexandria, *c.* 1915 (Werner Forman Archive/Musees Royaux, Brussels/ Heritage-Images/Imagestate)

69. The Italian occupation of Libya, 1911 (akg-images)

70. The attack on the French warships moored at Mers el-Kebir, October 1940 (Photograph: Bettmann/Corbis)

71. British troops land in Sicily, 1943 (Imperial War Museum, London, A17918)

72. Ship carrying Jewish refugees, Haifa, 1947 (akg-images/ Israelimages)

73. Charles de Gaulle in Algeria, 1958 (akg-images/Erich Lessing)

74. Beach scene, Lloret de Mar (Frank Lukasseck/Corbis)

75. Illegal migrants from Africa trying to land on Spanish soil (EFE/J. Ragel)

p. 597 Cartoon of 1936 from *Falastin* (Mark Levine, *Overthrowing Geography* (California, 2005))

ENDPAPERS *The Brig* by Gustave Le Gray (V&A Images/Victoria and Albert Museum, London)

System of Transliteration and Dating

Transliteration is a nightmare in a book that covers such a long period, and consistency is impossible. I have tried to combine authenticity with clarity. With Greek names, I have rejected the sometimes absurd latinized forms long used, unless, as with Aeschylus, the alternative is unrecognizable to non-experts. So I have Herodotos and Sophokles, and Komnenos for the great Byzantine dynasty, not Comnenus. This becomes more complicated in later centuries. Ancient Thessalonika becomes Ottoman Salonika and then modern Thessaloniki, while Epidamnos, Dyrrhachion, Dyrrachium, Durazzo, Durrës are all one place in Albania at different epochs; I have used the name current in the period about which I am writing. Comparable problems arise with Hebrew, Turkish and Arabic names. Along the Croatian and Montenegrin coast, I have favoured Slav forms, since they are now in general use, so I use Dubrovnik rather than Ragusa but (lacking an equally elegant word for the inhabitants) I have called its inhabitants 'Ragusans'.

Another contentious issue is whether to use the Christian labels for dates, BC and AD, or the modern substitutes, BCE and CE, or indeed (as Joseph Needham used to recommend) a simple '–' and '+'. Since these variants produce exactly the same dates as BC and AD I am not sure what advantage they bring; and those who are uncomfortable with *Before Christ* and *Anno Domini* are free to decide that BC and AD stand for some other combination of words, such as 'Backward chronology' and 'Accepted date'.

Preface

'Mediterranean history' can mean many things. This book is a history of the Mediterranean Sea, rather than a history of the lands around it; more particularly, it is a history of the people who crossed the sea and lived close by its shores in ports and on islands. My theme is the process by which the Mediterranean became in varying degrees integrated into a single commercial, cultural and even (under the Romans) political zone, and how these periods of integration ended with sometimes violent disintegration, whether through warfare or plague. I have identified five distinct periods: a First Mediterranean that descended into chaos after 1200 BC, that is, around the time Troy is said to have fallen; a Second Mediterranean that survived until about AD 500; a Third Mediterranean that emerged slowly and then experienced a great crisis at the time of the Black Death (1347); a Fourth Mediterranean that had to cope with increasing competition from the Atlantic, and domination by Atlantic powers, ending around the time of the opening of the Suez Canal in 1869; finally, a Fifth Mediterranean that became a passageway to the Indian Ocean, and found a surprising new identity in the second half of the twentieth century.

My 'Mediterranean' is resolutely the surface of the sea itself, its shores and its islands, particularly the port cities that provided the main departure and arrival points for those crossing it. This is a narrower definition than that of the great pioneer of Mediterranean history, Fernand Braudel, which at times encompassed places beyond the Mediterranean; but the Mediterranean of Braudel and most of those who have followed in his wake was a land mass stretching far beyond the shoreline as well as a basin filled with water, and there is still a tendency to define the Mediterranean in relation to the cultivation of the olive or the river valleys that feed into it. This means one must examine the often sedentary, traditional societies in those valleys that produced the food-stuffs and raw materials that were the staples of trans-Mediterranean commerce, which also means taking on board true landlubbers who never went near the sea. The hinterland – the events that took place there, the products that originated or came through there – cannot of course be ignored, but this book concentrates on those who dipped their toes into the sea, and, best of all, took journeys across it, participating directly, in some cases, in cross-cultural trade, in the movement of religious and other ideas, or, no less significantly, in naval conflicts for mastery over the sea routes.

Inevitably, in what is still a long book, difficult choices have had to be made about what should be included and what should be excluded. Words used less often than they should be are 'perhaps', 'possibly', 'maybe' and 'probably'; a great many statements about the early Mediterranean, in particular, can be qualified this way, at the risk of generating a fog of uncertainties for the reader. My intention has been to describe the people, processes and events that have transformed all or much of the Mediterranean, rather than to write a series of micro-histories of its edges, interesting as that might be; I have therefore concentrated on what I consider important in the long term, such as the foundation of Carthage, the emergence of Dubrovnik, the impact of the Barbary corsairs or the building of the Suez Canal. Religious interactions demand space, and plenty of attention is naturally given to the conflicts between Christians and Muslims, but the Jews also deserve close attention, because of their prominent role as merchants in the early Middle Ages and again in the early modern period. I have given roughly equal coverage to each century once I reach classical antiquity, since I wished to avoid writing one of those pyramid-shaped books in which one rushes through the antecedents to arrive at comfortably modern times as quickly as possible; but the dates attached to chapters are highly approximate, and separate chapters sometimes deal with events at the same time at different ends of the Mediterranean.

The Mediterranean we know now was shaped by Phoenicians, Greeks and Etruscans in antiquity, by Genoese, Venetians and Catalans in the Middle Ages, by Dutch, English and Russian navies in the centuries before 1800; indeed, there is some strength in the argument that after 1500, and certainly after 1850, the Mediterranean became decreasingly important in wider world affairs and commerce. In most chapters,

I have concentrated on one or two places which I believe best explain broader Mediterranean developments – Troy, Corinth, Alexandria, Amalfi, Salonika and so on – but the emphasis is always on their links across the Mediterranean Sea and, where possible, on some of the people who effected or experienced these interactions. One result of this approach is that I say less about fish and fishermen than some readers might expect. Most fish spend their time below the surface of the sea, and fishermen tend to set out from a port, make their catch (often at some distance from their home port) and return to base. By and large, they do not have a destination the other side of the water where they will make contact with other peoples and cultures. The fish they bring home may well be processed in some way, as salted or pickled food, or even as a strong-tasting sauce, and the merchants who carried these products abroad are often mentioned; fresh fish must very often have been standard food for naval crews. Frankly, though, the data are scanty; my attention has only switched to what happens beneath the surface of the Mediterranean with the arrival of submarine warfare in the early twentieth century.

My hope is that those who pick up this book will enjoy reading it as much as I have enjoyed writing it. For the invitation to do so and for their enthusiastic encouragement thereafter, I am deeply indebted to Stuart Proffitt at Penguin Books and my agent, Bill Hamilton, at A. M. Heath, and for further encouragement to Peter Ginna and Tim Bent at my American publisher, Oxford University Press in New York. One special pleasure has been the opportunity to visit or revisit some of the places I mention. I have benefited greatly from the hospitality of a number of hosts in the Mediterranean and beyond: Clive and Geraldine Finlayson, of the Gibraltar Museum, were as welcoming as ever, and enabled me not just to revisit Gibraltar but to make a foray across the Straits to Ceuta; Charles Dalli, Dominic Fenech, their colleagues in the History Department at the University of Malta, HE the British High Commissioner and Mrs Archer and Ronnie Micallef of the British Council were exemplary hosts in Malta; HE the Maltese Ambassador to Tunisia, Vicki-Ann Cremona, was also a superb host in Tunis and Mahdia; Mohamed Awad, rightly famous for his hospitality, opened my eyes to his city of Alexandria; Edhem Eldem revealed unsuspected corners of Istanbul (and Alexandria); Relja Seferović of the Croatian Historical Institute in Dubrovnik was enormously helpful there, in

Montenegro (at Herceg Novi and Kotor) and in Bosnia-Hercegovina (at Trebinje); Eduard Mira shared his knowledge of medieval Valencia *in situ*; Olivetta Schena invited me to Cagliari to commemorate my late friend and distinguished Mediterranean historian Marco Tangheroni, enabling me also to visit ancient Nora; further afield, the History Department of Helsinki University and the Finnish Foreign Ministry invited me to expound my views about Mediterranean history in a city whose great fortress is often called the 'Gibraltar of the North'; Francesca Trivellato allowed me to read her excellent study of Livorno in advance of publication. Roger Moorhouse identified a host of suitable illustrations, often difficult to run to earth; Bela Cunha was an exemplary copy-editor. My wife Anna explored Jaffa, Neve Tzedek, Tel Aviv, Tunis, Mahdia and large swathes of Cyprus with me. Anna tolerated growing mountains of books on the ancient and modern Mediterranean in a house already full of books on the medieval Mediterranean. My daughters Bianca and Rosa have been delightful companions on travels to various corners of the Mediterranean, and fed me material on diverse topics such as the Moriscos and the Barcelona Process.

I am also very grateful to audiences in Cambridge, St Andrews, Durham, Sheffield, Valletta and Frankfurt-am-Main who responded so helpfully to a lecture I hawked around on 'How to write the history of the Mediterranean'. In Cambridge, I received bibliographical and other advice from Colin and Jane Renfrew, Paul Cartledge, John Patterson, Alex Mullen, Richard Duncan-Jones, William O'Reilly, Hubertus Jahn and David Reynolds, among others, while Roger Dawe very kindly gave me a copy of his magnificent translation of and commentary on the *Odyssey*. Charles Stanton read the first draft and set me right on a number of points – needless to say, the errors that remain are mine. Alyssa Bandow engaged enthusiastically in lengthy discussions of the ancient economy which helped me clarify my ideas. No institution can compare with the colleges in Cambridge and Oxford in offering an opportunity to discuss one's ideas with people in a great variety of disciplines, and I owe more than I can say to the stimulus of having among my colleagues at Caius not just a host of History Fellows but Paul Binski, John Casey, Ruth Scurr, Noël Sugimura and (until recently) Colin Burrow, as well as Victoria Bateman, whose comments on the text I much appreciate, and Michalis Agathacleous, whose guidance around southern Cyprus was enormously helpful. The Classics Faculty Library was especially generous in providing for my needs, as were Mark Statham and the staff of Gonville and Caius College Library. When in the final stages of preparing the manuscript, I found myself unable to leave Naples owing to a volcanic eruption – not Vesuvius! – Francesco Senatore and his delightful colleagues (Alessandra Perricioli, Teresa d'Urso, Alessandra Coen and many more) offered magnificent hospitality including the use of an office at 'Frederick II University', and lively conversation. Soon after the skies cleared, I benefited enormously from a chance to discuss the themes of this book at a gathering at Villa La Pietra, the seat in Florence of New York University, thanks to the kindness of Katherine Fleming, and refined my 'Concluding Thoughts' further in Norway, following an invitation from the ever-courteous organizers of a symposium held in Bergen in June 2010 to celebrate the award of the Holberg Prize to Natalie Zemon Davis.

This book is dedicated to the memory of my ancestors who travelled back and forth across the Mediterranean over the centuries: from Castile to Safed and Tiberias in the Holy Land, with intervals in Smyrna; and then, with my grandfather, from Tiberias westwards again and after him, with my grandmother, back across the sea to Tiberias, also including my forebear Jacob Berab, who reached Safed from Maqueda in Castile, and sundry Abulafias, Abolaffios and Bolaffis in Livorno and across Italy. The title is of the book is taken from the Hebrew name for the Mediterranean, which appears in a blessing to be recited on setting eyes on it: 'Blessed are you, Lord our God, king of the Universe, who made the Great Sea'.

David Abulafia
Cambridge, 15 November 2010

Introduction: A Sea with Many Names

Known in English and the romance languages as the sea 'between the lands', the Mediterranean goes and has gone by many names: 'Our Sea' for the Romans, the 'White Sea' (*Akdeniz*) for the Turks, the 'Great Sea' (*Yam gadol*) for the Jews, the 'Middle Sea' (*Mittelmeer*) for the Germans, and more doubtfully the 'Great Green' of the ancient Egyptians. Modern writers have added to the vocabulary, coining epithets such as the 'Inner Sea', the 'Encircled Sea', the 'Friendly Sea', the 'Faithful Sea' of several religions, the 'Bitter Sea' of the Second World War, the 'Corrupting Sea' of dozens of micro-ecologies transformed by their relationship with neighbours who supply what they lack, and to which they can offer their own surpluses; the 'Liquid Continent' that, like a real continent, embraces many peoples, cultures and economies within a space with precise edges. It is important, then, to begin by defining its limits. The Black Sea washes shores from which grain, slaves, furs and fruit were exported into the Mediterranean since antiquity, but it was a sea penetrated by Mediterranean merchants rather than a sea whose inhabitants participated in the political, economic and religious changes taking place in the Mediterranean itself – its links across land, towards the Balkans, the Steppes and the Caucasus, gave the civilizations along its shores a different outlook and character to those of the Mediterranean. This is not true of the Adriatic, which has participated strongly in the commercial, political and religious life of the Mediterranean, thanks to the Etruscans and Greeks of Spina, the Venetians and Ragusans in the medieval and early modern period, and the businessmen of Trieste in more modern times. In this book, the boundaries of the Mediterranean have been set where first nature and then man set them: at the Straits of Gibraltar; at the Dardanelles, with occasional forays towards Constantinople since it functioned as a bridge between the Black Sea and the

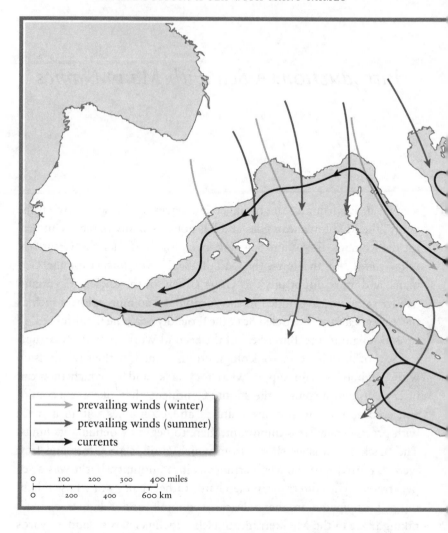

White Sea; and at the littoral running from Alexandria to Gaza and Jaffa. And then, within and along the Mediterranean, this book includes the port cities, particularly those where cultures met and mixed – Livorno, Smyrna, Trieste and so on – and the islands, mainly when their inhabitants looked outwards, which is why the Corsicans have a lower profile in this book than the Maltese.

This is perhaps a narrower vision of the Mediterranean than has been supplied by other writers, but it is surely a more consistent one. The subject-matter of books on Mediterranean history has been the history of the lands around the Mediterranean, allowing, naturally, for

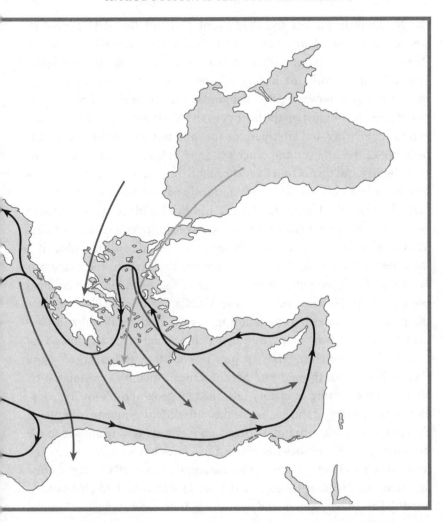

some attention to the interaction between these lands. Two works stand out prominently: Peregrine Horden and Nicholas Purcell's massive *Corrupting Sea* of 2000 is especially rich in ideas about the agrarian history of the lands bordering the Mediterranean, assuming that a history of the Mediterranean should include land bordering the sea to a depth of at least ten miles. They demonstrate some fundamental features of Mediterranean exchange: the 'connectivities' linking different points, the 'abatements' when contraction occurred. But, in the last analysis, they are essentially concerned with what happens on land rather than on the surface of the sea itself. And then, looming over all historians of the Mediterranean, lies the shadow of Fernand Braudel (1902–85), whose book *The Mediterranean and the Mediterranean World in the Age of Philip II*, first published in 1949, was one of the most original and influential works of history composed in the twentieth century. From the 1950s onwards, Braudel guided the researches of many dozens of scholars not just on the history of the Mediterranean in his chosen period, but earlier and later periods too, and not just of the Mediterranean but of the Atlantic and other seas; and in his latter days he reigned with dignity and distinction over the highly respected *Annales* school of historians from his base at the mysteriously named 'sixth section' of the École Pratique des Hautes Études in Paris. But his ideas had germinated slowly. French intellectuals such as the esteemed poet and essayist Paul Valéry, who died in 1945, had become fascinated with the idea of a 'Mediterranean civilization' shared among the French, the Spaniards and the Italians, present both on their native shores and in their colonial possessions in North Africa and the Middle East. Braudel's book was the product of lengthy rumination in France, Algeria, Brazil and German prisoner-of-war camps, during which Braudel made an intellectual journey from the close study of past politics that still engaged many French historians, through the Mediterranean identities postulated by Valéry, to the writing of history informed by geography. Showing encyclopaedic mastery of the history of the entire Mediterranean, not just in the sixteenth century, Braudel offered a novel and exciting answer to the question of how the societies around its edges have interacted. At the heart of Braudel's approach was his assumption that 'all change is slow' and that 'man is imprisoned in a destiny in which he himself has little hand'.[1] This book suggests the opposite in both cases. Whereas Braudel offered what might be called a horizontal history of the Mediterranean, seeking to capture its characteristics through the examination of a particular era, this book attempts to provide a vertical history of the Mediterranean, emphasizing change over time.

Braudel showed what almost amounted to contempt for political history, understood as 'events' (*histoire évènementielle*).[2] The geography of the Mediterranean was seen to determine what happened within its boundaries. He consigned politics and warfare to the very end of his book, and its real strength lay elsewhere, in its understanding of the landscape of the lands around the Mediterranean, and of important characteristics of the Mediterranean Sea itself – its winds and currents, which helped determine the routes people took to cross it. In fact, Braudel's Mediterranean extended far beyond the sea to encompass all the lands whose economic life was somehow determined by what was happening there: he managed at various points to bring Cracow and Madeira into his calculations. In his wake, John Pryor has laid a strong emphasis on the limitations imposed by winds and currents, arguing that medieval and early modern navigators found it difficult to navigate along the North African shore, and emphasizing the importance of the open season between spring and autumn when it was possible to sail the sea backed by suitable winds. Against this, Horden and Purcell have suggested that sailors were prepared to carve out additional shipping lanes where the winds and currents were less favourable, but where other interests – commercial or political – drew them along their new routes.[3] The forces of nature could, then, be challenged with skill and ingenuity.

The physical features of this sea certainly cannot be taken for granted. The Mediterranean possesses several features that result from its character as an enclosed sea. In remote geological time it was entirely closed, and between about 12 and 5 million years ago evaporation reached the point where the Mediterranean basin became a deep and empty desert; once breached by the Atlantic, it is thought to have been flooded with water in a couple of years. It loses water through evaporation more rapidly than river systems feeding into the Mediterranean are able to replace it, which is not surprising when it is remembered how puny some of the rivers are: the little rivers of Sicily and Sardinia, the historic but not substantial Tiber and Arno (the Arno becomes a trickle upriver from Florence in high summer). It is true that the Mediterranean draws down water from the massive river system of the Nile, and the Po and the Rhône also make some contribution. Among European rivers, the Danube and the Russian river systems make an indirect contribution, because the Black Sea draws in water from several great arteries stretching deep into the landmass. The result is that the Black Sea has an excess of unevaporated water, creating a fast current that rushes past Istanbul into the north-eastern Aegean. But this only compensates for 4 per cent of the water loss in the Mediterranean, and the principal source that replaces losses by evaporation is the Atlantic Ocean, which provides a steady inflow of cold Atlantic water, to some extent counterbalanced by an outflow of Mediterranean water which (because of the evaporation) is saltier and therefore heavier; the incoming water rides on top of the outgoing water.[4] The fact that the Mediterranean is open at its ends is thus crucial to its survival as a sea. The opening of a third channel, at Suez, has had more limited effects, since the sea route passes through narrow canals, but it has brought into the Mediterranean types of fish native to the Red Sea and Indian Ocean.

The inflow from the Atlantic deterred medieval navigators from making a regular passage out of the Straits of Gibraltar, though it did not deter Vikings, crusaders and others from entering the Mediterranean. The major currents follow the coasts of Africa eastwards from Gibraltar, swing past Israel and Lebanon and around Cyprus, and then round the Aegean, Adriatic and Tyrrhenian Seas and along the French and Spanish coasts back to the Pillars of Hercules.[5] These currents have had a significant impact on the ease with which ships have been able to move around the Mediterranean, at least in the days of oar and sail. It has even proved possible, tacking back and forth, to use the currents to sail in the face of the Mediterranean winds. The weather systems in the region tend to move from west to east, so that the winds could be profitably exploited to carry shipping in spring from the ports between Barcelona and Pisa towards Sardinia, Sicily and the Levant, though the major influence in the western Mediterranean during winter is the north Atlantic weather system, while in the summer it is the Atlantic subtropical high, stationed over the Azores. Wet and windy weather in the winter is characterized by the mistral bringing cold air into the valleys of Provence, but it has many close cousins such as the *bora* or *tramontana* of Italy and Croatia. John Pryor has pointed out that the 'Gulf of the Lion' off Provence is so named because the roar of the mistral resembles that of a lion.[6] No one should underestimate the unpleasantness or danger of a winter storm in the Mediterranean, despite the modern image of a sun-drenched sea. Occasionally low-pressure weather systems develop over the Sahara and are dragged north as the unsettling wind known as the *scirocco* (Italy), *xaloc* (Catalonia) or *hamsin* (Israel, Egypt); vast amounts of red Saharan dust may be dumped on the lands surrounding the Mediterranean. So long as ships relied on sail power, the prevailing northerly winds endangered navigation along the coast of North Africa, for they threatened to throw ships on to the sandbanks and reefs of the southern Mediterranean shores, while (as Pryor has also observed) the steeper inclination of most of the north Mediterranean shores made them much more attractive to navigators, as did their coves and beaches; however, these coves were also a long-standing temptation to pirates in search of a nook or cranny.[7] Passage from west to east, the famous Levant trade of the Middle Ages, was easier for ships setting out from Genoa or Marseilles in the spring and following the northern shores of the Mediterranean, past Sicily and Crete and around Cyprus to reach Egypt; it was not standard practice to cut across from Crete to the mouth of the Nile until the coming of the steamship. Of course, one cannot be completely sure that the winds and currents have remained the same. Yet there are enough references in classical and medieval sources to such winds as the *Boreas* from the north-west to make it clear that the *bora* has a very long history.

Changes in the climate could have important consequences for the productivity of lands close to the Mediterranean, with a knock-on effect on the trade in Mediterranean grain, which was so important in antiquity and the Middle Ages and then lost its primacy. A cooling of the climate in the sixteenth and seventeenth centuries helps explain why grain lands went out of cultivation and why imports of grain from northern Europe became surprisingly common, strengthening the hand of Dutch and German merchants in the Mediterranean. Desiccation of coastal regions may suggest climate change, though here, importantly, the human hand is often visible: in North Africa new waves of Arab invasion in the eleventh and twelfth centuries may have resulted in neglect of dams and irrigation works, so that agriculture suffered. Economic decline in Asia Minor during the period of the late Roman Empire was accentuated by the abandonment of vines and olive terraces that had held in place soil which now washed down into rivers and silted them up.[8] In modern times, dams, notably the Great Aswan Dam in Upper Egypt, have changed the pattern of flow of water into the Mediterranean, with effects on currents and humidity. It is man who has altered the seasonal cycle of the Nile, decisively changing the economic life of Egypt and putting to an end the annual floods which the ancient Egyptians attributed to their gods. On the other hand, the geographer Alfred Grove and the ecologist Oliver Rackham have suggested that human beings have had a less drastic effect on the Mediterranean environment than is often assumed, for nature in the Mediterranean lands shows a capacity to recover from climatic and other variations, and from the abuses imposed on it. Humans, they stress, do not determine the evolution of climate, or at least did not do so before the twentieth century; and erosion, even allowing for a human role, also takes place naturally – it happened in the age of the dinosaurs too. One area where human impact has often been reported is deforestation, which has had severe effects in Sicily, Cyprus and along the Spanish coast; demand for timber for ships has been succeeded by the clearance of land for new or expanding towns and villages, but here too an argument can be pressed that natural regeneration has often taken place. Grove and Rackham are less optimistic about the future the Mediterranean faces, as water resources and fish stocks are over-exploited and, in some areas, desertification threatens, likely to be rendered worse if credible prophecies about global warming are even partly valid.[9] To look back at the history of the Mediterranean is to observe a symbiosis of man and nature that may be about to end.

This book does not deny the importance of winds and currents, but aims to bring to the fore the human experience of crossing the Mediterranean or of living in the port towns and islands that depended for their existence on the sea. The human hand has been more important in moulding the history of the Mediterranean than Braudel was ever prepared to admit. The book is full of political decisions: navies setting out to conquer Syracuse or Carthage, Acre or Famagusta, Minorca or Malta. Why some of these places were strategically important did depend to a significant extent on geography – not just wind and waves but other limitations: fresh food and water might last a couple of weeks on a merchant vessel, but were too bulky to load in great quantities on a war galley that had little space to spare. This simple fact meant that control of the open sea was a very tough challenge, at least in the age of sail; without access to friendly ports where supplies could be taken on board and ships could be careened, no power, however many warships it possessed, could lord itself over sea routes. Conflicts for control of the Mediterranean thus have to be seen as struggles for mastery over its coasts, ports and islands rather than as battles over open spaces.[10] To manage the almost constant threat of piracy it was often necessary to enter into murky deals with the pirates and their masters, permitting free passage to merchant shipping in return for gifts and bribes. Advance positions were invaluable. The situation of Corfu ensured that it was coveted over many centuries by those who sought to control entry into the Adriatic. The Catalans and then the British constructed a line of possessions across the Mediterranean that served their economic and political interests well. Oddly, though, the places chosen as ports often provided poor harbours: physical advantages were by no means the only consideration. Alexandria was difficult of access through often choppy seas, medieval Barcelona offered little more than a beach, Pisa nothing but a few small roadsteads close to the Arno estuary, and even in the 1920s ships reaching Jaffa had to unload out at sea. The harbour at Messina lay close to the rushing waters of what classical commentators identified as the twin terrors of Scylla and Charybdis.[11]

Human history involves the study of the irrational as well as the rational, decisions made by individuals or groups that are hard to understand at a remove of centuries or millennia, and that may have been hard to understand at the time those decisions were made. Yet small decisions, like the flutter of a butterfly's wings, could have massive consequences: a pope's speech at Clermont in France in 1095, loaded with vague but impassioned rhetoric, could unleash 500 years of crusades; disputes between rival Turkish commanders, in contrast to charismatic leadership on the Christian side, could bring surprise defeat upon Ottoman armies and navies, as at Malta in 1565 – and even then Spain was slower to send aid than the emergency demanded, risking loss of command of the waters around one of its prize possessions, Sicily. Battles were won against the odds; the victories of brilliant naval commanders such as Lysander, Roger de Lauria and Horatio Nelson transformed the political map of the Mediterranean and frustrated the imperial plans of those in Athens, Naples or Napoleonic France. Merchant princes placed their own profit above the cause of the Christian faith. The roulette wheel spins and the outcome is unpredictable, but human hands spin the wheel.

PART ONE

The First Mediterranean,
22000 BC–1000 BC

I

Isolation and Insulation,
22000 BC–3000 BC

I

Carved out millions of years before mankind reached its coasts, the Mediterranean Sea became a 'sea between the lands' linking opposite shores once human beings traversed its surface in search of habitation, food or other vital resources. Early types of humans inhabited the lands bordering the Mediterranean 435,000 years before the present, to judge from evidence for a hunters' camp set up near modern Rome; others built a simple hut out of branches at Terra Amata near Nice, and created a hearth in the middle of their dwelling – their diet included rhinoceros and elephant meat as well as deer, rabbits and wild pigs.[1] When early man first ventured out across the sea's waters is uncertain. In 2010, the American School of Classical Studies at Athens announced the discovery in Crete of quartz hand-axes dated to before 130,000 BC, indicating that early types of humans found some means to cross the sea, though these people may have been swept there unintentionally on storm debris.[2] Discoveries in caves on Gibraltar prove that 24,000 years ago another species of human looked across the sea towards the mountain of Jebel Musa, clearly visible on the facing shore of Africa: the first Neanderthal bones ever discovered, in 1848, were those of a woman who lived in a cave on the side of the Rock of Gibraltar. Since the original finds were not immediately identified as the remains of a different human species, it was only when, eight years later, similar bones were unearthed in the Neander Valley in Germany that this species gained a name: Neanderthal Man should carry the name Gibraltar Woman. The Gibraltar Neanderthals made use of the sea that lapped the shores of their territory, for their diet included shellfish and crustaceans, even turtles

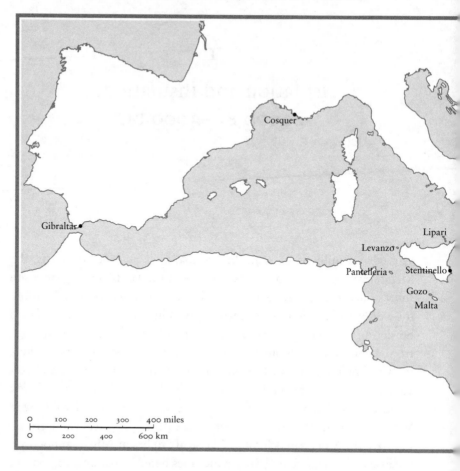

and seals, though at this time a flat plain separated their rock caves from the sea.[3] But there is no evidence for a Neanderthal population in Morocco, which was colonized by *homo sapiens sapiens*, our own branch of humanity. The Straits apparently kept the two populations apart.

In the long period of the Lower and Middle Palaeolithic ('Old and Middle Stone Age'), navigation across the Mediterranean was probably rare, though some present-day islands were accessible across land bridges later covered by the rising sea. The Cosquer grotto near Marseilles contains carvings by *homo sapiens* from as early as 27000 BC and paintings earlier than 19000 BC; it now lies well below sea level, but when it was inhabited the Mediterranean shore lay a few miles further out. The first good evidence for short sea-crossings comes during the Upper Palaeolithic (the late 'Old Stone Age'), that is, before about

11000 BC. At this point, visitors set foot on Melos in the Greek Cycla-des, in search of the volcanic glass obsidian, used in stone tools, and offering sharper edges than flint. Sicily has yielded dozens of Palaeo-lithic sites from the same period, very often along the coast, where settlers consumed large quantities of molluscs, though they also hunted foxes, hare and deer. They took care of the dead, covering the body with a layer of ochre and sometimes burying the corpses with decorated necklaces. On the western extremity of Sicily, they occupied what are now the easternmost Egadian islands (which were then probably small promontories connected to Sicily itself); on one of them, Levanzo, some-where around 11000 BC, they decorated a cave with incised and painted figures. The incised figures include deer and horses, drawn with liveli-ness and a degree of realism. The painted figures are more schematic, rough representations of human beings, and are thought to date to a later occupation of the cave. The drawings and paintings from the Sicilian caves demonstrate the existence of a hunter-gatherer society adept, as we know from other evidence, at the creation of effective tools out of flint and quartzite, whose rituals included sympathetic magic aimed at the winning of prey. They hunted with bows and arrows and with spears; they lived in caves and grottoes, but also inhabited camp sites in the open. They were thinly spread and, while their ancestors had reached Sicily on whatever simple boats were available to them, later generations did not explore the seas further.[4]

The style of life of the first inhabitants of Sicily was not markedly different from that of hundreds of generations of other Upper Palaeolithic people spread around the shores of the Mediterranean, from whom they were, nonetheless, isolated. This is not to say that their lives lacked complexity; a comparison with nomadic hunter-gatherers in Australia or the Amazon suggests that elaborate myths and rituals have for millennia bonded together families and groups, irrespective of their level of technology. Change, when it occurred, took place very slowly and did not necessarily consist of what might be called 'improvement', for skills such as those of the cave artists could be lost as well as gained. Around 8000 BC there was a very gradual warming, and this resulted in changes in flora and fauna that sometimes set these small groups of people on the move in search of their traditional prey, and sometimes encouraged a search for alternative types of food, especially that provided by the sea. The sea gradually rose, by as much as 120 metres, as the ice caps melted. The contours of the modern Mediterranean become more recognizable as isthmuses turned into islands and sea coasts retreated to roughly their current position; but all this was too slow a process to be readily visible.[5]

There was little social differentiation within these wandering bands of people, travelling in search of food, arriving at convenient hilltops and bays, moving from settlement to settlement, zigzagging back and forth. But as groups became familiar with particular areas, they adapted their diet and customs to that area. Possibly, as they buried their dead and decorated the caves, they acquired a real sense of attachment to the land. Occasionally stone tools passed from hand to hand and moved between communities, or were acquired in skirmishes between tribes. In essence, though, they were self-sufficient, relying on what the sea and land offered in wild animals, fish and berries. Although the human population remained tiny, maybe a few thousand in the whole of Sicily at any one time, the effect on the animal stock of climatic change and of human intervention was increasingly severe; larger animals began to disappear, notably the wild horses which had arrived before the humans arrived, when Sicily was still linked physically to Italy; these horses were recorded in the Levanzo cave drawings and provided massive feasts.

During the transitional period to about 5000 BC known as the Mesolithic ('Middle Stone Age'), when tools became steadily more refined but animal husbandry, ceramics or the cultivation of grain had yet to emerge, the diet of prehistoric Sicilians shifted towards products of the sea, from which they fished sea-bream and grouper; large numbers of mollusc shells have been found on archaeological sites, some incised and decorated with red ochre. By 6400 BC, in what would become Tunisia, the 'Capsian culture' emerged, which was heavily dependent on shellfish and has left large mounds or middens along the coast.[6] Further east, in the Aegean, Upper Palaeolithic and Mesolithic seafarers made their way occasionally along the island chain of the Cyclades to Melos, collecting its obsidian and transporting it back to cave sites on the Greek mainland such as the cave at Franchthi, 120 kilometres from Melos; their boats were probably manufactured from reeds, which could be shaped and cut using the small sharp-edged stones, or microliths, that they had developed. Since sea levels were still rising, the distance between islands was shorter than now.[7] Mesolithic Sicily also knew obsidian, which was obtained from the volcanic Lipari islands off Sicily's north-east shore. Movement across the open sea had begun. It was local; it was spasmodic; but it was deliberate: the aim was to collect precious materials in order to make superior tools. This was not 'trade'; there was probably no one living permanently on either Melos or Lipari, and even had there been, the settlers would not have expressed a proprietary right to the volcanic glass that lay about the islands. Those on Sicily or in Greece who acquired pieces of obsidian did not manufacture blades in order to send them inland to neighbouring communities. Autarchy was the rule. It is necessary to take a leap forward into the Neolithic period in order to find regular evidence for purposeful travel in search of desired products, in an age when societies were becoming more hierarchical and complex and the relationship between mankind and the land was changing in revolutionary ways.

I I

The 'Neolithic Revolution', which eventually encompassed all human communities across the globe, was really a series of independent discoveries of how to control food resources, from about 10,000 BC onwards. The taming of cattle, sheep, goats and pigs provided a consistent source of meat, milk, bone for tools, and in due course fibres for cloth; the realization that crops could be selected and sown in seasonal cycles resulted in the cultivation of various types of wheat, starting with semi-wild emmers, and culminating in the production (in the Mediterranean) of early wheat and barley. The earliest ceramics, at first moulded rather than wheel-thrown, began to be used as food containers; tools were still made of flint, obsidian and quartzes, but they became smaller and more specialized, a trend which was already visible by the Mesolithic period; this speaks for growing specialization, including a caste of skilled tool-makers whose training in what seems a deceptively simple craft was no doubt as long and as complex as that of a sushi chef. Neolithic societies were perfectly capable of creating complex, hierarchical political institutions such as monarchy, and of dividing society into castes defined by status and labour.

Concentrated settlements developed, permanent, walled, dependent on local supplies but also on goods brought across distances: the first, around 8000 BC, was Jericho, with about 2,000 inhabitants in the early eighth millennium; its obsidian was Anatolian rather than Mediterranean. From around 10,000 BC, the inhabitants of Eynan (Ayn Mallaha) in what is now northern Israel cultivated crops, ground flour and also had the time and inclination to produce schematic but elegant human portraits carved on stone. As the population of the eastern Mediterranean grew, fattening on the new sources of food, competition for resources led to more frequent conflict between communities, so that weaponry was used increasingly against fellow-humans rather than animal prey.[8] Conflicts generated migrations; folk from Anatolia or Syria moved towards Cyprus and Crete. By 5600 BC a community of several thousand people had settled in Cyprus, at Khirokitia, making pots not from clay but from carved stone; these first Cypriots imported some obsidian, but they mainly concentrated on their fields and flocks. They built houses out of mud-brick, on stone foundations, with bedrooms on a

8

first-floor gallery, and the graves of their ancestors under the hut floor. Less impressive was the first Neolithic settlement in Crete, at Knossos, dating to around 7000 BC; but it marked the beginning of the process of intensive settlement of the island which would dominate the eastern Mediterranean in the Bronze Age. The inhabitants arrived already equipped with seed grain and animals, from the coast of Asia Minor, for the animals they raised had no wild cousins on Crete itself. They grew wheat, barley and lentils. Pottery was a skill they did not develop for about half a millennium; weaving was practised by the first half of the fifth millennium. The lack of pottery suggests an isolated community which did not copy the methods of its neighbours further east; obsidian arrived from Melos, which lay not far to the north-west. Generally, though, the Cretans looked away from the sea: the relatively few sea shells that have been discovered in the lowest stratum of Knossos show water wear, indicating that they had been collected for decorative use long after the molluscs they once contained had died.[9] But external contacts started to transform the lives of early Cretans. When pottery began to be produced, around 6500 BC, it was of a dark, burnished variety that has some similarities to Anatolian styles of the period; the craft does not seem to have developed gradually, but to have been imported wholesale. During later Neolithic phases, further settlements emerged in other parts of the island, such as Phaistos in the south; but the process took 3,000 years, during which Crete turned increasingly outwards to the sea. The extraordinary civilization that eventually emerged in Crete can best be understood as an interplay between a slowly evolving native culture with a powerful local identity and growing contacts with the outside world which provided new technology and models, idiosyncratically adapted by the Cretans to meet their own uses.

Querns and mortars had to be fashioned; stone foundations were built for houses which now became permanent dwelling-places; potters needed equipment for moulding and firing their vessels. Specialization increased the demand for specific types of tool, and demand for obsidian grew. Its attractions were many, and compensated for the trouble involved in acquiring it: it was easy to flake, and the edges were exceedingly sharp. The obsidian quarries of Melos, which were exploited for about 12,000 years, reached their peak of popularity in the early Bronze Age, when one might expect metal tools to have become more fashionable. But obsidian was appreciated precisely because of its low value: in the early Bronze Age, metals were scarce and the technology to produce copper and bronze was not widely available, and difficult to set in place. Even allowing for increased specialization within Neolithic villages, quarrying on Melos long remained casual and lacked any commercial character. Although a settlement developed on the island, at Phylakopi, it emerged when the extraction of obsidian was already long established, and flourished just as the obsidian quarries began to decline; the first settlers were not obsidian merchants but tuna fishermen.[10] Melos offered no special port: those in search of obsidian found a suitable cove, beached their vessel, and came to the quarries, where they hacked off pieces of the volcanic glass.

III

For startling evidence of massive building projects from Neolithic Europe it is necessary to turn westwards, to the temples and sanctuaries of Malta and Gozo, which predate even the pyramids. The Maltese temples were created by people who crossed the sea and created an isolated culture with their own hands. The eminent British archaeologist Colin Renfrew has observed that 'something really exceptional was taking place in Malta more than five thousand years ago, something quite unlike anything else in the Mediterranean world or indeed beyond'; this society was in full ascendancy around 3500 BC.[11] The old diffusionist assumption that the temples were in some way imitations of the pyramids or ziggurats far to the east is patently false. But, although they were not imitations, neither did they become models followed by other cultures within the Mediterranean. Malta was settled by about 5700 BC, from Africa or more likely from Sicily, whose culture is reflected in the earliest Maltese rock-cut tombs. The early Maltese arrived quite well prepared: they brought with them emmer, barley and lentils, and they cleared parts of the island to create cultivable fields, for the archipelago had extensive tree cover, now completely lost. They acquired tools from the volcanic islands around Sicily, employing obsidian from Pantelleria and Lipari. The island culture began to develop in distinctive ways from 4100 BC. Then, very approximately in the millennium after 3600, great underground tombs or hypogea were carved out for collective burial, suggesting that the Maltese community had a strong sense of identity. Massive building works were already under way at Ġgantija on Gozo, and at Tarxien on Malta itself. With great concave decorated façades, and fronted by forecourts, these were enclosed structures, roofed buildings with hallways, passages and compartments, with a preference for a clover leaf arrangement of semi-circular rooms. The aim of the builders was to erect massive temples which could be seen from a great distance away, rising above the islands as one approached by sea, such as the temple at Ħaġar Qim in the south of Malta, where steep cliffs drop down to the Mediterranean.[12]

The buildings emerged slowly, over time, rather like medieval cathedrals, and with a less coordinated plan.[13] Oddly, there were no windows, but there must have been extensive wooden fittings, and the stone fittings, which are all that survives, are often handsomely decorated with carved designs, including spirals. For the culture of prehistoric Malta encompassed more than monumental buildings. The temples contained massive statues of which fragments survive, assumed to represent a Mother Goddess associated with childbirth and fertility. At Tarxien a female statue nearly two metres high was the focus of the cult; there is quite simply nothing similar anywhere in the western Mediterranean at this time. The chambers at Tarxien have left clear evidence of sacrificial ceremonies. An altar at Tarxien was found to contain, in a hollowed space, a flint knife; around the altar were the bones of cattle and sheep. Shells were unearthed, confirming that seafood was an important part of the local diet; and among the carvings are graffiti of ships.[14] All this building and carving was achieved without the use of metals, which reached Malta only around 2500 BC.

Culturally as well as physically this was an insular world. In the Neolithic period, the population of the islands has been estimated at less than 10,000. Yet the workforce was capable of building half a dozen large shrines and many smaller ones, suggesting the islands may have been divided into several little provinces. One might then expect evidence of warfare – spearheads, for instance. But virtually no such evidence survives: this was a community at peace.[15] Malta and Gozo were perhaps sacred islands that commanded the respect of the peoples of the central Mediterranean, rather like Delos in the classical Greek world. A hole in a slab in the temple at Tarxien may be proof that this was the site of an oracle. Yet it is remarkable that so little evidence has been found of foreign visitors. If these were sacred islands, part of their sacredness must have consisted in a rule that they were unapproachable, inhabited only by native Maltese in the service of the Great Goddess, who was represented not just in the statues and figurines the Maltese carved, but in the very shape of the temples, with their billowing exterior and womb-like internal passages.

The end of this culture is as perplexing as its creation. The long peace came to an end by the middle of the sixteenth century BC. There is no sign of a decline in the temple culture; rather, there was a sharp break, as invaders arrived, lacking the skills that had created the great monuments, but possessing one advantage: bronze weapons. Judging from finds of clay whorls and of carbonized cloth, they were spinners and weavers, who arrived from Sicily and south-eastern Italy.[16] By the fourteenth century they had been replaced by another wave of Sicilian settlers. But Malta had by now lost its distinctiveness: the migrants and their descendants squatted in the monuments left by people who had vanished from the face of the earth.

IV

Whereas on Malta nothing changed greatly over many hundreds of years, Sicily was more volatile, as one would expect of a large, accessible landmass with a great variety of resources. Settlers were drawn to the region by the availability of obsidian on the Lipari islands; they brought their culture with them ready-made, as can be seen at Stentinello, near Syracuse, which flourished at the start of the fourth millennium BC, while the Maltese temples were still being constructed. The site, filled with huts, had a perimeter of about 250 metres, and was surrounded by a ditch; within, pottery and simple animal-head figurines have been found. This was a busy village, with its own artisans and command of the surrounding countryside and shoreline, from which it could draw its food. The settlements of these people are very reminiscent of those found in south-eastern Italy, whence their ancestors clearly came.

As much as 3,000 years separate the very first Stentinello culture from the coming of copper and bronze; changes did not take place fast, and these migrations were spasmodic – as yet, there was no great wave of migrations that convulsed the Mediterranean. But it was precisely this slow, osmotic contact that created some elements of a common culture. The style of life of the Neolithic Sicilians from Stentinello shared many features with that of other Neolithic peoples in the Mediterranean; this does not mean they all spoke the same languages (lacking writing, they have left no traces of their language), nor that they shared a common ancestry. But they all participated in the great economic and cultural changes that resulted in the adoption of farming, the domestication of animals and the manufacture of pottery. A similar rough, incised pottery can be found on sites from Syria to Algeria, from Spain to Anatolia. In the same period, Lipari ceased to be simply a depot where obsidian could be collected at will, and was settled by people of similar tastes and habits to those of Stentinello. The open sea was no barrier: settlers headed southwards, and pottery similar to that from Stentinello has been found on sites in Tunisia, as has obsidian from Pantelleria, between Sicily and Africa.[17]

Lipari enjoyed an especially high standard of living as a result of its command of obsidian supplies. Whether the succession of different styles of pottery indicates changes in the composition of the settler population can be debated endlessly. Fashions change without populations changing, as any observer of modern Italy is well aware. Ceramics decorated with red flames characteristic of the sixth millennium BC were succeeded by others which were plain brown or black, remarkable for their smooth, polished surfaces, and carefully and precisely made. By the end of the fifth millennium BC these gave way to ceramics decorated with meandering patterns, zigzags or spirals, painted on the surface, very similar to items found in the interior of southern Italy and the Balkans. This too was succeeded by new fashions, as plain red pottery was introduced early in the fourth millennium BC, ushering in the long-lived 'Diana culture', as it has become known from the principal find-site. The important point is the slowness of change and the stability of these island societies.[18]

Mariners took advantage of their voyages across the Adriatic Sea, the Ionian Sea or the Sicilian Channel to carry and offer goods, most of them perishable – pottery and obsidian are simply what have tended to survive. It is only possible to guess at what sort of boats these early mariners used. On the open sea skin coverings probably provided insulation; nor can the boats have been tiny, since they were used to carry not just men and women but animals and pots.[19] Later evidence, crude drawings on ceramics from the Cyclades, suggests that the boats had a low draught, making them unstable in choppy seas, and that they were powered by oars. Practical experiments with a reed boat named the *Papyrella* have suggested that movement was slow – four knots at best – and that time was easily lost to bad weather. Reaching Melos in the Cyclades from the mainland of Attika, island-hopping along the way, may often have been a week's work.[20]

There were still Mediterranean islands where settlement was very limited, including the Balearics and Sardinia. Majorca and Minorca were already inhabited in the early fifth millennium, though pottery was not introduced until the middle of the third, and it is quite possible that there was an occasional hiatus, as early settlers gave up the battle against the environment. The earliest inhabitants of Sardinia appear to have been stock-raisers, who must have brought their animals with them.[21] Along the shores of North Africa, there were no monumental buildings, no efflorescence comparable to that on Malta. Most of those who inhabited the shores of the Mediterranean ventured no further than the fishing grounds within sight of their home. The emergence in the fifth millennium of farming communities in the Nile Delta and in the Fayyum to the west was a local rather than a Mediterranean phenomenon; that is to say, it marked a creative response by the inhabitants of well-watered, indeed waterlogged, lands to the environment in which they lived, and, for a few centuries at least, Lower Egypt was a closed world. Malta, Lipari, the Cyclades were still highly exceptional island communities that performed very specific roles, in two cases as the source of material for stone tools, and in one, very mysterious, case as the focus of an elaborate religious cult.

2

Copper and Bronze,
3000 BC–1500 BC

I

The development of prehistoric societies has always been viewed from one of two perspectives: a diffusionist approach, now largely out of fashion, which attributes the arrival of new styles and techniques to migration and trade; or an emphasis on the factors within a society that fostered change and growth. Alongside the tendency to look for internal explanations of change, interest in the ethnic identity of settlers has faded. Partly this reflects an awareness that easy identification of 'race' with language and culture bears no relation to circumstances on the ground: ethnic groups merge, languages are borrowed, important cultural traits such as burial practices mutate without the arrival of newcomers. Equally, it would be an error to see all social change as the result of internal developments merely enhanced by the effects of growing trade: the lightly populated shores and islands of the prehistoric Mediterranean provided broad spaces within which those in search of food, exiled warlords or pilgrims to pagan shrines could create new settlements far from home. If there were earlier settlers, the newcomers intermarried with them as often as they chased them away or exterminated them, and the language of one or the other group became dominant for reasons that are now beyond explanation.

The Cyclades became the home of a rich and lively culture, beginning in the early Bronze Age (roughly 3000 BC onwards). The main islands were by now all populated; villages such as Phylakopi on Melos were thriving; on several islands small villages developed out of an original core of a couple of small homesteads.[1] The obsidian quarries were still visited, and copper was available in the western Cyclades, whence it

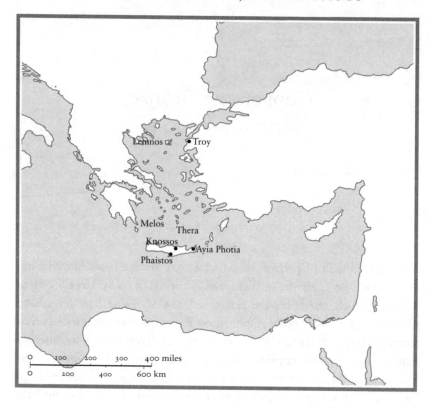

reached Crete; Cycladic products continued to flow outwards, though in quite precise directions: to the southern Aegean, but not, for some reason, northwards, suggesting that the opening of the seas was still partial and dependent on what other regions could offer the Cycladic islanders. The islanders appear to have imported little into their villages; very few eastern products have been found on excavated sites on the Cyclades. But this is to make the classic error of assuming that the archaeological record is reasonably complete; textiles, foodstuffs, slaves, objects made of perishable materials such as wood, all no doubt arrived, though whether their arrival can be formally described as 'trade' is still, in the third millennium BC, a moot point.

The Cycladic culture ceased to be defined solely by the Cycladic islands; it began to spread southwards. In what archaeologists call 'EB I', that is, the first stage of the Early Bronze Age, a new settlement developed at Ayia Photia in north-eastern Crete; to judge from the style of burial, it seems more Cycladic than Cretan. To describe this as a formal Cycladic 'colony' is to be too specific; rather, Cycladic natives installed themselves on Cretan soil, and continued to live in the style to which they were accustomed. By 'EB II', around 2500 BC, Cycladic goods were penetrating past Ayia Photia and even being imitated by Cretan artisans; in addition they began to radiate north-eastwards to the emerging town of Troy, close by the Dardanelles, which, with its gradually expanding links to the Anatolian interior and the Black Sea, was probably the major source of tin.[2]

For one product was gaining prestige, literally strengthening the hand of those who exercised political power: bronze; and it was demand for this alloy that would create a network of connections across the Aegean, linking Troy to the islands. Shiny containers and pedestals made of bronze or copper proclaimed their owners' wealth and prestige; but it was bronze weapons that assured safety from one's enemies. Those who owned these articles were doubtless successful warlords. Copper was to be found on the island of Kythnos in the westernmost Cyclades, or in Attika on the Greek mainland. Early metallurgists had learned they could strengthen the relatively soft metal copper by alloying it with tin. Bringing together the ingredients of bronze and establishing a system of exchanges meant that the network of connections across the Aegean developed into what can at last be described as trade routes: links established regularly according to the seasons, from one year to the next, for the purpose of exchange, in which the intermediaries travelled by boat, though it would be going too far to assume that they were professional merchants who lived entirely from the proceeds of trade. In consequence the Mediterranean was coming alive, criss-crossed by people of varied origins, in search of or anxious to dispose of goods that were of equally varied origins.

The Cyclades lay astride these routes. Rather than drawing in influences from several directions, they developed a distinctive art form of their own; the term 'art' should, however, be used with some qualification since the objects they produced had precise functions, even if those functions are now hard to decipher. 'Cycladic art' has been a powerful influence on modern artists – 'a simplicity of form that can be altogether breathtaking', in Colin Renfrew's words, for there was a growing concern with the proportions of the human body, a sense of 'harmony' that has no parallel in the other monumental sculptures of the period, in Malta, Old Kingdom Egypt or Mesopotamia.[3] Objects range in size from miniature figures, so stylized that to modern eyes they resemble a violin more than a human, to near lifesize statues of musicians; the violin figurines count among the earlier works, dating from roughly 3000 BC. Female figures predominate, hinting at the cult of a Great Goddess. The 'Fat Lady of Saliagos' with her generous buttocks may, like the Maltese idols, have some link to fertility cults. White marble from Paros provided the raw material, but enough stains survive to prove that these objects were highly coloured.[4]

The statues are associated with burials, and one grave was accompanied by fourteen 'idols'. Sometimes they are found broken, perhaps as part of an elaborate funeral ritual. Do they represent the deceased? They may have had several functions, especially as they were being produced over many hundreds of years (the Early Bronze Age on the Cyclades spans twelve centuries from 3000 BC onwards). Other explanations include the idea that they were *psychopompoi*, that is, guides to the souls of the dead in the Underworld, or substitutes for human sacrifices, or even companions who would offer sexual gratification or musical entertainment in the next world. The sculptures testify to the existence of a caste of skilled craftsmen. The graves indicate a stratified and complex society, with leaders and subordinates; the male workforce must also have been employed as oarsmen on board the small ships that increasingly plied the Aegean, though it is highly unlikely that they ranged any further, and sailing ships appear to have been introduced only during the second millennium BC. Images of their oared ships can be found on the so-called 'frying pans', engraved clay plates which carry pictures of centipede-like objects with raised prows.[5]

II

The impact of Troy on the history of the Mediterranean is twofold. On the one hand Troy functioned from the beginning of the Bronze Age as a staging-post linking the Aegean to Anatolia and the Black Sea; on the other, the tale of Troy lay at the heart of the historical consciousness not merely of the Greeks who claimed to have destroyed the city, but of the Romans who claimed to be descended from its refugees. The real Troy and the mythical Troy have been hard to disentangle since 1868, when the German businessman Heinrich Schliemann, obsessed with the veracity of the *Iliad*, identified the mound of Hisarlık, four miles from the point where the Dardanelles flow into the Aegean, as the site of Homer's city.[6] While some scholars have argued that there was no Trojan War, and that in consequence the identity of Troy is a non-question, discoveries in the Hittite archives further east have removed any serious doubt that Hisarlık contains the ruins of a city or statelet variously known to the classical Greeks as Troié and Ilios. Later settlers, including the Greeks who built the new city of Ilion in classical times, and Emperor Constantine, who thought at first of building the New Rome there rather than at Byzantion, were equally convinced of the attribution. More remarkably still, the site has an exceptionally long history reaching back long before the date ascribed to the Trojan War by classical authors (1184 BC). Its history began as bronze was first diffused across the eastern Mediterranean. It was rebuilt again and again; in 1961, one of the modern excavators of the mound, Carl Blegen, identified forty-six strata in nine main layers.[7]

Troy had no known Neolithic antecedents. It was settled by people who were familiar with copper, and probably traded in tin. The first Troy, 'Troy I' (*c.* 3000–*c.* 2500 BC), was a small settlement, about 100 metres across, but it grew into an impressively fortified site, with stone watchtowers and three lines of fortification.[8] Over this period there was much rebuilding, and in the last days of Troy I a great conflagration put an end to the fortress. But within the fortress a settled domestic life had proved possible, and the survival of spindle whorls shows that textiles were woven by the side of hearths whose remains have been unearthed; so it stands to reason that the early Trojans also traded in cloth, made from the fleeces of sheep reared in the plains below the citadel. The best-preserved house from Troy I was nearly twenty metres long, with a porch facing westwards; it may well have been inhabited by a leader of the community and his extended family. The early Trojans manufactured small figurines, mostly female, and they lived off shellfish, tuna and dolphin flesh as well as meat and grain. Metal weapons have not been recovered from this level; but the existence of whetstones indicates that copper and bronze tools were regularly sharpened. There is no evidence for luxury: surviving ornaments were made of bone, marble or coloured stone. The plentiful pottery is sombre in appearance, dull in colour and generally undecorated, though the shapes have a certain elegance.[9]

Early Troy formed part of a cultural world which extended beyond Anatolia; a similar community developed on the island of Lemnos, not far to the west, on the site of Poliochni, sometimes described as 'the oldest city in Europe', as also at Thermi on Lesbos.[10] But it is not profitable to speculate where the earliest inhabitants of these lands came from or what languages they spoke. Indeed, if Troy and Poliochni first emerged as trading stations guarding the routes across the Aegean and into the interior, it is likely that they began to attract people of varied origins, as have port cities ever after. Though Hisarlık now stands back from the sea, prehistoric Troy stood on the edge of a large bay (of which Homer seems to have been aware), which has gradually become full of silt.[11] Thus it was a maritime city, strategically situated: contrary winds could render entry into the Dardanelles impossible for weeks at a time; shipping was detained in the bay and the inhabitants of the citadel could profitably service the needs of those on board. All this did not happen immediately, and during the period of Troy I it is likely that navigation past the citadel was intermittent and not easy to control. What emerged in its place, Troy II (c. 2500–c. 2300 BC), was a grander and better defended citadel, a little larger, with a monumental gateway and a great hall or *megaron*, probably surrounded by wooden columns. These Trojans were also farmers and weavers – a spindle has been found to which a piece of carbonized thread still adhered.[12] They acquired or manufactured sophisticated armaments; it is thought that their bronze weapons were imports, but softer weapons made just of copper were available and may have been made locally, using metal brought across the Aegean.

Even though they had now graduated to wheel-thrown pottery (absent from Troy I), Blegen did not like their pots and assumed that they were 'a dour, austere people, with little fondness for gaiety and light';[13] it is a matter of taste whether the slender goblets the Trojans were now producing were really so dull and lacking in character. In addition, large pots arrived in Troy from as far away as the Cyclades, carrying oil or wine. Similar pottery to that made in Troy has been found around the shores of the Aegean and Anatolia, and the easy assumption is that these items were exported from Troy, though it is more likely that the style of pottery reflected a common culture of which Troy was one part. Indeed, Poliochni, with which Troy shared so many features, was twice the size of Troy. These Aegean settlements lagged far behind the cities of Egypt and Mesopotamia in wealth, and there is no evidence they had yet developed writing, a tool that would, in due course, greatly facilitate trade and accounting; nonetheless, Troy and Poliochni were becoming part of an intertwined trading world across which snaked regular commercial routes by sea and land; and the clearest evidence that this brought great wealth to the elite of Troy II is found in the famous 'Treasure of Priam' discovered by Schliemann.

The long disappearance of this treasure within Soviet vaults has deprived scholars of the opportunity to make sense of what sometimes seems to be a contrived creation of Schliemann himself.[14] Schliemann gathered together what he found in several hoards, one of which he characterized as the 'Great Treasure', attributing it to a siege which (if it ever occurred) took place a millennium later. The quality of workmanship was truly impressive. The collection of women's jewellery and gold and silver vessels is striking, including a golden 'sauceboat' and what he believed to be a woman's headdress made of gold filaments, as well as thousands of gold beads and several silver necklaces; there were plenty of items made of other materials, including jade ceremonial axes and rock crystal knobs that may have been attached to sceptres. Some items were apparently made locally; others, including the gold itself, must have been imports. All this speaks volubly for a society which was ruled by a prosperous elite that had accumulated considerable wealth from the profits of the trade passing through the city. Troy was not just a trade entrepôt but a centre of industry, most probably producing heavy wool fabrics; another export may have been timber from Mount Ida nearby, for shipbuilding and construction in nearby lands; the area was rich in farmland and livestock. Judging from finds of animal bones, it was not yet the famous centre for the rearing of horses that it would eventually become. But Troy was a peripheral settlement; the Mediterranean was never the focus of the interests of the great kings of Hatti further to the east, which were firmly directed towards the mountainous, mineral-bearing interior of western Asia.

The rise of Troy was not a straight trajectory. Troy III (built after Troy II was destroyed by fire around 2250 BC) was a poorer settlement than Troy II, and its inhabitants were squeezed together less comfortably on their hilltop. Turtle flesh featured prominently in their diet. On Lemnos, Poliochni apparently suffered attacks, and the town contracted in size and wealth by the end of the third millennium BC. Around 2100 BC Troy was destroyed again, perhaps in war, but in the rebuilt Troy IV conditions were not markedly better, and tight, tortuous streets wound between the houses. Wider changes in western Asia were affecting the eastern Mediterranean: in central and eastern Anatolia the empire of Hatti and then, from *c.* 1750 BC, the new empire of Anitta became the focus for trade up from the Tigris and Euphrates; business was diverted away from the trade routes that had been bringing metals to the northern edge of the Aegean.[15] After the age of gold, then, came a period of recession, lasting 300 years or more, though by the end of Troy V, around 1700 BC, conditions were improving; houses were cleaner, and the inhabitants preferred beef and pork to the turtle stews of their forebears. But the most striking developments in trade and culture were taking place once again in the islands of the eastern Mediterranean – on Crete and the Cyclades.

III

The Minoan civilization in Crete was the first major Mediterranean civilization, the first wealthy, literate, city-based culture with a vibrant artistic culture to emerge within the Mediterranean world. This claim might seem to be contradicted by the still earlier emergence of high civilization in Old Dynasty Egypt, but the Egyptians regarded the shores of the Mediterranean as the outer edge of their world, which was defined by the Nile, not by the sea beyond. By contrast, the Minoans actively navigated the Mediterranean and the sea featured in many striking ways in their culture – in the design of their pottery, in their ceramics, and, possibly, in the cult of the sea god Poseidon. The Minoans were almost certainly descended from migrants who had arrived from Anatolia. Yet what they created was a civilization distinctive in its style of art, religious cults, economic life and social organization. In addition, they left a memory of their achievements in the legends of the great king Minos, whose name has been attached to their civilization by modern archaeologists. Thucydides reported how King Minos had been the first to create a great naval empire, or *thalassokratia*, in the Mediterranean world; so some memory of early Crete lingered as late as fifth-century Athens. The Athenians also remembered a sacrificial tribute of young men which had been paid regularly to the king of Crete, of which echoes can be found in the ritual practices of the Cretans during the second millennium.[16]

The earliest settlement at Knossos, dating back to Neolithic times, was already developing its own artistic style before the end of the third millennium. Pottery designs of early Bronze Age Crete diverged more and more from those of neighbouring lands. Pottery of the period known as Early Minoan II (*c.* 2600–2300 BC) was characterized by a mottling effect, managed through tricks learned during firing; in addition, attention was paid to the outward form of vessels, achieving a delicacy of form and a liveliness in decoration (great swirls and flowing meanders) which increasingly distinguished the pottery of early Crete from that of contemporary Anatolia. There were influences from outside, too. By 2000 the Cretans were producing ivory and stone seals, a sign that an elite anxious to assert ownership of its goods had emerged; some themes, such as lions, are clearly of outside inspiration, while abstract patterns often recall Egyptian or Near Eastern seals – trade with Syria and the mouth of the Nile was already active.[17]

It is not necessary to make a stark choice between the early Minoans as an indigenous people of talent and the Minoans as migrants who brought with them elements of Near Eastern cultures; Crete was a crossroads of several cultures, and must have attracted settlers from many directions. Classical writers from Homer onwards enumerated the many different peoples who inhabited the island, including the 'great-hearted Eteo-Cretans', that is, 'true Cretans', and the 'noble Pelasgians', a term used for any number of wandering peoples. Place-names on Crete and on the mainland with pre-Greek endings such as *-nthos* and *-ssa* may have been left by peoples who were living in the region well before the coming of the Greeks; the most memorable *-nthos* word is 'labyrinth', which classical sources connected with the palace of Minos at Knossos, while *-ssa* words include the word for the sea itself, *thalassa*.[18] Language and genes are, however, separate issues, and better than any attempt to identify a 'native stock', with its own idiosyncratic genius, is an interpretation of the Minoans as cosmopolitan people whose easy openness to many cultures also left them free to devise art forms of their own that were unlike those anywhere else. They were not hidebound by traditions of style and technique which some neighbouring cultures, notably in Egypt, preserved little changed over many millennia.

The building of the palaces offers the clearest proof that what developed in Crete was a dynamic local civilization. Knossos, six miles from the seashore, was reconstructed as a great palace around 1950 BC, and around the same time ('Middle Minoan I') other palaces developed at Phaistos in the south and Mallia in the east. Knossos, however, was always the queen among the palaces; whether this reflected its political or religious pre-eminence, or simply the greater resources of the area under its command, is uncertain; theories that the island was divided into chiefdoms based at the various palaces are, indeed, theories. Even the term 'palace' is doubtful: possibly these structures were temple complexes, though it would be wrong to assume that the Minoans applied the same sharply defined categories as a modern observer.[19] There had been a small complex on the site of Knossos previously; so the building of the great palaces was not the initiative of a new immigrant people who had seized charge, but one that grew out of the existing culture of the island. It reflected an economic boom, as Crete confirmed its role as the crossroads of the eastern Mediterranean, as a source of wool and textiles. Imitation of foreign palaces was conscious: there were grand palaces and temples of comparable size in Egypt, with frescoed walls and colonnaded courts. But the design, style and function of the palaces in Crete was quite different.[20]

The palace at Knossos was repeatedly damaged by fires and quakes, and over its 200-year history there were many changes in its internal appearance. But a few snapshots of its contents can be shown. The so-called Vat Room, dug into the soil of the Old Palace, contained an impressive collection of goblets and artefacts from about 1900 BC, probably used in religious rites. Some of the pottery came from the highlands of Crete, but there were exotic objects too, such as pieces of ivory, faience and ostrich egg, revealing contact with Egypt and Syria. Predictably, there were quantities of obsidian from Melos. So it is clear that in the period of the Old Palace the Minoans were linked northwards to the Cyclades and south and eastwards to the Levant and the Nile. A distinctive type of loom-weight found in the Old Palace suggests that Knossos was a centre for the production of a special type of cloth which was exported to neighbouring lands; these weights appear outside Crete only after about 1750 BC. Enormous jars, *pithoi*, set into the ground were used to store oil, grain and other goods, whether for palace use or for trade. The Cretans perfected an eggshell-thin pottery, exported to Egypt and Syria. Some items were made in palace workshops; but around the palaces there stood real towns, for this was 'civilization' in the full sense, a culture that revolved in significant measure around cities, with all their specialized crafts. Knossos had satellite towns at Katsamba and Amnisos which functioned as its seaports, and Amnisos was mentioned in Egyptian texts. Here, the Minoan fleets were built and docked, and (to judge from pottery finds) trade expeditions set out for the Peloponnese and Dodecanese, including Rhodes, then up to Miletos and probably Troy.[21] The first Minoan shipwreck to be discovered by maritime archaeologists came to light only at the start of the twenty-first century, in north-eastern Crete. The ship was ten or fifteen metres in length and carried dozens of amphorae and large jars, used for carrying wine or oil along the coasts of Crete some time around 1700 BC. Its wooden structure has entirely decayed, but a Cretan seal shows a single-masted vessel with a beaked prow and high stern, and that is probably how it looked.[22]

Evidence for external links, and of the idiosyncratic response to them, comes with the appearance of writing in Crete. Seals in pictographic writing begin to appear from about 1900 onwards, so the development of a script seems to coincide quite neatly with the first phase of palace-building. By the end of the Old Palace period, large numbers of documents were pouring forth: inventories of goods received or stored, including tribute from those working the land to be paid to the ruler or deities of Knossos. The main function of writing was to maintain accounts; and behind the scribes there was evidently an efficient and demanding administration. A few of the symbols resembled Egyptian hieroglyphs, indicating that the Cretan script drew inspiration from Egyptian writing. Perhaps because the sound system of the Cretan language was different, most of the signs that actually developed were quite unEgyptian. So the idea of writing may have been borrowed; but the writing system was not.

Fires and massive earthquakes brought the first palace period to an end in the eighteenth century BC. Phaistos had to be totally reconstructed. At a sanctuary on Mount Jouktas, a priest, a priestess and a young man gathered to propitiate the earth-shaking gods; the young man was sacrificed, but then the roof collapsed, burying those who had vainly offered up his life.[23] Bearing in mind the story of the young men and women sent from Athens to feed the Minotaur, there is no reason to doubt that human sacrifice was practised in Minoan Crete. After some intermediate attempts at rebuilding, the New Palace complex emerged which – despite further fires and earthquakes – is still visible at Knossos, imaginatively reconstructed around 1900 by Sir Arthur Evans, with its vibrant frescoes, its maze of chambers, its 'royal quarters' on several levels, its great court and the ceremonies that can be dimly perceived: the ritual or sport of bull-leaping, and great processions bringing tribute to the goddess Potnia.[24] This New Palace period lasted from about 1700 BC to 1470 BC, ending spectacularly with earthquakes and volcanic eruptions that also put an end to the Cycladic civilization on the island of Thera. Some of the frescoes portray a lively palace-based culture: one shows the women of the court, often bare-breasted, sitting around what must be the central courtyard, though one should not be beguiled by these paintings, which are intelligent reconstructions from small fragments. Most commentators have revelled in this image of Minoan culture as happy, peaceful and respectful of women; but it is important not to impose modern values, and what we see in the frescoes is the life of the elite – a princely court, or colleges of priests and priestesses. The question whether the palaces were really, or also, temples is pertinent here. These buildings were home to a court culture that revolved around religious cults, in which the snake goddess played an especially important role, probably as a chthonic deity; as in other early Mediterranean cultures, female deities were dominant.

This was the period in which outside contacts grew significantly. An Egyptian alabaster lid found in Knossos dates from around 1640. Two hundred years later, the tomb of the Egyptian vizier Rekhmire outside Luxor was painted with images of the *Keftiu* bringing gifts; the visitors were dressed as Cretans, with their kilts and semi-naked bodies, and the name *Keftiu* recalls the 'Caphtor' of the Bible, which was Crete. The frescoes are labelled: 'gifts from the princes of the land of *Keftiu* and of the isles which are in the midst of the sea'. In return the Cretans received ivory, stone jars containing perfume, gold and chariots in panels ready for assembly – these were not crude self-assembly kits but prestigious decorated vehicles.[25] Yet no flood of foreign artefacts overwhelmed Crete; nor were Minoan artistic styles impregnated with foreign models. The Minoans were confident of their own styles, represented by some of the most famous finds at Knossos: the bare-breasted snake goddess figurines; the elegantly shaped goblets decorated with octopus designs. Indeed, it was Minoan culture that was being exported: fine pottery produced on the Greek mainland displays the same patterns and shapes, including the octopus designs.

It was in this period that the Cretans abandoned their hieroglyphs; they recorded their assets in the syllabic Linear A script, less handsome than the hieroglyphs, but quicker to write. It seems that the language they used in these documents was Luvian, an Indo-European language related to Hittite, which was also spoken along the western coast of Anatolia and, if an inscribed seal discovered there is any indication, in twelfth-century Troy.[26] Luvian was widely used for official correspondence between courts, and its use in Crete does not mean that some or all of the Cretans were descended from Anatolian Luvians; the fundamental point is that the Minoans (unlike the Trojans) created a civilization that was not simply Anatolian.

IV

The rebuilding of the Cretan palaces coincided with a new burst of energy in the Cyclades, especially Akrotiri on Thera, between about 1550 and 1400 BC. Thera may have been inhabited by natives of the Cyclades, by Cretans or by representatives of all the many peoples who lived around the shores of the Aegean Sea. They came for the obsidian of Melos. Saffron was grown on Thera: a fresco shows the harvesting of crocuses. Yet it was also via Crete and its dependencies such as Akrotiri that the Aegean lands received supplies of more exotic objects – scarabs, faience figurines and beads from Egypt and Syria. Akrotiri grew into an important centre and imported plenty of Cretan pottery. The buildings in Akrotiri followed Cretan designs; the remarkable frescoes on their walls portrayed fleets of vessels manned by kilted Cretans arriving in a port whose houses reached two or three storeys. The ships appear to be ferrying warriors dressed in the style favoured on the Greek mainland; Thera functioned as a bridge between the high civilization of Crete and the developing culture of the Mycenaean Greeks on the mainland, showing that the Minoans had extended their commercial, and probably their political, control beyond Crete.[27]

The years from about 1525 BC onwards saw troubling signs that the stability of the region was quite literally under threat. Akrotiri stood on the edge of the caldera of a great, partly submerged volcano. Tremors multiplied; an earthquake led to the evacuation of Akrotiri in good time, since around 1500 BC the island of Thera was blown apart in what was one of the greatest volcanic eruptions in human history, leaving the crescent-shaped island of Thera poking above the waves.[28] Seismic changes occurred in Crete too, in both the literal and the metaphorical sense. Earthquakes caused severe damage at Knossos around 1525, ushering in a period during which parts of the palace may have been abandoned. After Thera exploded, a rain of ash blotted out the sun, perhaps for years, and then fell to earth, so that as much as 10 centimetres of ash fell on eastern Crete. The severe disruption of agriculture resulted in long-term famine. In the small Minoan palace at Arkhanes on Mount Jouktas, chambers previously used for other purposes became storerooms. The need to protect supplies was rendered greater by the devastating effect of the eruption on the entire region, so that it was not possible to rely on trade with neighbours to make up any shortfall. The sense of crisis is conveyed by a gruesome discovery in a building at Knossos known as the North House; around this time four or five children were killed, and their flesh was scraped from their bones in what was surely an act of ritual sacrifice and cannibalism.[29] The Minoans wished to propitiate gods and goddesses who seemed increasingly wrathful.

The paintings of emissaries reaching the court of Pharaoh at Luxor date from this period. They came, perhaps, in the hope that not ivory, apes and peacocks but the grain of the Nile Valley would be made available to Pharaoh's Cretan allies. The eruption of Thera weakened but did not destroy the economy and society of Crete, and Knossos retained wealth and influence, if on a reduced scale, for about fifty years. This disruption marked only the first stage in a much wider series of changes that transformed the political, economic, cultural and ethnic identity of the eastern, and possibly parts of the western, Mediterranean.

3

Merchants and Heroes,
1500 BC–1250 BC

I

In the years around 1500 BC Crete experienced not just massive economic changes but very significant political changes. The arrival of a Greek dynasty on the island occurred around the time that many settlements such as Arkhanes were abandoned; Knossos alone survived among the great palaces, and one Minoan site after another was destroyed. Earthquakes and fires have been blamed; so too have invaders from Greece. Since no one really knows who was to blame, clever attempts have been made to integrate the explanations with one another, and to argue that the Greeks took advantage of chaos within Crete to seize charge; or perhaps the Cretans were in need of strong leaders who would take charge, and turned to the Greeks. Unarguably, though, Minoan Crete was drawn into the developing world of the Mycenaean Greeks. An area which had been of relatively minor importance in the trade networks of the Early and Middle Bronze Age now became the focus of political and possibly commercial power in the Aegean: the great centres of Mycenaean culture and power were a line of settlements along the edges of eastern Greece, and a little way inland, from Iolkos (Volos) in the north, through Orchomenos, Thebes, Mycenae, Tiryns, and down to Pylos in the south-west. Early signs of success were already visible in the early fifteenth century, when the kings of Mycenae were laid to rest in Grave Circle A (as it has come to be known), their faces covered by masks of hammered gold that seem to copy their bearded features, and which suggest an attempt to imitate the infinitely grander gold masks of the buried Pharaohs.[1] Still, Mycenae 'rich in gold' retained its special role and reputation. By the twelfth century BC, if we are to

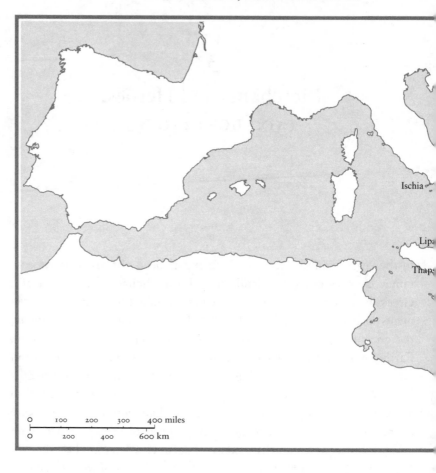

believe the evidence of Homer's 'Catalogue of Ships' (an archaic text incorporated in the *Iliad*), these statelets generally recognized as their leader the *wanax* or ruler of Mycenae.[2]

Descriptions of the Minoans merge imperceptibly with accounts of the Mycenaeans. In part this is because the imprint of Cretan art on that of the Greek mainland was so heavy; objects produced by the Mycenaeans, such as ceramics, only gradually acquired individuality as local potters tentatively developed their own shapes and designs. In part, too, the fuzzy boundary between Minoans and Mycenaeans is the result of the apparent Mycenaean conquest of Crete, and the occupation of Knossos by a Greek-speaking elite from the mainland; but even then the continuities are plain, and the writing system the Mycenaeans developed

to record their Greek dialect was an adaptation of the Linear A syllabic system created in Minoan Crete – the Linear B script triumphantly deciphered by Ventris and Chadwick in the 1950s.[3] At Knossos the Mycenaeans reconstituted, and at Pylos they developed, elaborate archives of clay tablets on which they recorded the tribute paid to their kings and gods by the subject population. Even in southern Greece, their religious cults were little different from those of the Minoans, to judge from the artefacts left behind: images on seals of goddesses and priests, a depiction on a cup and a panel of the sport or rite of bull-leaping (and even if these objects, though found in Greece, were really made in Crete, as some have argued, their presence in Greece reveals an interest in the bull rituals).[4] The names of gods and goddesses worshipped in classical Greece often betray pre-Greek roots, and these deities can sometimes be identified in the written records of the Mycenaeans. Trade, too, shows continuities, as Greek and Cretan goods were ferried to Rhodes, Syria and Troy, but longer voyages were now made deeper into the Mediterranean, as far as Sicily and Italy.

What distinguished the Mycenaeans was their warlike character. The Mycenaeans were good learners; they immersed themselves in the existing culture. The classical Greeks told how founding fathers such as Pelops had arrived in Greece from other lands, in his case Anatolia, though the ancestry of the Mycenaeans probably lay in the mountainous southern Balkans. They were great builders of fortifications. The lightly defended palaces characteristic of Minoan Crete became a rarity – Pylos on the south-western Peloponnese is the one significant example, and it almost certainly secured its protection by maintaining a large sea fleet – 'wooden walls', as the Delphic oracle would later describe the fleet of Athens. The sea had an important role in Mycenaean civilization; but so did land battles and sieges, represented in their art and even more dramatically by the massive retaining walls of the citadels of Mycenae and Tiryns. Parts of the walls of Mycenae were seven metres thick; at Tiryns narrow tunnels, which can still be visited, ran through the masonry, described by wondering classical writers as the work of Cyclopean giants. The Linear B tablets also reveal the importance to this warrior society of chariots, which were enumerated on the tablets, and which were described by Homer in archaic references to a vanished world full of bronze weapons and helmets made of boar's tusks.[5] Bronze weapons were buried, in quantity, in the tombs of their great war leaders, though they were also well acquainted with paper-thin arrow-heads made of obsidian brought to them from Melos and Lipari.

What the 'Mycenaeans' called themselves is an important question. 'Mycenaean' is a modern label for Bronze Age Greek civilization; in the fourteenth century BC, it would have conveyed only the sense of an inhabitant of the citadel and surrounding villages that made up the settlement (barely a town) of *Mukenai*. The plural form of this place-name, as of some others from this period (notably *Athenai*, Athens), may reflect the fact that these centres were conglomerations of villages.[6] Their rulers were a warrior caste, who by the fourteenth century BC lived very luxurious lives. They were buried not just with weapons but with gold and silver goblets, and with delicately inlaid ceremonial knives showing hunting scenes. When historians speak of 'Mycenaean trade' what they mean is the trade of those who lived within the political sphere of these early Greek warlords, though it is anybody's guess whether the merchants and peasants spoke Greek; many, in fact, must have been multilingual Cretans living in the Knossos and Phaistos of the Linear B tablets. References to neighbours known as *Ahhiyawa* in the Hittite archives, and to the *Ekwesh* in Egyptian documents, suggest that the name *Akhaiwoi*, in classical Greek *Akhaioi*, 'Achaeans', was used if not by themselves, at least by outside observers, who took them extremely seriously as a major regional power.[7] Building on the trading ties established by the Minoans, Mycenaean merchants maintained links with Cyprus, rich in copper (which continued to use a version of the Linear script right into classical times), as well as a trading presence on Rhodes, at Miletos on the Anatolian coast and on the Syrian coast. There may even have been some contact with the Black Sea, if the story of Jason's Argonauts has any historical basis. The 'Gelidonya wreck', a thirteenth-century shipwreck off the coast of southern Turkey, illuminates the trading world of the Mycenaeans. Most of the wreck was swept away by the waters, but its cargo was too heavy for the seas to shift: half a ton of big copper ingots, as well as bronze goods and seals that suggest the ship had visited Syria and Cyprus. Another slightly older wreck, found at Uluburun off the Turkish coast, contained even larger amounts of copper and, intriguingly, one tenth the amount of tin, the right proportion for the manufacture of bronze.[8]

One new feature of Mycenaean trade was the link to Italy, with which Minoan Crete did not engage. The first evidence of contact between the Greek mainland and Sicily may reach back as far as the seventeenth century BC, to judge from similarities between Greek ('Middle Helladic' period) pottery and that of eastern Sicily, where a handful of Middle Helladic pots have also been found. This does not necessarily indicate regular, direct contact, so much as spasmodic links through a series of intermediaries as these pots passed from Greece through the Ionian Sea, and then around the heel and toe of Italy to Sicily.[9] Hard evidence of regular contact comes a little later, when large numbers of Late Bronze Age ceramics were brought to Lipari, and large amounts of obsidian were sent back to Greece; the merchants also left behind faience beads, apparently of Egyptian origin, suggesting that a trade network had come into existence which encompassed great tracts of the eastern and central Mediterranean. By the time Knossos was in Mycenaean hands, however, obsidian was beginning to lose its attraction; new veins of copper and tin were being exploited across the Mediterranean and in Anatolia, and the search for metals was what now brought Mycenaean sailors as far as Ischia and its smaller neighbour Vivara, where they left their ceramics, before heading up the coasts of Tuscany (which offered tin) and Sardinia (where they left behind some copper ingots).[10] Representations of ships in the frescoes from Thera leave no doubt that shipping technology had made significant advances, with the use of sail as a supplement to oars and the building of larger vessels with higher bulwarks able to withstand more turbulent seas; to these must be added more detailed knowledge of the shoals, reefs and currents of the eastern and central Mediterranean, without which it was impossible to navigate between the Greek islands and towards Sicily. Coast-hugging routes still prevailed, for the passage taken by Mycenaean pottery traces a line linking the Dodecanese to the heel of Italy, and around the instep down to Sicily.

Close links to Italy resulted in the emergence of overseas trading-stations.[11] Although the Mycenaeans sent a great amount of pottery to Lipari, including large *pithoi*, there is no evidence that the Lipariots were under Mycenaean rule; but the inhabitants of Lipari did establish links with lands further north, as far as Luni in northern Tuscany.[12] The attraction of Lipari increasingly became not just its obsidian, but its role as a staging-post between the waters around Sicily and areas to the north. The *pithoi* were standard products, not objects of beauty, and they contained goods – oil, most likely, for that was one of the favoured exports of the Greek lands. An amber necklace found in a Lipari cemetery has been attributed to the northern Adriatic, not to the eastern Mediterranean. All this indicates that the Mycenaeans were the wealthiest but not the sole merchants who ventured across the waters of the central Mediterranean at this period. Meanwhile, the inhabitants of Lipari lived in wooden hut-like buildings clinging to the slopes of the island's volcano; for them, luxury consisted of amber and glass beads, not of gold and silver jewellery.

A settlement at Thapsos, an offshore island in eastern Sicily, offers evidence of a sophisticated, imported culture, Mycenaean in origin. The settlers created a grid-like town with streets up to four metres wide, spacious houses built round courtyards, and tombs full of Late Helladic wares from the Greek lands, suggesting 'a veritable foreign colony on the site'.[13] Indeed, the closest analogy to the layout of the houses in Thapsos is to be found at the other end of the Mycenaean world, on Cyprus, at Enkomi near Famagusta. It is almost as if a blueprint for a trading colony had been created and then transformed into reality at both ends of the Mycenaean world. Thapsos has yielded very many small perfume containers of Mycenaean origin.[14] For it was a centre of industry, specializing in the production of perfumed oils for an 'international' market. But Thapsos was not simply an offshoot of Mycenae. It produced plenty of coarse grey pottery in Sicilian styles, indicating that Thapsos contained a mixed population. In the same period, another Mycenaean settlement at Scoglio del Tonno near modern Taranto gave access to Adriatic goods, especially south Italian copper, and acted as a way-station for shipping bound for Sicily.[15] It was in the Mycenaean period, then, that the Mediterranean became significantly enlarged in the eyes of those who sailed across its surface.

II

Far more significant to the Mycenaean traders than the undeveloped west were the coasts of what are now Syria and Lebanon.[16] By the fourteenth century, traders were leaving large numbers of Mycenaean pots (in the style known as 'Late Helladic II') at Ugarit and Byblos, in Syria, and along the coast of Canaan at Gezer and Lachish. A Levantine trade network was coming into being, buoyant enough to sustain wealthy cities in which Aegean merchants mixed with Canaanites, Cypriots, Hittites, Egyptians and other residents and visitors.[17] The Levantine ports possessed even older links to the Nile Delta; the tomb of Kenamun at Egyptian Thebes, no longer extant, contained a wall-painting which showed the unloading of goods at an Egyptian port, under the oversight of Canaanite merchants, and these included textiles, purple dye (a speciality of the Levantine coast, made from the *murex* shellfish), oil, wine and cattle.

Ugarit was an important centre of trade, active since the third millennium; it fell for a time under Egyptian suzerainty, and one of its kings, Niqmadu, married into Pharaoh's family. The city supplied Egypt with cedar-wood from the mountains of Lebanon – supplies of timber within

Egypt were scanty. It acted as a bridge between the Mesopotamian world, from which it adapted its curious cuneiform alphabet, and the eastern Mediterranean lands – the Nile Delta, the Aegean, Crete (named as *Kabturi* in the Ugaritic tablets), and in particular Cyprus, 100 miles away, which functioned as a transit point to which goods from Egypt and the Greek lands were transferred.[18] Tablets in a Cypriot syllabic script have been found at Ugarit, suggesting that merchants from Cyprus lived in the city. The inhabitants of Ugarit were of very varied origins: there were mercenaries known to the Egyptians as *maryannu*, or 'young heroes', who came from Anatolia and the Greek world; there were administrators whose names are not local ones – the region around Ugarit was inhabited by speakers of Canaanite, the language out of which Phoenician and Hebrew evolved. A special official was appointed to look after the affairs of the foreign merchants, who were subject to restrictions on their right of residence and on their right to acquire houses in Ugarit. Minoan influence was felt in the art of Ugarit, to judge from an ivory box cover of the thirteenth century BC, portraying a goddess in a style that combines local features with those typical of Minoan artists.[19] Ugarit had a vibrant literary culture, and a number of the religious poems preserved on clay tablets display striking similarities to later Hebrew religious poetry. These contacts also had a revivifying effect on the art of the Aegean world. Once Knossos had been absorbed, the Mycenaean world had more to offer: the craft works of the Cretans, as well as items produced in Greece itself which now matched in mastery their Minoan models; the fine textiles of Crete too – the word *ri-no* which appears on the Linear B tablets is an early spelling of the classical Greek *linōn*, 'linen'. By now it is possible to think of little colonies of traders and settlers of Aegean origin, living in the port towns of the eastern Mediterranean; and along with the merchants and their goods, mercenaries arrived with their arms and armour. While trade was beginning to transform the character of the eastern Mediterranean, it was warfare that would alter it decisively, to the detriment of trade and the high cultures of these lands, ushering in (as will be seen) a long winter.

So far, more attention has been paid to impoverished Sicilian villagers than to the subjects of the Pharaohs, and their relative absence from the discussion needs an explanation. Following the unification of the marshlands of Lower Egypt with the long strip of naturally irrigated land bordering the Nile, the Egyptians created a complex, city-based society;

as early as the third millennium, with the building of the pyramids, they showed themselves able to organize massive labour forces. The works of art produced for the royal court, including magnificent objects made of gold and semi-precious stones, surpassed the finest works crafted in Minoan Crete. The influence of Egyptian art on the techniques, if not the subject-matter, of Cretan fresco painting is not in doubt; Egyptian objects were treasured in the early Greek world; the political influence of Egypt was felt along the shores of Canaan and Syria, notably at Byblos. The search for staple necessities such as tin, wood and copper prompted the Egyptians to extend their influence into and beyond Sinai. And yet, when thinking of Egyptian maritime trade, it is the links to the south that come to mind first of all: trading expeditions down the Red Sea towards the land of Punt, in the late second millennium, bringing luxuries such as ivory and ebony to the court of the Pharaohs.[20] Although some Pharaohs did build extensively in Lower Egypt – the Bible recalls the construction of a great store city named after Ramesses – the focus of their power in the period after about 1570 BC was generally Upper Egypt, though Ramesses (in ancient Egyptian, Piramesse) did serve as Egyptian capital at a point in the thirteenth century when the Pharaohs were actively pursuing their interests in Canaan and western Asia, and sought a base closer to their theatre of operations.

The year 1570 marks the expulsion of the Hyksos dynasty, who had ruled Lower and Middle Egypt for over a century. These rulers were later reviled as crude Asiatics (their exact identity remains a mystery); however, it was they who introduced important innovations into Egypt – chariots and bronze armour.[21] Whether they conquered Egypt in an armed invasion or trickled into the country and eventually seized power, they possessed a technological advantage over the native Egyptians; and they maintained ties with their neighbours in Syria and Crete, which was vital if they were to obtain the supplies they needed for their military machine. The end of Hyksos rule ushered in a period of extraordinary artistic vitality, best known from the discoveries in the tomb of Tut-ankhamun. Even when, around 1340 BC, the heretic Pharaoh Akhenaten built a new capital for his sun-god at Tell el-Amarna, he chose a site relatively close to the traditional centres of Pharaonic power in Upper Egypt. For the ancient Egyptians, the waters that mattered most were neither the Mediterranean nor the Red Sea, but the Nile; the Mediterranean was their horizon, and (though they drew on the resources of the eastern Mediterranean) Pharaonic Egypt cannot be described as a Mediterranean power, politically or commercially. It was only with the foundation of Alexandria in the fourth century BC that a major city was created on the shores of the Mediterranean, looking outwards to the Greek world. But in this period foreign merchants came to Egypt more often than Egyptian ones travelled overseas; the sailors depicted on reliefs at Sahure, dating to about 2400, are mostly Asiatic, and the design of sea-going vessels seems to have been copied from Levantine models – some may have been able to navigate upriver as well, functioning as warships as well as trading vessels. The overall impression is that the Egyptians relied on outside agents to build, manage and sail their ships, at least across the Mediterranean.[22]

The term 'Great Green' appears in Egyptian texts of this period, but it was used for a number of waters – Lake Fayyum was one, the Nile another; occasionally it was used to describe the Red Sea. In the second half of the second millennium BC the term Y-m was very occasionally used for the sea, including the Mediterranean, and the word itself was of Semitic origin (*yam* is 'sea' in Hebrew). The Mediterranean did not have such significance for them that it was assigned its own distinctive name.[23] There were ports in the Delta which were visited by shipping bound to and from Syria, such as Tjaru (Tell Hebua) at the end of the eastern arm of the Delta; it had been used by the Hyksos and was then rebuilt by the new rulers of the Eighteenth Dynasty. In the fifteenth century BC, under Thutmose IV, Tjaru was the seat of a governor who was also given the title 'royal messenger in all foreign lands', and one of his responsibilities was the exploitation of turquoise mines in the Sinai desert. Turquoise adorns much Egyptian jewellery of this period. But Tjaru also functioned as a base for trade with the outside world, as is demonstrated by finds of pottery originating in Syria and Cyprus, lands rich in the timber the Egyptians craved. More important, though, was Avaris, also in the eastern Delta. As early as the eighteenth century BC the population included many settlers of Canaanite origin, including soldiers, sailors and artisans. The Hyksos made it into their capital, and under their rule it occupied a space measuring over 200 square kilometres. The end of Hyksos rule did not spell the end of Avaris.[24] The palace constructed there after the fall of the Hyksos was decorated with frescoes in the Cretan style, further evidence of the ties between the *Keftiu* of Knossos and the court of the Pharaohs.[25]

Another port, one which grew in importance, was Tanis; from here an Egyptian emissary from Karnak in the deep south was sent on a frustrating mission to the Canaanite king of Byblos in the early eleventh century. His task was to secure a supply of timber, to be used to rebuild a river boat dedicated to the high god Amun; he was 'Elder of the Portal' or senior administrator of the god's temple. This man, Wenamun, left a report of his journey of which a copy on papyrus survived in an Egyptian tomb; there he described setting out from Tanis on 20 April 1075.[26] From the beginning he faced problems: the Nile Delta was to all intents independent of the weak Pharaoh Ramesses XI, and the local ruler, Smendes, did not feel it was worth the trouble of commissioning a ship to take Wenamun to Byblos, so he placed him on board the vessel operated by a local sea captain named Mengebet, who was about to set out on a trading expedition with a Syrian crew. The route taken followed the coastline, and they put in at Dor, south of present-day Haifa; this was a centre of the so-called Tjekker, one of the 'Sea Peoples' who will be discussed shortly.[27] There the governor was polite (he gave Wenamun bread, wine and meat). However, a sailor in Mengebet's crew was tempted by the fat treasure Wenamun had brought with him to pay for the timber: this consisted of several pounds' weight of silver and some golden vessels weighing over one pound. He carried all Wenamun's assets away with him, and disappeared. Wenamun went to the governor to complain; of course, the governor said, if the thief had been a man of Dor, he would have indemnified Wenamun, but all he could do was launch an investigation. This investigation lasted nine exasperating days, but nothing was found, and Wenamun decided his only option was to continue his journey northwards. On arriving at Byblos he managed to find nearly the amount of silver he had lost, squirrelled away on Mengebet's ship; this was evidently someone else's property, but he ungraciously insisted he would keep it until the owners of the boat recompensed him for the theft of his own goods by one of their crewmen.

The ruler of Byblos, Zekerbaal, was even more unhelpful than that of Dor. He would not receive Wenamun, whose messages sent up from the port received the terse reply that he should go away; 'the chief of Byblos sent to me saying, "Get out of my harbour!"'[28] This was repeated day after day, for twenty-nine days. September arrived; Wenamun was worried that he would not be able to leave until sailings resumed in the spring (so evidently there was a close season, which applied even to coast-hugging journeys along the coast of Canaan). Later on, the king reminded Wenamun that he had once kept similar emissaries waiting for seventeen years! Wenamun decided to reserve space on a ship that was ready to leave, for Mengebet had moved on to his next port of call and had left him behind. And then suddenly, while the royal court was sacrificing to Baal, one of the king's courtiers experienced a vision, and in the fervour of the moment the excited king decided that he must see the messenger of the Egyptian high-god Amun. This, at least, was the official explanation, but Wenamun thought the aim was to separate him from his property, miss his sailing, and pillage his silver while he was in the royal presence. Still, Wenamun had little choice; the papyrus describes how he entered the king's upper chamber, where Zekerbaal sat, 'and when he turned his back against the window, the waves of the great sea of Syria were breaking against the rear of his head'.[29] The king showed no politeness to Pharaoh nor to the high priest of Amun; he berated Wenamun for not being able to produce his credentials, which had been left behind at Tanis, and he dismissed Egyptian sailors as incompetent fools by comparison with his fellow-Syrians. The king insisted that twenty ships of Byblos traded with Egypt, and as many as fifty ships of Sidon, though Wenamun expressed the official Egyptian view that, by trading with Egypt, they were not really foreign vessels but ships sailing under the protection of Pharaoh. Thus there were constant attempts to score points, and the king clearly relished the opportunity to insult Egypt and its rulers at a time when they were weak. He admitted that earlier kings had supplied wood just as requested, but he expected payment; he ordered the accounts of the kingdom to be brought to him – an interesting sign of the sophistication of administration – and he proved from the accounts that the Egyptians had sent large quantities of silver in the past.[30] Wenamun lost his temper and began to berate the king for his disrespect to the great land of Egypt and to the king of the gods.

Wenamun knew, though, that angry words would achieve nothing, and sent a message to Egypt asking for handsome gifts for Zekerbaal. The Egyptians took his request seriously. They sent a mixture of luxury items such as gold and silver vases and supplies of basic materials such as ox-hides, linen, fish, lentils, rope and 500 rolls of papyrus, on which Zekerbaal would be able to record yet more financial accounts.[31] Still, what Wenamun was asking for was not to be given lightly. The king assigned 300 men and as many oxen to fell and move the timber. Zekerbaal processed down to the shore to watch it being loaded, and sent Wena-mun signs of his new goodwill: wine, a sheep and a female Egyptian singer to console him. Wenamun was allowed to depart on a ship manned by sailors from Byblos. He escaped pirates from Dor who tried to capture his vessel, but then it was driven by storms to Cyprus, where the inhabitants pounced upon him, and he was only saved from death by the kindly queen.[32] The surviving text does not go further. However, the whole tale has the flavour of a series of excuses for a mission that ended in failure – it is far from clear whether the wood arrived in Egypt. Of course, this account does not portray everyday trading contacts across the eastern Mediterranean; but it is extraordinarily precious as the first account of a trading voyage, and of the political difficulties which would ever after ensnare those who tried to conduct business at the courts of foreign rulers.

The Egyptians were the wealthiest power in the region, but they had serious rivals. The emergence of the Hittite empire in central Anatolia, with its formidable metal resources, threatened Egyptian interests in Syria. Ramesses II aimed to recover influence in the region, waning since the troubled reign of the heretic Pharaoh Akhenaten; the Hittites responded by mobilizing their allies, who included vassals in western Asia such as the Lycians and the Dardanians (a term Homer later used for the Trojans). Thousands of chariots were committed to battle at Kadesh in July 1274; although Ramesses, typically, claimed the contest as a great Egyptian victory, even so boastful a Pharaoh could not hide the massive destruction on both sides, for the Hittites had begun the battle by wiping out large segments of the Egyptian army.[33] By 1258 both sides at last admitted that the outcome had been at best a draw, and a treaty between them defined the boundaries of their spheres of influence in Syria, drawing a line near Damascus and creating half a century of stability. However, the battle of Kadesh can be seen as the beginning of a cataclysmic cycle of interlocked events, including the fall of Troy (sup-posedly ninety years later), the destruction of the Mycenaean strongholds and, not least, the arrival of the mysterious 'Sea Peoples'.

4

Sea Peoples and Land Peoples,
1250 BC–1100 BC

I

Both the fall of Troy and the Sea Peoples have been the subject of a vast literature. They were part of a common series of developments that affected the entire eastern Mediterranean and possibly the western Mediterranean too. Troy had been transformed at the end of the eighteenth century BC with the building of the most magnificent of the cities to stand on the hill of Hisarlık: Troy VI, which lasted, with many minor reconstructions, into the thirteenth century BC. The citadel walls were nine metres thick, or more; there were great gates and a massive watchtower, a memory of which may have survived to inspire Homer; there were big houses on two floors, with courtyards. The citadel was the home of an elite that lived in some style, though without the lavish accoutrements of their contemporaries in Mycenae, Pylos or Knossos.[1] Archaeological investigation of the plain beneath which then gave directly on to the seashore suggests the existence of a lower town about ten times the size of the citadel, or around 200 square kilometres, roughly the size of the Hyksos capital at Avaris.[2] One source of wealth was horses, whose bones begin to appear at this stage; Homer's Trojans were famous 'horse-tamers', *hippodamoi*, and even if he chose this word to fit his metre, it matches the archaeological evidence with some precision. In an age when great empires were investing in chariots, and sending hundreds of them to perdition at the battle of Kadesh (or, according to the Bible, in the depths of the Red Sea), horse-tamers were certainly in demand.

Opinion divided early on the identity of the Trojans. Claiming descent from Troy, the ancient Romans knew for sure that they were not

just a branch of the Greek people. Homer, though, made them speak Greek. The best chance of an answer comes from their pottery. The pottery of Troy is not just Trojan; it belongs to a wider culture that spread across parts of Anatolia. The Trojans acquired a little Helladic pottery from Greek lands, but only 1 per cent of the finds from Troy VI and VIIa consists of Mycenaean pottery (including local imitations). All the evidence suggests that they were members of one of the peoples who had developed on the outer edges of the Hittite world and spoke a language close to Hittite, Luvian, the language of the peoples who lived along the western flank of Anatolia and, as has been seen, possibly the language of the Linear A tablets from Crete.[3] The Hittite archives leave no doubt that they corresponded with the Hittite king, but none of their own correspondence has survived; only one minute written text has been found, a seal in Luvian hieroglyphs from the level of Troy VIIb (late twelfth century, though the seal itself may be older); its wording indicates that it belonged to a scribe and his wife.[4] Troy was an outpost not of Mycenae but of the Hittite world. Globally, it was not a place of enormous consequence; regionally, however, it occupied a commanding position on the trade routes of the northern Aegean, and for this reason it became a desirable prize.[5]

In the thirteenth century the Hittite rulers became increasingly anxious to maintain some degree of influence on the Mediterranean shores of Anatolia. They aimed to outflank the Egyptians, with whom they were competing for control of northern Syria; but they were also wary of other rivals, the kings of Ahhiyawa, that is, the high kings of Mycenae. Troy itself was a little out of the way, but its military aid could be useful, and it has been seen that the aid of western Asiatic vassals was summoned at Kadesh. Flashpoints between the Ahhiyawans and the Hittites included Milawanda or Miletos, once a centre of Minoan trade and now, at least intermittently, a Mycenaean ally on the coast of Asia Minor. Infuriated by this alliance, the Hittites descended on the city in 1320 BC and destroyed it.[6] The coast of Asia Minor was thus a troubled frontier zone, a region where allegiances changed back and forth and where Mycenaean warriors liked to interfere.

One source of trouble was a *condottiere* of unknown origin named Piyamaradu. Around 1250 BC he was the subject of a letter of complaint from the Hittite ruler to the king of Ahhiyawa, whom he now regarded as a friend following earlier disagreement about who should exercise influence over a place called Wilusa, a name that recalls the alternative Greek name for Troy, Ilios, or, originally, Wilios.[7] Evidently, the coastline of Asia Minor was divided among a bewildering mass of petty kings who were sometimes loyal to the Hittites but occasionally sheltered under the protection of the king of Ahhiyawa: there was Alaksandu, king of Wilusa, whose name sounds suspiciously similar to Alexander (Alexandros), the alternative name given for Helen's seducer Paris. Another *condottiere* who possessed a hundred chariots and many foot-soldiers was the 'man of Ahhiya' Attarssiya, whose name is strikingly similar to that of the father of Agamemnon and Menelaus, Atreus; he seems to have been aiming his small army at Cyprus, whose ownership was a matter of interest to both the Egyptians and the Hittites.[8] Neither of these names is proof of Homer's veracity; but somewhere there was a store of Anatolian names on which he or earlier tellers of tales drew. Having in the past opposed the Hittites, King Alaksandu of Wilusa entered into a treaty with them; Wilusa was one of the four lands of Assuwa, whose rulers often adopted different policies towards the Hittites and, by extension, towards the Mycenaeans, but which had supplied armies at Kadesh. Another entity within the region of Assuwa bore the name Taruisa, a name reminiscent of Troy.[9] Everything about the description of Assuwa indicates that it lay in the far west of Anatolia; and it is clear that both Wilusa and Taruisa stood near the site of Ilios/Troy. A poem from the Hittite capital, written in Luvian in the sixteenth century BC, refers to 'steep Wilusa'; and the same epithet was used by Homer to describe Ilios. Possibly Wilusa and Taruisa were one city or two neighbouring cities that at some stage shared a ruler, rather as Homer's Agamemnon was king of Argos as well as Mycenae; but Hisarlık was certainly Homer's *Ilios* and Virgil's *Troia*.

There is no reason to doubt that the Mycenaeans and the Anatolians fought wars for the possession of the lands and towns of western Asia Minor. The Trojan War was a later memory of these conflicts, which were collapsed into a single campaign aimed at one of several cities targeted by the Greeks. While some historians have stressed the implausibility of a ten-year siege, the reality was that this was not a war of one season or of ten but of many dozens of seasons, fought intermittently and punctuated by periods of peace recorded in the Hittite diplomatic correspondence. Generally, it was not a war between the great kings of Mycenae and of the Hittites, for much of the fighting was conducted by ambitious mercenary captains, who changed sides to secure their best advantage; there is no reason to suppose they were loyal to their own ethnic group. It was low-level, endemic conflict; but occasionally it resulted in major clashes, as when the Hittites felt obliged to assert their dominion over Miletos. The prosperity of Ilios/Troy was not undermined by these troubles; indeed, Troy VI risked drawing the attention of greedy conquerors because it sat astride the trade routes running from the Mediterranean into Anatolia, carrying metals, textiles and, very importantly, horses.

Troy VI was destroyed by another agency than human greed. Troy stands in a zone prone to violent earthquakes. In about 1250 BC, the south walls were thrown outwards and part of the east wall collapsed completely, as a powerful earthquake tore the city to pieces. Debris from the collapse of the buildings reached a depth, in some places, of a metre and a half.[10] The main circuit did, however, remain intact.[11] Whatever happened to the lower town, of which so little is known, it is plain that after these events the old elite no longer inhabited grand houses in the upper town. New houses were built atop the rubble of Troy VI, packed closer together to support a larger population at least within the citadel, and within these houses the Trojans sank storage vessels (pithoi), as they had never done in the past; so they were conscious of the need to build up their stocks in what seem to have been times of adversity. The decline in imports of Mycenaean pottery shows that trade connections had become weaker. Troy had passed its peak. But it was not alone. Mycenae was in difficulties; the lower town suffered an attack around 1250, and the citadel had to be strengthened; a wall was built across the isthmus of Corinth in the hope of keeping out the attackers, though whether these attackers were the kings of other cities within the Mycenaean world or invaders from outside is unclear.[12] By the end of the thirteenth century, watchtowers had been built along the coasts to alert the palace dwellers to invaders; even so, most of the great Mycenaean centres, including Tiryns and Pylos, had been ravaged by about 1200. At Pylos, sacrifices were offered to the gods as disaster loomed; a man and a woman mentioned on the Linear B tablets among a list of sacrificial beasts were probably intended for human sacrifice (a practice remembered in the Greek legend of Agamemnon and Iphigeneia). The damage reached the coasts of the Levant: the king of Ugarit sent his troops to serve the Hittites, and while they were away foreign fleets mustered off the Syrian coast; the king wrote a desperate letter on a clay tablet to warn his ally the king of Cyprus, but the letter was never sent – over 3,000 years later, it was found still waiting to be baked in the kiln, and within days or possibly hours the great trading centre at Ugarit was demolished, never to rise again.[13] The town of Alalakh, which lay a little way inland, close to the modern Turkish–Syrian border, was destroyed in 1194; the city never recovered, but its port, at al-Mina, was refounded, and Mycenaean wares have been found there from before and after the destruction of the mother-city.[14] Tossed between pro-Hittite and pro-Egyptian factions, the kingdom of Alalakh was always at political risk. The Hittite capital deep in the Anatolian interior at Boğazköy was destroyed at the same period, though this may have been the result of internal crises. Still, collapse at the centre meant that the Hittites were incapable of protecting their Mediterranean dependencies. And, despite the warnings from Ugarit, Cyprus suffered terribly; its towns were demolished – this was followed by the arrival of Greek refugees or invaders, bringing their archaic linear script and an early form of Greek. On Crete, part of the population moved inland to inaccessible points high above the island, at Karphi and Vrokastro.

And then, around the date assigned by the classical author Eratosthenes to the fall of Troy (1184), Troy was destroyed again, and this time the city went up in flames; the skeleton of one unfortunate Trojan who was trying to flee has been found beneath the debris of Troy VIIa.[15] Thus, if the Greeks did destroy Troy at this stage, their victory occurred when their own towns had also passed the peak of their prosperity. Rather than a clash between Mycenae rich in gold and the wealthy horse-tamers of Troy, the fall of Troy VIIa was a battle between declining powers. Nor can it be proved that the destroyers were the Greeks acting together under their Great King or *wanax* Agamemnon; it is just as probable that the destroyers were a mixed rabble of exiles and mercenaries of Greek and other origins. They could have been the people who also attacked Mycenae and Pylos, or armed refugees from Mycenae and Pylos. Seen from this perspective, the 'fall of Troy' was a gradual process, beginning with the wars between the Hittites and their surrogates and the Greeks and theirs; the calamity of the destruction of Troy VI weakened the capacity of the city to resist, even, apparently, to feed itself (witness the *pithoi*); the seizure of the citadel around 1184 left further massive damage; and thereafter Troy entered into a steady decline. That raises fundamental questions about what was happening in the eastern Mediterranean at this time: whether the disruptions that occurred during the Late Bronze Age marked a sharp break with the past, or whether decline, which undoubtedly occurred, was more gradual. The evidence from Crete and Troy of greater efforts to store food hints at frequent famines, setting peoples on the march towards lands richer in supplies. Moreover, 'decline' can mean many things: the loss of political unity as great empires dissolved; a reduction in trade as demand withered; a lowering of the standard of living not just among the political elite but across most of society. Once again the question revolves around invaders of uncertain identity and takes us to the boundaries between legend and history.

II

This was a period when talented soldiers could make careers in the armies that were fighting for control of the lands bordering the eastern Mediterranean; if no one wanted their services, they could turn themselves into proto-Viking raiders and seize what they wanted. In an inscription found at Tanis, Ramesses II claimed to have destroyed people known as the Shardana who had pounced on Egypt out of the sea, but before long they were integrated into his armies, and they were present at the great battle of Kadesh in 1274. In one papyrus, from 1189 BC, Ramesses III claimed grandiloquently to have turned those who raided his kingdom into ashes, and then admitted that he had resettled vast numbers of them in strongholds.[16] Excavation finds indicate that some Shardana were directed to the Bay of Acre, where they guarded the royal road through Canaan on Pharaoh's behalf. They were poachers turned gamekeepers. The Shardana raiders were skilled with sword and spear; they wore distinctive horned helmets.[17] While a welcome was extended to tough Shardana warriors, other groups were viewed with more suspicion: the *apiru* or *habiru* were seen as troublesome desert wanderers, occasionally employable as mercenaries; their name is possibly cognate with the term 'Hebrew', but it was not applied just to one small Semitic nation.[18] It is no surprise that poorer peoples – nomads, refugees, exiles – were attracted by the wealth of Egypt and sought to acquire a share of it. Their desperation to do so was enhanced by the deteriorating economic conditions in the Late Bronze Age Mediterranean; it would be surprising if Cretans and Anatolians had not gone looking for land, employment and new opportunities.

From the late thirteenth to the mid-twelfth century BC, at the time that Troy VI and VIIa were destroyed, Lower Egypt was beset by enemies from many directions. The first threat came from the lands of the western peoples. A great multitude of Libu, or Libyans, led by their king, Meryry, moved eastwards in the late thirteenth century, bringing with them whole families, flocks of animals, their gold, silver and furniture: 'they spend their day roaming the land and fighting to fill their bellies daily; they have come to Egypt to seek food for their mouths', as Pharaoh Merneptah proclaimed in a long inscription preserved in the temple at Karnak. They came with their North African allies the Meshwesh and with foreign mercenaries. They had arrived on the edges of the richest country in the world, and they intended to stay; if the Egyptians would not welcome them, they would force themselves into their kingdom. This was more than Merneptah could tolerate. In April 1220 his troops fought a lengthy and tough battle against the Libyans and their allies in the western Delta region; in the end King Meryry was soundly defeated and fled back to his homeland, 'leaving his bow and quiver and sandals on the ground behind him'. Merneptah claimed to have killed over 6,000 Libyans, and at least half that number of their allies.[19] Yet this was only the beginning of a cycle of invasions which were not so much raids as attempted migrations; within a few decades other groups would arrive with their ox-carts, this time from the east. The Sea Peoples who have attracted so much attention from historians of this period were only one element in much wider and larger population movements in which long-term migrants outnumbered opportunistic mercenaries, and in which Land Peoples outnumbered Sea Peoples.

The Libyans knew where to turn for help, and King Meryry secured the services of several foreign contingents from 'the countries of the sea', to cite one inscription. One group who arrived was the Lukka, Anatolians who gave their name to Lycia (though this does not prove they had already settled in that precise area); they had been making a nuisance of themselves as pirates and soldiers since at least the fourteenth century. There were some Shardana as well as other peoples: the Egyptians claimed that 2,201 Ekwesh, 722 Tursha and 200 Shekelesh died in the battle with Meryry.[20] Merneptah was now confident that he had solved the region's problems, and proudly recorded his violent pacification not just of the territory stretching west to Libya but of lands and peoples to the east, asserting that 'Israel is desolated and has no seed' (the first reference to Israel in an Egyptian document, and, he clearly hoped, the last); his uncompromising peace encompassed the land of Canaan as well, which he had 'plundered with every ill'; he had taken control of Ashkelon and Gezer. At last, he said,

> men can walk the roads at any pace without fear. The fortresses stand open and the wells are accessible to all travellers. The walls and the battlements sleep peacefully in the sunshine till their guards wake up. The police lie stretched out asleep. The desert frontier-guards are among the meadows where they like to be.[21]

He certainly employed an able propagandist. But there is no reason to believe his boast about a general peace, any more than his boast about Israel. Whatever peace he had achieved lasted only a very short while. Within thirty years, in 1182 BC, Pharaoh Ramesses III faced a new invasion from the west, but this time the Libyans could not muster their northern allies from across the sea. Still, the invading army was even more formidable than in the days of Merneptah: if the Egyptians slew 12,535 of the enemy, as they claimed, the Libyan army may well have exceeded 30,000 men, excluding dependants.[22] Egyptian reliefs portray a campaign in which some invaders are now part of the Egyptian army: there are Shardana, with their horned helmets; soldiers with feathered head-dresses which recall designs on small objects from twelfth-century Cyprus; kilted soldiers whose garments look similar to those worn by the Shekelesh on carvings elsewhere.[23]

This was, if Ramesses is to be believed, a great victory; but peace remained elusive: the northern peoples mobilized, in about 1179 BC (and the Libyans attacked again in 1176, losing over 2,175 Meshwesh warriors). A lengthy inscription from the temple at Medinet Habu set out the Egyptian version of events; what is remarkable is the picture of convulsions taking place not just on the Mediterranean shores of Egypt but across a much wider region:

> the foreign countries made a conspiracy in their islands. All at once the lands were on the move, scattered in war. No country could stand before their arms. Hatti, Kode, Carchemish, Arzawa and Alasiya [Cyprus] were cut off.

They turned the land into a desert, so that it was 'like that which has never come into being', and then from Syria and Canaan they advanced on Egypt itself.[24] The Egyptians were right to insist that this plague affected not just themselves but their old foes the Hittites, whose land-based empire disintegrated at this point. The peoples who invaded Egypt were the Peleshet, the Tjekker, the Shekelesh, the Denyen and the Weshesh, all united together; 'they laid their hands upon the lands to the entire circuit of the earth'. The image is intended to recall an invasion of locusts. The invaders came by both land and sea, and so they had to be confronted on the Mediterranean shores of Egypt and on its eastern frontier. The land battle brought the Egyptians and their Shardana auxiliaries face to face with charioteers mounted in Hittite style (three warriors to a vehicle); the invaders were thus capable of mobilizing considerable resources, including large numbers of expensive horses. Like the Libyans, they were also accompanied by women and children, travelling in large ox-carts.

Those who came by sea found themselves confronted with stockades and burning pyres: 'they were dragged ashore, hemmed in and flung down on the beach'.[25] Yet elsewhere in the Egyptian accounts the invaders are seen entering the mouths of the river channels running through the Delta; and there were some warships in Egyptian service which aimed to drive the attackers towards the shore, where they could be trapped in range of Egyptian archers. The Egyptian ships appear from the reliefs to be adapted river vessels, while the invaders' boats are similar to those of Syrian traders; all the vessels carry sails, though they would have depended on a combination of sail and oar-power. The ships of the Sea Peoples were decorated at bow and stern with birds' heads, a feature which can be seen on a twelfth-century Mycenaean pot from the island of Skyros. A persistent feature was attributed to the Peleshet, and sometimes to the Denyen, Tjekker and Shekelesh: as well as kilts, the Peleshet wore helmets topped with what look like feathers, somewhat like high crowns. The strength of the invaders – defeat in Egypt notwithstanding – came not from their navies but from their armies: they were by and large infantry troops, fighting with javelins and thrusting swords, and these weapons proved more efficient on the battlefield than the expensive but often fragile chariots of the Hittites and Egyptians. The round shields of the Shardana were well suited for close combat. The invaders did not yet have iron weapons, although the Hittites had already begun to produce iron goods in a small way. What they had was discipline, determination and (literally) a cutting edge. An image of these fighting men is preserved on a late Mycenaean vase, known as the Warrior Vase, which shows a squad of soldiers equipped with javelins, round shields, greaves and kilts; on their heads are the horned helmets typical of the Shardana and their allies.[26] Pharaoh showed some wisdom in employing Shardana, because it meant that he had the means to resist invaders with similar weapons and battle tactics.

If it were possible to identify the peoples mentioned in the Egyptian inscriptions and papyri, a much clearer idea of the turmoil in the Mediterranean could be gained. Modern sceptics fly from any attempt to identify the peoples mentioned in the documents, arguing (as with the Ahhiyawa in the Hittite documents) that a few consonants are not sufficient evidence, and that names in any case migrate even more easily than peoples.[27] But the number of similarities between the names in the Egyptian records and those known from Homer, the Bible and other later sources is too great for haphazard coincidence: one or two similarities might be coincidence, but more than half a dozen constitute evidence. The Denyen recall the *Danawoi* (*Danaoi*, Danaans), a term Homer sometimes used for the Greeks encamped at Troy; they also recall the Danites, a maritime people living near Jaffa, according to the books of Joshua and Judges, who evidently joined the covenant of Israel after the other eleven tribes.[28] These peoples scattered; in the ninth century there was a 'king of the Dannuniyim' at Karatepe in southern Turkey.[29] It has already been seen that we encounter *D-r-d-n-y*, Dardanians, on Egyptian inscriptions. The Tjekker sound similar to the Teucrians, Anatolian neighbours of the Dardanians, some of whom settled on the coast of what is now northern Israel, where Wenamun encountered them. Some scholars have seized on rough similarities in sound to assign Meryry's allies the Shekelesh to Sicily, the Ekwesh to Ahhiyawa, making them into Mycenaeans, and the Tursha (*T-r-s-w*) to Tuscany, assuming an identity with the *Tyrsenoi* or Etruscans five centuries later. These labels described peoples, tribes or places of origin, but by the time they had been rendered into hieroglyphics they lost their vowel sounds, and they are very difficult to reconstruct.[30] The overall impression is that by 1200 the eastern Mediterranean was being plagued by fluid and unstable alliances of pirates and mercenaries, able occasionally to form large enough navies and armies to pillage centres such as Pylos and Ugarit, possibly, indeed, to conduct a campaign against Troy which resulted in the fall of Troy VIIa. Sometimes they must have been attacking their own homeland, from which (to judge from later Greek legends) many a hero had been exiled. Sometimes the sack of their homeland led to an exodus of fighters who sought to recover their fortunes by attacking Cyprus, Ugarit or even the Nile Delta. Among them it is possible to identify the people of Taruisa, the area next to or fused with Wilusa. For that, and not the much later Etruscans, best explains the name Tursha; in other words, the Trojans were both Sea Peoples and victims of the Sea Peoples.

III

Egypt resisted conquest; but the Pharaohs lost control of the Nile Delta, which, as can be seen from Wenamun's tale, led a separate existence in the eleventh century under autonomous rulers who paid no more than lip-service to their suzerain lords in Upper Egypt. Further north, the events of around 1200 did not lead to an immediate and total collapse of Mycenaean cultural life, though if the Greek legends have any foundation, they did cause enormous political damage. In fact, there were places that escaped destruction. The most important was Athens: although it was not a town of the first rank in Mycenaean times, the acropolis was still inhabited, and burials continued in the Kerameikos cemetery down below; possibly it escaped destruction because of its natural defences – not just the steep sides of the citadel, topped with 'Cyclopean' walls, but a water supply which could help it withstand a long siege.[31] Even Mycenae was still inhabited for a while after the destruction of its larger buildings. In northern Greece, within Thessaly, and on several Aegean islands, conditions remained peaceful; Rhodes was the focal point of a trade route taking the good-quality 'Late Helladic IIIC' pottery of the Dodecanese to Greece, southern Italy and Syria; traditional designs, such as the octopus motif, were still strongly favoured. Emborio on Chios flourished as a centre of Mycenaean trade. The experience of Troy was very similar: after the destruction of Troy VIIa, a new, though less luxurious, city emerged.

The fact that an area in the north of Greece remained untouched by destruction suggests that those who attacked the great centres came from the south, across the sea; but the fact that not all the islands were affected suggests an invasion from the north. Greek tradition noted the remarkable survival of Athens in the face of an invasion from the north by Dorian Greeks. Since the Dorians were supposedly the ancestors of their Spartan rivals, the Athenians laid more emphasis on this tradition than the archaeological evidence allows. The leading authority on the end of the Mycenaean age commented: 'there should in this case, however, be evidence not only of invasion but also of invaders'.[32] He could find only two innovations: the cut-and-thrust sword and a type of safety-pin with a curved front known as the violin-bow fibula. The argument that new swords were arriving in the eastern Mediterranean may well explain the success of conquering forces pitted against Troy, Mycenae or the Syrian coastal towns; but it does not prove a massive invasion had occurred, and the Mycenaeans had access to the same swords. As for the safety-pins, very similar changes in design took place across the central and eastern Mediterranean in this period, and reflect changes in taste and perhaps greater skill in production, as far west as Sicily. And yet the evidence of dialect seems clear enough. Doric Greek dialects penetrated the Peloponnese. Meanwhile, refugees from Mycenaean Greece settled in Cyprus, marking the first injection of a substantial Greek population into the island and bringing their dialect (which otherwise survived only in remote Arcadia) with them. The philological evidence is for once neatly supported by the evidence of archaeology, for they carried with them the pottery styles of the area round Mycenae, which they long perpetuated, and a fashion for chamber tombs à la grecque.[33]

Yet the old culture was being transformed. The evidence is not easy to read, and one can debate whether the change from family chamber tombs to single or double slab-lined tombs ('cist tombs') betokened a change in population, a change in fashion or a lack of resources which made it impossible to organize a labour force able to build a family mausoleum. The signs that old skills were being lost can also be read in the pottery, which archaeologists class pejoratively as 'Sub-Mycenaean'. The Mycenaean civilization of the Aegean region was eventually affected too, and before 1000 the trading centres at Miletos and Emborio were wrecked; quantities of goods moving across the eastern Mediterranean were declining sharply, and what movement there was suffered constant harassment from pirates, known in later Greek tradition as 'Tyrsenians'. Although attention inevitably focuses on the eastern Mediterranean at this crucial moment, there is also evidence of a hiatus in the central Mediterranean. In Sicily, in the mid-thirteenth century BC, 'a time of war and fear began'; but the threat came from the Italian mainland, and not from distant Sea Peoples.[34] Judging from the finds of Late Helladic pottery in Sicily, contact with Greece began to decline around 1200 BC and may have come to an end by 1050 BC.[35]

When they came, the land migrations into southern Greece were not coordinated in the way that the raids on Egypt were. They were probably not even invasions, in the sense of hostile armed conquests, so much as a slow but continuous trickle of northern Greeks, living in and around modern Epeiros and Albania. They confirmed and consolidated a trend towards a simpler, more basic existence. But such an existence greatly lessened the role of the Greek lands in what remained of the trade of the Mediterranean world. Contacts did continue: by the eleventh century Athens, which was the major centre of the production of pottery in the linear 'proto-Geometric' style, sent its goods across the Aegean, and this pottery, some of it quite sophisticated in style and technique, has been found at Miletos (now reoccupied) and at Old Smyrna (a new settlement). Its presence there is an indication that Greeks were beginning to recreate a trading network linking Asia Minor to the Greek mainland by sea, out of which the vibrant civilization of Greek Ionia would emerge in the eighth century.

IV

A papyrus known as the Onomastikon of Amenope, discovered at the end of the nineteenth century, helpfully places the Peleshet in southern Palestine, the Tjekker in the middle (confirmed by Wenamun) and the Shardana in the north, according well with the archaeological evidence – Sea Peoples inhabited Acre, and Acre was possibly one of the bases set up by the Egyptians, using mercenary garrisons.[36] Their ties to this region were so intense that one group, the Peleshet, gave their name to the area. The word 'Peleshet', like the Ethiopian Semitic word 'Falasha' used of the Ethiopian Jews, signifies 'foreigner' or 'wanderer'; they became, in biblical Hebrew, *Pelishtim*; in Greek their land became *Palaistina*, whence the terms 'Philistine' and 'Palestine'. The term can also be linked to the word 'Pelasgian', an impossibly vague term used by later Greek writers to identify a variety of pre-Greek peoples in the Aegean, some of whom were said to live in Crete – foreigners or wanderers, as the Semitic term prescribes. With the help of archaeology, it is possible to go much further in identifying the Philistines. Pottery of the twelfth and eleventh centuries BC found on Philistine sites such as Ashdod in modern Israel is similar in style to Late Helladic pottery from the Mycenaean world; the closest parallels have been identified on Cyprus, although that does not prove their point of origin, since Cyprus was raided persistently by the Sea Peoples and settled by Mycenaeans.[37] This suggests a gradual process of migration which started about 1300 BC, punctuated by dramatic moments of destruction: if the migrants were not allowed to settle, they could take up arms, as the Pharaohs discovered; if they were welcomed, or even defeated by the Egyptians, they could be settled on the land, and many served alongside the Shardana in Pharaoh's armies.

The area of choice for Philistine settlement became the coastline northwards from Gaza; their four major centres were Gaza, Ekron, Ashkelon and Ashdod. 'Proto-Philistines' arrived in Ashdod and brought with them the techniques and styles of Mycenaean potters (their Mycenaean-looking pots were not imported but manufactured *in situ* from local clays). It was the Philistines (and Cypriots) who preserved longest the traditional designs of the Mycenaean world, when within Greece they had given way to simpler, more schematic decoration. A favourite design, found on wares from Gezer in Israel, Tell Aytun in the West Bank and other sites, shows a long-necked bird with its head sometimes turned to face behind; the design is elegantly combined with hatched lines, thin red stripes and other patterns.[38] Their pottery and their extraordinary anthropomorphic clay coffins, found in the Gaza Strip, also reveal influences from Egyptian art. It is hardly surprising that soldiers in Egyptian service should have borrowed Egyptian styles; but Mycenaean influence was overwhelming and betrays their original identity.

The home-made pottery in Mycenaean style proves that those who crossed the seas were not just soldiers and pirates. These migrations were on a grander scale, bringing whole families, taking along potters as well as fighters. The Philistine settlement at Tell Qasile, in what is now Tel Aviv, became a centre of agricultural trade in wine and oil. The coming of the Philistines did not result in a surge in commercial contact with the Aegean; rather, it had the opposite effect, as trading cities were destroyed and the old way of life along the Canaanite coast came to an end. Commerce in foodstuffs remained active, as deficiencies in one region were compensated by surpluses in another; but the luxury trade of the great days of Mycenaean civilization had shrunk and there no longer existed great palaces where travelling merchants could sell articles of prestige.

The Philistines came from the Greek world.[39] They were the kinsmen of Agamemnon and Odysseus, speakers, when they arrived, of Greek or possibly Luvian. A couple of seals carry scratched marks which resemble letters from the Linear A or B syllabaries. The constant biblical insistence that the Philistines came from Caphtor (Crete) clearly reflects local traditions. Jeremiah called the Philistines 'the remnant of the isle of Caphtor'. King David killed the Philistine giant Goliath, whose name recalls the Greek hero Alyattes (originally Wallyates); Goliath's armour, described in the Bible, is very similar to that of contemporary Greeks, illustrated on the Warrior Vase from Mycenae.[40] Having spent some time as an exile among the Philistines, David later employed what were clearly Cretan guards ('Cherethites').

Once settled in Palestine, many Philistines lost their maritime vocation, turned to farming and crafts and rapidly adopted Semitic speech and Canaanite gods; originally, they brought along their own gods and goddesses. Small painted figurines with raised arms, thought to represent an Aegean earth-goddess, have been found at Ashdod and are similar to clay idols found in the Mycenaean world.[41] At Ekron, in the interior, they built cult centres with hearths in the Aegean style which gradually modified their appearance to turn into Canaanite temples.[42] Here, knives with iron blades were discovered, for use in temple rituals; the Bible relates that they kept control of iron supplies so that the Israelites would not have the benefit of its use, mainly in fact confined to prized objects, such as iron bracelets, which were the height of fashion. The Philistines were not simply marauders and destroyers, Philistines in the modern sense of the word. They created a vibrant town-based civilization along the coast of Palestine which long retained the imprint of their Mycenaean origins. The Philistines show how a group of mercenaries and settlers could take charge of other people's lands, while the inhabitants of those lands, in the very long term, won a cultural victory by drawing them into Semitic Canaanite culture. They turned away from the Mediterranean towards the interior, occupying sites in the foothills of southern Canaan such as Ekron, which became famous for its olive-oil presses; and there they found themselves at odds with the Children of Israel.

V

Mention of Israel brings to the fore the question whether it was not just the Philistines but the Israelites who were set on the move during the convulsions of the Late Bronze Age: God asked through the prophet Amos, 'Did I not bring up Israel from the land of Egypt, and the Philistines from

Caphtor?'[43] Those who accept the historicity of the Israelite Exodus would generally assign it to the period between about 1400 and 1150; many of the details of the biblical account of the arrival of the Children of Israel in Egypt (if not their departure) match other evidence well – the arrival of Semitic travellers in search of food supplies and the occasional presence at court of Semitic viziers not too dissimilar to Joseph. The great Song of the Sea attributed to Moses after the Egyptian chariots had become stuck in the mud of the Red Sea is clearly very ancient and speaks of a style of chariot warfare which is consonant with the time of the Sea Peoples.[44] The presence of nomadic *apiru* or *habiru* in the lands to the east of Egypt has also been mentioned, and it is possible that they were involved in the fall of Ugarit; the king seems to mention them in one of his desperate last letters. Subject populations in Egypt, sometimes war captives, have also been encountered, and this is reminiscent of the long period of servitude the Israelites are said to have suffered in Egypt. A more cautious approach to the evidence would draw analogies with the way that Homer was able to refer back to features of a society hundreds of years before his time: oral histories, traditions, material from records of neighbouring peoples, could also have enabled the early Israelites to paint such a detailed and moving account of their long sojourn in Egypt and of their dramatic escape from Pharaoh's chariots. Equally, there is a powerful argument that the great movements of peoples described in this chapter set off many smaller movements, of which the migration of some Semitic tribes from Egypt was one, which went unnoticed (excepting Merneptah's brief reference) in the archives of the Near East; the Israelites were *apiru* nomads who returned for a while to their nomadism, cast away their subjection to Pharaoh and subjected themselves instead to their own God.

On entering Canaan the Children of Israel certainly did not destroy either Jericho or Aï, which had been demolished many hundreds of years earlier, but settled with their sheep and goats (but no pigs) in villages in the hills, entering into a mutual covenant under their own God, into which they also admitted other tribes and peoples such as the Danites.[45] Just as the Philistines became to all intents Canaanites, serving Dagon and other gods of local peoples, the Danites became Hebrews, serving the God of Israel. The contact of the Israelites with the Mediterranean at this period was slight, apart from the tribe of Dan, and apart from the growing tension with the Philistines, who had arrived from

Caphtor on the edge of the same small patch of land. As the Philistines began to cultivate the soil and merged with the local Canaanite population, they attempted to gain control of areas further inland, and clashed directly with the Israelites. If biblical sources are correct, the conflict peaked around 1000 BC. After King Saul and his son died in a ferocious battle with the Philistines, it fell to David, who had lived among the enemy, to crack Philistine power, using the newly conquered strongpoint of Jerusalem as the base from which he supposedly dominated the entire region. Despite these growing military successes, Israelite sites of the eleventh century have left few indications of luxury, and trade with the Mediterranean countries was slight. Even so, the Israelites need to be kept in view, since in the very long term they would have such a massive influence on the history of the Mediterranean peoples. The impression from the Bible is that there were plenty of restless tribes and peoples in the eastern Mediterranean; no one stood still for very long in the lands where Asia and Africa met one another.

The Sea Peoples may not all have come from the sea, and the scale of their migration may not have been as massive as the Egyptian record-makers wanted their readers to believe. But none of this should be taken to underestimate the impact of the Sea Peoples and the Land Peoples, who were evidently just as active. The calamities that occurred at this time were symptoms of a world already falling apart. Political chaos was accompanied by economic crisis, partly experienced in the form of biting famines. A brief mention of plague in the biblical account of the war with the Philistines may indicate that one reason for the disorder was the spread of bubonic plague or a similar disease, and that the roots of the catastrophe must be sought in the same places as the great plague of Justinian's time and the Black Death. In that case it would not be surprising if all the eastern Mediterranean were convulsed at once. But that, in a period when much is speculation, is perhaps a speculation too far. The end of the Bronze Age in the eastern Mediterranean has been described as 'one of history's most frightful turning points', more calamitous than the fall of the Roman Empire, 'arguably the worst disaster in ancient history'.[46] The First Mediterranean, a Mediterranean whose scope had extended from Sicily to Canaan and from the Nile Delta to Troy, had rapidly disintegrated, and its reconstruction into a trading lake which stretched from the Straits of Gibraltar to Lebanon would take several hundred years.

PART TWO

The Second Mediterranean,
1000 BC–AD 600

I

The Purple Traders,

1000 BC–700 BC

I

Recovery from the disasters of the twelfth century was slow. It is unclear how deep the recession in the Aegean lands was, but much was lost: the art of writing disappeared, except among the Greek refugees in Cyprus; the distinctive swirling styles of Minoan and Mycenaean pottery vanished, except, again, in Cyprus; trade withered; the palaces decayed. The Dark Age was not simply an Aegean phenomenon. There are signs of disorder as far west as the Lipari islands, for in Sicily the old order came to an end in the thirteenth century amid a wave of destruction, and the inhabitants of Lipari were able to preserve some measure of prosperity only by building strong defences.[1] The power of the Pharaohs weakened; what saved the land of the Nile from further destruction was the falling away of raids from outside, as the raiders settled in new lands, rather than any internal strength.

By the eighth century new networks of trade emerged, bringing the culture of the East to lands as far west as Etruria and southern Spain. What is astonishing about these new networks is that they were created not by a grand process of imperial expansion (as was happening in western Asia, under the formidable leadership of the Assyrians), but by communities of merchants: Greeks heading towards Sicily and Italy, consciously or unconsciously following in the wake of their Mycenaean predecessors; Etruscan pirates and traders, emerging from a land where cities were only now appearing for the first time; and, most precociously, the Canaanite merchants of Lebanon, known to the Greeks as *Phoinikes*, 'Phoenicians', and resented by Homer for their love of business and profit.[2] So begins the long history of contempt for those engaged in 'trade'. They took

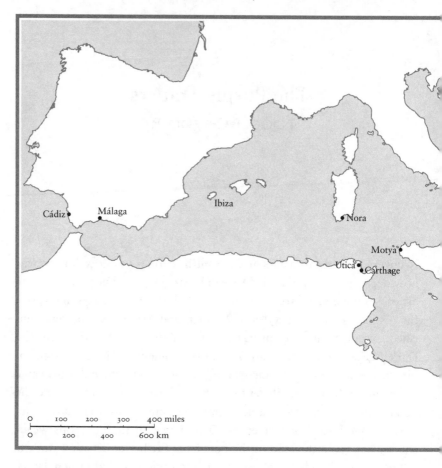

their name from the purple dye extracted from the *murex* shellfish, which was the most prized product of the Canaanite shores. Yet the Greeks also recognized the Phoenicians as the source of the alphabet which became the basis of their new writing system; and Phoenicia was the source of artistic models which transformed the art of archaic Greece and Italy in an age of great creative ferment.

Although the towns of the Lebanese coastline shared a culture and traded side by side, any sense of unity was limited: 'maritime trade, not territory, defined their sphere'.[3] However, the practice of archaeologists is to call the inhabitants of the Levantine littoral Canaanites up to about 1000, thereafter calling them Phoenicians.[4] This convention masks an important but difficult problem: when and how the Phoenician cities

became great centres of Mediterranean trade, and, more particularly, whether they were able to build on the success of the earlier trading centres of the Levantine coast such as Byblos and Ugarit.[5] Ugarit had, as has been seen, been destroyed around 1190 BC; the coast had been settled by people such as the Tjekker of Dor. Disruption undoubtedly occurred; old markets in the west were lost as Crete and the Aegean disappeared from the commercial map. Pirates mauled the traders. But important features of the old Canaanite world survived, sometimes with extraordinary strength.[6] The language of the Canaanites became the standard speech of the peoples who inhabited the Levantine lands: Aegean Philistines, Hebrew farmers, town-dwellers in Tyre and Sidon. The religion of the Canaanites was also adopted – with variations – by all but one of the peoples of the region, and even those who opted out – the Hebrews – were not quite so exceptional, for their prophets berated them for following Canaanite practices. The Israelites also knew the Phoenician practice of sometimes immolating their first-born children in sacrificial rituals that incurred the wrath and horror of the biblical prophets and subsequently of Roman writers: 'you shall not give any of your seed to set them apart for Molech'.[7]

There was, then, a greater degree of continuity in this corner of the Mediterranean than in Greece or Sicily. Prosperity declined but did not disappear in the eleventh century. But to say that the Phoenicians were a significant commercial presence in the tenth century BC is not to say that they already dominated the trade of the sea. They had other avenues to explore, and selling their purple dyes to the wealthy, militarily irresistible Assyrians in northern Iraq made more commercial sense than hawking it to impoverished peoples across the sea.[8] This was not, however, how the Greeks saw the early Phoenicians. Classical writers were convinced that Tyre was founded a few years before the fall of Troy, in 1191 BC; but Tyre itself is a far older site, and its king, Abi-milki, was a significant figure in the fourteenth century, to judge from the correspondence of the Egyptian Pharaohs. The Romans insisted that the Phoenicians were already founding settlements far to the west within a century of the supposed foundation of Tyre: Cádiz in 1104 BC, and Utica and Lixus in North Africa around the same time. This seemed to demonstrate that the early Phoenicians defied the onset of the Dark Age and carved out a network of trade routes, commemorated in the biblical references to a land far to the west, Tarshish, which sounds much like the Tartessos known to classical writers. Though several Roman writers mentioned the very early foundation of Cádiz, they were in fact parroting the opinions of the historian Velleius Paterculus, a contemporary of the Emperor Augustus, who lived 1100 years after the supposed event. Such early dates are not corroborated by archaeology. Even in Phoenicia the archaeological record from the eleventh and tenth centuries is surprisingly poor – this is partly because it is difficult to dig underneath the densely populated cities of modern Lebanon, but partly because the Levantine cities suffered so severely from raids by the Sea Peoples.

The Bible insists on the wealth and power of the kings of Tyre as far back as the tenth century BC. According to the Book of Kings, the alliances between Hiram, king of Tyre and Solomon, king of Israel (who acceded around 960) culminated in a treaty which assured the Tyrians of grain and oil supplies; in exchange they provided timber and crafts-men who built the Temple in the new Israelite capital of Jerusalem.[9] The biblical description of the Temple offers an unrivalled account of the appearance of an early Phoenician cult centre, and matches the founda-tions exposed at Hazor and elsewhere: an external altar, a shrine entrance flanked by two pillars, and then a progression through a larger outer chamber towards an inner Holy of Holies. Israelite amphorae found at Tyre, with a capacity of up to twenty-four litres, prove that the trade in foodstuffs from the lands settled by the early Hebrews continued throughout the ninth and eighth centuries.[10] In return for help with the Temple, Solomon is said to have given the king of Tyre a group of set-tlements in the north of Israel; the Bible calls them cities, but remarks that King Hiram did not like them when he saw them, so evidently Solo-mon's estate agents had shown a gift for exaggeration.[11] The Israelites had emerged as a force in their own right after centuries herding sheep and growing barley in the hill country east of the Philistine settlements. They knew that Tyre lacked a proper agricultural hinterland; this city, which may have contained 30,000 inhabitants a century or two later, could survive and grow only if it had regular access to grain supplies. The forests full of high-quality timber, rising to great heights behind the city, had to be exploited in trade and exchange if the city were to feed itself.[12] The Hebrews were also attracted by the *murex* shells; though forbidden to eat the shellfish within, they were commanded to colour the fringes of their garments with the dye extracted from these molluscs. This purple dye in fact varied in colour from a vivid blue to a rusty red, depending on how it was treated. Tyre and its neighbours therefore had two great advantages: a luxury product highly prized in the textile trade of western Asia; and a staple product without which house-building, ship construction and the production of countless small household objects was impossible. Thus Tyre and its neighbours did not flourish simply as intermediaries between Asia and Europe. They had something of their own to offer.

The great advantage the Phoenician cities possessed in the eleventh to early ninth centuries was independence from a higher power, and often from one another. The sharp decline in Egyptian influence over the Canaanite lands provided a marvellous opportunity for the Phoenicians to press ahead with their own schemes free from outside interference.

The arrival of Assyrian armies from the east in the ninth century acted as a brake: the 'wolf from the fold' swept up the coastal cities, just as it eventually absorbed the kingdom of Israel in the hinterland; but the Assyrians were wise enough to see that Phoenicia could remain a source of wealth, and extracted tribute from the continuing trade of Tyre and its neighbours. Until then, Tyre was only one of a series of independent cities along the Phoenician coast, but it became the best known to outsiders such as the Greeks and Hebrews, and it was the mother-city of the leading Phoenician settlement in the west, Carthage, supposedly founded in 814 BC. The rulers of Tyre sometimes exercised dominion over Sidon, and both in Homer and in the Bible they are actually called 'king of the Sidonians' (Homer never uses the term 'Phoenicians', always 'Sidonians').[13] This may appear to make Tyre exceptional, but Tyre was typical of Phoenician trading centres in several remarkable respects. Like several later Phoenician colonies, and like Arvad to the north, it stood on an island. Its well-defended position earned the site the name *Tzur*, for 'Tyre' means 'rock' or 'fortress'; only after Alexander the Great built a causeway to link Tyre to the mainland in the late fourth century BC did the city become permanently attached to the coast. These small islands possessed natural defences, but water supply was a constant worry, and late classical accounts describe a water pipe that supplied Arvad from the mainland, though water was also conveyed to the cities in tenders and rainfall was stored in cisterns.[14] By the time of Alexander, the island of Tyre had two harbours of its own, one facing Sidon to the north and the other facing Egypt; a canal linked them.[15] In the sixth century, the Hebrew prophet Ezekiel imagined Tyre as a fine ship made from the cypresses of Mount Hermon and the cedars of Lebanon; silver, iron, tin and lead arrived from Greece and the west, while the kingdom of Judah sent grain, wax, honey, tallow and balm.[16] He gloomily predicted that the magnificent vessel of Tyre was now heading for shipwreck. And yet he provided a periplus, or route map, of the Mediterranean and western Asia, seeing Tyre as the focal point in which all the goods of the world were concentrated – the wealth of Tarshish in the west, of Javan or Ionia in the north, of Tubal and other mysterious lands and islands.

Tyre only gradually became this glorious city. Short trips to Cyprus, Egypt and southern Anatolia continued even during the bleak period after the fall of Ugarit, though economic difficulties in eleventh-century Egypt weakened Tyre, which had relatively intimate ties with the Nile

Delta, while Sidon, looking more towards the Asiatic hinterland, was more successful.[17] It is not surprising that the artistic influences felt in Phoenicia came from the long-established cultures of western Asia and Pharaonic Egypt. What emerged was an eclectic amalgam of Assyrian and Egyptian styles.[18] Some eighth-century ivory fittings from King Omri's palace at Samaria, the capital of the kingdom of Israel, betray heavy Egyptian influence: two heavenly figures face one another, their wings facing forward; their faces are exposed, and they wear striped headdresses of typically Egyptian design. Though ivory mostly came up the Red Sea or by way of Egypt, it was sent westwards, and Phoenician silver and ivory objects appear in a noble tomb from Praeneste (Palestrina), south of Rome, dating from the seventh century. Gradually, then, the Phoenicians began to open up a new set of routes, into the central and western Mediterranean.

Some of the finest Phoenician products had to be presented to powerful rulers as tribute payments. The bronze gates of Balawat in northern Iraq, now in the British Museum, were built for Shalmanasar III of Assyria in the ninth century; they show Ithobaal, king of Tyre, loading a cargo of tribute on to ships standing in one of the harbours of Tyre, and an inscription solemnly announces: 'I received the tribute from the boats of the people of Tyre and Sidon'. Yet the tribute cannot have been sent from Tyre to northern Iraq on sea-going ships. The bronze panel portrays the fact that the Canaanites of the seaboard acquired their wealth from sailing the Mediterranean.[19] This is confirmed by the annals of Assurnasirpal, an Assyrian king, who died in 859 BC, and who claimed to have acquired from Tyre, Sidon, Arvad and other coastal cities 'silver, gold, lead, copper, vessels of bronze, garments made of brightly coloured wool, linen garments, a great monkey, a small monkey, maple-wood, boxwood and ivory, and a *nahiru*, a creature of the sea'. Here we can see a mixture of the exotic and the day-to-day, commodities carried across the Mediterranean and others produced in Phoenicia itself, as well as rare items such as the monkeys, which probably arrived via the Red Sea.[20] The Red Sea trade that fed into the Mediterranean was remembered in the biblical account of the ships of Ophir, sent out from Eilat by Solomon and Hiram.[21]

The Phoenicians traded without minting money, though they did not simply rely on barter.[22] For large payments they made use of ingots of silver and copper; sometimes too they paid or were paid in cups made of precious metals, presumably of standard weight (a memory of this is preserved in the biblical story of the cup that Joseph hid in the grain sack of his younger brother Benjamin, and in the story of Wenamun).[23] The employment of standardized weights such as the shekel provides clear evidence that, even without coinage, the Phoenicians were able to operate what might be called a market economy; or, put differently, they were familiar with a money economy, but money takes many forms other than coinage. Only much later, the Carthaginians began to mint coins; but their aim was to facilitate trade with the Greeks in Sicily and southern Italy, who were enthusiastic users of coin.[24] Metals, though, were the foundation of Phoenician trade in the Mediterranean: the first identifiable base of the Phoenicians was quite close to home, in copper-rich Cyprus, near Larnaka, and was established in the ninth century. Known to the Greeks as Kition and to the Hebrews as Kittim, among the Phoenicians the town generally went by the simple name 'New City', *Qart Hadasht*, the same name that would later be applied to Carthage in North Africa and Cartagena in Spain.[25] What was important at Kition was the attempt to create a colony and to gain dominion over the land that surrounded it; an inscription of the mid-eighth century indicates that the governor of the 'New City' was an agent of the king of Tyre, and he worshipped the *Baal Libnan*, the 'Lord of Lebanon', though Kition also contained a massive temple dedicated to the female deity Astarte.[26] The granaries of Cyprus were as great an attraction as its copper. Without regular supplies of food not just from the grain lands of Israel but from Cyprus they could not cope with the boom in their own city, whose increasing wealth was reflected by growth in population and greater pressure on resources. Unfortunately for the Tyrians, their success in Cyprus attracted the attention of the Assyrian king; Sargon II (d. 705 BC) acquired dominion over Cyprus, an event that marked the brief but significant arrival of the Assyrians in Mediterranean waters. An inscription recording Sargon's dominion was set up in Kition; he continued to receive tribute from the island over several years, without interfering in its internal affairs, because his aim was to exploit the island's wealth.[27] Its attractions as a source of copper were not, of course, lost on this warrior king. Later, the Assyrian hold on Cyprus weakened, for King Luli of Sidon and Tyre fled from Tyre to safety in Cyprus; the event was commemorated in a relief that portrayed the humiliated king scurrying away on a Phoenician boat.[28] But

Cyprus was only the most important place in a network of contacts that brought Phoenician merchants regularly to Rhodes and Crete.

By the end of the ninth century, then, Phoenician commerce across the Mediterranean had taken off. There is room for argument whether this take-off preceded that of the Greek merchants and of other mysterious groups such as the 'Tyrsenians' who are mentioned in the Aegean and Tyrrhenian Seas at this time. Whoever reached Italy first, the Phoenicians must be given credit for the elongated routes they created, stretching all the way along the coasts of North Africa.

II

The best way to trace the trading empire of the early Phoenicians is to take a tour of the Mediterranean some time around 800 BC.[29] This tour will also pass through the Straits of Gibraltar, to reach Cádiz and beyond, for one of the distinctive features of Phoenician trade in the Mediterranean was that these merchants from the extreme east of the Mediterranean also exploited the point of exit at the extreme west, giving access to the Atlantic Ocean. Taking into account the prevailing winds and currents in the Mediterranean, and the certainty that they travelled in a relatively short open season between late spring and early autumn, they must have taken a northerly route past Cyprus, Rhodes and Crete, then across the open expanse of the Ionian Sea to southern Sicily, southern Sardinia, Ibiza and southern Spain. Their jump across the Ionian Sea took them out of sight of land, as did their trajectory from Sardinia to the Balearics; the Mycenaeans had tended to crawl round the edges of the Ionian Sea past Ithaka to the heel of Italy, leaving pottery behind as clues, but the lack of Levantine pottery in southern Italy provides silent evidence of the confidence of Phoenician navigators. Once in the waters around Málaga, westward-bound Phoenician ships often stalled. Weather conditions in the Straits of Gibraltar can be treacherous; there is a strong inflow from the Atlantic, and fogs alternate with contrary winds. This could mean a lengthy wait before tentatively taking passage through the Straits towards Cádiz and other commercial outposts. Fortunately, it was easier to enter the Mediterranean from the Atlantic than to leave it, this time taking advantage of the winds and currents that blocked their exit. On the return journey to

Tyre the Phoenicians coasted along the great long flank of North Africa, but even then enormous care was needed: there were treacherous shoals and banks; nor, for long stretches, was there as much to buy as could be found in the metal-rich islands of Cyprus, Sicily and Sardinia.[30] On the other hand, Carthage, with its sizeable harbours, offered a refuge and helped to ensure the safety of waters very far from home in which Greek and Etruscan pirates abounded.

The ships can be reconstructed from carved bas-reliefs erected in the Assyrian palaces at Nineveh and elsewhere. Marine archaeologists have begun to expose the remains of Phoenician ships: there are some very late examples of Carthaginian vessels from western Sicily, of the third century BC; rather more fragmentary are two early Phoenician wrecks found thirty-three nautical miles west of the ancient Philistine port of Ashkelon, carrying pottery of the late eighth century.[31] The overall impression is that the Phoenicians and Carthaginians favoured heavier ships than those that were developed by the Greeks. There is a strong impression of continuity from the days when the ships of Byblos and Ugarit plied the eastern Mediterranean; and yet the Phoenicians have also been credited with important innovations. There were the sharp beak-like rams which were such fearful weapons in the naval warfare of the classical period, having been copied by the Greeks, Etruscans and Romans. By developing the keel the Phoenicians weighted their boats skilfully and made it possible to carry large cargoes in reasonably stable conditions across the open sea. The art of caulking ships with pitch is also supposedly a Phoenician invention, of obvious importance in making ships watertight during long voyages.

All this points to a real increase in carrying capacity in the trade of the Mediterranean at this period. The vessels themselves were not significantly larger than those of ancient Byblos: some ships of Ugarit, around 1200 BC, could carry forty-five tons of cargo, and the maximum capacity of Phoenician ships was only a little more.[32] What improved was the stability of the ships. It was this that made voyages as far as Atlantic ports such as Cádiz and Mogador realistic, and perhaps even enabled the circumnavigation of Africa, attributed by Herodotos to the sixth century BC. The rounded ships used for long- and medium-distance trade were three or four times as long as they were broad, and could achieve a length of as much as 30 metres, though the Ashkelon wrecks were about half that length.[33] Portrayed on the Balawat gates, they have high prows, decorated with the image of a horse's head (perhaps in homage to a god of the sea similar to Poseidon, who was also a horse-lover);[34] eyes might be painted on the bows, while at the stern, beyond the quarterdeck, the planking was gathered together in what looks like a fish-tail. A square sail was raised on a mast which, the biblical prophets say, was often made of cedarwood from Lebanon; some ships also made use of oar power. The rudder consisted of a broad oar attached to the port side. The impression is of sturdy boats with good carrying capacity, well suited to the trade in grain, wine and oil, and not simply fast flyers carrying small quantities of exotic luxury items. This is confirmed by the two early wrecks, which, between them, carried nearly 800 wine amphorae, making a cargo (if the amphorae were full) that weighed twenty-two tons. There were also smaller vessels, not greatly dissimilar, which serviced the short trade routes between the scattered ports of the Phoenician trading network; examples of these small vessels, about half the size of the Ashkelon ships, have been found in the waters of southern Spain, carrying lead ingots, wickerwork and local southern Spanish pottery.[35] These were the tramp steamers of the very early Mediterranean. Trade networks were dedicated as much to primary products such as foodstuffs as to high-value goods such as the ivory objects and silver bowls found in princely tombs in southern Spain and Etruria.[36] A different type of vessel evolved for use in warfare, characterized by the sharp bronze spike with which Phoenician captains tried to ram their opponents' ships. These ships were about seven times as long as they were wide, and they had a foremast as well. The warships also differed from the round cargo boats by making use of oar power for manoeuvring, especially at the battle scene.[37]

The earliest Phoenician object to have been found in the west is an inscribed tablet from southern Sardinia, the 'Nora stele', from the late ninth century; it mentions the building of a temple dedicated to the god Pumay, whose name appears in the common Phoenician name Pumayyaton (in Greek, Pygmalion). The inscription was made be-shardan, 'in Sardinia', so the island already possessed its name. Since the south of Sardinia offered a great medley of fine metals, including iron and silver, it is no surprise that Phoenicians appeared there. Possibly those who erected the inscription were pioneers, but the fact that they built a temple suggests they intended to stay in the area; building a temple was often one of the first acts of Phoenician settlers. And it was in the area of the Mediterranean due south of Nora that the Phoenicians were beginning to create substantial settlements of lasting importance.

III

Outstanding among these settlements was Carthage. Virgil happily backdated its foundation to the period of the Trojan War, when Aeneas visited its queen, Dido (also known as Elissa); but Virgil's *Aeneid* was a meditation on the past and future of Rome, and it is not surprising that he found in his book a role for the most potent enemy republican Rome had ever faced. Other classical writers, including the Jewish historian Josephus, provided alternative accounts of the birth of Carthage, in which once again Dido-Elissa appeared, fleeing from her tyrannical brother Pygmalion, who had assassinated her husband, the high priest of Herakles (the Greeks assimilated Herakles to the Canaanite god Melqart, *Melk-Qart*, that is, 'king of the city'). Her first port of call was Kition in Cyprus, another *Qart Hadasht* or 'New City'; then she decided to head westwards and gathered together eighty young women who were to serve as sacred prostitutes and ensure the continuation of the Phoenician cult in the lands the refugees would settle.[38] They made straight for North Africa, landing at the site of Carthage; they were not the first Phoenicians to arrive in the region, however, and the men of nearby Utica were on hand to greet them. They were also warmly welcomed by the Libyans who inhabited that area; it was these locals who first called Elissa Dido, meaning 'the wanderer'. The Phoenicians were not prevented from settling, but when it came to purchasing land, the Libyan king was less generous. He said that Dido-Elissa could buy as much land as could be covered by an ox-hide. The queen astutely countered this by cutting an ox-hide into very fine ribbons, which were laid out to trace the outline of the hill of Byrsa, the acropolis of Carthage. Attractive though this foundation legend is, it was no more than an attempt by Greek writers to explain the origin of the name of the hill at the heart of Carthage, for *byrsa* meant 'animal hide' in Greek. What they actually heard was the Canaanite word *brt*, meaning 'citadel'. Even after this deception, the Libyan king was still powerfully attracted by Dido. He insisted on marrying her; but she was intensely loyal to her husband's memory, and immolated herself on a pyre to avoid marriage, whereupon the settlers began to worship her as a goddess.[39] Tendentious though this account is, it has two important features. One is the persistence of the story of the self-immolating queen, which Virgil would pass into the mainstream of classical and subsequently European literature. The other feature is the apparent accuracy of some of the small details: the dating – about thirty-eight years before the first Olympiad (776+38=814) – accords with archaeological evidence that it was just at this period that the area was settled by Phoenicians. The Carthaginian elite continued to call themselves the 'children of Tyre', *bene Tzur*, or simply 'Tyrians', and later classical writers reported regular gifts from Carthage to the temple of Melqart in Tyre. Possibly, too, the self-sacrifice of Dido is a later attempt to portray something that was real enough in the Phoenician world, and was practised with especial fervour in Carthage: a human sacrifice, intended to secure the good grace of the god Melqart at the moment of the city's foundation.

It is disappointing that there are no objects from Carthage that can securely be dated to the first half of the eighth century; the archaeological record begins with burials, starting around 730 BC, and fragments of pottery from about 750 BC onwards. Strikingly, the earliest objects to survive are Greek, not Phoenician, geometric wares from Euboia in the Aegean, though, as will be seen, the Euboians had recently founded a colony of their own in the Bay of Naples, so some of this material could have come from there.[40] Early Carthage was not, then, sealed off from the developing world of Greek trade and colonial settlement. Homer's contempt for 'Sidonian' traders was the result of contact between the Phoenician and Greek trading spheres. Remarkably, the Greek pottery was deposited as a foundation offering underneath the shrine known as the *tophet*, where child sacrifices took place, of which more in a moment.

Carthage rapidly became the queen of the Phoenician colonies. The usual explanation for its rise is that the city was well placed for merchants travelling to and from southern Spain. However, objects of Spanish origin are hard to identify in the lowest levels of ancient Carthage. Other explanations would emphasize its origin as a place of refuge for Tyrian exiles, for migrants from Kition in Cyprus, and for the population overspill of the increasingly prosperous Levantine coastal cities; it also absorbed many local Berbers. But the real key to the success of Carthage lay not in Spain or in Phoenicia but at the gates of the city: the agricultural wealth of the region impressed classical writers, who described the villas and estates that surrounded the city, while a fifth- or fourth-century treatise on agriculture by the Carthaginian author Magon was translated into both Latin and Greek on the orders of the Roman Senate.[41] The aristocracy of Carthage derived its wealth from grain, olive oil and vineyards, not from purple dyes, cedar forests and ivory panels, as had the people of Tyre. All this accords well with the evidence from the round ships which, as has been seen, were much better suited to the carriage of jars full of oil and wine, and sacks of grain, than to the purveyance of costly luxuries. Carthage was clearly large and flourishing well before 600, and this would have been inconceivable without good local supplies of food. Carthage emerged so strongly because it became the focal point of a network of its own. This included other Phoenician settlements in the region; Utica lay not far away on the coast of North Africa, and was older, but it never managed to compete with Carthage. Motya in Sicily, on the other hand, was in certain respects more like Tyre or Arvad than Carthage; it has been described as 'a model of Phoenician settlement'.[42] Motya was founded in the eighth century on a small island a short distance from the western tip of Sicily, near modern Marsala; the island is well sheltered, lying between a reasonably substantial 'Isola Grande' and the Sicilian coast.[43] Another feature reminiscent of Tyre was the existence of purple dye factories, and so it was more than a trading station: it was a centre of industry, including the production of iron goods. Its boom period was the seventh century BC, and at this time child sacrifices became increasingly common, though why this should have been so is far from clear. The Motyans shared with the Tyrians the lack of an extensive hinterland under their own control. But this stimulated them to build friendly ties with the native Elymians of western Sicily, whose closest major centre was the great shrine of Eryx (Erice), standing on a peak towering above the western Sicilian coast. It was from the Elymians that they obtained the grain, oil and wine they needed, which was abundant in the west of Sicily. The Motyans also had access to the wide, white salt-pans of Trapani, on the coast below Eryx; and where there was salt there was also an opportunity to preserve fish, such as the abundant tuna that appears seasonally off the coasts of Sicily. Fish was a speciality of the Carthaginians, who are credited with inventing the foul-smelling fish-sauce, *garum*, which the Romans so loved. But the Phoenicians did not seek to conquer their neighbours. Their settlements were centres of

trade and industry; they made no attempt to establish political dominion over western Sicily.

Phoenician territorial ambitions did, however, extend beyond Sicily.
In southern Sardinia a cluster of colonies emerged from 750 onwards,
which aimed not just to provide safe harbours but to dominate the
countryside, probably so as to guarantee basic supplies. Most of these
settlements were classic Phoenician bases, built on isthmuses jutting
into the sea, as at Tharros and Nora; at Sulcis the lowest excavated levels,
just like those of Carthage, contained Greek pottery from Euboia.[44]
Heading inland, the Phoenicians occupied some of the ancient forts, or
nuraghi, while to all appearances maintaining peaceful relations with
the indigenous Sardinians, who welcomed the opportunity to trade
their metals and cereals with wealthy merchants based at Sulcis. The
hold of the Phoenicians and Carthaginians on Sardinia was confirmed
in about 1540 when the Carthaginians and Etruscans chased away the
Greeks of Phokaia in a great naval battle off Alalia in Corsica; this
ensured that Corsica and Sardinia remained outside the Greek sphere,
and, in view of the value of Sardinia as a source of all sorts of metals
and agricultural goods, the victory greatly strengthened Phoenician
power in the western Mediterranean. Although the Phokaian Greeks
established a base at Marseilles, the far west of the Mediterranean was
closed to intensive Greek penetration so long as Carthage remained a
major power; it was left to the Phoenicians to exploit the potential of
southern Spain and Morocco. The existence of these settlements tells us
where the Phoenicians went to live but not how far they actually travelled. Evidence for the impact of the Tyrians comes from tombs in Italy,
Spain and elsewhere, some containing the chased silver vessels decorated with animal designs which were greatly prized in central Italy
during the sixth century. But it is unclear whether the Phoenician and
Carthaginian merchants were free agents or agents of the state. Sometimes they were sent on missions by rulers and received commission for
their work, as when they operated in the service of the Assyrian monarch. Out in the west, they were able to operate as their own masters. At
first they were able to supply princely courts in Etruria and Carthage
itself. By 500 BC they had carved out trading networks that depended
on their own investment and provided them with direct profit; working
for others lost its attraction.

The far west became increasingly attractive. Greek writers such as

Strabo (writing early in the first century AD) insisted on the importance of southern Spain as a source of silver. There was a cluster of Phoenician bases in the Mediterranean approaches to the Straits of Gibraltar: at Montilla, Málaga, Almuñécar and other spots now buried beneath the concrete of the Costa del Sol. Some of these settlements were within a few hours' or even a few minutes' walking distance of one another; most were tied into the local economy and society, though finds of finely burnished early sixth-century Etruscan pottery at a site near Málaga indicate that wider connections also existed.[45] An early Phoenician settlement existed on Ibiza, within distant sight of the Iberian mainland; the usual exchanges of metals for oil and wine took place, though another asset of Ibiza throughout its history has been its gleaming salt-pans. On the Iberian mainland, the case of the little town of Toscanos, founded around 730 BC, is instructive. Toscanos was a community of as many as 1,500 people in the mid to late seventh century, whose artisans produced iron and copper goods, though it had been abandoned by about 550, for whatever reason. The impression is of a modest Phoeni-cian trading station, attuned to the needs of the local Iberian population, not particularly significant in the wider Phoenician trading networks, but quite important if one wants to understand how the Iberians were transformed through their contact with peoples from the east.

In fact, the major Phoenician base in this region lay beyond the Straits of Gibraltar, at Gadir or Cádiz; but because it fed its profits into the Mediterranean networks of the Phoenicians early Cádiz is also part of the history of the Mediterranean. Like so many Phoenician settlements, Gadir was founded on an offshore island, although the traditional date of 1104 BC is over 300 years too early. A temple of Melqart was estab-lished, and Cicero later recorded that human sacrifice was carried on here – probably a spring sacrifice in honour of the annual resurrection of Melqart recorded in Canaanite myth. This was a wealthy temple which functioned as a storehouse for precious objects as well as a cult centre, something which was seen as normal in the early Mediterranean trading world. And there was plenty to store in Melqart's shrine, for Gadir was the prime gateway to the wealth of the land known from the time of Herodotos as Tartessos. This is a place that has been argued over by scholars almost since antiquity. Some have seen Tartessos as a city, even as a river; now the name is taken to refer to a kingdom or region in southern Spain, inhabited by the native Iberian population. Its great attraction, or rather that of the lands bordering the river Guadalquivir, was its silver deposits: 'silver is synonymous with Tartessos'.[46] If Herodotos is to be believed, the Greek trader Kolaios of Samos was blown off course, arrived in southern Spain in the mid-seventh century and brought sixty talents of silver (maybe 2,000 kilograms) back from Tartessos. The name dubiously ascribed to the local king whom Kolaios met was Arganthonios, the first letters of which mean 'silver'.

It was the Phoenicians, not the Iberians, who transported the silver eastwards, both to Greece and Asia, according to the late testimony of Diodoros the Sicilian (first century BC). In exchange the Phoenicians brought olive oil and examples of their own craftsmanship such as jewellery, ivory objects, small perfume flasks and textiles; they taught the Tartessians how to extract, refine and process metals, beginning as far back as the eighth century. The methods used were sophisticated. This was not an exploitative 'colonial' relationship of 'unfair exchange', as one Spanish scholar has fashionably claimed.[47] It was the Tartessians who enthusiastically set to work, extracting and smelting not just silver but gold and copper at mining centres across southern Spain and Portugal, and, as even those addicted to a 'colonialist' interpretation admit, it was the local Iberians who controlled 'every facet of production' and were 'firmly in control of their own resources', from mining to smelting; the Iberian elites profited from the trade alongside the Phoenicians. Local artists began to adopt Phoenician styles, and the wealth that the Iberian princes acquired enabled them to live in a grand style. Here, contact with the East transformed a traditional society in the West, as was happening on an even greater scale in Etruria. The Phoenicians did not simply have a long reach; their activities also had the power to lift the political and economic life of a far-off land to a new level. They were beginning to transform the entire Mediterranean.

Tartessos has often been equated with the metal-rich land of Tarshish mentioned again and again in the Hebrew Bible. Jonah, fleeing from God, set out from Jaffa for Tarshish, which the author of this story clearly understood to be somewhere extremely remote, the furthest one could go across the seas. And Isaiah delivered a fearful prophecy concerning Tyre in which ships coming from Tarshish by way of Kittim (Kition in Cyprus) learn of the destruction of their home city: 'howl, ye ships of Tarshish, for it is laid waste, so that there is no house, no entering in'.[48]

IV

To make this system of trade work, the Phoenicians did not, as has been seen, have much use for coins. Far more important to them was their ability to record what they were doing. The merchants were literate and employed a simple, linear script that was easy to learn and rapid to write, the ancestor of most modern alphabets (in the strict sense of the term: a script with approximately one letter for each sound).[49] The art of reading and writing had mainly been a priestly craft, for the complex sound combinations in the three Egyptian scripts could be read only by the well-trained; even the syllabic scripts such as Linear B were clumsy, all the more so when imposed on a language like Greek which was not easily divided into simple consonant plus vowel syllables. In Phoenician script, a sign for a house represents 'b' because the word for house, *bet*, begins with a 'b'. Many, though not all, of the twenty-two Phoenician letters, beginning with *'aleph*, the 'ox', originated in the same way. The secret of success lay in the total exclusion of vowels, which were introduced only by the Greeks. *Mlk* could thus represent the word for 'he rules' or 'he ruled', depending on the vowels, which the attentive reader would have to supply from context. The first known example of this script survives on the coffin of King Ahiram of Byblos, from the tenth century. The important point is not whether the Phoenicians invented the alphabet from scratch (an earlier script used in Sinai may have provided some letters), but the fact that they diffused the alphabet across the Mediterranean, not merely to their settlements in the west, as the Nora stele proves, but to neighbours, the Greeks of Ionia, who converted letters they considered superfluous, such as the guttural stops absent from Greek, into vowel sounds, and subtly redesigned most of the signs.[50]

What the Phoenicians possessed in the way of literature is a mystery. The Canaanites of Ugarit produced impressive religious poetry not dissimilar to the psalms, and the Carthaginians wrote tracts on agronomy. There is a dismissive tendency to see much that the Phoenicians produced as derivative, and in the fine arts their dependence on Egyptian and Assyrian models is plain, as, for example, in their ivory carvings. This, of course, was what consumers across the Near East and the Mediterranean wanted: wares which carried the stamp not of the profit-hungry Canaanite towns, but of the great imperial civilizations of the

Nile, Tigris and Euphrates; and the Phoenicians knew how to satisfy that demand for clients as far west as Tartessos and Tuscany. The spread of Phoenician culture across the Mediterranean, as far as southern Spain, effected both through settlements and through trade with indigenous peoples, is important not just because it brought eastern styles so far to the West; this was also the first time that mariners from the East had reached so very far across the sea, ranging a long way beyond the Mycenaean navigators who had crept round from western Greece to southern Italy and Sicily.

Though the Phoenicians intermarried with native peoples, they did not lose their distinctive eastern Mediterranean culture, their identity and identification as 'Tyrians' or 'Canaanites'; nothing demonstrated this more forcibly than the practice of human sacrifice, which they carried with them from the land of Canaan. It was a practice that gave rise to deep abhorrence among biblical and classical authors: the story of the failed sacrifice of Isaac is one among many biblical invectives against child sacrifice. If anything this practice increased in intensity in the new settlements, especially Carthage, Sulcis and Motya. In the *tophet* at Carthage, which lay to the south of the city and can be visited today, children were offered to Baal for 600 years; in the last 200 years of the city, 20,000 urns were filled with the bones of children (and, occasionally, small animals), making an average of 100 urns a year, bearing in mind that one urn might contain the bones of several children. The *tophets* were special places of reverence. Very many urns contained the remains of what seem to have been stillborn, premature and naturally aborted infants, and in a society where infant mortality must have been high, many other remains must be those of children who died naturally. The *tophets* were thus graveyards for children who died prematurely; once adulthood was achieved, burial replaced cremation.[51] So, while human sacrifice did occur, as biblical and classical sources insist, it was less common than the vast number of jars containing infants' charred bones at first sight suggests, increasing in scale when great emergencies threatened, as the supreme way of appeasing the gods. Two Greek historians report that when Carthage was besieged by the tyrant of Syracuse in 310, the city fathers decided that they needed to appease Baal, whose displeasure noble families had incurred by sacrificing child slaves in place of their own firstborn; 500 noble children were then offered to their angry god. A fourth-century stele from the *tophet* at

Carthage portrays a priest in a flat, fez-like headdress and a transparent robe, carrying a child to the place of sacrifice. The practice, described by classical and biblical texts, was to place the living child on the extended arms of the statue of Baal; sacrificial victims then would drop, alive, from the arms down into the burning fiery furnace that raged beneath.[52] Child sacrifice was a way of affirming their identity as servants of Baal, Melqart and the Phoenician pantheon and as Tyrians hundreds of years after their forefathers had migrated from Lebanon to North Africa, Sicily and Sardinia. So, while the artistic output of the Phoenicians – and particularly of the Carthaginians – may appear lacking in originality, these were people with an overpowering sense of their identity.

2

The Heirs of Odysseus,
800 BC–550 BC

I

Whether the early Greeks possessed as powerful a sense of identity as the Phoenicians is far from clear. Only when a massive Persian threat appeared to loom from the east, in the sixth century, did the diverse Greek-speakers of the Peloponnese, Attika and the Aegean begin to lay a heavy emphasis on what they had in common; the sense of a Hellenic identity was further strengthened by bitter conflicts with Etruscan and Carthaginian navies in the west.[1] They knew themselves as distinct groups of Ionians, Dorians, Aeolians and Arcadians, rather than as Hellenes. There were the Spartans, proud inheritors of the Dorian name, who saw themselves as recent immigrants from the north. There were the Athenians, who insisted they were the unconquered descendants of more ancient Greeks. There were the Ionians, thriving in the new settlements across the Aegean, in Chios, Lesbos and on the Asian coast. The 'Greeks' cannot be identified simply as those who took delight in tales of the Greek gods and heroes, which were common currency elsewhere, especially among the Etruscans; nor would the Greeks have wished to recognize as fellow-Greeks all inhabitants of what we now call Greece, since they identified among the population of the islands and coasts strange remnants of earlier peoples, generically called 'Pelasgians' or 'Tyrsenians'; besides, the Greek-speakers were themselves moving outwards from the Aegean and Peloponnese towards Asia Minor, where they would remain for over two and a half millennia, and towards Sicily, Italy and North Africa.

How, when and why this great diaspora was created remains one of the big puzzles about the early Iron Age Mediterranean. What is certain is that it transformed the area, bringing goods and gods, styles and

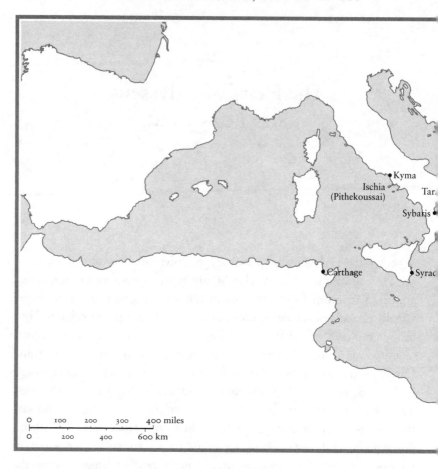

ideas, as well as people, as far west as Spain and as far east as Syria. The Greeks remembered these movements of people and things by way of often complex and contradictory tales of ancient ancestors who spread their seed across the Mediterranean: whole peoples at times reportedly boarded ships to be carried across distances of many hundreds of miles. The legends say more about the time when they were told and diffused than they do about a remote past in which these heroes supposedly lived.[2] There developed an obsession with identifying distant ancestors, and with linking the names of places and peoples to those ancestors, whose own movements could thus be mapped out by a series of what are now known to be false etymologies and fantastic facts.

For the ancient Greeks, the fall of Troy did not simply result in the collapse of the heroic world of Mycenae and Pylos. It was also remembered

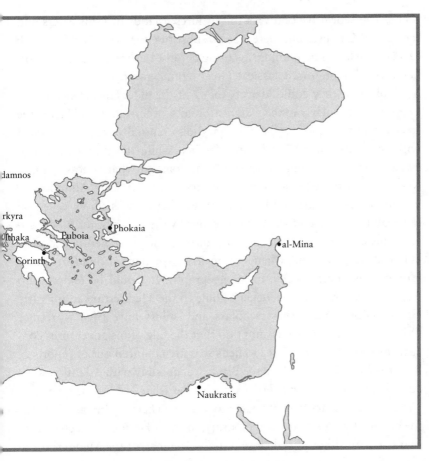

as the moment when Greeks set out to wander the Mediterranean and beyond; it was a time when sailors grappled with the dangers of the open seas – animate dangers, in the form of the singing Sirens, the witch Circe, the one-eyed Cyclops. The storm-tossed seas recorded in Homer's *Odyssey* and in other tales of heroes returning from Troy (a group of men known as the *Nostoi*, or 'returners') remained places of great uncertainty, whose physical limits were only vaguely described. Poseidon, god of the waves, conceived a great dislike for Odysseus, and constantly sought to dash his frail vessel to pieces in the open sea: 'all the gods pitied him apart from Poseidon, who was unrelentingly angry', all the more so when Odysseus killed his monstrous son Polyphemos the Cyclops.[3] The aim of the wanderers, whether Odysseus in the west, or Menelaos of Sparta in Libya and Egypt, was, ultimately, to return home. The world beyond was full of lures, islands of lotus-eaters and the cave of Calypso; but there was no substitute for the hearth by which Queen Penelope sat spinning, awaiting her lost husband and fending off her carousing suitors. Classical Greek commentators on Homer had no doubt that they could identify many of the places mentioned in the *Odyssey*, particularly in the waters around southern Italy and Sicily: the treacherous waters of Scylla and Charybdis eventually became identified with the fast-running Straits of Messina, while the island of Lotus-Eaters seemed to resemble Jerba, off the coast of what is now Tunisia. Kerkyra (Corfu) was assumed to be the realm of King Alkinoös, to whom Odysseus narrated his adventures after he was shipwrecked on the island's coasts, and was given succour by the king's beautiful daughter Nausikaä, who saw his nobility through his wretched nakedness.[4] Whoever he was, and whenever he lived (perhaps around 700 BC), Homer was never specific in his geography. It would be tempting to treat the *Odyssey* as a Baedeker's guide to the Mediterranean for early Greek sailors, and earnest scholars and sailors have tried to retrace Odysseus' route, on the assumption that the tale of his adventures conceals historical reality.[5] But Homer's seas are conjured out of reports of both the Mediterranean and the Black Sea, possibly with Atlantic waters stirred into the cocktail. For example, the island of Aiaia, on which Circe lived, appears from its name to lie somewhere in the east, towards the dawn. Homer's near-contemporary, the poet Hesiod, decided instead that Circe must have lived close to Italy. The map of the Mediterranean was infinitely malleable in the hands of the poets.[6]

The Greeks and their neighbours were aware of the convulsions that had set peoples on the move in the centuries after the fall of Troy, and they personalized the story of the migrations by identifying single persons whose progeny they were. It was a tale that was repeated time and again, culminating in the certain belief of the Romans that they were descended from the Trojan traveller Aeneas, whose own adventures were padded out with experiences copied from the life of Odysseus, most notably a visit to the Underworld. But there were also Etruscans who were convinced they were descended from Odysseus (known as *Uliśe*, hence the Latin form 'Ulysses'), or from Aeneas. The Greek and Trojan heroes became part of a Mediterranean body of legend, to which the Greeks lost exclusive copyright. Homer, after all, had told only a small part of the story: a few days during the siege of Troy, in the *Iliad*;

the lengthy travels of a single hero, and those of his son in search of his father, in the *Odyssey*. There was plenty of opportunity to fill in the gaps, and plenty of oral tradition that could be exploited by Greek writers, from Hesiod in the seventh century to the great dramatists of Athens, with their poignant accounts of the struggle for power in Mycenae following the return home of Agamemnon and his murder in the bath. The clearest evidence of the rapid spread of the Trojan cycle can be found in vase paintings, engraved mirrors and other items that illustrate not just the stories recorded by Homer but other aspects of the Trojan War and its aftermath – these appear as early as the seventh century BC, and scenes specifically from the *Odyssey* can be identified on Greek pottery from about 600 onwards, including the story of the Sirens and, a little later, the tale of the enchantress Circe.[7]

An unusual feature of the *Odyssey* is not just the misty location of the hero's landfalls, but the off-centre location of his home. Ithaka was on the furthest edges of the Mycenaean world, a jumping-off point, no doubt, for those early Mycenaean traders who ventured into southern Italy. Beyond Ithaka and the other Ionian isles stood Kerkyra; from there a short sea crossing carried ships to southern Italy, giving access to the Spartan colony at Taras, founded in 706 BC very close to the site at Scoglio del Tonno where native south Italians had acquired large quantities of Mycenaean pottery in earlier centuries. After 800, pottery from Corinth and Euboia in the western Aegean began to arrive in Ithaka, and the little town of Aetos, where many Corinthian pots have been found, was apparently a Corinthian staging-post; there was a shrine there at which sailors dedicated items such as amber beads, bronze amulets and golden ornaments from Crete.[8] Little survives to prove the presence of a flourishing Mycenaean centre on Ithaka, although Schliemann made every effort to find the palace of Odysseus. But the island was not rocked by revolution at the end of the Bronze Age; old cult centres continued to flourish, and the persistence of the old population and its habits may explain the survival of a richer fund of stories about this returning hero than exist for the other *Nostoi*. A shrine dedicated to Odysseus at Polis originated in the middle of the eighth century, and in later centuries the Greeks believed this site commemorated the dedication of bronze tripods by Odysseus on that spot when at last he returned to the island; his devotees left their own tripods there, which have been recovered from the soil.[9]

Homer was aware that the seas beyond the Aegean were being opened up by traders. He praised the daring of pirates and despised the mercenary methods of merchants; he described a Phoenician merchant as 'a man of deceitful mind, a weasel, who had done a lot of harm to people', for this was a 'very devious' nation of 'petty criminals'.[10] Homer nostalgically recalled days when the ideal form of exchange was not trade between merchants but gifts among noble warriors: 'he had given Menelaos two silver baths, a pair of tripods, and ten talents of gold'. Homer's image of a heroic society regulated by traditional codes of conduct led Moses Finley to conjure up a 'world of Odysseus' which preceded the commercialized world of the Greek traders.[11] But Homer himself was ambivalent. Princes could also be traders. Gods might even pose as merchants. At the start of the Odyssey Athena appeared before Odysseus' son Telemachos, posing as a princely trader: 'I call myself Mentes, son of the clever Anchialos, and I rule over the Taphians who are fond of rowing, and I have come here now with a ship and comrades, sailing over the sea that sparkles like wine, to foreign men, to Temese, to get bronze: I am bringing flashing iron.'[12] Temese is generally agreed to be a place in southern Italy; but, frankly, it could be anywhere. For the truth is that the Homeric radar barely extended to Italy. Homer occasionally mentioned Sicilians, though most of the references appear in the twenty-fourth book of the Odyssey, which is either a late, spurious, conclusion to the work, or a massively corrupted version of whatever came before.

In one of the most famous passages in the Odyssey, Homer described the encounter between Odysseus' crew and the Cyclopes. This can be read as an account of the deep fear that the Greeks, for all their veneer of culture, felt when they came into contact with strange and primitive peoples. Homer has no difficulty distinguishing the qualities of civilization from those of wildness. The Cyclopes are 'arrogant and lawless', they do not bother to sow the soil but gather what they need; 'they have no meetings for discussion and no code of law', living an unsociable life in caves, and paying no attention to their neighbours.[13] They are man-eaters, and they have no respect for the gods.[14] Above all, they do not know the benefits of commerce: 'the Cyclopes have not got crimson-cheeked ships, nor are there shipwrights among them, who could work on well-constructed ships, which could accomplish, in reaching every city of men, the many sorts of things for which men cross the sea to each other in ships'.[15] By contrast, Athena advised Telemachos to search for news of his father and to 'equip a ship with twenty rowers, the best one that you can', characterizing his island as a place where the craft of sea-manship was at everyone's fingertips.[16] This was a society in which movement by sea was natural and easy. It was a mobile society which was beginning to make contact with societies elsewhere in the Mediterranean; in combination or competition, the Greeks and the Phoenicians were beginning to generate not just a Renaissance in their own lands of origin, but vibrant city-based societies far from home; and, beyond the lands they themselves settled, their influence on the other peoples of the Mediterranean was profound.

II

The opening of contact between the Greeks of the Aegean (specifically, Euboia) and the lands facing the Tyrrhenian Sea has enthusiastically been described as a moment 'of greater lasting significance for western civilisation than almost any other single advance achieved in antiquity'.[17] It was an important moment not just for the Italian lands into which the first Greek traders and settlers penetrated, but for the lands back home which flourished as centres of trade: after the eclipse of the Euboian cities, Corinth came to dominate this traffic, sending its fine vases westwards in their thousands, and bringing back raw materials such as metals and foodstuffs; and after Corinth, Athens acquired a similarly dominant role in the fifth century. It was these outside resources and contacts that enabled the Greek lands to experience their great Renaissance after the collapse of Bronze Age civilization, and to disseminate objects in the distinctive styles favoured by Greek craftsmen and artists, with the result that the art of the Greeks became the point of reference for native artists among the Iberians and Etruscans in the far west. To write the history of Greek civilization as the story of the rise of Athens and Sparta without much reference to the waters of the central and western Mediterranean is like writing the history of the Italian Renaissance as if it all happened in Florence and Venice.

The first contact between Greeks and the Bay of Naples dates back to Mycenaean times, to judge from pottery finds on the island of Vivara. The Euboians established a base on the neighbouring island of Ischia around 750 BC. There is no sign that they were consciously following in the footsteps of their Bronze Age precursors; all the same, there is something strange about the fact that the first Greek settlement in Iron Age Italy lay so deeply within the Tyrrhenian Sea. A mainland settlement soon followed at Kyma (Cumae) in the same great bay.[18] A half-century later the Spartans founded a colony at Taras (Taranto) in the heel of Italy, within easy sailing distance of the Ionian islands and the Gulf of Corinth, and this seems a much more logical location for a first, tentative implantation on Italian soil. Still, the Phoenicians had reputedly been sailing to North Africa and out beyond Gibraltar to Tartessos even before this time. These long, ambitious routes found their rationale in the search for metals, whether the copper and iron of Tuscany and Sardinia or the silver of Sardinia and southern Spain. A late Greek account of the Phoenician voyages to Tartessos expressed wonder at the wealth that could be found in the far west, telling how these merchants took oil westwards and then returned with 'so great a quantity of silver that they were no longer able to keep or receive it, but were forced when sailing away from those parts to make of silver not only all the articles which they need, but also their anchors'.[19] And it will be seen that there is enough evidence of friendly contact between Greeks and Phoenicians in these waters to suggest that the opening of these sea routes was to some degree a joint enterprise, even if the major settlements, such as Carthage and Kyma, acquired a distinctive ethnic identity (in the case of the Greek cities not as Greek, but as Euboian, Dorian or Ionian).

There is a mystery at both ends of the route linking Euboia to Ischia. Why Euboia should have emerged as the first significant centre of overseas trade and settlement after the long recession of the 'Dark Age' is far from clear.[20] Euboia is a long, well-wooded island that flanks mainland Greece; the distance from the mainland is only a few miles at most, though Hesiod described his unreasonable terror at crossing even that narrow channel. The most likely explanation is that its two major cities, Chalkis and Eretria, commanded excellent natural resources and began to exploit them in local trade down to Athens and Corinth. Euboia was rich in timber, essential for its shipbuilders; indeed, one of the Homeric Hymns – a series of poems in praise of the gods written in the seventh or sixth century in what passes for a Homeric style – dedicated to Apollo, described it as 'famous for its ships'. Wine was another resource – the early Greek word *woinos* was transmitted to Italy, where the Etruscans transformed it into a word the Romans heard as *vinum*.[21] The name of one of its towns, Chalkis, suggests that the area was a source of copper (*khalkon*), and moulds for the casting of tripod legs, found at Lefkandi on Euboia, date from the late tenth century BC. Lefkandi was then a flourishing centre. A substantial building, with an apse at its end, has been excavated there; measuring 45 metres by 10 metres, it dates from before 950 BC, and was constructed out of mudbrick on stone foundations, while its roof was made of thatch. It was the mausoleum of a great warrior, who was found wrapped in a linen cloak of which fragments still survive, along with his iron sword and spear, and he had been accompanied to the next world by three horses. A woman was also buried within the building, along with gold jewellery and pins made of bronze and iron.[22]

The Euboians did not pour all their efforts into Ischia. Indeed, their aim was to make Chalkis and Eretria into mid-points between the trading networks of the western and the eastern Mediterranean. As early as the late eleventh century ceramics reached Lefkandi from the Syrian coast; ties to Syria were strengthened with the establishment of a trading counter at al-Mina around 825 BC. This site was excavated before the Second World War by Sir Leonard Woolley, who clearly demonstrated its importance as a centre of trade and industry looking out in all directions of the compass – towards the thriving empire of the Assyrians in the east, down the coast to Tyre and Sidon, but also across the open sea to the lands of *Yavan*, 'Ionia', the Greeks.[23] Closer still were the ties with Cyprus, which gave access to the towns of Syria, southern Anatolia and the Nile Delta. It was a place where all the cultures of the seaboard met; the Phoenician colony at Kition coexisted comfortably enough with the Greek settlers and merchants. Sites in Euboia have also yielded a bronze mace-head from Cyprus, and goods made of gold, faience, amber and rock crystal originating in Egypt or the Levant.[24] The fragments of fine cloth in the warrior's grave at Lefkandi indicate that high-quality textiles were another attraction; the reputation of the Syrian coast as a source of cloths and dyestuffs drew Greek eyes towards the Levant. All this made Euboia into the most prosperous part of the Greek world in the ninth century, apart from partly Hellenized Cyprus. Less clear is who brought these goods to Euboia. The boom there began before Chalkidian and Eretrian sailors established their settlement in Ischia, in the eighth century. Probably the merchants who arrived from Cyprus and the Levant were not Greeks at all, but Phoenicians; and this would account for the knowledge of Phoenician traders and of their sharp techniques among the earliest Greek poets.

The other mystery is what the Euboians were able to obtain in exchange for the goods they acquired from Cyprus and the Levant. As they opened up the routes to the west, they gained access to supplies of metals such as copper and iron, for local resources had apparently become inadequate to meet the excited demand among Euboians for oriental goods. Mostly, however, they met their obligations with items that leave no clear record in the soil: sacks of grain, amphorae filled with wine and oil, stoppered jars containing perfumes. When their pottery reached places as distant as the kingdom of Israel or Cilicia, in southern Anatolia, it may well have been appreciated for its design, but what mattered most were the contents. And then, as this commerce became regular, the strains of paying for more and more eastern luxuries stimulated further searches for metals and other goods that could be used in payment; and this brought the Euboians to the waters of the Tyrrhenian Sea. There was direct or indirect contact with Sardinia, documented in finds of pottery of Euboian origin, or at least in the Euboian style. Better still were the resources in iron of the Tuscan shores and hinterland, a region of prosperous villages which were about to coalesce into the rich city-based culture of the Etruscans. So, gradually at first, the Euboians began to make contact with the lands surrounding the Tyrrhenian Sea, first by way of Phoenician mediators, and then in their own ships.

Ischia was the base the Euboians chose, and they oddly called it *Pithekoussai*, 'the place of the monkeys'; one of the island's attractions was its vineyards, and another was its safe offshore location – it was a point from which Euboian traders could radiate outwards in search of the produce of southern and central Italy and the Italian islands.[25] Between about 750 and 700 BC there existed a flourishing commercial and industrial base at the site now known as Lacco Ameno, and two extraordinary finds there illuminate the links between this far-flung settlement and the Greek world. One is a drinking-cup, made in Rhodes, and deposited in the grave of a boy who died when he was only about ten years old. After its manufacture the cup was decorated with a light-hearted inscription:

Nestor had a fine drinking-cup, but anyone who drinks from this cup will soon be struck with desire for fair-crowned Aphrodite.[26]

Nestor's cup, the *Odyssey* relates, was made of gold, but the wine poured into it acquired a potency that gold alone could not confer.[27] There are many striking features of this inscription. It is written in the version of the Greek alphabet favoured by the inhabitants of Chalkis, supporting the argument that the inscription was not made along with the cup itself in Rhodes, but added by Euboian Greeks, who had learned the alphabet from Phoenician visitors to Euboia. It was the Euboians who carried the alphabet westwards to the peoples of Italy, and it was therefore their version (rather than the Attic version that came to triumph in the Greek world) that gave birth to the Etruscan alphabet, and, derived from that, the Roman one. These hexameter lines are the only eighth-century verses to have survived outside the Homeric canon. With their reference to Nestor, they offer further evidence of the central role of the Trojan War in the life and thought of the archaic Greeks. The link to Rhodes, whether directly or by way of Chalkis and Eretria, is confirmed by the discovery on Ischia of a good many *aryballoi*, small perfume jars, of Rhodian manufacture, discarded at the cemetery after being emptied during funerary rites.

The second remarkable find from Lacco Ameno is a shallow vase or *krater* that depicts on its rim a shipwreck. This too is the first object of its type, the first figured narrative painting to survive from an Italian site; and it was made locally. A ship, similar to those later depicted on Corinthian pottery, has capsized and its sailors are in the sea swimming for their lives, but one of them has drowned and another is about to be swallowed by an enormous fish. Since a further image shows a well-fed fish standing upright on its tail he seems not to have escaped. There is nothing here that is recognizable in the *Odyssey* or other tales of returning heroes; the story could be a local and very familiar one, about real men who went to sea and never returned. Other evidence from graves also testifies to the importance of sea traffic to the inhabitants of Pithekoussai. Some vases came south from Etruria, in the plain black style known as *bucchero*; it was their shape rather than their decoration that gave them elegance. Links to the east were particularly lively; about a third of the graves dating from the third quarter of the eighth century contained items of Levantine origin or produced under Levantine influence.[28] A scarab amulet found in a child's grave carries the name of Pharaoh Bocchoris, which provides a date somewhere around 720 BC, and there is a faience vase from the Etruscan site at Tarquinia which also mentions this Pharaoh, so we can deduce that traffic was moving from Egypt, probably via Phoenicia or the settlement at al-Mina in Syria, to Greece and then into the Tyrrhenian Sea; Pithekoussai was not by any means the end of the line, for merchants pressed on until they had arrived on the metal-rich Tuscan shore. Just as the Phoenicians overseas eventually became busier traders than the Phoenicians of the Levant, so too the Euboians in the far west built up their own lively trading world linking Syria, Rhodes, Ionia and eventually Corinth to Pithekoussai.

The people of Pithekoussai were traders, but they were also craftsmen and craftswomen. One fragment of iron slag is probably of Elban origin, underlining the importance of the link to Etruria, since Ischia could offer no metals. Crucibles have been found, and it is clear from the survival of small lengths of wire and of ingots that bronze goods as well as iron ones were manufactured. This was a hard-working community of expatriates, numbering, according to the best estimates, between 4,800 and 9,800 people in the late eighth century. What had been founded as a trading-post thus developed into a sizeable town, in which not just Greeks but some Phoenicians and mainland Italians made their home. A jar containing the remains of an infant carries what seems to be a Phoenician symbol.[29] Just because Pithekoussai was a Greek foundation we should not assume it was inhabited only by Greeks, or specifically Euboians. Foreign craftsmen were welcome if they could bring their styles and techniques with them, whether they were Corinthian potters, who began to settle in nearby Kyma by about 725 BC, or Phoenician carvers, who could satisfy the craving of the Italian peoples for oriental goods. Pithekoussai thus became the channel through which 'orientalizing' styles were funnelled through to the west. The Pithekoussans observed how hungry the growing village communities of southern Etruria, in places such as Veii, Caere and Tarquinia, were for eastern goods, and they sold the early Etruscans what they wanted, in exchange for the metals of northern Etruria. Whether they noticed a collection of villages grouped around seven hills, across the river Tiber just to the south of Etruria, is less certain.

III

Thucydides told of how the cities of Euboia became enmeshed in the 'Lelantine War', which in his view was the most serious internecine war among the Greeks before the Peloponnesian War. But the conflict is impossible to date, and there is little detail about what occurred; it may have been a contest for control of the copper and iron that lay beneath the Lelantine plain, or for the vineyards and pastures of the plain itself.[30] In any case, Euboia had passed its peak by 700. A precocious pioneer, Euboia was unable to sustain its lead once other centres such as Corinth became serious competitors. The trade to the west made the fortune of Corinth. Homer already described the city as *aphneios*, 'wealthy'.[31] The traditionalist fifth-century poet Pindar sang in his Olympian Odes of how 'I shall come to know fortunate Corinth, Poseidon's porch on the Isthmus'.[32] In the fifth century Corinth was only about a third the size of Athens in territory and population; but it was able to take advantage of its situation to draw great profit from commerce across the Aegean and, to an even greater degree, commerce from Greece westwards to the Adriatic, Ionian and Tyrrhenian Seas. Sitting astride the route linking northern Greece to the Peloponnese, the Corinthians could also draw benefit from the land trade that passed through the isthmus.[33] The inhabitants of what was probably still a collection of villages below the steep citadel of Acrocorinth had established contact with the wider world by about 900 BC, when Corinthian Proto-Geometric pottery reached Boiotia; by 800, a good amount of Corinthian pottery was reaching Delphi as votive offerings.[34] By the mid-eighth century much Corinthian pottery was arriving at Pithekoussai, and from there it was passed down the trade routes into the villages of early Etruria.[35] In the seventh century BC, the Corinthians developed ports on both sides of the isthmus, one at Lechaion on the Gulf of Corinth, and a second at Kenchreai, giving access to the Aegean through the Saronic Gulf – here the waters were calmer but access from Corinth took longer. No less important was the creation of a great slipway, the *diolkos*, across which teams of Corinthian slaves could heave boats overland from one port to the other. Only Aristophanes had the imagination to compare the *diolkos* to a sexual act: 'What is this business with the Isthmus? You are shoving your penis up and down more than the Corinthians shove ships across the *diolkos*!'[36] Evidence that lively contacts existed with both east and west – Chios, Samos, Etruria – can be found in the ceramics excavated within Corinth itself.[37] Thucydides confirms that Corinth was a centre of shipbuilding, for 'it is said that the first triremes ever built in Hellas were laid down in Corinth'.[38]

The Corinthian tyrant Periandros made a treaty with the ruler of Miletos on the coast of Asia Minor some time between 625 and 600, seeking a network of alliances as far away as Ionia and Egypt – the tyrant's nephew Kypselos was nicknamed Psammetichos, after a Pharaoh with whom Periandros had business ties. An Ionian trading settlement developed at Naukratis in the Nile Delta, where Corinthian pottery soon appeared.[39] By the middle of the sixth century BC the Greeks in Italy and Sicily bought Corinthian pottery in preference to all competitors. The Carthaginians copied Corinthian designs in the late eighth century, and then succumbed to a minor invasion of authentic Corinthian pottery. And the Etruscans had the discrimination to buy the best pieces, such as the Chigi vase of about 650 BC, regarded as the finest surviving product of the Corinthian potters. It was only in the course of the sixth century that Athens came to dominate the export of ceramics to Italy.[40]

No one really believes that these flourishing connections with east and west were sustained solely by demand for Corinthian pottery, however elegant it may have been; the areas given over to pottery production within the city were not large. Much of the pottery was carried as ballast on board ships full of perishable products, of which rugs, blankets and fine linen cloths, coloured crimson, violet, flame-red and sea-green, were probably the most prestigious items.[41] The manufacture of such items depended on the supply of dyestuffs, and here links to the Phoenician purple traders were of great importance. One point of contact was the emporium at al-Mina in the Levant, where Greeks, Phoenicians, Aramaeans and others mingled and traded.[42] But the strength of Corinth lay in its diversity. Its merchants handled agricultural produce, pastoral products, timber, fine wares, terracotta tiles (sent in quantity to the shrines at Delphi, so that nearly every structure there, apart from those roofed in marble, had Corinthian clay roof-tiles). Small bronzes were favoured exports, as were arms and armour made of bronze and iron, for which Corinth became famous as early as 700 BC.[43]

The price of success was envy, and there were occasions, during wars with Sparta, when Lechaion fell into the hands of Corinth's enemies. But the general trend in Corinthian policy was to try to keep the peace with as many of its neighbours as possible, until the outbreak of the Peloponnesian War in the late fifth century. After all, conflict at sea and on land would do a trading city no good. But it is less clear whether this trade was carried in Corinthian ships. The discovery in Corinth itself of large numbers of amphorae made in Carthage from about 460 BC onwards suggests that a lively trade in foodstuffs between Corinth and the western Mediterranean was shared between the Corinthians and the Carthaginians. It has been argued that the main product carried towards Corinth in these jars was the processed sauce *garon* (Latin *garum*), made from fish intestines and brought from as far away as the Phoenician trading-station at Kouass in Atlantic Morocco.[44] Amphorae made in Corinth between the late eighth and mid-third centuries BC have been found all over the western Mediterranean, as far west as Algeciras and Ibiza, as well as in southern Italy and in the Greek settlements in Cyrenaica. These jars were made in order to be filled with something, and what their presence reveals is a lively trade in grain, wine and oil; as the population of the maritime cities of the Greek mainland increased, demand for the grain of areas such as Sicily grew, and a lifeline linking the Greeks in the west to their ancestral lands was created through the Gulf of Corinth. Corinth responded by selling excess oil and wine from the area the city controlled to buyers in Sicily and beyond.[45]

The rise of Corinth raises wider issues about the ancient Mediterranean economy. For Moses Finley, the foundations of wealth lay in agriculture and local trade in the necessities of life. He insisted that the volume of luxury trade was simply too small to generate the economic growth visible at Corinth, and later at Athens. Finley seized hold of the insights of anthropologists into gift exchange to assign that relationship priority over the search for profit in this period. Yet the evidence points in the opposite direction.[46] For instance, the Corinthians began to use a silver coinage from the middle of the sixth century, and coin hoards discovered in southern Italy reveal that these coins were carried westwards as early as the late sixth century. Coinage in a recognizable form had originated across the Aegean, in Lydia, and it is still uncertain where Corinth acquired its silver, even if it is clear where it acquired the idea of coinage. It is possible, indeed, that the prime motive of the Corinthians in minting coins was to regularize tax payments by merchants using the two harbours and the *diolkos* slipway.[47] In any case, traders were something more than the agents of gift exchange by 600.

Two figures in the early history of Corinth confirm this view. One is Periandros, whose father had led a revolution against the Bacchiad dynasty that had previously ruled the city.[48] Periandros ruled Corinth from 627 to 585 BC; this was, in economic terms, a golden age. But Herodotos attributed to him many of the evil qualities of a true tyrant: he was supposed to have murdered his wife Melissa and to have made love to her corpse; enraged by the death of his son on the island, he enslaved 300 boys from Kerkyra and sent them to Lydia to be castrated. For Aristotle, he was a model example of the harsh tyrant. But Aristotle also reported elsewhere that Periandros relied on taxes from markets and harbours for his income, and acted justly; there were those who even included him among the Seven Sages of past time.[49] What are, admittedly, much later sources aver that he was an enemy of luxury; he was said to have burned the fine clothes beloved of rich Corinthian women, and to have legislated against the acquisition of slaves, preferring that his own subjects should be put to work.[50] He detested idleness. What is important here is the distant memory of someone whose policies were dedicated to wealth-making.

The other figure of note is the Bacchiad aristocrat Demaratos, whose career was reported in detail only much later, in the reign of the Emperor Augustus, by Dionysios of Halikarnassos, not the most reliable author. When his dynasty was overthrown, Demaratos supposedly fled to Tarquinia, in about 655 BC, and married a local noblewoman; she bore him a son named Tarquin, the first Etruscan king of Rome. Demaratos is said to have brought craftsmen with him.[51] There certainly was a Corinthian diaspora, and the Bacchiads were active in the foundation of Corinthian colonies overseas. In about 733 they established what became the most powerful Greek city in Sicily, Syracuse; around 709 they also established a colony at Kerkyra with which relations were sometimes difficult.[52] One of a group of Corinthian settlements along the coast of Epeiros and Illyria, Kerkyra itself generated a further colony at Epidamnos (modern Durrës in Albania). Kerkyra and Syracuse protected trade towards the Adriatic and across the Ionian Sea. The Adriatic colonies gave access to supplies of silver in the Balkan interior – this would explain where Corinth acquired the silver with which it minted its fine coinage. When, at the start of the fourth century, the tyrant Dionysios of Syracuse was trying to gain hold of the waters of the central Mediterranean he 'resolved to plant cities on the Adriatic Sea' and along the shores of the Ionian Sea 'in order that he might make the route to Epeiros safe and have there his own cities which could give haven to ships'.[53] A similar question has been raised in respect of the foundation of Syracuse and Kerkyra: was the aim to protect existing trade routes, or were they founded to absorb an excess population which Corinth could not feed?[54] As the colonists consolidated their hold on their new territory, they were able to develop a trade in primary products such as grain, further alleviating pressure on resources back home and, indeed, making it possible for the mother-city to grow without constraint.

In the end it is a chicken and egg question. There were many motives that might send a Greek city-dweller overseas in this period: at the top of the social scale, there were political exiles; lower down, there were merchants and shipowners with an eye on new markets; there were craftsmen who had become aware of surging demand for their products as far away as Italy and southern France; there were others in search of land to cultivate in the territories out to the west. Colonization was not a symptom of poverty at home, but of growing wealth and the wish to build further on the early successes of Corinth and the other cities which created daughter settlements in the Mediterranean. And yet, as the career of Demaratos of Corinth showed, there were also other lands over the horizon where the Greeks could settle only as guests of powerful indigenous peoples. The most important of these peoples were the Etruscans.

3

The Triumph of the Tyrrhenians,
800 BC–400 BC

I

The importance of the Etruscans does not simply lie in the painted tombs whose lively designs captivated D. H. Lawrence, nor in the puzzle of where their distinctive language originated, nor in the heavy imprint they left on early Rome. Theirs was the first civilization to emerge in the western Mediterranean under the impetus of the cultures of the eastern Mediterranean. Etruscan culture is sometimes derided as derivative, and the Etruscans have been labelled 'artless barbarians' by one of the most distinguished experts on Greek art;[1] anything they produced that meets Greek standards is classified as the work of Greek artists, and the rest is discarded as proof of their artistic incompetence. Most, though, would find common cause with Lawrence in praising the vitality and expressiveness of their art even when it breaks with classical notions of taste or perfection. But what matters here is precisely the depth of the Greek and oriental imprint on Etruria, the westward spread of a variety of east Mediterranean cultures, and the building of close commercial ties between central Italy, rarely visited by the Mycenaeans, and both the Aegean and the Levant. This was part of a wider movement that also embraced, in different ways, Sardinia and Mediterranean Spain.

With the rise of the Etruscans – the building of the first cities in Italy, apart from the very earliest Greek colonies, the creation of Etruscan sea power, the formation of trading links between central Italy and the Levant – the cultural geography of the Mediterranean underwent a lasting transformation. Highly complex urban societies developed along the shores of the western Mediterranean; there, the products of Phoenicia and the Aegean were in constant demand, and new artistic styles came into existence, marrying native traditions with those of the East. Along the new trade routes linking Etruria to the east came not just Greek and Phoenician merchants but the gods and goddesses of the Greeks and the Phoenicians, and it was the former (along with a full panoply of myths about Olympus, tales of Troy and legends of the heroes) that decisively conquered the minds of the peoples of central Italy. Mass markets were created for the fine vases of Corinth and later of Athens; indeed, the finest Greek vases have mostly been found not in Greece but inside Etruscan tombs. Carthage, too, owed much of its early success to the existence of markets close by in central Italy; it gained privileged access to the cities of Etruria, and this tie was confirmed by a series of treaties (which included one with Rome, in 509 BC). Whereas in North Africa and Sicily the Carthaginians traded with peoples whose culture they saw as relatively backward, in Etruria they found willing partners in trade, who also proved to be powerful allies in the struggle for control of the central Mediterranean between Carthage and the Greeks of Sicily.

The Etruscans have attracted attention because of the two 'enigmas' that are said to surround them: the question of their ethnic origins and the connected question of their language, unrelated to the other languages of the ancient world. Ancient historians produced their own confabulations concerning the migration of the Etruscans from the eastern Mediterranean; Herodotos' version offers a precious account of how an Ionian Greek of the fifth century BC saw the relationships between peoples and places in the Mediterranean, and had great currency.[2] He told how the migration took place in the reign of Atys, king of Lydia – in other words, in the very remote past. Herodotos relates that the Lydians invented board games, with the exception of draughts. The reason they did so was that they were afflicted by a severe famine. At first, their solution was to eat one day and spend the next day playing board games in the hope of forgetting their hunger: 'in this way they persevered for eighteen years'. But conditions simply worsened. So the king divided the hungry population into two parts, and drew lots. One half of the population was to stay in Lydia, and the other was destined to search for a new home, under the leadership of Atys' son Tyrsenos. The migrants went down to Smyrna, built ships, and sailed past many lands until they arrived in the land of the Umbrians, where they built cities and assumed the name *Tyrsenoi* after their leader Tyrsenos.[3] *Tyrsenos* (or in the Attic dialect of Athens *Tyrrhenos*) was the standard Greek

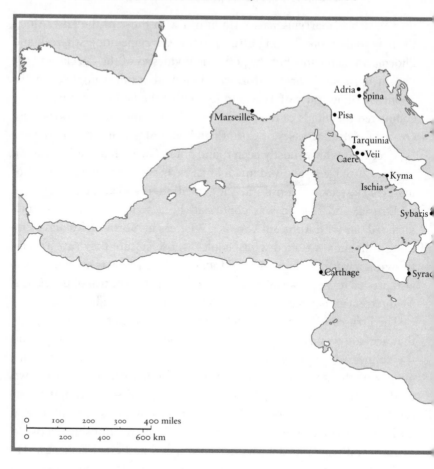

term for an Etruscan. Here, then, was another of those tales of travel to distant parts of which Greek writers were so fond. Among those who believed this story that the Etruscans had migrated from the east were the greatest Roman poets – Virgil, Horace, Ovid, Catullus – and the most influential prose-writers – Cicero, Tacitus, Seneca. This was apparently the firm belief of the Etruscans and of the Lydians. In AD 26 Emperor Tiberius decided to erect a grand temple in a city in Asia Minor; in the hope of convincing the Romans that Sardis was the natural home for such a temple, the city reminded the Senate that the Etruscans were their colonists, sent out centuries ago, which proved that Sardis had always possessed intimate ties with Italy.[4]

Writing under Augustus, the antiquary Dionysios, who like Herodotos

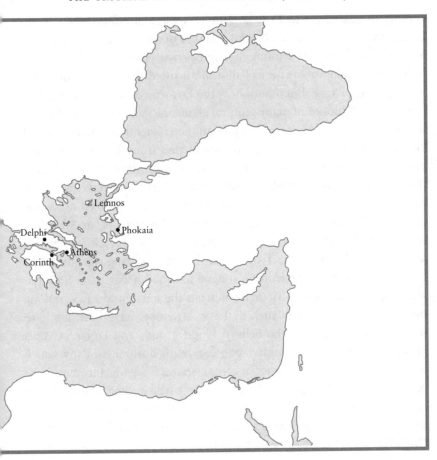

hailed from Halikarnassos, was determined to prove that the Etruscans were not oriental migrants, but that they were indigenous to Italy – 'autochthonous', born from the very soil of the land – as part of a complex argument which would demonstrate the close kinship of Greeks and Romans.[5] This view came into fashion among revisionist twentieth-century historians who were aware that Herodotos' account, still generally accepted, was only superficially satisfactory. On the one hand, Herodotos explained the extraordinary degree of oriental influence over early Etruscan art and culture. On the other hand, this influence was felt most profoundly around the time that the Phoenicians and Greeks began to penetrate into the Tyrrhenian Sea during the eighth and seventh centuries BC, a time far later than that hypothesized by Herodotos for the coming of easterners to Etruria. Nor was there any link between the Lydian language (of Luvian origin) and that of the Etruscans, as Dionysios had already noted.[6] Doffing his cap briefly to Dionysios, the modern Italian archaeologist Massimo Pallottino insisted that the real question was not that of 'race' but that of how the Etruscan civilization came into being as a composite of many cultural elements: native peoples of many origins and languages, alongside foreign merchants from Phoenicia and Greece.[7] At most, a few wandering *condottieri* from Asia Minor might have established themselves as rulers over communities in central Italy: this would explain the sudden passion of the elite of Tarquinia and Caere for grand tombs in the oriental style, beginning around 650 BC; while the name Tarquin (*Tarchna*) strongly recalls the name of an Anatolian storm god, Tarḫun, who in earlier centuries had given his name to people and places in Arzawa, near Troy. As for the Etruscan language, this must be a very ancient Mediterranean tongue that had persisted in Italy but was displaced elsewhere by invaders from the north and east speaking Indo-European languages such as Latin. Attempts have been made to solve this problem with the help of blood groups and DNA.[8] Claims have been made that the modern population of Murlo in Tuscany, which was once an important Etruscan centre, shares a significant number of genes with Levantine populations, and that cattle in central Tuscany are also more 'eastern' than might be expected, leading scientists to postulate the arrival of not just human migrants but their beasts as well.[9] However, since Etruscan times there have been plenty of opportunities for easterners to settle in Tuscan towns, as Roman legionaries or as medieval slaves. All this encourages the historian to concentrate on the real problem: not whence the Etruscans came, but how their distinctive culture came into being in Italy.

To say that Etruscan civilization emerged without a mass migration is not to say that the ties between Etruria and the eastern Mediterranean were insignificant. On the contrary, this explanation of the rise of Etruria places a heavy emphasis on the migration not of whole peoples but of objects, standards of taste and religious cults from east to west. Peoples may not have migrated; but there is good evidence from historical sources and from archaeology that individual people did so, for example Demaratos of Corinth, said to be the father of King Tarquin I of Rome (d. 579 BC), or the seventh-century Greek potter Aristonothos, who worked in Etruscan Caere.[10] The Greeks and Phoenicians brought not just ceramics and luxury goods but new models of social behaviour. Banquets and funerary feasts (including the custom of reclining on couches at banquets) may have been copied from Syrian models. Sexual behaviour combined Greek and native Etruscan customs: the word *katmite* was a typically Etruscan compression of the Greek name Ganymede, and it passed into Latin as *catamitus*, 'catamite', along with sharp accusations that the Etruscans enjoyed pederasty, though observers were also puzzled at the prominent role accorded to women at what elsewhere were all-male banquets.[11]

II

From an early date, these Etruscans were also accused of being pirates. One of the Homeric Hymns makes the connection plain. It tells how the god Dionysos was standing on a headland by the sea, in the appearance of a handsome young man, with long hair waving in the wind, wearing a fine purple cloak. But

> Soon men from a well-trimmed ship, pirates, came
> quickly over the wine-dark sea, Tyrsenians. An evil fate brought
> them. They saw him, nodded to each other, jumped quickly, seized
> him and took him to the ship, rejoicing in their hearts.[12]

But his bonds fell from his body, and the helmsman realized that he was a god, not a man, saying: 'Do not lay hands on him in case in his anger he summon fierce winds and heavy storms.' But the captain replied: 'I suspect he is going to Egypt or to Cyprus or to the Hyperborean land or even further. In the end he will tell us who are his friends and what is their wealth.' Dionysos responded by covering the ship with festoons of vines, and wine ran down the middle of the vessel. He summoned a bear into existence; the terrified sailors jumped into the sea and were transformed into dolphins, while the god mercifully spared the helmsman, revealing himself as 'loud-crying Dionysos'. The story of Dionysos and the pirates was a favourite theme of vase painters, including one of the most skilled Athenian painters, Exekias. A shallow cup from his hand depicts Dionysos lounging in a boat whose mast has become the support for an enormous vine that rises high above the ship's broad sail, while seven dolphins leap around the ship; the image is painted in black-figure on a red ground and dates from about 530 BC.[13] It carries his signature; most remarkably, it was found within the necropolis of one of the great Etruscan cities, Vulci. The inhabitants of Vulci possessed an almost insatiable appetite for the finest Greek pottery. The fact that the Etruscans were presented in such a negative way in the story did not prevent them from taking delight in Exekias' cup.

In the hymn Dionysos seems to be standing on a headland somewhere in the eastern Mediterranean, because the pirates imagine he may be trying to reach the Levant or the 'Hyperborean land' beyond the Black Sea. That Tyrsenians were present in Greek waters is confirmed by archaeological evidence from Lemnos and by the insistence of the ancient historians themselves that there were settlements consisting of these people on the islands and coasts of the Aegean.[14] Herodotos and Thucydides spoke of Tyrsenians and Pelasgians who lived on the northern shores of the Aegean, around Mount Athos, and on Lemnos, within sight of Athos, from which they were expelled in 511 following an Athenian invasion.[15] Out of this emerges a remarkable revision of the early history of Mediterranean trade and seafaring, in which the Greeks and Phoenicians have early competitors, somehow connected with the Etruscans. (According to an excessively ingenious French scholar, the story of Dionysos and the dolphins is really a tale about how the Etruscans tried to dominate the wine trade in the Mediterranean.)[16] All Etruscans were (in Greek) *Tyrsenoi*; but that is not necessarily to say that all *Tyrsenoi* were Etruscans. The term was clearly used in a generic sense to mean barbarian pirates.[17]

These comments might be easily dismissed as another example of ancient historians' fantasies about mysterious pre-Greek peoples. Yet the myths can be linked to reality. A gravestone discovered at Kaminia on Lemnos, and thought to date from around 515 BC, has a crude portrayal of a warrior carrying a spear and shield, accompanied by an extensive inscription in the Greek alphabet, but in a non-Greek language. Since a few other fragmentary inscriptions have also been found in the same language, the gravestone is evidently a record of the language spoken on Lemnos when the island was still inhabited by Thucydides' 'Tyrsenians'. This language was similar to, but not identical with, that of Etruscan inscriptions from far away in central Italy.[18] The Kaminia stone was erected in memory of Holaies the Phokaian (*Phokiasale*), who occupied high office and who died at the age of forty (some argue sixty). Holaies apparently served as a mercenary in Phokaia, on the Ionian coast, and in other lands around the Aegean.[19] But the Tyrsenians of the Aegean were in all respects, apart from language and love of piracy, unlike the Etruscans. Lemnos did not imitate Etruria in its art and crafts; but for the comments by classical historians and but for the inscriptions, there would be no suggestion that the inhabitants were linked to the Etruscans. There are no shards of Etruscan pottery, no signs of a direct link between these lands speaking similar tongues.[20] A seventh-century temple site outside Myrina (now somewhat oddly incorporated in a holiday hotel) consists of a maze of passages and rooms, and recalls nothing obvious in either Greece or Italy. Thus the Tyrsenians of the Aegean consisted of people who spoke a similar language to Etruscan, and probably shared their love of piracy, but retained a very conservative culture while, as will be seen, the Tyrsenians of Italy transformed Etruria into the seat of a pioneering civilization.

The Greeks might try to pigeon-hole each ethnic group they encountered, drawing sharp lines between them, but the reality was that places like Lemnos and Athos were the points where old and new cultures met. Sometimes ancient customs and even languages lingered in such places. The coasts and islands of the Mediterranean did not foster uniformity. Pockets of different peoples lived scattered around the islands and shores of the Mediterranean then and for millennia afterwards. The rigid compartmentalization of the peoples of the Mediterranean by Greek writers distorted the reality of what was there.

III

To move from conservative Lemnos to Tarquinia, in southern Etruria, is to enter a different world, one that was undergoing startling changes, the result of powerful impulses that had arrived from across the Mediterranean. This great transformation began as early as the tenth century; a sophisticated culture spread inland from the coast of western Italy, because the areas closest to the Mediterranean were the first to come into close contact with the cultures of the eastern Mediterranean. First of all, a series of village communities staked out land for huts on the top of the hill that would later be occupied by the great city known to the Romans as *Tarquinii*.[21] The plural form of this name, and that of other Etruscan city names (Veii, Volsinii, Vulci, Volaterrae), perhaps suggests a memory of these multiple origins. The pre-urban culture that came into existence in these villages is known as 'Villanovan', as entirely modern a name as it sounds: Villanova is a suburb of Bologna where the distinctive features of this culture were first recognized by archaeologists who excavated its rich cremation burials. Villanovan culture emerged simultaneously by the sea in southern Etruria, gradually spreading north into what is now Tuscany, and across the Apennines in Bologna. However, it was in the maritime cities of Etruria that the great leap towards urban civilization first occurred: these were rich cities, well organized, with literate elites, handsome temples and skilled craftsmen. Etruscan civilization spread inland from the coastal cities, and later centres such as Perugia emerged only as the inhabitants of the interior were gradually Etruscanized.[22] In that sense the Etruscan 'nation' did indeed emerge out of a migration, but it was a migration within Italy, from the Mediterranean coasts towards and over the Apennines, and a migration of styles more than of people.

The most striking examples of Villanovan technology are the impressive crested helmets made of bronze, whose method of production recalls that of bronzework in central Europe at the same period; the helmets are clear testimony to the role of warriors in the stratified village society of the Villanovans.[23] The shift among those of high birth from cremation to burial in long, narrow shaft graves was not the result of a great population shift but of a change in customs, influenced by contact with overseas. Eventually these shaft graves would turn into something much grander, the tumuli and painted tombs of Tarquinia and Cerveteri. One of the early warrior princes can be identified, though not by name, for there are no inscriptions in his praise, and there is no evidence the Villanovans used writing. In 1869 news circulated of the discovery of a vast sarcophagus in the necropolis outside Tarquinia; this late eighth-century burial became known as the 'Warrior's Tomb'.[24] Its contents demonstrate the arrival of goods from the eastern Mediterranean, which became the prized possession of a Tarquinian prince. Fourteen vases in the Greek style were found in the tomb; several were made in Italy by émigré Greek potters, though their design is reminiscent of goods produced in Crete, Rhodes and Cyprus.[25] This evidence of wider links with the eastern Mediterranean is confirmed by the discovery in the tomb of a scarab ring made of silver and bronze; engraved on the underside of the scarab is a lion in the Phoenician style.[26]

These connections to the outside world were made by sea. A number of pottery models of boats survive from the Villanovan period; their prow takes the form of a bird's head, and it has been surmised that they were placed in the graves of Villanovan pirates and merchants because it was impossible to bury an entire boat with the body or ashes of the deceased.[27] In the early seventh century the potter Aristonothos, who lived and worked in Caere, decorated a *krater* with a lively scene of a sea battle, possibly between Greeks and Etruscans, one group aboard a low-lying oared vessel and the others aboard a heavier merchant ship.[28] What the Villanovans brought back with them can be deduced from home-made objects as well as from imports, for there are echoes of the Aegean world in the design of bronze weapons, and nowhere more than in the style of pottery: traditional Villanovan forms were wedded with Greek styles to produce decorated jars that recall the Geometric style of ninth-century Greece. Jewellery began to be decorated with the fine granulation that was later to become the hallmark of Etruscan goldsmiths; this was a method that was learned from (and eventually surpassed) the Levant.[29] Some bronzework even has parallels with the fine bronze casting of Urartu, in modern Armenia.[30] The trade in base metals was the real foundation of Etruscan prosperity. It was mainly thanks to plentiful local supplies of copper, iron and other metals that the Etruscans could pay for the goods that they imported in increasingly massive quantities from Greece and the Levant, for they had little to offer in the way of finished goods (though they did find a market for their polished black *bucchero* wares, which turned up in Greece, Sicily and Spain). Elba, and the facing coast around Populonia, which was the only major Etruscan city actually situated on the sea, provided plentiful quantities of iron; a little inland, around Volterra and Vetulonia, copper mines were abundant.[31] By the seventh century a flourishing new settlement near the mouth of the river Arno came into existence at Pisa, through which much of this traffic flowed.[32] Via Pisa, the Etruscans exchanged metals with the inhabitants of Sardinia; Sard potters even settled in Vetulonia.[33] They may have arrived as slaves, for slave-raiding and slave-trading were further means to gain profit in the Tyrrhenian Sea as it opened up to commerce. Salt was another asset; the citizens of the Etruscan city of Veii and its very close neighbour Rome competed for control of the salt supplies at the mouth of the Tiber. Wine was a particular favourite of Etruscan traders; it was sent out of the Tyrrhenian Sea towards southern France.[34]

The exploitation of this material wealth became more intense once the Greeks had installed themselves close by in Ischia. And yet the arrival of the Greeks there follows by several decades the first evidence of close contact between central Italy and the Greek world, in the eighth century BC. Villanovan brooches and safety-pins appear on Greek sites, and there are also a good many fragments of shields and helmets made by Villanovan bronze-masters.[35] Perhaps they were carried on the 'Tyrsenian' ships mentioned by Greek authors. As links were forged to Ionia and to Corinth, the early Etruscans manufactured their own versions of Proto-Corinthian pottery. The most powerful inhabitants of Tarquinia and its neighbours sought the fine goods of the eastern Mediterranean, which loudly proclaimed their power and status: ostrich eggs brought by Phoenician traders, ivory and gold plaques showing sphinxes, panthers, lotuses and other 'oriental' motifs, objects made of faience and glass with Egyptian themes (though these were most often imitations made in Phoenicia).[36]

There was one import from the East that would transform the face of Italy. The alphabet reached the Etruscans from the Greeks, though it is uncertain whether the source was Greece itself or the first Greek settlements at Pithekoussai and Kyma. The form the Etruscan letters took indicates that they were derived from the Euboian version of the Greek alphabet. The alphabet came along the trade routes; and it came early. One of the most remarkable finds in Etruria is a seventh-century tablet unearthed in 1915 at Marsiliana d'Albegna. Around its edge is scratched an entire alphabet, in the traditional order of letters, the forms of which appear very archaic.[37] It was found with a stylus, and there were traces of wax on the tablet, so it was evidently obtained with the express purpose of learning the art of writing.[38] Out of the model alphabet a standard Etruscan alphabet developed, written generally from right to left (like Phoenician and some early Greek alphabets); and from this were derived the alphabets of many of the neighbouring peoples, notably the Romans.

Early inscriptions reveal a great deal about contacts across the sea. Greek and Etruscan merchants recorded their transactions, as can be seen on a lead plaque found at Pech Maho in south-western France, dating from the mid-fifth century BC. One side is written in Etruscan, and refers to *Mataliai* or Marseilles; later, the plaque was re-used, to record in Greek the purchase of some boats from men of Emporion, a

Greek base on the coast of Catalonia.[39] Three golden plaques found at Pyrgoi, the port of Caere, on the coast north of Rome, reveal the Phoenician (most probably Carthaginian) presence in the maritime cities of Etruria. Two of the tablets are in Etruscan and one is in Phoenician; they record a dedication by Thefarie Velianas, 'king over Cisra' (or Caere), around 500 BC; the king dedicated a temple to the Etruscan goddess Uni, generally identified with the Greek Hera and the Roman Juno, but here identified with Astarte, the goddess of the Phoenicians.[40] There were Greek visitors too: an inscription, of around 570 BC, appears on a stone made in the shape of half a crescent, representing an anchor, found near Tarquinia: 'I belong to the Aiginetan Apollo. Sostratos had me made.' The language is the Greek dialect of the island of Aigina near Athens; this is surely the Sostratos said by Herodotos to be the leading Greek merchant trading towards Tartessos.[41] The Etruscans did not try to erect barriers against foreign merchants and settlers, or against their gods; in fact, they welcomed them and sought to learn from them.[42]

IV

In the middle of the seventh century the culture, politics and even landscape of the Etruscans was transformed, as the intense influence of 'orientalizing' styles of art overwhelmed the ancient culture of the Villanovans. Greece had seen a similar process of transformation as its ties to the Levant were strengthened by way of Ionian and Phoenician merchants. Indeed, these Ionians formed part of the wave of influences from the East that crossed the sea to Etruria, so that the Greek and other eastern influences are hard to disentangle: sculpted winged creatures protect the tombs of the deceased, which were built in increasingly lavish styles, no longer as simple graves but as substantial chamber-tombs, often imitating the houses of the living. The earliest monumental tombs in Tarquinia stood above the ground, broad, circular constructions with a peaked roof; tufa slabs above the entrance portrayed the gods and spirits of the next world, but they also proclaimed the wealth of the new princely elite that could afford to build such impressive palaces for the dead. The source of inspiration was very probably similar tombs in the eastern Mediterranean, in regions such as Lydia, Lycia and Cyprus. Painted tombs for elite families became a Tarquinian speciality from the middle of the sixth century onwards, though earlier examples are known from neighbouring cities, and the discovery of a partly painted ante-chamber to what may be a royal tomb, dating to the middle of the seventh century BC, caused much excitement when it was announced in August 2010 – the closest comparison is with contemporary Greek tombs at Salamis in eastern Cyprus.[43] The earliest tombs betray such powerful influence from the art of Greek Ionia that it is legitimate to ask whether the artists themselves were Ionian Greeks; evidently there was no sharp line between foreign and native craftsmen. Sixth-century paintings from tombs in Caere, now preserved in the Louvre and the British Museum, with their strong delineation, formal arrangement and careful organiza-tion of space, are not merely Ionian in style but almost certainly portray scenes from Greek mythology: the judgment of Paris, the sacrifice of Iphigeneia. The painted tombs of Tarquinia were often decorated with scenes of family feasting, but there were also tales to be told from Greek mythology: Achilles appears in the Tomb of the Bulls, and the mysteri-ous processions of the Tomb of the Baron are painted in a style that is thoroughly Greek. A painted frieze shows youths leading horses and a meeting between a bearded man with a young companion and a mis-tress or goddess. Simply coloured, in red, green or black on a grey undercoat, each figure displays profound Ionian influence – in the cos-tume, which includes the Ionian *tutulus*, a peaked hat, and in the fleshy, rounded limbs. D. H. Lawrence, touring the tombs in the 1920s, was (like most visitors) enchanted by the unusual and very lively scenes in the Tomb of Hunting and Fishing, showing birds in flight, a naked man diving into the sea and a fisherman trailing a line; this, at least, seemed to be the expressive voice of Etruscan rather than Greek art. But the discovery of a painted tomb in the Greek colony at Poseidonia (Paes-tum) in southern Italy, showing a diving scene, suggests that these images were part of the general repertoire of Greek painters.

Much the same can be said for other branches of the arts and, more importantly, for the thought-world that they reveal. Etruscan potters began to imitate the black-figure pottery of Corinth and Athens with varying success. Later, painting in black on the red surface of the pot gave way to a still more delicate red-figure technique, by which the pot was painted black but figures were left largely unpainted on the red ground of the ceramic; and the Etruscans bought prodigious quantities of the new wares from Athens, also making their own imitations.[44] But the Etruscans had a strongly conservative outlook too. Their preference was for archaic or 'archaizing' styles even when, in Athens, the full classical style invested sculpture and painting with a greater sense of life and 'harmony'.[45] The pottery they bought from the Greeks was not always of the highest quality. At Spina, an Etruscan settlement on the mouth of the Po, virtually all the pottery so far discovered has been Greek, especially Attic Greek; but sometimes it is very poor Greek, as the name given to one Attic artist – 'the Worst Painter' – illustrates.[46] Most importantly, the subject-matter of the illustrations on these pots was consistently the stories of Greek mythology. The peoples of Italy were beginning to appropriate the myths and religious ideas of the Greek world; old cults of groves and water-sources remained very much alive, but the amorphous gods of the Italian peoples acquired the shape, form and indeed moodiness of the Olympians. The roof beam of a great temple at Veii was decorated around 500 BC with life-size painted figures of Apollo, Hermes and other gods, made of terracotta, the work of a celebrated Etruscan sculptor named Vulca. The fluid style of the sculptures was not simply borrowed wholesale from the Greeks; the practice of decorating the roof beam so dramatically was an Etruscan and not a Greek one. But what Vulca portrayed was Greek legend, not Etruscan. These works were the product of an Italo-Graeco-oriental syncretism, which in a sense is what we call Etruscan art. This syncretism was also expressed in the art of divination: here again Near Eastern practices merged with native Italian ones. No one was better at reading the spots on the liver of a sacrificial beast than an Etruscan soothsayer, or *haruspex*, and Etruscan soothsayers were still being consulted when the Goths attacked Rome in AD 410.

V

The relationship between the Greeks and the Etruscans also took a political form, and there relations were much less easy than in the spheres of culture, religion and trade. From at least the eighth century BC there had been sea battles between the peoples of central Italy and the Greeks. Evidence of this has been found on Greek soil at Olympia and at Delphi, where eighth-century Villanovan helmets, seized from defeated enemies, were dedicated to the gods.[47] Etruscan navigators often competed and sometimes cooperated with Phokaians from Greek Ionia in the waters off southern France, where the Phokaians founded a colony (the future Marseilles).[48] Herodotos reports a great battle between Phokaians and Etruscans, off the Corsican town of Alalia in around 540. Sixty Phokaian ships were ranged against sixty Carthaginian ships and sixty more from Caere. Despite this imbalance, the Phokaian ships won the battle, but their fleet was so crippled that the Phokaians had to evacuate Corsica. Herodotos tells how the Caeretans massacred their Phokaian prisoners by stoning them to death. Soon after, the Caeretans noticed that those who passed the site of the massacre suddenly became lame; this happened not just to human beings, but to their flocks. Perplexed, the Caeretans sent a mission to the priestess of Apollo at Delphi, and they were ordered to hold regular games in memory of the Phokaians, a practice that continued to Herodotos' time; similar funeral games are often shown on the walls of Etruscan painted tombs.[49] The Caeretans maintained their links with the shrine at Delphi, where the foundations of the treasury of the Caeretans have been identified; indeed, they were the first 'barbarians' to be admitted to what was primarily a Hellenic cult site.[50] Meanwhile the Etruscans were free to exploit Corsica for its iron, wax and honey. More important than its resources, though, was the fact that Etruscan shipping now faced no rivals in the northern Tyrrhenian Sea.[51]

The southern Tyrrhenian was another matter. The Greeks of Kyma were particularly conscious of the proximity of Etruscan power – land as well as sea power – since two Etruscan cities lay in the hinterland (Capua, Nola); and the Etruscans gained control over at least one coastal town, Pompeii.[52] Kyma had to rely on help from the Greek colonists in Sicily to triumph over the Etruscans. In 474 Hieron, tyrant of Syracuse, secured a victory that would transform not just the political but the commercial face of the western Mediterranean. He was well aware of this: at the time when Xerxes' Persian hordes had just been repelled by the might of Hellas, this was his contribution to the defeat of the barbarians. Moreover, Hieron's victory at Kyma followed another victory at Himera in Sicily, where six years earlier the Syracusan fleet under his predecessor Gelon had decisively defeated its other enemy in the western Mediterranean, Carthage; Gelon's victory was said to have occurred on the same day as one of the great battles against the Persians, the Greek victory at Salamis.[53] Writing not long afterwards, the

Greek poet Pindar took the defeat of the Etruscans at Kyma as one of the main themes of his ode in praise of Hieron 'of Etna, winner of the chariot race':

> Grant, I beg, O son of Kronos, that the Phoenician and the Tyrrhenians' war-cry keep quiet at home: it has seen what woe to its ships came of its pride before Kyma, and all that befell when the lord of Syracuse routed them, who out of their swift sailing ships cast down their youth in the sea – the dragger of Hellas from her weight of slavery.[54]

Hieron dedicated an Etruscan pot-helmet at Olympia inscribed: 'Hieron, son of Deinomenes and the Syracusans and Zeus: Tyrsenian from Kyma'; it is now preserved in the British Museum. However, Pindar's attempt to link the Etruscans and the Carthaginians ('the Phoenicians' war-cry') was anachronistic. For whatever reason, relations between the Carthaginians and the Etruscans had already begun to weaken in the two decades before the battle of Kyma. There is a clear archaeological break in Etruscan imports to Carthage not before 550 and not after 500.[55] Anaxilas of Rhegion, a Greek ally of Carthage, built a rampart specifically to prevent an Etruscan attack on his city, perched on the Straits of Messina. On their own and without success Etruscan ships sailed south to attack the Lipari islands, which still functioned, as they had done since prehistoric times, as a centre of exchange linking the western Mediterranean to the eastern Mediterranean.[56] During the early fifth century, then, the Etruscans became increasingly isolated within the western Mediterranean.

Even though Etruscan ships appear in action again at the end of the fifth century, the Syracusans had won access to the whole Tyrrhenian Sea. In 453–2, they raided the coast off Caere and installed themselves briefly on iron-bearing Elba, where they captured many slaves; at long last the Tyrsenian pirates were being paid back in their own coin.[57] The Etruscans maintained their grudge against Syracuse until the Peloponnesian War, which will be discussed in a later chapter. When they launched their own attacks on Syracuse, the Athenians were well aware of this hostility.[58] In 413 BC the Etruscans sent three large warships to Syracuse to help the Athenian fleet. As Thucydides laconically remarked: 'there were some Tyrrhenians fighting because of their hatred for Syracuse'.[59] They were few but they saved the day on at least one occasion. Several centuries later the Spurinna family, a noble clan of Tarquinia, proudly erected a Latin inscription in praise of their ancestors, one of whom was a naval commander in the Sicilian campaign of 413 BC.[60]

VI

The links between Greece and Etruria were effected by way of a city in southern Italy famed for its inhabitants' love of luxury. Until its destruction in 510 as a result of local jealousies, Sybaris was the great entrepôt at which products arrived from Corinth, Ionia and Athens, before being transported across country to Poseidonia (Paestum) and embarked on Etruscan ships.[61] Sybaris was especially famous, or notorious, for its friendship towards Etruria; according to Athenaios of Naukratis (who lived in the second century AD), its commercial alliances stretched far in two directions, north to Etruria and east to Miletos on the coast of Asia Minor:

> The Sybarites wore mantles made of wool from Miletos, and from this sprang the friendship between the states. The Sybarites loved the Etruscans above all other peoples of Italy and among those of the Orient had a special preference for the Ionians, because these, like themselves, were fond of luxury.[62]

The western Greeks functioned as intermediaries: it was not their own products but those of their brethren in the Aegean world that interested the Etruscans.

One way in which the Athenians managed to maintain their superiority over their rivals was by using new channels of communication when the old ones were rendered inaccessible by war and commercial disputes. The battle of Kyma marked the beginning of the end of the Etruscan thalassocracy in the western Mediterranean. The Tyrrhenian Sea was no longer their lake, but had to be shared with the Carthaginians, Greeks of Magna Graecia and new contenders such as the Romans and the Volscians, hill-people from central Italy who proved remarkably versatile and managed to launch their own pirate raids. The Etruscans responded to the loss of maritime opportunities by taking control of towns inland, including Perugia (previously a centre of the Umbrian people, related to the Latins), Bologna (previously inhabited by 'Villanovans' culturally similar to the very early Etruscans) and cities in the

Po Valley such as Mantua.[63] This meant that new routes could open up, carrying goods from the eastern Mediterranean across the peninsula from ports on the shores of the Adriatic. In the seventh and sixth centuries an extraordinary cultural florescence had occurred in what are now the Italian Marches, among the people known as the Picenes, who were open to Greek influences by sea and to Etruscan influences overland.[64] But after 500 the Adriatic became the main channel of communication with the Greek lands; the route was convenient for mariners, even if it entailed what must have been a costly overland journey through the Apennines. For ships could set out from the Gulf of Corinth, clearing the Ionian islands and calling in at the Greek colonies of Apollonia and Epidamnos, before working their way up past the lands of the Picenes to Adria and Spina, newly developed ports in the mud-flats and shallows of north-eastern Italy, close to the later cities of Ferrara and Ravenna. Just as the Este dukes of Renaissance Ferrara devoted great energy to the breeding of fine horses, so too in the archaic and classical Greek periods horse-breeding drew the Greeks to this region.[65]

Spina was either an Etruscan foundation that experienced heavy Greek immigration or a Greek foundation that experienced heavy Etruscan immigration; its population was a mix of Etruscans, Greeks, Veneti from north-eastern Italy and any number of other peoples. It may have been the outpost of the inland city of Felsina (Etruscan Bologna): a late fifth-century stele from Bologna portrays a warship that belonged to a member of the Kaikna family of Felsina, and it is hard to see where they could have based their ships except in the Adriatic ports such as Spina. Spina and Adria offered the Greeks and Etruscans large numbers of Italic and Celtic slaves; these numbers could only grow as Etruscan colonizers in the Po Valley and Celtic invaders coming across the Alps collided with one another. Spina was laid out on a grid plan, a design the Etruscans strongly favoured, but the water channels leading to the sea gave it something of the character of an Etrusco-Greek Venice. Over 4,000 tombs have been opened in its necropolis; massive quantities of Greek vases have been recovered, including many from the fifth and early fourth centuries, after which the link to Athens was sundered and the citizens of Spina had to rely on inferior pottery from Etruscan kilns.[66] The alluvial agricultural land of the Po delta was highly productive, but the problem with alluvial soils is that they do not stand still, and, as they advanced in the fourth century, the city found itself stranded further and further from the sea. Meanwhile, Celtic raids into Italy, which culminated in an attack on Rome in 390 BC, had severe effects in this region, which was heavily settled by the invaders.[67] Thus Spina's period of efflorescence was relatively short, but brilliant. Its rise to prominence formed part of a wider process which saw the entire Adriatic become a marketplace in which Greek wares were widely available.

The emergence of the Etruscan cities was thus much more than a phenomenon of the Tyrrhenian Sea; the Adriatic too was opened to the movement of people and goods. Along with the Greeks and the Phoenicians, the Etruscans refashioned the Mediterranean, helping to create interconnections that spanned the entire sea.

4

Towards the Garden of the Hesperides,
1000 BC–400 BC

I

The impact of contact with the eastern Mediterranean was felt in very different ways within what we now call Italy. Greek culture seeped more slowly into the everyday life of the native peoples of Sicily – Sikans, Sikels and Elymians – than into the life of the peoples of Tuscany and Latium. In Sicily, both the Greeks and the Carthaginians kept themselves largely apart from the native population. Sardinia, rich in minerals, had for centuries been the seat of a lively civilization characterized by the stone towers known as *nuraghi*, of which many thousands still dot the island; they were surrounded by what seem to have been prosperous villages, firmly rooted in the rich agricultural resources of the island. They began to be built around 1400 BC, but new *nuraghi* were still being constructed well into the Iron Age.[1] In the Mycenaean era, there had been some contact with the outside world, as eastern Mediterranean traders arrived in search of copper. The wealth of the native elite as far back as the second millennium BC can be measured from the tombs of Anghelu Ruju, near Alghero in north-western Sardinia; these are among the richest to have been unearthed in late Neolithic and early Bronze Age western Europe, and they indicate contact with Spain, southern France and the eastern Mediterranean.[2] The Spanish influence can be traced in the bell beaker jars found at this site. Another Spanish connection was linguistic. The Sardinians left no written records, whether because they did not use writing or because they used friable materials that have failed to survive. But place-names, many in current use, provide suggestive evidence, as does the Sard language, a distinctive form of late vulgar Latin that incorporates a number of pre-Latin words within its many dialects. It appears

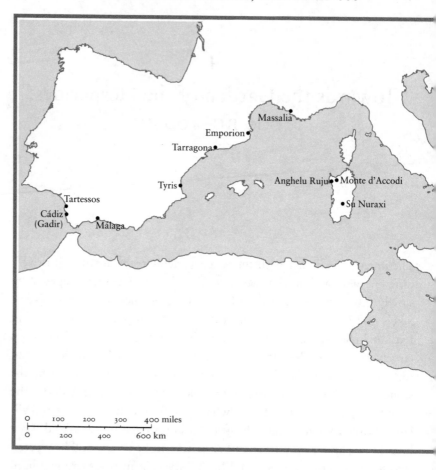

that the nuraghic peoples spoke a language or languages related to the non-Indo-European language Basque. Thus a Sard word for a young lamb, *bitti*, is very similar to a Basque term for a young goat, *bitin*.[3] Rather than revealing a large migration from Iberia to Sardinia, this is evidence for the existence of a group of western Mediterranean languages whose speakers could be found in Spain, southern France, some of the western Mediterranean islands and parts of North Africa.

As early as the second millennium the Sardinians were burying their dead in impressive rock-cut tombs, carved to resemble the houses of the living, containing several chambers joined by passages, and decorated with door jambs, cornices and other stone-carved imitations of what must have been, in the houses of the living, wooden accoutrements. In modern Sardinia these tombs are called *domus de janas*, 'houses of

Phokaia

fairies'. But the ancient Sardinians also constructed impressive sacred sites, as at Monte d'Accodi, in the north, near Sassari, where a truncated pyramid accessible along a great ramp was constructed, possibly in the fifteenth century BC, probably as a place of worship.

Most *nuraghi* stand back from the coast; many stood on the crests of hills, and everything suggests that their main purpose was defensive: to guard against sheep-rustlers, sea-raiders and, above all, troublesome Sardinian neighbours; they were also strongboxes in which copper and bronze, in raw form and manufactured into figurines and armaments, could be stored. A good example is provided by the massive complex at Su Nuraxi at Barumini in southern Sardinia, which flourished in the eighth to the sixth century; as well as its castle, Su Nuraxi contained about sixty huts, with stone foundations, arranged around a central piazza. One large structure is thought to have been a council chamber, equipped with a stone bench and recesses in which lamps were placed. Attacked and destroyed by the Carthaginians, whose base at Cagliari lay not far to the south, Su Nuraxi was rebuilt in the fifth century, and judging from the finds of objects in terracotta, bronze and iron it once again became a prosperous centre.[4] This was a highly fragmented society, in which every petty lord possessed his own castle. But influences from Phoenicia, Carthage and Etruria penetrated slowly: this was not a civilization that was rapidly and dazzlingly transformed by contact with the outside world, in the way that the early Etruscans were transformed by contact with the Greeks and the Phoenicians.[5] The interplay with Italy, Spain and Africa was more subtle, and Sardinian society leaves an impression of deep conservatism – nuraghi were still being constructed as late as the third century, by which time not just the Carthaginians but the Romans were often the enemy. The profusion of towers, staircases, secret passage-ways and ramparts at such sites as Palmavera, near Alghero, of about 750 BC, as well as the fortified villages clustering around the foot of the nuraghi, speak of a time when Phoenician invaders were installing themselves on Sardinia and more sophisticated constructions were needed to deal with more sophisticated enemies. The religious cults on ancient Sardinia also reveal the conservatism of this society; here, the gods of the Greeks or Phoenicians did not gain control, and the islanders focused their devotion on sacred wells and bull-cults.[6]

The Sards were not city-dwellers. Their characteristic settlements were villages around castles. The cities of Sardinia were those established by the Phoenicians and Carthaginians. Yet the sometimes difficult relationship between the Carthaginians and the Sardinians did not mean that nuraghic civilization was sealed off from the outside world. One exotic import was amber, which travelled down by some unknown route all the way from the Baltic, finishing its journey at Su Nuraxi. Gold did not greatly interest the Sards, and the full exploitation of the silver mines in southern Sardinia would wait until the fourteenth century AD. The oldest examples of Greek pottery found in Sardinia (setting aside some Mycenaean fragments) date from the eighth century. In the seventh century an Ionian vase reached Su Nuraxi. Some idea of the strength of outside contacts can be gained from the fact that Corinthian pottery has been found only on sites in southern Sardinia, whereas Etruscan pottery (including imitations of Greek pots) has been discovered across the island.[7] To the Sards these were evidently attractive, exotic items for which they could easily pay with copper ingots.

Finding copper was no problem for the Sards; but, to transform copper into its harder alloy bronze, tin had to be imported from Spain and southern France. And out of bronze the Sardinians manufactured statuettes whose influence spread in both place and time: the long-legged human figurines attracted the eye of the twentieth-century sculptor Giacometti, having already fascinated Etruscan metalworkers in Vetulonia, where their own long-limbed figurines were produced, often by Sard workmen. Several hundred of these statuettes survive from Sardinia itself, dating from the eighth to the sixth century BC. They seem to portray a real world of warriors, archers, craftsmen and shepherds, though female figures are rarer than male. Sometimes, too, they depict animals; on occasion they probably represent gods, and they were probably used in local cults.[8] The figurines provide direct evidence of navigation, for several model boats have been found in Etruscan ports. They are thought to date from the eighth century onwards; one has a prow in the form of a deer's head, and several animals and birds adorn the gunwales; another round-bottomed boat contains the crouching figure of a monkey, an animal the Carthaginians could have brought across from Africa.[9]

II

The Greeks in southern Italy acted as a bridge linking those of Ionia, Attika and the Peloponnese to the newly emergent cities of Etruria. In the same way a far-flung Ionian colony, Massalia, on the site of modern Marseilles, acted as a bridge between the metropolitan Greek world and the westernmost coasts of the Mediterranean.[10] Once again it was the Phokaians, from the coast of Asia Minor, who were the pioneers, establishing their settlement around 600 BC; about 600 adult settlers arrived, and they soon intermarried with the native population. Early Marseilles grew rapidly, and covered about fifty hectares during the sixth century.[11] Its true age of glory was its first half-century of existence. In the mid-sixth century, the invasion of Ionia by the Persians stimulated the Phokaians to emigrate as far from the Persian enemy as it was possible to go. Herodotos relates that the Persians demanded that one rampart of the city of Phokaia should be demolished and that one building should be symbolically handed over to the Persian satrap. The Phokaians indicated that they were interested in the proposal, and would like a day's truce during which they could think about it; but they took advantage of the truce to load their ships with all their possessions, sailing off to Chios to the far west – first Corsica, then Massalia. They thus handed the Persian king a ghost city.[12]

All this did not make Massalia into a hive of Ionian irredentists. Massalia was a special place, whose inhabitants managed to keep their heads down when their compatriots were fighting the Etruscans; and one explanation for this was the intimate relationship the Massaliots enjoyed with the peoples of the western Mediterranean – not just the Etruscans, but the Carthaginians in Africa and Spain and the less sophisticated Ligurians who inhabited north-western Italy and southern France.[13] Massalia became a point of contact with the Celtic peoples of western Europe, so that Greek and Etruscan pottery and other goods were funnelled northwards from there into the centre of Gaul. Meanwhile, the Greeks, Etruscans and Carthaginians traded side by side in the region; Pech Maho, which has been mentioned already, was used by Carthaginian merchants as a trading station, and yet was evidently visited by others as well, as the Etruscan inscription scratched on lead found there makes plain. Rather than lead, it was tin that attracted merchants to southern France, for they sought access to the tin supplies of north-western France and possibly even Britain, reached by Phoenician sailors out of Cádiz. Finds of Greek and Etruscan bronzes and pottery along the Seine, notably a massive Greek bronze *krater* found at Vix, dating from about 530 BC, give some clues to the lengthy routes that goods (though not necessarily individual merchants) followed deep into the interior of Gaul.[14] This great mixing bowl for wine serves as a reminder that the wine trade was one of the great strengths of Massalia. It could contain 1,100 litres of liquid, the custom among the Greeks being to mix one part of wine with two of water. Indeed, the sixth century was the golden age of Greek trade in the far west. Although an Ionian colony in Corsica was throttled at birth by the Etruscans and Carthaginians, small settlements came into being for a while at Málaga and elsewhere in southern Spain and, more illustriously, at Emporion, the emporium *par excellence*, now known as Empúries. Nearby, traders from Rhodes may have founded Rhode, the modern Roses in Catalonia. Massalia maintained its links to the eastern Mediterranean, whose bronze foundries were hungry for tin. Large quantities of sixth-century Greek pottery have been found during excavations in Marseilles, from Euboia, Corinth, Athens, Sparta, Ionia and, closer at hand, Etruria. The wealthy merchants of Massalia endowed a treasury at Delphi.[15] This was no colonial backwater. The culture of southern France became Hellenized. A late Roman writer, Justin, summarized the words of an earlier writer, Pompeius Trogus (whose *Philippic Histories* are now lost), as follows:

> From the people of Massalia, therefore, the Gauls learned a more civilised way of life, their former barbarity being laid aside or softened; and by them they were taught to cultivate their lands and to enclose their towns with walls. Then too, they grew accustomed to live according to laws, and not by violence; then they learned to prune the vine and plant the olive; and such a radiance was shed over both men and things, that it was not Greece which seemed to have immigrated into Gaul, but Gaul that seemed to have been transplanted into Greece.[16]

Of course, this encomium was written many centuries later, and it is doubtful whether the Greeks really introduced the olive and the vine.[17] Still, a good claim can be made that it was the Greeks and Etruscans who fostered the intensive exploitation of vineyards, and introduced a more advanced technology of olive-pressing and wine production. Sir John Boardman insisted that 'the first wine drunk in Burgundy was Greek wine from Marseilles', and the Athenian, Phoenician and Etruscan wine jars found on many sites in Languedoc and Provence support Boardman's contention.[18] Justin was right: it was not necessary to conduct a conquest in the style of the Roman legions to draw this region into the cultural orbit of Greece.

As elsewhere in the western Mediterranean, the years around 500 BC marked an important transition. Partly this was the result of the growing political tension between Greeks and Etruscans, which led to a decline in commercial contacts through the Tyrrhenian Sea. Meanwhile, the cultural centres in northern and eastern France (generally known as the Hallstatt culture) fell under a shadow, and it was Celtic lands further to the east that became the focus of a vibrant new continental culture, the so-called La Tène culture, which was heavily influenced by the Etruscans, by way of the passes over the eastern Alps. This meant that the trade routes linking the Mediterranean to northern Europe shifted eastwards, and demand for fine Mediterranean goods withered in the Rhône valley.[19]

Less Attic pottery arrived in Massalia, though by the end of the century this trade recovered. But, more importantly, the Greeks were no longer able to send wine and fine products inland from Marseilles, while in the far west, along the coast of Spain, it was the Carthaginians who dominated the conduct of commercial business. It has been seen that one response in the Greek world was to rely increasingly on a route up the Adriatic that linked them to the new town of Spina. Marseilles' loss was Spina's gain. Another response was for Massalia to become the mother-city to a new generation of colonies along the shores of Provence and Languedoc, including Agde, though its most famous offshoot, Nikaia (Nice), may have been founded only in the third century.[20]

III

One of the most remarkable cases of Hellenization can be observed in Spain. In early Greek literature, such as the works of Hesiod, the westernmost reaches of the Mediterranean were the home of fabulous creatures such as the three-headed monster Geryon; here lay the mysterious Garden of the Hesperides, and here at the Pillars of Hercules Atlas held up the sky.[21] The Phoenicians had, as has been seen, reached this region first, and had established an important base beyond the Mediterranean at Cádiz. Among the Greeks, the Phokaians and their neighbours were once again the pioneers, starting with the sailor Kolaios of Samos in the mid-seventh century; the king of Tartessos was even said to have invited the Phokaians to settle his lands.[22] Mistakenly, as events would prove, they went to Corsica instead. The Greek presence, as settlers and traders, in sixth- to fourth-century Spain was rather limited by comparison with the Carthaginians, and it is not clear that the Carthaginians were seen as competitors: the Greeks of Emporion traded in metals with them, and Emporion minted coins in the fourth century that combined Carthaginian motifs with those of Greek Sicily. The citizens of Emporion probably recruited mercenaries for the Carthaginian army fighting the Greeks in Sicily; nor did Emporion try to create a large territory under its direct control. Its wealth was based not on local resources but on its contact with the metal-rich lands of southern Spain, contacts that were mediated by Carthaginian merchants.[23] And yet the cultural influence of the Greeks easily surpassed that of Carthage. Although some of the Greek centres in Catalonia continued to flower, those of Andalucía, such as Mainake near modern Málaga, soon withered, and the region reverted to the Phoenician sphere. Silver-rich Tartessos may have passed its peak by 500 BC, but there were other opportunities, and the Carthaginians capitalized on their victories in the western Mediterranean, signing a treaty with the emerging city of Rome in 509 which politely but firmly forbade the Romans and their allies from entering large tracts of the western Mediterranean.

Attempts to close seas are often counterproductive; they invite piracy and are expensive to implement. It was probably before the Carthaginians established their Spanish monopoly that a Greek sailor compiled a sailing manual, or *Periplus*, that described the coasts of Spain from Galicia through the Straits of Gibraltar along the coast all the way to Marseilles, which was presumably his home base. No doubt his aim was to record the route that gave access to supplies of Galician tin. He was a precursor of the famous Greek sailor from Marseilles, Pytheas, who discovered the sea route to Britain in the fourth century.[24] This work of the sixth century BC, or possibly a little later, survived and was incorporated into a clumsily composed poem in Latin by a pagan writer of the late fourth century AD named Avienus.[25] Again and again Avienus indicates that his ancient text describes a place along the coast of Spain that has subsequently fallen into ruin, so there is a mixing of ancient material with observations by later travellers whom Avienus had also read. The omission of some places such as the Greek colony of Rhode suggests that they had not yet been founded by the time the Greek sailor wrote his *Periplus*, confirming its great antiquity. Avienus speaks at length about Tartessos, which had passed its peak by the fifth century BC, and confidently identifies it with Cádiz, while insisting that 'now it is small, now it is abandoned, now a heap of ruins';[26] he describes how the Tartessians traded with their neighbours, and how the Carthaginians reached these waters; he points out a glittering mountain rich in tin which would have greatly interested early traders.[27] The text also refers to decayed Phoenician cities in southern Spain, suggesting that Avienus' precursor travelled past these settlements in the late sixth century; and he mentions how some Phoenician settlements were now occupied by Carthaginian settlers.[28] In turning a Greek text into Latin verse and adding material from later sources, Avienus created a sort of palimpsest, but it is very hard to disentangle the layers.[29] Avienus does describe important native centres of settlement at Tarragona and Valencia, known to him as Tyris (a name that survives in the river Turia, which until recently flowed through the centre of Valencia), but in mentioning Barcelona, whose name is of Carthaginian origin, he refers to a relatively late foundation. He talks of fierce peoples along the Spanish coast who lived off milk and cheese 'like wild beasts', conjuring up an image of the great variety of peoples who fell under the Iberian label, and this is confirmed by archaeological evidence that there was no single Iberian 'nation' but many tribes and statelets.[30]

The Greeks and Carthaginians interacted closely with the Iberian peoples. The result was the emergence of a civilization that achieved a high level in the fine arts, built towns of reasonable size and adopted writing. Iberian civilization has received little attention outside Spain, yet the Iberians reached a level of sophistication surpassed among native peoples of the western Mediterranean only by the Etruscans.[31] They provide a second example of the penetration of Greek and Phoenician culture into the west, across lengthy routes of trade and migration, and of the melding of those cultural influences with native talent in stone sculpture and metalworking. But the Iberians are harder to identify than the Etruscans, who developed a sense of solidarity as a single people who called themselves *Rasna*. There were distinct cultural differences between the Iberians of Andalucía, the Valencian seaboard and Catalonia. There were many tribes and no political unity. It is not even clear that they all spoke the same or related languages, though the best candidates for surviving languages related to the ancient Iberian tongues are Basque and Berber. Inland, they merged with other populations, usually classed not just by modern scholars but by Avienus as Celtic (a very vague term, but one that emphasizes continental rather than Mediterranean cultural traditions).[32] The term 'Iberian' is thus something of a generalization, referring to various peoples between the seventh and second centuries BC, in a politically unstable world which Carthaginians, Greeks and finally Romans penetrated as traders and conquerors.

As in Sicily and southern Italy, Greek settlements such as Emporion sometimes stood apart from the native population, but with time, following intermarriage and other contacts, the towns probably became quite mixed in population. Not far from Emporion, at Ullastret, stood an important Iberian town, which was well planned with four gateways and an area, in the fourth century, of 40,000 square metres. But the

1. Mnajdra in Malta is the site of several temples from the fourth and third millennium BC, closely packed together, beside steep cliffs overlooking the sea; the large central temple here was the last to be built. The Maltese temples are the oldest large-scale buildings in the Mediterranean.

2. The 16 cm-long 'sleeping lady' preserved in the Archaeological Museum, Valletta, may represent an earth goddess, or is perhaps a personification of Malta and Gozo, with the humps representing the two islands.

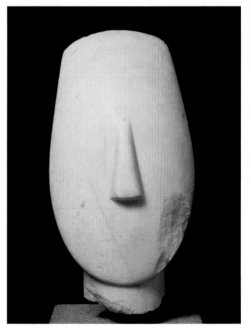

3. Most Cycladic figurines
are female and may portray
companions of the dead,
whether servants or spirits in
the next world.

4. A female head from Keros in the Cycladic
islands, made from local marble in the first
half of the third millennium BC. Its purity and
simplicity are deceptive, since it would have
been highly coloured.

5. Manufactured in Crete around 1500 BC, this vase is one of several
Minoan pots which uses the body and arms of an octopus to create a
fluid and naturalistic design, breaking away from Egyptian and Syrian
models to form a distinctive island style.

6. Fresco of *c.* 1420 BC from the tomb of Pharaoh's vizier Rekhmire in Upper Egypt. One of Rekhmire's functions was to arrange the arrival of tribute from neighbouring lands, portrayed here and boastfully labelled 'every land is subject to His Majesty'. Some tribute, such as jars of oil or wine, seems to come from Crete, other objects and animals from lands to the south.

7. Akrotiri on Thera was a major centre of trade and shipping before its destruction in a massive volcanic eruption in *c.* 1500 BC. This remarkable fresco from the sixteenth century BC shows the port and oared vessels bound for or returning from a Mediterranean voyage.

8. A gold death mask from Mycenae, from around 1500 BC, buried in a princely grave. 'Mycenae rich in gold', as Homer called it, was ruled by Greek-speaking warrior princes who eventually fell under the spell of Minoan culture. These masks may imitate the infinitely grander death masks of the Pharaohs.

9. Deprived of the gold with which their Aegean forebears had covered the faces of the dead, the early Philistines moulded clay images of their leaders. This face forms part of a sarcophagus found at Beth She'an in northern Israel.

10. The twelfth-century Warrior Vase from Mycenae shows a troop of soldiers wearing horned helmets typical of the invaders and mercenaries the Egyptians called the Shardana. Other parts of their equipment bear comparison with Homer's descriptions of his heroes' armour.

11. The Philistines appear on the walls of the early twelfth-century BC temple of Madinat Habu in Upper Egypt, whose friezes celebrate victories attributed to Rameses III over the so-called Sea Peoples.

12. In the late ninth century BC Phoenician merchants established a settlement at Nora in southern Sardinia. They commemorated the dedication of a temple with one of the earliest inscriptions in the Semitic alphabet to survive in the western Mediterranean.

13. This stone tablet or stele, engraved in Carthage around 400 BC, is thought to show a priest, identifiable from his distinctive headdress, carrying a child victim to the place of sacrifice.

14. A model of a Phoenician ship, converted into a lamp and dedicated in AD 232 in the temple of Zeus Beithmares in what is now Lebanon. Although late in date, it gives a good idea of the appearance of Phoenician and Carthaginian ships.

15. Phoenician silver coin portraying a Phoenician ship and the sea monster known to the Greeks as the hippocamp.

16. A battle between Greek foot soldiers or hoplites depicted on the Chigi Vase, found near Veii, north of Rome, and dating from around 600 BC. Prodigious quantities of often magnificent Corinthian pottery were acquired by Etruscan princes.

17. Panel from the bronze gates of the Assyrian royal palace at Balawat in northern Iraq, ninth century BC. The Phoenicians bring tribute across the Mediterranean and overland to the Assyrian court.

18. Late sixth-century BC *krater* decorated in black figure by the Athenian artist Exekias and exported to Vulci in Etruria, where it was discovered in a tomb. The bowl, used as a shallow wine cup, illustrates the story of the capture of the wine god Dionysos by Etruscan pirates, and the transformation of the pirates into dolphins.

19. Tomb of the Hunting and Fishing, Tarquinia, late sixth century BC. The delightful scenes on this Etruscan fresco betray strong influence from Ionian Greek art.

20. Tablet from Marsiliana d'Albegna, Etruria, seventh century BC. Probably used for teaching the alphabet, this tablet provides the earliest evidence for the importation of the archaic Greek alphabet into Etruria; the letters were written from right to left, as in Phoenician, and the alphabet contains several letters such as *delta* that were dropped from the Etruscan script because the sound did not exist in Etruscan speech.

21. 'This is the temple and this is the place of the statue which the king Thefarie Velianas has dedicated to Uni-Astarte ...' One of three gold tablets discovered in 1964 at Pyrgoi on the Etruscan coast, two in Etruscan and one in Phoenician, recording a dedication made by the king of Caere at the end of the sixth century BC.

22. Following his naval victory over the Etruscans at Kyma near Naples in 474 BC, the tyrant Hieron of Syracuse dedicated an enemy pot-helmet at the shrine of Zeus in Olympia inscribed: 'Hieron, son of Deinomenes and the Syracusans and Zeus: Tyrsenian from Kyma'.

relationship between Iberians and colonists should not be seen as one of inherent hostility. A few examples will illustrate how the Iberians combined lessons learned from the Greeks and others with their own expressions of individuality. Although there were variations in the south-west of Spain, there was rough uniformity in the scripts used by the Iberians, and the Greek derivation of many of the characters is not in doubt – Greek, not Phoenician. Oddly, having acquired an alphabet, the Iberians then added to it a number of syllabic symbols, *ba, be, bi, bo, bu* and similarly for the letters 'c' and 'd', after which, even more oddly, the inventiveness of the creators of this script evaporated. Two fundamental features of modern Spain came into existence as a result of Greek influence on the Iberians: both the vine and the olive became increasingly popular, though Catalan wines were decried by the Roman poet Martial for their poor quality; in any case, the Iberians had traditionally preferred beer, and often imported better wines from Etruria.[33]

Another example of cultural borrowing can be observed in their tombs; their consistent preference was for cremation. At Tutugi in Andalucía tombs from the fifth century onwards have been unearthed, varying from simple deposits of urns to sumptuous tumuli containing chambers with passages, and traces of painting on the walls. Architectonic motifs include supporting columns decorated in the Ionian style. These massive tombs, which evidently housed the remains of the elite, recall those of Etruria, suggesting influence from Italy. The practice of burying the rich and famous with impressive grave goods was followed, as in Italy and parts of the eastern Mediterranean: a triple-chambered tomb at Toya contained bronze buckets, gems and a chariot.[34] A third example of the mixing of native and external influences can be found in sculpture. Working with limestone, Iberian artists produced impressive near-lifesize representations of bulls, horses and deer, with the main features of the animal boldly expressed; their preference was for high relief, and many of the surviving sculptures must have been fitted as external decorations to temples and other cult centres.[35] The influence of Greek styles was felt gradually and resulted in a style that never appears wholly Greek. This is true even in the fourth century BC, the probable date of the most famous Iberian sculpture, the 'Dama de Elche', a bust of a priestess or goddess wearing elaborate jewellery. Although her face owes a great deal to classical Greek models, the rest of the figure bears close relation to other lifesize figures of women that have come to light in Spain.[36] Her jewellery may also owe something to Carthaginian models.[37] But the treatment of drapery in the Elche bust and other similar sculptures reflects Iberian canons. The Iberians did not share the Greek and Etruscan delight in portraying the naked body: only one Iberian vase painting shows naked men, and it was found at Emporion, where the Greeks predominated.[38]

Pottery reveals commercial connections and, in the case of painted vases, it exposes cultural influences, whether expressed through iconography or through the interest native peoples might show in Greek gods and heroes. Unlike the peoples of Italy, the Iberians were not overwhelmed by Greek or Phoenician religious ideas, though along the coast there is some evidence of shared cults dedicated to Demeter, Astarte and other foreign gods; an alabaster statuette from a tomb at Tutugi clearly represents a Phoenician goddess.[39] In the field of vase painting the Iberians showed particular originality, not simply trying to copy Greek models, as the Etruscans frequently did. Black-figured vases from Liria near Valencia portray scenes of dancing and war; human figures are outlined in a fluid semi-abstract style that readily conveys a sense of movement, and empty spaces are anxiously filled with curlicues, roundels, floral designs and anything else that would prevent a vacuum from being created.[40] In Andalucía, geometric designs with a sixth-century Greek paternity lingered as late as the fourth century, much adapted to meet the demands of Iberian buyers – a love of birds and animals, as also of foliage. Thus there was no single 'Iberian style', but the Iberians owed fundamental ideas to the Greeks, adapting what arrived on Greek and Phoenician ships from the eastern Mediterranean.

Finally, the Iberians made themselves known beyond the boundaries of Spain not as traders, but as formidable soldiers. They were recruited by the tyrant of Himera in Sicily, in 480 BC, but they also fought at the end of the fifth century in Carthaginian armies which were attacking the Greek cities in Sicily; after Carthage was defeated by the Greek tyrant of Syracuse in 395 many entered his service. They were even mentioned in one of the comedies of Aristophanes around this time, raising a laugh because they were said to be covered in body hair. Their famous sabres were adapted from Greek and Etruscan models which they learned to handle while serving as mercenaries.[41] Payment and loot from foreign wars must have made many fortunes in Iberia, and helps to account for the wealth of some of the Iberian tombs. On the other hand, it was the natural resources of Spain, particularly its metals, which were the real source of Iberian prosperity. The Iberians were ideally placed to benefit from the traffic that passed from the Spanish interior down to the coast, or that was carried on ships bound from Gadir and other Atlantic ports through Gibraltar and along the route described by Avienus. The entire Mediterranean was now being navigated by Greek, Etruscan or Carthaginian vessels; peoples from the far west were the subject of jokes in the Athens of Aristophanes; and the peoples of the west looked to Greece, first Corinth and later Athens, as the centre of style and fashion.

5

Thalassocracies, 550 BC–400 BC

The Mediterranean coasts might be expected to serve as the natural limit to imperial expansion by the great powers of the Middle East – the Hittites, Assyria, even Pharaonic Egypt. The Assyrians did occasionally try to browbeat Cyprus into submission, as did the Egyptians, for its resources in timber and metal were too precious to ignore. But no attempt to gain mastery over the eastern Mediterranean matched the Persian conquests in Anatolia and the Levant during the sixth century BC, and the Persian attempt to invade Greece; the defeat of Persia would be celebrated as the greatest Greek victory since the fall of Troy. The achievement was not just military but political, since a great many cities in Greece proper and the Aegean islands collaborated in the struggle against the Persians, and even Syracuse was asked to help (though it fought off a threat from Carthage, possibly instigated by Persia). The Greeks commemorated their triumph by erecting victory monuments such as the bronze serpent from Delphi, now in the Hippodrome at Istanbul; there, they inscribed the names of thirty-one cities that had helped resist the Persians at the great battle of Plataia in 479 BC, and even that list was not complete.[1] A 'Congress of the Hellenes' came into existence, and the name of Hellene, originally assigned by Homer to the followers of Achilles, was increasingly understood to refer to a common identity expressed through language, the cult of the gods and style of life.[2] The story that emerged, most resoundingly in the spirited account of these events by Herodotos, was that of the defence of Greek liberty against Persian tyranny. In his play *The Persians*, performed in Athens in 472, Aeschylus assumed that the future of Hellas directly depended on the fate of his home city:

QUEEN ATOSSA: Say where, in all this peopled world, a city men called
Athens lies?

LEADER: Far distant, where our Lord the sun sinks and his last effulgence
dies.

ATOSSA: And this far western land it is my son so craved to make his prey?

LEADER: Aye, for if Athens once were his, all Hellas must his word obey.[3]

Whether the Greeks were really fighting for liberty against Persian
tyranny is questionable. In the late fifth century, at the height of their
struggle against one another in the Peloponnesian War, the Spartans and
the Athenians were constantly trying to win the favour of the Persians;
submitting to the Persian king was not always seen as a despicable act.
The story grew in the telling, first with Herodotos and then, much later,
with the biographies of great Athenians and Spartans written in the
Roman period by Plutarch. Vast armies led by the Persian king invaded

Greece; yet among them there were many Greeks, reluctant or otherwise, who found themselves fighting other Greeks. Persian rule brought periodic irritations such as demands for troops and taxes, but the general policy of the Persians was to leave largely alone those cities that rendered without complaint a simple tribute of earth and water.

From a Greek perspective the Persian problem began with the destruction in 546 of the kingdom of Lydia, whose ruler Kroisos (Croesus) was renowned for his wealth. The Persian king, Cyrus, invited the Greek cities of Ionia, which owed Lydia nominal allegiance, to join him in overthrowing the Lydians, but the Ionians expressed interest only once Lydia had fallen, and that was too late: by then, Cyrus was no longer prepared to offer the easy terms under which the Ionians had lived as notional subjects of Lydia. Some did submit, and found themselves obliged to provide troops; the load was relatively light under Cyrus, but became more burdensome under later rulers, who sought funds to pay for grandiose wars. The citizens of other towns took advice from the Greeks of Hellas and emigrated en masse, notably the Phokaians. Miltiades, who was to become a distinguished general in Athenian service, set out from his native Ionia with five ships, a crowd of refugees and all the wealth of his town; unfortunately, one ship was seized by Phoenician pirates. Much more important to the Persians, at this stage, were the lands of the great Middle Eastern empires. The fall of Babylon to Cyrus in 539, later commemorated in the vivid tales of the biblical book of Daniel, was followed in 525 by the fall of Egypt to Cyrus's son Cambyses; in the meantime the Persians reduced the Phoenician cities to submission. For the Phoenicians this did not prove to be wholly bad news. The Persians stimulated new life into the trade routes that ran through Tyre and Sidon, bypassing Ionia. The Phoenicians provided the backbone of the Persian navy in the Mediterranean, though the Ionian Greeks were also expected to produce ships for the royal navy. Around 525 one Ionian ruler, Polykrates of Samos, who became an ally of Cambyses, could mobilize 100 penteconters (ships manned by fifty oarsmen) and forty triremes (ships with triple banks of oars); these vessels were also developed by the Phoenicians, who sent 200 triremes against Naxos in 499.[4] In other words, thousands of sailors were required to man an effective fleet, and it is likely that Polykrates drew on manpower well beyond Samos itself. Herodotos wondered whether to compare him with the thalassocrat Minos.[5]

The Greek cities of Cyrenaica accepted Persian overlordship after the fall of Egypt, so that the Persian empire now stretched as far as modern Libya; Carthage, like other Phoenician cities, seems to have viewed Persian successes with sympathy. This is not to say that the Persians sought to establish a Mediterranean dominion. The Greeks suggested to their brethren in Sicily that their island too was at risk. Yet the area within Europe that most worried the Persians was not Greece but the great swathe of lands in what is now Ukraine, inhabited by the nomadic Scythians, whom both Greeks and Persians regarded as wild barbarians; King Darius of Persia campaigned against them in 513. A few Greeks and others made trouble for the Persians in the northern Aegean, and the Persians responded with brutality, occupying Lemnos in 509, and massacring many of the inhabitants. The Persians greedily aspired to control Euboia, famous for its natural resources.[6] There was unrest in Ionia from 499 onwards, sometimes supported by cities in Greece itself, resulting in vicious reprisals as Phoenician sailors paid off their grudges against their Greek rivals in blood and pillage. Yet, as the Ionian revolt petered out, the Persians were surprisingly considerate, accepting democratic governments and attempting to remove a source of tension between cities by demanding that they make trade agreements with one another. The Persian Great King was conscious of his responsibility before his god Ahura Mazda to act mercifully towards his subjects and to promote stability. Even so, the prosperity of Ionia did not recover.[7]

II

The accession of Xerxes in 485 shifted Persian policy from tough accommodation with dissidents to vigorous suppression of Persia's foes; the Great King intended to punish the Greeks for supporting the Ionian rebels. The Phoenicians and Egyptians received orders for massive ropes out of which a pair of boat bridges could be constructed across the Hellespont; these cables must have been formidably strong to withstand the fierce currents. Because an earlier fleet had suffered severe damage off the great promontory of Mount Athos, the king ordered a canal to be dug through the neck of the mountain; and it was done. Food stores were established along the route the army would follow through Thrace.

The Greeks well understood that this war would be fought as much on sea as on land, and the Spartans were assigned the high command of the naval forces, further proof that Sparta's power at sea should never be underestimated. Not surprisingly, many Greeks were tempted to 'Medize', to submit to the Medes and Persians before Xerxes' armies obliterated their cities and enslaved their citizens. The Pythian Oracle at Delphi instructed the Athenians to abandon their homeland and migrate westwards; on further prompting she made some vague references to the Wooden Walls that would survive the Persian onslaught, and implied that something terrible would happen at Salamis, a little to the west of Athens.

The land campaign reached its most dramatic moment at the narrow pass of Thermopylai in 480 BC, when 300 brave Spartans fought to the death against overwhelming forces; thereafter, the Persians stormed through northern and eastern Greece, and Athens, now empty, was sacked, including the ancient temples on the Acropolis.[8] The sea campaign offered better opportunities for Greek success, for the Persian fleet was largely composed of Phoenician triremes, fast-moving and lightly constructed, against which the Greeks had some hope of mobilizing their own heavier triremes. The Phoenicians might have the advantage in numbers, but the Greeks knew these waters much better.[9] By holding the Persian fleet at Salamis in 480 BC the Greek allies were able to delay what seemed almost inevitable, a full-scale Persian invasion of the Peloponnese. Salamis is an island separated from the Attic mainland by narrow straits in the east, where the fleets faced one another, and broader straits beyond the bay facing Eleusis to the west. With more than 200 sea-worthy vessels (some estimates reach 380) the Greeks, mainly Athenians, faced between 800 and 1,200 enemy ships; the Greeks therefore needed to draw the Phoenicians into the narrow straits between Salamis and the Greek mainland and trap them there.[10] This they did by an Odyssean ruse: an Athenian spy reported to the Persians that the Greeks were planning to steal away westwards under cover of darkness. The Phoenicians were sent to patrol the western exit. But the Greeks stayed still, and when morning came the patrols sent to block a Greek exit were puzzled by the silence. Meanwhile, the Greeks engaged with that part of the Phoenician fleet that had remained in the eastern straits. Corinthian shipping hoisted sail and appeared to flee up the straits westwards towards Eleusis, acting as a magnetic draw to the enemy, who found themselves unable to manoeuvre in the narrow entrance. All the while, King Xerxes sat on a golden throne on the heights above the Bay of Salamis, expecting to watch an enjoyable day of pursuit and victory by the Persian navy. Instead, 200 Phoenician and other Persian ships were sunk or taken, and the Greeks lost about forty vessels.[11] The Ionian Greeks in Persian service avoided an engagement with their mainland cousins, and sailed off in a hurry. It was a curious sort of victory: the Persian navy was not smashed – perhaps 1,000 vessels of various types were still afloat, and there was a Persian army parked close by. But Salamis proved that Xerxes could not press on to conquer southern Greece. The Spartans and Athenians held the Aegean. They had prevented it from becoming a Persian sea. Victory on land at Plataia the next year confirmed the impregnability of the Greek alliance. With a certain amount of calendar adjustment, it was soon claimed that, on the same day as the victory at Salamis, the Syracusans under Gelon decisively defeated a Carthaginian invasion of Sicily. This invasion may have been launched in an attempt to create a second front for Persia and its Phoenician allies. The idea that the Persians had been defeated in both the east and the west had obvious appeal.

The Persian War confirmed the moral ascendancy of Sparta, heroic losers at Thermopylai, and of Athens, which, after sacrificing the city itself by abandoning it to the Persians, had won a victory in the waters of Attika. Both Athens and Sparta were able to follow through with further naval successes, notably in Samos, which they freed from Persian rule, and at the promontory of Mykale nearby, where they managed to set the Persian fleet on fire in 479, and helped stir up revolt in Ionia. Xerxes was thus left with less than he had started with; Aeschylus represented him as a tragic figure who over-reached himself by challenging the Greek gods and thus bringing misery on both Persians and Greeks. Aeschylus insisted that there was an underlying principle, liberty, for which the Greeks had fought:

> The right wing led the van, in order due,
> Behind it the whole fleet, prow after prow,
> Then one great shout: 'Now, sons of Hellas, now!
> Set Hellas free, set free your wives, your homes,
> Your gods' high altars and your fathers' tombs.
> Now all is on the stake!'[12]

III

Athens, spectacularly rebuilt, now became the ardent defender of democracy (democracy that was confined to the free male citizen body, excluding the many metics, or foreigners). It also became the seat of a regional empire, making use of its navy to exercise dominion over the islands of the Aegean.[13] Sparta concentrated on maintaining authority within the southern Peloponnese, where a small elite of highly trained Spartan soldiers (the hoplites) controlled a much larger population of enserfed dependants (the helots) and subordinate allies (or *perioikoi*). Sparta was 'simply a collection of villages', as Thucydides observed, without grand monuments, whereas Athens, he thought, gave the impression from its own monuments of being twice as powerful as it really was.[14]

Religious cults bound together the emerging Athenian empire. The most influential cult in these waters was the worship of Apollo on the sacred island of Delos. Delos stands in the middle of the Cycladic chain, about halfway across the Aegean, easily accessible from the lands inhabited by the Ionian Greeks: Samos to the east-north-east, Chios to the north-north-east. The great pirate Polykrates of Samos took a strong interest in Delos, and dedicated the island of Rheneia, very close to it, to Delian Apollo; he constructed a great chain to tie Rheneia to Delos not long before he died in 522 BC.[15] Delos attracted the attention of the inhabitants of several neighbouring islands, such as the Naxians, who installed a sculptured terrace (the 'Terrace of the Lions'), made of the fine marble for which Naxos was famous. By participating in the cult of Delian Apollo the Ionians expressed their bonds of solidarity with their fellow-Greeks around the Aegean. The cult of Apollo was expressed not just through sacrifices but through festivals that included athletic games, choral performances and dances; Thucydides cited an early poem addressed to the god Phoibos Apollo:

> Chiefly, O Phoibos, your heart found delight in the island of Delos.
> There, with their long robes trailing, Ionians gather together,
> Treading your sacred road, with their wives and children about them,
> There they give you pleasure with boxing and dancing, and singing,
> Calling aloud on your name, as they set in order the contests.[16]

A cult centre in the middle of the Aegean was an obvious place in which to create a sworn association of Greek cities, the Delian League, in 477 BC; its overt task was to maintain pressure on the Persians after the withdrawal of Xerxes. Apparently it was the Athenians who suggested Delos should be the headquarters of the league. This was not just in recognition of the sanctity of the place; it also drew attention away from the fact that Athens dominated the league. At first the treasury was based in the Athenian sanctuary on Delos, but in 454 it was transferred to Athens, for by then it was obvious that the Delian League was a tool of Athenian policy – the Athenians appointed the entire panel of administrators, who were supposed to be drawn from Ionia and the Aegean islands.[17] The Athenians both believed in and exploited the holy nature of the League.

Democracy at home and empire abroad have rarely been treated as inconsistent with one another; the historian Sir John Seeley's motto was *imperium et libertas*, 'empire and freedom'.[18] The Athenians knew why they needed an empire; it was not solely to keep the Persians at bay. There were essential resources on which the city had to call in order to ensure its survival; there were places from which to obtain supplies and, just as importantly, places that guarded the longer routes leading to sources of supply. The most important challenge was gaining access to grain supplies. There is some disagreement about how large Athens was in the fifth century; a good estimate for the late fifth century is 337,000 inhabitants in Athens and its dependent territory in Attika.[19] All these people could not be fed simply from local resources. Although the terrain is not at first sight promising, intensive agriculture was practised in parts of Attika, and Aristophanes described the enormous variety of products the Athenians could buy from the surrounding countryside: cucumbers, grapes, honey, figs, turnips, even managing to grow crops out of season so that you could no longer tell what time of year it was.[20] But classical evidence indicates that Attika could feed about 84,000 people from its own resources – in any case, not more than 106,000.[21] Athens therefore imported grain to feed itself, and much of this came from as far away as Euboia, the Black Sea (or Pontos) and Sicily. About half its grain supply was imported; there were shippers and grain-dealers (predictably, the butt of criticism) who ensured the city was fed.

The rhetorician Isokrates, writing in about 380 BC, described the *klerouchoi*, Athenian colonizers sent out to the territories Athens controlled in order to manage the estates from which it drew its supplies. They were a necessity because 'we had in proportion to the number of our citizens a very small territory, but a very great empire; we possessed not only twice as many warships as all other states combined, but these were strong enough to engage double their number'.[22] He stressed the importance of Euboia – 'we had greater control over it than over our own country', for as early as 506 the Athenians had seized the lands of the great families of Chalkis, and parcelled them out among 4,000 citizens, with a further distribution by Perikles sixty years later.[23] However, in 411, towards the end of the disastrous Peloponnesian War, Euboia escaped from Athenian control; Thucydides remarked that 'Euboia had been more useful to them than Attika itself', and the loss of Euboia caused more panic even than defeat in Sicily, which was another good source of grain.[24]

The common assumption that the Black Sea was always the major source of grain is based on evidence from the fourth century and later.[25] Earlier than this, references to Black Sea grain are occasional, reflecting the odd year when supplies were short within the Aegean. The obvious sources for Athens lay all around the Aegean, in Thrace, in Lemnos, in Euboia and in Lesbos, where land worked by 20,000 Lesbians was conveyed to 3,000 Athenian beneficiaries, who permitted part of the old population to remain as their serfs.[26] All this suggests a systematic and well-organized grain trade which was the creation of Athenian policy, and not simply a haphazard dependence on whatever supplies could be found by merchants in the Aegean and beyond.[27] Its main beneficiaries were the wealthy men who had been granted lands in the overseas territories (*chôra*) of the Athenian empire.[28]

IV

Athens did not tolerate dissent, and, when the Naxians tried to break free in 470, Athens imposed money payments in lieu of the ships Naxos had earlier provided; this was then extended more widely to Athens' allies, and a number of tribute lists survive that speak loudly for the way Athens was asserting itself in the Aegean. But the Delian League was well matched by a Peloponnesian League, embracing the towns of southern

Greece and dominated by Sparta. Thucydides commented on the difference between the two leagues:

> The Spartans did not make their allies pay tribute, but saw to it that they were governed by oligarchies who would work in the Spartan interest. Athens, on the other hand, had in the course of time taken over the fleets of her allies (except for those of Chios and Lesbos) and had made them pay contributions of money instead.[29]

Thus Sparta worked with allies; Athens asserted its dominion over dependants. On the other hand, the allies of Athens were impressed by the successful leadership it provided, often far from Greece – the Athenians well understood that foreign victories could be used to promote their own hegemony within the Aegean. In 466 the allies, led by the Athenian commander Kimon, literally smashed to pieces the Persian fleet, numbering 200 ships, off the coast of Asia Minor, at the mouth of the river Eurymedon. The allies struggled manfully against the Persians, sending 200 ships of their own to Egypt to support a revolt against Persian rule (459); this, however, resulted in humiliating defeat. Ten years later, the Delian League sent its fleet under Kimon to make trouble in Cyprus, where the Persians held sway. Meanwhile, Athens bullied rivals and rebels, tightening its grasp over Euboia, while also making peace with the most obvious competitor for hegemony, Sparta, in 446. Since Sparta and Athens had different obsessions, Athens seeking to hold on to its possessions in the Aegean, and Sparta to maintain supremacy in the Peloponnese, it was not difficult to separate their spheres of interest. The real difficulties would arise when lesser towns drew Athens and Sparta into their own squabbles.

The outbreak of the Peloponnesian War can be traced back to events in the Adriatic, in a small but strategically placed town founded on the edge of the land of the Illyrians: Epidamnos. It was a staging-post on the increasingly important trade route that carried goods up from the Gulf of Corinth towards the Etruscan and Greek colonies at Spina and Adria, a route in which Athens was taking an ever stronger interest. Epidamnos had been created by Corinthian colonists from Kerkyra (Corfu); it was thus a granddaughter of Corinth, and, like many Greek towns, it was riven by factional fighting between aristocrats and democrats (436–435 BC). The democrats, under siege from the aristocrats and their barbarian allies the Illyrians, appealed to Kerkyra for help; but the Kerkyrans were distinctly uninterested.[30] They saw themselves as a respectable naval power, with 120 ships (a fleet second in size to Athens), competing at sea with their mother-city of Corinth, with which relations were decidedly cool: the Corinthians were convinced that the Kerkyrans did not show the respect that was due to a mother-city, while the Kerkyrans claimed that 'their financial power at this time made them equal with the richest states in Hellas, and their military resources were greater than those of Corinth'.[31] Relations deteriorated further when Corinth responded to the appeal from its grandchildren in Epidamnos, and sent colonists to help the besieged town.[32] So an apparently pointless conflict broke out between Corinth and Kerkyra over Corinthian intervention in what the Kerkyrans were convinced were their waters. Kerkyra appealed to Athens for aid: the Kerkyrans argued that Athens, with its mighty fleet, could block the pretensions of Corinth; 'Corinth', they said, 'has attacked us first in order to attack you afterwards.'[33] They asked to be brought into the Athenian network of alliances, though they were aware that, under the terms of past treaties between Sparta and Athens, which had sought to balance the Delian and Peloponnesian Leagues, this might be viewed amiss:

> There are three considerable naval powers in Hellas – Athens, Kerkyra and Corinth. If Corinth gets control of us first and you allow our navy to be united with hers, you will have to fight against the combined fleets of Kerkyra and the Peloponnese. But if you receive us into the alliance, you will enter upon the war with our ships as well as your own.[34]

Judging from these words, there was a fatalism about the coming of war. In 433 the Athenians despatched ships to help the Kerkyrans, heading for Sybota, between Kerkyra and the Greek mainland, where 150 ships from Corinth and its allies faced 110 ships from Kerkyra. The main impact of the Athenian fleet was psychological: the Athenian squadron arrived as battle was joined, and, at sight of them, the Corinthian navy scuttled away, convinced that an even larger fleet was on its way, which was not in fact the case. Sparta wisely held itself aloof from these events.[35]

Thucydides was interested in war and politics, and especially in the rationale behind the political decisions of the Greek states during the conflict between Athens and Sparta. There are mysteries he does not resolve: why the Athenians, who had built an empire in the Aegean, should wish to become involved in the waters to the west of Greece, the Ionian and Adriatic Seas; and how significant the commercial interests of Athens, Corinth and Kerkyra were in the decisions to go to war. The Corinthians and Athenians were not blind to the new business opportunities that had been opening up in the Adriatic during the fifth century BC. Economic considerations surely lay behind another decision of the Athenian assembly: to besiege Potideia, a Corinthian colony (and Athenian ally) on the Chalkidian peninsula, not far from the modern city of Thessaloniki; Thessaly gave access to some of the grain lands from which Athens drew its supplies, and control of Thessaly would also determine control of the northern Aegean islands, such as Lemnos, which were dominated by Athens. Meanwhile, the Peloponnesian League was faced with a growing chorus of complaints against Athens, even from its own allies: Aigina, the island that lay between Attika and the Peloponnese, grumbled at the presence of an Athenian garrison, compromising its autonomy.[36] In other words, the other Greeks witnessed the way the Athenians had been turning their system of alliances into an empire, and wondered when and where the process would end. The Spartans decided they had to give a lead; many in Sparta were deeply reluctant to go to war, and, when the matter was put to a vote in the Spartan assembly, it was not at first obvious whether those in favour of the war were shouting louder than those who argued for appeasement.[37]

In the first phase of the conflict between Athens and Sparta, the so-called Archidamian War (431–421 BC), Athens was able to demonstrate its superior skill at sea; in 428, the Athenians responded vigorously to a rebellion in Lesbos, which began when the citizens of its capital, Mytilene, conspired to throw off Athenian rule over the island and expanded their navy.[38] They told Sparta that the Athenians 'felt some alarm about our navy, in case it might come together as one force and join you or some other power'; however, 'if you give us your whole-hearted support you will gain for yourself a state which has a large navy (which is the thing you need most)'.[39] The Peloponnesians admitted the Mytileneans to their league forthwith; but that did not save Mytilene from its recapture by the Athenians. In the famous, or infamous, debate that followed, the self-regarding, exclusive flavour of Athenian democracy can be detected: the Athenians agreed with the ruthless proposal of generals such as Kleon to put to death all male Mytileneans, and to enslave all women and children. A trireme was sent to Lesbos posthaste to enact this decree. The Athenians kept having second thoughts, however, and a second trireme was sent to rescind the sentence. It raced after the first one, never actually overtaking it; but it arrived just in time to save the population. This then was empire; as the rebels insisted, the Athenians had gradually deprived their own allies of independence, and no longer treated them as equals.

The Peloponnesian War saw massive loss of human life as a result of both disease and sheer human cruelty. Plague, possibly bubonic, arrived in Greece in 430, and devastated Athens. The sea routes of the Mediterranean have always provided a means for the transmission of pandemics, as the better documented cases of the plague under Justinian in the sixth century AD, or the Black Death in the fourteenth century, would dramatically reveal. Not much attention was paid to the pathology of this disease, which was seen as a punishment by the gods for human sins.

In 425, the Athenians attempted to bring the war into the Peloponnese by creating a base at Pylos, ancient Nestor's former capital, from where they could interfere with supplies bound for Sparta.[40] As a result, 440 Spartan hoplites found themselves stranded on the island of Sphakteria opposite Pylos, and for a time their fate seemed bound up with the future of this war. These men may have constituted one tenth of the elite Spartan army, so their recovery was an issue of great importance to Sparta. A local truce between the Spartans and the Athenian general resulted in the surrender to Athens of the Spartan fleet in these waters, about sixty vessels, as hostages to be held until negotiations between the two sides were complete. All this seemed to promise an end to the war itself; but, once Spartan delegates actually faced the Athenian assembly, they found it impossible to concede effective victory to their enemies.[41] So the war continued, and an Athenian commander, Kleon, surprised everyone by leading a taskforce to Pylos and obtaining the surrender of the hoplites on Sphakteria – this was no repeat of Thermopylai.[42]

The war soon spread beyond the Aegean and the waters around Kerkyra. Quite why the Athenians opened a new front in Sicily during 427 is a mystery. Thucydides thought that the Athenians hoped to prevent Sicilian grain from reaching the Peloponnesian cities, and that the Athenians were also beginning to wonder 'whether it would be possible for them to gain control of Sicily'.[43] Accustomed to rule over islands, the Athenians failed to realize how large this island was and how many rivals for its control existed: the Carthaginians were one potential enemy; the Syracusans were a more immediate threat, for they were Dorian colonists, well armed with a large fleet that might enter service on the Peloponnesian side.[44] Ancient loyalties came to the fore: according to Thucydides, the Sicilian colonists divided neatly between Ionians, who supported the Athenian alliance, and Dorians, who instinctively supported Sparta. Leontini, an Ionian colony in eastern Sicily that was at war with Syracuse, appealed to Athens for help, and the Athenians sent twenty ships; Athenian self-confidence was boosted by rapid successes, including the relief of Leontini and the establishment of Athenian mastery over the Straits of Messina. Syracuse seemed feebler than had been expected, and Sicily appeared to be a viable conquest. This was a disastrous assumption.

During the next phase of the conflict between Athens and Sparta the Sicilian Question re-emerged. The network of Athenian alliances in Sicily extended across the island, even encompassing the Hellenized Elymians of western Sicily. The inhabitants of Segesta or Egesta had recently started to build the splendid temple that still stands. They saw Athens as their protector against Syracuse and its allies; when Dorian Selinous, to the south, attacked Segesta the Segestans sent an embassy to Athens asking for aid (416/415 BC). Selinous (Selinunte) is another ancient Sicilian city whose sizeable temple still survives. The Segestan envoys stressed that this was just the start of an attempt by Syracuse and the Dorian Greeks to gain hegemony over the whole island, which is credible enough – several Syracusan tyrants had pan-Sicilian ambitions. All these arguments fed the enthusiasm of the Athenians for reopening their Sicilian front.[45] Segesta was prepared to pay the Athenians for their help, sending a substantial gift of sixty talents of uncoined silver; Athenian ambassadors to Segesta were wined and dined off gold and silver plates, and carried away the impression of a fabulously wealthy island whose acquisition would serve Athenian interests very well. But the Segestans had re-used their relatively small stock of fine plate, moving it from house to house as the Athenian ambassadors were passed from host to host.[46] All this, though, was more than enough to tempt the greedy Athenians, and the assembly voted to send sixty ships to Sicily; one of the commanders was Alkibiades, who was an outspoken supporter of a Sicilian expedition, and who would later shamelessly switch sides between Athens, Sparta and Persia, only to be greeted by Athens, towards the end of the war, as the city's potential saviour.[47] But Alkibiades was not given the chance to prove his worth; he was accused of involvement in a strange act of sacrilege, the nocturnal defacing of several herms, phallic sculptures, that were scattered across the city of Athens. Deciding that he was in greater danger in Athens than in Sparta, he defected to the enemy.

In 415 the Athenians at last launched an assault on Syracuse, a difficult place to master because the city stood on a spur blocking the entrance to the grand harbour, while to the north lay marshes, quarries and open land that the competing sides sought to enclose with walls – defensive walls built by the Syracusans to keep the Athenians away, and offensive walls built by the Athenians to hem in Syracuse and dry up its supplies. Yet this struggle was not fought in isolation: the Spartans sent reinforcements, and the Athenians appealed to non-Greeks – the Etruscans and Carthaginians – for naval support. The Etruscans sent a few ships, which proved their worth; the Carthaginians were happier to sit on the sidelines, for Athenian hegemony in Sicily offered as many disadvantages to them as Syracusan.[48] The arrival of a Spartan commander, Gylippos, with a small fleet and army, undermined these Athenian initiatives and, when battle was joined, the Syracusan fleet stood firm at the entrance to the Grand Harbour and was eventually able to smash the Athenian navy (including some newly arrived reinforcements).[49] This was soon followed by dramatic victories on land; 7,000 Athenian soldiers were captured and taken to the quarries near Syracuse where they were left to fester in the heat, so that thousands more now died of heatstroke and malnutrition. Many were sent into slavery, though according to Plutarch one route to freedom was an ability to recite the verses of Euripides, whose plays were passionately admired by the Sicilian Greeks.[50] The Sicilian expedition had therefore ended in a human disaster as painful as the plague; and it had ended in political disaster, with a tremendous loss of prestige, a sense that Athenian policy lacked direction, and the knowledge that the most capable Athenian politician of his generation, Alkibiades, was now the guest of the Spartans.

Having gone to war over Sicily in the hope of interfering in the flow of grain towards the Peloponnese, Athens now experienced the nightmare of threats to its own grain traffic. By 411 the Spartans were trying to activate an alliance with Persia that would, they hoped, bring Phoenician ships into the Aegean. The Persian stance was ambiguous, for the

Persians also parleyed with the Athenians: it would be better for them if the Greeks could fight each other to an exhausted standstill, and they could then take control of whatever they wanted. So the Phoenician fleet that was promised to Sparta in 411 never arrived, but the Peloponnesians used their own naval resources to gain control of the Hellespont and to foment revolt in the strategically vital city of Byzantion. A series of naval battles in the Hellespont demonstrated that Spartan inexperience gave the Athenian navy the edge in a pitched battle at sea; but these were not easy victories for Athens, and had it lost a single battle it would probably have had to concede the whole war.[51] In 406, at Arginoussai, between Chios and the Asian mainland, the Athenians won a spectacular victory at sea, losing only twenty-five out of 155 ships, but they then squandered the victory by putting the naval commanders on trial: they had committed sacrilege by failing to recover the bodies of drowned Athenian sailors from the sea.

The Spartans knew how to respond; they were busily building a fleet of their own.[52] Simply ravaging Attika would not bring them victory; this was a war that had to be won at sea. In the sixth century Sparta had already challenged Polykrates of Samos at sea, and Sparta's commitment to its navy must not be underestimated; the Spartans managed to mobilize their allies and dependants, making use of helot oarsmen. One of their most successful commanders in the last stages of the war with Athens was the naval commander (*nauarchos*) Lysandros or Lysander, who was regarded as so effective that, when his commission expired and he was no longer eligible to serve as *nauarchos*, he was appointed deputy to a nominal *nauarchos* and left to finish the task of defeating Athens. It was he who brought the war to its effective end in the battle of Aigospotamoi (405), where he captured or sank almost the entire Athenian navy.[53] Athens sued for peace and its empire crumbled; Sparta was now the Hellenic imperial power, even though it had to struggle hard on both land and sea in the first years of the fourth century to assert its supremacy.[54]

The Peloponnesian War resulted, then, in the transformation of the Aegean Sea from an Athenian to a Spartan lake. Yet this war had also had violent repercussions in the Adriatic and in Sicily. It was a war in which imperial ambitions became fatally intermeshed with economic questions, above all the issue of who would control the supply routes bringing grain to Athens and other cities from Sicily, the Aegean and the

Black Sea. And yet, by the end of the fourth century BC, the age of the city-states was drawing to a close; the political and economic geography of the eastern Mediterranean, including the flow of grain, altered decisively following the conquests of a Macedonian king obsessed with his own divinity. Moreover, it was in the west that the next great struggle for domination of Mediterranean waters would occur, as Carthage began to face ever more serious rivals to its regional hegemony. Two cities on the coast of Africa, Carthage and Alexandria, dominate the political and cultural history of the Mediterranean over the next couple of centuries.

6

The Lighthouse of the Mediterranean,
350 BC–100 BC

I

In 333 BC Alexander III, king of Macedon, whose claims to Greekness were treated with some scepticism down in Athens, wreaked vengeance on the Persian kings who had posed such a threat to Greece in past centuries, by defeating a massive Persian army at the battle of the Issos, beyond the Cilician Gates. Yet he did not pursue the Persian king, Darius III, into the Persian heartlands. He well understood the need to neutralize Persian power along the shores of the Mediterranean, and marched south through Syria and Palestine, where he ruthlessly took charge of the Phoenician cities that had in the past provided Persia with its fleets; Tyre resisted him for seven months, much to his fury, even after he built the great mole that for ever after joined the island city to the mainland. Once he had captured Tyre, most of its inhabitants were slaughtered, enslaved or crucified.[1] He bypassed Jerusalem, choosing the road through Gaza, since his real target at this stage was Egypt, ruled by a Persian satrap for nearly 200 years, since the days of Cambyses, and his conquest of this land transformed not just Egypt but the entire eastern Mediterranean. The result of his victory was that Egypt was turned around, looking outwards to the Mediterranean rather than inwards to the Nile valley.[2] In 331 BC he decided to found a city on the northernmost edge of Egypt, on a limestone spur separated from the alluvial lands of the interior by a freshwater lake – a city next to rather than actually in Egypt, as its designation in later Latin documents as *Alexandria ad Aegyptum*, 'Alexandria on the way to [or 'next to'] Egypt', affirms. This sense that Alexandria was more a city of the Mediterranean than of Egypt would persist for over two millennia, until the

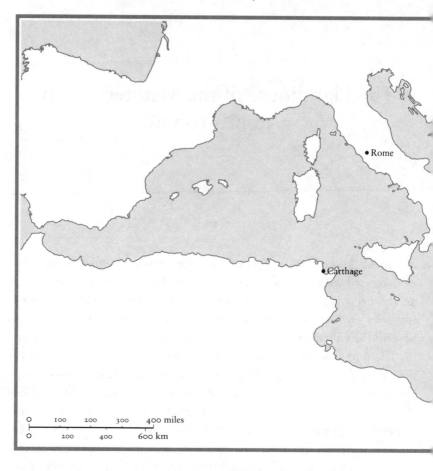

• Rome

• Carthage

| o | 100 | 200 | 300 | 400 miles |
| o | 200 | 400 | 600 km |

expulsion of its foreign communities in the twentieth century. For much of that period it was the greatest city in the Mediterranean.

Alexander's motives certainly included his own glorification.[3] He had recently been crowned as Pharoah in the ancient capital of Lower Egypt, Memphis, and after visiting the site of Alexandria he held an interview with the god Zeus Ammon; thereafter he liked to think that he was the son of this god rather than of the remarkable Philip II of Macedon whose own conquests in Greece had laid the basis for Alexander's empire. He was obsessed with Homer's works, and (according to Plutarch) Homer appeared in his dreams and reminded him of a passage in the *Odyssey* that described an island off the coast of Egypt called Pharos, possessed of a fine harbour. He understood the potential importance of Alexandria as a centre of trade, and his biographer Arrian insisted

that he was closely involved with its planning: unfortunately there was not enough chalk to hand with which to draw on the soil an outline of the city walls, so one of Alexander's architects suggested using barley meal instead, even though it had to be taken from the supplies the Macedonian soldiers were carrying with them. In the end it was flocks of birds attracted by the flour that marked out the boundaries of the city.[4] As in other new cities of the Mediterranean world the streets were laid out in a grid pattern that still to a significant extent survives, even though the broad avenues of early Alexandria have narrowed greatly, and little survives of the ancient city above the water line – nothing at all of the city as it was in the late fourth century BC. What was exceptional was its sheer scale: three miles (five kilometres) from west to east, and about half that from north to south: a long, narrow city, said to have resembled in shape a Greek cloak, or *chlamys*.[5] Its harbours featured prominently in the plans, separated from one another by a long mole that linked the new city to the island of Pharos of which Homer had spoken.

Alexander soon left Egypt behind, marching triumphantly through Persia towards India, and dying in Babylon eight years after the foundation of Alexandria, aged only thirty-two.[6] His dream of a Hellenic-Persian empire, bringing together the high cultures of two great nations, also died, and his empire was divided up among three competing generals, in Macedonia and Greece, Syria and the East, and Egypt. It was the dynasty of generals who took charge of Egypt that brought to fruition his dream of founding a great city on the edge of Egypt. Ptolemy I Soter ('the Saviour') assumed power as Pharaoh in his own right, fusing Hellenic and Egyptian ideas of rulership and government; statues of the Ptolemies represented them in a highly traditional style as Pharaohs (with an occasional concession to Greek hairstyles), and they built temples to Egyptian gods in archaic Egyptian styles.[7] It became customary for the Ptolemies to marry their sisters, as the Pharaohs had long done, a practice that did not appeal to the Greeks. But Alexandria also became one of the liveliest centres of a reinvigorated Greek culture that spread across the Mediterranean. What is distinctive about 'Hellenistic' culture is that it was not the preserve of Greeks; Hellenistic styles of art reached Carthage and Etruria, and Hellenistic ideas captivated Jews, Syrians and Egyptians. Hellenistic culture has often been treated as a demotic debasement of the classical culture of ancient Athens, characterized by florid styles of art and architecture – a sort of ancient Greek baroque. Yet it was the Hellenistic world, and Alexandria in particular (rather than Hellas itself), that produced some of the most famous names in Greek science and culture: the mathematician Euclid, the inventor Archimedes, the comedian Menander, followed in the early Roman period by the Alexandrian Jewish philosopher Philo and the physician Galen. Alexandria was of fundamental importance in the spreading of this new, open, version of Greek culture across the Mediterranean; it became the lighthouse of Mediterranean culture.

Particularly striking was the mixture of innovation and tradition in the religious policy of the Ptolemies. The early Ptolemies were men of extraordinary ambition, energy and inquisitiveness, open to many cultures and far-sighted in their management of the Egyptian economy. It was they, rather than Alexander the Great, who made Alexandria into

the vibrant city it became. Ptolemy I Soter (d. 283/2) and Ptolemy II
Philadelphos (d. 246) drew to Alexandria a mixed population of Greeks,
Syrians, Egyptians and Jews. Many of the Jews arrived as loyal soldiers,
greatly enamoured of Alexander the Great; 'Alexander' remained ever
after a favourite name among Jews. They, of course, possessed their own
distinctive cult, and the Ptolemies had no wish to interfere with it; a
significant area of eastern Alexandria, known as Delta, became the focus
of Jewish activity, and the first large Jewish settlement on the shores of
the Mediterranean came into being. The ancient Israelites had mainly
been a landlocked rural people, hemmed in by the Philistines and other
peoples who lived along the coast. For this reason they have not featured prominently in the history of the Mediterranean up to this point.
But with the founding of Alexandria, Jewish beliefs and culture began
to spread slowly across the Mediterranean. Philo emphasized the role of
Moses as lawgiver, and stressed the ethical value of the divine commandments handed down by Moses. The combination of a powerful
ethical message with a structured system of law, as well as the intellectual appeal of monotheism, brought Judaism increasing numbers of
converts and sympathizers over the next few centuries. Later Jewish
tradition would characterize this era as one of opposition, often violent,
between Hellenism and Judaism, culminating in the Maccabean revolt
against the Seleucid rulers of Syria and Palestine in the second century
BC. Yet these rulers signally failed to uphold the tradition of respect for
Judaism that their Ptolemaic rivals in Egypt understood so well: the
Seleucids tried to suppress Jewish practices such as circumcision and to
offer pagan sacrifices in the Temple. The festival of Hanukkah, which
commemorates the Jewish revolt, came to be treated as a celebration of
the decisive rejection of Hellenic ways. The revolt certainly gave expression to anti-Hellenic sentiments, but these sentiments themselves reveal
how Hellenized most Jews had become – criticized for attending games
and learning Greek philosophy. Greek, rather than Aramaic (the patois
of the Jews of Palestine), was so widely spoken among the Alexandrian
Jews that, as will be seen, a Greek version of the Bible was prepared.
Moreover, in the first two centuries of Alexandria, Greeks and Jews
lived side by side in harmony. The Jews commemorated the Ptolemies
in the dedicatory inscriptions of their many synagogues, loudly praising
the dynasty without conceding the claim made in pagan temples that
the Ptolemies were 'divine'.[8]

To the rest of the population, and especially the Greeks, Ptolemy I offered a new cult, that of the god Sarapis. Sarapis was partly of Egyptian origin, a fusion of the bull god Apis and the resurrected god Osiris (hence, indeed, the name, [O]sir-apis). But Sarapis acquired many of the characteristics of Greek gods as well: elements of Dionysos, of Zeus and – in parallel to the attributes of Osiris – even of Hades, the god of the Underworld. He was also linked to the Greek god of healing, Asklepios. He was often portrayed carrying on his head a grain measure, which signified his link to the fertility of Egypt and its growing trade in grain. This thoroughly eclectic figure could thus be represented in Greek or Egyptian styles.[9] When the Ptolemies erected a great temple to Sarapis, the Sarapeion or Serapaeum, at the god's supposed birthplace of Memphis, it was decorated with what have been described as 'purely Greek' sculptures, though the Serapaeum in Alexandria was surrounded by sphinxes in full Egyptian style, of which several still survive. Sarapis proved popular in Alexandria: 'the operation of creating a new deity, bizarre though it may seem to us, probably did not appear so at the time'.[10] For the Greeks did not regard their own gods as exclusively Hellenic, and could accept that they manifested themselves in different guises to different peoples. Thus the invention of Sarapis formed part of a process by which the Egyptian gods were accommodated to Greek observers. The Greek question was not 'How are your gods different from ours?' but 'How are your gods the same as ours?' The eclectic nature of Sarapis also reflected the sense that there were no sharp boundaries between the twelve Olympian gods, and that their personification (for example in Homer's works) was a way of making sense of a great jumble of divine attributes, an attitude that was also sometimes expressed by making Sarapis into the senior among a trinity of Greek or Egyptian gods. This culminated in much later attempts to portray Sarapis as the one true God of the Universe, in outright competition with the Christians of Alexandria.[11]

II

The second important innovation under Ptolemy I and II was the building of their great lighthouse on Pharos island; the word 'Pharos' survived in Greek, Latin and the romance languages with the simple meaning of lighthouse. It was immediately classed as one of the great wonders of the world, along with the Colossus of Rhodes, of which more shortly: both these monuments proclaimed the glory of the cities where they stood, but also emphasized how that glory was founded in significant measure upon trade. The lighthouse formed part of the early plans for Alexandria; work on the structure began in 297 BC and building lasted until 283. In part it was built out of necessity: shoals lay close to shore, invisible at night and hard to track by day. It was essential to make approaches to Alexandria safer if the city were to achieve its potential as a centre for trade across the Mediterranean. The massive structure the Ptolemies commissioned stood 135 metres (440 feet) above the waves; the building was constructed on three levels, the lowest part square tapering upwards to a platform on which stood an octagonal tower crowned by a circular colonnade, with a massive statue of Zeus at the very top. Great mirrors cast a light many miles out to sea – forty miles, at a reasonable guess. How the lighthouse was illuminated is a mystery. For, even though parts of the structure were re-used in the much smaller but impressive Mamluk fortress that was constructed on the site in the late fifteenth century, and even though sizeable fragments of the lighthouse have now been exposed by underwater excavations, the exact appearance and manner of operation of the Pharos remain elusive.

The building of the lighthouse and indeed of Alexandria was possible only because the Ptolemies had gained control of massive resources. Their achievement lay not just in capitalizing on those resources, but in magnifying them as Alexandria developed its trade. In fact some observers insisted that the wealth of Alexandria was derived at least as much from the Egyptian hinterland as from the Mediterranean: the geographer Strabo opined that 'the imports to the city by way of the canals greatly exceed those by sea, so that the lake harbour was far richer than that on the sea', though he was writing several centuries after the golden age of Ptolemy I and II, at the start of the first century AD.[12] The city looked two ways, linking Egypt to the Mediterranean as never before; and links beyond the Mediterranean – through the Red Sea to India – ensured Alexandria's role as the prime entrepôt between the Indian Ocean and the Mediterranean, which it would maintain with only occasional interruptions for two millennia. The Ptolemies possessed an acute sense of how to sustain the vigour of the Alexandrian, and Egyptian, economy. They knew that command of the sea routes did not simply depend on Alexandria. They worked hard to bring the cities of Phoenicia under their control, at the price of conflict with their rivals the Seleucids. If they were to maintain an effective fleet they would need to extend their political control far from Egypt, into lands rich in timber: Cyprus, Lebanon and southern Anatolia; equally, without such a fleet they would not be able to hold these lands.[13] A naval race began, and not just the size of the Egyptian and Syrian fleets grew, but the size of their ships. In the fourth century both sides could sometimes mobilize over 300 ships, and the Phoenician shipyards transformed the cedars of Lebanon into a substantial fleet for the Seleucid kings; under Ptolemy II a fleet of 336 warships included 224 quadriremes, triremes and smaller vessels, but it also included many monster ships – 17 quinquiremes and still larger ships identified by the supposed number of oarsmen on each bank: 5 'sixes', 37 'sevens', 30 'nines', 14 'elevens', and so on up to 2 great 'thirties'. Later, Ptolemy IV Philopator (d. 204) would build a 'forty', which may have been a massive catamaran.[14] Whether these names really reflect the number of rowers, or were simply a way of indicating 'even larger than the last large ship', is a moot point. The 'forty' of Ptolemy IV never entered battle, and was probably not fit to do so; on the other hand, it amply displayed the wealth and magnificence of the Greek Pharaohs of Egypt. Its length was over 130 metres, its width over 16 metres, and it is said to have been crewed by 4,000 oarsmen and over 3,000 marines and auxiliary crewmen. Simply providing food and water for such a ship would have necessitated a small fleet of supply boats.[15] Yet massive size was not all about display. A ship's ram of the second century BC found underwater near Atlit in Israel is 2¼ metres long and weighs 465 kilograms.[16]

In addition to timber for the fleet, the Ptolemies needed to find sources of gold, silver, tin and iron, the last of which had been strangely neglected in Egypt during the long centuries when Hittites, Philistines, Greeks and Carthaginians enthusiastically made weapons and implements out of iron. Maybe this was because the soil of Egypt was so tractable after the Nile floods that there was little call for heavy ploughs shod with iron. On the other hand, there did exist a flourishing metal industry, and exports of gold, silver and bronze plate became one of the strengths of Alexandria, along with the export of textiles, pottery and – a particular speciality – glass.[17] Papyrus was another Egyptian speciality that had been in demand in neighbouring lands since the era of Wena-mun, in the eleventh century BC; now, Egyptian papyrus was ever more widely diffused across the Mediterranean. One of the most enthusiastic markets for these goods was Carthage, which used the Ptolemaic weight standard for its coins; Carthage was valuable to the Ptolemies because Spanish and Sardinian silver was funnelled through the city.[18] There were also close relations with Rhodes, which in the third century BC was as important a hub of trade as Alexandria. Alexandria thus established itself as one of the major business centres of the entire Mediterranean; its strength rested not just on the extraordinary achievements of the early Ptolemies, but also in the way it rapidly became integrated into the Hellenistic trade network.

One of King Ptolemy II's administrators, named Apollonios, appears in a series of papyri from the Egyptian desert. Among them is a ship's manifest of the middle of the third century BC, recording a cargo sent to Apollonios' household from Syria to Alexandria, and it provides rich evidence of the variety of goods that were being traded: nuts from the Black Sea, always a favourite on Mediterranean trade routes; cheese from Chios; olive oil, figs, honey, sponges and wool. There was also wild boar meat, venison and goat's meat aboard. But what filled most of the hull was wine – 138 amphorae and 6 half-amphorae of ordinary wine, and 5 amphorae plus 15 half-amphorae of sweet dessert wine.[19] This commerce was carefully and accurately taxed. The Ptolemies inherited from the Pharaohs a tight system of control of trade that they had no intention of relaxing. Ships arrived at designated ports and their cargoes were closely examined. It was an ancient system of commercial taxation that continued under the Romans, Byzantines and Arabs: *ad valorem* taxes, representing a percentage of the estimated value of the cargo, sometimes as much as 50 per cent (on wine and oil), sometimes merely a third or a quarter; taxes were levied not just at the ports but at internal customs stations along the Nile, as goods moved up to Alexandria.[20] Although this forced up the price of goods by the time they reached the quayside at Alexandria, demand for Egyptian grain and other products was generally so strong that these goods could still find purchasers in the eastern Mediterranean. In addition, the Alexandrians profited hand-somely from their role as middlemen in the trade linking the Indian Ocean to the Mediterranean. Although in the past, at Naukratis and elsewhere, Greek merchants had been able to tap into this trade, the scale of contact was now vastly enlarged. Gold, frankincense and myrrh were three of the prized items carried up the Red Sea. In 270/269 Ptolemy II Philadelphos reopened a canal that linked the Nile Delta with the lakes to the west of Sinai (now traversed by the Suez Canal), and created a maritime route into the Red Sea. Indian goods became familiar in Alexandria, while the Ptolemies profited from access to African and Indian elephants for their army.[21] An Egyptian papyrus lists the cargo of a vessel named the *Hermapollo*, which had arrived from India carrying 60 cases of spikenard, 5 tons of general spices, and 235 tons of ivory and ebony.[22] The great Mediterranean spice trade had been founded, and Alexandria would remain its most important centre even beyond the opening of the Cape route to the Indies by the Portuguese at the end of the fifteenth century.

The product that came to dominate the business of Alexandria was, however, grain. This was partly so that the city itself could be fed. Channels had been constructed linking Lake Mareotis, behind Alexandria, to the Nile Delta, so access to grain was unproblematic. But the Ptolemies were well aware that there was always room on the international markets for grain; Athens might look to the Bosphorus for supplies, but Rhodes was keen to buy Egyptian wheat for itself and for its many trading partners.[23] The Ptolemies found themselves in an exceptionally strong position because they inherited a regime according to which most of the land in Egypt was the possession of Pharaoh. They were thus able to charge the peasants a steep rent and to demand as much as half of what was produced, for the fertility of the soil after the Nile floods did not make such demands entirely unreasonable. New opportunities arose on the export market: a series of invasions of the Black Sea region, by Celtic and Scythian tribes, was endangering the sources and supply route on which Athens and other Greek cities had been relying for food. Seeing a chance of enriching themselves from the grain trade, the Ptolemies worked hard to increase the quality and quantity of grain production. They also extended the areas under cultivation and encouraged the use of iron implements as a way of improving efficiency and yields: 'so extensive a use of iron in Egyptian agriculture almost amounted to a revolution'.[24] Irrigation was improved, and among the contraptions used to water the land appeared the Archimedes screw, still favoured by Egyptian *fellahin*, and known in those days as the *kochlias*, or 'snail'.[25] The Persians had introduced a new type of wheat, superior to traditional Egyptian varieties, and the advantages of this were seized upon while Alexander was still alive. The cultivation of vines was greatly extended on the shores opposite Alexandria, and some good wines were apparently produced; more important, perhaps, was the development of an oil industry, since before the Ptolemies olive trees had not been wide-spread in Egypt. In doing all this, the Ptolemies laid the foundations of a new prosperity that would last until the Byzantine period.

III

The Ptolemies had no difficulty spending their income. The glorification of the dynasty was achieved by seizing the body of Alexander the Great as it was being carried through Syria and burying it magnificently some-where in the centre of Alexandria (hunting for the site has long been a favourite Alexandrian pastime). But Alexandria was a living city, and its greatest buildings were not surprisingly those attached to the massive pal-ace complex on its northern side. There the Ptolemies created a linked pair of institutions that confirmed their deep dedication to scholarship and, at the same time, their determination that whatever they did should be the biggest and best: the Mouseion, or 'museum', and the Library of Alexan-dria, where the papyrus of Egypt was used to build the greatest collection of literature the world had ever seen. The idea of a Mouseion, a shrine to the Muses, was not new (there were famous Athenian models on which to draw, and Ptolemy I relied on the advice of a learned Athenian, Demetrios of Phaleron), but the scale of this enterprise, its longevity and its influence were all exceptional. This was not simply a cult centre where music, philosophy and the arts were graciously cultivated. It was an Institute of Advanced Study, an All Souls College, where scholars, largely free of teaching duties, could devote themselves fully to literature, science and philosophy. According to Strabo there was even a Common Room and the members dined together; the institution possessed an endowment and a priest appointed by the king presided over the community.[26]

The second great scholarly institution, the Library, is also quite mys-terious. It was not a public library, though access was clearly granted to serious scholars, and there were side rooms where scholars could hold discussions and work side by side. Its origins lay in a decision by Ptolemy I to 'equip the library with the writings of all nations so far as they were worthy of serious attention'.[27] Although it has been claimed that the Mouseion was concerned with Greek learning, it is clear that the Library, at any rate, extended its interests far beyond the Greek world, though it is likely that most non-Greek texts were translated before they were deposited – chronicles of the Egyptian Pharaohs, the Hebrew Bible, Indian tales. Under the direction of Demetrios of Phaleron (c. 350–c. 280) and his capable successors, the Library was accommodated somewhere within the great palace complex of the Ptolemies, though there soon developed a 'daughter library' at the Serapaion which seems to have been more accessible, even if its collection was perhaps a tenth of the size of that of the main library, 42,800 papyrus rolls as against 400,000 'mixed' books and 90,000 'unmixed' books in the central depository.[28] Some of the rolls held several texts, but longer works (of which the Alexandrian poet Kallimachos famously said *mega biblion, mega kakon* – 'big book, big evil') were divided into separate scrolls. The evidence suggests, though, that the question of quality competed with that of quantity. The Ptolemies were determined to lay their hands on the best possible texts of the great authors: they hoodwinked the Athenians into sending their master copies of the plays of Aeschylus, Sophokles and Euripides for copying, and then retained them, even though that meant sacrificing an enormous deposit in silver.[29] Meanwhile the scholars of the Mouseion concentrated many of their energies in classifying and editing the great poets of archaic and classical Greece, such as Sappho and Pindar, neglecting both lesser-known, but very capable, classical writers and their own talented contemporaries such as Kallimachos, whose works have often had to be recovered from small papyrus fragments found in the desert sands of Egypt.[30] Thus the Mouseion and the Library were of crucial importance in the creation of a canon of great classical writers, and the sanctification of archaic and classical Greece as the great age of literary production, at the expense of Hellenistic Alexandria itself.

It would be a mistake to disparage the literary productions of Ptolemaic Alexandria. Kallimachos of Cyrene and Apollonios of Rhodes served on the staff of the Library of Alexandria, and Kallimachos devised a cataloguing system for the Library. But they also composed work of lasting significance: Kallimachos was famous for his epigrams, while Apollonios' great contribution was an epic in the Homeric mould, the *Argonautika*, which recounted Jason's adventures in search of the

Golden Fleece and his love affair with Medea. But his style did not parody that of Homer: he had an unusual ability to present events as if he were an observer, addressing the audience directly, and his rather ornate style has charm. His description of the Mediterranean waters through which Jason supposedly passed, and of the European river system beyond, betrays the influence of contemporary Alexandrian geographers and ethnographers, even though he could never quite escape the influence of Homeric geography, with the result that Roman commentators laughed at his errors.[31]

The Alexandria Library was unique in size and comprehensiveness, but it had its rivals. The kings of Pergamon on the coast of Asia Minor amassed their own library; anxious to prevent it from growing, Ptolemy II is said to have placed an embargo on the export of papyrus to Pergamon. But the librarians of Pergamon came up with a solution: the use of animal-skin parchment (*pergamenon*) as a writing surface.[32] On the other hand, the Alexandrian collection grew quickly and then slowly declined. Wear and tear, illicit removal of texts (borrowing was forbidden) and periods of relative neglect meant that, even when Julius Caesar set alight some warehouses storing books on the quayside at Alexandria – probably an off-site library deposit of some sort – the Alexandria Library had passed its peak.[33] Although its destruction is traditionally associated with the Arab invasion in AD 642, it is generally accepted that by then there was little left to destroy, and, sadly, no original material from this great library now survives.[34]

The clearest proof that the Ptolemies were not closed to the wisdom of other peoples lies in the much repeated report by ancient authors that Ptolemy II commissioned a translation of the Hebrew Bible.[35] A famous story tells how seventy-two wise Jews were sent to Alexandria by the High Priest in Jerusalem, placed in seventy-two cubicles and ordered to translate the Pentateuch in isolation from one another. They emerged with seventy-two identical translations, the 'Septuagint', or 'Seventy'.[36] In fact, the Septuagint emerged gradually over several decades, and it met the needs not just of the curious Ptolemies and their scholars but of the Alexandrian Jews, who increasingly were Greek-speaking; it is not even clear that the great philosopher Philo had much command of Hebrew. Interestingly, the Septuagint was based on a Hebrew text that differed at several points from the standard, 'Masoretic' text of the Hebrew Bible preserved by the Jews, and included apocryphal material discarded in the Jewish Bible. Some of this material, such as the book known as 'The Wisdom of Solomon', betrays strong influences from Hellenistic philosophy – further proof that the Jews of Alexandria were not isolated from Hellenistic culture, but greeted it with enthusiasm. The Septuagint was one of the great contributions of Alexandria to the cultural history of the Mediterranean, adopted by the Christians of Constantinople as the text of the Old Testament; indeed, Byzantine Christianity preserved much more of Alexandrian Jewish culture than the Jews themselves, including the voluminous works of Philo.

It would be easy to produce a catalogue of the remarkable Greek scholars who studied in Ptolemaic Alexandria. Some of the most influential are also the murkiest: was Euclid a man or a committee of mathematicians? In the third century, Eratosthenes, who worked out with remarkable precision the diameter of the earth, served as librarian of Alexandria; another innovative scientist was Aristarchos, who deduced that the earth revolves around the sun, though he was not taken seriously, and his influence waned further in the Roman period when another Alexandrian, Claudius Ptolemy, published his own very influential description of the earth in which it remained at the centre of the universe. There was a vibrant medical tradition in Alexandria; understanding of the human body was enhanced by the practice not just of autopsy but of dissecting condemned prisoners while still alive. Archimedes probably spent only a relatively short part of his long life (287–212 BC) in Egypt, but he maintained contact with Alexandrian mathematicians such as Eratosthenes.[37] His career serves as a reminder of the fascination of the Ptolemaic court with ingenious machines. One of these has been recovered from the Mediterranean seabed off the island of Antikythera, and appears to be a mechanical model of the universe.[38] Alexandrian science was of more than local interest. The discoveries and inventions of many of these figures were of lasting importance, and provide further proof of the great vitality of Hellenistic culture, of which Alexandria established itself as the capital.

IV

Alexandria cannot be considered in isolation. Its commercial success depended on links to the eastern Mediterranean, and at least as far west as Carthage. There was another place in the eastern Mediterranean that also filled the vacuum left by the decline of Athens as a great maritime and commercial power: Rhodes, whose island aristocracy of Greek origin managed to maintain its independence from competitors even though the world beyond was fast being divided up among the Macedonian generals. The Rhodians successfully resisted an attempt by the Seleucid king Demetrios to seize their island in 305; he brought 40,000 men from Syria and harried Rhodes for a year, but in the end their determination forced him to withdraw – the first in a series of famous sieges of Rhodes. This victory was commemorated by the construction of a gigantic statue of the sun-god Helios, who bestrode the harbour of Rhodes, the famous Colossus, completed by about 280 BC. The Rhodians even managed to create their own territorial dominion in the eastern Aegean islands and on the coast of Asia Minor, which became an important source of goods and manpower.[39] They had great need for manpower because they launched large fleets and expended much energy clearing the seas of pirates, whose appearance was the inevitable consequence of the decline of Athenian sea power. In 206–203 BC the Rhodians worked hard to suppress pirates based in Crete.[40] The Rhodians dedicated themselves to the principle that no single power should dominate the seas where they navigated; they aimed to preserve a balance between competing forces. Thus, although they enjoyed close commercial and political ties to Ptolemaic Egypt, they were willing to support the Seleucids if the Egyptian navy threatened to dominate the eastern Mediterranean. All this was achieved without trying to build the preposterously vast vessels beloved of the Ptolemies and the Seleucids. One Rhodian favourite was the *triemiolia*, an adaptable version of the trireme that was able to make use of sail power and oar power at the same time, making these ships ideal for chasing pirates; the Rhodians also employed an early type of Greek fire, combustible flares lobbed from poles on to the decks of enemy ships.[41]

Although the Ptolemies had created such an imposing war fleet, the commercial traffic of Alexandria was dominated by the ships of Rhodes, which could reach Egypt in only three or four days when the wind was behind them, while even in winter return traffic to Rhodes was on the move, if much more slowly.[42] Diodoros wrote: 'the Rhodians derived the majority of their revenues from the merchants sailing to Egypt'; he added: 'one could even say that their city was sustained by that kingdom'.[43]

It was the Rhodians who shifted most of the Egyptian grain that was despatched northwards, and it was from Rhodes that large quantities of wine arrived in Egypt, for the Rhodians had developed extensive vineyards all over their island; the physical evidence for this trade survives in the stamped handles of over 100,000 Rhodian amphorae, discovered in and around Alexandria.[44] These wine jars can also be found on sites throughout the Aegean, up into the Black Sea, and westwards in Carthage and Sicily. Ancient sources provide an estimate of the annual value of Rhodian trade around 200 BC: 50,000,000 *drachmai*, based on a 2 per cent tax which was levied on incoming and outgoing traffic, and which produced 1,000,000 *drachmai* each year.[45] A web of Rhodian bankers existed across the eastern and central Mediterranean; they advanced credit, oiling the commercial networks of the Mediterranean. The weight standard of Rhodian coinage was adopted by towns and islands in the Aegean. All this earned appreciation rather than enmity: when Rhodes was devastated by an earthquake in 227 or 226 BC, offers of aid arrived from rulers in Sicily, Egypt, Asia Minor and Syria.

The other important centre of trade and banking in the Hellenistic world was Delos, which was at first used by the Rhodians as a clearing house for their regional trade.[46] From 168 BC onwards, the Romans, who had been imprudently fighting the king of Macedon to a stalemate, started to interfere in the trade networks of the Aegean. They began to treat the Rhodians not as allies (and valued trading partners) but as a satellite, expecting Rhodes to place its fleet at the service of Rome in its conflict with the kings of Macedon. In reprisal against Rhodian lack of enthusiasm, the Roman Senate encouraged a more submissive ally, Athens, to take charge of Delos, on two conditions: the native population must be expelled and the island must function as a free port. Delos was repopulated by a merchant community, including many south Italians who ensured links with the west were maintained and enhanced; its population grew to an estimated 30,000 around 100 BC. Business was dragged away from Rhodes, which experienced sharp decline; the commercial income of Rhodes is said to have quickly fallen to 15,000 *drachmai*. Delian success in trade boosted the already strong reputation of its sanctuary. Excavations on Delos have uncovered large commercial areas, which were unfortified, since they were protected by the island's sanctity. There were several *agorai* or marketplaces for the Italian merchants, containing not just colonnades, porticoes, shops and offices but shrines dedicated to the gods merchants favoured, such as Poseidon, master of the sea, or Hermes, the messenger god. The Italians encouraged the trade in perfumes and unguents, and indirect links were forged through Syria to the Nabataean trade routes that penetrated to sources of frankincense and myrrh in Arabia. There was also a busy trade in slaves, victims of the piracy that became more threatening by the end of the second century, with the resurgence of the Cilician pirates in the east (a reflection, surely, of the decline of Rhodes, which had policed the waters off Anatolia so effectively). By Roman times Delos was being described as 'the greatest emporium on the whole earth'.[47]

Although its fortune was built to some extent on the misfortune of Rhodes, the success of Delos is further proof of the way in which, during the third and second centuries BC, the eastern Mediterranean networks of trade and business became increasingly integrated into a coherent, well-managed system, first under the hegemony of Rhodes and then under that of Delos. Delos brought in new partners, enlarging the network to include the merchants of Puteoli in the Bay of Naples. The Hellenistic world was politically fragmented into three main units – Greece, Syria and Egypt – and yet what was beginning to emerge was a single domain of trade. One element was missing: the great city of Carthage had disappeared from the map in the middle of the second century BC. It is now necessary to step back in time and examine how this happened, and how the backwoodsmen of Rome came to dominate even Greek waters before 100 BC.

7

'Carthage Must Be Destroyed',
400 BC–146 BC

I

While the war between Athens and Sparta for control of the Aegean was at its peak, other conflicts, further to the west, embroiled Greek cities in struggles for their life. Carthage was as significant a naval power in its sector of the Mediterranean as Athens was further to the east. In 415, the Carthaginians were content to look on while the Athenians attacked Syracuse. They could see that the Greeks were divided among themselves and too busy squabbling to turn their attention against the Phoenician trading stations on Sicily. From their point of view, anything that weakened Greek power in Sicily was welcome. On the other hand, the destruction of the Athenian forces posed a new problem, to which they found themselves responding rapidly. Not for the first time the Syracusans threatened to dominate the island. However, the real troublemakers proved once again to be the Elymian inhabitants of Segesta, who, not content with the havoc they had wreaked by calling in the Athenians, now appealed to Carthage for help against their old rivals, the Greeks of Selinous. The Carthaginians had good reason to support Segesta. It lay in an area dotted with Punic, that is Phoenician, colonies, notably Panormos (Palermo) and Motya. When in 410 the Segestans offered to become dependants of Carthage in return for protection, the Carthaginian assembly realized that the time had come to consolidate their city's hold on western Sicily.[1] The Segestan appeal marked a decisive moment in the transformation from a loose confederation of allies and trading stations presided over by Carthage to a Carthaginian empire that included among its subjects not just fellow-Phoenicians but subject peoples – 'Libyans', as the Berbers of North Africa were called by Greek writers, Elymians, Sikels and Sikans in Sicily, not to mention Sards and Iberians.

There were other, personal factors at work among the Carthaginian elite, for the city was at this time controlled by a group of powerful dynasties that dominated its Senate. A prominent Carthaginian with the common name Hannibal is said to have conceived a passionate hatred for all Greeks after his grandfather Hamilcar was killed in battle against the Syracusan army at Himera in 480 BC. An easy victory in 410, under the redoubtable Hannibal, expelled the Selinuntines from Segestan territory, and was followed by a massive second invasion in 409, with troops drawn from southern Italy, North Africa, Greece and Iberia. Xenophon, in his somewhat lame continuation of Thucydides, claimed that Hannibal brought with him 100,000 men, maybe twice the real figure.[2] With the help of sophisticated siege engines modelled on those familiar to the Phoenicians in the Near East, the walls of Selinous were breached after a mere nine days. The inhabitants paid a horrific price for their resistance: 16,000 Selinuntines were put to the sword and 5,000 were taken into slavery. This was followed by the sack of Himera, where 3,000 male prisoners were sacrificed to the shade of Hannibal's grandfather on the spot where he had been killed in 480.[3] The Carthaginians had not simply gone on the rampage. They were now determined to forge a secure dominion over much of Sicily at the expense of Syracuse. This was not, however, an 'ethnic' war of Phoenicians against Greeks: the Carthaginians sent an embassy to Athens, and the Athenians, now in the final stages of the war with Sparta, showed themselves well disposed to the Carthaginians, for they were looking for any allies they could find.[4] Athens and Carthage could also hope to benefit from mutual trade, once peace was established in the Greek world.

Then in 407 the Carthaginians embarked 120,000 troops on 120 triremes, if Xenophon's rather incredible figure is to be believed, and invaded western Sicily; even with such a large force it took seven months to starve Akragas into surrender. The city was plundered of its fine works of art, which included a brazen bull inside which a sixth-century tyrant of Akragas was said to have roasted his victims.[5] These acquisitions turned the taste of the Carthaginians towards Greek styles; certainly, by the third century Greek art and architecture had gained a hold on Carthage. Western Sicily was now under its direct control, and Carthage began to look eastwards, to Gela on the southern coast, which

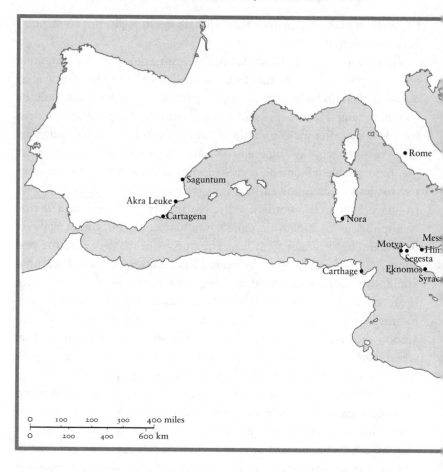

would open the road to Syracuse. The Gelans fled. Seeing one defeat after another for the Greeks, the Syracusans hurried to make peace, and the Carthaginians, who were expending vast sums on their army and navy, were ready to agree reasonably generous terms. The western and south-eastern Sicilian conquests were to remain under their control, but the Greek population was invited to return, while the eastern flank of Sicily, with its Greek and Sikel population, stayed independent of Carthage, which had achieved its main objectives.

One victim of the conflict was democracy. Syracuse once again fell under the control of a long-lived tyrant, Dionysios I (d. 367), the first of a much-feared dynasty. The story is told of one Sicilian tyrant who knew he was detested and was therefore amazed to find that an old

woman regularly offered prayers for his safety in a city temple. He summoned her and asked why she did this. She fearlessly replied that she
thought him a terrible despot. But she remembered the tyrant during
her distant youth; he had been dreadful, but was succeeded by someone even worse, and after him came someone worse still. So she prayed
for the life of this tyrant, knowing that, were he to die, he would be
succeeded by someone of unimaginable ghastliness. The tyrant was so
impressed by her honest answer that he gave her a bag of gold. These
tyrants relied on brute force and made no pretence to act as constitu-
tional monarchs. But they were also men of taste and culture; an earlier
generation of Sicilian tyrants had earned the praises of the poet Pindar,
and the new generation cultivated philosophers such as Plato, who

visited Syracuse in 388 or 387, and is said to have returned several times, in the hope of guiding the successors of Dionysios I towards policies properly informed by Platonic principles.[6] Although most of the remarkable correspondence between Plato and the Syracusan rulers is now discounted as later invention, the story of Plato's ties to the Syracusan court serves as a reminder that not just Greek goods but Greek ideas were travelling across the Mediterranean at this period.

It was Dionysios I who made peace with Carthage; but it was also Dionysios who revived the conflict with Carthage in 398, capturing the prize possession of the Phoenicians in western Sicily, Motya. The inhabitants were massacred, and not even the women and children were spared for the slave markets; those Greek traders who lived there were crucified as traitors.[7] That was the end of the history of Motya, but it was the beginning of a bitter conflict that brought a massive Carthaginian fleet to the harbour of Syracuse in 396. Once again the city was threatened with destruction; once again the Syracusans took advantage of the layout of their port to pick off the enemy fleet while also attacking the enemy land forces. Himilco, the Carthaginian commander, staring at defeat, made a secret deal with Dionysios and evacuated as many native Carthaginian soldiers as he could, abandoning his Iberian, Sikel and Libyan allies. The hairy Iberians, professional mercenaries, were absorbed into the Syracusan armed forces. More seriously still, there was uproar in the Carthaginian possessions in North Africa, and for a time it seemed that Carthage itself would be overwhelmed by a mass of slaves and rebels who gathered on the site of Tunis, hard by Carthage itself. The rebels dispersed, but Carthage had experienced a political earthquake. The only solution was to cede the Greek cities won under the earlier treaty to the tyrant of Syracuse, though the humiliation was not complete: the Punic settlements remained under Carthaginian control. Dionysios distracted himself with ambitious raids elsewhere in the Mediterranean – in 384 he raided Pyrgoi, the outport of Etruscan Caere, carrying away a vast treasure valued at 1,500 talents, which would pay for a substantial army. He probably needed the prestige this brought, because his envoys at the Olympic Games that year were mocked as the representatives of a tyrant no better than the Persian king. He did not seek to found a Syracusan empire but ruthlessly to establish his personal power, a point the Athenians tacitly recognized when they addressed him as 'archon [ruler] of Sicily'.[8] He had every intention of renewing the struggle for control of all Sicily, and a series of conflicts between Syracuse and Carthage in 375 culminated in the loss of a Carthaginian army of 15,000 – two-thirds dead, one-third enslaved. Carthage bounced back, defeating Dionysios and taking out 14,000 Syracusan troops. The end result was that Carthage did retain control of the parts of western Sicily it had long ruled, and even recovered title to some of the Greek cities captured by Hannibal.

II

Despite the hostility that had marked Carthaginian relations with Syracuse, the result of these wars was to tie Carthage more closely into the Greek world. The city was now to all intents detached from Phoenicia; it is doubtful how important trade with Tyre and Sidon was to late fourth-century Carthage, compared to the renewed intensity of contact between Carthage and the Greek cities of Hellas, Sicily and Italy. The Carthaginian god Melqart was identified with Herakles. The Carthaginians were convinced that they had offended Demeter by sacking one of her temples in Sicily, so they imported her cult into Carthage, even attempting to conduct the temple rituals according to the Greek liturgy, with the aid of Greek residents.[9] Carthaginians learned Greek – at one point when relations were particularly bad they were banned from learning or speaking the language, which is the surest proof that Greek had become the second language of the local elites. These elites actively exploited the fertile coastline of North Africa, often owning prosperous estates some distance away, abundant in grain, fruits and wine. The lesser towns that the Phoenicians had founded along the African coast were now subject cities. There was increased intermarriage with the local population, a trend that included the leading families of Carthage, who sometimes had family ties to local Berber kings, or indeed to prominent Greeks in Sicily. Carthage had become a cosmopolitan city numbering perhaps 200,000 inhabitants, with extensive suburbs and merchant and naval ports.

Throughout the fourth century the Carthaginians kept a close eye on Syracuse. They struggled for control over the seas between Africa and Sicily as well as over the island. The value of the straits became clear in 344–343 when the Corinthian admiral Timoleon became the saviour of

Syracuse. His fame rested on the fact that he had conspired to assassinate his brother for making himself tyrant of Corinth. Plutarch reported that Timoleon covered his own face and wept while his two co-conspirators killed his brother.[10] Timoleon therefore seemed an ideal ally for disaffected Syracusan nobles who opposed the ruthless policies of the dynasty of Dionysios. Since Corinth had originally founded Syracuse there still persisted a sense that Corinth was the place where aid should be sought, though it was no longer one of the political and economic leaders in the Greek world, and could provide only a small fleet. Carthage sent ships to block the arrival of Timoleon, who managed to find a way through, and Carthage found itself drawn into another destructive war: 3,000 Carthaginians died in battle in western Sicily in 341, and the Carthaginian general, Hasdrubal, was crucified when he returned home, the standard penalty for incompetence on the battlefield. Carthage did not lose its western Sicilian lands, but Timoleon established himself as the leading figure on the island, fostering the creation in nearly every Greek city of a system of aristocratic government. Tyrants went out of fashion for a couple of decades; more importantly, the Sicilian Greeks seemed to understand the need to work together.[11]

By the time of Plutarch, who died in AD 120, Timoleon was being hailed as the hero and favourite of the gods who had 'cut the nerves of tyranny' and had liberated Sicily from the power of the Punic barbarians. In reality, Timoleon was not very different from the tyrants who had preceded him. He had seized power with the help of mercenaries; and in suppressing petty tyrants across the island he was asserting the long-contested supremacy of Syracuse. One redeeming feature was that he had the good sense to resign office in old age, afflicted by cataracts and honoured by the Syracusan people. The other redeeming feature was that he presided over a period of economic recovery throughout much of Sicily. Cities were rebuilt, including several that had been devastated by the Carthaginian wars: Akragas and Gela revived; no less significantly, small centres of Greek settlement grew and prospered. Scornavacche in southeastern Sicily is the site of a small Greek town that had been destroyed by a Sikel attack in 405; now it became a centre of the ceramics industry.[12] This revival was the work of new settlers as well as the old Siculo-Greek population. Timoleon may have brought as many as 60,000 settlers from Greece itself and from the Greek cities of southern Italy. The grain trade between Sicily and Athens became increasingly regular in the late fourth century; to judge from the large number of Corinthian coins of the same period found in Sicily, there were particularly intense commercial contacts across the Ionian Sea to Corinth, through which Sicilian agricultural goods were funnelled into Greece.[13] It would be a mistake to attribute this new prosperity entirely to the efforts of Timoleon. The fourth century saw a wider revival of trade in the central Mediterranean. The plague that had erupted during the Peloponnesian War became less virulent and population revived. There were long enough stretches of peace for Carthage as well as the Greek cities of Sicily to rebuild trading contacts to east and west. Carthage enjoyed commercial ties with Athens and made the best use of its links to Spain as well.

The last major conflict between Carthage and Syracuse broke out in 311. Hamilcar, the Carthaginian commander in western Sicily, faced a formidable foe in Agathokles, who had managed to overturn Timoleon's constitution and to establish himself as tyrant of Syracuse. Agathokles, like his predecessors, aimed to bring all or most of Sicily under Syracusan control. Hamilcar reasoned that the best interest of Carthage would be served by an understanding that Syracuse could dominate eastern and central Sicily; the Carthaginians were worried to see Agathokles taking an unhealthy interest in Akragas, which lay close to their own settlements in western Sicily. In 311 Agathokles marched with a large army towards Akragas, but a Carthaginian fleet of fifty or sixty ships arrived and Agathokles was thwarted. The next year, Hamilcar disembarked 14,000 men (only one in seven was actually a citizen of Carthage). He swept through Sicily, supported by local forces resentful of Agathokles' ambitions. The tyrant of Syracuse realized that he had over-reached himself, and that he had lost the war in Sicily. His possessions were now confined to Syracuse itself. But what he also possessed was money and troops: 3,000 Greek mercenaries and another 3,000 Etruscan, Samnite and Celtic mercenaries lured from Italy. Adding another 8,000 men recruited locally, he fitted out a fleet of sixty warships and in August 310 the fleet headed through a Carthaginian naval barricade to the coast near Carthage. With outstanding temerity, Agathokles landed his men, burned his ships (because there were not enough men left to guard them) and marched his forces towards Carthage itself, camping nearby on the site of Tunis.[14] This meant that Carthage was under siege from the Syracusans while Syracuse was under siege from the Carthaginians.

Carthage, with its easy access to the sea, was impossible to invest without massive naval forces, so even the conquest of swathes of the North African coastline by Agathokles did not secure the surrender of Carthage. Still, the loss of its rich fields and orchards must have hurt the city badly. The moment Agathokles disembarked and launched a land attack on the Carthaginians, his Libyan allies deserted – perhaps 10,000 men – and 3,000 of his Italian and Greek mercenaries were killed in battle. Agathokles, it has been well said, 'was no Alexander either in genius or resources'.[15] He did at least understand that he must now make peace, and, predictably, the map of Sicily returned to its old appearance, with Carthage ruling the western end and the Greeks retaining control of the east and the centre.[16] Surprisingly, this defeat did not mark the end of Agathokles. He asserted his power as 'king of Sicily', taking this novel title in imitation of the Greek kings who, starting with Philip and Alexander of Macedon, had established themselves as rulers of the eastern Mediterranean. He now directed his imperial ambitions elsewhere, mainly towards the Adriatic, forging one marriage alliance with Pyrrhos of Epeiros, a cousin of Alexander the Great and a general of comparable talents, and another with the Ptolemies in Egypt. He took control of the islands of Kerkyra and Leukas in the Ionian Sea and extended his dominion into southern Italy, which he twice invaded. Yet he left no obvious legacy: he failed to establish a dynasty, as he had hoped, and his maritime empire did not outlive his assassination in 289 BC.[17]

The real legacy of Agathokles was the continued survival and prosperity of his bitterest enemy, Carthage. The Romans asked for a renewal of their commercial treaty with Carthage, first signed in 509 BC. Whereas in 509 the Carthaginians could see the Romans only as mildly useful neighbours of their Etruscan friends, they were now dealing with a significant power in Italy, which, within a few generations, would attempt to drive Carthage completely out of Sicily. To understand these developments it is necessary to step back in time once again.

III

The prominence, indeed pre-eminence, of Rome in the Italian peninsula by 300 BC was the result of wars fought on land; Rome had no ambition to become a naval power, and the treaties with Carthage, renewed in 348 BC, indicate that those Romans who crossed the seas travelled as merchants, not as men of arms. These treaties ensured that they did not wander into areas that lay within the Carthaginian sphere of influence, notably Sicily, though in times of severe famine, for example in 493, grain was brought all the way from Sicily to Rome.[18] The major pre-occupation of the early Romans was the defeat of neighbouring peoples such as the Volscians who were percolating down from the Appenines in the hope of settling the broad spaces of Latium, to the south of Rome. The Romans also faced a severe threat in 390 BC from Gallic invaders, from whom they were famously saved at night-time by cackling geese. Relations with the Etruscans, with whose culture they shared a great deal, were much more complex, but the complete destruction of one of the largest Etruscan cities, Veii, in 396 BC, marked the first stage in the submission of the southern Etruscan lands.[19] After the fall of Veii, which was within walking distance of Rome, the Etruscan cities were not destroyed but instead were drawn into a Roman web; wealthy Caere became a dependent ally following its defeat in 253, and lost control of part of its coastline, which included the port at Pyrgoi where in past times Greek and Carthaginian traders had gathered and settled. It is therefore no coincidence that, within a few decades of their expansion along the coast of southern Etruria, the Romans were able to launch massive fleets and defeat Carthaginian navies in the waters off Sicily. In addition to acquiring coastal stations in Etruria, the Romans began to develop their own outport at Ostia, though its original function was to channel goods from Greek Italy and Etruria into the Tiber and to supply Rome.[20]

Merchant shipping came and went, but the Roman war fleet almost seems to emerge fully armed out of nothing. The Romans responded passively to threats from the sea: in 338 BC Volscian pirates from Antium (Anzio) on the Latin coast raided the mouth of the Tiber, but they were beaten back, and the Romans took back home as trophies the *rostra* or 'beaks' of the ships they had destroyed. These *rostra* were displayed on the stage used for speeches in the Roman Forum, which explains the continuing use of the term 'rostrum' to mean a speaker's platform.[21] A few years later, around 320 BC, a treaty with the southern Italian city of Taras, founded by Spartan colonists, stipulated that Roman ships should not sail into the Gulf of Taranto, thereby defining a Tarentine sphere of influence and protecting the trading interests of what had become the dominant Greek city in southern Italy and leader of the 'Italiote League' of cities.[22] Although a treaty might be expected to bespeak amity, the more probable explanation for this agreement is that Roman land campaigns against the Samnites and other enemies were drawing Rome's armies closer and closer to the Greek cities; lines therefore needed to be drawn on the map. Treaties, contracts and other legal documents often mention possibilities that are not immediate or even real, and there is still no evidence that Rome was seeking to arm large fleets, though in 311 the *duumviri navales* or 'two naval men' were appointed to construct a *classis* or 'fleet' and ensure that it was kept in repair.[23] But this fleet was probably tiny.

The Samnite war drew the Roman armies further and further south, as they tried to outflank the large and vigorous Samnite armies. When ten ships under Roman command sailed into the Gulf of Taranto in 282 BC they were attacked by the Greeks of Taras, and the Romans lost half their flotilla; undeterred, they established a garrison in the town of Thourioi (Thurii), which also lay in the Gulf of Taranto, and which had appealed to Rome for help against raids by the inhabitants of the Lucanian hinterland. Taras had not turned against Rome because it feared for its control of the sea, for ten ships were no match for the hundreds Greek maritime cities could mobilize; the real threat was that a Roman presence on land would unravel the Italiote League and set one Greek city in southern Italy against another.[24] Fear of Rome led the Tarentines to look across the Adriatic and invite the aid of Pyrrhos of Epeiros; he claimed descent from Achilles, so there were echoes of the Trojan War in his campaign against Rome, which was by now vaunting its foundation by the descendants of the Trojan Aeneas. Whether Pyrrhos saw himself as future master of the Mediterranean, creating a western empire as vast as that his cousin Alexander had briefly brought into being in the East, is doubtful; he may simply have craved the payments the western Greeks were prepared to offer such a formidable mercenary army, organized in phalanxes and equipped with elephants. As the Tarentines feared, south Italian cities opted to join Rome as well as to join Pyrrhos, and as Pyrrhos made headway in Italy some of those cities that had supported Rome now opportunistically changed their mind. Pyrrhos dominated the affairs of southern and central Italy between 280 and 275; his Pyrrhic victories brought him little advantage, and within a few years of his exasperated withdrawal Rome had taken charge of Taras. The Greek cities in southern Italy continued to run their own affairs with an occasional nod in the direction of Rome (such as a special issue of coins showing the goddess

Roma).[25] The Romans had no desire or capacity to control the towns of the deep south so long as they saw themselves as a land power rooted in Latium. They established a few settlements: Paestum south of Naples, Cosa in Etruria and Ariminum (Rimini) were coastal stations intended to protect lines of communication by land and sea along the shores of Italy, but the emphasis lay on defending the interior, for instance the edges of Samnite country that would be tamed by the new colony of Beneventum (Benevento).[26]

The Punic Wars drew Rome out of its Italian shell. Carthage had joined in the war against Pyrrhos, and won a great naval victory in 276 BC, sinking two-thirds of his fleet of over 100 ships.[27] The First Punic War was fought in Sicily and Africa, and for the first time extended Roman influence across the open sea; the Second Punic War (dominated by land campaigns) drew the Romans towards Spain, though the main theatre of action was Italy itself, following Hannibal's invasion by way of the Alps; the brief Third Punic War drew Rome more deeply into African affairs and culminated in the destruction of Carthage in 146 BC. What is curious is the lack, at least at the start, of clear Roman intentions. The Romans did not set out to make an end of Carthage; they had ancient treaties with the city and there was no obvious conflict of interest.[28] Between the first and second wars there intervened a period of peace during which relations, if not trust, were restored. And yet at the end of the cycle Rome emerged as a Mediterranean power, extending its mastery over not just the ruined site of defeated Carthage but, in the same year, over large tracts of Greece. This is, perhaps, another example of an empire acquired in 'a fit of absence of mind'. Rome began to construct a large war fleet only when it became obvious that this was essential to the conduct of the First Punic War. Both cities were drawn into a series of conflicts that included the largest naval battles of antiquity and resulted in tens of thousands of casualties on land and sea. Not for nothing have historians compared the outbreak of these wars to the First World War, where a series of relatively small incidents lit a fuse that ignited vast regions.[29] Just as the First World War was much more than a conflict between Germany and the Anglo-French alliance, the Punic Wars were rather more than a conflict between Carthage and Rome, for other interests soon emerged: Iberian towns, North African kings, Sardinian chieftains and, during the First Punic War, the Greek cities of Sicily. The armies Hannibal set against Rome included Gallic, Etruscan and

Samnite recruits; the fleets Rome sent against the Carthaginians included large numbers of vessels, probably the great majority, supplied by Greek and other allies in central and southern Italy. To term these wars 'Punic' is mistakenly to assume that the conflicts were dominated by a continuous history of rivalry to the death between Carthage and Rome.[30]

IV

Ancient historians were astonished by the length, intensity and brutality of the Punic Wars. Polybios, the Greek historian of the rise of Rome, benefited from the patronage of one of the generals in the Punic Wars and opined that the First Punic War was the greatest war ever fought. Its time-span, from 264 to 241 BC, easily outlasted the Trojan War, and the Second Punic War (218–201) was also long and exhausting, leaving in its wake agricultural devastation.[31] The war with Carthage originated in quarrels far from Rome, and it was far from clear to either great city that intervention was in their best interests. The crisis began with the seizure of Messana on the tip of Sicily by a group of Campanian mercenaries who had earlier served Agathokles, tyrant of Syracuse, and who were known as the Mamertines, or 'men of Mars'. They arrived in the 280s and made thorough nuisances of themselves, raiding the towns of eastern Sicily; the Romans became involved because their own Italian campaigns had been proceeding so well that they had reached Rhegion (Reggio), the Greek city directly opposite Messana, which they occupied in 270. So Sicily was within the sights of the Romans; but that is not to say they intended to invade the island. When the new ruler of Syracuse, Hieron, defeated the Mamertines in battle the mercenaries panicked and sent messages both to Rome and to Carthage, asking for military help. Hieron was a power to be reckoned with; he had commercial and diplomatic ties to the Ptolemaic rulers of Egypt, and, following a great tradition, he not merely patronized the Olympic Games but competed in them.[32] As it happened, there was a Carthaginian fleet nearby, in the Lipari islands, and its admiral prevailed on the Mamertines to let him install a Carthaginian garrison in Messana.[33]

The Mamertines did not like to be under anyone's thumb, and now had second thoughts; they turned to Rome, asking for help against the Carthaginians. But the Senate was not easily convinced that Rome should become involved in a conflict beyond the peninsula. Polybios says that many Romans were afraid the Carthaginians would gain complete control of Sicily, and that they would then begin to interfere in Italy itself.[34] According to one version, the Senate was unwilling to act, and a popular assembly voted to fight. Even so, this was not a war against Carthage. The Roman general sent to Sicily attacked Hieron as well as the Carthaginians. His mission was to defend Messana against the enemies of the Mamertines. The idea that he intended to conquer Sicily and clear the island of Punic forces is preposterous. The aim was to restore the balance of power in the region. In the event, the Mamertines managed on their own to expel the Carthaginian garrison from Messana; back home, the Carthaginian commander was crucified *pour encourager les autres*. The Romans found it difficult to make headway across the Straits of Messina while there were substantial Carthaginian fleets in the Lipari islands, and the Roman general had no experience of the stormy waters between Italy and Sicily; so, not surprisingly, direct Roman help to the Mamertines was spasmodic. When it did arrive, it only forced Hieron of Syracuse and Carthage into an unholy alliance. The Romans were hampered by a severe lack of ships. Their commander Appius Claudius turned to Taras, Velia, Naples and other Greek cities for a fleet, made up of triremes and fifty-oared pentekonters.[35] The Carthaginians are said to have thrashed the Roman fleet, after which they sent a haughty message to Rome: come to terms or else you will not even be able to wash your hands in the sea.[36] Even so, Carthage was hoping for peace.

The Romans were too proud to pay attention, and by 263–262 they had at least 40,000 men under arms in Sicily. Hieron of Syracuse was impressed and decided to back the likely winner, switching sides from Carthage to Rome (for which he would eventually be handsomely rewarded). Even more significantly, the Romans had worked out how to transport large numbers of men by sea, not that all were Romans or Latins – many were confederate allies from Italy, while the Carthaginians encamped large numbers of Iberian, Gallic and Ligurian mercenaries at Akragas.[37] Rome prevailed, sacked the city, sold its 25,000 inhabitants into slavery, and embarked on what now seemed a realistic plan to remove the Carthaginians from Sicily.[38] Yet this is not to say that Rome saw itself as master of a colonial Sicily. Its ambitions were more modest. Rome would have been happy with guaranteed access to Sicilian grain, as its population grew prodigiously. Much as Roman optimates might, in later generations, scorn a life of commerce, there were sound commercial reasons for pursuing this war, once it began to look as if it could actually be won.[39]

Rome needed a proper war fleet. Polybios stated that it was only now that the Romans began to build a fleet of their own.[40] There was an important shift away from heavy reliance on ships provided by Greek allies or Etruscan clients, towards a war fleet much vaster than the ten or dozen vessels maintained by the 'two naval men'. How this was achieved is an even greater mystery than in the Spartan case. Sparta could draw on the expertise of neighbouring Greek cities, several of which were within its sphere of control. Now, in 261 or 260, it was resolved that Rome should construct 100 quinquiremes and twenty triremes. The Romans had captured a Carthaginian quinquireme and used it as a model.[41] How the Romans manned the fleet they built, how they acquired the essential navigational skills that would enable the vessels to be steered through the treacherous waters of the Tyrrhenian and Ionian Seas, how they managed to piece together the jigsaw puzzle of beams and shaped timbers, how, indeed, they managed to achieve this in sixty days from the cutting of the timber (as the Elder Pliny would later assert), is a mystery – the use of such fresh, unweathered wood would have generated hideous problems as it dried out and shrank. Polybios credibly remarked that the ships were 'poorly constructed and hard to move'.[42] Pitch and rigging had to be obtained or manufactured. Roman crews are said to have trained intensively on land, learning their oarsmanship in dry conditions before daring to set out on the sea. Evidence that adds plausibility to the story of the rapid building of the fleet is the discovery of the remains of a Carthaginian warship whose timbers bore letters of the Punic alphabet (which also functioned as numbers), so it seems that in Carthage ships were assembled by numbers. Whether the Roman assembly lines were at Ostia or in the Greek cities of southern Italy is unknown, but this was an enormously expensive operation. After its initial doubts, Rome had committed itself fully to the war with Carthage; and yet the Romans were still unclear about their objectives. Fighting the war had become a matter of honour.

How efficient this fleet was is also an open question. The first attempt to use it, at Lipari, was a disaster; the Roman commander was blockaded within the harbour of Lipari, and his crew were so alarmed that they ran away. Still, this was soon followed by a success in the same waters, at Mylai, enhanced by the invention of a short-lived but famous grappling device known as the *korax* or 'crow'. This device contained a raisable ramp that could swing in different directions, compensating for the lack of manoeuvrability of Roman ships; under the ramp was a heavy pointed spike made of iron, which would not merely grip an enemy ship but slice into its deck.[43] The aim was to enable Roman marines to board Carthaginian ships and do there what they did best, hand-to-hand fighting. The Romans still mistrusted the sea, and sought to transform sea battles conducted by ships with rams into ersatz land battles in which the boats provided platforms for men-at-arms. The fleets each side launched became bigger and deadlier year by year. Polybios says that at the great sea battle of Eknomos in western Sicily, in 256, 230 Roman ships faced about 350 (more probably 200) Carthaginian vessels and 150,000 men; it was 'possibly the biggest naval battle in history'.[44] Later in the war, at a crucial battle fought off the Egadian islands west of Sicily in 241, numbers were only a little smaller, indicating that, amid the awful destruction wreaked by battle and by storms, and the natural deterioration of ships kept too long at sea, the shipyards were working at full stretch to replace what had been lost. The figures of hundreds of ships are certainly very impressive, unmatched in later centuries, and yet the constant confusion about the figures among the classical authors suggests how easy it was for numbers to become inflated. Modern historians too have been seduced by figures that make sense only if they are totals for all vessels, not just the sleek triremes and quinquiremes – adding in the transport ships carrying marines, horses and, crucially, supplies, for the warships could not last more than a couple of days without fresh water and generous food supplies (further quantities of which were generally available from studiously neutral merchants who parked themselves on shore within sight of a battle, in the hope of quick profits).

Thanks in significant measure to the *korax* the battle of Eknomos was a great Roman triumph. The Roman fleet also learned very quickly how to form for battle in closely packed squadrons; the difficulty they then faced was that of holding the line together in the heat of battle. These formations were surely intended to follow the pattern of the Roman battle formations regularly employed on land. They gave the Romans an advantage over the more thinly spread Carthaginian navy, for what the Punic admirals counted on was the ease with which their ships could be manoeuvred and give chase. They had the advantage of speed and they preferred to descend rapidly on the side or even stern of enemy shipping, ramming and sinking their foes; at Eknomos the Punic fleet probably intended to surround the Roman fleet and to stab lethally at its sides and rear.[45] In other words, the battle of Eknomos is important in the history of naval strategy not simply because of the number of ships and sailors; it is also an intriguing example of a clash between navies with very different conceptions of how to fight a battle at sea.[46]

Victory at Eknomos opened the Sicilian Straits to the Roman fleet and gave Rome access to Africa. The great plan was now to invade the heartlands of the Carthaginian empire. But in attacking Carthage the Romans did not assume that they would capture the city, let alone destroy it. In 256 a Roman fleet landed more than 15,000 men at Aspis, a little to the east of Carthage, and raided the farms and townlets nearby, reportedly taking 20,000 slaves, though many were captive Romans and Italians who could now be released. But the Romans were unable to hold their position in Africa, and sailed away dejected in July 255, taking at least 364 ships back to Sicily.[47] Here inexperience with the seas brought the Romans a disaster far greater than anything the Carthaginian navy could have inflicted. The Roman commanders overruled their steersmen, evidently not Roman, who insisted that it was unsafe to sail close to the Sicilian shore at a time of the year famous for its sudden and violent storms. But the Romans wanted to show the flag and intimidate the towns along the south coast of Sicily into submission. Heavy storms swept water over the gunwales of the low-slung vessels and sank all but eighty of this great fleet, and up to 100,000 men drowned, maybe 15 per cent of Italy's manpower: 'a greater disaster than this has never been recorded as happening at sea at one time', according to Polybios.[48]

The final act of the war was the naval battle off the Egadian islands, west of Sicily, in 241 BC, in which the Roman navy, now rebuilt, sank or captured about 120 Carthaginian ships; Carthage realized it had to come to terms. Rome imposed heavy penalties, without suggesting that Carthage had no right to exist. The defeated city was required to pay an indemnity of eighty tons of silver (3,200 talents), spread over a period of ten years and, more importantly, Carthage had to renounce its interests in Sicily and Sicily's offshore islands. Carthage promised not to send warships into Italian waters, nor to attack Hieron of Syracuse, the turncoat who was now a firm ally of Rome.[49] Indeed, the main beneficiary was Hieron, who was entrusted by the Romans with the day-to-day supervision of Sicilian affairs. Rome had no appetite for extending direct dominion over Sicily. The aims of the war had developed slowly, but even at the end Rome foresaw no more than the neutralization of Carthage. Its merchant fleet could continue to ply the Mediterranean; indeed, it would have to do so if the vast sums in silver due to Rome were ever to be paid.

V

It has been necessary to dwell on the First Punic War because that conflict marks the moment when a Roman fleet emerged. The Second Punic War, ancient historians agreed, was a natural consequence of the First. Following its defeat, Carthage found itself under increasing pressure from Numidian rulers in the North African hinterland, and it also faced a serious mutiny among its mercenary army based in Sardinia. The mercenaries killed the Carthaginian commander as well as all the Carthaginians they could find on the island, and when new troops were sent to Sardinia to suppress the revolt, they joined the mutiny as well. In due course, though, the mercenaries were expelled, arrived in Etruria, and appealed to Rome for help, which the Senate was inclined to offer. The Romans were irritated that Carthage had arrested 500 Italian merchants who had been surreptitiously supplying the mutineers. Carthage would have preferred to restore its authority over the parts of Sardinia it had ruled, but, in the face of Roman determination, the Carthaginians buckled, and in 238 they offered the Romans not merely 1,200 talents of silver but Sardinia itself.[50] Rome had therefore rapidly established its claim to the two largest islands in the Mediterranean, and had acquired Sardinia merely through threats. Carthage was too exhausted to argue. Whether Rome could activate a claim to any more than a few harbours and coastal stations frequented by Punic merchants is doubtful. Sardinia was unconquerable, with its thousands of communities gathered under independent warlords around the *nuraghi*. The Sards were no more cooperative towards the Romans than towards the Carthaginians; Rome had to wait until 177 BC before it secured a major victory over the Sards.[51] Rome was mainly interested in Sardinia's strategic position, which would guarantee control of Tyrrhenian waters; it was not the island they craved, but its coastline with secure harbours free from pirates and Punic warships, from which their fleet could be supplied. Thus Rome had begun to develop a Mediterranean strategy consciously based on the principle of controlling the seas.

VI

The Roman acquisition of Sicily and Sardinia – or rather, the exclusion of Carthage from those islands – diverted Carthaginian ambitions westwards. All Carthage had been left with was Malta, Ibiza and some trading-posts in North Africa and southern Spain. It was in Spain that Hamilcar Barca built an empire that greatly surpassed in scale and ambition the network of trading settlements created by the Phoenicians many centuries earlier. Hamilcar sought a land dominion; the question, posed by the ancient historians themselves, is whether he saw it as his personal dominion or as a new theatre for Carthaginian expansion, which would include mastery of the silver mines of ancient Tartessos. Probably it was a mixture of both. Hamilcar's family, the Barcids, was exceptionally powerful within Carthage, even though its republican system of government meant that their influence did not go unchallenged. There is some debate whether the coins in the Greek style issued in Carthage's Spanish dominions show an image of a god such as Melqart or a wreathed ruler in the Hellenistic style; the Barcids were tempted to project themselves as new Alexanders who were creating a territorial monarchy in the west.[52] That Hamilcar was determined to emancipate Carthage from Roman shackles is made plain in a famous but possibly legendary tale: before leaving for Spain in 237 BC, Hamilcar prepared a sacrifice to the god Baal Hamon and, calling to his side his young son Hannibal, he told him to place his hand on the sacrificial beast and to swear 'never to bear goodwill to the Romans'.[53]

Not surprisingly, Hamilcar first concentrated his attention on winning control of the silver-bearing areas of southern Spain. As in Sardinia, the idea of 'control' must be handled with care. He made alliances with Iberian and Celtiberian chieftains, and he gradually increased his armies so that by 228 BC he had perhaps 56,000 men in the field. The other means of control adopted by the Barcids (for Hamilcar was succeeded in Spain first by his son-in-law Hasdrubal and then, after Hasdrubal's assassination, by his own son Hannibal) was city-foundation. Hamilcar was responsible for the foundation of Akra Leuke, generally agreed to lie under modern Alicante, and around 227 BC Hasdrubal was inspired to found a city further south along the coast and even closer to the sources of silver. The Carthaginians were strangely uncreative when naming people and places; there were countless Hannibals and Hasdrubals. Hasdrubal named his new city just that: 'New City', *Qart Hadasht*, now known as Cartagena, though, since the time of Polybios, historians, to avoid confusion with the mother-city, have often called it New Carthage, 'New New City'.[54] Hasdrubal ensured that his presence was felt by building a great palace for himself at the top of one of the hills on which this city stood. More importantly, Cartagena was easily accessible from North Africa, making it an essential link in the chain of ports and garrisons tying Carthage to Spain.

The conflict between Carthage and Rome actually resumed further north in Spain, at Saguntum, along the coast from modern Valencia. Following a lengthy siege, at the end of 219 Hannibal sacked this town, which had placed itself under Roman protection. That the Romans should take an interest in a place so remote from their political and commercial sphere suggests that they had become worried by eighteen years of Carthaginian consolidation in Spain. Once again, the real issue was strategic: the Romans did not want to be outflanked by the Carthaginians, and refused to allow them to strengthen their position to the point where they could re-establish themselves in Sardinia or Sicily. Hasdrubal had earlier entered into an understanding between Rome and Carthage about Punic control of parts of Spain, to the effect that the Carthaginians would remain south of the river Ebro, which lay a good way to the north of Saguntum.[55] Rome felt it had to act to prevent a resurgence of Carthaginian power. The decision by Hannibal to take his army across the Alps and bring the war to the gates of Rome was an inspired attempt to divert the conflict away from either Barcid Spain or the waters in which Carthage had been defeated twenty-three years earlier. This did not prevent a Roman attack on Spain, led by Cnaeus Publius Scipio, who had as many as 25,000 men under his command, and who reached Spain by sea, arriving at the ancient commercial station of Emporion. He managed to win a naval engagement against the Carthaginians, but the fleets were tiny by comparison with those that had fought in the first war: about thirty-five vessels under Roman command. Before long, though, the defection of their Celtiberian allies left the Romans floundering.

Another new theatre of war was northern Greece. The ruler of Macedon, Philip V, was so impressed by Hannibal's great victory over the Romans at Cannae in southern Italy (216 BC) that he took up arms against Rome. Rome found it impossible to fight on so many fronts at once, and Philip scored successes in the waters off the Albanian coast. Once again, the Romans viewed the Macedonian problem from the perspective of their strategy in Italy. They were seriously worried that they might lose control of the southern Adriatic coast, and sent an army to Brundisium (Brindisi) to head off the danger of a Macedonian landing.[56] The Macedonians stood their ground and Rome was unable to bully them into submission. Rome was learning that its growing Mediterranean dominions brought it into contact and even conflict with neighbours who had not previously been in their line of sight.

Cicero wrote of Sicily: 'it was the first jewel in our imperial crown, the first place to be called a province'. For the Romans began to think that the exercise of informal empire in areas such as Sicily no longer met their needs. Hieron of Syracuse was treated with honour, and was permitted to make a state visit to Rome in 237; significantly, he presented the Romans with 200,000 bushels of Sicilian grain. He was welcome to control the south and east of Sicily, but by 227 the north and west, which had been the scene of several of the most bitter naval engagements with Carthage, were placed under the authority of Roman praetors; military garrisons and fleets stood by on the island, but they needed to be fed, and the navies that patrolled the central Mediterranean also needed to be supplied with tack. Accordingly the Romans decided to set in place more formal systems of grain taxation. Trouble flared in 215 following the death of the aged Hieron, and the outbreak of turmoil in Syracuse.[57] Factions in the city hostile to Rome dreamed of a Punic alliance that would, improbably, ensure Syracusan domination over the entire island, as if Carthage would expect no prizes.[58] Carthage impressively managed to re-establish itself on the island, with tens of thousands of troops; Akragas became a major Punic base. But it was against Syracuse that the Romans unleashed the full force of their armies and navies in 213. It was by far the largest city on the island, and the source of the new difficulties Rome faced. When the Romans tried to blockade the port their ships stood so far apart that the Carthaginian fleet was able to sail past them with impunity, although in 212 a Carthaginian attempt to sail a massive convoy of 700 merchant ships into Syracuse under the protection of 150 warships not surprisingly proved too ambitious. Still, naval blockades were almost impossible to enforce in this period, especially against a city with a wide harbour mouth and extensive sea walls. The Syracusans and Carthaginians made mincemeat of the Roman fleet, benefiting from the advice of the great Archimedes, who took delight in designing new machines that lifted Roman vessels right out of the water, shaking them so hard that the crew fell into the sea, or mirrors that reflected the burning rays of the Sicilian sun on to the timbers of enemy ships, setting them alight. In the end, though, Roman tenacity resulted in the capture of Syracuse in 212, and Archimedes is said to have been slaughtered as he was sketching another of his ingenious designs in the dust.[59] The next year Akragas was prised from the Carthaginians, and Rome boasted the year after that that not a single free Carthaginian could now be found in Sicily.[60] The dividends were not just military and political but cultural: Syracuse was despoiled of its treasures, and Greek sculptures were carried in triumph to Rome, stimulating the growing taste of the Romans for the superior culture of the Hellenes.

The war continued for another decade and was decided by events beyond Sicily, although without these successes in Sicily much of what Rome achieved would have been impossible. In the west, Publius Cornelius Scipio captured New Carthage in 209 by realizing that a great lagoon bordering the town could be forded by a Roman army. The conflict was increasingly focused on Africa, however, where the Romans finally defeated Hannibal at the battle of Zama in 202 BC; he had failed to achieve his aims in Italy, after prowling around and wreaking havoc up and down the peninsula for many years. The ability of the Romans to transport thousands of men from Sicily to Africa was crucial, though alliances with the Numidian kings also ensured Roman success. The fact was that Rome had won command of the sea, and this was confirmed by the final humiliating treaty in which Carthage was allowed to retain only ten triremes – not even the big quinquiremes for which it was famous. Five hundred warships, Livy recounted, were taken out of the great round harbour of Carthage to be burned. A massive fine was once again levied and Carthage was deprived of all its possessions outside Africa, as well as some African lands which were assigned to the Numidians. The Spanish lands so carefully accumulated by Hamilcar Barca were lost to

Rome. Carthage was forbidden to fight wars outside Africa, and effectively reduced to the status of a client state of Rome. Such terms had often been imposed on Italian neighbours, but for Carthage this amounted to emasculation.[61] Once again Rome found itself in a commanding position, without having set out to achieve quite this degree of pre-eminence.

VII

The victory over Hannibal still left Rome facing many unresolved problems in the central Mediterranean. Two more wars were fought against the Macedonians, who were forced to accept Roman protection; further south, Rome battled the Aetolian League in central Greece; further east, it fought the armies of the Seleucids, the Greek generals who had gained power in Syria after the death of Alexander the Great.[62] By 187 BC the reach of Rome stretched from the ex-Barcid lands in Spain right across the Mediterranean to the Levant. There were still potential rivals, such as the Ptolemies in Egypt, with their massive fleets, but, for the first time, the entire Mediterranean felt the powerful political influence of a single state, the Roman Republic. Amid these conflicts Carthage stayed quiet and was loyal to the humiliating terms of its treaty with Rome. The Carthaginians willingly supplied their few remaining warships to serve in their distant ancestors' waters during the Syrian War. They provided grain to the Roman armies and navies from the broad estates that stretched across the horizon away from Carthage.[63] In 151 BC the Carthaginians completed payment of the indemnity they owed to Rome. It was just at this moment that they found themselves in conflict with the octogenarian king of Numidia, Masinissa. The Carthaginians had no doubt that they were by now free from Roman shackles, and could make their own decision to attack Masinissa. The mood in Rome was different. A prosperous, resurgent Carthage that conducted its own policies was now seen as an indirect threat to Roman dominion over much of the Mediterranean, even if there was no direct threat to Rome's possessions in Sicily, Sardinia or Spain. After a visit to Carthage, as an official mediator between the Carthaginians and Masinissa, the arch-traditionalist Cato became obsessively convinced that the future of Rome could be secured only by the city's annihilation. He constantly denounced Carthage in his speeches to the Roman Senate, and made sure that he ended every speech, even if it had nothing to do with Carthage, with the words: 'in addition, it is my opinion that Carthage must be destroyed'.[64] The bullying began. Carthage was first ordered to supply hostages, which it did, and next ordered to hand over its stock of arms, including 2,000 catapults, which once again it did. But the third demand made by Rome was simply unacceptable. The Carthaginians were ordered to abandon their city entirely and to migrate at least ten miles into the interior to a place of their own choosing.[65] If the Romans thought they were being generous in allowing the Carthaginians to choose where to live, they were deceiving themselves. The Carthaginians refused and war broke out; as the final demand made plain, this was now a war for the survival of Carthage, as neither of the previous wars had been. Under the command of Scipio Aemilianus, stepson of the great Scipio who had faced Hannibal, the Roman forces headed straight for North Africa. This time there was no shadow-boxing in Sicily or Spain, which were well outside the greatly constrained Carthaginian sphere of influence. Although the Carthaginians managed with extraordinary energy to construct a new war fleet, the city was blockaded by sea and besieged by land, and eventually fell to the Romans in spring 146. Scipio enslaved the inhabitants, and razed great parts of the city (though it is not actually clear whether he sowed salt into the ground as a sign that Carthage must never rise again).

The Punic Wars had stretched across nearly 120 years. Their significance extended far beyond the western and central Mediterranean: the year Carthage fell, Rome consolidated its hold on Greece, opening up the prospect of vigorous competition with the rulers of Egypt and Syria for mastery over the eastern Mediterranean. More than two decades of struggle with the Macedonians and then with Greek city-leagues culminated in the capture of Corinth, also in 146 BC. Corinth was seen as the focus of opposition to Rome, but its commercial attractions, with its two ports, were undeniable. The whole city was ruthlessly treated as booty. The entire population was enslaved. Its magnificent and often ancient works of art were auctioned. Shiploads of sculptures and paintings were despatched to Rome, resulting in a further surge of aristocratic interest in Greek art. The cultural effects of the destruction of a city thus varied enormously. Punic civilization lingered as the demotic culture of North Africa after the fall of Carthage, but Greek civilization was diffused westwards after the fall of Corinth.[66] These wars entered the Roman consciousness in other ways.

Writing under Augustus Caesar, Virgil described the fateful entanglement between Dido, foundress queen of Carthage, and Aeneas the Trojan refugee. It was a tumultuous relationship that could be resolved only if Dido's Carthage was destroyed on the funeral pyre:

> The groans of men, with shrieks, laments, and cries
> Of mixing women, mount the vaulted skies.
> Not less the clamour, than if – ancient Tyre,
> Or the new Carthage, set by foes on fire –
> The rolling ruin, with their loved abodes,
> Involved the blazing temple of their gods.[67]

8

'Our Sea', 146 BC–AD 150

I

The relationship between Rome and the Mediterranean was already changing significantly before the fall of Carthage and of Corinth. This relationship took two forms. There was the political relationship: it was clear before the Third Punic War that the Roman sphere of influence extended to Spain in the west and to Rhodes in the east, even when the Roman Senate did not exercise direct dominion over the coasts and islands. Then there was the commercial relationship that was creating increasingly close bonds between Rome's merchants and the corners of the Mediterranean. Yet the Senate and the merchants were distinct groups of people. Like Homer's heroes, Roman aristocrats liked to claim that they did not sully their hands in trade, which they associated with craft, peculation and dishonesty. How could a merchant make a profit without lies, deception and bribes? Rich merchants were successful gamblers; their fortune depended on taking risks and enjoying luck.[1] This condescending attitude did not prevent Romans as eminent as the Elder Cato and Cicero from commercial dealings, but naturally these were effected through agents, most of whom were Romans in a new sense.

As it gained control of Italy, Rome offered allied status to the citizens of many of the towns that fell under its rule, and also established its own colonies of army veterans. 'Romanness' was thus increasingly detached from the experience of living in Rome and, besides, only part of the population of the city counted as Roman citizens, with the right to vote, a right denied to women and to slaves. There may have been about 200,000 slaves in Rome around 1 BC, about one-fifth of the total population. Their experience forms an important part of the ethnic history

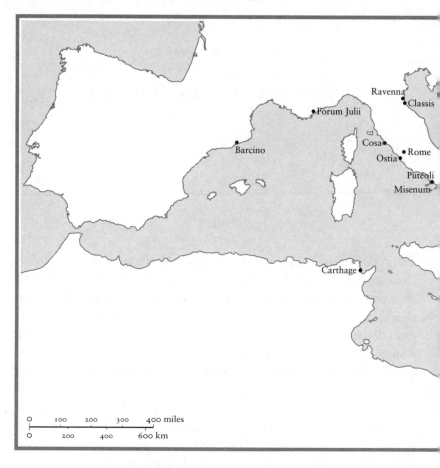

of the Mediterranean. Captives from Carthage and Corinth might be set to work in the fields, having to endure a harsh existence far from home, ignorant of the fate of their spouses and children. Iberian captives were put to work in the silver mines of southern Spain, in unspeakable conditions. But those who could demonstrate their talents might serve as Greek tutors in a noble household, or as commercial agents for their master, even travelling overseas to trade (despite the risk that they would disappear in the fleshpots of Alexandria). Accumulating funds in the *peculium*, the slave's private pot of money – though legally, like everything the slave had, this was the property of the slave's master – a slave might eventually be able to buy freedom, or a grateful master might free his favourite slaves, often under the terms of his will. Freedmen could prosper greatly as bankers and merchants, and their children

could aspire to Roman citizenship. Thus a massive immigrant population of Greeks, Syrians, Africans, Spaniards grew in Rome, and it is not
surprising that Greek, the standard means of communication in the
eastern Mediterranean, was the everyday language of many quarters of
the city. The poet Lucan, writing in the first century AD, grumbled: 'the
city population is no longer native Roman, but the refuse of humanity:
such a hodge-podge of races that we could not fight a *civil* war, even if
we wished'.[2] His snobbery possessed a tinge of self-hatred: he was born
in Córdoba in southern Spain, and had been brought to Rome as a
small child. Yet even the ranks of the Senate were infiltrated by the sons
of freedmen, not to mention well-born Etruscans, Samnites and Latins.[3]
The comedian Plautus livened up one of his plays, which were awash
with crafty merchants and clever slaves, with passages in the Punic

language of North Africa. The confusion of languages was made even greater because the city and its outports attracted large numbers of foreign merchants: Tyrians, for the merchants of the once great Phoenician city had recovered their role in trade by the time of Augustus; Jews, who at this period included a number of shippers and sailors; south Italians, for, as will be seen, the Bay of Naples occupied a special role in Rome's system of supply. The term 'Roman merchant' therefore means 'merchant under the protection of Rome' rather than 'merchant of Roman descent'.

The ascendancy of Rome in the Mediterranean Sea depended on three factors: provisions to feed the vast city, ports through which the provisions could arrive and protection of its merchants – the defeat of the pirates whose presence in the eastern Mediterranean threatened the stability of the trading systems built around Alexandria, Delos and other partners of Rome.

II

Pirates go in search of prosperity. The flourishing state of trade in the second century BC created the ideal circumstances in which pirates too could flourish, especially since neither the Rhodians nor the Delians had the naval strength to clear the eastern Mediterranean of rogue shipping, particularly after Rhodes set into decline. Pirates were as much a scourge in the west as in the east. In 123–121 BC Metellus 'Balearicus' earned his sobriquet after suppressing a particularly pestilential form of piracy practised in the Balearic islands, which now fell under Roman rule: its pirates would paddle out to sea on what were little better than rafts, but proved an enormous nuisance.[4] After the Punic capital was destroyed, there were no more Carthaginian merchants to police these waters. The Romans began to realize that they had responsibilities, and took them seriously. In 74 BC the young patrician Gaius Julius Caesar was captured by pirates while he was travelling to Rhodes, where he planned to study rhetoric (he was a man of considerable learning). A big enough prize to be worth a ransom, he was treated with honour by the pirates, but even before his release he had the courage to taunt them with the promise that he would return and destroy them. He gathered together a flotilla, captured his captors, and crucified them. Since they had been so polite, he graciously had their throats cut before they were raised on their crosses.[5]

Small, agile fleets preyed on the shipping routes from bases in Crete, Italy and the rocky shores of south-eastern Turkey, the precipitous area known appropriately as 'Rough Cilicia', lying due north of Cyprus and a couple of hundred miles east of Rhodes. As trade through the once-great Etruscan cities declined, the shipowners of Etruria turned to less orthodox ways of making a profit. An inscription from Rhodes commemorates the death of the three sons of Timakrates who were killed in engagements against Tyrrhenian pirates active in the eastern Mediterranean.[6] Sometimes, too, navies encouraged privateers to patrol the seas looking for particular enemies. This is what Nabis, king of Sparta, did around 200 BC, entering into an unholy alliance with Cretan pirates who raided supply ships heading towards Rome.[7] Rebel Roman generals in Sicily, such as Sextus Pompeius, the son of the famous Pompey, launched their own ships and tried to block grain supplies bound for Rome, which Sextus Pompeius could easily do – as well as Sicily he had Sardinia in his grasp.[8] The lords of islands and coastal ports demanded transit taxes from commercial shipping that passed through their waters, and responded to any refusal with violence. Pirates required places where they could unburden themselves of the money, goods and slaves they had seized, and their operations therefore depended on the willing collaboration of the inhabitants of several minor ports such as Attaleia that attracted innumerable fences, hustlers, traffickers and tricksters. The Cilician pirates managed to sustain whole communities on the southern edges of the Taurus Mountains. They were speakers of Luvian, living in clan-based societies in which both male and female descent was taken seriously, and they were governed by elders or *tyrannoi*.[9] The crews of the pirate ships were mountain men who migrated down to the coast and took to ships, though they cannot have learned the skills of seamanship without a great amount of help from the sailors of Side and Attaleia on the coast. According to the geographer Strabo, the people of Side allowed the Cilician pirates to hold slave auctions on the quayside, even though they knew that the captives were freeborn.[10] Plutarch described the lightly built boats that they used so effectively:

Their ships had gilded masts at their stems; the sails woven of purple, and the oars plated with silver, as if their delight were to glory in their iniquity. There was nothing but music and dancing, banqueting and revels, all along the shore.[11]

By 67 BC pirates had reached the doorstep of Rome itself, with attacks on the port of Ostia and along the coast of Italy.[12] Plutarch added:

> This piratic power having got the dominion and control of all the Mediterranean, there was left no place for navigation or commerce. And this it was which most of all made the Romans, finding themselves to be extremely straitened in their markets, and considering that if it should continue, there would be a dearth and famine in the land, determined at last to send out Pompey to recover the seas from the pirates.[13]

Pompey had already distinguished himself (or made enemies, depending on which side one supported) in the power struggles within Rome.[14] He intended to provide a permanent, global solution to the problem of piracy. In 66 BC he divided the Mediterranean into thirteen zones, each of which would be systematically cleared of pirates. First, he addressed the problem of piracy close to home, sweeping the Tyrrhenian Sea clean of pirates. He took a fleet to Sicily, North Africa and Sardinia, placing garrisons in what Cicero called 'these three granaries of the state' and guaranteeing the lifeline of Rome herself.[15] This work is said to have taken forty days. After that he was ready to pounce on Cilicia, but news of his achievements in the west outpaced his fleet, and as soon as he hove into sight of the Cilician coast towns began to surrender to him. Fighting at sea and on land was quite limited.[16] He had arrived with perhaps fifty warships and fifty transports: not a massive fleet, though the light boats of the Cilicians would be no match in battle, and the Roman People had voted him 500 ships if that was what he needed.[17] Pompey's aim was not to exterminate the pirates but to end piracy: instead of massacring his enemy he accepted their surrender and resettled them, offering them agricultural land.[18] The Senate had offered to support Pompey for three years; Pompey's campaign took three months. Piracy was henceforth a low-level irritant rather than a great scourge that threatened Rome's supply lines.

Pompey used the war against the pirates as a springboard for the creation of a large Roman dominion in Syria and Palestine, whose stability depended not just on Roman armies but on the recognition by local kings that an alliance with Rome was the best way to guarantee their own authority.[19] Pompey did not, however, intend to make the East his sole domain. Roman domination of the eastern Mediterranean was a by-product of the vicious civil wars that pitched Pompey the Great against Julius Caesar, Brutus against both Mark Antony and Octavian, and Mark Antony against Octavian, the future Augustus Caesar. In 48 BC the partisans of Pompey and those of Gaius Julius Caesar met in battle at Pharsalus in north-western Greece ('this is what they wished on themselves', Julius Caesar remarked as he contemplated the enemy dead).[20] Pompey fled to Egypt; lured into a trap, he was stabbed to death just as he reached what he imagined to be the safety of the shore. The one great territory in the eastern Mediterranean that still remained outside Roman control was Egypt: 'a loss if destroyed, a risk to annex, a problem to govern'.[21] But Julius Caesar arrived in hot pursuit of Pompey two days after his rival was killed; he immediately saw an opportunity to build Roman influence within Egypt, by offering his support to the charming, intelligent and wily (though probably not very beautiful) Queen Cleopatra in a struggle for power with her brother King Ptolemy XIII. As has been seen, Caesar achieved his aims by bombarding Alexandria and has been accused of destroying all or part of the Library. He was able to station Roman troops in Egypt, nominally for the protection of the still independent queen. Whether or not he had conquered Egypt, Cleopatra conquered him, and a son was born, named Ptolemy Caesar, whom the queen took with her to Rome and who was generally assumed to be Caesar's child. The sight of a Roman general whose son might be a future Pharaoh alarmed Roman politicians, suggesting that Caesar too had royal ambitions – even if most historians would argue that 'Caesar was slain for what he was, not for what he might become'.[22]

After Caesar's assassination in 44 BC, the rivalries of the Roman politicians threatened to take Egypt out of the Roman sphere once again. Although Caesar's heir, Octavian, and Caesar's friend Mark Antony wreaked revenge on his assassins at the battle of Philippi near the northern shores of the Aegean in 42, their own relations deteriorated. The victorious leaders appointed themselves as Triumvirs and divided the Roman world, Octavian taking charge of the west, Mark Antony of Egypt and the east, and Lepidus gaining rights in Africa. The idea was not to carve Rome's dominions into three but to assert the new regime and reorganize the provinces. Mark Antony granted Cleopatra several Phoenician cities, towns in 'Rough' Cilicia and the whole of Cyprus (annexed in 58 BC). Cilicia was worthwhile, because it had long been used as a source of timber, as were Phoenicia and Cyprus. Nonetheless,

Antony was the next great Roman to be seduced by the charms of Cleopatra, and his detractors insisted that he saw himself as a future king of Egypt. Or was it his wish that Alexandria would become the new capital of a pan-Mediterranean empire? After a campaign against the Armenians he conducted a Roman Triumph in the streets of Alexandria, an event without precedent there.[23] After this, the mistrust between Octavian and Antony was increasingly obvious, and their struggle for power became an open war.

Octavian's great public victory was won in 31 BC not in Egypt but in north-western Greece, at sea at Actium, close to the Ionian islands. Antony had the larger fleet and a good supply line all the way to Egypt; what he lacked was the loyalty of those he saw as his allies. They began to desert, and, faced by a blockade of Octavian's ships, Antony managed to break through with forty vessels and fled to Alexandria.[24] Whether this was really a great battle is far from certain, but Octavian was fully alive to its propaganda value.

> Young Caesar, on the stern, in armour bright,
> Here leads the Romans and their gods to fight:
> His beamy temples shoot their flames afar;
> And o'er his head is hung the Julian star.

And on the other side is the miscreant Antony:

> Ranged on the line opposed, Antonius brings
> Barbarian aids, and troops of eastern kings,
> The Arabians near, and Bactrians from afar,
> Of tongues discordant, and a mingled war:
> And, rich in gaudy robes, amidst the strife,
> His ill fate follows him – the Egyptian wife
> (*Sequitur, nefas, Aegyptia coniunx*).[25]

Actium has thus been celebrated for millennia as one of the decisive battles in world history. Its result was to win for Octavian the fame and approval back in Italy of which he had been short; his victory ensured that the eastern Mediterranean would remain tied to Rome for three centuries, until the founding of a New Rome at Constantinople created a new balance of power.

Antony survived for a year in Egypt, until Octavian's armies invaded from east and west; defeated in battle, he killed himself, and was followed a few days later by the last of the Pharaohs, Cleopatra. Whether she poisoned herself with an asp is a detail. What is important is that Octavian was now master of Egypt. He showed an immediate understanding of the heritage he had seized. He would rule like a Pharaoh, to all intents keeping Egypt as his personal domain, and governing through viceroys directly accountable to him rather than to the Senate and People of Rome who notionally exercised sovereign authority there.[26] He understood that Egypt's greatest treasure was not emeralds or porphyry, but ears of Nilotic wheat.

The war against piracy, the acquisition of large tracts of land in the eastern Mediterranean and the Roman civil wars therefore had dramatic political and economic consequences for the Mediterranean. The Romans henceforth guaranteed the safety of the seas from the Straits of Gibraltar to the coasts of Egypt, Syria and Asia Minor. The integration of the Mediterranean into a Roman lake was complete. The process had taken 116 years. The first phase stretched from the fall of Carthage and Corinth to the Cilician campaign of 66 BC. The second, much shorter, phase culminated in Octavian's acquisition of Egypt. Having defeated his rivals, Octavian transformed himself into Augustus Caesar, the *Princeps* or leader of the Roman world. His victory in the civil wars is often seen as the moment when a new order came into being and Imperial Rome was born, with the added help of propagandist poets and historians such as Virgil, Horace and Livy. But the new, imperial order was also created by the extension of Roman rule as far east as Egypt. The Mediterranean had become *mare nostrum*, 'our sea', but the 'our' referred to a much larger idea of Rome than the Senate and People of Rome itself, *Senatus Populusque Romanus*. Roman citizens, freedmen, slaves and allies swarmed across the Mediterranean: traders, soldiers and captives criss-crossed the sea. They carried with them a predominantly Hellenistic culture, which had penetrated deeply into Rome itself (the poets and dramatists such as Virgil, Plautus and Terence owed concepts, contents and metre to Greek models); it was a culture that was increasingly infused with themes of eastern origin, long familiar on the streets of Alexandria but now common currency in Rome herself: the cult of Isis, portrayed by Apuleius in his burlesque novel *The Golden Ass*; the cult of the God of Israel, brought to Rome by Jewish merchants and captives even before the destruction of Jerusalem by the Romans in AD 70. At the centre of the network lay Rome, a swarming, cosmopolitan city whose million inhabitants needed to be fed. The acquisition of Egypt assured supplies of grain, and thereby guaranteed the popularity of imperial rule.

III

The grain trade was not simply a source of profit for Rome's merchants. In 5 BC Augustus Caesar distributed grain to 320,000 male citizens; he proudly recorded this fact in a great public inscription commemorating his victories and achievements, for holding the favour of the Romans was as important as winning victories at sea and on land.[27] The era of 'bread and circuses' was beginning, and cultivating the Roman People was an art many emperors well understood (baked bread was not in fact distributed until the third century AD, when Emperor Aurelian substituted bread for grain).[28] By the end of the first century BC Rome controlled several of the most important sources of grain in the Mediterranean, those in Sicily, Sardinia and Africa that Pompey had been so careful to protect. One result may have been a decline in cultivation of grain in central Italy: in the late second century BC, the Roman tribune Tiberius Gracchus already complained that Etruria was now given over to great estates where landlords profited from their flocks, rather than from the soil.[29] Rome no longer had to depend on the vagaries of the Italian climate for its food supply, but it was not easy to control Sicily and Sardinia from afar, as the conflict with the rebel commander Sextus Pompeius proved. More and more elaborate systems of exchange developed to make sure that grain and other goods flowed towards Rome. As Augustus transformed the city, and as great palaces rose on the Palatine hill, demand for luxury items – silks, perfumes, ivory from the Indian Ocean, fine Greek sculptures, glassware, chased metalwork from the eastern Mediterranean – burgeoned. Earlier, in 129 BC, Ptolemy VIII, king of Egypt, received a Roman delegation led by Scipio, conqueror of Carthage, and caused deep shock when he entertained his guests to lavish feasts dressed in a transparent tunic made of silk (probably from China), through which the Romans could see not just his portly frame but his genitals. But Scipio's austerity was already unfashionable among the Roman nobility.[30] Even the equally austere Cato the Elder (d. 149 BC) used to buy 2 per cent shares in shipping ventures, spreading his investments across a number of voyages, and he sent a favoured freedman, Quintio, on these voyages as his agent.[31]

The period from the establishment of Delos as a free port (168–167 BC) to the second century AD saw a boom in maritime traffic. As has been seen, the problem of piracy diminished very significantly after 69 BC: journeys became safer. Interestingly, most of the largest ships (250 tons upwards) date from the second and first centuries BC, while the majority of vessels in all periods displaced less than 75 tons. Larger ships, carrying armed guards, were better able to defend themselves against pirates, even if they lacked the speed of the smaller vessels. As piracy declined, smaller ships became more popular. These small ships would have been able to carry about 1,500 amphorae at most, while the larger ships could carry 6,000 or more, and were not seriously rivalled in size until the late Middle Ages.[32] The sheer uniformity of cargoes conveys a sense of the regular rhythms of trade: about half the ships carried a single type of cargo, whether wine, oil or grain. Bulk goods were moving in ever larger quantities across the Mediterranean. Coastal areas with access to ports could specialize in particular products for which their soil was well suited, leaving the regular supply of essential foodstuffs to visiting merchants. Their safety was guaranteed by the *pax romana*, the Roman peace that followed the suppression of piracy and the extension of Roman rule across the Mediterranean.

The little port of Cosa on a promontory off the Etruscan coastline provides impressive evidence for the movement of goods around the Mediterranean at this time. Its workshops turned out thousands of amphorae at the instigation of a noble family of the early imperial age, the Sestii, who made their town into a successful industrial centre. Amphorae from Cosa have been found in a wreck at Grand-Congloué near Marseilles: most of the 1,200 jars were stamped with the letters SES, the family's mark. Another wreck lying underneath this one dates from 190–180 BC, and contained amphorae from Rhodes and elsewhere in the Aegean, as well as huge amounts of south Italian tableware on its way to southern Gaul or Spain. Items such as these could penetrate inland for great distances, though bulk foodstuffs tended to be consumed on or near the coasts, because of the difficulty and expense of transporting them inland, except by river. Water transport was immeasurably cheaper than land transport, a problem that, as will be seen, faced even a city such a short way from the sea as Rome.[33]

Grain was the staple foodstuff, particularly the *triticum durum*, hard wheat, of Sicily, Sardinia, Africa and Egypt (hard wheats are drier than soft, so they keep better), though real connoisseurs preferred *siligo*, a soft wheat made from naked spelt.[34] A bread-based diet only filled stomachs, and a *companaticum* ('something-with-bread') of cheese, fish or vegetables broadened the diet. Vegetables, unless pickled, did not travel well, but cheese, oil and wine found markets across the Mediterranean, while the transport by sea of salted meat was largely reserved for the Roman army.[35] Increasingly popular was *garum*, the stinking sauce made of fish innards, which was poured into amphorae and traded across the Mediterranean. Excavations in Barcelona, close to the cathedral, have revealed a sizeable *garum* factory amid the buildings of a medium-sized imperial town.[36] It took about ten days with a following wind to reach Alexandria from Rome, a distance of 1,000 miles; in unpleasant weather, the return journey could take six times as long, though shippers would hope for about three weeks. Navigation was strongly discouraged from mid-November to early March, and regarded as quite dangerous from mid-September to early November and from March to the end of May. This 'close season' was observed in some degree right through the Middle Ages as well.[37]

A vivid account of a winter voyage that went wrong is provided by Paul of Tarsus in the Acts of the Apostles. Paul, a prisoner of the Romans, was placed on board an Alexandrian grain ship setting out for Italy from Myra, on the south coast of Anatolia; but it was very late in the sailing season, the ship was delayed by the winds, and by the time they were off Crete the seas had become dangerous. Rather than wintering in Crete, the captain was foolhardy enough to venture out into the stormy seas, on which his vessel was tossed for a miserable fortnight. The crew 'lightened the ship and cast out the wheat into the sea'. The sailors managed to steer towards the island of Malta, beaching the ship, which, nevertheless, broke up. Paul says that the travellers were treated well by the 'barbarians' who inhabited the island; no one died, but Paul and everyone else became stuck on Malta for three months. Maltese tradition assumes that Paul used this time to convert the islanders, but Paul wrote of the Maltese as if they were credulous and primitive – he cured the governor's sick father and was taken for a god by the natives. Once conditions at sea had improved, another ship from Alexandria that was wintering there took everyone off; he was then able to reach

Syracuse, Reggio on the southern tip of Italy and, a day out from Reggio, the port of Puteoli in the Bay of Naples, to which the first grain ship had probably been bound all along; from there he headed towards Rome (and, according to Christian tradition, his eventual beheading).[38]

Surprisingly, the Roman government did not create a state merchant fleet similar to the fleets of the medieval Venetian republic; most of the merchants who carried grain to Rome were private traders, even when they carried grain from the emperor's own estates in Egypt and elsewhere.[39] Around 200 AD, grain ships had an average displacement of 340 to 400 tons, enabling them to carry 50,000 *modii* or measures of grain (1 ton equals about 150 *modii*); a few ships reached 1,000 tons but there were also, as has been seen, innumerable smaller vessels plying the waters. Rome probably required about 40 million measures each year, so that 800 shiploads of average size needed to reach Rome between spring and autumn. In the first century AD, Josephus asserted that Africa provided enough grain for eight months of the year, and Egypt enough for four months.[40] All this was more than enough to cover the 12,000,000 measures required for the free distribution of grain to 200,000 male citizens.[41] Central North Africa had been supplying Rome ever since the end of the Second Punic War, and the short, quick journey to Italy was intrinsically safer than the long haul from Alexandria.[42]

Large numbers of merchants travelled from the grain-exporting cities of the North African coast to Ostia, where they gathered around the portico now known as the Piazzale delle Corporazioni.[43] Desiccation and erosion had not yet spoiled the African soil, which benefited from an ideal cycle of winter rains followed by dry summers.[44] The emperor himself saw excellent opportunities there: Nero confiscated estates from six of the greatest landowners, and was credited by the Elder Pliny with acquiring half of the province of Africa (roughly modern Tunisia).[45] It was transformed from a prosperous region that mainly supplied its own cities, especially Carthage, into a region that supplied much wider areas of the central Mediterranean, especially Rome and Italy. Not just lands under Roman rule but the territories of the autonomous Mauretanian kings were drawn into this network, while other goods also reached Rome from Africa: figs (Cato the Elder alleged they arrived in three days), truffles and pomegranates for the tables of the richer Romans; lions and leopards for the Roman amphitheatres.[46] From the second century AD onwards, the emperors encouraged African peasants to occupy marginal lands, for Italian production was falling and was insufficient even for the Italian population, let alone the rest of the empire. Hadrian's officials in North Africa wrote: 'our Caesar, in the untiring zeal with which he constantly guards human needs has ordered all parts of land which are suitable for olives or vines, as well as for grain, to be cultivated'.[47] Irrigation and damming were practised, to capture and distribute the winter rains, and the system put in place disintegrated only in the eleventh century, following Arab raids; a mixed agricultural economy flourished, as did the pottery industry – 'African red-slip ware' exported overseas provides important evidence for patterns of trade in the later Roman Empire.[48] The intensification and commercialization of African agriculture was thus the result of Roman initiatives. The Mediterranean had become a well-integrated area of exchange as Roman power and influence spread to every corner of the sea.

From the perspective of the imperial fisc, Egyptian grain had some advantages over African. It was not directed solely towards Rome, for Egypt continued to supply large areas of the eastern Mediterranean and the Aegean. Alexandria was seen as a highly reliable source, guaranteed by the annual Nile floods, whereas the grain supplies of what are now Morocco, Algeria, Tunisia and Libya fluctuated, and had to be obtained from a large number of centres.[49] Most importantly, the grain supply of the Roman Empire did not depend on a single, fragile source in an age when famine occasionally struck fertile lands such as Sicily; there were even rare and frightening famines in Egypt.[50] With access to the supplies of the entire Mediterranean, these shortages became a minor anxiety. Rome was fed; the emperors celebrated the grain distribution on their coins. In AD 64–6, Nero alluded directly to the grain supply on some exceptionally elegant bronze coins (as one might expect from this self-proclaimed arbiter of taste). Ceres holds ears of wheat and faces another figure, Annona ('Harvest'), who holds a cornucopia; in the middle there is an altar on which a grain measure has been placed, and in the background the stern of a grain ship is visible.[51]

IV

Once the grain, oil and wine had arrived in Italy, they had somehow to be brought to Rome, whose position ten miles from the sea was compromised by the winding route of the river Tiber and the lack of good quays in Rome itself. The solution in the age of Augustus was to bring the grain first of all to the Bay of Naples, where a large, well-sheltered port existed at Puteoli, now the Neapolitan suburb of Pozzuoli. From there it was loaded on to smaller vessels that carried it up the Campanian and Latin coast to the Tiber, for there were no good harbours between Cosa in Etruria and Gaeta on the border between Latium and Campania. Accordingly, Nero (d. AD 68) planned to construct a great canal wide enough for two quinquiremes to pass one another, linking the port of Ostia to the Bay of Naples, so as to avoid cumbersome and sometimes perilous journeys along the Italian coast. When this massive project faltered, some impetus was given to the expansion of the ports at the mouth of the Tiber, most importantly Ostia, whose extensive remains bear witness to its business links with Africa, Gaul and the East: more of Ostia shortly.

Puteoli received advance news of the arrival of grain fleets:

> Today without warning the Alexandrian *tabellariae* came into view. These are the ships which they always send on ahead to give the news that the fleet is on its way. This is a very welcome sight for the Campanians; the whole population of Puteoli settles down on the quayside and tries to spot the Alexandrian ships by the type of rigging.[52]

This could be done because a special type of sail was reserved to the Alexandrian grain fleet, 'and all the ships hoist it high on their masts'. Emperor Gaius Caligula (d. AD 41) was proud of the Alexandria fleet based at Puteoli, and discouraged the Jewish prince Herod Agrippa from returning to Judaea by way of Brindisi, Greece and Syria, urging him to take ship from Puteoli – the Alexandria captains were famous for driving their ships like charioteers. Within days of his departure from Puteoli, Herod Agrippa had arrived in Egypt.[53] Puteoli became famous for its cement, made out of volcanic dust and used in concrete all over Italy. Most importantly, this cement was used in the building of jetties and moles to accommodate even the largest ships.[54] Puteoli was already a centre for trade in luxury goods such as Greek marble or Egyptian papyrus and glass when Egypt fell into Roman hands. Puteolan merchants were active at Delos, where there was a lively contingent of south Italian traders. The Delian connection brought many slaves to Italy by way of Puteoli. Like Rome itself, Puteoli was host to a very heterogeneous population, with little colonies of Phoenician merchants from Tyre, of Nabataeans from the desert lands beyond Palestine, of Egyptians who introduced the cult of Sarapis.[55] The Phoenicians had once been a great force in Puteoli, but by AD 174 they had fallen on hard times, and wrote to the city fathers in Tyre asking them to defray the large rent they had to pay for their offices and warehouses, which, they said, were grander than those of other nations:

> In former days the Tyrians living at Puteoli were responsible for its main-
> tenance; they were numerous and rich. But now we are reduced to a small
> number, and owing to the expenses that we have to meet for the sacrifices
> and the worship of our national gods, who have temples here, we have
> not the necessary resources to pay for the rent of the station, a sum of
> 100,000 *denarii* a year.[56]

A temple was also erected to Jupiter, Juno and Minerva by the merchants 'who trade in Alexandria, Asia and Syria'.[57] Fine public buildings were constructed, at the expense of the wealthiest families of the city. Puteoli was probably the unnamed Campanian city in which Petronius, a courtier of Nero, situated his scandalous novel the *Satyricon*. One of the central figures, Trimalchio, is a freed slave who has made his fortune at sea, lost it ('Neptune devoured 30,000,000 *sesterces* in a single day'), started again from scratch, and has now retired with assets of many millions of *sesterces*.[58]

Whether or not there existed freedmen as successful as the fictional Trimalchio, the evidence that freedmen played a major role in the business life of the port is clear. A remarkable series of wax tablets, discovered in Pompeii, bears witness to the financial affairs of the Sulpicii, bankers of Puteoli; 127 documents survive, mostly from between AD 35 and AD 55.[59] One of the documents is a loan of a thousand *denarii* made to Menelaus, a free-born Greek from Caria in Asia Minor, by the slave Primus, agent of the merchant Publius Attius Severus. Severus' name also appears in a completely different place: stamped on amphorae that contained fish-sauce exported from the Iberian peninsula to Rome. Menelaus owned his own cargo vessel, and the loan is thought to have been an advance payment for the carriage of a consignment of *garum* being shipped from Puteoli to Rome.[60] All this suggests how Puteoli was linked into the wider Mediterranean world – home to a Greek skipper, with links to a wealthy Roman trader in Spanish fish-sauce. The presence of a slave acting as Severus' trusted agent some way from his home base in Rome was far from unusual. Greek bankers in the heyday of Athens had been familiar with some of the banking techniques adopted at Puteoli. What is novel is the way such operations now encompassed the whole Mediterranean, from the *garum* factories of Spain to Egypt. Credit consisted not just of cash advances in hard coin or commodities: the word 'credit' (meaning 'he believes' in Latin) conveys a sense of trust. Cooperation and trust were easier and more effective in the era of Roman peace.

It was grain that really made the fortune of Puteoli; it has been estimated that 100,000 tons passed through it each year around this time.[61] Handling grain generated a myriad of tasks for slaves and paid labourers: whether grain was loaded in sacks or poured into containers, it had to be unloaded at its Italian port of arrival and reloaded on to smaller ships or barges for the journey to Rome. It was checked for quality and it was, of course, taxed. It had to be stored either in the ports or in Rome itself, and storing grain is not a straightforward operation, since it must be protected from dangerous moulds, insects and mice, meaning that it has to be aerated and kept at the right temperature.[62] The grain merchants had to rent rooms in storehouses, some of which were enormous: the Horrea Galbana in Rome offered over 140 rooms on the ground floor, and the Grandi Horrea on the coast at Ostia provided sixty ground-floor rooms.[63] Puteoli was also well placed for those in search of a market for eastern luxuries, such as the products of the India trade that passed through Alexandria, for it gave access to the summer retreats of the senatorial aristocracy at Baiae, Herculaneum and Stabiae; it stood close to Naples, still a thriving city, and the satellite towns of Naples such as Pompeii.

Ostia, at the mouth of the Tiber, gradually took the lead, replacing Puteoli as the principal port of call for the ships carrying goods intended for Rome. Its origins can be traced back to the fifth century BC when Rome and Veii competed for control of the saltpans at the Tiber mouth, but for long Ostia consisted of little more than a roadstead in an estuary. There were building programmes under Augustus and Tiberius, but only under Claudius was a real effort made to provide harbour facilities close to Rome, and in AD 42 a new harbour two miles north of the Tiber began to be constructed, known by the simple name Portus. The aim was not to undercut Puteoli, so much as to provide safe access for

Rome's grain. Unfortunately, Claudius' breakwaters and moles proved inadequate: in AD 62, 200 ships within the harbour were wrecked by a sudden tempest. Within a century, the Emperor Trajan enhanced Ostia's Portus by building a more secure and spectacular hexagonal harbour inside Claudius' harbour. Under his successor Hadrian large areas containing warehouses and shops were rebuilt. Ostia was full of solid brick-built apartment blocks on several floors – it had a somewhat middle-class atmosphere right through to the fourth century, and many of the poorer migrants who set foot on its quayside headed for the tenements of Rome instead.[64]

V

After Octavian won power, all the shores of the Mediterranean and all its islands were under Roman rule or within the Roman sphere of influence: it was indeed *mare nostrum*.[65] His victory ushered in a remarkable period of over 200 years of peace across the Mediterranean. Of course, there were occasional outbursts of piracy, for example by the Mauretanians in the far west of North Africa, an area where Roman control was relatively weak: in AD 171–2 Moorish pirates raided Spain and Africa, and the emperor, Marcus Aurelius, enlarged the Roman fleet to deal with this menace. But when Roman navies engaged in warfare, they generally did so away from the Mediterranean, for there were also large fleets as far away as Britain and along the Rhine and Danube, where they kept Germanic raiders at bay. Even instability at the very heart of the empire did not fundamentally destroy the peace of the Mediterranean. During the tumultuous 'Year of the Four Emperors' in AD 68–9, following the suicide of Nero, Emperor Otho recruited thousands of sailors to block the threat posed by his rival, and eventual supplanter, Vitellius. Otho could count on the support of the two Italian navies, based at Ravenna and at Misenum, very close to Puteoli. The final victor in 69, Vespasian, also used naval power, but differently: from his base in Egypt he first blocked the grain traffic to Rome, and then, as he approached Rome, he showed generosity by releasing these food supplies to the Roman People, fatally undermining Vitellius.[66] Later, navies served the emperors when armies had to be transported to (say) Africa, to quell regional revolts. Trajan sent fleets to Cyrenaica, Egypt and Syria to suppress a widespread

Jewish rebellion in 115–16.[67] Sailors were sometimes expected to fight on land once they reached their destination, but great naval battles similar to those of the Punic Wars were the stuff of literature, not something sailors could expect to experience.

It is not surprising that the Roman navy has received far less attention than Greek navies or that relentless, ruthless arm of the state, the Roman army. The assumption is that the navy did not do very much in the era of *pax romana*. Service in the navy was not rated as highly as army service. In the second century a legionary soldier transferred of his own volition to the navy; he was punished for unacceptable behaviour.[68] Yet there were many for whom service in the navy was a matter of pride. An Egyptian papyrus of the early second century AD records how a certain Sempronius was grieved to hear that his son Gaius had been persuaded not to join the fleet, as he had originally planned: 'see to it that you are not so persuaded, or else you will no longer be my son ... You will do well to enter a fine service.'[69] But recruitment to the fleet had important social consequences. Sailors in the Mediterranean hailed from right across the Roman world, including men from inland regions such as Pannonia (along the Danube); there were very many Greeks, not surprisingly, and also a large number of Egyptians, not just Greeks settled in Egypt but people of native Egyptian descent. These people brought their gods with them, and Sarapis was widely venerated by sailors in the Roman navy, whether or not the sailors were of Egyptian origin: 'Sarapis is great on the sea, and both merchantmen and warcraft are guided by him.'[70] The mixture of gods was entirely typical of the Roman world. But there were also pressures in the other direction. Entering a service where Latin was the language of command, recruits sought to Latinize and Romanize themselves, taking Latin names:

> Apion to Epimachos his father and lord, many greetings. Before all I pray that you are in good health and, prospering continually, fare well along with my sister and her daughter and my brother. I give thanks to the Lord Sarapis that he saved me at once when I was in danger on the sea ... I send you a little picture of myself by Eukremon. My name is now Antonius Maximus.[71]

A few years later he had married and had three children, two with Latin and one with a Greek name; 'Antonius Maximus' was now less interested in Sarapis, for he prayed for the welfare of his sister before 'the gods here'.[72]

The Roman navy had less prestige because it was less of a fighting force and more of a police force. Its existence ensured the safety of the civilian sea routes, even though convoys were not sent out to accompany merchant shipping – partly because merchant shipping was privately managed, and partly because there was rarely much need. The sheer presence of the fleet at Misenum near Naples, at Ravenna and at a number of coastal stations such as Forum Julii (Fréjus) in Provence was sufficient to ensure security. Carthage, rebuilt in 29 BC as a centre of trade and administration formally known as the *Colonia Iulia Concordia Carthago*, was not used by the fleet even though it became the principal Roman city in North Africa (setting aside Alexandria).[73] There was, however, a Roman naval presence at Caesarea (Cherchel) some way to the west, because beyond it lay the occasionally troublesome region of Mauretania.[74] This is what the *pax romana* meant for the Mediterranean: it was not an active process of suppressing foes to impose the peace of victors – 'they make a devastation and call it peace', as Tacitus ironically remarked of Roman armies in the north of Europe – so much as a benign presence. There was sufficient awareness, at least until the mid-third century, of the need to keep the fleet in good repair. The ships themselves were the traditional quadriremes and quinquiremes of the late classical world; there is no evidence of significant innovations in ship design until the Byzantine period, so navies faced the traditional problems of vessels with low gunwales, generally barely four metres above the water: an inability to expose themselves to choppy seas or to sail in winter.[75] The fleet was also available to convey officials around the empire, but (unlike medieval ships) these galleys did not double as trading vessels, partly because of their design and partly because the emperor did not wish to be a mere trader.

The idea of establishing Misenum and Ravenna as the prime command centres can be traced back to Augustus.[76] Misenum was the control hub for operations in the western Mediterranean, but its brief also extended much further to the east. Since the grain shipments from Egypt arrived at Puteoli, next door, Misenum kept an eye on movements along this sea route. An inland lake behind Misenum was dredged and connected to the coast, so that the fleet possessed a safe inner harbour; around the port were arrayed the villas of wealthy Romans; Tiberius spent some of his last days here.[77] From Ravenna, on the other hand, fleets were despatched to keep an eye on the Dalmatian coast, always a hideaway of pirates and brigands, and the Aegean also fell within its purview. Ravenna was surrounded by lagoons (the modern shoreline is several miles from the ancient one), and was not the ideal location for a harbour, so its port was constructed two miles away at a place called Classis, that is 'Fleet'; a canal linked Classis to Ravenna. This harbour is portrayed in the Ravenna mosaics of the sixth century, for it long retained its importance; all that remains of the glory of Classis is the mosaic-encrusted church of Sant'Apollinare in Classe, also of the sixth century.[78] The ability of the Romans to keep a watchful eye on the Mediterranean, principally from command posts in the Tyrrhenian Sea and the northern Adriatic, is very impressive.

A trader of the second century might well have wondered what could possibly shatter the unity of the Mediterranean. It was a political unity, under Rome; it was an economic unity, allowing traders to criss-cross the Mediterranean without interference; it was a cultural unity, dominated by Hellenistic culture, whether expressed in Greek or in Latin; it was even in many respects a religious unity, or unity in diversity, as the peoples of the Mediterranean shared their gods with one another, unless they were Jews or Christians. Single rule over *mare nostrum* ensured freedom of movement and resulted in cultural mixing in the Mediterranean on a scale never seen before or since.

9
Old and New Faiths, AD 1–450

I

As in any port city of the Roman world, the population of Ostia was very mixed. An extraordinary discovery was made on the outskirts of Ostia in 1961, while a road was being constructed linking Rome to its new door to the world, Fiumicino airport: the synagogue of Ostia, the oldest synagogue structure to have survived in Europe. The earliest part dates from the first century AD, but the building was repaired or partly rebuilt in the fourth century. It was in continuous use for Jewish prayer for at least 300 years. An inscription from the second century commemorates the building of the Ark for the scrolls of the Law, at the expense of a certain Mindis Faustos; the inscription is mainly in Greek, with a few Latin words, for the Jews of Rome, with their connections to the East, continued to use Greek as their daily language. The building and its annexes have an area of 856 square metres, and everything suggests that this was the major synagogue of a prosperous community of hundreds of Jews. More than a synagogue, by the fourth century the complex contained an oven, possibly for the baking of unleavened bread for Passover, and a ritual bath. There were side rooms that were probably used for teaching and for meetings of the Jewish council and of the rabbinical court. A carved architrave portrayed the great candlestick that had stood in the Temple, the ram's horn blown at New Year, and the symbols of the Feast of Tabernacles, the citron and decorated palm branch.[1] Nor was Judaism the only eastern cult with many followers in Ostia. A small brick-built temple elsewhere in the city has been identified as a shrine of Sarapis. Within the precinct there was a courtyard paved with a black-and-white mosaic of Nile scenes. Plenty of inscriptions refer to the cult of Isis; there were several shrines to Mithras, much favoured in the Roman army; during their wild ecstasies, male devotees of the mother-goddess Cybele, who was also worshipped at Ostia, were said to castrate themselves.[2]

Carried along the trade routes, ancient systems of belief transplanted themselves into Italy and other lands from Judaea or the Nile, and were modified by their own contact with the Hellenistic culture of the eastern Mediterranean. Sometimes individuals travelled across the Mediterranean bearing with them a new rather than an old faith. Paul of Tarsus has been encountered on his way to Rome, and in the same city a line of succession developed that traced itself back to another traveller from the East, his fellow-believer Simon Peter. On his travels in Syria, Asia Minor, Greece and Italy, Paul preached that a man acclaimed by his followers as the Jewish Messiah was actually God Incarnate. The slowly maturing seeds of a great religious revolution in the Mediterranean had been sown.

II

The two obvious transformations of the Mediterranean in the late Roman period were the Germanic invasions and the adoption of Christianity as the official religion of the Roman emperors. Christianization took place slowly in the teeth of vigorous opposition from pagans and Jews. Eastern cults spread easily across the surface of the Mediterranean, but neither Judaism nor Christianity could be compared to the pagan cults, as the Romans were aware. Jews and Christians were seen as 'atheists', in the sense that they straightforwardly denied the very existence of the pagan gods. They refused to sacrifice to the deified emperor. Yet the Romans, as they gained power in the eastern Mediterranean, were careful to make an exception of the Jews; the Jews were willing to sacrifice to their God in honour of the emperor, and were understood to have an eccentric way, therefore, of guaranteeing their loyalty. All other subjects were expected to make the required sacrifice to the deified emperor, and the refusal of Christians to do so placed them outside the law and exposed them to the risk of violent death in the amphitheatre. By vigorously preaching the word of Christ beyond the Jewish community, St Paul and his successors had created a growing

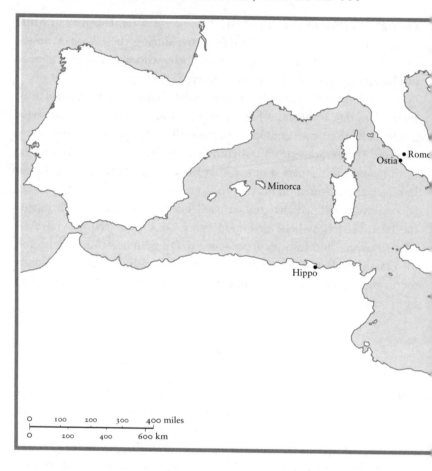

community of Christians whom the Romans could no longer classify as a branch of the Jewish people. Nor did they follow Jewish observances: circumcision was to be of the heart, not of the body; avoidance of pork was understood to mean avoidance of pig-like behaviour. The very fact of persecution strengthened the Christians in their resolve: they revered as martyrs those who were executed by the Romans and, discarding the Jewish concept that the bones of the dead were unclean, they developed a cult of the martyrs' remains. In the view of some enthusiasts, even their suffering was an illusion, for Christ would anaesthetize them against the claws of the lions, though others rejoiced in pain and suffering, as proof that they had won the mercy of Christ and the reward of eternal life.[3]

Although the Jews were generally guaranteed the right to practise

their religion, Roman policy was not consistent. As punishment for a fraud perpetrated in Rome, by four crooks who claimed to be collecting money for the Temple, Emperor Tiberius had already shunted 4,000 Roman Jews to Sardinia, a traditional land of exile. One of those they defrauded was the wife of a Senator, who (not unusually) was sympathetic to Judaism. Claudius agreed to restore to the Jews in Alexandria civil rights they had lost under the mad emperor Gaius Caligula, but there is no evidence that the Jewish communities of the diaspora were united in opposition to the powers-that-be; when there was trouble on the streets of Alexandria it was the result of a long-established dislike between Jews and Greeks, not of government policy, which the Greeks thought too favourable to the Jews. However, pressure on the Jews in Palestine resulted in both the forced and voluntary diffusion of the Jews across the Mediterranean. From the perspective of Mediterranean history the significance of the destruction of the Temple by Titus in AD 70, and of Jerusalem itself by Hadrian in AD 131, lies in the single word 'diaspora'. It is unlikely, as the Jewish historian Josephus pointed out, that the Romans intended to destroy the Jewish Temple when they quashed the Jewish revolt in 70; but, once it had been burned and pillaged, the new emperor Vespasian and his son Titus saw the political advantage of a great triumph in which they could parade the Temple treasures, and Titus commemorated this procession in the famous reliefs inside the arch of Titus which still stands at the southern end of the Roman Forum.[4] Large numbers of Jewish slaves were deported to Italy and beyond.

What was unusual was that Rome did not allow the Jewish sacrificial cult to resume in Jerusalem. It was not as if the capture of the Temple could have resulted in the complete destruction of the vast sanctuary and its colonnaded courts (large parts of the perimeter walls survive to this day). With extensive repairs, restoration of the cult could have begun. The kindly old emperor Nerva (d. 98) was happy to relieve the Jews of a special tax imposed after the Jewish War and it seemed that restoration of the cult was not far off.[5] But his soldier successor Trajan adopted a tough policy, and at the end of his reign he ruthlessly suppressed Jewish rebellions in Syria, Egypt and Cyrenaica (115–16): as Jews dispersed across the Mediterranean, tensions previously largely confined to Palestine and Alexandria became more widespread. Indeed, Palestine was relatively quiet during these revolts. His successor Hadrian had an uncompromising solution: he rebuilt Jerusalem as a city dedicated to Jupiter Capitolinus, under the name Aelia Capitolina; he banned circumcised males from entering the city. He set his mind against the Jews and the God of Israel in a manner completely at odds with traditional Roman respect for other religions. The revolt that followed in Palestine in 132–6 was fierce but hopeless; short-term successes, including the recovery of Jerusalem and possibly even the restoration of the sacrificial cult, culminated in massive defeat and in horrific massacres by Hadrian's armies, and as many as 600,000 Jews may have lost their lives.[6] Once again these events had a wider Mediterranean impact: very many Jews were dispersed westwards, as slaves or fugitives; Jews were certainly living in Spain a century later.[7] The effects of defeat in Jerusalem were not simply political and demographic. Judaism was already changing its character in the late Temple period, as sects such as the Pharisees challenged the authority of the old Temple priesthood. The loss of the Temple gave further impetus to these changes, led by the rabbis, learned laymen rather than Temple priests; and the synagogue, not in itself a novelty, became the focus of Jewish study and prayer.

Persecution of the Christians had also come in waves. In the first century, Nero had blamed Christians for the great fire that gave him the opportunity to rebuild parts of Rome in gilded magnificence. In the middle of the third century the emperors renewed the persecution of Christians across the empire. The emperor Decius was commemorated in the Tuscan port of Cosa as *restitutor sacrorum*, 'restorer of the holy things', a reference, apparently, to his enthusiastic hunt for Christians. One way to avoid persecution was to make outward compromises, worshipping in public but maintaining the faith behind closed doors. Disagreement about the validity of this policy, and, even more seriously, about the validity of the priestly orders of those who 'handed over' (*donaverunt*) the scriptures to the Roman authorities, generated bitter recriminations and schism: the Donatist Church, active in Africa in the fourth century, saw itself as the standard bearer of true belief in the face of the appeasers. Another way out of the dilemma presented by the Roman authorities was for Christians to pose as Jews: 'synagogue on Saturday, church on Sunday', a position condemned in vigorous anti-Jewish sermons at Antioch in the 390s.[8] By then, of course, the Christians had the upper hand, but throughout the Mediterranean the boundaries between Christianity and Judaism were less clear to observers (including even many Jews and Christians) than the angry prophets of Christian orthodoxy such as St Cyprian would have us believe. The vituperation expressed towards Judaism derived from a sense of bitter competition, not a wish to kick those who were already down. No quarter was given by either side. And yet the wider public was not much interested in the finer points of doctrine, and was probably attracted by ethical codes and religious aspirations that were not vastly different – love for one's neighbour, the hope that God would offer rewards in the next world if not in this one. Many Jews were probably quite liberal in their approach to the rules of the religion, which were still being finely honed in the academies of Babylonia, and this rendered movement back and forth between religions and sects much easier.

An account of the life and trial of the Christian martyr Pionius, who died at Smyrna in the Decian persecutions, constantly alludes to the 'Greeks, Jews and women' who formed a hostile crowd in the public squares of Smyrna when he was arrested; Pionius refused to take part in the pagan cult at a time when both Jews and pagans were celebrating their festivals (possibly the Jewish festival of Purim and the pagan Dionysia – both times when drunkenness was more than tolerated). On such occasions the celebrations of Jews and Gentiles merged impercept-ibly, despite any number of rabbinic injunctions.[9] In Smyrna and elsewhere there existed large and respected Jewish communities that attracted many converts, as well as the 'God-fearers' who attended Jew-ish rites without converting, so that the Jewish population was ethnically quite mixed.[10]

As galling to many Christians as the success of the Jews was the pres-ence of heretic Christians. Of course, one man's heretic was another man's orthodox Christian. Yet there were certainly some very radical movements. On his cross the dying Pionius found himself side by side with an adherent of the Marcionite creed, a movement of Christian ori-gin that regarded the God of the Jews as Satan, and rejected the Hebrew Bible.[11] For all their disagreement with the Jews, mainstream Christians accepted the Hebrew Bible and did not seek to emend its text; finding in it prophecies of the coming of Christ, they valued it highly but read it quite differently from the Jews. For St Augustine (d. 430), the Jews were the bearers of the holy books, occupying the place of servants ordered to look after their masters' property, though this did not mean that they understood what they preserved.[12]

Jews and Christians also came into contact on the surface of the Mediterranean Sea. There were Jewish shipowners. Ports frequented by Jews included Gaza. The rabbis debated whether the Jews of Gaza could take part in the local fair held in honour of a Greek god, a debate which once again reveals the often fuzzy boundaries between Jewish and pagan communities in the late Hellenistic and Roman world.[13] Yet some maritime Jews were very meticulous in their observance. In 404 a bishop from Asia Minor sailed to his see from Alexandria, where the Jews had their own guild of *navicularii* and owned and operated a good many ships. The captain of this ship was Amarantus, and he and his crew were Jews, whom the bishop lampooned; he feared for his life when the cap-tain let the ship drift after nightfall on Friday. It was the Sabbath eve and he was permitted (he said) to navigate the ship only when the passengers were in danger of their life. In that case, virtually all Jewish laws could be abrogated. Everything that is reported about the ship makes one wonder how it ever arrived: the rigging was broken, so its sails could not be unfurled; the captain had sold the spare anchor. In the same period, the discussions of the rabbis recorded in the Talmud reveal that Jews had become quite used to crossing the Great Sea. As well as examining issues in commercial law, they debated whether it is licit for Jews to travel across the sea on the Sabbath and what actions are permissible on the day of rest (such as the drawing of water, or even taking a stroll on the ship's deck).[14]

III

The conversion of Constantine to Christianity is traditionally supposed to have followed his victory over his rival Maxentius at the battle of the Milvian Bridge just outside Rome in October 312; it took him another thirteen years to establish himself as sole master of the Roman Empire. In fact he was baptized only on his deathbed in 337, but the Edict of Milan in 313 lifted the ban on Christian worship, and the New Rome he established at Constantinople was to be a Christian city, uncontaminated by pagan temples. He presided over a contentious Church Council at Nicaea in 325, which attempted to resolve difficult theological questions over the nature of the Trinity, mediated by the emperor (no theologian); the result was further schism in an already divided Church, even though the Nicaean Creed thereafter became the basis for Orthodox Christianity. He saw himself as 'bishop of those outside the Church'; but he was also the *pontifex maximus*, the chief priest of the empire. Whether through an awareness that religious change must be gradual, or through his own confusion of pagan and Christian ideas, Constantine paid attention to pagan as well as Christian practices, even – oddly – in the ceremonies of dedication of the New Rome, where the cross of Christ was placed above the chariot of the sun-god. In the Old Rome, his heavily decorated triumphal arch, which still stands, made no reference to his new faith, to which, in any case, the Senators were averse. But he also laid the foundations for the great Christian basilica dedicated to St Peter, ruthlessly cutting across a pagan cemetery that now lies underneath the Renaissance blunderbuss of St Peter's. To pursue the contradictions further: his coins carried the inscription SOL INVICTVS, 'the unconquered sun'. He banned under penalty of death the private use of the *haruspices*, Etruscan soothsayers who read the entrails of sacrificial beasts, while also requesting that *harsupices* should be consulted if lightning struck an imperial palace in Rome. There were attempts to bring together pagans and Christians: the army was commanded to use a prayer addressed to the god who had brought the emperor and his god-fearing sons victory, without specifying who that god might be. There were practical reasons for moving slowly; the worship of the emperor was well developed, and a ruler who had spent nearly twenty years engaged in a struggle for power could not release his pagan followers from a cult that vividly expressed their loyalty to the deified emperor.[15]

That the spread of Christianity across the Mediterranean was enormously eased by Constantine's policies goes without saying. There were, however, some constraints. One problem faced by the imperial 'establishment' was the emergence of non-Orthodox factions that rejected the Nicaean compromise dictated by Constantine: Monophysites in Syria and Egypt (notably the Coptic Church); Arians among the barbarian peoples of the European landmass – alternative Churches that, in the view of the Orthodox, denied the equal status of the Father and the Son in the Trinity. And then there were countless small groups such as the Marcionites and the Donatists, whose quarrel with their Christian neighbours was rooted in events that had taken place before Constantine's legalization of Christianity. All these movements were also represented in the Mediterranean and moved around it, sometimes in the baggage of barbarian mercenaries and invaders, sometimes with pilgrims and with fugitives from persecution, as one Church squeezed another in Carthage or Antioch or Alexandria.

Another problem was the persistence of pagan beliefs. Only one of Constantine's successors, the colourful Julian, abandoned Christianity. Julian studied Neo-Platonic philosophy in Athens and by the time he became emperor in 360 he had turned his back on Christianity. His aversion to it made him look favourably on Jewish requests to resume sacrifices in Jerusalem, and to demand that pagan temples be reopened.[16] He aimed to establish a pagan 'church' with its own high priest; this was a back-handed compliment to the Christian bishops, who had shown how to organize their own cult throughout the empire.[17] Julian's reign was brief, and it was dominated by wars with the Persians in the East;

but paganism did not lie down and die. It was only in the sixth century, with the suppression of the ancient schools and academies at Athens by Justinian I, that the study of philosophical texts from a pagan perspective came to an end. 'Paganism' is best understood not as a set of beliefs but as local cults of great variety, syncretistic, fluid, lacking any creed or divinely revealed texts.[18] These paganisms, in the plural, were hard for Christianity to defeat, despite the appeal of the ethical code Christianity offered, its emphasis on charitable work, and its willingness to include 'Jew and Greek, slave and free'. Locally, Christian cults accommodated pagan elements, as local gods were turned into Christian saints (the eastern warrior saints have more than a tinge of Herakles). The line between pagan and Christian was not a sharp one, and pagan cults remained a powerful force among local communities along the shores of the Mediterranean: they were well ensconced in North Africa and Spain at the time of the Islamic invasions, around 700.

A robust way of dealing with non-Christians was to destroy their temples and synagogues. Around 400, Gaza was a lively port and intellectual centre that benefited from its position on the trade route linking the Mediterranean through Beersheba and Petra to the Nabataean towns of the Arabian desert.[19] Imperial orders to close its temples were ignored here as elsewhere; local interests could override orders sent from Constantinople, and the great majority of Gazans remained pagan.[20] Its painfully ascetic bishop, Porphyry, suffered the humiliation of having to operate from a single church, while the pagans worshipped in any number of grand temples, dedicated to the Sun, Aphrodite, Athena and a god known as Marnas, a manifestation of Zeus whose temple, the Marneion, was particularly magnificent: a circular, domed structure surrounded by two sets of colonnades. When Porphyry complained about this state of affairs to the patriarch of Constantinople, the formidable John Chrysostom, an order was issued closing the temples, but the emperor's emissary happily accepted a bribe and permitted the Marneion to remain open. Porphyry felt obliged to petition the emperor directly; he travelled to Constantinople, where Empress Eudoxia took an interest, and troops were despatched to Gaza in 402. They spent ten vigorous days burning and demolishing the lesser temples and seizing their treasures. Then they turned their attention to the Marneion, where the pagans tried to defend the building, barricading its great doors. The imperial soldiers greased the doors with lard and pitch, and set them alight. The soldiers sacked the temple, before purging the city of all the idols they could find. Empress Eudoxia sent funds to build a church on the site of the ruined Marneion, and to the fury of the pagans marble slabs recovered from the Marneion were re-used as paving slabs, so pagans would have to walk on the remains of their sanctuary. Eudoxia provided thirty-two green marble columns from Euboia, and the church was consecrated at Easter 407. Meanwhile, many pagans converted, according to Porphyry's hagiographer.[21] The pagans also resorted to violence: on one occasion Porphyry was forced to flee across the flat rooftops of Gaza (he may have been an ascetic, but he lacked the inclination for martyrdom).[22] Christianity was only one of the cults in Gaza, a city that also teemed with pagans, Jews and Samaritans, and Christians were neither the most numerous nor the most powerful. The advantage they possessed was official sanction; the advantage pagans and Jews possessed was the sheer size of the empire. What happened in Gaza or the Balearic islands was generally well out of sight of Constantinople.

IV

The third constraint on Christian expansion was the continuing self-assertiveness of Judaism. There is a tendency to assume that Judaism was a spent force after the destruction of Jerusalem by Titus and Hadrian, and the choice of Christianity by Constantine. Yet its antiquity continued to impress. Its ethical code was not greatly different from that of Christianity: 'do not do to others what you would not have done to yourself; that is the whole Law and the rest is but a commentary', as Jesus' contemporary Rabbi Hillel observed. Converts were welcomed (including slaves, who were often made to convert), without a great fuss being made over how knowledgeable or observant the convert was.[23] It is thus no surprise to find that battles for supremacy between Judaism and Christianity continued to take place in the Mediterranean world as late as the fifth century. The Christian emperors attempted to prevent the circumcision of slaves, and to ban Jews from office-holding. Representing Judaism as a spent force, imperial legislation of the start of the fifth century denied the right of Jews to build new synagogues, though they could keep what they had.[24] Judaism would literally crumble away.

The nature of the battle for souls in the far corners of the Mediterranean is illustrated by a remarkable letter written by a friend of St Augustine of Hippo, Severus, bishop of Minorca, in which he describes the mass conversion of 540 Minorcan Jews in AD 418.[25] Severus insists that the Jews were the most powerful group in Minorcan society, not that Minorca was a place of much consequence: 'the most forsaken of all lands, due to its tiny size, dryness and harshness'. The Jews were based in the east of the island, at Magona, the modern Maó or Mahón, while the Christians were concentrated in the west at Jamona, now Ciutadella; Severus asserts that Jews were physically unable to live in Jamona – if they tried, they were struck down by disease or even by a thunderbolt. Be that as it may, the most prominent figures on the island were Jews, notably Theodorus, 'who was pre-eminent in both wealth and worldly honour not only among the Jews but also among the Christians' of Magona.[26] Theodorus' younger brother Meletius was married to Artemisia, the daughter of Count Litorius, a very prominent military commander who would become second-in-command to the greatest Roman general of the fifth century, Flavius Aetius, and would lead armies of Hunnish mercenaries to victory in Gaul.[27] That does not mean Litorius was a Jew, especially since current imperial legislation did not countenance the granting of such high office to Jews; whatever religion he observed, his daughter adhered to Jewish rites. Severus deliberately lays emphasis on the tension between Jews and Christians on the island, and yet it is abundantly clear that relations between the communities were peaceful enough until 400. Severus talks of 'our old habit of easy acquaintance', and of 'our longstanding affection', though he insists that this behaviour was in fact sinful.[28] Laws framed in Constantinople did not displace Theodorus and his Jewish family from leadership.

This was a time of deep uncertainty in the western Mediterranean. Alaric the Goth had sacked Rome in 410, and after that Visigothic armies had invaded Spain, and other barbarian peoples – Vandals, Suevi, Alans – were also on the march in the western Roman Empire. None of these groups was yet a naval power, but even in Minorca the sense of threat was powerful. The arrival of the newly discovered relics of St Stephen on Minorca in 416 triggered an outburst of enthusiasm among the Christians of Magona, who acted as host to the bones.[29] St Stephen was the 'first martyr' of the Christians, regarded as 'the first to wage the Lord's wars against the Jews'; he was engaged on a tour of the Mediterranean, from Jerusalem, where his bones had recently been found, to Spain and North Africa. Minorca was the one halt where he effected a revolution.[30] Their discovery was exploited by the Christians of Jerusalem to increase pressure on the local Jews; just before the bones were found Gamaliel, patriarch of the Jews of Jerusalem, had been stripped of his traditional precedence as the equal of an imperial prefect, and ordered not to allow further circumcision of converts nor the building of new synagogues. In 414 the patriarch of Alexandria is said to have expelled the Jews from his city, and across the eastern Mediterranean there were forced conversions and seizures of synagogues.[31] With the arrival of the relics of St Stephen in Minorca, the Christian population gained in confidence. Christians (including Severus) and Theodorus the Jew had dreams that the bishop knew must foretell the conversion of the Jews. There was an apocalyptic atmosphere: surely the conversion of the Jews would herald the Second Coming of Christ? Severus wrote:

> Perhaps that time predicted by the Apostle has indeed come when the fullness of the Gentiles will have come and all Israel shall be saved. And perhaps the Lord wished to kindle this spark from the ends of the earth, so that the whole breadth of the earth might be ablaze with the flame of love in order to burn down the forest of unbelief.[32]

The methods the Christians employed were not subtle. The Jews were accused of hoarding weapons for use against them. On 2 February 417, the Christians gathered in Jamona and marched across the length of the island, thirty miles, but we are assured it was a painless journey, because they had in mind their glorious purpose. Severus requested admission to the synagogue to look for weapons, and he was reluctantly admitted, but before an inspection could take place violence broke out. The Christians invaded and set fire to the synagogue, while taking care to seize its precious items – its silver (which they later returned) and the Torah scrolls (which they decided to keep). The weapons proved imaginary. Severus admits that the riot against the Jews was begun by a thieving Christian, 'drawn not by love of Christ, but by love of plunder'. The next day the first Jew, named Reuben, converted; the rest of the Jews deliberated for three days, and Theodorus tried to debate the truth of the two faiths with the Christians, but finally he was worn down by arguments that seem as much practical as theological, for Reuben urged him: 'if you truly wish to be safe and honoured and wealthy, believe in

Christ'. Theodorus was willing to convert only if the great majority of his people followed him to the font, as indeed happened.[33] Some delayed longer: Theodorus' sister-in-law Artemisia fled to a cave, intending to hold fast to her beliefs after her husband converted, but when the water her servant drew for her tasted of honey she realized that a miracle had happened, and she too conformed.[34]

Since Severus is the only source of information for these events, it is difficult to penetrate below the surface of what he says. Some points are striking: the political importance of the Jews, and the prominent role of Jewish women. A hint that even the long march from Jamona to Magona may not have begun with aggressive intentions comes from the remark that the Jews joined in 'with a wondrous sweetness' when they heard the Christians singing Psalm 9.[35] It is impossible to escape the conclusion that Jews and Christians had not just been on good terms until St Stephen arrived, but that the boundaries between Judaism and Christianity had been very permeable, which was exactly what bishops disliked. Violence prompted the Jews of Minorca to convert; but mutual familiarity lessened the shock of conversion.[36] Monotheism after the model of Nicaea was beginning to triumph in the Mediterranean, but its exclusive character left not just pagans but monotheists of a different persuasion in an embattled position.

IO

Dis-integration, 400–600

I

Ever since Edward Gibbon wrote his *Decline and Fall of the Roman Empire* the question why, when and indeed whether this great Roman Empire fell has been vigorously pursued by historians. It has been observed that at least 210 explanations have been offered, some frankly ridiculous ('Semitization', homosexuality, decline in manliness).[1] The argument that it was the barbarian invasions that destroyed Rome – both the city and its empire – lost favour and has returned to favour.[2] Some historians have insisted that the whole concept of the 'fall of Rome' is a misconception, and have emphasized the continuity of the Roman inheritance.[3] Yet from a Mediterranean perspective, it is abundantly clear that the unity of the Great Sea had been shattered by 800. That leaves several centuries in which to place the process of disintegration, and several suspects: the Germanic barbarians in the fifth century and after, the Arab conquerors in the seventh century, Charlemagne and his Frankish armies in the eighth century, not to mention internal strife as Roman generals competed for power, either seeking regional dominions or the crown of the empire itself. Evidently there was no single 'cause' for the decline of Rome, and it was precisely the accumulation of dozens of problems that brought the old order to an end, rupturing the 'Second Mediterranean'.

During the long period from 400 to 800, the Mediterranean split apart economically and also politically: the Roman emperors saw that the task of governing the Mediterranean lands and vast tracts of Europe west of the Rhine and south of the Danube exceeded the capacity of one man. Diocletian, ruling from 284 onwards, based himself in the east at

Nikomedeia, and entrusted the government of the empire to a team of co-emperors, first another 'Augustus' in the west, and then, from 293 to 305, two deputies or 'Caesars' as well, a system known as the Tetrarchy.[4] His residence in Nikomedeia was itself a prelude to the decision by Constantine to establish a 'New Rome' in 330; after looking at the site of Troy, the city from which the Roman people claimed its origins, he chose instead the emporium of Byzantion, with its fine harbour and its strategic position on the trade route linking the Black Sea to the Mediterranean. The other startling change that took place was, of course, Constantine's official recognition of Christianity, after centuries during which it had existed as an underground religion.

Italy remained the base for western emperors until 476, when the last, aptly named Romulus, 'the little emperor' (Augustulus), was deposed by the Germanic warlord Odoacer. But the centre of power had shifted eastward; and this was only to recognize the economic realities of the Mediterranean: it was in the east that the trading world of the Hellenistic and Ptolemaic eras still flourished, with busy ports such as Alexandria, Gaza and Ephesos, united by trade links and by their common Greek culture. Although it would be simplistic to contrast a predominantly urban East with a predominantly rural West, for the eastern lands were still mainly populated by farmers and pastoralists, the concentration of towns along the shores of the eastern Mediterranean and the variety of agricultural pursuits in the East created a more complex economy. The rich textiles of late Roman Egypt can still be appreciated in museums; and luxury goods circulated in greater volume east of Sicily. The pattern of distribution of more basic goods also changed. One consequence of the foundation of Constantinople was that the grain of Egypt was now diverted from the Old Rome to the New.[5] In 330 this appeared to be a harmless enough change. Africa in any case supplied two-thirds of Rome's grain. It was a prosperous area, and Carthage was now the largest city in the Mediterranean after Rome and Alexandria. If, as is possible, the population of the empire was declining in the late third and fourth centuries, as a result of disease, the continuing strength of the North African provinces ensured that the western capital would still be fed. Roman and Carthaginian senators and equestrians enlarged their African estates.[6] Hereditary guilds of shippers, or *navicularii*, were placed under imperial protection; members were entitled to tax reductions and were granted equestrian status. Although the imperial fisc did not intervene directly in

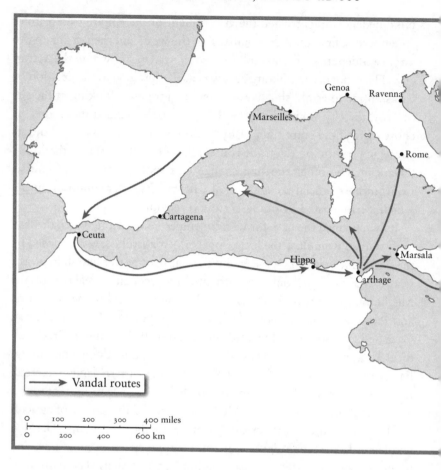

the management of shipping, its patronage of the *navicularii* ensured that the traffic in grain remained lively. African farmers also valued olives and vines as sources of income; the region flourished as an exporter of oil and wine towards Italy and elsewhere. 'African red-slip ware' became the staple pottery not just of the Mediterranean but of areas deep inland in Gaul and as far away as Britain. Among goods that arrived in return were Italian bricks. It was not that the Africans were ignorant of brick-making; but bricks provided excellent ballast in grain ships as they returned to Africa empty of their wheat.[7] It was a boom time in Africa, and especially for Carthage. The city was well laid out with a criss-cross pattern of streets, and it contained handsome buildings – the Carthaginians were especially fond of their amphitheatre and it was difficult to lure them from the games even when barbarian attackers threatened. Its

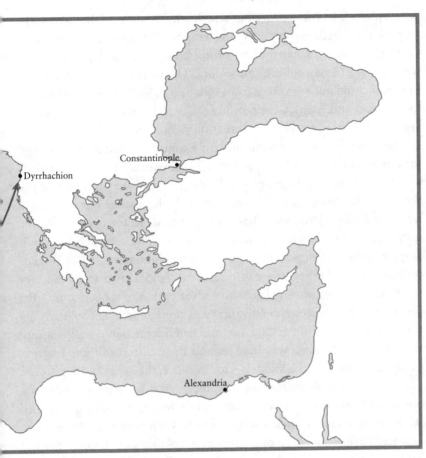

glory was the port, for the circular port of old Carthage was restored and a handsome hexagonal outer harbour was also built under Trajan. It was a twin of the hexagonal port he built at Portus near Ostia and the outline of the 'Punic Ports' can still be traced.[8]

Africa was also a peaceful place. From the third century onwards the outer frontiers of the empire had been under assault by barbarians; in far-off Britain the 'counts of the Saxon shore' organized the defence against Germanic raiders from across the North Sea. Even when hordes of Goths, Suevi and other Germanic peoples marched through Gaul, Italy and Spain in the years around 400, and even after Rome itself was sacked in 410, Africa seemed to be safe.[9] One African intellectual, Augustine, who became bishop of Hippo and died in 430, was, admittedly, so shocked by the sack of Rome that he was inspired to write his masterpiece, *The City of God*, in which a heavenly 'city' was shown to surpass the fragile earthly city and empire of Rome. Yet Hippo and Carthage, at least, seemed to be protected by the sea. The barbarians were known to be soldiers, not sailors. The Goths were bottled up in Italy and could not even cross from Calabria to Sicily. Other barbarians, the Vandals and Alans, were heading westwards, into the mountains of Spain. It was hard to see what threat they could pose.

The Vandals were Germanic and for a time inhabited areas that now form part of southern Poland; they were adherents of Arian Christianity, like most barbarian peoples, following a creed that argued that the Son was not co-equal and co-eternal with the Father but proceeded from the Father. Although it has become a byword for destruction, the term 'vandalism' was first coined only in 1794, by a French bishop in despair at the destruction wreaked by the revolutionaries.[10] The Vandals certainly enjoyed piling up treasure, and the Vandal kings were reluctant to release their accumulated gold and silver back into the economy – the process known to economic historians as *thésaurisation*. The Alans, by contrast, originated in the Caucasus and had migrated into south-eastern Europe; their language was Iranian, and their customs differed significantly from those of the Vandals – for instance, they did not keep slaves. These unlikely allies entered Spain and carved it up among themselves, but in 416 they were attacked and massacred by the Gothic warlord Wallia in the name of a newly forged, and very temporary, Gothic–Roman alliance. Barbarians were often better at fighting one another than at fighting the Romans. The Vandals in Baetica, roughly modern Andalucía, are said to have been virtually wiped out. But, after so momentous a defeat, the survivors needed to seek other lands. Their aim was to conquer and settle, not to plunder and vanish. The choice they made, Africa, may seem logical enough, since it lay so close by. In the summer of 429, led by their lame but ruthless king, Geiseric, they made their way to the Straits of Gibraltar.

The region around Tangier, Tingitania, was governed from Spain and was the one Roman base in an area that was otherwise controlled by Mauretanian kings, whose relationship with Rome had been, in general, cautiously polite. Rome saw less value in this region than in other parts of North Africa and was satisfied with loose alliances.[11] Geiseric, too, was more interested in gaining control of the wealthiest parts of Africa. Carthage lay in a promised land full of wheat and olive trees, conveying an even more opulent impression than southern Spain.[12] Yet he had to move as many as 180,000 soldiers, women and children across the Straits (a figure that suggests the story of near-annihilation in Baetica was greatly exaggerated).[13] But he had no ships, and many of the boats plying these waters would have been capable of carrying seventy people at best. If he did manage to gather together a few hundred smallish vessels, he could have ferried his people across the Straits in about a month. That still leaves the question of where he found all these boats. His route took him across the Straits of Gibraltar on the Atlantic side, from Tarifa, the southernmost point in Spain, to the beaches between Tangier and Ceuta. That short journey, repeated time after time in what are, even in summer, often inhospitable waters, brought the Vandals and Alans into Tingitania, but they did not linger, and marched eastwards overland, taking up to three months to reach Hippo in May or June 430.[14] Hippo resisted for fourteen months, for the Vandals were not greatly experienced at siege warfare and Hippo was well defended by its Roman walls – a good example of foresight, for during the long years of *pax romana* city defences could easily have been neglected. Among those looking out from the city was its bishop, Augustine, who passed away during the siege. He could reflect that the destruction that had been brought by the heretic barbarians to Rome now threatened his own province.

The conquest of Hippo was followed by the establishment of a new Arian order in which nearly 500 Catholic bishops were expelled from their often tiny sees for adhering to the teachings of the Council of Nicaea. This marked a departure from the Arian practice of tolerating Catholics.[15] The conquest of Carthage eventually followed, but Geiseric was very patient; the city fell in 439, though by then the lands around it were already in Vandal hands. It became the new capital of the kingdom. However, the Vandals in Africa were not destroyers; they owed much to the old order. Geiseric realized that he had to be more than king over his people – *rex Vandalorum et Alanorum*, 'king of the Vandals and the Alans', as his official title ran.[16] In 442, the Vandals entered into a treaty with the Romans, under the terms of which the king exercised full territorial sovereignty.[17] There is no evidence that Vandal rule led to economic decline, even if much of the gold Geiseric accumulated stayed in his treasury. Building programmes continued; oriental merchants arrived in Carthage, bringing Byzantine coins; North African merchants travelled to the East; the handsome commercial harbour of

Carthage was renovated.[18] There was a significant increase in the number of eastern Mediterranean amphorae imported into Carthage during the Vandal period. The Carthaginians also dined off the best pieces of local red-slip ware. The fact that North African grain was no longer requisitioned for export to Rome, but was handled by local merchants, stimulated economic enterprise.[19] The Vandals were fond of eastern silks, of bath-houses, banquets and theatres; they enjoyed punting. They acted as patrons of Latin poetry, and were as Romanized as the Goths who, settling in Italy, began the beautification of their centre of government at Ravenna.[20] Like the Goths, though, they kept their Germanic names (Gunthamund, Thrasamund, and so on) from generation to generation, though Latin and, to a lesser extent, Punic functioned as the *lingua franca* in Africa. Rural life was not interrupted by the conquest, as is shown in remarkable wooden estate records from the hinterland of the Vandal kingdom, the so-called Albertini tablets.[21] The old system did not just linger; it was full of its traditional energy. The Roman, Punic and Moorish population of north-west Africa provided the Vandals with the shipping that was needed to sustain the Vandal state.[22] Ships were used for trade or troop movements as circumstances demanded. In 533 King Gelimer possessed 120 vessels which he sent to Sardinia in the hope of defeating the island's rebellious governor. The Vandals did not require traditional warships; when they crossed the sea to conquer other lands, they simply needed to be transported with their horses and arms.[23]

The Vandal kingdom was much more than the African provinces of the Roman Empire. Even before the invasion of Africa, the Vandals had despatched raids to the Balearic Isles; in 455, they annexed them.[24] New opportunities opened up, following the death of the highly successful Roman general Aetius in 454 and the assassination of the distinctly less able western Roman emperor Valentinian III the year after.[25] Their most daring expedition took the Vandal army to Rome in June 455. The aim was not an Arian holy war against the Catholics, but plunder: the Vandals were under instructions not to destroy and kill, but to find treasure, especially imperial treasure. They carried off a vast booty, including very many slaves (whom they treated with no consideration, splitting apart husbands and wives, parents and children). According to some accounts the treasure included the great candlestick and other golden vessels seized by Titus from the Temple in Jerusalem, which were kept in Carthage as trophies until the Byzantines recovered the city in 534.[26] Geiseric also seized Corsica in 455 or 456, and used it as a source of wood for his ships – exiled Catholic bishops found themselves forced to work as woodcutters on the island. In the same period the Vandals attempted to conquer Sardinia, though it was lost around 468 and recovered by them only around 482. They settled the island with Moors deported from their African territory, the so-called *Barbarikinoi*, who gave their name to the wild mountains of Barbagia in north-eastern Sardinia. They were not shy of attempting to conquer Sicily as well, ruthlessly scouring the Sicilian Straits as early as 440, and again in 461 or 462, raiding the island each year after that. They managed to prise control of Sicily from the Romans for a time, but a little before the death of Geiseric (in 477, after half a century of war-mongering) they came to an agreement with the Germanic general Odoacer, who had deposed the last western emperor only a few months earlier, and now ruled as king of Italy. Odoacer paid tribute for Sicily but left only the western tip around Marsala under direct Vandal control. Still, it seemed for a time as if the Vandals would control the three granaries of the western Mediterranean: Africa, Sicily and Sardinia.[27] Then, after deciding they had extracted as much from Sicily and Italy as they could hope to do, they began to raid the coasts of Greece and Dalmatia as well, devastating Zakynthos, in the Ionian isles, in the last years of Geiseric's reign.

The Vandals had created a maritime empire of a very distinctive character. There is no evidence that they encouraged piracy on the high seas, nor that the kings took a direct interest in trade. They knew that they had placed their hands on the jugular vein of Rome when they gained control of the empire's granaries, and famines recorded in Italy, around 450, may have been accentuated or even caused by Vandal interference in the grain traffic. They did not often engage with the fleets of the Roman Empire, for that type of naval warfare was now rare (although in the 460s Geiseric did manage to destroy two Byzantine fleets). While the high point of the Vandal empire was the reign of its founder, Geiseric, the Vandals were still a significant force in the sixty years that followed his death in 477. By 500, Arian Ostrogoths ('eastern Goths') ruled Italy, Arian Vandals ruled Africa, Arian Visigoths ('western Goths') ruled Spain and southern Gaul. The political, ethnic and religious geography of the Mediterranean had changed decisively in the century and a half since the foundation of the New Rome. The process of dis-integration was under way.

II

This disintegration has to be understood several ways. There was a gradual detachment of the western Mediterranean from the eastern Mediterranean; and there was a series of crises in both, from which the eastern areas suffered badly but recovered more quickly and decisively than did the West. The era of the invasions also had dramatic effects on the early Byzantine state, but in the West the result was the disappearance of imperial authority, whereas in the East imperial authority survived massive incursions by Goths, Slavs, Persians and Arabs that even brought invaders to the impregnable walls of seventh-century Constantinople. Much of Greece was under the rule of Slav tribes in the seventh century. Yet the economy of the entire Mediterranean was also under assault from a very different attacker. The 540s saw the arrival of plague, possibly bubonic and pneumonic plague pathologically similar to the Black Death of the fourteenth century.[28] Like the Black Death, the plague of the era of Justinian carried away massive numbers of people, maybe 30 per cent of the population of Byzantium, particularly town-dwellers. Cold but dry winters in the eastern Mediterranean led to drought and famine, and possibly similar climatic changes much further east released plague from the lands in East Asia where it was residually endemic and allowed it to spread westwards.[29] In addition, a cool phase during the late Roman Empire may have resulted in deterioration of the soil, while the abandonment of terraces created for the cultivation of vines and olive trees would have led to landslips and erosion. But there is a chicken-and-egg problem here: the abandonment of vines and olives implies a decline in demand, and something must have caused that. Another view is that over-exploitation of the soil by a swollen population living on the edge of the Mediterranean, demanding more and more cereals, denuded the soil of trees and other cover, with the result that topsoil was carried away into river mouths, which silted up. A series of ecological accidents (for the people of the time were unable to appreciate the effects of their actions) thus damaged the soils from which they lived, and resulted in famines and droughts. One would then expect the population decline around the Mediterranean to have begun before the arrival of the plague, which hit the weakened population all the harder because of the lack of resilience to disease following food shortages and local epidemics of less virulent diseases.[30] All this may appear rather theoretical, but there is enough evidence, from North Africa, Ephesos in Asia Minor, Olympia in Greece, Nora in Sardinia and Luni in north-western Italy, to show that silting-up did occur.[31]

Under the Byzantine emperor Justinian I (527–65) vigorous efforts were made, notwithstanding the spread of disease, to re-establish Roman rule throughout the Mediterranean. Before the plague struck, Justinian had already recovered control of Carthage (534); money was then lavished on the city: a new portico was constructed in its famous circular harbour, and new walls and moats were set in place, for events a century earlier had shown that even a city in North Africa was vulnerable to land attack. The collapse of the Vandal kingdom was followed by Gothic Wars in Italy, led by Justinian's brilliant general Belisarios; Byzantine armies swept into Sicily, and a mere two years after the fall of Carthage they captured Naples by a classic ruse, entering through a tunnel. Justinian saw the recovery of Italy as a matter of special prestige; Ravenna, previously the base of the Ostrogothic kings, became once again the seat of imperial officials, the exarchs, and its outport at Classis resumed its role as the base for the Byzantine navy. The harbour of Naples was fortified, since the Gothic enemies of Justinian remained on the rampage after Belisarios had won the city back for the emperor.[32] The long arm of Byzantium even extended to the coastline around Genoa – the first signs of economic activity in an area that was to become one of the great centres of medieval Mediterranean trade.[33] Not afraid to fight on several fronts at once, Justinian also despatched armies to southern Spain, gaining control of the region around Cartagena in the teeth of Visigothic opposition. With Sardinia and the Balearic islands also under Byzantine rule, a chain of communication was created stretching from the heartlands of Byzantium towards Ceuta and the Straits of Gibraltar.

Justinian's attempt to re-establish a pan-Mediterranean Roman Empire stretched the resources of Constantinople at a time of economic crisis. Italy was severely damaged by war and disease.[34] Optimistic attempts to improve harbours and to bolster the defences of port cities continued despite the demographic collapse following the plague. In the hope of reinforcing the link between Constantinople and Italy, the city of Dyrrhachion (the old Epidamnos) was surrounded by an impressive series of walls and towers, parts of which still survive. Dyrrhachion stood at the end of the overland route to Constantinople, the Via Egnatia, but access to the Aegean by sea was also facilitated by similar works at Corinth, even though much of the population, already severely depleted by plague, decamped to the Aegean island of Aigina.[35] A similarly mixed story can be told of Carthage. The harbour works did not guarantee the city's economic vitality. The number of eastern amphorae dipped significantly following the Byzantine recovery of Carthage. Paradoxically, just as political control was imposed from the East, commercial links to the East weakened; the decline in trade may have been the result of renewed attempts to bring the grain trade under state control.[36]

The sixth century was also a time of very varied fortunes in the eastern Mediterranean; Ephesos experienced dramatic decline, as did Athens and Delphi, though Alexandria remained a lively city of about 100,000 inhabitants until the middle of the century. In some areas, however, there was new vitality: the city of Gortyna in Crete was adorned with handsome new buildings in the seventh century, following an earthquake, and became the centre of a successful pottery industry. One advantage Crete, and also Cyprus, had was that the Slav invasions did not reach these islands. Hoards of early seventh-century gold coins attest to their continuing prosperity. Several Aegean islands such as Samos and Chios acted as hosts to refugees from the Slavs, and were invigorated by the arrival of new settlers at a time of population decline elsewhere.[37] The 'Rhodian Sea Law' emerged as the standard code of maritime law in and beyond Byzantium.[38] As well as northern barbarians, Byzantium faced the sophisticated menace of the old rivals of the Greek world, the Persian emperors. Their invasions had a devastating effect on the cities of the Mediterranean coastline. Sardis was an imposing regional capital until 616, with marble-paved streets, porticoes and one of the largest synagogues in the Mediterranean; the city's destruction by the Persians left a pile of burned-out ruins, and it was never reconstructed. Pergamon, once famous for its library, shared a similar fate.[39]

Despite these calamities, some of the old trading networks remained alive, and were even reinvigorated. Po valley grain was exported from Classis when Byzantine rule resumed there. Naples, on the other hand, loosened its ties with Africa, which had once supplied it with large amounts of grain. This can be measured from the decline in the once plentiful African pottery found in sixth-century archaeological levels in Naples.[40] The decline of African red-slip ware contrasts with the arrival in Naples of noticeable quantities of pottery from the eastern

Mediterranean, including amphorae from Samos, one of the islands that had flourished while mainland Greece suffered catastrophic collapse under Slav rule.[41] In fact, around 600 Samian pottery appeared in Rome, Ravenna, Syracuse and Carthage, so the links between the eastern Mediterranean and the newly recovered lands in Italy and Africa were evidently maintained and possibly even strengthened. Southern Italy and Sicily retained ties to the outside world and the Lombard rulers of southern Italy were able to mint gold coins. The Adriatic was an outlying Byzantine lake, and it is in this period that the first stirrings of a group of muddy ports at its very top can be detected, the communities out of which Venice would emerge. Conditions were more difficult further west. Luni declined steeply and never recovered. Around 600 the inhabitants could only mint coins made of lead.[42] There were some ties between Genoa and Byzantium, but they are likely to have been more political than commercial. Marseilles retained a lead among the trading centres of the western Mediterranean, but was a pale shadow of the great Greek city of the past. The number of eastern amphorae shrank in the sixth century, so that by 600 it was only a quarter of the number around 500; in the seventh century these amphorae vanished. On the other hand, African amphorae staged a recovery in the sixth century, so medium-distance trade within the western Mediterranean continued through Marseilles. Nor were contacts with the East totally severed. Bishop Gregory of Tours, chronicler of the hideously brutal Merovingian kings of Gaul, mentioned wine from the Syro-Palestinian ports of Gaza and Laodicea.[43] Striking confirmation of this statement has been obtained from the wreck of a ship dating to Gregory's time, found near Port Cros off southern France. It carried wine amphorae from the Aegean and Gaza.[44]

About eighty shipwrecks from this period have been identified. Around 600 a vessel sank off the southern French coast carrying pitch, North African pottery, Gazan amphorae and pitchers with graffiti in Greek letters; the ship was poorly constructed, with thin planking and ill-fitting joints, so it is no surprise that it sank. The boat was not large; it displaced less than 50 tons and could carry at most 8,000 *modii* of wheat, a fraction of the capacity of Roman grain ships.[45] Sixth- and seventh-century ships were smaller than their Roman predecessors. A wreck found off Turkey, at Yassı Ada, from about 626, was built using lighter nails than the Romans would have employed; displacing over 50 tons, it was a cheaply built vessel, 'lasting just long enough to turn a good profit'.[46] On the other hand, it possessed a well-stocked galley with a tile roof, whose contents – bowls, plates and cups – suggest that it came from the Aegean or Constantinople.[47] Occasionally ships with more costly cargoes went down: the Marzameni wreck, from Sicily, dates from around 540 and carried up to 300 tons of green and white marble. The vessel was carrying the interior furnishings of an entire church, similar to those of churches in Ravenna and Libya. These fine pieces were sent across the sea as an advertisement for religious uniformity: one style of church design would reflect one theology under one emperor, Justinian the Great.[48] The eastern Mediterranean shipwrecks suggest more intensive contacts, linking the islands and the coasts. A ship wrecked off the south-west Turkish coast, at Iskandil Burnu, and dating from the late sixth century, was carrying wine from Gaza and what has been identified as a kosher casserole pot, so it is quite possible that the vessel was owned by a Jew (as in the story of Amarantus, the Jewish captain at the start of the fifth century).[49]

The balance sheet for Byzantium combines evidence for a serious economic depression with evidence for continued vitality, most marked in the eastern Mediterranean islands. This is only to be expected after the demographic earthquake of bubonic plague. The commercial map of the Mediterranean was recast, as old centres faded and new ones gained in vitality. Surviving nodes of economic vitality seeded the Byzantine Mediterranean, making possible the revival of the eighth and ninth centuries. Further west, recovery was much slower and more difficult.

PART THREE

The Third Mediterranean, 600–1350

I

Mediterranean Troughs,
600–900

I

By the sixth century, the unity of the Mediterranean had been shattered; it was no longer *mare nostrum*, either politically or commercially. There have been attempts to show that the fundamental unity of the Mediterranean as a trading space, at least, survived until the Islamic conquests of the seventh century (culminating in the invasion of Spain in 711), or even until the Frankish empire of the incestuous mass-murderer Charlemagne acquired control of Italy and Catalonia.[1] There have also been attempts to show that recovery began much earlier than past generations of historians had assumed, and was well under way in the tenth or even the ninth century.[2] It would be hard to dispute this in the case of the Byzantine East, which had already shown some resilience, or in the case of the Islamic lands that by then stretched from Syria and Egypt to Spain and Portugal, but the West is more of a puzzle. It is hardly an exaggeration to say that some historians observe decline at the same moments as others detect expansion. To this one can sensibly answer that there was enormous regional variation; but the question remains when and whether the Mediterranean lost, and then recovered, its unity. Just as in antiquity the integration of the Mediterranean into a single trading area, and subsequently into a single political area, had taken many centuries, from the Dark Age of the tenth century BC to the emergence of the Roman Empire, so in the era of the 'Third Mediterranean' the process of integration was painfully slow. Full political integration was never again achieved, despite the best efforts of invading Arabs and, much later, Turks.

The loss by Byzantium of so many of its mainland possessions to the

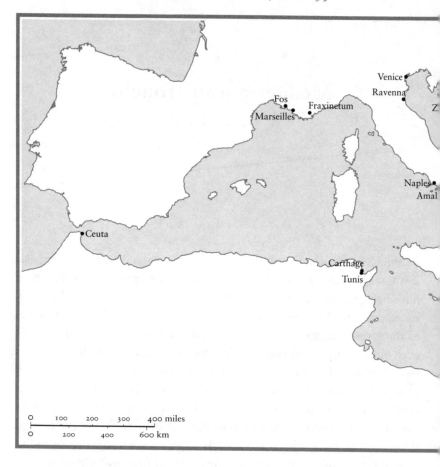

Slavs and other foes did leave the empire with several remarkable assets. Sicily, parts of southern Italy, Cyprus and the Aegean islands remained under Byzantine rule, and the empire drew wealth from gold and silver mines in several of these lands.[3] Even Sardinia and Majorca were under Byzantine suzerainty, but it is unclear whether a functioning network of communication across the Mediterranean still existed. Constantinople maintained control over Egypt, the source of much of its grain supply, though the city had shrunk considerably. 'Syrian' merchants, along with Jewish ones, were mentioned in western European chronicles, attesting to the continued role of the descendants of the Phoenicians in trans-Mediterranean trade networks. The Byzantines realized that they were gravely threatened not just by the barbarian peoples of the North but by enemies in the East. But, despite the temporary Persian occupation of

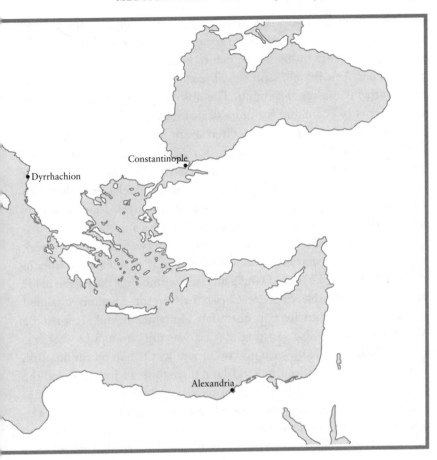

Jerusalem in the early seventh century, it was not the Persians who shattered Byzantine power in Syria and Egypt.

Far along the trade routes traversed by Syrian merchants in search of perfumes and spices for sale in the Mediterranean, beyond the lands of the desert-dwelling Nabataeans, a little way inland from the eastern shores of the Red Sea, a religious and political power was emerging that would permanently transform the relationship between the northern and southern shores of the Mediterranean. In the time of Muhammad (d. 632) the aim of the Muslims was to effect the conversion of the pagan peoples of Arabia, and the submission or conversion of the Arabian Jewish tribes. The unification of the tribes under the banner of Islam (meaning 'submission' – if not to Allah then at least to those who worshipped Allah) was followed by a tremendous release of military and political energy under the early 'deputies', or *khalifas* (caliphs), who succeeded Muhammad, and whose armies captured Jerusalem and Syria within a few years of his death, before pouring into Egypt under the commander 'Amr ibn al-'As in 641. Typically, ibn al-'As was already at odds with his master the caliph. The absolute unity of God was the central tenet of Islam, but the unity of its followers soon cracked.

Islam was not born in the Mediterranean but it interacted from the earliest days with the rival monotheistic religions of the Mediterranean, Judaism and Christianity (it also interacted with paganism, but in a negative way, since the Muslims refused to tolerate religions other than Judaism, Christianity and, in Persia, Zoroastrianism). Islam was able to win converts among the Christians of Syria because many were disaffected members of Monophysite churches persecuted by the Greek Church. The Monophysite treatment of Jesus not as an equal partner in the Trinity but as the Son of God generated within time may have made Islam more palatable to these Christians, for the Muslims accepted Jesus, or Isa, as the greatest prophet after Muhammad, and accepted the Virgin Birth, while also insisting that Isa was only human.[4] Other features of Islam recalled Jewish practices, notably the ban on eating pork, regular daily prayer (five times in Islam, three times in Judaism) and the lack of a priestly caste in charge of religious rites, for this was something that had virtually disappeared from post-Temple Judaism. The Muslim view was that the Hebrew Bible and the New Testament were corrupted texts out of which the foretelling of the arrival of the greatest prophet had been edited; on the other hand, it was recognized that Jews and Christians, the 'Peoples of the Book', worshipped the same God as the Muslims. What emerged from this was the concept of the *dhimmi*, the subject Christians and Jews who, in return for the poll-tax, or *jizyah*, were guaranteed the right to worship, so long as they did not attempt to convert Muslims to their faith. Indeed, the taxes paid by the *dhimmis* became one of the pillars of the Islamic state. Exempted from military service, which was the preserve of the Muslims, the *dhimmis* sustained the military machine through their tax payments. Therefore the rapid conversion of all the Copts in Egypt or all the Berbers in North Africa would be problematic. It would erode the tax base of the caliphate. It made sense to adopt a tolerant attitude to the *dhimmis*, who were, as the eminent historian of the Middle East Bernard Lewis has said, 'second-class citizens – but citizens'. In other words, they were seen as an integral part of society and were not regarded as alien minorities – indeed, outside Arabia they were, in the seventh and eighth centuries, majorities, all along the coast of Syria, in Egypt and in distant Spain, not to mention eastern lands such as Persia.

The fall of Egypt to an Arab army of perhaps 12,000 soldiers was rendered easier by the hostility of the Copts towards Orthodox Byzantium. The immediate effect on Constantinople was the sundering of the route carrying state grain from the Nile to feed the citizens of New Rome. Later, in 674 and 717, Constantinople would face Arab sieges, but for the moment the Arabs stayed within Africa, and they looked from Egypt not towards the Mediterranean but southwards to Nubia: the occupation of lands close to the Red Sea would enable them to consolidate their hold on Arabia. The main focus of Arab expansion immediately after the death of Muhammad was Iraq and Iran, since Persia was the greatest power in the region directly to the north of Arabia. Their initial aim was not, then, to create an empire that would stretch along the entire southern flank of the Mediterranean. Their Mediterranean conquests were a side-show. It was only after they were rebuffed in Nubia that they turned west to Cyrenaica, entering the lands of the Berber tribes.[5]

This proved to be a sensible decision. While Cyrenaica and the province of Africa remained under Byzantine rule, there was always the danger that they would serve as bases for a war of recovery aimed at Egypt. To prevent this, the Arabs needed to gain control of the coastlines and harbours of the North African coast, and this was possible only with the help of large contingents newly arrived from Yemen, and of the Berbers themselves, the native population of North Africa who consisted of a combination of Romanized town-dwellers and rural tribesmen of several religious allegiances. The Arabs also required a fleet, and an 'Arab' naval victory against the Byzantines off Rhodes as early as 654 can only mean that they were successful in hiring local Christian crews: the sea battle probably consisted of a tussle between Greeks on one side and Greeks, Syrians and Copts on the other. Relations with the Berbers were not always easy: pagan Berber tribes converted to Islam, and then slid back to their own beliefs once the Arabs had disappeared over the horizon; one tribe is said to have converted to Islam twelve times.[6] There were also large numbers of Christian and Jewish Berbers, and Queen Kahina, possibly a Jewish Berber, was remembered as a doughty warrior.[7] The Islamization of Berber North Africa in the seventh century was rapid, light and impermanent, but it was sufficient to carry along Berber troops in search of booty, as the Islamic armies began to face their real targets around the Byzantine city of Carthage. From the 660s onwards, they gained control of the lesser towns of the old Roman province of Africa, or, as they called it, Ifriqiya, and they established a garrison city of their own, set back from the Mediterranean, at Qaywaran; they were more interested in its proximity to land where they could graze their camels than in exploiting the sea. In 698, hemmed in by land, and without adequate support from Constantinople, Carthage was besieged by an Arab army of 40,000 troops brought from Syria and elsewhere; they were joined by perhaps 12,000 Berbers. It was the Arab capture of Carthage, rather than the Roman conquest nearly 750 years earlier, that marked the end of its extraordinary history as a centre of trade and empire. The Arabs had no use for it and built a new city close by, at Tunis. Byzantium had lost another of its richest territories; the sliver of Spain conquered by Justinian had already been absorbed by the Visigoths in the 630s, leaving little more than loose authority over Ceuta, Majorca and Sardinia. Byzantine power in the western Mediterranean had to all intents vanished.

II

The Islamic conquests present a paradox to historians of the Mediterranean. In one view, it was these conquests that sundered the unity of the Mediterranean; and yet it was also Islam that provided the foundation for the creation of a new unity across the Mediterranean, though not across the entire sea, for the Islamic networks of trade and communication were mainly confined to its southern and eastern shores. Close trading links developed with Constantinople, Asia Minor and the Byzantine Aegean, and with several Italian ports that lay under loose Byzantine suzerainty, notably Venice and Amalfi, but the inhabitants of southern Gaul and of Italy mainly experienced Muslim sailors in the unappetizing form of slave-raiders. Slaves became the main commodity that passed between western Europe and the Islamic world, generally through the Mediterranean (there also developed overland routes carrying slaves from eastern Europe to Spain, by way of castration clinics in the monasteries of Flanders). The persistence of piracy might be taken as evidence that trade continued, for there is no profit in piracy when there is no one on whom to prey; but most of the victims of the 'Saracens' were probably landlubbers picked off the shores of southern Italy and southern France by the slave-raiders. Three other commodities, papyrus, gold and luxury textiles, have been singled out as absentees, after many centuries in which they had supposedly been major articles of trade. On the basis of their disappearance, the great Belgian historian Henri Pirenne argued that the seventh and eighth centuries marked the fundamental break from antiquity in the Mediterranean; trade slowed to 'the merest trickle'.[8] Since most papyrus was produced in Egypt, the disappearance of this ancient product from western Europe and its replacement by locally manufactured parchment might be taken to indicate that it was no longer being traded across the Mediterranean. The papacy was one of the few institutions to continue to use papyrus as late as the tenth and eleventh centuries, and Rome had the advantage of proximity to the still-functioning ports of the Bay of Naples and Gulf of Salerno, which enjoyed links both to Constantinople and to the Islamic lands.

Evidence that trade remained active, if not exactly busy, does exist. In 716 the Frankish king of Gaul, Chilperic II, granted to the monks of Corbie handsome tax exemptions and permitted them to import papyrus and other eastern goods through Fos-sur-Mer in the Rhône delta, though he was merely confirming older privileges, so this does not prove that business through Fos was still lively.[9] In its heyday Fos channelled northwards not just Spanish leather and papyrus (fifty quires each year) but 10,000 pounds of oil, 30 drums of stinking fish-sauce, 30 pounds of pepper, five times as much cumin, as well as massive amounts of figs, almonds and olives, assuming these quantities ever actually arrived.[10] As has been seen, Marseilles, nearby, was one of the few ports in the north-western Mediterranean that had not withered completely. Archaeological investigations show that the city actually grew during the sixth century and that the ties to Carthage and its region remained strong after 600. There was even a local gold coinage, testifying to Mediterranean links, since there was no reliable source of gold within western Europe.[11] But by the end of the seventh century Marseilles was under pressure. The loss of Carthage to the Arabs meant that its ties to Africa were sundered. The supply of gold dried up and the coins could not be minted, while eastern amphorae no longer arrived.

One group of adventurous, multilingual Jewish merchants known as the *Radhaniyyah*, or 'Radhanites', was described by the ninth-century Arab writer ibn Khurdadbih.[12] He listed four routes along which these merchants travelled, some overland through Gaul and past Prague to the kingdom of the White Bulgars that stretched over vast open spaces north of the Black Sea, others by sea from Provence to Egypt and then down the Red Sea to India, or from Antioch in the Levant to Iraq, India, Ceylon and by sea once again to the Far East. Some, however, set out from Spain and made their way to the Levant by following the North African coast, a route easier to follow by land than by sea, because of shoals and contrary winds and currents.[13] Radhanite merchants returning from the Nile Delta might take ship for Constantinople, or they might find a route back to Gaul. These descriptions of their routes cast the Radhanites in the role of spice merchants, carrying condiments, perfumes and drugs, though their northern contacts enabled them to bring iron weapons, furs and slaves down to the Mediterranean, where Muslim buyers were short of iron and glad to purchase swords from the north.[14] Alongside the Radhanites there were many other slave traders, Christian and Muslim; by 961 there were 13,750 *Saqaliba*, Slav slaves, living in Muslim Córdoba. Warfare between Germanic and Slav peoples in the Wendish lands in what is now eastern Germany ensured a plentiful and regular supply of captives, and the terms *sclavus* and 'slave' recall the Slavonic origin of very many of these slaves. Slaves from the Slav borderlands arrived in Syria and Egypt as well, along with Circassians brought down from the Black Sea.[15] Though horrible, the fate of these slaves, even those who survived the trauma of castration, was not always comparable to the fate of the slaves carried in such vast numbers across the Atlantic towards the Americas in later centuries. Strong-looking young men were not emasculated but entered the emir's guard in Córdoba, sometimes rising to a high military command. On the other hand, women might enter the closed world of the harem; and handsome boys fell into the possession of pederast princes. One merchant who fits the Radhanite label well was Abraham of Saragossa, a Spanish Jew who benefited from the personal protection of the Frankish emperor Louis the Pious. He was active around 828 and was exempt from the payment of tolls; he was explicitly permitted to buy foreign slaves and to sell them within the Frankish lands, but in 846 Jewish merchants were accused by the archbishop of Lyons of looking no further than the cities of Provence for their source of supply, and of selling Christian slaves to buyers in Córdoba.[16]

Whereas Roman naval power had been based on the extinction of piracy, Muslim naval power was based on the exercise of piracy. It was this that made service in Muslim fleets palatable to the Greeks, Copts, Berbers and Spaniards who undoubtedly manned the ships. Western shipping was freely targeted by pirates in the service of Muslim rulers. A ninth-century Arab writer described how Christian ships in the Mediterranean could be treated as a legitimate target for Muslim pirates when the ships were heading for other Christian lands; if a ship was seized and its captain insisted that he was travelling under the protection of a Muslim ruler such as an Andalucían emir, written proof could be demanded.[17] Although the invasion of Spain by Arab and Berber armies in 711 had involved few naval operations – apart from the crucial one of crossing the Straits of Gibraltar – the rest of the eighth century saw Muslim fleets gain in confidence in the western Mediterranean. An outburst of piracy after the fall of Carthage in 698 was suppressed easily enough by the Byzantine navy, but the Byzantine loss of effective control of the seas west of Sicily allowed Muslim fleets a free hand off the islands and coastlines that still acknowledged, even if remotely, Byzantine overlordship: the Balearic islands, Sardinia, the Ligurian coast.[18]

The safety of this region deteriorated seriously around 800. Naval skirmishes erupted all over the surface of the western Mediterranean. These events are generally presented as a struggle to hold back Arab invaders who were trying to gain mastery of the Mediterranean islands. Often, though, the Muslim navies were more intent on grabbing booty (including captives, whom they would put on sale), than in trying to extend the dominion of Islam. The Christians too were keen to take slaves and to win booty, even though they were more obviously on the defensive. Moreover, precisely because there was now a great power in the west willing to fight back against the Muslim navies, tension increased and the pirates became ever more daring. In 798 Arab navies attacked the Balearic islands, which had not been a target of the original invasion of Spain. Knowing that Constantinople was incapable of offering any help, the islanders turned instead to the ruler of Gaul and northern Italy, Charlemagne, whom they acknowledged as their new overlord. Charlemagne sent some forces and the Arabs were repelled the next time they raided the islands.[19] He ordered his son Louis to build a fleet for the defence of the Rhône delta, and he commissioned new coastal defences to protect the ports of southern France and north-western Italy. Hadumar, the Frankish count of Genoa, led a fleet against Arabs invading Corsica, and was killed in the fray. Fighting continued off both Corsica and Sardinia, and a Frankish admiral named Burchard destroyed thirteen enemy ships. Meanwhile, the Venetians (of whom more shortly) patrolled the waters off Sicily and North Africa and they or other ships in Byzantine service scored notable victories against ships from al-Andalus, Islamic Spain. Thirteen Arab ships that attacked the small but strategically valuable island of Lampedusa, between Sicily and Africa, were wiped out by the Byzantines in 812. Before long the North Africans decided that events had gone far enough, and they arranged a ten-year truce with Gregorios, the governor of Byzantine Sicily.[20] Christian navies were now in command west of Sicily, while the Byzantines had gained a much needed respite in the central Mediterranean – the Arab raids on Sicily and Calabria had caused great damage to the exposed coastal towns and villages.

Unfortunately for the Byzantines, the Muslims decided that they wanted more from Sicily than slaves and booty, launching an invasion in 827 which slowly brought the entire island under the rule of the Aghlabid emirs of North Africa. They renewed their raids on Sardinia and Corsica, to which the Franks responded with an ambitious naval attack on the African coast. The problem was that the Frankish navy had no permanent base, and, even after winning a succession of engagements, a single defeat at Sousse was enough to force the Franks out of Africa. In any case, the Frankish empire had passed its peak with the death of Charlemagne in 814, and his successor Louis the Pious was distracted from the western Mediterranean by internal rivalries. In the 840s, the Arabs were free to raid Marseilles, Arles and Rome. To the extreme embarrassment of both the Byzantines and the Franks, who each claimed dominion over southern Italy, a Muslim navy captured the seaport of Bari in 847, establishing an emirate that lasted until 871, when finally the Franks and the Byzantines learned to work together long enough to expel the Muslims.[21] After tentative moves in the ninth century, Arab pirate bases were established in the tenth century along the coast of Provence, and a little way inland at Fraxinetum (La Garde-Freinet). Arab piracy gravely endangered Christian trade out of

Provence, while providing the Muslims with a supply of slaves and war booty.[22]

III

The Byzantines enjoyed mixed success in the face of the Muslim advance. Having held back the Arabs at the walls of Constantinople in 718, they mobilized their fleets in the Mediterranean in the early eighth century, and yet local revolts, particularly in Sicily, endangered their control of the sea routes across the Mediterranean. Since the sixth century the Byzantine navy had been dominated by the *dromôn*, a variant on the war galley that grew in size over time but became the standard warship used throughout the Mediterranean until the twelfth century; its characteristics included the use of a lateen instead of a square sail, banks of oars placed beneath the main deck and (possibly) skeletal hull construction instead of shell construction. Originally rowed by a small crew of fifty oarsmen, one on either side (making them 'monoremes'), they evolved into biremes, with each oar manipulated by pairs of rowers numbering up to 150 men.[23] Muslim fleets, equipped with similar ships, faced a great difficulty: the shoals, rocks and sandbanks of the North African shore made east–west movement along the coastline difficult. Shipping was forced to choose island-hopping routes further to the north, and this, as well as piracy and slaving, was a good reason why Muslim navies intruded into the waters around the Balearic islands, Sardinia and Sicily.[24] To say that these navies 'held waters' provides only a shorthand description of the way fleets operated: it was vital that galleys had access to friendly ports where they could take on supplies, if they were to patrol an area of sea effectively. Remote control in the form of fleets sent out from the heartlands of Byzantium was impossible, and the best option was to establish Byzantine bases on the maritime frontier.[25] The Byzantines managed to hold the waters north of Cyprus and Crete (which they lost for a time to the Arabs). This enabled them to maintain communications in the Aegean and a little way beyond, but the situation was more parlous on the fringes of the Byzantine Empire, notably in the Adriatic.

Their difficulties in this zone began not with the Arabs, whose seizure of Bari came relatively late, so much as with the Franks, rulers by the end of the eighth century of large tracts of Italy including (in 751) the former Byzantine province, or Exarchate, whose capital lay at Ravenna. Frankish armies were still active close to the Adriatic in the 790s, when Charlemagne crushed the great, wealthy empire of the Avars, annexing to his empire vast tracts of what are now Slovenia, Hungary and the northern Balkans. In 791 the Franks took charge of Istria, the rocky peninsula at the top of the Adriatic that was still under nominal Byzantine rule.[26] These campaigns brought Frankish and Byzantine interests into collision. Ill-feeling between the Franks and the Byzantines was compounded by the coronation of Charlemagne as western Roman emperor on Christmas Day 800 in Rome, even if the new emperor laughed off this event as of minor importance. Byzantium remained deeply sensitive about its claim to be the true successor to the Roman Empire until its fall in 1453. Reports that Charlemagne thought he might like to take over Sicily added to the unease. He even seemed to be conspiring with the Abbasid caliph of Baghdad, Harun ar-Rashid, who sent him an elephant as a sign of his esteem, along with the keys to the church of the Holy Sepulchre in Jerusalem, over which the Byzantines claimed protective authority.

From Constantinople, the Adriatic was seen as the first line of defence against hostile armies and navies that sought to penetrate the Byzantine heartlands. The defence of the Via Egnatia that ran from Dyrrhachion to Thessalonika had a military rationale, quite apart from its importance as a trade route.[27] The Byzantines therefore expended energy defending the Dalmatian and Albanian coastline from Franks, Slavs, Arabs and other invaders and raiders. Despite the survival of magnificent early Byzantine mosaics in towns such as Poreč, in Istria, this was a region where the Latin Church was dominant and where a form of Low Latin was spoken, developing into the now vanished Dalmatian language.[28] Byzantine influence also extended to the Italian side of the Upper Adriatic, stretching in a great crescent across the lagoons and marshes of Grado and down the Italian side past a series of sandbanks, or *lidi*, to the port of Comacchio, not far north of Ravenna. For the loss of the Exarchate of Ravenna had not entirely deprived Byzantium of an Italian dominion, and, even if it was inhabited more by fish than by humans, and produced more salt than wheat, it proved to be an unsuspected asset.

This was an unstable world in which water and silt jostled for control. It was here that the Piave, the Po and the Adige, as well as numerous smaller rivers, dumped their deposits. According to the sixth-century writer Cassiodorus, the early inhabitants of these marshlands lived 'like water birds, now on sea, now on land', and their wealth consisted only of fish and salt, though he had to admit that salt was in one sense more precious than gold: everyone needs salt but there must be people who feel no need for gold. Cassiodorus idealized the marshlanders, claiming that 'the same food and similar houses are shared by all, so they cannot envy each other's hearths, and they are free from the vices that rule the world'.[29] The barbarian invasions transformed this area, not by conquering the lagoons but by making them into a refuge for those escaping from the armies of the Germanic people known as the Lombards. This immigration did not happen all at once, but a number of villages emerged at Comacchio, Eraclea, Jesolo, Torcello, and a cluster of small islands around the 'high bank', or Rivo Alto, later abbreviated to Rialto. There were glass workshops in the little community of Torcello, going back to the seventh century. Comacchio received privileges from the Lombard rulers, perhaps as early as 715. One island, Grado, became the seat of a grandly titled patriarch whose ecclesiastical authority extended over all the lagoons, though individual bishops proliferated – every settlement of any size possessed one, and impressive churches began to be erected in the eighth and ninth centuries, strongly suggesting that trade was prospering.[30] As in Dalmatia, the bishops followed the Latin rite even though political allegiance was directed towards Constantinople. Before the fall of the Byzantine Exarchate, the inhabitants looked to Ravenna for immediate political guidance and military protection, and as early as 697 the Exarch appointed a military commander, or *dux*, to guard the lagoons.[31] After the fall of the Exarchate in 751, the value of the lagoons lay, paradoxically, in their remoteness. They were an assertion of the continuing presence of the true Roman Empire in northern Italy.

Following the arrival of the Franks in Italy in the late eighth century, the inhabitants of the lagoons were tempted to defect to the new Roman emperor Charlemagne. His armies were close by and he could lure them with promises of trading privileges in Lombardy and beyond. Moreover, the Franks had made themselves respectable with their interest in classical culture; they had begun to smooth the rough edges of their barbarian identity. Pro-Frankish and pro-Byzantine factions emerged in the lagoons and in Dalmatia. At the start of the ninth century, the

Byzantines were determined to hold their position and sent a fleet to the Upper Adriatic, clashing with the Franks in these waters. In 807 the Byzantines recovered most of the lagoons, and two years later they besieged Comacchio, still loyal to the Franks. This had the unfortunate effect of drawing a Frankish army and navy towards the region, led by Charlemagne's son Pippin, king of Italy. Pippin scared the Byzantine fleet away, which left the lagoons dangerously exposed, and he laid siege to the lido at Malamocco, hoping to break through to Rivo Alto and the settlements within the lagoon; accounts vary, but he seems to have failed. The fourteenth-century chronicle of Doge Andrea Dandolo described how the inhabitants bombarded the Franks with loaves of bread to prove that the siege was not hurting them and that they still had plenty to eat, a tale associated with so many sieges that it need not be believed.[32] Both the Franks and the Byzantines regarded this war as a distraction from more important issues, and had an appetite for peace. Charlemagne realized that if he made concessions he could secure grudging recognition as emperor from the Byzantines. In 812 a formula emerged that respected Byzantine claims to suzerainty over the lagoons, while expecting the inhabitants to pay the Franks an annual tribute of thirty-six pounds of silver and to provide naval help against the Slavs in Dalmatia. The tribute payment was no great burden, because peace brought privileged access to markets in Italy, and this corner of the Adriatic was able to function as a channel of communication between western Europe and Byzantium, enjoying the protection of the empires of East and West. This was a unique position, of which merchants took full advantage.

Out of the lagoons, and out of the Adriatic war with Charlemagne, emerged the city of Venice, as a physical, political and mercantile entity. The conflict with the Franks encouraged the scattered people of the lagoon to gather in a defensible group of islands, protected by a long lido from sea invaders, but far enough from the coastline to deter land invaders. Gradually the Venetians spread across the islands closest to Rialto, driving deep wooden piles into the sodden earth and constructing wooden houses out of timber brought from Istria. Early Venice was not a city of marble, and did not even possess a bishop of its own – the nearest bishop resided on the island of Castello, on the eastern fringe of the settlements around Rialto.[33] The Venetians were as expert in navigating barges and punts through the Po delta as they were in sailing the

Adriatic, but several families emerged that kept tight hold of the office of *dux*, or Doge, mainly families owning farms on the mainland, for Venice was not yet so dominated by trade that its elites had lost interest in cultivating the soil.[34]

Yet even before Venice began to coalesce into a single town, trading links with far afield had begun to develop. While the trade in salt, fish and timber must not be underestimated, the Venetians found a role as entrepreneurs in the limited luxury trade between East and West. Competitors were few: by the eighth century even Rome was receiving few goods from across the Mediterranean. The volume of luxury imports was small but the profits were high, because of the risks and because of the rarity of the articles the Venetians carried: silks, jewels, gold artefacts, saints' relics.[35] They sold these goods on to Lombard princes, Frankish kings and luxury-loving bishops, mainly in the Po Valley and neighbouring areas. Byzantine and occasionally Arab coins have been found on sites around the Upper Adriatic. A hoard of coins dating from the time of the Frankish–Byzantine naval war was discovered near Bologna, by the river Reno, one of the water-courses that debouches into the lagoons. It is a mixed bag of Byzantine, south Italian and Islamic gold coins; the Byzantine coins are from Constantinople, and the Islamic gold includes pieces from Egypt and North Africa. This suggests that the money was being carried on a river-boat by a merchant with connections across the Mediterranean. Venetian ships were sometimes commissioned to carry ambassadors back and forth to Constantinople.[36] Now that Marseilles was in decline, Venice had become the main port through which contact with the eastern Mediterranean was maintained – commercial, diplomatic, ecclesiastical.

Of all the travellers who reached Venice from the East by far the most important was a long-dead Judaean named Mark who was credited with authorship of one of the books of the Gospels and with founding the Church of Alexandria. In 828–9 some Venetian merchants in Alexandria stuffed his stolen remains into a barrel, covered the bones with pork and smuggled their cargo past Muslim customs officials who refused to poke beneath the pork – if a theft of relics succeeded, this was a sure sign that the saint approved.[37] St Mark was deposited in a chapel built next to the Doge's residence, though it was only in the eleventh century that the chapel was vastly enlarged to create the great basilica which until the nineteenth century was not a cathedral but the chapel of the Doge. This did not simply make Venice into a centre of pilgrim traffic, at the expense of Alexandria; it also meant that Venice was appropriating part of Alexandria's ancient identity as one of the patriarchal seats of Christianity.[38] By virtue of its close links with Constantinople, Venice also sought to uphold Byzantine culture amid the vanished glories of the western Roman Empire. The Venetians were beginning to create not just a distinctive city built in the water, but a distinctive culture and a distinctive polity, suspended between western Europe, Byzantium and Islam.

IV

The fact that Venice and a little later Amalfi became the principal centres of limited communication between East and West reveals the degree to which continuity had been broken. These were new towns. The scale of collapse in the late Roman Empire had been so great that the ancient trading centres of the western Mediterranean vanished off the commercial map. This was not true of the eastern Mediterranean, where Alexandria survived the sixth-century crisis and remained a vigorous centre of trade after the Islamic conquest of Egypt. By the late eighth century there are signs of general recovery in Byzantium, but the West was slow to recover, and what was lost was the intense trans-Mediterranean contact that had flourished when Rome ruled the entire sea. Under Rome, that contact had been more than commercial: religious ideas had flowed from the East towards the imperial capital; artistic styles had been copied; soldiers and slaves had arrived far from their place of birth. In the 'Dark Age' the slaves still moved back and forth, though in lesser quantity, but cultural influences from East to West took on an exotic character, as gifts from the court of Constantinople were passed across unsafe seas to reach the court of a barbarian king, pirates and leaking ships permitting.

When historians have tried to calculate the flow of traffic across the Mediterranean at this time, they have had to admit that there was far less movement in the eighth century than in the ninth, and this does not seem to be simply the result of the disappearance of written sources from the eighth century, since the evidence of shipwrecks is also less rich during that time.[39] Of 410 recorded movements in these two centuries,

23. The fortified tower (*nuraghe*) of Orolo in central Sardinia is one of the best-preserved examples of the prehistoric castles that once dotted the island in their thousands; many, such as this one, were surrounded by villages. Built between 1500 and 900 BC, it was occupied for many centuries thereafter.

24. The early Sards exploited the minerals on their island and were gifted copper workers. This bronze boat, made around 600 BC, may have been used as a lamp. Other examples have been found as far away as Vetulonia in Etruria.

25. Periandros ruled Corinth from 627 to 585 BC and actively promoted its economy. His reputation as a harsh tyrant was tempered by praise for his wisdom and justice.

26. A posthumous representation of Alexander the Great as the sun god. Alexander visited the temple of the Egyptian sun god Amun Ra in 331 BC and wanted the Egyptians to worship him as that god. After his death, ancient Egyptian and Greek religious ideas fused in Egypt during the rule of the Ptolemies.

27. The most famous ancient Iberian sculpture is the 'Dama de Elche', a bust of a priestess or goddess wearing elaborate jewellery, from the fourth century BC. It shows Greek influence, but also bears close comparison with other life size sculptures left by the remarkable civilization of the ancient Iberians.

28. The cult of Sarapis was promoted by Ptolemy I of Egypt. The god was an eclectic fusion of the bull god Apis, the god of rebirth Osiris and several Greek gods, including Zeus and Dionysos.

29. In the third century BC the Carthaginian general Hamilcar Barca, Hannibal's father, built a personal empire in Spain and issued coins which show either him or the god Melqart wreathed in Greek style; probably the intention was to identify Hamilcar with the Punic god, thought to be the same as the Greek Herakles.

30. Bronze coin of Nero (d. AD 68) celebrating the grain trade. The goddess Ceres holds ears of wheat and faces Annona ('Harvest'), who holds a cornucopia; also visible are an altar on which a grain measure has been placed, and the stern of a grain ship.

31. Cleopatra, the last of the Ptolemies, was a cultured though ruthless ruler of Egypt. Her affairs with Julius Caesar and Mark Antony eventually brought disaster on her dynasty and led to the Roman occupation of her country.

32. Coin marking the completion of a new harbour at Ostia, from the reign of Nero. The miniature portrayal of different kinds of ship, observed from various angles, is striking.

33. A large Roman warship or quinquireme, ready for battle at Actium in 31 BC. This relief comes from Praeneste, now Palestrina, south-east of Rome.

34. This striking fresco showing ships coming and going from a harbour near Naples, possibly Puteoli, decorated the walls of a house at Stabiae and was buried by the eruption of Vesuvius in AD 79.

35. Sixth-century mosaic from the basilica of Sant'Apollinare in Ravenna, showing the Byzantine fleet at Classis, Ravenna's outport, and its impressive harbour fortifications.

36. Cornice from the synagogue at Ostia, showing the seven-branched candlestick (*menorah*) that was one of the symbols of Judaism in the late Roman empire. The synagogue remained in use between the first and fourth centuries.

37. An inscription from the second century commemorates the building of the Ark for the scrolls of the Law in the Ostia synagogue, at the expense of Mindis Faustos; the inscription is mainly in Greek, the daily language of the Jews of Rome, together with a few Latin words

HIC DEFERTVRC ORPVS SCI MARCI

38. At the start of the twelfth century the magnificent altarpiece known as the Pala d'Oro, or Golden Standard, was installed on the high altar of St Mark's Basilica in Venice. This panel shows the ship carrying the relics of St Mark sailing towards Venice after the saint's bones were stolen from Alexandria in 828.

39. In a photograph from 1885 Amalfi can be seen clinging to the steep peninsula which was home to a lively community of early medieval merchants. It was little more than a village even at the height of its influence in the eleventh century, when its ships were run up on the beach, as here. It remains a tiny town, though the convent higher up the slopes has now become a luxury hotel.

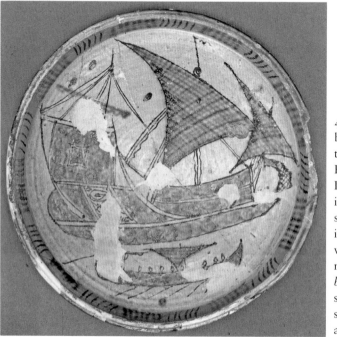

40. The highly glazed basins (*bacini*) that adorn the outside of several Romanesque churches in Pisa would have glistened in the sun, proclaiming the success of Pisan merchants in penetrating Muslim land where know how for their manufacture existed. This *bacino*, probably Majorcan shows a Muslim ship under sail, accompanied by a smaller boat.

only a quarter date from the eighth century, and these include voyages by missionaries, pilgrims, refugees and ambassadors, often engaged in special journeys. Only twenty-two merchant voyages can be identified; Muslim merchants did not want to enter infidel lands, and the merchants we hear about are either Jews or Syrians, even if these may eventually have become generic terms meaning little more than 'merchant'.[40] Ambassadors were sent back and forth between western Europe and Byzantium in the hope of opening up contacts, political, commercial, ecclesiastical and cultural, not because these contacts were already flourishing. Although Arab coins from the eighth and ninth centuries have been found in western Europe, they arrived in greater quantities at the end of the eighth century, when Charlemagne was carving out his new Frankish dominion that stretched into northern Spain and southern Italy, and Byzantine coins began to appear in quantity only from the middle of the ninth century.[41] In fact, many of these Arab coins were themselves European, produced in Muslim Spain.

The restoration of contact between the western and eastern Mediterranean lands, and between the northern and southern shores of the Mediterranean, would depend on the activities of groups of merchants who found it possible to move unhindered across the seas. Any number of factors would determine their ability to do this: their religious identity, the legal mechanisms they employed to control risk and to ensure profit, their ability to communicate with one another across vast spaces. By the tenth century such groups emerged both in the Islamic lands and in parts of Italy.

2

Crossing the Boundaries between Christendom and Islam, 900–1050

I

The enlargement of Muslim domination to include Morocco, Spain and eventually Sicily meant that the southern half of the Mediterranean became a Muslim-ruled lake, offering splendid new opportunities for trade. Jewish merchants emerge most prominently from the records. Whether this is an accident of survival, or whether they were more successful than Coptic and Syriac Christians or Muslim townsmen of North Africa, Spain and Egypt is uncertain. There are grounds for thinking that non-Muslim merchants had a distinct advantage. Muslims were constrained by legal rulings that forbade them from living or even trading in infidel lands. Over the centuries this meant that the rulers of Muslim cities in the Mediterranean opened their doors to Christian and Jewish traders, but their Muslim inhabitants were wary of venturing to Italy, Catalonia or Provence.

The reason so much is known about the Jewish traders is that hundreds of their letters and business documents have survived in the collection known as the Cairo Genizah. In the mid-seventh century, the Arab invaders of Egypt established their base at Fustat (meaning 'the Ditch') on the edge of modern Cairo, and only later moved their capital to the surroundings of the great citadel of New Cairo.[1] Old Cairo, or Fustat, became the base for the city's Jewish and Coptic population; in the eleventh century one group of Jews rebuilt the Ben Ezra synagogue, incorporating on the upper floor a storeroom, or Genizah, accessible only by ladder, into which they threw and stuffed their discarded papers and manuscripts. They wished to avoid destroying anything that carried the name of God; by extension they did not destroy anything written in Hebrew characters. It has been well said that the Genizah collection is 'the very opposite of an archive', because the aim was to throw away documents without destroying them, in effect burying them above ground, rather than to create an accessible room that could be used for systematic reference.[2] These manuscripts came to the attention of scholars in 1896 when a pair of Scottish women brought to Cambridge what appeared to be the Hebrew text of the Wisdom of Ben Sira, or Ecclesiasticus, previously known only from the Greek version preserved in the Septuagint, and consigned by the Jews (and later by the Protestants) to the non-canonical Apocrypha. Whether this was a lost Hebrew original, or a Hebrew translation from a Greek original, it was still a great discovery. In Cambridge, the Reader in Talmudic, Dr Solomon Schechter, was so excited that he travelled to Cairo and negotiated the sale of the contents of the synagogue storeroom, bringing back about three-quarters of all the manuscripts, often tiny scraps of torn, trampled, crumpled texts, jumbled together in a state of chaos that it has taken a hundred years to sort out (other fragments had already been sold piece by piece in the marketplace and ended up scattered from St Petersburg to New York).[3] The Genizah contained a vast number of merchant letters (often, alas, undated), as well as correspondence in the hand of many of the great figures of medieval Jewry, notably Moses Maimonides, the Spanish philosopher, and Judah ha-Levi, the Spanish poet.[4]

Until the merchant letters in the Genizah began to be examined, information about economic life in the medieval Islamic world had to be garnered from references in chronicles, records of legal cases and the evidence of archaeology. As important, therefore, as the discovery and preservation of this material was the decision by Shlomo Dov Goitein (who lived in Israel and then at Princeton) to explore this material in the hope of reconstructing the social and economic life of what he called 'a Mediterranean society'. This phrase begs the question of how typical the 'Genizah Jews' were of the trading societies of the Mediterranean world in the period for which most evidence survives, roughly 950 to 1150. It is not even certain that the members of the Ben Ezra synagogue were typical of Egyptian Jewry. Their synagogue followed the old 'Palestinian' liturgy, the ancestor of the liturgy later used by Jews in Italy and Germany. Another synagogue served the needs of the 'Babylonian'

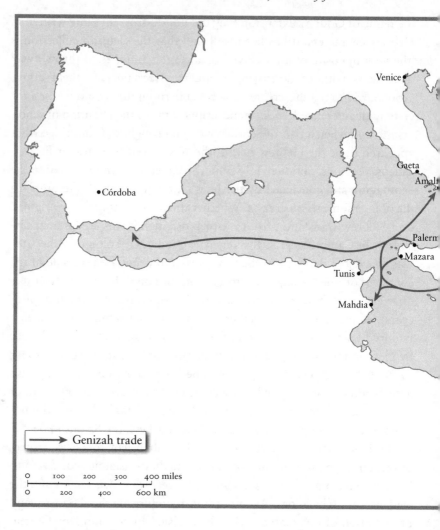

Jews, who included not just Iraqi Jews but all those who followed this rival liturgy, not least the Sephardic Jews of Iberia. There were also many Karaite Jews in Egypt, who rejected the authority of the Talmud, and there were some Samaritans. Still, by showering them with honours, the Ben Ezra Jews persuaded many wealthy Tunisian Jews living in Fustat to join their synagogue as well. This may explain why the Genizah documents are richer in information about links across the Mediterranean to Tunisia and Sicily than about links to Spain or Iraq.

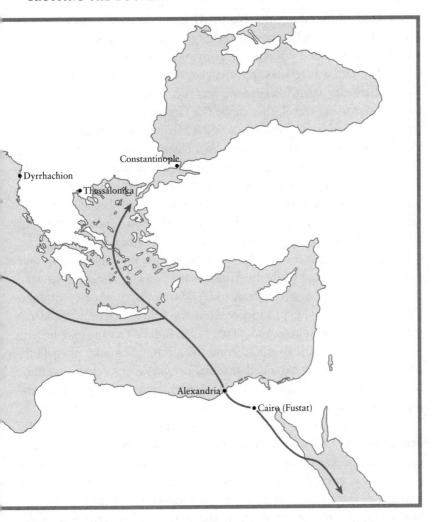

II

The Genizah documents do not simply record the life of those who lived within Fustat. These Jews corresponded with family, friends and business agents across most of the Mediterranean, including al-Andalus, Sicily and Byzantium, though contact with the cities of the Christian West was limited.[5] There are many references to Muslim merchants, who were often entrusted with goods being sent overland (there was heavy land traffic along the North African coast); this was because many Jews had scruples about travelling by land on the Sabbath, which was difficult to avoid when accompanying a caravan. Travelling by sea on the Sabbath was less complicated, so long as one did not set out on the Sabbath day itself.[6] Perhaps it was this simple fact, their religious preference for sea travel, that made the Genizah Jews into such enterprising merchants willing to traverse the Mediterranean. They created a closely interwoven society with its own elites and its customs, forming bonds with one another right across the Mediterranean – marriage alliances were made between families in Fustat and Palermo, and some merchants possessed houses, and even wives, in a number of ports. The range of these contacts is indicated by an eleventh-century letter sent from Fustat. A certain ibn Yiju wrote to his brother Joseph in Sicily, offering the hand of his daughter to Joseph's son and announcing that his only son had died while ibn Yiju was far away in Yemen.[7] This was, then, a distinctive Mediterranean society, but it also looked beyond the Mediterranean, for Egypt functioned as the bridge between the Mediterranean trading sphere and that of the Indian Ocean, to which it was linked by a short overland route to the Red Sea port of Aydhab. Merchants managed extended trading networks linking the western Mediterranean to Yemen and India. Eastern spices were pumped into the Mediterranean through Egypt.

The Genizah Jews were superbly situated to take advantage of the new prosperity that was developing in the Muslim parts of the Mediterranean. Egypt was the economic powerhouse of the region. Alexandria revived as a centre for trade and communication across the sea; Cairo boomed as the central link in the chain connecting Alexandria, by way of the Nile and the desert, to the Red Sea. Cairo also became a capital city when the Fatimid dynasty moved its power base eastwards from Tunisia to Cairo in 969, where they ruled as caliphs, challenging the claims of rival Abbasid caliphs in Baghdad and Umayyad caliphs in Córdoba. The Fatimids were Shi'ites but were aware that they ruled over a population that included rather more Sunni Muslims and many Christian Copts and Jews, all of whom they generally handled with consideration. When they flew the Shi'a flag it was to assert themselves against their Sunni rivals in the Mediterranean and in the East. The Fatimids gained primacy in the Middle East by channelling trade up the Red Sea through Egypt and drawing off handsome profits, reflected in their fine gold coinage. This was achieved at the expense of the Abbasids, who had in the past lived luxuriously off the trade routes that led up the Persian Gulf to the Tigris and Euphrates, and now saw their gold coins deteriorate as their profits contracted. It was these Red Sea routes that the Genizah merchants were able to exploit when they sold eastern luxury goods to their clients in the Mediterranean.[8]

These Jewish merchants specialized in certain goods; they did not involve themselves significantly in the grain trade. Yet there must have been a very lively grain trade, because one of the major effects of the creation of the Islamic world was that the cities of the Levant and North Africa began to revive – indeed some of them were brand new foundations, garrison cities such as Fustat and Qayrawan, ports through which the gold of the Sahara passed such as Mahdia (al-Mahdiyyah) and Tunis. Large numbers of townsfolk relied on outside supplies of basic foodstuffs and raw materials, including the textile fibres and metals they needed for their industries. Specialized groups of artisans flourished in the cities, manufacturing goods for export and buying in foodstuffs from far away. The Tunisians came to depend on Sicilian grain, but they (or the Genizah merchants acting on their behalf) exported linen and cotton textiles, themselves often made from raw cotton purchased in Sicily. This symbiosis between lands separated by the Mediterranean was found all over the sea: Islamic Spain derived grain from Morocco, and sold the Moroccans its finished goods – textiles, pottery, metalwork. When conditions allowed, the Egyptians turned, as they had in past centuries, to Byzantine Cyprus and Asia Minor for the wood they sorely lacked.[9]

The Genizah merchants took full advantage of the opportunities created by economic expansion. Unsatisfied by the commercial instruments whose use was prescribed in Jewish law, they generally followed Muslim commercial practices, which assigned the risk in a trading venture to the sleeping partner back home, rather than to the travelling agent, as required by the rabbis.[10] This meant that younger merchants could make their career as agents or factors of leading traders without fear of complete ruin if their venture miscarried.[11] Sophisticated methods were employed to transfer payments across the Mediterranean: types of credit note, bills of exchange and cheque were known, which were vital if travelling merchants were to settle debts, acquire goods when needed and cover expenses.[12] They traded vigorously in flax and in silk, and bolts of silk were often used as a form of investment, stored away in a drawer until the time came to raise some cash. Flax came from Egypt and was sent to Sicily and Tunisia, while silk sometimes came from Spain or Sicily; in Sicily imitations of Persian silk were made – the practice of imitating the original trade mark was common in the Islamic world, and should be seen not as forgery but as a mark of respect.[13] The Genizah merchants were masters at distinguishing different grades of silk, and knew that the best Spanish silk could fetch 33 dinars per pound-weight at the port of entry into Egypt, while poor-quality Sicilian silk could sink below 2 dinars per pound.[14] Flax was traded in much larger quantities, both spun and unspun, and there was a type of cloth made partly of linen that was actually named after Fustat – 'fustian', a term Italian merchants would adopt for linen and cotton weaves made anywhere, even Germany, and that would pass into modern European languages.

The world of the Genizah stretched to the western edges of the known world. Although al-Andalus, Muslim Spain, was not a major focus of the business conducted by the Genizah merchants, there are still plenty of references to colleagues who originated in Spain. Some, given the labels *al-Andalusi* or *ha-Sefardi*, 'the Spaniard', moved around the Mediterranean, like the family of Jacob al-Andalusi, which was living in Sicily, Tunisia and Egypt in the middle of the eleventh century.[15] The great merchant Halfon ben Nethanel was in Spain in 1128–30, then in India between 1132 and 1134, returning to al-Andalus in 1138–9.[16] Sicily was one of the hubs of the Genizah network. When it was conquered by the Muslims in the ninth century, the first town to fall to the invaders was Mazara in the west of the island. It became the grand terminal for shipping bound from Egypt, and small boats would ferry goods across from Mahdia and other Tunisian ports; once in Mazara, the goods were loaded on to bigger vessels for despatch eastwards. Some of the ships that travelled between al-Andalus, Sicily and Egypt were large; around 1050 ten large ships, each carrying about 500 passengers, reached Palermo from Alexandria. There was a famous market for Egyptian flax in Mazara, and traders in Egypt anxiously awaited news of the flax prices there so that they would know how much flax should be sent westwards. In the other direction travelled silk, used extensively in the trousseaux of Egyptian brides, along with many other fine textiles: pillows, bed covers, carpets and an object called a *mandil*, or mantilla, to cover the bride's hair.[17] Sicily had large areas given over to pasture, and it is no surprise that good-quality leather, sometimes gilded, and sheep's cheese were among prized exports from the island.[18] The cheese was carried as far as Egypt, even though some of it was young and fresh.

This is not to suggest that all was calm in Muslim Sicily; there were Byzantine attacks on eastern Sicily (the emperor was determined to recover this jewel for Constantinople) and there was fighting between rival emirs. A poignant letter sent to Egypt in the early eleventh century describes the miserable experiences of a certain Joseph ben Samuel at a time of renewed Byzantine attack on Sicily. He was born in Tunisia but lived in Egypt, where he married; he possessed a house in Palermo as well. Shipwreck threw him naked and penniless on the shores of North Africa. Fortunately he found a Jew in Tripoli who owed him some money, with which he bought new clothes and set out for his house in Palermo, only to find that a neighbour had pulled it down. He complained that he did not have the funds to take this man before the law-courts. All the same, he was able to send ten pounds of silk to Egypt as well as a handful of gold coins. He was willing to run the gauntlet of Byzantine navies; he wanted to go back to Egypt to collect his wife and son and bring them to Palermo, but he wondered whether she would agree to this, or whether he might have to divorce her instead. It was customary for travelling merchants to make out a conditional bill of divorce in case they died without witnesses and their wives were left in limbo, prevented by Jewish law from remarrying. This divorce could, if she wished, be put into effect now, but Joseph protested that he did love his wife and had written the bill of divorce only out of fear of God and the fate that might await him overseas. He plaintively continued:

> And, oh God, oh God, my Lord, the little boy! Concern yourself with him in accordance with your religious observance, which is so well known to me. When he becomes stronger, let him pass time with a teacher.[19]

The Genizah documents are rich in information about shipping. Most shipowners were Muslim. It was a good idea to board early and to keep a close eye on one's cargo before the vessel sailed; it was customary to board a day before sailing, and to spend the night before departure immersed in prayer and writing last-minute letters and instructions. Of course, timetables were inconceivable, and ships might be forced to stay in harbour as a result of storms, news of pirates or even government interference, as when a ship in the port of Palermo which was about to leave for Spain at the end of the sailing season was seized by the government, and all the passengers were stranded for the entire winter. One complained that he was stuck in Palermo 'with my hands and feet cut off' – not to be understood literally. The length of a voyage was also unpredictable; in 1062 a ship travelled from Alexandria to Mazara in seventeen days, but another letter describes a good week spent hopping from point to point as a merchant named Perahya Yiju tried to sail from Palermo to Messina (which he deeply disliked and found filthy). A small vessel took over two months to reach Almería from Alexandria; another ship took fifty days to sail as far as Palermo, but thirteen days was also possible.[20] Passengers carried their own bedding, cutlery and crockery, and sometimes slept on top of their cargo, which, if it consisted of flax, may not have been too uncomfortable; there were no cabins, and the voyage was spent on deck. Little information is provided in the letters about food, which was probably very simple.[21] Goitein's impression was that shipwrecks were uncommon – they have been seized on by historians because descriptions of them are inevitably graphic. Ships did arrive and the people of the Genizah were not scared of the sea. It was probably no more dangerous than travelling by land. Captains tried to stay in sight of land when navigating the North African coast, and there were watchtowers that monitored the movement of ships, apparently for their own good and not simply to control customs dues. Messages were sent back to Alexandria confirming shipping movements, and businessmen seized on the news that their shipments were properly under way.[22]

There is plentiful evidence for the movement of books and scholars, in the nature of the evidence Jewish ones, revealing how the trade routes carried ideas as well as flax. Around 1007, a query about a point of religion was sent from Morocco to Baghdad with Muslim merchants travelling eastwards by camel caravan.[23] What was possible for Jews was also very easy for Muslims, and texts of works of Greek medicine and philosophy filtered through to southern Spain across the wide expanse of the Mediterranean. It is true that no one understood the medical text of Dioskorides when it reached tenth-century Córdoba, though the caliph's physician, the Jew Hasday ibn Shaprut, is said to have worked with a Greek monk, and together they produced a version in Arabic. Some degree of economic, cultural and religious unity had been achieved along the line linking Spain to Egypt and Syria. The lands of Islam, despite the sectarian division between Shi'ite and Sunni and the political divisions between Umayyads, Fatimids and Abbasids, interacted in trade and culture. This was aided by the constant movement of Muslim pilgrims across the Mediterranean on their way to Mecca, just as much as by the activities of merchants of several faiths. Those who were largely left out were the inhabitants of Christian western Europe. In the tenth and eleventh centuries the Latin merchants of Italy and Provence still ventured cautiously into these waters. Only a small number of Christian cities sent their ships into Muslim seas, knowing that the secret of success was collaboration with the Muslim enemy. One of these cities was Venice, whose early history has been examined already. Another was the no less remarkable port of Amalfi, in its improbable position clinging to the mountains of the Sorrentine peninsula.

III

Amalfi is one of the great mysteries of Mediterranean history. If any town to the south of Rome were to emerge as a great Italian trading centre, it would surely be the teeming city of Naples, with its linen industry, its access to the interior and its sheer physical size; moreover, Naples had a continuous trading history, having suffered recession but not collapse during the sixth and seventh centuries. And yet during the centuries of Amalfitan ascendancy, roughly between 850 and 1100, Amalfi surpassed Naples as a centre of international trade, even though it was a town without any past history, growing up around a watchtower in the sixth and seventh centuries.[24] With a single main street winding upwards, and tiny alleyways that duck under and through its buildings, Amalfi seems an unpromising rival to Venice.[25] It was almost impossible to catch a wind in the morning, and this must have constrained navigation quite significantly.[26] This has led some historians to speak of the 'myth of Amalfi', and to reject the consistent description of Amalfi by Christian, Jewish and in particular Muslim writers as the great entrepôt of the West in the tenth and eleventh centuries. An Italian historian has portrayed Amalfi as a city 'without merchants': in this view, the Amalfitans cultivated their vineyards and gardens on the rocky slopes, and saw trading just as a way of gaining some additional income.[27] Yet building ships capable of reaching other continents was an expensive business, and created the momentum for commercial expansion.

Tiny Amalfi is only part of the story. The label 'Amalfitan' was really a brand name, applied generically to a mass of merchants and sailors from all over southern Italy, especially the inhabitants of a host of tiny towns that clung to the vertices of the Sorrentine peninsula. Hanging above Amalfi, without ports of their own, Ravello and Scala sent their own merchants across the sea in ships of Amalfi; Atrani is five minutes' walk from Amalfi, from which it is separated by an outcrop; Maiori and Minori lie on the short coastal route to Salerno; Cetara became the base of a fishing fleet. In short, the whole southern shore of the Sorrentine peninsula, from Positano to the great monastery of the Santissima Trinità at La Cava, founded in 1025, was 'Amalfi'. The analogy with Venice in its marshes is closer than may at first appear. Venice had originated as a congeries of little communities, separated by sea water rather than by steep mountains and sheer precipices, all of which conferred a sense of impregnability. Both communities believed themselves to have originated as sanctuaries for refugees from the barbarian invasions. Amalfi, under its dukes, who like the doge very loosely recognized remote Byzantine authority, formed a scattered, fragmented city. In an age of Saracen raids from North Africa, this dispersal gave it similar strength to the dispersal of the Venetians across the lagoons.

The first signs that the Amalfitans were able to launch a navy can be found as early as 812, when, along with sailors from Gaeta, another town that became active in Mediterranean trade, they were summoned by the Byzantine governor of Sicily to resist Muslim incursions that reached as far as the offshore islands of Ischia and Ponza. The danger grew as Muslim armies invaded Sicily, and as Muslim navies impudently raided as far as Rome, sacking both St Peter's Basilica and St Paul's-without-the-Walls; three years later a south Italian fleet managed with difficulty to defeat the enemy in a naval battle off Ostia, and for centuries this event was seen as the salvation of Rome – it was commemorated in Raphael's frescoes in the Vatican palace, for his patron, Leo X, shared his name with the pope at the time of the victory, Leo IV.[28] The pope tried to win Amalfi to his side, and granted it free access to the ports of Rome. But what use, its merchants must have asked themselves, was trade with Rome when they needed first of all to penetrate to Sicily, Tunisia and beyond in search of the luxury goods the papal court in Rome still craved? So the Amalfitans and Gaetans made a deal with the Muslims, despite papal threats of excommunication, and this brought material if not spiritual salvation. By 906 the consul of Gaeta possessed gold, silver and bronze coins, jewels, silk and marble fittings for a church, as well as land and animals, all described in his will.[29] The Amalfitans also supplied the great mother-abbey of the Benedictine order at Montecassino in the south Italian interior, acting as its agents as far away as Jerusalem. They were the patrons of a Benedictine monastery situated amid the holy convents of Mount Athos, at a time when the Greek and Latin churches retained some semblance of amity.

Distant Constantinople was happy to issue grandiloquent letters conferring titles such as *protospatarius* (notionally, the title of a military commander) on the duke and leading citizens of Amalfi.[30] However, there was one family, the Pantaleoni, who gained the emperor's ear. During the eleventh century one of the Pantaleoni brought magnificent sets of bronze doors to the abbey of Montecassino, Amalfi Cathedral and St Paul's-without-the-Walls.[31] These were only the most magnificent of the many luxury items the Pantaleoni brought from the East. The Amalfitans wanted bases on Byzantine soil from which they could trade, and possessed wharves and warehouses in Constantinople during the tenth century.[32] Across the Adriatic, they, along with the Venetians, were the main inhabitants of the mightily fortified Byzantine stronghold of Dyrrhachion.[33] Both Venetian and Amalfitan traders were keen to take advantage of the great road that ran from Dyrrhachion through Thessalonika to Constantinople.

Amalfi left a lasting imprint further east, in Fatimid territory. Men of Amalfi established a hospice in Jerusalem, a city which offered little commercial advantage beyond the trade in increasingly improbable relics. But, as agents of the abbey of Montecassino, they made it possible for the Benedictine monks to provide care for the pilgrims who in growing numbers set out from Europe – often by way of the ports of southern Italy – for the Holy Land. From its small beginnings this hospice developed into the Hospitaller Order of St John of Jerusalem and its fighting monks later defended Rhodes and Malta from the Turks. A continuous line stretches from the eleventh century to the Sovereign Military Order of Malta, now based in Rome.[34] A legend reports that

Amalfitans were within Jerusalem when it was besieged by the armies of the First Crusade in 1099. Ordered by the Muslims to throw stones at the crusading rabble, they were forced to comply; miraculously, the stones were transformed in mid-air into bread rolls, and fed the famished Christian army. The truth was, of course, that the Amalfitans flourished when they avoided taking sides in conflicts between Christians and Muslims.

In the tenth century an Amalfitan colony existed in Fustat; in 996 its members were accused of setting fire to the shipyards of the Fatimid caliphs, and up to 160 Italian merchants were killed in the riot that followed.[35] Living in Fustat, the Amalfitans struck up relations with Jewish merchants, and a place called 'Malf' appears now and again in the Genizah letters. Genizah merchants travelled to Amalfi to sell pepper. The link with the Fatimids, the pogrom notwithstanding, made the fortune of the Amalfitans.[36] They were able to mint a gold currency created out of the melted-down profits of their trade in Africa.

Recovery was under way in the West, producing profits for those like the Amalfitans who were willing to do a deal with the Muslim enemy. Two other Italian cities, Genoa and Pisa, were, however, beginning to demonstrate that a more aggressive policy paid even higher dividends.

3

The Great Sea-change,

1000–1100

I

The rise of Pisa and Genoa is almost as mysterious as that of Amalfi, and the mystery is compounded by the startling success of these cities in clearing the western Mediterranean of pirates and in creating trade routes, sustained by colonies of merchants and settlers, as far east as the Holy Land, Egypt and Byzantium. Pisa and Genoa had strikingly different profiles. Genoa had been the seat of a Byzantine governor in the seventh century, but after that two or three hundred years of quiet descended, savagely interrupted by the sack of the city by Saracen raiders from North Africa in 934–5.[1] It has no obvious resources; it perches by the side of the Ligurian Alps and is cut off from grain-producing plains. The favoured products of its coastline are wine, chestnuts, herbs and olive oil, and it was out of its herbs and oil that Genoa perfected the basil sauce known as *pesto*, a product that speaks for poverty rather than wealth. Its harbour became adequate by the end of the Middle Ages, after many centuries of improvements, but its ships were best protected from the weather by being beached along the sandy shores to east and west of Genoa itself, and it was there that most of them were put together.[2] Genoa was not a centre of industry, with the exception of shipbuilding. The Genoese had to struggle to survive, and came to see their trading voyages as the key to the city's survival. As their city grew, so did their dependence on outside supplies of wheat, salted meats and cheese. From these modest beginnings emerged one of the most ambitious trading networks in the pre-industrial world.

Pisa looked quite different. The city stands astride the river Arno, several miles from the sea; the final muddy, marshy exit of the river into

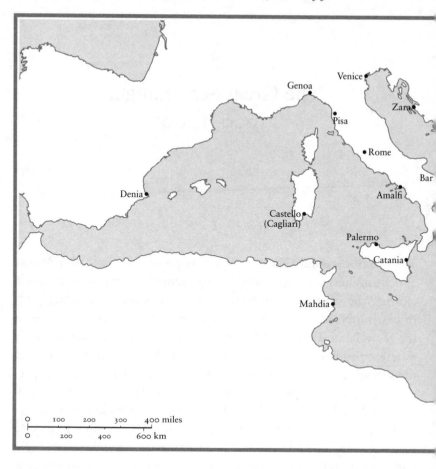

the sea deprived Pisa of a good port. Its obvious assets lay in the flat fields stretching down to the coast, sown with grain and, closer to the shoreline, inhabited by the sheep that supplied Pisa with wool, leather, meat and dairy products. The citizens of Pisa had less reason to worry about how they might feed themselves than those of Genoa. On the other hand, the low-lying Tuscan coast was more exposed than rocky Liguria to sea-raiders from Muslim hideouts in Provence and Sardinia, and, by the time Pisa's navy first appeared, its prime enemy had become the Muslims. In 982 Pisan ships accompanied the army of the German emperor Otto II as he marched far south into Calabria, hoping to suppress Muslim raids from Sicily. During the next century Pisa and Genoa concentrated on clearing the Tyrrhenian Sea of Saracen

pirates. The obvious way to achieve this was to establish command positions in Sardinia, and Pisa and Genoa responded with precocious vigour to the arrival in Sardinia of the army and navy of the Spanish Muslim warlord Mujahid, ruler of Denia and Majorca, in 1013.[3] Mujahid's power almost certainly reached no further than some coastal stations in Sardinia, whether or not he aspired to conquer the whole island. Chasing Mujahid out of Sardinia by 1016 greatly enhanced the credentials of the Pisans and Genoese as exponents of Christian holy war against the Muslim enemy. The power balance between Christians and Muslims was slowly changing; as central power in the Muslim lands became more fragmented, the fleets of Pisa and Genoa seized their opportunity.

II

The better the two cities came to know Sardinia, the more they saw that it was valuable in its own right. The island had a vast sheep population, and by the twelfth century the Pisans and Genoese began to see Sardinia as an extension of their own countryside or *contado*. There was plenty of grain, of middling quality; there were big lagoons in the south that could be turned into saltpans; the Pisans and Genoese also had no compunction about enslaving Sards, whom they regarded as primitive folk. These Sards spoke a form of late Latin, preserved in curious estate documents listing the sheep, cattle and horses of a society that had changed remarkably little since the days of the *nuraghi*. Sardinia remained a pastoral society that looked away from the sea: it was insular but not really Mediterranean. The political and religious institutions were archaic. Petty kings or 'judges' had emerged in the tenth century as the last representatives of now vanished Byzantine authority. But Byzantium lingered in another form. The churches of the island followed a version of the Greek rite, and before 1100 some at least of them were built in the cruciform Greek style. The papacy inveighed against these customs, and supported the arrival of monks from the mainland, including Benedictines from Montecassino.[4] All these changes helped transform life in Sardinia; members of the leading families, the so-called *maiorales*, took Genoese and Pisan wives or husbands, and they could now easily buy the products of the mainland, for even pots and pans were imported. But the standard of living of Sardinian peasants, suffering from disease, poor diet and high mortality, remained extremely depressed. This meant fewer mouths to feed, and more grain to export. There is only one word for the way Pisa and Genoa treated Sardinia: exploitation.

During the twelfth century the Genoese regularly sent ships to the island, whose cheap but vital products ensured a safe return on investments. Anyone with a little spare cash – widows with a modest inheritance, for instance – could quite safely invest five or ten pounds of Genoese silver money in a trading expedition to Sardinia and hope to receive six or twelve pounds back a few months later.[5] Sardinia gave Pisa and Genoa their first colonial experience. The two cities attempted to maintain control by securing the loyalty of the judges. In the years around 1100, this was often achieved through the agency of the great churches of the two cities. Mariano Torchitorio, judge of Cagliari in the south, gave the cathedral of San Lorenzo in Genoa lands in southern Sardinia. But he was a far-sighted man, because he also ensured that Pisa received some gifts.[6] Even so, playing off one side against another achieved only short-term results. Pisa and Genoa were too powerful to be resisted. The Pisans built cathedrals and convents in the striking Pisan style of architecture, their exterior covered in bands of black and white marble; no clearer statement could be made of Pisan ascendancy. The abbey of Santa Trinità di Saccargia, built at the beginning of the twelfth century, is a typical northern Sardinian example of this architecture, with its zebra façade and flanks. It was the Pisans and Genoese who built the first well fortified towns since the days of the *nuraghi*: in the judgeship of Cagliari the Pisans occupied the steep hill simply known as Castello that still hangs over the city of Cagliari, surrounding it with high walls and making out of it a Pisan enclosure, where their soldiers and merchants could abide in safety. The Doria family of Genoa is credited with founding Alghero, in north-western Sardinia, around 1102. In the twelfth and thirteenth centuries Genoa and Pisa were able to consolidate their hold on Sardinia, despite attempts by popes and Holy Roman Emperors to insist that it was (at least in theory) their own property. Yet what mattered was who was there on the ground. The problem was that Genoa and Pisa both aspired to dominion over as much of the island as they could grab for themselves. Bitter conflict between the two cities was the result. It was Sardinia, rather than disagreements in the Italian mainland, that brought them most often to war. By 1200, the waters around Sardinia were largely clear of Muslim pirates; but Italian pirates abounded – Pisans preying on Genoese, and vice versa.

III

One reason the Pisans and Genoese were able to launch their own fleets was the collapse of central authority in northern Italy. The 'kingdom of Italy' had little more than a notional existence, and its ruler was, since the tenth century, the German king, who was also entitled to claim the crown of the western Roman Empire, revived in 962 with the papal coronation of Otto I. The power of the local imperial viscounts withered;

the day-to-day government of these and other towns fell into the hands of the local patricians. By the beginning of the twelfth century they began to organize themselves into self-governing communities – historians use the terms 'commune' and 'city-republic', but they adopted a variety of terms including, in Genoa, 'company' (*compagna*), which literally meant 'those who break bread (*pane*) together'. Indeed, the government of Genoa after 1100 was very like the management of a business partnership. The *compagna* was formed for a limited period of a few years, to resolve a specific problem such as the building of a crusade fleet, or political tensions that, in Genoa, sometimes resulted in assassinations and street-fighting. The commune was in some respects a public institution, embracing the whole community, but in other very important respects it was a private league, though the distinction between 'public' and 'private' was not clear in the minds of twelfth-century Genoese. The city was littered with private enclaves, the property of monasteries and nobles, little pieces of exempt territory that were only very gradually brought under the control of the presiding officers of the *compagna*. These officers took the resounding title of 'consul', proving an awareness of the Roman republican model, though there were as many as six consuls when the first *compagna* came into being.[7] As in ancient Rome, the system of election was carefully manipulated by those with real power, and in this period they were always drawn from the patrician class.[8]

These patricians created the trading empire of Genoa, and similar developments occurred in Pisa. The difficult question is who they were – not their names, such as Doria and Spinola at Genoa, or Visconti and Alliata at Pisa, which are recorded again and again – but whether their wealth and power originated in trade or from the land. The Italian city communes brought together the petty nobility of the region around the town, who had long been accustomed to taking up residence there, and a body of relatively newly made men whose status depended on the wealth derived from commerce, textile workshops or banking. By the early twelfth century, in Pisa and Genoa, these groups were well mixed together, by marriage alliances that brought new money into old families in need of extra cash. The prestige of entry into families whose members had earned a record on the battlefield or in naval combat appealed to the richest members of the merchant community. A new solidarity emerged. This patriciate was certainly not willing to share its power with the artisans and sailors who made up a large part of the citizen body. The rise of the commune did not indicate that the cities had become democratic republics; rather, it indicated that oligarchy had triumphed – hence, indeed, the bitter struggles between factions on the streets of Genoa. Between these outbreaks of violence, however, there were opportunities to make money on an unprecedented scale. The elite invested in overseas trade directed to ever more distant destinations; they bought urban property and they continued to manage their country estates, even extending them by acquiring lands across the water in Sardinia. The city government interfered little in these activities, except when international alliances affected trade, and those alliances were determined by the same people who dominated trade.[9]

These were trends that could be observed right across northern Italy in the years around 1100, though Pisa and Genoa were among the first cities to form an aristocratic commune. The growth of towns in the interior, particularly in the great Lombard plain, had an important effect on what was happening in the Mediterranean, because they became centres of demand for luxury goods from overseas, while their own elites organized the production of increasingly fine cloths and metal goods that could be carried across the Mediterranean in payment for the silks and spices they now demanded. Genoa and Pisa and, on the eastern side of Italy, Venice found themselves able to supply consumers with whom the older generation of merchants from Amalfi had not been able to make close and regular contact. Besides, these cities began to look beyond the Alps. Courts and cities in southern Germany welcomed goods that arrived by way of Venice, and in the twelfth century German merchants arrived there, laying the foundations for the German warehouse, or Fondaco dei Tedeschi, that would for many centuries act as the commercial agency of the German merchants based there.[10] Genoese merchants began to wend their way up the Rhône towards the emerging fairs of Champagne, where they could buy the finest Flemish woollen cloths, for transport down the Rhône to the Mediterranean. A vast network was emerging, focused on the maritime trade of Genoa, Pisa and Venice, but with ramifications that stretched across western Europe.

This commercial revolution was backed up by impressive developments in business methods and in record-keeping. Indeed, the reason so much is known about the economy and society of Genoa in this period is that, from 1154 onwards, large volumes survive containing contracts, wills, land sales and other transactions, recorded by the city notaries.[11] The first of these notarial registers to survive is a bulky book written on thick, smooth paper imported from Alexandria by a certain Giovanni Scriba ('John the Scribe'), whose clients included the most powerful families in mid-twelfth-century Genoa.[12] Business methods became increasingly sophisticated, which was partly made necessary by the public disapproval of the Catholic Church towards anything that smelled of 'usury', a term whose meaning varied enormously, from extortionate rates of interest to simple commercial profits. Mechanisms had to be developed to escape ecclesiastical censure, which in its sternest form could lead to excommunication. Loans could be made in one currency, to be repaid in another, so that interest was hidden in the exchange rate. Often, though, merchants engaged in what they simply called a *societas*, or 'partnership', where a sleeping partner would invest three-quarters of the total and his (or her) colleague would invest one quarter, while also agreeing to travel to whichever destination had been agreed, and to trade there. On his return, the profits would be divided in half. This was a good way for a young merchant to begin to build up capital, but another arrangement became even more common: the *commenda*, where the travelling partner invested nothing apart from his skills and services, and received a quarter of the profits. These arrangements helped to spread wealth beyond the patrician elite; a busy, ambitious merchant class was developing, unafraid of the dangers of the sea and of ports in foreign lands.[13] The Genoese and Pisans looked across the Mediterranean and saw opportunities in every corner.

IV

Mastering the waters near home was the essential prelude to more ambitious ventures in Byzantium and the Islamic lands. Venice needed to clear Muslim fleets from the Adriatic while Bari was held by Muslim emirs (between 847 and 871); in 880 it was rewarded for its efforts with a privilege from the grateful Byzantine emperor. In 992 Venice once again came to the help of Byzantium, and on this occasion received a grant of trading rights.[14] The Pisans and Genoese did not possess as powerful a patron as the Greek emperor, and relied on their own efforts.

In 1063 a Pisan fleet raided the port of Muslim Palermo, destroying some enemy ships and seizing the great chain that stretched across the harbour to keep away intruders such as themselves. They did not penetrate beyond the quayside, but they still carried off vast amounts of booty.[15] They used their profits to glorify God, for they donated part of them to the great cathedral of Santa Maria that the Pisans were beginning to construct, and if anything was a sign of the city's growing prosperity it was this magnificent marble church.

These forays generated a sense that they were engaged in a holy struggle against the Muslims. God would reward their efforts with victory, with booty and with what were as yet ill-defined spiritual benefits. There was no sharp line dividing material and spiritual rewards. This is abundantly clear from the events of 1087, when the Pisans and Genoese launched an attack on the city of Mahdia on the coast of Tunisia.[16] Standing on a promontory, Mahdia had been founded by the Fatimid rulers who eventually took charge of Egypt, and was one of the major towns through which passed the gold dust gathered in the bend of the river Niger, beyond Timbuktu; carried by caravan across the Sahara, it reached the Mediterranean and was pumped into the economy of the Islamic lands. Control of Mahdia might also be seen as the key to control of the Sicilian Straits, and therefore to free passage between the eastern and the western Mediterranean. Thus it would long remain the target of Christian conquerors – Norman kings in the twelfth century, French crusaders in the fourteenth. But in the late eleventh century it was at the height of its prosperity. It was frequented by the Genizah merchants, who sold products such as eastern pepper and Egyptian flax there.[17] From 1062 to 1108 Mahdia was ruled by a single vigorous emir, Tamin, who enriched himself not just from trade but from pirate attacks on Nicotera in Calabria and Mazara in Sicily.[18] He was a thorough nuisance to his close neighbours. The Fatimids foolishly unleashed Bedouin armies (the Banu Hillal and the Banu Sulaym) who, they thought, would bring Tunisia back to Egyptian allegiance. In the end the Bedouins merely increased the disorder, and damaged the countryside beyond repair, so that the inhabitants of North Africa became dependent on Sicilian grain, after so many centuries during which Tunisia had been a bread basket of the Mediterranean.[19] According to an early thirteenth-century Arab writer, ibn al-Athir, the Christians tried to involve Roger, the Norman count of Sicily, in their campaign against Mahdia (he had

t the last quarter-century extending Christian control over the
ld); but 'Roger lifted his thigh, made a great fart' and complained
ut all the trouble that would result: 'commerce in foodstuffs will
ss into their hands from those of the Sicilians, and I shall lose to them
what I make each year on grain sales'.[20]

Even without Count Roger, the Italian allies were happy to press
ahead in 1087. Pope Victor III welcomed members of the expedition in
Rome, where they acquired pilgrims' purses, showing they had visited
the shrine of St Peter. This has excited modern historians of the crusades
who have insisted, rightly, that from the preaching of the First Crusade
in 1095 onwards, crusaders were treated as pilgrims: 'pilgrimage and
holy war were evidently drawing together'.[21] As in Palermo, the Italians
did great damage, raiding Mahdia, but did not take the city, and probably never expected to do so. With their spoils they were able to pay for
the construction of the church of San Sisto in Cortevecchia in the heart
of Pisa, whose façade they decorated with ceramics seized from Mahdia.[22] In addition, the Pisans commissioned a victory poem in Latin. The
'Song about the victory of the Pisans' (*Carmen in victoriam Pisanorum*)
is full of biblical imagery recalling the struggle of the Children of Israel
against their heathen neighbours. The Mahdians, *Madianiti*, were transformed in the poet's version into ancient Midianites, while the Pisans
saw themselves as the heirs of the Maccabees and, even more, of Moses:
'Lo! Once again the Hebrews despoil Egypt and rejoice in having
defeated Pharaoh; they cross the Great Sea as if it is the driest land;
Moses draws water out of the hardest stone.'[23] The poem conjures up a
febrile atmosphere in which the holy cause of fighting the Infidel super-
sedes merely commercial considerations.

That the relations between Pisa and the Muslims were not always
antagonistic is demonstrated by the Islamic ceramics used by the Pisans
to decorate their churches.[24] These ceramics, highly glazed and colourfully decorated, were quite different in style to the plainer wares
produced in western Europe, and, when inserted in church exteriors,
they glistened in the sun like jewels.[25] The large bowls, or *bacini*, inserted
in the towers and façades of churches in Pisa tell an intriguing tale not
just of war but of trade and of fascination with objects from the East.
Churches constructed in the eleventh century displayed fine Egyptian
ceramics on their exterior. There were pots from Sicily and Tunisia
before and well after the Mahdia campaign; Morocco sent to Pisa large

amounts of rather plainer pottery in green and brown, covered with a bluish glaze. The Pisans became so accustomed to this type of decoration that they continued to insert *bacini* in church towers long after they had developed their own glazed ceramics industry, in the thirteenth century. For it was not just the pottery that the Italians acquired from the Muslim world; they also borrowed the technology, laying the foundations of the maiolica industry of Renaissance Italy.

A bowl inserted in the façade of the church of San Piero a Grado near Pisa displays a three-masted vessel with triangular sails, a sharply curved prow and a steep poop; this is a ship from Muslim Majorca, and the design is very stylized.[26] Even so, the image conveys a blurred impression of the sort of bulky sailing ship that carried goods between Spain, Africa and Sicily in the days of Islamic hegemony in the southern waters of the Mediterranean. It matches the description in the Genizah letters of very capacious ships, known as *qunbar*, that carried both heavy cargoes and passengers.[27] Another bowl shows a smaller boat furnished with oars as well as a sail, side by side with a two-masted ship, and this could be a representation of a fast, long, low, sleek galley.[28] Once again, the Genizah letters come to our aid. There, light galleys called *ghurabs* appear; the word signified the sharp edge of a sword, in view of their ability to cut through the waves. Alternatively, the long low boat could be a *qarib*, a sea-going barge, capable of travelling all the way from Tunisia to Syria.[29]

V

The challenges to Muslim domination of the Mediterranean became critical at the end of the eleventh century. Christian expansion into the Muslim Mediterranean was well under way in the 1060s, following the invasion of Sicily by the armies of Robert Guiscard and his brother Roger de Hauteville, Norman knights who had already carved out for themselves dominions in the Lombard and Byzantine territories in southern Italy. In 1061, ten years before they took control of Bari, the capital of the Byzantine province known as 'Longobardia', they were tempted to cross the Straits of Messina and to intervene in the bitter quarrels among the three emirs who dominated Sicily, and were largely oblivious of the Norman threat. One of these emirs, ibn al-Hawas, held his own sister in protective custody in the hilltop city of Enna; she was the much abused wife of the powerful and unlovable emir of Catania, ibn ath-Thimnah, whose attempts to win her back by force failed. In desperation, ibn ath-Thimnah begged the Normans to come to his aid, and Robert and Roger de Hauteville agreed to do so. They arrived, outwardly at least, not as invaders but as military support for the emir of Catania, and used this alliance as the basis for their gradual takeover of the entire island, beginning with the capture of Messina and continuing with the capture of Palermo in 1072 (though the conquest was not complete till Noto fell in 1091). Their ability to move men and horses across the Straits of Messina is impressive. Roger became count of Sicily and married a noblewoman from Savona, in north-western Italy; she was followed to Sicily by large numbers of settlers from Liguria and other parts of Italy, who became known as the *Lombardi*. With this immigration the slow process of the Latinization of Sicily began, and speakers of dialects related to Ligurian Italian could still be found in several eastern Sicilian towns in the twentieth century.[30]

Still, the island's character did not change quickly. For much of the twelfth century Sicily remained home to a mixed population of Muslims, in the majority around 1100, Greeks, only a little less numerous, and Jews, perhaps 5 per cent of the whole population, with the Latin settlers, whether Norman or 'Lombard', accounting for less than 1 per cent. The Greeks were concentrated more in the north-east of Sicily, in the area round Etna known as the Val Demone, and in particular in Messina, which became the main shipyard of Norman Sicily. Each group was allowed considerable autonomy: freedom to practise its religion, which had been enshrined in the 'surrender treaties' conferred on conquered towns such as Enna; its own law-courts for cases between co-religionists; a guarantee of the count's protection, subject to payment by Muslims and Jews of the *gesia*, or poll-tax, which was simply a continuation of the Muslim *jizyah* tax payable by the Peoples of the Book, except that now Christians were exempt and Muslims were liable.

Robert Guiscard's conquest of the Byzantine province in southern Italy and the neighbouring Lombard principalities had, meanwhile, aroused the intense ire of the Byzantine emperor. The relationship between the papacy and the Greek Orthodox Church had been steadily deteriorating in the eleventh century, as the popes began to emphasize their authority over all Christendom, and the Norman victories threatened to draw southern Italy away from Greek ecclesiastical allegiance as well. Although the 'Eastern Schism' of 1054 is often seen as the decisive moment in the break between a Catholic West and an Orthodox East, the events of that year were another moment in a long catalogue of quarrels: the papal legate Humbert of Silva Candida slammed a bull of excommunication directed at the patriarch of Constantinople and his master, the emperor, on the high altar of Hagia Sophia in Constantinople. The Byzantines had adroitly balanced Latin and Greek in the coastal towns of Apulia, where Latin bishops were often keener to accept the authority of Constantinople, at least in political matters, than that of western rulers, including the pope. The arrival of the Normans turned Latin against Latin and Greek against Greek; the Norman conquest of the toe of Italy, Calabria, and then of Sicily, brought many thousands of Greeks under the rule of Robert's brother Roger. After the fall of Bari in 1071 Norman enmity only became more intense, as Robert planned the invasion of the Byzantine territories facing Italy across the Adriatic. He saw Dyrrhachion and the Ionian isles as a gateway through which he could penetrate deeply into Byzantine territory, with the help of his son, the blond giant Bohemond. Robert's excuse for campaigning against Byzantium was that he was acting on behalf of the deposed and exiled emperor Michael Doukas; he welcomed into his entourage a fugitive monk whom he declared to be Michael. He paraded this monk in imperial finery in front of the walls of Dyrrhachion, whereupon (the historian Anna Komnene insists) 'Michael' was immediately and raucously denounced as an impostor by the citizens ranged along the battlements. One might expect Anna to say this, as she was the daughter of the reigning emperor, Alexios Komnenos, founder of a vigorous dynasty whose military and political successes generated a great revival in the fortunes of Byzantium. Anna suspected, and it is hard not to agree, that Robert aspired to the throne of Constantinople. The attack on Albania was only the first stage in a war he intended to carry along the Via Egnatia to the very heart of Byzantium.

In 1081–2 Robert built a fleet of ships capable of carrying massive siege towers covered in animal hides, intending to launch a naval assault on Dyrrhachion while Bohemond would advance overland after disembarking at Valona further down the coast. It was summer and the seas should have remained calm, but Anna Komnene reported that God showed favour to the Byzantines by sending a great tempest that scattered and destroyed Robert's fleet. As the clouds emptied themselves, the towers built on the ships were weighed down by the sodden hides and collapsed on to the deck. The ships were swamped and Robert and a few of his men were lucky to survive, cast up on the shore. Even in the face of such adversity the obstinate Robert Guiscard did not see this as divine judgment, but was determined to renew the attack.[31] Robert gathered his remaining forces together and besieged Dyrrhachion, even bringing forward some more massive siege towers that topped the walls. These walls were so solidly built that two chariots could, according to Byzantine writers, pass one another on top – an image that owes more to Homer than to the realities of eleventh-century warfare, from which chariots had long since disappeared. For Dyrrhachion could only be won by treachery and deceit. Eventually, an Amalfitan merchant opened the gates of the city to the invaders.[32]

Alexios had a clever solution to the problem of how to manage a war with a potent foe at the western extremity of his empire. His fleet lacked the capacity to fight and win so far from home. Byzantine sea power was confined to the Aegean, and Byzantium had sufficient problems on land: Seljuk Turks attacking its eastern borders in Asia Minor, Slavs in the Balkans, not to mention faction fighting within Constantinople itself. The Byzantines preferred diplomacy to conflict, but clearly diplomacy alone would not tame Robert Guiscard. Instead, the diplomacy was directed elsewhere, to Venice, whose merchants lived in dread of conflicts that would make the Adriatic exit impassable. A Norman victory in Albania would enable south Italian fleets to control access to the Adriatic. Venice was always happiest if the power that controlled the western coast of the southern Adriatic did not control the eastern coast as well. So the Venetians agreed to provide naval help against Guiscard's fleet off Dyrrhachion. They set sail carrying piles of heavy beams studded with nails, and they pounced on enemy ships, punching holes in them. In the end, the Byzantines recovered Dyrrhachion and Robert (facing trouble back home in Italy) was forced to withdraw, though Bohemond continued for a while to wreak havoc in Albania. When Robert returned to the attack he was old and sick, and he died on campaign in 1085, in Kephalonia, in the little port of Fiskardo that still carries his nickname of Guiscard, 'the wily one'. Although Alexios and his court heard the news with relief, this was by no means the last attempt by the rulers of southern Italy to invade Byzantium through Albania.

Meanwhile, the Venetians sent messengers to Emperor Alexios, and in 1082 he issued a Golden Bull that showered them with gifts, while emphasizing that they were his *duli*, or subjects. The most precious and controversial of his presents was a grant of the right to trade free of taxation anywhere in the Byzantine Empire, excluding the Black Sea and Cyprus. The emperor wanted to preserve the special role of Constantinople as the link between the Mediterranean, from which it received spices and luxury goods, and the Black Sea, down which merchants brought furs, amber and other northern products. The Venetians were even granted bits and pieces of land by the Golden Horn, including a wharf and their own church (with its own bakery).[33] The privilege of 1082 set a gold standard in the Mediterranean; and, whenever the Italian cities negotiated an alliance with a trading partner in need of naval assistance, they had a model to emulate.

There are different views about the extent to which the Byzantine economy came to be dominated by Venetian and other Italian merchants. In the longer term, the presence of the Italians probably stimulated the production of agricultural goods and of cloths for export.[34] Clearly, in the years around 1100 the Venetian presence in Byzantium was still very limited. The main destinations of Venetian traders within the Byzantine world were surprisingly close to home: Dyrrhachion, once it was recovered from the Normans; Corinth, to which access could be gained without entering the Aegean, using the ancient port at Lechaion on the Gulf of Corinth. Thence the Venetians carried wine, oil, salt and grain back home to their booming city, where demand for these relatively humble foodstuffs was constantly increasing.[35] For most Venetian traders, Constantinople, with its silks and gems and metalwork, lay over the horizon. But they began to think of realizing the full potential of the privileges they had been granted. This was a matter of entitlement, for they still saw themselves as inhabitants of a far-flung fragment of the Eastern Roman Empire, and took pride in their status as imperial subjects: no clearer indication of this can be found than the architecture and decoration of the Basilica of St Mark, which had been rebuilt in the second half of the eleventh century in an overtly Byzantine style, derived from the Basilica of the Apostles in Constantinople. St Mark's was intended to recall a whole catalogue of eastern connections, for it also proclaimed with pride the link to Alexandria, the patriarchal seat of the saint whose bones it conserved.[36]

By the end of the eleventh century, then, Pisa and Genoa had taken up arms with increasing vigour to clear the western Mediterranean of Muslim pirates, and had carved out a dominion of their own in Sardinia; meanwhile, the Venetians had won what would become a unique position within the Byzantine Empire. Muslim domination of the Mediterranean could no longer be taken for granted, especially once the armies and navies of the First Crusade began to move.

4

'The Profit That God Shall Give',

1100–1200

I

In 1095, preaching at Clermont in central France, Pope Urban II set in motion a movement that would transform the political, religious and economic map of the Mediterranean and Europe. His theme was the shame heaped on Christendom by the oppression of Christians in the Muslim East, the defeat of Christian armies fighting the Turks and the scandal that the Church of the Holy Sepulchre in Jerusalem, the site of Christ's crucifixion and resurrection, should now be in Infidel hands.[1] What Pope Urban intended as a recruitment speech summoning southern French volunteers to go east and aid Byzantium against the Turks was understood as an appeal to the knighthood of Christendom to cease fighting one another (which they did in peril of their souls), and to direct their force against the Infidel, united in a holy pilgrimage, under arms, in the sure knowledge that those who died on the great journey would earn eternal salvation. Here was an opportunity to substitute for acts of penance imposed by the Church an act for which no one was better suited than the knightly class – warfare, but this time in the service of God. Only gradually did the concept of remission of all past sins for those who joined a crusading campaign become official doctrine. But popular understanding of what the pope had offered, in the name of Christ, leaped ahead of the more cautious formulations of the canon lawyers.

The principal route followed by the First Crusade bypassed the Mediterranean and took the army overland through the Balkans and Anatolia; many crusaders never saw more of the sea than the Bosphorus at Constantinople until, much reduced in numbers through war, disease

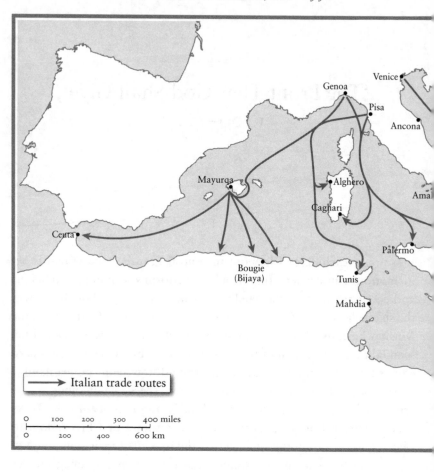

Italian trade routes

and exhaustion, they reached Syria.² And even in the East their target was not a maritime city but Jerusalem, so that its conquest in 1099 created an enclave cut off from the sea, a problem which, as will be seen, only Italian navies could resolve. Another force left from Apulia, where Robert Guiscard's son Bohemond brought together an army. The Byzantines wondered whether he was really planning to revive his father's schemes for the conquest of Byzantine territory, and so, when he reached Constantinople, he was pressed to acknowledge the emperor's authority, becoming his *lizios*, or liegeman, a western feudal term that was used because Bohemond was more likely to feel bound by oaths made according to his native customs than by promises made under Byzantine law. When in 1098 he established himself as prince of Antioch, a city

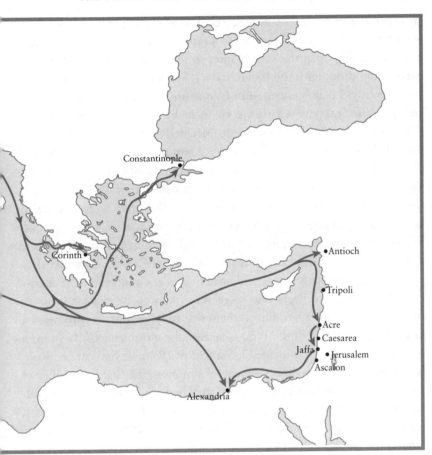

only recently lost by the Byzantines to the Turks, the imperial court made every effort to insist that his principality lay under Byzantine suzerainty. It was amazing that a vast rabble of men, often poorly armed, proved capable of seizing Antioch in 1098 and Jerusalem in 1099, though the Byzantines were more inclined to regard this as a typical barbarian stroke of fortune than as a victory masterminded by Christ. Seen from Constantinople, the outcome of the crusade was not entirely negative. Western knights had installed themselves in sensitive borderlands between Byzantine territory and lands over which the Seljuk Turks and the Fatimid caliphs were squabbling.

Bohemond's religious motives in joining the crusade should not be underestimated, but he was a pragmatist: he saw clearly that the crusader armies would be able to retain nothing without access to the Mediterranean, and without naval support from Christian fleets capable of keeping open the supply-lines to the West. He would therefore need to build ties with the Italian navies. He could count on the enthusiasm that had been generated in Genoa and Pisa by the news of Pope Urban's speech, conveyed to the Genoese by the bishops of Grenoble and of Orange. The citizens of Genoa decided that the time had come to bury their differences and to unite in a *compagna* under the direction of six consuls; the aim of the *compagna* was primarily to build and arm ships for the crusade. Historians have long argued that the Genoese saw the crusade as a business opportunity, and that they were hoping to secure trade privileges in whatever lands the crusaders conquered comparable to those the Venetians had recently acquired in the Byzantine Empire. Yet they could not foresee the outcome of the crusade; they were willing to suspend their trading activities and pump all their energy into the building of fleets that were very likely to be lost far away in battles and storms. What moved them was holy fervour. According to a Genoese participant in the First Crusade, the chronicler Caffaro, even before it, in 1083, a Genoese ship named the *Pomella* had carried Robert, count of Flanders, and Godfrey of Bouillon, the first Latin ruler of Jerusalem, to Alexandria; from there they had made their way with difficulty to the Holy Sepulchre, and had begun to dream of recovering it for Christendom.[3] The story was pure fancy, but it expresses the sense among the Genoese elite that their city was destined to play a major role in the war for the conquest of Jerusalem.

Twelve galleys and one smaller vessel set out from Genoa in July 1097. The crew consisted of about 1,200 men, a sizeable proportion of its male population, for the overall population of the city of Genoa may have been only 10,000.[4] Somehow the fleet knew where the crusaders were, and made contact off the northern coast of Syria. Antioch was still under siege, and the Genoese fleet stood off Port St Symeon, the outport of the city that had functioned as a gateway to the Mediterranean since the Bronze Age.[5] After the fall of Antioch in June 1098, Bohemond rewarded the Genoese crusaders with a church in Antioch, thirty houses nearby, a warehouse and a well, creating the nucleus of a merchant colony.[6] This grant was the first of many that the Genoese were to receive in the states created by the crusaders. In the early summer of 1099 members of a prominent Genoese family, the Embriachi, anchored off Jaffa, bringing aid to the crusader army besieging Jerusalem – they dismantled their own ships, carrying the wood from which they were built to Jerusalem for use in the construction of siege engines. And then in August 1100 twenty-six galleys and four supply ships set out from Genoa, carrying about 3,000 men.[7] They made contact with the northern French ruler of the newly established kingdom of Jerusalem, Baldwin I, and began the slow process of conquering a coastal strip, since it was essential to maintain supply-lines from western Europe to the embattled kingdom. They sacked the ancient coastal city of Caesarea in May 1101.[8] When the Genoese leaders divided up their loot, they gave each sailor two pounds of pepper, which demonstrates how rich in spices even a minor Levantine port was likely to be. They also carried away a large green bowl that had been hanging in the Great Mosque of Caesarea, convinced that it was the bowl used at the Last Supper and that it was made of emerald (a mistake rectified several centuries later when someone dropped it, and it was found to be made of glass).[9] Since the bowl is almost certainly a fine piece of Roman workmanship from the first century AD, their intuitions about its origins were not entirely wrong. It was carried in triumph to the cathedral in Genoa, where it is still displayed, attracting attention as one of several candidates for the title Holy Grail.[10]

The green bowl was, for the Genoese, probably as great a prize as any of their commercial privileges, all of which were celebrated in the city annals as signs of divine bounty. The Genoese made friends with the rulers of each of the crusader states (Jerusalem, Tripoli, Antioch) that needed help in gaining control of the seaports of Syria and Palestine. In 1104 their fortunes were further boosted by the capture of the port city of Acre, with an adequate harbour and good access into the interior. For most of the next two centuries, Acre functioned as the main base of the Italian merchants trading to the Holy Land. The Genoese produced documents to show that the rulers of Jerusalem promised them one-third of the cities they helped conquer all the way down the coast of Palestine, though not everyone is convinced all these documents were genuine; if not, they are still evidence for their vast ambitions.[11] They were even promised a third of 'Babylonia', the current European name for Cairo, for there were constant plans to invade Fatimid Egypt as well. To all this were added legal exemptions, extending from criminal law to property rights, that separated the Genoese from the day-to-day exercise of justice by the king's courts.[12] The Genoese insisted that they were permitted to erect an inscription in gilded letters recording their special privileges inside the Church of the Holy Sepulchre in Jerusalem. Whether or not this inscription was ever put in place, the demand for such a public record indicates how determined the Genoese were to maintain their special extra-territorial status in the kingdom of Jerusalem, which never developed a significant navy of its own.[13]

II

The Genoese had competitors. The Pisans were also enthusiastic about the crusade, sending out a fleet in 1099 under their archbishop, Daimbert. They were rewarded for their help in seizing Jaffa, in 1099, and were able to set up a trading base there.[14] The slowest of the three Italian cities to provide aid to the crusaders was Venice. The Venetians were aware that the Byzantine emperor did not view with equanimity the arrival in Constantinople of hordes of western crusaders, hungry and ill-equipped. They also did not want to place at risk the Venetian merchants trading in Fatimid Alexandria. Yet, seeing what bounty the crusade had brought the Genoese, they eventually sent up to 200 ships eastwards. The first stop was the small, decayed town of Myra in southern Asia Minor, where they dug for the bones of St Nicholas, the patron saint of sailors. The Venetians were jealous that in 1087 a group of sailors from Bari had managed to steal away from Myra with the bones of St Nicholas, around which they erected a magnificent basilica of white stone. Thereafter Bari, which was well placed as a departure point for pilgrims wishing to reach the Holy Land, had become an important pilgrim centre in its own right. The Venetians found enough human remains to build the Church of San Niccolò around them on the Venetian lido.[15] After Myra, they turned their attention back to the crusade. Their main task was to help the crusaders attack Haifa; its sack in 1100 was accompanied by horrific massacres of its Muslim and Jewish population.[16] This gave the crusaders control of the whole bay curving round from Mount Carmel to Acre. Most of the coast of Palestine was in their hands by 1110, though Ascalon was held by the Egyptians until as late as 1153.[17] Egyptian tenure of Ascalon actually served the interests of the Italians, since their navies were needed so long as enemy forces persisted along the coast of the Holy Land, and the greater the need for their fleets, the better the privileges they could hope to squeeze out of the royal court in Jerusalem.

The Italians could congratulate themselves. Trade obviously flourished in times of peace, but in war too there were excellent business opportunities: the seizure of booty and of slaves, the provision of armaments (often to both sides), pirate raids against enemy shipping. It was not, however, easy to balance support for the Latin kings of Jerusalem against other ties and commitments, especially in Egypt and Byzantium. The Byzantine emperor began to wonder whether he had given the Venetians too much. In 1111 the Pisans were granted a limited set of commercial privileges, and then in 1118 Alexios Komnenos' son and successor, John II, refused to renew the Golden Bull granted to Venice in 1082. He should not have been surprised when the Venetians looked elsewhere; they showed a new burst of enthusiasm for crusading, and responded to an appeal for naval help by sending a massive fleet to the Holy Land. In 1123, off Ascalon, much of the Fatimid navy was sent to the bottom of the sea.[18] This enabled the Venetians to blockade Tyre, which was still in Muslim hands but fell the next year. Here the Venetians established themselves in a highly privileged position, acquiring not merely one-third of the town but estates outside it, and the right to a church, a square, an oven and a street in every town they helped capture in future. They were to be exempt from all trade taxes; it was proclaimed that 'in every land of the king or his barons, each Venetian is to be as free as within Venice itself'.[19] Tyre became their major base along the Syro-Palestinian coast. This did not prevent occasional razzias by the Fatimid fleet, but the Egyptian navy now found that it had no bases where it could call in for supplies. On one occasion some Egyptian sailors who tried to land in the hope of taking on water were chased away by loyal bowmen of the Latin kingdom.[20] The Fatimids lost access to the forests of Lebanon, for millennia a vital resource of Levantine shipbuilders. Although the sea battle at Ascalon did not mark the destruction of the entire Fatimid navy, it did mark a turning-point: Muslim shipping was no longer able to challenge the supremacy of Christian fleets. Command of the eastern Mediterranean sea-lanes had fallen into the hands of the Pisans, Genoese and Venetians. Participation in the early crusades had brought these cities not just quarters in the cities of the Holy Land but domination over movement across vast swathes of the Mediterranean.

Finally, even the Byzantine emperor realized that he could not stand in the way of the Venetians. He reluctantly confirmed their privileges in 1126.[21] The Venetian presence stimulated the Byzantine economy.[22] Even if the Venetians paid no taxes to the imperial fisc, the Byzantine subjects with whom they conducted business did so, and in the long term revenue from commercial taxation rose rather than fell. But the emperors could not always see beyond their immediate fiscal concerns. The existence of a highly privileged group who paid no taxes aroused xenophobia.[23] In the 1140s Emperor Manuel I Komnenos renewed the attack on the Venetians, adopting different tactics: he noticed that the Italians had flooded into Constantinople, some becoming denizens of the city and integrating themselves into city life (the *bourgesioi*, or bourgeois), while others, who were more troublesome, had come mainly to trade overseas. He created an enclosed area next to the Golden Horn, taking away land from German and French merchants, so as to create a Venetian quarter and control the Venetian traders more easily.

III

The rise of the north Italians led to the eclipse of other groups of merchants who had successfully conducted business in the eleventh-century Mediterranean: the Amalfitans and the Genizah merchants. Amalfi lost favour at the Byzantine court, and its citizens based in Constantinople were even made to pay taxes to the Venetians. One obvious reason was that Amalfi could not supply what Venice offered: a large fleet able to defeat the navy of Robert Guiscard. Although Amalfi managed to remain largely independent of Norman rule until 1131, its status in Byzantine eyes was gravely compromised by its location so very close to the strongholds of the Norman conquerors of southern Italy – Salerno lies a short boat-ride away.[24] But Amalfi still counted. In 1127 Amalfi and Pisa entered into a treaty of friendship. But in 1135 the Pisans joined a German invasion of the newly established Norman kingdom in southern Italy and Sicily. Roger of Sicily permitted Amalfitan ships to leave port and attack any enemy vessels they could find – no doubt his new subjects dreamed of finding stray Pisan merchantmen piled high with expensive goods. While the Amalfitans were away, the Pisan navy entered the harbour of Amalfi and sacked the city, carrying away a great

booty; they attacked again in 1137.[25] Amalfi's maritime trade contracted into the waters of the Tyrrhenian Sea, including Palermo,
Messina and Sardinia, while its landward trade in southern Italy
developed healthily, so that very many inland towns, such as Benevento,
came to possess little nuclei of Amalfitans.[26] By 1400 Amalfi had become
a source of unexciting but basic goods such as wine, oil, lard, wool and
linen cloth, though it also became known for its fine paper.[27] Underneath these changes, there existed a striking continuity. The Amalfitans
had always understood that the sea was not their only source of a livelihood. They continued to cultivate vines on the steep hillsides of the
Sorrento peninsula, and did not simply see themselves as professional
merchants.[28]

Wider changes that were affecting the Mediterranean in the twelfth
century left Amalfi on the margins; it stood too far from the new centres
of business in northern Italy and across the Alps. The Genoese, Pisans
and Venetians could gain easy enough access to France and Germany,
not to mention the Lombard plain, and were able to forge links with the
great cloth cities far away in Flanders, so that selling fine Flemish woollen cloth to purchasers in Egypt became a regular source of profit to the
Genoese. Amalfi represented an older order of pedlar trade, in which
small numbers of merchants carried limited quantities of expensively
priced luxury goods from the centres of high civilization in the Islamic
world and in Byzantium to equally small numbers of wealthy princes
and prelates in western Europe. Henceforth, the elite of Amalfi, Ravello
and neighbouring towns used the knowledge of record-keeping and
accounting passed down by their forebears to enter the civil service of
the kingdom of Sicily, where several followed very successful careers.
This elite did not lose its taste for eastern motifs. The Rufolo family of
Ravello built a palace in the thirteenth century which borrowed from
Islamic architectural styles, and the cathedral of Amalfi, with its famous
'Cloister of Paradise', recalls elements of both Islamic and Byzantine
style.[29] The decision to borrow eastern motifs did not indicate particular
openness to other religions and cultures. As in Venice, exotic styles pro-
claimed wealth, prestige and family pride, as well as nostalgia for the
days when Amalfi (with Venice) dominated communications between
East and West.

The same period saw the eclipse of another group of traders and
travellers, the Genizah merchants. Around 1150 the stream of merchant

letters deposited in the Cairo Genizah began to dry up;[30] after 1200, non-Egyptian matters largely disappeared from it. That vast world, stretching from al-Andalus to Yemen and India, had now contracted to the Nile Valley and Delta. Political calamities included the rise of the Almohad sect in Morocco and Spain, which was intolerant of Judaism; among the Jewish refugees from the Almohad West was the philosopher and physician Moses Maimonides.[31] Yet the greatest difficulty faced by the Genizah merchants was the rise of the Italians. Venice and Genoa discouraged Jewish settlement – according to a Spanish Jewish traveller, there were only two Jews in Genoa around 1160, who had migrated from Ceuta in Morocco.[32] As the Italians gained greater control over communications across the Mediterranean, and as Muslim merchant shipping became more than ever exposed to Christian attack, the old sea routes became less attractive to the Genizah merchants. And, as Italian naval power grew, even the sea routes between Byzantium and Egypt, along which the Genizah Jews had travelled in the past, fell into the hands of Italian shipowners, who benefited from grants of privilege by both the Byzantine emperors and the Fatimid caliphs.

There was another important reason why the Jewish merchants lost influence. In the late twelfth century a consortium of Muslim merchants known as the Karimis emerged and took command of the routes running down the Red Sea towards Yemen and India, along which the Jews had been extremely active in the previous two centuries. These routes fed into the Mediterranean: eastern spices and perfumes arrived at Aydhab on the Red Sea coast of Egypt, were transported overland to Cairo, and then by water up the Nile to Alexandria. Following attempts in the 1180s by a maverick crusader lord, Reynaud de Châtillon, to launch a fleet in the Red Sea (in the hope of raiding Madina and Mecca), the Red Sea was closed to non-Muslim travellers. The Karimis continued to dominate business there until the early fifteenth century.[33] A grand partnership, mediated by the rulers of Egypt, joined the Italians and the Karimis and ensured the regular flow of pepper and other spices into the Mediterranean. Trading networks that had carried a single individual all the way from southern Spain to India were now fragmented in two: the Mediterranean sector was Christian, the Indian Ocean sector was Muslim.

The Fatimid rulers and their successors, the Ayyubids (of whom the most famous was the Kurdish warlord Saladin), became increasingly interested in the revenues they could raise from trade. This was not out of a mercantilist spirit, but because they saw the spice trade, in particular, as a source of funds to cover their war expenses. During twelve months in 1191–2 the so-called one-fifth tax (*khums*) raised 28,613 gold dinars from Christian merchants trading through the Nile ports. This means that exports through these ports reached well over 100,000 dinars even at a difficult time – Saladin had captured Jerusalem, the Third Crusade was under way and the Italian cities, as well as southern French and Catalan towns, were sending fleets to the Holy Land.[34] Despite the name of the tax, it was levied at a higher rate than one-fifth on spices such as caraway, cumin and coriander, for the Egyptian government was well aware how keen the western Europeans were to acquire these products. In the late twelfth century, an Arab customs official, al-Makhzumi, compiled a handbook on taxation in which he listed the goods that passed through Egyptian ports. He mentions a much wider range of products than the Genizah letters reveal: Damietta exported chickens, grain and alum, the last of which was a government monopoly in Egypt. Alum was required in increasing quantities by European textile producers, who used this dull grey powder as a fixative and cleansing agent.[35] Egypt was also a source of flax, heavily taxed by the government; emeralds, over which the government took increasing control; gold, looted from the tombs of the Pharaohs; and a much-prized drug, known in the West as *mommia* – powdered mummy. The Nile Delta ports received timber, which was in very short supply within Egypt; Alexandria acquired iron, coral, oil and saffron, all carried eastwards by Italian merchants.[36] Some of these commodities could be classified as war materials, and the papal court was becoming increasingly worried at the role of the north Italian fleets in supplying armaments to the Muslims while acting, or posing, as the main naval defence force of the Latin kingdom of Jerusalem. Arabic writers refer to a type of shield known as the *janawiyah*, that is, 'Genoa', suggesting that some at least of these shields were brought illicitly from Italy.[37]

Occasionally tensions boiled over and Italian merchants were arrested, but the Fatimids and Ayyubids could not risk undermining their finances. On one occasion, Pisan sailors attacked Muslim passengers on board a Pisan ship; they killed the men and enslaved the women and children, as well as stealing all the merchandise. In reprisal, the Egyptian government imprisoned the Pisan merchants who were in

Egypt. Soon after, in 1154–5, the Pisans sent an ambassador to Fatimid Egypt. Relations were mended and a promise of safe-conduct for merchants was obtained.[38] The Pisans were not alone in preferring Egypt to the Holy Land. Out of nearly 400 Venetian trade contracts that have survived from before 1171, it is no surprise that over half concern trade in Constantinople, but seventy-one concern Egypt, rather more than concern trade with the Latin kingdom of Jerusalem.[39] These are only accidental survivals from a mass of documents mostly now lost, but they suggest how strong was the lure of the East.

North-west Africa also lured Italian merchants when access to Constantinople, Alexandria, Acre or Palermo was obstructed by quarrels with their rulers. The Pisans and Genoese visited the ports of the Maghrib to acquire leather, wool, fine ceramics and, from Morocco, increasing quantities of grain. Particularly important was the supply of gold, in the form of gold dust, that reached the towns of the Maghrib along the caravan routes that stretched across the Sahara.[40] In the middle of the twelfth century these lands fell under the rule of the uncompromising Almohad sect of Islam. Almohad Islam had its own Berber caliph, and was viewed by Sunni Muslims (such as the Almoravids they largely replaced) as rank heresy. Its principal feature was an attempt to return to what was seen as a pure and unadulterated Islam, whose fundamental principle was the absolute Oneness of God – even to name his attributes, such as mercy, was to misunderstand God's true being. Although hostile to their Jewish and Christian minorities, the Almohad caliphs in Spain and North Africa welcomed foreign merchants, whom they saw as a source of income. In 1161 the Genoese sent an embassy to the Almohad caliph in Morocco; a fifteen-year peace was agreed, and the Genoese were assured that they could travel throughout the Almohad territories with their goods, free of molestation. In 1182 Ceuta took 29 per cent of recorded Genoese trade, a little ahead of Norman Sicily, but, if one includes Bougie and Tunis, North Africa dominated the trade of Genoa, with nearly 37 per cent.[41]

The Genoese acquired a fonduk – a warehouse and headquarters with living quarters – in Tunis, Bougie, Mahdia and other cities along the coast of North Africa. The remaining fonduk buildings in Tunis are of the seventeenth century and belonged to the Italian, German, Austrian and French merchants.[42] The fonduks of the Italians and Catalans could expand into a whole merchant quarter. The acts of the Genoese notary

Pietro Battifoglio, of 1289, portray a large and vibrant Genoese community in Tunis, consisting of merchants, soldiers, priests and fallen women, who took great pride in their tavern filled with wine casks, from which even the Almohad ruler was happy to draw taxes.

IV

Using the trade contracts, the life and career of several successful Genoese and Venetian merchants can be reconstructed. At the top of the social ladder stood the great patrician families such as the della Volta of Genoa, whose members often held office as consul, and who directed the foreign policy of the republic – whether to make peace or war with Norman Sicily, Byzantium, the Muslims of Spain, and so on. Since they were also active investors in overseas trade, they operated at a great advantage, able to negotiate political treaties that brought commercial dividends they were keen to exploit.[43] The great Genoese families were grouped together in tight clans, and the common interest of the clan overrode the immediate interest of the individual.[44] The price that Genoa paid was acute factional strife, as rival clans tried to gain mastery of the consulate and other offices. At the other extreme the Venetian patriciate generally managed to keep strife in check, by accepting the authority of the doge as first among equals; once again great families such as the Ziani, Tiepolo and Dandolo dominated both high office and trade to the really profitable destinations, such as Constantinople and Alexandria. Their success had a knock-on effect on the fortunes of an urban upper middle class that included many very successful merchants. Not just ancestry differentiated the great patrician houses from the plebeian merchants; the patricians could also call on much more diverse assets, so that if trade dried up during a period of warfare they still had revenues from urban and rural property or tax farms. Their position was less fragile than that of the ordinary merchants; they had greater staying-power. So, while the commercial revolution made many fortunes, it also further enriched the elite and strengthened rather than weakened their commanding position in the great maritime cities of twelfth-century Italy.

Two 'new men' are well documented. Romano Mairano, from Venice, started in a small way during the 1140s with trading expeditions into Greece, operating mainly from the Venetian colony in Constantin-ople.[45] He then turned to more ambitious destinations, including Alexandria and the Holy Land. His career illustrates how the Venetians had taken charge of the sea routes linking Byzantium to the Islamic lands. They were well ensconced in internal Byzantine trade too, main-taining contact between Constantinople and the lesser Greek cities.[46] By 1158 Romano prospered greatly, supplying 50,000 pounds of iron to the Knights Templars in the Holy Land. He was not simply a merchant; he became a prominent shipowner. His star still seemed to be rising when the Byzantine emperor turned against the Venetians, whom Manuel I suspected of showing sympathy for his foe the king of Sicily, and who were, in any case, increasingly the focus of Greek resentment at the powerful position they occupied (or were imagined to occupy) in the Byzantine economy. Aware of this trend, Mairano began to build up his business in Venice during the late 1160s. After his first wife died, he remarried and found himself richer thanks to his new wife's fat dowry. Working with Sebastiano Ziani, a future doge, he built the largest ship in the Venetian merchant fleet, the *Totus Mundus* or (in Greek) the *Kosmos*, which he sailed to Constantinople. Relations with the emperor seemed to be improving, and Manuel I even issued a decree in which he declared he would hang anyone who molested the Venetians. But his aim was to create a false sense of security, and in March 1171 the emperor unleashed a *Kristallnacht* against the Venetians, knowing he could count on public support. Thousands of Venetians were arrested within the confines of their quarter, hundreds were killed and their property was seized. Those who could escaped to the wharves, where the *Kosmos* stood ready to sail, protected against flaming arrows and catapult stones by a covering of animal hides soaked in vinegar. The *Kosmos* managed to reach Acre, carrying news of the disaster, but Romano Mairano had lost all his other assets, and was probably deeply in debt after building his great ship. Two years later his vessel reap-peared off Ancona, which had proclaimed its allegiance to Manuel Komnenos and was under siege from Manuel's rival, the German emperor Frederick Barbarossa. Not surprisingly the Venetians now pre-ferred Barbarossa to Manuel, quite apart from their concern that Ancona was becoming a commercial rival within the Adriatic. They obligingly helped bombard Ancona, though the city held out against the Germans.[47]

By now, Mairano was about fifty years old, and had to rebuild his business from scratch. He could only do this by turning once again to the patrician Ziani family; the late doge's son Pietro invested £1,000 of Venetian money in a voyage Romano was to make to Alexandria. Romano carried with him a large cargo of timber, paying no attention to papal condemnation of the trade in war materials. While relations between Venice and Constantinople were so bad, he sent ships to North Africa, Egypt and the kingdom of Jerusalem, trading in pepper and alum. He was ready to return to Constantinople when a new emperor readmitted the Venetians on excellent terms in 1187–9. Even in old age Romano continued to invest in trade with Egypt and Apulia, though funds ran low again in 1201, when he borrowed money from his cousin; he died not long after.[48] It was, then, a career marked by ups and downs, as notable for its successes as for the disastrous collapse of his business and his dramatic escape in mid-career.

Another uneven career was that of Solomon of Salerno. Though he came from southern Italy he traded from Genoa, where, like Mairano, he was close to the patrician families.[49] He also had personal ties to the king of Sicily, whose faithful subject, or *fidelis*, he was said to be. He showed he wanted to be counted as Genoese when he bought some land just outside the city, and he tried to forge a marriage alliance between his daughter and one of the patrician families; he had turned his back on Salerno. He recognized that Salerno, Amalfi and neighbouring towns had been greatly overtaken by the more aggressive trading cities of Genoa, Pisa and Venice, and it was in Genoa that he made his fortune. He brought with him from Salerno his wife Eliadar, who was another keen merchant, for there was nothing to prevent women in Genoa from investing money in trading ventures. Solomon and Eliadar made a formidable pair, casting their eyes over the entire Mediterranean. Like Romano Mairano, Solomon was willing to travel to its furthest corners in pursuit of wealth. Golden opportunities beckoned in 1156, in Egypt, Sicily and the West. In summer of that year he decided to capitalize on the more open mood of the Fatimids. He agreed to travel out to Alexandria on behalf of a team of investors, and then to follow the Nile down to Cairo, where he would purchase oriental spices including lac, a resin that could be used as a varnish or dyestuff, and brazilwood, the source of a red dye. Solomon also had plenty of interests that pulled him in other directions. The same year he was trying to recover 2⅔ pounds of Sicilian gold coinage, a formidable sum at the time, from a Genoese who had absconded with the money in Sicily while Genoese ambassadors were negotiating a treaty with its king.[50] He was away nearly two years in the East, leaving Eliadar at home to manage a triangular trade network linking Genoa, Fréjus and Palermo.

After his return from the East, Solomon looked westwards, trading with Majorca and Spain as well as Sicily and his old favourite, Egypt, where he invested very substantial amounts of money. One document describes a roundabout voyage he commissioned that was typical of the more ambitious ventures of the time: 'to Spain, then to Sicily or Provence or Genoa, from Provence to Genoa or Sicily, or if he wishes from Sicily to Romania [the Byzantine Empire] and then to Genoa, or from Sicily to Genoa'.[51] Great Genoese patricians eagerly invested money in Solomon's expedition to Egypt, ignoring a clause in the documents that implied the ship might be sold in Egypt. For not merely did the Italians send timber to the shipyards of Alexandria, they sent whole ships, ready for use in the Fatimid fleet. Solomon was at the peak of his success; although he was an outsider, his daughter Alda was betrothed to the son of a powerful member of the Mallone clan. Solomon had his own notary to record his business, and documents grandly speak of the 'court of Solomon', suggesting that he lived in a lavish style. Like Romano Mairano, however, he lay at the mercy of political changes over which he had no control. Having made friends with the king of Sicily in 1156, Genoa was forced in 1162 to abandon what had been a very lucrative alliance that gave access to vast amounts of wheat and cotton; the German emperor Frederick Barbarossa was breathing down the necks of the Genoese, and they felt obliged to join his army of invasion directed against Sicily. Ansaldo Mallone broke off the advantageous engagement between his son and Solomon's daughter. Suddenly the business empire of Solomon and Eliadar seemed very fragile.

However, some contact with Sicily was still possible. In September 1162, a few months after the Genoese abandoned Sicily for Germany, Solomon received the emissaries of an eminent Sicilian Muslim, ibn Hammud, the leader of the Muslim community in Sicily, who advanced him funds against the security of an ermine mantle, silver cups and other fine goods. A Sicilian Arab writer eloquently said of ibn Hammud: 'he does not suffer his coin to rust'. He was very wealthy: taking advantage of accusations that he was disloyal, the king of Sicily fined him

250 pounds of gold, an enormous fortune.[52] Contacts such as these enabled Solomon to stay in business, but conditions were bleak for someone with his interests and expertise. Quarrels between Genoa and the king of Jerusalem inhibited trade to the Holy Land, and access to the eastern Mediterranean was rendered more difficult by the breach with the king of Sicily, whose fleets controlled the passages between the western and the eastern Mediterranean. Like other Genoese merchants, Solomon and his wife now turned from the eastern to the western Mediterranean, trading with the important port of Bougie in what is now Algeria. Solomon must have died some time around 1170. His ambition of anchoring himself to the Genoese patriciate by a marriage alliance had been frustrated by political events. Until he and his heirs entered the ranks of the patriciate, his position would always be fragile. The land he acquired outside Genoa was worth only £108 of Genoese silver, and his wealth was mainly built on cash, loans, investments and speculations, whereas the wealth of the city aristocracy was firmly rooted in urban and rural property. It was this that gave them the staying-power that men such as Solomon of Salerno and Romano Mairano lacked. And yet it was by working together that the patricians and the merchants created the commercial revolution that was taking place.

5

Ways across the Sea, 1160–1185

I

There are no diaries or log-books of sea captains from the twelfth century, but there are vivid accounts of crossing the Mediterranean written by Jewish and Muslim pilgrims journeying from Spain to the East. Benjamin of Tudela was a rabbi from a town in Navarre, and he set out on his travels around 1160.[1] The aim of his diary was to describe the lands of the Mediterranean, large areas of Europe, and Asia as far as China, in Hebrew for a Jewish audience, and he carefully noted the number of Jews in each town he visited. His book reports genuine travels across the Mediterranean, through Constantinople and down the coast of Syria, though his descriptions of more remote areas beyond the Mediterranean are clearly based on report and rumour, which became more fantastic the further his imagination ventured. He evidently did go to Jerusalem, though, and expressed his wonderment at the supposed tomb of King David on Mount Zion. As Christian passions about the Holy Land became more intense, the attention of Jewish pilgrims was also directed there, under the influence of the crusaders whom they scorned.[2] Benjamin's route took him down from Navarre through the kingdom of Aragon and along the river Ebro to Tarragona, where the massive ancient fortifications built by 'giants and Greeks' impressed him.[3] From there he moved to Barcelona, 'a small city and beautiful', full of wise rabbis and of merchants from every land, including Greece, Pisa, Genoa, Sicily, Alexandria, the Holy Land and Africa. Benjamin provides precious and precocious evidence that Barcelona was beginning to develop contacts across the Mediterranean.[4] Another place that attracted merchants from all over the world, even, he says, from England, was

Montpellier; 'people of all nations are found there doing business through the medium of the Genoese and Pisans'.[5]

It took four days to reach Genoa by sea from Marseilles.[6] Genoa, he wrote, 'is surrounded by a wall, and the inhabitants are not governed by any king, but by judges whom they appoint at their pleasure'. He also insisted that 'they have command of the sea'. He was thinking here of piracy no less than trade, for he mentioned their raids on Muslim and Christian lands (including Byzantium), and was impressed by the booty they brought back. Two days' journey away lay Pisa, but the Genoese were constantly at war with the Pisans, who, he claimed, had 'ten thousand' towers in their city from which they fought one another.[7] He travelled to Bari, but found it desolate, following its destruction by King William I in 1156 (of which more later).[8] He crossed to Corfu, which he said was also under Sicilian rule at this time, and then, full of energy, he tackled overland routes by way of Thebes to Constantinople, returning to the Mediterranean only when he reached Gallipoli. From there he hopped across the islands of the Aegean, and then over to Cyprus, where he was shocked by the behaviour of some 'heretical Jews called *Epikursin* [Epicureans], whom the Israelites have excommunicated in all places', for their Sabbath day excluded Friday night but included Saturday night.[9] Their presence is a reminder that within the eastern Mediterranean a myriad of small sects still flourished – as Benjamin travelled down the coast of Lebanon he encountered a more dangerous sect, the Ismaili Assassins, but he was able to avoid them and to reach Gibellet, one of the Genoese bases in the Levant, governed, as he rightly observed, by a member of the noble Embriaco family. He was fascinated by the discovery there of an ancient temple, with a statue seated on a throne and two female statuettes at each side. This was evidence of ancient pagan practices with which the ancient Israelites had contended, but there were modern pagans too, he believed: setting off again, he had to pass the territory of the Druze warriors, whom he described as lawless pagans, supposedly practising incest and swapping wives among themselves.[10]

Benjamin reached Egypt at some stage in his travels, and was very impressed by the harbour facilities at Alexandria: there was the lighthouse, which could be seen from 100 miles away, and there were the merchants from all over the world: 'from all the Christian kingdoms', including Venice, Tuscany, Amalfi, Sicily, from Greece, Germany, France

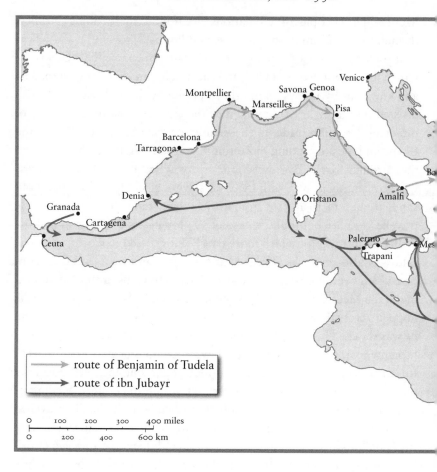

route of Benjamin of Tudela
route of ibn Jubayr

and England, from Spain and Provence, and from many Muslim lands, such as al-Andalus and the Maghrib.[11] 'Merchants of India bring thither all kinds of spices, and the merchants of Edom [Christendom] buy from them.' Moreover, 'each nation has an inn of its own'.[12] Benjamin travelled back by way of Sicily, and his description of the glories of the Sicilian court will be mentioned in the next chapter.

II

Benjamin might be described nowadays as an antiquarian. He was fascinated by ancient buildings in Rome, Constantinople and Jerusalem.

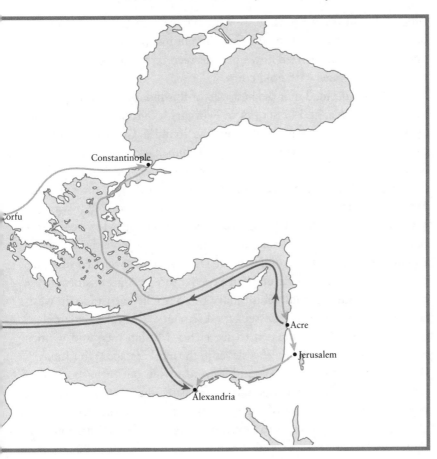

His compulsion to list every Jewish community he encountered was matched by an eye for detail and a fascination with the many peoples he encountered. When writing about the Holy Land he not surprisingly turned himself into a guide to the Jewish shrines and graves of the rabbis in Jerusalem, Hebron and Tiberias, and left the Christian holy places out of the account. His private purpose in travelling was most likely to visit the Holy Land as a pilgrim, and yet his other interests kept surfacing. Much the same is true of Muhammad ibn Ahmad ibn Jubayr, who wrote about twenty-five years later.[13] He was born in 1145 in Valencia, but became the secretary to the governor of Granada, who was the son of the Almohad caliph, 'Abd al-Mu'min. Notwithstanding his excellent Almohad credentials, the governor liked a tipple, and insisted that ibn

Jubayr should try some wine. Ibn Jubayr was mortally afraid of disobeying his master, and for the first time in his life drank alcohol. But once the governor realized how upset his secretary had become, he filled the cup seven times with gold coins.

Ibn Jubayr decided that the best use for this money was to pay for his journey to Mecca, and he set out in February 1183; he was away from Spain for over two years.[14] In Ceuta he found a Genoese ship ready to sail to Alexandria. The first leg took him back along the coast of al-Andalus, as far as Denia, from where the boat struck out to Ibiza, Majorca and Minorca, reaching Sardinia a fortnight after leaving Morocco: 'it had been a crossing remarkable for its speed'.[15] It was also a voyage across political boundaries: from Almohad Morocco to the Balearics, ruled by the inveterate enemies of the Almohads, the Sunni Almoravids, and up to Sardinia, where Pisan sea power reigned supreme. Yet it was not man but nature that posed a threat. A great storm arose off Sardinia, but eventually ibn Jubayr's ship reached Oristano, in western Sardinia, where some passengers disembarked to take on supplies; one, a Muslim, was distressed to see eighty Muslim men and women who had been put up for sale as slaves in the marketplace.[16] Ibn Jubayr's ship took advantage of a favourable wind to slip out of harbour. This was a mistake. Another tempest arose, so fierce that the ship could not use its mainsails, and one of these was then ripped by the strong wind, along with one of the spars to which the sails were fixed. 'Christian sea-captains who were present, and Muslims who had gone through journeys and storms at sea, all agreed that they had never in their lives seen such a tempest. The description of it diminishes the reality.'[17] Yet even in this foul weather they reached their target, Sicily, for the ship was following what is often called 'the route of the islands', a westward route that took best advantage of the currents and winds.[18] Had they lasted, the north-westerly winds of the winter would have favoured their journey, but the weather in early spring was unpredictable as the prevailing winds changed direction.[19] They skirted Sicily, observing Etna, and headed for Crete, where they arrived at night about four weeks after setting out from Ceuta. From there they jumped across the Libyan Sea to North Africa, and on 29 March the lighthouse of Alexandria came into distant view. The whole journey took thirty days, which was not excessive compared to journeys recorded in the Genizah letters.[20]

There were tribulations on land as well as on the high sea. When they arrived in Alexandria customs officials boarded, and personal details of each passenger were written down, as well as a list of all the cargo. The Muslims were made to pay the charitable tax known as the *zakat*, even if all they possessed was the provisions they needed for the *hajj*. Another eminent passenger, Ahmad ibn Hassan, who was a physician from Granada, was led under guard to the government offices, to be interviewed about what was happening in the West, and to answer questions about the goods being carried on board. This questioning of important passengers was standard practice in the Mediterranean ports – ibn Jubayr submitted to even closer questioning when he arrived in Palermo on his way back to Spain.[21] Then the passengers were subjected to humiliating searches by excessively thorough customs officers:

> The Customs House was packed to choking. All their goods, great and small, were searched and confusedly thrown together, while hands were thrust into their waistbands in search of what might be within. The owners were then put to oath whether they had anything else that had not been discovered. During all this, because of the confusion of hands and the excessive throng, many possessions disappeared.[22]

If only, ibn Jubayr complained to himself, this had been brought to the attention of the just and merciful sultan Saladin: he would surely put a stop to such behaviour.

Yet ibn Jubayr greatly admired Alexandria. Today, very little remains above ground of either the ancient or the medieval city. Even in ibn Jubayr's time, underground Alexandria was more impressive than Alexandria above ground: 'the buildings below the ground are like those above it and are even finer and stronger', with wells and water-courses that ran below the houses and alleys of the city. In the streets, he observed great columns 'that climb up and choke the skies, and whose purpose and the reason for whose erection none can tell'; he was told that they were used by philosophers of past times, but was convinced that they were part of an astronomical observatory. Memories of the Library of Alexandria had turned into fables. He was enormously impressed by the lighthouse; there was a mosque on its top level, where he went to pray. He heard that there were up to 12,000 mosques – in other words, a very great many – whose imams received their salary from the state. As befitted a great city of the Islamic world, it was full of madrasas, hospices and bath-houses; the government supervised a scheme under which the sick were visited at home and were then reported to physicians, who were answerable for their care. Two thousand loaves of bread were distributed each day to travellers. When public funds were inadequate for this, Saladin's own funds covered the cost.[23] Taxes were very low, though the Jews and Christians had to pay the standard *dhimmi* taxes. Ibn Jubayr was strangely fulsome in praise of the Ayyubid sultan, whose Sunni Islam was some way removed from Almohad beliefs, and whose relations with the Almohads were not easy.

From Alexandria ibn Jubayr made his way down the Nile to the Red Sea and Mecca, and he returned to the Mediterranean only in September 1184, coming down to the coast from Damascus and over the Golan Heights to Acre in the Latin kingdom of Jerusalem. He passed through lands inhabited by Muslims but owned by Franks: Tibnin, he says, 'belongs to the sow known as queen who is the mother of the pig who is lord of Acre', that is, to the Queen Mother of the Latin kingdom of Jerusalem.[24] Firmly resolved to resist temptation, ibn Jubayr and his fellow-pilgrims entered Acre on 18 September, and he expressed the fervent hope that Allah would destroy the city. Here too visitors were sent to the Customs House, whose great courtyard offered space in which to accommodate newly arrived caravans; there were stone benches at which Christian clerks sat, and they spoke and wrote in Arabic, dipping their pens in inkstands made of ebony and gold. They worked for a tax-farmer who paid the king a vast sum of money for the concession of running the Customs House. This was standard practice in the medieval Mediterranean, and the building ibn Jubayr visited was almost certainly the Khan al-'Umdan, a substantial arcaded structure arranged around a court that still stands close to the harbour, though largely rebuilt in the Turkish period.[25] There was space on the upper floors in which to store goods once they had been checked, but the customs officers were thorough, and even inspected the luggage of those who said they were not carrying any merchandise; by contrast with Alexandria, 'all this was done with civility and respect, and without harshness and unfairness'.[26]

Even in 1184 Acre was a great port, and it would become greater still following a shower of new privileges for Italian and other European merchants from 1190 onwards. These privileges were offered as a reward for sending naval help during the great emergency that followed the capture of Jerusalem and of most of the crusader kingdom by Saladin in 1187. The Pisans were able to move their business from Jaffa, which was too far to the south to bring them the full benefits of the Levant trade, northwards to Acre, with its easy links to Damascus and the interior. It was not that Acre possessed a particularly good harbour. Ships anchored at the entrance to the harbour, which (as in most Mediterranean ports) could be closed off by a chain, and goods had to be ferried across from the shore: it 'cannot take the large ships, which must anchor outside, small ships only being able to enter'. When the weather was bad ships would need to be beached. Good harbours were not a prerequisite when medieval merchants chose their trading station – witness also Barcelona, Pisa and Messina. Yet ibn Jubayr took the view that 'in its greatness it resembles Constantinople', referring not to the size of Acre but to the way in which Muslim and Christian merchants converged there, arriving by ship and caravan, so that 'its roads and streets are choked by the press of men, and it is hard to put foot to ground'. As ever, ibn Jubayr was quick to mask his admiration for what he saw with imprecations: 'unbelief and unpiousness there burn fiercely, and pigs and crosses abound', the pigs being impure Christians as well as unclean animals. 'It stinks and is filthy, being full of refuse and excrement.'[27] Naturally, he deplored the conversion of mosques into churches by the crusaders, but he did note that within the former Friday Mosque there was a corner Muslims were permitted to use. For the relationship between the Frankish settlers and the local population was less tense than either the Almohad ibn Jubayr or newly arrived crusaders may have wished. These new crusaders were perplexed by the easy attitudes they found. The elderly sheikh of Shayzar in northern Syria, Usamah ibn Munqidh (1095–1188), left a memoir of his times that reveals friendly relationships across the Christian–Muslim divide. He came to know well a Frankish knight of whom he wrote, 'he was of my intimate fellowship and kept such constant company with me that he began to call me "my brother"'.[28] The Franks of the kingdom of Jerusalem borrowed little from Muslim culture, by comparison with the extensive cultural contacts taking place at this time in Spain and Sicily, and yet a practical *convivencia* was achieved. Ibn Jubayr was very uneasy at the presence of Muslims in this Christian kingdom. 'There can,' he wrote, 'be no excuse in the eyes of God for a Muslim to stay in any infidel country save when passing through it, while the way lies clear in Muslim lands.'[29]

Still, Christian shipping was regarded as safest and most reliable, and for his return to the west ibn Jubayr chose a ship under the command of a Genoese sailor 'who was perspicacious in his art and skilled in the duties of a sea-captain'. The aim was to catch the east wind that blew for about a fortnight in October, because for the rest of the year, apart from mid-April to late May, the prevailing winds came from the west. On 6 October 1184 ibn Jubayr and other Muslims embarked alongside 2,000 Christian pilgrims who had arrived from Jerusalem, though his estimate of numbers sounds impossibly high for one ship. Christians and Muslims shared the space on board, but they kept out of one another's way: 'the Muslims secured places apart from the Franks', and ibn Jubayr expressed the hope that God would soon relieve the Muslims of their company. He and the other Muslims stowed their goods, and, while the ship awaited a favourable wind, they went every night on land, to sleep in greater comfort. The decision to do this almost resulted in disaster. On 18 October the weather did not seem fair enough for the vessel to depart, and ibn Jubayr was still in his bed when the ship set sail. Desperate to catch up with it, he and his friends hired a large boat with four oars and set off in pursuit of the ship, which, after all, contained their belongings, and on which they had paid for their passage. It was a dangerous journey through choppy waters, but by the evening they had caught up with the Genoese ship. They had five days of suitable winds, making good progress until a west wind began to blow; the captain tacked back and forth to avoid its worst effects, but the full force of the wind fell on the ship on 27 October, and a spar with sails attached broke off and collapsed into the sea, though the sailors managed to make a new one.[30] When the wind dropped, the sea was like 'a palace made smooth with glass', words ibn Jubayr quoted from the Koran.[31] At nightfall on 1 November the Christians celebrated the Feast of All Saints; all of them, old and young, male and female, carried a lighted candle, and listened to prayers and sermons: 'the whole ship, from top to bottom, was luminous with kindled lamps.'[32] Once again, ibn Jubayr was clearly impressed, but as usual did not want to admit this.

Ibn Jubayr's diary provides an unrivalled account of shipboard life at this period. He describes how Muslims and Christians who died at sea were buried in the time-honoured fashion of being dropped overboard. Under Genoese maritime law the captain acquired the goods of those who had died at sea: 'there is no way for the true heir of the dead to gain his inheritance, and at this we were much astonished'.[33] The ship made no stops for revictualling, and many of the pilgrims of both faiths found themselves short of supplies after several days. Yet, he insists, there was plenty of fresh food available to buy on board, and 'in this ship they were as if in a city filled with all commodities'. There was bread, water, fruit (including watermelons, figs, quinces and pomegranates), nuts, chickpeas, beans, cheese, fish, and much else besides; well-practised Genoese sailors evidently knew that they had a captive market for any extra supplies they could load. Blown towards an island under Byzantine control, the passengers obtained meat and bread from the inhabitants. More storms accompanied the ship on its way past Crete, and the passengers began to fear that they would have to winter on one of the Greek islands or somewhere on the African coast, providing they even survived; in fact they were simply blown back towards Crete. Ibn Jubayr was moved to cite some verses from an Arab poet beginning: 'the sea is bitter of taste, intractable'.[34] Having noted that there was a period in the autumn when safe passage was possible from east to west, ibn Jubayr now opined that:

> all modes of travel have their proper season, and travel by sea should be at the propitious time and the recognised period. There should not be a reckless venturing forth in the months of winter as we did. First and last the matter is in the hands of God.[35]

His pessimism was unwarranted. Before long, five more ships coming from Alexandria hove into view; this little flotilla entered the harbour of one of the Ionian isles and took on meat, oil and overbaked black bread made of wheat and barley, yet 'people rushed for it, despite its dearness – and indeed there was nothing cheap for sale – and thanked God for what he had granted'.[36]

When the boats left harbour, November was drawing to a close; travelling became still more difficult as winter set in. Off southern Italy 'the swollen waves beat incessantly upon us, their shocks making the heart leap'. But they made landfall in Calabria, where many of the Christians decided that they had had enough, for in addition to the storms they were all now smitten by hunger. Ibn Jubayr and his friends were living off little more than a pound of moistened ship's biscuit each day. Those who landed sold any food they still possessed to those who remained on board, and the Muslims were prepared to pay a single silver *dirham* for a mere biscuit.[37] Whatever relief they felt at arriving close to Sicily soon dissipated. The Straits of Messina were like boiling water, as the sea was forced between the mainland and Sicily. Strong winds propelled the ship towards the shore close to Messina, and one of the sails was stuck, so that it could not be lowered; the ship careered forward towards shallow water with the wind behind it, and its keel struck the seabed and became stuck. A rudder broke; the anchors were useless; all those on board, Muslim and Christian, submitted themselves to the will of God. Some passengers of high status were taken off on a longboat, but this was smashed as it tried to return from the shore. Small boats came out to aid the stranded passengers, though not with the best motives: their owners demanded a high price for the privilege of being rescued. News of the shipwreck reached the king of Sicily, who had recently arrived in Messina to supervise the building of his war fleet, and he came to watch. Displeased at the behaviour of the boatmen, he ordered that 100 *tarí* (small gold coins) should be dispensed to them so that they would bring to shore a number of Muslims who were too poor to pay what they were demanding. Ibn Jubayr marvelled at God's prescience in bringing the king to Messina, 'which proved a saving mercy to us'.[38] King William had truly saved those who were still on board, because the day after the ship was grounded it broke up.

Despite his terrifying experience, ibn Jubayr was struck by how accessible the port of Messina was. Ships could approach right up to the shore, and there was no need for lighters to transport passengers and goods to shore – all that was needed was a plank. The ships were 'ranged along the quay like horses lined at their pickets or in their stables'.[39] In order to reach Andalucía, however, he had to travel across the island to Trapani, where he looked for a Genoese ship bound for Spain. Normally this would have been no problem, but the king had imposed an embargo on all sailings: 'it seems that he is preparing a fleet, and no ships may sail until his fleet has left. May God frustrate his designs, and may he not achieve his ends!' He began to realize that the destination of this fleet was the Byzantine Empire, for everyone in Sicily was talking about the young man whom King William kept at his court and whom he intended to set on the Byzantine throne, in a reprise of Robert Guiscard's plans a century earlier.[40] The embargo was a nuisance, but it was always possible to influence the king's officials, using time-honoured ways. Ibn Jubayr managed to find a place on one of three vessels that were travelling together to the west, and the Genoese owners bribed the royal officer, who turned a blind eye to their departure. The ships departed on 14 March 1185. Passing through the Egadian isles to the west of Sicily, they stopped in the little port of Favignana, where they crossed the path of the ship of Marco the Genoese bringing North African pilgrims from Alexandria, people ibn Jubayr had met months ago in Mecca itself. Old friends were reunited and they all feasted together. Four ships now set out for Spain, but the wind seemed to be playing games with them, as they were blown to Sardinia, then southwards, and eventually made headway back past Sardinia to Ibiza, Denia and Cartagena, where ibn Jubayr set foot on Spanish soil once again, finally reaching his home in Granada on 25 April 1185. He concluded his narrative with the weary words of an Arab poet, 'she threw away her staff and there she stayed, as does the traveller at his journey's end'.[41]

Ibn Jubayr was deeply unfortunate with the weather, and the shipwreck off Messina was not a daily calamity. He no doubt exaggerated the dangers he had faced and the numbers and travails of those on board. Yet in many respects his voyage was probably quite typical of the times, notably the use of Genoese ships by both Muslim and Christian pilgrims. He writes about Genoese captains who 'ruled' their ships, but these large ships would not usually be owned by their captain. Genoese investors bought shares, often as little as one sixty-fourth part, so that ownership of trading vessels was spread widely. An active investor would spread the risk and buy shares in several vessels. The word used for these shares was *loca*, 'places', and they could be traded and inherited rather like modern equities.[42] There was no fixed price, since each ship was different, as was the number of shares into which it was divided; shares could often be bought for around £30 of Genoese money, which was the sort of sum a middle-class Genoese might receive in an inheritance and decide to invest for profit. Shareholders included a small number of women; very many shareholders were involved in the government of Genoa, including members of the greatest families of that city such as the della Volta and the Embriachi. Holding these shares would generate revenue from the fees paid by passengers and from the rental of storage space by merchants. The total value of the shares might be as high as £2,480, an example from 1192, or as low as £90, which no doubt represented a ship nearing the end of its life or in need of extensive repair.[43]

There were two main categories of vessel. Light galleys were used in warfare and for sending ambassadors to foreign courts, but, as in antiquity, they were ill-adapted to choppy waters and had generally to sail in sight of land, using their oars as ancillary power when winds were light or when they manoeuvred into port. The galleys had a mast with a single lateen sail, and a beak or spur rather than a ram at the prow. They were manned by between twenty and eighty oarsmen, who were free citizens. Rather than sharing one massive oar, as was common from the sixteenth century onwards, the oarsmen sat two to a bench, each manipulating an oar of a different length, a system that became known in Venice as rowing *alla sensile*.[44] Their virtue was their speed, for they easily overtook the round ships. Many galleys were privately owned, but were requisitioned by the Commune in time of war, presumably with ample compensation.[45] The Genoese documents mention tubby sailing ships, simply known by the Latin word for ship, *navis*, far more often than they mention galleys, and they do not say much about smaller boats called by names such as *barca*, because these boats went on short journeys along the coast or across to Corsica and Sardinia on which few goods were carried and in which little money was invested.[46] Large *naves* could reach 24 metres in length and 7.5 metres in width. By the early thirteenth century they might carry two or even three masts, lateen rigged, though ibn Jubayr makes it plain that they would adjust to square rigging when the winds called for this. After 1200 these ships began to be built higher, with two or even three decks, but the lower decks were very cramped, and the aim was to increase storage space rather than to improve conditions for passengers.[47] Sternpost rudders were not yet in use in the Mediterranean, where the traditional steering oar favoured by Greeks and Etruscans still held sway. How long the ships lasted is doubtful. Sturdy Roman galleys had enjoyed a long life as grain transports, but medieval vessels were more lightly constructed, and plenty of attention was needed to their careening and repair.

Most ships did arrive safely at their destination, so they were not bad investments, if spread around several ventures. This meant that towns that were only sending small numbers of ships across the sea, such as Amalfi and Savona (not far from Genoa) stood at a disadvantage: their merchants could not spread their investments widely. So some of them, like Solomon of Salerno, went to Genoa, Pisa or Venice and realized that they would do better business there. This had a multiplier effect. The trade of these three cities boomed and potential rivals proved unable to compete. The triumph of the Genoese and Pisans in their part of the Mediterranean was capped by their insistence in the late twelfth century that ships from Provençal ports that sailed to the Levant should be allowed to carry only pilgrims and other passengers, not cargoes.[48]

Everything and everyone on board was tightly packed together, and travellers slept under the stars, using their possessions as pillow and mattress. By the thirteenth century goods might be kept below deck and cabins were built up at each end of the ship, so there was space for those willing to pay for a more comfortable journey in medieval club class.[49] In the dire conditions of sea travel, what carried many of the sea voyagers across the Mediterranean was faith: the faith of the pilgrims, for whom adversity at sea was a test of their devotion that would earn them God's approval; and the faith of the merchants in their ability to take calculated risks and to emerge with profit from expeditions to the sometimes dangerous lands of the southern and eastern Mediterranean. The merchants too were aware that any profit they made was made thanks to a merciful God – it was *proficuum quod Deus dederit*, 'the profit that God will have given'.

6

The Fall and Rise of Empires,
1130–1260

I

The fleets of Pisa, Genoa and Venice were not the only navies that plied Italian waters. The conquest of Sicily by Roger I, the 'Great Count', was complete by 1091. Under Norman rule, the island flourished: Messina attracted Latin merchants, acting as a staging-post on the trade routes linking Genoa and Pisa to Acre and Alexandria; ibn Jubayr called it 'the mart of the merchant infidels, the focus of ships from the world over', and noted that it was a great arsenal, where the Sicilian fleet was constructed.[1] The ruler reserved to his own use much of the pitch, iron and steel produced in his lands, for it was vital to control the raw materials required for ship construction.[2] Roger I's ruthless and talented son Roger II gained control of large tracts of southern Italy ruled by his cousins; no less importantly, he obtained the newly created crown of Sicily from the pope in 1130. He was a man of Mediterranean ambitions, seeing himself as the successor to the Greek tyrants and arguing that he was not a usurper but the reviver of an ancient kingdom.[3] He appeared in public in Byzantine imperial costume or in the robes of an Arab emir. He decorated his palace chapel with the finest Greek mosaics and a superb wooden roof, the work of Arab craftsmen. He commissioned from Idrisi, a refugee prince from Ceuta, a geography of the world that enabled him (with its accompanying map) to contemplate the Mediterranean and the world beyond in extraordinary detail.

Propaganda was matched by action. In 1147–8, at the time of the Second Crusade, he turned his attention to the Byzantine Empire. The crusade was summoned by the pope in 1147, following the fall to the Muslims of the crusader principality of Edessa in northern Syria;

Roger offered his fleet, but under pressure from his enemy the German ruler, Conrad III, the offer was rejected. Roger had other uses for his fleet. In 1148 he took advantage of the fact that Manuel Komnenos, the Byzantine emperor, was distracted by the passage of the armies of the Second Crusade through his lands. Roger's navy seized Corfu and attacked Corinth and Athens, while his troops penetrated inland, carrying away from Thebes dozens of Jewish silk-weavers, who were put to work in his palace ateliers. A Byzantine chronicler eloquently remarked of the returning Sicilian galleys:

> If anyone had seen the Sicilian triremes laden with so many beautiful objects, and submerged down to the oars, he would truly have said they were not pirate ships but merchant ships carrying goods of every sort.[4]

Not surprisingly, there was a backlash. The Venetians, alarmed that Roger now controlled the Adriatic exit, sent naval aid to Manuel Komnenos, who had no option but to renew the trade privileges that he already considered excessive. His distrust of the Venetians strengthened when he received reports of how they spent their time during the siege of Corfu: making fun of Manuel's swarthy features, they dressed a black African in magnificent robes, installed him on one of the imperial flagships, and mockingly acted out the sacred ceremonies of the Byzantine court.[5] Unwittingly, Roger was forcing the Byzantines and the Venetians to realize how much they disliked one another. Roger's attacks on Greece were lightning raids, but he attempted to create a lasting empire overseas as well, in North Africa.[6] He ably exploited political and economic disorder there: during a period of severe famine, Sicilian grain was used to pry recognition of his authority from one African emir after another, and he sent a fleet against Tripoli in 1146, capturing it without difficulty.[7] Two years later, when al-Hasan, the emir of Mahdia, proved insubordinate, he launched a fleet under the command of Admiral George of Antioch, a highly mobile and exceptionally able Greek Christian who had earlier served the ruler of Mahdia. Off the little island of Pantelleria the Sicilian fleet encountered a Mahdian ship and discovered that there were carrier-pigeons on board. George forced the captain to send a message to Mahdia telling the emir that, while it was true a Sicilian fleet had sailed, it was bound for the Byzantine Empire. Al-Hasan thought this was highly plausible, and was horrified when he saw the Sicilian ships crossing the horizon at dawn on 22 June

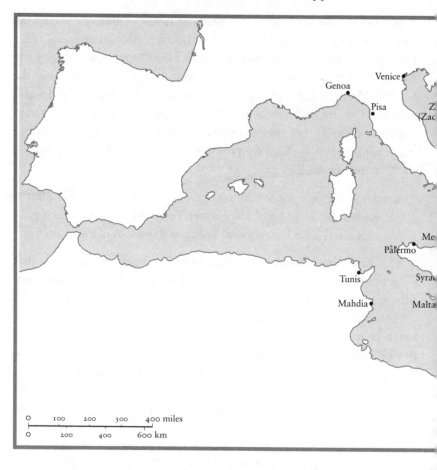

1148. Al-Hasan fled; the city was taken with ease, and George allowed his troops two hours in which to pillage.

After that, he extended royal protection to the Mahdians, and even arranged loans to local merchants so that business could resume as quickly as possible. Judges were appointed from among the local community, to ensure that the Muslims could continue to live under their own laws; foreign merchants arrived; prosperity returned. Roger saw this series of conquests as the first stage in the establishment of a partly rechristianized 'kingdom of Africa'. He attempted to settle Christians in Mahdia, for Christianity had gradually disappeared over the past five centuries.[8] But he also had a wider strategic plan, aiming to gain control of the seas around his kingdom – in 1127 he had already reoccupied

Malta (first occupied by his father in 1090), and he was keen to establish his influence over the Ionian islands off western Greece.[9] Possession of all these points would enable him to create a naval *cordon sanitaire* around his kingdom, ensuring that enemy fleets – whether Venetians in the service of Byzantium, or Pisans in the service of the German emperor – could not lead an invasion of his lands. He took an interest in plans for naval campaigns off the coast of Spain. By the time he died in 1154, he was thus on the verge of creating a great thalassocracy.[10] Roger did not sail with his fleet but placed it under the command of his chief administrator George of Antioch, who now flaunted the title 'emir of emirs'. Later, in 1177, a certain William of Modica was appointed emir, or *amiratus*, 'of the fortunate royal fleet', and it was in this specifically naval sense that the word *amiratus*, or 'admiral', came to be used in France, Spain and elsewhere in the thirteenth century. It was a term of Sicilian Arabic derivation that reflected the supremacy of the Sicilian navy in the twelfth-century central Mediterranean.[11]

After 1154, Roger's son William 'the Bad' was far less successful in holding together the fabric of the kingdom than his father. Faced with a Byzantine invasion of Apulia, to which the Venetian navy lent its support, William probably showed good judgement when he accepted that the African possessions were untenable. The North African cities sensed the difficulties William faced at home, and linked their fortunes to the rapidly expanding Almohad movement in Morocco; the Almohad caliph himself led the assault on Mahdia in 1159. In January 1160, the Almohads breached its walls, offering its Christians and Jews the choice between death and Islam.[12] William was roundly blamed for this great reverse, but in fact he (or his advisers) showed some skill in foreign relations. William defeated the Byzantine invasion and came to terms with Manuel Komnenos, the first time a Byzantine emperor gave grudging recognition to the kingdom's legitimacy.

Just when the Genoese, Pisans and Venetians gained control of the elongated routes carrying goods and pilgrims between west and east, the Sicilians established control over the vital passage-ways between the Tyrrhenian Sea and the East, and between the Adriatic and the East. Sicilian naval supremacy in these waters presented the north Italians with a dilemma. Unless they wished their ships to be at the mercy of the Sicilian navy, they had to make friends with the court in Palermo. Yet they were constantly pulled in other directions by their wish to placate the Byzantine and German emperors. In 1156 the Genoese made a treaty with King William I, of which the city chronicler wrote: 'it was for a long time and widely said by wise people throughout the world that the Genoese received greater and better things than they gave'.[13] King William needed an assurance that the Genoese would not allow their fleet to be used by his enemies in an invasion of his kingdom.[14] The Genoese were granted reduced taxes on cargoes carried from Alexandria and the Holy Land through Messina, for the treaty was concerned with the security of the routes to the East as much as it was with the right to take certain goods out of Sicily. Equally, the Genoese needed the produce of Sicily. The city had to feed itself as it grew, and Sicilian wheat was more plentiful and of higher quality than Sardinian, for which, in any case, the Genoese competed with the Pisans. The treaty describes how the Genoese would acquire wheat, salted pork (from north-western Sicily, a largely Christian area), wool, lambskins and cotton (mainly from the area around Agrigento).[15] For centuries Genoa would depend on the grain of Sicily, which could be bought cheaply and carried at low cost to their booming home-town; and by bringing large quantities of raw cotton from Sicily to northern Italy, the Genoese laid the basis for a cotton industry that would flourish throughout the Middle Ages.[16] Some of the best cotton came from Malta, which was ruled by the king of Sicily, and Maltese cotton is already recorded in Genoa in 1164.[17] Gradually, the trade of Sicily was being turned around, so that the traditionally close links to North Africa were replaced by close links to northern Italy. Under Norman rule, Sicily was entering the European economic network. For the moment, it was still an exotic land where merchants could find not just grain but sugar and indigo, traditional products of the Islamic Mediterranean that went out of fashion after 1200 to be replaced by yet more wheat, as their Muslim cultivators declined in numbers. As the Genoese brought increasing amounts of Italian and even Flemish woollen cloth south to Sicily, to help them pay for their wheat, cotton and other goods, the bonds between North and South became increasingly close, and a complementary relationship between northern and southern Italy began to develop, in which Sicily provided raw materials and foodstuffs, and northern Italy provided finished goods. The ruler of Sicily, as master of large grain estates in Sicily, was able to draw great wealth from his humble but vital assets.[18]

King William II 'the Good' (1166–89) took a strong interest in wider Mediterranean affairs, capitalizing on the existence of a large and powerful fleet. He extended his authority across the Adriatic, bringing under his protection the Dalmatian town of Dubrovnik (Ragusa), which was beginning to emerge as a port of significance.[19] But he was looking far beyond the Adriatic. In 1174 he launched a massive attack on Alexandria in Egypt; in 1182 he set his sails in the direction of Majorca, though his fleet achieved nothing. Three years later Byzantium was his target, and when he died he was planning to send help to the beleaguered crusader states. He saw himself as a fighter for Christ against both the Muslims and the Greeks. His most ambitious campaign, in 1185, took the Sicilian fleet deep into the Byzantine Empire. He could hope for support from the Italian merchants for, in 1182, in an ugly outburst of violence openly encouraged by the new emperor, Andronikos Komnenos, the Latins in Constantinople were massacred. News spread when a Venetian ship entering the Aegean encountered other Venetian ships off Cape Malea, whose crews shouted: 'Why do you stop here? If you do not flee you are all dead, for we and all the Latins have been exiled from Constantinople.'[20] Yet most victims were Pisans and Genoese – the Venetians were still embroiled in one of their perennial arguments with Constantinople, and were not much in evidence there.

By 1185 William had the excuse he needed: a wandering impostor had arrived at his court, claiming to be a deposed emperor, and William took on the noble task of restoring this unconvincing figure to the imperial throne.[21] When the time came for action, his fleet followed the pattern laid down by Robert Guiscard a century earlier: Dyrrhachion was taken, and an army landed; it penetrated as far as Thessalonika, which was captured and sacked with the help of the royal fleet, sent all the way round the Peloponnese. The fall of the second city in the Byzantine Empire electrified the Greeks.[22] The Sicilians proved unable to hold Thessalonika, but their attack only deepened Byzantine hatred for westerners.[23] While William's ambitions embraced the entire Mediterranean, what was missing was lasting success. Here the north Italians performed much better.

II

The final years of the twelfth century and the beginning of the thirteenth saw a series of political cataclysms that changed the political geography of the Mediterranean in enduring ways, even though the Italian maritime republics exploited these changes to gain an increasingly secure hold over the Mediterranean sea passages. In 1169 the king of Jerusalem, Amaury, made a serious miscalculation in allying himself to Manuel Komnenos with the aim of attacking Fatimid Egypt. Manuel was to provide a massive Byzantine fleet, which suggests that when they had the willpower the Byzantines could still put together a large navy. Amaury would summon the Frankish army, and together they would attack the Nile Delta and Cairo. In the event, a Frankish army did reach

Cairo, but its attempts to establish a puppet government there led to a popular backlash. The Fatimids were toppled and Egypt became not a submissive ally but the focus of opposition to the Latin kingdom.[24] Before long a new Ayyubid sultan, Saladin, a Sunni Muslim of Kurdish origin, would see in the struggle for the third holiest city of Islam a cause that would unite the Muslims of the Middle East against the Franks.[25] The threat to Frankish Jerusalem was all the greater since Saladin combined rule over Muslim Syria with control of Egypt, throwing off balance the traditional Frankish strategy of playing off the rulers of Syria against the Fatimids. His massive defeat of a badly managed Frankish army at the Horns of Hattin, near Tiberias, in 1187 led to the capture of Jerusalem and the seizure of the coast of Palestine, including the great port of Acre; only Tyre held out.

The western reaction was decisive, but failed to secure its objectives. The Third Crusade, launched in 1189, relied heavily on sea power: ships of Marseilles helped transport the army of Richard I, king of England and duke of Normandy, to the Levant by way of Sicily, where his interference (largely connected with sordid attempts to recover the dowry of his wife, who had been married to the late King William II) caused upheaval and fighting between Greeks and Latins in Messina. Richard did succeed in capturing Cyprus, which was in the hands of a rebel member of the Komnenos dynasty, and in the end Acre was recovered, together with a sliver of land along the coast of what is now Israel and Lebanon, but not Jerusalem. Acre's streets teemed more than ever with Italian sailors and merchants: their desperate need for naval support prompted the Frankish rulers to shower foreign merchants with commercial privileges in Acre and Tyre – the merchants of Marseilles, Montpellier and Barcelona were granted the 'Green Palace', a building in Tyre, as their base, as well as exemption from customs dues.[26]

Acre became a city divided among many masters, who insisted heavily on their rights: there were self-governing quarters for the Venetians and the Pisans close to the harbour, and a substantial Genoese section was tucked behind these enclaves. By the middle of the thirteenth century the Venetian quarter, enclosed by walls, contained churches dedicated to St Mark and St Demetrius; there was a palazzo for the governor, or *bailli*, of the community, a cistern, a fonduk with sixteen shops on the ground floor, storerooms on three levels, and living accommodation for the priest of St Mark's church. The Italian quarters were very crowded – the Genoese may have had about sixty houses.[27] Armed conflict between the different communities erupted: the War of St Sabas (1256–61) started with a quarrel over the boundaries between the Genoese and Venetian districts that flew out of control and resulted in the evacuation of Acre by the Genoese. They transferred their headquarters to Tyre, while the Venetians, previously dominant in Tyre, ensconced themselves even more firmly in Acre. The rival republics became so obsessed with one another that they seemed to be ignoring the constant threat from the kingdom's Muslim enemies, though in this they were no worse than the quarrelsome Frankish nobility of the Latin East. The Military Orders of the Temple and Hospital (or St John) also possessed large quarters in Acre, and they too insisted on their political autonomy.[28] Allowing for the lands of the patriarch of Jerusalem and other lords, there was not a great deal of Acre left for the Frankish king, but what he did have was the booming income from trade taxes – even the exempt merchants had to do business with merchants from the interior who paid the full rate of taxation, including a standard tax at the rather odd rate of $11\frac{5}{24}$ per cent. Medieval Mediterranean rulers well understood that lowering taxes would stimulate trade, earning them more, not less.[29]

Saladin was as keen as his Frankish rivals to encourage Italian visitors. They were simply too valuable as a source of revenue – and, when no one else was looking, of armaments.[30] Egypt was buying more and more European goods, especially fine cloths from Lombardy and Flanders. Demand was not simply generated by a wish to dress in luxurious and (for an Egyptian) exotic clothes, often made with the finest and softest English wools and coloured with expensive eastern indigo or Spanish *grana*, a red dye similar to cochineal. The industries of the Middle East were in decline. Why this should have happened is not clear; the Islamic Mediterranean was still heavily urbanized, and several cities such as Cairo, Damascus and Alexandria were massive. What is, however, clear is that the Italians seized the advantage.

Pisa acted as the portal for other Tuscan traders, who could live in Pisan quarters overseas so long as they submitted to Pisan judges and paid the taxes required of Pisan residents there; they then counted as Pisans and could enjoy whatever exemptions the local ruler had conferred on Pisa itself. One city that was well placed to sell its produce in the East was the many towered town of San Gimignano, in the Tuscan hinterland, which was the greatest centre of saffron production in the West. Saffron, made from the fragile stamens of a species of crocus, was a rare example of a spice that could be produced to higher quality in the West than in eastern lands. It was used as a dyestuff, condiment and drug, and its production was very labour-intensive, with the result that it was extremely expensive.[31] Men from San Gimignano carried this product to Acre, and then crossed into Muslim territory, reaching as far as Aleppo. The commercial revolution initiated by Genoa, Pisa and Venice was beginning to encompass the inhabitants of other towns away from the Mediterranean coast. Florence was also very successful: its merchants hawked fine French and Flemish textiles that were finished off in its workshops, and, later, they began to produce their own excellent imitations of these cloths. Florentine businessmen started to accumulate large quantities of gold from their trade in Tunis, Acre and elsewhere, not just from cloth sales but from the exchange of gold for silver, more suited to medium-value payments but in very short supply in the Islamic West. In 1252 both the Genoese and the Florentines had a large enough stockpile of gold to start minting their own gold coins, the first to be produced in western Europe (apart from Sicily, southern Italy and parts of Spain) since the days of Charlemagne.[32] By 1300, the presence of the florin of Florence in every corner of the Mediterranean demonstrated the primacy of the Italians and the increasing integration of the Great Sea into a single trading zone.

III

Even more dramatic than the fall of the Fatimids was the collapse of the kingdom of Sicily. While Saladin was able to maintain the old system of government, including the exercise of lucrative monopolies, Sicily and southern Italy fell prey to rapacious barons in the 1190s, creating enormous instability in the central Mediterranean. In the face of bitter opposition from most Sicilian barons, the German emperor, Henry VI of Hohenstaufen, invaded the kingdom, which he claimed in right of his wife (Roger II's posthumous daughter), with the opportunistic support of fleets from Pisa and Genoa.[33] He was only able to enjoy his conquest for three years, between 1194 and 1197, all the while planning a crusade and a war for the conquest of Constantinople. Then his widow

Constance attempted, in the year of life that was left to her, to return Sicily to its old equilibrium, but disintegration had begun: the Muslims were in revolt in western Sicily, and would remain in rebellion for a quarter of a century. After she died her small son Frederick became the plaything of competing factions in Palermo, and the barons and bishops on the south Italian mainland seized the opportunity to take over crown lands without serious opposition.

Control of Sicilian waters passed into the hands of north Italian pirates. The Genoese and Pisans decided to make real some of the generous promises Emperor Henry had made when he lured them into an alliance. The Genoese had been promised possession of Syracuse and so, in 1204, a Genoese pirate, Alamanno da Costa, took charge there as 'count of Syracuse'. Pisan shipping was subject to constant raids by Genoese pirates in Sicilian waters, who acted with the approval of the Genoese Commune.[34] Meanwhile, Alamanno's Genoese friend Enrico Pescatore ('the fisherman'), installed himself as count of Malta. Henry, count of Malta, was one of the most dangerous privateers on the high seas, with his own flotilla and broad ambitions – in 1205 he sent two galleys and 300 Genoese and Maltese sailors to raid Greek waters, where they seized two Venetian merchantmen bound for Constantinople laden with money, arms and 200 bales of European cloth. Having created one international incident, they then penetrated as far as Tripoli in Lebanon, where they besieged the town until its Christian count came to terms, promising trading rights for the Genoese in return for aid against the Syrian Muslims.[35] Henry's achievements were celebrated in verse by the great troubadour Peire Vidal, who served in his entourage:

> He is generous and intrepid and chivalrous, the star of the Genoese, and makes all his enemies tremble throughout the land and the sea . . . And my dear son Count Henry has destroyed all his enemies and is so safe a shelter to his friends that whosoever wishes may come or go without doubt or fear.[36]

Even when pursuing private ambitions, then, the Genoese pirates tried to produce benefits for their mother-city, which was unlikely to abandon them if they were thought to be working in the republic's interests.

Henry's next venture, his attempt to conquer Crete, followed the collapse of yet another great power in the Mediterranean. After the death of Manuel I Komnenos in 1180 succession disputes consumed the political energies of the Byzantine aristocracy; these energies were further sapped by a great Turkish military victory at Myriokephalon in Asia Minor four years earlier, from which Manuel had been lucky to escape alive.[37] Italian pirates acquired bases in the Aegean; Corfu fell into the hands of a Genoese pirate who was now free to raid Venetian shipping as it passed through the Adriatic exit.[38] The Pisans and Genoese were keen to wreak revenge on the Greeks for the massacre of their citizens in Constantinople in 1182, which was mentioned earlier in this chapter.[39] One of the worst outrages was committed by the Genoese pirate Guglielmo Grasso, who was in league with a Pisan pirate named Fortis. After raiding Rhodes with impunity in 1187, they attacked a Venetian ship sent by Saladin to Isaac Angelos, the Byzantine emperor; as well as Saladin's ambassadors it carried wild beasts, fine woods, precious metals and, as a special gift from the sultan, a piece of the 'true cross'. The pirates killed everyone on board, apart from some Pisan and Genoese merchants, and Fortis gained possession of the relic, which he carried off across the Mediterranean to the rock-girt town of Bonifacio, in southern Corsica, then held by his fellow-Pisans. The Genoese were convinced they had a better claim to the true cross, and raided Bonifacio, capturing both the relic and the town, which they held thereafter and used as a base for their trading operations in northern Sardinia.[40] Western regrets at the attack on Saladin's envoys were few, for their journey was seen as proof that the Byzantines and the Ayyubids were in league against the kingdom of Jerusalem.

Crisis afflicted Byzantium on all fronts. In south-eastern Europe, Byzantine power was challenged by warlords in Bulgaria and Serbia. Members of the Komnenos family, which had lost control of the imperial crown, set up states of their own in Trebizond on the Black Sea and in Cyprus. Byzantium was fractured even before it was conquered. When a new crusade to the east was planned in 1202, it was assumed that its target would be Saladin's economic power base, Alexandria. If Alexandria could be captured, it could then be traded for the lost cities of the kingdom of Jerusalem, or used as a forward position from which to destroy Ayyubid power. The story of the Fourth Crusade has been told many times: how the crusaders hired ships in Venice; how they could not pay the fees demanded of them, how the Venetians persuaded them to help capture Zara (Zadar) on the Dalmatian coast in part-payment; how the crusaders then agreed to head for Constantinople in the hope of installing their own protégé, Alexios Angelos, on the imperial throne; how the relations between the crusaders, in particular the Venetians, and the Greeks turned sour during 1203 as hostility to Alexios increased among the Greeks; how Alexios IV was overthrown and the crusaders responded with an assault on Constantinople; and how in April 1204 the great walls of the city were scaled and the previously impregnable city was taken and then sacked in a matter of days.[41] The Venetians filled the treasury of the church of St Mark with jewelled bowls, rock-crystal ewers, gilded and enamelled book covers, saints' relics and other gorgeous loot from the imperial palace and the great city churches. Many of these objects are still in St Mark's, most notably the lifesize bronze horses from the Hippodrome of Constantinople. The city of St Mark was now the new Constantinople as well as the new Alexandria.[42]

The most obvious beneficiaries of the fall of Constantinople were the Venetians, who gained control of the trade routes of Byzantium and could exclude their rivals at will. The empire was carved up: Thessalonika and the title to Crete were granted to a leading crusader, the north-west Italian aristocrat Boniface of Montferrat, while the crown of Constantinople went to Baldwin, count of Flanders. Greek princes continued to resist in Asia Minor, at Nikaia (Nicaea), and in the western Balkans, in Epeiros. Emperor Baldwin had to spend much of his time fighting the Bulgarians, with limited resources. The Greek rump states fought tenaciously to recover the Byzantine heartlands, and the impoverished Latin empire of Constantinople was finally dismantled by Michael Palaiologos, ruler of Nikaia, who recaptured Constantinople in 1261.[43] Venice, on the other hand, proclaimed itself 'lord of a quarter and half a quarter of the empire of Romania' (that is, the Byzantine Empire). The Venetian share grew, at least in theory, when Boniface, who was under as much pressure as Emperor Baldwin, decided to raise 1,000 silver marks by selling Crete to the republic. He did not actually control the island, so Venice would have to take possession. Its excellent reasons for wishing to do so were that it lay astride the routes to the East, and that it was a source of grain, oil and wine, already known to Venetian merchants.

Before the Venetians could act, Henry, count of Malta, launched an ambitious naval attack on Crete, seeking to make himself king of the island, and the Genoese, excluded from the booty of the Fourth Crusade, surreptitiously backed him. In 1206 he occupied Candia (Heraklion) and fourteen strongholds on the island. He boldly sent an envoy to Pope Innocent III, asking to be made king of Crete, though the pope demurred. Genoa had pretended not to be involved in Henry's great enterprise, but began to take a direct interest from 1208, supplying him with ships, men and food, and before long they were promised warehouses, ovens, baths and churches in the towns of the island. After a slow start, the Venetians riposted with men and arms; a member of the great Tiepolo family was appointed duke of Crete, a post that would often serve as an apprenticeship for the office of doge of Venice. The Genoese had no appetite for a long war with Venice, and concluded a treaty in 1212, though it took another six years to suppress piracy by the Genoese counts of Malta and Syracuse.[44] After that, Henry blithely offered his services to Frederick, king of Sicily and (from 1220) Holy Roman Emperor, becoming his admiral; the poacher had turned gamekeeper.

The importance of this brief conflict should not be underestimated. It was the first major confrontation between Genoa and Venice, which became rivals along the routes to Acre where, as has been seen, they squabbled viciously between 1256 and 1261. The Genoese deeply resented Venetian control over the trade of the former Byzantine Empire, and it is no surprise that they offered their naval support to Michael Palaiologos when he recaptured Constantinople in 1261, in return for handsome favours. But after 1212 Crete passed into Venetian hands, and the Venetians found themselves masters of a Greek population that had no great love for the republic (there was a great rebellion in 1363). On the other hand, Venice had secured its supply lines in the eastern Mediterranean; gradually, Greeks and Venetians learned to cooperate, and a mixed culture developed on the island, as Venetians married native Cretans – even the boundaries between Catholic and Orthodox Christian were blurred.[45]

IV

Despite these local interactions within Crete, the importance of the Italian communities in cultural developments within the Latin East or across the Mediterranean is hard to measure. Several illuminated manuscripts from the thirteenth-century kingdom of Jerusalem have been identified, proving that artists in the East borrowed Byzantine imagery in ways similar to those working in Tuscany and Sicily. The fall of Constantinople in 1204 injected more Byzantine objects into the West, strengthening Byzantine influence on Italian art, as well as creating a means by which Venetians interested in classical texts could obtain and study them.[46] Islamic motifs were of decorative interest, and appeared in Venetian and south Italian buildings, but curiosity about the culture that produced them was very limited. Interest in Eastern cultures was largely practical. There were one or two Pisan interpreters in twelfth-century Constantinople, whose attempts to translate works of Greek philosophy extended beyond what must have been their main task – rendering official correspondence to and from the West into or out of Latin. Jacob the Pisan acted as interpreter for the emperor Isaac Angelos in 1194.[47] The Pisan Maimon, son of William, whose name suggests mixed parentage, helped negotiate with the Almohads of North Africa; Pisan scribes corresponded with the Almohads in Arabic. The Pisans even learned some useful lessons in accounting from North Africa. The Pisan merchant Leonardo Fibonacci lived for a time in Bougie, and wrote a famous treatise on Arabic numerals at the start of the thirteenth century.[48] But innate conservatism among notaries meant that calculations were still a wearisome task conducted in Latin numerals.

The Mediterranean trade routes may also have carried a very different set of ideas that would set alight southern France for decades after 1209. During the eleventh century, the Byzantine emperors had actively suppressed the Bogomil heresy, which preached a dualist view of the universe in which a good God of the spiritual realms was battling against Satan, who controlled the world of the flesh. Historians have argued that crusaders passing through Constantinople on the First and Second Crusades, or Italian merchants from Pisa and elsewhere, made contact with the Bogomils and exported their beliefs to Europe, where they developed into the Cathar heresy of twelfth-century Languedoc.[49] Italian Cathars, generally more moderate in their views, seem to have fallen under the influence of heretics in the Balkans who brought their ideas across the Adriatic, by way of Dubrovnik and its neighbours.

However, the difficulty with the argument that these ideas reached western Europe along the main maritime trade routes is that they did not implant themselves in the port cities: Montpellier was an important centre of Mediterranean trade, but was considered generally clean of heresy, and it is very hard to find Genoese Cathars. Genoese and Venetians make unlikely Cathars. The Genoese were too busy making money and immersing themselves in the world of the flesh – *Genuensis, ergo mercator*, as the saying went, 'Genoese, therefore a merchant'.

7

Merchants, Mercenaries and Missionaries, 1220–1300

I

The collapse of empires in the central and eastern Mediterranean was matched in the far west by the disintegration of Almohad power. The caliphs lost their enthusiasm for the extremist doctrines of Almohadism, and were accused of betraying the principles of their movement. Following military defeat at the hands of Christian kings of Spain at Las Navas de Tolosa in 1212 the caliph is said to have been strangled by one of his slaves. The Almohad territories in Spain and Tunisia fell into the hands of a new generation of local kings who only paid lip-service to Almohadism. The Hafsid rulers who gained control of Tunis proclaimed themselves successors to the Almohad caliphate, though more as a way of asserting their legitimacy than out of deep commitment to Almohad beliefs. The Berber Marinids broke Almohad power in Morocco in the mid-thirteenth century, after a long struggle. At the same time the Nasrid dynasty established itself in Granada, where it would last until 1492; it adhered strictly to Sunni Islam, not Almohadism. The thirteenth century also saw a major transformation in the Christian western Mediterranean: Pisa's rivalry with Genoa for mastery over the waters around Corsica and Sardinia culminated in Pisan defeat at the battle of Meloria and the loss of iron-rich Elba in 1284.[1] Although the Pisans did not yet lose control of the large areas of Sardinia they ruled, and even recovered Elba, a new rival to both Pisa and Genoa emerged, not a maritime republic but a group of cities led by Barcelona and backed by the growing power of the king of Aragon and count of Catalonia, James I 'the Conqueror'.

The Mediterranean vocation of the kings of Aragon was not obvious before the thirteenth century. Lords of a small, mountainous kingdom that only toppled the Muslim emirate of Saragossa in 1118, they dissipated much of their energy in attempts to interfere in Christian Castile and Navarre. But in 1134 King Alfonso 'the Battler' of Aragon died, having failed to produce an heir; his brother, a monk, was forced out of his convent in order to breed. A daughter was born who eventually married the count of Barcelona. As a result, the county of Barcelona and the kingdom of Aragon remained joined together from the middle of the twelfth century onwards, but the union was a personal one, embodied in the ruler, who remained a count (notionally under the overlordship of the king of France) in Catalonia, and a king only in highland Aragon. Moreover, the count of Barcelona was distracted by regional conflicts within Catalonia, where he was at best the first among equals. The count's horizon did extend further than Catalonia, though, since he had a number of allies and vassals across the Pyrenees in Languedoc and Roussillon. In 1209 the involvement in southern French affairs of the count-king of Aragon-Catalonia (as he is often called) dragged him into the great crusade preached by the papacy against the Cathar heretics, the Albigensian Crusade. Although several of his southern French vassals were accused of protecting the heretics, or even being heretics themselves, the count-king, Peter II, placed his obligations as overlord first and came to their aid against the northern French army of invasion led by Simon de Montfort. Peter was killed in battle at Muret near Toulouse in 1213, leaving a young heir, James, in Montpellier; these events further destabilized Catalonia.[2]

Barcelona was still, in the days of Benjamin of Tudela, 'a small city and beautiful', though he insists that around 1160 it was visited by merchants from Italy and all over the Mediterranean.[3] This was a low point in the city's fortunes, however, for if there was one Spanish city on the shores of the Mediterranean that had seemed, in the eleventh century, to be on the verge of a boom it was Christian Barcelona.[4] Under its energetic and warlike counts, who enjoyed making threats against and raiding the Muslim kingdoms dispersed through southern Spain, vast amounts of tribute were received, pumping gold into the economy and encouraging prosperous businessmen like Ricart Guillem to invest in vineyards, orchards and other properties on the western edge of Barcelona (close to the modern Ramblas). Ricart, the son of a castellan, was a rising star in Barcelona: he fought against the troublesome mercenary

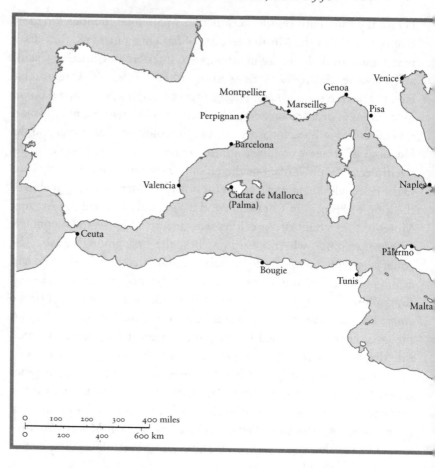

El Cid in 1090 and travelled to Muslim Saragossa to trade silver for gold. But this first flowering of Barcelona was brief and was followed by a long winter; tribute payments dried up at the end of the eleventh century after the Almoravids established themselves in southern Spain.[5] Then, with the rise of Genoa and Pisa, Barcelona was sidelined, because it lay a little way from the routes Italian ships took when bound for such desirable havens as Ceuta and Bougie: they preferred to descend past Majorca and Ibiza and make contact with the Iberian coast at Denia, on its spur a little to the south of Valencia. Barcelona did not have a fine port, for what seems today such an excellent harbour is modern. The Catalans still had to rely on the Genoese navy when their army attacked Tortosa in 1148. Yet the Catalans began to build their

own small fleets, setting up a shipyard by the Regomir Gate in Barcelona, the southern portal of the city, where the road running down from the cathedral debouched on the beach (this is now well within the city, in the southern reaches of the 'Gothic Quarter').[6] Barcelona was also a capital city, in which the count-king's palace dominated its north-eastern quarter. For, although Barcelona developed a well-regulated system of government, it was never a free republic, and the city fathers lacked the freedom of manoeuvre the Pisans and Genoese possessed.[7] But that was one of the reasons for Barcelona's success. In the thirteenth century, the interests of its patricians and of the count-king increasingly converged. They all began to see the benefits of overseas trade and of naval campaigns right across the Mediterranean.

II

During the long minority of James I, absent in his mother's city of Montpellier, the great Catalan lords squabbled among themselves; even so, royal rights were not fatally undermined, for James's supporters included grandees such as the count of Roussillon, who saw that the defence of royal authority would bolster his own position. By the 1220s the young king was keen to establish his credentials as a crusading hero. He revived long-standing schemes for the conquest of Muslim Majorca, briefly held by his ancestor Ramon Berenguer III in 1114, thanks to Pisan naval support. On this occasion, though, he proposed to attack Majorca using a fleet composed of his own subjects' ships. Indeed, the Genoese and Pisans were firmly ensconced in Majorca, where they had trading stations, so they were unsympathetic to James's ambitions.[8] The king began by consulting his subjects at a great banquet in Tarragona, offered to him by a prominent shipowner, Pere Martell, who acclaimed the enterprise as a just and profitable one:

> So please you, we hold it right that you conquer that island for two reasons: the first, that you and we will thereby increase in power; the other, that those who hear of the conquest will think it a marvel that you can take land and a kingdom in the sea where God pleased to put it.[9]

From that moment, it was clear that the interests of the king and the merchants coincided.

As well as Catalan ships, James could call on the resources of Marseilles, for the counts of Provence were members of a cadet branch of the house of Barcelona. In May 1229 he gathered together 150 large ships, besides a great many smaller ones. James asserted that 'all the sea seemed white with sails, so large a fleet was it'.[10] After a troublesome crossing the Catalans and their allies landed, and by the end of the year they had captured the capital city, Madina Mayurqa (known to the Catalans as Ciutat de Mallorca, the modern Palma). The Catalan cities, as well as Marseilles and Montpellier, were rewarded for their help by the award of urban properties and lands outside the city walls. Aware of Genoese and Pisan sensitivities, the king bestowed trading privileges on the Italian merchants in Majorca, even though they had opposed his great enterprise. These acts laid the foundation for the commercial expansion of Ciutat de Mallorca. However, it took many more months to quell the rest of the island. In 1231 James scared Minorca into surrender by a bluff: he gathered his troops in eastern Majorca, within sight of Minorca, and at nightfall each soldier was given two torches, so that when the Muslims of Minorca saw the flares in the distance they were convinced a massive army was ready to descend on them, and sent a message of submission. They paid an annual tribute in return for a guarantee of the right to govern themselves and to practise Islam.[11] Ibiza was captured in 1235 by a private expedition sanctioned by the king but organized by the archbishop of Tarragona.

As the conquest of Ibiza suggests, James took little direct interest in the affairs of these islands. He happily placed the government of Majorca in the hands of an Iberian prince, Pedro of Portugal, in exchange for strategically valuable territories in the Pyrenees to which Pedro had a claim. James was still looking landward more than seaward. Yet the result of his Majorcan campaign was that the Balearic islands had suddenly become a forward position for Christian navies, and James celebrated his victory by recording his deeds in an autobiography, the first such work to survive from the hand of a medieval king. It was written in Catalan, a language merchants and conquerors now carried across the sea and down the coast of Spain to Majorca, and then, when James conquered Valencia in 1238, into yet another new Christian dominion. At the end of his life, with two surviving sons, he thought it right to reward the elder one, Peter, with Aragon, Catalonia and Valencia, but created an enlarged kingdom of Majorca for his younger son, James. This new kingdom, which lasted from 1276 to 1343, included valuable lands James held on the French side of the Pyrenees: Roussillon, Cerdagne and Montpellier, an important centre of trade linking the Mediterranean to northern France. Intentionally or otherwise, he had created a kingdom that would live from the sea.

One problem with his conquests was what to do with the Muslim population. James saw the Muslims as an economic asset. In Majorca many remained on the land, subject to Christian overlords. The Muslim community slowly seeped away, some emigrating, others converting. This did not leave the land empty: Christians migrated across the sea, whether from Catalonia or Provence, and the character of the island population changed quickly, so that by 1300 the Muslims were a beleaguered minority.[12] In Valencia, on the other hand, the king tried to present himself as a Christian king over a Muslim kingdom: although the core of Valencia City was depopulated of Muslims, a flourishing Muslim suburb developed, and across the old Muslim kingdom of Valencia Muslim communities were guaranteed the right to practise their laws and religion, and even (as also happened in Minorca) to ban Christians and Jews from settling in their small towns and villages. These were important centres of production, often specializing in those crops and crafts that the Arabs had brought westwards in the early days of the Islamic conquests: ceramics, grain (including rice), dried fruits and fine cloths were all available, and brought the king and noble land-lords valuable income through taxes on trade, overland or across the Mediterranean.[13] The surrender agreements that were offered to the Muslims sometimes barely indicated that they had been defeated; they read almost like treaties between equals.[14] But that seemed a good way to secure stability, at least until the Valencian Muslims rebelled, and tougher conditions were imposed in the 1260s. Royal tolerance was real, but conditional and fragile.

James saw special potential in the Jews, even though the large Jewish community in Barcelona was not greatly interested in maritime trade (or, contrary to facile stereotypes, in moneylending).[15] He invited Jews from Catalonia, Provence and North Africa to settle in Majorca. He had his eye on one particular Jew from Sijilmasa, the town on the northern edge of the Sahara where many of the caravans bringing gold from the bend of the Niger arrived. This was Solomon ben Ammar, who was active in trade and finance around 1240, and acquired property in Ciu-tat de Mallorca. Such a figure could penetrate with ease into the markets of North Africa, making Majorca into a bridge between Catalonia and the Islamic Mediterranean. Like many of the Jews in Spain itself, he had the advantage of fluency in Arabic. It is no coincidence, then, that in the next century Jews and converts from Judaism based in Majorca set up cartographic studios that exploited exact geographical knowledge from both Muslim and Christian sources, and produced the famous portolan charts that still astonish with their fine detail as they trace the coastlines of the Mediterranean and the seas beyond.[16]

Within Spain, the encounter between the three Abrahamic faiths took on various guises. In Toledo, deep within Castile, King Alfonso X sponsored translations of Arabic texts (including Greek works put into Arabic), using Jewish intermediaries. By the shores of the Mediterranean such activities were more limited. The uppermost questions in the mind of James I of Aragon were a practical one: how to maintain control over a potentially restive Muslim population in Valencia and other lands he ruled; and a religious one: whether and how to offer his Jewish and Muslim subjects the opportunity to convert to Christianity. Since he benefited enormously from special taxes imposed on these communities he faced the same dilemma as the early Muslim conquerors of the southern Mediterranean littoral: too many conversions would erode his tax base. So, when he insisted that his Jewish subjects must attend synagogue to listen to sermons delivered by missionary friars, he was secretly glad that they preferred to pay him a special tax so that they would be exempted from this demand. Still, he made a public show of supporting the friars. Ramon de Penyafort, General of the Dominican Order, gave high priority to missions among the Catalan Jews and to the Muslims of North Africa. One of his achievements was the creation of language schools where missionaries could learn Arabic and Hebrew to the very highest standard and study the Talmud and the *hadith*, so they could argue with rabbis and imams on their adversaries' terms.[17] In 1263, King James acted as host to a public disputation in Barcelona, where the eminent rabbi Nahmanides, from Girona, and Paul the Christian, a convert from Judaism, argued furiously over whether the Messiah had come; each side claimed victory, but Nahmanides knew that he was now a marked man and would have to leave Catalonia. Fleeing to Acre, he lost his seal-ring on the beach. It has now been found and is displayed in the Israel Museum in Jerusalem.[18]

Something of the quality of day-to-day encounters between people of different faiths can be gathered from a report of a second, more modest, disputation between a Jew and a prominent Genoese merchant, Ingheto Contardo, that took place in the Genoese warehouse in Majorca in 1286. A local rabbi used to come to the Genoese loggia to spar with his Genoese acquaintance. Contardo treated the rabbi not as an enemy but as a friend in need of enlightenment and salvation. He said that if he found a Jew freezing in the cold, he would happily take down a wooden cross, smash it into fragments and burn it to provide warmth.[19] The Jew taunted Contardo with the question: why, if the Messiah has come, is the world at war, and why are you Genoese fighting the Pisans so bitterly? These years of bitter conflict also provide a setting in which to try to understand the career of a charismatic kabbalist who travelled back

h across the Mediterranean and who knew something about
1 and Muslim mysticism: Abraham ben Samuel Abulafia, born
ossa in the Hebrew year 5000 (1239–40).[20] Abulafia was pre-
l by the coming of the End of Days – the theme of a Messiah
..... ould declare himself in the presence of the pope had been
mentioned in the Barcelona disputation of 1263.[21] He travelled the
Mediterranean from end to end. Setting out from southern Italy, he
attempted to penetrate beyond Acre in 1260, but his way through
the Holy Land to the legendary river Sambatyon where dwelled the
Twelve Lost Tribes of Israel was barred by fighting between Franks,
Muslims and Mongols. Abulafia returned to Barcelona, but restlessly set
out again in the 1270s, teaching his doctrines at Patras and Thebes in
Greece, arousing the ire of the Jews of Trani in southern Italy, and heading for the papal court where he planned to reveal his Messianic mission,
writing visionary books all the while. In his writings he developed a distinctive, ecstatic kabbalistic system, characterized by his belief that the
letters of the Hebrew alphabet could be used, in elaborate combinations, to provide a spiritual pathway to God. He was convinced he
could show how the soul, immersed in contemplation of God, would
leave its material presence and witness God's ineffable glory. Fortunately for him, the pope died a few days before his proposed audience,
and (after a month in prison, where he succeeded only in puzzling his
Franciscan captors) he headed back to southern Italy and Sicily, surrounded by his devoted followers; his last appearance was on the island
of Comino, between Malta and Gozo, in 1291, a violent time to be
living in those waters.

Abulafia's career illustrates how radical religious ideas were spread
by travel across the Mediterranean, sometimes by the innovator himself, sometimes by his followers. His career also shows how, among
mystics, ideas of how to approach God were shared and exchanged
between adherents of all the revealed religions. One prolific Catalan
author and missionary, Ramon Llull (1232–1316), attempted to harness
together the common beliefs of Jews, Christians and Muslims, his own
mystical theories, and Trinitarian theology, and produced a system or
'Art' that he carried across the Mediterranean on travels as ambitious
as those of Abraham Abulafia. Llull hailed from the Majorcan branch
of a respectable Barcelona family; in the new society of Majorca he
prospered as a royal courtier but, he insisted, he led a life of sin and

debauchery; a mystical experience on Mount Randa in Majorca in 1274 convinced him that he must turn his talents to the conversion of unbelievers.[22] He attempted to learn Arabic and Hebrew, and established a language school for missionaries at Miramar in the Majorcan mountains. He composed hundreds of books and visited North Africa several times (only to be expelled for denouncing the Prophet), but there is no evidence he ever converted anyone. Perhaps his 'Art' was too complicated for anyone but a small coterie of followers. One way of explaining the 'Art' is to see it as an attempt to categorize everything that exists and to understand the relationship between each of the categories. Thus he defined nine 'absolutes' (though the number varied in his works), including Goodness, Greatness, Power and Wisdom, and nine 'relatives', such as Beginning, Middle and End. The profusion of codes, diagrams and symbols makes some of his books impenetrable at first sight, though he also wrote novellas on the theme of conversion aimed at a more popular audience.[23]

Llull was unusual among Christian missionaries in insisting that Jews, Christians and Muslims worshipped the same God, and he set his face against the growing trend to see in the rivals of Christianity adherents of Satan. In his *Book of the Gentile and the Three Wise Men* he offered a generally fair and well-informed account of the beliefs of Judaism, Christianity and Islam, and allowed a Jewish interlocutor to set out the proofs for the existence of God. His book argued that 'just as we have One God, One creator, One Lord, we should also have one faith, one religion, one sect, one manner of loving and honouring God, and we should love and help one another'.[24] He attempted to put into practice what he preached. He wrote a short handbook for merchants visiting Alexandria and other Muslim lands, setting out how they should engage in discussion with the inhabitants about the relative merits of Christianity and Islam. But they were much more interested in engaging in discussion about pepper prices; they knew, too, that any criticism of Islam could lead to arrest and deportation or even execution. Llull's first attempt to cross from Genoa to Africa in 1293 failed because even he lost courage. He had already loaded his books and other effects on the ship when he was paralysed by fear and refused to sail, scandalizing those he had been impressing with his fine words. Soon after, though, he did set out for Tunis, and there he announced to the Muslims that he was ready to convert to their faith if they could convince him of its truth – a ploy to draw them into debate. His verbal battles brought him to the sultan's attention, and he was placed on board a Genoese ship and sternly ordered never to return, under penalty of death. Such threats to missionaries often made them dream of martyrdom.[25] After carrying his teachings to Naples and Cyprus he returned to North Africa in 1307, this time to Bougie, standing up in the marketplace to denounce Islam. When he was arrested he told the authorities: 'the true servant of Christ who has experienced the truth of the Catholic faith should not fear the danger of physical death when he can gain the grace of spiritual life for the souls of unbelievers'. Ramon Llull had, however, charmed the Genoese and Catalan merchants, who possessed some influence at court and ensured that he was not executed. He returned to Tunis in 1314, at a time when the sultan was playing a time-honoured game: to strengthen his hand against his rivals he sought the support of the Catalans, and let whispers circulate that he was interested in converting to Christianity. Llull was therefore welcome, at last, but he was an old man, and he probably died on board a ship returning to Majorca in spring 1316.[26]

The sultan was more interested in mercenaries than in missionaries. Catalan militias helped sustain the rulers of the Maghrib, but the kings of Aragon valued their presence too: they provided a guarantee that the North African sultans would not become sucked into the bitter rivalries that, as will be seen, convulsed the Christian monarchies of the western Mediterranean in the late thirteenth and early fourteenth centuries. Some mercenaries, such as Henry, prince of Castile, were adventurers who had failed to secure lands in Europe.[27] They were not a new phenomenon. In the late eleventh century Pope Gregory VII had written appeasing letters to North African emirs, in the hope of providing for the religious needs of Christian soldiers in Muslim armies. In Spain, Christians joined Muslim armies and Muslims joined Christian ones. By 1300, however, the mercenaries formed part of a wider strategy that made areas of North Africa into virtual protectorates of Aragon-Catalonia.

III

Another area of Catalan expertise was sailing the sea. By the end of the thirteenth century Catalan ships had a good reputation for safety and reliability; if a merchant was in search of a ship in, say, Palermo on which to load his goods, he knew he would do well to choose a Catalan vessel, such as the substantial *Sanctus Franciscus*, owned by Mateu Oliverdar, which was there during 1298.[28] Whereas the Genoese liked to divide up the ownership of their boats, the Catalans often owned a large ship outright. They rented out space to Tuscan wheat merchants or slave dealers, and sought out rich merchants who might be willing to lease all or part of the ship.[29] The shipowners and merchants of Barcelona and Majorca inveigled themselves into the places where the Italians had long been dominant. In the 1270s, the middle-class widow Maria de Malla, from Barcelona, was trading with Constantinople and the Aegean, sending out her sons to bring back mastic (much valued as chewing-gum); she exported fine cloths to the East, including linens from Châlons in northern France. The great speciality of the de Malla family was the trade in furs, including those of wolves and foxes.[30] The Catalans were granted the right to establish fonduks governed by their own consuls in Tunis, Bougie and other North African towns. There were big profits to be made from the overseas consulates. James I was outraged when he discovered in 1259 how low was the rent paid to him by the Catalan consul in Tunis. He promptly tripled it.[31] Another focus of Catalan penetration was Alexandria; in the 1290s the de Mallas were seeking linseed and pepper there. In the fourteenth century, King James II of Aragon tried to persuade the sultan of Egypt to grant him protective authority over some of the Christian holy places in Palestine, and the sultan promised him relics of Christ's Passion if he would send 'large ships containing plenty of goods'.[32] The papacy, with the outward support of the king of Aragon, attempted to ban the lively trade of the Catalans and Italians in Egypt; those who traded with the Muslim enemy were to be excommunicated. But the king ensured that two Catalan abbots were to hand who could absolve merchants trading with Egypt, subject to payment of a swingeing fine. These fines developed into a tax on trade, and produced handsome revenues: in 1302 fines on trade with Alexandria accounted for nearly half the king's recorded revenues from Catalonia. Far from suppressing the trade, the Aragonese kings became complicit in it.[33]

Naturally the Catalans wanted to challenge the Italian monopoly over the spice trade to the East. Yet their real strength lay in the network they created in the western Mediterranean. Catalans, Pisans and

Genoese jostled in the streets of the spacious foreign quarter of Tunis, a concessionary area full of fonduks, taverns and churches. Access to the ports of North Africa meant access to the gold-bearing routes across the Sahara; into these lands, the Catalans brought linen and woollen cloths from Flanders and northern France and, as their own textile industry expanded after 1300, fine cloths from Barcelona and Lleida. They brought salt too, which was plentiful in Catalan Ibiza, and in southern Sardinia and western Sicily, but was in short supply in the deserts to the south, and was sometimes used there as a currency in its own right. As thirteenth-century Barcelona began to boom, they ensured that there were sufficient food supplies for a growing city. Sicily early became the focus of their trade in wheat, carried in big, round, bulky ships, and they were so successful that as early as the 1260s they began to supply other parts of the Mediterranean with Sicilian wheat: Tunis, which had never recovered from the devastation of the North African countryside by Arab tribes in the eleventh century; Genoa and Pisa, which might have been expected to look after their own supplies; the towns of Provence.[34] A business contract of the late 1280s simply demanded that the ship *Bonaventura*, recently in the port of Palermo, should sail to Agrigento where it was to be filled up with 'as great a quantity of wheat as the said ship can take and carry'.

The Catalans specialized in another important cargo: slaves. These were variously described as 'black', 'olive' or 'white', and were generally Muslim captives from North Africa. They were put on sale in Majorca, Palermo and Valencia, and sent to perform domestic work in the households of their Catalan and Italian owners. In 1287 the king of Aragon decided that the Minorcans were guilty of treachery, declared the surrender treaty of 1231 void and invaded the island, enslaving the entire population, which was dispersed across the Mediterranean – for a time there was a glut in the slave market.[35] The luckier and better-connected slaves would be ransomed by co-religionists – Muslims, Jews and Christians all set aside funds for the ransoming of their brethren, and the two religious orders of the Trinitarians and Mercedarians, well represented in Catalonia and Provence, specialized in ransoming Christians who had fallen into Muslim hands.[36] The image of the young woman plucked off the shores of southern France by Saracen raiders was a stock theme in medieval romance, but the Catalans were perfectly ready to respond in kind; they muscled into the Mediterranean trade networks through piracy as well as honest business.

Meanwhile, Majorcan ships kept up a constant flow of traffic towards North Africa and Spain. A remarkable series of licences issued to sailors intending to leave Majorca in 1284 reveals that ships set off from the island almost every day of the year, even in the depths of January, and there was no close season, even if business was livelier in warmer months. Some of these ships were small vessels called *barques*, crewed by fewer than a dozen men, able to slip quickly across to mainland Spain time and again. More typical was the larger *leny*, literally 'wood'; *lenys* were well suited to the slightly longer run across open water towards North Africa.[37] The Majorcans were pioneers, too. In 1281 two Genoese ships and one Majorcan vessel reached the port of London, where the Majorcan ship loaded 267 sacks of fine English wool, and the Majorcans continued to trade regularly with England well into the fourteenth century. The Phoenicians had never had much difficulty in escaping through the Straits of Gibraltar, bound for Tartessos, but medieval ships battled with the incoming flow from the Atlantic and the fogs and contrary winds between Gibraltar and Ceuta. They also battled, literally, with the rulers of the facing shores – Marinid Berbers in Morocco, the Nasrid rulers of Granada in southern Spain. These were not hospitable waters, and the opening of the sea route out of the Mediterranean was as much a diplomatic as a technical triumph. Raw wool and Flemish textiles could now be brought directly and relatively cheaply from the north straight into the Mediterranean, bound for the workshops of Florence, Barcelona and other cities where the wool was processed and the textiles were finished. Alum, the fixative most easily obtained from Phokaia on the coast of Asia Minor, could be ferried to cloth workshops in Bruges, Ghent and Ypres, avoiding the costly and tedious trek by road and river through eastern France or Germany. The navigation of the Mediterranean and the Atlantic began slowly to be tied together, even if there were constant crises, and Catalan war fleets often patrolled the Straits. By the early fourteenth century, Mediterranean shipbuilders were imitating the broad, round shape of the northern cogs, big cargo vessels that tramped the Baltic and the North Sea – they even adopted the name, *cocka*. Down the coast of Morocco, too, Catalan and Genoese ships found markets full of the grain they craved, where the inhabitants were keen to acquire Italian and Catalan textiles; by the 1340s these boats had penetrated as far as the Canary Islands, which the Majorcans tried (and failed) to conquer.[38]

Predictably, the Majorcan merchants, subject to their own king after 1276, decided they wanted their own consuls and fonduks. This was one of many sources of tension between the two brothers, Peter of Aragon and James of Majorca, who divided up James I's realms. Sailors and merchants were not slow to exploit these tensions. In 1299 a scoundrel named Pere de Grau, who owned a ship, was accused of stealing a tool box from a Genoese carpenter in the western Sicilian port of Trapani. Tit-for-tat, Pere insisted that in fact the carpenter had stolen his longboat. The matter was brought before the Catalan consul, but Pere scathingly stated: 'this consul does not have any jurisdiction over citizens of Majorca, only over those who are under the dominion of the king of Aragon'.[39] As fast as the Catalans extended their trading network across the Mediterranean, it threatened to fragment into pieces.

IV

This fragmentation extended across the Mediterranean. In the mid-thirteenth century dramatic political changes once again altered the regional power balance. Crusading expeditions vainly tried to protect the fragile, narrow coastal strip ruled from Acre that called itself the kingdom of Jerusalem. The smaller it became the more it was contested between baronial factions, for the monarchy was very weak and other contentious forces, including the Italian communes and the Military Orders of the Hospital and Temple, were very strong. Western rulers were well aware of the danger Egypt posed to the kingdom, and a series of ship-borne crusades targeted Egypt: the Fifth Crusade briefly gained control of Damietta in the Nile Delta, in 1219–21; Louis IX of France also invested Damietta in a disastrous crusade in 1248; on both occasions, the crusaders hoped to trade their Egyptian conquests for Jerusalem, or even to hold both Egypt and the Holy Land, a vain dream. Increasingly, though, Christian kings were distracted from crusading by quarrels nearer home, such as the battle for Sicily that will be discussed later in this chapter. There was plenty of crusading rhetoric, and there were small naval expeditions, but after 1248 the age of large-scale expeditions to the Holy Land came to an end.[40] Military commanders of slave origin seized power in the Ayyubid dominions, controlling Egypt and Syria from 1250 to 1517; these Mamluks perpetuated the commercial arrangements between the Italian merchants and the Egyptian government, but they were also determined to wipe the Latin kingdom of Jerusalem off the map. Acre fell to the Mamluks in 1291 amid horrific massacres, though many refugees crowded on to the last departing ships and found safety in Cyprus. Acre disappeared as a centre of international trade, and Latin rule in the East became confined to the kingdom of Cyprus.

We have already seen that one legacy of the Fourth Crusade was a weak Frankish regime in Constantinople, which the Greeks of Nikaia recovered with Genoese help in 1261 – the reward for Genoa was handsome trading privileges that included access to the grain, slaves, wax and furs of the Black Sea. There was also violent change in Sicily, where Frederick II revived and reinvigorated the Norman system of government; one of his achievements was the rebuilding of the Sicilian fleet, which he launched on a campaign against Jerba in North Africa, in 1235.[41] When the papacy opposed his combined rule over Germany, Sicily and parts of northern Italy, Frederick put his fleet to good use in 1241, capturing an entire delegation of cardinals and bishops as they travelled aboard Genoese ships to Rome to attend a papal council.[42] Ironically, Frederick's admiral was another Genoese, Ansaldo de' Mari, for the Genoese were as divided as ever about whether to support or oppose Frederick. While the bitter wars between Frederick and the papacy are not strictly part of the history of the Mediterranean, the years following his death in 1250 had major repercussions for the Mediterranean as a whole. In 1266–8, Frederick's heirs in Sicily and southern Italy were defeated and all but exterminated by the papal champion Charles, count of Anjou and Provence, and brother of the crusading king of France, Louis IX.

Charles attempted to create a Mediterranean empire, not just for himself but for his Angevin heirs. At the centre of it, he envisaged the kingdom of Sicily and southern Italy, surrounded by a maritime *cordon sanitaire* ensuring control of the waters between Sicily and Africa and between southern Italy and both Albania and Sardinia. As a young man he had already snatched Provence away from the Aragonese, by marrying one of the heiresses to the county; under his rule the rebellious patricians of Marseilles were forced to accept his authority, and its port became his great arsenal.[43] He plotted to ensure that his son Philip was elected king of Sardinia in 1269, in the face of the opposition of King James I of Aragon.[44] He bought the title to the shrinking kingdom of Jerusalem from Princess Maria of Antioch in 1277, even though the king of Cyprus possessed a widely recognized counter-claim. Charles saw himself as a crusader against the Muslims, whether in Tunis or the East, but his primary concern in the East was the former Byzantine Empire. He claimed lands acquired in Albania by the Hohenstaufen, and seized Dyrrhachion; then, with the approval of a number of Albanian warlords, he assumed the title 'king of Albania'.[45] Following the restoration of the Greeks to Constantinople, he dreamed of setting the Frankish dynasty back on the imperial throne it had seized after the Fourth Crusade, and of winning the hand of the Frankish emperor for his daughter. He was convinced that the Greek emperor, Michael VIII Palaiologos, was not seriously interested in the reunification of the Greek and Latin Churches under papal control. For him, the only way to bring the schismatic Greeks under the authority of Rome was by force.

Charles planned to send a great fleet against Constantinople, in conjunction with the Venetians; Dyrrhachion would provide a base from which he could penetrate deep into Byzantium along the Via Egnatia. The old battle plans of Robert Guiscard and William the Good were taken out of a drawer and dusted off. Charles committed half of his very plentiful revenues to the building of his fleet of fifty or sixty galleys and maybe thirty auxiliary vessels. These galleys were magnificent ships, large, sturdy and supposedly capable of staying afloat in high seas.[46] Operating such a fleet would cost at least 32,000 ounces of gold, possibly 50,000 ounces.[47] It was an extraordinary misjudgement of what his heavily taxed subjects would tolerate. The pressure cooker exploded. In Palermo, descendants of the Latin settlers who had been migrating to the island since the late eleventh century turned on Charles's Angevin soldiers in the great uprising of the Sicilian Vespers, of March 1282.[48] Their cry was 'Death to the French!', but just as important a focus of their hostility was the group of bureaucrats from Amalfi and the Bay of Naples who, having been pushed out of Mediterranean trade by the Genoese and Pisans, now placed their skills in accounting at the service first of Frederick II and then of Charles I.[49] Their enthusiasm for the minutiae of the tax system helped antagonize the island elites. The rebels rapidly conquered the island in the hope of creating a federation of free republics there. Rebuffed by Charles's great ally the pope, to whom they naively appealed for support, they turned instead to the husband of Frederick II's granddaughter, the last survivor of the Hohenstaufen dynasty: King Peter III of Aragon, the son of James the Conqueror.

In August 1282, Peter and his fleet happened to be close by, campaigning on what Peter insisted was a holy war against the North African town of Alcol. Whether this was a façade, and he was really plotting to seize Sicily, has been much debated. The events in Palermo, beginning with riots after a French soldier made sexual advances to a young Sicilian housewife, seem quite uncoordinated, even chaotic. When Peter arrived in September, he, or rather, his wife Constance, won the support of most of the Sicilian elite. He came, after all, to vindicate her claim to Sicily, and would have seized southern Italy as well if its inhabitants had joined in the rebellion and if he had possessed the resources to defeat Charles of Anjou's well-funded armies (Charles benefited from the loans of the Florentine bankers, whose support guaranteed supplies of Apulian grain to the growing city of Florence).[50] The Angevins persuaded the French king to invade Aragon in 1283 (a disaster for France); the Aragonese supported the anti-papal factions in Italy, providing a focus of loyalty in the internecine strife of pro-Angevin Guelfs and pro-Aragonese Ghibellines within the Tuscan and Lombard cities.[51] The result was stalemate: by 1285, when both Peter III and Charles I died, the Aragonese king held Sicily and the Angevin king held southern Italy, but both called themselves 'king of Sicily'. (The mainland kingdom is often conveniently referred to as the 'kingdom of Naples'.) Despite papal attempts at mediation in 1302 and after, the rivalry between Angevins and Aragonese continued throughout the fourteenth century, consuming precious financial resources and occasionally exploding outwards.

The conflict was fought out on the sea as well as on land. Charles of Anjou probably regarded the smaller Catalan fleet as a puny rival. This was a mistake, particularly after King Peter appointed Roger de Lauria, a nobleman from Calabria, Admiral of the Fleet. He was one of the greatest naval commanders in the history of the Mediterranean, a new Lysander.[52] In contrast to the compact, well-run Catalan fleet, Charles's navy was impressively equipped but lacked cohesion; it was a motley assortment of south Italians, Pisans and Provençaux. In October 1282 Roger de Lauria overwhelmed Charles's fleet off the coast of Calabria, at Nicotera, capturing twenty Angevin and two Pisan galleys, and forcing Charles on to the defensive in mainland southern Italy.[53] However, if Charles were ever to recapture Sicily, he would also need to gain mastery over the Sicilian Straits dividing the island from Africa. Here again he was stymied by Roger de Lauria, and the battleground was the waters around Malta, which was contested between an Angevin garrison and an Aragonese invading force. In June 1283 a Provençal fleet of eighteen galleys arrived in what was to become the Grand Harbour of Malta, but it was pursued there by Lauria's fleet of twenty-one galleys. The two navies fought all day, and by nightfall the Angevins had been forced to surrender many of their ships and to scuttle several others. No less serious were the Angevin casualties: perhaps 3,500 Angevin troops were slaughtered, and the Aragonese took several hundred captives, including noblemen. Most of the victims were probably from Marseilles, which may have lost nearly one-fifth of its population in the battle.[54] When the French launched their invasion of Catalonia in 1283, Catalan fleets were also on hand, capturing half the French fleet off Roses. Roger asserted: 'no galley or ship, nor even, I believe, any fish goes about on the sea unless it carries the arms of the king of Aragon'.[55]

The Angevins were now unable to defend the shores of southern Italy from constant Catalan raids, and their loss of mastery over the Tyrrhenian Sea was confirmed in June 1284, when Charles I's son, Charles, prince of Salerno, was foolhardy enough to lead an Angevin fleet against Roger de Lauria's ships off Naples. Many Neapolitan sailors knew better than to engage with the Catalans, and had to be forced at sword-point to embark. This time disaster took a different form. The Neapolitan fleet was not destroyed, but several Provençal galleys were captured, and on board one of them was Charles of Salerno.[56] He was to remain an Aragonese captive until 1289, even though his father died in 1285 and (at least in Angevin eyes) he then became king of Sicily and count of Provence. In the years that followed, the Catalan fleet impudently extended its operations across the Mediterranean, raiding Kephalonia (a Neapolitan possession), the Cyclades and Chios; Jerba and Kerkennah, off the coast of Tunisia, were brought back under Sicilian control. No one could withstand Roger de Lauria. His unbroken series of naval victories ensured that Sicily remained in Aragonese hands.

Majorca was a different problem. Peter III had from the start resented his father's division of his lands between the king of Aragon and the king of Majorca. When his younger brother, James II of Majorca, treacherously embraced the Angevin cause, Peter invaded Roussillon, marched into the royal palace in Perpignan, and, finding himself locked out of his brother's bedroom, hammered on the door in frustration while James escaped down a filthy manhole and fled across country. He won back his crown only in 1298, following papal mediation.[57] Yet Peter made a similar decision to his father when he divided the newly conquered island of Sicily from his other lands, bequeathing it to his second son as a separate entity. This recognized an awkward fact: the Sicilians had not been fighting for the house of Barcelona but for the house of Hohenstaufen. Moreover, Sicily was far from home and difficult or impossible to control from Barcelona. Yet the island was enormously desirable. Well before the Vespers, Catalan merchants were coming en masse to Palermo, Trapani and other ports, seeking grain and cotton. Peter's aim was, however, to redeem his wife's dynastic claim, not to defend the interests of his merchants. After Peter's death, opportunities for the merchants were compromised by strife among the three Aragonese kings – the rulers of Aragon-Catalonia, Majorca and Sicily.

Despite the political divisions, and despite occasional embargoes within the Catalan-Aragonese world, the Catalans had carved out a place for themselves alongside the Italians. They entered the competition for mastery over the Mediterranean at the right moment: the Genoese, Pisan and Venetians had not yet gained complete control over the sea routes when Barcelona began to compete for access to Africa, Sicily and the East. The Catalans possessed impressive expertise in the arts of navigation, including cartography. But they also had one advantage their rivals entirely lacked: under the protection of the kings of Aragon, they gained easy access to the courts of rulers in Tunis, Tlemcen and Alexandria. Later generations would look back on the age of James the Conqueror and Peter the Great as the heroic age of Catalonia.

8

Serrata – Closing, 1291–1350

I

The fall of Acre in 1291 shocked western Europe, which had in fact done little to protect the city in its last decades. Plans to launch new expeditions abounded, and among the greatest enthusiasts was Charles II of Naples, after his release from his Catalan gaol. But this was all talk; he was far too preoccupied with trying to defeat the Aragonese to be able to launch a crusade, nor did he have the resources to do so.[1] The Italian merchants diversified their interests to cope with the loss of access to eastern silks and spices through Acre. Venice gradually took the lead in Egypt, while the Genoese concentrated more on bulky goods from the Aegean and the Black Sea, following the establishment of a Genoese colony in Constantinople in 1261. But the Byzantine emperors were wary of the Genoese. They favoured the Venetians as well, though to a lesser degree, so that the Genoese would not assume they could do whatever they wished. Michael VIII and his son Andronikos II confined the Genoese to the high ground north of the Golden Horn, the area known as Pera, or Galata, where a massive Genoese tower still dominates the skyline of northern Istanbul, but they also granted them the right to self-government, and the Genoese colony grew so rapidly that it soon had to be extended. By the mid-fourteenth century the trade revenues of Genoese Pera dwarfed those of Greek Constantinople, by a ratio of about seven to one. These emperors effectively handed control of the Aegean and the Black Sea to the Genoese, and Michael's navy, consisting of about eighty ships, was dismantled by his son. It was assumed that God would protect Constantinople as a reward for the rejection of all attempts at a union of the holy Orthodox Church with the unholy Catholic one.[2]

The Genoese generally tolerated a Venetian presence, for war damaged trade and ate up valuable resources. Occasionally, as in 1298, pirate attacks by one side caused a crisis, and the cities did go to war. The battle of Curzola (Korčula) that year pitted about eighty Genoese galleys against more than ninety Venetian ones. The Venetians were on home territory, deep within the Adriatic. But Genoese persistence won the day, and hundreds of Venetians were captured, including (it is said) Marco Polo, who dictated his extraordinary tales of China and the East to a Pisan troubadour with whom he shared a cell in Genoa.[3] The real story of the Polos was not simply one of intrepid, or foolhardy, Venetian jewel merchants who set out via Acre for the Far East, accompanied by the young Marco. The rise of the Mongol empire in the thirteenth century led to a reconfiguration of the trans-Asiatic trade routes, and opened a route bringing eastern silks to the shores of the Black Sea, although the sea-lanes through the Indian Ocean and Red Sea continued to bring spices to Alexandria and the Mediterranean from the East Indies. Once they had gained access to the Black Sea in the 1260s, the Genoese and Venetians attempted to tap into this exotic trans-Asia trade. True to form, the Venetians were more interested in the expensive luxury items, while the Genoese concentrated on slaves, grain and dried fruits, local products of the shores of the Black Sea. Good-quality wax was also in high demand, to illuminate churches and palaces across western Europe. The Genoese set up a successful trading base at Caffa in Crimea, while the Venetians operated from Tana, in the Sea of Azov. In Caffa the Genoese collected thousands of slaves, mostly Circassians and Tartars; they sold them for domestic service in Italian cities or to the Mamluks in Egypt, who recruited them into the sultan's guard. The spectacle of the Genoese supplying the Muslim enemy with its crack troops not surprisingly caused alarm and displeasure at the papal court.

The Genoese despatched Pontic grain far beyond Constantinople, reviving the Black Sea grain traffic that had helped feed ancient Athens. As the Italian cities grew in size, they drew their grain from further and further afield: Morocco, the shores of Bulgaria and Romania, the Crimea, Ukraine. Production costs there were far lower than in northern Italy, so that, even after taking into account the cost of transport, grain from these lands could be put on sale back home at prices no higher than Sicilian or Sardinian imports. Of those too there was still a great need. The Genoese distributed grain from all these sources around the

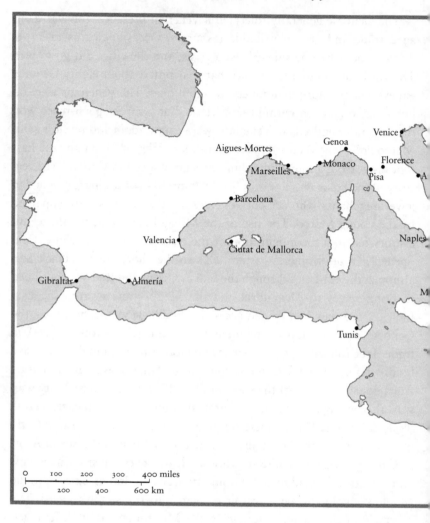

Mediterranean: they and the Catalans supplied Tunis; they ferried grain from Sicily to northern Italy.[4] One city where demand was constant was Florence, only now emerging as an economic powerhouse, a centre of cloth-finishing and cloth-production. Although it lies well inland, Florence depended heavily on the Mediterranean for its wool supplies and for its food; it controlled a small territory that could produce enough grain to feed the city for only five months out of twelve. The soil of Tuscany was generally poor, and local grain could not match the quality of the hard wheats that were imported from abroad. One solution was

regular loans to their ally the Angevin king of Naples, which gave access to the seemingly limitless grain of Apulia.[5]

These developments reflected massive changes in the society and economy of the lands surrounding the Mediterranean. By 1280 or 1300, population was rising and grain prices were rising in parallel. Local famines became more frequent and towns had to search ever further afield for the food they needed. The commercial revolution in Europe led to a spurt in urban growth, as employment prospects within towns drew workers in from the countryside. Cities began to dominate the economy of Mediterranean western Europe as never before in history: Valencia, Majorca, Barcelona, Perpignan, Narbonne, Montpellier, Aigues-Mortes, Marseilles, Savona, Genoa, Pisa and Florence, with its widely used and imitated gold florins, to name the major centres in the great arc stretching from the Catalan lands to Tuscany. Aigues-Mortes, rich in salt, whose appearance has changed little since the early four-teenth century, was founded in the 1240s as a commercial gateway to the Mediterranean for the kingdom of France, which had only recently acquired direct control over Languedoc. King Louis IX eyed with con-cern the flourishing city of Montpellier, a centre of trade, banking and manufacture that lay, as part of a complex feudal arrangement, under the lordship of the king of Aragon. He hoped to divert business to his new port in the salt lagoons, which he also used as a departure point for his disastrous crusade in 1248. In the event, Aigues-Mortes soon became an outport for Montpellier, which avoided French royal control for another century.[6] The Venetians had their own distinctive answer to the problem of how to feed the 100,000 inhabitants of their city. They attempted to channel all grain that came into the Upper Adriatic towards the city; the Venetians would have first choice, and then what remained would be redistributed to hungry neighbours such as Ravenna, Ferrara and Rimini. They sought to transform the Adriatic Sea into what came to be called the 'Venetian Gulf'. The Venetians negotiated hard with Charles of Anjou and his successors to secure access to Apulian wheat, and were even prepared to offer support to Charles I's campaign against Constantinople, which was supposed to depart in 1282, the year of the Sicilian Vespers.

As well as food, the big round ships of the Genoese and Venetians fer-ried alum from Asia Minor to the West; the Genoese established enclaves on the edge of the alum-producing lands, first, and briefly, on the coast of Asia Minor, where the Genoese adventurer Benedetto Zaccaria tried to create a 'kingdom of Asia' in 1297, and then close by on Chios, which was recaptured by a consortium of Genoese merchant families in 1346 (and was held till 1566). Chios not merely gave access to the alum of Phokaia; it also produced dried fruits and mastic. More important than Chios was Famagusta in Cyprus, which filled the gap left by the fall of Acre. Cyprus lay under the rule of the Lusignan family, of French origin, though the majority of its inhabitants were Byzantine Greeks. Its rulers were often embroiled in faction-fighting, but the dynasty managed to survive for two more centuries, supported by the prosperity Cyprus derived from its intensive trade with neighbouring lands.[7] Massive communities of foreign merchants visited and settled: Famagusta was the base for merchants from Venice, Genoa, Barcelona, Ancona, Narbonne, Messina, Montpellier, Marseilles and elsewhere; its ruined Gothic churches still testify to the wealth its merchants accumulated.[8]

From Cyprus, trade routes extended to another Christian kingdom, Cilician Armenia, on the south-east coast of modern Turkey. Western merchants supplied wheat to Armenia by way of Cyprus, and they used Armenia as a gateway to exotic and arduous trade routes that took them away from the Mediterranean, to the silk markets of Persian Tabriz and beyond. Cyprus enjoyed close links to Beirut, where Syrian Christian merchants acted as agents of businessmen from Ancona and Venice, furnishing them with massive quantities of raw cotton for processing into cloth in Italy and even in Germany, a clear sign that a single economic system was emerging in the Mediterranean, crossing the boundaries between Christendom and Islam. Some of the cotton cloth would eventually be conveyed back to the East to be sold in Egypt and Syria. Trade and politics were fatefully intertwined in the minds of the Lusignan kings. When King Peter I of Cyprus launched an ambitious crusade against Alexandria in 1365, his grand plan included the establishment of Christian hegemony over the ports of southern Anatolia (of which he had already captured a couple) and Syria, but a sustained campaign in Egypt was far beyond his resources; the expedition turned into the unwholesome sack of Alexandria, confirming that what had been proclaimed as a holy war was motivated by material considerations. Soon after his return to Cyprus, King Peter, who knew how to make enemies, was assassinated.[9]

II

The commercial supremacy of the Italian and Catalan merchants was based on their naval supremacy. The big round sailing ships could cross freely from Christian to Muslim shores only because long, oared galleys patrolled the seas. The galleys were about eight times as long as they were broad, and combined oar and sail power. Under oar, four or six men sat abreast of one another, two or three per oar. As trading vessels, they were best suited to carrying small quantities of high-value goods such as spices, for hold space was very limited. They were fast and man-oeuvrable, but they were still liable to be swamped by high seas. As the Flanders route developed, ships bound for the Atlantic were built longer, broader and (most importantly) higher, so the new 'great galleys' could face the winds and currents of the Bay of Biscay.[10] The round ships included a very few Venetian and Genoese vessels the size of the *Rocca-forte*, built in the 1260s: this was a massive ship of about 500 tons, more than twice the displacement of most round ships.[11]

Some fleets, notably those sailing from Venice to the Levant or to Flanders, moved in convoy and had armed protection (what the Vene-tians called the *muda* system). Even so, rampant piracy by Muslim or Christian corsairs could interrupt traffic for long periods. In 1297 a rebel faction from Genoa, led by a member of the Grimaldi family whose habit of wearing a hood supposedly earned him the nickname 'the Monk', seized the rock of Monaco at the extreme west of the Genoese land dominion (in fact, the name *Monoikos* originated with Phokaian settlers in antiquity and has nothing to do with a monk, or *monaco*). The sailors of Monaco made thorough nuisances of themselves for many decades, posing as supporters of the Angevin king of Naples, Robert the Wise, who had become overlord of Genoa in 1318. In 1336 Monegasque pirates seized two galleys returning from Flanders laden with merchan-dise. The Senate felt obliged to suspend all its Flanders sailings, which did not resume for twenty years. The Grimaldi stayed put, remained a nuisance, and are still rulers of Monaco, though they found slightly more respectable ways to make money than piracy.[12]

While trade created a successful merchant class, it also enhanced the power of the patrician families. In Venice, the nobility dominated the most profitable trade routes, leaving the commerce in grain, salt and wine to middle-class merchants in their round ships. Defining who qualified as noble was not straightforward, though there were some ancient families, such as the Dandolos, who had stayed at the top of the social ladder for centuries. The question was who was to be allowed to ascend that ladder at a time of growing prosperity, when many new men had acquired great wealth and claimed the right to determine where the galley convoys should sail and with which foreign kings treaties should be made, decisions that (in the early fourteenth century) were made by the aristocratic Senate. The solution that was offered in 1297 was to limit membership of the Great Council, from which the Senate and higher committees were drawn, to those who were already members and their descendants – about 200 families, many of them leading trading families such as the Tiepolos. This 'closing', or *Serrata*, was intended to be more or less final, although, over the years, some families were admitted to noble ranks through the back door.[13] The *Serrata* was thus an opportunity to reaffirm the supremacy of the aristocracy in politics, trade and society.

III

The Catalans too were enjoying their successes at the start of the fourteenth century. The formal end to the War of the Vespers in 1302 reopened the routes linking Sicily, Majorca and Barcelona. Most importantly, the king of Aragon decided to vindicate a claim to Sardinia, which the pope had granted to James II of Aragon in 1297, in exchange, the pope hoped, for Sicily.[14] James's brother Frederick responded aggressively by holding on to Sicily as its independent monarch, and it was only in 1323 that King Alfonso IV launched an invasion of Sardinia. While his motives were primarily dynastic, the Catalan merchant community thought it would gain substantially from the conquest of an island so rich in grain, salt, cheese, leather and – most importantly – silver.[15] The would-be conquerors failed to take into account the eternal reluctance of the native Sards to accept outside rule. The Catalans bunkered down in the towns, mainly along the coast (their Catalan-speaking descendants still live in Alghero), and kept the Sards outside the town walls. Meanwhile, the Genoese and Pisans regarded the Catalan invasion as an infringement of their own rights of lordship. The Pisans were in the end allowed to retain estates in southern Sardinia, but Pisa was a spent force – not long before, the city had even considered voluntary submission to James II of Aragon. The Genoese posed a more serious problem. They responded with vicious attacks on Catalan shipping, while the Catalans were just as brutal. The seas around Sardinia became perilous. This was a contested isle – contested between its would-be masters and its ancient inhabitants, contested between one would-be master and another. In the late fourteenth century native resistance culminated in the creation of a dynamic kingdom based at Arborea, in the centre-west of the island; its queen, Eleonora, is much celebrated as a lawgiver.[16]

Following the accession of the ambitious, pint-sized king known as Peter the Ceremonious (Peter IV) to the throne of Aragon in 1337, the Aragonese court began to develop what might be called an imperial strategy. At the start of his reign he resolved to deal with the problem of his cousin's behaviour in Majorca. King James III of Majorca gives the impression of being mentally unstable. He deeply resented the insistence of Peter IV that the king of Majorca was a vassal of the king of Aragon, but he came to Barcelona to discuss their fraught relationship. His ship docked by the walls of a seaside palace, and at his insistence a covered bridge was built linking the ship to it; he then tried to lure Peter on board, and the story circulated that he had an insane plan to kidnap the king of Aragon. The Majorcan business community found all this very trying. They wanted and needed to maintain close links to their opposite numbers in Barcelona. It was a relief when the king of Aragon declared James contumacious and seized Majorca in 1343; the Catalan fleet contained 116 ships, including twenty-two galleys.[17] James died soon after, attempting to recover his lands. At the end of his long life (he reigned for fifty years) Peter was trying to negotiate a marriage alliance that would return Aragonese Sicily to the fold. His imperial dream began to turn into reality: at last, a Catalan-Aragonese 'empire' was coming into existence, from which the Catalan merchants hoped to make big profits. In 1380 Peter explained the importance of these trans-Mediterranean connections while pondering the need to retain control of the war-torn island of Sardinia:

> If Sardinia is lost, it will follow that Majorca will also be lost, because the food that Majorca is accustomed to receiving from Sicily and Sardinia will stop arriving, and as a result the land will become depopulated and will be lost.[18]

A network was emerging that would tie together Sicily, Sardinia, Majorca and Catalonia, in which the Italian islands regularly provisioned Majorca and Barcelona with vital food supplies.

Maintaining the fleet was a headache. During the thirteenth century, a large arsenal was built in Barcelona, the shell of which is now the Maritime Museum. Here the shipwrights worked under cover, and large iron rings were suspended from the arches, enabling them to use block and tackle to raise the hull. But the cost of building an arsenal to house twenty-five galleys was estimated by a royal counsellor as 2,000 gold ounces, which was more than the kings of Aragon could afford. This was before taking into account the cost of maintaining ships in good order and of supplying the sailors with food, armaments and other equipment. The diet of sailors aboard Catalan galleys was a monotonous one of hard biscuit, salted meat, cheese, beans, oil and wine, as well as chickpeas and broad beans; the main difference from the diet of Genoese, Venetian and Neapolitan sailors was the balance of elements, with the Venetians receiving rather less biscuit and cheese and much more salted meat, while the Neapolitan fleet was awash with free wine (does this explain its poor performance in battle?).[19] With the help of garlic, onions and spices it was possible to mix together a reasonably tasty topping for the biscuit, and it was understood that garlic and onions protected against diseases such as scurvy. Biscuit was exactly that – *biscoctus*, 'twice-cooked', so that it was hard but light, easily preserved and nutritious.[20] The lack of salted fish seems odd. Salted fish was an important part of the diet in Barcelona; there were plenty of local anchovies and fish was also brought from the Atlantic, especially in Lent, when consumption of meat was forbidden to Christians. On the other hand, there was no reason for the crown to pay for fish when an abundance was available underneath the ship's keel. Salted foods would increase demand for water, which was a constant problem. Each man would need at least eight litres a day, especially when rowing in hot weather. Ships could carry over 5,000 litres of water, which spoiled easily and had to be purified and flavoured with vinegar. But supplies needed to be replenished, and, as in antiquity, frequent landfalls were the solution.[21] Mastering these supply problems was one of the chores the admiral had to perform. He was much more than a naval commander.

Some areas of the western Mediterranean were off-limits. Around 1340, command of the Straits of Gibraltar was disputed between the Genoese, the Catalans and the Marinids of Morocco.[22] The problem was compounded by fears of a Moroccan invasion of southern Spain, a reprise of the invasions from Morocco that had posed such a threat to the Christian kingdoms of Iberia in the eleventh and twelfth centuries. Fortunately for the Christian powers, the Muslim kings of Granada were generally as anxious to avoid Marinid domination as were the

Christians, but in the late 1330s they allied themselves with the Moroccans, greatly endangering passage through the Straits. Not for the first time, the king of Castile attempted to win control of the Straits by besieging Gibraltar, but was himself besieged by Muslim forces and reluctantly pulled back.[23] In 1340 the Castilian fleet was defeated by a renascent Moroccan fleet off Gibraltar, losing thirty-two warships. The shock of the defeat of fellow-Christians prompted the Aragonese to make peace with the Castilians, with whom they had long been squabbling. The king of Aragon hoped to equip at least sixty galleys, but he had to beg his parliaments or *Corts* for funds; the Valencian *Corts* offered twenty galleys and even the quarrelsone king of Majorca offered fifteen. Meanwhile, the Moroccans were free to enter Spain, but the Castilians, this time with Portuguese help, crushed a Moroccan army at the battle of Salado in southern Spain, in October 1340. The captured Marinid battle-standards can still be seen in the treasury of Toledo Cathedral. The victory did not end the war, however, and squadrons of ten or twenty galleys were repeatedly sent to the Straits. This was rather little by comparison with the Moroccans, who had somehow managed to float 250 ships, including sixty galleys, in 1340.[24] The war came to an end in 1344 when King Alfonso XI of Castile marched into Algeciras, with the result that a Christian king held the northern side of the Straits, even though Gibraltar next door remained unconquered.[25]

Muslim naval activity revived in the eastern Mediterranean, too. To some degree this was in response to Christian successes in the waters off Turkey. In 1310 the Knights Hospitallers, displaced from Acre nearly two decades earlier, set out from their current base in Cyprus and seized Rhodes, which for several years had been the target of Turkish raids and lay under nominal Byzantine suzerainty.[26] The Hospitallers now made Rhodes their base, building a large fleet and engaging actively in piracy. They also negotiated endlessly with western rulers – the kings of France, Naples and other lands – in the hope of securing the help of a massive crusading fleet. But the target of this fleet was no longer just the Holy Land and the Mamluk state in Egypt and Syria. Increasingly, attention turned to the Turks, whose arrival on the shores of Asia Minor changed the rules of the game: the Turks had broken through the long-established Byzantine cordon that confined them to the Anatolian plateau, and, just as the Hospitallers adapted to the sea, so did the Turks, with the help of Greek manpower drawn from the imperial navy. Michael VIII had disbanded the Byzantine fleet in 1284 to save money, thinking that the Italian navies would protect him and that he was now safe from Charles of Anjou, who was tied up fighting the rebels in Sicily. A number of small Turkish principalities emerged along the coast of Asia Minor, most importantly the emirate of Aydın, which bordered the Aegean. Fortunately for the Christians, these Turkish emirates spent as much time quarrelling among themselves as they spent raiding Christian lands. Even so, Aydın was becoming a severe nuisance to its Christian neighbours by 1318, when its emir, Umur Pasha, entered into an alliance with Catalan mercenaries who had gained control of Athens a few years earlier and placed themselves under the nominal authority of the Aragonese king of Sicily.[27] A curious alliance came into being between these Catalans and the Turks of Aydın, to the intense irritation of the Venetians – the island of Santorini, which was the feudal possession of a Venetian nobleman, was attacked twice, and the Venetians feared that the allies would next threaten Crete.[28]

The solution to the Turkish threat seemed to lie in a properly equipped, well-funded naval crusade in which the Hospitallers, the Italian navies, the Angevins of Naples and the French would work together to establish complete mastery over the Aegean. This was compromised by the ambitions of the Venetians and the Genoese, whose primary concern was the protection of their trade routes and of the lordships they possessed in the region. A 'Holy League' of western navies, to which Venice eventually adhered, temporarily cleared the Aegean of pirates in 1334.[29] But the problem did not go away and the pope eagerly promoted another crusade which managed to seize Smyrna from Umur Pasha in 1344. The Smyrna crusade was only superficially a success. The Christians had succeeded in collecting a fleet of only about thirty galleys: western enthusiasm had been more theoretical than real.[30] Having occupied the citadel, which, remarkably, they held until the great Timur captured it in 1402, the crusaders failed to conquer the hinterland, and a valuable trading centre was transformed into a beleaguered garrison town. The truth was that the crusaders were under-resourced. Rulers such as Robert the Wise, the Angevin king of Naples, had long been raising crusade taxes and even equipping crusade fleets, which then magically turned in the other direction, being put to use in the king's wars against the Genoese Ghibellines or the Aragonese of Sicily.

The instability of this region was enhanced by the strengthening of the Genoese presence, following the conquest of Chios by a Genoese joint-stock company in 1346; the island was shared out among the Genoese investors and administered by the company or *Mahona*. Their main sources of profit were alum, mastic and dried fruits, and they were not keen on further adventurism by western fleets; even the Hospitallers gradually lost their crusading fervour and capitalized on the superb position of Rhodes on the trade routes. Just to the east, the defeat of Aydın left a power vacuum in Anatolia that was rapidly filled by a parvenu group of Turks tucked away in the north-west. The Osmanlı, or Ottoman, Turks were enthusiasts for the holy *jihad* against Byzantium (they conquered Nikaia in 1331), but, like all the Turks of this period, they were also willing to offer their services to Christian rulers in need of mercenaries. So it was that the Greek emperor John VI Kantakouzenos allowed them to settle on the European side of the Dardanelles, at Gallipoli, their first Balkan bridgehead.

The ascendancy of the Christian fleets thus did not remain unchallenged, even as late as the middle of the fourteenth century. The Catalans struggled to mobilize fleets of the size they would need if Muslim contenders for domination of the Straits of Gibraltar were to be held in check. Even so, the alliance of the king of Aragon with the Catalan merchants had created a well-integrated network capable of supplying the western Mediterranean lands with both necessities and luxuries. Despite minor interruptions and many moments of foreboding, peace was maintained between Venice and Genoa from 1299 to 1350. Genoese admirals in search of a good war found other clients. They had already served Frederick II in the thirteenth century; by 1300 they were teaching the Castilians how to mobilize fleets in the Mediterranean and the Atlantic, and they laid the foundations of the Portuguese fleet. But they were incapable of resisting another murderous invader which returned to the Mediterranean after seven or eight hundred years.

IV

The Black Death has sometimes been seen as a natural check on the excessively rapid expansion of the economy of Europe and the Mediterranean lands in the high Middle Ages: population grew so fast that intolerable pressure was placed on the land, forcing up grain prices, and forcing out the production of up-market foodstuffs such as eggs and chickens. Marginal lands that produced poor yields were brought into cultivation; every stalk of grain counted. Famines occurred more and more often, especially in highly urbanized areas such as Tuscany, though the shortages were far worse in northern Europe, especially the Great Famine of 1315 onwards, which had little effect south of the Alps.[31] Yet a more optimistic picture can also be painted. By 1340, population had peaked, at least in western Europe and Byzantium. Between 1329 and 1343 the urban population of Majorca shrank by 23 per cent, and similar figures can be produced for towns in Provence and elsewhere.[32] Greater specialization stimulated trade networks, bringing vital necessities to the cities in return for commercial products. As early as 1280, the Pisans abandoned indifferent grain lands in the mouth of the Arno to sheep; they traded leather, meat, cheese and wool for grain from overseas, for there is hardly a part of a sheep that cannot be put to good use. The little Tuscan town of San Gimignano, specializing in commercial crops such as saffron and wine, was able to support a population denser than at any time before the twentieth century. Its commercial network extended into the Mediterranean, where, as has been seen, its merchants traded local saffron as far east as Aleppo. This trend to 'commercialization', visible also in northern Europe, anticipated many of the developments that followed the Black Death.

Whether or not the economy was emerging from a crisis around 1340, the Black Death knocked Europe and the Islamic world off balance. The death of up to half of the population of the lands around the Mediterranean was bound to have dramatic effects on the social, economic, religious and political life of the peoples of the Mediterranean. It was a psychological shock as much as an economic one.[33] Yet the plague did not induce a long Dark Age comparable to the bleak periods that marked the end of the Bronze Age and the collapse of Roman unity in the Mediterranean. The coming of the plague had accentuated the troubles of the late Roman Empire and had delayed recovery, but it was not the sole cause of the massive recession that occurred. But the plague of the fourteenth century was the main agent in transformations within the Mediterranean and the lands beyond that led to the creation of a new order.

The Genoese were unwittingly responsible for the arrival of the Black Death in the Mediterranean. Bubonic plague was brought to their trading base at Caffa in the Crimea not by merchants but by Mongol armies, who besieged Caffa in 1347.[34] Several Italian ships managed to flee from the war in the Crimea; their route took them to Constantinople, but, even if they were not infected, there were stowaways on board who were – black rats, who relished the grain that filled the holds of the Black Sea fleets, and who carried plague fleas, which also found a home in bales of cloth in the cargo hold. By September 1347 bubonic plague was raging in the Byzantine capital, and as its citizens began to flee they carried the infection with them. A slave ship set out for Alexandria from the Black Sea, carrying over 300 people; according to the Arab historian al-Maqrizi only forty-five were still alive when the ship reached Egypt, and all soon died.[35] It is no surprise that Alexandria became a hub from which bubonic plague spread across the eastern Mediterranean, infecting Gaza in spring 1348. The first port in the western Mediterranean to be infected was Messina. A Sicilian chronicler placed the blame for the arrival of the disease on twelve Genoese galleys fleeing from the East, which arrived in October 1347. The inhabitants of Messina fled all over their island, carrying the germs with them, and the infection crossed the Straits to Reggio as well, reaching Naples by May 1348.[36] By spring 1348 the Black Death had gained a firm grip on Majorca, and from there it spread along the classic trade routes across the Catalan world, towards Perpignan, Barcelona and Valencia, and down into the Muslim kingdom of Granada, reaching Almería by May 1348.[37] In the same month, the citizens of Barcelona processed with their relics and statues beseeching divine intercession to end the plague; such processions naturally did more to spread the disease than to end it.[38] Tunis was infected in April 1348, most likely from Sicily, while a further source of infection lay in the Catalan ships travelling down to the ports of Morocco and Algeria from Majorca.[39] The urban boom of the twelfth to fourteenth century meant that the western shores of the Mediterranean were just as susceptible to plague as the teeming cities of the Middle East. Everywhere, it carried away astonishing numbers of people: a third to a half of the population, possibly as much as 60 or 70 per cent in some parts of the western Mediterranean, such as Catalonia.[40] As it spread it intensified, taking on a pneumonic form that could kill within hours of breath-borne infection.

The loss of up to half of the population of Europe and the Mediterranean had dramatic effects on economic relationships. Demand for foodstuffs contracted greatly, even though in the immediate aftermath of the plague many went hungry as fields in Sicily and elsewhere were left uncultivated, since the labour force was dead or dispersed. The population of the great trading cities collapsed, for the disease spread easily down the alleyways and canals of Genoa, Venice and other trading towns.[41] The Black Death was not a single occurrence: recurrent bouts of plague in the late fourteenth century pushed the overall population down again just as it was poised to recover; new plagues hit the young particularly hard, for the older generations had lived through plague years and had built up some resistance. In the century after the revolt of the Vespers Sicily may have lost 60 per cent of its population, falling from 850,000 to 350,000 inhabitants; two events of capital importance were the plague of 1347 and a further plague that erupted on the island in 1366.[42] Nothing could be the same again after the devastations and horror of the Black Death. Yet the plague, though it had transformed the Mediterranean, had not produced a lasting recession. Old institutions such as the merchant fonduk remained in place; the Genoese, Venetians and Catalans continued to snipe at one another; Christians drew up elaborate plans for crusades against the Mamluks, whose power remained for the moment firm. Underneath all this, there were subtle but important changes in the way that the old networks operated, and the first signs emerged that a rival trading zone was emerging beyond the Straits of Gibraltar. Out of this recovery the Fourth Mediterranean was born at the end of the fourteenth century.

PART FOUR

The Fourth Mediterranean, 1350–1830

I

Would-be Roman Emperors,
1350–1480

I

Following the arrival of the plague, and the dramatic fall in population, pressure on food supplies within the Mediterranean diminished. This did not mean that the old Mediterranean grain trade withered. In fact, it flourished: as inferior lands were abandoned and turned over to pasture, and as other areas became dedicated to products such as sugar and dyestuffs, the economic life of the lands bordering the Great Sea became more varied. As specialization increased, trade in all manner of goods was stimulated. The Mediterranean economy began to take on a new shape. Local contacts came to the fore: products such as timber were ferried down the coasts of Catalonia; wool was sent across the Adriatic from Apulia to the burgeoning towns of Dalmatia, and from Minorca (famous for its sheep) to Tuscany, where around 1400 the 'Merchant of Prato', Francesco di Marco Datini, obsessively ensured that every bale was recorded and every piece of correspondence was preserved – about 150,000 letters – to the great advantage of historians.[1] One of his agents in Ibiza complained: 'this land is unhealthy, the bread is bad, the wine is bad – God forgive me, nothing is good! I fear I shall leave my skin here.'[2] But the demands of business came before personal comfort.

The Merchant of Prato also had Tuscan agents based in San Mateu on the Spanish coast, where they could collect the best Aragonese wools, while deep within the Spanish interior sheep were conquering the Meseta, as millions of animals grazed the high ground in summer and the plateau in winter. Datini's reach extended to the Maghrib and eastwards to the Balkans and the Black Sea. In the 1390s, he was involved in the slave trade, at a time when Circassians from the Black Sea and

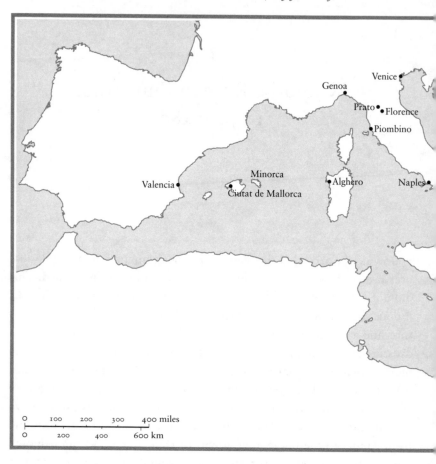

Berbers from North Africa were being sold in the slave markets of Majorca and Sicily.[3] From oriental lands beyond the Mediterranean he obtained indigo, brazilwood, pepper, aloes, zedoary and galingale, as well as cotton, mastic and refined sugar from within the Great Sea. From Spain and Morocco, he imported, besides vast amounts of raw wool, ostrich feathers, elephant ivory, rice, almonds and dates. He ordered a dinner service from Valencia, decorated, as was common practice, with his coat-of-arms, and was irritated when he made a repeat order a few years later and no record of the design had been kept.[4]

Datini was an oligarch, and not typical of late fourteenth-century businessmen, but his career provides an excellent illustration of the continuing vitality of trade and exchange. He managed to conduct business

374

in the most adverse circumstances, even while the duke of Milan prowled around Tuscany in 1402, sweeping under his belt every major city apart from Florence. Mediterranean merchants had always known how to profit from war as well as peace. Yet there was one very significant change. In the early fourteenth century, the three great Florentine banks of the Bardi, Peruzzi and Acciaiuoli had built close ties to the kings of Naples, the Knights of Rhodes and rulers deep within Europe, who relied all too heavily on the credit they provided; but the banks crashed on the eve of the Black Death when it became obvious that they had accumulated too many toxic debts (notably loans to the English king). The international banks that eventually replaced them were careful not to over-extend themselves and were more modest operations;

375

this was true of the Medici Bank despite the political power and fame of the controlling family.[5] Greater caution ensured stable profits. Ambitions were more modest, too: the Catalans sent fewer galleys all the way to Flanders and England, and Marseilles, once an important trading centre, faded in significance. Thus new structures emerged, bound together with new mental attitudes.[6] Urban life was stimulated not just by the increasing specialization, reflected in the development of craft guilds, but by the migration into the towns of country-dwellers whose villages had ceased to function through lack of manpower. In Egypt, abandonment of the soil led to neglect of the irrigation works that had maintained the ecological stability of the Nile Delta. The Delta became impoverished, and wages fell, whereas on the European shores they tended to rise in reponse to the limited availability of labour.[7] However, city populations grew, in many cases recovering to pre-plague levels by 1400, and this encouraged the Genoese, Venetians and Catalans to continue to explore the granaries of the Mediterranean and the Black Sea.

Even if the coming of the plague stimulated a sense that Christians needed to repent of their sins, these sins clearly did not include fighting one another: Venice and Genoa were at each other's throats in 1350–55, and again in 1378–81 (the War of Chioggia). On both occasions the cause of conflict was disagreement over access to the Black Sea from the Aegean. During the first conflict, the Venetians entered into an alliance with the king of Aragon, who was competing with the Genoese for control of Sardinia. The Venetians sent their fleet into the western Mediterranean, scoring a victory against the Genoese off Alghero in northern Sardinia in 1353, while the Catalans sent a fleet as far as the Bosphorus, losing one of their admirals in battle. Yet the war brought benefit to neither side: Venice was forced to accept the loss of the duchy of Dalmatia to Hungary after 350 years, and Genoa descended into civil strife – the city fell under the dominion of the Visconti lords of Milan, who decided that Genoese resources were exhausted, and made peace with an equally exhausted Venice in 1355.[8]

When war broke out again in 1378, attention focused initially on the small island of Tenedos, dominion over which was thought to guarantee mastery over the route through the Dardanelles. A couple of years earlier a Byzantine usurper had donated the island to the Genoese, in return for their aid, but Venice secured promises from one of his rivals that it could take control of the island.[9] The willingness of Genoa and Venice to fight is all the more surprising since the Black Death had greatly reduced available manpower, and the Venetians had to recruit large numbers of oarsmen from Dalmatia. There were other serious troubles, too. In between these wars, the Venetians faced a rebellion in Crete in 1363, in which not just the native Greeks were implicated but also some Venetian nobles, such as members of the great and ancient Gradenigo family.[10] The rebellion placed in doubt the Venetian supply network, for Crete was exploited – or, as these events suggested, over-exploited – for its grain, wine, oil and vegetables, compensating for the lack of a sufficiently extensive hinterland in north-eastern Italy. During the two wars Venice was placed at severe risk in a different and even more perilous way, when Genoa and Venice clashed within the Adriatic, which Genoese navies had rarely dared enter. In 1378–80 Venice was dangerously exposed, now that the king of Hungary controlled the eastern flank of the Adriatic. Venice faced the constant problem that its imperial ambitions in the eastern Mediterranean could be guaranteed only if the seas closest to Venice were dominated by the republic.

When the Genoese were able to call on aid from the king of Hungary and Venice's close neighbour, the Carrara lord of Padua, Venice found itself surrounded. In 1379, the Genoese burned the villages that lay along the Venetian Lido and the allied forces stormed the town of Chioggia, at the southern end of the Venetian lagoon. The allies boasted that they would not rest until they had bridled the four bronze horses that stood over the portico of St Mark's Basilica. The city faced its greatest danger since the Carolingians had besieged the lagoons at the start of the ninth century. Venice managed to hold out under siege; eventually it was the Genoese who felt under siege, as their provisions became exhausted. By June 1380 the Genoese realized that their position was unsustainable, and made peace. One important feature of this conflict is that the Venetians made extensive use of gunpowder, using cannon mounted on the forecastles of their ships. The Genoese commander, Pietro Doria, died when a cannon-ball hit a tower that collapsed on top of him.[11]

Historians of Venice would like to classify the War of Chioggia as a Venetian victory, but the arrival of the Genoese on the sandbanks of the Lido was an enormous humiliation. Venice lost Tenedos, failed to recover Dalmatia, had to recognize Genoese rights in Cyprus (and therefore the Genoese role in the sugar trade), and even had to hand its mainland dependency of Treviso to the Austrian duke, thereby losing such grain lands as it possessed in north-eastern Italy – a Habsburg shadow would fall over parts of north-eastern Italy until the end of the First World War.[12] From both the war of 1350 and the war of 1378 Venice lost more than it gained, in territory and reputation. But, serious as these conflicts were, they were dramatic interruptions in otherwise reasonably peaceful relations, as the ships of the two cities traded side by side in the Aegean, through Constantinople, and onwards to the grain lands of the Crimea. After 1381, the two cities took care to avoid entanglements by defining their trading spheres and commercial interests with care: Venice remained the prime centre of the Levant trade, sending its galleys to Alexandria and Beirut in search of spices; the Genoese laid more emphasis on bulk goods carried in round ships – alum, grain and dried fruits – searching out these products in Asia Minor, Greece and the Black Sea; 'currants' took their name from Corinth, while the independent Greek state of Trebizond, on the southern shores of the Black Sea, was the unrivalled source of hazelnuts. Ambitious trading ventures which, around 1300, had sent Genoese and Venetian travellers deep into Persia and even as far as China were no longer pursued; merchants decided to concentrate on restoring vital links across the sea.[13]

One element of stability was the efficient Venetian shipbuilding industry, the largest industry in the city and perhaps the best organized one in the entire Mediterranean. The Arsenal, which stood alongside the great rope workshop known as the Tana, was already well established in the early fourteenth century, when Dante heard in its dark depths the echoes of Hell itself.

> As in the Arsenal of the Venetians
>> Boils in the winter the tenacious pitch
>> To smear their unsound vessels o'er again,
> For sail they cannot; and instead thereof
>> One makes his vessel new, and one recaulks
>> The ribs of that which many a voyage has made;
> One hammers at the prow, one at the stern,
>> This one makes oars and that one cordage twists,
>> Another mends the mainsail and the mizzen . . .[14]

There was an Old Arsenal with docking space for twelve galleys and a New Arsenal three times larger. By the late fourteenth century an efficient system of production under an admiral had evolved: the Arsenal could produce about three large merchant galleys a year, which may not seem many, except that the size of galleys had grown significantly as sailings to the Levant and Flanders became more regular from the 1340s onwards. These great galleys were lateen-rigged triremes that could load up to 150 tons of cargo, though they also carried very large crews of maybe 200 sailors. Only Venetian citizens could load goods on these ships, which travelled in convoy, often accompanied by smaller armed galleys, along routes carefully approved by the Senate; it took twenty-five years to qualify for citizenship, and, as has been seen, the most profitable voyages, handling silks and spices, were dominated by the investments of Venetian noblemen. For more modest goods, the Venetians used round merchant cogs with square sails, constructed in private shipyards and subject to less restriction on design. The largest cog known from the fifteenth century was nearly thirty metres long and displaced 720 tons.[15] Skills in shipbuilding were matched by skills in navigation, and Venice vied with Genoa and Majorca as a major centre of cartography. Venetian sailors thus had plenty of exact information about the coasts of the Mediterranean. Moreover, with the increased use of compasses it was possible to navigate with greater confidence and to extend the sailing season across most of the year.[16]

II

One business enterprise that kept sailors busy was ferrying pilgrims to the Holy Land. The loss of the last Christian outposts in Palestine did not put an end to pilgrimage; the kings of Aragon vied with others to secure vague rights of protection over Christian sanctuaries in the Holy Land, and the Mamluk sultans knew that they could play the Holy Land card when negotiating political and commercial agreements with western rulers. Pilgrimage was, and was supposed to be, physically demanding. Felix Fabri was a Dominican friar who travelled from Germany to the Holy Land in 1480, and left a vivid account of the smells, discomfort and squalor on board ship: meat swarming with maggots, undrinkable water, vermin everywhere. His return voyage from Alexandria, out of season, exposed him to the winds and waves that had battered earlier pilgrims such as ibn Jubayr. He learned, though, that the best place to sleep was under cover, on top of the hard bales of spices.[17] But, at least for a scholarly minority, pilgrimage was taking on a new shape. In 1358 Petrarch was invited by a friend, Giovanni Mandelli, to travel with him to the Holy Sepulchre. Deciding that it was immeasurably safer to stay behind, he favoured Mandelli with a little book in which he described the route across the Mediterranean. He noted all the places that had been visited by Ulysses; he pointed out the temple of Juno Lacinia in Crotone, in the far south of Italy; he observed that Cilicia was where Pompey had defeated bands of pirates; he paused briefly to contemplate the place of the crucifixion of Christ ('you would not have undertaken such an arduous labour for any other reason than to see with your own eyes . . . the things that you have already seen with your mind'); but he finally left Mandelli standing not in Jerusalem but in Alexandria, and not among sacks of spices but by the tomb of Alexander and the urn of Pompey.[18] Cultural tourism around the sites of classical antiquity was about to begin. Over forty manuscripts of Petrarch's *Itinerary* survive, showing how popular it was, above all in fifteenth-century Naples, for Mandelli was showered with information about classical sites along the coasts of southern Italy, and it was this (rather than interest in the holy places) that appealed to readers.

Petrarch's classical tourism was turned into reality in the 1420s by a merchant of Ancona who found himself transfixed by the sight of classical monuments, first in his home city and then around the Mediterranean. Cyriac of Ancona had political motives too: he made himself known to the Ottoman sultan, who did not realize that one of Cyriac's aims was to collect information that could be used in a crusade against the Turks. But he took a genuine delight in physical remains from the classical past, travelling to Delphi where, to the amazement of the inhabitants of a greatly overgrown site, he spent six days in 1436 enthusing over what he wrongly believed to be its main temple and over the theatre and stadium, copying inscriptions and drawing plans.[19] Although most of those who interested themselves in the classical past would remain comfortably in their armchair, like Petrarch, Cyriac's career indicates that the allure of Mediterranean travel was no longer exclusively religious or commercial.

A very few of those who travelled 'went native', immersing themselves in the religion and customs of the peoples who lived on the opposite shore. There is the extraordinary Anselmo Turmeda, a Majorcan friar who discovered the teachings of Islam in Bologna, travelled to North Africa, where he converted and became a noted early fifteenth-century Muslim scholar under the name of 'Abdallah at-Tarjuman; his tomb still stands in Tunis. A century later the scholar and diplomat al-Hasan ibn Muhammad al-Wazzan, or Leo Africanus, who was of Granadan birth, was captured by Christian pirates, taken to Rome and became a protégé of the Pope Leo X, and wrote a geography of Africa: here we have someone who could also convey to western audiences the physical realities of the Islamic world way beyond the Mediterranean, and who switched back and forth from Islam to Christianity and back to Islam.[20]

III

The fortunes of the kings of Aragon, and of the many kingdoms under their rule, provide an excellent guide to the wider fortunes of the Mediterranean in the late fourteenth and fifteenth centuries. Catalan influence extended right across the Mediterranean, as far as the marketplaces of Alexandria and Rhodes; and, at the end of the century, the king of Aragon was a dominant figure both in the Iberian peninsula and in wider European politics. Martin the Younger, the son and heir of King Martin of Aragon, married the heiress to Sicily after she was to all intents kidnapped and despatched to Spain, giving him ample excuse to invade the island in 1392; in the fifteenth century the island was ruled by viceroys held to account by island parliaments, and the separate line of increasingly ineffective Aragonese kings of Sicily disappeared. Peace was obviously good for the Sicilians, and it was also good for those who wanted to buy their grain. Catalan nobles began to acquire extensive estates in Sicily and to settle there.[21] The final achievement of Martin the Younger, before he was felled by malaria in Sardinia, was the recovery of Catalan-Aragonese control over large swathes of that island as well, after which Catalan cultural influence dominated, for instance in the arts.[22]

The new assertiveness of the rulers of Aragon was demonstrated most forcefully by Alfonso V, who succeeded to the throne in 1416 and was to become one of the great monarchs of the fifteenth century.[23] The male line of the house of Barcelona had died out, and Alfonso came from Castile; nonetheless, he looked outwards to the Mediterranean, and his schemes encompassed the entire sea. Like all the Aragonese kings he earned a sobriquet, and Alfonso's, 'the Magnanimous', perfectly expresses his desire to be seen as a generous patron, endowed with the princely qualities he read about in the works of his fellow-Spaniard Seneca, the philosopher of the ancient Roman emperors, for he was a passionate student of classical texts, with a strong interest in heroic accounts of ancient warfare. He knew that two of the most successful Roman emperors, Trajan and Hadrian, were Spaniards.[24] Alfonso aspired to restore the Roman Empire in the Mediterranean, in the face of the growing Turkish threat. Early in his reign he attacked Corsica, which the papacy had offered to the kings of Aragon at the same time as Sardinia, far back in 1297. He failed to secure much beyond the stronghold of Calvi, but his campaign reveals that his ambitions were by no means limited to the lands he had inherited in Spain. Pursuing his Roman imperial dreams, he looked towards Italy, and offered his services to the confused queen of Naples, Joanna II, even securing a promise that she would nominate him as her heir (despite a colourful private life she had no sons). Unfortunately she also promised to leave her increasingly turbulent kingdom to the duke of Anjou and count of Provence, René of Anjou. *Le bon roi René* shared with Alfonso a passion for chivalric culture and the patronage of the arts; he also shared a wish to accumulate kingdoms, though by the end of his life in 1480 he was left with none, compared to the six or seven kingdoms and one principality over which Alfonso ruled when he died in 1458.[25] The intermittent battle with René for control of southern Italy took over twenty years, and consumed royal resources, for maintaining a powerful fleet was extraordinarily costly. The financial reserves of the monarchy were perilously low, and Alfonso was therefore forced to go cap-in-hand to his parliaments, giving them a chance to bargain for the privileges they valued most.[26] Fortunately, René of Anjou was even poorer, but he did manage to mobilize the Genoese fleet: Genoese hostility to the Catalans had not waned since the Catalan invasion of Sardinia over a century earlier.

Alfonso faced moments of intense danger. In 1435 he led his fleet against the Genoese off the island of Ponza; he was defeated, captured and carried off to Genoa. The Genoese then found themselves obliged to hand their prisoner over to their overlord, the duke of Milan, Filippo Maria Visconti, who was charmed by Alfonso and turned events upside down when he decided to enter into an alliance with him. The duke of Milan even contemplated bequeathing his duchy to Alfonso, whose plans for the domination of Italy distracted him from Iberian affairs. The long and costly war with René culminated in Alfonso's capture of Naples by tunnelling under its walls, in 1442. Even after his expulsion from what he always regarded as his own kingdom of Naples, René maintained pressure on the conquering Aragonese, and Genoa remained the base for hostile expeditions into southern Italy well into the 1460s.[27] Nor did Italian campaigns cease with the fall of Naples. In 1448 Alfonso was knocking at the gates of the small but strategically valuable statelet of Piombino, which incorporated the iron-rich island of Elba, and which had its own fleet, trading and raiding as far as Tunis.[28] From Piombino he could exercise control over the movement of ships between Genoa and Naples, while the town also provided a springboard for the invasion of Tuscany. Piombino proved too hard a nut to crack, though the lord of Piombino wisely began to render an annual tribute, in the form of a golden goblet, to assure himself of Alfonso's goodwill, and over the years bases along the coast either side of Elba fell under Aragonese and, in the sixteenth century, Spanish control.[29] By the middle of the fifteenth century most of Italy was divided between five great powers: Milan, Florence, Venice, the papacy and the king of Aragon. Although the king of Aragon controlled much the largest territory (even vaster if the two Italian islands are included), he was forced to abandon his dream of domination over the peninsula when the four other powers adhered to the Peace of Lodi in 1454, to which Alfonso added his signature early the next year. This treaty guaranteed peace (with some notable interruptions) for the next half-century, and one of its aims was to divert the energies of the signatories to the urgent task of fighting the Turks.

Constantinople had fallen to Mehmet the Conqueror one year before the peace agreement. All the talk about resisting the Turks had achieved nothing; indeed, they were advancing with ever greater confidence through the Balkans. Already, in 1447, Alfonso had promised help to the embattled king of Hungary, John Hunyadi. Alfonso raised the promised troops and then sent them to fight his Tuscan war instead. He was not, however, simply a cynic about the crusade against the Turks.[30] Alfonso rejoiced in his self-image as a king-redeemer and warrior for Christ – as the new Galahad, a theme that was taken up in the magnificent sculptures of his triumphal arch in Naples. He offered warm support to Scanderbeg, the great Albanian rebel against the Turks, for the loss of Albania to the Ottomans would bring their fleets and armies within sight of southern Italy.[31] Alfonso's ambitions extended as far as Kastellórizo, a tiny island to the east of Rhodes, which became a base for Aragonese naval operations deep inside the eastern Mediterranean (it is now the farthest flung possession of Greece).[32] Shortly before the fall of Constantinople he and the Greek prince Demetrios Palaiologos were fabricating plans to seize power in Constantinople from the last Byzantine emperor, Constantine XI, and Alfonso had his own viceroy in the Peloponnese. These grandiose aims of defeating the Turks and recovering the eastern Mediterranean lands were commemorated after Alfonso's death in the lively novel by Joannot Martorell, *Tirant lo Blanc*.[33] In many ways the swashbuckling hero Tirant is an Alfonso-figure, or rather the figure the king had aspired to become, and (amid the often explicit love scenes) the book was filled with advice about the best way to defeat a Turkish army, along with the Genoese, whom Alfonso regarded as secret allies of the Ottomans.[34] In *Tirant lo Blanc* the Genoese try to frustrate the Hospitaller army defending Rhodes from the Turks:

> Your Lordship should know that two Genoese friars of our order have betrayed us, for on their advice the villainous Genoese sent all those ships with many soldiers but little cargo. The traitors in our castle have done a foul deed, removing the notches from our crossbows and replacing them with soap and cheese.[35]

Genoese behaviour during the final siege of Constantinople in 1453 aroused similar suspicions.[36]

IV

By 1453, aided by a strong administration and a devotion to the holy cause of the *jihad*, the Ottomans had already extinguished rival Turkish statelets along the coast of Asia Minor, notably the pirate stronghold of Aydın. Despite a massive defeat at the hands of the central Asian warlord Timur (Tamerlane) in 1402, the Ottomans revived quickly. By the 1420s they had once again become active in the Balkans. The Byzantine emperor sold Thessalonika to Venice in 1423; but, having hankered so long after its dominion, the Venetians were able to hold the city for only seven years before it fell to the armies of Sultan Murad II. The succession of the young Mehmet II resolved the dispute between those relatively cautious advisers who opposed rapid expansion for fear of over-extension, and the more adventurous faction that saw Mehmet as the leader of a revitalized Roman Empire controlled by Muslim Turks who would combine Roman-Byzantine, Turkic and Islamic concepts of rule. His aim was to restore and fulfil, rather than destroy, the Roman Empire. His Greek scribes issued documents describing him as Mehmet, *Basileus* and Autocrat of the Romans, the title by which the Byzantine emperors had been known.[37] But his imperial dream was not satisfied with the New Rome; he sought to make himself master of the Old Rome too. Practical politics also drew western affairs to his attention. The rebellion of Scanderbeg in Albania made the sultan realize that there were defects in the traditional policy of allowing independent Christian vassals to rule the Balkan lands. Even those who had been educated as Muslims at the Ottoman court, like Scanderbeg, could become renegades. Ottoman authority thus needed to be imposed directly, and Ottoman power edged forwards to the shores of the Adriatic. Scanderbeg died in 1468, after which the Albanian rebellion petered out; by 1478 Mehmet had gained control of Valona (Vlorë) on the Albanian coast, and over the next few months he wrested the city of Scutari (Shkodër), dominated by the great fortified hill of Rozafa, from the Venetians.[38] Durazzo, the ancient Dyrrhachion, remained in Venetian hands till the start of the next century, and the port of Kotor (Cattaro), deep within its fjord in Montenegro, enjoyed Venetian protection; but the rest of the Venetian dominion in this part of the Adriatic was whittled away.[39]

The Venetians had been lukewarm about Scanderbeg, anxious that support for rebels would compromise their trading position at Constantinople. Yet to lose the coast of Albania was to pay a heavy price, not just because of its usefulness as a source of salt, but because the Venetians needed to navigate past the Albanian shore on their way out of the Adriatic. Routes inland from the coast were valued too, as they gave access to the silver, slaves and other products of the mountainous Balkan interior. The difficulties were compounded by Turkish assaults on the Venetian naval bases in the Aegean: Lemnos and Negroponte fell into Ottoman hands. Wise to the implications, the Sublime Porte (as the

Ottoman court was often known) still issued the Venetians with trading privileges. The message was clear: the Ottomans could tolerate Christian merchants from overseas, just as Muslim rulers all around the Mediterranean had done for centuries; but they regarded Venetian or Genoese territorial dominion within the *Akdeniz*, or White Sea, as unacceptable.[40]

By the end of his reign Mehmet was determined to confront the Christian powers in the Mediterranean. An obvious focus of Turkish attention was the headquarters of the Knights Hospitallers on Rhodes, which they had occupied since 1310, and from which they had launched pirate raids against Muslim shipping, as well as gaining control of a few coastal stations in Asia Minor, most notably Bodrum, whose Hospitaller castle was built out of the stones of the great Mausoleum of Halikarnassos. Rhodes also attracted Mehmet as one of the famous cities of the ancient world.[41] A Saxon cannon founder named Meister Georg who had been domiciled in Istanbul offered the Turks precious information about the layout of the fortress, but in 1480 the defences of Rhodes proved too strong even for massive Turkish cannon cast by the finest experts. Neither side showed any mercy: the Hospitallers sent out sorties at night-time, and brought back the heads of the Turks they had killed, which were carried in procession through the city to encourage its defenders. Frustrated by the resolute resistance, the Turks made peace with the Knights, who promised to cease interfering with Turkish shipping.[42] The sultans did not forget their defeat, but Rhodes remained the property of the Knights of St John for another forty-two years. Nor did western Europeans forget what happened at Rhodes, since it brought some cheer at a time when the Turkish threat was so severe. Immediately afterwards, a woodcut history of the siege was an early bestseller in Venice, Ulm, Salamanca, Paris, Bruges and London.

At the same time, Turkish fleets were threatening the West. Southern Italy was an obvious target, because of its proximity to Albania and because Ottoman control of both sides of the Adriatic entrance would force Venice to obey the sultan's will. Venice did not want to be seen to oppose the Turks. When they attacked Otranto in 1480, Venetian ships helped ferry Turkish troops across to Italy from Albania, though this met with official disapproval in Venice itself. One hundred and forty Ottoman ships carrying 18,000 men crossed the Straits, including forty galleys. After the inhabitants of Otranto refused to surrender, the

Turkish commander, Gedik Ahmet Pasha, made clear what would happen to the survivors and pressed on with his assault; the town possessed poor defences and no cannon, and the outcome was predictable. On capturing the city Ahmet Pasha slaughtered the entire male population, leaving 10,000 people alive out of about 22,000; 8,000 slaves were sent across the Straits to Albania. The elderly archbishop was struck down at the high altar of Otranto Cathedral. The Turks then fanned out across southern Apulia, raiding neighbouring cities. The king of Naples, Alfonso V's son Ferrante, had sent his armies into Tuscany, but once his troops and ships were ready he was able to launch a successful counter-assault. Even when the Turks withdrew, they made plain their intention of returning and conquering the Apulian ports, while rumour enlarged this into a grand army ready to attack both Italy and Sicily from Albania.[43]

The siege of Otranto was an enormous shock to western Europe. All the Christian powers in the Mediterranean offered help against the Turks, notably Ferdinand II, king of Aragon and cousin of Ferrante of Naples. The conspicuous exception was Venice, claiming to be too tired after decades of conflict with the sultan's armies and navies. Turkish raiding parties had started to penetrate into Friuli, an area of northeastern Italy partly under Venetian dominion – on land as on sea the Turks were threateningly close, and the Venetians preferred appeasement.[44] The Venetian consul in Apulia was advised that he should express his satisfaction at the Christian victory to the Neapolitan king orally and not in writing; written messages were often stolen by spies, and the Serenissima Repubblica was fearful that the sultan might see a purloined letter of congratulations and blame Venice for its two-faced outlook.

The immediate danger of a further attack on southern Italy disappeared with the death of Mehmet in May 1481. He was only forty-nine years old. During the coming years western rulers such as Charles VIII of France and Ferdinand of Aragon would make the war against the Turks a central area of policy. Both these rulers took the view that, if they controlled southern Italy, they would be able to lay their hands on the resources needed for a grand crusade and use Apulia as a convenient launching-pad for attacks on Ottoman lands, which now lay so close; both also had controversial claims to the throne of Naples, notwithstanding the presence of a local dynasty of Aragonese origin. Charles

VIII's invasion of southern Italy, in 1494–5, brought him mastery over Naples, but his position proved unsustainable, and he soon had to withdraw. Venice now felt threatened on all sides. Crusades against the Turks would only endanger traffic through the waters facing Ottoman Albania. At the end of the fifteenth century Venice therefore took control of a number of Apulian ports, to guarantee free passage through the Straits.[45] In 1495, amid scenes of gory massacre and brutal rape, the Venetians seized Monopoli from the French; they then persuaded the king of Naples, Ferrante II, to grant them Trani, Brindisi and Otranto without bloodshed, holding them until 1509. The king needed allies, and they needed the produce of Apulia, exporting grain, wine, salt, oil, vegetables and saltpetre for their cannons.[46] However, the loss of Durazzo to the Turks in 1502 deprived Venice of its most important listening station on the Albanian side of the Straits. They had only just built new fortifications, which still stand. The Mediterranean was becoming divided in two: an Ottoman East and a Christian West. One obvious question was which side was likely to win the contest; but another question was which Christian power would dominate the waters of the western Mediterranean.

V

A few bridges were created between these two worlds. The Ottoman court was fascinated by Western culture, understandably in view of the claim to mastery over the old Roman Empire; meanwhile western Europeans sought to understand the Turks, and continued to acquire exotic oriental goods.[47] The artist Gentile Bellini travelled from Venice to Constantinople, where he painted a famous portrait of Mehmet II that now hangs in the National Gallery in London.[48] Pressure on the West was rarely relaxed (mainly when the sultans turned their attention to Persia instead), but the Ottomans realized the importance of creating a neutral territory between their lands and western Europe, whose merchants could gain entry into the contrasting worlds of western Christendom and the Turks. This territory was the small but vibrant trading republic of Dubrovnik, known to western Europeans as Ragusa. Its origins, like those of Venice and Amalfi, lay in a group of refugees from barbarian invasions who occupied a rocky promontory in southern Dalmatia, protected by a wall of mountains from Slav incursions. The Latin Ragusans were soon joined by a Slav population, and by the late twelfth century the town was bilingual, some speaking south Slav dialects and some speaking Dalmatian, a romance language closely related to Italian; in Slavonic, the inhabitants were known as the *dubrovčani*, 'those of the woods'. Although they entered into treaties with assertive Serbian and Bosnian princes in the interior, the Ragusans needed protectors, and found them in the Norman kings of Sicily and then in Venice, which consolidated its hold on southern Dalmatia after the Fourth Crusade of 1202–4.[49]

Once the Hungarian king had wrested Dalmatia from Venice following his intervention in the war of 1350 between Venice and Genoa, the city fell under Hungarian suzerainty (from 1358).[50] This allowed the Ragusans to develop their own institutions and their own commercial network without a great amount of external interference. A trading patriciate emerged, able to benefit from access to the Bosnian interior, rich in silver and slaves; Dubrovnik became the main centre in the region for the purchase of salt.[51] Demand for silver in the eastern Mediterranean had always been strong, for lack of local supplies, and Ragusan merchants made some headway in the Byzantine and Turkish lands of the East.[52] Dubrovnik was able to benefit greatly from new opportunities following the Black Death. Local trade flourished – indeed, without the wheat, oil, salted meat, wine, fruit and vegetables that were regularly carried across to Dalmatia from Apulia, neither Dubrovnik nor its neighbours could have survived; even fish was imported from southern Italy, unlikely as this may seem in a maritime city.[53] There was very little land fit for growing anything. A fifteenth-century writer, Philippus de Diversis, explained the essential features of his home city:

> The territory of Ragusa, because of its sterility as much as because of the large number of people, lives off a small income, so that nobody could live with his family from his possessions unless he had other riches, and this is why it is necessary to engage in commerce.[54]

He felt embarrassed at the involvement of the city patricians in trade, which he knew was a taboo shunned by the patriciate of ancient Rome. On the other hand, the lack of local resources stimulated the emergence of important industries: raw wool from southern Italy and Spain was manufactured into woollen cloth, and by the mid-sixteenth century Dubrovnik had become a notable textile centre. The link across the Adriatic to the towns of southern Italy was of crucial importance. Dubrovnik provided the kings of Naples with valuable information about what was happening in the Ottoman lands. In return, these kings helped suppress piracy in the Adriatic and exempted the Ragusans from port taxes.[55] Ragusan ships were allowed to dominate the waters off Apulia. This was the beginning of a phase of expansion which would see the Ragusan fleet emerge as one of the largest merchant navies in the Mediterranean; Dubrovnik, not the Argonauts of Jason, provided the English language with the word *argosy*, a corruption of 'Ragusa'. A Ragusan patrician, Benedetto Cotrugli, or Kotruljević, became mintmaster in Naples, but he is best known for his tract on the art of commerce that set out the business skills that guaranteed success. Among his sage advice to merchants was that they should avoid gambling and card games, nor should they drink and eat too much.[56]

A maritime republic that lay within walking distance of the territories ruled by the great Slav princes could not escape their attempts at interference, and it was for this reason that the Ragusans preferred protectors who lived some distance away – even the Turks. The city's difficulties multiplied in the middle of the fifteenth century, when enemies, Slav and Turkish, closed in from several directions. The city was firmly enclosed within its impressive set of walls, which still stand. One enemy was Stjepan Vukčić, *herceg* (or duke) of lands to the rear of Dubrovnik that became known as Hercegovina. His title was confirmed by the Ottoman court, though he was independent-minded and saw submission to the Sublime Porte as a way of guaranteeing rather than compromising his authority. He decided to raise funds by establishing a trading settlement that would, he hoped, outrival Dubrovnik, at Herceg Novi, by the entrance to the Bay of Kotor. The source of profit would not be exotic goods from the Orient; it would be salt, traditionally traded through Dubrovnik.[57] The Ragusans were not innocent of territorial ambitions. They of course wanted to acquire Herceg Novi and even the Serbian town of Trebinje, a little way into Hercegovina. In 1451 Ragusan heralds proclaimed that the reward for assassinating the Herceg (who was also suspected of heresy) would be 15,000 ducats and elevation to the Ragusan patriciate.

This threat frightened Vukčić enough to make him withdraw his armies from Ragusan territory, but Dubrovnik almost at once had to confront a new threat, as Mehmet the Conqueror triumphantly extended his power over the Balkan principalities. So in 1458 Ragusan ambassadors toiled their way to the sultan's court at Skopje with an offer of submission in return, they hoped, for confirmation of their commercial privileges. Some haggling was necessary, but by 1472 they were sending 10,000 ducats as annual tribute – and it continued to rise thereafter.[58] Regular tribute payments were a better guarantee of safety than the city's massive walls. A curious situation developed. The Ragusans traded with the Ottoman-ruled lands, and yet they gave support to enemies of the Turks such as Scanderbeg, as he passed from Albania to southern Italy to enter the service of the beleaguered King Ferrante of Naples; they looked after Vukčić when he was dispossessed by the Turks, having evidently forgotten their wish to do away with him. Yet the Turks rarely oppressed Dubrovnik, seeing advantage in its role as a commercial middleman that supplied the Sublime Porte with goods and tribute. Around 1500 the Ragusans were able to benefit from the discomfiture of the Venetians who struggled to hold back Ottoman advances along the coast of Albania. Venice could no longer trade with Constantinople, but Ragusan ships could fly their flag with impunity in Turkish waters, and carry goods between East and West. Putting out of their mind the tribute they paid to the Ottoman sultan, the Ragusans flaunted the myth of the city's freedom, encapsulated in the simple motto LIBERTAS.

2

Transformations in the West,
1391–1500

I

While the Ragusans benefited from their special relationship with the Turks, the Genoese and Venetians were more cautious in building ties to the Ottoman court. The sultan was anxious not to turn them away, but they viewed the eastern Mediterranean as increasingly dangerous. Difficulties were compounded by occasional arguments between the Venetians and the Mamluk sultans of Egypt, who required ever larger amounts in taxes in order to prop up their regime. The Mamluks were also a regional threat. In 1424–6 they invaded Cyprus and carried away its king, Janus, along with 6,000 captives; a ransom of 200,000 ducats had to be paid before Janus was restored to the throne, and it is said that he never laughed again. In 1444 they besieged Rhodes. In 1460 they supported a claimant to the throne of Cyprus, sending eighty ships against the island, to the horror of Christendom, for no one could understand why James of Lusignan, a bastard, would wish to enlist Egyptian aid in a bid for a throne to which he was not entitled.[1]

As Ottoman and Mamluk pressure on these areas became intolerable, the Genoese and their rivals increasingly turned their attention towards the West, buying sugar in Sicily and Spain and grain in Sicily and Morocco. The mid-fifteenth century saw a veritable economic renaissance in Genoa, at first sight against all the odds: the city was still consumed by internal strife, but large segments of the population were able to benefit from trade and investment, and the city boomed. Especially attractive were shares in the new public bank, the Banco di San Giorgio, which eventually acquired dominion over Corsica.[2] The loss of easy access by the Genoese to the alum mines of Phokaia in Asia Minor was compensated by the discovery in 1464 of alum mines on the door-step of Rome itself, at Tolfa; Pope Pius II described the discovery as 'our greatest victory against the Turk'. It reduced dependence on 'the Turk', and yet it did not reduce dependence on the Genoese, who switched their attention to central Italy, and built a new alum monopoly there. The technology of sugar production travelled westwards ahead of the merchants, and the eastern sugar industry began to decline.[3] Sophisticated sugar-mills, or *trappeti*, were developed in Sicily. In Valencia, the furthest north sugar cane could be made to grow, businessmen from as far away as Germany set up plantations; the need for ceramic vessels used in processing raw sugar stimulated the local pottery industry as well, bringing further fame to Valencia in the form of its 'Hispano-Moresque' pottery that can be found in many modern museums.[4] The drive to the west was so powerful that it continued through the Straits of Gibraltar, reaching Madeira in the 1420s, and then the Azores, the Canaries, the Cape Verde islands and São Tomé – most of these were Portuguese acquisitions, but the capital and know-how came from the Genoese, while the first sugar-stocks in Madeira are said to have come from Sicily.[5]

Stopping-points on the way out to the Atlantic acquired new importance. Granada, though a Muslim state until 1492, became a centre of operations for Genoese, Florentine and Catalan businessmen, who regularly visited Almería and Málaga, buying silk, dried fruits and ceramics. It is hard to see how the Nasrid sultans of Granada could have maintained themselves in power (or built the Alhambra palaces) without the financial support they gained from the Christian merchants. They liked to think it was their fervent Islam that held Granada together, but foreign funds were no less important.[6] Granada was further neutralized by the occasional success of the kings of Castile in imposing tribute payments on the sultans. Border warfare between the Castilians and the Granadans did not cease, though it took on the character of a long-running tournament, and was more successful in generating Spanish ballads about beautiful Moorish princesses than in winning territory.

This fragile stability was placed at risk in August 1415 when the Portuguese sent 100 ships against Ceuta and captured the city after a brief siege in which the king's son Henry, later known as 'the Navigator', earned his spurs. It was a remarkable victory: the Portuguese showed little understanding of the complex currents in the Straits and their fleet

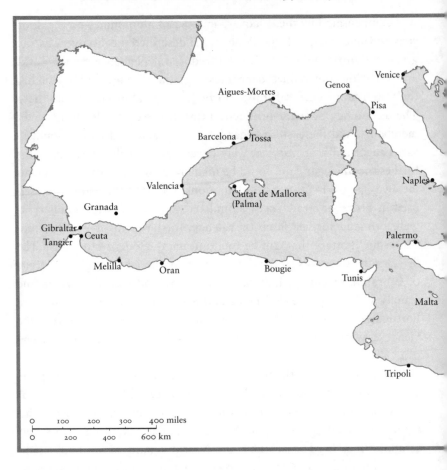

was battered by summer storms, so that part of it was blown back towards Spain. This allowed the governor of Ceuta time to summon Moroccan reinforcements, though he then stupidly cancelled his request. The Portuguese dithered about whether to follow their original plans or whether to attack Gibraltar, on Granadan territory, instead; in many ways Gibraltar was the obvious choice, because it had been tossed back and forth between Fez and Granada, following a rebellion on the rock in 1410. But Ceuta was larger, far richer and stands in a less forbidding position, astride a narrow peninsula connecting the low eminence of Monte Hacho to the African continent. Its conquest astonished contemporary Europeans. No one could quite understand what was in the mind of the Portuguese court. The astonishment was compounded by

the secrecy of the Portuguese: everyone knew they were building a fleet and hiring foreign ships, but it was widely assumed they planned to attack Granadan territory, despite Castilian insistence that attacks on Granada were reserved to Castile.[7]

Thus the Portuguese arrived in the Straits as an unwelcome fourth force alongside Marinid Morocco, Nasrid Granada and Castile. Even if the Portuguese aspired to the wealth of Ceuta, they failed to secure it: Muslim merchants avoided the city, which became an empty ghost town inhabited mainly by a Portuguese garrison and by convicts sent there as punishment. The Portuguese presumably hoped that their capture of Ceuta would open up access to the wheatfields of Atlantic Morocco, but the campaign had exactly the opposite effect. Ceuta became a millstone around the necks of the Portuguese. Yet they were too proud to relinquish it and even hoped to gain more Moroccan lands: in 1437 the Portuguese attempted to seize Tangier, and met with ignominious failure (much later, in 1471, they did occupy the town). Prince Henry's brother Fernando was sent to Fez as a hostage, to be released after the Portuguese handed back Ceuta; Henry agreed and then, to his eternal shame, reneged on the agreement, so that his brother was left to die in prison.[8] The long-term result was that Ceuta has remained in Portuguese and, since 1668, Spanish hands.[9] Since the sixteenth century, when Luis de Camões wrote his great epic of Portuguese expansion, the *Lusiads*, the conquest of Ceuta has been seen as the first step towards Portuguese expansion along the coast of Africa:

> A thousand swimming birds, spreading
> Their concave pinions to the winds,
> Parted the white, turbulent waves
> To where Hercules set his pillars.[10]

Evidently, though, the Portuguese could not yet predict the opening of the trade route round Africa to India – the possibility of entering the Indian Ocean from the Atlantic was strenuously denied in Ptolemy's *Geography*.

The Mediterranean, not the distant oceans, was the immediate target of Portuguese sailors.[11] One of the features of the great restructuring that followed the Black Death was the emergence of new centres of business and new groups of traders; visitors to the Mediterranean from the Atlantic, such as the Portuguese, became more frequent. Much of this trade was confined to short, regular routes, intensively exploited. The Portuguese, Basques, Cantabrians and Galicians plied their trade in salted fish as far as Valencia and Barcelona.[12] There were some more ambitious long-distance voyages too: an English ship is recorded at Ibiza in 1412; in 1468 King Ferrante of Naples entered into a commercial pact with Edward IV of England.[13] The most ambitious English expeditions were launched by merchants of Bristol. In 1457 Robert Sturmy sailed with three vessels for the Levant, but on the return voyage the Genoese attacked his ships off Malta, sinking two of them. When news of this attack reached England, there was a great outcry against the Genoese for blocking north European attempts to compete in the trade of the Mediterranean. The mayor of Southampton summarily arrested all the Genoese he could find.[14] These were the violent beginnings of the ties between England and the Mediterranean that would transform the sea in later centuries.

It is no surprise that French ships attempted to create a niche for themselves in the spice trade to Alexandria, launching ships from ports on the Mediterranean.[15] Jacques Cœur of Bourges, the son of a prosperous furrier, travelled from Narbonne to Alexandria and Damascus in 1432, and became fascinated by the trading opportunities in the Levant. He entered royal service, where his great talents were quickly recognized; he served King Charles VII as quartermaster, or *argentier*, responsible for the supply of goods, including luxuries, to the royal court; in the 1440s and 50s he began to fulfil his dream of building ties between France and both Egypt and North Africa. He operated at least four galleys, and, according to a contemporary writer, he was 'the first of all the French of his time to equip and arm galleys that, loaded with woollen garments and other products of the workshops of France, travelled up and down the coasts of Africa and the East'.[16] He began to see Aigues-Mortes, stuck in its stagnant pools near Montpellier, as the obvious base for an ambitious programme of shipbuilding; the city council of Barcelona was worried that he was diverting the spice trade there, and trying to establish a French royal monopoly. Indeed, it is not entirely clear whether the French galleys were owned by the king of France or his hugely ambitious *argentier*; perhaps it was a matter of little consequence, for the king and his financier shared the profits. Jacques Cœur's network of agents was bolstered by attempts to gain favours from the Mamluk sultans of Egypt, permitting him to trade on preferential terms. He has been seen as a prototype mercantilist, well attuned to the political advantages of an active trading policy within the Mediterranean.[17] His success brought envy, while his contacts with foreign powers as varied as the Mamluk sultan and René of Anjou, ruler of Provence, seemed to suggest he was conducting his own foreign policy. In 1451 his enemies turned against him; he was arrested on charges of peculation and treason, tortured and exiled. Although this trading network did not survive his arrest, the career of Jacques Cœur amply illustrates the new opportunities that ambitious businessmen were able to seize in the mid-fifteenth-century Mediterranean.

II

All the traffic through the Straits of Gibraltar had to work its way past the great rock itself. Castilian adventurers were determined to recover the town, which had been briefly held by their compatriots in the four-teenth century. In 1436 the count of Niebla was drowned with forty companions while retreating from a failed attack on Gibraltar; his remains were ignominiously displayed in a wicker basket, or *barcina*, which still gives its name to one of Gibraltar's gateways. Finally, the duke of Medina Sidonia captured the rock in 1462, taking advantage of the absence of its leading citizens, who had gone to pay homage to the sultan in Granada. Enormously powerful nobles, operating their own war fleet, the dukes of Medina Sidonia took the view that they could do what they wished with the rock, including replacing its inhabitants with a new population. In 1474, 4,350 *conversos*, New Christians of Jewish origin, settled in Gibraltar; they hoped to escape the tribulations they had experienced in their native Córdoba, and they offered to maintain the town garrison from their own resources. However, the duke soon became convinced that the *conversos* would offer the town to the king and queen, who were regarded as sympathetic to *conversos*. He had been planning an expedition against Portuguese Ceuta (such was his love for his Christian neighbours), but he diverted his flotilla against Gibraltar instead, which he easily recovered. This time it was the *con-versos* who were forced to leave. The rock remained in the hands of the Medina Sidonia family until 1501, when Queen Isabella of Castile insisted that so important a strategic position had to lie under royal control.[18]

Castile had only a limited Mediterranean coast, mainly consisting of the old Muslim kingdom of Murcia, conquered in the thirteenth cen-tury. During the fifteenth century, both Castile and Aragon experienced periods of intense internal strife, culminating, during the 1470s, in a struggle between Isabella and the king of Portugal for control of the Castilian Crown. By then, Isabella was married to Ferdinand II, king of Aragon and Sicily. The Crown of Aragon, like Castile, had only recently emerged from a period of civil war. Alfonso V of Aragon, who died in Naples in 1458, regarded his south Italian kingdom as disposable prop-erty and bequeathed it to his illegitimate son Ferrante; all the other lands – those on the Spanish mainland, the Balearic islands, Sardinia and Sicily – passed to Alfonso's brother John, who was already king of Navarre by marriage. He refused to cede Navarre to his popular heir Charles, prince of Viana, whose supporters within Navarre and then within Catalonia held him up as their hero, all the more so when he died in suspicious circumstances, possibly poisoned. Civil war in Navarre was the prelude to civil war in Catalonia. The causes of this conflict lay in social tensions within town and country that were rooted in the great economic transformations that resulted from the Black Death.[19]

In Barcelona, the popular factions, known as the *Busca*, demanded lower taxes, participation in the city government, tighter limits on the fees charged by lawyers and physicians, and restrictions on the importation of foreign cloths and on the use of foreign ships.[20] Their message (which appealed to the cash-strapped monarchy) was summed up in the single word *redreç*, best translated as 'economic recovery'. The *Busca* gained power on the City Council, but proved unable to solve the problems of Barcelona. By the time of Alfonso V, the *Busca* was constantly jockeying for power with the *Biga*, which was a loose party of old patrician families; at the outbreak of the Catalan civil war in 1462, the city was still a divided community. Majorca too was a divided society. During the fifteenth century, there were repeated political explosions, expressed in the rivalry between the inhabitants of the capital and the *forenses* ('outsiders') who inhabited the rest of the island. While Alfonso was absent from his Spanish lands conflict became very intense; Majorca City was placed under siege by the *forenses*. In addition, plague continued to afflict the island throughout the second half of the fifteenth century (in 1467, 1481 and 1493).[21]

Yet the picture is not as bleak as all this suggests. In Majorca, wealthy patrons were commissioning impressive works of art. This was the period in which the citizens of Majorca, Valencia, Barcelona and Perpignan erected impressive *llotjas*, or loggias, which acted as seats of the commercial tribunal known as the Consulate of the Sea, and in which all sorts of commercial business was conducted – the registering of insurance contracts for overseas voyages, the sale of bonds, the exchange of currency.[22] The *llotja* in Majorca, erected in the 1430s, was the work of the eminent Catalan architect Guillem Sagrera, who also designed Alfonso's great hall in the massive fortress of Castelnuovo in Naples, carrying the late Gothic styles of Spain across the Mediterranean. His breathtaking design for the *llotja*, with its soaring columns, was partly followed when Pere Compte erected the no less impressive *llotja* in Valencia between 1483 and 1498. A remarkable Latin inscription running around the top of the inside walls of the *llotja* in Valencia states:

> I am an illustrious house built in fifteen years. Fellow-citizens, rejoice and see how good a thing is business, when it does not give rise to lies in speaking, when it keeps faith with one's neighbour and does not deceive him, when it does not dedicate money to usury. The merchant who acts in this way will prosper galore and eventually will enjoy eternal life.

At first sight it does not seem that this was an age when the lands of the Crown of Aragon could 'prosper galore'.[23] Banking failures in the 1380s dampened financial initiatives, and Italian capital, largely discouraged in earlier decades, began to dominate the trade of the Spanish seaboard.[24] The Barcelona business elite tired of trade, with all its dangers, and increasingly preferred to invest in bonds with reasonably safe returns; this was stimulated further when a new public bank, the *Taula de Canvi* ('table of exchange'), was established in the *llotja* of Barcelona, hard by the waterfront, in 1401. On top of this, the king's financial demands, made in order to sustain Alfonso's Mediterranean campaigns, drained funds out of his Spanish lands. And yet there was also good news. The commercial networks of the Crown of Aragon did not disintegrate; if anything, they experienced new vitality. Ships set out for the eastern Mediterranean from Barcelona nearly every year between 1404 and 1464, and most of them were Catalan, not foreign. In 1411 eleven Catalan ships sailed to the Levant, in 1432 seven, in 1453 eight. The numbers may appear small, but these were vessels sent to collect high-value items such as spices, which were traded in small quantities. Having built up their Levant trade with care over many decades, the Catalans took third place in the great Levant trade behind the Venetians and the Genoese; they traded in Beirut and maintained a consulate in Damascus.[25] There were also regular departures (mainly by foreign ships) for Flanders and England.[26]

These were the prestige routes followed by the great galleys, but there was an especially lively trade in the sturdy round cogs that carried grain, dried fruits, oil, salt and slaves. Records survive of nearly 2,000 voyages from Barcelona between 1428 and 1493, about a quarter to Sicily, about 15 per cent to Sardinia and over 10 per cent to southern Italy – in other words, to the Italian possessions of the Crown of Aragon. Rhodes was visited by large numbers of Catalan ships too (129 in this period), for it was not simply the fortress of the Knights; it also served as the hub of a distribution network that gave access to Turkey, Egypt and Syria.[27] Catalan control of the textile trade of southern Italy owed much to the patronage of King Alfonso. After he captured Naples in 1442, he expelled the Florentine merchants who had dominated the city's business under the Angevin kings. The Catalans leaped at the opportunity to replace their rivals. By 1457 Aragonese Naples teemed with Catalan merchants, who exceeded all others in numbers.[28] They were so successful in flooding the south of Italy with cheap woollen cloths that King Ferrante of Naples, even though he was the nephew of the current king of Aragon, tried to ban their import in 1465.[29]

There were other subtle but important changes in the character of Catalan trade during the fifteenth century. Well-integrated local trade networks became increasingly important; ships generally travelled less far, seeking out supplies in convenient destinations close at hand. There was a constant traffic between the little town of Tossa (with perhaps 300 inhabitants) and Barcelona, carrying large amounts of timber from the Catalan forests to Barcelona.[30] An even more important source of wood was Mataró, whose church contained a remarkable model of a round ship, or *nau*, now preserved in Rotterdam; it provides unique testimony to the shipbuilding skills of the Catalans in the fifteenth century.[31] Another active line of trade, humble but important, was the transport of fish. Tax records for 1434 show how salted sardines were carried in vast numbers from the Bay of Biscay to Barcelona during Lent; Barcelonans were also eager consumers of hake, tuna and eels. Along the Spanish coasts came oil, honey, wood, metals, leather, skins, dyestuffs – a whole range of local products which provided the basis for economic recovery after the assaults of the plague.[32]

The ten years after 1462 saw the trade of Barcelona crippled by the Catalan civil war, but after 1472 recovery was surprisingly fast.[33] During the 1470s, consuls were nominated to look after Catalan affairs in ports large and small all over the Mediterranean, including Dubrovnik and Venice in the Adriatic, Trapani, Syracuse and Malta in the kingdom of Sicily. German and Savoyard merchants came to Barcelona.[34] Opportunities once again abounded. Majorca, too, remained surprisingly buoyant, despite internal crises. Ships fanned out from Majorca towards

North Africa, Barcelona, Valencia, Naples, Sardinia, and even occasionally as far as Rhodes and Alexandria. Out of nearly 400 voyages between Majorca and North Africa recorded in the first half of the fifteenth century, 80 per cent of the ships were Majorcan. As in previous centuries, Majorca was a focal point for Catalan trade with North Africa, a highly desirable market because of its access to gold supplies. In Majorca, the Jewish businessman Astruch Xibili did lively business as an insurance broker for trade with the Spanish mainland, southern France and North Africa.[35] Here, as in Barcelona, maritime insurance was taken increasingly seriously, reflecting the realities of the time: Muslim piracy aimed at Christian shipping, conflicts between Christian states, upheavals within towns. Yet what is striking is the resilience, indeed optimism, of those who did business across the sea in this period.

One city in the lands of the Crown of Aragon was a veritable boom town: Valencia. The eminent British historian John Elliott has written that 'for Valencia the fifteenth century was something of a golden age', an appropriate term if one takes into account its gold coinage, which remained 'as steady as a gyroscope' during the fifteenth century.[36] The city was the favoured residence of Alfonso V before he abandoned Spain for Italy, and this is reflected in the large number of works of art produced within the city and in ambitious building programmes. Valencia played an important part in the development of commercial institutions. Inside the magnificent *llotja* the Consuls of the Sea, who had the status of royal judges, met to determine cases in maritime and commercial law. They were to be drawn from 'the most able, the most competent and the most experienced' members of the merchant community, and they were to issue their judgments speedily and without pompous ceremonies, impartially doing justice to both the rich and the poor. However, they preferred out-of-court settlements, for the aim was to promote harmony in the community rather than to encourage confrontation.[37] The Valencian consulate became particularly famous because its highly comprehensive law-code was printed in the city in 1494, and was widely diffused.

The code addressed age-old problems in maritime law:

> If any property or merchandise is damaged by rats while aboard a vessel, and the patron had failed to provide a cat to protect it from rats, he shall pay the damage; however, it was not explained what will happen if there were cats aboard the vessel while it was being loaded, but during the

journey these cats died and the rats damaged the cargo before the vessel reached a port where the patron of the vessel could purchase additional cats. If the patron of the vessel purchases and puts aboard cats at the first port of call where such cats can be purchased, he cannot be held responsible for the damages since this did not happen owing to any negligence on his part.[38]

During a storm, the master of a vessel was required to call together the merchants on board his ship if he was convinced it would sink unless some of the cargo was jettisoned. He was to proclaim:

'Sirs, merchants, if we do not lighten the load we will find ourselves in danger and expose all on board, plus the cargo and other merchandise and possessions, to a total loss. If you, gentleman merchants, consent that we reduce the load we have aboard, we will be able with the aid of God to save all the people on board as well as most of the cargo . . .' It is obviously more sensible to get rid of some of the cargo than to sacrifice human life, the vessel and all the cargo.[39]

The fundamental principle that shines through the often meticulous legislation of the Consulate of the Sea is that responsibilities must be recognized and that all parties to an agreement must be protected. Thus if the ship's master tells a prospective passenger that he is leaving at a later date than in fact happens, the full fare will have to be returned, along with compensation for consequential damages. Passengers also had their responsibilities, not least the observance of these customs and regulations.[40] Since Valencia exported high-quality ceramics (including dinner sets for King Edward IV of England and the Medici of Florence), it is no surprise that careful attention was paid to the hiring of skilled stevedores who knew how to load pottery on board. If they did a good job, and there were still some breakages, the merchants and not the shipowner were liable.[41] Sailors were guaranteed meat on Sundays, Tuesdays and Thursdays, with a stew on the other days; each evening they were to receive ship's biscuit with cheese, onions, sardines or other fish. There was a wine ration too, and this could be provided from wine manufactured on board from raisins or even figs (steeped in water, to produce a sweet mud-coloured brew).[42]

Valencia benefited from the difficulties in Barcelona – the banking crises, the political strife between *Biga* and *Busca*, and, above all, the frequent attempts by the Barcelona patriciate to exclude foreign bankers from the city.[43] It also benefited from its more advantageous position along the trade routes linking northern Italy to the Atlantic.[44] Genoese and Florentine galleys would head down past Ibiza, bypassing Barcelona. Calling in at Valencia, they could load the up-market agricultural produce that was a speciality of the still substantial Muslim population of the Valencian *horta*, or countryside: dried fruits, sugar and rice, much favoured at the English court, where rice was mixed with minced chicken and sugar in a white concoction known as blancmange.[45] Foreign capital dominated Valencia, stimulating the economy and increasing its advantage over the more xenophobic Barcelona. There were lively communities of Genoese, Milanese, Venetians, Tuscans, Flemings and Germans who used Valencia as their base in the western Mediterranean.[46] The Milanese imported armaments and other metal goods. Merchants from Languedoc took an interest in the large quantities of wool that were brought down from the Castilian plateau, a trade partly conducted by the Jews of Toledo.[47] Muslim merchants from Valencia traded with the Nasrid kingdom of Granada.[48] King Ferdinand's greedy attempts to extract higher taxes from the city slowed growth at the end of the fifteenth century.[49] Still, the balance sheet for the Crown of Aragon is remarkably positive, even more so if recovery in the Italian possessions is taken into account: Sicily, rich in wheat and sugar, Sardinia, rich in wheat and salt.[50] The Catalan-Aragonese commonwealth flourished, and benefited from the radical restructuring of the economy that followed the Black Death.

III

There was one oddity in the success of Valencia: the lack of practising Jews. A unique feature of the fifteenth-century Iberian kingdoms, by comparison with other western European states, was the presence in each of them of Christians, Jews and Muslims. Within Spain, day-to-day relations between Jews, Christians and Muslims were sometimes cordial, with Christians attending Muslim and Jewish weddings, and Muslims and Christians setting up joint workshops in Valencia. But by the late fourteenth century *convivencia* had been replaced by an atmosphere of mistrust. The spread of the Black Death was blamed on the

Jews, leading to violent attacks on Jewish quarters in Barcelona and elsewhere.[51] One effect of the plague was the emergence of a new middle class, whose members sometimes looked upon the Jews as business rivals. In the late fourteenth century, Ferran Martínez, archdeacon of Ecija in southern Spain, preached with intense passion against the Jews, attempting to demolish synagogues and to despoil them of their scrolls and books. The Castilian Crown proved unable to restrain the forces he unleashed, and in 1391 popular riots in the archdeacon's support began in Seville and then spread northwards and eastwards into the lands of the Crown of Aragon, accompanied by slaughter of the Jews and mass conversions.

The infection spread across the western Mediterranean, leading to attacks on the Jews in Aragonese Sicily during 1392.[52] In Valencia City the Jewish quarter ceased to exist, for only about 200 professing Jews survived the killing or conversion of the remaining 2,500 Jews of the city. The shock was as great in Barcelona, where Jews had lived since the eighth century. The Jewish quarter or *Call*, in the north-west corner of the old city, was invaded and devastated. In Majorca a rural protest against the lieutenant-governor grew out of control: failing to break into Bellver Castle outside Majorca City, the peasants turned on the *Call*, which they invaded, murdering many of those they found. Further pressure came from above when King Ferdinand I of Aragon and Pope Benedict XIII organized a public disputation between Jews and Christians at Tortosa in 1413–14. This was not a debate between equals but an opportunity to bully many Jewish leaders into conversion.[53] The numbers professing Judaism within the lands of the Crown of Aragon shrank, though among the converts there were many who maintained their ancestral religion behind closed doors. Secrecy was to become even more important by the 1480s, with the re-establishment of the Inquisition within the Spanish kingdoms. Jewish life in the Crown of Aragon seemed to be drawing to an end, not as a result of a mass expulsion but because of intolerable pressures within Iberia.

The mass conversions of 1391 and 1413–14 seemed to suggest that, under pressure, most Jews would convert. After Ferdinand II acceded to the throne of Aragon in 1479, he gradually reverted to the tough policies of his grandfather and namesake. In order to address the issue of converted Jews who kept up their old religious practices (often known as 'Marranos'), he revived the Aragonese Inquisition, and extended it across Spain, where it was seen as a tool of royal interference even by Old Christian families.[54] The Dominican friars who manned the Inquisition convinced Ferdinand that its job would never be done unless converts and Jews were totally separated, by the removal of all professing Jews from Spain.[55] Ferdinand's great hope was that most of the Jews would convert rather than depart (he had no antipathy to people of Jewish descent and favoured sincere *conversos*). Yet the decrees led to a mass migration. Very many Jews – perhaps 75,000 – abandoned Spain, though the great majority, by now, were Jews from Castile, given the disappearance of so many Catalan and Aragonese communities after the convulsions of 1391. Still, it was from the ports of the Crown of Aragon that many Spanish Jews from both Aragon and Castile set out in search of refuge.

The refugees were sometimes treated quite well and sometimes execrably: there is no reason to disbelieve stories of shiploads of Jews who were thrown into the sea by captains and crews.[56] The sultan of Morocco did not want them, so the nearest Muslim land was a poor option. Although many of the ships that carried them were Genoese, Genoa was unwelcoming, for it had never encouraged Jewish settlement within the city: the Jews who landed there were confined to a spit of land full of discarded rocks and debris; facing a harsh winter many were tempted to convert.[57] It made more sense to head for new homes in southern Italy, where Ferdinand's cousin Ferrante welcomed them with open arms, ensuring that his officials checked each immigrant to see what that person's special skills were as a craftsman or merchant, and insisting that the Jews should be treated *humanamente*. A few months later Ferrante welcomed a second surge of Jewish immigrants from Aragonese Sicily, from which they had also been expelled, despite the objections of the city council of Palermo, which feared for the economic effects.[58] Ferdinand remained passionate about expelling Jews as he conquered new lands across the sea – banishing them from Oran in 1509 and from Naples in 1510.[59]

More important than their number is the impact the exiles had on the wider Mediterranean world. They moved through southern Italy and then, as they were expelled from there, they fanned out: some went a little way north, reaching the courts of friendly princes in Ferrara and Mantua; others penetrated the Ottoman lands, where the sultan could not believe his good fortune in acquiring their skills as textile-workers, merchants and physicians. A sixteenth-century French agent at the Ottoman court wrote that the Jews

> have among them workmen of all artes and handicrafts most excellent, and specially of the Maranes of late banished and driven out of Spain and Portugale, who to the great detriment and damage of the Christianitie, have taught the Turkes divers inventions, craftes and engines of warre, as to make artillerie, harquebuses, gunne powder, shot and other munitions; they have also there set up printing, not before seen in those countries, by the which in faire characters they put in light divers bookes in divers languages as Greek, Latin, Italian, Spanish and the Hebrew tongue, being to them naturell.[60]

The Ottomans, ruling over vast areas where Muslims were a minority, were easy in their minds about the presence of the Jews in their domains, subject to the usual limitations imposed by *dhimmi* status. Salonika (Thessalonika) became a particular focus of settlement.

Many of the exiles saw the expulsion from Spain as a sign that the tribulations of Israel were not about to increase but that they would soon end, with the redemption of the Jews under the leadership of the Messiah. In this spirit, some headed for the land of their distant ancestors, settling in Safed in the hills of Galilee, where they were also eager to set up weaving workshops and other enterprises. At the same time they immersed themselves in kabbalistic texts and produced liturgical poetry which was widely diffused across the Mediterranean and beyond. One of their rabbis, Jacob Berab, had made his way from Maqueda, near Toledo, to Fez, then to Egypt and finally to Safed, where he dreamed of re-establishing the ancient Jewish council of sages, the Sanhedrin, as a prelude to the Messianic Age.[61] As the exiles travelled eastwards, they carried with them memories of Spain or, in Hebrew, *Sepharad*. Many of these Sephardic Jews continued for centuries to speak fifteenth-century Spanish, which they spread within the Jewish communities of the Ottoman lands and North Africa – the language often called 'Ladino', though it acquired vocabulary from other languages as well, such as Turkish. The widespread adoption of Ladino among the Mediterranean Jews was part of an act of cultural imperialism that also saw the Sephardim impose their liturgy and practices on the Jews of Greece, North Africa and much of Italy. For the Sephardim insisted that they were descended from the Jewish equivalent of *hidalgos*, and that they were the aristocracy of the

Jewish people who had lived in Spain in splendour. Had not the prophet Obadiah referred to 'the exile of Jerusalem that is in Sepharad'?

The year 1492 also saw the final extinction of Muslim rule in Spain, when, on 2 January, Boabdil, king of Granada, surrendered his city to Ferdinand and Isabella after a long and painful war, which helped to confirm Isabella's dubious claim to the throne of Castile. The surrender treaty preserved the right of the Muslims to stay in their former kingdom; if they did wish to leave, their shipping costs would be covered by the king and queen. They were expelled from Granada and all the Castilian lands only in 1502, following an uprising in the Granadan Sierra three years earlier. Yet nothing similar happened in the lands of the Crown of Aragon, whose Muslim population was concentrated in the kingdom of Valencia and in southern Aragon. Maybe a third of the population of the Valencian kingdom was Muslim in the fifteenth century, diminishing as Christian settlement advanced and as Muslim families converted to the dominant faith. The famous water tribunal which still meets every Thursday outside Valencia Cathedral to adjudicate the distribution of water in the fields outside the city perpetuates some of the principles and methods of the Muslim farmers of the late Middle Ages.[62] But isolation from the Muslim world and the loss of their elite meant that the Muslims of Aragon and Valencia struggled to maintain their knowledge of Islam or, in some areas, of the Arabic language.[63] Ferdinand was a canny ruler who realized that the expulsion of the Muslims would lead to depopulation and economic chaos in kingdoms whose prosperity had already been placed at risk by the civil war under his father. It was only in 1525, nine years after he died, that an attempt was made to convert every Spanish Muslim to Christianity, and it was only from 1609 onwards that the 'Moriscos', as they became known, were ruthlessly expelled en masse from Spain.[64]

IV

Within Castile and Granada, Ferdinand possessed near-equal status with his wife Isabella, though she was only queen consort in Aragon. But after her death in 1504, Ferdinand was denied the regency of Castile by the Cortes for several years, prompting him to turn his attention more decisively towards the Mediterranean, and the revival of his uncle

Alfonso's Mediterranean empire. His concern became the fortunes of the Crown of Aragon, and he assumed that Castile and Aragon would once again go their separate ways after his death. With the help of the 'Great Captain', the brilliant military commander Fernando González de Córdoba, he restored direct Aragonese rule over Naples in 1503, after a short struggle with the French, who had returned to Italy under King Louis XII, less with the intention of crushing the Turks than in the hope of anchoring down Louis's claim to the duchy of Milan.[65] As with Alfonso, Naples was not an end in itself: Ferdinand, whose politics often had a strong Messianic flavour, aspired to lead a crusade for the defeat of the Turks and for the recovery of Jerusalem, and a few expeditions headed eastwards, such as a flotilla sent under the Great Captain's command to Kephalonia – not, admittedly, very far from the heel of Italy.[66] These daydreams were further stimulated by the insistence of an eccentric Genoese sailor, Christopher Columbus, that he would find enough gold in the Indies to pay for everything Ferdinand's heart desired.[67]

Ferdinand preferred to see his Catalan subjects sailing the Mediterranean rather than the Atlantic, and here he was inspired by the same idea that his uncle Alfonso had developed, of a Catalan Common Market encompassing Sicily, Sardinia, Naples, Majorca and newly won possessions in North Africa. In 1497, the duke of Medina Sidonia had already shown how easy it was to capture Melilla on the coast of Morocco; it remains Spanish to this day. With the help of the powerful cleric Cardinal Cisneros, Ferdinand added Oran to his possessions in 1509. Riding a mule and brandishing a silver cross, the aged cardinal processed in front of the Spanish army, urging the men to fight for Christ. His ardour had not been dimmed by the conquest of Granada, where in his contempt for Islam he made great bonfires of Arabic books, happily depriving humanity of vast amounts of knowledge. The fall of Oran was followed by the capture of Bougie and Tripoli in 1510.[68] The presence of Spanish garrisons along the coast of North Africa as far east as Libya strengthened the grip of Christendom on the western and central Mediterranean, but also drew the fire of a variety of Muslim foes intent on recovering the cities held by Spain. While Ferdinand was delighted to score points in the holy war he was fighting against Islam, there was a practical dimension to his African ambitions. Control of the coastline of the Maghrib would offer protection to Catalan and other shipping bound for the East, not because

European shipping made use of routes along the African coast, but because a Spanish presence deterred Muslim piracy.

Ferdinand demonstrated how important the Mediterranean was in his thinking when, after Isabella's death, he spent several months in Naples setting the war-damaged south Italian kingdom back on its feet. He took a new wife, the capable and cultured Pyrenean princess Germaine of Foix, in the hope of producing a male heir to the lands of the Crown of Aragon.[69] Yet all his grandiose policies were compromised by the extinction of the male line. The son of Ferdinand and Isabella, the Infante Juan, predeceased his parents. Nor did Germaine of Foix produce a surviving heir. Thus both Castile and Aragon passed through Ferdinand's demented daughter Juana to his grandson, the Habsburg prince Charles of Ghent.[70] Under Charles power within Spain shifted decisively away from Aragon and back towards Castile. With the opening of the New World trade routes, Castile, and especially Seville, boomed, while the Catalan networks in the Mediterranean settled into torpor. Traditional Aragonese interests continued to be prosecuted in Italy, but Castilians increasingly took charge of the Mediterranean empire once ruled from Barcelona and Valencia.[71]

3

Holy Leagues and Unholy Alliances, 1500–1550

I

The reshaping of the Mediterranean in the wake of the Black Death was a slow process. In addition to political changes within the Mediterranean, notably the expansion of Ottoman power, events taking place beyond the Straits of Gibraltar would, in the long term, greatly transform the life of those who lived on its shores and in its islands. The opening of the Atlantic had already begun in the decade before plague arrived, with voyages down the coast of Africa to the Canary Islands, and it continued with the discovery and settlement of Madeira and the Azores by the Portuguese in the early fifteenth century.[1] As sugar plantations developed on Madeira, it became possible to supply Flanders and other parts of northern Europe directly from the Atlantic with one of the costly products that had previously been obtained within the Mediterranean. By 1482, with the establishment of a Portuguese fortress at São Jorge da Mina ('the Mine') in West Africa, not far north of the Equator, gold was beginning to reach Europe without being channelled across the Sahara and through the Muslim ports of the Maghrib; the opening of this Guinea trade compensated for disappointment at the failure of Ceuta to pay for its upkeep. The Atlantic also became a source of slaves for Mediterranean masters: Canary Islanders, Berbers from the opposite shores of Africa and, increasingly, black slaves carried north from the Mine. Many of these eventually reached Valencia, Majorca and other Mediterranean ports, after passing through Lisbon.[2]

Then, with Columbus's entry into the Caribbean islands in October 1492, Castile also acquired a source of precious metal that was ruthlessly exploited by imposing heavy taxes in gold on the Indians, even

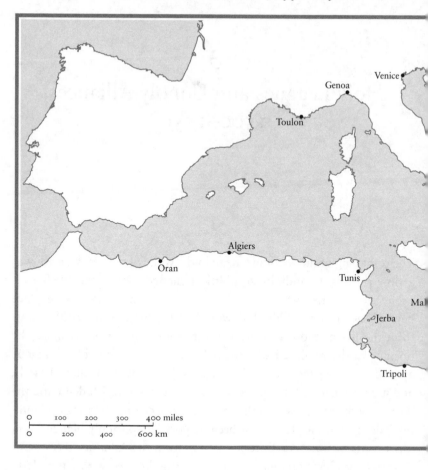

though they were supposedly free subjects of the Crown. The Genoese, despite their unpopularity in Spain, installed themselves in Seville and, with royal approval, ran the trans-Atlantic trading operations. At the same time, they turned their hands to finance. Turkish pressure on the Genoese possessions in the eastern Mediterranean increased, and so the Genoese allied themselves more insistently with Spain, the power that seemed best able to stand up to the Turks. As Mediterranean navigation became more dangerous, the Venetians also reconsidered their options. By the middle of the fifteenth century, Venice had become embroiled in the tortured politics of Renaissance Italy, acquiring, under Doge Francesco Foscari, a mainland dominion far in excess of the small tracts it controlled a century earlier. The writ of Venice reached as far

west as Bergamo, where the lion of St Mark brushed against the serpent of Milan. This is not to say that Venice abandoned its Mediterranean interests, but the Serenissima Repubblica was beginning to acquire the assets on the Terraferma, or Italian mainland, that would enable it to turn in that direction in the sixteenth and seventeenth centuries, as it gradually lost its eastern Mediterranean dependencies to the Ottomans.[3] Venice felt itself increasingly exposed, and its leaders were aware that their reluctance to use their navy to challenge the Ottomans exposed them in western Europe to accusations of hypocrisy and opportunism.

The sense that the seas were less safe was not an illusion. From the end of the fifteenth century onwards pirates ranged across the Mediterranean, raiding ships, coasts and islands from which they carried off thousands of slaves each year.[4] Among the Christian lands most severely affected by Muslim piracy were Calabria, Sicily and Majorca; these regions had not experienced Muslim piracy on this scale since the Saracen raids of the ninth and tenth centuries. Piracy became endemic; the long-standing control of the seas by Italian and Catalan merchants was turning into a memory. There were both Christian and Muslim pirates; among the Christians, the Knights of St John on Rhodes were the most active. They remained committed to the ideal of a holy war against Islam, and they could draw on their estates in western Europe to pay for the upkeep of perhaps half a dozen well-equipped galleys. On the other side, the Barbary corsairs threatened Christendom for three centuries. They had the backing of the Ottoman court; they established secure bases in North Africa; they were led by energetic and talented commanders; and they brought the war between Christian and Muslim navies deep into the western Mediterranean.[5]

The eastern Mediterranean became an Ottoman lake during the first quarter of the sixteenth century. An obvious explanation for Ottoman expansion is the desire to spread the faith, and the sultans did not forget their ancestors who had waged war against the Byzantines as *ghazis*, holy warriors for Islam; however, in the Balkans they preferred to leave most of their subjects as Christians or Jews, reasoning, as had the Arab caliphs of the early Middle Ages, that the Peoples of the Book were a valuable source of tax revenue. They sought to protect trade, partly in order to supply their magnificent court and their teeming capital city with silks, jewels, gold and humbler supplies such as grain, and partly because they understood that functioning trade routes were another source of plentiful revenue – hence their willingness to protect the Ragusans and to offer trade treaties to the Venetians and Genoese.[6] Elsewhere, they tried to impose their will. In 1516 Ottoman armies crushed the Mamluks in Syria, opening the way for a quick and easy occupation of Egypt. This left the Christians in charge of a scattering of islands: in the isles of the Aegean, sundry Italian lords (themselves often pirates) were picked off by the Turks over several decades; Cyprus remained in Venetian hands, and Chios in Genoese hands, but Rhodes was subjected to a long and harsh siege in 1522. This provided the new Ottoman sultan, Süleyman, with an opportunity to prove his military abilities. He was there in person to avenge the defeat at Rhodes in 1480. The citadel had been impressively strengthened in anticipation of a Turkish siege, but the active defenders were few – only 300 Knights, though there were many others of lesser rank. Süleyman refused to abandon his siege even as the weather turned, and battered Rhodes into submission. The Knights surrendered in December 1522, and were granted generous terms, for the Ottomans sometimes showed respect to those who had fought gallantly against them.[7]

Now homeless, the Hospitallers were determined to renew the fight against the Muslims. Fortunately, Charles V, Holy Roman Emperor and ruler of the lands of the Crown of Aragon (including Sicily), had a ready answer. He granted the Knights a magnificent charter in March 1530, in which he pointed out that they had 'wandered for several years' and sought a 'fixed residence'; he was ready to dispose in their favour of several dependencies of the kingdom of Sicily: Tripoli, on the coast of Africa, along with Malta and Gozo. In return, all that was required in recognition of Sicilian sovereignty was a gift of a falcon to the viceroy of Sicily each All Saints' Day. Ferdinand the Catholic had installed a Spanish garrison in Tripoli in 1510, though it was proving difficult to hold the town against the Berbers who pressed in from each landward side.[8] For Charles, holding Tripoli was what mattered; it was lost in 1551, after which it became obvious that holding Malta was no less important.

The Barbary corsairs at first sight seem very different from the highly organized Knights Hospitallers. Yet the corsairs too were warriors who had travelled far to earn their reputation. A number were the descendants of Greeks, renegades who had themselves renounced the Christian faith; others were of Calabrian, Albanian, Jewish, Genoese, even Hungarian origin.[9] They were not, or not all, roving psychopaths dedicated solely to their own profit and amusement. They included skilled navigators, notably Piri Reis, whose detailed maps of the Mediterranean and the world beyond furnished the Ottoman court with precise information in the age of discovery.[10] But the most famous corsair was Barbarossa, so called in the West because of his red beard. In fact he was not one but two pirates, Uruj, or Oruc, and his younger brother Hizr, or Khizr. Around these men there developed a whole series of stories, and it is not always clear what is fable. It is generally agreed that the brothers were born in Lesbos in the days of Mehmet the Conqueror, who conquered the island from its Italian duke, Niccolò Giustiniani. Their father had probably been born a Christian, had served in the Ottoman army as a Muslim janissary and had then settled down with a Christian wife; he traded in ceramics all round the Aegean, as far north as Constantinople itself, and often took his sons along with him. It was on these journeys that the Barbarossa brothers acquired their skill as seamen. On one journey Uruj collected timber from the shores of Anatolia, only to find his vessel pursued by *Our Lady of the Conception*, a Hospitaller galley out of Rhodes. Uruj was captured and sent to toil as a galley slave, though after a couple of years he was ransomed, which was not unusual; nonetheless, a story of heroic escape began to be told. He happily returned to the sea, spending time in the waters between Spain and the Maghrib in the company of Hizr; it is claimed that they helped ferry Jewish and Muslim refugees out of Spain in 1492.[11]

Their original equipment was a light galley, crewed by about 100 volunteers, all in search of booty and glory, and around 1502 their base became Jerba, long a nest of pirates and the scene of conflict between Christian invaders and Muslim defenders. They built ties to the court in Tunis, operating as licensed pirates of the Hafsid sultan; in 1504, they set sail for Elba, whose deep coves favoured corsairs, and swooped on two galleys which proved to be sailing in the service of Pope Julius II, as well as a Spanish ship carrying 300 soldiers and sixty Aragonese noblemen to Naples. They easily took the galleys, enormously enhancing their reputation as heroes in Tunis and as fearsome enemies in Rome. By 1506 they possessed eight ships, but their successes had earned them so much fame that the Ottoman sultan bestowed on them the honorific title 'Protector of the Faith', *khayr-ad-din*, or, in Turkish, 'Hayrettin'. A war of attrition was being fought between Muslim corsairs and their Christian foes; these were not just Genoese and Catalan sailors (whether merchants or corsairs) but the Portuguese and the Spaniards, who insistently intruded themselves into coastal forts along the Mediterranean and Atlantic shores of Morocco. Despite their successes at Melilla and Oran, the best the Spaniards could achieve at Algiers was the capture of some isolated rocks guarding the port, which were fortified with cannon in 1510 but were no substitute for control of the city.[12]

During these conflicts, the Muslims had one great advantage: they could call on the support of warrior chieftains in the Moroccan hinterland around Tetuan. They spent their summers on the sea, raiding towards Spain and carrying off thousands of slaves, whom they put to work building up the defences of Tetuan. Hizr claimed to have captured twenty-one merchant vessels and 3,800 Christian slaves (including women and children) in a single month. The brothers raided relentlessly towards Majorca, Minorca, Sardinia and Sicily, and the impact of their raids can be measured in the number of towns and villages that moved away from the dangerously exposed coasts of the western Mediterranean islands, to be rebuilt several miles inland.[13] Uruj acquired a thoroughly bloodthirsty reputation as the sort of man who would bite out a victim's windpipe like a mad mastiff, but he was an astute politician, and utilized his reputation to achieve political ends. He created his own realm, starting with the town of Jijelli on the Algerian coast. Its inhabitants were impressed when he seized a Sicilian galley laden with wheat at a time when their own supplies were very low. They invited him to take charge, and before long he launched a coup in Algiers. He exploited a succession crisis in Tlemcen, an important city situated a little way back from the sea, and made himself its master in 1517. All of this was of deep concern to the Spaniards based at Oran, who had been trying to develop friendly links with local chieftains.[14] Spain's new ruler, Charles of Habsburg, understood the need to mobilize troops in his North African possessions. Fortunately, the problem of Tlemcen was resolved by the inhabitants, who saw Uruj as an agent of Turkish rule; chased out, he was trapped by Spanish troops and killed in battle.

The second Barbarossa, Hizr, more often known as Hayrettin, now acquired an even more fearsome reputation than Uruj. To emphasize his succession to the elder, red-bearded, Barbarossa, he dyed his own beard red. He consolidated his hold over the coastal towns of the Maghrib, managing to prise from the Spaniards the forts on the islands at the entrance to Algiers in 1529.[15] The same year he defeated a Spanish flotilla off Formentera in the Balearic islands, which were now easily within range, carrying off seven galleys along with their captains; when he became irritated with the captains he had them sliced up with sharp knives.[16] Algiers became Barbarossa's capital, but he took care to seek the protection of the Ottoman sultan. He was far enough from Constantinople to retain autonomy, and he was valuable enough to the Ottoman sultan to benefit from the material support of the Sublime Porte. The Ottoman sultans switched their attention back and forth from the Mediterranean to the Balkans to Persia, and their struggles with the Safavid shahs in the East often distracted them from Mediterranean affairs. It made good sense to work through the agency of

Hayrettin Barbarossa rather than to commit all their resources to one of these theatres of war. Barbarossa received official recognition as emir of Algiers, and liked to call himself *kapudan pasha*, 'captain general'. Sultan Selim I sent him a Turkish standard, cannons and war munitions, along with 2,000 janissaries.

By the early 1530s Hayrettin had won the trust of Selim's successor, Süleyman, and was even summoned to the court in Constantinople to advise on strategy in the western Mediterranean, for the great question was how intensely the Turks should maintain pressure on their Spanish rivals. The Grand Vizier, Ibrahim Pasha, is said to have encouraged Barbarossa to launch a daring attack on Fondi, on the Italian coast south of Rome, in the hope of capturing the beautiful widow Giulia Gonzaga, whose husband had been lord of the region. According to legend, she escaped half-naked as the Turks battered on the gates of Fondi, though in reality she was not even in Fondi that night.[17] The viceroy of Naples took the gloomy view that southern Italy was the new Rhodes, the last frontier post on the edge of Turkdom.[18] Not surprisingly, it was Hayrettin who commanded a fleet the Ottoman sultan sent to Tunis in 1534 after its king, known for his suspicion of the Turks, died and a succession struggle broke out. Barbarossa pounced on the city, though Charles V then counter-attacked, pressing on despite Barbarossa's threat to exterminate 20,000 Christian slaves held inside Tunis. Charles recaptured Tunis in 1535, pragmatically entrusting it to the youngest son of the previous king, though he demanded a heavy tribute: 12,000 gold pieces, twelve falcons and six fine steeds.[19] But if Charles felt he earned the congratulations of his subjects on his victory at Tunis, he was soon to realize that he had been over-optimistic. Within a few months a flotilla slipped out of Algiers and headed for Minorca, where Barbarossa's men impudently raised Spanish flags on their masts and brazenly entered the massive natural harbour of Mahón. They sacked the town and acquired 1,800 slaves.[20]

II

Christian reactions to the extension of Turkish influence into the western Mediterranean took two forms: confrontation and accommodation. The French king, Francis I, proved willing to cooperate with the Turks, to the scandal of his many rivals; in Spain, though, the struggle with the Ottomans was seen as a continuation and accentuation of the great crusade that Christians had long been fighting against the Moors. Charles V sought 'the aid and guidance of our Creator', in the hope that with divine assistance he would manage to do 'what seems most effective against Barbarossa'.[21] Under the Genoese admiral Andrea Doria a Christian counter-attack began.[22] Doria's family had produced many of the great Genoese admirals of the previous centuries, and Andrea was his own master: he showed his independence by failing to participate in person in an attack on Naples launched by Francis I in 1528, and then switched sides from Francis to Charles V. But it is likely that he was lured into the service of Charles V more by money than by principle. He operated his own fleet, though he had access to the dockyards of his native city; he employed volunteer crews, to whom were added an assortment of convicts; his run of successes made him popular with the volunteers, even though he imposed a moral regime in which blasphemy was strictly forbidden.[23] In many ways he is a mirror image of Hayrettin Barbarossa, combining a degree of independence with willingness to work for a cause. Sent against Greece in 1532, he amply proved his worth to his new master with the brilliantly executed capture of the naval base of Coron on the southern tip of the Peloponnese. Doria penetrated a Turkish cordon and landed his own troops, to the amazement of his enemies. In their heyday Coron and Modon had been 'the two eyes of the Venetian Empire', protecting the trade routes running east from the Ionian Sea. Recovering Coron from the Turks was a great strategic victory; Süleyman despatched sixty galleys in the expectation of winning it back again, but Doria saw them off.[24]

Concern in the West grew in 1537 when Süleyman sent 25,000 men under Hayrettin against Corfu. A Turkish siege of Corfu was an obvious threat to the West: the Ottomans would acquire a launch-pad for attacks on Italy, and would be able to control traffic into the Adriatic. A Holy League was formed at Nice under papal patronage, bringing together Doria, the Spaniards and Venice, which was traditionally so cautious in its dealings with the Sublime Porte. Early in 1538, Hayrettin responded with a series of assaults on the Venetian bases in the eastern Mediterranean, which included Nafplion and Monemvasia in the Peloponnese. This was not simply tit-for-tat warfare: taken together, the Venetian islands and coastal stations offered supply lines and protection to western shipping. The Ottomans claimed to have taken twenty-five islands out of the hands of Venice, sometimes by sacking them and sometimes by imposing tribute.[25] The impression that Doria was ultimately his own master was confirmed, however, by his lacklustre performance when the massed forces of the Holy League – 36 papal galleys, 10 Hospitaller ships, 50 Portuguese ships, as many as 61 Genoese ships – met the Ottoman fleet, commanded by Hayrettin, at the battle of Preveza, off Corfu, on 28 September 1538.[26] Once he saw that the western fleet was suffering losses, he pulled back rather than continuing to fight. As a Genoese he had no great interest in protecting Venetian interests, and – though well aware of the threat from Süleyman and Hayrettin – his priority was the defence of the western Mediterranean. A contemporary French observer compared Doria and Barbarossa to wolves who do not eat each other or crows 'who do not peck out each other's eyes'.[27]

III

The king of France offered a different solution to the question of how to deal with the Turks. Francis I was locked in conflict with Charles V over historic claims to parts of Italy – the duchy of Milan, to which his predecessor Louis XII had possessed a claim, and the kingdom of Naples, already invaded by both Charles VIII and Louis XII. Whereas Charles had seen the conquest of Naples in 1495 as the first step on a victorious crusade to Constantinople and Jerusalem, Louis XII, who reigned from 1498 to 1515, looked towards a narrower horizon. He did launch a naval expedition to Lesbos, but this was a disaster, and cured him of any ambitions in the eastern Mediterranean. He became involved in the ever-turbulent affairs of Genoa in 1507, suppressing a revolt within the city, but his aim was, once again, to consolidate his hold in north-western Italy rather than to launch a great French enterprise against the Turks. He underestimated the ability of Ferdinand of Aragon to mobilize opposition within northern Italy. Defeat at Ravenna in 1511 forced Louis to withdraw from Italy; nevertheless, his successor, Francis, resolved to avenge France on its Habsburg foes, first recovering Milan and then unfurling ever more ambitious plans, which culminated in his humiliating defeat and capture at the great battle of Pavia in 1525.[28] After his release from prison in Madrid, Francis rapidly abandoned his promise to live in peace alongside his Habsburg neighbours, for France was flanked on all its frontiers by lands owing allegiance in various degrees to Charles V. Some of these neighbours were not particularly loyal to Charles, and Francis had less reason to fear encirclement than he may have imagined, but he also knew that he could pursue his dream of an empire in Italy only by maintaining pressure on the Habsburgs.[29]

The French king attempted to resolve his difficulties within western Europe by meddling in the Mediterranean wars between the Spaniards and the Turks.[30] Ultimately, his aim in seeking an alliance with the Turks was not peace but mischief. In 1520 he sent an emissary to Tunis, urging the corsairs 'to multiply the difficulties of the emperor in his kingdom of Naples', a plan that showed scant regard for the interests of the inhabitants in southern Italy, whose sovereign Francis aspired to become.[31] For the moment, the alliance between the French and the Turks was a secret one, and much of the interference took place within the Balkans, where French agents encouraged Christian warlords to work alongside the Turks in attacking the Habsburg territories. Francis sent embassies to Süleyman in 1529, keen to avenge himself against Andrea Doria following the admiral's defection; the same year the French supplied cannons that were used in the reduction of the Spanish fort at the entrance to Algiers harbour. Seven years later Charles V heard reports of an understanding between the French and Ottoman courts to attack the Habsburg dominions simultaneously. Charles tried to box Francis into a corner by appealing for the creation of a Holy League against the Turks, since if it came into being the French king would be forced to choose publicly between Christian unity and a Turkish alliance; for Francis what mattered was the balance of power, since the Ottomans could be used, he imagined, as a counterweight against the Habsburgs.[32] One wonders how Francis would have reacted had Süleyman's attack on Vienna in 1529 succeeded. An embassy to the sultan in 1532 expressed Francis' priorities with ruthless clarity: Süleyman was urged to concentrate on Italy rather than Hungary and Austria. Francis imagined that Süleyman's troops could chase the Habsburgs out of the peninsula, upon which he would raise the banner of Christ and enter Italy as its divinely appointed saviour. Süleyman, however, was increasingly distracted by conflict with the Shah of Persia, and left the management of the Mediterranean war to Hayrettin Barbarossa in North Africa. The impression is of pure cynicism on the French king's part. By 1533 the alliance was no secret: embassies from Hayrettin were received in France, and a few months later eleven fine Turkish galleys arrived, bringing the emissaries of the sultan himself. Negotiations culminated in a trade treaty, the 'Capitulations', which masked a political alliance.[33]

French support for the Turks was shameless. In 1537 twelve French galleys set out to resupply 100 Turkish ships, chasing around the central Mediterranean in search of Hayrettin's fleet, and dodging the ships of the Maltese Knights. In 1543 a French ambassador accompanied Hayrettin's fleet as it savaged the coasts of southern Italy, carrying off the daughter of the governor of Reggio. The sultan even offered to lend Barbarossa's ships to the French king. Barbarossa's fleet arrived in Marseilles amid fanfares and public celebrations. Francis was happy to offer food not just for the great feast held in honour of the Turkish navy, but also to supply Hayrettin's war fleet, so that 'he would be master of the sea'. The Turks then amused themselves with raids along the coast to the east, which lay under the dominion not of France but of the duke of Savoy, an imperial vassal: Nice was besieged and the nuns of Antibes were carried into slavery.

At this point the most extraordinary event in the curious history of the Franco-Turkish alliance occurred. Francis opened up Toulon to the Turkish ships, inviting Hayrettin's men to spend the winter there. Francis presented Barbarossa with a clock and silver plate. Thirty thousand Turks were dispersed within the town and its suburbs, and Toulon Cathedral was transformed into a mosque. A slave market was established, for the Turks continued to pick up men and women from the surrounding countryside, pressing some of the men into galley service. Turkish coin circulated in place of French money. The city council complained that the Turkish troops consumed too many olives, and supplies of food and fuel became short in a region not bountifully endowed with natural resources. Barbarossa was well aware of the controversy that had developed over his presence in France, and he was also worried by the failing provisions; he persuaded the king to give him 800,000 gold écus, and sailed away in May 1544. Further depredations resumed, on a savage scale, when Barbarossa left Toulon, having persuaded the French fleet to join him: Talamone on the Tuscan coast was sacked; Ischia was devastated after refusing to pay off the attackers with money, boys and girls; and all this was witnessed by Francis's embarrassed ambassador, le Paulin.[34] Later in 1544 Francis shamefacedly made peace with Charles V, promising to unite with Spain against the Turks, but in reality Francis and his successor Henry III had no compunction about collaborating with Turkish fleets, including the Barbary corsairs, in raids on the territory of the common Habsburg enemy. In the late 1550s, for instance, the navies of France and Algiers joined in attacks on Minorca, always exposed and vulnerable, and on Sorrento, within sight of Naples.

Charles V was not so principled that he was unwilling to collaborate occasionally with Muslim rulers within the Mediterranean, most obviously the rulers of Tunis. Venice, too, had a tradition of appeasing the Ottomans in order to serve its commercial interests. The neutrality of Dubrovnik was assured by tribute payments to the Sublime Porte. But King Francis pursued his own interests more ruthlessly than his Christian rivals, and did so in the hope that this would win him territories in Italy and glory as a military commander. Charles V was a more sober figure, careful in framing his policies, which in large measure were reactive: he saw Islam expanding in the Mediterranean at the same time as Protestantism was expanding in Europe, while France was challenging the supremacy of the Holy Roman Empire and of the Spanish kingdoms that now lay under his rule. Charles's political passions were determined by the confrontation with Süleyman the Magnificent and with Martin Luther and his successors. When he abdicated in 1556, not long before he died, the balance of forces within the Mediterranean remained delicate. Three events within the next sixteen years would confirm the division of the Great Sea between a partly Christian West and a mainly Muslim East: the siege of Malta, the Ottoman conquest of Cyprus and the battle of Lepanto.

IV

A glance at the naval forces arrayed in the sixteenth-century Mediterranean reveals that the coming of the Ottomans had created a new order, reminiscent, if anything, of the early days of Islam. Now that a Muslim empire was once again seeking to expand its power by land and sea in all directions, navies under Muslim command gained control of the waters of the eastern Mediterranean and challenged Christian navies in the western Mediterranean by means of their proxies, the rulers of the Barbary coast. It was an extraordinary transformation. After centuries in which Muslim navies had exercised tentative control of waters close to the Islamic states – Mamluk fleets off Egypt and Syria, Moroccan ships in the far west, Turkish emirs within the Aegean – Muslim sea power had expanded outwards on a massive scale.[35] Constantinople became the command centre of an enormous fleet, in great contrast to the Byzantine era, when naval power had increasingly fallen into the hands of the Genoese and Venetians. Skilled admirals became expert in the art of war at sea. This was not just a fighting force; the sultans were also keenly interested in provisioning their capital, both with wheat for its ever-expanding population and with luxuries for its imperial court.[36] Meanwhile, in the West, Spanish naval power came to rely on Italian resources. Most of the 'Spanish' ships that will appear in the next chapter, fighting the Turks at Malta and Lepanto, were supplied by Spanish Naples and Sicily.[37] The arsenal at Messina had been active for centuries; but the role of Sicily and southern Italy in the struggle for naval command within the Mediterranean had not been so significant since Charles of Anjou attempted to create a maritime empire in the thirteenth century.

Alongside these changes there was conservatism. One of the extraordinary features of the history of the Mediterranean is the longevity of the galley. The ships themselves, especially when built by the Ottomans out of unseasoned or 'green' timber, did not last as long as the great Roman grain ships of antiquity. But the basic design of the galley had changed rather little, if one sets aside the massive galleasses built by the Venetians – slow and cumbersome vessels that had to be towed to their stations, and that developed out of the large merchant galleys built to service the late medieval trade to Flanders and the Levant.[38] The length of a Spanish galley might be about forty metres and the width only five or six, making a ratio of roughly 8:1. As in antiquity, there was a raised deck running along the length of the ship, with rowing benches placed at a lower level. A vessel of this size would have about twenty-five benches down each side, typically seating five oarsmen.[39] Sail-power was also used when appropriate, and in the western Mediterranean there was a preference for larger sails than in Venice and the Ottoman Empire. This may have suited navigation across the more open seas of the western Mediterranean, while in the Adriatic, Ionian and Aegean

Seas galleys tended to hop from island to island and to crawl along the sharply indented coastlines – there existed quite an intense network of communication by galley in the Ottoman Aegean.[40] Under sail, speeds were respectable, and might reach ten or even twelve knots, but a mere three knots was a normal cruising speed under oar, which could be more than doubled when a quick spurt was needed, in pursuit or escape. Naturally, the men could not maintain high speeds for long; a rate of twenty-six strokes per minute could probably be kept up for only twenty minutes. The old problems remained: low freeboards were easily swamped in high seas, and it was difficult to supply the rowers with sufficient water and food without making frequent halts.[41] These problems could be resolved by not sailing too far out of sight of land in squally weather, so galleys still hugged the shores. Yet they had the advantage of manoeuvrability precisely because they were not entirely dependent on the vagaries of the Mediterranean winds, and a well-trained crew could turn the vessel about in a narrow space.

These crews were typically a combination of slaves and free men. The art in managing a crew was, of course, to instil an awareness of the need for teamwork. It was common practice to seat free and unfree oarsmen side by side; free oarsmen had greater privileges and could be used to watch over their unfree neighbours, who were generally shackled. Ottoman fleets, though, might be composed of a mixture of ships, some manned by slaves and others by volunteers. A sixteenth-century report refers to a fleet of 130 ships, of which forty were rowed by slaves, sixty by free Muslim conscripts, who received a stipend, and another forty by Christian volunteers, who were paid as well; the report also stresses that in time of war care was taken to recruit free Muslims because they alone were fully trusted. Villages were expected to send conscripts and to pay for their maintenance – about one oarsman for every twenty to thirty households.[42] Venice had its *Milizia da Mar*, a government agency established in 1545 to organize conscription in Venice and its dependencies; nearly 4,000 oarsmen were owed by the Venetian guilds and confraternities, and at any time over 10,000 conscripts were on the books, from whom galley crews would be selected by lot.[43] Free and unfree rowers were subjected to tight discipline, whether they served on Christian or Muslim ships. It was obviously essential that all rowers kept time and carried the weight of the oar (some galleys had individual oars, but many were quinquiremes, where five men manipulated one massive oar). Conditions on board were very unpleasant when under way: oarsmen had to relieve themselves where they sat, though a sensible commander would make sure that faeces and other rubbish were washed away every couple of days. In the meantime, the air became fetid. There was a little space in which to store goods and curl up for the night under the benches and in the gangways. Shackled slaves had no chance of escaping when a galley was swamped and sank; this was the fate of enormous numbers on both sides at the great battle near Lepanto in 1571. Under way, many rowed almost naked; dehydration was a problem in the summer heat of the Mediterranean, and some died at their niches, but a captain with an ounce of sense knew that he could not afford to lose his oarsmen. A shift system meant that oarsmen had time to recover their energy. Those who proved most cooperative would be promoted up the ship's command structure, and released from the tedium and squalor below decks to help keep time or to perform other vital functions. Up to a point, then, the stark picture of misery on board the galleys needs to be modified, though it would be equally erroneous to try to present the treatment of the slaves, or indeed the volunteers, as positive and considerate. Iron discipline ruled.

Galley slaves in the Ottoman fleet were marked out by their shaven heads, with one lock left dangling in the case of Muslim slaves; they wore an iron ring on one foot as a symbol of their captivity. They were therefore easily identifiable on land. And it was on land that they spent much of their time. Although winter voyages were not rare (ferrying embassies, carrying out lightning raids, and so on), galley slaves were mostly laid off in the winter, and were often employed in activities that had nothing to do with the sea, for instance as spare hands in market gardens and workshops; some would trade on their own account, technically against the rules (at least in Venice), but important if they aimed to raise money with which to purchase their freedom. Even during the sailing season, they had to spend time on land awaiting orders to sail, and quarters, or *bagni*, were provided, often consisting of caverns and cells built deep within city walls and forming a reserved area with its own shops and markets. Conditions within the *bagni* varied from tolerable to miserable; homosexual rape was common. On the other hand, *bagni* often contained prayer-spaces: a mosque in the *bagno* of Livorno; room for church services in the *bagno* of Algiers. Tolerance of different religions was counterbalanced by a trend in some areas, such as North

Africa, to change religion in order to win freedom, and Christian renegades played a major role in the Barbary fleets, often winning command.[44]

The oarsmen seem to have been well enough fed to carry out their
arduous duty, accentuating the need for frequent landfalls. Different
fleets supplied different combinations of diet, as in earlier centuries: in
1538 the rations for an oarsman, or *ciurma*, in the Sicilian galleys of the
Spanish navy were 26 ounces of ship's biscuit each day, with four ounces
of meat on three days a week, substituted by stew (mainly vegetable) on
the remaining four days. Ships out of Spain favoured chickpeas and the
amount of meat on offer declined during the sixteenth century. Over
this period, galleys were built to larger and larger measurements, while
the cost of food was rising across western Europe. This meant that the
cost of supplying the galleys became prohibitive by the late sixteenth
century: 'the appetite of the Mediterranean war galley, like that of *Tyr-
annosaurus rex*, had outgrown the capability of its environment to
support it'.[45] The enormous expense of the land campaigns of the Turks
in the Balkans and Persia, and of the Spaniards in the Netherlands,
which rose in revolt under Charles V's son and successor, the dour
Philip II, left little money to spare for the Mediterranean fleets of both
sides, which became locked in stalemate.

4

Akdeniz – the Battle for the White Sea, 1550–1571

Jean de Valette was a Knight of St John who had led slave raids in the days when the Hospitallers were based on Rhodes. Several years after the evacuation of Rhodes, whose capitulation he had witnessed, he was appointed governor of Tripoli, granted to the Knights along with Malta; then in 1541 his galley, the *San Giovanni*, had an altercation with Turkish pirates, and he was captured and put to work as a galley slave at the ripe age (for those times) of forty-seven. He survived the humiliation for a year, until the Knights of Malta and the Turks effected a prisoner exchange. Back in Malta he rose up the hierarchy of the Order; he was known for his occasional bursts of temper, but he was also admired as a brave, imposing figure. He was emerging as a potential leader of the Order just as Turkish power edged ever closer to Malta, and indeed Sicily. In 1546, Turgut, or Dragut, one of the most capable naval commanders in Turkish service, captured Mahdia on the Tunisian coast, though the Spaniards recaptured it in 1550. Turgut clashed with Andrea Doria's fleet off Jerba, but he escaped just when Doria seemed to have trapped him; he sailed to Malta and Gozo, laying waste the home islands of the Knights, before a victorious assault on Tripoli, lost after over forty years of Christian occupation.[1] The Spaniards attempted to swing the balance back in their favour, and in 1560 they despatched a fleet of about 100 ships (half of them galleys) in the hope of finally capturing Jerba. Andrea Doria was now elderly, and command was entrusted nepotistically to his heir and great-nephew, Gian Andrea Doria, who was unable to impose on his captains the strict discipline that was needed to hold the line in the face of the Turkish naval counter-attack led by Piyale, a talented young admiral of Christian ancestry. It has been claimed that Piyale's order to hoist sail and run down the Spanish fleet 'ranks among the great snap decisions in naval history'.[2] Few Spanish galleys escaped the destruction that followed at Jerba.[3] The Sicilian and papal fleets took years to recover from the defeat. As damaging as the loss of ships was the loss of life among the Spanish and Italian officer class and among skilled seamen and artisans (coopers, boatswains, marines) – about 600 of Spain's best men.[4] The victory boosted the confidence of the Turks. They had good reason to feel that they were on the verge of a breakthrough.

What was at stake was command of the entire Mediterranean. Any ruler who aspired to control passage from the eastern to the western Mediterranean had to be able to control the Sicilian Straits. With Tripoli gone, and control of Tunisia in question, the importance of holding Malta became ever more apparent to Christendom. Turkish writers showed their impatience at what they called the 'cursed rock', and urged the sultan to take it quickly, so that communication between the Maghrib and the Aegean could flow smoothly.[5] The urge to capture Malta became more intense following pirate attacks by the Hospitaller fleet. Among commanders in Maltese service, the most notorious was Romegas. In early June 1564, off western Greece, he led an attack on a large Turkish galleon, the *Sultana*, heading towards Venice; Romegas appropriated merchandise worth 80,000 ducats. Next, he captured the governors of Cairo and Alexandria, as well as an ancient and much loved nurse from the imperial harem, who was said to be 107 years old. Süleyman set out his aims with clarity:

> I intend to conquer the island of Malta and I have appointed Mustafa Pasha as commander of this campaign. The island of Malta is a headquarters for infidels. The Maltese have already blocked the route utilised by Muslim pilgrims and merchants in the eastern part of the White Sea, on their way to Egypt. I have ordered Piyale Pasha to take part in the campaign with the Imperial Navy.[6]

A massive Turkish fleet sailed out of Constantinople on 30 March 1565 in the confident expectation that the gates to the western Mediterranean would soon be unlocked; 170 warships and over 200 transport ships, bearing 30,000 men, hove into sight off Malta on 18 May.[7] This looked like an invincible armada; the horizon was white with sails.[8] Further

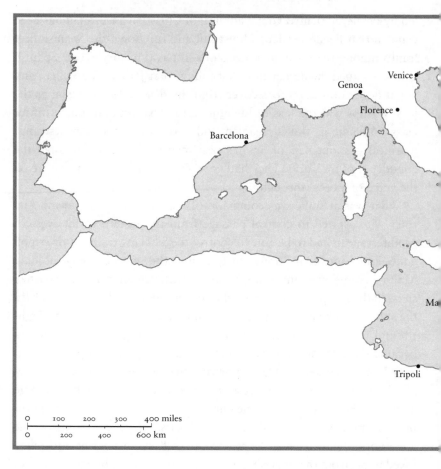

ships were on their way under the command of the elderly Turgut, based in Tripoli. The Ottoman pincers would surely seize and crush Malta.

That this did not happen was partly the result of a series of bad decisions by the Turks, and partly the result of the attachment of the Maltese themselves to their new Hospitaller masters. The Maltese nobility bunkered down in their stone palaces in the ancient capital at Mdina, in the centre of the island. But Maltese of lesser standing identified enthusiastically with the cause of Christendom, acting as scouts and swimming across dangerous waters to carry messages to beleaguered garrisons. The conflict centred on the Grand Harbour and its inlets. The modern capital, Valletta, was built only after the siege, and where it now stands there was a rocky promontory, Mount Sciberras, at the end of which stood the

fort of St Elmo, defended by a rather low set of walls. Opposite St Elmo, the Knights were based in Vittoriosa, the old port of Malta – now called Birgu – where they replicated their style of life in Rhodes, building head-quarters for each of the divisions, or *langues*, into which the Order of St John was divided (the *langue* of England, now ruled by a Protestant queen, could muster only a single knight). Beyond the tip of Vittoriosa, the massive castle of St Angelo stood guard over the harbour. Opposite lay its suburb, Senglea, from which it was divided by a narrow inlet. These were mostly well-fortified areas, and not surprisingly the Turks were drawn towards them. An Italian soldier who helped defend Malta, Francisco Balbi di Correggio, wrote a memoir of the siege, and described, apparently accurately, the discussions between the two commanders,

Mustafa Pasha, in charge of the land forces, and the much younger Piyale, in charge of the naval forces. Balbi stated baldly that if Mustafa's advice to take Mdina had been followed, 'we should certainly have been lost, for all our reliefs reached us by way of Mdina. But Almighty God did not permit that it should be so, for it was his will that the two pashas in their jealousy should disagree violently with one another – as we learned from deserters'.[9] Instead, the Turks resolved to seize St Elmo, on the grounds that they would then be able to break the Knights' hold on the Grand Harbour, as well as gaining entry into the northern inlet of Marsamuscetto (the channel between modern Valletta and modern Sliema), where they hoped to dock much of their fleet. They were full of confidence. St Elmo would be theirs in no more than a dozen days.

The Turks underestimated the determination of their opponents, and they were taken aback by the desolate setting in which they found themselves: a rocky island, denuded of tree cover, which would be able to support their vast army only with great difficulty. Fort St Elmo was defended by 800 troops, amply supplied with meat (including live cattle), biscuits, wine and cheese.[10] It was battered relentlessly; the Knights answered Turkish attempts to storm the citadel with deadly hoops that were set ablaze and sent into their midst. The Turks began to see that Malta was far less vulnerable than they had supposed. St Elmo held out, remarkably, until 23 June. In part this was due to the dedication of the Knights to the Christian cause they sought to defend. They were willing to fight to the death amid appalling scenes of carnage; Balbi testifies that the water of the Grand Harbour was red with blood. Eighty-nine Knights were killed during the siege, but they were only the elite of a much larger force: 1,500 French, Italian and Spanish soldiers died with them. Ottoman losses were even more severe: about four Turkish soldiers for each western European one.[11] Jean de Valette, now Grand Master, boosted morale by appearing, as it seemed, everywhere, and never apparently sleeping. Christian relief ships from Sicily managed, as yet, to achieve little, though by early July 700 men from the relief force were able to enter Vittoriosa. Much greater assistance would be required if the Turks were to be chased away from the island, and yet the European courts only gradually saw the implications of an Ottoman victory. De Valette was constantly sending messages to Sicily appealing for aid, but the Spanish king was afraid he would lose his fleet at sea, as had already happened at Jerba. Sometimes Philip viewed the conflict with the beady eyes of an accountant, even though he was thoroughly convinced that it was his duty to throw the Ottoman advance back into the eastern Mediterranean. The king finally agreed to the proposal by Don García de Toledo, viceroy of Sicily, that a large navy should at once be sent to Malta; but poor communications between Madrid and Palermo accentuated the delay, as did the shortage of available galleys in Sicily (Don García could call on twenty-five in late June, 100 two months later).[12]

The fall of St Elmo enabled the Turks to launch a much delayed assault on the Knights' strongholds of Senglea and Vittoriosa, using cannon Mustafa Pasha had drawn up on higher ground behind these towns. There followed weeks of intense bombardment and hideous slaughter. Quite simply, the defenders were lucky or rather, in their view, God saved them and the island. At a desperate point in early August a Maltese detachment ravaged the Turkish camp near Senglea. Those they killed were already too sick to fight, but the havoc they created was enhanced by the assumption that they were the long-awaited relief force from Sicily. In fact, they had ridden out from Mdina, to which they returned; and when the Turks sent their own detachment to Mdina, they were shocked to see how well defended the ancient capital was. This and other events led to further quarrels between Piyale and Mustafa Pasha, reported by Balbi. Piyale insisted that he had heard of the arrival of a great Christian relief force. 'If such were the case, he felt it was his duty to save the fleet. "The sultan", he said, "thinks much more of the fleet than he does of an army like this one." With this reply he walked off.'[13] The ruthless slaughter continued for another month, as the Turks tried to mine Vittoriosa and turned the town into a pile of rubble; Mustafa was embarrassed by letters from Süleyman demanding information about the siege, which, the sultan insisted, should have drawn to a victorious conclusion by now.

For a brief moment, it seemed that luck favoured the Turks: late summer storms sent the relief force from Sicily in a vast arc from Syracuse past the island of Pantelleria to Trapani, after which it at last made headway towards Gozo, reaching Malta on 6 September 1565. The news of the landing from Sicily set off further disagreements between Mustafa Pasha and Piyale:

> After a bitter and protracted argument, Mustafa gave it as his opinion that, since they were sure a strong relief force had landed, the best thing

was to leave immediately. But Piyale said: 'What excuse will you give, O Mustafa, to the sultan? If you leave without even seeing the enemy, will he not cut off your head? If you have not seen them, you cannot even tell him from what forces you have fled.'[14]

So Mustafa agreed to stand and fight, but his troops were not of a like disposition: 10,000 men from the relief force routed Mustafa's army near Mdina, and the Turkish army fled towards Piyale's ships. By 12 September those Turks who were still alive had all gone. Many thousands had been left behind in makeshift graves on Mount Sciberras. Balbi reported that 35,000 Turkish troops had died in the siege, which would be a larger number of men than the initial invading force.[15]

The impact of the siege of Malta on morale in the West should not be underestimated. The news of the Turkish defeat reached the papal court in about a week. The pope announced at an audience that the victory had been achieved by God and the Knights, giving no credit to King Philip.[16] Victory in Malta broke a cycle of defeats at the hands of Süleyman and the Barbary pirates: the loss of Rhodes; the battle of Preveza; the embarrassment at Jerba. The Spaniards felt rejuvenated and started to build a new fleet in Catalonia, southern Italy and Sicily, for they were convinced that the Ottomans would return in force; but they now had the energy and confidence to try to block rather than evade a Turkish counter-assault. The Ottomans seem to have regarded the defeat as an inconvenient reversal, rather than as the end of a period of Turkish ascendancy in the Mediterranean. The sultan could still call on massive reserves of manpower. He had not actually lost his fleet. Neither Piyale nor Mustafa Pasha lost his head, though Mustafa was deprived of his command. But, against all expectations, the Hospitallers had managed to prevent the Ottomans from breaking decisively into the western Mediterranean. Of course, the Turks already possessed allies there, among the Barbary emirs who recognized Ottoman sovereignty. The Ottomans hoped, too, to find allies on the very soil of Spain, among the converted Muslims, or Moriscos, many of whom still adhered to Islam and deeply resented attempts to suppress 'Moorish practices' in religion and daily life. The Moriscos erupted in rebellion at the end of 1568, and were defeated only after two blood-filled years, during which aid was supplied by the Barbary states – easily done, since 'in Spain at this time there were no galleys at all, for the king's forces were fully occupied in many distant places'.[17] An Ottoman breakthrough might well have forced the Spanish monarchy on to the defensive in what it still, despite the presence of the Muslim corsairs, regarded as its own maritime space. Instead, the Sublime Porte turned its attention to the eastern Mediterranean, contemplating the fact that three of the most important islands, Chios, Cyprus and Crete, still lay in Genoese and Venetian hands.

II

The Knights were remote from the people over whom they ruled. They were French, Spanish and Italian noblemen; officially at any rate they did not procreate; it has been remarked that the lowliest Knight was regarded as more important than the most noble Maltese.[18] After 1565 they were lauded as the saviours of Christendom, for their grit and determination in horrific circumstances had earned them respect as far away as Protestant Europe and even, grudgingly, in Ottoman Constantinople. However, Malta's strategic position at the heart of the Mediterranean was expressed in other ways than as the target of Ottoman armies and navies. The coming of the Knights and their choice of Vittoriosa rather than Mdina as their centre of government greatly stimulated the life of what had previously been a small fishing port. Piracy had been a major source of income for the Knights since their days in Rhodes, but they also encouraged Maltese captains to apply for privateering licences; they were allowed to fly the flag of the Order (a white cross on a red field), and had to pay 10 per cent of their profits to the Grand Master. Still, fitting out a ship, which would need to be armed with efficient cannon, was an expensive business; a pirate flotilla might contain a combination of ships owned by the Grand Master and vessels owned by local pirates.[19] Corsairs such as Romegas often brought captured ships to Malta and put them up for auction.[20] And among the booty brought back from raids, the most precious was often the cargo of slaves who, if male, could be put to work in the galleys of the Knights. There was a massive slave market in late sixteenth-century Malta. As the port of Vittoriosa developed into an important stopping-point on trans-Mediterranean voyages, Christian navigators increasingly relied on its slave market to replace captives who had died or escaped earlier in their voyage. As in previous centuries, there was also profit to be made from ransoming those slaves about whom someone cared back in their homeland.[21]

In times of relative peace, the Maltese conducted trade in the surrounding waters, mainly to Sicily, which accounted for 80 per cent of voyages from the island between 1564, the eve of the Great Siege, and 1600. Since this amounts to nearly 4,700 voyages to Sicily, the intensity of this activity is clear. But there were also nearly 300 recorded trips to Marseilles and nearly 250 to Naples, as well as occasional trading visits to Egypt, Syria, Libya, Constantinople, Algiers, Dalmatia and out into the North Sea as far as England and Flanders. Meanwhile, the presence of the Knights made Malta into a pole of attraction for settlers from across the Mediterranean. There were Greek merchants from Rhodes, following in the wake of the Knights themselves. Further down the scale there were local Maltese businessmen who would have counted for little in international affairs, small cogs in the great machine that distributed food around the Mediterranean. Villagers from Naxxar, Zebbug and other places in the interior invested small sums of gold in trading ventures whose aim was to bring Sicilian grain to Malta. Another product in very short supply on Malta was wood, and the presence of the Knights vastly increased demand for timber, for they were above all a naval power.[22] Their ability to keep the island supplied with timber is almost as impressive as the massive building projects initiated by de Valette, which resulted in the creation of the Grand Harbour as it is today. As the heirs to the Hospitaller Order of St John of Jerusalem, the Knights of Malta did not forget their duty to care for the sick: the great ward of their infirmary was the largest hall in early modern Europe. Care for their patients demanded a ready supply of often expensive and exotic spices, and even of luxury metals: the practice of serving food on silver plates reflected not inordinate luxury but a sense that silver was more hygienic than earthenware.

Malta was not the only location in the central Mediterranean that experienced an economic boom in the sixteenth century. This was the age when 'free ports' came into existence on either side of Italy. Two types of free port developed: ports where people of all religions and origins were made welcome, and protected from the interference of the Inquisition; and ports that were free in the modern sense, places where taxes were reduced or abolished in order to encourage trade. A good example of the former is the western Adriatic port of Ancona, within the Papal States.[23] Despite concentrating on trans-Adriatic exchanges, notably with Dubrovnik, Ancona managed to maintain a limited trans-Mediterranean trade during the later Middle Ages, jealously observed by the monopolistic Venetians but protected by Ancona's papal over-lords. Around 1500 two or three ships were sent each year to the Levant, bringing back raw silk and cotton as well as spices, which were then distributed outwards both from Ancona and Dubrovnik. Among the goods sent from Ancona to the East were soap, oil and wine, but cloths sent overland from Florence and Siena were also loaded, as well as a famous by-product of the cloth business, Fabriano paper, made from rag according to techniques the Italians had learned from the East – evidence for the way the technology of western Europe supplanted that of the East by 1500.[24] By that date the Florentines were concentrating their eastbound cloth traffic through Ancona; this consisted not simply of silks and velvets produced in Florence, but of goods acquired from right across western Europe: linen arrived from Rheims, whence it was car-ried along rivers and roads to Lyons, now a flourishing business centre linking northern and southern Europe. The aim was to supply the rich markets of Constantinople and the Ottoman Empire. From the 1520s the Florentines were able to meet their Balkan clients closer to home, as Turkish, Ragusan, Greek and Jewish merchants congregated in Ancona, which rapidly developed into a free port for all nations and religions. The Jewish merchants consisted of two groups: the *Ponentini*, Sephardim of the western Mediterranean largely descended from Marrano con-verts (and in some cases still notionally Catholic, under the ambiguous label 'Portuguese'); and the *Levantini*, Sephardim who had settled in the Ottoman Empire and traded out of Constantinople, Salonika and Smyrna. One group had acculturated more to western styles of living, the other to Turkish manners.

From the Balkans, hides arrived in great quantities; and, as Ancona grew and flourished, the city had to turn beyond the Italian Marches for supplies of grain, which the Ragusans willingly provided from their sources of supply in Sicily, southern Italy, the Aegean and Albania (a source of millet).[25] Grain supplies came under increasing pressure in the late sixteenth century: land was being given over to vines and olives, in reaction to local population decline in Italy and Iberia, but the inevit-able result was that estates produced grain for local consumption only, and lost interest in supplying the international market. This posed a

problem for those city communities that could survive only by importing surplus food from elsewhere in the Mediterranean. The problem
formed part of a wider series of difficulties that was changing the character not just of trade across the Great Sea, but of the cultivation of the
lands close to its shores.[26] When Florentine cloth supplies dwindled in
the late sixteenth century, following political strife in central Italy,
Ancona reached further afield and imported woollen cloth from as far
away as London, which it then passed on to Dubrovnik, Herceg Novi
and Kotor, for distribution within the Balkans.[27] The rise of Ancona was
not, then, simply a phenomenon of a small corner of Italy. A whole network of Anconitan 'connectivities' came into being; it was densest in the
Adriatic but extended far beyond. Ancona was a 'true frontier' between
Islam and Christendom, where merchants from many nations met face
to face.[28]

Ancona's business partner Dubrovnik reached the high point of its
fortunes precisely during this period of bitter tension between the Ottomans and the Spaniards, for its Senate steered with agility between the
opposing navies. Tribute continued to flow to the Sublime Porte, and yet
Ragusan ships were content to join the Spanish Armada in its disastrous
attempt to invade England in 1588; the 'Tobermory wreck' found in
Scotland is thought to have been a ship of Dubrovnik.[29] It was an extraordinary achievement that a republic whose territory consisted mainly
of a compact walled town was able to maintain a fleet of 180 ships as
early as 1530. Its total capacity by the 1580s has been estimated at
40,000 tons.[30] Dubrovnik drew full benefit from being both a Catholic
city and an Ottoman vassal. But it also began to open its doors to non-
Christian merchants. The city fathers had at first wanted to ban Jewish
settlement, as the number of Jews in the city increased following expulsion from Spain and southern Italy either side of 1500. Then, by 1532,
they began to see the Jewish merchants as a vital link on the route to
Ancona, where Jewish settlement had been strongly encouraged. Now
the city fathers lowered customs duties for Jewish merchants, in the
hope of stimulating business. Among the influx of Sephardic settlers
were a number of physicians. A small ghetto was established in 1546,
but the area in which it was placed was not unpleasant or remote, like
the ghetto of Venice: it lay close to the Sponza Palace, which was the
customs house, just off the Stradun or Placa, the attractive main street
of Dubrovnik. Although a massive earthquake in 1667 led to the recon-

struction of much of this area, the ghetto can still be identified, with its ancient synagogue.[31]

Dubrovnik became a cosmopolitan city. This was a period of cultural efflorescence, in which the study of Latin texts was matched by the growth of literature in Croatian – the dramatist Marin Držić was influenced by the ancient Roman playwright Plautus, and has attracted much attention, not just from nationalist Croatians but from Titoist Yugoslavs who saw in him a harbinger of socialism. Meanwhile, the Franciscans and Dominicans accumulated sizeable libraries, which still survive; and artistic styles, rather dependent on those of the Italian Marches and Venice, are further testimony to the profound influence of Italian culture alongside Croatian.[32] Italian, indeed, continued to be the language of government. The port cities of the Adriatic (including Venice) were places where the cultures of East and West created a kaleidoscopic mix.

Dubrovnik looked both to the sea and to the land. It was a source of skins from the Bosnian interior, importing hides from the nearby town of Trebinje, and further afield from Mostar and Novi Pazar, but the Ragusans also brought hides down from the coast of Bulgaria through the Sea of Marmara, the Aegean and the Ionian Sea.[33] The Ragusans were great specialists in the trade in European woollen cloths during the early sixteenth century (including their own, manufactured from Balkan wool), although in the second half of the century they found they had to divert much of their wool trade to overland routes across the Balkans. This was partly the result of competition with the Venetians, who directed their own business away from Dubrovnik and towards their new outpost at Split, of which more shortly. The other difficulty faced by both the Ragusans and the Venetians was the arrival of competitors from the North Sea: the Dutch and the English, of whom more in a moment.[34] The flourishing Ragusan colony in London withered in the second half of the sixteenth century as the sea route through the western Mediterranean became increasingly insecure; even their neutral status could not protect the Ragusans against prohibitive charges for maritime insurance.[35] And, as will be seen, the piracy of their fellow-Croatians, the Uskoks, based in narrow inlets and islands a little way to the north of Dubrovnik, was a constant irritation.

There was, however, a decline in traffic by sea during the sixteenth century, and land routes acquired greater importance instead.[36] Fernand

Braudel saw this largely as a late sixteenth-century development, but the trend began rather earlier, as Ancona, Dubrovnik and a few other centres became the interface between the Ottoman world and western Europe, for each side, even in times of conflict, remained hungry for the other's goods. Braudel insisted that one factor was the mass breeding of mules in Cyprus, Andalusia, Naples and elsewhere; but that might be (to mix metaphors) to put the cart before the horse. Why should mules rather than ships have become the preferred means of transport? One answer is that the security of the seas had declined to a point where land transport, long regarded as slow and costly, gained a comparative advantage over sea transport. For instance, at the end of the sixteenth century raw silk was sent from Naples to Livorno and then on to Germany and Flanders by land. Dubrovnik became more involved in Balkan business through Bosnia-Hercegovina and less enthusiastic about its long-distance sea trade as far as England, the Black Sea and the Levant.[37] Even the emergence of new trading centres on the shores of the Mediterranean was seen by Braudel as evidence for the vitality of land rather than sea routes: the rise of Smyrna, at the start of the seventeenth century, giving access across Anatolia to the riches of Persia; the attempts by Venice to develop its trade through Kotor and then across the 'black mountain' of Montenegro. Most remarkable was the proposal of the Marrano Daniel Rodriguez that Split should became Venice's staple town on the eastern coast of the Adriatic, which led to the rebuilding of this ancient city and the creation by 1600 of a vigorous centre of trade that specialized in eastern products such as silks, carpets and wax.[38] The Ottomans complied enthusiastically with such schemes, setting guards along the roads through the Balkans. The Venetian great galleys were now sent on a modest journey one third of the way down the Adriatic to Split, rather than out of the Adriatic towards Alexandria and Southampton; but even the brief voyage they now undertook was liable to interruptions from Croatian pirates.[39] This trend towards shorter, more local sea routes had already begun after the Black Death (cases from Spanish waters have been cited already). The eclipse of the long-distance routes was a gradual process; the importance of the Mediterranean Sea as a means of communication was beginning to wane.[40]

Quite apart from the effects of warfare and piracy, the opening of the Atlantic stimulated into new life the economies of the northern European lands; Baltic rye became the great article of trade in the North. The scourge of inflation in Spain and western Europe has sometimes been attributed to the massive influx of American silver at this period.[41] The Fourth Mediterranean was not merely fractured, as a result of the conflict between Habsburgs and Ottomans; it was also marginalized, as a result of the vigorous expansion of the Atlantic economy. Yet the picture was not all bleak. Barcelona, for instance, had not been wiped off the trading map, even though most histories of the city seem to lose interest once its medieval glory days come to an end. Shipbuilding contracts abounded, to meet the needs of the fleets launched against the Turks and the Barbary corsairs. Catalan cloths found a new market in a New World. The trade of Barcelona may well have expanded during the sixteenth century, though it turned more towards the Spanish interior and focused less on the sea, fitting into the general pattern of a shift from sea to land routes. At sea, it was the merchants of Genoa and southern France who increasingly took the lead in trade out of Barcelona, and the Genoese came to dominate the commerce of the western Mediterranean islands, where the Catalans had occupied the first place for three centuries. There were calls for the expulsion of the Genoese from Barcelona in 1591, though hostility to Italian merchants in Spain was nothing new. On the other hand, large numbers of French settlers came to Barcelona, so that, according to one estimate, 10 per cent of the population was of French origin by 1637.[42] In southern Italy, the Genoese took charge of long-distance contacts as well as running the finances of Spanish Naples.[43] Indeed, Genoa became banker to the Spanish empire, advancing loans on which the Spanish Crown finances heavily depended, against anticipated receipts of American silver.[44]

III

Those who found a new vocation on the surface of the Mediterranean included the exiled Jews from Spain and Portugal. Two of them achieved international fame, and became directly involved in the sequence of events that culminated in the loss of Cyprus to the Ottomans and the great sea battle of Lepanto. Beatrice Mendes de Luna was born in Portugal around 1510, several years after the mass conversion of the Portuguese Jews in 1497. Living in Flanders, which shared its ruler, Charles V, with Spain, her family fell under suspicion of heresy, even though several members consorted with the imperial family; the problem in accumulating so much wealth was that it brought false security – whether for holy or unholy reasons wealthy Marranos became easy targets.[45] Charles V was convinced that all these dubious converts from Judaism must have something to do with the spread of Protestantism in his German realms. In 1545 Beatrice de Luna and her close relatives precipitately left Flanders for Venice, though there too she fell under suspicion of judaizing, and then found a more secure haven in Ferrara, where the Este princes adopted an easy attitude to the New Christian settlers, who had brought prosperity, medical skills and fine music to their increasingly magnificent city. Beatrice de Luna restored her fortunes and reinvented, or rediscovered, herself as Gracia Nasi, living openly as a Jew, and supporting Marrano refugees from the Inquisition; the first Spanish translation of the Hebrew Bible to be printed, the 'Ladino Bible of Ferrara', was dedicated to her, and was aimed at both Jewish and Christian readers.[46] By 1552 she had once again attracted enough attention from Inquisitors to feel uncomfortable in Italy; she set off in great style for Constantinople, with a retinue of forty horsemen to accompany her across the Balkans. The Ragusan government showed foresight in welcoming her, for once she was in Constantinople her commercial agents in Dubrovnik brought plenty of business to the town.[47] The sultan permitted her and her entourage to continue to dress in Venetian style, rather than requiring them to adopt the costume accorded to the Jews. She had not turned her back on the West, however; Doña Gracia maintained an interest in Italy and the Mediterranean, informed by her determination to defend her co-religionists.

How strong this determination was became obvious when the Papal Inquisition descended on Ancona in 1555, searching out heretics among the hundred-odd 'Portuguese' who traded through the city and who had been encouraged to settle there in the past. The persecution of the Marranos signalled a newly aggressive policy under Pope Paul IV, who also enclosed the Jews of Rome in a narrow ghetto; he was shocked at the spread of what he saw as unbelief in a trading city that lay under papal jurisdiction. In this spirit, his agents arrested the Portuguese, confiscated their goods (said to be worth 300,000 ducats) and burned twenty-six of them at the stake. Doña Gracia gained access to the sultan's ear, and in March 1556 Süleyman the Magnificent sent a resounding letter to Pope Paul by way of an emissary of his ally the French king, in which he demanded the release of those Jewish prisoners who were his subjects; the sultan insisted that his treasury had lost 400,000 ducats, but he expressed himself politely enough, describing himself as 'Great Emperor of all other emperors', and conceding that the pope was 'High and Mighty Lord of the Generation of the Messiah Jesus'.[48] The pope, in reply, said he was prepared to save the lives and property of Turkish subjects, but the burnings of other New Christians would continue; he argued that his good disposition to unconverted Jews was to be seen in his creation of a ghetto specially for them in Ancona (no irony was intended). As news of this reached Constantinople, the circle of Doña Gracia began to coordinate a boycott of trade with Ancona. A number of Marranos had fled northwards to the port of Pesaro, in the dominions of the duke of Urbino; so, to the intense irritation of the Anconitans, business was diverted away from their own port, which had been so successful over the last half-century, to a previously insignificant rival.[49]

Pesaro, however, had much inferior harbour facilities, and those Jews in Ancona who were not Marranos were seriously afraid that they would suffer along with their Christian neighbours from a Turkish boycott. Arguments also erupted within the Ottoman Empire, where the Sephardic rabbis refused to be guided by a wealthy, domineering woman who had been brought up as a Portuguese Christian. They did not see her as a new Esther who would protect and save Jewish merchants, despite all her munificence in setting up synagogues and schools across the empire. The boycott fizzled out. Ancona survived. One woman could not strangle Ancona; but the city fathers knew that a Turkish boycott led by the Sephardic merchants would mean the end of their prosperity. They recognized the great influence that this worldly-wise group exercised, with its ability to cross political, cultural and religious boundaries, despite the risk of becoming trapped in local bouts of persecution. The exiles from Spain and Portugal had moved eastward (and in some cases northward to the Low Countries), but their diaspora took the form not just of new settlements in lands far from Iberia. A whole maritime network came into existence, which at its peak reached as far as Brazil and the West Indies in one direction, and Goa and Calicut in the other.[50] They inhabited a larger trading world than their forebears the Genizah merchants five centuries earlier. The expulsion of the Jews from Spain had been a tragedy and disaster for those who experienced it; the next generation turned destruction into regeneration.

Doña Gracia was joined in Constantinople by her nephew and son-in-law, João Miguez; after circumcision he took the name Joseph Nasi, modestly signifying 'prince'. His career was even more dramatic than that of his aunt. He had the good fortune to support the winning candidate in the struggle for power that followed the death of Süleyman the Magnificent in 1566, and became a trusted adviser of Sultan Selim II, 'Selim the Sot', who, it has been said, preferred bottles to battles.[51] Wine made the fortune of Joseph Nasi, just as it hastened the downfall of his master. Although Süleyman had forbidden the sale of wine in Constantinople, in accordance with Islamic law, Joseph Nasi was granted a monopoly on the carriage of wine from Venetian Crete past Constantinople to Moldavia. This produced handsome taxes of 2,000 ducats per annum for the Ottoman government, and his income grew when the ban on wine in the capital was relaxed in order to permit Jews and Christians to deal in it, which of course meant that it seeped into the wider economy (it already flooded into the Topkapı Palace).[52] One place that had been celebrated in classical antiquity for its wine was Dionysos' isle of Naxos in the Cyclades, and it was therefore appropriate that Joseph was granted the title of duke of Naxos when Selim ascended to the throne. The island had remained under loose Venetian suzerainty until 1536, after which the Turks took charge but permitted its Latin duke to remain so long as he paid tribute; the Greek Orthodox inhabitants of Naxos complained to the Sublime Porte about misgovernment, and Selim thought that appointing a Jewish duke would be no less suitable than having a Catholic one. In reality, the Naxians were hostile to any government imposed from outside, though Nasi spent most of his time in Constantinople, where he lived in a very grandiose style and took great pride in his title.

Joseph looked beyond the Aegean. He developed a scheme to encourage Jewish settlement in Tiberias, in Galilee.[53] The mystically inclined Sephardic Jews of nearby Safed lacked a solid source of income, though they attempted to promote a textile industry and even printing; the duke of Naxos saw their salvation in silk, and proposed to plant mulberry trees. He also arranged for Spanish wool to be sent across the Mediterranean to Tiberias, in the hope of stimulating a woollen cloth industry in imitation of the expanding cloth industry of Venice.[54] He wanted to attract settlers from as far away as Italy, for a renewed bout of persecution in the Papal States stimulated hundreds of Jews to set out for the more tolerant Ottoman lands of the East. A letter that circulated among Jewish communities in the Mediterranean stated in rotund language:

> We have heard from the corner of the land the songs of glory addressed to the righteous one, the Nasi [prince], the aforementioned lord, that he has lavished money from his purse and arranged in many places, such as Venice and Ancona, ships and help, in order to put an end to the groaning of the captive.[55]

Reaching Tiberias was not easy. One shipload of immigrants was captured by the Knights of St John, and the passengers were enslaved. By repopulating the ancient holy cities of Palestine, Jewish settlers hoped to accelerate the coming of the Messiah; neither they nor Joseph Nasi possessed a coherent notion of building a Jewish state or principality. In the event, the Tiberias initiative withered, for the region was still insecure, and it was only in the mid-eighteenth century that Jewish settlers returned, this time permanently.[56]

IV

The duke of Naxos was able to exert considerable influence at the Ottoman court. In 1568 he became exasperated with attempts to recover massive amounts of his property and funds that had been seized in France, and he persuaded Selim to issue a decree that one third of the goods on board French ships should be expropriated until the duke's claims were met. Its target was the Levant trade through Alexandria, but the decree caused unexpected disruption when Egyptian tax officials assumed that it also applied to ships from Venice and Dubrovnik. Meanwhile, the French court was shocked by what was seen as a breach in its long-standing alliance with Turkey, all in the private interests of one man (a Jew, to boot) who claimed to have been wronged. Although relations between the French king and the Ottoman sultan were gradually patched together again, Joseph Nasi never received full satisfaction for his claims.[57] The sultan was prepared to listen to him once again, though, in 1569, while the Ottomans were planning the invasion of Cyprus. When a massive explosion destroyed the powder dump in the Venetian Arsenal in September of that year, along with four galleys, colourful rumours attributed what was almost certainly an accident waiting to happen to the malign machinations of the Jew of Naxos. Still, he had grudges against Venice, which had treated his famous aunt badly, and which aspired to control his islands in the Cyclades. Selim the Sot, in his cups, is said to have promised Nasi the ultimate prize: the crown of Cyprus, which the Ottomans decided to pluck from Venetian hands, and the story was embroidered further with tales that he commissioned a crown for the great day of triumph, and had a banner made bearing the inscription 'Joseph Nasi, king of Cyprus'. More precisely, Venetian observers considered that Joseph Nasi was pressing for an attack on Cyprus, even though the Grand Vizier, Mehmet Sokollu, advised against.[58] As usual, Turkish policy took time to be formulated, and there were eloquent war and peace parties. Even so, the rumour of an attack on Cyprus was already being disseminated in January 1566, when the Venetian *bailo* in charge of his fellow-nationals in Constantinople reported that plans were being drawn up; in September 1568 the Venetians were further alarmed by the arrival of a Turkish fleet of sixty-four galleys in Cyprus, notionally on a goodwill visit. The Turks unselfconsciously examined the fortifications of the two cities they would need to capture: Nicosia in the interior, and Famagusta on the east coast. Among the visitors was the duke of Naxos.[59]

Cyprus was an obvious target, a Christian possession isolated in the far corner of the eastern Mediterranean. The Turks had recently (in 1566) cleared the Genoese out of their last base in the Aegean, Chios. The presence of these Christian enclaves distracted the Ottomans from other pressing needs, such as the struggle against the Safavid Shahs of Persia and the wish to keep the waters of the Indian Ocean clear of their new rivals, the Portuguese India fleet. Cyprus offered refuge to Christian pirates who preyed on grain ships, and, now that grain production was in decline, the routes carrying grain towards Constantinople and other major centres needed to be protected. Interference by Christian pirates in the pilgrim traffic that led across these waters to the holy cities of Islam in Arabia was another genuine grievance. Islamic apologists for war could argue that there had been earlier occasions when the island was occupied and governed by the Muslims, or at least paid them tribute; it was a fundamental rule that lands that had once formed part of the *dar al-Islam* should be recovered when possible. Indeed, when the Venetians objected to the growing threat to Cyprus, Sokollu said the matter now lay in the hands of the experts in Islamic law, led by the Grand Mufti, and was not moved by the reminder that the Turks had cultivated good relations with Venice over many decades.[60] Now, however, the Sublime Porte delivered an ultimatum requiring Venice to hand over the island if it wished to avoid war.

Just as Ottoman attitudes hardened, so did the attitude of Philip II, though as usual he was worried about where he could find the funds to pay for a fleet; his troops were literally bogged down in Flanders, fighting the Protestants and other rebels against the Spanish Crown. Philip hoped the pope could raise money to pay for this war. He could offer half the costs of the campaign, Venice a quarter.[61] Endless bargaining followed, not just about finance but about the chain of command. Philip II became less distracted by events in the Low Countries after the duke of Alva imposed a harsh and uneasy peace there.[62] Within Spain itself, rebellion among the Moriscos, many of whom remained attached to their ancestral religion, used up Spanish resources and delayed Philip's response to the appeal for a Holy League; it also made the League seem more urgent, for the danger of a Turkish strike on Spain, supported by the Barbary rulers and the Moriscos, aroused fears that Islamic armies were about to return to Spanish soil.

All this wavering left the Turks free to swoop down on Cyprus. In early July 1570 they brought a massive army of around 100,000 men on a fleet of 400 ships, including 160 galleys.[63] The Turks decided that their first target should be Nicosia, in the interior, though the Venetians had set to work repairing and extending its earthworks and stone walls. Nicosia held out for a while, but after desperate fighting within the walls, the Turkish soldiers obtained their distasteful prize: the right to kill, rape and despoil the inhabitants. All the while the western powers were still arguing, in ignorance of events in Cyprus. Eventually a fleet of fewer than 200 warships set out for Cyprus, in mid-September, only to hear the news of the defeat at Nicosia as they sailed east; uncertainty about what to do next led to new arguments between Philip's admiral, Gian Andrea Doria, and the papal commander, Marcantonio Colonna. Nothing was done to challenge the Turks at Nicosia, and sensibly so, since Doria was surely right: there was no hope of recapturing an inland city without massive armies and a much larger navy. The siege of Malta had concentrated on the outer edge of a small island; Cyprus was a very different proposition.[64] The one source of hope was Famagusta, not yet taken by the Turks, for it possessed its own sturdy line of defences, and could in theory be supplied from the sea. An opportunity seemed to arise in winter 1571, when the Turkish fleet had largely withdrawn from the waters around Famagusta; a Venetian squadron broke through the weak Turkish defences, but left only 1,319 soldiers behind, making a total of 8,100 defenders. Mehmet Sokollu in Constantinople calculated that this might be a good opportunity to talk peace with the Venetians, though of course they would have to surrender Famagusta. He doubted whether they really had the means or the will to fight.[65] Venice was in a bullish mood, however – the Venetians even succeeded in capturing Durazzo, which they had lost at the start of the century, and which was strategically as valuable to them as Cyprus was to the Turks. Venice declined an offer of a trading station in Famagusta in return for the cession of the island. In any case, negotiations in another quarter were reaching their end. The Holy League was formed, a highly ambitious crusading force that brought together the pope, Venice and Spain, and that won for Philip an agreement that some of the objectives that were dearest to his heart, notably the war in north-west Africa, should be permanent objectives of the League.[66] Its commander was to be the youthful but energetic bastard son of Charles V, Don John of Austria.

The building of the great fleet required for the Holy League continued as Famagusta held out. The Turks sent a fleet by way of Venetian Crete, which they raided, into the Ionian Sea and southern Adriatic, diverting the Venetian navy from its wider concerns. Among coastal fortresses that now fell into Turkish hands was Ulcinj, just to the north of the modern border between Montenegro and Albania. Turkish ships harried their foes as far north as Korčula and Dubrovnik (though the Ragusans managed to preserve their neutrality, carefully respected by both sides).[67] Then the Turks homed in on Zadar, in the northern Adriatic, and dangerously close to Venice itself, where memories of the War of Chioggia 180 years earlier must have been revived. Still, the aim was to scare rather than smash Venice – to convince the Venetians that their empire was fragile and that resistance to Ottoman power was futile. Moreover, after months of bombardment, the wrecked city of Famagusta was ready to surrender. In early August the Venetian commander, Bragadin, presented himself at the tent of the Turkish commander, Lala Mustafa. The mood soured when Mustafa learned that fifty Muslim pilgrims whom the Venetians had incarcerated had now been executed.

Lala Mustafa's displeasure turned into fury. Bragadin's companions were killed on the spot, Bragadin was mutilated; ten days later, he was flayed alive and his stuffed skin was borne triumphantly around Cyprus, then despatched to Constantinople.[68] This was as much a message to the Ottoman court, and particularly to Mehmet Sokollu, as it was to Venice: by his foul behaviour, Lala Mustafa hoped to undermine those who thought peace with Venice was still possible.[69] There was no need for this rough persuasion: the fleet of the Holy League was all but ready to sail. At sea off Corfu the Christian navy learned that Famagusta had fallen. If anything, this news strengthened their resolve.[70]

The great battle of Lepanto that followed, at the entrance to the Gulf of Corinth, has long been regarded as one of the decisive sea battles in history: 'the most spectacular military event in the Mediterranean during the entire sixteenth century', according to Fernand Braudel, whose study of the Mediterranean world in the age of Philip II culminated in an account of the battle. 'There is no doubt that on this occasion Don John was the instrument of destiny,' Braudel proclaimed, sententiously and mysteriously. A struggle close to the mouth of the Adriatic had different implications from a siege in the Sicilian Straits. The Turks had revealed in the months before the battle that they aspired to win the Adriatic, and had accompanied their sea-raids with land-raids from Turkish Bosnia towards the Venetian possessions at the head of the Adriatic. These raids were not simply motivated by empire-building or the wish to spread Islamic rule. As will become clear, the Turks were also goaded by Slav Christian pirates and bandits in northern Dalmatia, the crusading Uskoks.

The balance between the rival forces was very delicate. The number of soldiers on board the ships of each side was similar: somewhere around 30,000 troops, though it is possible the Turkish marines had greater experience.[71] There were more Turkish ships than Christian ones: just 200 on the Christian side, and maybe 300 on the Turkish, which the Ottoman admiral, Müezzinzâde Ali, organized in a crescent shape in the hope of wrapping his fleet around the Christian navy, while the centre of his line would attempt to break the Christian navy into digestible chunks.[72] Western ships, though, were built to last, whereas part of the Ottoman fleet was constructed out of 'green' wood and was regarded as disposable – suitable for a couple of seasons before replacement. The Ottoman fleet consisted mainly of light galleys that sat low in the water, increasing their vulnerability but also enabling them to handle shallower in-shore waters in which they could hope to outflank the heavier Christian craft; Venice also favoured relatively light galleys.[73] The Christian navy possessed about twice as many cannon as the Turkish, but the Turks had brought along very many archers; guns were devastating, but slow to load, while archers could reload in an instant.[74] Both sides also used matchlock arquebuses, hand-held guns which were not terribly accurate, but which could be reloaded reasonably fast, and had replaced the deadly crossbows of the late Middle Ages.[75] The Spanish flagship, the *Real*, carried 400 Sardinian arquebusiers; the Ottoman flagship, the *Sultana*, only half that number.[76] Added to this there were problems created by the tight location, the Kurzolaris islands, to the east of Ithaka, where narrow channels impeded the quick deployment of the Christian galleys.[77]

In these circumstances, it is no surprise that the battle resulted in horrific casualties. The navy of the Holy League was convinced that the crucial moment in the struggle against the Turks had come, and impressive acts of bravery under Turkish fire led to many deaths. The Venetian commander, Agostino Barbarigo, showed almost complete disregard for his vessel's safety when he directed the flagship of the Most Serene Republic towards advancing Ottoman galleys, and tried to stand in their way. One Venetian captain after another was killed – members of the great Venetian dynasties such as the Querini and the Contarini. Barbarigo pressed on regardless, though he foolishly lifted his visor as a hail of arrows descended on his ship, and he was struck in the eye, dying down below soon afterwards. But papal and Neapolitan galleys attached to the Venetian squadrons came up from behind, and, minute by minute, the Turks were edged back.[78] Heavy gunfire from the bows of the Venetian galleasses tore Turkish ships apart, and the galley-slaves shackled to their positions were dragged down to the bottom of the sea with the smashed remains of their galley. Smoke from the constant cannon fire impeded Turkish bowmen. The slaughter was relentless, hideous and fanatical.[79] Finally Christian marines boarded the flagship of Müezzinzâde Ali, who died fighting manfully; his head was raised on a pike to the great benefit of Christian morale.[80] This did not end the fighting, for Algerian ships also entered the fray. But as dusk fell the fleet of the Holy League pulled away from the blood-coloured waters and took shelter from an approaching thunderstorm. The next morning it became apparent from the sheer evidence of death and destruction that the Holy League had not just won a massive victory, but that the number of Turkish dead was almost beyond counting. Maybe 25,000 or even 35,000 had died on the Turkish side, including not just galley-slaves but captains and commanders, while Christian losses were much lighter, though still very considerable: 8,000 dead and a larger number wounded (of whom a further 4,000 soon died); about two-thirds of the casualties were Venetian, a blow to its skilled manpower the city cannot have found it easy to bear. On the other hand, at least 12,000 Christians found on board the Turkish galleys were freed.[81]

Back in Venice the news of the victory, despite the massive casualties, alleviated the despair felt at the loss of Cyprus. The scale of the victory was brought home to the Venetians when a ship arrived from Lepanto trailing the banners of the defeated enemy; victory was celebrated in Venice, Rome and across Italy and Spain, not just by bonfires and fiestas but, more permanently, in vast frescoes and canvases in the Doge's Palace and other public places.[82] And yet the victory was, in strategic terms, no more than a stalemate, for in the coming years neither side would have the manpower, timber and supplies to fit out new fleets on this scale, or at least to risk them in great sea battles.[83] Don John of Austria, in the flush of success, would have liked to press on towards Constantinople itself, but Philip II, with characteristic caution, thought that it was best if the surviving galleys wintered in Italy.[84] It is true, as Braudel asserted, that victory at Lepanto helped protect Italy and Sicily from further attack, but the siege of Malta had already preserved Christian mastery over the waters off Sicily. The political map of the Mediterranean had been drawn in the years and weeks leading up to 7 October 1571. Famagusta had fallen and the Venetians had no hope of recovering Cyprus; Malta had stood firm, and the Turks would need to think again before they attacked the stronghold of the Knights, even though they did return to those waters, and secured their position at Tunis in 1574. What was important, Braudel insisted, was that 'the spell of Turkish supremacy had been broken'.[85] Lepanto consolidated a position that had already come into being: the Mediterranean was now divided between two naval powers, the Turks in the east, holding all major coasts and islands apart from Venetian Crete; the Spaniards in the west, with the support of fleets from Malta and Italy.

5

Interlopers in the Mediterranean, 1571–1650

I

The period between the battle of Lepanto and the middle of the seventeenth century has a certain unity. Barbary pirates did not go away – indeed, they became more piratical, in the sense that the Ottomans allowed them a freer hand, for the Sublime Porte no longer expected to extend its direct authority deep into the western Mediterranean.[1] The western Mediterranean was also exposed to vicious raids by Christian corsairs – to the Knights of Malta could now be added the Knights of Santo Stefano, Tuscan pirates and holy warriors whose order was founded in 1562 by the Medici duke of Tuscany. Like the Venetians, they brought some of the Ottoman banners back in victory from Lepanto; they still hang incongruously in their church in Pisa, daily proclaiming the faith of Islam amid the incense of Catholic ritual. It would be otiose to repeat the endless saga of attacks and reprisals as Christian Knights of Malta or Santo Stefano scored points against Barbary corsairs; the most unfortunate victims were always those who were carried away into slavery from the decks of captured merchant ships, or from the shores of Italy, Spain and Africa (the French were relatively immune to Muslim raiders as a result of their ties to the Ottoman court). Galleys out of Sicily continued to patrol the seas in the hope of defending the Spanish king's Italian possessions from sea-raiders, but large-scale galley warfare had come to an end, not just because new ship-types were seen as more efficient but because the cost of building and maintaining galleys was prohibitive. Even so, the Ottomans reconstructed their war fleet in the immediate aftermath of Lepanto. There were alarums in the West: it was confidently assumed that the Ottomans would launch a second great assault on a Christian target.

Yet the Sublime Porte had lost its taste for naval warfare, and was content to leave the Spaniards alone, while pursuing its traditional rivalry with the Shi'ite emperors of Persia. This was extremely convenient, since Spanish preoccupations also now turned away from the Mediterranean; Philip II's great ambition was to defeat the new type of Infidel who was crawling all over northern Europe: the Protestants. Philip was ensnared by wars with Elizabeth of England and his rebellious subjects in the Low Countries. He had seen off not just the Ottomans but the Moriscos, whose lands in Andalucía were depopulated and abandoned.[2] In addition, he had received an unexpected prize in the form of Portugal and its overseas empire. Filled with crusading bravado, the youthful King Sebastian of Portugal led his forces to a massive defeat in Morocco in 1578, whereupon he was succeeded by the last member of the house of Aviz, Cardinal Henry, and after he died without an heir in 1580 the Portuguese crown passed to Philip of Spain, who did not actively pursue the old Portuguese dream of taming Morocco.[3] The Mediterranean looked quite small within the massive conglomeration of lands Philip ruled in the Old World and the New. An Italian political theorist, Giovanni Botero, published a work on *Reason of State* in 1589 that was to prove especially popular in Spain. He argued that dispersed states are inherently weak, but that the Spaniards had managed to overcome this through the flexible use of their fleet. Within the Spanish Empire, 'no state is so distant that it cannot be aided by naval forces', making it possible for Catalan, Basque and Portuguese sailors to join together Iberia, King Philip's Italian states and even the Low Countries in a single unit: 'the empire, which might otherwise appear scattered and unwieldy, must be accounted united and compact with its naval forces in the hands of such men'.[4]

The calming of the Mediterranean resulted from the tacit settlement between the Ottomans and the Spaniards. But crossing the sea became all the more dangerous once Spanish patrols limited themselves to protecting the coastal waters of southern Italy, Sicily and Spain. Jewish and Muslim merchants regularly saw their goods seized by Christian pirates. The dangers were increased as newly disruptive seamen took to the waters of the Mediterranean. As the Atlantic economy began to develop

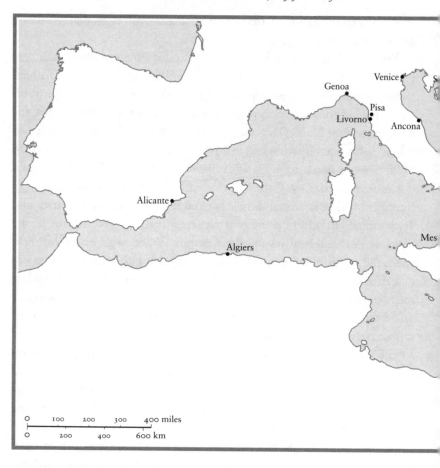

a new vigour, Dutch, German and English seamen made their way deep into the Mediterranean, whether for trade or piracy; once north European merchants appropriated a large share of the traffic in grain and spices within the Mediterranean as well as the Atlantic, the relationship between the two great seas, developing gradually since before 1300, became much more intense. More will be said shortly about these visitors; yet there were also interlopers from within the Mediterranean who posed a severe threat to the navigation of the traditionally dominant powers. The Uskoks of Senj operated from a base tucked away among the islets and inlets of northern Dalmatia, behind the islands of Cres, Krk and Rab. What is now seen as a coastline of great beauty inspired fear in the late sixteenth century. This was a borderland between the

Ottoman territories in the Balkan interior and the Habsburg domains in what are now Slovenia and northern Croatia, not to mention the Venetian possessions along the Adriatic coast. In such a setting it was possible for wilful, independently minded bandits and corsairs to flourish, especially if they presented themselves as standard-bearers of the Christian crusade against the Turks, working for the good of Christendom and Habsburg Austria.[5]

The Uskoks became the Robin Hood figures of Croatian folk epics and, though few in number and reliant on small ships, they succeeded in boxing Venice into a corner of the Adriatic. This made them into the heroes of a school of nationalist and then socialist historians in modern Yugoslavia.[6] But one should not be too romantic about the Uskoks.

They had their own patrician leaders, and were not very different from bands of corsairs and robbers along both the Christian and the Muslim shores of the Great Sea. The term *uskok* means 'refugee', and, like the Barbary pirates, they were ethnically diverse, with recruits from the Venetian colonies along the Adriatic, Dubrovnik and Albania, as well as Italian sailors and occasional renegade Muslims. Some had been born as Habsburg, some as Ottoman, and some as Venetian subjects; and their background changed slightly over time, so that in the 1590s a high proportion hailed from the Dalmatian hinterland behind Zadar and Split, an area under intense pressure during the lengthy land conflict between the Ottomans and the Habsburgs.[7] The Venetian view was that the Uskoks were 'former subjects of the Turk, who have fled to Senj, unable to bear the tyrannies of the Turkish ministers'.[8] Senj seemed to offer the chance to make good again: men 'taken from the hoe and the plough, badly dressed and barefoot, have become fat and prosperous in a short time'.[9]

Senj did not offer a natural harbour. When the strong wind known as the *bora* blew, ships had to be beached and tied down firmly so that they were not torn away. But the town was well protected by steep mountains and thick forests at its rear.[10] At the peak of their influence, between Lepanto and about 1610, the Uskoks were able to set up outposts some way from Senj, as far south as the mouth of the river Neretva, which is no great distance from Dubrovnik.[11] They were an incorrigible bunch. If the Austrian authorities were at peace with their enemies, that did not deter them from attacking Venetian or Turkish ships, as opportunity dictated.[12] In the 1590s, far from welcoming the Uskoks as Christian refugees from the Ottomans, the Venetians continued to treat them as dangerous criminals, blockading Senj and executing large numbers (though in 1596 the total number of armed men in Senj was only about 1,000, and generally around 600).[13] The Venetians would tolerate them only if they agreed to abandon their evil ways and to serve loyally on the galleys of the Most Serene Republic.[14]

As early as the 1520s, raiders from Senj had begun to threaten Turkish ships in the Adriatic. The Venetians too were easy prey because of their willingness to enter into treaties with the Turks, and because of occasional hostilities between Venice and the Habsburgs in the Slovenian borderlands. In the early days the Uskoks were content to seize cargoes of fish, wine, oil and cheese carried on local boats, but they soon graduated to attacks on large roundships bound for Dubrovnik and Ancona, threatening the line of communication that stretched by land and sea from Tuscany to Constantinople.[15] In 1599 the Venetians were so exasperated by the Uskoks that they sent a cargo of poisoned wine into Uskok-infested waters, let it be captured, and hoped to hear that the Uskoks had all died from drinking it. Since they remained full of life, however, the ruse obviously failed. The relationship with Dubrovnik was also fraught. The Ragusans were seen as collaborators with the Turks, and the Ragusan city fathers knew that the Turks would not tolerate collaboration between Dubrovnik and the Uskoks. On one occasion the Ragusans decorated one of the city gates with the heads of executed Uskoks, making a clear point both to the Uskoks and to the Ottomans. The result was predictable: a Ragusan report stated that 'they regard us as they do the Turks themselves'.[16]

Still, they were generally more interested in cargoes owned by Jews and Muslims than in those of Christians, and would board ships simply to confiscate 'infidel' goods; as a result, Jewish merchants were about seven times more likely to enter an insurance claim than Christian ones. Muslims also fared badly: a captain from Perast, a flourishing port in the Bay of Kotor, reassured his Muslim passengers when his ship was boarded by Uskoks in 1581, saying he would look after them, but he sailed to Senj and feasted with the Uskoks while his passengers were enslaved and taken away.[17] Jewish and Muslim merchants trading out of Italy tried various subterfuges. Marking cargoes with a cross was perhaps too obvious; keeping a secret account book along with a falsified one was another trick. Meanwhile, the bishop of Senj was happy to confirm that Christian merchants who collaborated with the Turks, especially in the armaments trade, deserved to be excommunicated – or, reading this differently, no objection could be made if holy warriors from Senj seized their cargo.

II

These developments confirmed a broad trend in the political and economic life of Venice, visible since the mid-fifteenth century: withdrawal from the great Levant trade, and the integration of the city into the life of northern Italy. Quite apart from the consequences of piracy, the

Venetians had to cope with the effect of the new route to the East opened up by the Portuguese in 1497. A strong Venetian presence remained in Constantinople, where twelve merchant houses had established themselves by 1560, even though numbers had shrunk significantly since the heyday of medieval trade.[18] Besides the patricians who had traditionally dominated Venice's Levant trade, other businessmen were active, notably the Jews who had settled in Venice in the sixteenth century. They were a mixed community. There were German and Italian Jews who concentrated on pawnbroking, under licence from the city government, and who were required to live in the 'new foundry', or Ghetto Nuovo, tucked away in the north of the city. Next door to them, there were communities that were more involved in Mediterranean commerce, notably the overland trade through the Balkans towards Salonika and Constantinople – the Sephardim, divided (as at Ancona) between the 'Levantines' from the Ottoman Empire and the 'Ponentines', or westerners, mainly Portuguese Marranos, who had often spent much of their lives, at least outwardly, as Christians. The Ponentines faced the threat of investigation by the Venetian Inquisition, but on balance the need Venice felt for its Levant traders outweighed any scruples about imposing Christian orthodoxy.[19] The pragmatism of the Venetians was also visible in the willingness of the government to sanction the erection of a Greek Orthodox church, San Giorgio dei Greci, for all the other Greek churches in Italy up to this point were Uniate, that is, they recognized papal authority.[20]

'The decline of Venice' is too easily identified simply with the decline of Venetian sea power.[21] In fact, Venice proved remarkably adaptable in the sixteenth century. This was a period of economic expansion in continental western Europe, and the Venetians claimed their share of the proceeds. Old industries, such as glass-making, expanded, and production of woollen cloth inflated massively. In 1516 the city was producing fewer than 2,000 cloths per annum, but in 1565 Venice was producing over ten times that amount.[22] The city benefited from a decline in the production of similar cloths in Florence, and from the regular supply of Spanish raw wool. This placed greater emphasis on its trade routes to the west, with stocks arriving by land across Lombardy as well as by sea, though there was still every need to keep the city supplied with grain, oil and wine from its possessions in the Ionian isles and Crete. The loss of Cyprus contracted the range of Venetian sailings, but renewed peace with the Ottomans ensured that, for the moment, Crete was still safely under Venetian rule – the principal threat there was not from the Turks but from its restive native population.

The reshaping of Venice (a more suitable expression than 'decline') left others freer to intrude themselves into the Levant trade. The withdrawal of Venice was compensated by a revival of commercial activity among the Greeks, who serviced the trade of the Ottoman Empire in the Aegean, and between Asia Minor and Egypt.[23] On the other hand, the coming of the English was a by-product of the great rivalry between the king of Spain and the queen of England, between the Catholic monarch and his Protestant opponent. Elizabeth was tempted to make contact with the Sublime Porte, partly for political reasons – seeing in 'the Turk' a fellow-opponent of Philip II – but also for commercial motives. In 1578 her minister Walsingham wrote a tract on 'the trade into Turkey' in which he opined that the time had come to send an 'apt man' secretly to the Ottoman sultan, with letters from Queen Elizabeth. A Turkey Company was founded in 1580, to promote trade with Ottoman lands.[24] Yet it also reflected a new aggressiveness among English merchants in markets traditionally dominated by the Italian merchants who had long supplied England with exotic wares. By increasing tariffs on Venetian ships and their goods, the queen made clear her intention of favouring native-born merchants in trade with the Mediterranean, though she did renew her agreements with Venice in 1582, and Venetian galleons were still reaching England until the end of her reign.[25] One target of the English was Morocco, where tradesmen of the Barbary Company were making their presence felt even before Elizabeth ascended the English throne in 1558. Exports included armaments, which English merchants were happy to think might be used against the Spaniards and the Portuguese.[26]

None of this prevented the English from trying to develop other routes that would bypass the Mediterranean entirely, bringing spices to northern Europe via a north-west or north-east passage, colder but supposedly quicker than the Portuguese route around Africa; as a result the English became involved with the Muscovy trade. Since this failed to produce the spices they sought, they turned back to the Mediterranean, utilizing that combination of piracy and commerce for which the Elizabethan privateers have become so famous; many of those involved in the Turkey Company (soon known as the Levant Company) had also invested in the Muscovy Company.[27] The Venetians were in a sombre mood about these developments. As English trading vessels penetrated into Turkish waters, they deprived Venice of the revenue it had traditionally received through forwarding English cloths from Venice into Ottoman territory. An agreement between the English queen and the Ottoman sultan was bad news. Nor did the Venetians approve of Elizabeth's religious policy; Venice was hardly the most whole-hearted supporter of the papacy, but was still unwilling to send a formal ambassador to England until 1603, the year Elizabeth died.[28] And yet there were some developments from which the Serenissima benefited. English ships began to sail as far as Venice itself, with the result that the city was supplied with basic northern products on which its survival increasingly depended, notably grain: the trade in northern grain grew in volume, as grain lands went out of cultivation in the Mediterranean and as shortages were accentuated by a series of famines, which were already beginning to bite as early as 1587. Dried and salted fish from the Atlantic was also a firm favourite – *stoccafisso* ('stockfish') became and remains an essential ingredient in popular Venetian cuisine.

The English and Dutch came to buy as well as to sell.[29] Initially, the focus of English attention was not the trade in spices such as pepper and ginger, but products grown on islands that lay under Venetian rule: Zante and Kephalonia, in the Ionian isles. Since the late Middle Ages the English had been obsessed with currants, raisins and sultanas, and competition with the Venetians for access to what the Italians call *uva passa*, 'dried grapes', caused many ugly incidents. English merchants intruded themselves so successfully into the Ionian isles that they were soon carrying off the greater part of its dried fruit. The Venetian government attempted to prevent the islanders from doing business with the foreign merchants, a prohibition about which the inhabitants complained volubly, and which they largely ignored.[30]

Meanwhile, the English had no compunction about attacking Venetian ships, especially if they were trading with Spain, which supplied the wool they needed for their looms. In October 1589 an English captain fell out with a Venetian captain in the harbour of Corfu; the Italian challenged the Englishman to a duel, and called him an insolent dog. When the Venetian ship slipped out of port the English captain impudently gave chase. After a brief exchange of gunfire the Italian decided he had had enough and abandoned ship, but even then the

English captain pursued his longboat part of the way back into Corfu harbour. These pirates respected no one. In 1591 English pirates who had been made welcome in the port of Algiers plundered a Ragusan ship in the channel between the Balearic islands and Barcelona as it was sailing west from Livorno. The North African rulers were often content to let the pirates use their ports so long as they shared their booty with the rulers of Barbary. Crews might be half-Muslim, half-English.[31] One English exile, John Ward, brought 300 men under his command; in 1607 he terrified the captain of a Venetian spice galleon into surrender, and sold its cargo in Tunis for 70,000 crowns, only to follow this with the seizure of goods worth 400,000 crowns.[32] Irate at the treatment Protestants received when they fell into the hands of the Inquisition, English pirates also defiled Catholic churches on islands held by Venice.[33]

The pirates owed much of their success to new technology. They brought with them into the Mediterranean high-sided sailing ships that the Italians called *bertoni*. They looked fairly similar to the galleons that were coming into fashion in the Spanish and Venetian navies, but they possessed a deep, strong keel and functioned well with three square-rigged sails. They were not especially large and they carried crews of around sixty, with one cannon for about every three men. When their rivals within the Mediterranean managed to capture these ships, they made every use of them; they even purchased them from English and Dutch captains. Yet Venice was strangely conservative. Lateen-rigged galleys had defended the city's trade and empire for many centuries, and attempts to convince the Venetian government that the new type of ship was vital to the defence of the republic fell on deaf ears. The Venetian elite could not understand why what had worked in the thirteenth century would not work in the seventeenth. *Bertoni* became a common sight in Venice only in the early seventeenth century, when the republic begged England and Holland to support its struggle against the Austrian Habsburgs. By 1619 the Venetian navy possessed fifty *bertoni* alongside fifty galleys. Yet even when Venetian captains sailed *bertoni*, they seemed unable to challenge the superior skill of northern seamen. In 1603 the *Santa Maria della Grazia*, a Venetian *bertone*, was heading for Alexandria when it was captured off Crete – Venetian territory. Then, once released, it was seized at night-time while sailing up the Adriatic, and deprived of its guns. The Italians were no longer near-invincible at sea.

Northerners also attacked northerners; the relationship between the English and the Dutch oscillated violently in the late sixteenth and early seventeenth centuries. In 1603 Thomas Sherley, in command of a motley crew of English, Italian and Greek sailors, attacked two Dutch ships carrying Aegean grain from the Cyclades to Genoa. Sherley was content to pose as the agent of the Medici duke of Tuscany, and as a sort of crusader against the Turks, though quite how an attack on the Dutch fitted into this is a mystery. Sherley had to write to the duke to explain himself, because he had clearly over-reached himself. The Medici were happy to buy English *bertoni* and to employ English sailors. The duke even obtained his gunpowder from England. He wondered whether it might be a good idea to lure John Ward into his service, since he seemed such an effective corsair. The duke of Savoy, whose territory extended down to Nice, was happy to make his flag and his port at Villefranche available to all sorts of dubious sailors.³⁴ As Alberto Tenenti pointed out, 'in the Mediterranean at the end of the sixteenth century, a real change was taking place, psychological as well as naval and commercial': the spirit of the crusade had been replaced by a cynicism which was occasionally masked by the language of holy war, but among the pirates that was belied by their willing cooperation with Turks and Moors.³⁵ The clearest indication of this was provided by the Knights of Santo Stefano: by the seventeenth century they were freebooters able to benefit from the handsome concessions made to them by the Medici dukes of Tuscany.

The northerners found that the tough shipboard life of the seventeenth century – fetid water, biscuits full of weevils, tough discipline – was alleviated a little when sailing in Mediterranean waters. John Baltharpe was an English sailor who recounted in doggerel his voyage around the Mediterranean in 1670. Putting in at Messina, 'a market was on board each day' and he could buy

> Silk-stockings, Carpets, Brande-wine,
> Silk Neckcloaths, also very fine:
> Cabidges, Carrets, Turnips, Nuts,
> The last a man may eat from Sluts:
> Lemmons, Orenges, and good Figs,
> *Seracusa* Wine also, and Eggs.

In Livorno, Baltharpe was delighted to find excellent fish, 'which 'mongst *Italians* is a good dish', while at 'Cales', or Cagliari, 'nothing was scant'.

Even at Alicante, where meat was scarce and 'instead of *English* Cheese, and Butter, A little Oyl we get, God wot, far worser', there was the consolation of plenty of red wine – 'this blood of *Bulls* ... 'Tis sweet, Delicious, very tempting, The Bottle is not long a emptying'.[36] Looking into the future, the efforts of Lord Nelson around 1800 to keep his men supplied with Sicilian lemons – 30,000 gallons a year, made available to the entire British Navy – ensured that his crews in the Mediterranean and beyond did not suffer from scurvy.[37]

The interest of northerners in the Mediterranean was accentuated by the rising standard of living in the sixteenth century, and, even though this stalled in the seventeenth century, the northerners became a permanent presence after Lepanto. Their identity varied: the Hanseatic Germans were pioneers (arriving when Mediterranean harvests failed in 1587), but did not maintain a strong presence, while the 'Flemish' increasingly consisted of mainly Protestant Dutch from the rebellious northern provinces of the Spanish Netherlands, rather than the Catholics of Flanders proper.[38] The rise of the Dutch navies began with the emergence of Antwerp as the hub of the Portuguese spice trade with the East, but Dutch prosperity was based on profits from expanding trade and piracy in the Mediterranean just as much as it was based on the proceeds of its Atlantic and Indian Ocean traffic.[39] When the United Provinces established their de facto independence from Spain, business shifted increasingly to the shipyards of Holland. Within the Mediterranean there was some cooperation, at first, with the French merchants who were beginning to make headway in North Africa, and occasionally allowed Dutch ships to fly the French flag (guaranteeing their safety in Ottoman waters).[40] The phrase 'flag of convenience' is especially apt: captains switched back and forth, to gain whatever protection a particular nation could claim from the rulers of the Mediterranean shores and islands.

III

Among all those that sailed this sea, the 'Portuguese nation', mostly Marranos, attracted special curiosity. The Portuguese Inquisition had (by royal command) held back from persecuting the New Christians in the years after the suppression of Judaism in Portugal (1497); but it turned against them in 1547, with the result that many started to move to more welcoming lands. The indistinct status of the Ponentine Jews was exploited by rulers such as the dukes of Tuscany, ever happy to offer their patronage to any merchants who might help them maximize their income. In extending their favours to the 'Portuguese', the dukes did not intend to emancipate all the Jews of their dominions; indeed, they enclosed the Jews of Florence within a ghetto in 1570.[41] Gradually, though, they began to see the advantages of creating an open port in which not just Marranos of doubtful religious allegiance but Levantine Jews, Muslims and northern Europeans could take advantage of rights of settlement and special tax provisions. Duke Cosimo I, who died in 1574, transformed Livorno from a sleepy fishing village into one of the great centres of Mediterranean trade. Towards the end of his life, the harbour was greatly improved, and a canal was dug that linked the town to the river Arno, facilitating the transfer of goods to and from Pisa and Florence; under his successor Francesco I, Livorno was surrounded with its impressive pentagonal set of walls. Within this area a rectangular Roman-style street plan was laid out, in accord with the best principles of Renaissance town-planning.[42] Gradually the population grew: in 1601 there were nearly 5,000 inhabitants, including 762 soldiers, 114 Jews and 76 young prostitutes, the last group a sad reminder of the sexual services in demand in every Mediterranean port. After this, as the port infrastructure developed, the city boomed.[43]

The right of aliens to live in Livorno was confirmed by a series of privileges, the *Livornine*, which determined the relationship between the Medicean government and its non-Catholic subjects for over two centuries. In the most famous of these privileges, of 1593, the duke extended a welcome to 'merchants of all nations, Levantine and Ponentine, Spanish and Portuguese, Greeks, Germans and Italians, Jews, Turks and Moors, Armenians, Persians and others'.[44] It is noticeable how low down the list were the Italians, in an Italian city. It is also significant that the document repeated again and again the welcome to the Marranos: as Ponentines, as Iberian merchants, as Jews. Ponentine merchants needed to declare themselves as Jews, despite their mask of Christianity, thereby ensuring exemption from interference by the Inquisition – which meant that they had to keep switching their identity, especially if they traded intensively with Spain and Portugal, but they were adept at doing this.[45] Few restrictions were placed on their economic activities;

uniquely in Italy, they were permitted to acquire landed property. Although they generally lived close to the synagogue, which, by the eighteenth century, was a grand and opulent building, there was no official Jewish quarter. There was also a church for Armenian merchants from the eastern Mediterranean. Three mosques existed within the *bagno*, the quarters reserved for galley slaves, though free Muslim merchants certainly came to Livorno in growing numbers; permission was granted for the creation of a Muslim cemetery.[46]

All this reflected the opening of trade routes between Livorno and Islamic lands: ships were arriving from Alexandria in the years around 1590, but the real success story was the opening of routes to North Africa between 1573 and 1593, a period during which Braudel and Romano identified forty-four voyages to Livorno from a great swathe of territory between Larache in Morocco and Tunisia. These contacts could not have been effected without investment by the Sephardic merchants, or without cooperation between the rulers of Barbary and the Medici; the Dutch also became involved in this traffic, providing insurance and additional shipping capacity. The routes were vital for the provisioning of Tuscany, which drew wheat from North Africa, as well as wax, leather, wool and sugar.[47] Other basic products such as tin, pine-nuts, tunny and anchovies were brought from Spain and Portugal, often on ships originating in the ports of southern France. Something, however, had changed in the geography of Spanish trade. Barcelona had few contacts with Livorno, and Valencia had only a modest role, but Alicante, which had an excellent port and which gave access by good-quality roads to the produce of the Spanish hinterland, was the favoured port within Mediterranean Spain. Alicante itself produced little apart from soap, made with local olive oil, and wine; 'it retained into modern times something of the air of a colonial factory, of the kind which might have been found in the somnolent hinterlands of Asia or Africa'.[48] Along the route between Alicante and Livorno (and a rival one between Alicante and Genoa), the Ragusans were the dominant intermediaries, carrying cochineal and kermes, the red dyes made from tiny insects, rice, silk, honey, sugar and, above all, wool, and Jewish merchants played a major role in this commerce, even though it was forbidden for them to practise their religion within the Spanish kingdoms.[49]

Livorno also established relations with places beyond the Straits of Gibraltar – with Cádiz, which was emerging as a major Spanish trading centre in the Atlantic, with Lisbon and with the North Sea lands. The Dutch were attracted there like bees to a flower. Although the *Livornine* did not specifically encourage Protestant settlement in Livorno, Dutch merchants found they could live there in peace with a certain amount of discretion. Livorno was the hub of the Dutch network within the Mediterranean as well as the target for many Dutch ships arriving from Atlantic waters. Despite the intensification of trade with North Africa, and despite occasional good harvests, Tuscany remained hungry for Baltic grain. Its quality was often prized above that of the Mediterranean, and at the same time – even allowing for transport costs – it was usually cheaper. As has been seen, this reflects the retreat of cultivation around the shores of the Mediterranean in this period. The Italians developed a taste for northern rye: in 1620, around one in five of the Dutch ships that brought grain to Livorno carried a cargo solely of rye. The Medici dukes negotiated favourable prices in Holland so that their subjects could afford sufficient food; and when grain was plentiful in the Mediterranean it was always possible to substitute smoked and dried herrings, pilchards and cod, even caviar.[50] The Dutch merchants who brought this grain did not simply carry goods to and from northern Europe. They intruded themselves into the carrying trade within the Mediterranean, willingly finding space in their holds for south Italian grain and salt, which they ferried to northern Italy. If there was a famine in northern Europe, as in 1630, Dutch captains were willing to pick up provisions for Livorno in the Aegean, defying Ottoman orders that anyone found exporting grain illegally was to be tied to a stake and allowed to die by starvation. When supplies of grain within the Mediterranean were adequate, they shopped around, picking up wool and salt in Alicante, wine and dried fruits in the Ionian isles, silk in the Aegean, and so on, and they sought to develop their relations with the great centres of trade in the Levant – Aleppo had emerged as the main emporium in Syria, and there was a Dutch consul there who also looked after trade in Palestine and Cyprus. Since Aleppo lies inland ships would dock at Alexandretta, and goods would then have to be carried overland; they included such exotic products as indigo and rhubarb, which was prized for its medical properties.[51]

In 1608 Duke Ferdinand permitted the 'Flemish-German nation' to build a Catholic chapel dedicated to the Madonna containing a vault in which Flemish and Dutch merchants could be buried. Inevitably, many

Protestants preferred to be buried outside Catholic precincts; they were allowed to use private gardens. On the other hand, some prominent members of the 'nation' were devout Catholics, like Bernard van den Broecke, who was treasurer of the chapel of the Madonna, and who ran his business from a large house on the principal street, the Via Ferdinanda. His house contained ten bedrooms and a reception room adorned with a dozen paintings, a parrot in a cage, a backgammon table and fine furniture; in the garden there was a fountain and a spacious orangery. From Livorno, van den Broecke operated a whole network of business, encompassing the court of the duke of Tuscany, Naples, Sicily and Venice, as well, of course, as northern Europe. In 1624, he even laid plans for the creation of a trade route bringing cod directly from Newfoundland to Naples, but was frustrated by English interference – his cod was confiscated because the English king was once again at war with Spain, which ruled Naples. Even so, the English and the Dutch (including van den Broecke) occasionally cooperated in trade with Spain, using the Tuscan banner as a flag of convenience. Van den Broecke had no qualms about becoming involved in the slave trade within the Mediterranean, though here his aim was to extort ransom money from the families of well-connected captives. He ensured that slaves in his household were well cared for, so they could be returned in top condition; they must have 'enough to live on and to be clothed without being spoilt'.[52] Van den Broecke's business house flourished until the 1630s, when political difficulties with Spain, competition from the English and epidemics made life increasingly difficult. But the city maintained its primacy in Mediterranean trade, especially because the Sephardic Jews continued to use it as their link to other focal points of Sephardic settlement: Aleppo, Salonika and, increasingly, Smyrna.

IV

The great success of Livorno was not exceptional. The Genoese also attempted to create their own free port in the seventeenth century, beginning in 1590 with foodstuffs, and extending tariff exemptions to all goods in 1609. This was a different type of free port from Livorno: in Genoa, the emphasis was on free passage of merchandise, whereas in Livorno the emphasis lay on attracting merchants who would be free from restrictions on the right to reside and conduct business. The character of the city and its business had changed enormously since Genoa had competed with Pisa, Venice and Barcelona for mastery over the Mediterranean. The shift from active interest in trade to the provision of finance to the Spanish court had effects throughout Genoese society, even though those who serviced the Spanish royal debt were members of the elite families. By the 1560s they had lost interest in shipowning.[53] Genoese ships became a minority among those arriving in the port of Genoa: from 1596 onwards, more than 70 per cent of the ships passing through it were foreign. Predictably, the Ragusans were very active, but so were Hanseatic vessels from Germany and the Low Countries, with the Dutch assuming an ever more important role in the seventeenth century.[54] In the late sixteenth century, Genoese merchants often bought shares in Ragusan ships, but this only underlines the great change that had taken place: the idea that a small Adriatic republic could outclass 'la Superba', the proud Genoese republic, would have been laughed to scorn two centuries earlier.

The Genoese saw themselves as allies of the Spanish Crown; the king of Spain would rather have seen them as his subjects, but insistence on this point only weakened Genoese affection for the Spanish alliance. Just to show where Genoa fitted into their scheme of things, in 1606 and 1611 the Spaniards ensured that their tributaries the Knights of Malta were given precedence in battle orders over the Genoese, which Genoa rightly understood to mean that Spain saw it as its dependency. Disputes over this issue sometimes reached the point where Genoese and Maltese galleys, arrayed for battle, threatened to turn their guns on each other, and Spanish admirals had to force them to back down. But Spanish finances depended heavily on the Genoese, whose galleys carried bullion from Spain to Genoa – nearly 70,000,000 pieces of eight in the period 1600 to 1640. The principle underlying Genoese loans to the Spanish Crown was that advances would be repaid from the income in silver and gold arriving from the New World.[55] Other galleys were dedicated to the lucrative trade in raw silk from Messina; silk had become one the foundations of Genoa's revived prosperity a century earlier, and it symbolized the intense but troubled relationship with Spain, since it came from Sicily, a Spanish possession, along with Sicilian grain, at the same time as being heavily taxed by a Spanish government anxious to squeeze every penny from the merchants.[56]

The Genoese shared with the Venetians a nostalgia for past times, for an era in which Genoa had achieved greatness through sending its galleys across the Mediterranean and even into the seas beyond. A Genoese nobleman, Antonio Giulio Brignole Sale, wrote a treatise in 1642 in which he examined the arguments for and against the building of a new galley fleet, which the city fathers hoped would restore Genoese fortunes. He was convinced that the Mediterranean was the ideal theatre of operations, for 'the provinces are more numerous, and more distinct, where many put in to port, so that everyone can find employment more easily'. By building galleys, it would be possible to renew 'the ancient Levant routes', which were the 'special theatre of the acquisitions and glories of the Genoese', a point upon which he insisted while admitting that opponents of his scheme argued that the Mediterranean no longer looked the same as it did in medieval days, and building galleys in the medieval fashion would not bring back that lost world.[57]

In the late sixteenth and seventeenth centuries, the Mediterranean suffered from a sort of disorientation. Despite attempts by the Genoese to reconstitute the Levant trade, the Mediterranean lost its primacy in the traffic of western Europe to the Atlantic merchants, for whom the Mediterranean was one, and not necessarily the most interesting or important, of their concerns, which stretched from Holland to Brazil and the East Indies, or from England to Newfoundland and Muscovy.[58] The initial promise of the fifteenth and early sixteenth centuries had not been fulfilled.

6

Diasporas in Despair, 1560–1700

I

Ottoman sultans and Spanish kings, along with their tax officials, took a strong interest in the religious identity of those who crossed the areas of the Mediterranean under their control. Sometimes, in an era marked by the clash of Christian and Muslim empires, the Mediterranean seems to be sharply divided between the two faiths. Yet the Ottomans had long accepted the existence of Christian majorities in many of the lands they ruled, while other groups navigated (metaphorically) between religious identities. The Sephardic Jews have already been encountered, with their astonishing ability to mutate into notionally Christian 'Portuguese' when they entered the ports of Mediterranean Spain. This existence suspended between worlds set off its own tensions in the seventeenth century, when many Sephardim acclaimed a deluded Jew of Smyrna as the Messiah. Similar tensions could also be found among the remnants of the Muslim population of Spain. The tragic history of the Moriscos was played out largely away from the Mediterranean Sea between the conversion of the last openly practising Muslims, in 1525, and the final act of their expulsion in 1609; it was their very isolation from the Islamic world that gave these people their distinctive identity, once again suspended between religions.

The world inhabited by these Moriscos differed in important respects from that inhabited by the other group of *conversos*, those of Jewish descent. Although some Moriscos were hauled before the Inquisition, the Spanish authorities at first turned a blind eye to the continued practice of Islam; it was sometimes possible to pay the Crown a 'service' that bought exemption from interference by the Inquisition, which was

470

mortified to discover that it could not boost its income by seizing the property of exempt suspects.[1] Many Morisco communities lacked a Christian priest, so the continued practice of the old religion is no great surprise; even in areas where christianization took place, what sometimes emerged was an islamized Christianity, evinced in the remarkable lead tablets of Sacromonte, outside Granada, with their prophecies that 'the Arabs will be those who aid religion in the last days' and their mysterious references to a Christian caliph, or successor (to Jesus, not Muhammad).[2] In many respects, the Crown's major concern was political, rather than religious: a Spanish Christian writer reported that the leaders of the Granadan Moriscos had secretly negotiated with the rulers of the Barbary states and with the Turks, in the hope of establishing a statelet under their protection, but this was a hopeless cause since they lacked ships or supplies; besides, the Spanish coastal stations in North Africa acted as a partial barrier to contact between the Barbary states and the Moriscos, while 'the Algiers corsairs are much better at piracy and trading along the coasts than they are at mounting difficult expeditions on land'.[3] Even so, there was no room for complacency. The Moriscos might support the Ottoman sultans by creating a diversion within Spain while the armies and navies of the Catholic king were engaged in faraway lands – not just at Lepanto or Malta, but in the Netherlands. Philip II, like his father, Charles V, was tempted to see the problem of Unbelief in black-and-white, so that, for Philip, the presence within Spain of unruly Moriscos was, ultimately, part of the same problem as the presence within his northernmost possessions of unruly Calvinists: 'I have such a specific obligation to God and the world to act,' Philip wrote, for 'if the heretics were to prevail (which I hope God will not allow) it might open the door to worse damages and dangers, and to war at home'.[4]

These fears seemed to be realized in the final days of 1568, when violence erupted among the Moriscos of Granada, who were exasperated at recurrent attempts by the government and the Inquisition to turn them into proper Christians. The Moriscos had been ordered to speak Castilian instead of Arabic; they were forbidden to wear 'the Moorish robes in which they took such pride'; women were ordered to abandon the veil and to show their faces; they were ordered not to gather at the public baths, and Moorish dancing was banned at weddings and other celebrations.[5] For two years a hideously bloodthirsty war was waged between

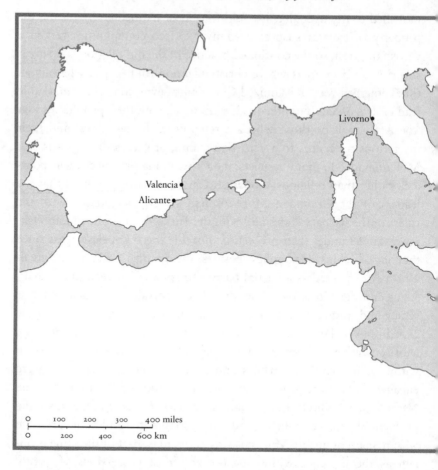

contestants who were unwilling to give any quarter; as feared, Turks and Berbers arrived from North Africa to offer support to the rebels, and diplomatic links were forged with the Sublime Porte and the North African rulers.[6] And yet this support was never enough to crack the resolve of the Spanish troops, led by Don John of Austria, whose ruthlessness soon won him the command of the Christian navy at Lepanto. The problem for the Moriscos was that 'instead of relying on their own efforts, they persisted in deluding themselves (against all the evidence) that large armies would arrive from Barbary to help them or, failing that, huge fleets would arrive, miraculously to waft them, their families and their possessions out of our grasp'.[7] In fact the Turkish court decided that Spain was beyond its reach, and turned its attention to the much

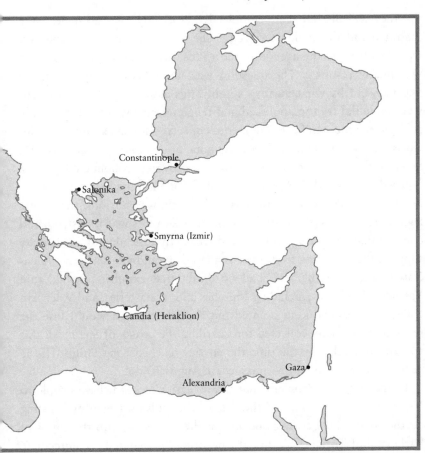

more accessible and feasible prize of Cyprus.[8] The difficulties of the Moriscos were made all the greater because the rebellion was centred in the Alpujarras mountains and Granada, away from the coastline. Following defeat, 50,000 Moriscos found themselves dispersed across Castile, leaving the only large concentration of Muslims in the kingdom of Valencia.[9] This, however, was seen as a temporary solution; when Philip II acquired the throne of Portugal in 1580, the chance seemed to have arrived for the imposition of complete religious uniformity throughout all Iberia. One possibility that was mooted was to send the Moriscos out to sea in ships that would then be scuttled, for it made no sense to add to the population of hostile North Africa. The bishop of Segorbe chillingly suggested that the Moriscos should be sent to Newfoundland, for 'they will die out there completely', especially after all males were castrated and all females sterilized.[10] The possibility of a mass expulsion was therefore on the agenda in the 1580s, nearly thirty years before it was finally resolved. The question was not whether they should be expelled, but by what means. Notably, this assumed that all Moriscos were potential traitors, political and religious enemies of Christendom, and ignored the significant number of converts who had assimilated into Christian society (some, indeed, becoming priests); nor was any account taken of the effects on Spain at a time of growing economic difficulties, especially within the Morisco heartlands of the kingdom of Valencia. For by now the decline of the city of Valencia was obvious; there were legitimate worries about the state of the silk and sugar industries, and concern that irrigation works would fail, so that the already inadequate supplies the city drew from the countryside would vanish.[11] The Valencian *Corts*, or parliament, had no doubt that expulsion would ruin Valencian landlords, including churches and monasteries, and Valencian envoys sent to the king pointed out that the Crown would lose the revenue it normally collected for guarding the coasts of Spain. All this was of no avail – by the time the envoys reached King Philip III, the decree of expulsion had been issued, in August 1609.[12]

In the end the argument that it was easier to send these people to North Africa had won, and the decree of expulsion began by insisting on the treasonable correspondence of the Moriscos with the rulers of Barbary and Turkey.[13] Although the decree demanded an immediate evacuation, on ships provided by the Crown, the process inevitably proved much slower, and the expulsions continued until 1614. The economic arguments against expulsion were partly heeded: six in every 100 Moriscos were allowed to stay, so long as they were farmers and were thought to show Christian sympathies; they would be expected 'to show those who took over the properties how to work, among other things, the sugar mills and irrigation systems'. The decree set out in painstaking detail (to a modern reader, reminiscent of the infamous Wannsee conference in Nazi Berlin) the exact categories of people who were to go, for there were mixed families and questions arose concerning children who had one Old Christian parent.[14] The ports from which they were to depart were carefully assigned, and included Alicante, Valencia and Tortosa. A preaching campaign was set in train, to argue that the Moriscos were about to bring the Ottoman fleet to Spain, and that they had offered 150,000 troops to aid the Turks. The Moriscos were tempted to resist, but abandoned any hope of doing so when they saw how large were the Spanish forces sent to usher them out of their homeland. Indeed, the Moriscos decided that no one should volunteer to join the special category of those who were permitted to remain and teach the Christians how to exploit the land. The solidarity of the Moriscos is impressive. In the kingdom of Valencia, the duke of Gandía was desperate when he learned that nobody would stay behind to cultivate his sugar estates. For him, as for the Moriscos, what was happening was a disaster. On 2 October 1609 nearly 4,000 Moriscos embarked at Denia, many on Neapolitan galleys sent specially to take them to the Barbary coast; the number of those who embarked swelled, and 28,000 were carried in a short space of time to North Africa. It was not difficult for Spanish ships to leave them there: the first shipment was taken to Oran, still a Spanish possession, and on their arrival the Moriscos negotiated with the ruler of Tlemcen for the right to settle in Muslim territory. Other refugees spurned the initial Spanish offers of free transport and arranged their own passage: 14,500 embarked at Valencia, in sight of the Christian citizens, who came to buy their silks and laces at bargain prices in what became, perforce, 'a giant flea market'.[15] Some Moriscos made it plain that this was, for them, an act of liberation rather than persecution: the princes of Barbary 'will let us live as Moors and not as slaves, as we have been treated by our masters'.

There is evidence for over 150,000 departures, though some contemporary estimates were lower: the Valencian Inquisition produced a figure of 100,656, including 17,766 who embarked at the port of Valencia itself, and of these 3,269 were less than twelve years old, and 1,339 were unweaned babies.[16] Soon it was time to turn attention to the ancient kingdom of Aragon, from which 74,000 Moriscos departed, and a lesser number from Catalonia; many left by sea via Tortosa, though others took a land route through the Pyrenees into France, enduring terrible conditions. King Henry IV of France insisted they must nearly all be shipped to North Africa.[17] The Franco-Ottoman alliance did not extend to the protection of the Spanish Muslims, and Henry, who had triumphed after bitter wars between Protestants and Catholics, was reluctant to introduce further religious diversity into the kingdom he had won by abandoning Protestantism.[18] Still, the French were taken aback by what they saw. Cardinal Richelieu later described these events as 'the most fantastic, the most barbarous act in the annals of mankind', though he was probably more interested in condemning the Spanish Christians than in defending the Spanish Muslims.[19] Meanwhile, the Spanish Crown turned its attention to Castile, and in early 1614 the Council of State informed Philip III that the work was done.[20] Adding together all the Spanish kingdoms, perhaps 300,000 Moriscos were expelled.[21]

From the Spanish Christian perspective, the expulsion was an act against unbelievers, though some well-assimilated Christians of Muslim descent were swept up despite assurances that those who willingly took the sacrament would be permitted to stay. The curious effect of the Crown's brutality was that a mixed population, resentful of Spanish policy, had now been installed on the Barbary coast, and Moriscos lent their energies to the corsair raids on the Spanish coastline. Alongside the spirit of revenge, there persisted nostalgia for a romantically remembered past. The music of al-Andalus was preserved partly among the Moriscos and partly among earlier groups of exiles – refugees from troubles in Granada and elsewhere who had already settled in the North African towns. The indigenous inhabitants of North Africa were less welcoming than the exiles hoped. Many Moriscos seemed to be impossibly Hispanicized in language, dress and customs, after decades of Christian campaigns against 'Moorish practices'; they held themselves aloof from the Maghribi population. Most of the Moriscos who settled in Tunisia spoke Spanish and many carried Spanish names; they even introduced American fruits such as the prickly pear into North Africa, products they had come to know in Spain between 1492 and 1609.[22] If they wanted to find comrades who would understand their ways, they sometimes decided that they were better understood by the Sephardic Jews, who shared their nostalgia for the old Spain of the three religions, maintained a distance of their own from the native Jewish communities, and continued to speak a form of Castilian. Thus an emotional kinship in exile was formed between Sephardic Jews and Andalusi Muslims in North Africa.

II

The Sephardic Jews also underwent a sharp crisis later in the same century. Its starting-point was the city of Smyrna, or Izmir. Smyrna and

Livorno formed part of a binary system that linked Italy to the Ottoman world.[23] Neither had been a place of great significance in the early sixteenth century. But the Baron de Courmenin visited Smyrna in 1621 and wrote:

> At present, Izmir has a great traffic in wool, beeswax, cotton and silk, which the Armenians bring there instead of going to Aleppo. It is more advantageous for them to go there because they do not pay as many dues. There are several merchants, more French than Venetian, English or Dutch, who live in great freedom.[24]

As with the dried fruit of the Ionian isles, it was local produce that brought Smyrna to the attention of foreign merchants; other contemporary merchants also noted the arrival of increasing quantities of Persian silk, brought across Anatolia by the Armenians. The Turks had less difficulty with European silk traders than with European merchants who sought out grain and fruits, since Constantinople was also hungry for those items.

After 1566, European trade with the Aegean was thrown off balance by the loss of the last Genoese possession in the region, Chios. Without a strong Genoese base offshore, Smyrna began to develop, offering locally produced cotton and newer commodities such as tobacco, about which the Sublime Porte had doubts – not because of a generic dislike of its fumes, but because the more tobacco the region produced, the less foodstuffs could be grown, and the Ottoman capital was always in need of a regular food supply.[25] Almost immediately after the fall of Chios, Charles IX of France secured trading rights in Smyrna for French merchants (in 1569), and Elizabeth I secured a charter of privileges for trade there in 1580, which became the preserve of the English Levant Company; then the Dutch received privileges in 1612.[26] The foreign merchants appreciated Smyrna's position, tucked inside a gulf, which prevented lightning raids by corsairs, and their presence also drew to the city countless Jews, Greeks, Arabs and Armenians.[27] A traveller's report from 1675 speaks, somewhat implausibly, of a Jewish population of 15,000, which should probably be scaled down to a couple of thousand. These Jews came from all over the Mediterranean and beyond: there were Sephardim, both Levantine and Portuguese, Romaniotes (Greek Jews) and Ashkenazim from eastern Europe. The legal status of the Portuguese Jews varied, for they sought protectors from whose tax exemptions they could benefit: at one moment at the end of the seventeenth century they (along with the Danes and the Venetians) accepted English protection, then they turned to the Ragusans, and finally the sultan took them under his own protection, which denied them a good many tax breaks, and therefore pleased their rivals – as the Levant Company asserted in 1695, 'it is the Jews who are our greatest rivals in Smyrna'.[28]

The special nature of seventeenth-century Smyrna was particularly obvious along the harbour front, on the Street of the Franks. It was there that the elegantly furnished houses of the Europeans could be found. Gardens at the back of them gave access to the quayside, and were used as passage-ways for goods; terraces led upwards to the roofs of European warehouses.[29] A French visitor observed in 1700:

> The Turks are seldom seen in the Franks' Street, which is the whole length of the city. When we are in this street, we seem to be in Christendom; they speak nothing but Italian, French, English or Dutch there. Everybody takes off his hat when he pays his respects to another.

But of all the languages heard on the Street of the Franks, the most common was the Provençal of the merchants of Marseilles, 'because there are more from Provence than any other parts'. The Christians were free to operate their own taverns, but they did so rather tactlessly, leaving them open all day and all night. Remarkable too was their freedom of worship: 'they sing publicly in the churches; they sing psalms, preach and perform Divine Service without any trouble'.[30] A functioning port city had come into being, in which the needs of trade allowed Muslims, Jews and a variety of Christian sects to coexist side by side: there were three churches used by western Europeans, two for the Greeks and an Armenian church as well. There were several synagogues too, but it was events in the Portuguese synagogue that would set the Jewish world alight in the 1660s; the heat of these flames would be felt by Christians and Muslims as well as Jews.

The different ethnic and religious groups in Smyrna worked together in business. The merchants of the English Levant Company often employed Jewish agents, and among these there was a decrepit and gouty broker named Mordecai Zevi (often spelled Sevi, Tzvi or Sebi), a Greek Jew who had devoted his early career to the humble task of dealing in eggs.[31] He had three sons; two also became brokers, but the third,

Shabbetai, began to have extraordinary visions, and became immersed in some of the more abstruse areas of Jewish scholarship. Kabbalistic studies had long flourished, first among the Jews of Spain and, since 1492, among the Sephardim of Safed in Palestine. The rabbis took the view that it was dangerous to study Kabbalah before the age of forty, by which time one should possess the necessary background knowledge and maturity; but this opinion did not dissuade Shabbetai Zevi, who taught himself while still a very young man: 'he learned everything for himself, for he was one of the four to arrive at the knowledge of the Creator by themselves', the others being the patriarch Abraham, Hezekiah, king of Judah and Job.[32] Descriptions of Shabbetai's mood swings and conduct leave little doubt that he possessed a bi-polar personality. Self-doubt and introspection were counterbalanced by ecstasy and megalomania. When he declaimed Isaiah's words, 'I will ascend above the heights of the clouds', he imagined that he was doing just that, and invited his friends to confirm that he had the power to levitate. They denied having seen him do so. He then ticked them off: 'You were not worthy to behold this glorious sight because you were not purified like me.'[33]

The time seemed right for the coming of the salvation of the people of Israel. In the 1640s, terrible massacres wreaked by the Cossacks in eastern Europe induced a sense of deep crisis among Jews as far away as the Mediterranean, and refugees brought tales of what had happened to the safe havens they found in the Ottoman Empire. The sense of crisis was almost as acute as it had been in 1492, when expulsion from Spain had unleashed earlier Messianic fervour. Shabbetai, now in his twenties, began to reveal himself as a Messianic figure, though there was some ambiguity about who exactly he claimed to be. He set aside centuries of tradition and began to pronounce the four-letter Name of God in synagogue (Jews always substitute the word *Adonai*, 'my Lord'), and he began to contradict commandments found in the Torah itself, for example the commandment not to eat the fat around an animal's kidneys, which had been reserved for the Temple sacrifices. He even uttered this prayer when eating the forbidden food: 'Blessed are You, Lord our God and king of the universe, who permits that which is forbidden.' His private life was complicated: his wife Sarah was, frankly, a whore and had earned a little money as a fortune-teller, but this was only to re-enact the career of the prophet Hosea, who had married a prostitute.[34]

Spending some time in Salonika, he began to recruit followers who were impressed by his prophetic skills and self-assurance. He travelled around the eastern Mediterranean, clearly hoping to win the approval of the Palestinian rabbis whose opinions would be respected across the Jewish world; his most prominent recruit was a noisy Jew from Gaza named Nathan, who became his most persistent advocate. Unfortunately, Shabbetai refused to perform any miracles, even for his followers in Hebron, where the leading Sephardic rabbi, Haim Abulafia, declared: 'I do not believe the Messiah will come in this way.'[35] After all, Shabbetai lacked the credentials of a member of the royal house of David.

Back in Smyrna, he and his 'Sabbatian' followers stormed the Portuguese synagogue in Smyrna on 12 December 1665 and ejected the old leadership. Once he and his adherents had acquired a base for their activities, new festivals were instituted and old ones were cancelled (notably the summer fast commemorating the fall of the Temple, for which there was surely no need if the redemption for which Jews had been praying on that day was now at hand). He called women to the reading of the Torah, a practice then unknown, and entertained the congregation by declaiming an erotic romance in Judaeo-Spanish called *Meliselda* in which the beautiful daughter of an emperor meets and makes love to a young man: 'her face a gleaming sword of light, her lips like corals red and bright, her flesh as milk so fair and white'.[36] Not that anyone had noticed before, but this song was evidently an allegory of the bond between the Messiah and the Torah, which represented the Divine Presence. The Messiah would be a real king and not just a religious leader, so Shabbetai assumed imperial authority and began to nominate his followers as kings and emperors of such lands as Portugal, Turkey and Rome (the last two posts being reserved for his brothers); it goes without saying that he appeared magnificently arrayed and delighted in the office of 'king of the Jews'; news of his achievements, if they can be called that, reached Amsterdam in the correspondence of both Sephardic and Christian merchants.[37] Far from generating anger, these acts confirmed the belief of his followers that he was the promised Messiah.

For Christians the meaning of these events, which they assiduously noted, was rather different: 'God alone knows whether he may be a means of the Conversion of that stiff-necked Generation.'[38] The interest of Christian merchants in the growing ferment among the Jews of the eastern Mediterranean (which soon spread to Italy as well) is easier to understand when the roots of Shabbetai's movement are traced. The way he projected himself as a Messiah who had the power and authority to set aside parts of the old law is reminiscent of the portrayal of Jesus of Nazareth in the Gospels. The young Shabbetai had contact, through his father's business, with English and other Christian merchants in Smyrna. Among them too, apocalyptic ideas had been spreading, for in the 1640s England was a place of religious ferment, as enthusiastic Protestant sects jostled for position, some of them adopting Messianic ideas of their own (to which Oliver Cromwell was by no means immune); these sects read their Old Testaments very closely, and paid careful attention to passages thought to prophesy the Second Coming of Christ. Among these groups were the Fifth Monarchy Men, precursors of the Quakers, whose own origins were full of apocalyptic expectation.[39] Another movement that influenced Christian merchants, and, indirectly, Shabbetai Zevi, was the 'Rosicrucian enlightenment', a system of abstruse knowledge, including alchemy, which was spread by the printed word in the early seventeenth century.[40] The origins of this movement lay in Germany, wracked by the Thirty Years' War, but its tenets attracted men of science across northern Europe. The trade routes that carried Smyrna cotton to England brought esoteric ideas in return.

Yet Shabbetai Zevi's activities were centred on the Ottoman parts of the Mediterranean, and it is no surprise that his name came to the notice of the sultan. Here was a Jewish subject who had made his own brother 'king of Turkey'; and in the synagogues of his followers the traditional prayer for the sovereign had been modified so that, instead of asking for God's blessing on the sultan, the congregation prayed for 'our Messiah, the anointed of the God of Joseph, the celestial lion and celestial stag, the Messiah of righteousness, the king of kings, the sultan Shabbetai Zevi'.[41] The vizier, Fazıl Ahmet Pasha, had fallen under the influence of a puritanical branch of Islam that scorned other religions; he had been occupied with war against the Venetians in Crete, but now turned his master's attention to this troublesome prophet.[42] Shabbetai had plans of his own, which brought him closer to Fazıl Ahmet. On 30 December 1665 Shabbetai and his followers took a ship from Smyrna for Constantinople, where he would establish his realm. A voyage out of season was risky, even within a short span of the Aegean, but the words of Psalm 107 were sufficient to calm the storm they encountered: 'He makes the storm a calm so that the waves are still.' He was at sea for nearly forty days. The Jews of the Ottoman Empire had gathered in vast numbers to greet him; but the Turkish authorities also awaited him. He was carried off to prison, yet even his journey into captivity was treated by his adherents as a great public procession; and, once in prison, he was still able to hold court. The sultan, Mehmet IV, was at Adrianople (Edirne) on the road into the Balkans, and it took a while for the prophet to be brought to the imperial presence. There, he was offered the choice between proving himself to be the Messiah through a miracle and converting to Islam. The miracle required was that Turkish archers should aim their arrows at his naked body, and that the arrows should pass miraculously through him without doing him any harm. Shabbetai demurred. He would rather 'turn Turk', and did so without more ado.[43]

The apostasy of Shabbetai Zevi was all the more dramatic because the Jews of Adrianople had gathered to witness his arrival at the sultan's court with such high expectations. Instead, he appears to have denounced his followers. He accepted the honorary office of keeper of the palace gates, and the name Mehmet Effendi. The shock to the Jewish communities of Turkey, Italy and elsewhere was immense. Throughout the Jewish world there were those who argued that all this simply proved he was an impostor, those who were deflated and discouraged by the course of events, and those who saw in his actions a further stage in his revelation to the world: maybe the Messiah must appear to turn Turk before finally revealing himself – some of his adherents followed in his path and accepted Islam, while keeping up their Jewish practices in secret, forming the Dönme sect that still persists in parts of Turkey. Even though a Jesuit writer insisted that Shabbetai kept a hoard of biscuits with which he fortified himself during his long fasts, there is no reason to suppose he was a rank impostor. He was self-deluded, megalomaniac and unwise, but even his opponents acknowledged that he and his advocate, Nathan of Gaza, were learned men.[44] Still, 'a little learning is a dangerous thing', and nowhere more so than in the esoteric universe of Kabbalah. His travels and the spread of the movement he founded reveal important facets of the networks that linked together the ports of the Mediterranean: from the trading base at Smyrna his ideas percolated to Salonika, Livorno and then into the Balkan and Italian interior. His ideas did not grow simply out of Jewish soil but were irrigated by the apocalyptic enthusiasm of Protestant merchants who had carried their ideas to Smyrna from England, Holland and central Europe. The northerners helped redraw the religious as well as the commercial map of the Mediterranean.

III

The seventeenth-century Mediterranean, with its renegade corsairs, its displaced Moriscos, its Sabbatian converts, its 'Portuguese' merchants, was therefore a place in which religious identities were constantly distorted and reshaped. Christian communities also experienced strong pressures, as the case of Crete illustrates. Here, the Venetians faced a long struggle to maintain control over their last major overseas possession. Crete was becoming a substantial financial burden to Venice, and the republic wondered when, rather than whether, it would have to send a massive fleet there to defend the island against the Turks, for the capture of Cyprus in 1571 would inevitably be followed by a Turkish assault on Crete. This was not simply a struggle with the Turks. The Cretans themselves – the descendants of both Greeks and Venetians who had intermarried with the Greek population – seized the opportunities offered by the wine and oil trades in the late sixteenth century to plant vines and olive trees across the island; by the middle of the seventeenth century olive oil had become the staple export of Crete, and Cretan wine slaked the thirst of consumers in the Ottoman Aegean and the Nile Delta. The production of grain fell to a point where Crete had difficulty feeding itself, a transformation all the more astonishing since it had long been a major source of wheat for Venice itself. The Cretans began to import their grain from Ottoman lands, which worked well enough so long as the Venetians continued to pay court to the Turkish sultan, and so long as the sultan did not feel that supplies were under strain within his own empire. Thus the ties between Crete and the Ottoman world were becoming closer even before the Turks acquired control of Crete in the mid-seventeenth century.[45] The only reason the Turks tolerated Venetian control of Crete was the desire to keep business flowing between Venice and the Ottoman lands; but, as Venice gradually turned its face away from the Levant trade, the Sublime Porte became less interested in its special relationship with the Serenissima Repubblica. The Turks observed, too, that the European powers were all at each other's throats during what became the Thirty Years' War, and so there was little chance of a united Christian response to an assault on Crete. Moreover, the Ottomans were no longer distracted by war with Persia, which had consumed their energies between 1624 and 1639.[46]

The *casus belli* for the lengthy Cretan War was the seizure, late in 1644, of a Turkish ship travelling from Constantinople to Rhodes and then on to Egypt, which was carrying the chief eunuch of the harem and the new judge of Mecca. The pirates were Maltese; they killed the chief eunuch and held the judge captive. They seized a vast booty. Even though the Venetians had played no role in the attack, the Turkish court insisted that the Maltese had been making use of Venetian ports in Crete and Kephalonia. By the end of June 1645, a large Ottoman fleet stood off Crete.[47] The Christian navies of the western Mediterranean were duly mobilized, and a few ships were sent from Naples, Malta and the Papal States. Venice naturally made its own fleet ready, and the republic appointed the eighty-year-old doge as commander, but all these efforts were useless: over the next few months, the Turks captured the second and third cities of Crete, Chania and Rethymnon, as well as much of the interior.[48] Fortunately for Venice, the capital, Candia, was stoutly defended by ditches, walls, fortresses and ravelins; this was state-of-the-art military architecture capable of resisting all that the Turks cared to throw at it. The broad strategy of the allies was to draw the Ottoman navy into engagements far from Crete and close to the heartland of the empire: the Dardanelles became a flashpoint early in the conflict, and from 1654 onwards several bitter engagements took place in which the Venetians tried to prevent Turkish fleets from entering the Aegean in support of the Cretan campaign.[49] Still, the pressure on Candia grew, and by 1669 the situation had become critical. The Spanish king promised aid, which never materialized, because he was more worried about possible attacks from France than about the Turks. The French king did send aid, but his fleet was no match for the Ottoman navy, and a quick and easy naval victory by the Turks sent the allies scuttling away, leaving Candia exposed. On 6 September 1669 the Venetians surrendered the city and recognized Ottoman sovereignty over Crete; they also, typically, seized the chance to enter into a peace treaty with the Ottomans.[50] It was obvious to the Venetians that a great epoch in their history had come to an end, for they had ruled Crete since the early thirteenth century. When they capitulated, the Venetian envoys stated: 'We have come to surrender a fortress whose equal does not exist in the entire world. It is a priceless pearl the like of which no sultan possesses.' Within hours a sultan did indeed possess it.

The coming of the Ottomans did not effect a revolution in Crete.[51] Candia became the centre of a regional trading network, while Chania, to the west, became the favoured port of international trade. Where Venetians had once traded, the French were very willing to replace them, exploiting their history of warm ties to the Sublime Porte. Even with the spread of Islam in Crete wine production did not cease. Both French and Cretan merchants extracted sweet Malmsey wine, oil, dried fruits, cheese, honey and wax from the island; occasionally wheat was exported, notably when famine struck the opposite coasts of North Africa. The monks of the Arkadi monastery produced a 'rich, racy, strong-bodied, deep-coloured' wine with an excellent perfume, according to a French visitor writing in 1699. The Cretans meanwhile developed a taste they have never lost for coffee, which arrived from the Yemen by way of Ottoman Egypt, henceforth the main market for Cretan produce. Striking, too, is the emergence of native merchants, who had been pushed into a modest position under Venetian rule but had begun to assert themselves even before the Turkish conquest. This meant that there existed a solid base of local business expertise when the Turks took over the island, consisting of traders keen to keep Ottoman lands supplied with the island's goods.[52]

Greek sailors and merchants were becoming a more common sight, but in conquered Candia the majority of the merchants were Muslims. It would be easy to assume that the city had been repopulated, but most of these Candiote Muslim traders were in fact indigenous Cretans who had changed religion, not location. By 1751 Muslims owned nearly all of the forty-eight vessels that comprised the merchant navy of Candia.[53] The ready acceptance of Islam throughout the Cretan towns is remarkable. The indigenous population ensured that the past was not obliterated: Greek, not Turkish, was the common language of the island, used by Muslims as well as Greek Orthodox. Cretans were cut off from regular contact with the Latin Church which in Venetian days had controlled the island hierarchy. The Venetians had banned Orthodox bishops from setting foot on the island, although Orthodox churches and monasteries continued to function under government protection – Cretan monks were admired beyond the island, and several became abbot of St Catherine's in Sinai. The Ottoman conquerors exploited the opportunity to win support among the Orthodox, appointing an archbishop of Crete even before they had taken control of Candia.[54] As important, then, as the coming of Islam to Crete was the reassertion of the primacy of Orthodoxy among those who did not adopt the new faith. Crete, with its close links to Sinai, became the centre for a revival of Greek Orthodoxy in the eastern Mediterranean.

IV

The sense that a single community of inhabitants of the harbours, coasts and islands of the Mediterranean existed is reinforced by the evidence for the use of a common tongue, the so-called *lingua franca* or 'Frankish speech'.[55] Languages that enabled people from the different shores to communicate go back to very ancient times, when Punic, Greek and eventually Low Latin were deployed across wide swathes of the Mediterranean.[56] Many must have communicated in rough pidgins that owed as much to gesticulation as to sound. Among the Sephardic Jews, Judaeo-Spanish was spoken widely enough, from the Levant to Morocco, to enable easy communication between merchants, pilgrims and other travellers, and came to be adopted even by the Greek-speaking Romaniote Jews. While speakers of romance languages generally had no great difficulty communicating (as anyone who has been present at a meeting in Spain attended by Italian-speakers can testify), there were much higher barriers between Latin-based languages and the Arabic or Turkish of the Muslim lands. In the early modern period the Turks made use of a large nautical vocabulary derived from Italian and Greek, which says something about the sources from which they copied their ships and equipment.[57] The need for sailors and merchants to communicate was matched by the wish of slave-owners to be able to give orders to their captives, and the *bagni*, or slave quarters, were also places where Turks or Europeans, as the case may be, barked commands in this strange mixture of tongues, the core of which was, however, generally a combination of Italian and Spanish. Tunisian *lingua franca* was closer to Italian, while the *lingua franca* of Algiers was closer to Spanish; both proximity and politics determined their different character.[58] Of an eighteenth-century pasha of Algiers it was asserted that 'he understood and spoke *lingua franca*, but he considered it beneath his dignity to use it with free Christians'. It was commonly used by renegade corsairs, who sometimes found it difficult to acquire fluent Turkish and Arabic. Words in *lingua franca* underwent etymological shifts, so that among the Turks the Italian-derived *forti* meant not 'strongly' but 'gently', and *todo mangiado* meant not just 'all eaten' but, more generally, 'disappeared'.[59] It would be a mistake to think of *lingua franca* as a language with formal rules and an agreed vocabulary; indeed, it was its fluidity and changeability that expressed most clearly the shifting identities of the people of the early modern Mediterranean.

7

Encouragement to Others,
1650–1780

I

In the course of the seventeenth century the character of the relationship between the European states changed dramatically, with important repercussions in the Mediterranean. Until the end of the Thirty Years' War in 1648, Catholic confronted Protestant, and confessional identity was an issue of surpassing significance for the competing powers in Europe. After 1648, a greater degree of political realism, or cynical calculation, began to intrude. Within a few years, it was possible for the English arch-Protestant Oliver Cromwell to cooperate with the Spanish king, while English suspicion of the Dutch led to conflict in the North Sea. The character of English involvement in the Mediterranean changed: royal fleets began to intervene and the English (after union with Scotland in 1707, the British) sought out permanent bases in the western Mediterranean: first Tangier, then Gibraltar, Minorca and, in 1800, Malta. The period from 1648 to the Napoleonic Wars was marked, therefore, by frequent about-turns as the English switched from Spanish to French alliances, and as the whole question of the Spanish royal succession divided Europe and opened up the prospect of spoils from a declining Spanish empire in the Mediterranean. While Spain's difficulties were obvious, it was less clear that the Ottomans had passed their peak: the Ottoman siege of Vienna in 1683 was unsuccessful, but in the Mediterranean Turkish galleys still posed a serious threat, and their Barbary allies could be relied upon to give support when naval conflict broke out.

Even so, the Venetians managed to gain control of the Morea or Peloponnese for several years, and, interestingly, it was they who were the aggressors. Bolder than they had been for some time, the Venetians ambitiously aimed to crack Turkish power in the regions closest to their navigation routes. In 1685 and 1686 they captured and demolished a number of Turkish fortresses on either side of the Morea, culminating in the capture of Nafplion on 30 August 1686. This was only the prelude to an attempt to clean up the Dalmatian coast, starting with the Turkish base at Herceg Novi, which they captured in September 1687. The Ottomans came to terms in 1698, recognizing Venetian control of both Dalmatia and the Morea. This did not produce lasting peace, for Venice lost most of the Morea by July 1718, when its fleet confronted a large Turkish navy off western Greece, at Cape Matapan. Both sides suffered serious damage, but the Turks realized they could never gain the upper hand and withdrew. A new treaty ensured half a century of peace with the Ottomans, and this was something Venice needed, at a time when its power and influence were fading. The major issue for Venice was no longer the protection of the Levant trade, in which non-Mediterranean rivals now played so significant a role; rather, it was the protection of the republic's dominions in Dalmatia. But the Serenissima Repubblica had shown it was not a spent force, while the Turks had to fight for every inch of land.[1]

II

During the late seventeenth and eighteenth centuries, events far to the west also had repercussions in the Mediterranean, setting off conflicts between the English and the Spaniards, and, later, between the British and the French. In 1655, the English capture of Jamaica, occupied by Spain in the aftermath of Columbus's voyages, turned Spanish friendship towards the Lord Protector of the Commonwealth into Spanish fury at his support for an action that threatened the security of the treasure fleets. As the war clouds gathered, English ships sailed down to Cádiz to spy out King Philip IV's navy. There were two worries: that the Spanish king would try to relieve Jamaica with a massive fleet, and that access to the Mediterranean for English merchant shipping would be cut off by Spanish aggression. If it could be established, an English base at the mouth of the Mediterranean would have any number of strategic advantages. Cromwell's spy, Montague, reported that the obvious prize

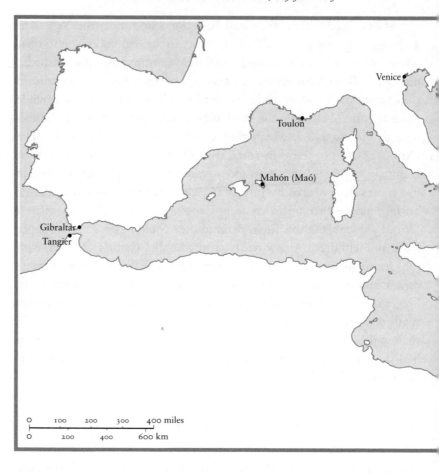

was Gibraltar, but it was very strongly fortified. Maybe, then, it made more sense to look at the Barbary coast instead. He opined that, with the help of 'a dozen or 15 sail of nimble frigates' and a fort, the Straits could be held open for English trade. Possible candidates for dispossession were Ceuta, which the Spaniards now controlled, and Tangier, which was a Portuguese command post. Cromwell remained fond of the idea of taking Gibraltar, and Samuel Pepys, later secretary of the navy, insisted that he send a ship to the Straits loaded with wheelbarrows and spades, the aim being to cut across the isthmus linking the rock of Gibraltar to the mainland; but the ship was captured.[2]

Even after the monarchy was restored in England under Charles II,

the idea of planting the English flag at the entrance to the Mediterranean was not forgotten. The perfect opportunity arose almost immediately, in 1661, with a renewal of the ancient alliance between England and Portugal, once again independent of Spain, which not merely brought Catherine of Braganza to England as Charles's long-suffering queen, but, in her dowry, offered England Bombay and Tangier. A base was thus acquired without a shot being fired, though the Portuguese governor was peeved by the order to hand over Tangier, and believed that by doing so he would dishonour his distant ancestors, who had held the city since 1471.[3] Foreign observers were also dismayed. King Louis XIV wrote to the French ambassador in London, complaining that the English were trying to gain control of the Straits of Gibraltar – they might attempt, he thought, to levy taxes on vessels passing through the Straits, just as the Danes did at the entrance to the Baltic.[4]

For their part, the English were disappointed by the run-down appearance of the town, and were worried about securing an adequate water supply: 'no water but Fountain Fort at this time, which the Moors if they knew and would, might prevent us of', as Samuel Pepys reported.[5] They had wrongly imagined that this would be a bright new jewel in Charles II's crown. The town was virtually empty of people and needed to be repopulated. One idea, used centuries earlier when the Portuguese captured nearby Ceuta, was to transport criminals there; another more bizarre idea was to dump one third of the population of Scotland there. It was assumed that its acquisition would foster trade with both Atlantic Morocco and the Barbary states within the Mediterranean.[6] If this were to be achieved, it was vital to develop a good rapport with the ruler of the area beyond the city walls. This was Abdallah Ghaylan, whom the English called Gayland; his authority embraced four Arab tribes in the plains and eighteen Berber tribes in the hills. He is said to have been plump, sly, lustful, 'careful and intemperate: a contradiction in nature'.[7] He oscillated between friendship, or at least promises of friendship, and hostility; for instance, he rejected a request by the English to collect wood for fuel in the outskirts of Tangier. His pusillanimous attitude won him plenty of concessions from the English governor, who did not want to risk the safety of the new colony before it had even been properly established. Eventually his demands became too outrageous (he required fifty barrels of gunpowder and the use of English ships), and before long the Moroccan troops were engaged in cattle-rustling and in skirmishes with English soldiers: more than 600 English troops were killed in these engagements, including the governor, Lord Teviot, before the wind shifted and Ghaylan made friends with the English once again.[8]

English Tangier developed into a lively port city. The empty spaces found by its first governor were soon filled with people of the most varied origins: alongside the garrison of 1,200 to 2,000 men, there were about 600 civilian inhabitants, including at various times Dutch merchants, Portuguese friars, Muslim slaves, and European and North African Jews. The Jews were suspect because of their contact with the Muslims, with whom they traded actively. Samuel Pepys recorded the story of 'a poor Jew and his wife that came out of Spain to avoid the Inquisition'; the commander-in-chief of the English garrison showed no sympathy, 'swearing, "God damn him, he should be burned!", and they were carried into the Inquisition and burned'.[9] Other visitors were made more welcome. Pepys described the arrival of Turkish or Armenian merchants from as far away as Smyrna, who laid their goods on the sand 'to be by them carried into Fez for sale'.[10] Merchants in search of a safe haven could take encouragement from the impressive new fortifications that surrounded the city; the mole was also impressive, though Christopher Wren had refused an invitation to design it.[11]

Opinions in England about the usefulness of Tangier varied, but when Lord Belasyse arrived as Teviot's successor in 1665 he insisted on the town's virtues:

> His Majesty would have a greater esteeme off it than any other off his dominions weare he heare to see the prospects off the Streights upon Spaine, the shipps that pass, the frutefull mountaynes off Affrique, the fragrent perfumes off flowers, rare frutes and salads, excellent ayre, meates and wines which this place most seemingly affords, or shall doe.[12]

This was optimistic. War with the Dutch loomed; the Dutch were trying to put together a Mediterranean fleet, and the English riposted by strengthening their political and commercial bonds with Tunis and Tripoli. Then the Dutch destroyed the flotilla bringing desperately needed supplies to Tangier, and a few months later, in early 1666, Louis XIV decided to support Calvinist Holland against the English. His chief minister, Colbert, who was working hard to promote French trade and manufacture, sent ships against the English in the Mediterranean. But English 'Tangerine' pirates proved remarkably successful against the French and the Dutch, and brought the ships they captured and their cargoes to Tangier, where they were put up for sale.[13] The colony showed itself to be quite resilient. In many respects, its most serious problem lay in London, not around the Straits of Gibraltar. The cost of the Tangier enterprise was a source of constant worry to a court engaged in conflicts on several fronts. So long as Tangier contributed to the war with the Dutch, the English presence there made sense. It was also apparent that Tangier was an effective base for cooperation with the Barbary rulers, notably in Algiers, or for operations against Barbary corsairs who did not respect treaties with England. But not everyone was convinced that

England required a base at the gates of the Mediterranean, especially when Ghaylan was such an unpredictable neighbour, forcing the Tangier garrison to consume resources in armaments and manpower that England needed to employ elsewhere.

It was these considerations that led Charles II to rethink his policy in 1683. By now he was financially dependent on his erstwhile enemy Louis XIV, who had long been hostile to the English colony, and he simply could not afford further campaigns against the Moroccans. Charles II decided to pay for the Tangier garrison out of his own resources, costing him up to £70,000 each year, and £1,600,000 in all, but he knew he could not maintain this indefinitely.[14] Ideas were mooted of returning the town to the Portuguese (who, along with many English merchants, insisted on its value in the struggle against piracy) or of handing it over to Charles's new French allies (whose fleet was growing dangerously large – 276 ships in 1683). But in the end the last governor, Lord Dartmouth, was sent out in 1683 with explicit instructions to level the town and destroy the mole. So, in 1684, the English finally evacuated Tangier, leaving behind a pile of ruins.[15] What survived was the aspiration to hold the Straits of Gibraltar. Charles II had abandoned Tangier with real regret, and only twenty years passed before England acquired the Mediterranean town over which the British flag still flies.

III

The acquisition of Gibraltar was not, however, a carefully planned attempt to make real the idea of an English base at the entrance to the Mediterranean. It was an acquisition made 'in a fit of absence of mind', to cite again Sir John Seeley's famous phrase. By the 1690s it was obvious that a succession crisis would tear Spain apart. The last of the Spanish Habsburgs, Charles II (who died in 1700), had no heir and was regarded as an idiot; inbreeding among the Habsburgs had done their health no good over the last two centuries. His will nominated Philip de Bourbon, duke of Anjou, grandson of Louis XIV, as his heir; not surprisingly, France's neighbours considered that the inheritance by a French prince of the vast Spanish empire in Europe, the Mediterranean and the Americas would have disastrous consequences, turning France into a world power even greater than Spain had been at the height of its influence. The alternative appeared to be the preservation of the Habsburg line in Spain, by placing a member of the Austrian branch on the Spanish throne. Since the English king was now a Dutchman, William of Orange, Dutch and English interests converged, though the English insisted, as the Dutch might equally have done, that they 'were moved by no other interest than that of their commerce and navigation'; were a French prince to become Spanish king 'the Mediterranean trade would be absolutely lost whenever a French king might think proper, since he would be master of the Straits and of all the countries and ports of the sea, assisted or supported by France'.[16] King William went further, arguing:

> With regard to the Mediterranean trade, it will be requisite to have the ports on the coast of Barbary; for example Ceuta or Oran, as well as some ports on the coast of Spain, as Mahón, in the island of Minorca which is said to be a very good port; perhaps we ought to have the whole island to be more sure of the port.

But Louis XIV was adamant that Spanish territories such as Ceuta, Oran and Minorca must not be occupied by England, which had no claims upon the Spanish inheritance. Minorca was not, to be sure, part of the Iberian peninsula, but 'it would render them masters of all the commerce of the Mediterranean and would absolutely exclude all other nations' apart from Holland. English or Dutch possession of Mahón would undermine the standing of Toulon as command base of the French navy, which was all the more serious an issue since Colbert was now dead and the French navy was less energetically managed.[17]

The English saw the War of the Spanish Succession (1701–14), between the Bourbon Philip of Anjou and the Austrian Habsburg Charles III, as an opportunity to take advantage of the crisis in Spain: there were Caribbean islands open to conquest and treasure ships ripe for capture. The English wondered whether to attack Cádiz or Gibraltar, but the motive was interference with Spain's Atlantic communications no less than the much vaunted protection of English trade in the Mediterranean. Cádiz was a bigger and wealthier town; Gibraltar was a very small one but its strategic position was more tempting.[18] In July 1704, a War Council held aboard the flagship of the English admiral Rooke decided that an army under the command of Prince George of Darmstadt-Hesse should assault Gibraltar. The aim was 'to reduce it to the king of Spaines obedience', not to conquer Gibraltar for England.[19] Of course, only one king of Spain was meant, the Austrian claimant. The inhabitants of Gibraltar were invited in a grandiose royal letter to accept Charles III as their king, but they very politely but equally obstinately insisted that they were the 'faithful and loyal subjects of King Philip V', the French claimant, before wishing George of Hesse long life. Gibraltar was splendidly defended by its lines of walls and by good-quality guns, but what the defenders lacked, and the invaders possessed, was manpower. After the attackers trapped the women and children of the town at their point of refuge, the shrine of Our Lady of Europa on the southern tip of the rock, the city council and the military governor concurred that it was 'more pleasing to His Majesty that they should seek such terms and surrender than that they should hold out to no purpose, and occasion severe loss to the city and his vassals'.[20] By 'His Majesty' they meant, once again, Philip and not Charles. So Gibraltar surrendered, and was offered guarantees: the conquerors would not impose Protestantism – after all, they had seized it on behalf of a Catholic king. The local population decamped to San Roque a little way inland, a town that still regards itself as the home of the original Gibraltarians.[21]

Discussions about who should govern the rock expressed clearly and consistently the view that the conquest had been achieved by English troops on behalf of the rightful king of Spain: 'England would not wish to claim that she had made a conquest' for herself.[22] Hesse hoped to use Gibraltar as the gateway into Spain: a plan to attack Catalonia, setting out by sea from Gibraltar, was approved, and King Charles III arrived in Gibraltar to implement it. There is some irony in the fact that he had now taken possession of his first few inches of Spain, when before long Gibraltar would be permanently lost to the British queen. The argument now began to be pressed that Gibraltar 'will not protect a fleet against a superior one, but 'twill be of use and safety for single ships, or four or five men-of-war, and in that respect of great advantage to our trade'.[23] The English began to see that possession of Gibraltar opened up larger possibilities for control of the western Mediterranean. The English ambassador in Lisbon, Methuen, warned that should Charles III fail in his bid for the Spanish throne, 'England must never part with Gibraltar, which will always be a pledge of our commerce and privileges in Spain'. Propagandists in England extolled the virtues of Gibraltar, 'situate as it

41. Fonduks were generally arcaded buildings on two floors built around a quadrangle. The royal fonduk in crusader Acre, now called the Inn of the Columns (*Khan al-'Umdan*), where taxes on merchandise were collected, was rebuilt by the Turks but preserves its form well. The Italian merchants possessed their own fonduks in other parts of the city.

42. Four magnificent horses of ancient Greek workmanship adorned the hippodrome in Constantinople and formed part of the loot carried away by the Venetians after they stormed the city during the Fourth Crusade. Until they began to deteriorate, they stood proudly above the entrance to St Mark's Basilica.

43. The Muslim scholar and prince Idrisi, from Ceuta, served the Norman kings of Sicily as their geographer. Although twelfth-century manuscripts of his work do not survive, this late-medieval world map is probably a copy of one drawn by Idrisi. South is at the top and so the Mediterranean is in the bottom right segment, with the Adriatic cutting deep into the European landmass.

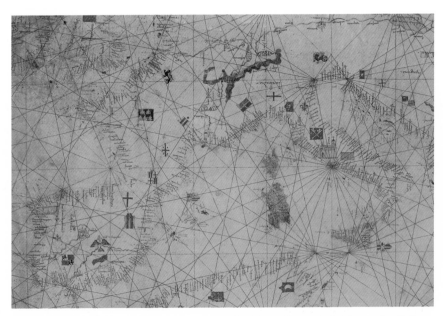

44. Detail of an early fourteenth-century portolan chart drawn in Majorca. Sardinia stands in the centre, and Majorca is flamboyantly distinguished by the flag of its Catalan king. Place-names crowd the coasts.

45. Thirteenth-century wall-paintings showing the capture of the City of Majorca in 1229 by the troops of King James I of Aragon. These events were also celebrated in King James's *Book of Deeds*, written in Catalan, the first royal autobiography from the Middle Ages.

46. Aigues-Mortes, meaning 'dead waters', was founded on the edge of the Carmargue as a base for French trade into the Mediterranean and as a departure point for crusaders bound for the East. Most of its well-preserved buildings date from the start of the fourteenth century, by which time it was functioning as the outport of its former rival Montpellier, which lay under Majorcan rule.

47. Genoa is squeezed between the Ligurian Alps and the sea, and Hartmann Schedel's *Nuremberg Chronicle* printed in 1493 conveys well the mass of buildings, towers and churches clustered together beside the port, including (*top centre*) the imposing gateway built when the city was under threat from the German emperor Frederick Barbarossa in the mid-twelfth century.

48. Dubrovnik seen from the south-east, with its imposing line of fifteenth-century walls. The harbour, just visible, lay on the other side and one of the tall buildings on the right was the grain store. The town is bisected by the street known as Placa or Stradun, ending on the right next to the weighing-house or Sponza Palace, which now houses the city's rich archives; the Jewish quarter lay to the left of the palace.

49. In the fifteenth century, Manises in the Valencian hinterland was the great centre for the production of glazed ceramics with lustre decoration. This bowl bears the coat-of-arms of the degli Agli family of Florence; Italian patricians were keen purchasers of these Hispano-Moresque wares. Inspired by Moorish technology, Christian potters came to dominate production, but there were some joint workshops where Muslims and Christians worked side by side.

50. This votive model of a cargo ship, a unique survival from the Middle Ages, originally stood in a church in Mataró in Catalonia. Nearly 120 cm long and over 50 cm broad, it dates from around 1420 and is made partly of mulberry wood from the Mediterranean, its hull constructed out of planks laid flush, in Mediterranean style.

51. The magnificent Exchange (*llotja*) in Valencia, built between 1483 and 1498. This hall with its soaring columns was used for the transaction of business, while in another room the commercial court of Valencia sat. The inscription glorifying honest trade can be seen running around the cornice.

52. The code of maritime law known as the *Consulate of the Sea* determined commercial law in Valencia and among Catalan merchants overseas. A printed edition appeared in 1494. This earlier manuscript copy portrays King Alfonso the Magnanimous (d. 1458) surrounded by his courtiers, a reminder that the king and the merchants worked closely together to create a political and commercial empire in the Mediterranean.

53. Mehmet II, Ottoman sultan, known as 'the Conqueror' (*Fatih*) in recognition of his capture of Constantinople. Fascinated by Italian culture, he summoned the Italian artist Giovanni Bellini to his court, where this portrait was painted not long before Mehmet's death in 1481.

54. At the end of his life, Mehmet launched ambitious expeditions against Latin Christendom, sending his fleet to Otranto in southern Italy, which was occupied, but failing in 1480 to capture Rhodes. Here, a French miniaturist celebrates the defeat of the Turks, forced to come to terms with the Knights Hospitallers, whose flags can be seen along the walls and atop the maritime fortress.

55 & 56. Hisr (*left*), also known as Hayrettin and as Barbarossa (d. 1546), was one of the most ruthless Barbary corsairs; based in Algiers, he launched attacks on Minorca and Italy and wintered in Toulon at the invitation of King Francis I of France. This painting was the work of Nakkep Reis Haydar, who had himself served at sea. Andrea Doria (*right*) came from one of the most eminent Genoese families. He entered the service of the king of France but then abandoned him in 1528 for Charles V. He was a tough rival to Hayrettin Barbarossa and scored significant victories, such as the recovery of Coron in southern Greece in 1532.

57. Hayrettin commanded an Ottoman fleet sent to Tunis after a succession struggle broke out in 1534. Charles V intervened and recaptured Tunis in 1535; the Spaniards built a fort in the Lac de Tunis near Goleta that still stands. This cartoon for a series of tapestries shows the Spanish capture of Goleta.

were in the very centre of our business, in the very mouth of the Straits, commanding from shore to shore, and awing by our cruisers all the intercourse betwixt East France and Cádiz'.[24] Hyperbole was king: Gibraltar was in fact a small, abandoned town and its dockyards were still undeveloped.

In 1711 the balance of power shifted significantly with the death of the Holy Roman Emperor, Joseph I, the brother of Charles III. Charles could expect to be elected to the imperial throne, and would be able to commit even more resources from the Habsburg lands of the east into the Spanish war. But no one wanted a return to the dual empire of Emperor Charles V. It was not too difficult to lure the British government into a deal whereby Philip would be accepted as Spanish king so long as this insignificant notch in the far south of Spain (as it seemed from Paris) remained in English hands. The arguments were endless, and very complicated. At one moment the French objected on behalf of Philip V to the idea that 'the most minutest part' of Spain could ever be ceded to anyone else; then they started to argue about what the cession of Gibraltar actually meant – the minimalist view was that it involved no more than the castle, town and port, and no land round about, not even the rock.[25] The question was, what exactly was Gibraltar?

The Treaty of Utrecht of 11 April 1713 supposedly settled all these matters. Under article 10, Philip V, now recognized by the British as king of Spain, handed over

> the full and intire propriety of the Town and Castle of Gibraltar, together with the port, fortifications, and forts thereunto belonging; and he gives up the said propriety, to be held and enjoyed absolutely with all manner of right for ever, without any exception or impediment.

Catholics could exercise their religion freely within Gibraltar; but the British queen agreed, at the petition of King Philip, that Jews and Moors might not live in Gibraltar, though merchant ships from Morocco could dock there.[26] The ban was only a breakable promise by the town's new sovereign, and Jewish brokers had already arrived from Morocco in the brief interval between the seizure of Gibraltar in 1704 and the treaty of 1713. They were increasingly valued for their work in supplying the navy with food and equipment. Even so, it took several decades for the potential of Gibraltar to be realized and appreciated: complaints abounded that the rock possessed insufficient stores and inadequate facilities for the repair of ships. The Jews were joined by increasing numbers of Genoese during the eighteenth century. A distinctive society came into being, largely consisting of brokers, hawkers and ships' chandlers; but Gibraltar was dominated by its shifting population of up to 5,000 seamen, and many of the civilian population lived in what can only be described as squalor.[27]

I V

The Treaty of Utrecht conferred another piece of Spanish soil on Great Britain: Minorca. British ships engaged in skirmishes with the Barbary corsairs had used it as a victualling station in the 1670s, with Spanish permission, but facilities were poor – there were no warehouses and too many rats, although 'Bread, Wine, Hens, Eggs, all things were cheap, One piece of Eight, would buy a Sheep'.[28] In 1708 the British occupied the island, but their ally Charles III was unwilling to cede its sovereignty; when the British decided to make terms with Philip V instead, the Bourbon claimant agreed to give away the island despite the disadvantages for France, a concession he rapidly came to regret.[29] The duke of Marlborough recognized the importance of Minorca, to which Gibraltar could serve as a way-station – a grand strategy for the creation of permanent British bases in the Mediterranean was beginning to evolve.[30] But the island's lack of resources was an immediate problem. Once an army was camped on its shores, Minorca proved incapable of feeding everyone, for it produced barely enough grain to feed its native inhabitants, and its animals provided tough meat. Parts of the island were treeless, so supplies of wood were hard to find. It was difficult even to find billets for the troops.[31] Service in hot, arid Minorca was seen as a trial. And yet, at Mahón, the island possessed the finest natural harbour in the Mediterranean: it is three miles long, and at some points over half a mile wide; its entrance is about 200 metres wide, making it difficult for enemy ships to enter the port and wreak havoc. Moreover, the entrance was protected by a solid fort, St Philip's. As important as the harbour was the strategic value of holding a base close to southern France: the French fleet at Toulon lay 220 miles to the north-east. The commander of the British forces in Spain, Stanhope, wrote that 'England ought never to part with the island which will give the law to the

Mediterranean both in time of war and peace', and he stressed its importance in keeping the French at bay – just as the British held Dunkirk, in order to tame the French in the English Channel, they needed to hold Minorca to tame the French in the Mediterranean.[32]

The British began to wonder whether Minorca possessed some unrealized potential. With such a good port, the island could become an entrepôt for Mediterranean trade. The Minorcans might become 'a rich and flourishing people' if commerce were encouraged.[33] Richard Kane, the most able of the island's lieutenant-governors, set in train major works that brought new prosperity. Marshes were drained and turned into orchards (a plum called *quen*, that is, 'Kane', is still grown on the island), and cattle were imported from North Africa in the hope of improving the size and quality of the island's animals. Kane shared the spirit of the eighteenth-century English innovators who were leading an agricultural revolution in his homeland. By 1719 a road was completed that ran between Mahón and Ciutadella – the work took two years and the road is still known as the *Camí d'En Kane*, 'the road of Mr Kane'.[34] Mahón was designated as the new capital, in place of its rival Ciutadella (ancient Jamona) on the western coast. This deepened the divide between the native Minorcans, especially the island nobility, and the British authorities, who often saw the islanders as ungrateful and uncooperative: Lieutenant-Governor Murray wrote to the island magistrates, or *jurats*, in 1777 asking them whether they were keen to see the return of the Inquisition or the Barbary pirates, from both of which they were now protected, while the British had also lifted them out of their ancient poverty.[35] Mahón itself became the focus of British efforts at improvement: new dockyards were built, and the straight streets that still characterize the town were laid out. The impress of English architecture remains visible in the sash windows of the houses, recalling the coastal towns of southern England rather than those of Spain.

All these wise projects could not, in themselves, propel Minorca into the front rank of Mediterranean trading ports; the town remained primarily a naval base. Anglo-French (and Anglo-Dutch) rivalry was fought out in trade as well as in war, and, though Britain's Mediterranean trade held up well, the French were the market leaders during much of the eighteenth century. French cloth producers were better at meeting demand in Levantine markets, offering lighter and brighter cloths more suited to Turkish taste and climate. English trade in Turkey contracted greatly, after the successes of the previous century, with exports falling in value from £233,000 to £79,000 between 1700 and 1774. The French took the lion's share of trade with Smyrna during the eighteenth century, by way of Marseilles, making Smyrna the principal centre of Ottoman trade with the West, though they were also very busy in Syria, Cyprus, Alexandria, Salonika, the Barbary regencies and Constantinople (allowing for interruptions, such as a severe outbreak of bubonic plague in Marseilles in 1720). British trade with the Mediterranean as a whole did rise during this period, but not as fast as with America, Africa and Asia. Moreover, trade was hampered by conflicts within the Mediterranean, whether with France or Spain. Admirable policies to make Minorca the grain store of the western Mediterranean, or to develop a local cotton industry, or to create saltpans never had much effect.[36]

The wish to encourage commerce had other important effects on island society. From the beginning of the British occupation, a place was found for Protestants, Jews and Greeks. The British promised to protect the rights of the Catholic Church, despite a lingering suspicion that Catholics were bound to be disloyal to the British Crown (an argument undermined by the presence in British service of large numbers of Irish Catholic soldiers). The Catholic authorities nonetheless resented Britain's insistence that age-old institutions such as the Inquisition had no place in a territory under British rule. In 1715 and again in 1721 Governor Kane issued decrees in which he excluded foreign Catholic priests from the island and placed limits on Church courts. Eventually, Kane decided that the time had come to build Anglican churches on Minorca, which (it was pointed out) would be the first ever built within the Mediterranean. The British had never promised, as they did at Gibraltar, to exclude Jews and Moors from Minorca, and by 1781 a community of 500 Jews had come into being, with their own synagogue. The ethnic and cultural variety of Minorca was further enhanced by the arrival of a couple of hundred Greeks, though they had come from nearby: there was a Greek refugee community in Corsica. The Greeks were granted the right to build a church, but the hostile Catholics initially refused to sell them a plot of land for it, even though their religious leaders were Uniate Greeks who acknowledged papal authority but followed the Greek liturgy. After several centuries of the Inquisition, the native Minorcans had no patience with different practices, and in attempting to protect freedom of worship the British inevitably caused new tensions.[37]

The Minorcan elite, organized in several communities, or *universitats*, continued to regard the British as a morally disruptive army of occupation. Minorcan noblemen made sure that their daughters avoided contact with British officers, some of whom had an irritating habit of visiting the convents to converse with pretty nuns. In 1749 three nuns in search of romance stole away from a convent in Ciutadella and hid in the house of a British officer. They converted to Anglicanism and married British officers, to the great scandal of the native magistrates, though the governor merely issued an order that his men should not befriend the island's nuns.[38] Otherwise, social mixing between the colonial power and the islanders was limited. Yet British occupation lasted long enough to leave an imprint (literally: one import from London was a printing press). Minorcan Catalan acquired words from the shipyard: *móguini* for 'mahogany', *escrú* for 'screw', *rul* for 'ruler'. Even the diet of the Minorcans took on an English flavour with its gravy, or *grevi*, and a juniper-flavoured spirit based on London gin. The war cry of small Minorcan children, *faitim!*, is derived from the English 'fight him!'[39]

The English did not take the defence of Minorca for granted. St Philip's was one of the strongest fortresses in the British Empire, with a network of deep tunnels in which men could hide, or stores be kept dry, but there remained one overriding problem that could be resolved only by the government in London: a shortage of troops.[40] This, and a lack of adequate naval support, would prove fatal to British rule (and, eventually, to himself) in 1756, when Admiral Byng realized he could not save Minorca from French invasion. The subsequent trial and execution of Admiral Byng has overshadowed the events that brought Minorca under French rule. The Seven Years War started not in the Mediterranean but on the Ohio river, where the French were attempting to build a line of forts linking Louisiana, in the south, to the Great Lakes, in the north; the effect would have been to confine the thirteen British colonies to the eastern seaboard of North America. The French sought to tie down Britain in the Mediterranean as well, turning their attention to the waters off Toulon, the seat of its Mediterranean navy. Reports reached London that the French were fitting out sixteen or seventeen men-of-war there. The British consul in Cartagena seemed to know what was going on:

> I have received intelligence that 100 battalions are marching into Roussillon with great diligence, and that those troops are designed against Minorca

and are to be transported thither by merchant ships now at Marseilles, and to be convoyed by all the men-of-war at Toulon.[41]

Initially, then, the Mediterranean was a secondary theatre of the Seven Years War, but it rapidly became obvious that the British hoped to use Minorca as a base from which to interfere with the Levant trade of the French.

The British government, partly for lack of funds, responded feebly to the French threat. Admiral Byng was a perfectly competent commander, but he knew his task was well-nigh impossible when he was assigned a squadron of only ten ships and was short of 722 men. Then there were delays while other battleships were sent to sea on missions in the Atlantic. Byng's mission was to see if Minorca had been occupied by the French and to relieve the island, or, if it had not been attacked, he was to blockade the harbour at Toulon.[42] He was barely out of Portsmouth on his way to the Mediterranean, in April 1756, when the French fleet descended on Minorca, under the naval command of the marquis de Galissonnière and the military command of the duc de Richelieu. Richelieu was the great-nephew of the brilliant and unscrupulous cardinal who had served Louis XIII; Galissonnière was a capable naval man whose career had advanced slowly (probably because he was small and hunchbacked). Galissonnière ensured that the French fleet was of the size needed for the enterprise: he had 163 transport ships for 15,000 troops. The ships of the line included the *Foudroyant*, with eighty-four guns, with which nothing in the British squadron (now counting fourteen ships) could compare, not even the flagship, the *Ramillies*.[43] The French had no difficulty in landing at Ciutadella and in winning over the Minorcans, who were only too anxious to be rid of the Protestant British. There was the good road, built by Lieutenant-Governor Kane, that promised to carry these men east to Mahón, though the British sent out a workforce of Jews and Greeks who broke up its precious surface, making the progress of the French, who came with heavy cannon, very difficult. Even so, within days all the British troops held was St Philip's Fort.[44]

So, by the time Byng stood off the Balearic islands, in mid-May 1756, the task that he faced was the relief of St Philip's. At a council of war with his senior officers, he outlined the key questions that would determine his squadron's strategy: was there any chance of relieving Minorca by an attack on the French fleet? Clearly not. Even if there were no French fleet in these waters, could Minorca be prised from French control? Again, they thought not. But if they were defeated, would Gibraltar be under threat? It would. They concluded, 'we are unanimously of the opinion that the fleet should immediately proceed for Gibraltar'.[45] The lieutenant-governor was left to defend St Philip's Fort, which he did manfully for as long as was possible. As for Byng, he was made the scapegoat for the dilatory and parsimonious policy of the British government, which had to explain to an infuriated public why a British possession in the Mediterranean had fallen to the old enemy. After a court martial in which he defended himself ably against the accusation that he had deserted the field of battle, he was nonetheless found guilty and executed on 14 March 1757. It was certainly not his fault that Minorca was lost.[46] Among those who tried to intercede for him were the duc de Richelieu, as a gallant enemy, and the duke's correspondent Voltaire, who in his most famous work described the arrival of Candide at Portsmouth, where he witnessed the execution of a British admiral: 'in this country it is considered good to kill an admiral from time to time, so as to encourage the others'.

The French held Minorca for only a few years; peace with England brought the island back under British rule between 1763 and 1782, and again, after a brief Spanish interlude, between 1798 and 1802, when the struggle against Napoleon gave the island renewed strategic significance. Yet the British were never entirely at ease in Minorca, despite their awareness of the strategic advantage of a western Mediterranean base. Partly this was because they found the island dry and desolate, strangely remote despite its proximity to France, Spain and Africa (as, many centuries before, Bishop Severus had complained). Partly, too, they wondered whether they could use it as a lure, ceding it to a potential ally in the hope of creating a firm friendship with another Mediterranean power.[47] Such discussions took place in 1780, and they took place with Russia. In order to understand how Russia had suddenly become a Mediterranean power it is necessary to step back a few years.

8

The View through the Russian Prism, 1760–1805

I

The increasing debility of the Ottoman Empire brought the Mediterranean to the attention of the Russian tsars. From the end of the seventeenth century Russian power spread southwards towards the Sea of Azov and the Caucasus. Peter the Great sliced away at the Persian empire, and the Ottomans, who ruled the Crimea, felt threatened.[1] For the moment, the Russians were distracted by conflict with the Swedes for dominion over the Baltic, but Peter sought free access to the Black Sea as well. These schemes had the flavour of the old Russia Peter had sought to reform, just as much as they had the flavour of the new technocratic Russia he had sought to create. The idea that the tsar was the religious and even political heir to the Byzantine emperor – that Muscovy was the 'Third Rome' – had not been swept aside when Peter established his new capital on the Baltic, at St Petersburg. Equally, the Russians could now boast hundreds of vessels capable of challenging Turkish pretensions in the Black Sea, even if they were far from capable of mounting a full naval war, and the ships themselves were badly constructed, notwithstanding Peter the Great's famous journey to inspect the shipyards of western Europe, under the alias Pyotr Mikhailovich. In sum, this was a fleet that was 'poor in discipline, training, and morale, unskilful in manoeuvre, and badly administered and equipped'; a contemporary remarked that 'nothing has been under worse management than the Russian navy', for the imperial naval stores had run out of hemp, tar and nails. The Russians began to hire Scottish admirals in an attempt to create a modern command structure, and they turned to Britain for naval stores; this relationship was further bolstered by the intense trading relationship between Britain and Russia, which had continued to flourish throughout the eighteenth century while England's Levant trade withered: in the last third of the eighteenth century a maximum of twenty-seven British ships sailed to the Levant in any one year, while as many as 700 headed for Russia.[2] For the economy of the North Sea, Baltic and Atlantic had continued to grow, while the Mediterranean was becoming, relatively speaking, a backwater.

It is therefore no surprise that it was not events in the Mediterranean, nor even in the Black Sea, that brought Russian navies into Mediterranean waters. Far away in north-eastern Europe, the Russian empress Catherine the Great intruded her own candidate on to the contested throne of Poland; raids on the opponents of the new king spilled over into Ottoman territory, and in 1768 they set off a Turkish-Russian war.[3] The British had entered into a commercial treaty with Catherine in 1766, and were convinced that, handled with care, Empress Catherine could bring them many a bonus. The British government assumed that Russian maritime expansion would actually increase dependence on Britain, because expansion could be achieved only with British aid. The government also believed that French merchants would eventually break into the Black Sea if they were not checked by a successful Russian campaign against the Turks. The idea of a proxy war began to develop in the British political imagination, in which Russian fleets would clear the Mediterranean of threats to British interests. Louis XV's minister de Broglie viewed the problem in much the same way: he argued that a Russian naval victory over the Turks would endanger French trade in the Levant.[4]

Still, the chances of the Russians achieving anything in the Mediterranean appeared slim. The Black Sea fleet would not be able to brave the passage of the Bosphorus past the Ottoman capital, so the Russians decided to send five squadrons from the Baltic into the Mediterranean, through the Straits of Gibraltar. It was thus imperative, both within the North Sea and the Mediterranean, that the Russians could make use of the naval facilities of a friendly power – some of their ships were, frankly, not in a fit state to spend many months at sea (as soon as they arrived at the English port of Hull, two large vessels had to undergo major repairs, and one of them then ran aground off the southern English

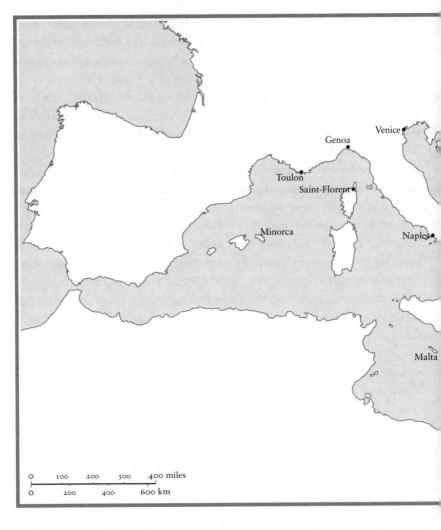

coast). The British were anxious to protect their supposed neutrality, but the Admiralty issued orders that Russian ships could buy what they needed in Gibraltar and Minorca. In January 1770 four Russian battleships were being made ready at Mahón, and the Russians appointed a Greek businessman as their consul there.[5]

While the Turks grumbled at British aid to the Russian fleet, the Russians advanced eastwards, engaging the Turkish navy on 6 July 1770 off Çesme, tucked behind Chios. At the start of the battle the Russians found themselves in difficulty: one of their ships exploded when the

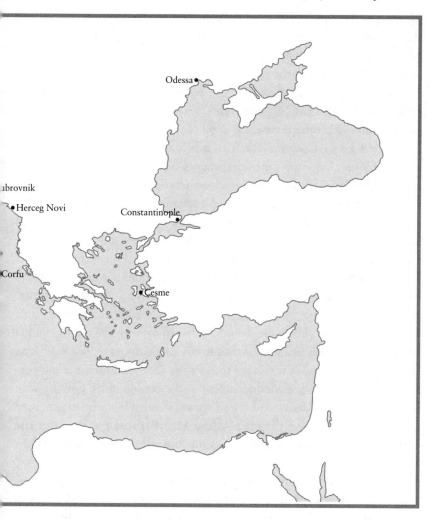

blazing mast of a Turkish vessel fell on to its deck. In the end, the Russians were simply lucky: a strong west wind favoured their use of fireships within the straits between Chios and the Turkish mainland, and many Turkish ships were burned in the water. The Austrian emperor was impressed and worried: 'all Europe will be needed to contain those people, the Turks are nothing compared to them'.[6] Although they had scored a victory, and in a sense had won command of the sea, the Russians had no idea what to do next; however, they established some supply-stations, and for several years skirmishes and raids took place within the Aegean and as far south as Damietta, where they captured the governor of Damascus. But, as the British had discovered with Minorca, what was really valuable was the possession of a substantial, strategically placed, harbour, and this the Russians lacked.

Even so, there was a sense that the balance of power in the Mediterranean had shifted in unpredictable ways. The decline of Ottoman power, along with the increasing debility of Venice, had left a vacuum, and, as will be seen, not just the Russians but the Danes, the Swedes and eventually the Americans intruded themselves into the Mediterranean, even if their primary interests lay elsewhere. That, indeed, was part of the problem: everyone, except the Venetians and the Ragusans, who were old-timers, saw the Mediterranean as one among many political and commercial spheres in which they had to operate – even the Barbary pirates raided Atlantic waters with impunity. French inactivity in the face of British counter-threats gave the Russians a free hand in the eastern Mediterranean.[7] Indeed, by 1774 there was little fighting, because the Russians had, against the odds, gained effective control of Levantine waters. They had, though, failed to capture the major islands of the Aegean, such as Lemnos and Imbros, which controlled access to the Dardanelles, and it was hard to see how they could maintain a permanent presence in the Mediterranean if they could enter only by way of Gibraltar.[8] The Russians still had to work out what advantages they could draw from their presence in the Mediterranean: control of the eastern Mediterranean was not an end in itself, as was shown when the Russians made peace with the Turks in 1774. Under the terms of the Treaty of Küçük Kaynarca the Turks recognized for the first time Russian control of part of the Black Sea coast; Russia also secured the right to send merchant ships through the Bosphorus into the Mediterranean, and this raised the prospect of a revival of the ancient trade routes linking the northern shores of the Black Sea to the Mediterranean. Catherine II now began to consider the duty of Orthodox Russia to the Christian peoples of eastern Europe, especially the Greeks. The Russians fomented a serious but futile Greek rebellion in the Morea during 1770. The ideal of helping the oppressed Orthodox of Ottoman-ruled Greece formed part of a grander ideal: the recovery of Constantinople for Orthodox Christendom, the 'Great Idea' which the Russian tsars would ponder for a long while.[9]

II

A few years of success in the Aegean whetted the appetite of the Russian court for further Mediterranean adventures. A consistent feature of these projects was the way they originated beyond the Mediterranean. In 1780 the British government was embroiled in its war with the rebellious American colonies, rendered more dangerous by the support the French and Spanish gave the United States. From 1779 to 1783, Gibraltar once again faced Spanish blockades, and, finally, relentless bombardment, through all of which it was stoutly defended by Governor Eliott.[10] With Britain under such pressure, it was important to find allies, preferably allies with ships, and Russia emerged as the obvious friend. Still, friendship would have to be bought. The British minister Stormont tried to lure Catherine into a joint attack on Majorca, arguing that 'the advantage to Russia of such a port so situated is too obvious to be dwelt upon'. He insisted that 'Peter the Great would at once have caught at the idea' and that the British government would feel nothing but joy at the Russian acquisition of Majorca. Stormont was worried by rumours that Britain's enemies had been trying to tempt Russia into their camp with offers of Puerto Rico or Trinidad. The British understood that the Mediterranean was the sea that mysteriously attracted Russia. The Russians were scathing about offers of islands in the Caribbean, whether they were made by Spain or Britain. Catherine II's minister Potyomkin looked down from his great height and told Sir James Harris, the British envoy to St Petersburg: 'You would ruin us if you give us distant colonies. You see our ships can scarce get out of the Baltick, how would you then have them cross the Atlantick?' Sir James was left with the clear impression 'that the only cession which would induce the Empress to become our ally, was that of Minorca'; it would become 'a column of the empress's glory'. Potyomkin's vision was not calculated to win the support of the Minorcans: they were all to be expelled, and the island was to be settled with Greeks. Minorca would become a bastion of Orthodoxy in the western Mediterranean, an advance post in the Russian struggle against the Ottomans.

Harris's problem was that this was simply a proposal in which Potyomkin and his own government had expressed interest; the British government had not actually authorized an explicit offer, and the Russians were greatly enjoying the opportunity to act as power brokers in a divided Europe. On the one hand Catherine genuinely coveted Minorca, but on the other she realized that Britain expected something very substantial in return, Russian naval support. She knew, too, that Minorca would be hard to defend from Spanish and French incursions. For once she commented, 'I will not be led into temptation.' She decided that her mission was to make peace between the warring parties, rather than to exacerbate the conflict in the Atlantic and the Mediterranean. Her practical common sense had triumphed, and her judgement was vindicated within a year, since the Spaniards were now turning their attention to Minorca, and wrenched the island from British control in February 1782.[11] A terse commentary on these approaches to the tsarina was provided by an anonymous writer, possibly Edmund Burke:

> England had had full leisure to ruminate upon, and sufficient cause to reprobate, that absurd and blind policy, under the influence of which she had drawn an uncertain ally, and an ever-to-be-suspected friend, from the bottom of the Bothnic Gulf to establish a new naval empire in the Mediterranean and the Archipelago.[12]

This was written a few years later, when the British government was beginning to rue its past support for Russia. Now, in 1788, the British government was wondering whether Louis XVI would be interested in a joint blockade of the English Channel, to prevent the Russians from reaching the Mediterranean.[13]

Despite Catherine's rejection of the offer of Minorca, these negotiations, and the eventual cooling of British affection for the Russians, demonstrate that Russia had won for itself a significant role in Mediterranean war and diplomacy, which it would try to retain ever after. The annexation of Crimea in 1783 and the further extension of Russian authority along the Black Sea coast (leading to the foundation of Odessa) furthered Russian ambitions in the Mediterranean, since the tsarina now possessed a base for commercial and naval ventures towards the Dardanelles. Much would depend on relations with the Turks; in 1789, while Catherine was at war with the Sublime Porte, Greek corsairs licensed by the Russians harried Turkish shipping in the Adriatic and Aegean. They had the willing support of Venice, engaged in its final acts of defiance as an independent republic: a Greek captain,

Katzones, was permitted to use Venetian Corfu as his base, prompting the Russians to think of the island as a possible vantage point in the Mediterranean. Katzones made life difficult for the Turks: he captured the castle at Herceg Novi in the Bay of Kotor and raided as far away as Cyprus. By 1789 three 'undisciplined, largely unorganised, and semi-piratical squadrons' under the Russian flag were proving a real irritant to the Ottomans.[14] Their predations made plain the instability of the Mediterranean.

The way to bring stability was obvious: at least in the short term, peace treaties resolved grievances over territories and gave merchant shipping safe passage. So, once peace was signed with the Turks in 1792, Russian trade in the Mediterranean began to expand, partly because Odessa was so well situated – it was largely free from ice and had good access to the open spaces of the Ukraine and southern Poland. In the year of its official foundation, 1796, Odessa already acted as host to forty-nine Turkish ships, thirty-four Russian ships and three Austrian ones, and it attracted settlers from Greece, Albania and the southern Slav lands. Merchants arrived from Corfu, Naples, Genoa and Tripoli. Looking to the future, by 1802–3 Odessa was importing massive amounts of olive oil, wine, dried fruit and wool from Greece, Italy and Spain, mainly on Greek and Italian vessels flying Turkish, Russian and Austrian flags of convenience; meanwhile, the Russian Black Sea ports exported grain worth nearly twice as much as the imports (indeed, in 1805 grain exports were worth a staggering 5,700,000 roubles).[15] All this commercial success was impossible without free passage through the Bosphorus and Dardanelles, which could be guaranteed only by a Turkish treaty with Russia, or, more ominously, by a Russian victory over the Ottomans that would wrest Constantinople from the Turks and return it to Orthodox masters.

In the year of the foundation of Odessa, Catherine was succeeded by her son Paul, whose ambitions easily outstripped those of his mother, for she had been clever enough to know the limits of Russian power. He had already travelled to the Mediterranean in 1782, notionally incognito as 'the count of the North', on a grand tour that encompassed Naples, Venice and Genoa, and his experiences aroused his interest in establishing a Russian foothold in the region.[16] In his short five-year reign he once more propelled Russia into the heart of the Mediterranean. The Russians still sought an island base in the Mediterranean; but

Tsar Paul's attention wandered eastwards from Minorca, and focused instead on Malta. Yet, as before, it was circumstances far from the Mediterranean that prompted Russian intervention, and Paul's initial interest lay not in the island but in its Knights. Links between the Knights of Malta and Russia went back many years. Peter the Great had sent his general Boris Cheremetov to the island in 1697, to propose a joint campaign against the Ottomans. Russian ships would engage the Turkish navy in the Black Sea, while the small but potent Maltese fleet would attack the Turks in the Aegean. The Grand Master was not willing to throw in his lot with the still little-known Russian empire, which remained, after all, the bastion of Orthodox Christianity. Still, Cheremetov greatly impressed the Knights by his tearful devotion to the relic of the arm of St John the Baptist, brought into the magnificent Conventual Church in Valletta during the service for Pentecost, which was attended, to the great fascination of the Knights, by this visitor from another Christian world.[17]

Under Catherine, too, there were matters arising between the Knights and the Russian court. These turned on a complex legacy by a Polish nobleman which resulted in the establishment of a Hospitaller priory in Russian-controlled areas of Poland.[18] Catherine imagined that she could use the Knights against her opponents in Poland, and welcomed an old acquaintance, Michele Sagromoso, an Italian Knight of Malta, to her court in 1769, aware that he brought messages from the Grand Master and from the pope, who, naturally, was keen to set up Catholic institutions in the Russian empire. Religious questions intruded, however, when Catherine sent a dubious Italian protégé, the burlesque marquis of Cavalcabó, to Malta as her agent. Things did not start well: the Knights objected to the presence of a *chargé d'affaires* appointed by a non-Catholic power, and Cavalcabó was an untrustworthy figure who was suspected of conspiring with the strong pro-French party among the Knights. For many of the Knights were French, and the Order of Malta held vast estates in France.[19] Cavalcabó's aim was to gain access to Malta for the Russian fleet, which at this stage was still wandering the eastern Mediterranean. By 1775 the frustrated imperial agent was scheming with the ancient Maltese nobility, who had long been pushed to the margins by the Knights, in the vain hope that they would lead an uprising against their tyrannical masters and confer their island on Empress Catherine. The Knights became increasingly irritated at the bizarre behaviour of Catherine's agent. They raided his house in Floriana, the suburb of Valletta, only to find it full of arms. Cavalcabó was kicked out, and he spent his last days in disgrace, living in France in fear of arrest for fraud.[20]

Tsar Paul's approaches to the Knights of Malta were not, then, a total surprise.[21] Paul had studied the history of the Knights as a young man, and he romantically saw the Order as a potential bulwark against revolution: here were noblemen of pure blood, united by common Christian zeal, transcending the petty differences between the European states of his day. He was unworried by its Catholic identity, and never had any doubt that he, as the greatest Orthodox prince, could work closely with the Order.[22] He imagined that the Knights of Malta would be able to support him on two fronts: a Polish-Russian priory would contribute money and manpower to the fight against the Turks in mainland eastern Europe, while the Knights based in Malta, working together with Russian squadrons, would squeeze the Turks in the Mediterranean. Before long, Orthodox rule would be restored in the old Byzantine lands. There was one insuperable obstacle to this grand dream. The name of this obstacle was Napoleon Bonaparte.

III

The Revolutionary War, and the Napoleonic Wars that followed, affected the entire Mediterranean. In 1793, not long after the revolutionary government declared war on Britain, it seemed for a moment that the British fleet would be able to prevent the French navy from making any use of Mediterranean waters. As the war between France and its neighbours intensified, to the accompaniment of the ruthless suppression of those who opposed the Jacobin radicals, rebellions broke out in the French provinces. The citizens of Toulon ejected the Jacobins from office, and appealed to the British to save their city from the revolutionary armies that were advancing southwards. Refugees flooded in and supplies were short. Fortunately, British ships, commanded by Lord Hood, had already placed Toulon under a blockade; this had only accentuated the shortages within Toulon. On 23 August Hood agreed to take charge of Toulon if the inhabitants recognized the heir to the throne as King Louis XVII. The citizens swallowed hard and agreed to this, for their fear of the Jacobins compensated for their lack of enthusiasm for the monarchy. The occupation brought about half the French fleet under British control. But Hood was poorly supplied with ground troops, and once the revolutionary army, commanded by Napoleon Bonaparte, captured the fort at the mouth of the harbour entrance known as 'Petit Gibraltar' (17 December 1793), Hood realized that the British position was untenable. As they withdrew, the British destroyed nine French ships of the line as well as three frigates, and blew up stocks of timber on which the future of the French fleet depended. They also towed away twelve more ships, which were taken into the British and Spanish navies.[23]

This was one of the severest blows against the French navy during the entire war with France, at least as serious as the destruction unleashed at Trafalgar. And yet the loss of Toulon created a mountain of problems for the British. Every British commander in the Mediterranean obsessively watched Toulon as long as Napoleon was active.[24] British commanders had to devise new ways of confronting the French fleet there. One solution was the recovery of Minorca, which was re-occupied in 1798 as a forward position close to southern France. Before that, though, another tempting possibility offered itself. In 1768 the French Crown had taken Corsica off the hands of the Genoese, who had in any case lost control of the island to the nationalist forces led by the eloquent and inspiring Pasquale Paoli. And then, before France declared war on Britain, reports circulated in Livorno that the revolutionary government had no interest in Corsica and that the island was up for sale. The Russians were said to be keen to fund a bid by the Genoese government to buy back Corsica, seeing it as a potential naval base in the western Mediterranean.[25] These rumours stimulated British interest in Corsica, which grew once Great Britain found itself at war with France.

While Toulon was in British hands, Pasquale Paoli became more and more enthusiastic about a Corsican alliance with Britain. He understood the significance of the loss of Toulon by the British, noting: 'the capture of Toulon is fortunate; it obliges the English to liberate us.' What Paoli overestimated was the usefulness of Corsica. The island has not featured in this book as often as Sardinia, Majorca, Crete or Cyprus simply because it offered fewer facilities for trans-Mediterranean shipping, and fewer products of its own than the other islands. There was some grain available in the Balagne, an area in the north that had been exploited ever since it had fallen under Pisan rule in the twelfth century, but this was a society that looked inwards, isolated, conservative, whose interior was of difficult access. It was therefore not surprising that the Genoese eventually gave up their attempts to hold the island.[26] The British, however, began to imagine that Corsica possessed untapped potential as a naval base. Maybe, it was wildly suggested, Ajaccio could eventually become a port to rival Livorno, and Corsica could become 'an emporium which may command all the markets of the Mediterranean and Levant'. In 1794 Saint-Florent in the Balagne was stormed by the British, and within a few weeks a Corsican parliament voted for union with Great Britain; the island was to be a self-governing community under the sovereign authority of King George III. The Corsicans were granted their own flag, carrying a Moor's head alongside the royal arms, as well as a motto: *Amici e non di ventura*, 'friends and not by chance'.[27]

The relationship between the British and the Corsicans turned sour, however: Paoli became disillusioned, and revolutionary committees became increasingly active, as Napoleon infiltrated activists into his native island. During 1796 William Pitt's government decided that the British position in Corsica was untenable; the Corsican union with Britain was dissolved, and British troops were withdrawn. The hopes that had been raised about the value of the island had been rapidly disappointed. Pitt wondered whether Catherine the Great might be willing to take on Corsica, in return for a promise of special access for British shipping; he wanted her to believe that she could hold the island with no more than 6,000 troops and the goodwill of the Corsican parliament. Catherine died before the proposal ever reached her. The British view of a Russian presence in the Mediterranean was, then, that the Russians might serve as useful idiots who could perform secondary tasks for Britain, while Britain's major effort and expense were dedicated to the war against revolutionary France and, subsequently, Napoleon.

It became the task of Nelson and his very capable colleagues – Hood, Collingwood, Troubridge and others – to prise control of the Mediterranean from the French. One important purpose was to block Napoleon's attempts to establish a French base in Egypt, from which he could interfere with British imperial projects still further to the east, in India, for the British had been building their power out there since the mid-eighteenth century. A French letter intercepted by the British set out the arguments behind an Egyptian campaign:

> The Government have turned their eyes towards Egypt and Syria: countries which by their climate, goodness and fertility of soil may become the Granaries of the French Commerce, her magazine of abundance, and by the course of time the depository of the riches of India: it is almost indubitable that when possessed of & regularly organized in these countries we may throw our views still farther, & in the end destroy the English Commerce in the Indies, turn it to our own profit, & render our selves the Sovereigns also of that, of Africa, & Asia. All these considerations united, have induced our Government to attempt the expedition to Egypt.[28]

Nelson was a commander of exceptional brilliance, but it was his opponent, Napoleon, who drew the conflict between Britain and France deep into the Mediterranean and, once again, a good, though unorthodox, way of viewing the course of events is from the Russian and Maltese perspective.

Bonaparte could see from the start that Malta was a prize worth winning. While still an employee of the revolutionary Directory, in 1797, he wrote to his masters that 'the island of Malta is of major interest for us', arguing that France needed a sympathetic Grand Master. This could be arranged, in his view, for at least half a million francs: the current Grand Master had never recovered from a stroke, and his successor was expected to be the German von Hompesch:

> Valletta has 37,000 inhabitants who are very well disposed towards the French; there are no longer any English in the Mediterranean; why should not our fleet or the Spanish, before going into the Atlantic, sail to Valletta and occupy it? There are only 500 Knights and the regiment of the Order is only 600 strong. If we do not, Malta will fall into the power of the king of Naples. This little island is worth any price to us.[29]

These were very acute comments, even if he overestimated the value of Malta as a supply base, given its shortage of wood and water. The magnificent fortifications of Valletta were a mask behind which sat an inadequate army of defenders, men who were, in any case, often seduced by fine living – the passionate, even fanatical, ideals of the earlier Hospitallers had become greatly diluted, even if the war against the infidel

Turk remained the set purpose of the Maltese corsairs.[30] Moreover, the danger of a Neapolitan takeover of Malta had more than local signifi-cance. The 'king of the Two Sicilies' enjoyed close ties to Nelson and to Britain, and his historic claim to be the ultimate suzerain of the Maltese archipelago was recognized in the tribute of a falcon paid each year by the Grand Master.

Von Hompesch was duly elected Grand Master in July 1797. He saw in the Russian tsar an ally who could restore the Order's fortunes through the Polish-Russian priory, while also hoping for support from the Austrian emperor, in whose lands he had been born, and from the French Knights, who were appalled by what had been happening in France, where the Order held many lands.[31] Von Hompesch rightly assumed that Napoleon's real concerns lay elsewhere; but Napoleon was convinced that in order to achieve his objectives in the eastern Mediterranean he must control Malta. When a massive French fleet left Toulon in May 1798, bound for Egypt by way of Malta, von Hompesch continued to place his trust in the Russians and the Austrians, as if they were really in a position to offer him any help. Doublet, who had served as secretary to the previous Grand Master, observed that 'never had Malta seen such a numberless fleet in her waters', and the leaders of the native Maltese community reflected on the irony that it was a western European and not a Turkish navy that was now poised to take the island from the Order.[32] Once the French fleet reached Malta, von Hompesch cautiously insisted that ships could enter the harbour only four at a time, and Napoleon's emissary complained: 'what length of time, indeed, would it not take for 500 to 600 sail to procure in this way the water and other things they urgently need?' The emissary went on to complain that much better favours had been shown in the recent past to the British.[33] Still, this was the answer Bonaparte had wanted. He now had ample excuse to unload 15,000 men and take charge of the island. Von Hompesch realized that he had no chance of holding out against massively superior forces. He surrendered the island, and on 13 June Napoleon expelled the Knights; he melted down great quantities of silver plate and appropri-ated their archives, not in order to read the documents, but because ammunition shells were usually packed with paper. Thus the Knights were stripped of their identity and thrown on the mercy of the Christian powers, as they had been after the fall of Acre and after the fall of Rhodes. Once again the survival of the Order was much in doubt.

The capture of Malta only strengthened the determination of Tsar Paul to bring Russian navies back into the Mediterranean. That he over-estimated its usefulness as a source of wood and water is undeniable. But he fully expected to move on from Malta to more substantial conquests.[34] His first move was to persuade the Russian priory of the Order to declare von Hompesch deposed, and to elect the tsar as their new Grand Master, in November 1797.[35] He proceeded to appoint a number of Russian Orthodox nobles as Knights of Malta, and he wore his magisterial robes every day, giving the impression that he was as proud of his (contested) position as Grand Master as he was of his position as Russian emperor. He saw himself as a paragon of chivalry. 'Just now,' an Austrian minister observed, 'the Tsar's sole preoccupation is with Malta.'[36]

One of the many surprises Paul gave his contemporaries was his alliance with the Ottomans. This followed Admiral Nelson's great victory over Napoleon's fleet at Aboukir Bay, close to Alexandria, in summer 1798 (the Battle of the Nile); after this, the British were able to expel French armies from Egypt, though not before Napoleon had despoiled the country of vast numbers of its antiquities.[37] The Sublime Porte had remained broadly content with its French alliance since the sixteenth century. A French landing in Ottoman Egypt could not, however, be tolerated. Besides, there were troublemakers in the Balkans who seemed dangerously sympathetic to France, notably the great Albanian warlord Ali Pasha, lord of Ioannina. Now, clearly, it was time for the sultan to turn against a France which had shown itself more ambitious in the Levant than the Ottomans could allow, and at the same time had shown itself more vulnerable than observers of Napoleon's fleets and armies might have expected. The most important feature of the Russo-Turkish alliance was the preliminary agreement, signed only a few weeks after Aboukir, which permitted the Russian navy to sail through the Bosphorus into the Mediterranean.[38] Fortunately, the Turks and the Russians could agree on a common objective: the Ionian isles, which Napoleon had seized shortly before, while he was sweeping up the remnants of the Venetian empire following his capture of Venice in May 1797. The Turks suspected that Ancona was to be used as a base for a French invasion of the Balkans, and saw control of Corfu and its neighbours as a necessary step towards a blockade of the Adriatic. Each side managed to put aside deep distrust for its new ally. Indeed, the Russian naval commander, the boorish, monolingual Ushakov, reserved his jealousy for Nelson, since he did not want the British to win all the glory, and Nelson, for his part, was determined to keep these unlikely allies within the eastern Mediterranean, while winning Malta and Corfu for Britain. 'I hate the Russians', he wrote, describing Ushakov as 'a blackguard'.[39] The Turks possessed a finely constructed fleet of modern French ships, but their sailors, many of whom were in fact Greek, were not well disciplined, while the Russian shipyards in the Black Sea were incapable of producing ships that would have the stamina for a long war far from home.[40] Still, the combined forces of Turkey and Russia had taken control of the Ionian islands by early March 1799. Typically, the tsar remembered the Order of St John when he rewarded Ushakov, who now became a Knight of Malta. The provision made for the government of the Ionian isles was distinctive. The seven islands would constitute an aristocratic 'Septinsular Republic', under the sovereignty of Turkey; however, Russia would exercise special influence as the protecting power.[41]

Setting aside his real doubts about the seaworthiness of the Russian fleet and about its commander, Nelson wrote to Ushakov proposing a joint attack on Malta, a prospect that seemed more real now that a Russian army was advancing southwards from Turin. Nelson was worried that this would turn into a Russian invasion achieved with British support. He insisted: 'although one Power may have a few more men in the Island than the other, yet they are not to have a preponderance. The moment the French flag is struck, the colours of the Order must be hoisted and no other.'[42] According to one historian, 'Russian prospects in the Mediterranean never looked more promising than in October 1799'. Ushakov knew this too, and in December he was shocked to receive an imperial *ukaz* telling him that the tsar had changed his mind: he was to leave the Mediterranean forthwith, and retreat with the entire Russian fleet to the Black Sea; Russian positions in Corfu were to be handed over directly to the Turks, in the expectation that this would lead the sultan to favour the passage of a Russian fleet from the Aegean into the Black Sea. Withdrawal came none too soon. Russian intervention in the Ionian isles threatened to interfere with Habsburg control of the Adriatic, and the Austrians were just growing comfortable in the possession of Venice, which Napoleon had handed over to them as a piece of candy. Paul's calculations were out of touch with reality, and he grandly offered the Holy Roman Emperor a choice between Venice and the Low Countries, as he imaginatively carved up post-revolutionary Europe among the reluctant allies who faced Napoleon.[43]

How far Paul's ambitions were from reality was further revealed when Ushakov found it impossible to sail his decaying fleet into the eastern Mediterranean, and was obliged to winter in Corfu. The Russians impotently sat out the siege of Malta by the British, only leaving Corfu for the Black Sea in July 1800. Napoleon had no hope of holding on to Malta, and, so as 'to cast an apple of discord among my enemies', he offered it as a gift to Paul; the tsar fell into the trap by accepting the offer, only to learn in November 1800 that it had been seized by the British a couple of months earlier.[44] The British decided to forget that their avowed intention had been the restoration of the Knights, nor did they bother to raise the flags of any of their allies when they captured Valletta: neither that of the tsar-cum-Grand Master, nor that of the Order of St John, nor that of the king of Naples, ancient overlord of Malta. The Foreign Office in London murmured, in best Foreign Office style, about the irregularity, and expressed timid fears about the offence caused to the tsar as 'acknowledged Grand Master' (something of an exaggeration). But the British army and navy, *in situ* in Malta, would have none of this.[45] It was the British flag that would fly over Malta for more than a century and a half. Napoleon could only have dreamed of what happened next: the tsar created an 'Armed Neutrality of the North' with the help of Denmark, Sweden and Prussia, and placed an embargo on British ships. Then Napoleon's dream developed into a nightmare. Conflict erupted in the Baltic and North Sea; Nelson, though technically only second-in-command, once again emerged as the brilliant victor at the battle of Copenhagen in April 1801, when the Danish fleet was smashed to pieces.[46] About a week earlier disgruntled Russian officers forced their way into the tsar's bedchamber and throttled him. The British were relieved to learn of the fate of this unpredictable ally; Napoleon, recognizing another megalomaniac, was deeply moved, and decided that a British conspiracy lay behind the assassination. But Paul was his own worst enemy.

IV

Paul's successor, Alexander I, began his reign more cautiously. When Russia was proposed as guarantor of Malta's autonomy under a restored government of the Knights, following pan-European peace negotiations with France in 1801, the tsar politely demurred: who else but the king of the Two Sicilies should guarantee Malta, in his capacity as suzerain of the island?[47] On the other hand, Alexander was keen to reactivate Russian interest in the Ionian isles, especially since the Ottoman Empire seemed to be tottering (it would be a long totter). The imperial counsellor Czartoryski called Turkey 'rotten and gangrenous in its principal and vital parts'.[48] Were the Ottoman Empire to dissolve, Czartoryski envisaged a division of Turkey-in-Europe between the Romanovs and the Habsburgs, with shares for Britain and France in the Aegean, Asia Minor and North Africa, as well as independence for the Greeks. The Habsburg emperor would gain the Dalmatian coast, including Dubrovnik, while Russia would hold on to Kotor and Corfu, as well, of course, as Constantinople itself. Practical actions were taken: the defence of the Ionian isles was strengthened, in the face of a French threat from southern Italy, and consuls were sent to towns such as Kotor, in the hope of winning them over to Russian sympathies.[49] But the Peace of Amiens arranged with France fell apart in 1803 (partly over Britain's refusal to surrender Malta), and Napoleon, soon to become self-crowned emperor of France, began to flex his muscles again on the mainland.[50] These events persuaded Alexander to return his ships to the Mediterranean. The task was rendered easier with the 'glorious victory' obtained by Lord Nelson at Trafalgar, just outside the Mediterranean, on 21 October 1805.[51] The Mediterranean was made safer for anti-French shipping, but the dead hero Nelson was no longer there to warn against the unreliable Russians, who had, in fact, been working hard to improve the seaworthiness of their fleet.

Under Alexander, as under his predecessors, Russian interest in the Mediterranean was closely tied to Russian sympathy for the Orthodox Slavs, over whom the tsar sought to extend his protection. It was for this reason that the Russians sent ships to the Bay of Kotor, which gave access to the mountain-girt Orthodox principality of Montenegro, a region the Turks had never bothered to bring fully under their dominion. The importance of Montenegro to the Russians was ideological, not practical, even if Kotor was said to be home to 400 trading vessels, though this must include some that were no larger than skiffs.[52] The religious question also came to the fore in Russian dealings with Dubrovnik. For fear of the Serbs, the Ragusans had traditionally discouraged the

Orthodox Church within their narrow domains, and in 1803 the Senate even closed down the chapel of the Russian consulate. By March 1806 a French army was advancing down the Dalmatian coast, and the Ragusan government reluctantly agreed to let Russian soldiers man the defences of Dubrovnik if and when the French arrived. But at the end of May, as the French entered Ragusan territory, the Senate decided that French Catholics were preferable to Russian Orthodox, setting off a struggle that took place over their heads between French troops and Russian ones, aided by Montenegrin Slavs. Although the Russians managed for a time to extend their influence along the Dalmatian coast, Dubrovnik remained a French base, and in 1808 its republican government went the way of the Venetian republic, with barely a whimper. A representative of the French commander Marmont declared: 'my lords, the republic of Ragusa and its government are dissolved and the new administration is installed'. Dubrovnik was placed under the authority first of Napoleonic Italy and then of the new province of Illyria. Marmont was rewarded with the novel title *duc de Raguse*.[53] The collapse was not merely political, for, even though Dubrovnik was home to 277 sailing ships in 1806, only forty-nine were still in use in 1810.[54] The republic had become caught up in wars that could not possibly serve its interests. The fading power of the Ottomans left the Ragusans without the traditional Turkish guarantee of their neutrality and safety; an attempt to secure Turkish support was fruitless, because the Ottomans were, at this stage, largely beholden to the French.[55] It was an ignominious end to a republic that optimistically took LIBERTAS as its motto.

It was also the beginning of the end for Russian intervention in the Mediterranean. The Russians still found it difficult to maintain control over operations so far from St Petersburg. Operations were compromised by the collapse of the Russian-Turkish entente late in 1806, following deep disagreements with the Turks about the affairs of Wallachia, in modern Romania. The Russians and the Turks were surprised to find themselves at war. With misgivings, Great Britain gave some support to the Russians, but it was the Russian fleet that fought one of the great naval battles of the Napoleonic Wars off Mount Athos at the end of June and start of July 1807, hoping to break open the mouth of the Dardanelles.[56] On paper, this was a Russian victory, but in reality the Turkish fleet was still able to block the Dardanelles, and the tsar had in any case had more than enough. The lucrative trade from the Black Sea into the Mediterranean had dried up during the conflict; following reverses in Europe the tsar made his peace with Napoleon at Tilsit in 1807 and abandoned his Mediterranean ambitions. He also abandoned his fleet in the Mediterranean. The Russian ships were simply stuck there. Those that tried to escape into the Atlantic were easily captured by the British. Several ships made for Trieste, Venice and Corfu, but there was nothing for them there, and they were surrendered, abandoned or even scuttled; others reached Toulon and joined the French navy: Napoleon had been hoping that one advantage of peace with Russia would be the acquisition of its fleet. French officers raced to Corfu to raise the French flag there in place of the Russian.[57] Mediterranean intervention had cost Russia a great deal of money and in the end brought it no permanent advantage.

9
Deys, Beys and Bashaws,
1800–1830

I

The battle of Trafalgar left the Mediterranean open to British shipping, but Great Britain had not yet gained incontestable mastery over the sea-lanes. The bitter struggle for control of Sicily and southern Italy between Britain, acting in support of King Ferdinand of Naples, and Napoleon's armies, acting in support of Marshal Murat, who was trying to usurp the Neapolitan throne, reached a high point in July 1806 at the battle of Maida (a British victory, deep in Calabria).[1] Maida demonstrated that Napoleon had been foolish in allowing so many troops to be pinned down in miserable conditions far from the areas in northern and central Italy he most wished to control. Earlier dreams of using Taranto as a base for controlling southern Italy and the entrance to the Adriatic and Ionian seas evaporated.[2] Yet the British fleet was far more stretched than the story of its victories suggests. The British needed to keep open the channel of communication linking Malta to Trieste, for Trieste had become an important source of supplies from the Austrian empire, now that routes through Germany were blocked by Napoleon's armies.[3] And by 1808 the French seemed to be clawing back their control of the Mediterranean; they had re-established their fleet at Toulon, and there were fears of a naval attack on Naples and Sicily.

The British government wondered whether there was any point pursuing war in the Mediterranean. Other concerns intruded: the French were trying to take control of Spain, and with the outbreak of the Peninsular War attention shifted to formidably tough land campaigns in Iberia. How difficult conditions were can be seen from the size of the British fleet, which had plenty of other duties to perform close to England, in the

Caribbean and elsewhere. On 8 March 1808 fifteen ships of the line lay under the control of Admiral Collingwood, Nelson's capable successor; one at Syracuse, one at Messina and one off Corfu; twelve stood guard at Cádiz. These large warships were supported by thirty-eight frigates, sloops, brigs and bomb-vessels within the Mediterranean, most of which were patrolling and reconnoitring as far afield as Turkey and the Adriatic. In earlier stages of the Napoleonic Wars British naval strength had been even smaller: eleven ships of the line in July 1803, ten in July 1805.[4] Compared to the massive war fleets of antiquity, or at Lepanto, the fleets of the competing navies at the start of the nineteenth century seem minute. On the other hand, British ships were demonstrably superior to French and Spanish ones, especially in fire-power.[5] The British government constantly had to make choices about where to concentrate naval resources, and yet these decisions were made at a great remove in time and space from the fleets in the Mediterranean: proposals to blockade Tuscany, Naples and Dubrovnik brought its deliberations into the realms of fantasy.[6]

The British needed allies. Russian ambitions had been useful in providing naval help. By 1809 the British tried to harness the Albanian warlord Ali Pasha, in the hope that he would take the Ionian isles for them. They also tried to win the support of Greek rebels against the Ottomans, who were, though, instinctively hostile to Ali Pasha. And the British government was also afraid that excessive trouble in the western lands of the Ottoman Empire would weaken the Turks so much that their empire would implode. They did not want that to happen just yet, during a war with Napoleon on which the very survival of the United Kingdom depended. In the Mediterranean, the only way out of this conundrum was to occupy the Ionian isles and to place the Septinsular Republic under the protection of Great Britain. Admiral Collingwood landed with 2,000 men, whose mere arrival in the Ionian isles was sufficient to scare the French into abject surrender. Count Stadion, an Austrian minister, believed that Britain had now become 'master of the Adriatic'.[7]

Great Britain had gained the prizes by the end of the Napoleonic Wars – Malta, Corfu, Sicily. Sicily became to all intents a British protectorate in the last phases of the Napoleonic Wars, between 1806 and 1815. King Ferdinand resented his dependence on British aid, but the British kept a tight hold on Sicily: they required naval bases there and they needed to obtain essential supplies for their fleet.[8] The British presence on the island ensured that Murat did not dare invade in 1810, even

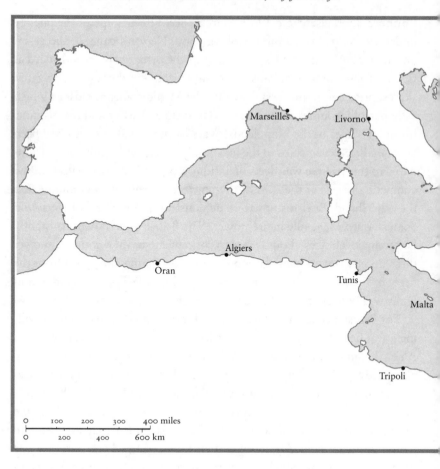

though Napoleon had ordered him to do so, and even though he marched as far as the Straits of Messina.[9] The British understood the need for a permanent presence in the Mediterranean in order to hold back the French, and especially to keep them out of Egypt and the routes leading to India. Despite a general fall in Mediterranean trade, a commercial mentality was also at work, and the markets of the Mediterranean would be even more attractive if Britain had unimpeded access to them. The Napoleonic Wars brought other dramatic changes. Napoleon's extinction of the Venetian republic in 1797 was not greatly mourned in the rest of Europe; nor could the Ragusans persuade anybody to restore their privileges once Bonaparte had been defeated. The old Mediterranean commercial powers disappeared off the map.

II

The waning of Venetian and Ragusan commerce provided opportunities for the ships of other, non-Mediterranean, nations. Trade may have declined, but plenty of commercial opportunities remained. Sicily, it is true, had lost its age-old position as a great granary servicing the needs of the entire Mediterranean. The island's population grew by about half during the eighteenth century, but much of this growth was concentrated in the cities, notably Palermo. Meanwhile, grain production fell, partly through a failure to maximize output and partly because land was going out of cultivation. The Sicilians had been exporting as much as 40,000 tons of grain each year in the seventeenth century, but climatic conditions worsened; the wetter climate of what has been termed a 'Little Ice Age' was only one factor, since Mediterranean producers faced competition from the Baltic and other regions.[10] In the nineteenth century, British entrepreneurs such as Woodhouse and Whitaker encouraged vine cultivation in western Sicily, for the production of heavy Marsala wines. There were still goods that could most easily be acquired in the Mediterranean – coral from Sardinia and North Africa, dried fruits from Greece and Turkey, coffee exported via the Ottoman lands. The Danes, Norwegians and Swedes, fat from the proceeds of their northern trade, made their appearance off the coasts of North Africa, in the Barbary 'regencies' (so called because their rulers, variously known as deys, beys and bashaws, or pashas, were nominally the deputies of the Ottoman sultan). From 1769 the Danes had delivered 'presents' to the dey of Algiers, in return for protection of their shipping, though periodically the dey would decide he wanted larger donations, which he obtained by harrying Scandinavian shipping, and around 1800 these demands brought the Algerians and the Danes to the edge of war. Meanwhile, the bey of Tunis felt so insulted at the inferior quality of their presents that he seized some Danish ships in May 1800, and the next month sent some men to chop down the flagpole of the Danish consulate, setting off a brief war in which the Danes, and before long the Swedes, largely found themselves at his mercy.[11]

These problems were resolved through diplomacy. The beys and deys wanted presents, which kept their finances afloat. Their policy, the United States Congress was informed, was to tempt each nation into Mediterranean waters with new commercial treaties, and then to 'break friendship with every nation as often as possible'.[12] Too many agreements with European powers deprived the Barbary regencies of the chance to seize merchandise and captives from foreign ships. Captives could be ransomed, but they could also be used as diplomatic pawns, to secure presents; and while they lingered in filthy conditions in Barbary jails, they could be used as free labour (though officers were generally treated much better). Ratings were chained to the floor at night and, in Tripoli, received a daily allowance consisting of a biscuit made of barley and beans, full of impurities, some goat's meat, some oil and water. Put to work building the walls of Tripoli, enslaved captives might be forced to work bare-headed in the hot sun, berated as 'Christian dogs' and lashed with whips.[13] The North African rulers were aware, of course, that the Christian states would go to great lengths to gain the freedom of these men, and of the women who continued to be picked off the shores of Sardinia, Sicily and the Balearic islands.

There was a new nation whose ships provided novel opportunities for Barbary extortion: the United States of America. The American conflict with Tripoli was the first war fought by the fledgling union against a foreign power, and it led to the creation of an American navy.[14] American writers presented the North Africans as uncivilized 'barbarians', which was easy to do when the commonly used name for the Maghrib was 'Barbary'.[15] The reports sent by American consuls in Tunis and elsewhere confirmed the belief that the beys, deys and bashaws were uncontrolled tyrants, whose attitude to the art of government could be judged from the beheadings and amputations that American envoys witnessed. George Washington expressed strong views about the Barbary corsairs in a letter sent to Lafayette in 1786:

> In such an enlightened, in such a liberal age, how is it possible the great maritime powers of Europe should submit to pay an annual tribute to the little piratical States of Barbary? Would to heaven we had a navy able to reform those enemies to mankind, or crush them into non-existence.[16]

He failed to foresee that the United States would soon join the powers of Europe in making such payments to the Barbary states.

The idea, mooted by several historians, that the American war against the Barbary states was fought as a Christian struggle against Islamic 'barbarism' does not match the evidence. As Frank Lambert has written, 'the Barbary Wars were primarily about trade, not theology'; the treaty of 1797 between the United States and Tripoli stated explicitly that the United States was not constitutionally a Christian country, and President Madison was convinced that this statement had eased relations with Muslim North Africa, by removing religious differences from the issues under contention.[17] For, 'rather than being holy wars, they were an extension of the American War of Independence'.[18] On paper, the War of Independence had ended in 1783 with the British recognition that the thirteen colonies had broken loose from the Crown. In reality, there were many unresolved issues, especially the right of American shipping to trade freely across the Atlantic and within the Mediterranean. The principle that citizens of the new nation should be greeted in foreign ports on the same terms as the old European nations was one for which the Americans were willing to fight. Great Britain had seen the American colonies as an integral part of a closed colonial system in which its trans-Atlantic possessions would provide Britain with raw materials and at the same time absorb the growing output of British industry. The whole system was protected by a web of commercial taxation typical of the mercantilist outlook of the eighteenth century. American opposition was expressed in the famous Boston Tea Party of 1773; it proved very difficult for either side to disengage from this relationship. In 1766, ten years before the American Revolution, the *Pennsylvania Gazette* reported that 'a Bond for a Mediterranean Pass' approved by the British authorities was contemptuously set alight in a coffee house in Philadelphia.[19]

For the Americans, trading towards the Mediterranean posed two sets of problems, though they were intertwined. Even after 1783, British ports such as Gibraltar might be reluctant to host American ships, and British captains might seize any opportunity to arrest American shipping – British captains were especially keen to press American crews into British service, especially while Great Britain was at war with France. British politicians such as Lord Sheffield saw the Americans as potential trade rivals who could undermine Britain's commercial supremacy, though it was noted that their chances of making a success of Mediterranean trade were limited, thanks to the Barbary corsairs. The second problem was that of relations with the rulers of North Africa: the Americans sought free access to their ports, and they also sought assurances that their ships would not be attacked on the high seas by corsairs from Algiers, Tunis and Tripoli. Jefferson to all intents agreed with Lord Sheffield, observing that the Europeans already had a large presence in the Mediterranean, but the Americans would have to creep in through narrow straits where pirates 'could very effectually inspect whatever enters it'.[20]

It was clear, then, that American trade with the Mediterranean could never compete in volume with that of the established European powers, especially France, which played the leading role in Mediterranean commerce at the end of the eighteenth century. Nevertheless, American intervention had very significant consequences for the Barbary states, reshaping their relationship with the non-Muslim naval powers. The Barbary Wars were the first phase in a series of events that culminated in the French conquest of Algeria from 1830 onwards. Among the principal actors was the Bacri family, Jewish financiers who operated out of Algiers; as well as bankrolling the dey, the Bacris traded towards Livorno and maintained close commercial ties with co-religionists in the British bases at Gibraltar and Minorca. Their influence at the court of the dey is all the more surprising because American observers acknowledged that the Jews were ill-treated in Algeria. But the dey realized that he could use the Jewish bankers as intermediaries in his dealings with the Europeans, and that they were totally at his mercy. The dey of Algiers executed David Coen Bacri in 1811, after a rival Jewish leader, David Duran, whose ancestors had arrived from Majorca following the pogroms of 1391, ruthlessly accused him of treason. Duran hoped to lever himself into Bacri's seat of honour, but soon met a similar fate.

Thus a small elite of Jewish families remained close to the dey, occasionally attracting hostile comment from figures such as the American consul in Tunis, William Eaton.[21] In 1805 Eaton addressed an appeal to the inhabitants of Tripoli, informing them that the Americans had given their support to a rival claimant to the office of bashaw. He begged them to realize that the Americans were 'people of every nation, every tongue and every faith', who lived 'at the uttermost limits of the West'. The present bashaw, Yussuf Karamanli, was, he said, a 'base and perjured traitor, whose naval commander is a drunken renegade, and whose principal counsellor is a grasping Jew'. The naval commander, Murad Reis, was virulently anti-American; he arrived in Algiers as Peter Lisle, a Scot with a fondness for liquor, converted and married the bashaw's daughter, without, however, abandoning strong drink.[22] 'Be assured,' Eaton wrote, 'that the God of the Americans and of the Mahometans is the same; the one true and omnipotent God.'[23] He found Tunis and its neighbours an impenetrable world. In one sense it was an enlightening one, however. He questioned the justice of slavery when he saw the white and black slaves who abounded in Muslim North Africa:

> Remorse seizes my whole soul when I reflect that this is indeed but a copy of the very barbarity which my eyes have seen in my own native country. And yet we boast of liberty and natural justice.[24]

Eaton noted that in Tunis, as in Algiers, there were Jewish merchants who seemed to dominate trade. He described a Jewish trading company, the *Giornata*, that paid the bey of Tunis 60,000 piastres each year and possessed a 'factory', or warehouse, at Livorno. He asserted that

250,000 hides were exported from Tunis each year, as well as vast amounts of wax. In addition, oil, wheat, barley, beans, dates, salt and livestock (including horses) were sent to Europe; while the war between France and England was at its height, the Ragusans acted as carriers, benefiting from the special status of Dubrovnik in its last years as a tributary of the Sublime Porte. Meanwhile, the souks of Tunis were hungry for exactly the goods the Americans could bring to North Africa: 'muslins, stuffs, fine cloths, iron, coffee, sugar, pepper, and spices of all kinds, bleached wax candles, cochineal, dried fish, and lumber'. He predicted that they would fetch three times the price in Tunis that they would command in the United States.[25] His comments show that he had in mind not just direct trade between the United States and North Africa, but a role in the carrying trade of the Mediterranean and the Atlantic. His account confirms the lack of manufacturing industry in Tunis, Algiers and Tripoli; even candles needed to be imported, despite the export of prodigious amounts of wax. However, the lack of good quality wood in North Africa remained a serious problem, especially for states that launched their own pirate fleets. To some extent this was resolved by the purchase or seizure of foreign ships, but the Barbary fleets had been shrinking since the late seventeenth century, under British and Dutch pressure; by 1800, each state was lucky if it could mobilize a dozen corsair ships. To the trade in North Africa could be added trade in other corners of the Mediterranean, only possible while the United States enjoyed peace with the Barbary regencies. Thomas Jefferson recorded substantial exports of American wheat and flour into the Mediterranean, as well as rice and pickled or dried fish, enough to furnish the cargo of up to 100 ships each year; but 'it was obvious to our merchants, that their adventures into that sea would be exposed to the depredations of the piratical States on the coast of Barbary'.[26]

III

From the moment of independence, the United States tried to address the problem of the Barbary corsairs. In May 1784 Congress authorized negotiations with the Barbary states. The Moroccan sultan was the first ruler to recognize the independence of the United States. The Americans signed agreements with Morocco, Algiers, Tripoli and Tunis between

1786 and 1797. In the agreement with Algiers, of December 1794, the United States promised the dey $642,500 at once and naval stores each year worth $21,600, including powder and shot, pine masts and oak planking; they also presented him with a golden tea-set. This was a marked change from the terms originally demanded by the dey: $2,247,000 in cash and two frigates with hulls sheathed in copper. Even so, difficulties continued when the dey complained that the money he was owed had not arrived, so it became necessary to offer him a new gift – 'a new American ship of 20 guns, which should sail very fast, to be presented to his daughter' – but the dey successfully demanded a 36-gun ship instead.[27] The North African rulers constantly berated the Americans and Europeans for the poor quality and insufficient quantity of the goods they were supposed to receive. The Christian powers did cut corners, for they saw these demands as nothing but bare-faced robbery.

In 1800 the *George Washington*, a bulky American man-of-war converted from an East India trading vessel, arrived in Algiers harbour carrying the gifts expected by the local ruler, along with sugar, coffee and herrings. Following the usual complaints that American presents were in arrears, the dey summarily demanded that the captain should sail to Constantinople with an Algerian envoy; the captain felt too intimidated to refuse. His bizarre cargo has been described as a 'Noah's ark': it included not just horses, cattle and 150 sheep but four lions, four tigers, four antelopes and twelve parrots, and he also carried 100 black slaves who were being sent to the Ottoman sultan as tribute, as well as an ambassadorial entourage of as many people. The captain was ordered to fly the Algerian flag, though he soon reverted to that of the United States; it was reported that the sailors, in mockery of Islam, swung the vessel about during Muslim prayers so that the worshippers could no longer tell in which direction Mecca lay.[28] The Americans were mortified to learn of their humiliation in their own newspapers, but, precariously, relations with the dey had been preserved. While relations with Algiers remained afloat, even if low in the water, those with Tripoli deteriorated as the bashaw demanded further tribute. On failing to receive any, he sent his men to the American consulate to chop down the flagpole bearing the Stars and Stripes, and then sent out ships to hunt for prizes; as well as a captured Swedish vessel, his flotilla included the *Betsy* of Boston, seized from the Americans a few years earlier and renamed the *Meshuda*.[29]

This was a period, between October 1801 and May 1803, when France and Great Britain were at peace, and the Americans and Scandinavians were seeking to exploit the relative quiet of the Mediterranean for purely commercial reasons. But the Barbary states again and again stood in their way, and the United States, for the first time, felt itself being pushed towards war with a foreign power. In 1802 the Swedes, with grievances of their own, gladly joined the Americans in a blockade of Tripoli. This conflict was already spilling over into something larger, and its range was extended still further when the Moroccan emperor, irate at an American refusal to guarantee free passage for his ships carrying grain to Tripoli, declared war on the United States.[30] Then, in October 1803, the frigate USS *Philadelphia*, which was taking part in the blockade of Tripoli, ran aground while pursuing a Tripolitanian vessel. It was captured by the bashaw's men, along with its crew of 307. The bashaw thought he could use this opportunity to extract $450,000 in ransom money. The commander of the American fleet, Preble, was still committed to a military solution, and was convinced that possession of the *Philadelphia* by his foes would give them the advantage they needed at sea: even in peacetime the *Philadelphia* would be used in corsair raids, or as a bargaining counter to squeeze more money out of the Americans and Europeans. The ship had to be destroyed or, better still, recaptured. A daring plan was drawn up for a night-time attack on the ship, and the ketch *Intrepid* was sent into Tripoli after nightfall on 16 February, impudently flying the British flag, under the command of Lieutenant Stephen Decatur. The *Intrepid* argued its way into Tripoli harbour: the harbour pilot was hailed in *lingua franca* and told that the vessel was bringing in provisions. Meanwhile, the Tripolitanian fleet remained sleepily unaware of what was happening. Decatur fought his way into American legend by leading the attack, rendered easier by the rapid flight of most of the enemy. Realizing that they had no chance of sailing it back to their own lines, the Americans set the *Philadelphia* alight within a quarter of an hour of taking it. All of Tripoli is said to have been illuminated by the blaze.[31] A later attack on Tripoli harbour, in August 1804, brought Decatur still greater fame: he was said to have searched out a vast Turkish Mamluk who had killed his brother earlier that day; he grappled with the giant, not giving way even when his cutlass broke, and finally (after his life was saved by a selfless sailor who parried the mortal blow intended for Decatur) he managed to shoot the

Turk at close quarters. The event was celebrated in paint and print throughout the United States. It showed how American courage triumphed over brute force, the small, free and resolute Decatur over the dark and ugly Mamluk slave. This small victory in Tripoli added immeasurably to American self-confidence.[32]

Even so, they were unable to break the bashaw's will, and the Americans now adopted a very different plan, long advocated by William Eaton. Eaton sailed to Alexandria in search of Hamet, the claimant to the throne of Tripoli, who had been pushed aside by his younger brother Yusuf. Eaton found himself leading an army of men (mainly Arabs) overland from Egypt to Tripoli, in tough conditions. It took six weeks to march 400 miles, as far as Derne, a coastal city thought likely to accept Hamet as its ruler. In the end, the United States failed to install him in Tripoli, but the mere threat of Hamet's return forced the bashaw to negotiate. He was willing to agree to modest terms, in no way comparable to the fortune other North African rulers had extorted – a $60,000 ransom payment.[33]

IV

Algiers proved more intractable. In 1812, aware that war had broken out between the United States and Great Britain, the dey of Algiers decided to place further pressure on the Americans, who would not now be able to mobilize a fleet in the Mediterranean. He insisted that the presents brought on board the *Allegheny* were of poor quality: for example, he had asked for twenty-seven large-diameter ropes and was only given four. He demanded $27,000, and, when the Americans refused, he expelled them, subject to payment of that amount, which the consul, Lear, had to borrow at 25 per cent interest from the Bacris.[34] The Algerians had meanwhile brought home the captured American brig *Edwin*, engaged in contraband trade through Gibraltar in support of the British army in Spain (and in ignorance of the severe deterioration in Anglo-American relations). The crew of the *Edwin* was held in Algiers along with the ship, and the United States government, preoccupied with war on its Atlantic seaboard and in Canada, resolved to send an envoy to the Maghrib, in the hope that negotiations might still succeed. Mordecai Noah was appointed consul at Tunis. He was a remarkable figure, keen to show his fellow-Jews that they had a place in American society, who talked of encouraging the 'Hebrew nation' to bring its funds across the Atlantic from the Old World, to the general benefit of all Americans. The American administration knew all about the Bacri family, and Noah might provide a valuable means of access to the dey through his co-religionists. In winter 1814 he passed through the Straits of Gibraltar, cultivating links with the Jewish community of Gibraltar, and obtaining from one of its leaders a letter of introduction to the Bacris. But he was able to secure the release of only a handful of the American captives.[35]

President Madison was not a warmonger, but the United States had tasted blood in the war against Tripoli, and saw war against Algiers as the second phase in a conflict that would put an end to the importunings of the Barbary rulers. On 17 February 1815 the United States and Great Britain made peace; a week later, Madison requested Congress to declare war on Algiers, and the Americans assembled the largest fleet they had ever put together (numbering only ten warships). The national hero Stephen Decatur was placed in charge of the expedition.[36] He amply fulfilled expectations, seizing several Algerian ships well before he reached Algiers. He was thus in an excellent position to dictate terms to the dey, who was quite new to office (the two previous deys having been assassinated). When the dey's envoy asked Decatur for time to think about the terms of the treaty the Americans wished to impose, Decatur answered: 'Not a minute!'[37] A treaty with Algiers was followed in swift succession by treaties with Tunis and Tripoli. The Algerian treaty provided for the return of American captives, and it regulated the functions of the American consul, but its real importance in the history of the Mediterranean lies in the second article: there were to be no presents or tribute payments ever again. This was the great achievement of Decatur's expedition. A precedent had been set and its importance was well understood by the European powers; they viewed the United States with far greater respect than ever before. The Americans congratulated themselves – John Quincy Adams wrote: 'our naval campaign in the Mediterranean has been perhaps as splendid as anything that has occurred in our annals since our existence as a nation'. That was not very long, but this made the victory with a brand-new navy all the more impressive.[38] The victories against the men of Barbary were a defining moment in the emergence of an American identity.

V

A new order was coming into being in the East as well. By 1800, the Ottoman sultan found that his Egyptian and Greek subjects were becoming unmanageable. The warlord Muhammad Ali took advantage of the chaos created in Egypt by Napoleon's arrival and withdrawal to overthrow the Mamluk functionaries of the Ottoman state and to install himself as ruler in 1805. Although he acknowleged Ottoman suzerainty and officially functioned as viceroy, he was very much his own master. He was an Albanian who spoke Albanian and Turkish, not Arabic, and he looked beyond the Ottoman world, seeking to draw on the learning and technology of western Europe, especially France – he was for Egypt what Peter the Great had been for Russia. He saw economic improvement as the key to the success of his plans, taking the land into state ownership and building a war fleet. These policies recall in almost uncanny detail the policies of the Ptolemies 2,000 years earlier. He encouraged new agricultural schemes, including irrigation projects, for he recognized the strength of demand in western Europe for good-quality cotton, but he was also keen to establish an industrial base, so that Egypt did not simply become an exporter of raw materials to richer nations.[39] His ambition was to bring to Egypt the benefits of the economic expansion that was transforming Europe at the start of the nineteenth century. He could see, for instance, to what poverty Alexandria had been reduced: the city had shrunk in size and population so that it was now little more than a village; its long-distance trade was not very significant. Its revival began under Muhammad Ali with the arrival of immigrants from all around the eastern Mediterranean: Turks, Greeks, Jews, Syrians.[40]

Muhammad Ali's growing assertiveness was expressed during the 1820s in his attempts to gain recognition of his authority over Crete and Syria. If he wished to make Egypt into a modern naval power, the viceroy would need access to good supplies of timber and, as in past millennia, this meant he would have to gain control of well-forested lands. The difficulty that faced him in the 1820s was that the Ottomans were proving even less successful in managing their European lands than they were in managing their African ones. In 1821 revolts broke out in the Morea, where geography favoured the rebels, who soon controlled the countryside, leaving the Turks in charge of naval bases at Nafplion, Modon and Coron. Even so, the Turks did not maintain command of the seas. Islands such as Hydra and Samos became the new focuses of resistance. The Greek merchant communities, increasingly active since the seventeenth century, cobbled together a war fleet mainly consisting of merchant ships armed with cannon. One Greek fleet possessed thirty-seven vessels, another a dozen, both under commanders from Hydra. By late April these Greek sea-dogs had captured four Turkish warships, including two men-of-war, giving the Greeks the confidence to patrol the Aegean and to confront the Turkish fleet in the approaches to the Dardanelles; although the Greek fleet proved no match for the Turks, the Greeks retreated without serious loss. By 1822 the Turkish government had become exasperated by Greek sea-raids, and mobilized a much larger Turkish fleet mainly brought from the Barbary states. In April the Turks intervened in Chios, where a Greek expeditionary force was trying to capture the citadel. The Greek force was chased away and the Turks went on to massacre much of the population, in a bloodbath that understandably found its way into the heroic history of Greek opposition to the Turks, and provided a powerful theme for a painting by Eugène Delacroix.[41] The Greeks riposted in kind: they massacred the Muslims and Jews of Tripoli in the Morea five and a half months later. Over the centuries many Greeks had turned Muslim and many Turks had become Hellenized. The massacres and ethnic cleansing of the Graeco-Turkish wars, which continued for a century and a half, were thus based on a tragic denial of the common heritage of Greeks and Turks in the eastern Mediterranean.

This did not, however, impede observers in Great Britain, France and Germany from celebrating the success of the Greeks, seeing in them the heirs of the classical world whose history, philosophy and literature they studied at school. Governments might be more cautious about giving their support to the rebels: the British government, pragmatically, wondered whether the disintegration of the Ottoman Empire was desirable just yet, a view shared by Muhammad Ali, though few imagined it had very long to last. The problem was that the break-up of the Balkans would alter the whole balance of power in Europe, the delicate mechanism known as 'the Concert of Europe' created in the aftermath of Napoleon's final defeat at Waterloo. One source of concern was Austria, which protected its commercial interests by maintaining a larger fleet of warships (twenty-two) in the eastern Mediterranean than did Great Britain. The Austrians were compromised in the eyes of the Greeks by their willingness to trade with the Turks, though all they were doing was continuing the age-old commerce between Dalmatia and the eastern Mediterranean by way of Dubrovnik and its neighours.[42] Only in 1827 did the European powers send substantial aid to the Greeks. Meanwhile, Muhammad Ali saw the Greek rebellion as a chance to pick some ripe plums for himself, and decided to send a fleet towards Greece early in 1825. He intended to win Crete, Cyprus, Syria and the Morea for his personal empire, and imagined that he could hold Greece if he summarily expelled the Greeks and repopulated southern Greece with Egyptian *fellahin.* His aim, then, was domination over almost the entire eastern Mediterranean. He spared no expense, sending sixty-two vessels to the waters east of Crete, in the hope of knocking out Greek naval forces in the southern Aegean.[43]

In October 1827, when negotiations between the contending parties were already under way, a fleet of twelve British, eight Russian and seven French ships standing off Navarino became entangled almost by accident with an Ottoman fleet of about sixty vessels drawn from Turkey, Egypt and Tunis, including three large battleships (their opponents possessed ten). Despite an armistice, the Turks refused the allied fleet entry into Navarino Bay. The allies decided that a show of force was needed, and this developed into a full-scale battle within the bay, in which the Turkish fleet was smashed to pieces. Some Turkish boats escaped towards Alexandria; others were scuttled. The allied fleet, especially the British, Russian and French flagships, suffered damage too, and 182 men were killed. The allies did not quite know what to do with their victory – the Ottoman sultan riposted by declaring holy war against the unbelievers, and the British and the French, aware of chaotic infighting among the Greeks, sent their own ships against independent-minded Greek captains who continued to make a nuisance of themselves.[44] But the battle of Navarino was a vital step towards securing a treaty in which the independence of southern Greece, under loose Ottoman suzerainty, was recognized in 1828. Muhammad Ali now realized that the best hope for the future lay in the reinvigoration of trade with Britain and France through Alexandria, so in the next few years he improved the shipyards and capitalized on the Mahmudiyya canal linking Alexandria to the Nile Delta. It had been constructed ten years earlier.[45] Now it was time to enjoy its benefits.

VI

The French invasion of Algeria was also the result of unpredicted events, at the heart of which lay not, as might be expected, the activities of the Barbary corsairs, but the finance house of the Bacri. The French had never taken much interest in the accumulated arrears in payment owed for Algerian grain, which had fed the French army since the start of the Revolutionary War. By 1827, the Bacris were short of money and insisted that the Algerian government should cover their debts until the French paid what was due. The dey was convinced that the Bacris and the French were colluding in an attempt to squeeze money out of him.[46] Recent history showed, of course, that the deys were much more enthusiastic about squeezing money out of other people. The dey was also suspicious of the French because they had started to fortify two of their trading stations in Algeria. So on 29 April 1827 an argument between the dey and the consul broke out, during which the dey became so irritated that he hit the French consul in the face with a fly-swatter. The French reaction was to demand a gun salute in honour of the French flag, but the dey was unwilling even to contemplate this symbolic act, and unleashed his privateers against French shipping. By summer 1829 the French were blockading the port of Algiers. Even so, they did not see the conquest of Algeria as the obvious solution to their problems, thinking at first that it might be best to let Muhammad Ali take charge, in view of his pro-French leanings.

The merchant community of Marseilles pressed several commercial arguments in favour of the conquest of Algiers: during the blockade trade with Algeria suffered, while the Greek rebellion against the Turks had interfered with French business in the Levant. The Marseilles businessmen wanted a safe and secure trading partner, lying under French control. It was obvious that Algiers, due south of Marseilles, should be the target. And it proved a very easy conquest. The dey went into exile in Naples in July 1830, though he had to leave most of his money behind. The lesser cities of the Algerian regency, Oran and Constantine, were assigned to friendly Tunisian princes – after nearly 300 years of occupation, the Spaniards had decided that Oran was too expensive to hold, selling it to the Muslims in 1792.[47] Still, the French were far from clear in their own minds about what they wanted to do with Algeria. They found themselves attacking targets in western and eastern Algeria: the ruler installed in Constantine had his own ideas about how his town could develop as a centre of trade with the Europeans, and there was trouble in Annaba, east of Algiers. In the 1830s, they were being dragged deeper into Algeria than they had anticipated. The Ottomans were unwilling to offer any comfort to North African rulers who appealed for support, partly through lack of resources and willpower. And yet, despite endemic conflict in several provinces, Algeria attracted coloniz-ers from France and Spain: in 1847 there were nearly 110,000 settlers, and they did not simply hide themselves in the cities, for many hoped to acquire estates carved out of the state lands of the old regime.[48] The cities themselves saw massive construction projects throughout the next decades, and Algiers was transformed into a new Marseilles with broad streets and solid, stately buildings. The conquest of Algiers was the first phase in a series of colonial conquests that divided up many of the key strategic positions in the Mediterranean between France, Great Britain, Spain and (though it was still unborn in 1830) Italy.

The history of the Fourth Mediterranean had begun in an era when Venetian, Genoese and Catalan galleys had breasted their way across the sea to reach Alexander's city. It ended as Egypt became the gateway to the East in ways of which past rulers had only dreamed. By the time the last dredging machines had finished their task and the Suez Canal was opened not just to sailing ships but to steamboats, a new era in the history of the Mediterranean had also opened: the Fifth Mediterranean had come into being.

PART FIVE

The Fifth Mediterranean, 1830–2010

I

Ever the Twain Shall Meet,
1830–1900

I

The English poet of empire Rudyard Kipling penned the much quoted lines, 'East is East and West is West, and never the twain shall meet'. Even if, by the early twentieth century, European observers had become overwhelmed by what they saw as fundamental differences between attitudes and styles of life in East and West, this was not true of the nineteenth century. Then, the ideal became the joining of East and West: a physical joining, through the Suez Canal, but also a cultural joining, as western Europeans relished the cultures of the Near East, and as the rulers of Near Eastern lands – the Ottoman sultans and their highly autonomous viceroys in Egypt – looked towards France and Great Britain in search of models they could follow in reviving the languishing economy of their dominions. This was, then, a reciprocal relationship: despite the claims of those who see 'orientalism' as the cultural expression of western imperialism, the masters of the eastern Mediterranean actively sought cultural contact with the West, and saw themselves as members of a community of monarchs that embraced Europe and the Mediterranean.[1] Ismail Pasha, viceroy of Egypt between 1863 and 1879, always dressed in European clothes, though he would occasionally top his frock-coat and epaulettes with a fez; he spoke Turkish, not Arabic. Equally, the Ottoman sultans, and more particularly their courtiers (like Ismail, frequently Albanian), often sported western dress. They would, of course, be selective in their use of western ideas. The Egyptian viceroys were happy to send clever subjects to study at the École Polytechnique in Paris, a Napoleonic foundation; at the same time they discouraged excessive mixing in the French salons: they wished to import radical

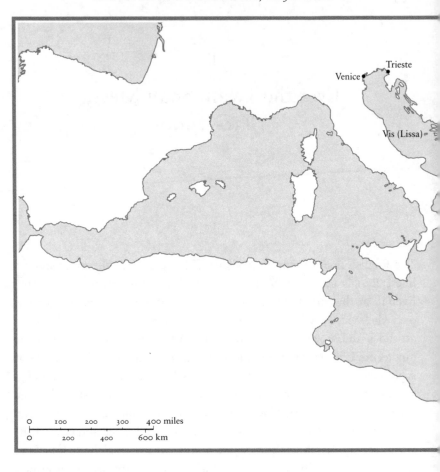

ideas, but about technology, not government. What had almost entirely disappeared by the early nineteenth century was the idea of the Ottoman realms as the seat of conquering warriors of the faith. Having lost their military and naval superiority in the East, the Ottomans were no longer the subject of fear but of fascination. Traditional ways of life caught the attention of western artists such as Delacroix, but other westerners, notably Ferdinand de Lesseps, the builder of the Suez Canal, were keen to promote modernization. The Egyptian rulers themselves were anxious to bring Egypt into Europe. They saw no contradiction between its location in an African corner of the Levant and a European vocation: Europe was (and is) an idea and an ideal rather than a place.[2]

Napoleon's campaigns in the East had already aroused enormous

interest in Egypt among the French: just as ancient Egypt had been the seat of a magnificent and wealthy empire, modern France was now equipped to play the same role in Europe, the Mediterranean and the wider world. The underlying concept was that of 'civilization', a concept that still maintains a hold on how the French think of their place in the world. This fascination with ancient Egypt began with the careful recording of ancient monuments by draughtsmen in Napoleon's army; far from being a luxurious indulgence, this was a task which expressed the central aims of the French enterprise in the eastern Mediterranean, in which France posed as the heir to the empires of the Pharaohs and the Ptolemies. Egyptian motifs did not lose their fascination after the first Napoleon: under the rule of his nephew, Napoleon III, between 1848 and 1870, the 'Second Empire style' canonized Egyptian decorative forms in elegant furnishings and architectural details. The difficulty in making contact with the mental world of the ancient Egyptians was that their scripts were unreadable. But even this problem was eventually resolved, once French troops had uncovered an inscription in hieroglyphics, hieratic script and Greek at Rosetta, which Napoleon appropriated (though it now rests in the British Museum). The decipherment of the Egyptian scripts by the young French genius Champollion, in 1822, opened new windows on to ancient Egypt and was as important as the acquisition of Algiers, a few years later, in convincing France that it possessed a mission in the lands of Ottoman allegiance within the Mediterranean.

There were enthusiasts who were obsessed by the attractions of the East. Around 1830 Barthélemy-Prosper Enfantin became the self-appointed prophet of a new sect dedicated to the creation of a link between the Mediterranean and the Red Sea. This was not simply a question of trade and engineering. Enfantin saw in the physical meeting of East and West the creation of a new world order in which the male principle, embodied in the rationally minded West, would enter into union with the female principle, embodied in the mysterious life forces of the East: 'to make the Mediterranean the nuptial bed for a marriage between the East and West and to consummate the marriage by the piercing of a canal through the isthmus of Suez'. Out of this intercourse a world of peace would emerge in which the semi-divine Enfantin would be acclaimed as the heir to St Paul, not to mention Moses, Jesus and Muhammad. This was only one feature of his thinking that attracted attention. His insistence on showing proper honour to women puzzled many in Constantinople and Cairo; his bizarre sky-blue costume with flared trousers might easily have made him a figure of fun in Paris. Yet he gained entrée into French salons, and he surveyed the terrain between the Mediterranean and Suez before he was received by Muhammad Ali, who listened politely to his plans for a canal linking East and West.[3] The viceroy of Egypt was as enthusiastic as anybody about the need to bring economic improvement to his land, but he saw a canal through the desert as a drain on his resources, not as an asset: he suspected that a canal would divert trade past the Egyptian heartlands, bringing no benefit to Alexandria or Cairo (now linked by the Nile and the Mahmudiyya canal), but plenty of profit to western European businessmen attempting to trade between France or England and India.

Enfantin's eccentricities seemed more tolerable back home in France because he colourfully expressed an assumption that began to guide French thinking about society and the economy. Under the influence of Saint-Simon's writings, Enfantin and his contemporaries insisted on the need for progressive improvement of both material and moral conditions. New technology, including railways and steamships, was beginning to transform the European economy, although the darker side of industrialization soon became visible in England. In the salons of Paris, however, theory reigned, and it continued to be nourished by the ethos of revolutionary France. Progress had become an ideal. Significantly, it had become an ideal in the Egypt of Muhammad Ali no less than in the France of Louis-Philippe. Transforming the ideal into reality, in the case of the Suez Canal, was the work of Ferdinand de Lesseps. He combined extensive diplomatic experience with mastery of the detail needed to form a Canal Company, to sell many (but not quite enough) of its shares, and, most importantly, to persist in his project until he had worn down the resistance of those who objected to his plans. His tireless travels back and forth by steamship between France and the Levant, as well as to Spain, England and elsewhere, even to Odessa, ensured that he was constantly in touch with developments throughout the complex network of politicians, investors and specialist engineers on whom the canal project depended. He had the great advantage of family ties to Louis-Napoléon, president of the Republic from 1848 and emperor from 1852 to 1870: his cousin was the empress's mother.

There were many who claimed that the canal was their idea, though there still remained, carved into the stony desert of western Sinai, traces of ancient canals built to join the Mediterranean and the Red Sea. In the third century BC, Ptolemy II Philadelphos extended what remained of a canal built by the Persians in the years around 500 BC. Links between the Nile and the Red Sea remained open, with interruptions, until the early Arab period. The aims, however, were quite limited: 'Amr ibn al-'As, the Arab conqueror of Egypt, used the canal system to convey Egyptian wheat to Mecca.[4] The idea that a canal might link the trade routes of the Mediterranean with those of the Indian Ocean was not seriously broached before the nineteenth century, for good reason: Egypt was to all intents the Nile waterway, and a parallel waterway through the desert would deprive its rulers of the tax revenues on which the Ptolemies, Fatimids and Mamluks had depended so heavily.

There were other ideas about how to create a trade route linking the two seas. In the 1820s the young English entrepreneur Thomas Waghorn noticed the long delays incurred when sending mail from India to England, and saw the potential of a route from Bombay to Suez, which could also carry those passengers who were willing to endure the heat and discomfort of a journey by carriage across the desert from the Red Sea to the Nile. Relief at reaching the Nile was tempered by consternation at the plague of rats, cockroaches, flies and fleas that infested the steamers and sailing vessels that carried passengers up river. After that, it was reasonably easy to take passage to England, since a monthly steam packet service linked Alexandria to Malta and Falmouth in Cornwall – these steamship services will be discussed later.[5] When de Lesseps met Waghorn, he was impressed, writing that 'he served as an example' – not merely of enterprise and courage but of the need to create an effective link between the Red Sea and the Mediterranean.[6] The British position remained that a Nile route was preferable. Lord Palmerston, while he was prime minister, strongly opposed de Lesseps's plans. There were technical problems that any number of land surveys failed adequately to resolve. Was the level of the Red Sea the same as that of the Mediterranean? The aim was to build a canal, not a cascade. The variety of soils – sandy desert, rocky desert, swamp – further complicated the operation. But the reasons behind Palmerston's opposition were not simply technical. Should the project succeed, the French would acquire a passage to India, their prestige in Egypt would increase immeasurably, and British interests in the Mediterranean and the Indian Ocean would suffer.

The Ottoman sultan was also far from convinced that he wanted a canal to the Red Sea to be built. In part this was a political issue. De Lesseps urged the viceroys to make their own decision about the canal, and to ignore those who argued that the canal required the permission of the Ottoman sultan himself. The first viceroy to be seduced by de Lesseps's project was Said, the obese son of Muhammad Ali, who had despaired at his child's inordinate love for macaroni. Said was in fact a canny politician who was willing to commission ground surveys, to invest heavily in de Lesseps's shares, and even to pay for the newspaper of the Suez Canal Company. Said did, it is true, waver, but the more he became involved in the schemes the more obvious it became that the losses he would incur if it collapsed were intolerable. Money was, of course, the problem, especially after de Lesseps failed to agree terms with Jacob de Rothschild in 1856.[7] De Lesseps turned to another source of finance, announcing a worldwide shares offer in which only the Egyptian viceroy and the French participated with any enthusiasm. De Lesseps was a persuasive man, as Said discovered when unsold shares had to be offloaded on the viceroy. There were rewards for Said: the new port at the northern end of the canal was named Port Said; even if at the start it was only a rough encampment, it grew rapidly as the canal progressed, and in time for the opening it acquired an impressive mole made of great concrete blocks dumped in the sea. By the time Said died, in January 1863, considerable progress had been made with the project, even if it was still far from certain that the target date of 1869 could be met: vast amounts of earth needed to be moved, and the higher ground along the designated route of the canal needed to be breached. So far, the solution was to rely on forced labour recruited by Said, corvée labour of the type that had been practised in Egypt since the days of the Children of Israel. The corvées aroused unease in Europe, because they seemed something like slavery, and because they were inefficient, with men constantly in transit from the Nile to the canal and back again.

All this changed with the accession of a new viceroy, Said's capable and efficient nephew Ismail. He had not previously favoured the canal, for he was a great landowner and disliked the corvée system, which took *fellahin* away from the fields, often in the months when they were needed most. He was a graduate of the military academy of St Cyr and was aware of Western ideas. He had no intention of democratizing his monarchy, but (rather like Tsar Alexander II) he viewed the labour system as anachronistic in a modernizing society. It was he who said: 'Egypt must become part of Europe.'[8] His suspension of the corvées left de Lesseps with the problem of where to find labour, and appeals as far east as China produced little manpower. The answer, entirely appropriate to the modernizers, was mechanization, and at the end of 1863 Borel, Lavalley and Company set to work to design a great array of machines suitable for the different soils along the canal route. About three-quarters of the soil removed to create the canal was dug up by these machines, mainly in the final two years of the building of the canal, from 1867 to 1869, but nothing was predictable: on the very last day an enormous rock was found to be protruding into the canal, threatening any ship of reasonable draft, and had to be blasted out of existence.[9] The use of machines doubled the cost of the enterprise, but without mechanization the project would never have finished on time, and swift delivery was vital if the canal were to win the approval of the viceroy, the sultan and the French emperor.

Ismail was convinced that he could use his handsome revenues from cotton to pay his contribution to the building of the canal. Egypt was well placed in the 1860s to benefit from world demand for cotton, which had boomed because the traditional supplier across the Atlantic, the United States, was immersed in civil war. In the long term, prospects were not as good as Ismail assumed, but, like too many politicians, he assumed there would be no bust after boom; in 1866 he was already short of funds, and de Lesseps arranged a loan in Paris at a hefty rate of interest without even consulting him. By the time the canal was completed Ismail Pasha had paid 240,000,000 francs towards its construction, nearly £10,000,000 at then current exchange rates.[10] Politically, Ismail found he had to steer a careful course. He persuaded the Sublime Porte to grant him a new title and the automatic right of succession through eldest sons, and saw this, with some justice, as recognition that he was now to all intents an independent sovereign. The Turks reluctantly dredged up an old Persian title, 'khedive', whose exact meaning was apparent to no one, but which seemed to be an assertion of regal authority. On the other hand, Ismail had good reason to be alarmed at the development of the powers of the Suez Canal Company, which acted, at least towards European settlers in the canal zone, as an autonomous government. The erosion of Egyptian control over the canal was already under way.

The ceremonies for the opening of the canal in November 1869 neatly expressed the desire of the khedive to be accepted among the rulers of Europe. Among the guests were Empress Eugénie of France in the paddle-steamer *L'Aigle*, Franz Josef, emperor of Austria, and princes from Prussia and the Netherlands. Religious ceremonies were held to mark the event, according to both Muslim and Christian rites. The empress's father-confessor proclaimed that 'today two worlds are made one'; 'today is a great festival for all of humanity'. This message of the brotherhood of mankind, of which Enfantin would certainly have approved, was exactly the one Ismail wished to promote. The confessor also delivered a eulogy of de Lesseps, comparing him to Christopher Columbus, while de Lesseps was convinced that no such joint ceremony of Muslims and Christians had ever before been held.[11] On 17 November a great procession of more than thirty ships set out from Port Said along the canal, and the grandees' journey was interrupted by lavish stops for refreshment and entertainment along the route. The empress's paddle-boat reached the Red Sea on 20 November and was greeted by a 21-gun salute. De Lesseps had 'converted Africa into an island', as *The Times* reported.[12]

Everything now would depend on the volume of traffic through the canal, from which the khedive optimistically hoped to derive great benefit; he was entitled to a 15 per cent share in the profits from the canal. It is no surprise that shippers and traders took a few years to adjust to the existence of a new express route to the Orient. In 1870 over 400,000 tons of goods were shipped through the canal, on nearly 500 vessels. In 1871 this rose to 750,000 tons. But the khedive had been led to believe that he would be receiving revenue from 5,000,000 tons a year, and it took a while to reach that figure. While the canal was being built, Port Said attracted plenty of French steamships (sixty-four) and many Egyptian ones too, as well as great numbers of Turkish sailing ships. Austrian sailing vessels brought coal from Wales and southern France, wood from Corsica and Istria, and wine from Provence to solace the European settlers on the barren edges of Sinai.[13] The contrast between these raw figures and those from the years following the inauguration of the canal provides a real sense of the changes that took place once the passage was opened. In the long term, there was massive growth: 486 ships passed through the canal in 1870, 765 in 1871, and for the rest of the decade the figure hovered around 1,400, breaking beyond 2,000 in 1880 and reaching a high point of over 3,600 in 1885, after which the number fell back only slightly. Despite the coolness of the British government towards the project, British businessmen were quick to take advantage, and by 1870 two-thirds of the traffic was owned by British investors. In the twenty years from 1870, the British ascendancy became stronger and stronger, so that by 1889 the United Kingdom accounted for well over 5,000,000 tons of goods, out of nearly 6,800,000 tons; this left France with a tiny proportion (362,000 tons) and smaller shares for shipping from Germany, Italy and Austria (mainly Trieste). The Board of Trade in London asserted: 'the trade between Europe and the East flows more and more through the Canal, and the British Flag covers an ever increasing proportion of this trade'.[14]

This was a bright future, but in 1870 shareholders could only hope, and their uncertainty grew as the Canal Company proved unable to produce a dividend, or, as a French pamphlet proclaimed: 'The agony of the Suez Canal – Zero results – Next comes ruin!'[15] De Lesseps decided to focus his attention on another canal project, through Panama (which was beyond his technical and financial capacity), and the French emperor, defeated in war by Prussia, was forced into exile while Paris was taken over by its communards. Once order was restored in Paris, the Third Republic proclaimed its firm support for the canal, but was unable to help the hapless investors. Ismail had been largely abandoned, and in 1872, out of funds, he was forced to raise a loan of 800,000,000 francs (£32,000,000); by 1875 his debts were approaching £100,000,000, and simply servicing them, at about £5,000,000 per annum, was draining away his resources faster than he could accumulate them – in 1863 the Egyptian government had received less than that in tax revenues. His attraction to lenders lay in his collateral: he possessed large numbers of Suez Canal shares, including those dumped on Egypt by de Lesseps when foreign investors had proved reluctant to buy. He had steered Egypt towards greater political independence, but the financial cost was so great that he risked compromising that independence. In 1875 the only option seemed to be the sale of the Egyptian shares. French buyers were ready to pounce. Then Benjamin Disraeli received intelligence of what was happening and saw that, for £4,000,000, he had the opportunity to gain partial control of the Mediterranean route to the Indies. He informed Queen Victoria that purchase of the shares, 'an affair of millions', 'would give the possessor an immense, not to say preponderating, influence in the management of the Canal. It is vital to Your Majesty's authority and power at this critical moment, that the Canal should belong to England.' By the end of 1875 the British government found itself the owner of 44 per cent of all canal shares, making it the largest shareholder. Disraeli informed the queen: 'it is just settled: you have it, Madam'.[16]

This purchase had enormous consequences for Egypt and the Mediterranean. An Anglo-French Dual Control Commission was set in place to administer the Egyptian state treasury and to impose proper discipline on the khedival budget, vastly increasing the influence of Great Britain in Egyptian affairs. However, the commission authorized the sale of the khedive's right to 15 per cent of the canal revenues to a

French bank for a knockdown sum, which hardly bolstered his position. The Ottoman sultan, with good reason, saw this as the first step towards an Anglo-French takeover of Egypt, while Ismail's dependence on foreign loans would endanger the annual tribute the khedive paid to Constantinople. Ismail dreamed of finding new assets within Sudan, but sending armies to the south cost more money than he could afford. He became increasingly isolated: in 1879 the sultan removed him from office, though in these kinder times he suffered no worse a penalty than exile in the Bay of Naples. Yet in deposing Ismail, the sultan was in reality bowing to pressure from the Dual Control Commission, and the succession of Ismail's son Tawfiq, who was friendly to the European powers, only brought Egypt deeper into the British web. By 1882 Tawfiq was under immense pressure at home: an army coup installed an Arab-led government that was hostile to the old Turkish-Albanian elite. In late summer 1882, with the help of an army despatched from England, British forces bombarded Alexandria, where a massacre of foreigners had taken place, to European disgust; the British secured the Suez Canal and advanced towards Cairo, with the public aim of restoring Tawfiq to his throne.[17] Egypt now became to all intents a British protectorate, even if the khedive (and his successors, the kings of Egypt) were allowed considerable autonomy. In deposing Ismail, the sultan had set off a series of events that led to the final loss of Egypt by the Ottoman Empire, but in reality the sequence of events had begun when de Lesseps's labourers turned the first sod of the Suez Canal.

II

The other transformation that took place in the Mediterranean in the middle of the nineteenth century was the coming of steamships, followed by the arrival of ironclad vessels. The first attempts to build steamboats can be dated as far back as the 1780s, in the United States and France. The fundamental new features of steam navigation were speed, reliability and regularity. Speed should not be exaggerated; eight knots was considered fast. Nonetheless, the steamship route from Trieste to Constantinople, instituted in 1837, took two weeks, as against a month or even forty days by sailing ship, and by the end of the century larger, ironclad, screw-driven steamships reached the Turkish capital in less than a week. Steamships did not need to tack in the face of contrary winds and could face the Mediterranean in all seasons. Shipping was less constrained by the traditional routes that followed prevailing winds and currents; in other words, routes from point to point became more direct, and it became possible to predict with a fair degree of accuracy when a ship would arrive. On the other hand, steamships were very expensive, and – whereas sailing ships were empty of machinery down below – the hold of a steamship was full of fuel (in the form of coal), not to mention the engines and boilers, which occupied the prime position amidships, as well as the quarters provided for the crew and passengers; they also carried sail to augment or replace steam power when appropriate. One report explained that 'steamships cannot be and never will be cargo ships'; because they provided an express service, they did not linger in ports loading and unloading cargoes in the rather casual way a sailing vessel might.[18]

It became obvious that steamships would be most useful for transporting mail, including bank transfers; in other words, steamships could play a vital ancillary role in trade, accelerating the speed of payments and the spread of commercial information, as well as providing space for passengers who found steam packet ships more comfortable. The French government was planning steam packet routes as early as 1831, when steamships opened a route from Marseilles to southern Italy.[19] Timetables could be constructed: in 1837 the Austrian government entered into a contract with the Austrian Lloyd Company, based in Trieste, for two voyages a month from Trieste to Constantinople and Alexandria, visiting Corfu, Patras, Athens, Crete and Smyrna, and carrying coin, mail and passengers.[20] Four years earlier a group of insurance underwriters in Trieste had established the organization known as Lloyd Austriaco, taking the name from the London coffee house where a similar cooperative organization of underwriters had emerged in the eighteenth century. In 1835 Austrian Lloyd created a steamship company, in the realization that their work as insurers would benefit enormously from access to up-to-date information; 60 per cent of stock in Austrian Lloyd was snapped up by the Rothschilds in Vienna, and the London branch of the Rothschild bank helped supply ships and engines from England.[21] In 1838 the Austrian Lloyd fleet consisted of ten steamships, the largest of which, the *Mahmudié*, was, significantly, named after the canal linking Alexandria to the Nile, and displaced 410 tons; its engines produced

120 horsepower. The fleet was decribed by the British consul in Trieste as 'well-constructed, well-equipped, and well-manned'.[22]

Outside the Mediterranean, the Peninsular Steam Navigation Company established services from England through the Straits of Gibraltar; it had already begun to specialize in a packet service between England and Iberia (this was the 'peninsular' part of the title of the firm that became Peninsular and Oriental, or P & O), and took as its colours the red and gold of the Spanish flag and the blue and white of the Portuguese flag then current. P & O rivalry with Austrian Lloyd caused some annoyance: in 1845 the British company established a route right across the Mediterranean and into the Black Sea, as far as Trebizond – once in the Black Sea, the British threatened to clash further with the commercial interests of Austrian steamships that plied up and down the Danube and along the Black Sea coasts.[23] Steam navigation had turned into a success story: European powers competed to gain ascendancy along the trade routes, and yet the competition remained remarkably peaceful: some naval conflicts did break out in the mid-nineteenth-century Mediterranean, but the threat of piracy had been very greatly reduced since the American and French victories in Barbary, and clashes between armed fleets were rare after the Greek War of Independence.

One exception is provided by the conflict that culminated in an Austrian naval victory over the newly established Italian fleet at Lissa, now known as Vis, in July 1866. The Austrian acquisition of Venice after the Napoleonic Wars brought the Venetian fleet under Austrian command, and for a period the Austrians also controlled fleets in Tuscan lands briefly ruled by the Habsburgs – until 1848, Italian was the language of command in the Habsburg navy and the majority of sailors were Italian, though by 1866 Germans accounted for 60 per cent of manpower.[24] The Habsburg fleet was well managed; the emperor's brother Ferdinand Maximilian, later to meet a tragic fate in Mexico as Emperor Maximilian, served as commander-in-chief between 1854 and 1864, and appreciated the advantages not simply of steam power but of cladding the hulls of his ships in iron. He found the fleet to consist of sailing ships and a few paddle-steamers; he commissioned screw-driven schooners, followed later by armour-plated frigates, which were particularly expensive – in 1861 Austrian foundries were not up to the task of producing iron plates at sufficient speed and in sufficient quantity, and the plates had to be ordered from the Loire Valley and exported from Marseilles in strict secrecy. Engines, though, were constructed at a new factory in Trieste, in which the emperor had a financial stake. He let his brother spend whatever he thought was necessary.[25]

Rule over lands in northern Italy had brought the Habsburg emperor into conflict with the forces that sought to unify the peninsula under the house of Savoy. An alliance between Prussia and the kingdom of Italy threatened Austrian control of Venice and north-eastern Italy. When the Austrian and Italian fleets met off the Croatian coast at Lissa the Austrian fleet was outnumbered – the Italians possessed twelve ironclad steamships, while the Austrians had only mobilized seven. The number of unarmoured steamships in the Italian side was also slightly higher. On the other hand, the Italians had clearly given little thought to the form action would need to take. An engagement between ironclads was a novelty, and the Austrians decided that the correct tactics (in a throwback to classical antiquity) would be to ram the enemy. Although this did no favours to their ships, the Austrians did manage to sink two Italian ironclads. The Austrian commander admitted: 'the whole thing was chaos . . . It is a miracle we did not lose a single ship.' Against the odds, the Austrians had won.[26] The victory did not assure them of Venice, which they lost to the Italian kingdom, but it did prevent Italy from gaining control of the Dalmatian coast (from which a number of the 'Austrian' sailors originated).[27] If anything, the loss of Venice after Lissa only enhanced the importance of Trieste as the gateway of the Habsburg empire in the Mediterranean.

Trieste boomed under Habsburg rule. Thirty years before the Suez Canal opened, an American diplomat in Vienna reported to the Secretary of State in Washington in glowing terms:

> Trieste itself is a beautiful and for the greater part a new city – and, as in new cities generally, there is much activity and business. Its harbour is excellent with a sufficient depth of water for almost any vessel. It contains 50,000 inhabitants mostly engaged in commerce which is said to be lucrative and rapidly increasing. Its imports amount to 50 millions of Florins [over $100,000,000] and its exports to 40 millions.[28]

Trieste faced many challenges: the quality of goods coming down from the Habsburg hinterland around Vienna and Prague was not especially high, making it difficult for Trieste to sell Austrian products in the Mediterranean, while access to the Austrian heartlands was blocked by the

Alps. On the other hand, Trieste was a free port able to enjoy generous exemptions from standard commercial taxes. As early as 1717 the city had received privileges from Emperor Charles VI of Austria, and behind that lay an even longer tradition of trade within the Adriatic – Charles V had granted the merchants of Trieste special rights in southern Italy in 1518. In these centuries Trieste was still very small, greatly overshadowed by Venice, from whose political tutelage it had escaped in the fourteenth century. It took much longer to escape Venice's economic domination: at the end of the eighteenth century Venetian merchants were trans-shipping goods via Trieste to benefit from its status as a free port. Further privileges, along with maritime law codes, were acquired at the end of the eighteenth century under Empress Maria Theresa, and Trieste was able to exploit its position even more when Venice lost its independence in 1797: in 1805 537 ships were registered at Trieste, the vast majority owned by Venetians.[29]

There was another side to Trieste that was distinctive. Aware of the success of Livorno, Charles VI created an enclave in which buinessmen of all faiths could settle and prosper. After Joseph II proclaimed his Edicts of Toleration in the 1780s, the Jews and other ethnic groups were guaranteed their security.[30] The ghetto of Trieste, squeezed on to the hillside beneath the castle, was abolished in 1785. One Jewish writer, Elia Morpurgo, who was also a silk producer, praised Maria Theresa as the 'woman of valour' described in the Book of Proverbs, for she had caused commerce to flourish to the advantage of her subjects: 'open ports, roads made short, convenient and easy, the flag at sea respected and secure'. The other religious groups to be found in Trieste included Armenians, Greek Orthodox, Lutherans, Calvinists, Serbian Orthodox. Each group was organized as a *nazione* which was expected to consider the well-being of the city before admitting more settlers, who should be economically useful, not vagabonds. Behind the religious labels could be found any number of ethnic groups, notably Slovenes and Croats from close by, but also German, Dutch, English, Albanian and Turkish migrants or visitors, a *guazzabuglia*, or disordered mix of peoples and tongues, though the languages that dominated public life were Italian and German.[31]

The city of Italo Svevo is particularly famous for its Jewish community, which was well integrated into local society by the 1830s, while it retained its own schools and institutions. Indeed, the rabbis became very exercised about standards of religious observance, whether breaches of the Sabbath or a casual attitude to the Jewish dietary laws.[32] The Jewish population grew substantially, from just over 100 in 1735, when the town had a total population of fewer than 4,000, to 2,400 in 1818, when Trieste had grown to contain over 33,000 inhabitants. Freer from restrictions than elsewhere in the Habsburg dominions, the Jews of Trieste played a significant role in the economic development of the city. Theory as well as practice appealed to them – G. V. Bolaffio wrote a book about currency exchange, and Samuel Vital wrote about insurance, while in later decades Triestino Jews were prominent in the development of the study of accounting, economics and commercial law. Jews also took an active part in the *Borsa*, or Stock Exchange, and were involved in the foundation of Austrian Lloyd: the founders included the Jews Rodrigues da Costa and Kohen, the Greek Apostopoulo, the Slav Vučetić, the Rhinelander Bruck and the Ligurian Sartorio, the last two of whom pleased the monarchy so much that they were ennobled.[33] This mixing of peoples provided a cultural stimulus as well. By the end of the century Trieste was famous for its literary cafés, beginning with the Caffé degli Specchi, 'of the mirrors', founded in 1837, and intellectual and political life at the end of the nineteenth century was dominated by the question whether Trieste belonged in Italy or Austria, quite apart from the presence within the city of an increasingly self-conscious Slovene population.[34]

Viewed from Vienna, another city where many peoples managed to coexist in varying degrees of tension, Trieste appeared the ideal gateway to the East. The thirty years after 1830 saw a gradual expansion of business through its port: the tonnage of imports more than doubled, while the number of steamships began to increase at the expense of sailing vessels, showing that steamships gradually found space for merchandise. In 1852 nearly 80 per cent of goods arrived on sailing ships, but by 1857 only about two-thirds did so. The major trading partner of Trieste was the Ottoman Empire, accounting for around one third of exports in the 1860s, but the United States, Brazil, Egypt, England, Greece all enjoyed regular contact with Trieste; its shipping took third place after Great Britain and France in the commerce of Alexandria, ahead of Turkey and Italy, nor did this business slacken in the late nineteenth century. The range of goods is also impressive, though most were simply forwarded to Vienna and the Habsburg heartlands: coffee, tea and cocoa, large quantities of pepper, rice and cotton.[35] Between the year the canal opened and 1899, the quantity of goods transported almost quadrupled.[36]

The history of Trieste and of Austrian Lloyd reveals the opportunities and frustrations faced by those seeking to exploit the new conditions in the Mediterranean during the nineteenth century. Mediterranean navigation had changed beyond recognition: the Great Sea was now a passage-way to the Indian Ocean, and making the passage was an entirely different experience from anything in past times; information shuttled back and forth as the mail networks developed; there was a greater degree of peace and safety than at any time since the heyday of the Roman Empire. Yet it was not the Austrians, nor the Turks, nor even the French, who dominated the Mediterranean, but imperial Britain.

2

The Greek and the unGreek,
1830–1920

I

An important feature of the Fifth Mediterranean was the discovery of the First Mediterranean, and the rediscovery of the Second. The Greek world came to encompass Bronze Age heroes riding the chariots described by Homer, and the Roman world was found to have deep roots among the little-known Etruscans. Thus, during the nineteenth and early twentieth centuries entirely new perspectives on the history of the Mediterranean were opened up. An early lead was given by the growth of interest in ancient Egypt, discussed in the previous chapter, though that was closely linked to traditional biblical studies as well. In the eighteenth century, the Grand Tour introduced well-heeled travellers from northern Europe to classical remains in Rome and Sicily, and Englishmen saw it as an attractive alternative to time spent at Oxford or Cambridge, where those who paid any attention to their studies were more likely to be immersed in ancient texts than in ancient objects.[1] On the other hand, aesthetic appreciation of ancient works of art was renewed in the late eighteenth century, as the German art historian Winckelmann began to impart a love for the forms of Greek art, arguing that the Greeks dedicated themselves to the representation of beauty (as the Romans failed to do). His *History of Art in Antiquity* was published in German in 1764 and in French very soon afterwards, and was enormously influential.

In the next few decades, discoveries at Pompeii and Herculaneum, in which Nelson's cuckolded host, Sir William Hamilton, was closely involved, and then in Etruria, further enlarged northern European interest in ancient art, providing interior designers with rich patterns, and collectors with vast amounts of loot – 'Etruscan vases', nearly all in reality

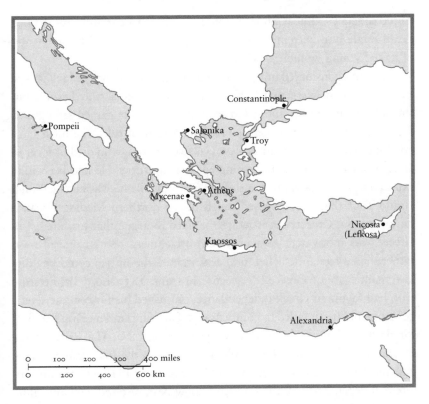

Greek, were shipped out of Italy as the Etruscan tombs began to be opened up. In Greece, it was necessary to purchase the consent of Ottoman officials before excavating and exporting what was found; the most famous case, that of the Parthenon marbles at the start of the nineteenth century, was succeeded by other acquisitions for northern museums: the Pergamon altar was sent to Berlin, the facings of the Treasury of Atreus from Mycenae were sent to the British Museum, and so on. The survival of so many sculptures of naked men and women aroused aesthetic and, not surprisingly, erotic passions. It became possible to make proxy visits to the ancient sites of the Mediterranean by wandering through the great museums of England, France and Germany, where the ancient collections were suffused with the principles of Winckelmann: to understand classical art, it was vital to appreciate its beauty.[2] The Mediterranean world was also imported into northern Europe by way of the imaginative reconstructions of the classical past painted by artists such as Lawrence Alma-Tadema and J. W. Waterhouse in England.

Alma-Tadema's almost photographic attention to carefully researched detail made him extremely popular, as, undoubtedly, did the inclusion of naked young women in several of his canvases.[3]

It was not considered important to tread the soil of ancient Hellas. The legends of Troy were myths about nonexistent gods and heroes, but romantic assumptions about Greece and the Greeks gained strength as the Greeks emancipated themselves from Ottoman rule. The most famous exponent of this romantic view was Lord Byron, who died of fever in 1824 in Greece while campaigning against the Turks. He had been fully exposed to the classical past a decade earlier, while he was engaged on a Grand Tour that encompassed much of the northern Mediterranean – Italy, Albania, Greece. Yet it would be hard to argue that his interest in Greece was motivated by a profound attachment to its classical past, rather than a romantic belief in liberty. Indeed, the British could be quite unromantic about Greece. Between 1848 and 1850 Lord Palmerston, who had favoured Greek independence, unleashed his fury on the Greek government after it failed to compensate a Gibraltarian Jew, Don Pacifico, for damage done to his property by a rioting mob. The Royal Navy blockaded Athens until the Greeks gave way, to the fury of the French and the Russians, who, with Great Britain, were the co-guarantors of Greek independence. But Palmerston knew best, resoundingly appealing to the classics against, not in favour of, the behaviour of the Greeks:

> As the Roman, in days of old, held himself free from indignity, when he could say, *civis Romanus sum*, so also a British subject, in whatever land he may be, shall feel confident that the watchful eye and the strong arm of England will protect him from injustice and wrong.

Something of the spirit of ancient Hellas could be assumed to have persisted in the Greek love of liberty, but it was not easy to see the descendants of Perikles and Plato in the Greeks of the early nineteenth century. And if one wanted true Romans, one needed only to turn to the British.

II

There were a few who believed literally in the tales of Troy. The discovery of the civilizations of the Aegean Bronze Age began, as has been seen, with the literalist obsessions of Heinrich Schliemann, who first visited Troy in 1868 and who, five years later, unearthed what he declared to be the 'Treasure of Priam'. At a time when the principles of stratigraphy and dating were still undeveloped, Schliemann happily applied instinct in the identification of whatever he found. Passing through Ithaka, he pulled out of the ground a score of ancient urns; the problem was not whether they were the urns of Odysseus' family, but which member's ashes lay in which urn.[4] In 1876 he was already digging at Mycenae, which was easier to identify than Troy, for the Lion Gate had remained partially visible over the millennia. There, predictably, he found the tombs of Agamemnon and family. He was more interested in validating Homer than in the political implications of his discoveries, but racial theorists soon began to capitalize on his revelations, arguing that the founders of the first Greek civilization, and therefore of high European culture, had been blond, blue-eyed Aryans.[5] In scholarly circles, though, it took a long while – eighty years – to convince anyone that the Mycenaeans were closely related to later Greeks and even spoke an early form of Greek. And here the arguments turned on the peculiar scripts that excavators began to find in Greece and Crete: it was tiny hieroglyphs to which his short-sighted eyes were well suited that drew Sir Arthur Evans to Crete, and led him to uncover and, no less importantly, reconstruct what he called the 'palace of Minos at Knossos'.

Evans's career in Crete is best understood against the background of political and social changes that were taking place on the island at the end of the nineteenth and start of the twentieth centuries. By 1900 around 30 per cent of Cretans were Muslim, mostly Greek-speaking and of Greek descent. The Muslims included the major landholders and a high proportion of merchants, and the Muslim population was concentrated in the towns, while the Christians were traditionally scattered in the countryside.[6] The winning of independence by the Greeks of the mainland raised hopes among Christian Cretans that they would be able to enter the new kingdom. Their aim was *enôsis*, 'union'; and following a Greek rebellion against the Ottomans in 1821, which lasted a good nine years, trouble simmered in Crete throughout the century. Greek historians note the ruthless reprisals of the Turks, though neither side had clean hands – at the end of the century the Muslims of eastern Crete suffered horribly. The European powers recognized that Crete could not simply be added to the Greek kingdom; with Turkish consent, it was conferred on Muhammad Ali, and for ten years from 1830 the island was governed from Egypt. A committee of Greeks offered the island to Great Britain, which had no interest in governing Crete or in upsetting the eastern Mediterranean apple-cart.[7] The Ottomans were perfectly aware of the need to compromise, and permitted the Cretans ever greater autonomy from 1868 onwards, though this did not satisfy the advocates of *enôsis*, and by 1897 they were recruiting volunteers to their cause from as far away as Scandinavia, Britain and Russia.

In 1898 the war-torn island was finally granted complete autonomy under a High Commissioner, Prince George of Greece, under French, Italian and British protection, but the sultan in Constantinople remained the nominal suzerain, for he simply would not let go of his lands, still less when the beneficiaries would mainly be Greek Christians. The island government, on which both communities were represented, tried with all its energy to stimulate the economy, but many Muslims left Crete now peace had come, and many had already fled while civil war was being waged. Reconstructing the economy was understood to involve a reconstruction of Cretan identity as well. In 1898 Arthur Evans required plenty of hands to help him excavate Knossos, and among its first acts the Cretan government obligingly passed a series of laws encouraging foreign archaeological projects and even permitting the export of artefacts.[8] The Cretans saw this as a public relations exercise, a chance to make Crete's presence known through revealing its past in the museums of the protecting powers.

Here was an island in search of peace, and, as his diggers exposed Knossos, Evans conjured up an image of a peaceful Crete in his attempt to interpret the puzzling ruins that he found. Evans's Crete was a kingdom ruled by someone he assumed to be named Minos. His interpretation reflected his sincere wishes for the future of Crete as much as his assumptions about its past; he viewed Minoan Crete as a gentle, nature-loving matriarchal society, in which even the king's male courtiers became feminized: dedicated followers of fashion whose delight, like that of the court women, was in pirouetting on the great 'Dancing Floor' he had identified. He made his workmen dance for him in an attempt to recover the magic of Minoan Crete.[9] Out of small fragments of Minoan frescoes big, bold paintings of peace-loving princes and chattering court ladies were reconstructed. The reconstructed palace at Knossos, which owed so much to his fertile imagination, was thus a modernist temple of peace.

III

Cyprus, whose history in many respects mirrored that of Crete, was another island where the Turks found themselves under increasing pressure, although the Muslim proportion of the population remained a little lower. There, events within mainland Greece had a great impact: from 1821 onwards the Greek Cypriots became restive, and the Turkish governor prohibited non-Muslims from carrying arms. Up to 25,000 Cypriots left for Greece in the 1830s, aiming to acquire Greek citizenship before returning to the island as subjects of the Greek king, which brought them the protection of the British, Russian and French consuls as guarantors of Greek independence, to the irritation of the Ottoman authorities.[10] Even so, the sense of 'Greekness' of the Orthodox majority on Cyprus should not be exaggerated: ideas of union with a Greek motherland were generated more in Greece than in Cyprus, where for long periods inter-community relations had been quite peaceful. The British consulate in Cyprus cooperated with the Turkish authorities to ensure that Greek advocates of *enôsis* were kept under control: in 1854 the British vice-consul supplied the governor with information about a treasonable pamphlet attributed to the principal of the Greek high school in Nicosia. The warm ties between the vice-consul and the governor were also expressed in an invitation from the governor to a party in honour of his son's circumcision in 1864: 'I beg to invite you for the whole duration of the festival, which will begin on Monday and continue until Thursday, and also to dinner on the four days.'[11] Given its position between Anatolia, Syria and Egypt, the value of Cyprus was primarily strategic. It produced a surplus of some basic agricultural goods such as barley, exported to Syria, and carob, exported to Alexandria, but the standard of living was not high, and – to cite a late eighteenth-century visitor – 'imports were of very small consequence, because Cyprus imported just enough for the wants of its own scanty inhabitants': some fine cloths, tin, iron, pepper and dyestuffs.[12] By the late nineteenth century dyes were put to good use in local industry: white English calico cloths were brought across from Beirut and dyed in local workshops, and quite an active silk industry developed. But Cyprus formed part of a local, eastern Mediterranean, network, and its international connections were rather limited.[13] However, with the growth in interest in antiquities, a new and largely illicit trade out of Cyprus began to grow. Between 1865 and 1875, the American consul, General Louis Palma di Cesnola, was one of the most assiduous collectors of what he called 'my treasures'; much of his plunder from the magnificent site at Kourion reached the Metropolitan Museum in New York.[14]

The weakness of Ottoman power in the eastern Mediterranean became ever more obvious when the British prevailed upon the sultan to cede the administration of the island to Great Britain in 1878. The sultan, Abdülhamid II, understood that he needed British support if he were to keep the Russians at bay, for the Russians still hoped to establish a permanent presence in the Mediterranean, which could be achieved only if they were able to maintain free access through the Bosphorus and Dardanelles. British support for the Ottomans was ebbing away as news reached Great Britain of massacres of Armenians and others who opposed Turkish authority; British sympathy for the Greeks living beyond the boundaries of the independent kingdom also remained very strong.[15] So Cyprus was seen as a down-payment for continuing friendship. In the typical Ottoman style, the Sublime Porte retained notional sovereignty over the island, and the British were supposed to remit any profits from their administration to Constantinople (it was only when Britain and Turkey faced one another on opposite sides during the First World War that the island was annexed by Great Britain, and only in 1925 that Cyprus became a Crown Colony). British interest in Cyprus was purely strategic, following the acquisition of the massive British share in the Suez Canal, and its value was enhanced when Great Britain established its ascendancy over Egypt in 1882. Tenure of Cyprus granted Britain control of bases all the way from Gibraltar to the Levant, by way of Malta, but Britain had acquired a cauldron in which anatagonism between Cypriots of the two faiths was not eased but exacerbated by living under the rule of a third party: the Greek islanders became increasingly insistent that the destiny of the island lay within Greece, while the Turkish islanders feared that what was happening to the Turks in Crete would begin to happen in Cyprus as well. By the start of the twentieth century, Turkish Cypriots were following with avid interest the reform movement of the Young Turks in the Ottoman Empire, and a sense of national identity began to develop, which was further accentuated by competition with Greek nationalism.[16] The erosion of the

Ottoman Empire was, then, accompanied by increasingly assertive expressions of national identity that threatened to tear apart societies where once different ethnic and religious groups had lived in some degree of harmony.

IV

National identities were developing in Ottoman lands where ethnic and religious groups were scattered and intermingled. It is no surprise that the greatest jumble of peoples and faiths could be found in Mediterranean port cities such as Salonika, Alexandria and Smyrna. Salonika, in particular, became the battleground between Turks, Slavs and Greeks, even though the Jews were the largest single group in the city in 1912, and there were so many Jewish stevedores that the docks closed on Saturdays.[17] As Mark Mazower has observed, four main scripts were in use in the city, and four calendars, so the question 'At what time is noon today?' made a sort of sense.[18] In large parts of the city the main language was Judaeo-Spanish, brought by the Sephardic exiles after 1492. The names of the synagogues still recalled the places of origin of the Salonika Jews: there was a synagogue of the Catalans, of 'Saragossa' (in reality Syracuse in Sicily), and one nicknamed *Macarron*, because it was frequented by Jews of Apulian descent, who were believed to share the Italian love of macaroni.[19]

It would be a mistake to romanticize Salonika. In 1911 the view was expressed in a Ladino newspaper, *La Solidad Ovradera*, that

> Salonika is not one city. It is a juxtaposition of tiny villages. Jews, Turks,
> Dönmehs [followers of Shabbetai Zevi], Greeks, Bulgarians, westerners,
> Gypsies, each of these groups that one today calls 'nations', keeps well
> away from the others, as if fearing contagion.[20]

Admittedly, a newspaper entitled *Workers' Solidarity* might not have been offering the most objective view of relations between ethnic groups, wishing, rather, to transcend national feeling and to create a single proletarian community. Some sense of easy daily interaction between Jews, Turks and others can be gathered from Leon Sciaky's account of his childhood in late nineteenth-century Salonika; here, a prosperous Jewish family is shown enjoying warm relations with Bulgarian peasants who supplied Sciaky's father with the grain he traded, while on the streets of the city the young Sciaky received many kindnesses from Muslim and Christian neighbours, who were often willing to help members of other communities when rioting broke out.[21]

Sephardic Judaism has always been more open to surrounding cultures than the often stricter forms of Judaism practised in Ashkenazi eastern Europe, and, as western European influences became increasingly powerful within the Ottoman world, the Jewish elites became westernized in manners and speech. There was ambivalence about Sephardic identity. Ideally, it would combine western sophistication with a touch of eastern exoticism, a view shared by Disraeli in Britain. Even as a child, Leon Sciaky wore western clothes, a clear sign of his family's social and economic status and of their cultural aspirations, while Salonika's wealthiest Jewish family, the Allatini, surrounded themselves at home with the finest furnishings from both East and West.[22] From 1873, channelled through the new schools of the Alliance Israélite Universelle, French began to make massive inroads among the Salonika Jews, edging out Ladino, which some saw as the language of the lower classes (in Alexandria too French was becoming *de mode*, even *de rigueur*, among the Jewish elite). By 1912 the AIU possessed over 4,000 pupils, more than half the children in the city's Jewish schools.[23] The Salonikans and Alexandrians were unworried about the French cultural imperialism to which they were succumbing; not just Jews but all prosperous city-dwellers across the Ottoman Empire saw French as a badge of distinction.

While they still ruled Salonika, the Turks knew that, though a minority, they had the upper hand. Sciaky reported how in 1876 riots broke out when a Bulgarian father appealed to the foreign consuls to prevent the wedding of his daughter to a Turk; the French and German consuls made the cardinal error of entering a mosque while tempers were flaring, and were lynched.[24] Unrest among the different communities became more intense by 1900. The Greeks were fired by the spread of education: children were now taught their own language in proper schools, and they could look southwards and observe the fact that their brethren lived in an independent Greek kingdom. The Slavs became very restive. In the 1890s radical Macedonian Slavs, who spoke a form of Bulgarian, organized themselves around the Internal Macedonian Revolutionary Organization (IMRO), seeking autonomy for the wide swathe of Ottoman provinces between Salonika and Skopje, but they saw Salonika as the obvious capital, and they were intent on giving these lands a Bulgarian cultural identity. This was intolerable to the Greeks of Salonika, who obliged the Turks with information they picked up about the activities of IMRO.[25] Before long IMRO decided that the time had come for drastic action. In January 1903 its agents acquired a small grocery shop opposite the Ottoman Bank, staffed by a dour Bulgarian who seemed unwilling to sell the exiguous stock he displayed. At night, though, the shop came to life, as an IMRO team burrowed under the road, placing mines under the handsome edifice of the Ottoman Bank. The tunnellers were almost caught, because they had blocked off one of the city sewers that lay across their path, and the Hotel Colombo, nearby, complained that its plumbing had ceased to work. On 28 April they set off their bombs, demolishing the bank and several neighbouring buildings.[26]

Salonika felt the strong ripples of change within the Turkish government, as the Young Turks asserted themselves and political reform was in the air. Political troubles in the Mediterranean were depriving Salonika of its livelihood: Italian goods were boycotted after the Italians invaded Tripolitania in 1911, and trade with Trieste was boycotted because the Austrians had, controversially, taken control of Bosnia. The wealthy Allatini had had enough and decamped to Italy. Ottoman power was crumbling faster than ever, and it was no great surprise when the Greeks marched into Salonika in 1912, claiming it for the motherland. Unfortunately, Bulgarian troops also arrived, and were unwilling to leave; even when they were persuaded to depart, skirmishes broke out between Greek and Bulgarian units beyond the walls. So the Greeks held Salonika, but the Bulgarian threat was real, and the city was deprived of the fertile hinterland from which Leon Sciaky's father had obtained grain. In 1913, the city was still home to nearly 46,000 Muslims and over 61,000 Jews, as against 40,000 Orthodox Christians, but Greek activists intended to make them feel unwelcome.[27] Cemeteries were desecrated and shops were ransacked. The prime minister, Venizelos, a hero of the Cretan revolution, was a strong believer in the idea of a Greece populated by Orthodox Greeks. Quite where this left the Jews, of whom Venizelos remained suspicious, was unclear. In August 1917, a great fire destroyed vast tracts of the city, wrecking the Jewish and Muslim districts. The fire, along with increasing Jewish and Muslim emigration, gave the Greek authorities the opportunity to forge ahead with the rebuilding of Salonika as a Greek city, populated by Greeks. The aim was clear: Salonika would again become the Christian city of St Demetrios. Salonika would be reborn as Thessaloniki.

3
Ottoman Exit,
1900–1918

The history of the Mediterranean has been presented in this book as a series of phases in which the sea was, to a greater or lesser degree, integrated into a single economic and even political area. With the coming of the Fifth Mediterranean the whole character of this process changed. The Mediterranean became the great artery through which goods, warships, migrants and other travellers reached the Indian Ocean from the Atlantic. The falling productivity of the lands surrounding the Mediterranean, and the opening of high-volume trade in grain from Canada or tobacco from the United States (to cite two examples), rendered the Mediterranean less interesting to businessmen. Even the revived cotton trade of Egypt faced competition from India and the southern United States. Steamship lines out of Genoa headed across the western Mediterranean and out into the Atlantic, bearing to the New World hundreds of thousands of migrants, who settled in New York, Chicago, Buenos Aires, São Paulo and other booming cities of North and South America in the years around 1900. Italian emigration was dominated by southerners, for the inhabitants of the southern villages saw none of the improvement in the standard of living that was beginning to transform Milan and other northern centres.

For the French, on the other hand, opportunities to create a new life elsewhere could be found within the Mediterranean: Algeria became the focus of French emigration, for the ideal was to create a new France on the shores of North Africa, while keeping the wilder interior under colonial rule. Two manifestations of this policy were the rebuilding of large areas of Algiers as a European city, and the collective extension of French citizenship to 35,000 Algerian Jews, in 1870. The Algerian Jews

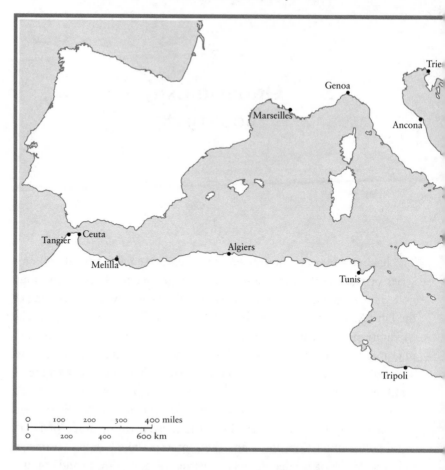

were seen as *évolué*, 'civilized', for they had embraced the opportunities provided by French rule, opening modern schools under the auspices of the Alliance Israélite Universelle, founded to promote Jewish education on the European model, and transforming themselves into a new professional class.[1] From the 1880s onwards, after it fell under French control, Tunisia also attracted French colonists, though more slowly; around 1900 it was a more popular target for Italian settlers than for French ones. The kingdom of Italy also looked towards North Africa, as its political leaders saw opportunities to establish their country as a colonial power within the Mediterranean comparable to France. The Italians were not yet articulating the idea of the Mediterranean as *Mare Nostrum*, as Mussolini would do in the 1930s, for it was obvious that

Great Britain dominated the sea, but Italian public opinion, and Italian democrats, were convinced that Italy possessed an imperial destiny. In part, the arguments were moral: as in French Algeria, there was an opportunity to bring European civilization to peoples condescendingly regarded as backward. In part they were political: Italy would lose influence within Europe if it could not show itself capable of grandiose achievements. To a large extent the arguments were economic: the strength of the Italian state would depend on its economic advancement, and that was possible only if one could take advantage of the raw materials supplied by a colonial territory. Spain, which by 1904 had extended its control of the Moroccan coastline to include Tetuán and the hinterland of Ceuta and Melilla, was only a minor competitor.[2]

The collapse of state finances in Tunisia during the 1860s provided opportunities for both France and Italy. Large numbers of French creditors would suffer if the bey and his government could not meet their obligations. The situation was not vastly different from that in the Egypt of Said and Ismail. An international financial commission was established, which the French aimed to dominate. The Italian government was not happy with this: the heavy involvement of Italians in the Tunisian economy, and the large number of Italian settlers encouraged Italy to demand control over whole areas of the Tunisian economy, such as the production and export of tobacco, and the running of the railways. By 1883, however, the French had managed to secure a dominant position, and the bey agreed to the creation of a French protectorate over Tunisia.[3] The Italian government was forced to look in other directions, and rapidly saw that similar opportunities existed close by, in Ottoman-ruled Libya; by 1902 the French and the British, intent on carving up the Mediterranean, had agreed that Italy could do what it liked there – a useful way of coaxing Italy into a wider political alliance against future enemies. Who those enemies might be was rapidly made plain: German banks began to invest in Libya in competition with the Banco di Roma. In 1911, Germans, but not Italians, were permitted to acquire lands in Libya. As tension between Rome and Constantinople grew, the Turks attempted to appease Italy with commercial concessions. But it was too late. The Italians had decided that an imperial mission was an integral part of Italy's entry into the ranks of the European nations. The weakness of Ottoman power, especially in the outlying provinces, daily became more obvious. In late September 1911 the Italian government declared war on Turkey, and by the end of October Italian fleets had smoothly moved an occupying force of 60,000 troops into Tripoli, Benghazi and other major towns. That was the easy part; local resistance flared, and, as Italian casualties mounted, the Italian government agreed to discuss peace terms with Constantinople. As ever, the Ottoman sultan was unwilling to renounce nominal Turkish sovereignty over his former subjects. A year after the invasion, he recognized Italian rule over a notionally Ottoman Libya.[4] The Italians were unable to control the hinterland, but, as in Algiers, they were determined to Europeanize those parts they did control, and began to rebuild Tripoli as a modern Italian city.

By the time the First World War broke out, then, the entire line of towns from Ceuta in the west to Port Said in the east lay under the rule or protectorate of Spain, France, Italy and Great Britain. The German Kaiser visited Tangier in 1905, and made noises about the growth of French influence in Morocco, but Germany did not gain a foothold in Morocco, any more than in Libya. Indeed, Tangier became a special enclave, in which the sultan of Morocco shared power with the foreign consuls. One particularly important figure was the chief inspector of police, who acted as a liaison between the sultan and the consuls; he provides a rare example of a Swiss presence in the Mediterranean, for what was vital was to employ someone whose neutrality was assured. So the Turks had lost what remaining authority they possessed in North Africa; the Germans had not gained a foothold anywhere; the Austrians remained confined to Trieste and the coast of Dalmatia, and took no part in the scramble for North Africa; and Great Britain dominated the sea-ways between Gibraltar and the Suez Canal.

II

An additional, valuable prize for Italy was Rhodes, along with the Dodecanese islands. The islanders, mainly Greek, had tried to emancipate themselves from Ottoman control, and the prospects for a 'Federation of the Dodecanese Islands' had seemed good: the islands were well placed along the trade routes, bringing prosperity to the local Greeks and Jews. The Italians, however, appreciated the strategic value of islands that lay so close to the centre of Ottoman power, and took advantage of the war with Turkey over Libya to seize the islands in 1912. Italy tried to promote the economy of its new colony. The Dodecanese were a very different proposition to Libya, or to the empire the Italians also dreamed of creating in Abyssinia, and the Italians were more willing to treat the Dodecanesians as humans on the same level as they believed themselves to be.[5] This conquest marks the first stage in an attempt by the European powers finally to dismantle the Ottoman Empire. It was hardly a coordinated process; indeed, much of the initiative came from within the Ottoman territories, for even Albania, traditionally quite loyal to Constantinople, had become a focus of discontent by 1912. The First World War only accentuated a fast-growing trend towards the detachment of the Ottoman provinces. The adherence of Turkey to the German side was by no means inevitable. As the war clouds gathered over Europe, the Turks showed themselves keen to discuss a new treaty with Great Britain, which they continued to see as their obvious ally against attempts by the Russians to break through from the Black to the White Sea; they were aware, too, that Greek adventurism, which had brought King George of Greece as far as Salonika, remained a threat to their capital – the *Megalé Idea* or 'Great Idea' of Venizelos involved nothing less than the substitution of Constantinople for Athens as Greek capital. But the most striking feature of the Mediterranean in August 1914 was the extreme volatility of all political relationships: would Britain cut a deal with Turkey? Or rather with Russia? What was to be done with Greece? It seemed that the sultan was being drawn into the Kaiser's net, but nothing was certain. Two German warships were permitted to sail into the Golden Horn on 10 August 1914, and the Turkish government agreed that, if they were pursued by British ships, Turkish batteries would open fire on the British. Meanwhile, two ships being built in Britain for the Ottoman fleet, at a cost of £7,500,000, were commandeered by the Royal Navy, setting off fierce denunciations of Britain in the Turkish press.[6]

One of those who turned decisively against the Turks was Winston Churchill, now First Lord of the Admiralty. The prime minister, Asquith, noted on 21 August that Churchill was 'violently anti-Turk'. Yet underneath his rhetoric there lay a distinctive and bold policy. Victory over the Ottoman Empire would ensure the safety of British interests not simply in the Mediterranean, but within the Indian Ocean, where Persia was emerging as an important source of oil, shipped through the Suez Canal. Once Russia joined the war against Germany, the Dardanelles became a vital passage-way through which Russia could be supplied with arms and through which it could export Ukrainian grain, which was important for its balance of payments.[7] In March 1915, fearful of a Russian-German truce, the British government accepted that Russia should be allowed to control Constantinople, the Dardanelles, southern Thrace and the Aegean islands closest to the Dardanelles.[8]

Churchill's impassioned advocacy of a campaign to force the Dardanelles resulted in the most important naval offensive to take place in the Mediterranean during the Great War. This war, unlike the Second World War, saw relatively limited action within the Mediterranean, and the Austrian fleet, as will be seen, made few ventures beyond the Adriatic, which it was determined to defend. Around the edges of the

Mediterranean, though, some important land campaigns took place, notably in Palestine and north-eastern Italy. A Turkish military threat to the Suez Canal was enough to make the British impose their own nominee as khedive of Egypt and to denominate the country as a British protectorate – from now on, both here and in Cyprus, the fiction that these lands still lay under the sultan's umbrella was forgotten.[9] The surface of the Mediterranean remained rather unruffled, even though beneath it there now lurked increasing numbers of submarines, whose capacity for doing harm to imperial navies was most clearly demonstrated out in the Atlantic. Part of the explanation for this relative quiet was that British and German ships were required for what were seen as more important duties in northern seas.

The highly controversial exception was the Gallipoli campaign of 1915. In January 1915 Fisher, the First Sea Lord, complained to his colleague Lord Jellicoe:

> The Cabinet have decided on taking the Dardanelles solely with the Navy, using 15 battleships and 32 other vessels, and keeping out there three battle cruisers and a flotilla of destroyers – *all urgently required at the decisive theatre at home!* There is only one way out, and that is to resign! But you say '*no!*', which simply means I am a consenting party to what I absolutely disapprove. *I don't agree with one single step taken.*[10]

And, even when Fisher had given way, he sent a message to Churchill saying: '*the more I consider the Dardanelles the less I like it!*'[11] He firmly believed that the naval conflict had to be resolved in the North Sea. The Gallipoli campaign is best remembered for the bitterly fought battles in which the Turks confronted British, Australian and New Zealand troops on the tongue of land commanding the European flank of the Dardanelles. The original plan had been for British ships, supported by the French, to force the passage. When it became obvious that this could not be done, the decision was made to ferry 50,000 troops to the bay of Mudros, a massive natural harbour on the south side of Lemnos, suitably close to the Gallipoli peninsula. Mudros lacked the harbour installations the Royal Navy needed, and there was neither sufficient water for the troops nor anywhere to accommodate them. Since they arrived in February, they had to endure unpleasant winter conditions.[12] A British naval attack on the entrance to the Dardanelles on 18 March 1915 resulted in the loss of three British battleships, though the Turks firing down on the fleet used up all their ammunition, and mines in the straits proved a greater danger.[13] The British had been hoping that the Russian Black Sea fleet would head for Constantinople with 47,000 troops, but the Russians did no more than bombard Turkish positions at the mouth of the Bosphorus from a safe distance. They could see that the time for the recovery of Constantinople by Orthodoxy had not come.[14] Further disasters resulted in the sacking of Churchill from the Admiralty, but by then the troops were bogged down in impossible positions:

Upon the margin of a rugged shore
There is a spot now barren, desolate,
A place of graves, sodden with human gore
That Time will hallow, Memory consecrate.
There lie the ashes of the mighty dead,
The youth who lit with flame Obscurity,
Fought true for Freedom, won through rain of lead
Undying fame, their immortality.[15]

Total losses were 265,000 troops from Britain, the British Empire and France, and perhaps 300,000 on the Turkish side; but, despite their dreadful losses, it was the Turks who held the ground, and after less than nine months the attacking forces retreated. Gallipoli had some positive effects from the British perspective: the Turks were forced to withdraw many of their best troops from Palestine, taking pressure off Egypt and the Suez Canal.[16]

III

During the Great War, large parts of the Mediterranean remained quiet. On the eve of the conflict, the British and French hoped to draw King Alfonso of Spain into an alliance, and the British Admiralty eyed Ceuta as a base suitable for submarines and torpedo boats, while the French hoped that the Balearic islands could be used as a way-station for troops transferring from French North Africa. Perhaps negotiations would have gone further had the Spanish king not recklessly raised the possibility of receiving the disordered republic of Portugal as compensation for any support he might offer France and Britain.[17] But at least he stayed neutral, and Spanish waters remained safe for shipping. In the centre the main focus of naval activity was the Adriatic, where the Austrian fleet was stationed. Italian irredentists were casting covetous eyes on the coasts of Istria and Dalmatia, and the Austrians saw Kotor as the vital naval station on which their ability to hold the eastern Adriatic shores depended. A mutiny at Kotor in February 1918 proved that more thought should have been given to the conditions under which sailors had to work while they were deployed there. Sailors complained that officers lived in some style, often accompanied by their wife or mistress, and one sailor claimed that he was expected to use up his soap ration washing the captain's dog. Worse still, ratings had to make do with threadbare clothes and suffer an evil diet of rotting meat and underweight loaves, while officers were properly fed with good-quality meats, vegetables and fruit. Given the novelty of flying, it is no surprise that officers who wanted to impress young nurses would take them on plane trips, or that seaplanes occasionally carried Austrian officers to an elite brothel in Dubrovnik. Once the mutiny was suppressed, the authorities shot only the obvious ringleaders, realizing that the time had come for serious reorganization of the navy (under the newly promoted Admiral Horthy, who years later continued to wear his title with pride even as 'regent' of the landlocked state of Hungary).[18]

At the start of the war conditions at Kotor were not as bad. The harbour lies deep within its fjord, beyond the narrows of the Bocche di Cattaro; behind lie the precipitous mountains of Montenegro. To ensure maximum safety, the Austrians would need to tame Montenegro, whose ruler, out of sympathy for his fellow-Serbs, had declared war against Austria-Hungary soon after the assassination of Franz Ferdinand. In late summer 1914 the Austrian navy started to bombard the Montenegrin port of Bar, and the French responded with a sizeable fleet sent out from Malta: fourteen battleships and several smaller vessels. The French fleet cleared the Austrians away from Bar and bombarded the outer fortifications of the Bocche di Cattaro, without denting Kotor. But it was a parlous situation: until Italy declared war on Austria-Hungary in May 1915, the French had no closer base than British Malta, and French troops were fully committed fighting on the Marne, far to the north.[19] Then the Austrians became bolder, brazenly attacking Italian coastal towns such as Senigallia, Rimini and Ancona, where they wreaked havoc by destroying the railway station and stores of coal and oil, and damaging several public buildings, including a hospital; there were sixty-eight deaths. Even so, the Austrians kept well clear of Taranto, which was the main Italian naval base. They were not seeking a sea battle. The Italians responded by sending their navy from Apulia to southern Dalmatia; they broke the railway line from Dubrovnik to Kotor. This game of tit-for-tat continued with torpedo attacks by German U-boats on Italian shipping; since Italy was not yet at war with Germany, only with Austria, the U-boats shamelessly flew the Austrian flag. In November 1915 the surreptitious German presence had ugly consequences: a German U-boat sank the Italian liner *Ancona*, with heavy loss of life, off the coast of North Africa, while it was heading from Sicily to New York, and the American president protested volubly to Austria about an act the Austrians were, of course, only too keen to blame on the Germans.[20] Finally, after renewed bombardment from the sea, Austrian troops ascended the heights of Montenegro and captured Cetinje, the capital, early in 1916.[21]

This was, then, a struggle for mastery of just one corner of the Mediterranean. In spring 1917 action was concentrated on the narrow passage-way between Otranto and Albania, where the Austrians now held Durazzo. All the new technology that was to hand was put to the fullest possible use. Each side mobilized seaplanes that lobbed bombs at enemy ships without doing any noticeable damage, and the British established a new base for seaplanes at Brindisi. Nets were deployed against the Austrian and German submarines, but, even if they could stop a submarine, they could not stop a torpedo. Reinforcements arrived, in support of the British, Italians and French: fourteen Japanese destroyers and one cruiser played an especially significant role in defeating German submarines; six Australian cruisers also arrived, and, once Greece tardily entered the war, in July 1917, a respectable Greek fleet became available.[22] The importance of the relatively limited conflict with the Austrians lies in the appearance of new methods of fighting for control of the sea: aeroplanes, which still had to prove their worth, and submarines, which rapidly did so. Some new dangers had become obvious: merchant shipping was at risk from enemy submarines, and by 1917 the British and French had introduced an effective system of convoys to accompany vessels eastwards from Gibraltar.[23] In time of war, a more insidious enemy than the Barbary corsairs had arrived, after a century of relative peace: invisible, deadly and wantonly destructive in a way that the corsairs, who sought booty and captives, had never been.

4

A Tale of Four and a Half Cities, 1900–1950

I

From a Mediterranean perspective, the First World War was only part of a sequence of crises that marked the death throes of the Ottoman Empire: the loss of Cyprus, Egypt, Libya, the Dodecanese, then the war itself with the loss of Palestine to British control, soon followed by a French mandate in Syria. All these changes had consequences, sometimes drastic, in the port cities where different ethnic and religious groups had coexisted over the centuries, notably Salonika, Smyrna, Alexandria and Jaffa. At the end of the war, the Ottoman heartlands were carved up between the victorious powers, and even Constantinople swarmed with British soldiers.[1] The sultan was immobilized politically, providing plenty of opportunities for the Turkish radicals, in particular Mustafa Kemal, who had acquitted himself with great distinction fighting at Gallipoli. Allied mistrust of the Turks was compounded by public feeling: the mass deportation of the Armenians in spring and summer 1915 aroused horror among American diplomats based in Constantinople and Smyrna. Marched across the Anatolian highlands in searing heat, with harsh taskmasters forcing them on, men, women and children collapsed and died, or were killed for fun, while the Ottoman government made noises about the treasonable plots that were said to be festering among the Armenians. The intention was to 'exterminate all males under fifty'.[2] The worry among Greeks, Jews and foreign merchants was that the 'purification' of Anatolia would not be confined to persecution of the Armenians. In its last days, the Ottoman government had turned its back on the old ideal of coexistence. In Turkey too, as the radical Young Turks often revealed, powerful nationalist sentiment was overwhelming the tolerance of past times.

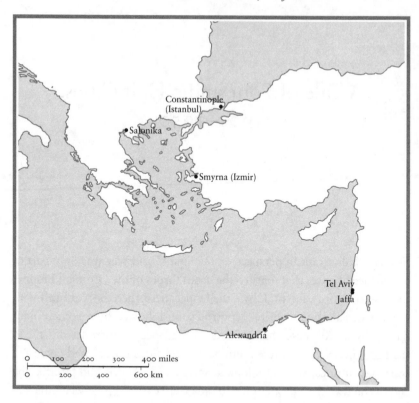

Smyrna survived the war physically intact, with most of its population protected from persecution, partly because its *vali*, or governor,
Rahmi Bey, was sceptical about the Turkish alliance with Germany and
Austria, and understood that the prosperity of his city depended on its
mixed population of Greeks, Armenians, Jews, European merchants
and Turks.[3] When he was ordered to deliver the Armenians to the Ottoman authorities, he temporized, though he had to despatch about a
hundred 'disreputables' to an uncertain fate.[4] The Greeks formed the
majority in Smyrna; indeed, there were more Greeks there than in Athens, and they remained very attached to Orthodoxy, which played an
important role in the Greek school system and in public festivals, while
nationalist ideas from Greece had also begun to filter into the community. The Greeks were very active in the trade in dried fruits, and the
arrival of the fig harvest from the interior was a great event on the quayside of Smyrna. The Ladino-speaking Jewish community was less
prominent than in Salonika, but in Smyrna as in Salonika western fash-

ions were gaining hold. The governor once visited the school of the Alliance Israélite Universelle and commented that he wanted the Jews to wear fezzes, not the western-style hats they were now adopting: 'You are not in France or Germany, you are in Turkey, you are subjects of His Majesty the sultan.'[5]

Smyrna possessed an excellent harbour and had continued to flourish from the late eighteenth century onwards, when other Ottoman ports found business was contracting. France dominated Ottoman trade with Europe around 1800, and supplied the city not just with European cloths but with colonial products such as sugar, coffee, cochineal and indigo. The Turks of Smyrna actually bought fezzes made in France.[6] Among the Europeans, there was a lively community of business families of British, French and Italian origin, who helped keep Smyrna's business alive throughout the nineteenth century, when families such as the Whittalls, major fruit exporters, and the Girauds, whose carpet factories employed 150,000 people, dominated economic life. Among newer arrivals were the Americans, who used Smyrna as a staging-post for the traffic of the Standard Oil Company of New Jersey.[7] Spacious suburbs containing the grand houses of the Levantine families, such as the aptly named Paradise, were laid out a few miles from the city, connected by railway line or boat services to the heart of Smyrna.[8] Even during the war, these 'Levantines', as they were known, managed to continue their life of ease, since Rahmi Bey saw no reason to treat the foreign merchants as enemy aliens – most had been born in Smyrna and had never visited the country whose passport they carried.

Back in London, the victorious British government was blind to the interests of the Levantine merchants of Smyrna. There was bitter hostility to the Turks: Lord Curzon, the foreign secretary, described the Ottomans as one of Earth's 'most pestilent roots of evil', and Lloyd George, the prime minister, had for several years been enthusing about the noble achievements of ancient Greek civilization, in contrast to the miserable failings of the Turks – in the wildest of misjudgements, he dismissed Kemal as 'a carpet seller in a bazaar'. This led him to embrace Venizelos' dream of a restored Greek dominion that would stretch across the Aegean to include the coast of Asia Minor. For Venizelos this was the very heartland of Greek civilization: ancient Ionia, whose Greek inhabitants, he insisted, 'constitute the purest part of the Hellenic race', optimistically numbered at 800,000 souls.[9] Great Britain valued Greek military support during 1919 in the struggle against the Bolshevik revolutionaries in Russia. These Greek freedom-fighters surely needed to be rewarded. The British were happy to offer the Greeks Smyrna and its hinterland, though the Americans and the continental powers, gathered for their Peace Conference in Paris in 1919, were less sure, and the Whittalls of Smyrna submitted evidence that the inhabitants of the city did not want to be ruled by the Greek government, for all of them, Greek, Turk, Jew, Armenian, valued the harmony that existed within the city and wanted no more than local self-government. Lloyd George convinced most of his allies that Smyrna and its hinterland should be granted forthwith to Venizelos, who should be urged to send Greek ships there and occupy the Ionian coast without delay. Among those who bitterly opposed these developments was the American High Commissioner in Constantinople, Admiral Bristol, a man whose prejudices hardly suited him for the tasks ahead: he asserted that 'the Armenians are a race like the Jews; they have little or no national spirit and have poor moral character', but he reserved his greatest anger for the British, for he did not believe that Lloyd George was motivated by high moral concerns – it was all about competition for oil.[10]

In May 1919 13,000 Greek troops arrived. After a quiet start, incidents began to multiply: Turkish villages were ransacked and about 400 Turks and 100 Greeks were killed within Smyrna alone. The new Greek governor, Aristides Sterghiades, was a remote figure who preferred to stand above the social life of the Smyrna elite. He tried to be fair and would often favour Turks over Greeks in disputes; the price he paid was the contempt of the Greeks, whose triumphalism threatened all that was special about the city. On the other hand, his policies brought trade back to Smyrna. It was in the hinterland that problems became ever more serious; the Red Cross collected evidence of the ethnic cleansing of Turkish-inhabited areas by Greeks. One Greek officer was asked by the Red Cross why he let his men kill Turks, to which he replied, 'because it gave me pleasure'. In fact, violence was the trademark of both sides. But Mustafa Kemal was gathering his forces, and, when, in 1921, the Greeks attempted to penetrate into the highlands to the east, in the hope of drawing a frontier between Greece and Turkey in the western plateau, early successes were met with a dramatic Turkish counter-attack – the Greeks had allowed themselves to be drawn far too deeply into Anatolia. The rout of the Greeks brought Turkish armies cascading westwards towards Smyrna, which they entered on 9 September 1922, but not before about 50,000 defeated Greek soldiers and 150,000 Greeks from the interior began to converge on the city.

This was the beginning of a disaster that seared itself into the Greek memory. Although the first Turkish troops to enter Smyrna were well-disciplined cavalry, they were accompanied by *chettes*, Turkish irregulars who had already tasted a great amount of Greek blood during rampages in western Anatolia. As the refugees crowded into the city, massacres, rape and looting, mainly but not exclusively by the irregulars, became the unspoken order of the day, starting with the favourite enemy – not the Greeks but the Armenians. Neither the new Turkish governor nor, when he arrived, Mustafa Kemal, appeared worried by something they seemed to regard as a fact of war; there was apparently no longer any room for Greeks and Armenians in the new Turkey that was coming into existence. The thorough sacking of the Armenian quarter was followed by violence across the city, though the Turkish quarter was respected. The suburban villas of the Levantine merchants were pillaged; most Levantines (if they survived) lost everything they owned, and their trading companies went out of business. Finally, the streets and houses of Smyrna were soaked in petrol (beginning, again, with the Armenian quarter), and on 13 September the city was set alight. This swelled the refugee population to 700,000, for now the Greeks and Armenians of Smyrna itself were forced to flee to the quayside. There, a tantalizing spectacle awaited them: British, French, Italian and American warships were in harbour, all nervously protecting the interests of their own mother-country. The fire spread closer to the quayside, wrecking the warehouses and offices of the great trading firms, and the centre of the city was reduced to ashes, while a desperate mass of people, many of whom were dying of wounds, thirst and exhaustion, prayed for deliverance.

The attitude of the Great Powers was chillingly unsympathetic. Admiral Bristol had already instructed two American journalists that they were not to write of Turkish atrocities, and the French and Italians insisted that their 'neutrality' prevented them from taking on board refugees – so much so that people who swam out to the warships were left to drown in the sea. When a boy and a girl were found in the water off an American ship, the sailors told Asa Jennings, an employee of the Young Men's Christian Association who was trying to organize large-scale evacuation, that, much as they wished to help, this was against orders, as it would compromise American neutrality. He refused to accept this – the children were recovered and turned out to be brother and sister.[11] On board the British warships, bands were ordered to play rousing sea shanties while the officers dined in the mess, to drown out the terrified screams that were coming from the quayside a few hundred yards away. Eventually the British admiral gave way to the impassioned pleas, and the admirably persistent Jennings was able to secure the help of the Greek navy based nearby in Lesbos as well. Twenty thousand were saved on allied ships, and very many more on Jennings's Greek flotilla. Even so, something like 100,000 people were killed in Smyrna and its hinterland, and at least as many were deported into the Anatolian interior, where most vanished.

The callousness of the commanders in Smyrna Bay, and the sheer hostility of Admiral Bristol in Constantinople, reflected a different way of thinking about humanitarian catastrophes from that of the early twenty-first century. 'Neutrality' was understood to mean that one should stand aside, rather than that neutral powers were best placed to offer aid to the dispossessed and dying victims of ethnic violence. This unwillingness to intervene was compounded by awareness that Lloyd George's support for Venizelos had set off a train of events over which neither Greece nor Great Britain had any control. Most of the people of Smyrna had gone; Smyrna too had ceased to exist, wrecked by fire, and the new Turkish city of Izmir never recovered its long-standing commercial primacy. The gap left by the Greeks and Armenians was filled as Turks expelled from Crete and northern Greece flooded into Turkey. Eventually, under the Treaty of Lausanne of 1923, a massive exchange of population between Greece and Turkey took place – 30,000 Muslims left Crete alone. The flight from Istanbul of the last sultan, in November 1922, removed the final, very feeble, barrier to the creation of a new, westward-inclined Turkey, with a new capital, a new alphabet and a secular constitution. In Greece, the *Megalé Idea* was dead, but the multinational character of the Turkish empire was also discarded. Despite the tensions and even hatreds that erupted between peoples and religions, and despite frequent attempts to humiliate Christians and Jews by imposing on them a variety of financial and social disabilities, the Ottoman system had managed to hold together disparate peoples for several centuries. It was replaced by a group of nations whose leaders proclaimed strident nationalism, and found it difficult to accommodate those they now deemed outsiders – Greeks and Armenians in Turkey, Jews and Muslims in Greece.

II

Alexandria was another port city in which cultures met and mixed. The city began to take its modern shape in the late nineteenth and early twentieth centuries, when an elegant Corniche road along a new water-front was created, and wide streets with apartment blocks and offices came into being. These buildings included the pseudo-Coptic Anglican cathedral, built as early as the 1850s, as well as the extraordinary group of buildings designed by the architect Alessandro Loria, who was born in Egypt, trained in Italy and then lionized in Alexandria in the 1920s. His National Bank of Egypt looks like a Venetian palazzo; he also built the Jewish and Italian hospitals, appropriately since he was both a Jew and an Italian; his most visited building is the famous Cecil Hotel, a favourite of Winston Churchill and Lawrence Durrell, and indeed of Durrell's own creation, Justine.[12] The Greek, Jewish, Italian, Coptic and Turkish inhabitants of the city were immensely proud of Alexandria, interpreting the classical phrase *Alexandria ad Aegyptum* to mean that it was a European city beside, not in, Egypt.[13] Jasper Brinton, an Ameri-can who served as appeal judge of the Mixed Courts of Egypt in the early twentieth century, enthused about Alexandria, which, he said, was 'brilliant and sophisticated, far beyond any city in the Mediterranean'; music-lovers were entertained in the city's great theatres by Toscanini, Pavlova and the best voices from La Scala.[14] It was said that the streets were so clean you could eat food off them, something definitely not to be tried nowadays.

Of course, cosmopolitan Alexandria was not all Alexandria, and the life of the elite, which will be discussed shortly, was not the life of the majority of the Greeks, Italians, Jews and Copts who lived along the northern shore of the city. On late nineteenth-century maps, the south-ern flank of the long, narrow city was labelled *Ville arabe*, but it did not greatly intrude on the life of the Alexandrian middle classes, except to provide cooks, maids and tram-drivers. The Europeans accounted for only 15 per cent of the population, even if it was they who exercised most of the economic power; in 1927 there were about 49,000 Greeks in the city, 37,000 of whom had Greek citizenship, 24,000 Italians and 4,700 Maltese. Overlapping with various nationalities there were 25,000 Jews (nearly 5,000 with Italian passports, though many remained stateless); a good many Greeks also held non-Greek passports, whether as Cypriots (making them British) or as Rhodians (making them Italian) or, even after 1923, as Turkish subjects.[15] The majority of influential Muslim families, including the royal family, hailed from Turkey, Albania, Syria or Lebanon. As in Salonika and Smyrna, French made great inroads, even though Egypt was a British protectorate. One Alexandrian exile confessed that his reading knowledge of Arabic was limited to menus and newspaper headlines: 'I have always considered English and French as my mother tongues.' His wife told a different story: 'My mother was entirely Francophone, and my father spoke only Italian. I don't know how they understood one another, but they did.'[16] A smattering of Arabic was mainly thought useful for communicating with servants. In an age of rising nationalism, this rejection of any 'Eastern' identity would eventually prove fatal to the survival of these communities.

A fictionalized memoir of life in Alexandria by André Aciman shows the direction of thinking of many Alexandrians. Aciman's family arrived from Constantinople in 1905, but his uncle Vili attached himself both to Alexandria and to Europe:

> Like most men born in Turkey towards the end of the century, Vili disparaged anything that had to do with Ottoman culture and thirsted for the West, finally becoming 'Italian' the way most Jews in Turkey did: by claiming ancestral ties to Livorno, a port city near Pisa where escaped Jews from Spain had settled in the sixteenth century.[17]

The architect Loria liked to dress himself and his family in the black shirts of the Fascists; he was also a benefactor of the Alexandria synagogue. The most influential Jewish family was that of Baron Félix de Menasce, who held an Austrian imperial title, although his grandfather, who was born in Cairo, had acquired his wealth after becoming the banker to Khedive Ismail; by Félix's time not just banking but commerce with Trieste sustained the fortunes of this glittering family. He founded schools and hospitals, and even established his own synagogue and cemetery, for he fell out with the leaders of the imposing new synagogue on Nebi Daniel Street. Even though he led a secular life in which Jewish observance counted for little, he was deeply upset when he learned that his son Jean, who was studying in Paris, had been baptized a Catholic. Worse still, in his eyes, his son joined the Dominican Order and came to Alexandria to preach. Félix de Menasce was a close friend of the Zionist leader Chaim Weizmann, who visited the city in March 1918, staying at the imposing Menasce residence. Interestingly, Baron Félix used his contacts with the Arabs in Palestine to attempt to negotiate a bilateral agreement between Jews and Arabs over the future of Palestine, but the British, now in charge of Palestine, were uninterested.[18]

These connections provided the inspiration for Lawrence Durrell's description of the enormously rich Alexandrian banker Nessim, whom he cast as a Copt rather than a Jew. Durrell wrote the first volume of his *Alexandria Quartet* in Bellapais, in Cyprus, in the early 1950s, but he had close links with the Alexandrian Jews through his second wife, Eve Cohen, and even more through his third wife, Claude Vincendon, who was the granddaughter of Félix de Menasce.[19] The Menasces mixed socially with another eminent family, the Zoghebs, who were Melkite Christians from Syria, members of a community that included many prosperous traders in silk, timber, fruit and tobacco.[20] There was no comparison between the *haut bourgeois* life of the Smyrna Levantines and the truly grand style of the Menasces and their peers, especially since the Alexandrian elite had the ear of the king and, in particular, of Omar Toussoun, a much admired member of the royal family who understood the importance of associating himself with the different communities of Alexandria. He might be found giving out the prizes at a Jewish school, or to children of the Alexandrian elite at Victoria College, which was modelled on an English public (i.e. private) school. He was honorary president of the Coptic Archaeological Society and donated handsomely towards the building of the Coptic hospital. At the same time he took a great interest in the local economy, working hard to stabilize cotton prices.[21]

The daily life of the foreign communities revolved around commerce and coffee houses, among which the most famous were those of the Greeks, notably the Café Pastroudis. And within these cafés might be found members of the Greek intelligentsia, of whom the most accomplished was the poet Cavafy.[22] The English novelist E. M. Forster, who spent most of the First World War in the city (falling in love with an Arab tram-conductor), spread awareness of Cavafy's poetry beyond Alexandria, while the poet himself returned again and again to the theme of his home city. The problem was that it was ancient Alexandria to which his mind kept returning, rather than the modern city, which had no great appeal for him.[23] Alexandria, of all the port cities in the eastern Mediterranean, was damaged least by the political changes that followed the fall of the Ottomans, for it owed its revival to foreign settlers attracted by the initiatives of the khedives, not the sultans.

III

Alexandria was a newly rebuilt city; not far away there emerged a brand new one, in Palestine. There, the British found themselves in a very different political environment from Egypt. The Arab revolt during the First World War, in part fostered by T. E. Lawrence, had brought Britain valuable allies against the Turks; simultaneously, Zionist demands for a Jewish homeland led to increasing tension between Jews and Arabs in Palestine, particularly after the British government indicated its sympathy for the idea of a Jewish National Home in the Balfour Declaration of 1917. Jewish aspirations were expressed in the idea of a return to the land, as idealistic settlers from central and eastern Europe created agricultural settlements – the kibbutz movement aimed to take Jews out of cities and into the fresh air of the countryside – but there was another strand to Zionism, according to which the creation of a westernized city in Palestine, inhabited by Jews, was a fundamental task. In 1909 a group of Jews, mainly European Ashkenazim, acquired the title to some sandy dunes a mile north of the ancient port of Jaffa, and divided the land into sixty-six plots, which were assigned by lot – a sign of their idealism, since a lottery ensured that no one could bid for a better position and rich and poor would have to live side by side.[24] Their intention was to create a well-spaced garden city, or rather a garden suburb, since initially they refused to include any shops in their plans. They assumed that the residents would travel down to Jaffa for whatever supplies they needed. Looking for a name, the settlers argued about any number of alternatives, including the staunchly Zionist Herzliya and the delightfully mellifluous Yefefia ('most beautiful'). In the end Theodor Herzl won, because the name Tel Aviv was the Hebrew title of his novel about re-establishing Zion, *Altneuland*, 'old-new land': *tel* signified the ancient remains which reminded visitors of the Jewish presence in past millennia, and *aviv*, the first green shoots of the wheat harvest, and, by extension, springtime.[25]

Thus was born what was to become the first major city to emerge on the shores of the Mediterranean since the early Middle Ages, when Tunis had been founded to replace Carthage and Venice had emerged from its lagoons. The emergence of Tel Aviv offers a different, Mediterranean perspective to the tortuous history of the foundation of Israel, and the new city aroused intense passions among its Arab neighbours – it still does not feature on many maps of the Middle East produced in Arab countries.[26] The founders of Tel Aviv were clear in their minds that they wished to create a Jewish settlement, and that it would possess a European character distinct from Jaffa, which they saw as distressingly 'oriental'. This wish for European modernity was not new to Jaffa. With a strong sense of German propriety, a Protestant sect known as the Templars had created two orderly settlements outside Jaffa in the 1880s: 'with its broad streets and elegant buildings, a person might forget he was walking in a desolate land and imagine himself in one of the civilised cities of Europe'.[27] The wealthier Arabs of Jaffa also built comfortable villas in its suburbs. Nor was Tel Aviv the first Jewish suburb of Jaffa. In the 1880s a prosperous Algerian Jew, Aharon Chelouche, who had lived in Palestine since 1838, bought land on which there arose the Jaffa suburb of Neve Tzedek. What impressed those who saw Neve Tzedek was its clean and relatively spacious layout, and its homes were thought to be among the most beautiful in Jaffa.[28] Neve Tzedek attracted settlers from a variety of origins – as well as the North African Chelouches, there were Ashkenazim arriving from central Europe, while Solomon Abulafia, who became its mayor, came from no further away than Tiberias – he and his Ashkenazi wife, Rebecca Freimann, decamped in 1909 to join the founders of Tel Aviv. Not surprisingly he is portrayed in photographs in a morning coat, cravat and striped trousers, emblems of modernization that were also worn by his Turkish and Arab peers in Jaffa.[29] The writer Agnon lived for a time in the Abulafia house in Neve Tzedek, and, before Tel Aviv became a centre of Hebrew culture, a writers' and artists' colony gathered here.

Jaffa too was on the ascendant. It was the major port in Palestine and Jerusalem's main outlet to the sea, even though ships of any respectable size could not come close in to shore, and travellers had to disembark on to lighters, or were carried ashore piggy-back by Jaffan porters. The

Ottoman sultan bestowed an eloquent symbol of modernization on Jaffa by building the clock tower that still stands. By the eve of the First World War, Jaffa was host to over 40,000 inhabitants, Muslim, Christian and Jewish (the last group roughly a quarter of the whole). Then, during the war, the city was evacuated of Arabs and Jews, under orders from the Turks, who suspected collusion between the Jaffans and the advancing British army; but Jaffa and its Jewish suburbs were not pillaged by the Turks (more damage was done by Australian troops who squatted for a while in the empty city), and Jaffa bounced back thereafter.[30] From its railway station one could travel northwards to Beirut and south and west to Cairo – even to Khartoum. Jaffa drew its income not just from trade passing from the Mediterranean into the interior but from its excellent oranges, which were distributed around the Ottoman lands and to western Europe. Jaffa, rather than Jerusalem, was also the prime cultural centre of Palestine, and a growing sense of identity among the Arab population was reflected in the title and contents of a Christian-owned newspaper, *Falastin*, 'Palestine'.[31] This is not to suggest that its cultural life rivalled that of Alexandria. Setting aside the dour German Protestants, it was an Arabic-speaking city, and the Chelouches mixed on easy terms with their Arab friends and neighbours.[32] But the emergence of Tel Aviv set off new tensions. In the 1920s, Jaffan Christians and Muslims often enjoyed visiting the new settlement – there were attractions such as the Eden Cinema, not to mention the gambling dens and brothels that began to sprout there. However, outbreaks of violence between Jews and Arabs soured relations from 1921 onwards; the first riot began when the Jaffa Arabs, already tense, mistakenly assumed that a Communist demonstration in Tel Aviv was a rabble about to descend on Jaffa; forty-nine Jews were killed, including the inhabitants of a writers' colony on the outskirts.[33]

The underlying cause of tension was the arrival from across the Mediterranean of shiploads of Jewish immigrants. Towards the end of 1919 the Russian ship *Ruslan* arrived in Jaffa from Odessa with 670 passengers. Even if these Ashkenazi migrants were not changing the inner character of old Jaffa, because they went to live in Tel Aviv or the Palestinian hinterland, the balance between Jaffa and Tel Aviv was shifting perceptibly and rapidly. In 1923 Tel Aviv already contained 20,000 inhabitants, almost all Jews. After that, it began to overtake Jaffa proper: a year later, Tel Aviv contained 46,000 inhabitants, 150,000 in

1930, and in 1948, the year of Israel's creation, 244,000. Gradually it became emancipated from the municipality of Jaffa, enjoying internal autonomy from 1921, absorbing the other Jewish quarters on the edge of Jaffa, such as Neve Tzedek, and becoming a separate municipality in 1934.[34] One early development within Tel Aviv was the foundation of a school, the Herzliya Gymnasium, whose imposing modern building (now, unbelievably, swept away and replaced by a hideous tower block) functioned as an important cultural centre.[35] On the other hand, this drew Jewish children away from the mixed schools in Jaffa, often operated by nuns, where Jews, Christians and Muslims had been educated side by side.

One of the most important developments was the creation of a harbour. The port of Jaffa serviced Tel Aviv until the outbreak of a new and even more serious round of violence in 1936. Then, amid Arab boycotts of Jewish shops and Jewish boycotts of Arab ones, the town council petitioned the British authorities for permission to establish a port in the north of their growing city. The Jewish leader David Ben Gurion stated: 'I want a Jewish sea. The sea is a continuation of Palestine.' The impact of the rival port was quickly felt in Jaffa: in 1935 Jaffa imported goods worth £7.7 million, which fell the following year to £3.2 million, with Tel Aviv catering for £602,000; but by 1939 Jaffa was importing goods worth only £1.3 million, and Tel Aviv had expanded to £4.1 million. Since Arab labour was not available during the crisis of 1936, the port was staffed from Salonika, the city that was famous for its Jewish stevedores.[36] A series of Levant Fairs also brought wealth to Tel Aviv, beginning modestly in 1924, but expanding to a point where, in 1932, 831 foreign companies exhibited their products. The vision that was being promoted was one of Tel Aviv as the new crossroads between the Mediterranean and the Middle East, and (proving that this might yet be possible) the fairs attracted displays from Syria, Egypt and the newly created kingdom of Transjordan.[37]

This growth was accompanied by the emergence of Tel Aviv as a real city, even while its boundaries with Jaffa remained indistinct and the subject of bickering. The building of the city was a mixture of uncoordinated private enterprise and a certain amount of central planning – enough to create a broad tree-lined avenue named after the Rothschilds (in the hope of greater financial support than was received). In the 1930s, a master-plan was devised by the Scottish architect Geddes, who sought to tie the city more firmly to its long seafront. In the core of the city striking Bauhaus buildings expressed the wish of its wealthier inhabitants to be seen as the carriers of modern western culture; the 'White City' they built was considered remarkable enough to earn UNESCO World Heritage status in 2003. Other expressions of the search for a western, European identity could be found in the Habima Theatre and in the literary, artistic and musical culture of the city. Similar trends were taking place in Alexandria, Salonika and Beirut, as well as in Jaffa; what was different here, as observers often remarked, was that Tel Aviv seemed at times to have more in common with eastern European cities such as Odessa and Vienna than with Mediterranean ones such as Naples and Marseilles.

The puzzlement of the Jaffans at the behaviour of their Jewish neighbours, even in less tense times, can be seen in a cartoon from the Arabic newspaper *Falastin*, of 1936 (opposite). An Anglican archbishop stands in a pulpit admonishing a corpulent John Bull, who has ended up with two wives, the first a demure Palestinian Arab whose face and hair are exposed, but who wears traditional Palestinian dress and carries a cage containing a dove; the second is a long-legged Jewish pioneer in very short shorts and a tight blouse, smoking a cigarette. John Bull explains that the pressure of the Great War led him to marry twice, and the archbishop insists he must divorce his Jewish wife. The political message is clear, but so is the mixture of fascination and unease at the manners of the new Jewish settlers.[38] The casual familiarity between Jew and Arab in the days when the Chelouches had established Neve Tzedek had vanished. Those who built Tel Aviv had come to insist too hard on the difference between what they proposed to create and what they left behind in Jaffa. The mere modernizers who founded Neve Tzedek had been swamped by immigrants for whom the ways of the East were entirely alien. Such changes grew naturally out of the pressures placed on Tel Aviv by the thousands of newcomers who were escaping from persecution in central and eastern Europe. At the same time, several Zionist leaders vaunted the advantages of creating a Jewish city – the first all-Jewish city, they averred, for 1,900 years. Ironically, just as this happened, the waves of persecution within Europe reached a new and unprecedented intensity, devastating the eastern European cities where Jews constituted a near or real majority. One of those cities was Salonika.

The man of the two wives

JOHN BULL :— My Lord, I married first an Arab woman and then a Jewess and for the last 16 years I have had no peace at home...

THE ARCHBISHOP :— How did you manage to have two wives, are you not a Christian ?

JOHN BULL :— It was the pressure of the Great war, my Lord ...

THE ARCHBISHOP :— Well my son, if you are sincerely looking for peace you must divorce your second wife, because your marriage to her is illegal ...

الرجل ذو المرأتين

جون بول : اتى يا سيدنا تزوجت امرأة عربية اولا ثم تزوجت عليها امرأة يهودية ومنذ ١٦ سنة حتى الان والخصام قائم عندي بيتي...

رئيس الاساقفة : • وكيف تزوجت اثنتين ألست مسيحيا ؟؟

جون بول : كان ذلك تحت ضغط الحرب العظمى يا سيدنا...

رئيس الاساقفة : اذن عليك يا ولدي اذا كنت حقيقة ترغب في السلام ان تطلق الثانية لان زواجك بها غير شرعي ....

IV

It has already been seen how Salonika found itself caught up in the disintegration of the Ottoman Empire; it even found itself on the front line from 1915 onwards, when British and French troops arrived, in the hope (soon abandoned) of supporting Serbian armies fighting against Austria; the allies bedded down in Salonika and its surroundings, an area the British called 'the Birdcage'. The allied presence had unsettling political results: Britain and France deepened an existing schism in Greek politics when they gave their support to Venizelos against the king of Greece – Venizelos came to Salonika in 1916, and fighting broke out between royalists and Venizelists, while the allies seized some of the ships of the Royal Hellenic Navy.[39] Then, after the fire of 1917 and the end of the war, Salonika attracted the attention of the Greek and Turkish governments because it retained such a large Muslim population: in July 1923 there were about 18,000 Muslims still in Salonika. A million Christians arrived in Greece from Turkey, refugees from the warfare that destroyed Smyrna, followed by those who were expelled under the terms of the population exchange agreed at Lausanne; 92,000 of these would settle in Salonika. The city and the surrounding countryside were denuded of Muslims, while the Christians from Asia Minor were settled in the vacant houses and lands of the Turks, or in areas rebuilt after the fire. Ironically, the Salonikans found that many Anatolian refugees spoke Turkish; their badge of identity was the Greek Church, not the Greek language, and their customs were almost indistinguishable from those of the Turkish Muslims among whom they had lived for as much as 900 years.[40]

There were still 70,000 Jews in Salonika. The Greek government encouraged their Hellenization, notably through the teaching of Greek in schools. Sometimes this led to tensions, as when the government, challenging what were seen as 'narrow religious conceptions', removed the provision that Jewish shops could close on Saturdays but open on Sundays.[41] And yet the Day of Atonement was made a general public holiday in Salonika, and everyone understood that the economic stability of the city depended on Greeks and Jews working together. There was some Jewish emigration to France, Italy and the United States; in Haifa and Tel Aviv, Jewish dockworkers were valued. But the overall sense was that, despite massive political changes, there was no threat. If anything, threats had receded now that the borders between Greece, Turkey, Bulgaria and Yugoslavia had been defined.

It became clear how mistaken this view was during the Second World War, after the Germans occupied the city in April 1941. There were occasional outrages such as the seizure of valuable Jewish manuscripts and artefacts, but for nearly two years restrictions on the Jews were less stringent than elsewhere in Hitler's empire. This was partly because the economy of the city was near collapse, with severe food shortages, and the Germans were unwilling to disrupt what commercial activity there was.[42] The Nazis treated the Spanish-speaking Sephardim no differently from the Ashkenazim of central and eastern Europe. Once the Nazis had decided to act, they did so quickly and efficiently – behind these acts lay the malign hand of Adolf Eichmann. In February 1943 the Jews were confined in ghettoes. Tales that they would be deported to Cracow to work in rubber factories were disseminated; and on 15 March the first train packed with victims departed for Poland. By August the city was almost entirely *Judenrein*, to cite contemporary German usage. Within a matter of weeks 43,850 Salonikan Jews were put to death, most gassed immediately on arrival in Auschwitz and elsewhere.[43] The Italian consul saved some, and individual Greeks, including clerics, often did what they could; the Spanish authorities were sometimes willing to help those they saw as fellow-Spaniards of very long standing. Even so, in Greece the Nazis succeeded in wiping out 85 per cent of the Jewish community.

So, after three and a half centuries, old Salonika ceased to exist. Smyrna was the first of the great port cities to succumb. The fall of Smyrna had led to perhaps 100,000 deaths. Salonika experienced the added horror of an industrialized killing machine. The destruction of the port cities of the eastern Mediterranean would continue after the Second World War, though without such staggering loss of life. Each acquired an exclusive identity as a Greek, Turkish, Jewish or Egyptian city. Further west, too, port cities that brought together people of different cultures and religions were in decline. Livorno had entered united Italy long before these events and, as early as the mid-nineteenth century, its elite, identifying (whatever a person's ancestry) with *Italia*, looked increasingly towards the professions and non-commercial careers, as the city lost its special privileges and ceded primacy to Genoa and other rivals.[44] After the First World War, Trieste was detached from Austria-Hungary and a geographical position that had once been its advantage now became an embarrassment, as the city was boxed in by the new kingdom of Serbs, Croats and Slovenes, with Austria a small and inconsequential state across the Alps, uncertain of its cultural and political identity. Then, after the Second World War, it became a bone of contention between Italy and Yugoslavia, acquiring the ambiguous status of 'Free City' until 1954. Its distinctive cultural identity, or rather plurality of identities, proved unable to survive these political and economic changes.

Jaffa changed more suddenly, even though it had already lost its plural identity as Tel Aviv developed into a separate, non-Arab, city. Over a number of weeks in spring 1948, on the eve of the birth of Israel, tens of thousands of Jaffan Arabs fled by ship or overland, seeking refuge in Gaza, Beirut and elsewhere. The United Nations had designated Jaffa as an exclave of the proposed Arab state that would coexist with a Jewish state in Palestine. Following bombardment by Jewish forces in late April, the population of Jaffa dwindled. The leaders of the Arab community, which had now contracted to only about 5,000, surrendered the city on 13 May, the day before the state of Israel was proclaimed down the road on Rothschild Avenue, Tel Aviv.[45] Thereafter, Jaffa became a suburb of Tel Aviv with an Arab minority, in what was almost a reversal of the situation forty years earlier, while those who had left found themselves unable to return. In Alexandria, the final act was delayed until 1956, when the nationalization of the Suez Canal was followed by the expropriation and expulsion of Italians, Jews and others at the orders of Gamal Abdel Nasser. The city reconstituted itself as a massive Muslim Arab city, but its economy nose-dived. Something remains of the old Alexandria, but mainly in the form of cemeteries – of Greeks, Catholics, Jews and Copts. As for the cemeteries of Salonika, the massive Jewish one had already been despoiled, graves and all, by the Nazis. It is now covered by the vast campus of the Aristotle University of Thessaloniki: 'and some there be, which have no memorial'.[46]

5

Mare Nostrum – Again,
1918–1945

I

While most naval action within the Mediterranean during the First
World War took place in the east and in the Adriatic, in waters that
lapped the shores of the disintegrating empires of the Ottomans and the
Habsburgs, the entire Mediterranean became the setting for rivalry
between 1918 and 1939.[1] At the centre of the struggle for mastery of the
Mediterranean lay the ambitions of Benito Mussolini, after he won control of Italy in 1922. His attitude to the Mediterranean wavered. At
some moments he dreamed of an Italian empire that would stretch to 'the
Oceans' and offer Italy 'a place in the sun'; he attempted to make this
dream real with the invasion of Abyssinia in 1935, which, apart from its
sheer difficulty as a military campaign, was a political disaster because
it lost him whatever consideration Britain and France had shown for
him until then. At other times his focus was on the Mediterranean itself:
Italy, he said, is 'an island which juts into the Mediterranean', and yet,
the Fascist Grand Council ominously agreed, it was an imprisoned
island: 'the bars of this prison are Corsica, Tunisia, Malta and Cyprus.
The guards of this prison are Gibraltar and Suez.'[2]

Italian ambitions had been fed by the peace treaties at the end of the
First World War. Not merely did Italy retain the Dodecanese, but the
Austrians were pushed back in north-eastern Italy, and Italy acquired
much of *Italia irredenta*, 'unredeemed Italy', in the form of Trieste, Istria
and, along the Dalmatian coast, Zara (Zadar), which became famous
for the excellent cherry brandy produced by the Luxardo family. Fiume
(Rijeka) in Istria was seized by the rag-tag private army of the nationalist
poet d'Annunzio in 1919, who declared it the seat of the 'Italian Regency

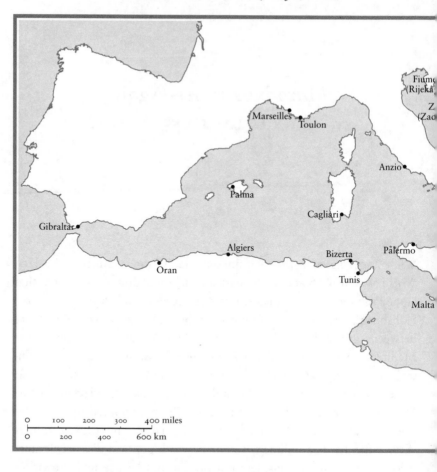

Gibraltar

Marseilles
Toulon

Palma

Cagliari

Anzio

Algiers

Oran

Bizerta

Palermo

Tunis

Malta

Fium(
(Rijeka

Z
(Za

0	100	200	300	400 miles
0	200		400	600 km

of Carnaro'; despite international opposition, by 1924 Fascist Italy had incorporated it into the fatherland. One strange manifestation, which reveals how important the past was to the Fascist dream, was the creation of institutes to promote the serious study (and *italianità*, 'Italianness') of Corsican, Maltese and Dalmatian history. Anyone who wandered along the great ceremonial avenue carved out alongside the Roman Forum, through the heart of ancient Rome, could admire large maps of the Roman Empire that showed how it had grown from a tiny settlement on the Palatine Hill to the empire of Trajan, encompassing the entire Mediterranean and lands far beyond. Albania, precariously independent since 1913, also came within Italian sights: the central bank of Albania was based in Rome; its new ruler, King Zog, was des-

perate for financial and political support from Italy, an issue impatiently resolved with the Italian invasion of Albania in April 1939. Even before then, Italy operated an important submarine base at Saseno, a small island off the Albanian coast. Submarines were seen as the key to future Italian success in the Mediterranean, when the time came to challenge the ascendancy of Great Britain. In 1935 Marshal Badoglio, commander of the Italian armed forces, asserted that Italy would have no need for heavy battleships, but could win command of the sea by more modern means. In fact, the Italian fleet was unimpressive: 'it lagged in practically every category of naval warfare, being technologically backward, operationally off balance and unimaginatively led'.[3]

The invasion of Albania and continued repression of rebels in Libya

proved that talk of a Mediterranean empire was not mere bluster, however much observers saw Mussolini as a semi-comic figure with his
jutting jaw out of which poured grandiose statements about the restoration of the Roman *Mare Nostrum*. The acquisition of Libya had created
a north–south axis across the Mediterranean, and North Africa was to
constitute Italy's 'fourth shore'. British Malta, commanding the seas
between Sicily and the 'fourth shore', was therefore more than an inconvenience; it was an obstacle. Mussolini staged a triumphal visit to Tripoli
in 1937, celebrating the creation of the first proper road running for
1,000 miles along the Libyan coast, and the rebuilding of parts of the
capital as a modern European city.[4] Further proof of the Fascist ambition
to displace Great Britain, by whatever means, emerged when the Italians
extended financial support to the Grand Mufti of Jerusalem, a highly
disruptive figure who exploited the Arab riots in Palestine in 1936 to
increase his political influence as religious leader of the Sunni Muslims in
Palestine. Fascist militias – Green Shirts and Blue Shirts (who naturally
detested one another) – were created in Egypt, where, in any case, there
were many Black Shirts within the Italian community of Alexandria.[5]

Then, in 1936, the Italians offered active help to the Falangist forces
fighting in Spain under the ruthless, uncharismatic but effective command of General Franco. As well as 50,000 troops, Fascist Italy provided
air and sea support and played a major role in the battle for the Balearic
islands. Mussolini made no claims to the Spanish mainland, but the
islands were a different matter. The Italians landed in Majorca, from
where by September 1936 they had chased out the Republicans; they
executed about 3,000 Majorcans accused of sympathy for the Commu-
nists. Over the next two years the island became a base for savage
Italian air raids on major Republican centres such as Valencia and Barcelona. Mussolini would probably have liked to hold on to Majorca,
but he had acquired what he wanted: a centre of operations in the western Mediterranean, close enough to Toulon and Oran to serve as a
warning to the French fleets based there, although his major obsession
remained the British navy. In reality, though, the Italians made their
presence felt: the main street of Palma de Mallorca was renamed Via
Roma, its entrance adorned with statues of youths on whose shoulders
Roman eagles were perched.[6] After fifteen centuries, *Mare Nostrum*
once again extended from Italy into Spanish waters.

Great Britain was not sure what it wanted in the Mediterranean. By

1939, only 9 per cent of British imports passed through the Suez Canal, while Malta was not, in fact, a particularly useful supply base, despite its magnificent harbour, since the lack of local resources (beginning with water) meant that it constantly had to be resupplied. It did provide a useful staging-post for aircraft flying the length of the Mediterranean, enabling them to refuel between Gibraltar and Alexandria. Apart from its superb sixteenth-century fortifications, Malta was not well defended. At the start of the war the island was protected by three single-engine biplanes known as *Faith*, *Hope* and *Charity*, carrying light .303 machine-guns.[7] Strategically, Malta had the advantage, and disadvantage, of lying only a few minutes by air from Sicily: it was dangerously exposed, but Britain would not give up lightly a position that commanded the sea passages of the central Mediterranean. It was at Alexandria, though, that Britain chose to concentrate its Mediterranean fleet, despite having to use a harbour much inferior to Valletta.[8] As for Britain's other Mediterranean holdings, Cyprus had not been much used as a naval base since it was acquired from the Ottomans, while the bay of Haifa possessed a special strategic value as the terminal of the great oil pipeline from Iraq. Gibraltar was to prove slightly less of a problem in relations with Spain than the British government expected, even after war with Germany broke out: Franco, to Hitler's disgust, refused to be drawn into the war, partly for fear that Britain would then occupy the Canaries. Hitler denounced Franco for his ingratitude after years of support during the civil war, suggesting that he must have Jewish blood.[9] Still, what Britain required was easy access from west to east, particularly towards the Suez Canal.

Even when Britain and France declared war on Nazi Germany in September 1939 there was no reason to suppose that a war in defence of Poland would convulse the Mediterranean. Most of those involved expected a reprise of the hard-fought land battles in Flanders during the First World War. Mussolini was reticent about joining Hitler's side, though his propaganda ministry routinely churned out empty boasts: on 21 April 1940 his spokesman declared that 'the whole Mediterranean was under the control of Italy's naval and air forces, and if Britain dared to fight she would at once be driven out'.[10] It was only when France was about to fall that he opportunistically decided to join the rout, on 10 June. This brought him a small slice of occupied France, though not yet the port he coveted, Nice.

II

France, not Italy, was Britain's first problem in the Mediterranean. Most French commanders, stunned by defeat, saw the salvation of their country in Pétain's humiliating deal with Hitler; they masked the shame they felt with an intense patriotism that was turned not so much against Germany as against Britain, for had not Britain sent too few men to fight, exposing *la Patrie* to a defeat it did not deserve? Before it could come to grips with the Italians, who were beginning to threaten British convoys, the British navy needed to know where it stood in relation to the French fleet, part of which, under the title 'Force X', was parked at Alexandria. There, in what was effectively British territory, the French refused to offer their vessels to Britain but did agree to mothball their ships, and little trouble ensued, despite the professed loyalty of the French sailors to the Pétain regime at Vichy.[11] But the pride of the French fleet lay at Oran, mainly in the harbour of Mers el-Kebir, and included two of the world's best-equipped battle cruisers, the *Dunkerque* and the *Strasbourg*. Admiral Darlan proved to be an impassioned defender of what he saw as French interests, and it would be several years before his loyalty to Vichy wavered. The British offered Darlan a variety of options, from bringing his fleet into the British navy to sailing the ships to the Caribbean where they would be immobilized for the rest of the war. Darlan's view was that French they were and French they would remain. The only option left, the British made clear, was for the Royal Navy to attack, which it did on 3 July 1940, giving no quarter. Although the *Strasbourg* managed to make its escape, the British achieved their main military objectives: the French ships were wrecked, though at a cost of about 1,300 French lives.[12] But Britain paid a political cost: vestigial diplomatic ties with Vichy France were broken. Darlan's loathing of Britain was amply confirmed. Hitler could now see that the French navy and army in North Africa and French Syria were led by men who would remain tenaciously loyal to the Vichy regime. They might be of some use against the British, but the edges were fuzzy: France considered itself out of the war. Mers el-Kebir confirmed Hitler's sense that he should concentrate his war in northern Europe. Mussolini could be allowed the scraps he sought in the Mediterranean, though Tunisia was out of the question: the Germans considered that North Africa was safer in the hands of a compliant Vichy France, and they laughed at Foreign Minister Ciano's demand for Nice, Corsica, Malta, Tunisia and part of Algeria.[13]

So Britain's next clashes in the Mediterranean were with the Italians, who seized Sidi Barrani, at the extreme west of Egypt, though not for long. In November 1940 the British won their spurs at Taranto, where an air attack launched from the decks of the aircraft-carrier *Illustrious* holed the *Littorio*, the most powerful ship the Italians possessed, and sank the battleship *Cavour*.[14] This quick and easy victory discouraged the Italians from seeking battle at sea and, more importantly, it confirmed that even limited air power could overwhelm the pride of an enemy fleet. The question now was whether air raids could help conquer an island. Malta had been suffering Italian air attacks almost from the outbreak of war between Great Britain and Italy, though with the help of newly developed radar the little planes *Faith*, *Hope* and *Charity* proved surprisingly effective against the Italian Regia Aeronautica, until a squadron of modern Hurricane aircraft arrived to boost British air defences. At the start of 1941, German and Italian aircraft crippled the *Illustrious* as she made her way east from Gibraltar, though she managed to limp into the Grand Harbour of Malta.[15] The bombing of Malta intensified, with daily air raids by the Germans that devastated Valletta and the Three Cities on the opposite side of the Grand Harbour, as well as killing hundreds of Maltese civilians who, along with British troops stationed on the island, were constantly short of food and other basic supplies. The situation became even worse after December 1941. By now the Germans were taking the Mediterranean more seriously. The fanatical Kesselring was appointed commander in the Mediterranean and made a concerted effort to destroy British convoys heading for Malta; as the German presence grew, though, pressures from other directions also grew, once Nazi Germany and the Soviet Union were at war. By autumn 1941 the British were able to respond with bombing campaigns against Sicily and North Africa, and British submarines targeted Italian and German shipping supplying the Axis forces in North Africa. The Germans and Italians were so irritated that they consulted the third major Axis power, Japan, about the best way to seize an island, given Japanese experience in the Pacific; one method they proposed to employ was starvation.[16]

Malta now possessed a Grand Harbour filled with debris, the bodies of drowned sailors and oil from sunken vessels (which threatened to catch fire). Part of its defenders' achievement was to keep Malta functioning as a base for aircraft and submarines capable of needling the enemy and interfering with their deployment of forces and supplies in North Africa. It is hardly surprising that the second Great Siege of Malta has seared itself as deeply in the Maltese consciousness as the Great Siege of 1565.[17] Churchill was worried that conditions had reached a point where the Axis powers would not even need to invade: Malta would simply be bombed into submission. British convoys were under enormous pressure from submarines in the waters south of Majorca, and then from Italian cruisers and German and Italian aeroplanes on the approach past Tunis – in August 1942 only five ships out of a convoy of fourteen, heading from Gibraltar, reached safe anchorage in Malta.[18] Fortunately, the Germans themselves could not decide whether they wanted to take the island, especially since that would mean a joint exercise with the Italian army, which recent experiences in North Africa had led them to respect less and less; and Mussolini assumed that the island would be his for the asking once Great Britain was forced to surrender on all fronts.[19] Fortunately, too, the Germans became increasingly obsessed by their ambitions in North Africa, as Rommel advanced eastwards to Tobruk, and so, by May 1942, Malta seemed to be a peripheral consideration. The Axis powers were convinced that the war in the Mediterranean would be won on land, and not by conquering a small, dusty island. British commanders too thought that 'it is better to lose Malta than Egypt'.[20] Yet what also saved Malta was undoubtedly the stalwart refusal of those on the island to allow constant bombardment and months of utter misery to break their resolve, and this was duly recognized when King George VI awarded the entire island the George Cross. The medal is still borne on the Maltese flag as a reminder of the island's heroic resistance: 30,000 buildings had been damaged or destroyed, and 1,300 civilians had been killed by bombs.[21]

Malta held out, but in 1941 the British were beaten in the battle for Crete, even if its strategic value to the Germans was not entirely obvious.[22] The German High Command had only a disjointed appreciation of the importance of the Mediterranean. The Germans viewed the *Mittelmeer* from the perspective of the Balkans. Who in the long term would control routes across the sea was seen as an issue between Italy and Britain. With German forces fighting alongside the Italians in North Africa, the Axis powers aimed to secure the north–south supply route across

the Mediterranean. But the way the Führer chose to do so was controversial. When Hitler decided to send U-boats into the Mediterranean – a
hazardous exercise, since it meant passing Gibraltar – Admiral Raeder
expostulated that this would harm the German war effort in the Atlantic. The Axis powers knew that the Mediterranean gave access to the oil
supplies of the Middle East, via the Suez Canal, although it was unreal-
istic to expect that route to be opened up quickly. But Axis oil stocks
were running short; by summer 1942, the Italian fleet was marooned without oil, and the Germans refused to supply any in view of all their other
commitments. So Hitler pointed to a different route to the oil, across the
vast open plains of Russia into Persia, which made more sense to him
once the war with Russia was under way in 1941. This took his army to
Stalingrad, where it stalled and then suffered a massive defeat. The
growing importance of the Mediterranean took the Germans by surprise. Its real importance became much clearer when, in November
1942, the Allies, now including the Americans, landed on the same
beaches the French had used in 1830 to invade Algeria.[23]

The attack on Algeria ('Operation Torch') was accompanied by landings in Morocco and a drive eastwards to Tunisia. The Germans had
already been checked at El Alamein in July 1942, and were pushed back
decisively in November by Montgomery's army of 'Desert Rats'. However, the presence in North Africa of Vichy commanders, notably Darlan,
enormously complicated the situation. Darlan was only really interested
in supporting the winning side. He regarded himself as heir-apparent to
Pétain. He was willing to treat with the Allies, however much contempt
they felt for a man many saw as a craven traitor. But he was worried
that the Allies might yet be beaten back, and then he would be exposed
as a double-dealer. In November 1942 General Eisenhower met Darlan
at Algiers, where the admiral lived in spectacular style. Eisenhower
hoped to persuade him to bring the French home fleet from Toulon to
North Africa and join the American effort. Darlan made murmurs of
assent, but he knew that the admiral in charge at Toulon, an old rival,
would not dream of so doing, and even the French ships at Alexandria
demurred, despite the good relations their crews enjoyed with the British. A messy compromise allowed Darlan to remain as Pétain's deputy in
North Africa, creating outrage in Britain and the United States: Darlan
was denounced as a quisling and anti-Semite; the CBS anchorman Ed
Murrow asked: 'Are we fighting Nazis or sleeping with them?' Darlan's

predicament was resolved when, on Christmas Eve, a fanatical monarchist sneaked into the government offices in Algiers, waited for him to return from an agreeable lunch, and shot the self-righteous admiral dead.[24]

The contest for mastery over the Mediterranean was becoming more bitter; Allied success seemed far from certain. In December 1942 the Vichy commander in Tunisia handed the Axis powers the finely equipped French naval base at Bizerta. Meanwhile, during November, Hitler had decided to end the divided status of France by occupying the areas under the control of Vichy; Mussolini was allowed to claim Nice as his prize, while for good measure he also sent some squadrons across to Corsica, on which they raised the Italian flag. Vichy commanders played a murky role in Mediterranean war and politics, and used their indeterminate status as the representatives of a country not officially at war to oscillate between both sides. When the Allies smuggled a little-known French general, Henri Giraud, by submarine from Vichy France to Algiers, they discovered that he possessed all Darlan's pride and prejudices – he did not want to be an Allied poodle, he had no interest in abolishing the anti-Semitic laws, he arrested the 'usual suspects' and interned them in concentration camps out of sight of the Allies. His great hope was to lead a massive assault to free his mother-country from the humiliation of German occupation.[25] The lines between the opposing sides were far clearer in the Atlantic or the Pacific than in the Mediterranean.

III

Political confusion in the Mediterranean increased still further in 1943. Allied forces crushed the Germans at Medenine in Tunisia in March, and Rommel's Germans pulled out of Tunisia. On 8 May Tunis and Bizerta fell to the Allies, along with 250,000 Italian and German troops. The fall of Tunisia rendered the Mediterranean safer for Allied shipping, and super-convoys of as many as 100 ships now passed Malta to reach Gibraltar or Alexandria – the unity of the Mediterranean as a largely British-controlled sea was, if not restored, at least in prospect. In June 1943 King George VI sailed across the open sea from Tripoli to Malta, where he was greeted by masses of jubilant Maltese. The intention was not just to boost the morale of the Maltese, but to show the whole empire that Great Britain was making ineluctable progress towards final victory.[26]

There was further bleak news for the Axis. Greece descended into civil war, and resistance was building up in Yugoslavia.[27] Within the Axis, suspicion grew that Sardinia was being targeted as the gathering point for a massed Allied invasion of Europe by way of southern France; Cagliari paid a high price for this disinformation, and the marks of allied bombing are still visible there. The real question was whether Mediterranean France or Italy was (to use Churchill's phrase) 'the soft underbelly' of Axis Europe. In June 1943 the Allies captured their first piece of Italy: the small but strategically placed island of Pantelleria west of Malta, where 12,000 demoralized Italian troops succumbed to intense bombardment.[28] When the Allies confounded earlier expectations by landing in Sicily, in July, a special meeting of the Fascist Grand Council turned on Mussolini. At his next audience with King Victor Emmanuel he was not asked to resign – he was informed that he had already been replaced by Field Marshal Badoglio, and on leaving the Quirinale Palace he was hustled into a police van and placed under arrest. Even though the direction Badoglio's government would take was not clear, the Germans began to build up their own strength in Italy, awaiting the day when Allied forces crossed to the mainland. On 22 July Palermo was occupied by the Americans, led by General Patton; by the time the Allies arrived at Messina, on 17 August, the city had been reduced to rubble and 60,000 German troops with 75,000 Italian troops had escaped. These Italians were not keen to carry on fighting, and their mood matched that of the nation; in early September Badoglio was cajoled into signing an armistice agreement with the Allies. When German planes bombed the Italian battleship *Roma*, causing a great many deaths, the Italian navy sailed the pride of the home fleet to Malta, handing the ships over to Britain. The great harbour at Taranto was willingly ceded to the Allies. On the other hand, the situation in the islands was more confused. British forces managed to occupy the smaller islands in the Dodecanese; in Kephalonia the Germans wantonly killed 6,000 Italian troops; in Corsica there was complete chaos, as Germans, Italians, Free French and Corsican resistance fighters all staked claims to pieces of the island.[29] The capitulation of Italy thus introduced new uncertainties across the Mediterranean.

The first attempts to gain an Allied toehold in Italy in late 1943 were succeeded by the surprise landing of masses of Allied troops at Anzio, south of Rome. Thereafter the Allies would have to fight their way up

the rest of the peninsula; the political situation in Italy had been complicated by the escape of Mussolini and his acquiescence in the creation of
the 'Italian Social Republic' in the north, under Nazi control. Despite
slow progress, the Free French (not surprisingly) and the Americans
were keen to go ahead with landings in southern France, to balance the
Allied landings in Normandy during June 1944: Toulon fell to the Allies
on 26 August, earlier than they had believed possible, and this released
manpower for the attack on Marseilles, which crumbled on 28 August.[30]

Before long, thoughts turned to the future of the Mediterranean after
the German defeat. Live issues included Palestine, Yugoslavia and
Greece, where Communist insurgency was beginning to tear the country apart. In October 1944 Churchill was in Moscow and put to Stalin
the British position: Britain 'must be the leading Mediterranean Power'.
Stalin saw the point, sympathizing with the difficulties Britain had faced
when the Germans interfered with its transit routes across the Mediterranean; he even assured Churchill that he would not rock the boat in
Italy. This was because Stalin was primarily interested in gaining British
acquiescence to a Soviet ascendancy in Slav Europe, including Serbia.[31]
The moment had not yet come for the Russians to reassert their own
claim to be a Mediterranean power.

6

A Fragmented Mediterranean,
1945–1990

I

The Allied victory over Germany in the Second World War, like that in the First, left the Mediterranean unsettled. After Greece emerged from its civil war with a pro-western government, there were ever louder rumbles in Cyprus, where the movement calling for *enôsis*, union with Greece, was gathering pace again. Precisely because the Greeks sided with the West, and because Turkey had kept out of the war, during the late 1940s the United States began to see the Mediterranean as an advance position in the new struggle against the expanding power of the Soviet Union. The explicit theme was the defence of democracy against Communist tyranny.[1] Stalin's realism had prevented him from supporting Communist insurgency in Greece, but he was keen to find ways of gaining free access to the Mediterranean through the Dardanelles. In London and Washington, the fear that Soviet allies would establish themselves on the shores of the Mediterranean remained real, since the partisan leader in Yugoslavia, Tito, had played the right cards during the last stages of the war, even winning support from the British. Moreover, the Italians had lost Zadar along with the naval base at Kotor and chunks of Dalmatia they had greedily acquired during the war, while Albania, after an agonizing period of first Italian and then German occupation, had recovered its independence under the Paris-educated Communist leader Enver Hoxha, whose uncompromising stance was to bring his country into ever-greater isolation.

When he took power, Hoxha imagined that his country would form part of a brotherly band of socialist nations, alongside Tito's renascent Yugoslavia and the Soviet Union. Close ties with the Yugoslavs were

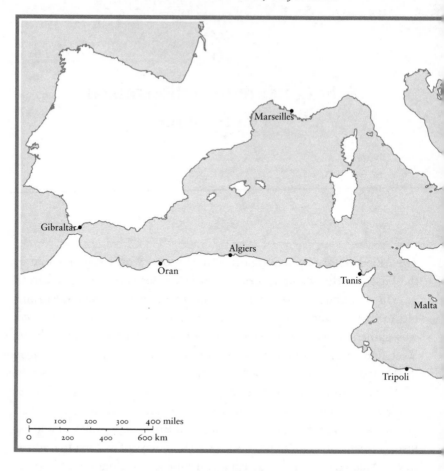

sealed by economic pacts which reveal Tito's hope of drawing Albania into the Yugoslav federation. Hoxha had other aspirations, and in his view Albania's right to defend every square inch of the national territory extended into the waters off the Albanian coast: the Corfu Channel, long used as a waterway linking Greece to the Adriatic, was mined to prevent foreign incursions. Britain decided to send warships through the channel, asserting its right to police the Mediterranean on behalf of the nations of the world. On 22 October 1946 two British warships passing close to Sarande, an Albanian port north-east of Corfu, struck mines and forty-four sailors were killed.[2] Who provided the mines is a controversial question; a subsequent sweep of the channel showed that those that remained in the water were free of rust and newly greased,

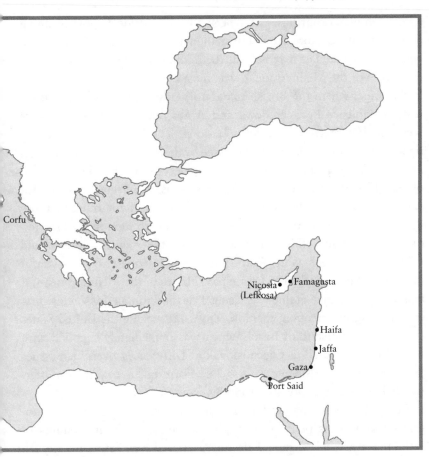

Corfu

Nicosia• •Famagusta
(Lefkosa)

•Haifa

•Jaffa

Gaza•
Port Said

even though they were not brand new, and there is a strong suspicion that they were laid by Tito's navy on Hoxha's behalf. The Albanians lacked any boats suitable for mine-laying.[3] Hoxha made no apologies and pointed his finger at the Greeks, highly unlikely culprits. That was the end of attempts to establish diplomatic relations between Britain and Hoxha's Albania. On the other hand, Tito took offence at Soviet attempts to treat Yugoslavia as a satellite, denying the Soviet Union the naval bases it craved in Dalmatia.

On paper, British influence in the Mediterranean was still strong: Libya had been taken away from Italy and placed under a British man-date, though Britain, impoverished by the war, was keen to rid itself of the country as soon as possible. The Americans were granted full use of

a vast complex of air bases at Wheelus Field, outside Tripoli, meaning
that they gained more from Libya than the British – oil exploration
began only in the late 1950s.[4] But the inability of the British to mould
the future of the Mediterranean was most clearly revealed by the crisis
in Palestine, where the British mandatory authorities could no longer
restrain violence between Jews and Arabs, and British troops were
increasingly targeted by extremist factions.[5] The American Defense Secretary, James Forrestal, became obsessed by the idea of the Mediterranean
as an advance position against the Soviet Union, but he was also
obsessed by Palestine, and indeed by the Jews, and argued that American interests in the Mediterranean were being fatally harmed by those
in America who were pressing President Truman to support the creation
of a Jewish state within Palestine. He took the view that this would
alienate others, such as the Arab states, whose cooperation was vital if
the United States wished to create naval bases in the Mediterranean. It
was clear, too, that Stalin was using Palestine for his own ends, first
encouraging insurrection, then, in May 1948, racing the United States
to recognize the state of Israel, which was immediately supplied with
arms from his satellite Czechoslovakia. Differences over such issues
exasperated the president, who sacked Forrestal in 1949; soon afterwards Forrestal, a depressive, took his own life.[6]

In a Mediterranean setting, the significance of Israel was demographic as well as political. It has been seen how the inhabitants of
Jaffa, the largest Arab city in Palestine, scattered even before the city fell
to the Haganah, the future army of Israel. The other important port was
Haifa, a mixed city of Arabs and Jews, which possessed a population of
about 70,000 Arabs at the start of 1948. By the end of the war of independence there were only 4,000 Arabs, at most, left in the city. The
circumstances were, inevitably, very confused: some of the Arab leaders
gave up the fight early and left in April 1948, demoralizing those who
remained behind; the Arab Higher Command seemed to want the Arabs
to leave, fearing they could be used as hostages after the British finally
left Palestine in May; the Haganah shelled the city, inducing panic and
flight under fire to Acre and Beirut. The aim of the bombardment was
to push the Arab leaders in Haifa towards a quick surrender. This tough
policy was opposed by some Jewish leaders, who argued that the future
of the city must be as a joint enterprise of Jews and Arabs – a Jewish
delegation went to the Arab quarters of Haifa urging people not to

leave, and British military intelligence noted that 'the Jews have been making extensive efforts to prevent wholesale evacuation, but their propaganda appears to have had very little effect'.[7] As news of the evacuation spread, other Arabs began to leave areas on which the Haganah was advancing: most notably Jaffa, but also the towns of the Galilee interior. There was, a Haganah report suggested, a 'psychosis of flight' rendered more severe by reports of expulsions from villages in the interior.[8]

Whereas the Jewish settlers earlier in the twentieth century had been guided by Zionist ideals, most of the later ones were guided by the search for a refuge, before, during and in the wake of the Nazi persecution of the Jews. British restrictions on immigration since 1938 were determined by the relentless opposition of Arab leaders, and made it a difficult refuge to reach. The vehement Arab hostility to a Jewish state was not confined to Palestine itself, and had the curious effect of bolstering the population of Israel, as a new exodus, that of Jews from Arab lands, gathered pace from 1948 onwards. Within a dozen years the Jewish communities of the Mediterranean were heavily concentrated in Israel. In North Africa, the creation of Israel resulted in anti-Jewish riots, leading to a steady exodus of hundreds of thousands of Jews from Morocco, Algeria, Tunisia and Libya, though the wealthier and more westernized families often shunned the Middle East for France or Italy. Thus there was a south–north flow of Jews as well as a west–east flow. By 1967 the only major centre of Jewish population in the Mediterranean apart from Israel was southern France, as a result of migration from North Africa. Otherwise, 1,900 years of the Mediterranean diaspora had suddenly been reversed.

It was now that Britain, France and Italy began to lose control over their possessions in the eastern and southern Mediterranean. The Lebanese had already started agitating for independence from France in 1943 (not the best moment), but in 1946 a curious constitution, guaranteeing the rights of both Christians and Muslims, was enacted; with independence came an economic boom, as Beirut, with its westernized ways, became the major port and banking centre in the Arab Levant. In Egypt, the break with the past took a different form: in 1952 a cabal of Arab army officers seized power and King Farouk went into exile, marking the first stage in the dissolution of the mixed society of Alexandria over which his dynasty had presided all too lavishly. Agitation in French and Spanish Morocco, Algeria and Tunisia placed further pressure on the colonial powers. Direct British control was contracting inwards to the line from Gibraltar through Malta to Cyprus and the Suez Canal. This mattered less than it would have done during the war years; India obtained its independence two years after the war ended, and, even with the retention of Malaya, Singapore and Hong Kong, the military and political importance of Suez was declining. All this meant that Churchill's hopes of restoring British mastery over the Mediterranean were becoming irrelevant, with one proviso: that the Soviet Union did not, after all, find allies within the Mediterranean. By 1956 it had done precisely that.

II

The revolution that overthrew King Farouk aroused new worries. The new Egyptian leader, Gamal Abdel Nasser, began to present himself to the Arab world as the figure who would restore self-respect to the Arab nations (this was accompanied by the standard insistence that they were all ultimately a single pan-Arab nation). Even though Nasser had encouraged behind-the-scenes dialogue with Israel in 1954, neither side trusted the other, and hesitant attempts at rapprochement turned into hostility.[9] Britain and France had agreed to withdraw troops from the Canal Zone in 1954, and should not have been greatly surprised by Nasser's speech in Alexandria in July 1956 announcing the nationalization of the canal; perhaps what disturbed them most was the ranting tone in which he denounced the colonial powers. The British prime minister, Anthony Eden, decided that he faced a 'Hitler on the Nile'. Behind these fears lay other, global worries: when the United States withdrew its support for the building of the Aswan High Dam, which was supposed to bring prosperity to Egypt, Nasser turned to the Soviet Union. The danger that he might offer his new ally a naval base within the Mediterranean could not be ignored.

The British and the French assumed that the Egyptians would make a mess of running the canal, while the Israelis were increasingly anxious to show that Egyptian bombardment of settlements in the Negev and raids into Israel by Arab *fedayin* from Egyptian-occupied Gaza must be stopped by force. In October 1956 Nasser built up his army within Gaza, and launched scathing verbal attacks on Israel, threatening to wipe it off the map – thereby raising further his prestige in the Arab world.[10] At a secret meeting near Paris in October 1956, the Israeli prime minister, David Ben Gurion, encouraged France and Britain to make common cause against Egypt, setting out some fantastic ideas about restabilizing the Middle East with a friendly Christian Lebanon, a semi-autonomous West Bank under Israeli protection and a British ascendancy in Jordan and Iraq. The British foreign secretary, Selwyn Lloyd, thought this was all far too ambitious, and still believed that jaw-jaw was better than war-war, if only Nasser would listen. On the other hand, if there were to be war, then, he insisted, the aims must be 'the conquest of the Canal Zone and the destruction of Nasser'. If Israel attacked Egypt, the French and British would intervene to protect the canal, giving them the chance to reoccupy what they had lost, but there was no possibility of siding openly with Israel.[11]

So the scene was set for the great fiasco that announced to the world the end of British and French power within the Mediterranean. Israel attacked Egypt, quickly seizing Gaza and Sinai; British and French troops landed in the Canal Zone, supposedly to protect the canal and separate the belligerents; but President Eisenhower's disapproval brought the campaign to an early end, and Israel was required to withdraw from Sinai, securing little more than promises of free access up the Red Sea to Eilat (but not through the Suez Canal), and a tacit agreement that *fedayin* raids encouraged by Egypt would end. Nasser looked stronger than ever, while Eden lasted only a few more months as prime minister. European fears about the maintenance of the canal proved groundless, but the crisis had shaken the old master of the Mediterranean to its core.[12] In the next eleven years Soviet influence in Egypt greatly increased, as it did in Syria, which was briefly joined to Egypt in the 'United Arab Republic'. The USSR provided Nasser with 'advisers', while Egyptian invectives against Israel became ever more tasteless, including a host of anti-Semitic cartoons in the government-controlled press.

Nasser's rhetoric against Israel worked well as a means to assert his dominance in the Arab world, but he became carried away by his own words as crowds throughout the Middle East gathered to acclaim him and denounce Israel. By early summer 1967 he was promising a maritime blockade of Israel, though in the Red Sea, not in the Mediterranean.[13] A pre-emptive strike by Israel on 5 June culminated after only six days in the occupation of Gaza, Sinai, the Golan Heights and (after King

Hussein of Jordan made the mistake of taking part) the Jordanian parts of Palestine. As a result the Suez Canal was blocked for ten years, becoming the front line of the opposing Israeli and Egyptian armies, which then fought a war of attrition across its banks until the Egyptians launched a surprise attack in October 1973 – the Yom Kippur War – whose aim was not, this time, to 'throw Israel into the sea' but, more realistically, to recover Sinai. Despite early successes, the Egyptians were finally pushed back across the canal, and it took four years for serious peace negotiations to begin, following President Sadat's brave decision to enter the lion's den and address the Israeli parliament, for which, before long, he paid with his life. After this, the canal was reopened to the shipping of all nations, including at last Israel. But a second result of the Six-Day War was the hardening of Soviet attitudes towards Israel; during the war the Soviet bloc, apart from unpredictable Romania, finally broke off diplomatic relations with Israel, a move designed to win approval within the Arab world and to emphasize that Israel's friends were the bourgeois capitalist powers of Great Britain, France and, above all, the United States. The Yom Kippur War had, indeed, something of the character of a proxy war between the Soviet Union and the United States: the Soviets supplied large quantities of arms to the Egyptians and Syrians, while the Americans ferried in armaments by way of US bases in the Azores. Further Soviet mischief was created by support for violent Palestinian radicals, some of whom, like the Popular Front for the Liberation of Palestine, were comfortably ensconced in Damascus, where they proclaimed a version of Marxist doctrines.

III

The Soviet entry into Mediterranean politics was not all plain sailing. Stalin had accepted that Italy and Greece would remain in the western sphere, and in 1952 both Greece and Turkey were drawn into the new alliance the United States, Britain and France had created three years earlier, the North Atlantic Treaty Organization, a misnomer for a body that also included Italy. But NATO came to see the Mediterranean as a front line against Soviet expansion: both France, with its North African empire, and Britain, with its bases in Gibraltar, Malta and Cyprus, were Mediterranean powers. And the United States, still present at Wheelus

Field in Libya, had its own ideas about how to defend the Mediterranean against Soviet ambitions. In 1952 the US Sixth Fleet visited eight Spanish ports, including Barcelona and Palma de Mallorca, thereby bringing Generalissimo Franco respectability while he was still merrily despatching the regime's enemies to the next world. Although Spanish entry into NATO would have to await the dictator's death in 1975, the United States began to establish air bases within Spain well before then.

In the 1950s France increasingly looked away from the Mediterranean. This was partly because the centre of gravity within Europe now lay, more clearly than ever, within northern Europe: the creation of the European Economic Community in 1957 was seen not just as an instrument to promote economic cooperation, but as a means to prevent new conflict between France and Germany. The adhesion of Italy appeared to give the EEC a Mediterranean dimension, but this should not be exaggerated: Italy qualified for entry thanks to Milan and Turin, industrial cities away from the Mediterranean, and during the first fifteen years of the EEC it was the poorest state in the community, with a poverty-stricken south bedevilled by low literacy, agricultural backwardness and lack of industrialization.[14] Further evidence of a turning away from the Mediterranean can be found in the troubled history of French decolonization. France conceded first autonomy and then independence to the troublesome Moroccans and Tunisians, and then imagined it could hold Algeria, the northern coast of which had been incorporated into metropolitan France. The already vicious war between French troops and the nationalist *Front de Libération Nationale* was complicated by the intervention of the activists of the *Organisation de l'armée secrète*, fighting both the Algerian nationalists and the French government to protect what they saw as French interests in Algeria. The Algerian question convulsed public opinion and French politics. The generals' coup that led to the overthrow of the Fourth Republic and the assumption of power by General de Gaulle in 1958 began when French settlers in Algeria occupied government buildings in Algiers; it continued with landings by troops in Corsica. De Gaulle came to power arguing that Algeria must stay French, but before long he conceded that this was impossible, and several of his fellow-generals decided he had betrayed their cause and launched a conspiracy against him. Undeterred by these threats, de Gaulle let Algeria go in 1962. The consequences were predictable: another mass movement of population. Those Europeans who had not already left Algeria were encouraged to do so by the 'massacre of Oran' on 5 July 1962: on the day the country became independent the European quarter of Oran was raided by nationalists who killed a disputed number of people (the lowest estimates hover around 100) but succeeded in their aim of scaring away hundreds of thousands of Europeans. French troops, still in Oran, stood aside, under orders to maintain neutrality. Perhaps 900,000 French Algerians left in the months before and after independence, including both the descendants of settlers and Algerian Jews, with vast numbers settling in southern France. They were followed by a wave of native Algerian immigration, and immigration from Morocco and Tunisia, transforming the heart of Marseilles and other cities. Rather than creating a new *convivencia*, the presence of a teeming North African population unlocked ugly, xenophobic sentiments in southern France, accentuated by memories of the terrorism of the FLN.

Britain too faced emphatic demands for independence from its Mediterranean possessions. The Maltese faced three options: to join Italy, an idea fashionable before the war but unthinkable after the siege; to strengthen the bond with its master by union with Great Britain; to gain independence. The second option attracted extensive support, but it became obvious that the Royal Navy had less and less use for the Malta dockyards, as Britain reduced its presence within the Mediterranean, and by 1964 the independence movement had triumphed, though Malta retained Queen Elizabeth as its head of state for another ten years, and remained within the Commonwealth. Later, under the socialist government of Dom Mintoff, Malta would vaunt its non-aligned status and would seek allies in the region, including the highly unpredictable Colonel Gaddafi, who seized power in Libya in 1969. The island retained a strange legacy: fish and chips, sticky buns and the English language, though now in second place to Maltese. Successive Maltese governments were left with a headache, for it was unclear how the assets of the Grand Harbour could be deployed to good advantage without the presence of the British fleet. The island's non-aligned status meant that the Soviet fleet could not expect much benefit from Malta, but the Chinese began to see an opportunity as their relations with the USSR deteriorated into ideological name-calling. Diplomatic relations were solemnly established between tiny Malta and the vast People's Republic, and the Chinese invested in improvements to Malta's dry docks. On the other hand, until the late 1970s, China enjoyed access to naval facilities in Albania, its one close European ally, which now delighted in denying facilities to the 'revisionist social Fascists' of Moscow.[15]

To Britain, Malta was an irritating mosquito, but Cyprus was a giant hornets' nest. The Greek Cypriot demand for *enôsis* with Greece, and a growing divide between Greek and Turkish Cypriots, had a predictable result: the Turkish government insisted that a Greek-owned Cyprus was a strategic threat in the waters to the south of Turkey. Yet the focus of opposition was not simply the other community. The colonial power was targeted by violent Greek nationalists, who included increasingly radicalized high-school pupils. They imagined that they were reliving the Greek struggle for independence from the Ottomans, and a number joined the thousand-odd members of the *Ethniki Organôsis Kypriôn Agonistôn* (EOKA), the 'National Organization of Cypriot Fighters'. Its youth wing required members to swear in the name of the Trinity that they would 'work with all my power for the liberation of Cyprus from the British yoke, sacrificing for this even my life'.[16] But this was no game. The EOKA commander, George Grivas, was a fanatical national- ist who gave no quarter. At the height of the emergency, the streets of Nicosia saw daily killings of British troops (over 100 in all) and of Turks, and the Greek and Turkish communities bunkered down in dis- tinct areas, separated by barbed wire or guarded by armed irregulars.[17]

Lawrence Durrell, who taught in a Greek high school in Nicosia and then became a British information officer in Cyprus, remembered the indecisiveness of the British colonial authorities as the troubles began:

> Should one for example behave as if the Greeks were Greeks? The Greek National Anthem – should it be played on Independence Day while Athens was broadcasting scurrilous and inflammatory material, inciting Greeks to rise? There seemed to be no clear line on this so I was forced to steer a course between vague amiabilities and reproaches for the time being.[18]

The invocation of the Trinity in the EOKA oath underlined the role of Greek Orthodoxy in the struggle for *enôsis*, for the Greek Church, not a sense of being the heirs of Perikles, was the focus of Greek identity – the Turks were more casual about their attachment to Islam. Archbishop Makarios functioned as 'Ethnarch' at the head of the Greek community, though the British authorities shipped him out of the island in 1956, detaining him in the Seychelles for three years. He was a staunch advocate of decolonization, to be followed by *enôsis*, and the Turks countered with the argument that the only way to ease tensions between Turk and Greek was to divide the island. It was difficult to see how this could be done, since the Turks were scattered all over it. Moreover, the Greeks tended to occupy the commanding economic positions, and Turkish areas within mixed villages often remained poor.

The republic of Cyprus came into existence in 1960, with Makarios as president, but required careful nurturing. Greece, Turkey and Great Britain were the guarantor powers, with the right to intervene if Cyprus was under threat. Britain retained two irregularly shaped bases at Dhekelia and Akrotiri, encompassing nearly 100 square miles (250 square kilometres), and constituting sovereign British territory; they became important Middle Eastern listening-stations for NATO. Under the Cypriot constitution the Turks provided a vice-president and had (the Greeks maintained) stronger political influence than their numbers warranted. But of course the intention of the constitution was to make sure that the Greeks did not haul the island into union with Greece. Although in 1960 Makarios had accepted that Cyprus would become a separate republic, *enôsis* remained on the Greek Cypriot agenda even after 1967, when a brutal, intensely nationalistic military regime seized power in Athens. Greek officers stationed in Cyprus became a source of trouble in summer 1974, and Makarios was overthrown in a coup. It seemed that the Greek colonels intended to achieve *enôsis* by force. The Turkish government intervened in late July, claiming the right to do so as a guarantor power; Turkey landed 30,000 troops on the island and occupied the northern third, while the junta in Athens, thoroughly discredited, fell from power. Within Cyprus, the human effects were predictable. As many as 190,000 Greek Cypriots fled south from Kyrenia, Famagusta and smaller towns and villages into the Greek-controlled areas, and tens of thousands of Turkish Cypriots hurried northwards to seek the protection of the Turkish army. The island was thus at last ethnically divided, but there were deep scars, physical and mental: close to the Turkish front line, the seashore of Famagusta, bristling with hotels built by Greeks to take advantage of the relative peace that had followed independence, became a deserted ghost town, complementing old Famagusta, a ghost town of ruined Gothic churches ever since it had been bombarded by the Turks 400 years earlier. Across the island, stretches of no-man's-land under United Nations supervision separated the two

58. About 150,000 Spaniards of Muslim descent, the Moriscos, were expelled between 1609 and 1614, even though some protested that they were devout Christians. This painting shows their departure by sea from Vinaròs, a flourishing port north of Valencia City.

59. Venetian painting recording the victory of a small Venetian squadron over seventeen Turkish ships off Crete in May 1661. By this time the Venetians had lost the second and third cities of Crete and were holding on to Candia (Heraklion) by their fingernails; they lost the island in 1669.

60. French assault on Mahón in British-held Minorca, 1756. St Philip's Fort, guarding the entrance to the largest natural harbour in the Mediterranean, can be seen in the foreground. France saw the British presence close to Toulon as a direct threat to its Mediterranean fleet.

61. The execution of Admiral Byng on 14 March 1757 on the quarterdeck of HMS *Monarch*. Byng was the scapegoat for the British government and Admiralty, which had sent him on an impossible mission to relieve Minorca with inadequate numbers of ships and men. As Voltaire famously said, he was executed *pour encourager les autres*.

62. Admiral Fyodor Ushakov (1744–1817), commander of the Russian fleet in the Mediterranean, who captured the Ionian islands from France. In 2000 he became the patron saint of the Russian navy.

63. Viscount Hood, commander of the British fleet in the Mediterranean from 1793. Like Nelson, he was the son of a clergyman. Under his command the British occupied Toulon and brought Corsica under the British Crown.

64. The German nobleman Ferdinand von Hompesch was the last Grand Master of the Sovereign Military Order of Malta, or Knights of St John, to rule Malta. Elected in July 1797, his rule lasted only a year before Napoleon seized the island.

65. Stephen Decatur was the first American naval hero, and his name is still borne by US warships. In 1803 and 1804 he led celebrated attacks on Tripoli harbour in Libya; his acts of bravery symbolized the victory of American courage over the brute strength of the Barbary pirates.

66. Port Said was a new town built to service the Suez Canal. In this photograph from 1880 ships wait to enter the Canal. The ship at centre left is an ironclad vessel combining sail and steam power.

67. Trieste, with its mixed population of German-speakers, Italian-speakers and Slav-speakers, of Christians and Jews, gave the Austro-Hungarian empire access to the Mediterranean. This photograph of around 1890 shows the quayside belonging to Austrian Lloyd, the city's most important navigation company, whose leading shareholders were drawn from a variety of ethnic backgrounds.

68. The Grand Square, also known as Place Mehmet Ali, in Alexandria in the 1910s. The square neatly expressed the wish to make Alexandria into a European city perched next to Africa. Here stood the multinational court that dealt with commercial cases, and here Colonel Nasser delivered a rousing speech in 1956 announcing the nationalization of the Suez Canal.

69. Italian attempts to portray the occupation of Turkish Libya as part of a European civilizing mission were reinforced by illustrations such as this one from a French magazine of October 1911. The mere presence of Italian officers, inspired by the goddess bearing the flame of liberty, is sufficient to scare away the cowardly and primitive natives.

70. The refusal of the French navy to join the British fleet or to withdraw to neutral waters led Churchill to authorize the attack on the French warships moored at Mers el-Kebir in October 1940. Resentment at British actions not only led to a final break in diplomatic relations but soured relations between the defeated French and Great Britain throughout much of the Second World War.

71. In July 1943 British troops landed in Sicily in the first stage of a campaign that would take Allied armies slowly up the Italian peninsula. Feint attacks on Sardinia had led the Germans to imagine that it rather than Sicily was the intended target.

72. Ship carrying 4,500 Jewish refugees from central and eastern Europe, seen docking at Haifa on 7 October 1947 after its seizure by the British authorities. Many of those attempting to reach Palestine were sent to camps in Cyprus.

73. Charles de Gaulle, having led Free French forces during the Second World War, seized power in 1958 as the Third Republic grappled with the problem of French rule over Algeria, which he initially promised to maintain. Here he is seen visiting Algeria in June 1958, to the delight of the French settlers.

74. From the 1960s onwards, Spain exploited the rise of the package holiday and then came to regret some of its effects: concrete hotels, restaurants and bars on the Costas, along with impossibly crowded beaches, such as this one at Lloret de Mar in Catalonia. Similar scenes now regularly appear in parts of France, Italy, Greece, Cyprus and Israel.

75. By the end of the twentieth century the Mediterranean lands of the European Union had become a tightly guarded frontier across which the movement of migrants from Africa and Asia was strictly controlled. Here a group of migrants from Africa is trying to land on Spanish soil near the Straits of Gibraltar.

sides. Nicosia had already become divided between Turks and Greeks in 1963, with barricaded areas inhabited by the Turks.[19] The frontier between Turks and Greeks cut right through the middle of the old city. Only in April 2008 was a crossing-point opened within old Nicosia.

The Turks went on to enact the policy they had been advocating in response to *enôsis*. In 1983 the 'Turkish Republic of North Cyprus' was created, unrecognized internationally except by Turkey, which maintained large forces there and encouraged tens of thousands of Anatolian Turks to find a new life in Turkish Cyprus. The political changes in Cyprus can be measured in changes to place-names, in the abandonment of disused places of worship and, of course, in the presence of flags everywhere – in northern Cyprus the Turkish flag fluttering alongside its variant, the northern Cypriot flag, white with a red crescent; in the south the Greek flag alongside that of the Republic of Cyprus. *De facto*, Cyprus falls under four separate authorities: the Greek Cypriot republic, the Turkish Cypriot republic, Great Britain and the United Nations. The adhesion of Greek Cyprus to the European Union in 2004 was accompanied by attempts to bring the sides together, and, since the EU regards the Greek republic as the government of all Cyprus, EU investment has also benefited projects in Turkish Nicosia, Kyrenia and other parts of northern Cyprus. The admission of Cyprus to the Union was, not surprisingly, fervently urged by Greece, which saw this as a chance to gain a second Hellenic voice at the EU table, to involve the EU more deeply in Graeco-Turkish rivalries, and to bring the issue of a divided Cyprus into the international arena.[20] While the Turkish population is generally ready to accept plans for a united federal Cyprus, the Greek Cypriots have refused to countenance the loss of their properties in the north, and hopes that the problem would or could be resolved around the time Cyprus joined the EU were over-optimistic. The most important factor pressing North Cyprus towards a resolution has been the difficult economic position of an unrecognized state that depends so heavily on Turkish economic, not to mention military, support.[21]

The third and smallest British territory in the Mediterranean had no chance of decolonization – nor any wish to be decolonized. Britain still saw Gibraltar as a vital naval base immediately after the Second World War, though its importance faded as British commitments in the Mediterranean declined, and the Americans had no use for it once they had contracted with Franco for the use of bases in southern Spain. Franco imagined that he could have Gibraltar if he made enough noise. But around 1950 Britain was not very interested in developing ties with the Spanish government, which was badly tarnished by its record of oppression; nor could Spain make its voice heard at the UN, which it was not permitted to join until 1955.[22] One year before that, the new queen, Elizabeth, visited Gibraltar at the end of her six-month world tour, which gave Franco the excuse to mobilize crowds on the streets of Madrid. Spain argued that it had a right to every inch of its national territory, and that many of the Gibraltarians were as alien as the British, claiming that the true Gibraltar lived on among the inhabitants of San Roque, the Spanish town nearby which had been settled by the original inhabitants of the rock in 1704.[23] Unlike other decolonization arguments, the issue was not the right of the inhabitants to govern themselves, but a more traditional one about natural frontiers (how this applied to Moroccan claims to the Spanish outposts at Ceuta and Melilla was not clearly explained). Following the royal visit, Franco imposed increasingly severe restrictions on movement between Spain and the rock. A former pilot in the USAF writes:

> I flew into Gibraltar from Naples and Sicily on several occasions in the late 70s and early 80s. It was one of the most difficult approaches I was required to make because Spanish Air Traffic Control imposed extremely tight approach corridors on aircraft landing to the east.[24]

Britain wavered over the issue, seeing less use for Gibraltar than in the glory days of the Royal Navy, but impressed by the constantly stated loyalty of the Gibraltarians to Britain.[25]

Britain insisted that what mattered was not territorial integrity but the wishes of the Gibraltarians. In May 1969, the British government made it plain that 'Her Majesty's Government will never enter into arrangements under which the people of Gibraltar would pass under the sovereignty of another state against their freely and democratically expressed wishes.'[26] Frustrated and outraged, Franco, who had never lost his capacity to bully, completely closed the border between Spain and Gibraltar. It remained so for thirteen years, well into the era of democratic Spain, and was fully opened only when Spain joined the European Community in 1986. During that time, Spanish workers with jobs in Gibraltar were cut off from their place of work, and Gibraltarians were able to visit Spain only by a roundabout route through Tangier.

Spanish sensitivity reached extraordinary levels: in 1965 Spain threatened to boycott the Miss World contest if Miss Gibraltar were allowed
to compete; but any temptation in the Foreign Office to let Spain have
its way has been consistently blocked by the refusal of nearly all the
inhabitants to dissolve the tie to Great Britain.[27] With its mixed population of British, Spanish, Genoese, Maltese, Jewish, Hindu and latterly
Muslim inhabitants, Gibraltar can be seen as one of the last survivors of
a once widespread phenomenon, the Mediterranean port city.

7

The Last Mediterranean,
1950–2010

I

The late twentieth century was one of the great periods of Mediterranean migration. Migrations out of North Africa and into and out of Israel have been discussed in the previous chapter. The history of migration out of Sicily and southern Italy began as far back as the late nineteenth century, and it was largely directed towards North and South America. In the 1950s and 60s it was redirected towards the towns of northern Italy. Southern Italian agriculture, already suffering from neglect and lack of investment, declined still further as villages were abandoned. Elsewhere, colonial connections were important; for example, British rule over Cyprus brought substantial Greek and Turkish communities to north London. Along with these migrants, their cuisines arrived: pizza became familiar in London in the 1970s, while Greek restaurants in Britain had a Cypriot flavour. Not surprisingly, the food of the south of Italy took a strong lead among Italian émigrés: the sublime creation of Genoese cooks, *trenette al pesto*, was little known outside Italy, or indeed Liguria, before the 1970s. But the first stirrings of north European fascination with Mediterranean food could be felt in 1950, when Elizabeth David's *Book of Mediterranean Food* appeared.[1] It drew on her often hair-raising travels around the Mediterranean, keeping just ahead of the enemy during the Second World War. Initially, the book evoked aspirations rather than achievements: Great Britain was still subject to post-war food rationing, and even olive oil was hard to find. With increasing prosperity in northern Europe, the market for unfamiliar, Mediterranean produce expanded and finally, in 1965, Mrs David found the confidence to open her own food shop. By 1970 it was not too difficult to find aubergines and avocados in the groceries of Britain, Germany or Holland; and by 2000 the idea that a Mediterranean diet rich in fish, olive oil and vegetables is far healthier than traditional north European diets often based on pork and lard took hold. Interest in regional Mediterranean cuisines expanded all over Europe and North America – not just Italian food but Roman food, not just Roman food but the food of the Roman Jews, and so on.[2] Interest also grew in Mediterranean wines from as far south as Apulia and Alicante, under the influence of sophisticated Californian viticulture, with constant talk of promising new areas along the Croatian coast or in Turkey, not to mention vineyards old and new in the Bekaa Valley and the Golan Heights. Bland northern European menus (France and Belgium apart) became a distant memory. These changes in diet are of far more than anecdotal significance: old ethnic identities have been broken down as the cuisine of the Mediterranean has become globalized.

In a sense, then, the Mediterranean has become everyone's cultural possession. But population movements that originated far beyond its shores have also had a significant political and social impact. New, non-Mediterranean populations became temporarily or permanently installed in its cities or employed as cheap labour in the countryside. Many of the African or Asian migrants who reached the Mediterranean in the years either side of 2000 aimed only to set foot on European soil, and then to head northwards, to France, Germany or England, though the big Italian cities have also been a magnet; but it is the Mediterranean members of the European Union who have had to deal with the influx first of all, as numbers swelled. As well as Ceuta, the small islands between Sicily and North Africa – Lampedusa, Pantelleria, Malta – have become favoured entry points. The UN refugee agency, UNHCR, berated Italy in May 2009 for sending boatloads of refugees back to Libya. In 2008 36,900 asylum-seekers arrived in Italy, 75 per cent more than in 2007; in 2008 2,775 reached Malta, equivalent to one migrant for every 148 Maltese; but this was the peak in the nine-year period from 2002 to 2010. Indeed, in 2010 the number fell sharply, because Malta benefited from an asylum agreement between Libya and Italy, the intended destination of many migrants, and perhaps because Europe itself seemed less attractive once it was in the grip of an economic crisis.[3] The issue is not simply one for the western Mediterranean states: the Dodecanese islands have become a favourite entry point for migrants arriving from Asia by way of Turkey.

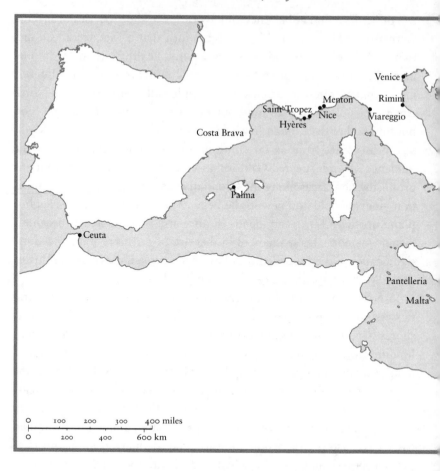

One striking feature of this new migration has been the predominance of Muslims, leading to arguments about the construction of mosques – old sensitivities, or indeed prejudices, are still powerful in Andalucía and Sicily, not helped by occasional extremist calls for all formerly Islamic lands, including al-Andalus, to be recovered for a revived caliphate. Against this, there is the old reality of migration: as living standards have improved in western Europe, menial tasks have been offloaded on to the migrants, who can find employment in hotels as chambermaids, waiters or cleaners, or as construction workers building these very hotels. For the one area in which the economy of the Mediterranean has experienced an unprecedented boom during the post-war period is tourism, along with the opportunities it has created for employment.

II

In the second half of the twentieth century the Mediterranean, no longer a vital seat of commercial or naval power, found a new vocation: mass tourism.[4] Mass tourism first took off in the Mediterranean, and it now attracts over 230 million visitors each year.[5] The temporary migration of millions of northern Europeans, Americans and Japanese in search of sun, or culture, or both, has taken place alongside the more permanent immigration of retired Germans, Britons and Scandinavians who hope to spend their last days in apartments and villas along the Spanish coast or in Majorca, Malta and Cyprus, forming distinctive communities with their own clubs, pubs and beer cellars – even, in Majorca, a political party for Germans.[6] Unlicensed building and, in the case of northern Cyprus, contested title deeds have not always made retirement to the Mediterranean a happy experience, especially when houses have been summarily demolished by irate Spanish authorities. This southward migration has had serious environmental consequences, placing heavy demands on limited water and energy supplies (notably in Cyprus), and replacing sweeping vistas of coasts and hillsides with poorly designed, monotonous blocks of white concrete houses (notably in Spain).

To understand how the tourist industry took off in the Mediterranean it is necessary to look back at developments well before the Second World War. The age of the Grand Tour, which took English or German travellers to the Bay of Naples and other Mediterranean sites (and sights) met the needs of a small elite. The Mediterranean became more accessible once railways crossed France and once Queen Victoria made Menton and Hyères into fashionable winter resorts in the late nineteenth century. Monumental hotels were built along the promenades at Nice and Cannes, and a small part of the Mediterranean shores, the Côte d'Azur, became a playground for the rich in summer as well as winter, though the rise to prominence of Monte Carlo took longer and followed the creation by the prince of Monaco of a *Société des Bains de Mer* that was rather more concerned with gambling than with bathing, which the British promoted for its health-giving properties.[7] Italian spas began to develop inland at Montecatini, Abano and on the coast at Rimini, serving an Italian clientèle in the main – streams of English tourists, chronicled in the novels of E. M. Forster, arrived in Florence, taking up residence in *pensioni* for months at a time, but the sea had not yet become a significant attraction for them.[8] What changed dramatically in the late twentieth century was the number and aims of the visitors, and the ease with which they could reach most corners of the Mediterranean. Tourists replaced travellers.

The expansion of tourism was led by three agents: within the Mediterranean, there were governments – national, regional or municipal – that saw in tourism a way to attract foreign currency and to promote local industry. In Israel, for example, three master-plans were produced in the hope of encouraging tourism, in 1976, 1987 and 1996; this country had the advantage of four tourist constituencies: Jewish visitors, Christian pilgrims, domestic tourists and foreign holidaymakers attracted by the country's beaches and monuments. By 2000 the Tel Aviv littoral from the edge of Jaffa northwards was lined with massive new hotels offering four- or five-star service, but little in the way of beautiful architecture.[9] Outside the Mediterranean there were giant travel companies such as Thomson and Hapag Lloyd that aggressively marketed the Mediterranean, sending their representatives along the shores of Spain, Italy, Greece and Tunisia, in a search for hotels that would appeal to visitors from England, Germany and elsewhere. Finally, just as importantly, there were the clients, who saw in two weeks on the shores of the Mediterranean a release from the greyness of northern Europe in the 1950s and 60s – many wanted little more than a sunlounger on the beach or by the hotel pool, and some were unsure whether they even wanted to eat the food the locals laid before them. In Greek Cyprus British holidaymakers can easily find Cadbury's chocolate and British sliced bread.[10] Dutch holidaymakers are known to take bags of native potatoes with them. The French, with their own Mediterranean coastline, have been much more creative than their north European neighbours. Club Méditerranée pioneered inclusive holidays from 1950 onwards, starting with beach huts in Majorca which were intended to conjure up romantic images of desert islands. Its Mediterranean destinations included many places little visited by mass tourism, such as the Mediterranean coast of Morocco. Innovative methods included an emphasis on direct sales to customers, but its peak lay in the years before 1990; economic conditions and management problems subsequently weakened the organization.[11]

At first the northern invasion was gentle. Rimini possessed an airport as early as 1938. At this period, though, Rimini attracted wealthy clients, air travel was still very costly, and war soon interrupted the trickle of foreign tourists. After the war, Rimini adopted a populist approach.[12] There and elsewhere business blossomed, as travel by air, rail and road became ever cheaper and easier. Trainloads of Germans and Britons began to descend on Rimini in the 1950s; satellite towns swelled in size, so that Riccione and Milano Marittima began to compete with Rimini itself. Their trademark has long been the serried ranks of sunbeds and umbrellas marking out the domain of each concrete hotel. Similar developments occurred near Pisa, where Viareggio became a major centre for the Tuscan tourist traffic, satisfying a clientèle apparently less interested in the artistic wonders of Florence and other Tuscan cities than in a seaside holiday (allowing for the odd day-trip to Pisa to gawp at the Leaning Tower). Mass tourism, with new hotels and other infrastructure, became a significant route to economic recovery in Italy, Spain and Greece.

But the real transformation occurred with the arrival of the aeroplane.[13] Cheap, safe, rapid air travel took time to arrive. Here, England was a pioneer, because of the sheer inconvenience of having no direct rail link to the Mediterranean. Britain was a major centre of the aeronautical industry, capitalizing on new aircraft technology developed during the war to construct the efficient, smooth airliners of the late 1950s and early 60s such as the Vickers Viscount and the Britannia. So the British, and later the Germans and Scandinavians, took to the air. In the 1950s Thomson Holidays inaugurated regular flights to Majorca, which was to become the first target of intensive air tourism. Otherwise a journey to Majorca was tediously slow, by train, ship, train, another train (on wider Spanish gauge) and finally ship again.[14] By the late 1960s, with the introduction of faster, smoother jet aircraft such as the BAC 1-11, traffic was burgeoning; and the airport at Palma remains, at least in summertime, one of the busiest in Europe. Between 1960 and 1973 the number of annual visitors to Majorca rose precipitously from 600,000 to 3,600,000.[15] By the start of the twenty-first century, tourism accounted for 84 per cent of the Majorcan economy. Whole concrete towns such as Palma Nova were created for the tourist industry. But the roots of this success went back to Franco's time. Majorca and Spain (excluding the Canaries) accounted for 25 per cent of British foreign holidaymaking in 1967, and 36 per cent in 1972, while holidays to Italy fell from 16 per cent to 11 per cent.[16] No country could compete with Spain, which was exactly what Franco's regime wanted: in 1959 a new 'Stabilization Plan' for the Spanish economy envisaged not so much the stabilization as the expansion of tourism in Mediterranean Spain, the Balearics and the Canaries.[17] Along the coast of Spain vast swathes of concrete brought a degree of prosperity, but also showed little consideration for the natural beauty of the Costa Brava and the rest of Mediterranean Spain. For the moment, the astonishing cultural assets of Spain – Toledo, Segovia, Córdoba, Granada – took second place to the coastline, which benefited from new access roads, proper lighting and other vital improvements, even if the railways long remained painfully slow.

Travel became democratized as well as globalized. The idea of travelling from Britain to Spain began to appeal to a wide range of people of all backgrounds, aided by the creation of the package holiday. The tourist ceased being an adventurer who navigated a way across the towns and countryside of Mediterranean lands, since it was now possible to choose flights, hotels, meals, even daytrips, from a catalogue in the secure comfort of a sitting room in England or Germany, knowing that representatives who spoke one's own language would be there to confront any difficulties with the natives. What people wanted was a 'holiday from the assembly line'.[18] And in case the idea of being abroad seemed too threatening, there was comfort in numbers, and there was the willingness of the natives themselves to accommodate the eccentric needs of foreign visitors: fish and chips for the English, *Bratwurst* for the Germans.

Those who took Mediterranean holidays were keen to display the fact conspicuously, returning from Spain or Italy with a suitably deep tan. By 1947 French brochures advertising the Côte d'Azur were laying stress on the joys of the beach.[19] Tanned skin became a badge indicating both prosperity and health, since more was known about the advantages of Vitamin D than about the disadvantages of UVA and UVB rays. Pallor was now associated with consumptives and office clerks. The great arbiter of taste, Coco Chanel, decided to make a fashion accessory of her suntan after cruising the Mediterranean in the 1920s, setting a standard for generations of women. However, this interest in bronzed flesh was also associated with changing moral standards.[20] Even before the Second World War parts of the body could be displayed on the beach that remained carefully hidden in other public places. The display of the female (and male) body became gradually more extensive. Named after a Pacific atoll used for nuclear testing, the bikini was shown at a fashion show in Paris in 1946, though it took a couple of decades for it to be widely adopted – even its designers expected something like a nuclear reaction among those opposed to it. Over time, it became increasingly daring, so that the navel, originally covered, was invariably exposed.[21] The supposed immorality of the bikini led both the Italians and the Spaniards to ban them in 1948 (with vocal support from the Vatican), but this could simply not be sustained as foreign tourists flooded into the country. Part of its appeal could be found in the material used to make it by the 1960s, Spandex or Lycra, a blend of synthetic and natural materials that does not retain water. Even when used for one-piece swimsuits, the tight, clinging quality of Lycra revealed more of the female body than conservatives would have wished. Display is an important part of how people make use of swimwear, and the pool is often a place where there is plenty of silent watching and little swimming.[22] Thus the aeroplane and the bikini, two inventions as far apart in technology as could be imagined, transformed the relationship between the Mediterranean and the north of Europe in the second half of the twentieth century.[23]

Naturally, the arrival of tourists in search of a suntan puzzled inhabitants of the Mediterranean for whom the sun was something to be avoided at midday. Puzzlement was compounded by the behaviour of tourists: physical contact between men and women, especially when they were not wearing very much, could shock Greeks, Tunisians and others. In Communist Albania the behaviour of tourists was seen as a sign of western decadence: Enver Hoxha complained about the antics of tourists in neighbouring countries 'with pants or no pants at all'. Whatever he meant (probably it was an attack on Yugoslav liberalism) he ensured that very few western tourists were allowed to enter, apart from members of Marxist-Leninist-Maoist parties. The hedonism and permissiveness of north Europeans, especially from the 1960s onwards, affected the attitude of those they encountered, beginning with local young men who were fascinated by what they saw.[24] The clash of cultures became even more obvious in the 1980s as it became more common for women to bare their breasts on the beach. The cult of physical beauty in France, with its large cosmetics industry, made it inevitable that Saint-Tropez should be the pioneer in this; Italian and Spanish resorts followed suit. Liberalization for some meant a dilemma for others, and responses varied. A nun charged with turning away vistors to St Mark's Basilica in Venice who were improperly dressed found the job so stressful that she had a nervous breakdown. In Spain, Ibiza has become well known as a centre for gay tourism, a sign of how far the country has moved since Franco's time. One country that seized the opportunity to profit from tourism with marked success was Yugoslavia, which determinedly built a reputation for cheap, well-organized hotel-based holidays, particularly favoured by Germans, one speciality being naturist resorts, which the Tito regime had quite cleverly encouraged, knowing that this would appeal specially to the eager adherents of German and Scandinavian *Frei-Korps-Kultur* seeking an all-over tan.

Cheap flights and cheap alcohol can also ruin tourism: Mallia in Crete and Ayia Napa in Greek Cyprus have acquired horrific reputations, and young British tourists have done most to damage their standing. They are not interested in local culture but want to seize 'the opportunity to have more fun in a short space of time than might be possible at home'. 'Fun' is mainly concerned with sex and alcohol, and in 2003 the British press claimed that both had been actively promoted by representatives of the tour company Club 18–30.[25] It is no surprise that in Majorca there have been attempts to move upmarket; for, even if this means the number of tourists will fall, more prosperous visitors will spend more per head. Some areas, such as Apulia and parts of Sardinia, have been consciously marketed as 'quality' destinations, and boutique hotels have started to take business away from giant complexes. Tourism has brought prosperity to areas that were previously impoverished and unproductive. Yet the environmental price has been very high. The strain on water resources, the contribution to carbon emissions from air-conditioning units, let alone aeroplanes, and pollution of the sea close to hotel complexes have all contributed to the deterioration of the Mediterranean environment. Local traditions have also suffered, as festivals have become commercialized: the long moribund Venetian carnival was reinvented and marketed as the high point of the Venetian calendar – it is no coincidence that it falls in a lean season when the city used to be empty of tourists. The impact of the media on demand can be detected in Kephalonia, promoted after the publication of Louis de Bernières's bestseller *Captain Corelli's Mandolin*, or in the Greek islands after the runaway success of the film *Mamma Mia* in 2008.[26]

For long the Mediterranean was almost the exclusive beneficiary of this expansion of mass summer tourism, along with Portugal and the Canary Islands; only in the 1990s did long-haul holidays to Cuba, Florida or the Dominican Republic become significant competitors in the mass market. The late 1990s also saw a very substantial expansion of short holidays, 'city breaks', as price wars among airlines resulted in the creation of budget airlines, led by British and Irish entrepreneurs. Irish-owned Ryanair developed hubs in Britain, Belgium, Germany and Italy, becoming Europe's largest airline. These airlines appealed not just to the price-conscious but to those with holiday homes in southern France, Tuscany or Spain. Alongside air travel, sea travel has been boosted, sometimes cynically, by shipping companies arguing that a cruise is more environmentally friendly than a flight. Dubrovnik is so overwhelmed by cruise ships that traffic police are employed in high season to control the flow of tour groups through the old city.

Tourism in the Mediterranean is not, of course, just for Europeans. Two 'invasions' from further afield have been particularly significant: the American and the Japanese. Americans were far from unknown in the watering-holes of the Mediterranean before the Second World War (D. H. Lawrence visited the Etruscan tombs with an American friend), but the inclusion of historical monuments in Italy, Greece, southern France and Egypt on the tourist circuit once again reflects ease of movement as cheap fares and elaborate communications networks made the Mediterranean easily accessible by air from the other side of the Atlantic. The Japanese have sought the explanation for the economic successes of western Europe in European culture and history; in addition, these contacts have accelerated the already rapid westernization of Japan. Japanese visitors have waxed and waned as the economy of Japan has expanded and contracted. Another constraint on tourism has been political turmoil: the once flourishing resorts of the beautiful Dalmatian coast have recovered slowly from the disintegration of Yugoslavia during the 1990s. However, as with the trade routes of the medieval Mediterranean, so also with the holiday trails of the modern tourist: if Croatia or Israel is unsafe, then other places gain a comparative advantage – Cyprus, Malta, Turkey, and so on.

III

The fall of Communism and the disintegration of the Soviet Union eased some tensions, because Moscow was no longer trying to create a vigorously anti-American faction based in Syria, Libya and other allies, even if these countries remained generally hostile to Israel, which, for its part, seemed half-hearted in its offers of peace and reluctant to let go of its settlements in the West Bank, despite the evacuation of Gaza in 2005 (after which the territory fell under the rule of the Islamist Hamas movement). Strong military and economic ties binding Turkey and Israel together disintegrated in 2010, nominally over an Israeli attack on ships bringing aid to Gaza while it was under a strict Israeli blockade; but it was also clear that Turkey was seeking a new mission, which some defined as 'new Ottomanism', within the Middle East, and that this was partly the consequence of rebuffs from the European Union, some of whose most powerful members opposed Turkish entry, and none of whom could offer a solution to the Cyprus question that would satisfy the Turks.

The search for greater stability within the Mediterranean has increasingly turned away from political rivalries towards ecological issues that can be addressed only if all the nations of the Mediterranean agree to transcend political differences and work together. Whether the series of initiatives launched at the start of the twenty-first century will have any effect depends on a willingness to limit economic growth so as to preserve the Mediterranean environment for future generations. Beginning with the 'Barcelona Process' in 1995, the European Union has attempted to steer all the Mediterranean countries towards common political, economic and cultural objectives. Out of the agreements of 1995 there evolved in 2008 a *Union pour la Méditerranée* in which the entire EU and every state in the Mediterranean participates. Although the first objective, political stability, seems to be blocked by continuing tensions, notably between Israel and its neighbours, the inclusion of Israel, the Palestinian Authority, Syria and Lebanon in the Mediterranean Union is intended to provide a framework within which they can begin tentatively to recognize common interests rather than differences. Among economic objectives, the idea of a pan-Mediterranean free trade area conjures up images of the great days of Roman or early Islamic trade across the Mediterranean. Its principal drawback is that it is seen by Mediterranean states outside the EU, especially Turkey, as a weak substitute for membership of the EU itself, and some European politicians who have opposed Turkish entry into Europe, such as President Sarkozy of France, have been noticeably enthusiastic about the Mediterranean Union. Others have looked forward to the day when the EU will become a Euro-Mediterranean Union offering membership to all the Mediterranean lands, but there are quite enough problems to resolve concerning political rivalries and economic disparities within the Mediterranean, not to mention the future of Europe, to make this sound a Utopian dream – a severe warning against over-hasty integration was provided early in 2010 by the dramatic collapse of government finances in Greece, a member of the Eurozone that irresponsibly spent far beyond its means. And a consequence of the Greek crisis was that the Chinese government was able to purchase one of the docks at Peiraieus later that year, giving the People's Republic easier access within the Mediterranean for its industrial goods – a sign of how much China has changed since it dreamed of naval bases in Hoxha's Albania. Other very worthy objectives include a solar energy plan and the cleaning of the seas, where pollution and over-exploitation have wreaked havoc with (for instance) the tunny-fishing industry – three-quarters of tuna fished in the Mediterranean go to Japan. Yet in March 2010 the Convention on International Trade in Endangered Species meeting in Doha refused to act when it was clear that over-fishing, in and beyond the Mediterranean, threatens the bluefin tuna with extinction.

On the cultural front, results will be easier to show: a Euro-Mediterranean University has been founded in Slovenia, and ever more intense cultural exchanges are proposed between Mediterranean countries. The aim, of course, is to break down barriers – to recreate, within a fresh mould, the 'integrated' Mediterranean of past times and to recover some elements of the lost *convivencia* of Jew, Christian and Muslim. Yet what is most striking about the Union for the Mediterranean is that most of its members, who include Finland, Estonia, Slovakia, Holland and Ireland, are remote from the Mediterranean. The centre of gravity of Europe still lies in the north, despite the accession to the EU of a few more Mediterranean countries (all small) at the start of the twenty-first century. This confirms the impression that the Mediterranean has lost its place at the centre of the western world, a process that began as early as 1492 when new opportunities beckoned in the Atlantic; and, early in the twenty-first century, it has become clear that the great economic powerhouse of the future will be China. In the world-wide economy of the twenty-first century, an integrated Mediterranean has local rather than global significance. Ease of contact across the globe – physical contact by air, virtual contact through the Web – means that political, commercial and cultural contacts can be sustained rapidly across vast distances. In this sense, the world has become one big Mediterranean, and the Fifth Mediterranean is the last Mediterranean in which, in any meaningful sense, the world has revolved around the Great Sea.

Conclusion: Crossing the Sea

It is tempting to try to reduce the history of the Mediterranean to a few common features, to attempt to define a 'Mediterranean identity' or to insist that certain physical features of the region have moulded human experience there (as Braudel strongly argued).[1] Yet this search for a fundamental unity starts from a misunderstanding of what the Mediterranean has meant for the peoples who have inhabited its shores and islands, or have crossed its surface. Rather than searching for unity, we should note diversity. At the human level, this ethnic, linguistic, religious and political diversity was constantly subject to external influences from across the sea, and therefore in a constant state of flux. From the earliest chapters of this book, where the first settlers in Sicily were described, to the ribbon developments along the Spanish costas, the edges of the Mediterranean Sea have provided meeting-points for peoples of the most varied backgrounds who have exploited its resources and learned, in some cases, to make a living from transferring its products from better-endowed to ill-endowed regions. From within its waters came fish and salt, two ingredients of the much-traded *garum* sauce of ancient Rome, and the basis for the early prosperity of one of the greatest of Mediterranean cities, Venice. As predicted in the preface, fishermen have not featured prominently in this book, in part because the evidence they have left behind is often very slight, but in part too because fishermen seek what is by definition under the surface of the sea and are less likely to make contact with communities on the opposing shores of the Mediterranean. The great exceptions are within the narrows near Malta, where the Genoese established a colony at Tabarka on the coast of Tunisia between 1540 and 1742 specializing in coral-fishing, and where Tunisian fishermen have now joined Sicilian fleets in the *matanza*, the great seasonal slaughter of tuna. Even more than fish, which keeps well

641

only after salting or drying, grain has long been the major product car-ried across the sea, originally grown around its shores or brought down from the Black Sea, but, by the seventeenth century, increasingly of north European origin. Access to supplies of vital foodstuffs and other primary materials enabled cities to grow, whether Corinth, Athens or Rome in antiquity, or Genoa, Venice and Barcelona in the Middle Ages. For these cities and many others, denial of access to basic supplies by one's enemies meant strangulation. Less glamorous than the famous and better documented spice trade, the trade in wheat, wood and wool provided a sure foundation on which it was then possible to build com-merce in silk, gold and pepper, items often produced far from the shores of the Mediterranean itself. The struggle for access to all these com-modities set off bloody conflicts between rivals, while the more the Mediterranean was criss-crossed by ships full of rich cargoes, the more these vessels were likely to be preyed upon by pirates, whether ancient Etruscans or early modern Barbary corsairs and Uskoks.

Keeping the sea safe was thus an important function of governments. It could be achieved the Roman way, by actively suppressing pirates in a series of vigorous campaigns, and then policing the sea; or, in times when no one was master of great tracts of the sea, merchant fleets could demand the protection of armed convoys, such as the Venetian *muda*. Pirate states in Barbary and elsewhere could be the object of eager nego-tiation, in the hope of securing guarantees for the safety of those with whom the ruler had treaties, or they could be confronted aggressively, as the Americans successfully chose to do at the start of the nineteenth century. There were bigger dangers to shipping as well, when great land empires reached the shores of the Mediterranean and began to interfere with movement across its surface: the Persians in antiquity, the Otto-man Turks from the late fourteenth century onwards, and (though attempts to acquire permanent bases failed) the Russians in the eight-eenth century. Perhaps the most extraordinary case of imperial expansion within the Mediterranean is that of Great Britain, a kingdom with no Mediterranean shores, which, thanks to its acquisitions stretching from Gibraltar to Suez, managed to exercise a degree of control that aroused the ire and envy of powers whose lands actually bordered the Mediter-ranean, notably France. This book has been a history of conflict as well as contact.

Control of the Mediterranean must be understood as control of the key routes across the sea. To achieve this, it was essential to establish bases from which ships could be supplied with fresh food and water, and from which patrols could be sent out against pirates and other interlopers. Thus from very early times settlements on offshore islands provided merchants with vital staging-posts as they ventured deeper into Mediterranean waters. Equally, loss of control of the shoreline could mean loss of access to timber and other materials essential for the building of a war fleet or merchant navy, as the rulers of Egypt were apt to find. Maintaining control of sea-lanes was especially difficult when competing powers dominated the shores and islands of the Mediterranean. Under Rome, a single political dominion created a single economic zone. But it was a unique occurrence.

The history of the Mediterranean is also the story of the port cities of very varied political loyalties in which merchants and settlers from all over the sea and far beyond gathered and interacted. One port city that has featured again and again in these chapters is Alexandria, which from the very start possessed a mixed identity, and which only lost that identity in the second half of the twentieth century, as rising nationalism destroyed the cosmopolitan communities of the Mediterranean. These port cities acted as vectors for the transmission of ideas, including religious beliefs, bringing Greek gods to Etruscan Tarquinia, and much later acting as focal points for the spread of proselytizing Judaism, Christianity and Islam, each of which left an extraordinarily powerful imprint on the societies of the lands around the Mediterranean.

Those individuals who transformed the Mediterranean world were sometimes visionaries, such as Alexander the Great or St Paul, to cite two very different cases. It is noticeable that they always seem to be men. At a time when gender has become the focus of so much historical debate, one might ask: how male is the Mediterranean? Sedentary merchants might be women, as among the Jews of eleventh-century Egypt and the Christians of twelfth-century Genoa. In that era, at least, wives did not accompany their husbands on trading expeditions, let alone travel for trade in their own right, though attitudes to participation in business varied between Jews, Christians and Muslims. A few European women could be found in the Genoese trading colony in late thirteenth-century Tunis, mainly offering sexual services to the Christian business community. Female participation in naval warfare, a twenty-first-century phenomenon, has not been tested within the Mediterranean. But among

migrants, whether the Alans and Vandals invading Africa at the time of
St Augustine, or the Sephardim expelled from Spain in 1492, there was
often, though not invariably, a large female component – even the
armies of the early crusades were accompanied by both noblewomen
and bands of prostitutes. Female pilgrims appear in the record as early
as the first decades of the Christian Roman Empire: a fragment from the
late fourth-century records the travels of the intrepid Egeria (or Aetheria) from either Gaul or northern Spain to the Holy Land. It is less clear
whether the Bronze Age raiders known as the Sea Peoples came accompanied by women to the lands in Syria, Palestine and elsewhere that
they settled; indeed, a likely explanation for the rapid abandonment of
their Aegean culture by the early Philistines is that they intermarried
with the Canaanites, adopted their gods and learned their language. Yet
one group of women has a particular importance for the history of the
Mediterranean: female slaves, whose fortune varied enormously, from
the extraordinary power it might be possible to exercise within an Ottoman harem to the sad exploitation and debasement of those used for
sexual purposes or assigned lowly work in the villas of prosperous
Romans. During the Middle Ages, many of these slaves, both male and
female, were brought out of the Black Sea, but those who inhabited the
shores of the Mediterranean in the age of the Barbary corsairs (and at
many other periods) also knew the horror of raiding parties that picked
people off the shore – Christians off the coasts of Italy, France and
Spain, Muslims off the coasts of Morocco, Algeria and Tunisia. When
King Francis I of France permitted the Turks to visit Marseilles and
occupy Toulon in 1543, they kidnapped the nuns of Antibes, among
other victims. Still, the relative maleness of the traversed Mediterranean
is something to ponder – the Italians seem to be right to say *il mare*, as
opposed to the French *la mer* or indeed the neutral Latin *mare*; and the
principal Greek, Etruscan and Roman sea gods – Poseidon, Fufluns and
Neptune – were male.

Among all those who traversed the Mediterranean, merchants generally reveal most, for several reasons. One is simply that ever since
Phoenician merchants spread the art of alphabetic writing across the
Mediterranean, traders have been anxious to record their transactions;
we therefore know a great deal about them, whether in Roman Puteoli,
near Naples, in medieval Genoa and Venice, or modern Smyrna and
Livorno. But the merchant pioneer is almost by definition an outsider,

someone who crosses cultural and physical boundaries, encountering new gods, hearing different languages, and finding himself (much more rarely, herself) exposed to the sharp criticisms of the inhabitants of the places he visits in search of goods unavailable at home. This ambiguous image of the merchant as a desirable outsider is there in our earliest sources. It has been seen that Homer was uneasy about merchants, showing contempt for mere traders of Phoenicia, and suggesting that they were deceitful and unheroic, despite glorying, paradoxically, in the trickery of Odysseus; the somewhat hypocritical sense that trade dirtied one's hands remained strong among patrician readers of Homer in ancient Rome. It was the Phoenicians, however, who ventured as far as southern Spain, establishing colonies side-by-side with but often apart from the native populations of the western Mediterranean – typically on offshore islands that were easy to guard, for one never knew how long relations with neighbouring peoples would remain warm. Then, as the Phoenician colony at Carthage became an economic and political power in its own right, this booming city became the hub of new networks of communication, a cosmopolitan meeting-point between Levantine and North African cultures, a place where divergent cultures fused and a new identity may be said to have emerged, even if the city elite continued to describe themselves as 'people of Tyre'. Greek culture too gained a purchase in Carthage, whose citizens identified the Phoenician god Melqart with Herakles. Gods and goddesses as well as merchants criss-crossed the ancient Mediterranean. Additionally, the presence on the shores of Italy of Phoenicians and Greeks, individuals with a distinct cultural identity, acted as a yeast that transformed the villages of rural Etruria into cities whose richer inhabitants possessed an insatiable hunger for the foreign: for Greek vases, Phoenician silver bowls, Sardinian bronze figurines. Alongside merchants who came for the metals of Italy, we can soon detect artisans who travelled west to settle in the lands of the *barbaroi*, knowing that their skills would probably earn them greater esteem than at home, where each was one of many.

There are striking parallels in later centuries. Alien traders are an obvious feature of the medieval Mediterranean, where we have the intriguing phenomenon of the ghettoized merchant visiting Islamic or Byzantine territory, enclosed in an inn or fonduk that also functioned as a warehouse, chapel, bakehouse and bath-house, with one inn for each major 'nation': Genoese, Venetian, Catalan and so on. The sense that the merchant might be a source of religious contamination and political subversion led the rulers of Egypt to lock the doors of these inns at night-time (the keys being held by Muslims on the outside). This only enhanced the solidarity and sense of community that held these merchants together, while underlining the differences between the various groups of Italians and Catalans, who coexisted in a rivalry Muslim emirs proved adept at exploiting. The Byzantines too set the Italian merchants apart in a walled compound during the twelfth century, feeding xenophobia in their capital city, with the ugly consequences of anti-Latin pogroms. The idea of enclosing distinct communities behind walls was not, then, particularly novel when the king of Aragon first segregated the Majorcan Jews around 1300, and was quite venerable by the time the government of Venice enclosed the Jews in the *ghetto nuovo* in 1516; these merchant communities provided a useful model for the ghetto. The enclosed areas, whether of Jews or of European merchants, were places where a certain amount of privilege – self-government, freedom to practise one's religion, tax exemptions – was counter-balanced by constraint – limitations on free movement and reliance on often capricious public authorities for protection.

To speak of the Jews is to speak of traders who had an unusual ability to cross the boundaries between cultures, whether in the early days of Islam, during the period of ascendancy of the Genizah Jews from Cairo, with their trans- and ultra-Mediterranean connections, or in the period of Catalan commercial expansion, when they could exploit their family and business ties to their co-religionists and penetrate deep into the Sahara in search of gold, ostrich feathers and other African products that were beyond the reach of their Christian compatriots still stuck within their trading compounds. The prominence and mobility of a minority group is intriguing. These Jewish merchants were able to bring back information about the world beyond the Mediterranean ports that was recorded and disseminated across Mediterranean Europe and further afield in the remarkable portolan charts and world maps produced in late medieval Majorca. As merchants moved around, so did information about the physical world.

The concept of the Mediterranean as a 'faithful sea', to cite the title of a recent collection of essays, needs to take into account its role as a surface across which moved not merely poor and anonymous pilgrims but also charismatic missionaries such as Ramon Llull, who died in

1316 after writing hundreds of books and pamphlets on how to convert Muslims, Jews and Greeks to the true faith, without, it must be said, ever converting anyone.[2] Yet Llull's career is a reminder that religious friction and confrontation are only part of the picture. He imitated Sufi verses and hobnobbed with kabbalists; he was at once a keen missionary and an exponent of old-fashioned Iberian *convivencia*, recognizing the God of the three Abrahamic religions as the same single God. A different sort of *convivencia* existed in the minds of members of the religious communities that were expelled or forced to convert as Spain asserted its Catholic identity in 1492 and afterwards: the Marranos and Moriscos, Jews and Muslims who might or might not adhere to their ancestral religion in private, while being expected to practise the Catholic faith in public. The ascendancy of the Sephardic merchants in the early modern Mediterranean is astonishing in any number of ways: their ability to acquire and shed different identities, as 'Portuguese' able to enter Iberia and as Jews resident in Livorno or Ancona – an ability to cross cultural, religious and political boundaries reminiscent of their forebears in the Cairo Genizah six centuries earlier. These multiple identities are an extreme case of a wider Mediterranean phenomenon: there were places where cultures met and mixed, but here were individuals within whom identities met and mixed, often uneasily.

There is an understandable tendency to romanticize the Mediterranean meeting-places, and the darker reality of trans-Mediterranean contact in (say) the early modern period also needs to be born in mind: the ascendancy, between the fifteenth and the early nineteenth centuries, of the Barbary corsairs, and the close intersection between piracy and trade. Before the final suppression of the Barbary corsairs, the Mediterranean had only ever really been free of a serious threat from piracy under Roman imperial rule, as a result of Rome's political control of more or less all its shores and islands. But piracy reveals some of the most extraordinary cases of mixed identity: corsairs from as far away as Scotland and England who, outwardly at least, accepted Islam and preyed on the shipping of the nation from which they came. This darker side of Mediterranean history also encompasses the history of those already mentioned whom the pirates carried back and forth: male and female slaves and captives, though they too, like the historian Polybios, could play a notable role in cultural contact between the opposing shores of the Mediterranean.

The unity of Mediterranean history thus lies, paradoxically, in its swirling changeability, in the diasporas of merchants and exiles, in the people hurrying to cross its surface as quickly as possible, not seeking to linger at sea, especially in winter, when travel became dangerous, like the long-suffering pilgrims ibn Jubayr and Felix Fabri. Its opposing shores are close enough to permit easy contact, but far enough apart to allow societies to develop distinctively under the influence of their hinterland as well as of one another. Those who cross its surface are often hardly typical of the societies from which they come. If they are not outsiders when they set out, they are likely to become so when they enter different societies across the water, whether as traders, slaves or pilgrims. But their presence can have a transforming effect on these different societies, introducing something of the culture of one continent into the outer edges, at least, of another. The Mediterranean thus became probably the most vigorous place of interaction between different societies on the face of this planet, and it has played a role in the history of human civilization that has far surpassed any other expanse of sea.

Further Reading

A bibliography based on this book would be enormous and shapeless. This short note simply points out several works that have looked at the Mediterranean as a whole, though more often the surrounding lands than the sea itself. Peregrine Horden and Nicholas Purcell's *The Corrupting Sea: a Study of Mediterranean History* (Oxford, 2000) is the first part of an ambitious and richly textured account of the localities around the Mediterranean and their interaction. Its main focus is antiquity and the early Middle Ages. A valuable set of essays edited by William Harris ponders their conclusions: *Rethinking the Mediterranean* (Oxford, 2005). Fernand Braudel's *The Mediterranean and the Mediterranean World in the Age of Philip II*, translated by Siân Reynolds, 2 vols. (London, 1972–3), shaped research on the Mediterranean not just in the late medieval and early modern periods for a whole generation. Braudel's thought-world is well explained by E. Paris, *La genèse intellectuelle de l'œuvre de Fernand Braudel: 'La Méditerranée et le monde méditerranéen à l'époque de Philippe II' (1923–1947)* (Athens, 1999). Further perspectives on the historiography of the Mediterranean are provided by S. Guarracino, *Mediterraneo: immagini, storie e teorie da Omero a Braudel* (Milan, 2007). A rich study of the economic and ecological changes in the Mediterranean between about 1350 and 1900 was provided by F. Tabak, *The Waning of the Mediterranean 1550–1870: a Geohistorical Approach* (Baltimore, MD, 2008) – the dates do not do justice to the timespan he covered. On the Mediterranean environment, A. Grove and O. Rackham, *The Nature of Mediterranean Europe: an Ecological History* (New Haven, CT, 2001) is especially worthwhile and thought-provoking. A short but important book within the Braudelian tradition is J. Pryor, *Geography, Technology, and War: Studies in the Maritime History of the Mediterranean 649–1571* (Cambridge, 1988).

Several volumes of collected essays should be added to that edited by Harris: my own *The Mediterranean in History* (London and New York, 2003; also French, Spanish, Turkish and Greek editions), with excellent chapters by Torelli, Balard, Greene and many others; and J. Carpentier and F. Lebrun's *Histoire de la Méditerranée* (Paris, 1998), which is rather skewed towards modern times but contains some vivid source material. On the religious setting, see the essays collected by A. Husain and K. Fleming, *A Faithful Sea: the Religious Cultures of the Mediterranean, 1200–1700* (Oxford, 2007). More specialized is A. Cowan, *Mediterranean Urban Culture 1400–1700* (Exeter, 2000), with fine studies by Sakellariou, Arbel, Amelang and others; and *Trade and Cultural Exchange in the Early Modern Mediterranean*, edited by M. Fusaro, C. Heywood and M.-S. Omri (London, 2010). There is a marvellous collection of sources in English translation, edited by miriam cooke (spelt thus), E. Göknar and G. Parker: *Mediterranean Passages: Readings from Dido to Derrida* (Chapel Hill, NC, 2008).

More popular accounts of the Mediterranean, often well illustrated, include Sarah Arenson, *The Encircled Sea: the Mediterranean Maritime Civilisation* (London, 1990), making good use of marine archaeology, and David Attenborough, *The First Eden: the Mediterranean World and Man* (London, 1987), whose real strength is the illustrations; both books were based on television series. Captivating musings on the Mediterranean are offered by P. Matvejević, *Mediterranean: a Cultural Landscape* (Berkeley and Los Angeles, CA, 1999). John Julius Norwich, *The Middle Sea: a History of the Mediterranean* (London, 2006), wanders rather far from the shores of the Mediterranean and is not my favourite book by this author. P. Mansel, *Levant: Splendour and Catastrophe on the Mediterranean* (London, 2010) looks at Smyrna, Alexandria and Beirut, in the era of ethnic and religious coexistence.

Lively travel accounts of the whole Mediterranean have been provided by the always readable Paul Theroux, *The Pillars of Hercules: a Grand Tour of the Mediterranean* (London, 1995), by Eric Newby, *On the Shores of the Mediterranean* (London, 1984), and by Robert Fox, *The Inner Sea: the Mediterranean and its People* (London, 1991). Lastly, no one with affection for the Mediterranean can ignore Elizabeth David, *A Book of Mediterranean Food* (London, 1950) and more recent accounts of Mediterranean cuisine such as Claudia Roden's *Mediterranean Cookery* (London, 1987).

Notes

INTRODUCTION

1. F. Braudel, *The Mediterranean and the Mediterranean World in the Age of Philip II*, trans. S. Reynolds, 2 vols. (London, 1972–3), vol. 2, p. 1244; P. Horden and N. Purcell, *The Corrupting Sea: a Study of Mediterranean History* (Oxford, 2000), p. 36.

2. E. Paris, *La genèse intellectuelle de l'œuvre de Fernand Braudel: 'La Méditerranée et le monde méditerranéen à l'époque de Philippe II' (1923–1947)* (Athens, 1999), pp. 64, 316.

3. J. Pryor, *Geography, Technology, and War: Studies in the Maritime History of the Mediterranean 649–1571* (Cambridge, 1988), pp. 7, 21–4; Horden and Purcell, *Corrupting Sea*, pp. 138–9.

4. Pryor, *Geography, Technology, and War*, pp. 12–13.

5. Ibid., p. 14, fig. 2.

6. Ibid., p. 19.

7. Ibid., pp. 12–24; C. Delano Smith, *Western Mediterranean Europe: a Historical Geography of Italy, Spain and Southern France since the Neolithic* (London, 1979).

8. See F. Tabak, *The Waning of the Mediterranean 1550–1870: a Geohistorical Approach* (Baltimore, MD, 2008), and Braudel, *Mediterranean*, vol. 1, pp. 267–75; C. Vita-Finzi, *The Mediterranean Valleys: Geological Change in Historical Times* (Cambridge, 1969).

9. A. Grove and O. Rackham, *The Nature of Mediterranean Europe: an Ecological History* (New Haven, CT, 2001); O. Rackham, 'The physical setting', in D. Abulafia (ed.), *The Mediterranean in History* (London and New York, 2003), pp. 32–61.

10. Pryor, *Geography, Technology, and War*, pp. 75–86.

11. S. Orvietani Busch, *Medieval Mediterranean Ports: the Catalan and Tuscan Coasts, 1100–1235* (Leiden, 2001).

PART ONE
THE FIRST MEDITERRANEAN, 22000 BC–1000 BC

1. Isolation and Insulation, 22000 BC–3000 BC

1. D. Trump, *The Prehistory of the Mediterranean* (Harmondsworth, 1980), pp. 12–13.
2. E. Panagopoulou and T. Strasser in *Hesperia*, vol. 79 (2010).
3. C. Finlayson, *The Humans Who Went Extinct: Why Neanderthals Died out and We Survived* (Oxford, 2009), pp. 143–55.
4. L. Bernabò Brea, *Sicily before the Greeks* (London, 1957), pp. 23–36; R. Leighton, *Sicily before History: an Archaeological Survey from the Palaeolithic to the Iron Age* (London, 1999).
5. Trump, *Prehistory of the Mediterranean*, p. 19.
6. Ibid., p. 20.
7. S. Wachsmann, 'Paddled and oared ships before the Iron Age', in J. Morrison (ed.), *The Age of the Galley* (London, 1995), p. 10; C. Perlès, *The Early Neolithic in Greece: the First Farming Communities in Europe* (Cambridge, 2001), p. 36; R. Torrence, *Production and Exchange of Stone Tools: Prehistoric Obsidian in the Aegean* (Cambridge, 1986), p. 96; C. Broodbank, *An Island Archaeology of the Early Cyclades* (Cambridge, 2000), pp. 114–15.
8. W. F. Albright, *The Archaeology of Palestine* (Harmondsworth, 1949), pp. 38, 62; Trump, *Prehistory of the Mediterranean*, pp. 24–6.
9. C. F. Macdonald, *Knossos* (London, 2005), p. 3.
10. Torrence, *Production and Exchange*, pp. 96, 140–63.
11. C. Renfrew, in *Malta before History: the World's Oldest Freestanding Stone Architecture*, ed. D. Cilia (Sliema, 2004), p. 10.
12. A. Pace, 'The building of Megalithic Malta', in Cilia, *Malta before History*, pp. 19–40.
13. J. Evans, *Malta* (Ancient Peoples and Places, London, 1959), pp. 90–91.
14. A. Pace, 'The sites', and A. Bonanno, 'Rituals of life and rituals of death', in Cilia, *Malta before History*, pp. 72–4, 82–3, 272–9.
15. Evans, *Malta*, p. 158.
16. D. Trump, 'Prehistoric pottery', in Cilia, *Malta before History*, pp. 243–7.
17. Bernabò Brea, *Sicily*, pp. 38–57; Leighton, *Sicily before History*, pp. 51–85.
18. Leighton, *Sicily before History*, p. 65.
19. Trump, *Prehistory of the Mediterranean*, p. 80.
20. Wachsmann, 'Paddled and oared ships', p. 10; C. Broodbank and T. Strasser, 'Migrant farmers and the Neolithic colonization of Crete', *Antiquity*, vol. 65 (1991), pp. 233–45; Broodbank, *Island Archaeology*, pp. 96–105.
21. Trump, *Prehistory of the Mediterranean*, pp. 55–6.

2. Copper and Bronze, 3000 BC–1500 BC

1. R. L. N. Barber, *The Cyclades in the Bronze Age* (London, 1987), pp. 26–33.
2. C. Broodbank, *An Island Archaeology of the Early Cyclades* (Cambridge, 2000), pp. 301–6; Barber, *Cyclades*, pp. 136–7.
3. C. Renfrew, *The Cycladic Spirit* (London, 1991), p. 18; J. L. Fitton, *Cycladic Art* (London, 1989).
4. F. Matz, *Crete and Early Greece* (London, 1962), p. 62.
5. Broodbank, *Island Archaeology*, pp. 99–102; Renfrew, *Cycladic Spirit*, p. 62.
6. C. Moorehead, *The Lost Treasures of Troy* (London, 1994), pp. 84–6; J. Latacz, *Troy and Homer: Towards a Solution of an Old Mystery* (Oxford, 2004).
7. C. Blegen, 'Troy', *Cambridge Ancient History*, vols. 1 and 2, rev. edn, pre-print fascicle (Cambridge, 1961), p. 4.
8. D. Easton, 'Introduction', in C. Blegen, *Troy* (2nd edn, London, 2005), p. xxii.
9. Blegen, *Troy*, pp. 25–41; T. Bryce, *The Trojans and Their Neighbours* (London, 2006), pp. 39–40.
10. Blegen, *Troy*, p. 40; Bryce, *Trojans*, p. 40; Matz, *Crete and Early Greece*, p. 37; L. Bernabò Brea, *Poliochni, città preistorica nell'isola di Lemnos*, 2 vols. (Rome, 1964–71); S. Tiné, *Poliochni, the Earliest Town in Europe* (Athens, 2001).
11. Latacz, *Troy and Homer*, p. 41.
12. Blegen, *Troy*, pp. 47–8, 55.
13. Ibid.
14. Moorehead, *Lost Treasures*, pp. 128–30.
15. Bryce, *Trojans*, pp. 51–6; Blegen, *Troy*, pp. 56–61, 77–84, noting Easton's comments, ibid., p. xvii.
16. Thucydides 1:4.
17. Matz, *Crete and Early Greece*, pp. 57–8, 69.
18. A. Morpurgo Davies, 'The linguistic evidence: is there any?' in *The End of the Early Bronze Age in the Aegean*, ed. G. Cadogan (Leiden, 1986), pp. 93–123.
19. R. Castleden, *Minoans: Life in Bronze Age Crete* (London, 1990), pp. 4–7; C. F. Macdonald, *Knossos* (London, 2005), pp. 25–30.
20. Matz, *Crete and Early Greece*, p. 57; Castleden, *Minoans*, p. 29; Macdonald, *Knossos*, pp. 43–7.
21. Macdonald, *Knossos*, pp. 50–52; Castleden, *Minoans*, p. 69, fig. 18 (plan of Gournia), p. 112.
22. Reported in *Archaeology* (Archeological Institute of America), vol. 63 (2010), pp. 44–7.
23. Macdonald, *Knossos*, pp. 58–9, 87–8; Castleden, *Minoans*, pp. 169–72.
24. C. Gere, *Knossos and the Prophets of Modernism* (Chicago, IL, 2009), and the discussion in part 5, chap. 2 below.

25. Macdonald, *Knossos*, pp. 134, 173; Castleden, *Minoans*, p. 12.
26. Morpurgo Davies, 'The linguistic evidence'; L. R. Palmer, *Mycenaeans and Minoans: Aegean Prehistory in the Light of the Linear B Tablets* (2nd edn, London, 1965).
27. L. Casson, 'Bronze Age ships: the evidence of the Thera wall-paintings', *International Journal of Archaeology*, vol. 4 (1975), pp. 3–10; Barber, *Cyclades*, pp. 159–78, 193, 196–9.
28. Barber, *Cyclades*, pp. 209–18.
29. Macdonald, *Knossos*, pp. 171–2, 192.

3. Merchants and Heroes, 1500 BC–1250 BC

1. W. D. Taylour, *The Mycenaeans* (London, 1964), p. 76.
2. Homer, *Iliad*, 2:494–760.
3. J. Chadwick, *The Decipherment of Linear B* (Cambridge, 1958).
4. F. Matz, *Crete and Early Greece* (London, 1962), p. 134, plate 32; Taylour, *Mycenaeans*, plates 3–4.
5. Taylour, *Mycenaeans*, pp. 139–48.
6. Ibid., p. 100.
7. T. Bryce, *The Trojans and Their Neighbours* (London, 2006), pp. 100–102; J. Latacz, *Troy and Homer: Towards a Solution of an Old Mystery* (Oxford, 2004), p. 123; cf. O. R. Gurney, *The Hittites* (London, 1952), pp. 46–58; A. Yasur-Landau, *The Philistines and Aegean Migration and the End of the Late Bronze Age* (Cambridge, 2010), p. 180.
8. G. F. Bass, 'Cape Gelidonya: a Bronze Age shipwreck', *Transactions of the American Philosophical Society*, vol. 57, part 8 (1967); G. F. Bass, 'A Bronze Age shipwreck at Ulu Burun (Kas): 1984 campaign', *American Journal of Archeology*, 90 (1986), pp. 269–96.
9. R. Leighton, *Sicily before History: an Archaeological Survey from the Palaeolithic to the Iron Age* (London, 1999), pp. 141, 144, 147–8; cf. L. Bernabò Brea, *Sicily before the Greeks* (London, 1957), pp. 103–8.
10. Taylour, *Mycenaeans*, pp. 152–3.
11. W. D. Taylour, *Mycenaean Pottery in Italy and Adjacent Areas* (Cambridge, 1958); R. Holloway, *Italy and the Aegean 3000–700 BC* (Louvain-la-Neuve, 1981).
12. Bernabò Brea, *Sicily*, pp. 138–9; cf. Holloway, *Italy and the Aegean*, pp. 71–4.
13. Holloway, *Italy and the Aegean*, pp. 87, 95.
14. Taylour, *Mycenaean Pottery*; Holloway, *Italy and the Aegean*, pp. 85–6.
15. Holloway, *Italy and the Aegean*, pp. 67, 87–9.
16. F. Stubbings, *Mycenaean Pottery from the Levant* (Cambridge, 1951).
17. W. Culican, *The First Merchant Venturers: the Ancient Levant in History and Commerce* (London, 1966), pp. 46–9.

18. Ibid., pp. 41–2, 49–50; W. F. Albright, *The Archaeology of Palestine* (Harmondsworth, 1949), pp. 101–4.

19. Taylour, *Mycenaeans*, pp. 131, 159.

20. D. Fabre, *Seafaring in Ancient Egypt* (London, 2004–5), pp. 39–42.

21. A. Gardiner, *Egypt of the Pharaohs: an Introduction* (Oxford, 1961), pp. 151–8.

22. Fabre, *Seafaring in Ancient Egypt*, pp. 158–73.

23. Ibid., pp. 12–13.

24. Ibid., pp. 65–70.

25. Bryce, *Trojans*, p. 89.

26. H. Goedicke, *The Report of Wenamun* (Baltimore, MD, 1975).

27. Ibid., pp. 175–83.

28. Ibid., p. 51.

29. Ibid., p. 58.

30. Ibid., pp. 76, 84, 87.

31. Ibid., p. 94.

32. Ibid., p. 126.

33. Gardiner, *Egypt*, pp. 252–7; Gurney, *Hittites*, p. 110; N. Sandars, *The Sea Peoples: Warriors of the Ancient Mediterranean 1250–1150 BC* (London, 1978), pp. 29–32; R. Drews, *The End of the Bronze Age: Changes in Warfare and the Catastrophe ca. 1200 BC* (Princeton, NJ, 1993), pp. 130–34.

4. Sea Peoples and Land Peoples, 1250 BC–1100 BC

1. C. Blegen, *Troy* (2nd edn, London, 2005), pp. 92–4; T. Bryce, *The Trojans and Their Neighbours* (London, 2006), pp. 58–61.

2. J. Latacz, *Troy and Homer: Towards a Solution to an Old Mystery* (London, 2004), pp. 20–37; cf. Bryce, *Trojans*, pp. 62–4.

3. Bryce, *Trojans*, p. 117.

4. Latacz, *Troy and Homer*, pp. 49–51, 69.

5. Ibid., pp. 46–7, fig. 10 (map of trade routes).

6. Bryce, *Trojans*, pp. 104, 111.

7. O. R. Gurney, *The Hittites* (London, 1952), pp. 49–50; Bryce, *Trojans*, pp. 110–11.

8. Gurney, *Hittites*, pp. 51–2; Bryce, *Trojans*, p. 100.

9. Latacz, *Troy and Homer*, pp. 92–100.

10. Blegen, *Troy*, pp. 124–8.

11. For an argument favouring subsidence as a major cause of damage, see M. Wood, *In Search of the Trojan War* (2nd edn, London, 1996), pp. 203–11.

12. V. R. d'A. Desborough and N. G. L. Hammond, 'The end of Mycenaean civilisation and the Dark Age', *Cambridge Ancient History*, vols. 1 and 2, revised edn, pre-print fascicle (Cambridge, 1964), p. 4; N. Sandars, *The Sea Peoples:*

Warriors of the Ancient Mediterranean 1250–1150 BC (London, 1978), p. 180.

13. Sandars, *Sea Peoples*, pp. 142–4; R. Drews, *The End of the Bronze Age: Changes in Warfare and the Catastrophe ca. 1200 BC* (Princeton, NJ, 1993), pp. 13–15.

14. L. Woolley, *A Forgotten Kingdom* (Harmondsworth, 1953), pp. 163–4, 170–73.

15. Blegen, *Troy*, p. 142.

16. Sandars, *Sea Peoples*, p. 133; also A. Gardiner, *Egypt of the Pharaohs: an Introduction* (Oxford, 1961), pp. 284, 288; A. R. Burn, *Minoans, Philistines, and Greeks BC 1400–900* (2nd edn, London, 1968).

17. Sandars, *Sea Peoples*, pp. 106–7.

18. Ibid., pp. 50–51; Gardiner, *Egypt*, p. 198; B. Isserlin, *The Israelites* (London, 1998), p. 55.

19. Sandars, *Sea Peoples*, p. 105; Gardiner, *Egypt*, pp. 265–6.

20. Drews, *End of the Bronze Age*, p. 20; A. Yasur-Landau, *The Philistines and Aegean Migration and the End of the Late Bronze Age* (Cambridge, 2010), p. 180.

21. Sandars, *Sea Peoples*, p. 114; Gardiner, *Egypt*, p. 266; Isserlin, *Israelites*, p. 56, and plate 34 opposite p. 81.

22. Drews, *End of the Bronze Age*, p. 21.

23. T. and M. Dothan, *People of the Sea: the Search for the Philistines* (New York, 1992), p. 95; cf. Sandars, *Sea Peoples*, pp. 134–5.

24. Sandars, *Sea Peoples*, p. 119; Gardiner, *Egypt*, pp. 276–7.

25. Sandars, *Sea Peoples*.

26. Ibid., pp. 124, 134–5, 165, 178, plate 119; p. 189, plate 124; F. Matz, *Crete and Early Greece* (London, 1962), supplementary plate 22; W. D. Taylour, *The Mycenaeans* (London, 1964), plate 7.

27. Gurney, *Hittites*, p. 54.

28. Joshua 18:1 and 19:40–48; Judges 5; Dothan, *People of the Sea*, pp. 215–18; Sandars, *Sea Peoples*, pp. 163–4.

29. Dothan, *People of the Sea*, p. 215.

30. Sandars, *Sea Peoples*, pp. 111–12, 200; Yasur-Landau, *Philistines and Aegean Migration*, pp. 180, 182; cf. Gardiner, *Egypt*, p. 264.

31. C. Whitman, *Homer and the Heroic Tradition* (Cambridge, MA, 1958), pp. 51–2.

32. Desborough and Hammond, 'End of Mycenaean Civilisation', p. 5; also V. R. d'A. Desborough, *The Last Mycenaeans and Their Successors* (Oxford, 1964).

33. Desborough and Hammond, 'End of Mycenaean Civilisation', p. 12.

34. L. Bernabò Brea, *Sicily before the Greeks* (London, 1967), p. 136.

35. R. Leighton, *Sicily before History: an Archaeological Survey from the Palaeolithic to the Iron Age* (London, 1999), p. 149; also R. Holloway, *Italy and the Aegean 3000–700 BC* (Louvain-la-Neuve, 1981), p. 95.

36. Dothan, *People of the Sea*, pp. 211–13.

37. W. Culican, *The First Merchant Venturers: the Ancient Levant in History and Commerce* (London, 1966), pp. 66–70.

38. Dothan, *People of the Sea*, plates 5 and 6, and pp. 37–9, 53.

39. Yasur-Landau, *Philistines and Aegean Migration*, pp. 334–45.
40. I Samuel 17:5–7.
41. Yasur-Landau, *Philistines and Aegean Migration*, pp. 305–6.
42. Dothan, *People of the Sea*, pp. 8, 239–54.
43. Amos 9:7.
44. Exodus 15:1–18; Isserlin, *Israelites*, p. 206.
45. Isserlin, *Israelites*, p. 57.
46. Drews, *End of the Bronze Age*, p. 3.

PART TWO
THE SECOND MEDITERRANEAN, 1000 BC–AD 600

1. The Purple Traders, 1000 BC–700 BC

1. L. Bernabò Brea, *Sicily before the Greeks* (London, 1957), pp. 136–43.
2. M. E. Aubet, *The Phoenicians and the West: Politics, Colonies, and Trade* (2nd edn, Cambridge, 2001), p. 128; S. Moscati, 'Who were the Phoenicians?', in S. Moscati (ed.), *The Phoenicians* (New York, 1999), pp. 17–19.
3. G. Markoe, *The Phoenicians* (2nd edn, London, 2005), p. xviii.
4. D. B. Harden, *The Phoenicians* (2nd edn, Harmondsworth, 1971), p. 20.
5. S. Filippo Bondì, 'The origins in the East', in Moscati, *Phoenicians*, pp. 23–9.
6. Aubet, *Phoenicians in the West*, pp. 23–5.
7. Leviticus 18:22.
8. Markoe, *Phoenicians*, pp. 38–45, 121.
9. B. Isserlin, *The Israelites* (London, 1998), pp. 149–59, for Israelite agriculture.
10. Aubet, *Phoenicians and the West*, pp. 48–9, and fig. 19.
11. I Kings 9:11–14; S. Moscati, *The World of the Phoenicians* (London, 1968), p. 33.
12. Markoe, *Phoenicians*, p. xx, but missing the importance of grain.
13. Ibid., p. 37 (King Ithobaal, early ninth century); Moscati, *World of the Phoenicians*, p. 35.
14. Harden, *Phoenicians*, p. 25; cf. Tyre: Markoe, *Phoenicians*, p. 73.
15. Aubet, *Phoenicians and the West*, pp. 34–5; Markoe, *Phoenicians*, p. 73.
16. Ezekiel 27.
17. Markoe, *Phoenicians*, pp. 15–28.
18. M. L. Uberti, 'Ivory and bone carving', in Moscati, *Phoenicians*, pp. 456–71.
19. Harden, *Phoenicians*, p. 49 and plate 48.
20. Moscati, *World of the Phoenicians*, p. 36; Aubet, *Phoenicians and the West*, p. 91, fig. 27, a later bas-relief from Nimrud showing two monkeys.
21. I Kings 9:26–8; I Kings 10:22, 10:49; Markoe, *Phoenicians*, pp. 31–4; Isserlin, *Israelites*, pp. 188–9.
22. Markoe, *Phoenicians*, p. 122.

23. Genesis 44:2.
24. Aubet, *Phoenicians and the West*, pp. 80–84.
25. Moscati, *World of the Phoenicians*, pp. 137–45.
26. V. Karageorghis, 'Cyprus', in Moscati, *Phoenicians*, pp. 185–9.
27. Ibid., p. 191; Markoe, *Phoenicians*, pp. 41–2.
28. Harden, *Phoenicians*, p. 49 and plate 51; Moscati, *World of the Phoenicians*, pp. 40–41.
29. Cf. Ezekiel's account of Tyre: Ezekiel 27; Isserlin, *Israelites*, p. 163.
30. Aubet, *Phoenicians and the West*, pp. 166–72, 182–91; P. Bartoloni, 'Ships and navigation', in Moscati, *Phoenicians*, pp. 84–5.
31. Markoe, *Phoenicians*, pp. 116–17; R. D. Ballard and M. McConnell, *Adventures in Ocean Exploration* (Washington, DC, 2001).
32. Markoe, *Phoenicians*, p. 117; cf. Aubet, *Phoenicians and the West*, p. 174.
33. Bartoloni, 'Ships and navigation', pp. 86–7; Markoe, *Phoenicians*, p. 116.
34. Aubet, *Phoenicians and the West*, pp. 173–4.
35. Markoe, *Phoenicians*, pp. 118–19.
36. Ibid., p. xxi.
37. Bartoloni, 'Ships and navigation', pp. 87–9; Aubet, *Phoenicians and the West*, pp. 174–8.
38. S. Ribichini, 'Beliefs and religious life', in Moscati, *Phoenicians*, p. 137.
39. Aubet, *Phoenicians and the West*, pp. 215–16; R. Miles, *Carthage Must Be Destroyed: the Rise and Fall of an Ancient Civilization* (London, 2010), pp. 58–9.
40. Aubet, *Phoenicians and the West*, pp. 221–6, and figs. 49 and 51.
41. Miles, *Carthage Must Be Destroyed*, p. 81.
42. Aubet, *Phoenicians and the West*, p. 232.
43. Harden, *Phoenicians*, pp. 35–6, figs. 6–7; Markoe, *Phoenicians*, pp. 81–3; popular account: G. Servadio, *Motya: Unearthing a Lost Civilization* (London, 2000).
44. Aubet, *Phoenicians and the West*, p. 238.
45. Ibid., pp. 311, 325; also Miles, *Carthage Must Be Destroyed*, pp. 49–54.
46. Aubet, *Phoenicians and the West*, p. 279.
47. Ibid., pp. 279–81, 288–9.
48. Jonah 1; Isaiah 23:1; cf. 23:6, 23:14.
49. G. Garbini, 'The question of the alphabet', in Moscati, *Phoenicians*, pp. 101–119; Markoe, *Phoenicians*, pp. 141–3; Moscati, *World of the Phoenicians*, pp. 120–26.
50. Harden, *Phoenicians*, p. 108 and fig. 34; also plates 15 and 38; Markoe, *Phoenicians*, pp. 143–7.
51. Markoe, *Phoenicians*, pp. 173–9; Aubet, *Phoenicians and the West*, pp. 245–56 (though the biblical references there are confused); Miles, *Carthage Must Be Destroyed*, pp. 69–73.
52. Aubet, *Phoenicians and the West*, p. 249; Harden, *Phoenicians*, plate 35;

Ribichini, 'Beliefs and religious life', in Moscati, *Phoenicians*, pp. 139–41; Miles, *Carthage Must Be Destroyed*, p. 70.

2. The Heirs of Odysseus, 800 BC–550 BC

1. I. Malkin, *The Returns of Odysseus: Colonisation and Ethnicity* (Berkeley and Los Angeles, CA, 1998), p. 17.
2. Ibid., p. 22; also D. Briquel, *Les Pélasges en Italie: recherches sur l'histoire de la légende* (Rome, 1984); R. Lane Fox, *Travelling Heroes: Greeks and Their Myths in the Epic Age of Homer* (London, 2008).
3. *Odyssey* 1:20, 5:291, 5:366, in the translation of Roger Dawe.
4. Malkin, *Returns of Odysseus*, pp. 4, 8.
5. Notably in the works of the French Homer scholars Victor Bérard and his son Jean Bérard: J. Bérard, *La colonisation grecque de l'Italie méridionale et de la Sicile dans l'antiquité* (Paris, 1957), pp. viii, 304–9.
6. Malkin, *Returns of Odysseus*, p. 186.
7. Ibid., p. 41; M. Scherer, *The Legends of Troy in Art and Literature* (New York, 1963).
8. Malkin, *Returns of Odysseus*, pp. 68–72.
9. Ibid., pp. 68–9, 94–8; Lane Fox, *Travelling Heroes*, pp. 181–2.
10. *Odyssey* 14:289; 15:416, trans. Dawe.
11. M. Finley, *The World of Odysseus* (2nd edn, London, 1964).
12. *Odyssey* 1:180–85, trans. Dawe.
13. Ibid., 9:105–115.
14. Ibid., 9:275.
15. Ibid. 9:125–9.
16. Ibid. 1:280.
17. D. Ridgway, *The First Western Greeks* (Cambridge, 1992) (revised edn of *L'alba della Magna Grecia*, Milan, 1984). Subsequent literature on the western Greeks: G. Pugliese Carratelli (ed.), *The Western Greeks* (London, 1996); V. M. Manfredi and L. Braccesi, *I Greci d'Occidente* (Milan, 1996); D. Puliga and S. Panichi, *Un'altra Grecia: le colonie d'Occidente tra mito, arte e memoria* (Turin, 2005); also Lane Fox, *Travelling Heroes*.
18. Lane Fox, *Travelling Heroes*, p. 160.
19. Cited by Ridgway, *First Western Greeks*, p. 99.
20. Lane Fox, *Travelling Heroes*, pp. 52–69.
21. Ibid., p. 159.
22. Ridgway, *First Western Greeks*, p. 17; Lane Fox, *Travelling Heroes*, pp. 55–9.
23. L. Woolley, *A Forgotten Kingdom* (Harmondsworth, 1953), pp. 172–88.
24. Ridgway, *First Western Greeks*, pp. 22–4.
25. Lane Fox, *Travelling Heroes*, pp. 138–49.

26. Ridgway, *First Western Greeks*, pp. 55–6, figs. 8–9; Lane Fox, *Travelling Heroes*, pp. 157–8.
27. *Odyssey* 3:54, trans. Dawe.
28. Ridgway, *First Western Greeks*, pp. 57–9, 115.
29. Ibid., pp. 111–13, and fig. 29, p. 112.
30. Lane Fox, *Travelling Heroes*, pp. 169–70.
31. *Iliad* 2:570 – cf. Thucydides 1:13.5; J. B. Salmon, *Wealthy Corinth: a History of the City to 338 BC* (Oxford, 1984), p. 1; M. L. Z. Munn, 'Corinthian trade with the West in the classical period' (Ph.D. thesis, Bryn Mawr College, University Microfilms, Ann Arbor, MI, 1983–4), p. 1.
32. Pindar, Olympian Ode 13; C. M. Bowra (trans.), *The Odes of Pindar* (Harmondsworth, 1969), p. 170.
33. Thucydides 1:13.
34. Salmon, *Wealthy Corinth*, pp. 84–5, 89.
35. Ridgway, *First Western Greeks*, p. 89.
36. Aristophanes, *Thesmophoriazousai*, ll. 647–8.
37. L. J. Siegel, 'Corinthian trade in the ninth through sixth centuries BC', 2 vols. (Ph.D. thesis, Yale University, University Microfilms, Ann Arbor, MI, 1978), vol. 1, pp. 64–84, 242–57.
38. Thucydides 1:13; Siegel, *Corinthian Trade*, p. 173.
39. Herodotos 1:18.20 and 5:92; A. Andrewes, *The Greek Tyrants* (London, 1956), pp. 50–51; Siegel, *Corinthian Trade*, pp. 176–8; also M. M. Austin, *Greece and Egypt in the Archaic Age* (supplements to *Proceedings of the Cambridge Philological Society*, no. 2, Cambridge, 1970), especially p. 37.
40. Salmon, *Wealthy Corinth*, pp. 105–6, 109–10.
41. Munn, *Corinthian Trade*, pp. 6–7; Salmon, *Wealthy Corinth*, pp. 101–5, 119.
42. Woolley, *Forgotten Kingdom* pp. 183–7.
43. Salmon, *Wealthy Corinth*, pp. 99, 120.
44. Munn, *Corinthian Trade*, pp. 263–7, 323–5.
45. Salmon, *Wealthy Corinth*, p. 136.
46. K. Greene, 'Technological innovation and economic progress in the ancient world: M. I. Finley reconsidered', *Economic History Review*, vol. 53 (2000), pp. 29–59, especially 29–34.
47. Munn, *Corinthian Trade*, pp. 78, 84, 95–6, 111; cf. M. Finley, *The Ancient Economy* (London, 1973).
48. Andrewes, *Greek Tyrants*, pp. 45–9.
49. Herodotos 5:92; Aristotle, *Politics*, 1313a35–37; Salmon, *Wealthy Corinth*, p. 197; also Andrewes, *Greek Tyrants*, pp. 50–53.
50. Salmon, *Wealthy Corinth*, pp. 199–204.
51. C. Riva, *The Urbanisation of Etruria: Funerary Practices and Social Change, 700–600 BC* (Cambridge, 2010), pp. 70–71; A. Carandini, *Re Tarquinio e il divino bastardo* (Milan, 2010).

52. A. J. Graham, *Colony and Mother City in Ancient Greece* (Manchester, 1964), p. 220.
53. Diodoros the Sicilian 15:13.1; Munn, *Corinthian Trade*, p. 35.
54. Graham, *Colony and Mother City*, pp. 218–23.

3. The Triumph of the Tyrrhenians, 800 BC–400 BC

1. J. Boardman, *Pre-classical: from Crete to Archaic Greece* (Harmondsworth, 1967), p. 169.
2. D. Briquel, *Origine lydienne des Étrusques: histoire de la doctrine dans l'antiquité* (Rome, 1991).
3. Herodotos 1:94.
4. Tacitus, *Annals* 4:55; R. Drews, 'Herodotos I. 94, the drought ca. 1200 BC, and the origin of the Etruscans', *Historia*, vol. 41 (1992), p. 17.
5. D. Briquel, *Tyrrhènes, peuple des tours: Denys d'Halicarnasse et l'autochtonie des Étrusques* (Rome, 1993).
6. Dionysios of Halikarnassos 1:30.
7. M. Pallottino, *The Etruscans* (2nd edn, London, 1975), pp. 78–81; but the point about Tarhun is mine.
8. Beginning with *Ciba Foundation Symposium on Medical Biology and Etruscan Origins*, ed. G. E. W. Wolstenholme and C. M. O'Connor (London, 1958).
9. G. Barbujani et al., 'The Etruscans: a population-genetic study', *American Journal of Human Genetics*, vol. 74 (2004), pp. 694–704; A. Piazza, A. Torroni et al., 'Mitochondrial DNA variation of modern Tuscans supports the Near Eastern origin of Etruscans', *American Journal of Human Genetics*, vol. 80 (2007), pp. 759–68.
10. C. Dougherty, 'The Aristonothos krater: competing stories of conflict and collaboration', in C. Dougherty and L. Kurke (eds.), *The Cultures within Ancient Greek Culture: Contact, Conflict, Collaboration* (Cambridge, 2003), pp. 35–56.
11. C. Riva, *The Urbanisation of Etruria: Funerary Practices and Social Change, 700–600 BC* (Cambridge, 2010), pp. 142–6; R. Lane Fox, *Travelling Heroes: Greeks and Their Myths in the Epic Age of Homer* (London, 2008), pp. 142–6.
12. Homeric Hymn no. 8, to Dionysos; see also M. Iuffrida Gentile, *La pirateria tirrenica: momenti e fortuna*, Supplementi a *Kókalos*, no. 6 (Rome and Palermo, 1983), pp. 33–47.
13. M. Cristofani, *Gli Etruschi del mare* (Milan, 1983), pp. 57–8 and plate 37 – cf. plate 68 (late 4th c.); G. Pettena, *Gli Etruschi e il mare* (Turin, 2002); Iuffrida Gentile, *Pirateria tirrenica*, p. 37.
14. M. Torelli, 'The battle for the sea-routes, 1000–300 BC', in D. Abulafia (ed.), *The Mediterranean in History* (London and New York, 2003), pp. 101–3.
15. Herodotos 1:57; also 4:145, 5:26; Thucydides 4:14.

16. M. Gras, *Trafics tyrrhéniens archaïques* (Rome, 1985), pp. 648–9; cf. Iuffrida Gentile, *Pirateria tirrenica*, p. 47.

17. Dionysios of Halikarnassos 1:30; they called themselves *Rasna*.

18. Gras, *Trafics tyrrhéniens*, p. 629; Lemnian *aviz* = Etruscan *avils*, 'years'.

19. Ibid., generally, and pp. 628, 637, 650; *Il commercio etrusco arcaico* (Quaderni del Centro di Studio per l'Archeologia etrusco-italica, vol. 9, Rome, 1985); G. M. della Fina (ed.), *Gli Etruschi e il Mediterraneo: commercio e politica* (Annali della Fondazione per il Museo Claudio Faina, vol. 13, Orvieto and Rome, 2006); cf. Cristofani, *Etruschi del Mare*, pp. 56–60.

20. Gras, *Trafics tyrrhéniens*, p. 615.

21. Riva, *Urbanisation of Etruria*, p. 67; H. Hencken, *Tarquinia and Etruscan Origins* (London, 1968), pp. 78–84.

22. Pallottino, *Etruscans*, pp. 91–4.

23. Hencken, *Tarquinia and Etruscan Origins*, p. 99 and plates 54, 90–93.

24. R. Leighton, *Tarquinia: an Etruscan City* (London, 2004), pp. 56–7; Hencken, *Tarquinia and Etruscan Origins*, pp. 66–73.

25. Hencken, *Tarquinia and Etruscan Origins*, plates 139–41.

26. Ibid., p. 72, fig. 31c, and p. 119.

27. Dougherty, 'Aristonothos krater', pp. 36–7; Hencken, *Tarquinia and Etruscan Origins*, pp. 116, 230, and plates 76–7.

28. Cristofani, *Etruschi del Mare*, pp. 28–9 and plate 15.

29. Hencken, *Tarquinia and Etruscan Origins*, p. 122, and plate 138.

30. Ibid., p. 123.

31. G. Camporeale et al., *The Etruscans outside Etruria* (Los Angeles, CA, 2004), p. 29.

32. S. Bruni, *Pisa Etrusca: anatomia di una città scomparsa* (Milan, 1998), pp. 86–113.

33. Camporeale et al., *Etruscans outside Etruria*, p. 37; also Riva, *Urbanisation of Etruria*, p. 51 (Bronze Age contact).

34. Gras, *Trafics tyrrhéniens*, pp. 254–390.

35. Cristofani, *Etruschi del Mare*, p. 30.

36. Hencken, *Tarquinia and Etruscan Origins*, pp. 137–41.

37. E.g. Pallottino, *Etruscans*, plate 11.

38. D. Diringer, 'La tavoletta di Marsiliana d'Albegna', *Studi in onore di Luisa Banti* (Rome, 1965), pp. 139–42; Lane Fox, *Travelling Heroes*, p. 159.

39. A. Mullen, 'Gallia Trilinguis: the multiple voices of south-eastern Gaul' (Ph.D. dissertation, Cambridge University, 2008), p. 90; H. Rodríguez Somolinos, 'The commercial transaction of the Pech Maho lead: a new interpretation', *Zeitschrift für Papyrologie und Epigraphik*, vol. 111 (1996), pp. 74–6; Camporeale et al., *Etruscans outside Etruria*, p. 89.

40. E. Acquaro, 'Phoenicians and Etruscans', in S. Moscati (ed.), *The Phoenicians* (New York, 1999), p. 613; Pallottino, *Etruscans*, p. 221.

41. Pallottino, *Etruscans*, p. 112 and plate 11 (original in Museo Nazionale Etrusco, Tarquinia); Herodotos 4:152.

42. Gras, *Trafics tyrrhéniens*, pp. 523–5.

43. Announced in *Corriere della Sera*, 5 August 2010; *La Stampa*, 6 August 2010.

44. J. D. Beazley, *Etruscan Vase-Painting* (Oxford, 1947), p. 1.

45. Ibid., p. 3.

46. So named by J. D. Beazley, *Attic Red-figure Vase-Painters* (2nd edn, Oxford, 1964).

47. Cristofani, *Etruschi del Mare*, p. 30 and plate 13.

48. Gras, *Trafics tyrrhéniens*, pp. 393–475; Torelli, 'Battle for the sea-routes', p. 117.

49. Herodotos 1:165–7.

50. Cristofani, *Etruschi del Mare*, p. 83 and plates 54, 58; cf. O. W. von Vacano, *The Etruscans in the Ancient World* (London, 1960), p. 121.

51. L. Donati, 'The Etruscans and Corsica', in Camporeale et al., *Etruscans outside Etruria*, pp. 274–9.

52. Cristofani, *Etruschi del Mare*, pp. 70, 84.

53. A. G. Woodhead, *The Greeks in the West* (London, 1962), p. 78.

54. Pindar, *Pythian Odes*, 1:72–4, trans. M. Bowra.

55. C. and G. Picard, *The Life and Death of Carthage* (London, 1968), p. 81.

56. Gras, *Trafics tyrrhéniens*, pp. 514–22.

57. Diodoros the Sicilian 11:88.4–5; Cristofani, *Etruschi del Mare*, pp. 114–15.

58. Thucydides 6:88.6.

59. Thucydides 7:57.11.

60. Leighton, *Tarquinia*, p. 133 and fig. 56, p. 140; Gras, *Trafics tyrrhéniens*, pp. 521, 686; Cristofani, *Etruschi del Mare*, p. 115.

61. Cf. T. J. Dunbabin, *The Western Greeks: the History of Sicily and South Italy from the Foundation of the Greek Colonies to 480 BC* (Oxford, 1968), p. 207.

62. Cited by J. Heurgon, *Daily Life of the Etruscans* (London, 1964), p. 33.

63. Cristofani, *Etruschi del Mare*, p. 95.

64. C. Riva, 'The archaeology of Picenum', in G. Bradley, E. Isayev and C. Riva (eds.), *Ancient Italy: Regions without Boundaries* (Exeter, 2007), pp. 96–100 (for Matelica).

65. Cristofani, *Etruschi del Mare*, p. 93.

66. Ibid., p. 101 and plate 66, p. 103, pp. 128–9; Heurgon, *Daily Life*, p. 140; cf. J. Boardman, *The Greeks Overseas: their Early Colonies and Trade* (2nd edn, London, 1980), pp. 228–9; Cristofani, *Etruschi del Mare*, pp. 103, 129.

67. Cristofani, *Etruschi del Mare*, p. 128.

4. Towards the Garden of the Hesperides, 1000 BC–400 BC

1. M. Guido, *Sardinia* (Ancient Peoples and Places, London, 1963), pp. 59–60; cf. M. Gras, *Trafics tyrrhéniens archaïques* (Rome, 1985), pp. 87–91.

2. M. Pallottino, *La Sardegna nuragica* (2nd edn, with an introduction by G. Lilliu, Nuoro, 2000), pp. 109–14.

3. Ibid., pp. 91–102.

4. Ibid., p. 162; Guido, *Sardinia*, pp. 106–7, 142.

5. Guido, *Sardinia*, p. 156.

6. Ibid., pp. 112–18; Pallottino, *Sardegna nuragica*, pp. 141–7.

7. Gras, *Trafics tyrrhéniens*, pp. 113–15, and fig, 19, p. 114, also pp. 164–7, figs. 29–30, and pp. 185–6.

8. Guido, *Sardinia*, pp. 172–7; Gras, *Trafics tyrrhéniens*, p. 145 (Vulci).

9. Guido, *Sardinia*, plates 56–7; Gras, *Trafics tyrrhéniens*, pp. 115–19, 123–40; Bible Lands Museum, Jerusalem, *Guide to the Collection* (3rd edn, Jerusalem, 2002), p. 84.

10. V. M. Manfredi and L. Braccesi, *I Greci d'Occidente* (Milan, 1966), pp. 184–9; D. Puliga and S. Panichi, *Un'altra Grecia: le colonie d'Occidente tra mito, arte a memoria* (Turin, 2005), pp. 203–14.

11. Gras, *Trafics tyrrhéniens*, p. 402.

12. Herodotos 1.163–7; A. J. Graham, *Colony and Mother City in Ancient Greece* (Manchester, 1964), pp. 111–12; M. Sakellariou, 'The metropolises of the western Greeks', in G. Pugliese Carratelli (ed.), *The Western Greeks* (London, 1996), pp. 187–8; Manfredi and Braccesi, *Greci d'Occidente*, pp. 179–81, 184–5; Puliga and Panichi, *Un'altra Grecia*, pp. 203–4.

13. G. Pugliese Carratelli, 'An outline of the political history of the Greeks in the West', in Pugliese Carratelli, *Western Greeks*, pp. 154–5.

14. M. Bats, 'The Greeks in Gaul and Corsica', in Pugliese Carratelli, *Western Greeks*, pp. 578–80, and plate, p. 579; V. Kruta, 'The Greek and Celtic worlds: a meeting of two cultures', in Pugliese Carratelli, *Western Greeks*, pp. 585–90; Puliga and Panichi, *Un'altra Grecia*, pp. 206–7.

15. J. Boardman, *The Greeks Overseas: their Early Colonies and Trade* (2nd edn, London, 1980), pp. 216–17; Manfredi and Braccesi, *Greci d'Occidente*, p. 187.

16. Justin, *Epitome* of Pompeius Trogus, 43:4; Boardman, *Greeks Overseas*, p. 218; Manfredi and Braccesi, *Greci d'Occidente*, p. 186.

17. L. Foxhall, *Olive Cultivation in Ancient Greece: Seeking the Ancient Economy* (Oxford, 2007), and other studies by the same author.

18. Boardman, *Greeks Overseas*, p. 219.

19. Ibid., p. 224.

20. Kruta and Bats in Pugliese Carratelli, *Western Greeks*, pp. 580–83; Boardman, *Greeks Overseas*, p. 224.

21. P. Dixon, *The Iberians of Spain and Their Relations with the Aegean World* (Oxford, 1940), p. 38.

22. Ibid., pp. 35–6.

23. A. Arribas, *The Iberians* (London, 1963), pp. 56–7.

24. B. Cunliffe, *The Extraordinary Voyage of Pytheas the Greek* (London, 2001).

25. Avienus, *Ora Maritima*, ed. J. P. Murphy (Chicago, IL, 1977); L. Antonelli, *Il Periplo nascosto: lettura stratigrafica e commento storico-archeologico del-*

l'Ora Maritima *di Avieno* (Padua, 1998) (with edition); F. J. González Ponce, *Avieno y el Periplo* (Ecija, 1995).

26. Avienus ll. 267–74.
27. Ibid. ll. 80–332, especially ll. 85, 113–16, 254, 308, 290–98.
28. Ibid. ll. 309–12, 375–80, 438–48, 459–60.
29. Cunliffe, *Extraordinary Voyage*, pp. 42–8; Dixon, *Iberians of Spain*, pp. 39–40.
30. Avienus ll. 481–2, 485–9, 496–7, 519–22.
31. Dixon, *Iberians of Spain*; Arribas, *Iberians*; A. Ruiz and M. Molinos, *The Archaeology of the Iberians* (Cambridge, 1998).
32. Avienus l. 133.
33. Arribas, *Iberians*, pp. 89, 93, 95, figs. 24, 27, 28, and pp. 102–4, 120, bearing in mind Foxhall, *Olive Cultivation*.
34. Arribas, *Iberians*, pp. 146–9.
35. Ibid., plates 35–8, 52–4.
36. Ibid., p. 160; also plates 22–3; Dixon, *Iberians of Spain*, pp. 106–7, 113–15 and frontispiece.
37. Dixon, *Iberians of Spain*, p. 107.
38. Ibid., p. 82 and plate 12b.
39. Arribas, *Iberians*, p. 131 and plate 21; also Dixon, *Iberians of Spain*, p. 11.
40. Dixon, *Iberians of Spain*, pp. 85–8, plates 10, 11a and b.
41. Ibid., pp. 54–60; Arribas, *Iberians*, pp. 73–87.

5. Thalassocracies, 550 BC–400 BC

1. N. G. L. Hammond, *A History of Greece to 322 BC* (Oxford, 1959), p. 226.
2. Thucydides 1:5.
3. Aeschylus, *The Persians (Persae)*, trans. Gilbert Murray (London, 1939), ll. 230–34, p. 30.
4. A. R. Burn, *The Pelican History of Greece* (Harmondsworth, 1966), pp. 146, 159; Hammond, *History of Greece*, pp. 176, 202; J. Morrison and J. Oates, *The Athenian Trireme: the History and Reconstruction of an Ancient Greek Warship* (Cambridge, 1986).
5. Thucydides 1:21; Herodotos 3:122; C. Constantakopolou, *The Dance of the Islands: Insularity, Networks, the Athenian Empire and the Aegean World* (Oxford, 2007), p. 94.
6. Herodotos 5:31.
7. Burn, *Pelican History*, p. 158.
8. P. Cartledge, *The Spartans: an Epic History* (London, 2002), pp. 101–17.
9. Burn, *Pelican History*, p. 174 – cf. Hammond, *History of Greece*, p. 202.
10. On numbers: W. Rodgers, *Greek and Roman Naval Warfare* (Annapolis, MD, 1937), pp. 80–95.
11. Ibid., p. 86.

12. Aeschylus, *Persians*, ll. 399–405, p. 39.
13. J. Hale, *Lords of the Sea: the Triumph and Tragedy of Ancient Athens* (London, 2010).
14. Thucydides 1:14.
15. Ibid. 1:13 and 3:104; Constantakopolou, *Dance of the Islands*, pp. 47–8.
16. Thucydides. 3.104 (trans. Rex Warner); cf. Homeric Hymn to Delian Apollo, ll. 144–55.
17. Constantakopolou, *Dance of the Islands*, p. 70.
18. Displayed on the modern doors of the library that commemorates his name in the History Faculty, Cambridge University.
19. A. Moreno, *Feeding the Democracy: the Athenian Grain Supply in the Fifth and Fourth Centuries BC* (Oxford, 2007), pp. 28–31.
20. Aristophanes, *Horai*, fragment 581, cited in Moreno, *Feeding the Democracy*, p. 75.
21. Cf. P. Garnsey, *Famine and Food Supply in the Graeco-Roman World: Responses to Risk and Crisis* (Cambridge, 1988), and M. Finley, *The Ancient Economy* (London, 1973).
22. Isokrates 4:107–9, cited in Moreno, *Feeding the Democracy*, p. 77.
23. Moreno, *Feeding the Democracy*, p. 100.
24. Thucydides 8:96; cf. Moreno, *Feeding the Democracy*, p. 126.
25. Herodotos 7:147.
26. R. Meiggs, *The Athenian Empire* (Oxford, 1972), pp. 121–3, 530; Moreno, *Feeding the Democracy*, p. 318.
27. Moreno, *Feeding the Democracy*, p. 319; cf. P. Horden and N. Purcell, *The Corrupting Sea: a Study of Mediterranean History* (Oxford, 2000), p. 121.
28. P. J. Rhodes, *The Athenian Empire* (*Greece and Rome*, New Surveys in the Classics, no. 17) (Oxford, 1985).
29. Thucydides 1 (trans. Rex Warner).
30. Ibid. 1:2; J. Wilson, *Athens and Corcyra: Strategy and Tactics in the Peloponnesian War* (Bristol, 1987); D. Kagan, *The Peloponnesian War: Athens and Sparta in Savage Conflict 431–404 BC* (London, 2003), p. 25.
31. Thucydides 1:2 (adapted from version by Rex Warner).
32. Kagan, *Peloponnesian War*, p. 27.
33. Thucydides 1:3.
34. Ibid.
35. Thucydides 1:4; Kagan, *Peloponnesian War*, pp. 34–6, and map 8, p. 35.
36. Thucydides 1:67.2; Kagan, *Peloponnesian War*, p. 41, n.1.
37. Thucydides 1:6.
38. Kagan, *Peloponnesian War*, pp. 100–101; Constantakopolou, *Dance of the Islands*, pp. 239–42.
39. Thucydides 3:13.
40. Ibid. 4:1.
41. Kagan, *Peloponnesian War*, pp. 142–7.

42. Thucydides 4:2.
43. Ibid. 3:86.4.
44. Ibid. 6:6.1; Kagan, *Peloponnesian War*, pp. 118–20.
45. Cf. Thucydides 6:6.1.
46. Ibid. 6:46.3.
47. W. M. Ellis, *Alcibiades* (London, 1989), p. 54.
48. Kagan, *Peloponnesian War*, p. 280.
49. Rodgers, *Greek and Roman Naval Warfare*, pp. 159–67.
50. Kagan, *Peloponnesian War*, p. 321.
51. Ibid., pp. 402–14.
52. Ibid., pp. 331–2.
53. Xenophon, *Hellenika*, 2:1; Cartledge, *Spartans*, pp. 192–202.
54. Xenophon, *Hellenika*, 3:2, 3:5, 4:2, 4:3, 4:4, 4:5, 4:7, 4:8, 4:9, etc.

6. The Lighthouse of the Mediterranean, 350 BC–100 BC

1. R. Lane Fox, *Alexander the Great* (3rd edn, Harmondsworth, 1986), pp. 181–91.
2. Serious account: P. M. Fraser, *Ptolemaic Alexandria*, 3 vols. (Oxford, 1972), vol. 1, p. 3; popular account: J. Pollard and H. Reid, *The Rise and Fall of Alexandria, Birthplace of the Modern Mind* (New York, 2006), pp. 6–7.
3. Lane Fox, *Alexander the Great*, p. 198.
4. Pollard and Reid, *Rise and Fall of Alexandria*, pp. 2–3.
5. Strabo, *Geography*, 17:8; J.-Y. Empereur, *Alexandria: Past, Present and Future* (London, 2002), p. 23.
6. Lane Fox, *Alexander the Great*, pp. 461–72.
7. S.-A. Ashton, 'Ptolemaic Alexandria and the Egyptian tradition', in A. Hirst and M. Silk (eds.), *Alexandria Real and Imagined* (2nd edn, Cairo, 2006), pp. 15–40.
8. J. Carleton Paget, 'Jews and Christians in ancient Alexandria from the Ptolemies to Caracalla', in Hirst and Silk, *Alexandria Real and Imagined*, pp. 146–9.
9. Fraser, *Ptolemaic Alexandria*, vol. 1, p. 255; Empereur, *Alexandria*, pp. 24–5.
10. Fraser, *Ptolemaic Alexandria*, vol. 1, p. 252; also pp. 116–17.
11. Ibid., p. 259.
12. Strabo, *Geography*, 17:7; cf. Fraser, *Ptolemaic Alexandria*, vol. 1, pp. 132, 143.
13. M. Rostovtzeff, *The Social and Economic History of the Hellenistic World*, 3 vols. (Oxford, 1941), vol. 1, p. 29.
14. L. Casson, *The Ancient Mariners: Seafarers and Sea Fighters of the Mediterranean in Ancient Times* (2nd edn, Princeton, NJ, 1991), pp. 131–3.
15. Ibid., p. 130.
16. Ibid., p. 135, and pl. 32.

17. Rostovtzeff, *Social and Economic History*, vol. 1, pp. 367, 387; Fraser, *Ptolemaic Alexandria*, vol. 1, pp. 137–9.

18. Rostovtzeff, *Social and Economic History*, vol. 1, pp. 395–6.

19. Casson, *Ancient Mariners*, p. 160; cf. Rostovtzeff, *Social and Economic History*, vol. 1, pp. 226–9.

20. Fraser, *Ptolemaic Alexandria*, vol. 1, p. 150.

21. Ibid., pp. 176, 178–81.

22. Empereur, *Alexandria*, p. 35.

23. Bosphoran grain: G. J. Oliver, *War, Food, and Politics in Early Hellenistic Athens* (Oxford, 2007), pp. 22–30.

24. Rostovtzeff, *Social and Economic History*, vol. 1, pp. 359–60, 363.

25. Diodoros the Sicilian 1:34.

26. Fraser, *Ptolemaic Alexandria*, vol. 1, p. 315; H. Maehler, 'Alexandria, the Mouseion, and cultural identity', in Hirst and Silk, *Alexandria Real and Imagined*, pp. 1–14.

27. Irenaeus, cited in M. El-Abbadi, 'The Alexandria Library in history', in Hirst and Silk, *Alexandria Real and Imagined*, p. 167.

28. El-Abbadi, 'The Alexandria Library in history', p. 172; Fraser, *Ptolemaic Alexandria*, vol. 1, p. 329.

29. Empereur, *Alexandria*, pp. 38–9.

30. Maehler, 'Alexandria, the Mouseion, and cultural identity', pp. 9–10.

31. Comments by E. V. Rieu in his translation of Apollonius of Rhodes, *The Voyage of Argo* (Harmondsworth, 1959), pp. 25–7; cf. Fraser, *Ptolemaic Alexandria*, vol. 1, p. 627.

32. Pollard and Reid, *Rise and Fall of Alexandria*, p. 79.

33. Empereur, *Alexandria*, p. 43.

34. El-Abbadi, 'The Alexandria Library in history', p. 174.

35. N. Collins, *The Library in Alexandria and the Bible in Greek* (Leiden, 2000), p. 45: Philo, Josephus (Jewish authors); Justin, Tertullian (Christian authors – also Irenaeus and Clement of Alexandria, attributing the work to the reign of Ptolemy I).

36. Carleton Paget, 'Jews and Christians', pp. 149–51.

37. Fraser, *Ptolemaic Alexandria*, vol. 1, pp. 331, 338–76, 387–9.

38. Pollard and Reid, *Rise and Fall of Alexandria*, pp. 133–7.

39. N. K. Rauh, *Merchants, Sailors and Pirates in the Roman World* (Stroud, 2003), pp. 65–7.

40. P. de Souza, *Piracy in the Graeco-Roman World* (Cambridge, 1999), pp. 80–84.

41. Casson, *Ancient Mariners*, pp. 138–40.

42. Rauh, *Merchants*, p. 66.

43. Diodoros the Sicilian 22:81.4, cited by Rauh, *Merchants*, p. 66.

44. Rauh, *Merchants*, p. 68.

45. Casson, *Ancient Mariners*, p. 163.

46. Rostovtzeff, *Social and Economic History*, vol. 1, pp. 230–32; for its early development, see G. Reger, *Regionalism and Change in the Economy of*

Independent Delos, 314–167 BC (Berkeley, CA, 1994); later developments in: N. Rauh, *The Sacred Bonds of Commerce: Religion, Economy, and Trade Society at Hellenistic-Roman Delos, 166–87 BC* (Amsterdam, 1993).

47. Rauh, *Merchants*, pp. 53–65, 73–4; Casson, *Ancient Mariners*, p. 165.

7. 'Carthage Must Be Destroyed', 400 BC–146 BC

1. B. H. Warmington, *Carthage* (London, 1960), pp. 74–5, 77; R. Miles, *Carthage Must Be Destroyed: the Rise and Fall of an Ancient Civilization* (London, 2010), pp. 121–3.

2. Xenophon, *Hellenika*, 1:1.

3. A. Andrewes, *The Greek Tyrants* (London, 1956), p. 137; Miles, *Carthage Must Be Destroyed*, pp. 123–4.

4. Warmington, *Carthage*, p. 80.

5. M. Finley, *Ancient Sicily* (London, 1968), p. 71; Andrewes, *Greek Tyrants*, p. 129; Miles, *Carthage Must Be Destroyed*, p. 126 (for a Carthaginian inscription commemorating the fall of Akragas).

6. Warmington, *Carthage*, pp. 83, 87; Finley, *Ancient Sicily*, pp. 71–2, 91–3.

7. Warmington, *Carthage*, p. 91; Miles, *Carthage Must Be Destroyed*, pp. 127–8.

8. Warmington, *Carthage*, pp. 93–5; Finley, *Ancient Sicily*, pp. 76, 78, 80, 82.

9. Warmington, *Carthage*, p. 94.

10. Plutarch, *Parallel Lives*, 'Timoleon'; Finley, *Ancient Sicily*, p. 96.

11. Warmington, *Carthage*, pp. 102–3; Miles, *Carthage Must Be Destroyed*, pp. 136–7.

12. R. J. A. Talbert, *Timoleon and the Revival of Greek Sicily, 344–317 BC* (Cambridge, 1974), pp. 151–2; Finley, *Ancient Sicily*, p. 99.

13. Plutarch, 'Timoleon'; Talbert, *Timoleon*, pp. 156–7, 161–5; Finley, *Ancient Sicily*, p. 99.

14. Finley, *Ancient Sicily*, p. 104; Warmington, *Carthage*, p. 107.

15. Warmington, *Carthage*, p. 113.

16. Finley, *Ancient Sicily*, p. 105.

17. J. Serrati, 'The coming of the Romans: Sicily from the fourth to the first centuries BC', in *Sicily from Aeneas to Augustus: New Approaches in Archaeology and History*, ed. C. Smith and J. Serrati (Edinburgh, 2000), pp. 109–10.

18. Livy 2:34.4; B. D. Hoyos, *Unplanned Wars: the Origins of the First and Second Punic Wars* (Berlin, 1998), p. 28; G. Rickman, *The Corn Supply of Ancient Rome* (Oxford, 1980), p. 31.

19. R. Cowan, *Roman Conquests: Italy* (London, 2009), pp. 8–11, 21–5.

20. R. Meiggs, *Roman Ostia* (2nd edn, Oxford, 1973), p. 24.

21. Rickman, *Corn Supply*, p. 32.

22. K. Lomas, *Rome and the Western Greeks 350 BC–AD 200* (London, 1993), p. 50.

23. Livy 9:30.4.

24. Disagreeing with Lomas, *Rome and the Western Greeks*, p. 51.

25. Lomas, *Rome and the Western Greeks*, p. 56.

26. Hoyos, *Unplanned Wars*, pp. 19–20.

27. J. F. Lazenby, *The First Punic War: a Military History* (London, 1996), p. 34; Miles, *Carthage Must Be Destroyed*, pp. 162–5.

28. Miles, *Carthage Must Be Destroyed*, pp. 107–11, 160–61.

29. E.g. A. Goldsworthy, *The Fall of Carthage* (London, 2000), pp. 16, 65, 322.

30. Hoyos, *Unplanned Wars*, pp. 1–4; Goldsworthy, *Fall of Carthage*, pp. 19–20.

31. Polybios 1:63; Hoyos, *Unplanned Wars*, p. 1; on devastation: Goldsworthy, *Fall of Carthage*, pp. 363–4.

32. J. Serrati, 'Garrisons and grain: Sicily between the Punic Wars', in *Sicily from Aeneas to Augustus*, ed. Smith and Serrati, pp. 116–19.

33. Lazenby, *First Punic War*, pp. 35–9; Goldsworthy, *Fall of Carthage*, pp. 66–8; Miles, *Carthage Must Be Destroyed*, pp. 171–3.

34. Polybios 10:3; Lazenby, *First Punic War*, p. 37; Hoyos, *Unplanned Wars*, pp. 33–66.

35. Polybios 20:14; Lazenby, *First Punic War*, p. 48; Miles, *Carthage Must Be Destroyed*, p. 174.

36. Diodoros 23:2.1.

37. Lazenby, *First Punic War*, pp. 51, 55.

38. Polybios 20:1–2; Hoyos, *Unplanned Wars*, p. 113; Lazenby, *First Punic War*, p. 60; Goldsworthy, *Fall of Carthage*, p. 81.

39. Cf. though Miles, *Carthage Must Be Destroyed*, p. 175.

40. Polybios 20:9; Lazenby, *First Punic War*, pp. 62–3.

41. Polybios 20:9–12.

42. Ibid. 22:2.

43. Lazenby, *First Punic War*, pp. 64, 66 and 69, fig. 5.1; Miles, *Carthage Must Be Destroyed*, pp. 181–3.

44. J. H. Thiel, *Studies on the History of Roman Sea-power in Republican Times* (Amsterdam, 1946), p. 19; Goldsworthy, *Fall of Carthage*, pp. 109–15; also Lazenby, *First Punic War*, pp. 83, 86–7.

45. Cf. Lazenby, *First Punic War*, p. 94.

46. J. Morrison, *Greek and Roman Oared Warships, 339–30 BC* (Oxford, 1996), pp. 46–50.

47. Goldsworthy, *Fall of Carthage*, p. 115.

48. Polybios 37:3; Lazenby, *First Punic War*, p. 111; Miles, *Carthage Must Be Destroyed*, p. 181.

49. Polybios 62:8–63.3; Lazenby, *First Punic War*, p. 158.

50. Warmington, *Carthage*, pp. 167–8; Hoyos, *Unplanned Wars*, pp. 131–43.

51. M. Guido, *Sardinia* (Ancient Peoples and Places, London, 1963), p. 209.

52. B. D. Hoyos, *Hannibal's Dynasty: Power and Politics in the Western Mediterranean, 247–183 BC* (London, 2003), pp. 50–52, 72, 74–6; Miles, *Carthage Must Be Destroyed*, pp. 214–22.

53. Hoyos, *Hannibal's Dynasty*, p. 53.
54. Ibid., pp. 55, 63–7, 79–80; Miles, *Carthage Must Be Destroyed*, p. 224, citing Polybios 10:10.
55. Hoyos, *Unplanned Wars*, pp. 150–95, especially p. 177 and p. 208.
56. Goldsworthy, *Fall of Carthage*, pp. 253–60.
57. Serrati, 'Garrisons and grain', pp. 115–33.
58. Finley, *Ancient Sicily*, pp. 117–18; Goldsworthy, *Fall of Carthage*, p. 261.
59. Thiel, *Studies on the History of Roman Sea-power*, pp. 79–86; Goldsworthy, *Fall of Carthage*, pp. 263, 266.
60. Finley, *Ancient Sicily*, p. 119.
61. Goldsworthy, *Fall of Carthage*, p. 308.
62. Thiel, *Studies on the History of Roman Sea-power*, pp. 255–372.
63. Goldsworthy, *Fall of Carthage*, p. 331.
64. Warmington, *Carthage*, pp. 201–2.
65. Goldsworthy, *Fall of Carthage*, pp. 338–9.
66. Rauh, *Merchants*, pp. 38–53.
67. Virgil, *Aeneid*, 4:667–71, in Dryden's translation.

8. 'Our Sea', 146 BC–AD 150

1. N. K. Rauh, *Merchants, Sailors and Pirates in the Roman World* (Stroud, 2003), pp. 136–41.
2. Lucan, *Pharsalia*, 7:400–407, trans. Robert Graves.
3. R. Syme, *The Roman Revolution* (Oxford, 1939), pp. 78, 83–8.
4. P. de Souza, *Piracy in the Graeco-Roman World* (Cambridge, 1999), pp. 92–6.
5. L. Casson, *The Ancient Mariners: Seafarers and Sea Fighters of the Mediterranean in Ancient Times* (2nd edn, Princeton, NJ, 1991), p. 191; de Souza, *Piracy*, pp. 140–41, 162, 164.
6. Cited in de Souza, *Piracy*, pp. 50–51.
7. Livy 34:32.17–20; Polybios 13:6.1–2; both cited in de Souza, *Piracy*, pp. 84–5.
8. de Souza, *Piracy*, pp. 185–95.
9. Rauh, *Merchants*, pp. 177, 184; but maybe these *tyrannoi* (and not Etruscans) were the *Tyrrhenoi* active near Rhodes – an easy etymological confusion.
10. Strabo, *Geography*, 14.3.2; Rauh, *Merchants*, pp. 171–2.
11. Plutarch, *Parallel Lives*, 'Pompey', 24.1–3, trans. John Dryden.
12. de Souza, *Piracy*, pp. 165–6.
13. Plutarch, *Parallel Lives*, 'Pompey', 25:1, trans. John Dryden.
14. Syme, *Roman Revolution*, p. 28.
15. Cicero, *Pro Lege Manilia*, 34; G. Rickman, *The Corn Supply of Ancient Rome* (Oxford, 1980), pp. 51–2.
16. de Souza, *Piracy*, pp. 169–70.
17. Rickman, *Corn Supply*, p. 51; Syme, *Roman Revolution*, p. 29.

18. Plutarch, *Parallel Lives*, 'Pompey', 28:3; de Souza, *Piracy*, pp. 170–71, 175–6.

19. Syme, *Roman Revolution*, p. 30.

20. *Hoc voluerunt*: Suetonius, *Twelve Caesars*, 'Divus Julius', 30:4.

21. Syme, *Roman Revolution*, p. 260.

22. F. Adcock in *Cambridge Ancient History*, 12 vols. (Cambridge, 1923–39), vol. 9, *The Roman Republic, 133–44 BC*, p. 724; Syme, *Roman Revolution*, pp. 53–60.

23. Syme, *Roman Revolution*, pp. 260, 270.

24. Ibid., pp. 294–7; C. G. Starr, *The Roman Imperial Navy 31 BC–AD 324* (Ithaca, NY, 1941), pp. 7–8; J. Morrison, *Greek and Roman Oared Warships, 339–30 BC* (Oxford, 1996), pp. 157–75.

25. Virgil, *Aeneid*, 8:678–80, 685–8, in Dryden's rather loose version.

26. Syme, *Roman Revolution*, pp. 298–300; Rickman, *Corn Supply*, pp. 61, 70.

27. *Res Gestae Divi Augusti*, ed. P. A. Brunt and J. M. Moore (Oxford, 1967), 15:2.

28. Rickman, *Corn Supply*, pp. 176–7, 187, 197, 205–8.

29. Ibid., p. 12.

30. Rauh, *Merchants*, pp. 93–4.

31. Plutarch, *Parallel Lives*, 'Cato the Elder', 21.6; Rauh, *Merchants*, p. 104.

32. Rauh, *Merchants*, p. 105.

33. Rickman, *Corn Supply*, pp. 16, 121.

34. Ibid., pp. 6–7; also P. Erdkamp, *The Grain Market in the Roman Empire: a Social and Political Study* (Cambridge, 2005); P. Garnsey, *Famine and Food Supply in the Graeco-Roman World: Responses to Risk and Crisis* (Cambridge, 1988).

35. Rickman, *Corn Supply*, p. 16.

36. Museu de la Ciutat de Barcelona, Roman section.

37. Rickman, *Corn Supply*, pp. 15, 128.

38. Acts of the Apostles, 27 and 28.

39. Rickman, *Corn Supply*, pp. 17, 65.

40. Josephus, *Jewish War*, 2:383–5; Rickman, *Corn Supply*, pp. 68, 232.

41. Rickman, *Corn Supply*, pp. 61, 123.

42. Ibid., pp. 108–12; S. Raven, *Rome in Africa* (2nd edn, Harlow, 1984), pp. 84–105. Other sources included Sicily: Rickman, *Corn Supply*, pp. 104–6; Sardinia: ibid., pp. 106–7; Spain: ibid., pp. 107–8.

43. Rickman, *Corn Supply*, pp. 67, 69.

44. Raven, *Rome in Africa*, p. 94.

45. Pliny the Elder, *Natural History*, 18:35; Rickman, *Corn Supply*, p. 111.

46. Raven, *Rome in Africa*, pp. 86, 93.

47. Ibid., p. 95.

48. Ibid., pp. 95, 100–102.

49. Rickman, *Corn Supply*, pp. 69–70 and Appendix 4, pp. 231–5.

50. Ibid., p. 115 (AD 99).

51. Ibid., pp. 76–7, and Appendix 11, pp. 256–67.
52. Seneca, *Letters*, 77:1–3, cited in D. Jones, *The Bankers of Puteoli: Finance, Trade and Industry in the Roman World* (Stroud, 2006), p. 26.
53. Jones, *Bankers of Puteoli*, p. 28.
54. Ibid., pp. 23–4; and Strabo, *Geography*, 5:4.6.
55. Jones, *Bankers of Puteoli*, p. 33.
56. Cited in R. Meiggs, *Roman Ostia* (Oxford, 1960), p. 60.
57. Jones, *Bankers of Puteoli*, p. 34.
58. Petronius, *Satyricon*, 76; Jones, *Bankers of Puteoli*, p. 43.
59. Jones, *Bankers of Puteoli*, p. 11.
60. Ibid., pp. 102–17.
61. Ibid., Appendix 9, p. 255.
62. Rickman, *Corn Supply*, pp. 21–4, 134–43; G. Rickman, *Roman Granaries and Store Buildings* (Cambridge, 1971).
63. Rickman, *Corn Supply*, p. 23; Rickman, *Roman Granaries*, pp. 97–104.
64. Meiggs, *Roman Ostia*, pp. 16–17, 41–5, 57–9, 74, 77.
65. M. Reddé, *Mare Nostrum: les infrastructures, le dispositif et l'histoire de la marine militaire sous l'empire romain* (Rome, 1986).
66. Tacitus, *Histories*, 3:8; Starr, *Roman Imperial Navy*, pp. 181, 183, 185, 189; Rickman, *Corn Supply*, p. 67.
67. Starr, *Roman Imperial Navy*, p. 188.
68. Ibid., p. 67.
69. Cited ibid., p. 78.
70. Aelius Aristides, cited ibid., p. 87.
71. Oxyrhyncus papyrus cited ibid., p. 79.
72. Ibid., pp. 84–5.
73. Reddé, *Mare Nostrum*, p. 402.
74. Raven, *Rome in Africa*, pp. 75–6; Reddé, *Mare Nostrum*, pp. 244–8.
75. Reddé, *Mare Nostrum*, pp. 139, 607, and more generally pp. 11–141.
76. Tacitus, *Annals*, 4:5; Suetonius, *Lives of the Caesars*, 'Augustus', 49; Reddé, *Mare Nostrum*, p. 472.
77. Reddé, *Mare Nostrum*, pp. 186–97; Starr, *Roman Imperial Navy*, pp. 13–21.
78. Reddé, *Mare Nostrum*, pp. 177–86; Starr, *Roman Imperial Navy*, pp. 21–4.

9. Old and New Faiths, AD 1–450

1. B. de Breffny, *The Synagogue* (London, 1978), pp. 30–32, 37.
2. R. Meiggs, *Roman Ostia* (Oxford, 1960), pp. 355–66, 368–76.
3. R. Lane Fox, *Pagans and Christians in the Mediterranean World from the Second Century AD to the Conversion of Constantine* (London, 1986), pp. 428, 438, 453.

4. M. Goodman, *Rome and Jerusalem: the Clash of Ancient Civilisations* (London, 2007), pp. 26–8, 421, 440–43.

5. Ibid., pp. 469–70: coins inscribed FISCI IVDAICI CALVMNIA SVBLATA.

6. Ibid., pp. 480, 484–91.

7. S. Sand, *The Invention of the Jewish People* (London, 2009), pp. 130–46, seriously underestimates the scale of this diaspora.

8. Lane Fox, *Pagans and Christians*, pp. 450, 482.

9. Ibid., p. 487.

10. Sand, *Invention*, pp. 171–2.

11. Lane Fox, *Pagans and Christians*, p. 492.

12. A. S. Abulafia, *Christian-Jewish Relations, 1000–1300: Jews in the Service of Christians* (Harlow, 2011), pp. 4–8, 15–16.

13. R. Patai, *The Children of Noah: Jewish Seafaring in Ancient Times* (Princeton, NJ, 1998), pp. 137–42.

14. Ibid., pp. 70–71, 85–100.

15. Lane Fox, *Pagans and Christians*, pp. 609–62.

16. G. Bowersock, *Julian the Apostate* (London, 1978), pp. 89–90, 120–22; P. Athanassiadi, *Julian the Apostate: an Intellectual Biography* (London, 1992), pp. 163–5.

17. Bowersock, *Julian*, pp. 79–93; R. Smith, *Julian's Gods: Religion and Philosophy in the Thought and Action of Julian the Apostate* (London, 1995).

18. Lane Fox, *Pagans and Christians*, p. 31.

19. G. Downey, *Gaza in the Early Sixth Century* (Norman, OK, 1963), pp. 33–59 – much of this book is the most dreadful waffle.

20. Lane Fox, *Pagans and Christians*, p. 270.

21. Downey, *Gaza*, pp. 17–26, 20–21, 25–9.

22. For his career, see Mark the Deacon, *Life of Porphyry Bishop of Gaza*, ed. G. F. Hill (Oxford, 1913); Marc le Diacre, *Vie de Porphyre, évêque de Gaza*, ed. H. Grégoire and M.-A. Kugener (Paris, 1930).

23. Sand, *Invention*, pp. 166–78, though overstated.

24. Severus of Minorca, *Letter on the Conversion of the Jews*, ed. S. Bradbury (Oxford, 1996), editor's introduction, pp. 54–5; J. Amengual i Batle, *Judíos, Católicos y herejes: el microcosmos balear y tarraconense de Seuerus de Menorca, Consentius y Orosius (413–421)* (Granada, 2008), pp. 69–201.

25. C. Ginzburg, 'The conversion of Minorcan Jews (417–418): an experiment in history of historiography', in S. Waugh and P. Diehl (eds.), *Christendom and its Discontents: Exclusion, Persecution, and Rebellion, 1000–1500* (Cambridge, 1996), pp. 207–19.

26. Severus of Minorca, *Letter*, pp. 80–85.

27. Bradbury, ibid., pp. 34–6.

28. Severus of Minorca, *Letter*, pp. 84–5.

29. Ibid., pp. 82–3.

30. Bishop John II of Jerusalem, ibid., p. 18; also Bradbury's comments, pp. 16–25.

31. Ginzburg, 'Conversion', pp. 213–15; Bradbury in Severus of Minorca, *Letter*, pp. 19, 53.

32. Severus of Minorca, *Letter*, pp. 124–5.

33. Ibid., pp. 94–101.

34. Ibid., pp. 116–19.

35. Ibid., pp. 92–3; but cf. Bradbury's comment, p. 32.

36. Bradbury, ibid., pp. 41–2.

10. Dis-integration, 400–600

1. B. Ward-Perkins, *The Fall of Rome and the End of Civilisation* (Oxford, 2005), p. 32.

2. Ibid., pp. 1–10; P. Heather, *The Fall of the Roman Empire: a New History* (London, 2005), p. xii.

3. C. Wickham, *The Inheritance of Rome: a History of Europe from 400 to 1000* (London, 2009).

4. Heather, *Fall of the Roman Empire*, p. 130.

5. G. Rickman, *The Corn Supply of Ancient Rome* (Oxford, 1980), pp. 69, 118.

6. B. H. Warmington, *The North African Provinces from Diocletian to the Vandal Conquest* (Cambridge, 1954), pp. 64–5, 113.

7. Ward-Perkins, *Fall of Rome*, pp. 103, 131.

8. Heather, *Fall of the Roman Empire*, pp. 277–80.

9. Warmington, *North African Provinces*, p. 112; S. Raven, *Rome in Africa* (2nd ed, Harlow, 1984), p. 207.

10. H. Castritius, *Die Vandalen: Etappen einer Spurensuche* (Stuttgart, 2007), pp. 15–33; A. Merrills and R. Miles, *The Vandals* (Oxford, 2010).

11. Raven, *Rome in Africa*, p. 171.

12. C. Courtois, *Les Vandales et l'Afrique* (Paris, 1955), p. 157.

13. Ibid., p. 160; cf. H. J. Diesner, *Das Vandelenreich: Aufstieg und Untergang* (Leipzig, 1966), p. 51 for lower estimates.

14. Courtois, *Vandales*, pp. 159–63; Castritius, *Vandalen*, pp. 76–8.

15. Courtois, *Vandales*, pp. 110, 170; Wickham, *Inheritance of Rome*, p. 77.

16. A. Schwarcz, 'The settlement of the Vandals in North Africa', in A. Merrills (ed.), *Vandals, Romans and Berbers: New Perspectives on Late Antique North Africa* (Aldershot, 2004), pp. 49–57.

17. Courtois, *Vandales*, p. 173; A. Merrills, 'Vandals, Romans and Berbers: understanding late antique North Africa', in Merrills (ed.), *Vandals, Romans and Berbers*, pp. 4–5.

18. Merrills, 'Vandals, Romans and Berbers', pp. 10–11.

19. R. Hodges and D. Whitehouse, *Mohammed, Charlemagne and the Origins of Europe* (London, 1983), pp. 27–8; also Wickham, *Inheritance of Rome*, p. 78: 'the Carthage-Rome tax spine ended'.

20. J. George, 'Vandal poets in their context', in Merrills (ed.), *Vandals, Romans and Berbers*, pp. 133–4; D. Bright, *The Miniature Epic in Vandal North Africa* (Norman, OK, 1987).

21. Merrills, 'Vandals, Romans and Berbers', p. 13.

22. Diesner, *Vandalenreich*, p. 125.

23. Courtois, *Vandales*, p. 208.

24. Ibid., p. 186.

25. Heather, *Fall of the Roman Empire*, p. 373.

26. Castritius, *Vandalen*, pp. 105–6.

27. Courtois, *Vandales*, pp. 186–93, 212.

28. Some authors reject the bubonic explanation; see W. Rosen, *Justinian's Flea: Plague, Empire and the Birth of Europe* (London, 2007).

29. A. Laiou and C. Morrisson, *The Byzantine Economy* (Cambridge, 2007), p. 38; C. Morrisson and J.-P. Sodini, 'The sixth-century economy', in A. Laiou (ed.), *Economic History of Byzantium from the Seventh through the Fifteenth Century*, 3 vols. (Washington, DC, 2002), vol. 1, p. 193.

30. C. Vita-Finzi, *The Mediterranean Valleys: Geological Change in Historical Times* (Cambridge, 1969); Hodges and Whitehouse, *Mohammed, Charlemagne*, pp. 57–9.

31. C. Delano Smith, *Western Mediterranean Europe: a Historical Geography of Italy, Spain and Southern France since the Neolithic* (London, 1979), pp. 328–92.

32. Morrisson and Sodini, 'Sixth-century economy', p. 209; P. Arthur, *Naples: from Roman Town to City-state* (Archaeological Monographs of the British School at Rome, vol. 12, London, 2002), pp. 15, 35; H. Ahrweiler, *Byzance et la mer* (Paris, 1966), p. 411; J. Pryor and E. Jeffreys, *The Age of the Δρομων: the Byzantine Navy ca 500–1204* (Leiden, 2006).

33. Morrisson and Sodini, 'Sixth-century economy', p. 173.

34. Arthur, *Naples*, p. 12.

35. Morrisson and Sodini, 'Sixth-century economy', pp. 173–4; G. D. R. Sanders, 'Corinth', in Laiou (ed.), *Economic History of Byzantium*, vol. 2, pp. 647–8.

36. Hodges and Whitehouse, *Mohammed, Charlemagne*, p. 28.

37. Morrisson and Sodini, 'Sixth-century economy', pp. 174, 190–91; C. Foss, *Ephesus after Antiquity: a Late Antique, Byzantine and Turkish City* (Cambridge, 1979); M. Kazanaki-Lappa, 'Medieval Athens', in Laiou (ed.), *Economic History of Byzantium*, vol. 2, pp. 639–41; Hodges and Whitehouse, *Mohammed, Charlemagne*, p. 60.

38. W. Ashburner, *The Rhodian Sea-law* (Oxford, 1909).

39. C. Foss and J. Ayer Scott, 'Sardis', in Laiou (ed.), *Economic History of Byzantium*, vol. 2, p. 615; K. Rheidt, 'The urban economy of Pergamon', in Laiou (ed.), *Economic History of Byzantium*, vol. 2, p. 624.

40. Hodges and Whitehouse, *Mohammed, Charlemagne*, p. 38; J. W. Hayes, *Late Roman Pottery* (Supplementary Monograph of the British School at Rome, London, 1972) and *Supplement to Late Roman Pottery* (London, 1980);

C. Wickham, *Framing the Early Middle Ages: Europe and the Mediterranean, 400–800* (Oxford, 2005), pp. 720–28.

41. Arthur, *Naples*, p. 141; Morrisson and Sodini, 'Sixth-century economy', p. 191.
42. Hodges and Whitehouse, *Mohammed, Charlemagne*, p. 72.
43. Morrisson and Sodini, 'Sixth-century economy', p. 211.
44. F. van Doorninck, Jr, 'Byzantine shipwrecks', in Laiou (ed.), *Economic History of Byzantium*, vol. 2, p. 899; A. J. Parker, *Ancient Shipwrecks of the Mediterranean and the Roman Provinces* (British Archaeological Reports, International series, vol. 580, Oxford, 1992), no. 782, p. 301.
45. Parker, *Ancient Shipwrecks*, no. 1001, pp. 372–3.
46. Van Doorninck, 'Byzantine shipwrecks', p. 899.
47. Parker, *Ancient Shipwrecks*, no. 1239, pp. 454–5.
48. Van Doorninck, 'Byzantine shipwrecks', p. 899.
49. Parker, *Ancient shipwrecks*, no. 518, p. 217.

PART THREE
THE THIRD MEDITERRANEAN, 600–1350

1. Mediterranean Troughs, 600–900

1. H. Pirenne, *Mohammed and Charlemagne* (London, 1939) – cf. R. Hodges and D. Whitehouse, *Mohammed, Charlemagne and the Origins of Europe* (London, 1983); R. Latouche, *The Birth of the Western Economy: Economic Aspects of the Dark Ages* (London, 1961).
2. M. McCormick, *The Origins of the European Economy: Communications and Commerce AD 300–900* (Cambridge, 2001), pp. 778–98.
3. A. Laiou and C. Morrisson, *The Byzantine Economy* (Cambridge, 2007), p. 63.
4. T. Khalidi, *The Muslim Jesus: Sayings and Stories in Islamic Literature* (Cambridge, MA, 2001).
5. Hodges and Whitehouse, *Mohammed, Charlemagne*, pp. 68–9; D. Pringle, *The Defence of Byzantine Africa from Justinian to the Arab Conquest* (British Archaeological Reports, International series, vol. 99, Oxford, 1981); on Byzantine ships: J. Pryor and E. Jeffreys, *The Age of the Δρομων: The Byzantine Navy ca 500–1204* (Leiden, 2006).
6. X. de Planhol, *Minorités en Islam: géographie politique et sociale* (Paris, 1997), pp. 95–107.
7. S. Sand, *The Invention of the Jewish People* (London, 2009), pp. 202–7.
8. Pirenne, *Mohammed and Charlemagne*; A. Lewis, *Naval Power and Trade in the Mediterranean A.D. 500–1100* (Princeton, NJ, 1951); McCormick, *Origins*, p. 118; P. Horden and N. Purcell, *The Corrupting Sea: a Study of*

Mediterranean History (Oxford, 2000), pp. 153–72 (p. 154 for 'the merest trickle'); also C. Wickham, *Framing the Early Middle Ages: Europe and the Mediterranean, 400–800* (Oxford, 2005), pp. 821–3.

9. McCormick, *Origins*, p. 65; Horden and Purcell, *Corrupting Sea*, p. 164.

10. Horden and Purcell, *Corrupting Sea*, p. 163.

11. Ibid., pp. 164–5; S. Loseby, 'Marseille: a late Roman success story?' *Journal of Roman Studies*, vol. 82 (1992), pp. 165–85.

12. E. Ashtor, 'Aperçus sur les Radhanites', *Revue suisse d'histoire*, vol. 27 (1977), pp. 245–75; Y. Rotman, *Byzantine Slavery and the Mediterranean World* (Cambridge, MA, 2009), pp. 66–8, 74.

13. Cf. J. Pryor, *Geography, Technology, and War: Studies in the Maritime History of the Mediterranean 649–1571* (Cambridge, 1988), p. 138.

14. M. Lombard, *The Golden Age of Islam* (Amsterdam, 1987), p. 212: Rotman, *Byzantine Slavery*, pp. 66–7.

15. D. Abulafia, 'Asia, Africa and the trade of medieval Europe', *Cambridge Economic History of Europe*, vol. 2, *Trade and Industry in the Middle Ages*, ed. M. M. Postan, E. Miller and C. Postan (2nd edn, Cambridge, 1987), p. 417.

16. McCormick, *Origins*, pp. 668, 675; Rotman, *Byzantine Slavery*, p. 73.

17. P. Sénac, *Provence et piraterie sarrasine* (Paris, 1982), p. 52.

18. Pryor, *Geography, Technology*, pp. 102–3.

19. J. Haywood, *Dark Age Naval Power: a Reassessment of Frankish and Anglo-Saxon Seafaring Activity* (London, 1991), p. 113.

20. Ibid., pp. 114–15.

21. G. Musca, *L'emirato di Bari, 847–871* (Bari, 1964); Haywood, *Dark Age Naval Power*, p. 116.

22. Sénac, *Provence et piraterie*, pp. 35–48; J. Lacam, *Les Sarrasins dans le haut moyen âge français* (Paris, 1965).

23. Pryor and Jeffreys, *Age of the Δρομων*, pp. 446–7.

24. J. Pryor, 'Byzantium and the sea: Byzantine fleets and the history of the empire in the age of the Macedonian emperors, *c.*900–1025 CE', in J. Hattendorf and R. Unger (eds.), *War at Sea in the Middle Ages and Renaissance* (Woodbridge, 2003), pp. 83–104; Pryor and Jeffreys, *Age of the Δρομων*, p. 354; Pryor, *Geography, Technology*, pp. 108–9.

25. Pryor and Jeffreys, *Age of the Δρομων*, pp. 333–78.

26. Haywood, *Dark Age Naval Power*, p. 110.

27. McCormick, *Origins*, pp. 69–73, 559–60.

28. M. G. Bartoli, *Il Dalmatico*, ed. A. Duro (Rome, 2000).

29. F. C. Lane, *Venice: a Maritime Republic* (Baltimore, MD, 1973), pp. 3–4.

30. Wickham, *Framing the Early Middle Ages*, pp. 690, 732–3; McCormick, *Origins*, pp. 529–30.

31. Lane, *Venice*, pp. 4–5.

32. Sources in Haywood, *Dark Age Naval Power*, pp. 195, nn. 88–94.

33. Wickham, *Framing the Early Middle Ages*, p. 690.

34. Lane, *Venice*, p. 4.

35. Cf. Wickham, *Framing the Early Middle Ages*, pp. 73, 75.

36. McCormick, *Origins*, pp. 361–9, 523–31.

37. P. Geary, *Furta Sacra: Thefts of Relics in the Central Middle Ages* (Princeton, NJ, 1978).

38. D. Howard, *Venice and the East: the Impact of the Islamic World on Venetian Architecture 1100–1500* (New Haven, CT, 2000), pp. 65–7.

39. McCormick, *Origins*, pp. 433–8.

40. Cf. Lewis, *Naval Power and Trade in the Mediterranean*, pp. 45–6.

41. McCormick, *Origins*, pp. 436, 440, 816–51.

2. Crossing the Boundaries between Christendom and Islam, 900–1050

1. S. Reif, *A Jewish Archive from Old Cairo: the History of Cambridge University's Genizah Collection* (Richmond, Surrey, 2000), p. 2 and fig. 1, p. 3.

2. S. D. Goitein, *A Mediterranean Society: the Jewish Communities of the Arab World as Portrayed in the Documents of the Cairo Geniza*, vol. 1, *Economic Foundations* (Berkeley, CA, 1967), p. 7; cf. the puzzling title of Reif's *Jewish Archive*.

3. S. Shaked, *A Tentative Bibliography of Geniza Documents* (Paris and The Hague, 1964).

4. Reif, *Jewish Archive*, pp. 72–95.

5. On Byzantium: J. Holo, *Byzantine Jewry in the Mediterranean Economy* (Cambridge, 2009).

6. R. Patai, *The Children of Noah: Jewish Seafaring in Ancient Times* (Princeton, NJ, 1998), pp. 93–6; Goitein, *Mediterranean Society*, vol. 1, pp. 280–81.

7. Shaked, *Tentative Bibliography*, no. 337.

8. D. Abulafia, 'Asia, Africa and the trade of medieval Europe', *Cambridge Economic History of Europe*, vol. 2, *Trade and Industry in the Middle Ages*, ed. M. M. Postan, E. Miller and C. Postan (2nd edn, Cambridge, 1987), pp. 421–3.

9. Mercantile contacts: Holo, *Byzantine Jewry*, pp. 201–2.

10. Goitein, *Mediterranean Society*, vol. 1, p. 429.

11. Shaked, *Tentative Bibliography*, nos. 22, 243 (wheat), 248, 254, 279, 281, 339, etc., etc.

12. Goitein, *Mediterranean Society*, vol. 1, pp. 229–48, 257–8.

13. S. Goitein, 'Sicily and southern Italy in the Cairo Geniza documents', *Archivio storico per la Sicilia orientale*, vol. 67 (1971), p. 14.

14. Abulafia, 'Asia, Africa', p. 431; Goitein, *Mediterranean Society*, vol. 1, p. 102.

15. O. R. Constable, *Trade and Traders in Muslim Spain: the Commercial Realignment of the Iberian Peninsula 900–1500* (Cambridge, 1994), pp. 91–2.

16. Ibid., p. 92.

17. Goitein, 'Sicily and southern Italy', pp. 10, 14, 16.
18. Goitein, *Mediterranean Society*, vol. 1, p. 111; Goitein, 'Sicily and southern Italy', p. 31.
19. Goitein, 'Sicily and southern Italy', pp. 20-23.
20. Goitein, *Mediterranean Society*, vol. 1, pp. 311-12, 314, 317, 325-6; Goitein, 'Sicily and southern Italy', pp. 28-30.
21. Goitein, *Mediterranean Society*, vol. 1, pp. 315-16.
22. Ibid., pp. 319-22.
23. Reif, *Jewish Archive*, p. 167.
24. P. Arthur, *Naples: from Roman Town to City-state* (Archaeological Monographs of the British School at Rome, vol. 12, London, 2002), pp. 149-51.
25. D. Abulafia, 'Southern Italy, Sicily and Sardinia in the medieval Mediterranean economy', in D. Abulafia, *Commerce and Conquest in the Mediterranean, 1100-1500* (Aldershot, 1993), essay i, pp. 8-9; B. Kreutz, 'The ecology of maritime success: the puzzling case of Amalfi', *Mediterranean Historical Review*, vol. 3 (1988), pp. 103-13.
26. Kreutz, 'Ecology', p. 107.
27. M. del Treppo and A. Leone, *Amalfi medioevale* (Naples, 1977), the views being those of del Treppo.
28. G. Imperato, *Amalfi e il suo commercio* (Salerno, 1980), pp. 38, 44.
29. C. Wickham, *Early Medieval Italy: Central Power and Local Society 400-1000* (London, 1981), p. 150; on Gaeta: P. Skinner, *Family Power in Southern Italy: the Duchy of Gaeta and its Neighbours, 850-1139* (Cambridge, 1995), especially pp. 27-42 and p. 288.
30. Imperato, *Amalfi*, p. 71.
31. H. Willard, *Abbot Desiderius of Montecassino and the Ties between Montecassino and Amalfi in the Eleventh Century* (Miscellanea Cassinese, vol. 37, Montecassino, 1973).
32. Abulafia, 'Southern Italy, Sicily and Sardinia', p. 12.
33. Anna Komnene, *Alexiad*, 6:1.1.
34. J. Riley-Smith, *The Knights of St John in Jerusalem and Cyprus, 1050-1310* (London, 1967), pp. 36-7.
35. C. Cahen, 'Un texte peu connu relative au commerce orientale d'Amalfi au Xe siècle', *Archivio storico per le province napoletane*, vol. 34 (1953-4), pp. 61-7.
36. A. Citarella, *Il commercio di Amalfi nell'alto medioevo* (Salerno, 1977).

3. The Great Sea-change, 1000-1100

1. S. A. Epstein, *Genoa and the Genoese, 958-1528* (Chapel Hill, NC, 1996), p. 14.
2. Ibid., pp. 10-11 (with a rather more positive view of its harbour).
3. Ibid., pp. 22-3.

4. D. Abulafia, 'Southern Italy, Sicily and Sardinia in the medieval Mediterranean economy', in D. Abulafia, *Commerce and Conquest in the Mediterranean, 1100–1500* (Aldershot, 1993), essay i, p. 24.

5. Ibid., pp. 25–6.

6. J. Day, *La Sardegna sotto la dominazione pisano-genovese* (Turin, 1986; = J. Day, 'La Sardegna e i suoi dominatori dal secolo XI al secolo XIV', in J. Day, B. Anatra and L. Scaraffia, *La Sardegna medioevale e moderna*, Storia d'Italia UTET, ed. G. Galasso, Turin, 1984), pp. 3–186; F. Artizzu, *L'Opera di S. Maria di Pisa e la Sardegna* (Padua, 1974).

7. Epstein, *Genoa*, pp. 33–6.

8. Cf. A. Greif, *Institutions and the Path to the Modern Economy: Lessons from Medieval Trade* (Cambridge, 2006), p. 229; also L. R. Taylor, *Party Politics in the Age of Caesar* (Berkeley, CA, 1949).

9. Epstein, *Genoa*, pp. 19–22, 41; Greif, *Institutions*, p. 230.

10. G. Rösch, *Venedig und das Reich: Handels- und Verkehrspolitische Beziehungen in der deutschen Kaiserzeit* (Tübingen, 1982).

11. S. A. Epstein, *Wills and Wealth in Medieval Genoa, 1150–1250* (Cambridge, MA, 1984).

12. D. Abulafia, *The Two Italies: Economic Relations between the Norman Kingdom of Sicily and the Northern Communes* (Cambridge, 1977), pp. 11–22.

13. Q. van Dosselaere, *Commercial Agreements and Social Dynamics in Medieval Genoa* (Cambridge, 2009).

14. D. Abulafia, 'Gli italiani fuori d'Italia', in *Storia dell'economia italiana*, ed. R. Romano (Turin, 1990), vol. 1, p. 268; repr. in D. Abulafia, *Commerce and Conquest in the Mediterranean, 1100–1500* (Aldershot, 1993); D. Nicol, *Byzantium and Venice: a Study in Diplomatic and Cultural Relations* (Cambridge, 1988), pp. 33, 41.

15. Abulafia, *Two Italies*, p. 52.

16. H. E. J. Cowdrey, 'The Mahdia campaign of 1087', *English Historical Review*, vol. 92 (1977), pp. 1–29, repr. in H. E. J. Cowdrey, *Popes, Monks and Crusaders* (London, 1984), essay xii.

17. S. D. Goitein, *A Mediterranean Society: the Jewish Communities of the Arab World as Portrayed in the Documents of the Cairo Geniza*, vol. 1, *Economic Foundations* (Berkeley, CA, 1967), pp. 196–200, 204–5.

18. Cowdrey, 'Mahdia campaign', p. 8.

19. D. Abulafia, 'Asia, Africa and the trade of medieval Europe', *Cambridge Economic History of Europe*, vol. 2, *Trade and Industry in the Middle Ages*, ed. M. M. Postan, E. Miller and C. Postan (2nd edn, Cambridge, 1987), pp. 464–5.

20. Abulafia, *Two Italies*, p. 40.

21. Cowdrey, 'Mahdia campaign', pp. 18, 22.

22. D. Abulafia, 'The Pisan *bacini* and the medieval Mediterranean economy: a historian's viewpoint', *Papers in Italian Archaeology, IV: the Cambridge Conference*, part iv, *Classical and Medieval Archaeology*, ed. C. Malone and

S. Stoddart (British Archaeological Reports, International Series, vol. 246, Oxford, 1985), pp. 290, repr. in D. Abulafia, *Italy, Sicily and the Mediterranean, 1100–1400* (London, 1987), essay xiii.

23. Cowdrey, 'Mahdia campaign', p. 28, verse 68; also p. 21.
24. G. Berti, P. Torre et al., *Arte islamica in Italia: i bacini delle chiese pisane* (catalogue of an exhibition at the Museo Nazionale d'Arte Orientale, Rome; Pisa, 1983).
25. Abulafia, 'Pisan *bacini*', p. 289.
26. Ibid., pp. 290–91; J. Pryor and S. Bellabarba, 'The medieval Muslim ships of the Pisan *bacini*', *Mariner's Mirror*, vol. 76 (1990), pp. 99–113; G. Berti, J. Pastor Quijada and G. Rosselló Bordoy, *Naves andalusíes en cerámicas mallorquinas* (Palma de Mallorca, 1993).
27. Goitein, *Mediterranean Society*, vol. 1, p. 306.
28. Pastor Quijada in *Naves andalusíes en cerámicas mallorquinas*, pp. 24–5.
29. Goitein, *Mediterranean Society*, vol. 1, pp. 305–6.
30. D. Abulafia, 'The Crown and the economy under Roger II and his successors', *Dumbarton Oaks Papers*, vol. 37 (1981), p. 12; repr. in Abulafia, *Italy, Sicily and the Mediterranean*.
31. Anna Komnene, *Alexiad*, 3:12.
32. Ibid., 4:1–5:1.
33. R.-J. Lilie, *Handel und Politik zwischen dem byzantinischen Reich und den italienischen Kommunen Venedig, Pisa und Genua in der Epoche der Komnenen und der Angeloi (1081–1204)*, (Amsterdam, 1984), pp. 9–16; Abulafia, *Two Italies*, pp. 54–5; Abulafia, 'Italiani fuori d'Italia', pp. 268–9.
34. J. Holo, *Byzantine Jewry in the Mediterranean Economy* (Cambridge, 2009), pp. 183–6.
35. Abulafia, 'Italiani fuori d'Italia', p. 270.
36. D. Howard, *Venice and the East: the Impact of the Islamic World on Venetian Architecture 1100–1500* (New Haven, CT, 2000), pp. 65–109.

4. 'The Profit That God Shall Give', 1100–1200

1. For earlier plans, see H. E. J. Cowdrey, 'Pope Gregory VII's crusading plans', in *Outremer: Studies in the History of the Crusading Kingdom of Jerusalem Presented to Joshua Prawer*, ed. R. C. Smail, H. E. Mayer and B. Z. Kedar (Jerusalem, 1982), pp. 27–40, repr. in H. E. J. Cowdrey, *Popes, Monks and Crusaders* (London, 1984), essay x.
2. J. Prawer, *Histoire du royaume latin de Jérusalem*, 2 vols. (Paris, 1969), vol. 1, pp. 177–238.
3. S. A. Epstein, *Genoa and the Genoese, 958–1528* (Chapel Hill, NC, 1996), pp. 28–9.
4. Ibid., p. 29.

5. L. Woolley, *A Forgotten Kingdom* (Harmondsworth, 1953), pp. 190–91, plate 23.

6. M.-L. Favreau-Lilie, *Die Italiener im Heiligen Land vom ersten Kreuzzug bis zum Tode Heinrichs von Champagne (1098–1197)*, (Amsterdam, 1989), pp. 43–8.

7. Epstein, *Genoa*, p. 30.

8. Prawer, *Histoire*, vol. 1, pp. 254, 257.

9. Favreau-Lilie, *Italiener im Heiligen Land*, pp. 94–5.

10. R. Barber, *The Holy Grail: Imagination and Belief* (London, 2004), p. 168.

11. Favreau-Lilie, *Italiener im Heiligen Land*, pp. 88–9, 106.

12. Epstein, *Genoa*, p. 32.

13. D. Abulafia, 'Trade and crusade 1050–1250', in *Cultural Convergences in the Crusader Period*, ed. M. Goodich, S. Menache and S. Schein (New York, 1995), pp. 10–11; repr. in D. Abulafia, *Mediterranean Encounters: Economic, Religious, Political, 1100–1550* (Aldershot, 2000); J. Pryor, *Geography, Technology, and War: Studies in the Maritime History of the Mediterranean 649–1571* (Cambridge, 1988), pp. 122, 124.

14. Favreau-Lilie, *Italiener im Heiligen Land*, pp. 51–61; Prawer, *Histoire*, vol. 1, p. 258.

15. Abulafia, 'Trade and crusade', pp. 10–11.

16. Prawer, *Histoire*, vol. 1, pp. 258–9.

17. R. C. Smail, *The Crusaders in Syria and the Holy Land* (Ancient Peoples and Places, London, 1973), p. 17; R. C. Smail, *Crusading Warfare (1097–1193)*, (Cambridge, 1956), pp. 94–6.

18. Pryor, *Geography, Technology, and War*, p. 115.

19. J. Prawer, *Crusader Institutions* (Oxford, 1980), pp. 221–6; J. Richard, *Le royaume latin de Jérusalem* (Paris, 1953), p. 218.

20. Pryor, *Geography, Technology, and War*, pp. 115–16.

21. R.-J. Lilie, *Handel und Politik zwischen dem byzantinischen Reich und den italienischen Kommunen Venedig, Pisa und Genua in der Epoche der Komnenen und der Angeloi (1081–1204)*, (Amsterdam, 1984), pp. 17–22.

22. J. Holo, *Byzantine Jewry in the Mediterranean Economy* (Cambridge, 2009), pp. 183–6.

23. Abulafia, 'Italiani fuori d'Italia', pp. 207–10.

24. A. Citarella, *Il commercio di Amalfi nell'alto medioevo* (Salerno, 1977).

25. D. Abulafia, *The Two Italies: Economic Relations between the Norman Kingdom of Sicily and the Northern Communes* (Cambridge, 1977), pp. 59–61.

26. G. Imperato, *Amalfi e il suo commercio* (Salerno, 1980), pp. 179–235.

27. D. Abulafia, 'Southern Italy, Sicily and Sardinia in the medieval Mediterranean economy', in D. Abulafia, *Commerce and Conquest in the Mediterranean, 1100–1500* (Aldershot, 1993), essay i, pp. 10–14.

28. M. del Treppo and A. Leone, *Amalfi medioevale* (Naples, 1977).

29. J. Caskey, *Art and Patronage in the Medieval Mediterranean: Merchant Culture in the Region of Amalfi* (Cambridge, 2004).

30. S. D. Goitein, *A Mediterranean Society: the Jewish Communities of the Arab World as Portrayed in the Documents of the Cairo Geniza*, vol. 1, *Economic Foundations* (Berkeley, CA, 1967), pp. 18–19.

31. D. Corcos, 'The nature of the Almohad rulers' treatment of the Jews', *Journal of Medieval Iberian Studies*, vol. 2 (2010), pp. 259–85.

32. Benjamin of Tudela, *The Itinerary of Benjamin of Tudela*, ed. M. N. Adler (London, 1907), p. 5; Abulafia, *Two Italies*, p. 238.

33. D. Abulafia, 'Asia, Africa and the trade of medieval Europe', *Cambridge Economic History of Europe*, vol. 2, *Trade and Industry in the Middle Ages*, ed. M. M. Postan, E. Miller and C. Postan (2nd edn, Cambridge, 1987) pp. 437–43; cf. the misconceptions in Holo, *Byzantine Jewry*, p. 203.

34. H. Rabie, *The Financial System of Egypt*, AH 564–741/AD 1169–1341 (London and Oxford, 1972), pp. 91–2.

35. Abulafia, 'Asia, Africa and the trade of medieval Europe', p. 436.

36. C. Cahen, *Makhzūmiyyāt: études sur l'histoire économique et financière de l'Égypte médiévale* (Leiden, 1977).

37. C. Cahen, *Orient et occident au temps des croisades* (Paris, 1983), pp. 132–3, 176.

38. K.-H. Allmendinger, *Die Beziehungen zwischen der Kommune Pisa und Ägypten im hohen Mittelalter: eine rechts- und wirtschaftshistorische Untersuchung* (Wiesbaden, 1967), pp. 45–54; Cahen, *Orient et occident*, p. 125.

39. Cahen, *Orient et occident*, p. 131.

40. L. de Mas Latrie, *Traités de paix et de commerce et documents divers concernant les relations des Chrétiens avec les arabes de l'Afrique septentrionale au Moyen Âge* (Paris, 1966).

41. D. Abulafia, 'Christian merchants in the Almohad cities', *Journal of Medieval Iberian Studies*, vol. 2 (2010), pp. 251–7; Corcos, 'The nature of the Almohad rulers' treatment of the Jews', pp. 259–85.

42. O. R. Constable, *Housing the Stranger in the Mediterranean World: Lodging, Trade, and Travel in Late Antiquity and the Middle Ages* (Cambridge, 2003), p. 278.

43. Abulafia, *Two Italies*, pp. 50–51.

44. D. O. Hughes, 'Urban growth and family structure in medieval Genoa', *Past and Present*, no. 66 (1975), pp. 3–28.

45. R. Heynen, *Zur Entstehung des Kapitalismus in Venedig* (Stuttgart, 1905); J. and F. Gies, *Merchants and Moneymen: the Commercial Revolution, 1000–1500* (London, 1972), pp. 51–8.

46. D. Jacoby, 'Byzantine trade with Egypt from the mid-tenth century to the Fourth Crusade', *Thesaurismata*, vol. 30 (2000), pp. 25–77, repr. in D. Jacoby, *Commercial Exchange across the Mediterranean: Byzantium, the Crusader Levant, Egypt and Italy* (Aldershot, 2005), essay i.

47. D. Abulafia, 'Ancona, Byzantium and the Adriatic, 1155–1173', *Papers of the*

British School at Rome, vol. 52 (1984), p. 208, repr. in D. Abulafia, *Italy, Sicily and the Mediterranean, 1100–1400* (London, 1987), essay ix.

48. Gies, *Merchants and Moneymen*, pp. 57–8.
49. Abulafia, *Two Italies*, pp. 237–54, showing he was not a Jew; cf. E. H. Byrne, 'Easterners in Genoa', *Journal of the American Oriental Society*, vol. 38 (1918), pp. 176–87; and V. Slessarev, 'Die sogennanten Orientalen im mittelalterlichen Genua. Einwänderer aus Südfrankreich in der ligurischen Metropole', *Vierteljahrschrift für Sozial- und Wirtschaftsgeschichte*, vol. 51 (1964), pp. 22–65.
50. Abulafia, *Two Italies*, pp. 102–3, 240.
51. Ibid., p. 244.
52. Ibn Jubayr, *The Travels of ibn Jubayr*, trans. R. Broadhurst (London, 1952), pp. 358–9; Abulafia, *Two Italies*, pp. 247–51 – in the Genoese documents he appears as 'Caitus Bulcassem'.

5. Ways across the Sea, 1160–1185

1. Benjamin of Tudela, *The Itinerary of Benjamin of Tudela*, ed. M. N. Adler (London, 1907); also *The Itinerary of Benjamin of Tudela*, ed. M. Signer (Malibu, CA, 1983); references here are to the original Adler edition.
2. J. Prawer, *The History of the Jews in the Latin Kingdom of Jerusalem* (Oxford, 1988), especially pp. 191–206.
3. Benjamin of Tudela, *Itinerary*, p. ב
4. Ibid., p. 2.
5. Ibid., p. 3; cf. H. E. Mayer, *Marseilles Levantehandel und ein akkonensisches Fälscheratelier des XIII. Jahrhunderts* (Tübingen, 1972), pp. 62–5.
6. Cf. M. Soifer, '"You say that the Messiah has come . . .": the Ceuta Disputation (1179) and its place in the Christian anti-Jewish polemics of the high Middle Ages', *Journal of Medieval History*, vol. 31 (2005), pp. 287–307.
7. Benjamin of Tudela, *Itinerary*, p. 3.
8. Ibid., p. 9.
9. Ibid., pp. 14–15.
10. Ibid., pp. 17–18.
11. Ibid., p. 76, n. 1: twenty-eight groups in one MS, forty in another.
12. Ibid., pp. 75–6.
13. Ibn Jubayr, *The Travels of ibn Jubayr*, trans. R. Broadhurst (London, 1952).
14. Broadhurst, ibid., p. 15.
15. Ibn Jubayr, *Travels*, p. 26.
16. Ibid., p. 27.
17. Ibid., p. 28.
18. Roger of Howden, cited in J. Pryor, *Geography, Technology, and War: Studies in the Maritime History of the Mediterranean 649–1571* (Cambridge, 1988), p. 37.
19. Pryor, *Geography, Technology, and War*, pp. 16–19, and p. 17, figs. 3a–b.

20. Ibn Jubayr, *Travels*, p. 29.
21. Ibid., pp. 346–7; also J. Riley-Smith, 'Government in Latin Syria and the commercial privileges of foreign merchants', in *Relations between East and West in the Middle Ages*, ed. D. Baker (Edinburgh, 1973), p. 112.
22. Ibn Jubayr, *Travels*, pp. 31–2.
23. Ibid., pp. 32–5.
24. Ibid., p. 316.
25. R. C. Smail, *The Crusaders in Syria and the Holy Land* (Ancient Peoples and Places, London, 1973), p. 75.
26. Ibn Jubayr, *Travels*, pp. 317–18.
27. Ibid., pp. 318, 320.
28. Usamah ibn Munqidh, *Memoirs of an Arab-Syrian Gentleman or an Arab Knight in the Crusades*, ed. and trans. P. Hitti (2nd edn, Beirut, 1964), p. 161.
29. Ibn Jubayr, *Travels*, pp. 320–22.
30. Ibid., pp. 325–8.
31. Koran, 27:44.
32. Ibn Jubayr, *Travels*, p. 328.
33. Ibid., p. 329.
34. Ibid., pp. 330–31.
35. Ibid., p. 332.
36. Ibid., p. 333.
37. Ibid., p. 334; Pryor, *Geography, Technology, and War*, p. 36.
38. Ibn Jubayr, *Travels*, pp. 336–8.
39. Ibid., p. 339.
40. Ibid., pp. 353, 356.
41. Ibid., pp. 360–65.
42. H. Krueger, *Navi e proprietà navale a Genova: seconda metà del secolo XII* (= *Atti della Società ligure di storia patria*, vol. 25, fasc. 1, Genoa, 1985).
43. Ibid., pp. 148–9, 160–61.
44. J. Pryor and E. Jeffreys, *The Age of the Δρομων: the Byzantine Navy ca 500–1204* (Leiden, 2006), pp. 423–44.
45. Pryor, *Geography, Technology, and War*, p. 64; Krueger, *Navi*, p. 26.
46. Krueger, *Navi*, pp. 24–7.
47. Pryor, *Geography, Technology, and War*, pp. 29–32; R. Unger, *The Ship in the Medieval Economy, 600–1600* (London, 1980), pp. 123–7.
48. D. Abulafia, 'Marseilles, Acre and the Mediterranean, 1200–1291', in *Coinage in the Latin East: the Fourth Oxford Symposium on Coinage and Monetary History*, ed. P. Edbury and D. M. Metcalf (British Archaeological Reports, Oxford, 1980), pp. 20–21, repr. in D. Abulafia, *Italy, Sicily and the Mediterranean, 1100–1400* (London, 1987), essay x.
49. Unger, *Ship in the Medieval Economy*, p. 126.

6. The Fall and Rise of Empires, 1130–1260

1. Ibn Jubayr, *The Travels of ibn Jubayr*, trans. R. Broadhurst (London, 1952), p. 338; D. Abulafia, *The Two Italies: Economic Relations between the Norman Kingdom of Sicily and the Northern Communes* (Cambridge, 1977), pp. 116–19.

2. D. Abulafia, 'The Crown and the economy under Roger II and his successors', *Dumbarton Oaks Papers*, vol. 37 (1981), p. 12; repr. in D. Abulafia, *Italy, Sicily and the Mediterranean, 1100–1400* (London, 1987), essay i.

3. H. Wieruszowski, 'Roger of Sicily, *Rex-Tyrannus*, in twelfth-century political thought', *Speculum*, vol. 38 (1963), pp. 46–78, repr. in H. Wieruszowski, *Politics and Culture in Medieval Spain and Italy* (Rome, 1971).

4. Niketas Choniates, cited in Abulafia, *Two Italies*, p. 81.

5. D. Nicol, *Byzantium and Venice: a Study in Diplomatic and Cultural Relations* (Cambridge, 1988), p. 87.

6. D. Abulafia, 'The Norman Kingdom of Africa and the Norman expeditions to Majorca and the Muslim Mediterranean', *Anglo-Norman Studies*, vol. 7 (1985), pp. 26–41, repr. in D. Abulafia, *Italy, Sicily and the Mediterranean, 1100–1400* (London, 1987), essay xii.

7. Ibn al-Athir, in ibid., p. 34.

8. Abulafia, 'Norman Kingdom of Africa', pp. 36–8.

9. C. Dalli, *Malta: the Medieval Millennium* (Malta, 2006), pp. 66–79.

10. C. Stanton, 'Norman naval power in the Mediterranean in the eleventh and twelfth centuries' (Ph.D. thesis, Cambridge University, 2008).

11. L.-R. Ménager, *Amiratus-'Αμηρᾶç: l'Émirat et les origines de l'Amirauté* (Paris, 1960); L. Mott, *Sea Power in the Medieval Mediterranean: the Catalan-Aragonese Fleet in the War of the Sicilian Vespers* (Gainesville, FL, 2003), pp. 59–60.

12. Abulafia, 'Norman Kingdom of Africa', pp. 41–3.

13. Caffaro, in Abulafia, *Two Italies*, p. 97.

14. Cf. G. Day, *Genoa's Response to Byzantium, 1155–1204: Commercial Expansion and Factionalism in a Medieval City* (Urbana, IL, 1988).

15. Abulafia, *Two Italies*, pp. 90–98.

16. M. Mazzaoui, *The Italian Cotton Industry in the Later Middle Ages, 1100–1600* (Cambridge, 1981).

17. Abulafia, *Two Italies*, p. 218; Dalli, *Malta*, p. 84.

18. See Abulafia, *Two Italies*, pp. 255–6, 283–4; D. Abulafia, 'Southern Italy, Sicily and Sardinia in the medieval Mediterranean economy', in D. Abulafia, *Commerce and Conquest in the Mediterranean, 1100–1500* (Aldershot, 1993), essay i, pp. 1–32; colonial economy: H. Bresc, *Un monde méditerranéen: économie et société en Sicile, 1300–1450*, 2 vols. (Rome and Palermo, 1986); another view in S. R. Epstein, *An Island for Itself: Economic Development and Social Change in Late Medieval Sicily* (Cambridge, 1992).

19. D. Abulafia, 'Dalmatian Ragusa and the Norman Kingdom of Sicily', *Slavonic and East European Review*, vol. 54 (1976), pp. 412-28, repr. in D. Abulafia, *Italy, Sicily and the Mediterranean, 1100-1400* (London, 1987), essay x.

20. C. M. Brand, *Byzantium Confronts the West 1180-1204* (Cambridge, MA, 1968), pp. 41-2, 195-6.

21. Ibid., p. 161.

22. Eustathios of Thessalonika, *The Capture of Thessaloniki*, ed. and trans. J. R. Melville-Jones (Canberra, 1988).

23. Brand, *Byzantium Confronts the West*, p. 175.

24. G. Schlumberger, *Les campagnes du roi Amaury Ier de Jérusalem en Égypte au XIIe siècle* (Paris, 1906).

25. E. Sivan, *L'Islam et la Croisade: idéologie et propagande dans les réactions musulmanes aux Croisades* (Paris, 1968).

26. D. Abulafia, 'Marseilles, Acre and the Mediterranean 1200-1291', in *Coinage in the Latin East: the Fourth Oxford Symposium on Coinage and Monetary History*, ed. P. Edbury and D. M. Metcalf (British Archaeological Reports, Oxford, 1980), p. 20, repr. in D. Abulafia, *Italy, Sicily and the Mediterranean, 1100-1400* (London, 1987), essay xv.

27. J. Prawer, *Crusader Institutions* (Oxford, 1980), pp. 230-37, 241.

28. R. C. Smail, *The Crusaders in Syria and the Holy Land* (Ancient Peoples and Places, London, 1973), pp. 74-5 (with map); M. Benvenisti, *The Crusaders in the Holy Land* (Jerusalem, 1970), pp. 97-102; Prawer, *Crusader Institutions*, pp. 229-41; P. Pierotti, *Pisa e Accon: l'insediamento pisano nella città crociata. Il porto. Il fondaco* (Pisa, 1987).

29. J. Riley-Smith, 'Government in Latin Syria and the commercial privileges of foreign merchants', in *Relations between East and West in the Middle Ages*, ed. D. Baker (Edinburgh, 1973), pp. 109-32.

30. C. Cahen, *Orient et occident au temps des croisades* (Paris, 1983), p. 139.

31. D. Abulafia, 'Crocuses and crusaders: San Gimignano, Pisa and the kingdom of Jerusalem', in *Outremer: Studies in the History of the Crusading Kingdom of Jerusalem Presented to Joshua Prawer*, ed. R. C. Smail, H. E. Mayer and B. Z. Kedar (Jerusalem, 1982), pp. 227-43, repr. in Abulafia, *Italy, Sicily and the Mediterranean*, essay xiv.

32. D. Abulafia, 'Maometto e Carlo Magno: le due aree monetarie dell'oro e dell'argento', *Economia Naturale, Economia Monetaria*, ed. R. Romano and U. Tucci, *Storia d'Italia, Annali*, vol. 6 (Turin, 1983), pp. 223-70.

33. Abulafia, *Two Italies*, pp. 172-3, 190-92.

34. D. Abulafia, 'Henry count of Malta and his Mediterranean activities: 1203-1230', in *Medieval Malta: Studies on Malta before the Knights*, ed. A. Luttrell (London, 1975), p. 111, repr. in Abulafia, *Italy, Sicily and the Mediterranean*, essay iii.

35. Ibid., pp. 112-13.

36. Cited in ibid., pp. 113-14, nn. 43, 46.

37. Brand, *Byzantium Confronts the West*, p. 16.

38. Abulafia, 'Henry count of Malta', p. 106.
39. Brand, *Byzantium Confronts the West*, p. 209.
40. Ibid., pp. 210–11; Abulafia, 'Henry count of Malta', p. 108.
41. J. Phillips, *The Fourth Crusade and the Sack of Constantinople* (London, 2004); J. Godfrey, *1204: the Unholy Crusade* (Oxford, 1980); D. Queller and T. Madden, *The Fourth Crusade: the Conquest of Constantinople* (2nd edn, Philadelphia, PA, 1997).
42. D. Howard, *Venice and the East: the Impact of the Islamic World on Venetian Architecture 1100–1500* (New Haven, CT, 2000), pp. 103, 108.
43. J. Longnon, *L'Empire latin de Constantinople et la principauté de Morée* (Paris, 1949); D. Nicol, *The Despotate of Epiros* (Oxford, 1957); M. Angold, *A Byzantine Government in Exile: Government and Society under the Laskarids of Nicaea (1204–1261)* (Oxford, 1975).
44. Abulafia, 'Henry count of Malta', pp. 115–19.
45. S. McKee, *Uncommon Dominion: Venetian Crete and the Myth of Ethnic Purity* (Philadelphia, PA, 2000).
46. Howard, *Venice and the East*, p. 93.
47. Brand, *Byzantium Confronts the West*, p. 213.
48. *Leonardo Fibonacci: il tempo, le opere, l'eredità scientifica*, ed. M. Morelli and M. Tangheroni (Pisa, 1994).
49. C. Thouzellier, *Hérésie et hérétiques: vaudois, cathares, patarins, albigeois* (Paris, 1969).

7. Merchants, Mercenaries and Missionaries, 1220–1300

1. D. Herlihy, *Pisa in the Early Renaissance* (New Haven, CT, 1958), pp. 131–3.
2. D. Abulafia, *The Western Mediterranean Kingdoms 1200–1500: the Struggle for Dominion* (London, 1997), pp. 35–7.
3. Benjamin of Tudela, *The Itinerary of Benjamin of Tudela*, ed. M. N. Adler (London, 1907), p. 2.
4. S. Bensch, *Barcelona and its Rulers, 1096–1291* (Cambridge, 1995).
5. J.-E. Ruiz-Domènec, *Ricard Guillem: un sogno per Barcellona*, with an appendix of documents edited by R. Conde y Delgado de Molina (Naples, 1999); but cf. Bensch, *Barcelona*, pp. 85–121, 154–5.
6. S. Orvietani Busch, *Medieval Mediterranean Ports: the Catalan and Tuscan Coasts, 1100–1235* (Leiden, 2001).
7. Abulafia, *Western Mediterranean Kingdoms*, p. 52.
8. Bernat Desclot, *Llibre del rey En Pere*, in *Les quatre grans cròniques*, ed. F. Soldevila (Barcelona, 1971), chap. 14; D. Abulafia, *A Mediterranean Emporium: the Catalan Kingdom of Majorca* (Cambridge, 1994), pp. 7–8.
9. James I, *Llibre dels Feyts*, in *Les quatre grans cròniques*, ed. F. Soldevila (Barcelona, 1971), chap. 47, cited here with modifications from the translation of

J. Forster, *Chronicle of James I of Aragon*, 2 vols. (London, 1883); Abulafia, *Mediterranean Emporium*, p. 7.

10. James I, *Llibre dels Feyts*, chaps. 54, 56.

11. Abulafia, *Mediterranean Emporium*, pp. 78–9, 65–8.

12. Ibid., pp. 56–64.

13. See A. Watson, *Agricultural Innovation in the Early Islamic World: the Diffusion of Crops and Farming Techniques, 700–1100* (Cambridge, 1983).

14. R. Burns and P. Chevedden, *Negotiating Cultures: Bilingual Surrender Treaties on the Crusader-Muslim Frontier under James the Conqueror* (Leiden, 1999).

15. L. Berner, 'On the western shores: the Jews of Barcelona during the reign of Jaume I, "el Conqueridor", 1213–1276' (Ph.D. thesis, University of California, Los Angeles, 1986).

16. Abulafia, *Mediterranean Emporium*, pp. 78–9, 204–8; A. Hernando et al., *Cartogràfia mallorquina* (Barcelona, 1995).

17. R. Vose, *Dominicans, Muslims and Jews in the Medieval Crown of Aragon* (Cambridge, 2009).

18. R. Chazan, *Barcelona and Beyond: the Disputation of 1263 and its Aftermath* (Berkeley, CA, 1992).

19. Best edition: O. Limor, *Die Disputationen zu Ceuta (1179) und Mallorca (1286): zwei antijüdische Schriften aus dem mittelalterlichen Genua* (Monumenta Germaniae Historica, Munich, 1994), pp. 169–300.

20. H. Hames, *Like Angels on Jacob's Ladder: Abraham Abulafia, the Franciscans, and Joachimism* (Albany, NY, 2007).

21. Ibid., pp. 33–4.

22. H. Hames, *The Art of Conversion: Christianity and Kabbalah in the Thirteenth Century* (Leiden, 2000); D. Urvoy, *Penser l'Islam: les présupposés islamiques de l'"art" de Lull* (Paris, 1980).

23. D. Abulafia, 'The apostolic imperative: religious conversion in Llull's *Blaquerna*', in *Religion, Text and Society in Medieval Spain and Northern Europe: Essays in Honour of J. N. Hillgarth*, ed. L. Shopkow et al. (Toronto, 2002), pp. 105–21.

24. Ramon Llull, 'Book of the Gentile and the three wise men', in A. Bonner, *Doctor Illuminatus: a Ramon Llull Reader* (Princeton, NJ, 1993), p. 168.

25. 'Vita coetanea', in Bonner, *Doctor Illuminatus*, pp. 24–5, 28–30.

26. Bonner, *Doctor Illuminatus*, p. 43.

27. C.-E. Dufourcq, *L'Espagne catalane et le Maghrib au XIIIe et XIVe siècles* (Paris, 1966), pp. 514–20.

28. D. Abulafia, 'Catalan merchants and the western Mediterranean, 1236–1300: studies in the notarial acts of Barcelona and Sicily', *Viator: Medieval and Renaissance Studies*, vol. 16 (1985), pp. 232–5, repr. in D. Abulafia, *Italy, Sicily and the Mediterranean, 1100–1400* (London, 1987), essay viii.

29. Ibid., pp. 235, 237.

30. Ibid., pp. 220–21.

31. A. Hibbert, 'Catalan consulates in the thirteenth century', *Cambridge Historical Journal*, vol. 9 (1949), pp. 352–8; Dufourcq, *L'Espagne catalane et le Maghrib*, pp. 133–56.

32. J. Hillgarth, *The Problem of a Catalan Mediterranean Empire 1229–1327* (English Historical Review, supplement no. 8, London, 1975), p. 41; A. Atiya, *Egypt and Aragon* (Leipzig, 1938), pp. 57–60.

33. Hillgarth, *Problem*, p. 41; J. Trenchs Odena, '*De alexandrinis* (el comercio prohibido con los musulmanes y el papado de Aviñón durante la primera mitad del siglo XIV)', *Anuario de estudios medievales*, vol. 10 (1980), pp. 237–320.

34. Abulafia, 'Catalan merchants', p. 222.

35. Ibid., pp. 230–31.

36. J. Brodman, *Ransoming Captives in Crusader Spain: the Order of Merced on the Christian-Islamic Frontier* (Philadelphia, PA, 1986); J. Rodriguez, *Captives and Their Saviors in the Medieval Crown of Aragon* (Washington, DC, 2007).

37. Abulafia, *Mediterranean Emporium*, pp. 130–39.

38. Ibid., pp. 188–215; A. Ortega Villoslada, *El reino de Mallorca y el mundo atlántico: evolución político-mercantil (1230–1349)* (Madrid, 2008); also Dufourcq, *L'Espagne catalane et le Maghrib*, pp. 208–37.

39. Abulafia, 'Catalan merchants', pp. 237–8.

40. N. Housley, *The Later Crusades: from Lyons to Alcázar 1274–1580* (Oxford, 1992), pp. 7–17.

41. D. Abulafia, *Frederick II: a Medieval Emperor* (London, 1988), pp. 164–201.

42. Ibid., pp. 346–7.

43. G. Lesage, *Marseille angevine* (Paris, 1950).

44. Abulafia, *Mediterranean Emporium*, pp. 240–45.

45. P. Xhufi, *Dilemat e Arbërit: studime mbi Shqipërinë mesjetare* (Tirana, 2006), pp. 89–172.

46. J. Pryor, 'The galleys of Charles I of Anjou, king of Sicily, ca. 1269–1284', *Studies in Medieval and Renaissance History*, vol. 14 (1993), pp. 35–103.

47. L. Mott, *Sea Power in the Medieval Mediterranean: the Catalan-Aragonese Fleet in the War of the Sicilian Vespers* (Gainesville, FL, 2003), p. 15.

48. Abulafia, *Western Mediterranean Kingdoms*, pp. 66–76; S. Runciman, *The Sicilian Vespers: a History of the Mediterranean World in the Thirteenth Century* (Cambridge, 1958).

49. H. Bresc, '1282: classes sociales et révolution nationale', *XI Congresso di storia della Corona d'Aragona* (Palermo, 1983–4), vol. 2, pp. 241–58, repr. in H. Bresc, *Politique et société en Sicile, XIIe-XVe siècles* (Aldershot, 1990).

50. D. Abulafia, 'Southern Italy and the Florentine economy, 1265–1370', *Economic History Review*, ser. 2, 33 (1981), pp. 377–88, repr. in Abulafia, *Italy, Sicily and the Mediterranean*, essay vi.

51. Abulafia, *Western Mediterranean Kingdoms*, pp. 107–71.

52. J. Pryor, 'The naval battles of Roger de Lauria', *Journal of Medieval History*, vol. 9 (1983), pp. 179–216.
53. Mott, *Sea Power*, pp. 29–30.
54. Ibid., pp. 31–2.
55. From the chronicle of Bernat Desclot: see ibid., pp. 39–40.
56. Mott, *Sea Power*, pp. 33–4.
57. Abulafia, *Mediterranean Emporium*, pp. 10–12.

8. *Serrata* – Closing, 1291–1350

1. S. Schein, *Fideles Cruces: the Papacy, the West and the Recovery of the Holy Land, 1274–1314* (Oxford, 1991).
2. A. Laiou, *Constantinople and the Latins: the Foreign Policy of Andronicus II 1282–1328* (Cambridge, MA, 1972), pp. 68–76, 147–57.
3. F. C. Lane, *Venice: a Maritime Republic* (Baltimore, MD, 1973), p. 84.
4. D. Abulafia, 'Sul commercio del grano siciliano nel tardo Duecento', *XI° Congresso della Corona d'Aragona*, 4 vols. (Palermo, 1983–4), vol. 2, pp. 5–22, repr. in D. Abulafia, *Italy, Sicily and the Mediterranean, 1100–1400* (London, 1987), essay vii.
5. D. Abulafia, 'Southern Italy and the Florentine economy, 1265–1370', *Economic History Review*, ser. 2, 33 (1981), pp. 377–88, repr. in Abulafia, *Italy, Sicily and the Mediterranean*, essay vi.
6. G. Jehel, *Aigues-mortes, un port pour un roi: les Capétiens et la Méditerranée* (Roanne, 1985); K. Reyerson, *Business, Banking and Finance in Medieval Montpellier* (Toronto, 1985).
7. P. Edbury, *The Kingdom of Cyprus and the Crusades 1191–1374* (Cambridge, 1991); very helpful studies in B. Arbel, *Cyprus, the Franks and Venice, 13th–16th Centuries* (Aldershot, 2000).
8. D. Abulafia, 'The Levant trade of the minor cities in the thirteenth and fourteenth centuries: strengths and weaknesses', in *The Medieval Levant. Studies in Memory of Eliyahu Ashtor (1914–1984)*, ed. B. Z. Kedar and A. Udovitch, *Asian and African Studies*, vol. 22 (1988), pp. 183–202.
9. P. Edbury, 'The crusading policy of King Peter I of Cyprus, 1359–1369', in P. Holt (ed.), *The Eastern Mediterranean Lands in the Period of the Crusades* (Warminster, 1977), pp. 90–105; Edbury, *Kingdom of Cyprus*, pp. 147–79.
10. R. Unger, *The Ship in the Medieval Economy, 600–1600* (London, 1980), pp. 176–9; J. Robson, 'The Catalan fleet and Moorish sea-power (1337–1344)', *English Historical Review*, vol. 74 (1959), p. 391.
11. Lane, *Venice*, p. 46.
12. D. Abulafia, 'Venice and the kingdom of Naples in the last years of Robert the Wise, 1332–1343', *Papers of the British School at Rome*, vol. 48 (1980), pp. 196–9.

13. S. Chojnacki, 'In search of the Venetian patriciate: families and faction in the fourteenth century', in *Renaissance Venice*, ed. J. R. Hale (London, 1973), pp. 47-90.

14. Another project involved an exchange with Albania: D. Abulafia, 'The Aragonese Kingdom of Albania: an Angevin project of 1311-16', *Mediterranean Historical Review*, vol. 10 (1995), pp. 1-13

15. M. Tangheroni, *Aspetti del commercio dei cereali nei paesi della Corona d'Aragona*, 1: *La Sardegna* (Pisa and Cagliari, 1981); C. Manca, *Aspetti dell'espansione economica catalano-aragonese nel Mediterraneo occidentale: il commercio internazionale del sale* (Milan, 1966); M. Tangheroni, *Città dell'argento: Iglesias dalle origini alla fine del Medioevo* (Naples, 1985).

16. F. C. Casula, *La Sardegna aragonese*, 2 vols. (Sassari, 1990-91); B. Pitzorno, *Vita di Eleanora d'Arborea, principessa medioevale di Sardegna* (Milan, 2010).

17. D. Abulafia, *A Mediterranean Emporium: the Catalan Kingdom of Majorca* (Cambridge, 1994), pp. 15-17, 54.

18. Ibid., pp. 14, 248.

19. L. Mott, *Sea Power in the Medieval Mediterranean: the Catalan-Aragonese Fleet in the War of the Sicilian Vespers* (Gainesville, FL, 2003), p. 216, table 2, and p. 217; J. Pryor, 'The galleys of Charles I of Anjou, king of Sicily, ca. 1269-1284', *Studies in Medieval and Renaissance History*, vol. 14 (1993), p. 86.

20. Mott, *Sea Power*, pp. 211-24.

21. Tangheroni, *Aspetti del commercio*, pp. 72-8.

22. Robson, 'Catalan fleet', p. 386.

23. G. Hills, *Rock of Contention: a History of Gibraltar* (London, 1974), pp. 60-72; M. Harvey, *Gibraltar: a History* (2nd edn, Staplehurst, Kent, 2000), pp. 37-40.

24. Robson, 'Catalan fleet', pp. 389-91, 394, 398.

25. Harvey, *Gibraltar*, pp. 44-5.

26. J. Riley-Smith, *The Knights of St John in Jerusalem and Cyprus, 1050-1310* (London, 1967), p. 225; Edbury, *Kingdom of Cyprus*, p. 123.

27. K. Setton, *The Catalan Domination of Athens, 1311-1388* (2nd edn, London, 1975).

28. E. Zachariadou, *Trade and Crusade: Venetian Crete and the Emirates of Menteshe and Aydın (1300-1415)* (Venice, 1983), pp. 13-14.

29. Ibid., pp. 27-37.

30. N. Housley, *The Later Crusades: from Lyons to Alcázar 1274-1580* (Oxford, 1992), pp. 59-60; Zachariadou, *Trade and Crusade*, pp. 49-51.

31. W. C. Jordan, *The Great Famine: Northern Europe in the Early Fourteenth Century* (Princeton, NJ, 1966); cf. D. Abulafia, 'Un'economia in crisi? L'Europa alla vigilia della Peste Nera', *Archivio storico del Sannio*, vol. 3 (1998), pp. 5-24.

32. O. Benedictow, *The Black Death 1346–1353: the Complete History* (Woodbridge, 2004), p. 281.

33. B. Kedar, *Merchants in Crisis: Genoese and Venetian Men of Affairs and the Fourteenth-century Depression* (New Haven, CT, 1976).

34. M. Dols, *The Black Death in the Middle East* (Princeton, NJ, 1977); Benedictow, *Black Death*, pp. 60–64, 69; for the view that it was not bubonic and pneumonic plague, see B. Gummer, *The Scourging Angel: the Black Death in the British Isles* (London, 2009).

35. S. Borsch, *The Black Death in Egypt and England: a Comparative Study* (Cairo, 2005), pp. 1–2.

36. Benedictow, *Black Death*, pp. 70–71, 93–4.

37. Ibid., pp. 77–82, 89–90, 278–81.

38. Ibid., pp. 82–3.

39. Ibid., pp. 65–6.

40. Ibid., pp. 380–84.

41. D. Abulafia, 'Carestia, peste, economia', *Le epidemie nei secoli XIV–XVII* (Nuova Scuola Medica Salernitana, Salerno, 2006).

42. S. R. Epstein, *An Island for Itself: Economic Development and Social Change in Late Medieval Sicily* (Cambridge, 1992).

PART FOUR
THE FOURTH MEDITERRANEAN, 1350–1830

1. Would-be Roman Emperors, 1350–1480

1. D. Abulafia, *A Mediterranean Emporium: the Catalan Kingdom of Majorca* (Cambridge, 1994), pp. 217–21; F. Melis, *Aspetti della vita economica medievale (studi nell'Archivio Datini di Prato)* (Siena and Florence, 1962); I. Origo, *The Merchant of Prato* (2nd edn, Harmondsworth, 1963).

2. Origo, *Merchant of Prato*, p. 128.

3. I. Houssaye Michienzi, 'Réseaux et stratégies marchandes: le commerce de la compagnie Datini avec le Maghrib (fin XIVe–début XVe siècle)', (doctoral dissertation, European University Institute, Florence, 2010).

4. Origo, *Merchant of Prato*, pp. 97–8.

5. R. de Roover, *The Rise and Decline of the Medici Bank 1397–1494* (Cambridge, MA, 1963).

6. B. Kedar, *Merchants in Crisis: Genoese and Venetian Men of Affairs and the Fourteenth-century Depression* (New Haven, CT, 1976), arguing that a supposed economic depression was matched by psychological depression among merchants.

7. O. Benedictow, *The Black Death 1346–1353: the Complete History* (Woodbridge, 2004), pp. 118–33.

8. F. C. Lane, *Venice: a Maritime Republic* (Baltimore, MD, 1973), pp. 176–9; S. A. Epstein, *Genoa and the Genoese, 958–1528* (Chapel Hill, NC, 1996), pp. 220–21.

9. Lane, *Venice*, p. 186; Epstein, *Genoa*, pp. 219–20.

10. S. McKee, *Uncommon Dominion: Venetian Crete and the Myth of Ethnic Purity* (Philadelphia, PA, 2000), pp. 145–61.

11. Lane, *Venice*, pp. 189–201; Epstein, *Genoa*, pp. 237–42.

12. Lane, *Venice*, p. 196.

13. Cf. Kedar, *Merchants in Crisis*.

14. Dante Alighieri, *Divina Commedia*, 'Inferno', 21:7–15; Lane, *Venice*, p. 163.

15. Lane, *Venice*, pp. 122–3, 163–4; F. C. Lane, *Venetian Ships and Shipbuilders of the Renaissance* (Baltimore, MD, 1934).

16. Lane, *Venice*, p. 120.

17. H. Prescott, *Jerusalem Journey: Pilgrimage to the Holy Land in the Fifteenth Century* (London, 1954); H. Prescott, *Once to Sinai: the Further Pilgrimage of Friar Felix Fabri* (London, 1957).

18. *Petrarch's Guide to the Holy Land: Itinerary to the Sepulcher of Our Lord Jesus Christ*, ed. T. Cachey (Notre Dame, IN, 2002).

19. Cyriac of Ancona, *Later Travels*, ed. E. Bondar (Cambridge, MA, 2003); M. Belozerskaya, *To Wake the Dead: a Renaissance Merchant and the Birth of Archaeology* (New York, 2009); B. Ashmole, 'Cyriac of Ancona', in *Art and Politics in Renaissance Italy*, ed. G. Holmes (Oxford, 1993), pp. 41–57.

20. N. Z. Davis, *Trickster Travels: a Sixteenth-century Muslim between Worlds* (New York, 2006).

21. P. Corrao, *Governare un regno: potere, società e istituzioni in Sicilia fra Trecento e Quattrocento* (Naples, 1991).

22. J. Carbonell and F. Manconi (eds.), *I Catalani in Sardegna* (Milan, 1994); G. Goddard King, *Pittura sarda del Quattro-Cinquecento* (2nd edn, Nuoro, 2000).

23. A. Ryder, *Alfonso the Magnanimous, King of Aragon, Naples, and Sicily, 1396–1458* (Oxford, 1990).

24. P. Stacey, *Roman Monarchy and the Renaissance Prince* (Cambridge, 2007).

25. J. Favier, *Le roi René* (Paris, 2009); M. Kekewich, *The Good King: René of Anjou and Fifteenth-century Europe* (Basingstoke, 2008).

26. W. Küchler, *Die Finanzen der Krone Aragon während des 15. Jahrhunderts (Alfons V. und Johann II.)* (Münster, 1983); L. Sánchez Aragonés, *Cortes, monarquía y ciudades en Aragón, durante el reinado de Alfonso el Magnánimo* (Saragossa, 1994).

27. A. Gallo, *Commentarius de Genuensium maritima classe in Barchinonenses expedita, anno MCCCCLXVI*, ed. C. Fossati (Fonti per la storia dell'Italia medievale, Rerum italicarum scriptores, ser. 3, vol. 8, Rome, 2010); and C. Fossati, *Genovesi e Catalani: guerra sul mare. Relazione di Antonio Gallo (1466)* (Genoa, 2008).

28. D. Abulafia, 'From Tunis to Piombino: piracy and trade in the Tyrrhenian Sea, 1397–1472', in *The Experience of Crusading*, vol. 2: *Defining the Crusader Kingdom*, ed. P. Edbury and J. Phillips (Cambridge, 2003), pp. 275–97.

29. D. Abulafia, 'The mouse and the elephant: relations between the kings of Naples and the lordship of Piombino in the fifteenth century', in J. Law and B. Paton (eds.), *Communes and Despots: Essays in Memory of Philip Jones* (Aldershot, 2010), pp. 145–60; G. Forte, *Di Castiglione di Pescaia presidio aragonese dal 1447 al 1460* (Grosseto, 1935; also published in *Bollettino della società storica maremmana*, 1934–5).

30. M. Navarro Sorní, *Calixto II Borja y Alfonso el Magnánimo frente a la cruzada* (Valencia, 2003); cf. A. Ryder, 'The eastern policy of Alfonso the Magnanimous', *Atti dell'Accademia Pontaniana*, vol. 27 (1979), pp. 7–27.

31. D. Abulafia, 'Scanderbeg: a hero and his reputation', introduction to H. Hodgkinson, *Scanderbeg* (London, 1999), pp. ix–xv; O. J. Schmitt, *Skënderbeu* (Tirana, 2008; German edn: *Skanderbeg: der neue Alexander auf dem Balkan*, Regensburg, 2009); F. Babinger, *Mehmed the Conqueror and his Time*, ed. W. Hickman (Princeton, NJ, 1979), pp. 390–96.

32. D. Duran i Duelt, *Kastellórizo, una isla griega bajo dominio de Alfonso el Magnánimo (1450–1458), colección documental* (Barcelona, 2003); C. Marinescu, *La politique orientale d'Alfonse V d'Aragon, roi de Naples (1416–1458)* (Institut d'Estudis Catalans, Memòries de la Secció Històrico-Arqueològica, vol. 46, Barcelona, 1994), pp. 203–34.

33. D. Abulafia, 'Genoese, Turks and Catalans in the age of Mehmet II and Tirant lo Blanc', in *Quel mar che la terra inghirlanda. Studi sul Mediterraneo medievale in ricordo di Marco Tangheroni*, 2 vols. (Pisa, 2007), vol. 1, pp. 49–58; English translations: C. R. La Fontaine, *Tirant lo Blanc: the Complete Translation* (New York, 1993), a full literal translation, and D. Rosenthal, trans. *Tirant lo Blanc* (London, 1984), an abridged version.

34. E. Aylward, *Martorell's* Tirant lo Blanch: *a Program for Military and Social Reform in Fifteenth-century Christendom* (Chapel Hill, NC, 1985).

35. *Tirant lo Blanc*, chapter 99.

36. Doukas, *Decline and Fall of Byzantium to the Ottoman Turks by Doukas: an Annotated Translation of* Historia Turco-Byzantina, ed. H. Magoulias (Detroit, 1976), chap. 38:5, p. 212.

37. H. İnalcık, *The Ottoman Empire: the Classical Age 1300–1600* (London, 1973).

38. Babinger, *Mehmed the Conqueror*, pp. 359–66.

39. P. Butorac, *Kotor za samovlade (1355–1420)* (Perast, 1999), pp. 75–115.

40. L. Malltezi, *Qytetet e bregdetit shqiptar gjatë sundemit Venedikas (aspekte te jetës së tyre)* (Tirana, 1988), pp. 229–41 (French summary); O. J. Schmitt, *Das venezianische Albanien (1392–1479)* (Munich, 2001).

41. L. Butler, *The Siege of Rhodes 1480* (Order of St John Historical Pamphlets,

no. 10, London, 1970), pp. 1–24; E. Brockman, *The Two Sieges of Rhodes 1480–1522* (London, 1969); Babinger, *Mehmed the Conqueror*, pp. 396–9.

42. Butler, *Siege of Rhodes*, pp. 11, 22.

43. H. Houben (ed.), *La conquista turca di Otranto (1480) tra storia e mito*, 2 vols. (Galatina, 2008); Babinger, *Mehmed the Conqueror*, pp. 390–91, 395.

44. Babinger, *Mehmed the Conqueror*, pp. 390–96.

45. C. Kidwell, 'Venice, the French invasion and the Apulian ports', in *The French Descent into Renaissance Italy 1494–1495: Antecedents and Effects*, ed. D. Abulafia (Aldershot, 1995), pp. 295–308.

46. Ibid., p. 300.

47. N. Bisaha, *Creating East and West: Renaissance Humanism and the Ottoman Turks* (Philadelphia, PA, 2004); R. Mack, *Bazaar to Piazza: Islamic Trade and Italian Art, 1300–1600* (Berkeley, CA, 2002).

48. C. Campbell, A. Chong, D. Howard and M. Rogers, *Bellini and the East* (National Gallery, London, 2006).

49. D. Abulafia, 'Dalmatian Ragusa and the Norman Kingdom of Sicily', *Slavonic and East European Review*, vol. 54 (1976), pp. 412–28, repr. in D. Abulafia, *Italy, Sicily and the Mediterranean, 1100–1400* (London, 1987), essay x.

50. R. Harris, *Dubrovnik: a History* (London, 2003), pp. 58–63.

51. F. Carter, 'Balkan exports through Dubrovnik 1358–1500: a geographical analysis', *Journal of Croatian Studies*, vols. 9–10 (1968–9), pp. 133–59, repr. in F. Carter's strange *Dubrovnik (Ragusa): a Classic City-state* (London, 1972), pp. 214–92, much of the rest of which is an unattributed reprint of L. Villari, *The Republic of Ragusa* (London, 1904).

52. B. Krekić, *Dubrovnik (Raguse) et le Levant au Moyen Âge* (Paris, 1961).

53. B. Krekić, 'Four Florentine commercial companies in Dubrovnik (Ragusa) in the first half of the fourteenth century', in *The Medieval City*, ed. D. Herlihy, H. Miskimin and A. Udovitch (New Haven, CT, 1977), pp. 25–41; D. Abulafia, 'Grain traffic out of the Apulian ports on behalf of Lorenzo de' Medici, 1486–7', *Karissime Gotifride: Historical Essays Presented to Professor Godfrey Wettinger on his Seventieth Birthday*, ed. P. Xuereb (Malta, 1999), pp. 25–36, repr. in D. Abulafia, *Mediterranean Encounters: Economic, Religious, Political, 1100–1550* (Aldershot, 2000), essay ix; M. Spremić, *Dubrovnik i Aragonci (1442–1495)* (Belgrade, 1971), p. 210.

54. Filip de Diversis, *Opis slavnogo grada Dubrovnika*, ed. Z. Janeković-Römer (Zagreb, 2004), p. 156; B. Krekić, *Dubrovnik in the Fourteenth and Fifteenth Centuries: a City between East and West* (Norman, OK, 1972), p. 35.

55. Spremić, *Dubrovnik i Aragonci*, pp. 207–11 (Italian summary).

56. B. Cotrugli, *Il libro dell'arte di mercatura*, ed. U. Tucci (Venice, 1990); B. Kotruljević, *Knjiga o umijeću trgovanja* (Zagreb, 2005); also, on winds, waves and navigation: B. Kotruljević, *De Navigatione – O plovidbi*, ed. D. Salopek (Zagreb, 2005).

57. Harris, *Dubrovnik*, pp. 88–90.
58. Ibid., pp. 93, 95; N. Biegman, *The Turco-Ragusan Relationship according to the firmāns of Murād III (1575–1595) extant in the State Archives of Dubrovnik* (The Hague and Paris, 1967).

2. Transformations in the West, 1391–1500

1. N. Housley, *The Later Crusades: from Lyons to Alcázar 1274–1580* (Oxford, 1992), pp. 196–7.
2. J. Heers, *Gênes au XVe siècle: civilisation méditerranéenne, grand capitalisme, et capitalisme populaire* (Paris, 1971).
3. E. Ashtor, 'Levantine sugar industry in the late Middle Ages: a case of technological decline', *The Islamic Middle East, 700–1900*, ed. A. L. Udovitch (Princeton, NJ, 1981), pp. 91–132.
4. These include the Wallace Collection (London), the Hispanic Society of America (New York) and the Israel Museum (Jerusalem).
5. D. Abulafia, 'Sugar in Spain', *European Review*, vol. 16 (2008), pp 191–210; M. Ouerfelli, *Le sucre: production, commercialisation et usages dans la Méditerranée médiévale* (Leiden, 2007).
6. A. Fábregas Garcia, *Producción y comercio de azúcar en el Mediterráneo medieval: el ejemplo del reino de Granada* (Granada, 2000); J. Heers, 'Le royaume de Grenade et la politique marchande de Gênes en Occident (XVe siècle)', *Le Moyen Âge*, vol. 63 (1957), p. 109, repr. in J. Heers, *Société et économie à Gênes (XIVe-XVe siècles)* (London, 1979), essay vii; F. Melis, 'Málaga nel sistema economico del XIV e XV secolo', *Economia e Storia*, vol. 3 (1956), pp. 19–59, 139–63, repr. in F. Melis, *Mercaderes italianos en España (investigaciones sobre su correspondencia y su contabilidad)* (Seville, 1976), pp. 3–65; R. Salicrú i Lluch, 'The Catalano-Aragonese commercial presence in the sultanate of Granada during the reign of Alfonso the Magnanimous', *Journal of Medieval History*, vol. 27 (2001), pp. 289–312.
7. P. Russell, *Prince Henry 'the Navigator': a Life* (New Haven, CT, 2000), pp. 29–58.
8. Ibid., pp. 182–93.
9. B. Rogerson, *The Last Crusaders: the Hundred-year Battle for the Centre of the World* (London, 2009), especially pp. 399–422.
10. Luis Vaz de Camões, *The Lusiads*, trans. L. White (Oxford, 1997), canto 4:49, p. 86.
11. F. Themudo Barata, *Navegação, comércio e relações políticas: os portugueses no Mediterrâneo Ocidental (1385–1466)* (Lisbon, 1998); J. Heers, 'L'expansion maritime portugaise à la fin du Moyen-Âge: la Méditerranée', *Actas do III Colóquio internacional de estudios luso-brasileiros*, vol. 2 (Lisbon, 1960), pp. 138–47, repr. in Heers, *Société et économie*, essay iii.

12. R. Salicrú i Lluch, *El tràfic de mercaderies a Barcelona segons els comptes de la Lleuda de Mediona (febrer de 1434)* (Anuario de estudios medievales, annex no. 30, Barcelona, 1995).

13. D. Abulafia, 'The Crown and the economy under Ferrante I of Naples (1458–94)', in T. Dean and C. Wickham (eds.), *City and Countryside in Late Medieval and Renaissance Italy: Essays Presented to Philip Jones* (London, 1990), pp. 135, 140, repr. in D. Abulafia, *Commerce and Conquest in the Mediterranean, 1100–1500* (Aldershot, 1993).

14. A. Ruddock, *Italian Merchants and Shipping in Southampton 1270–1600* (Southampton, 1951), pp. 173–7.

15. K. Reyerson, *Jacques Coeur: Entrepreneur and King's Bursar* (New York, 2005), pp. 3, 90–91; J. Heers, *Jacques Cœur 1400–1456* (Paris, 1997), taking a different view from M. Mollat, *Jacques Cœur ou l'esprit de l'entreprise au XVe siècle* (Paris, 1988) and C. Poulain, *Jacques Cœur ou les rêves concrétisés* (Paris, 1982).

16. Cited by Reyerson, *Jacques Coeur*, p. 87.

17. Ibid., pp. 90, 92, 162; Mollat, *Jacques Cœur*, pp. 168–80.

18. D. Lamelas, *The Sale of Gibraltar in 1474 to the New Christians of Cordova*, ed. S. Benady (Gibraltar and Grendon, Northants, 1992); M. Harvey, *Gibraltar: a History* (2nd edn, Staplehurst, Kent, 2000), pp. 48–53.

19. P. Wolff, 'The 1391 pogrom in Spain: social crisis or not?', *Past & Present*, no. 50 (1971), pp. 4–18.

20. C. Carrère, *Barcelone: centre économique à l'époque des difficultés, 1380–1462*, 2 vols. (Paris and The Hague, 1967); C. Batlle, *Barcelona a mediados del siglo XV: historia de una crisis urbana* (Barcelona, 1976).

21. J. M. Quadrado, *Forenses y Ciudadanos* (Biblioteca Balear, vol. 1, Palma de Mallorca, 1986, repr. of 2nd edn, Palma, 1895); plague: M. Barceló Crespi, *Ciutat de Mallorca en el Trànsit a la Modernitat* (Palma de Mallorca, 1988).

22. R. Piña Homs, *El Consolat de Mar: Mallorca 1326–1800* (Palma de Mallorca, 1985); R. Smith, *The Spanish Guild Merchant: a History of the Consulado, 1250–1700* (Durham, NC, 1972), pp. 3–33.

23. Classic negative views in: J. Elliott, *Imperial Spain 1469–1714* (London, 1963), pp. 24, 30–31; P. Vilar, 'Le declin catalan au bas Moyen Âge', *Estudios de Historia Moderna*, vol. 6 (1956–9), pp. 1–68; J. Vicens Vives, *An Economic History of Spain* (Princeton, NJ, 1969), with relevant sections republished in R. Highfield (ed.), *Spain in the Fifteenth Century 1369–1516* (London, 1972), pp. 31–57, 248–75.

24. A. P. Usher, *The Early History of Deposit Banking in Mediterranean Europe* (Cambridge, MA, 1943).

25. D. Coulon, *Barcelone et le grand commerce d'Orient au Moyen Âge: un siècle de relations avec l'Égypte et la Syrie-Palestine, ca. 1330–ca. 1430* (Madrid and Barcelona, 2004).

26. M. del Treppo, *I Mercanti Catalani e l'Espansione della Corona d'Aragona nel Secolo XV* (Naples, 1972), figure facing p. 16; D. Pifarré Torres, *El comerç*

internacional de Barcelona i el mar del Nord (Bruges) al final del segle XIV (Barcelona and Montserrat, 2002).

27. There were 154 voyages from Barcelona to Rhodes between 1390 and 1493: del Treppo, *Mercanti Catalani*, p. 59.

28. Del Treppo, *Mercanti Catalani*, pp. 211, 213, 231–44.

29. Abulafia, 'The Crown and the economy under Ferrante', pp. 142–3.

30. D. Abulafia, 'L'economia mercantile nel Mediterraneo occidentale (1390ca.–1460ca.): commercio locale e a lunga distanza nell'età di Alfonso il Magnanimo', *Schola Salernitana. Dipartimento di Latinità e Medioevo, Università degli Studi di Salerno, Annali*, vol. 2 (1997), pp. 28–30, repr. in D. Abulafia, *Mediterranean Encounters: Economic, Religious, Political, 1100–1550* (Aldershot, 2000), essay viii; M. Zucchitello, *El comerç maritime de Tossa a través del port barceloní (1357–1553)* (Quaderns d'estudis tossencs, Tossa de Mar, 1982).

31. H. Winter, *Die katalanische Nao von 1450 nach dem Modell im Maritiem Museum Prins Hendrik in Rotterdam* (Burg bez. Magdeburg, 1956); *Het Matarò-Model: een bijzondere Aanwist* (Maritiem Museum Prins Hendrik, Rotterdam, 1982).

32. Salicrú, *Tràfic de mercaderies*.

33. M. Peláez, *Catalunya després de le Guerra Civil del segle XV* (Barcelona, 1981), p. 140; cf. del Treppo, *Mercanti catalani*, pp. 586–7.

34. Peláez, *Catalunya*, pp. 145, 153–9.

35. P. Macaire, *Majorque et le commerce international (1400–1450 environ)* (Lille, 1986), pp. 81–91, 411; O. Vaquer Bennasar, *El comerç marítim de Mallorca, 1448–1531* (Palma de Mallorca, 2001).

36. Elliott, *Imperial Spain*, p. 24; 'gyroscope' cited from E. Hamilton, *Money, Prices and Wages in Valencia, Aragon and Navarre 1351–1500* (Cambridge, MA, 1936), pp. 55–9.

37. S. Jados (ed. and trans.), *Consulate of the Sea and Related Documents* (Tuscaloosa, AL, 1975), pp. 3–18; Smith, *Spanish Guild Merchant*, pp. 20–25.

38. Jados, *Consulate of the Sea*, p. 38; also pp. 35–8, 54–7, 204–8.

39. Ibid., pp. 56–7; O. R. Constable, 'The problem of jettison in medieval Mediterranean maritime law', *Journal of Medieval History*, vol. 20 (1994), pp. 207–20.

40. Jados, *Consulate of the Sea*, pp. 65, 68–9.

41. Ibid., pp. 135–7; on ceramics: *Valenza-Napoli: rotte mediterranee della ceramica/València-Nàpols; les rutes mediterrànies de la ceramica* (Valencia, 1997).

42. Jados, *Consulate of the Sea*, p. 79.

43. M. Teresa Ferrer i Mallol, 'Els italians a terres catalanes (segles XII–XV)', *Anuario de Estudios Medievales*, vol. 19 (1980), pp. 393–467.

44. J. Guiral-Hadziiossif, *Valence, port méditerranéen au XVe siècle (1410–1525)* (Publications de la Sorbonne, Paris, 1986), pp. 281–6; D. Igual Luis, *Valencia y Italia en el siglo XV: rutas, mercados y hombres de negocios en el espacio económico del Mediterráneo occidental* (Bancaixa Fundació Caixa Castelló, Castellón, 1998).

45. P. Iradiel, 'Valencia y la expansión económica de la Corona de Aragón', in D. Abulafia and B. Garí (eds.), *En las costas del Mediterráneo occidental: las ciudades de la Peninsula Ibérica y del reino de Mallorca y el comercio mediterráneo en la Edad Media* (Barcelona, 1997), pp. 155–69; E. Cruselles, *Los mercaderes de Valencia en la Edad Media, 1380–1450* (Lleidà, 2001); E. Cruselles, *Los comerciantes valencianos del siglo XV y sus libros de cuentas* (Castelló de la Plana, 2007).

46. See the studies by P. Mainoni, V. Mora, C. Verlinden collected in A. Furió (ed.), *València, mercat medieval* (Valencia, 1985), pp. 83–156, 159–73, 267–75.

47. E.g. Gentino Abulafia: G. Romestan, 'Els mercaders llenguadocians en el regne de València durant la primera meitat del segle XIV', in Furió, *València*, p. 217.

48. Salicrú, 'Catalano-Aragonese commercial presence', pp. 289–312.

49. E. Belenguer Cebrià, *València en la crisi del segle XV* (Barcelona, 1976).

50. S. R. Epstein, *An Island for Itself: Economic Development and Social Change in Late Medieval Sicily* (Cambridge, 1992); C. Zedda, *Cagliari: un porto commerciale nel Mediterraneo del Quattrocento* (Naples, 2001).

51. O. Benedictow, *The Black Death 1346–1353: the Complete History* (Woodbridge, 2004), p. 281.

52. Wolff, '1391 pogrom', pp. 4–18.

53. H. Maccoby, *Judaism on Trial: Jewish-Christian Disputations in the Middle Ages* (Rutherford, NJ, 1982), pp. 168–215.

54. A. Y. d'Abrera, *The Tribunal of Zaragoza and Crypto-Judaism, 1484–1515* (Turnhout, 2008).

55. R. Conde y Delgado de Molina, *La Expulsión de los Judíos de la Corona de Aragón: documentos para su estudio* (Saragossa, 1991), doc. §1, pp. 41–4.

56. Samuel Usque, *Consolation for the Tribulations of Israel (Consolaçam as Tribulaçoens de Israel)*, ed. M. Cohen (Philadelphia, PA, 1964); Joseph Hacohen and the Anonymous Corrector, *The Vale of Tears (Emek Habacha)*, ed. H. May (The Hague, 1971).

57. G. N. Zazzu, *Sepharad addio – 1492: I profughi ebrei della Spagna al 'ghetto' di Genova* (Genoa, 1991).

58. N. Zeldes, 'Sefardi and Sicilian exiles in the Kingdom of Naples: settlement, community formation and crisis', *Hispania Judaica Bulletin*, vol. 6 (5769/2008), pp. 237–66; D. Abulafia, 'Aragonese kings of Naples and the Jews', in B. Garvin and B. Cooperman (eds.), *The Jews of Italy: Memory and Identity* (Bethesda, MD, 2000), pp. 82–106.

59. D. Abulafia, 'Insediamenti, diaspora e tradizione ebraica: gli Ebrei del Regno di Napoli da Ferdinando il Cattolico a Carlo V', *Convegno internazionale Carlo V, Napoli e il Mediterraneo = Archivio storico per le province napoletane*, vol. 119 (2001), pp. 171–200.

60. Cited in M. Mazower, *Salonica, City of Ghosts: Christians, Muslims and Jews 1430–1950* (London, 2004), p. 48; *Maranes* signifies 'Marranos', a term more often used for *conversos*.

61. A. David, *To Come to the Land: Immigration and Settlement in Sixteenth-century Eretz-Israel* (Tuscaloosa, AL, 1999).

62. T. Glick, *Irrigation and Society in Medieval Valencia* (Cambridge, MA, 1970).

63. L. P. Harvey, *Islamic Spain 1250 to 1500* (Chicago, 1990).

64. M. Meyerson, *The Muslims of Valencia in the Age of Fernando and Isabel: between Coexistence and Crusade* (Berkeley, CA, 1991); L. P. Harvey, *Muslims in Spain, 1500 to 1614* (Chicago, IL, 2005).

65. J.-E. Ruiz-Domènec, *El Gran Capitán: retrato de una época* (Barcelona, 2002); C. J. Hernando Sánchez, *El Reino de Nápoles en el imperio de Carlos V: la consolidación de la conquista* (Madrid, 2001); D. Abulafia, 'Ferdinand the Catholic and the kingdom of Naples', in *Italy and the European Powers: the Impact of War, 1503-1530*, ed. Christine Shaw (Leiden, 2006), pp. 129-58; F. Baumgartner, *Louis XII* (Stroud, 1994).

66. J. M. Doussinague, *La política internacional de Fernando el Católico* (Madrid, 1944), pp. 91-106.

67. D. Abulafia, *The Discovery of Mankind: Atlantic Encounters in the Age of Columbus* (New Haven, CT, 2008); M. A. Ladero Quesada, *El primer oro de América: los comienzos de la Casa de la Contratación de las Yndias, 1503-1511* (Madrid, 2002).

68. A. Hess, *The Forgotten Frontier: a History of the Sixteenth-century Ibero-African Frontier* (Chicago, IL, 1978), pp. 37-42; Doussinague, *Política internacional*, pp. 194-209, 212-28, 346-52; R. Gutiérrez Cruz, *Los presidios españoles del Norte de África en tiempo de los Reyes Católicos* (Melilla, 1998).

69. R. Ríos Lloret, *Germana de Foix, una mujer, una reina, una corte* (Valencia, 2003).

70. B. Aram, *Juana the Mad: Sovereignty and Dynasty in Renaissance Europe* (Baltimore, MD, 2005).

71. T. Dandelet and J. Marino (eds.), *Spain in Italy: Politics, Society, and Religion, 1500-1700* (Leiden, 2007); T. Dandelet, *Spanish Rome, 1500-1700* (New Haven, CT, 2001).

3. Holy Leagues and Unholy Alliances, 1500-1550

1. D. Abulafia, *The Discovery of Mankind: Atlantic Encounters in the Age of Columbus* (New Haven, CT, 2008), pp. 33-44, 82-6.

2. D. Blumenthal, *Enemies and Familiars: Slavery and Mastery in Fifteenth-century Valencia* (Ithaca, NY, 2009).

3. B. Pullan (ed.), *Crisis and Change in the Venetian Economy in the Sixteenth and Seventeenth Centuries* (London, 1968).

4. F. Braudel, *The Mediterranean and the Mediterranean World in the Age of Philip II*, trans. S. Reynolds, 2 vols. (London, 1972-3), vol. 2, p. 880 dates the phenomenon too late.

5. J. Heers, *The Barbary Corsairs: Warfare in the Mediterranean, 1480–1580* (London, 2003); G. Fisher, *Barbary Legend: Trade and Piracy in North Africa 1415–1830* (Oxford, 1957); also J. Wolf, *The Barbary Coast: Algiers under the Turks, 1500 to 1830* (New York, 1979).

6. P. Brummett, *Ottoman Seapower and Levantine Diplomacy in the Age of Discovery* (Albany, NY, 1994), pp. 123–41.

7. Lively accounts in R. Crowley, *Empires of the Sea: the Final Battle for the Mediterranean 1521–1580* (London, 2008), pp. 11–27; and B. Rogerson, *The Last Crusaders: the Hundred-year Battle for the Centre of the World* (London, 2009), pp. 261–5.

8. A. Hess, *The Forgotten Frontier: a History of the Sixteenth-century Ibero-African Frontier* (Chicago, IL, 1978), pp. 21, 42, 75–6.

9. Ö. Kumrular, *El Duelo entre Carlos V y Solimán el Magnífico (1520–1535)* (Istanbul, 2005), p. 126.

10. M. Özen, *Pirî Reis and his Charts* (2nd edn, Istanbul, 2006), pp. 4, 8–9.

11. Fisher, *Barbary Legend*, p. 42; Heers, *Barbary Corsairs*, p. 61; Özen, *Pirî Reis*, p. 4; Rogerson, *Last Crusaders*, p. 156.

12. Heers, *Barbary Corsairs*, p. 63; Rogerson, *Last Crusaders*, pp. 160–63; Hess, *Forgotten Frontier*, pp. 63–4.

13. R. Davis, *Christian Slaves, Muslim Masters: White Slavery in the Mediterranean, the Barbary Coast and Italy, 1500–1800* (Basingstoke, 2003); Crowley, *Empires of the Sea*, p. 34.

14. Heers, *Barbary Corsairs*, pp. 64–5.

15. Kumrular, *El Duelo*, p. 119; also Ö. Kumrular, *Las Relaciones entre el Imperio Otomano y la Monarquía Católica entre los Años 1520–1535 y el Papel de los Estados Satellites* (Istanbul, 2003).

16. Heers, *Barbary Corsairs*, p. 68.

17. Ibid., pp. 70–71.

18. Kumrular, *El Duelo*, p. 119.

19. Heers, *Barbary Corsairs*, p. 71.

20. Crowley, *Empires of the Sea*, p. 63.

21. Wolf, *Barbary Coast*, p. 20 (1535).

22. P. Lingua, *Andrea Doria: Principe e Pirata nell'Italia del '500* (Genoa, 2006).

23. Crowley, *Empires of the Sea*, p. 49; Heers, *Barbary Corsairs*, p. 69.

24. Crowley, *Empires of the Sea*, p. 55; Rogerson, *Last Crusaders*, p. 288.

25. Crowley, *Empires of the Sea*, p. 69.

26. Lingua, *Andrea Doria*, pp. 94–101.

27. Wolf, *Barbary Coast*, p. 20.

28. D. Abulafia, 'La politica italiana della monarchia francese da Carlo VIII a Francesco I', in *El reino de Nápoles y la monarquía de España: entre agregación y conquista*, ed. G. Galasso and C. Hernando Sánchez (Madrid, 2004).

29. Heers, *Barbary Corsairs*, pp. 73–4.

30. R. Knecht, *Renaissance Warrior and Patron: the Reign of Francis I* (Cambridge,

1994), p. 296; J. Luis Castellano, 'Estudio preliminar', in J. Sánchez Montes, *Franceses, Protestantes, Turcos: los Españoles ante la política internacional de Carlos V* (2nd edn, Granada, 1995), pp. ix–xlvi.

31. Heers, *Barbary Corsairs*, p. 73.

32. Hess, *Forgotten Frontier*, p. 73; Sánchez Montes, *Franceses, Protestantes, Turcos*, p. 52.

33. Knecht, *Renaissance Warrior*, pp. 296, 299, 329.

34. Ibid., p. 489; Heers, *Barbary Corsairs*, pp. 83–90; Hess, *Forgotten Frontier*, p. 75.

35. Brummett, *Ottoman Seapower*, pp. 89–121.

36. Ibid., pp. 131–41.

37. G. Hanlon, *The Twilight of a Military Tradition: Italian Aristocrats and European Conflicts, 1560–1800* (London, 1998), pp. 29–30; D. Goodman, *Spanish Naval Power, 1589–1665: Reconstruction and Defeat* (Cambridge, 1997), pp. 13, 132.

38. J. Guilmartin, *Gunpowder and Galleys: Changing Technology and Mediterranean Warfare at Sea in the 16th Century* (2nd edn, London, 2003), pp. 245–7.

39. N. Capponi, *Victory of the West: the Story of the Battle of Lepanto* (London, 2006), pp. 179–81; Guilmartin, *Gunpowder and Galleys*, pp. 209–34; H. Bicheno, *Crescent and Cross: the Battle of Lepanto 1571* (London, 2003), p. 73 (plan of galley).

40. Capponi, *Victory of the West*, pp. 183–4.

41. Guilmartin, *Gunpowder and Galleys*, pp. 78–9, 211–20; J. Pryor, *Geography, Technology, and War: Studies in the Maritime History of the Mediterranean 649–1571* (Cambridge, 1988), p. 85.

42. Guilmartin, *Gunpowder and Galleys*, pp. 125–6.

43. Capponi, *Victory of the West*, pp. 198–9.

44. Davis, *Christian Slaves, Muslim Masters*, pp. 42–3 (renegades), 115–29 (*bagni*).

45. Guilmartin, *Gunpowder and Galleys*, pp. 237–9.

4. *Akdeniz* – the Battle for the White Sea, 1550–1571

1. F. Braudel, *The Mediterranean and the Mediterranean World in the Age of Philip II*, trans. S. Reynolds, 2 vols. (London, 1972–3), vol. 2, pp. 919–20.

2. J. Guilmartin, *Gunpowder and Galleys: Changing Technology and Mediterranean Warfare at Sea in the 16th Century* (2nd edn, London, 2003), p. 143.

3. Braudel, *Mediterranean*, vol. 2, pp. 973–87.

4. Guilmartin, *Gunpowder and Galleys*, pp. 137–47.

5. E. Bradford, *The Great Siege: Malta 1565* (2nd edn, Harmondsworth, 1964), p. 14.

6. A. Cassola, 'The Great Siege of Malta (1565) and the Istanbul State Archives', in A. Cassola, I. Bostan and T. Scheben, *The 1565 Ottoman/Malta Campaign Register* (Malta, 1998), p. 19.

7. Braudel, *Mediterranean*, vol. 2, pp. 1014–17.

8. R. Crowley, *Empires of the Sea: the Final Battle for the Mediterranean 1521–1580* (London, 2008), p. 114.

9. F. Balbi di Correggio, *The Siege of Malta 1565*, trans. E. Bradford (London, 1965), pp. 51–3.

10. Ibid., pp. 55, 61–4.

11. Ibid., p. 91.

12. Braudel, *Mediterranean*, vol. 2, p. 1018; Crowley, *Empires of the Sea*, pp. 155–6, 165–6.

13. Balbi, *Siege of Malta*, pp. 145–7, 149–50; Crowley, *Empires of the Sea*, pp. 176–7.

14. Balbi, *Siege of Malta*, p. 182.

15. Ibid., p. 187.

16. Braudel, *Mediterranean*, vol. 2, p. 1020.

17. D. Hurtado de Mendoza, *The War in Granada*, trans. M. Shuttleworth (London, 1982), p. 58.

18. R. Cavaliero, *The Last of the Crusaders: the Knights of St John and Malta in the Eighteenth Century* (2nd edn, London, 2009), p. 23.

19. J. Abela, 'Port Activities in Sixteenth-century Malta' (MA thesis, University of Malta), pp. 151–2, 155.

20. Ibid., pp. 161, 163.

21. G. Wettinger, *Slavery in the Islands of Malta and Gozo* (Malta, 2002).

22. Abela, 'Port Activities', pp. 104, 114, 122, 139–42.

23. P. Earle, 'The commercial development of Ancona, 1479–1551', *Economic History Review*, 2nd ser., vol. 22 (1969), pp. 28–44.

24. E. Ashtor, 'Il commercio levantino di Ancona nel basso medioevo', *Rivista storica italiana*, vol. 88 (1976), pp. 213–53.

25. R. Harris, *Dubrovnik: a History* (London, 2003), p. 162.

26. F. Tabak, *The Waning of the Mediterranean 1550–1870: a Geohistorical Approach* (Baltimore, MD, 2008), p. 127.

27. Earle, 'Commercial development of Ancona', pp. 35–7; M. Aymard, *Venise, Raguse et le commerce du blé pendant la second moitié du XVIe siècle* (Paris, 1966).

28. Earle, 'Commercial development of Ancona', p. 40.

29. V. Kostić, *Dubrovnik i Engleska 1300–1650* (Belgrade, 1975).

30. Harris, *Dubrovnik*, pp. 163–4; F. Carter, 'The commerce of the Dubrovnik Republic, 1500–1700', *Economic History Review*, 2nd ser., vol. 24 (1971), p. 390.

31. V. Miović, *The Jewish Ghetto in the Dubrovnik Republic (1546–1808)* (Zagreb and Dubrovnik, 2005).

32. Harris, *Dubrovnik*, pp. 252–60, 271–84.

33. Carter, 'Commerce of the Dubrovnik Republic', pp. 369–94; repr. in his unsatisfactory *Dubrovnik (Ragusa): a Classic City-state* (London, 1972), pp. 349–404; Harris, *Dubrovnik*, p. 160.

34. Carter, 'Commerce of the Dubrovnik Republic', pp. 386–7.

35. Harris, *Dubrovnik*, p. 270.
36. Braudel, *Mediterranean*, vol. 1, pp. 284–90.
37. Ibid., p. 285.
38. Harris, *Dubrovnik*, p. 172.
39. Braudel, *Mediterranean*, vol. 1, pp. 286–7; A. Tenenti, *Piracy and the Decline of Venice 1580–1615* (London, 1967), pp. 3–15.
40. Tabak, *Waning of the Mediterranean*, pp. 173–85.
41. E. Hamilton, *American Treasure and the Price Revolution in Spain, 1501–1650* (Cambridge, MA, 1934).
42. J. Amelang, *Honored Citizens of Barcelona: Patrician Culture and Class Relations, 1490–1714* (Princeton, NJ, 1986), pp. 13–14; A. García Espuche, *Un siglo decisivo: Barcelona y Cataluña 1550–1640* (Madrid, 1998), generally, and pp. 62–8 for French settlers.
43. A. Musi, *I mercanti genovesi nel Regno di Napoli* (Naples, 1996); G. Brancaccio, '*Nazione genovese': consoli e colonia nella Napoli moderna* (Naples, 2001), pp. 43–74.
44. R. Carande, *Carlos V y sus banqueros*, 3 vols. (4th edn, Barcelona, 1990); R. Canosa, *Banchieri genovesi e sovrani spagnoli tra Cinquecento e Seicento* (Rome, 1998); Braudel, *Mediterranean*, vol. 1, pp. 500–504.
45. C. Roth, *Doña Gracia of the House of Nasi* (Philadelphia, PA, 1948), pp. 21–49.
46. M. Lazar (ed.), *The Ladino Bible of Ferrara* (Culver City, CA, 1992); Roth, *Doña Gracia*, pp. 73–4.
47. Miović, *Jewish Ghetto*, p. 27.
48. Roth, *Doña Gracia*, pp. 138–46, 150–51.
49. Ibid., pp. 154–8.
50. D. Studnicki-Gizbert, *A Nation upon the Ocean Sea: Portugal's Atlantic Diaspora and the Crisis of the Spanish Empire 1492–1640* (Oxford and New York, 2007).
51. C. Roth, *The House of Nasi: the Duke of Naxos* (Philadelphia, PA, 1948), pp. 39–40.
52. Ibid., pp. 46–7.
53. Ibid., pp. 75–137.
54. J. ha-Cohen, *The Vale of Tears*, cited ibid., p. 137.
55. Roth, *Duke of Naxos*, p. 128.
56. Under the leadership of Haim Abulafia: J. Barnai, *The Jews of Palestine in the Eighteenth Century under the Patronage of the Committee of Officials for Palestine* (Tuscaloosa, AL, 1992), pp. 152–3.
57. Roth, *Duke of Naxos*, pp. 62–74.
58. Ibid., pp. 138–42; N. Capponi, *Victory of the West: the Story of the Battle of Lepanto* (London, 2006), p. 127.
59. Capponi, *Victory of the West*, pp. 119–23.
60. Ibid., pp. 121, 124–5.

61. Ibid., pp. 128–30.
62. Braudel, *Mediterranean*, vol. 2, p. 1105.
63. Capponi, *Victory of the West*, p. 137; A. Gazioğlu, *The Turks in Cyprus: a Province of the Ottoman Empire (1571–1878)* (London and Nicosia, 1990), pp. 28–35.
64. Capponi, *Victory of the West*, pp. 150–54; Gazioğlu, *Turks in Cyprus*, pp. 36–48.
65. Capponi, *Victory of the West*, pp. 160–61.
66. Ibid., p. 170.
67. Ibid., pp. 229–31.
68. H. Bicheno, *Crescent and Cross: the Battle of Lepanto 1571* (London, 2003), p. 208; Gazioğlu, *Turks in Cyprus*, pp. 61–6.
69. Capponi, *Victory of the West*, pp. 233–6.
70. Guilmartin, *Gunpowder and Galleys*, p. 252.
71. Capponi, *Victory of the West*, pp. 263–4; Bicheno, *Crescent and Cross*, pp. 300–308.
72. Capponi, *Victory of the West*, pp. 259–60; Bicheno, *Crescent and Cross*, pp. 252, 260 (plan of deployment and opening stages).
73. Guilmartin, *Gunpowder and Galleys*, pp. 253, 255, 257.
74. Crowley, *Empires of the Sea*, p. 272.
75. Guilmartin, *Gunpowder and Galleys*, pp. 158–60.
76. Crowley, *Empires of the Sea*, p. 279.
77. Capponi, *Victory of the West*, p. 256.
78. Ibid., pp. 268–71; Bicheno, *Crescent and Cross*, p. 263.
79. Crowley, *Empires of the Sea*, pp. 284–5.
80. Capponi, *Victory of the West*, p. 279.
81. Bicheno, *Crescent and Cross*, pp. 319–21; Capponi, *Victory of the West*, pp. 289–91.
82. Bicheno, *Crescent and Cross*, plates 6a, 6b, 7.
83. Guilmartin, *Gunpowder and Galleys*, pp. 247–8.
84. Braudel, *Mediterranean*, vol. 2, p. 1103.
85. Ibid., pp. 1088–9.

5. Interlopers in the Mediterranean, 1571–1650

1. G. Hanlon, *The Twilight of a Military Tradition: Italian Aristocrats and European Conflicts, 1560–1800* (London, 1998), pp. 26–7.
2. D. Hurtado de Mendoza, *The War in Granada*, trans. M. Shuttleworth (London, 1982), p. 259.
3. B. Rogerson, *The Last Crusaders: the Hundred-year Battle for the Centre of the World* (London, 2009), pp. 399–422.

4. G. Botero, *The Reason of State*, trans. D. and P. Waley (London, 1956), p. 12; D. Goodman, *Spanish Naval Power, 1589–1665: Reconstruction and Defeat* (Cambridge, 1997), pp. 9–10.

5. C. W. Bracewell, *The Uskoks of Senj: Piracy, Banditry, and Holy War in the Sixteenth-century Adriatic* (Ithaca, NY, 1992), p. 8; A. Tenenti, *Piracy and the Decline of Venice 1580–1615* (London, 1967), pp. 3–15.

6. E. Hobsbawm, *Primitive Rebels* (Manchester, 1959), and *Bandits* (London, 1969); cf. T. Judt, *Reappraisals: Reflections on the Forgotten Twentieth Century* (London, 2008); Bracewell, *Uskoks of Senj*, pp. 10–11.

7. Bracewell, *Uskoks of Senj*, pp. 51–2, 56–62, 67–8, 72–4.

8. Ibid., p. 70, n. 43 (1558).

9. Venetian report cited in ibid., p. 83.

10. Bracewell, *The Uskoks of Senj*, p. 2; Tenenti, *Piracy and the Decline of Venice*, p. 3.

11. Tenenti, *Piracy and the Decline of Venice*, p. 6.

12. Bracewell, *Uskoks of Senj*, p. 8; Tenenti, *Piracy and the Decline of Venice*, p. 8.

13. Tenenti, *Piracy and the Decline of Venice*, p. 10.

14. Bracewell, *Uskoks of Senj*, pp. 63–4; Tenenti, *Piracy and the Decline of Venice*, p. 10.

15. Bracewell, *Uskoks of Senj*, pp. 103–4; Tenenti, *Piracy and the Decline of Venice*, p. 8.

16. Bracewell, *Uskoks of Senj*, pp. 202–3.

17. Ibid., pp. 210, n. 109, 211–12.

18. E. Dursteler, *Venetians in Constantinople: Nation, Identity and Coexistence in the Early Modern Mediterranean* (Baltimore, MD, 2006), p. 24.

19. B. Pullan, *The Jews of Europe and the Inquisition of Venice, 1550–1670* (Oxford, 1983), especially pp. 201–312; R. Calimani, *The Ghetto of Venice* (New York, 1987).

20. D. Geanakoplos, *Byzantine East and Latin West: Two Worlds of Christendom in Middle Ages and Renaissance, Studies in Ecclesiastical and Cultural History* (Oxford, 1966).

21. E.g. Tenenti, *Piracy and the Decline of Venice*, p. 56; cf. R. Rapp, 'The unmaking of the Mediterranean trade hegemony: international trade rivalry and the commercial revolution', *Journal of Economic History*, vol. 35 (1975), pp. 499–525.

22. F. C. Lane, *Venice: a Maritime Republic* (Baltimore, MD, 1973), pp. 309–10.

23. M. Greene, 'Beyond northern invasions: the Mediterranean in the seventeenth century', *Past and Present*, no. 174 (2002), pp. 40–72.

24. J. Mather, *Pashas: Traders and Travellers in the Islamic World* (New Haven, CT, 2009), pp. 28–32; M. Fusaro, *Uva passa: una guerra commerciale tra Venezia e l'Inghilterra (1540–1640)* (Venice, 1996), pp. 23–4.

25. Tenenti, *Piracy and the Decline of Venice*, pp. 59–60.

26. T. S. Willan, *Studies in Elizabethan Foreign Trade* (Manchester, 1959), pp. 92–312.

27. Fusaro, *Uva passa*, p. 24.

28. Tenenti, *Piracy and the Decline of Venice*, pp. 60, 72.

29. Rapp, 'Unmaking of the Mediterranean trade hegemony', pp. 509–12.

30. Fusaro, *Uva passa*, pp. 25–6, 48–55; Tenenti, *Piracy and the Decline of Venice*, p. 61.

31. Tenenti, *Piracy and the Decline of Venice*, pp. 74–5.

32. Ibid., pp. 77–8; C. Lloyd, *English Corsairs on the Barbary Coast* (London, 1981), pp. 48–53; A. Tinniswood, *Pirates of Barbary: Corsairs, Conquests and Captivity in the Seventeenth-century Mediterranean* (London, 2010), pp. 19–25, 30–42.

33. Tenenti, *Piracy and the Decline of Venice*, pp. 63–4.

34. Ibid., pp. 64–5, 70–71, 74, 85, 138–43.

35. Ibid., p. 82.

36. J. Baltharpe, *The Straights Voyage or St David's Poem*, ed. J. S. Bromley (Luttrell Society, Oxford, 1959), pp. 35, 45, 58–9, 68–9; N. A. M. Rodger, *The Command of the Ocean: a Naval History of Britain, 1649–1815* (London, 2004), pp. 132–3.

37. Rodger, *Command of the Ocean*, p. 486.

38. M.-C. Engels, *Merchants, Interlopers, Seamen and Corsairs: the 'Flemish' Community in Livorno and Genoa (1615–1635)* (Hilversum, 1997), pp. 47–50.

39. Rapp, 'Unmaking of the Mediterranean trade hegemony', pp. 500–502.

40. Engels, *Merchants, Interlopers*, pp. 50–51.

41. S. Siegmund, *The Medici State and the Ghetto of Florence: the Construction of an Early Modern Jewish Community* (Stanford, CA, 2006).

42. F. Trivellato, *The Familiarity of Strangers: the Sephardic Diaspora, Livorno, and Cross Cultural Trade in the Early Modern Period* (New Haven, CT, 2009), p. 74; L. Frattarelli Fischer, 'La città medicea', in O. Vaccari et al., *Storia illustrata di Livorno* (Pisa, 2006), pp. 57–109; more generally: D. Calabi, *La città del primo Rinascimento* (Bari and Rome, 2001).

43. F. Braudel and R. Romano, *Navires et merchandises à l'entrée du port de Livourne* (Ports, Routes, Trafics, vol. 1, Paris, 1951), p. 21; Engels, *Merchants, Interlopers*, p. 41.

44. Trivellato, *Familiarity of Strangers*, p. 76; Engels, *Merchants, Interlopers*, p. 40.

45. Y. Yovel, *The Other Within: the Marranos, Split Identity and Emerging Modernity* (Princeton, NJ, 2009).

46. Trivellato, *Familiarity of Strangers*, pp. 78, 82.

47. Braudel and Romano, *Navires et merchandises*, p. 45; Engels, *Merchants, Interlopers*, p. 180.

48. Braudel and Romano, *Navires et merchandises*, p. 46; J. Casey, *The Kingdom of Valencia in the Seventeenth Century* (Cambridge, 1979), pp. 80–82.

49. Braudel and Romano, *Navires et merchandises*, p. 47.

50. Engels, *Merchants, Interlopers*, pp. 67, 91–9, 206–13; K. Persson, *Grain Markets in Europe 1500–1900: Integration and Deregulation* (Cambridge, 1999).

51. Engels, *Merchants, Interlopers*, pp. 65, 67–73, 96; on Aleppo: Mather, *Pashas*, pp. 17–102.

52. Engels, *Merchants, Interlopers*, pp. 179, 191, 195, 201.

53. T. Kirk, *Genoa and the Sea: Policy and Power in an Early Modern Maritime Republic, 1559–1684* (Baltimore, MD, 2005), pp. 45, 193–4; E. Grendi, *La repubblica aristocratica dei genovesi* (Bologna, 1987), p. 332.

54. Grendi, *Repubblica aristocratica*, pp. 339–43, 356–7.

55. Kirk, *Genoa and the Sea*, pp. 34–5, 84–7, 91–6.

56. Grendi, *Repubblica aristocratica*, p. 207.

57. Kirk, *Genoa and the Sea*, pp. 119–23.

58. F. Tabak, *The Waning of the Mediterranean 1550–1870: a Geohistorical Approach* (Baltimore, MD, 2008), pp. 1–29.

6. Diasporas in Despair, 1560–1700

1. L. P. Harvey, *Muslims in Spain, 1500 to 1614* (Chicago, IL, 2005), pp. 206–7; M. Carr, *Blood and Faith: the Purging of Muslim Spain, 1492–1614* (London, 2009), pp. 109–17.

2. Texts in Harvey, *Muslims in Spain*, pp. 382–98.

3. D. Hurtado de Mendoza, *The War in Granada*, trans. M. Shuttleworth (London, 1982), p. 42.

4. Cited in G. Parker, *Empire, War and Faith in Early Modern Europe* (London, 2002), p. 33.

5. Hurtado de Mendoza, *War in Granada*, p. 41; Carr, *Blood and Faith*, pp. 153–8.

6. Hurtado de Mendoza, *War in Granada*, pp. 150–51, 217–18, etc.; Harvey, *Muslims in Spain*, pp. 337–40; Carr, *Blood and Faith*, pp. 159–79.

7. Hurtado de Mendoza, *War in Granada*, p. 218 (with emendations).

8. Harvey, *Muslims in Spain*, p. 339.

9. Carr, *Blood and Faith*, p. 182.

10. Harvey, *Muslims in Spain*, pp. 295–6, revising H. C. Lea, *The Moriscos of Spain: their Conversion and Expulsion* (Philadelphia, PA, 1901), p. 296.

11. J. Casey, *The Kingdom of Valencia in the Seventeenth Century* (Cambridge, 1979), pp. 79–100.

12. Lea, *Moriscos*, pp. 318–19; Casey, *Kingdom of Valencia*, pp. 228–9, 234; Carr, *Blood and Faith*, p. 256.

13. Lea, *Moriscos*, p. 320; partial text in Harvey, *Muslims in Spain*, pp. 310–11.

14. Lea, *Moriscos*, pp. 322–5, n. 1.

15. Carr, *Blood and Faith*, p. 263.

16. Lea, *Moriscos*, pp. 326–33 (figures: p. 332, n. 1); Harvey, *Muslims in Spain*, pp. 314–16.

17. Harvey, *Muslims in Spain*, p. 317; Carr, *Blood and Faith*, p. 286.
18. Lea, *Moriscos*, pp. 340–41.
19. Cited in J. Casey, 'Moriscos and the depopulation of Valencia', *Past and Present*, no. 50 (1971), p. 19.
20. Harvey, *Muslims in Spain*, pp. 320–31.
21. M. García Arenal, *La diaspora des Andalousiens* (Aix-en-Provence, 2003), p. 103.
22. Ibid., pp. 123, 137, 139.
23. M. Greene, 'Beyond northern invasions: the Mediterranean in the seventeenth century', *Past and Present*, no. 174 (2002), pp. 40–72.
24. Cited in D. Goffman, *Izmir and the Levantine World, 1550–1650* (Seattle, WA, 1990), p. 52.
25. Ibid., pp. 61–4, 74–5.
26. E. Frangakis-Syrett, *The Commerce of Smyrna in the Eighteenth Century, 1700–1820* (Athens, 1992), pp. 74–9.
27. Goffman, *Izmir*, pp. 67, 77.
28. Ibid., pp. 81–4; Frangakis-Syrett, *Commerce of Smyrna*, pp. 80–81, 106.
29. Frangakis-Syrett, *Commerce of Smyrna*, p. 35.
30. Passages cited in Goffman, *Izmir*, p. 137; also J. Mather, *Pashas: Traders and Travellers in the Islamic World* (New Haven, CT, 2009), pp. 94, 213.
31. G. Scholem, *Sabbatai Sevi, the Mystical Messiah 1626–1676* (London, 1973), pp. 106–7, 109, n. 17; and the often inaccurate J. Freely, *The Lost Messiah: in Search of Sabbatai Sevi* (London, 2001), pp. 14–15.
32. Moses Pinheiro of Smyrna, cited by Scholem, *Sabbatai Sevi*, p. 115.
33. Scholem, *Sabbatai Sevi*, pp. 126–7.
34. Freely, *Lost Messiah*, pp. 50, 61.
35. Scholem, *Sabbatai Sevi*, pp. 358–9; Freely, *Lost Messiah*, p. 76.
36. Scholem, *Sabbatai Sevi*, pp. 396–401; Freely, *Lost Messiah*, p. 85.
37. Scholem, *Sabbatai Sevi*, pp. 374–5; Freely, *Lost Messiah*, p. 84.
38. Letter to England, cited by Scholem, *Sabbatai Sevi*, p. 383.
39. Scholem, *Sabbatai Sevi*, p. 101.
40. F. Yates, *The Rosicrucian Enlightenment* (London, 1972).
41. Freely, *Lost Messiah*, p. 93.
42. Ibid., pp. 133–4.
43. Scholem, *Sabbatai Sevi*, pp. 673–86.
44. Haim Abulafia, ibid., p. 359.
45. M. Greene, *A Shared World: Christians and Muslims in the Early Modern Mediterranean* (Princeton, NJ, 2000), pp. 62–7, 110–19.
46. Ibid., p. 17.
47. Ibid., p. 14; R. C. Anderson, *Naval Wars in the Levant 1559–1853* (Liverpool, 1951), pp. 121–2.
48. Anderson, *Naval Wars in the Levant*, pp. 122–5.
49. Ibid., pp. 148–67.
50. Ibid., pp. 181–4; Greene, *Shared World*, pp. 18, 56.

51. Greene, *Shared World*, p. 121.

52. Ibid., pp. 122–40, 141–54; Greene, 'Beyond northern invasions'.

53. Greene, *Shared World*, p. 155.

54. Ibid., pp. 175–81.

55. J. Dakhlia, *Lingua franca: histoire d'une langue métisse en Méditerranée* (Arles, 2008).

56. J. Wansborough, *Lingua Franca in the Mediterranean* (Richmond, Surrey, 1996).

57. H. and R. Kahane and A. Tietze, *The Lingua Franca in the Levant: Turkish Nautical Terms of Italian and Greek Origin* (Urbana, IL, 1958).

58. G. Cifoletti, *La lingua franca mediterranea* (Quaderni patavini di linguistica, monografie, no. 5, Padua, 1989), p. 74; *Dictionnaire de la langue franque ou petit mauresque* (Marseilles, 1830), p. 6, repr. in Cifoletti, *Lingua franca*, pp. 72–84.

59. R. Davis, *Christian Slaves, Muslim Masters: White Slavery in the Mediterranean, the Barbary Coast and Italy, 1500–1800* (Basingstoke, 2003), pp. 25, 57, 114–15; A. Tinniswood, *Pirates of Barbary: Corsairs, Conquests and Captivity in the Seventeenth-century Mediterranean* (London, 2010), pp. 58–61; Cifoletti, *Lingua franca*, p. 108.

7. Encouragement to Others, 1650–1780

1. R. C. Anderson, *Naval Wars in the Levant 1559–1853* (Liverpool, 1951), pp. 194–211, 236, 264–70.

2. G. Hills, *Rock of Contention: a History of Gibraltar* (London, 1974), pp. 142–6.

3. E. Routh, *Tangier: England's Lost Atlantic Outpost 1661–1684* (London, 1912), p. 10; A. Tinniswood, *Pirates of Barbary: Corsairs, Conquests and Captivity in the Seventeenth-century Mediterranean* (London, 2010), p. 204.

4. Routh, *Tangier*, p. 27.

5. S. Pepys, *The Tangier Papers of Samuel Pepys*, ed. E. Chappell (Navy Records Society, vol. 73, London, 1935), p. 88; A. Smithers, *The Tangier Campaign: the Birth of the British Army* (Stroud, 2003), pp. 31–2.

6. Routh, *Tangier*, pp. 21, 28.

7. Cited in ibid., pp. 23–4; Bromley in J. Baltharpe, *The Straights Voyage or St David's Poem*, ed. J. S. Bromley (Luttrell Society, Oxford, 1959), pp. xxvii–viii.

8. Routh, *Tangier*, pp. 66–9; Smithers, *Tangier Campaign*, pp. 49–53.

9. Pepys, *Tangier Papers*, p. 97; Routh, *Tangier*, pp. 272–6.

10. Pepys, *Tangier Papers*, p. 41.

11. Tinniswood, *Pirates of Barbary*, pp. 211–15.

12. Routh, *Tangier*, p. 81; also Sir Henry Sheres's opinion in Tinniswood, *Pirates of Barbary*, p. 205.

13. Routh, *Tangier*, pp. 82–6.

14. Pepys, *Tangier Papers*, p. 77; Hills, *Rock of Contention*, p. 150; Routh, *Tangier*, pp. 242–4.

15. Pepys, *Tangier Papers*, p. 65; Routh, *Tangier*, pp. 247–66; also plate facing p. 266; Smithers, *Tangier Campaign*, pp. 142–9; Tinniswood, *Pirates of Barbary*, pp. 242–53.

16. Earl of Portland, cited by Hills, *Rock of Contention*, pp. 157–8; M. Alexander, *Gibraltar: Conquered by No Enemy* (Stroud, 2008), p. 45.

17. Hills, *Rock of Contention*, pp. 158–9.

18. S. Conn, *Gibraltar in British Diplomacy in the Eighteenth Century* (New Haven, CT, 1942), p. 5.

19. Hills, *Rock of Contention*, pp. 167–9, and appendix A, pp. 475–7; M. Harvey, *Gibraltar: a History* (2nd edn, Staplehurst, Kent, 2000), p. 65; S. Constantine, *Community and Identity: the Making of Modern Gibraltar since 1704* (Manchester, 2009), p. 12.

20. Cited in Hills, *Rock of Contention*, p. 174 from council minutes.

21. Ibid., pp. 176–7.

22. Ibid., pp. 183, 195.

23. Cited in Conn, *Gibraltar in British Diplomacy*, p. 6.

24. Passages cited in Hills, *Rock of Contention*, pp. 204–5.

25. Ibid., p. 219.

26. Utrecht clauses, ibid., pp. 222–3; Conn, *Gibraltar in British Diplomacy*, pp. 18–22, 25–6.

27. Constantine, *Community and Identity*, pp. 14–34.

28. Baltharpe, *Straights Voyage*, pp. xxv, 61.

29. D. Gregory, *Minorca, the Illusory Prize: a history of the British Occupations of Minorca between 1708 and 1802* (Rutherford, NJ, 1990), pp. 206–7; Conn, *Gibraltar in British Diplomacy*, pp. 28–111; M. Mata, *Conquests and Reconquests of Menorca* (Barcelona, 1984), pp. 129–60.

30. Gregory, *Minorca*, p. 26.

31. J. Sloss, *A Small Affair: the French Occupation of Menorca during the Seven Years War* (Tetbury, 2000), pp. 40–43; Gregory, *Minorca*, pp. 35–6, 144–6.

32. Cited by Gregory, *Minorca*, p. 26.

33. Mata, *Conquests and Reconquests*, p. 160.

34. Ibid., p. 163; J. Sloss, *Richard Kane Governor of Minorca* (Tetbury, 1995), p. 224; Gregory, *Minorca*, pp. 59–60, 151.

35. Gregory, *Minorca*, pp. 90, 156; Mata, *Conquests and Reconquests*, p. 164.

36. E. Frangakis-Syrett, *The Commerce of Smyrna in the Eighteenth Century, 1700–1820* (Athens, 1992), pp. 119–21, 131; Gregory, *Minorca*, pp. 144, 149–55, and p. 247, n. 1, summarizing figures from R. Davis, *The Rise of the English Shipping Industry in the Seventeenth and Eighteenth Centuries* (Newton Abbot, 1962), p. 256; R. Davis, 'English foreign trade', in W. Minchinton (ed.), *The Growth of English Overseas Trade in the Seventeenth and*

Eighteenth Centuries (London, 1969), p. 108 and table opposite p. 118; Gregory, *Minorca*, pp. 144, 149–55.

37. Sloss, *Richard Kane*, p. 210; Gregory, *Minorca*, pp. 71, 119, 122, 132–4.
38. Gregory, *Minorca*, pp. 126–7; Mata, *Conquests and Reconquests*, p. 164.
39. Mata, *Conquests and Reconquests*, pp. 237–8.
40. Sloss, *Small Affair*, pp. 2–4.
41. Mr Consul Banks, in H. W. Richmond (ed.), *Papers Relating to the Loss of Minorca in 1756* (Navy Records Society, London, 1913), vol. 42, p. 34, and see also pp. 38, 50; B. Tunstall, *Admiral Byng and the Loss of Minorca* (London, 1928), pp. 22, 32, 39; D. Pope, *At 12 Mr Byng Was Shot* (London, 1962), pp. 36, 38 and p. 315, n. 6.
42. Pope, *At 12 Mr Byng Was Shot*, pp. 59–60, 65.
43. Tunstall, *Admiral Byng*, p. 103.
44. Sloss, *Small Affair*, pp. 7–16.
45. Text in Pope, *At 12 Mr Byng Was Shot*, appendix v, p. 311; Tunstall, *Admiral Byng*, pp. 137–9.
46. Pope, *At 12 Mr Byng Was Shot*, pp. 294–302.
47. I. de Madariaga, *Britain, Russia, and the Armed Neutrality of 1780: Sir James Harris's Mission to St Petersburg during the American Revolution* (New Haven, CT and London, 1962), pp. 239–63, 295–300.

8. The View through the Russian Prism, 1760–1805

1. R. C. Anderson, *Naval Wars in the Levant 1559–1853* (Liverpool, 1951), pp. 237–42, 270–76.
2. M. S. Anderson, 'Great Britain and the Russian fleet, 1769–70', *Slavonic and East European Review*, vol. 31 (1952), pp. 148–50, 152, 154.
3. N. Saul, *Russia and the Mediterranean 1797–1807* (Chicago, IL, 1970), p. 4.
4. Anderson, 'Great Britain and the Russian fleet', p. 150; M. S. Anderson, 'Great Britain and the Russo-Turkish war of 1768–74', *English Historical Review*, vol. 69 (1954), pp. 39–58.
5. Anderson, 'Great Britain and the Russian fleet', pp. 153, 155–6, 158–9; Anderson, 'Great Britain and the Russo-Turkish war', pp. 44–5; Anderson, *Naval Wars in the Levant*, p. 281; D. Gregory, *Minorca, the Illusory Prize: a History of the British Occupations of Minorca between 1708 and 1802* (Rutherford, NJ, 1990), p. 141.
6. Anderson, *Naval Wars in the Levant*, pp. 286–91; E. V. Tarlé, *Chesmenskii boy i pervaya russkaya ekspeditsiya v Arkhipelag 1769–1774* (Moscow, 1945), p. 105, n. 1; F. S. Krinitsyn, *Chesmenskoye srazhenye* (Moscow, 1962), pp. 32–4 (maps).
7. Anderson, 'Great Britain and the Russo-Turkish war', pp. 56–7.
8. Anderson, *Naval Wars in the Levant*, pp. 286–305.

9. Saul, *Russia and the Mediterranean*, pp. 7–8; Anderson, 'Great Britain and the Russo-Turkish war', p. 46.

10. S. Conn, *Gibraltar in British Diplomacy in the Eighteenth Century* (New Haven, CT, 1942), pp. 174–6, 189–98; T. H. McGuffie, *The Siege of Gibraltar 1779–1783* (London, 1965); M. Alexander, *Gibraltar: Conquered by No Enemy* (Stroud, 2008), pp. 92–114.

11. I. de Madariaga, *Britain, Russia and the Armed Neutrality of 1780: Sir James Harris's Mission to St Petersburg during the American Revolution* (New Haven, CT and London, 1962), pp. 240–44, 250–52, 258, 263, 298–9; Gregory, *Minorca*, pp. 187–99.

12. Cited by Saul, *Russia and the Mediterranean*, p. 12, from *Annual Register of 1788, or a View of the History, Politics, and Literature for the Year 1788* (London, 1789), p. 59.

13. M. S. Anderson, 'Russia in the Mediterranean, 1788–1791: a little-known chapter in the history of naval warfare and privateering', *Mariner's Mirror*, vol. 45 (1959), p. 26.

14. Ibid., pp. 27–31.

15. Saul, *Russia and the Mediterranean*, pp. 178–9.

16. Ibid., p. 27.

17. R. Cavaliero, *The Last of the Crusaders: the Knights of St John and Malta in the Eighteenth Century* (2nd edn, London, 2009), p. 103.

18. Ibid., pp. 144–9.

19. Ibid., pp. 181–201.

20. D. Gregory, *Malta, Britain, and the European Powers, 1793–1815* (Cranbury, NJ, 1996), p. 105; Cavaliero, *Last of the Crusaders*, pp. 155, 158.

21. Cf. Saul, *Russia and the Mediterranean*, p. 35.

22. Gregory, *Malta, Britain*, p. 106; Saul, *Russia and the Mediterranean*, pp. 36–8.

23. M. Crook, *Toulon in War and Revolution: from the* Ancien Régime *to the Restoration, 1750–1820* (Manchester, 1991), pp. 139–48; D. Gregory, *The Ungovernable Rock: a History of the Anglo-Corsican Kingdom and its Role in Britain's Mediterranean Strategy during the Revolutionary War (1793–1797)* (Madison, WI, 1985), pp. 52–7; N. A. M. Rodger, *The Command of the Ocean: a Naval History of Britain 1649–1815* (London, 2004), p. 429.

24. P. Mackesy, *The War in the Mediterranean 1803–1810* (London, 1957), pp. 5, 7, 13.

25. Gregory, *Ungovernable Rock*, pp. 30–31, 47.

26. D. Carrington, *Granite Island: a Portrait of Corsica* (London, 1971).

27. Gregory, *Ungovernable Rock*, pp. 63, 73, 80–84.

28. Huntingdon Record Office, Sismey papers 3658/E4 (e).

29. Cited by Saul, *Russia and the Mediterranean*, p. 39, from J. E. Howard, *Letters and Documents of Napoleon*, vol. 1, *The Rise to Power* (London, 1961), p. 191.

30. Cavaliero, *Last of the Crusaders*, pp. 9–101.

31. Saul, *Russia and the Mediterranean*, pp. 39–40.

32. Cavaliero, *Last of the Crusaders*, pp. 223, 226.

33. Ibid., pp. 223–4; Saul, *Russia and the Mediterranean*, pp. 41–2.

34. Cf. Saul, *Russia and the Mediterranean*, p. 45.

35. Cavaliero, *Last of the Crusaders*, pp. 236, 238, 242.

36. Count Philip Cobenzl, cited ibid., p. 238; Gregory, *Malta, Britain*, p. 108.

37. R. Knight, *The Pursuit of Victory: the Life and Achievement of Horatio Nelson* (London, 2005), pp. 288–303; P. Padfield, *Maritime Power and the Struggle for Freedom: Naval Campaigns That Shaped the Modern World 1788–1851* (London, 2003), pp. 147–71.

38. Saul, *Russia and the Mediterranean*, p. 65.

39. Knight, *Pursuit of Victory*, p. 675.

40. Saul, *Russia and the Mediterranean*, pp. 79, 87; Gregory, *Malta, Britain*, p. 109.

41. Saul, *Russia and the Mediterranean*, p. 99.

42. Cited ibid., pp. 124–9.

43. Ibid., p. 128.

44. Gregory, *Malta, Britain*, pp. 113, 115.

45. Saul, *Russia and the Mediterranean*, pp. 145–6.

46. Knight, *Pursuit of Victory*, pp. 362–84.

47. Saul, *Russia and the Mediterranean*, pp. 162–3; Gregory, *Malta, Britain*, pp. 116–40.

48. Cited by Saul, *Russia and the Mediterranean*, p. 185.

49. Ibid., p. 186.

50. Knight, *Pursuit of Victory*, pp. 437–50.

51. Ibid., pp. 501–24.

52. Saul, *Russia and the Mediterranean*, p. 198.

53. R. Harris, *Dubrovnik: a History* (London, 2003), pp. 397–401.

54. Anderson, *Naval Wars in the Levant*, pp. 431–7; Saul, *Russia and the Mediterranean*, pp. 198–206.

55. Harris, *Dubrovnik*, p. 397.

56. Anderson, *Naval Wars in the Levant*, pp. 449–53.

57. Anderson, *Naval Wars in the Levant*, pp. 457–8; Mackesy, *War in the Mediterranean*, p. 211; Saul, *Russia and the Mediterranean*, pp. 216–20, 222; L. Sondhaus, *The Habsburg Empire and the Sea: Austrian Naval Policy 1797–1866* (West Lafayette, IN, 1989), p. 19.

9. Deys, Beys and Bashaws, 1800–1830

1. P. Mackesy, *The War in the Mediterranean 1803–1810* (London, 1957), pp. 121–53.

2. In 1803: ibid., p. 21.

3. Ibid., pp. 98, 319.

4. Ibid., appendices 1 and 5, pp. 398, 403–4.

5. R. Knight, *The Pursuit of Victory: the Life and Achievement of Horatio Nelson* (London, 2005), p. 555.

6. Mackesy, *War in the Mediterranean*, p. 229.

7. Ibid., pp. 352–5; L. Sondhaus, *The Habsburg Empire and the Sea: Austrian Naval Policy 1797–1866* (West Lafayette, IN, 1989), p. 42; M. Pratt, *Britain's Greek Empire: Reflections on the History of the Ionian Islands from the Fall of Byzantium* (London, 1978).

8. D. Gregory, *Sicily, the Insecure Base: a History of the British Occupation of Sicily, 1806–1815* (Madison, WI, 1988); Knight, *Pursuit of Victory*, pp. 307–27.

9. Mackesy, *War in the Mediterranean*, p. 375.

10. F. Tabak, *The Waning of the Mediterranean 1550–1870: a Geohistorical Approach* (Baltimore, MD, 2008), pp. 221–5; D. Mack Smith, *A History of Sicily*, vol. 3, *Modern Sicily after 1713* (London, 1968), pp. 272–4; Gregory, *Sicily*, p. 37.

11. L. Wright and J. Macleod, *The First Americans in North Africa: William Eaton's Struggle for a Vigorous Policy against the Barbary Pirates, 1799–1805* (Princeton, NJ, 1945), pp. 66–8; F. Lambert, *The Barbary Wars: American Independence in the Atlantic World* (New York, 2005), p. 91; R. C. Anderson, *Naval Wars in the Levant 1559–1853* (Liverpool, 1951), pp. 394–5.

12. Lambert, *Barbary Wars*, p. 90.

13. Testimony of Elijah Shaw in M. Kitzen, *Tripoli and the United States at War: a History of American Relations with the Barbary States, 1785–1805* (Jefferson, NC, 1993), pp. 97–101.

14. J. London, *Victory in Tripoli: How America's War with the Barbary Pirates Established the U.S. Navy and Shaped a Nation* (Hoboken, NJ, 2005).

15. J. Wheelan, *Jefferson's War: America's First War on Terror 1801–1805* (New York, 2003), pp. xxiii, 1, 7, etc.; Lambert, *Barbary Wars*, pp. 106–7.

16. F. Leiner, *The End of Barbary Terror: America's 1815 War against the Pirates of North Africa* (New York, 2006), p. ix.

17. Lambert, *Barbary Wars*, p. 118.

18. Ibid., p. 8; also pp. 109–13.

19. Ibid., pp. 9, 11, 23.

20. Ibid., pp. 47, 50, 76.

21. Wright and Macleod, *First Americans*, p. 48.

22. Kitzen, *Tripoli*, pp. 49–50.

23. Cited *in extenso* in R. Zacks, *The Pirate Coast: Thomas Jefferson, the First Marines, and the Secret Mission of 1805* (New York, 2005), pp. 189–90.

24. Leiner, *End of Barbary Terror*, p. 19.

25. Wright and Macleod, *First Americans*, pp. 54–5; Lambert, *Barbary Wars*, p. 31.

26. Lambert, *Barbary Wars*, pp. 30, 34.

27. Kitzen, *Tripoli*, pp. 19–20; Lambert, *Barbary Wars*, p. 87.

28. Lambert, *Barbary Wars*, pp. 100–103; Kitzen, *Tripoli*, pp. 40–42; Wheelan, *Jefferson's War*, pp. 96–7; Anderson, *Naval Wars in the Levant*, p. 396.

29. Lambert, *Barbary Wars*, p. 101; Anderson, *Naval Wars in the Levant*, pp. 397, 403.

30. Lambert, *Barbary Wars*, pp. 133–4; Anderson, *Naval Wars in the Levant*, p. 407.

31. Lambert, *Barbary Wars*, pp. 140–44; Kitzen, *Tripoli*, pp. 93–113.

32. Lambert, *Barbary Wars*, pp. 146–8; Kitzen, *Tripoli*, p. 122, and plates on pp. 123–4.

33. Lambert, *Barbary Wars*, pp. 130–54; Kitzen, *Tripoli*, pp. 135–76.

34. Leiner, *End of Barbary Terror*, p. 23.

35. Ibid., pp. 26–36.

36. Navy orders to Decatur: ibid., appendix i, pp. 183–6.

37. Lambert, *Barbary Wars*, pp. 189–93; Leiner, *End of Barbary Terror*, pp. 87–122, and appendix iii, pp. 189–94 for the Algiers treaty.

38. Leiner, *End of Barbary Terror*, appendix iii, pp. 189–94 (p. 189 for article 2); Lambert, *Barbary Wars*, p. 195.

39. G. Contis, 'Environment, health and disease in Alexandria and the Nile Delta', in A. Hirst and M. Silk (eds.), *Alexandria, Real and Imagined* (2nd edn, Cairo, 2006), p. 229.

40. O. Abdel-Aziz Omar, 'Alexandria during the period of the Ottoman conquest to the end of the reign of Ismail', in *The History and Civilisation of Alexandria across the Ages* (2nd edn, Alexandria, 2000), pp. 154, 158–9.

41. Anderson, *Naval Wars in the Levant*, pp. 483, 486–7.

42. Ibid., p. 508; Sondhaus, *Habsburg Empire and the Sea*, p. 63.

43. Anderson, *Naval Wars in the Levant*, pp. 492–3.

44. Ibid., pp. 523–36.

45. K. Fahmy, 'Towards a social history of modern Alexandria', in Hirst and Silk (eds.), *Alexandria, Real and Imagined*, pp. 283–4.

46. J. Abun-Nasr, *A History of the Maghrib in the Islamic Period* (Cambridge, 1987), p. 249.

47. Ibid., pp. 164, 166, 251, 254.

48. Ibid., p. 261.

PART FIVE

THE FIFTH MEDITERRANEAN, 1830–2010

1. Ever the Twain Shall Meet, 1830–1900

1. Cf. E. Said's tendentious *Orientalism* (London, 1978).

2. Z. Karabell, *Parting the Desert: the Creation of the Suez Canal* (London, 2003), pp. 147, 183.

3. Ibid., pp. 28–37; J. Marlowe, *The Making of the Suez Canal* (London, 1964), pp. 44–5.

4. Marlowe, *Making of the Suez Canal*, pp. 1–3.

5. Karabell, *Parting the Desert*, pp. 56–7; Lord Kinross, *Between Two Seas: the Creation of the Suez Canal* (London, 1968), pp. 20–30.

6. Kinross, *Between Two Seas*, pp. 32–3; R. Coons, *Steamships, Statesmen, and Bureaucrats: Austrian Policy towards the Steam Navigation Company of the Austrian Lloyd 1836–1848* (Wiesbaden, 1975), pp. 148–61.

7. Karabell, *Parting the Desert*, pp. 131–2; Kinross, *Between Two Seas*, pp. 98–9.

8. Karabell, *Parting the Desert*, p. 183.

9. Ibid., pp. 208–11; Kinross, *Between Two Seas*, pp. 222–5.

10. Marlowe, *Making of the Suez Canal*, pp. 227, 231.

11. Karabell, *Parting the Desert*, p. 254; Kinross, *Between Two Seas*, p. 246.

12. Kinross, *Between Two Seas*, p. 253.

13. G. Lo Giudice, *L'Austria, Trieste ed il Canale di Suez* (2nd edn of *Trieste, l'Austria ed il Canale di Suez*, Catania, 1979) (Catania, 1981), pp. 163–7, 180–81; Kinross, *Between Two Seas*, p. 287; Karabell, *Parting the Desert*, p. 269.

14. Lo Giudice, *Austria, Trieste*, p. 180, table 20; p. 181, graph 7; Board of Trade report cited in Marlowe, *Making of the Suez Canal*, p. 260.

15. Karabell, *Parting the Desert*, p. 260; Kinross, *Between Two Seas*, p. 287.

16. Marlowe, *Making of the Suez Canal*, pp. 255–75; Karabell, *Parting the Desert*, pp. 262–5; R. Blake, *Disraeli* (London, 1966), pp. 581–7.

17. Marlowe, *Making of the Suez Canal*, pp. 255–75, 313–20; Kinross, *Between Two Seas*, pp. 293–309, 313–14; Karabell, *Parting the Desert*, pp. 262–5.

18. Cited in Coons, *Steamships, Statesmen*, p. 55: 'Dämpschiffe warden und können niemals Frachtschiffe seyn'.

19. Ibid., pp. 26–7, 35, 63.

20. Ibid., p. 61.

21. L. Sondhaus, *The Habsburg Empire and the Sea: Austrian Naval Policy 1797–1866* (West Lafayette, IN, 1989), p. 95.

22. Cited by Coons, *Steamships, Statesmen*, p. 63.

23. U. Cova, *Commercio e navigazione a Trieste e nella monarchia asburgica da Maria Teresa al 1915* (Civiltà del Risorgimento, vol. 45, Udine, 1992), p. 171, n. 13; Coons, *Steamships, Statesmen*, pp. 129–32.

24. Sondhaus, *Habsburg Empire and the Sea*, pp. 5–7, 13, 36.

25. Ibid., pp. 184–7, 209–13.

26. Ibid., pp. 252–9, 273 (battle diagram).

27. Ibid., pp. 36–8, 129, 151, 178–9, 259; L. Sondhaus, *The Naval Policy of Austria-Hungary, 1867–1918* (West Lafayette, IN, 1994), pp. 6–7.

28. Cited in Coons, *Steamships, Statesmen*, p. 3; see also Lo Giudice, *Austria, Trieste*, p. 221.

29. Cova, *Commercio e navigazione*, pp. 10, 28–9, 74–5; Sondhaus, *Habsburg Empire and the Sea*, pp. 2–3, 12–13.

30. L. Dubin, *The Port Jews of Habsburg Trieste: Absolutist Politics and Enlightenment Culture* (Stanford, CA, 1999), pp. 44–5.

31. Ibid., pp. 3–4, 10–17, 43.

32. Ibid., pp. 164–73.
33. Ibid., p. 32; Coons, *Steamships, Statesmen*, p. 9; Cova, *Commercio e navigazione*, p. 153.
34. C. Russell, 'Italo Svevo's Trieste', *Italica*, vol. 52 (1975), pp. 3–36; A. J. P. Taylor, *The Habsburg Monarchy 1809–1918: a History of the Austrian Empire and Austria-Hungary* (London, 1948), pp. 201–3.
35. Lo Giudice, *Austria, Trieste*, pp. 135, 137, 142, 145–6, tables 8, 9, 10, 14, 16.
36. Ibid., pp. 205–6, table 29 and graph 13.

2. The Greek and the unGreek, 1830–1920

1. J. Black, *The British Abroad: the Grand Tour in the Eighteenth Century* (Stroud, 1992).
2. R. Jenkins, *The Victorians and Ancient Greece* (Oxford, 1980), pp. 133–9.
3. Ibid., pp. 313–15, 318–24; C. Wood, *Olympian Dreamers: Victorian Classical Painters 1860–1914* (London, 1983), pp. 106–30; *J. W. Waterhouse: the Modern Pre-Raphaelite* (Royal Academy of Arts, London, 2009).
4. C. Gere, *Knossos and the Prophets of Modernism* (Chicago, IL, 2009), p. 20.
5. Ibid., pp. 38–44.
6. T. Detorakis, *History of Crete* (Iraklion, 1994), pp. 368–72.
7. Ibid., pp. 295–6, 320–26, 349 (very biased).
8. Gere, *Knossos*, p. 73.
9. Ibid., pp. 67, 82–5.
10. A. Gazioğlu, *The Turks in Cyprus: a Province of the Ottoman Empire (1571–1878)* (London and Nicosia, 1990), pp. 220, 242–8.
11. Ibid., pp. 216–17.
12. Giovanni Mariti (1769), cited ibid., p. 155.
13. Archduke Louis Salvator of Austria, ibid., pp. 164–5.
14. Ibid., pp. 225–34.
15. R. Rhodes James, *Gallipoli* (2nd edn, London, 2004), p. 4.
16. A. Nevzat, *Nationalism amongst the Turks of Cyprus: the First Wave* (Acta Universitatis Ouluensis, Humaniora, Oulu, 2005).
17. M. Mazower, *Salonica, City of Ghosts: Christians, Muslims and Jews 1430–1950* (London, 2004), p. 6.
18. Ibid., p. 194.
19. Ibid., p. 242.
20. Ibid., p. 253.
21. L. Sciaky, *Farewell to Ottoman Salonica* (Istanbul, 2000), p. 37 (another edition, as *Farewell to Salonica: a City at the Crossroads*, London, 2007).
22. R. Patai, *Vanished Worlds of Jewry* (London, 1981), pp. 90–91; Mazower, *Salonica*, p. 237.
23. Mazower, *Salonica*, p. 234; also Sciaky, *Farewell to Ottoman Salonica*, pp. 92–3.

24. Sciaky, *Farewell to Ottoman Salonica*, p. 37.
25. Mazower, *Salonica*, pp. 264–5; Sciaky, *Farewell to Ottoman Salonica*, pp. 73–4.
26. Mazower, *Salonica*, pp. 266–8; Sciaky, *Farewell to Ottoman Salonica*, pp. 75–81.
27. Mazower, *Salonica*, p. 303.

3. Ottoman Exit, 1900–1918

1. R. Patai, *Vanished Worlds of Jewry* (London, 1981), p. 120.
2. J. Abun-Nasr, *A History of the Maghrib in the Islamic Period* (Cambridge, 1987), pp. 309, 376–81.
3. Ibid., pp. 281–93.
4. Ibid., pp. 319–23.
5. N. Doumanis, *Myth and Memory in the Mediterranean: Remembering Fascism's Empire* (Basingstoke, 1997).
6. R. Rhodes James, *Gallipoli* (2nd edn, London, 2004), pp. 9–11; P. Halpern, *The Mediterranean Naval Situation 1908–1914* (Cambridge, MA, 1971), pp. 357–8; M. Hickey, *The First World War*, vol. 4: *The Mediterranean Front 1914–1923* (Botley, Oxon, 2002), pp. 33–4.
7. Hickey, *Mediterranean Front*, p. 36.
8. Rhodes James, *Gallipoli*, pp. 23, 33–7.
9. Ibid., pp. 16–17; P. Halpern, *A Naval History of World War I* (London, 1994), pp. 106–9.
10. Cited by Rhodes James, *Gallipoli*, p. 33.
11. Ibid., p. 38.
12. Ibid., pp. 40–41; Halpern, *Naval History*, pp. 112, 118.
13. Rhodes James, *Gallipoli*, pp. 61–4; Halpern, *Naval History*, p. 115.
14. Halpern, *Naval History*, p. 113.
15. J. W. Streets, 'Gallipoli', in L. Macdonald (ed.), *Anthem for Doomed Youth: Poets of the Great War* (London, 2000), p. 45.
16. Rhodes James, *Gallipoli*, p. 348; Halpern, *Naval History*, pp. 106–9.
17. Halpern, *Mediterranean Naval Situation*, pp. 287–90.
18. L. Sondhaus, *The Naval Policy of Austria-Hungary, 1867–1918* (West Lafayette, IN, 1994), pp. 318–24.
19. Ibid., pp. 258–9; Halpern, *Mediterranean Naval Situation*, p. 365; Halpern, *Naval History*, pp. 142–3.
20. Sondhaus, *Naval Policy of Austria-Hungary*, pp. 275–9, 286; Halpern, *Naval History*, pp. 148, 381–5; P. Halpern, *The Naval War in the Mediterranean, 1914–1918* (London, 1987), pp. 107–19, 132–3.
21. Sondhaus, *Naval Policy of Austria-Hungary*, pp. 285–6.
22. Halpern, *Mediterranean Naval Situation*, pp. 329–30, 337–42; Sondhaus,

Naval Policy of Austria-Hungary, pp. 307–8; Halpern, *Naval History*, p. 393; Halpern, *Naval War*, p. 344.

23. Halpern, *Naval History*, p. 396; Halpern, *Naval War*, pp. 386–94.

4. A Tale of Four and a Half Cities, 1900–1950

1. M. Housepian, *Smyrna 1922* (London, 1972), p. 83.
2. G. Milton, *Paradise Lost – Smyrna 1922: the Destruction of Islam's City of Tolerance* (London, 2008), pp. 84–8.
3. H. Georgelin, *La fin de Smyrne: du cosmopolitisme aux nationalismes* (Paris, 2005); M.-C. Smyrnelis (ed.), *Smyrne: la ville oubliée? Mémoires d'un grand port ottoman, 1830–1930* (Paris, 2006).
4. Milton, *Paradise Lost – Smyrna 1922*, pp. 86–7, 98–9; Housepian, *Smyrna 1922*, pp. 124–5.
5. H. Nahum, 'En regardant une photographie: une famille juive de Smyrne en 1900', in Smyrnelis, *Smyrne: la ville oubliée?*, p. 103.
6. E. Frangakis-Syrett, *The Commerce of Smyrna in the Eighteenth Century, 1700–1820* (Athens, 1992), pp. 121, 207–14; E. Frangakis-Syrett, 'Le développement d'un port méditerranéen d'importance internationale: Smyrne (1700–1914)', in Smyrnelis, *Smyrne: la ville oubliée?*, pp. 23, 37, 45–9; and in the same volume, O. Schmitt, 'Levantins, Européens et jeux d'identité', pp. 106–19.
7. Milton, *Paradise Lost – Smyrna 1922*, pp. 16–19; Frangakis-Syrett, 'Développement d'un port', p. 41.
8. Georgelin, *Fin de Smyrne*, pp. 44–50.
9. Milton, *Paradise Lost – Smyrna 1922*, pp. 36–8, 121, 127–8, 155, 178.
10. Ibid., pp. 128–34; Housepian, *Smyrna 1922*, pp. 63–4, 76.
11. Milton, *Paradise Lost – Smyrna 1922*, pp. 176, 322, 332, 354; Housepian, *Smyrna 1922*, pp. 191–2.
12. M. Haag, *Alexandria Illustrated* (2nd edn, Cairo, 2004), pp. 8–20; M. Haag, *Alexandria, City of Memory* (New Haven, CT, 2004), pp. 150–51.
13. Haag, *Alexandria, City of Memory*, p. 17; E. Breccia, *Alexandria ad Aegyptum: a Guide to the Ancient and Modern Town and to its Graeco-Roman Museum* (Bergamo and Alexandria, 1922); K. Fahmy, 'Towards a social history of modern Alexandria', in A. Hirst and M. Silk (eds.), *Alexandria Real and Imagined* (2nd edn, Cairo, 2006), p. 282.
14. Haag, *Alexandria, City of Memory*, pp. 136–7.
15. R. Mabro, 'Alexandria 1860–1960: the cosmopolitan identity', in Hirst and Silk, *Alexandria Real and Imagined*, pp. 254–7.
16. J. Mawas and N. Mawas (*née* Pinto) speaking in M. Awad and S. Hamouda, *Voices from Cosmopolitan Alexandria* (Alexandria, 2006), p. 41.
17. A. Aciman, *Out of Egypt* (London, 1996), p. 4; K. Fahmy, 'For Cavafy, with love and squalor: some critical notes on the history and historiography of

modern Alexandria', in Hirst and Silk, *Alexandria Real and Imagined*, pp. 274–7.

18. Haag, *Alexandria, City of Memory*, pp. 139–50.

19. L. Durrell, *Justine* (London, 1957); also his *Bitter Lemons of Cyprus* (London, 1957).

20. M. Awad and S. Hamouda (eds.), *The Zoghebs: an Alexandrian Saga* (Alexandria and Mediterranean Research Center monographs, vol. 2, Alexandria, 2005), p. xxxix.

21. S. Hamouda, *Omar Toussoun Prince of Alexandria* (Alexandria and Mediterranean Research Center monographs, vol. 1, Alexandria, 2005), pp. 11, 27, 35.

22. Cited by M. Allott in E. M. Forster, *Alexandria: a History and Guide and Pharos and Pharillon*, ed. M. Allott (London, 2004), p. xv.

23. Cavafy's 'The gods abandon Antony', trans. D. Ricks, 'Cavafy's Alexandrianism', in Hirst and Silk, *Alexandria Real and Imagined*, p. 346; E. Keeley, *Cavafy's Alexandria* (2nd edn, Princeton, NJ, 1996), p. 6; Fahmy, 'For Cavafy', p. 274; also N. Woodsworth, *The Liquid Continent: a Mediterranean Trilogy*, vol. 1, *Alexandria* (London, 2009), p. 175.

24. Y. Shavit, *Tel Aviv: naissance d'une ville (1909–1936)* (Paris, 2004), pp. 9, 44–6.

25. J. Schlör, *Tel Aviv: from Dream to City* (London, 1999), pp. 43–4; M. LeVine, *Overthrowing Geography: Jaffa, Tel Aviv, and the Struggle for Palestine, 1880–1948* (Berkeley and Los Angeles, CA, 2005), pp. 60, 72.

26. Schlör, *Tel Aviv*, p. 211.

27. Cited in A. LeBor, *City of Oranges: Arabs and Jews in Jaffa* (London, 2006), p. 30; Shavit, *Tel Aviv*, p. 31.

28. LeVine, *Overthrowing Geography*, p. 285, n. 2.

29. *Bare Feet on Golden Sands: the Abulafia Family's Story* (Hebrew) (Tel Aviv, 2006), pp. 18–21.

30. Shavit, *Tel Aviv*, pp. 81–4.

31. LeBor, *City of Oranges*, pp. 12–13; LeVine, *Overthrowing Geography*, pp. 33–4.

32. LeBor, *City of Oranges*, pp. 38–41; Schlör, *Tel Aviv*, p. 208.

33. Shavit, *Tel Aviv*, pp. 90–91.

34. Ibid., pp. 9, 34.

35. Ibid., pp. 55–6.

36. LeVine, *Overthrowing Geography*, p. 88; LeBor, *City of Oranges*, pp. 46–7; Schlör, *Tel Aviv*, pp. 180, 183–5.

37. Schlör, *Tel Aviv*, pp. 191–9.

38. LeVine, *Overthrowing Geography*, p. 138, fig. 8.

39. P. Halpern, *The Naval War in the Mediterranean, 1914–1918* (London, 1987), pp. 295–300; M. Hickey, *The First World War*, vol. 4: *The Mediterranean Front 1914–1923* (Botley, Oxon, 2002), pp. 65–9.

40. M. Mazower, *Salonica, City of Ghosts: Christians, Muslims and Jews 1430–1950* (London, 2004), pp. 345, 359–60.

41. Ibid., pp. 402–8.

42. Ibid., pp. 423–4.
43. R. Patai, *Vanished Worlds of Jewry* (London, 1981), p. 97.
44. C. Ferrara degli Uberti, 'The "Jewish nation" of Livorno: a port Jewry on the road to emancipation', in D. Cesarani and G. Romain (eds.), *Jews and Port Cities 1590–1990: Commerce, Community and Cosmopolitanism* (London, 2006), p. 165; D. LoRomer, *Merchants and Reform in Livorno, 1814–1868* (Berkeley and Los Angeles, CA, 1987), p. 15.
45. LeBor, *City of Oranges*, pp. 2, 125–35; B. Morris, *The Birth of the Palestinian Refugee Problem, 1917–1949* (Cambridge, 1997), pp. 95–7, 101.
46. Ecclesiasticus 44:9.

5. *Mare Nostrum* – Again, 1918–1945

1. D. Porch, *Hitler's Mediterranean Gamble: the North African and the Mediterranean Campaigns in World War II* (London, 2004), pp. xi, 5, 661; S. Ball, *The Bitter Sea: the Struggle for Mastery in the Mediterranean, 1935–1949* (London, 2009), p. xxxiii.
2. Cited by Ball, *Bitter Sea*, pp. 10–11.
3. Porch, *Hitler's Mediterranean Gamble*, p. 48.
4. Ball, *Bitter Sea*, pp. 7, 18–19.
5. Ibid., pp. 20–23; M. Haag, *Alexandria, City of Memory* (New Haven, CT, 2004), p. 151.
6. H. Thomas, *The Spanish Civil War* (London, 1961), p. 279 and n. 2.
7. T. Spooner, *Supreme Gallantry: Malta's Role in the Allied Victory 1939–1945* (London, 1996), p. 14; C. Boffa, *The Second Great Siege: Malta, 1940–1943* (Malta, 1992).
8. Porch, *Hitler's Mediterranean Gamble*, pp. 12–16, 40–46.
9. Ibid., pp. 59–60; C. Smith, *England's Last War against France: Fighting Vichy 1940–1942* (London, 2009), p. 142.
10. Cited in Ball, *Bitter Sea*, p. 41.
11. Porch, *Hitler's Mediterranean Gamble*, p. 63; Ball, *Bitter Sea*, pp. 48, 50.
12. Smith, *England's Last War*, pp. 57–94; Porch, *Hitler's Mediterranean Gamble*, pp. 62–9.
13. Ball, *Bitter Sea*, p. 51; Porch, *Hitler's Mediterranean Gamble*, p. 358.
14. Porch, *Hitler's Mediterranean Gamble*, pp. 93–5; Ball, *Bitter Sea*, pp. 56–63.
15. Ball, *Bitter Sea*, p. 68.
16. Spooner, *Supreme Gallantry*, pp. 27, 40–42, 92, 187–205.
17. See e.g. Admiral of the Fleet Lord Lewin in Spooner, *Supreme Gallantry*, pp. xv–xvi.
18. Ball, *Bitter Sea*, p. 149.
19. Spooner, *Supreme Gallantry*, p. 17.
20. Porch, *Hitler's Mediterranean Gamble*, pp. 259–65; Ball, *Bitter Sea*, p. 133.

21. Spooner, *Supreme Gallantry*, p. 11.
22. Porch, *Hitler's Mediterranean Gamble*, pp. 158–76.
23. Ball, *Bitter Sea*, pp. 109, 148–9; Porch, *Hitler's Mediterranean Gamble*, pp. 348–51.
24. Porch, *Hitler's Mediterranean Gamble*, pp. 360–62; Ball, *Bitter Sea*, pp. 170–73; Smith, *England's Last War*, pp. 246–7, 424–5.
25. Ball, *Bitter Sea*, pp. 160–61, 167, 178, 186–7; Smith, *England's Last War*, pp. 350–51, 361–2, 366, 372–3, 402, 416.
26. Spooner, *Supreme Gallantry*, p. 281; Ball, *Bitter Sea*, p. 261.
27. Ball, *Bitter Sea*, pp. 200–209; Porch, *Hitler's Mediterranean Gamble*, p. 566.
28. Ball, *Bitter Sea*, p. 220; Porch, *Hitler's Mediterranean Gamble*, pp. 424, 429.
29. Ball, *Bitter Sea*, pp. 219–33, 239–40; Porch, *Hitler's Mediterranean Gamble*, pp. 430–52.
30. Porch, *Hitler's Mediterranean Gamble*, p. 597.
31. Ball, *Bitter Sea*, pp. 272–7, and for Moscow meeting, p. 280.

6. A Fragmented Mediterranean, 1945–1990

1. S. Ball, *The Bitter Sea: the Struggle for Mastery in the Mediterranean, 1935–1949* (London, 2009), pp. 303–6.
2. E. Leggett, *The Corfu Incident* (2nd edn, London, 1976), pp. 28–100.
3. Ibid., pp. 113, 128–30.
4. Ball, *Bitter Sea*, pp. 309, 323.
5. See, e.g., N. Bethell, *The Palestine Triangle: the Struggle between the British, the Jews and the Arabs 1935–48* (London, 1979); M. Gilbert, *Israel: a History* (London, 1998), pp. 153–250; A. Shlaim, *The Politics of Partition: King Abdullah, the Zionists and Palestine 1921–1951* (Oxford, 1990: 2nd edn of his *Collusion across the Jordan*, Oxford, 1988).
6. Ball, *Bitter Sea*, pp. 295, 305–14.
7. Cited by B. Morris, *The Birth of the Palestinian Refugee Problem, 1917–1949* (Cambridge, 1997), p. 87.
8. A. LeBor, *City of Oranges: Arabs and Jews in Jaffa* (London, 2006), p. 122.
9. A. Shlaim, *The Iron Wall: Israel and the Arab World* (London, 2000), pp. 118–19; Gilbert, *Israel*, pp. 306–11; see also Shlaim, *Politics of Partition*, p. 172.
10. Gilbert, *Israel*, pp. 297–8, 311–12, 317.
11. Shlaim, *Iron Wall*, pp. 172–3.
12. H. Thomas, *The Suez Affair* (London, 1967); Shlaim, *Iron Wall*, p. 184.
13. M. Oren, *Six Days of War: June 1967 and the Making of the Modern Middle East* (London, 2002), pp. 60–116.
14. G. Schachter, *The Italian South: Economic Development in Mediterranean Europe* (New York, 1965).
15. H. Frendo, *Malta's Quest for Independence: Reflections on the Course of*

Maltese History (Malta, 1989); B. Blouet, *The Story of Malta* (3rd edn, Malta, 1987), pp. 211–22.

16. L. Durrell, *Bitter Lemons of Cyprus* (London, 1957), pp. 193–4.

17. J. Ker-Lindsay, *Britain and the Cyprus Crisis 1963–1964* (Peleus: Studien zur Archäologie und Geschichte Griechenlands und Zyperns, vol. 27, Mannheim and Möhnesee, 2004), pp. 21, 51–65.

18. Durrell, *Bitter Lemons*, p. 159.

19. Ker-Lindsay, *Britain and the Cyprus Crisis*, p. 37.

20. M. Gruel-Dieudé, *Chypre et l'Union Européenne: mutations diplomatiques et politiques* (Paris, 2007), pp. 160, 165–6.

21. D. Ioannides, 'The dynamics and effects of tourism evolution in Cyprus', in Y. Apostolopoulos, P. Loukissas and L. Leontidou (eds.), *Mediterranean Tourism: Facets of Socioeconomic Development and Change* (London, 2001), p. 123.

22. M. Harvey, *Gibraltar: a History* (2nd edn, Staplehurst, Kent, 2000), pp. 167–8.

23. M. Alexander, *Gibraltar: Conquered by No Enemy* (Stroud, 2008), p. 237.

24. Private communication from Dr Charles Stanton.

25. Note the ambiguities in the approach of G. Hills, *Rock of Contention: a History of Gibraltar* (London, 1974).

26. Alexander, *Gibraltar*, p. 241.

27. S. Constantine, *Community and Identity: the Making of Modern Gibraltar since 1704* (Manchester, 2009), pp. 414–15.

7. The Last Mediterranean, 1950–2010

1. E. David, *A Book of Mediterranean Food* (London, 1950).

2. C. Roden, *Mediterranean Cookery* (London, 1987); J. Goldstein, *Cucina Ebraica: Flavors of the Italian Jewish Kitchen* (San Francisco, 1998).

3. Information kindly supplied by Dr V. A. Cremona, Maltese ambassador in Tunis, and by Julian Metcalf, Ministry of Justice and Home Affairs, Valletta.

4. L. Segreto, C. Manera and M. Pohl (eds.), *Europe at the Seaside: the Economic History of Mass Tourism in the Mediterranean* (London, 2009); Y. Apostolopoulos, P. Loukissas and L. Leontidou (eds.), *Mediterranean Tourism: Facets of Socioeconomic Development and Change* (London, 2001); P. Obrador Pons, M. Craig and P. Travlou (eds.), *Cultures of Mass Tourism: Doing the Mediterranean in the Age of Banal Mobilities* (Aldershot, 2009); N. Theuma, *Le tourisme en Méditerranée: une perspective socio-culturelle* (*Encyclopédie de la Méditerranée*, vol. 37, Malta and Aix-en-Provence, 2005).

5. P. Obrador Pons, M. Craig and P. Travlou, 'Corrupted seas: the Mediterranean in an age of mass mobility', in Obrador Pons et al. (eds.), *Cultures of Mass Tourism*, pp. 163, 167.

6. K. O'Reilly, 'Hosts and guests, guests and hosts; British residential tourism in the Costa del Sol', in Obrador Pons et al. (eds.), *Cultures of Mass Tourism*, pp. 129–42.

7. M. Boyer, 'Tourism in the French Mediterranean; history and transformation', in Apostolopoulos et al. (eds.), *Mediterranean Tourism*, p. 47.

8. P. Battilani, 'Rimini: an original mix of Italian style and foreign models', in Segreto et al. (eds.), *Europe at the Seaside*, p. 106.

9. Y. Mansfeld, 'Acquired tourism deficiency syndrome: planning and developing tourism in Israel', in Apostolopoulos et al. (eds.), *Mediterranean Tourism*, pp. 166–8.

10. P. Obrador Pons, 'The Mediterranean pool: cultivating hospitality in the coastal hotel', in Obrador Pons et al. (eds.), *Cultures of Mass Tourism*, pp. 98, 105 (fig. 5.3); D. Knox, 'Mobile practice and youth tourism', in the same volume, p. 150.

11. E. Furlough, 'Club Méditerranée, 1950–2002', in Segreto et al. (eds.), *Europe at the Seaside*, pp. 174–7.

12. Battilani, 'Rimini', pp. 107–9.

13. P. Blyth, 'The growth of British air package tours, 1945–1975', in Segreto et al. (eds.), *Europe at the Seaside*, pp. 11–30.

14. C. Manera and J. Garau-Taberner, 'The transformation of the economic model of the Balearic islands: the pioneers of mass tourism', in Segreto et al. (eds.), *Europe at the Seaside*, p. 36.

15. Ibid., p. 32.

16. Blyth, 'Growth of British air package tours', p. 13.

17. V. Monfort Mir and J. Ivars Baidal, 'Towards a sustained competitiveness of Spanish tourism', in Apostolopoulos et al. (eds.), *Mediterranean Tourism*, pp. 18, 27–30.

18. Blyth, 'Growth of British air package tours', pp. 12–13.

19. P. Alac, *The Bikini: a Cultural History* (New York, 2002), p. 38.

20. I. Littlewood, *Sultry Climates: Travel and Sex since the Grand Tour* (London, 2001), pp. 189–215.

21. C. Probert, *Swimwear in Vogue since 1910* (London, 1981); Alac, *Bikini*, p. 21.

22. Alac, *Bikini*, pp. 54, 94; Obrador Pons, 'Mediterranean pool', p. 103.

23. D. Abulafia, 'The Mediterranean globalized', in D. Abulafia (ed.), *The Mediterranean in History* (London and New York, 2003), p. 312.

24. Theuma, *Tourisme en Méditerranée*, p. 43.

25. Knox, 'Mobile practice', pp. 150–51.

26. M. Crang and P. Travlou, 'The island that was not there: producing Corelli's island, staging Kefalonia', in Obrador Pons et al. (eds.), *Cultures of Mass Tourism*, pp. 75–89.

CONCLUSION

1. E. Paris, *La genèse intellectuelle de l'œuvre de Fernand Braudel: 'La Méditerranée et le monde méditerranéen à l'époque de Philippe II' (1921–1947)* (Athens, 1999), pp. 315–16, 323.

2. A. Husain and K. Fleming (eds.), *A Faithful Sea: The Religious Cultures of the Mediterranean, 1200–1700* (Oxford, 2007).

Index

Abano 632
Abbasids 263
Abdülhamid II, Ottoman sultan 568
Abi-milki 66
Aboukir Bay 518
Abraham of Saragossa 248
Abulafia, Abraham ben Samuel 342
Abulafia, Haim 480
Abulafia, Solomon 593
Abyssinia 601
Acciaiuoli Bank 375
Aciman, André 590
Acre 55, 291, 300, 310–11, 325–6, 327, 331, 349, 616
    fall of (1291) 354
    Military Orders of the Temple and Hospital 326
Actium 198
Adams, John Quincy 536
Adria 117
Adrianople 482
Adriatic Sea xxiii, xxx, 13, 98, 117–18, 126, 237, 385, 448
    and marshlands in the eighth century 251–4
    Turkish ships in 456
    Venetian–Genoese clashes in 377
    'Venetian Gulf' 358
    in World War I 580–81
Aegean
    Bronze Age 16–22, 27–8
    Byzantine 246
    Crete see Crete
    Cyclades see Cyclades

eastern 163
    Euboia see Euboia; Euboians
    Genoese control of 354
    grain sources 140
    Greek civilizations see Greek civilizations/cultures
    Levantine trade network 35
    Mesolithic 7
    northern 44, 135, 143
    pottery 20
    Rhodians and the Aegean islands 163
    Sea xxvii, 18, 27, 147, 365, 439;
        defended against the Persians 136–7; and the Peloponnesian War 147
    southern 16, 539
    struggle of islands against the Persians 132
    trade routes 17, 22, 44
    Turkish assaults on Venetian naval bases in 385
    'Tyrsenians' see 'Tyrsenians'
    Upper Palaeolithic 7
    western 87
    see also specific islands
Aelia Capitolina 216
    see also Jerusalem
Aeneas 74, 86, 189–90
Aeneid (Virgil) 74
Aeschylus 132–3, 137, 160
Aetheria 644
Aetius, Flavius 223, 232
Aetolian League 188
Aetos 87

Africa, North *see* North Africa
Agamemnon 45, 47, 565
Agathokles 173, 174
Agde 126
Aghlabid emirs 250
Agnon, Shemuel Yosef 593
agriculture
    and the Black Death 367, 368–9
    and economic complexity 227
    grain trade *see* grain trade
    kibbutz movement 592
    Neolithic 8, 9, 14
    North Africa 203–4
    over-exploitation of soil 234–5
    vineyards *see* vines/vineyards
Ahhiyawa 44
Ahiram, King, coffin 80
Ahmad ibn Hassan 309
Ahmet Pasha, Fazıl 481
Ahmet Pasha, Gedik 387
Ahura Mazda 135
Aï 58
Aigina 111, 143, 236
Aigospotamoi, battle of 147
Aigues-Mortes 358, 397
air travel 634, 637
Ajaccio 515
Akdeniz see White Sea
Akhenaten, Pharaoh 37
Akra Leuke 185
Akragas 167, 172, 173, 179, 186, 187
Akrotiri 27
al-Mahdiyyah *see* Mahdia
al-Mina 46, 91, 96
Alaksandu, king of Wilusa 44–5
Alalakh 46
Alalia 114
Alamanno da Costa 328
Alans 223, 230, 231
Alaric the Goth 223
Albania 55, 283, 350, 385, 391, 577, 613,
    614–15
    and China 623
    Italian invasion of 602–4
    tourists 636
Albertini tablets 232

Albigensian Crusade 335
alchemy 481
alcohol
    and the tourist industry 636–7
    wine *see* wine
Alcol 351
Aleppo 327, 367
Alexander I of Russia 520–21, 523
Alexander the Great 68, 149–52, 153, 159,
    174, 643
Alexander/Alexandros (Paris) 44
Alexandria xxxi, 38, 149–64, 197, 198,
    204, 236, 305–6, 569, 643
    attack by William II 323
    British bombardment of 555
    British fleet at 605
    bubonic plague 368
    Catalans in 345
    Church of 255
    cosmopolitan, early twentieth century
    589–92
    cult of Sarapis 154
    Delta settlement 153
    French in 606, 609
    grain trade 157, 158–9
    Greeks in 589–90
    Jews 153, 161, 162, 215, 218, 224,
    590–91
    Library 159–61, 197
    lighthouse of 154–5, 305, 309
    medical tradition 162
    Mouseion 159, 160
    and Peter I of Cyprus 359
    Ptolemaic 152–4, 155–62
    reconstituted from 1956 as a Muslim
    Arab city 600
    and Rhodes 157, 163–4
    science 162
    and the Septuagint 161–2
    trade with India 158, 207
    travel accounts of 256, 309–10
    and Venice 255–6, 292
    Victoria College 591
Alexios I Komnenos 283, 284–5, 293
Alexios IV Angelos 330
Alfonso I, 'the Battler' of Aragon 335

Alfonso IV of Aragon 361
Alfonso V, 'the Magnanimous' of Aragon
381–4, 398, 401, 402
Alfonso X of Castile 340
Alfonso XI of Castile 364
Alfonso XIII of Spain 580
Algeciras 97, 364
Algeria 528, 617–18
and the French 530, 540–41, 573–4,
621–2
Jews 531, 573–4
Operation Torch (World War II) 609
Alghero 275
Algiers 416, 417, 423, 461, 493
and America 533, 535–6
dey of 528, 531, 535, 540
and the French 573
French conquest of 540–41
in World War II 609–10
Ali Pasha of Ioannina 518, 525
Alicante 465
Alkibiades 145–6
Allatini family 570, 571
Allegheny, USS 535
Alliance Israélite Universelle (AIU) 570,
574, 585
Alma-Tadema, Lawrence 563–4
Almería 368, 393
Almohads 296, 298, 299, 310, 322, 332
disintegration of Almohad power 334
Ibn Jubayr 307–15
Almoravids 298, 336
Almuñécar 78
alphabet 36, 64
carried by Euboians 93
Etruscan 93, 110
Iberian 129
Phoenician 80, 644
alum 297, 347, 358, 366, 392–3
Alva, duke of 447
Alyattes 57
Amalfi 246, 256, 267–70, 294–5, 301, 316
merchants 294–5
Amarantus 218–19
Amaury, king of Jerusalem 324
amber 34, 91, 122, 285
America see United States of America

American School of Classical Studies,
Athens 3
American War of Independence 529
Amiens, Peace of 521
Amnisos 25
Amos 57–58
'Amr ibn al-'As 244, 549
Anatolia xxix, 8, 9, 83
Anatolian refugees in Salonika 598
Bronze Age 22, 34, 44–5
coast of Asia Minor 9, 27, 44, 96, 116,
123, 141, 161, 163, 202, 347, 358,
364–5, 384, 585
Hittites see Hittites
and the Mycenaeans 44–7
pottery 20
'purification' of 583
trading network 55
Troy see Troy
Turks in 364–5, 366
Anaxilas of Rhegion 115
Ancona 300, 436–8, 440, 442–3, 518
Ancona (Italian ship) 582
Andalucía 127, 129, 130, 453, 630
al-Andalus (Islamic Spain) 250, 258, 261,
263, 264, 306, 308, 476, 630
Andronikos I Komnenos 324
Andronikos II Palaiologos 354
Angevins 349–52, 353, 357, 360, 365, 401
Anghelu Ruju 119
Anglicanism 501
Anglican churches, Minorca 500
Anglo-French Dual Control Commission
554–5
animal hides see hides, animal
animal husbandry Neolithic 8
Anitta 22
Annaba 541
Annales school xxvi
Anne, Queen 497
Ansaldo de' Mari 349
Antibes 422, 644
Antikythera 162
Antioch 288–9, 290
Antium (Anzio) 175
'Antonius Maximus' 209
Antony, Mark 197–8

Antwerp 463
Anzio 175, 611
Aphrodite 221
apiru 48, 58
Apollo 138
Apollonia 117
Apollonios, administrator of Ptolemy II
157
Apollonios of Rhodes 160–61
Apuleius 199
Apulia 283, 288, 301, 322, 373, 387, 388
grain 351, 357, 358
tourism 637
trade with Dalmatia 389
Turkish raids 387
and the Venetians 388
Arab Higher Command 616
Arabs
and the Byzantine Empire 243–51
capture of Carthage 246
and Charlemagne 249–50
coinage 255, 257
conquest of Egypt 245; 1952 revolution
617
conquest of North Africa 245–6
early Arab expansion after death
of Muhammad 245
invasions xxix, 161, 234
Islam *see* Islam
of Jaffa 593, 594, 600
Muslim merchants 257, 258, 261–2,
266, 296, 404, 453, 457, 465
Muslim naval power/piracy 249,
250–51, 268, 278–9, 402, 414,
423–4
and Nasser 618–19
in Palestine 592, 594, 595, 616–17
revolt in the Great War 592
Aragon 335, 351
and Castile 398, 408–10
kings of 334–5, 338–41, 344, 345,
351, 353, 361–2, 364, 376, 379,
381–4, 387, 398–9, 401, 405,
420, 646
Moriscos of 475
Aragonese 351, 352, 364, 365
Angevins and 351–2

Catalan-Aragonese commonwealth
353, 361–3, 381, 404, 409
Inquisition 405–6
rule over Naples 401, 409
see also Aragon
Arborea 361–2
Archidamian War 143
Archimedes 152, 162, 187
Arganthonios 79
Arginoussai 147
Arians 220, 230, 231–3
Ostrogoths 233
Ariminum 177
see also Rimini
Aristarchos 162
Aristonothos 104, 109
Aristophanes 95, 130, 139
Aristotle 98
Arkadi monastery 485
Arkhanes 28, 29
Arles 250
Armenia, Cilician 359
Armenians 198, 583, 584, 586, 587
Arno, river xxvii, 271–2, 464
art
Athenian 105–6
Byzantine influence on Italian art 332
cave paintings 4, 5–6, 7
Cretan fresco painting 37
Cycladic 17–18
Egyptian 37
Etruscan 100, 103, 111, 112
Greek 89, 167, 562–3
Hellenistic styles 152
Iberian 129–30
Ionian 112
in Majorca 399
Minoan 36, 37
Phoenician 69
of Ugarit 36
see also pottery/ceramics
Artemisia, wife of Meletius 223, 225
Arzawa 104
Ascalon 292–3
Ashdod 55, 56, 57
Ashkelon 56
Ashkenazi Jews 592, 593, 599

Asia Minor *see* Anatolia
Asquith, H. H., 1st Earl of Oxford and
　　Asquith 578
Assurnasirpal 69
Assuwa 45
Assyrians 63, 66, 68, 69, 70, 132
Astarte 70, 111, 130
Aswan High Dam xxix, 618
asylum-seekers 629
Atatürk, Mustafa Kemal 583, 585, 586,
　　587
Athena 221
Athenaios of Naukratis 116
Athenians 22, 25, 53, 83
　　Archidamian War 143
　　Athenian empire 138, 139, 140, 143
　　attacks on Syracuse 115, 146
　　and Carthaginians 167, 173
　　communication channels 116–17
　　and the Delian League 139
　　grain trade 139–40, 146, 147–8, 158,
　　　172–3
　　klerouchoi 139–40
　　navy 115, 142, 146, 147
　　Peloponnesian War 133, 141–8
　　and the Persians 133, 136–7
　　pottery/ceramics 96, 101, 105–6
　　and the Ptolemies 160
　　and Sicily 144–6
　　trade routes 116–17, 141
　　see also Athens
Athens 25, 53, 55, 89, 131, 138–44
　　attack by Roger II 319
　　and Carthage 167, 173
　　decline during sixth century 236
　　and Delos 164
　　and Euboia 140, 141
　　people of *see* Athenians
　　Persian sacking of 136
　　plague 144
　　Romans and 164
　　Royal Navy's blockade of 564
Athos 107
Atlantic economy 440–41, 453–4, 505
Atlantic Ocean xxvii–xxviii, 71, 347, 411,
　　440, 454
　　trans-Atlantic trade 411–12

Atlas 126
Atrani 268
Atreus, Treasury of 563
Attaleia 195
Attarssiya 44
Attic pottery 113, 126
Attika 17, 137, 139
Atys, king of Lydia 101
Augustine of Hippo 218, 229–30,
　　231
Augustus Caesar 199, 200, 207, 210
　　Octavian 197, 198–9, 208
Aurelian 200
Auschwitz 599
Australians, Gallipoli campaign 579
Austria 600
　　people of *see* Austrians
Austrian Lloyd 556, 557, 560, 561
Austrians 456
　　in Bosnia 571
　　and Greeks 539
　　Habsburgs *see* Habsburgs
　　in Italy 601
　　and Montenegro 581, 582
　　and Ottomans 539
　　and Venice 519, 557, 558
　　war fleets 539, 558, 578, 580–82
　　World War I 581–2
　　see also Austria
autarchy 7
Avaris 38
Avars 252
Avienus 127–8
Axis powers 605, 606–11
Aydhab 296
Aydın 365, 366, 384
Ayia Napa 636
Ayia Photia 16–17
Ayyubids 296–7, 325, 329
Azores 393, 620

Baal Hamon 184
Baal worship 70, 81–2
Babylon 134
Bacchiad dynasty 97–8
Bacri family 531, 535, 540
Badoglio, Pietro 603, 611

Baetica 230
Balagne 515
Balawat gates 69, 72–3
Balbi di Correggio, Francisco 431–2, 433, 434
Baldwin I of Constantinople 330
Baldwin I of Jerusalem 291
Balearic islands 14, 194, 232, 235, 246, 249–50, 339, 417, 604
    see also Ibiza; Majorca; Minorca
Balfour Declaration 592
Balkans 383, 384, 385, 391, 437
    Franco-Turkish alliance in 421
    Ottomans in 414, 421
    silver 98
    trade in the late sixteenth century 437–40
Baltharpe, John 462–3
Baltic 520
    economy 505
    grain 440, 466
Banco di Roma 576
Banco di San Giorgio 392
bankers
    Florentine 351
    Greek 207
    Rhodian 164
    Sulpicii of Puteoli 206
banks 392, 400, 556, 576
    Florentine 375
    international 375–6
Banu Hillal 279
Banu Sulaym 279
Bar 581
Barbarigo, Agostino 450
Barbarossa, Frederick 300, 302
Barbarossa, Hizr/Khizr/Hayrettin 415–18, 419–20, 421–2
Barbarossa, Uruj/Oruc 415–17
Barbary corsairs 414, 415–18, 419–20, 421–2, 423, 452, 493, 498
    and America 529, 530, 532–6
Barbary states 434, 471, 492, 528–36
    and America: the Barbary Wars 529–36
    corsairs of see Barbary corsairs
    regencies 500, 528, 532; see also
        Algiers; Tripoli; Tunis

see also Algiers; Maghrib; Morocco;
    Tripoli; Tunisia
Barcelona xxxi, 128, 202, 304, 325, 334, 335–7, 340, 341, 342, 346, 358
    attacks on Jews 405
    Biga 399, 403
    and the Black Death 368
    Busca 399, 403
    business elite 400
    and the Catalan civil war 401
    French in 441
    and Genoese 441
    llotja 399, 400
    merchants/shipowners 345
    shipbuilding 441
    shipping 400–401
    trade in the sixteenth century 441
    trade with Catalonia 401
    and Valencia 403–4
Barcelona Process 639
Barcids 184
Bardi Bank 375
Bari 250, 251, 278, 281, 283, 292, 305
bashaws 528, 529, 531, 534
Battifoglio, Pietro 299
beachwear 635–6
Beatrice de Luna (Gracia Mendes/Gracia
        Nasi) 441–2, 443, 444
Bedouins 279
Beirut 359, 400, 616, 617
Belasyse, John, 1st Baron 493
Belisarios 235
Bellini, Gentile 388
Ben Ezra synagogue, Cairo 258–9
Ben-Gurion, David 595, 619
Benedict XIII 405
Benedictines 269
    Montecassino 269, 274
Benevento 295
Benjamin of Tudela 304–7, 335
Berab, Jacob 407
Berbers 75, 166–7, 374, 411, 472
    Barbary corsairs see Barbary corsairs
    Islamization of 245–6
    Marinid 334, 347, 363–4
    see also Libyans
Bergamo 413

Betsy (US ship) 533
beys 528, 529
Bible 52, 66–7, 69, 79, 134
    account of Paul's winter voyage to
        Rome 202–3
    Greek version 153
    Ladino Bible of Ferrara 442
    and the migrations of the Sea Peoples
        56–58
    Muslim view of 244
    Septuagint 161–2
Biga 399, 403
bikinis 635–6
Birgu *see* Vittoriosa
Bizerta 610
Black Death/bubonic plague 59, 144, 234,
        238, 366–9, 377, 500
    blamed on Jews 404–5
    changes after 373, 389, 396, 399, 401,
        404, 411
Black Sea xxiii, xxvii, 17, 86, 140, 285,
        355
    and the British 557
    Celtic and Scythian invasions of area
        158
    Genoese control of 354
    grain traffic 140, 355, 511; and
        bubonic plague 368
    Mycenaean contact with 33
    and the Napoleonic Wars 522–3
    and the Russians 505, 508, 510, 511,
        519
    slaves 349, 355, 373–4, 644
    trade routes 227, 355, 508, 557
Blakeney, William, Ist Baron, Lieutenant-
        Governor of Minorca 503
blancmange 404
Blegen, Carl 19, 20
bluefin tuna 640
Boabdil, king of Granada 408
Boardman, Sir John 125
Bocche di Cattaro 581
Bocchoris, Pharaoh 93
Bodrum 386
Bogomils 332
Bohemond I of Antioch (Bohemond of
        Taranto) 283, 284, 288–90

Bolaffio, G. V. 560
Bologna 108, 116
    see also Felsina
Bombay 491
Bonaparte, Napoleon *see* Napoleon I
Bonaventura (Italian ship) 346
Boniface of Montferrat 330
Bonifacio 329
bora xxviii, xxix, 456
Boreas xxix
Borel, Lavalley and Company 551
Bosnia 449, 571
Bosnia-Hercegovina 440
Bosphorus 158, 376, 505, 508, 511, 518,
        568, 580
Boston Tea Party 530
Botero, Giovanni 453
Bougie 303, 344, 345, 409
Bourbon, Philip de *see* Philip V of Spain
Bragadin, Marco Antonio 448, 449
Braudel, Fernand xxv–xxvii, 439–40, 449,
        451, 465, 641
brazilwood 301, 374
Brignole Sale, Antonio Giulio 469
Brindisi 205, 388, 582
    Brundisium 186
Brinton, Jasper 589
Bristol, Admiral Mark L. 586, 587, 588
Britain/the British
    aeronautical industry 634
    in Alexandria 555
    choice of Mediterranean ports xxx–
        xxxi
    contraction of control in Mediterranean
        617–18, 619, 622–7
    and Corsica 514–15
    and Cyprus 567, 568, 605, 623–4, 628,
        633
    decolonization 622–5; and Gibraltar
        625–7
    and Egypt 550, 554–5, 579, 619
    England *see* England
    the English *see* English
    and the French 606
    and the French Revolutionary War
        513–16
    and Gibraltar 605, 625–7

and the Greeks 564, 586–7
imperial expansion within the
    Mediterranean 642
and the Italians 607
and Malta 519, 520, 525, 607–8,
    622–3
and the Mediterranean in World War II
    605–12
and Minorca 498–503, 514
Napoleonic Wars 522, 524–6
and NATO 620
navy/fleets see Royal Navy
and the Ottomans 525, 538–40, 568,
    578–80, 585
and Palestine 592, 616–17, 619
and the Russians 504–6, 509–10, 515,
    522, 523, 612
in Salonika 598
and the Seven Years War 501–3
and Sicily 525–6, 607
and Smyrna 585–6, 588
steam shipping 557
and the Suez Canal 550, 553, 554–5,
    605, 619
tourists 633, 634
and the US 529–30, 535, 536
World War I 578–80, 582
World War II 605–12
Broecke, Bernard van den 467
Broglie, Victor-François, 2nd duc de 505
bronze 12, 17, 19, 94
    Alexandrian 156
    Etruscan bronzes 124
    gates of Balawat 69
    serpent from Delphi 132
    Villanovan 108
    weapons 12, 17, 20, 32, 109
Bronze Age
    Early 9–10, 15–23
    Late 27–8, 29–41, 42–6, 47, 48; Sea
        Peoples 42, 49–54, 55–59, 66, 644
    Melos obsidian 9–10
    metal work 10
    Middle 24–6
Bruges 347
Brundisium 164
    see also Brindisi

Brutus, Marcus Junius 197
bubonic plague see Black Death/bubonic
    plague
Bulgaria 355, 439, 599
    people of see Bulgarians
Bulgarians 329, 330
    and Salonika 571
    see also Bulgaria
Burchard (Frankish admiral) 250
burial practices 10–11, 15, 16, 81, 108
    Iberian 129
    at sea 312
    see also cremation; funerary rites;
        tombs
Busca 399, 403
Byblos 35, 37, 39
Byng, Admiral John 501, 502–3
Byron, George Gordon, 6th Baron 564
Byzantine Christianity 162
Byzantine Empire/Byzantium 234, 246,
    319
    economy 238, 285, 294
    fracturing in late twelfth and early
        thirteenth centuries 329–30
    and the Franks 251–4
    integration process 241
    and Islamic conquests 243–51
    jihad against 366
    under Justinian I 234–8
    Komnenos dynasty see Komnenos
        dynasty
    loss of trans-Mediterranean contact
        241–2, 256–7
    navy/fleets 233, 235, 249, 251, 324
    and the Normans 281–4, 288–9, 319,
        322, 323–4
    and Sicily 235, 242, 265
    and the Slavs 234, 236, 241–2
Byzantion 147, 227
    see also Constantinople

Cádiz 66, 72, 78, 126, 465–6, 489, 525
Caere 94, 104, 108, 111, 112, 170, 175
Caeretans 114
Caesar, (Gaius) Julius 194, 197
Caesarea 210, 291
Café Pastroudis, Alexandria 591

Caffa 355, 367–8
Caffaro di Rustico da Caschifellone 290
Caffé degli Specchi, Trieste 560
Cagliari 122, 275, 462, 611
Cairo 324–5
  'Babylonia' 291
  Fustat 258–60, 263, 270
  Genizah Jews 258–9, 262, 263–4, 266,
    279, 295–6, 646
Cairo Genizah collection 258–9, 260–61,
    265, 281, 296
Calabria 272, 279, 283, 313, 414
Caligula, Gaius 205, 215
Calvi 382
Cambyses 134
Camões, Luis de 396
Canaan 35, 37, 48, 49, 57, 58–59
  see also Palestine
Canaanites 80–81, 644
  language 36, 65, 644
  Philistines see Philistines
  Phoenicians see Phoenicians
  poetry 80
  religion 57, 65–6, 644
Canaries 348, 393, 411, 634, 637
Candia 331, 484, 485
Cannae 186
Cannes 632
cannibalism 28
Cantabrians 396
Cape Verde islands 393
Caphtor 56–57
  see also Crete
Capitulations (trade treaty) 422
Capsian culture 7
carbon emissions 637
Caribbean islands 411
Carmen in victoriam Pisanorum 280
Cartagena (New Carthage) 185, 187
Carthage 68, 72, 74–6, 77, 90, 114, 227,
    228–9, 645
  Arab capture of 246
  and Athens 167, 173
  Byzantine recovery of 235, 236
  Colonia Iulia Concordia Carthago 210
  as a cosmopolitan city 171
  destruction of 165, 177
  people of see Carthaginians
  and the Persians 135
  and the Ptolemies 157
  Punic Wars see Punic Wars
  Vandal conquest of 230–32
Carthaginians 70, 72, 74–6
  and Athenians 167, 173
  child sacrifice 81–2
  and Corinthian pottery 96
  and Iberians 128, 130–31
  invasion of Sicily 137, 166–74
  massacre of Motya 170
  and Massaliots 124
  and the Peloponnesian War 146
  pre-Punic War battles with Romans 175
  Punic Wars see Punic Wars
  rise of Carthaginian empire 166–7
  in Sardinia 77, 122
  Segestan appeal to 166
  and the Selinuntines 166, 167
  trade and settlement along coast of
    Spain 126, 127–8
  trade with Corinthians 97
  trade with Etruscans 101, 115
  treaties with Rome 127, 174–5, 188
  under Vandal rule 232
  warships 114, 167, 173, 178, 180, 181,
    186–7
  see also Carthage
cartography 340, 353, 379
Cassiodorus 253
Castelnuovo fortress, Naples 399
Castile 335, 364, 393, 398, 410
  and Aragon 398, 408–10
  gold 411
  Moriscos 473, 476
  people of see Castilians
Castilians 364, 366, 393, 395, 398, 404,
    405, 410
  expulsion of Muslims from Castilian
    lands 408
  see also Castile
castration 98, 213, 248, 474
  clinics 246–7
Catalans xxx, 298, 336–7, 338, 353, 376
  Catalan-Aragonese commonwealth
    353, 361–3, 381, 404, 409

and Genoese 361, 382
grain trade 346, 347–8, 356
Jews 341
and the kings of Aragon 334–5,
    338–41, 344, 345, 351, 353, 361,
    362, 376, 381–4
Levant trade 400
merchants 344, 353, 359–60, 400
militias 344
and Pisans 361
rise of a Catalan-Aragonese 'empire'
    361–3
and Sardinia 361, 381
shipping 344–8, 359–60, 400
in Sicily 381
slave trade 346–7
textile trade 401
trade in the fifteenth century 400, 401,
    402
trade networks 344–8, 401, 410
trade with North Africa 402
and the Turks of Aydın 365
war fleets 347, 352, 359, 362–3, 366,
    434
see also Catalonia
Catalonia 111, 127, 335, 352
    Catalan wine 129
    civil war 399, 401
    fleet built after siege of Malta 434
    Moriscos 475
    people of see Catalans
Cathars 332–3
    Albigensian Crusade 335
Catherine II, the Great, empress of Russia
    505, 508, 510, 512
Catherine of Braganza, queen of England
    491
Catholic Church 278, 354, 500
    and confessional identity 488
    in Gibraltar 497
    Inquisition see Inquisition
    in Minorca 500
    papacy see papacy
    and Russian Orthodox Church 522
Cato, Marcus Porcius, the Elder 188–9,
    191, 200–201, 203
Cattaro see Kotor

Catullus 102
Cavafy, Constantine P. 591–2
Cavalcabó, marquis of 512–13
cave paintings 4, 5–6, 7
Cavour (Italian battleship) 607
Cecil Hotel, Alexandria 589
Celtiberians 184, 185
Celtic peoples 117, 118, 124, 125, 128,
    158, 173
    Celtiberians 184, 185
ceramics see pottery/ceramics
Cerdagne 339
Cerveteri see Caere
Cesnola, Louis Palma di 568
Cetara 268
Cetinje 582
Ceuta 246, 298, 308, 393–5, 495, 575, 629
Chalkis 90, 91, 93, 140
Champagne 277
Champollion, Jean-François 548
Chanel, Coco 635
Chania 484, 485
Charlemagne 249–50, 252, 253, 254
Charles I of Anjou 349–52, 358, 365
Charles I of Naples, prince of Salerno 352,
    354
Charles II of England 490, 492, 494
Charles II of Spain 494
Charles III of Spain, later Charles VI, Holy
    Roman Emperor 495, 496–7, 498
Charles V, Holy Roman Emperor 410, 415,
    417, 418, 419, 441, 442, 559
    and Francis I 420–23
Charles VI of Austria 559
    see also Charles III of Spain
Charles VII of France 397
Charles VIII of France 387–8, 420
Charles IX of France 477
Charles, prince of Viana 399
Chelouche, Aharon 593
Chelouche family 594
Cherchel see Caesarea
Cheremetov, Boris 512
Chigi Vase 96
child sacrifice 66, 75, 76, 81–2
Chilperic II 247
China 378, 622–3, 639–40

Chioggia, War of 376–8
Chios 53, 83, 95, 236, 352, 358, 477
    and Genoese 366, 414, 446
    Turks in 538
Christendom
    Christian pirates 381, 414, 429, 435,
        446, 449, 453
    crossing the boundaries with Islam
        258–70
    and the Crusades see Crusades
Christianity
    Anglicanism see Anglicanism
    Arian 220, 230, 231; see also Arians
    and Judaism 222–5
    attempted conversion of Muslims to
        408
    Byzantine 162
    Catholic Church 278, 354, 500; see
        also papacy
    Christian relations with Jews and
        Muslims in Spain 340–41, 404–6
    Christians viewed by Romans as
        atheists 213
    churches see churches
    Constantine's conversion to 219–20
    Coptic 245
    Eastern Schism (1054) 283
    Greek Orthodox Church 282–3, 354,
        458, 485–6
    and 'heretics' 218, 220
    and Islam 244, 273, 281–2, 340–41;
        Crusades see Crusades; and the
        fragmentation of trade networks
        296; mixture of Christian and
        Muslim soldiers in armies 344; Pisa
        and the Muslims 279–81
    martyrs 214, 217–18, 223–4
    Melkites 591
    Minorcan Christians 224–5
    New Christians: converted from Islam
        see Moriscos; converted from
        Judaism 398, 443, 463–4
    and Paganism 220–22
    papacy see papacy
    persecution of Christians 214, 217–18,
        443

    Protestantism see Protestantism
    relationships between Catholic West
        and Orthodox East 282–3
    rift with Judaism 213–14, 217
    Roman legalization of 213, 219–20, 227
    Russian Orthodox Church 522
    spread across Mediterranean 213–14,
        220
Chrysostom, John 221
churches
    on Grado 253
    Greek style 274
    Monophysite 244
    of Pisa and Genoa 275
    relations between Greek and Latin 269,
        274
    Sardinian 274
Churchill, Winston 578, 580, 589, 608, 612
Cicero 78, 102, 186, 191, 196
Cid, El 336
Cilicia 92, 196, 197, 380
    Cilician Armenia 359
    pirates 165, 195
    Rough Cilicia 195, 197
Circassians 248, 355, 373–4
Cisneros, Cardinal 409
Ciutadella, Minorca 499
    Jamona 223, 224, 225
Ciutat de Mallorca 338–9, 340
Classis, Ravenna 211, 236
Claudius, Emperor 207, 215
Claudius, Appius 179
Cleopatra 197–8, 199
climate changes xxix, 6, 7
Club 18–30 637
Club Méditerranée 633
cochineal 465, 532, 585
cocoa 560
Cœur, Jacques, of Bourges 397
coffee 485, 528, 560, 585
Cohen, Eve 591
coinage 70, 97
    Amalfitan 270
    Arab 255, 257
    Byzantine 231, 255
    Corinthian 97

Florentine 327, 358
gold 236, 237, 247, 255, 263, 270, 302,
    308, 327, 358, 402
lead 237
Rhodian 164
Roman 204, 220
Valencian 402
Colbert, Jean-Baptiste 493
Collingwood, Admiral Cuthbert, 1st Baron
    Collingwood 515, 525
Colonna, Marcantonio 447
Colossus of Rhodes 155, 163
Columbus, Christopher 409, 411
Comacchio 252, 253, 254
commercialization 367, 637
Communism 604, 612, 613
    fall of 638
Comnenus dynasty see Komnenos dynasty
Compte, Pere 400
Concert of Europe 538
Conrad III, king of Germany 319
Constance, queen of Aragon 351
Constance, queen of Sicily 327–8
Constantine I, Roman emperor 19,
    219–20, 227
Constantine XI, Byzantine emperor 384
Constantine, Algeria 540–41
Constantinople 219, 221, 227, 234, 235,
    242, 349, 354
    1453 siege 384
    after the Great War 583
    and Alfonso V of Aragon 384
    and Amalfi 269
    as a centre of Muslim sea power 424
    fall in the Fourth Crusade (1204)
        329–30, 332
    fall to Mehmet the Conqueror 383
    Gracia Nasi and 443
    Hagia Sophia 283
    and the Islamic world 245, 246, 247,
        251
    as link between Mediterranean and the
        Black Sea 285
    massacre of Italians (1182) 324, 329
    Michael Palaiologos's recapture 330,
        331

Gracia Nasi and 442
Joseph Nasi and 444
Russian 'Great Idea' for 508
Venetians in 458
and Venice 256, 330
Contardo, Ingheto 341
Convention on International Trade in
    Endangered Species 640
Copenhagen, battle of 520
copper 12, 15–16, 17, 19, 33, 34, 35, 92
    from Cyprus 70
    Etruscan 109
    Phoenician 69
    Sardinia 123
    Tartessian 79
    weapons 20
Coptic Archaeological Society 591
Copts 245
    of Cairo 258
Córdoba 248, 249
Corfu xxx, 305, 319, 329, 525
    Channel 614–15
    and the Ottomans 419, 518
    see also Kerkyra
Corinth 89, 95–9, 110, 189, 236
    attack by Roger II 319
    Gulf of 97, 285, 449
    people of see Corinthians
    and Syracuse 98, 172
    trade routes 95, 98–9
    Venetian trade with 285
Corinthians
    and the Kerkyrans 141–2
    pottery 87, 95, 96, 101; in Sardinia 122
    slaves 95
    trade with Carthaginians 97
    see also Corinth
Coron 419, 538
Corsica 114, 382, 514, 621
    Arab invasion 250
    and the British 514–15
    Geiseric in 233
    and the Genoese 514, 515
    Ionian colony in 124
    Phokaians and 126
    in World War II 610, 611

Cosa 177, 201, 217
Cosimo I, Duke 464
Cosquer grotto 4
Cossacks 479
Côte d'Azur 632, 635
Cotrugli, Benedetto 390
cotton 323, 359, 374, 437, 477, 560, 573
Courmenin, Louis des Hayes, Baron de 477
cremation 81, 108, 129
Cretans
    Cretan War (1645–1669) 484–5
    fresco painting 37
    grain 483
    Greek 565–6; Orthodox 458, 485–6
    hand-axes 3
    pirates 163, 195
    pottery 236
    trade networks 485
    see also Crete
Crete
    1368 rebellion 377
    after the fall of Constantinople 330–31
    Bronze Age 16–17, 22–8
    Byzantium and 236
    Caphtor and the Philistines 56–57
    Cretan War (1645–1669) 484–5
    Evans and the 'palace of Minos at Knossos' 565, 566
    governed by Egypt (1830–40) 565–6
    Greek Orthodoxy in 458, 485–6
    Islam in 485–6
    Minoan 22–7, 28, 29–31, 566
    Mycenaean 29–35, 47
    Neolithic 8, 9
    and the Ottomans 448, 483–6, 565–6, 588
    people of see Cretans
    and Pharaonic Egypt 38
    and the Venetians 331, 377, 483–5
    World War II 608
Crimea 355, 368, 378, 510
Croatians
    pirates 439, 440
    Uskoks 439, 449, 454–7
Croesus (Kroisos), king of Lydia 134
Cromwell, Oliver 481, 488, 490

cruises 637
crusaders 280, 348
Crusades 287–93
    First Crusade 270, 287–91
    Second Crusade 318–19
    Third Crusade 297, 325
    Fourth Crusade 329–30, 331, 349
    Fifth Crusade 348
    and commercial revolution 293–303
cuisines 628–9
Cumae see Kyma
Curzola, battle of 355
Curzon, George Nathaniel, Marquis 585
Cybele 213
Cyclades 7, 13–14, 352
    Bronze Age 15–18, 27–8
Cycladic art 17–18
Cyclopes (Homer) 88
Cyprus 35, 55, 305, 358–9, 414, 623–5
    under the Assyrians 70, 132
    and the British 567, 568, 605, 623–4, 628, 633
    Byzantium and 236
    Cleopatra and 197
    deforestation xxx
    Delian League in 141
    Egyptians and 132
    and the EU 639
    Euboian ties 91
    foreign retirement problems in 632
    Genoese rights in 377
    granaries 70
    and Greece, enôsis movement 613, 623, 624
    Greek Cypriots 567–9, 623, 624–5
    invasion by Mamluks 392
    and Joseph Nasi 446
    Komnenos family in 329
    Mycenaean refugees 54
    Mycenaean trade with 33
    Mycenaeans, Hittites and 47
    Neolithic 8–9
    and the Ottomans 446–51, 567–9
    pottery 38
    refugees from Acre 349
    Richard I's capture of 325
    and the Sea Peoples 52

tourism 631, 632, 633, 636–7
as a trading transit point 36
Turkish Cypriots 568–9, 623, 624–5
and the Venetians 446–7, 451,
458
Cyrenaica 97, 135, 245
Jewish rebellion in 208–9, 216
Cyriac of Ancona 380
Cyrus, king of Persia 134
Czartoryski, Adam Jerzy 521
Czechoslovakia 616

Daimbert of Pisa 292
Dalmatia 210–11, 233, 252, 253, 254, 373,
376, 377, 389, 539, 613, 615
Dubrovnik *see* Dubrovnik
Uskoks 439, 449, 454–7
Dama de Elche 129–30
Damascus 620
Damietta 297, 348, 508
damming, North Africa 204
Danawoi 52
Dandolo, Andrea 254
Dandolo family 299, 360
Danes 478, 492, 528
Daniel, book of 134
Danites 52, 58–59
d'Annunzio, Gabriele 601–2
Dardanelles (Hellespont) 20, 135, 147,
376, 484, 522, 538, 578–80
and the Russians 510, 511
Dardanians 41, 52
Darius I, king of Persia 135
Darius III, king of of Persia 149
Darlan, Admiral Jean François 606,
609–10
Dartmouth, William Legge, 1st Earl 494
Datini, Francesco di Marco 373–5
David, Elizabeth 628
David, king of Israel 57, 59
de Gaulle, Charles 621
de Lesseps, Ferdinand *see* Lesseps,
Ferdinand, Vicomte de
de Malla family 345
Decatur, Stephen 534–5, 536
Decius, Gaius Messius 217
decolonization

British 622–5; Gibraltar 625–7
French 621
deforestation xxx, 234
Delacroix, Eugène 538, 546
Delian League 139, 140–41, 142
Delos 138, 139, 164–5, 201, 205
Delphi 95, 96, 113, 114, 125, 132, 380
decline during sixth century 236
Oracle 32, 136
Demaratos of Corinth 98, 99, 104
Demeter 130, 171
Demetrios of Phaleron 159, 160
Demetrios Palaiologos 384
Demetrios, Seleucid king 163
democracy 135, 138, 139, 613
democrats and aristocrats,
Peloponnesian War 141–2
lost to tyrants 168–70
Denia 336
Denmark 520
Denyen 50–51, 52
Derne 535
'Desert Rats' 609
deys 528, 529, 531, 535, 540
dhimmis 244–5
Diana culture 13
Dido, queen of Carthage 74–5, 189–90
diet *see* food
Diocletian, Roman emperor 226–7
Diodoros the Sicilian 79, 163
diolkos (slipway) 95, 97
Dionysios I of Syracuse 98–9, 130, 168,
170–71
Dionysios of Halikarnassos 98, 102–3, 104
Dionysos (god) 105–6
Dioskorides 266–7
Disraeli, Benjamin 554, 570
Diversis, Philippus de 389
divination 113
Dodecanese islands 577, 601, 611, 629
Dominicans 341, 379–80, 406, 439
Don John of Austria 448, 449, 451, 472
Donatists 217, 220
Dönme sect 482
Dor 39, 41
Doria, Andrea 419, 420, 421, 428
Doria, Gian Andrea 428–9, 447

Doria, Pietro 377
Doria family of Genoa 275
Dorians 53, 83
  and the Peloponnesian War 145
Doublet, Pierre Jean 517
Dragut (Turgut) 428, 430
dried fruits 340, 355, 358, 366, 378, 393,
    400, 404, 460, 466, 485, 511, 528,
    584
Druze warriors 305
Držić, Marin 439
Dual Control Commission, Anglo-French
    554–5
dualism 332
Dubrovnik (Ragusa) 323, 332, 388–91,
    401, 423, 438–9, 440, 442, 448,
    532, 539
  and Ancona 437, 438
  inhabitants see Ragusans
  and the Russians 521–2
  tourism 637
  and the Uskoks 457
  wool trade 389–90, 439
Dunkerque (French ship) 606
Duran, David 531
Durazzo 385, 388, 448, 582
  see also Dyrrhachion; Epidamnos
Durrell, Lawrence 589, 591, 623
Durrës see Durazzo; Dyrrhachion;
    Epidamnos
Dutch 463 see also Holland
  and English 462, 467, 488, 493, 495
  and Genoa 468
  grain trade 466
  and Livorno trade 465, 466
  navies 463
  seamen 454
  tourists 633
  and Venetians 460, 461
Dyrrachium see Durazzo; Dyrrhachion;
    Epidamnos
Dyrrhachion 235–6, 269, 283, 285, 324,
    350
  see also Durazzo; Epidamnos

early man, pre-Neolithic 3–8
earthquakes 27–8, 45, 164, 438–9

Eaton, William 531–2, 535
ebony 37, 158, 310
Ecija 405
economy
  agricultural 204
  Alexandrian 155–6
  Atlantic 440–41, 453–4, 505
  Baltic 505
  and the Black Death 366–9
  boom in the sixteenth century 436–9
  Byzantine 238, 285, 294
  and China 640
  domination by cities 357–8
  economic recovery (redreç) 399, 401
  Egyptian 155–6, 537
  European economic crisis 629
  European economic network 323
  Genoese 392
  global 640
  Greek 639
  Italian capital 400
  and the Japanese 638
  Mediterranean 97; growing complexity
      and disintegration 226, 227
  Mediterranean Union economic
      objectives 639
  North Sea 505
  northern European economies 440
  redreç/economic recovery 399
  of Salonika 598
  Spanish 634; Genoa and Spanish
      finances 468
  specialization and the Mediterranean
      economy 373
  and tourism 633–4
  transformations after the Black Death
      373, 399, 401, 404
  Tunisian 576
  Valencian 404
  Venetian 457–8
  voluntary limitation of economic
      growth 639
Eden, Anthony 618, 619
Edessa 318
Edicts of Toleration 559
Edward IV, king of England 396, 403
Edwin (US ship) 535

EEC (European Economic Community) 621
Egadian islands 5
  Punic naval battle off 182
Egeria 644
Egesta *see* Segesta
Egypt xxix, 14, 22
  and Alexander the Great 149–52
  Alexandria *see* Alexandria
  Arab seizure of power (revolution of
    1952) 617, 618
  under Ayyubids 296–7
  and the British 550, 554–5, 579, 619
  Cairo *see* Cairo
  and Constantinople 227, 242
  economy 155–6, 537
  European imports in the thirteenth
    century 326
  Fatimid 291, 296–8, 324–5; *see also*
    Fatimids
  French fascination with ancient Egypt
    547–8
  government of Crete (1830–40) 565–6
  grain trade 157, 158, 164, 203, 204,
    227, 242
  incident with Pisan merchants 297–8
  irrigation 376
  under Ismail Pasha 551–2
  Israel and: ancient Israelites 58; modern
    state of Israel 618–20
  and James II of Aragon 345
  Jewish rebellion in 208–9, 216
  and the Karimis 296
  and the kingdom of Jerusalem 348
  late Roman 227
  Libyan invasions of 48–50
  Mamluks in 349, 355, 392, 397
  Muhammad Ali and 537–40
  Muslim conquest 245
  and Napoleon 515–16
  under Nasser 618–20
  Ottoman 485, 518, 545–8
  people of *see* Egyptians
  Pharaonic 36–41, 48–53, 63, 132; and
    Crete 38; Hyksos dynasty 37, 38
  Ptolemaic 152–64, 188, 197–200
  and the Romans 197–200, 208–9
  Sea Peoples' invasion of 50–53, 55
  Suez Canal *see* Suez Canal
  and Syria 35–6, 38, 39–41
  taxation 297
  timber 37, 39, 40, 263, 297, 537, 643
  and Tyre 68–9
  and Ugarit 35–6
Egyptians
  in Ascalon 292–3
  ceramics 280
  and Cyprus 132
  navy/warships 51, 156, 163, 293
  papyrus 156–7, 161
  in Puteoli 206
  trade routes to Tyrrhenian Sea 93–4
  see also Egypt
Eilat 619
Eisenhower, Dwight D. 609, 619
Eknomos, battle of 181–2
Ekron 56, 57
Ekwesh 49, 52
El Alamein 609
Elba 109, 115, 334, 383, 416
Elche bust 129–30
Eleonora of Arborea 362
Eliadar, wife of Solomon of Salerno 301,
  302
Eliott, George Augustus 509
Elissa (Dido) 74–5
Elizabeth I, queen of England 453, 459,
  477
Elizabeth II, British queen 622, 626
Elliott, John 402
Elymians 76, 145, 167
Emborio 53, 54
Embriaco family 290–91, 305, 315
emperor worship 213, 220
Emporion 110–11, 124, 126, 128, 185
Empúries *see* Emporion
Enfantin, Barthélemy-Prosper 546–8
England
  and Catholic Spain 453, 459
  and the Genoese 396–7
  Mediterranean trade with 347
  people of *see* English
  Philip II's wars with Elizabeth I 453
  trade in the sixteenth century 459–61
  see also Britain/the British

English
   changing alliances between Spain and
      France 488
   conflicts with Spaniards 489–90
   and Dutch 462, 467, 488, 493, 495
   and Gibraltar 490, 494–8
   pirates 461
   shipping 396–7
   and Tangier 491–4
   trade in Turkey 499–500
   and Venetians 459, 460–61
   war fleets 488
   see also Britain/the British; England
Enkomi 35
Enna 282
Enrico Pescatore 328
environmental pollution 637, 640
EOKA (Ethniki Organôsis Kypriôn
      Agonistôn) 623
Epeiros 55, 330
Ephesos 236
Epicureans 305
Epidamnos 98, 117, 141–2
   see also Durazzo; Dyrrhachion
Epirus see Epeiros
Eraclea 253
Eratosthenes 47, 162
Eretria 90, 91
Eryx (Erice) shrine 76
Ethniki Organôsis Kypriôn Agonistôn
      (EOKA) 623
Etruria 63, 77, 79, 94, 95, 100, 107, 183,
      562
   Eastern influences 111
   engagements against pirates 195
   people of see Etruscans
   Tarquinia see Tarquinia
   trade routes 95, 101, 110
Etruscans 52, 63, 72, 77, 83, 90, 94,
      100–118
   alphabet 93, 110
   art 100, 103, 111, 112
   bronzes 124
   and Corinthian pottery 96
   ethnic origins 101–5
   influence on La Tène culture 125
   language 104
   migration 101–5, 108, 117
   and the Peloponnesian War 146
   Phoenician trade 111
   and Phokaians 114
   pirates 63, 72, 105–6, 109
   political relations with Greeks 113–16,
      125
   pottery 78, 109, 110, 112–13; in
      Massalia 124; in Sardinia 122
   and Romans 175
   sexual behaviour 105
   soothsayers 113, 220
   tombs 100, 101, 104, 108, 111–12,
      114, 117, 563
   trade with Carthaginians 101, 115
   trade with Greeks 110–11
   Villanovan culture 108–10, 113
   see also Etruria
EU (European Union) 625, 629, 638–9,
      640
Euboia 75, 77, 90–91, 94–5, 135
   Athens and 140, 141
   marble 222
Euboians 75, 89–95
   Lelantine War 94–5
   pottery 87, 92
Euclid 152, 162
Eudoxia, Empress 221, 222
Eugénie of France, Empress 552
Euripides 146, 160
European Economic Community (EEC)
      621
European Union (EU) 625, 629, 638–9,
      640
Evans, Sir Arthur 26, 565, 566
Exarchate of Ravenna 252, 253
Exekias 105–6
Eynan (Ayn Mallaha) 8
Ezekiel 68

Fabri, Felix 379–80
Fabriano paper 437
Falangists 604
Falastin (newspaper) 594, 596
Famagusta 358, 359, 446, 447–8, 449,
      451, 624
famines 367

Farouk, king of Egypt 617
Fascism 601–4, 611
'Fat Lady of Saliagos' 18
Fatimids 270, 279, 289, 293, 296–8, 301, 324–5
fauna 6, 7
Fayyum 14
Fayyum, Lake 38
Felsina 117
   see also Bologna
Ferdinand I, duke of Tuscany 466–7
Ferdinand I, king of Aragon 405
Ferdinand II, king of Aragon 387, 398, 405, 406, 408–10, 415, 420
Ferdinand IV, king of Naples 524, 525
Fernando, brother of Henry the Navigator 396
Ferrante I, king of Naples 387, 396, 398
Ferrante II, king of Naples 388, 406
Ferrara 358, 406, 442
fertility cults 11, 18, 154
Fibonacci, Leonardi 332
Fifth Monarchy Men 481
Finley, Moses 88, 97
fish xxviii, 76, 641
   of the Adriatic marshlands 252, 253
   and the Mediterranean diet 629
   over-fishing 640
   preservation 76, 641–2
   sauce 76, 97, 202, 206, 247, 641
   stocks xxx
   trade in 389, 396, 460
   transport 401
   tuna-fishing 10, 19, 76, 640, 641
Fisher, John Arbuthnot, 1st Baron 579
Fiskardo 284
Fiume (Rijeka) 601–2
Flanders 295, 346, 411, 441–2, 447
   Venetian trade with 379
flax 263, 264, 279, 297
FLN (*Front de Libération Nationale*) 621, 622
flora 6
Florence 327, 356–7, 358, 383, 632
   Jewish ghetto 464
   people of *see* Florentines

Florentines 327, 437
   bankers 351
   banks 375
   cloth trade 437, 438
   Jews 464
   Medici 403
   shipping 404, 437
   see also Florence
Fondi 418
fonduks 298–9, 325, 345, 346, 348, 369, 645
food
   dried fruits *see* dried fruits
   grain *see* grain trade
   Mediterranean cuisines 628–9
   on package holidays 635
   rationing 628
   and sea transport 202
   spice trade *see* spice trade
   warship diets 427, 463
Forrestal, James 616
Forster, E. M. 591–2, 632
Fortis (Pisan pirate) 329
Forum Julii 210
   see also Fréjus
Fos-sur-Mer 247
France
   Charlemagne's defence of 250
   dominating Ottoman trade 585
   and the EEC 621
   French Revolutionary War 513–20
   Hellenization of southern France 125
   Jewish emigration to 598, 617
   and NATO 620
   people of *see* French
   Provence *see* Provence
   spice trade 397
   tin of southern France 123, 124
   tourism 636
   Vichy 606–7, 610
Francesco I, duke of Tuscany 464
Franchthi cave 7
Francis I, king of France 418–19, 420–23, 644
Franciscans 342, 439
Franco, Francisco 604, 605, 621, 625–6
frankincense 158, 165

Franks 247, 250, 251–4, 255, 311, 324–5, 326, 342, 349
Franz Josef, emperor of Austria 552, 558
Fraxinetum 250
Frederick I, Barbarossa, German emperor 300, 302
Frederick II of Hohenstaufen, German emperor and king of Sicily 328, 331, 349, 350, 361, 366
free ports 164, 201, 436–7, 464–8, 559
Fréjus 302
    Forum Julii 210
French
    and Aigues-Mortes 358
    and Algeria 530, 540–41, 573–4, 621–2
    alliance with Italians against Turkish threat 365
    in Barcelona 441
    and the British 606
    contraction of control in Mediterranean 617–18, 619
    cultural imperialism 570
    decolonization 621
    and Egypt's threat to Israel 619
    fascination with ancient Egypt 547–8
    Franco-Turkish alliance 418–19, 420–23, 475
    Hallstatt culture 125
    and the ideal of progress 549
    invasion of Catalonia 352
    in Italy under Louis XII 409
    Levant trade 499
    and Minorca 498, 501–3
    Napoleonic Wars 513, 522–3, 524–6
    navy/fleets 423, 514, 523, 581, 606
    and the Ottomans 418–19, 420–23, 475, 539, 546–8
    Revolutionary War 513–20
    in Salonika 598
    Seven Years War 501–3
    and Smyrna 585
    and the Suez Canal 548–9, 550, 553, 554–5
    tourism 633
    trading networks 397
    in Tunisia 574, 576, 621
    World War I 581

World War II 606–7, 609, 610, 611–12
    xenophobia in southern France 622
    see also France
Friuli 387
Front de Libération Nationale (FLN) 621, 622
Fufluns 644
funerary rites 18, 93, 105, 114
Fustat (Old Cairo) 258–60, 263
    Amalfitans in 270

Gaddafi, Muammar al- 622
Gadir 78
Gaeta 268, 269
Galata 354
Galen 152
Galicians 396
Galilee 407
Galissonière, Roland-Michel Barrin de la 502
galley slaves 425–7, 435
Gallipoli 366
    campaign 579–80
Gamaliel 224
García de Toledo, Don 433
garon/garum sauce 76, 97, 202, 206, 247, 641
Gaul 246, 247
    Visigothic rule of southern Gaul 233
Gaza 56, 221–2, 237, 618–19, 638
    bubonic plague 368
Gaza Strip 56
Geddes, Patrick 595–6
Geiseric 230–31, 233
Gela 167–8, 172
Gelidonya wreck 33
Gelimer, King 232
Gelon 114, 137
gender 643–4
Genizah collection 258–9, 260–61, 265, 281, 296
Genizah Jews of Cairo 258–9, 262, 263–4, 266, 279, 295–6, 646
Genoa 237, 271, 301, 346, 358, 420
    as banker to the Spanish empire 441
    Black Death 369
    economy 392

as a free port 467–8
government of 276–7
and the Jews 296, 406
people of *see* Genoese
and the Visconti lords of Milan 376
War of Chioggia 376–8
Genoese 272–8, 286, 305, 467–9
in Acre 325–6
and Alfonso V of Aragon 382–3
alliance with Spain 412, 468
and the Almohads 298
alum 392–3
in Barcelona 441
and the Black Death 367–8, 369
and Catalans 361, 382
and Chios 366, 414, 446
compagna 276–7, 290
cooks 628
and Corsica 514, 515
and the Crusades 290–92, 331, 349
and the English 396–7
and Frederick II of Sicily 349
on Gibraltar 497
grain trade 347–8, 355–6, 392
and Henry, count of Malta 331
in Majorca 338
massacre in Constantinople (1182) 324,
  329
merchants 277, 278, 298–9, 301–3,
  341, 344, 358, 441
in North Africa 298–9
and the Ottomans 392–3
pirates 328–9, 331
and Pisans 273, 274, 275, 278–9, 305,
  334
and Sardinia 273, 274–5
in Seville 412
shipping 315, 316–17, 347–8, 360,
  378, 404
and Sicily 322–3, 328
slave trade 355
and Syracuse 328
trade networks 271, 354
and Venetians 325–6, 331, 355, 366,
  376–8
see also Genoa
Georg, Meister 386

George I, king of Greece 578
George III, British king 515
George VI, British king 608, 610
George of Antioch, admiral 319, 321
George of Darmstadt-Hesse, Prince 495,
  496
George, prince of Greece 566
George Washington (US ship) 533
Germaine of Foix, queen of Aragon 410
Germanic peoples
  barbarians 208, 226, 229, 230–33
  Lombards 237, 253
  warfare with Slav peoples 248
Germans
  at the beginning of the twentieth
    century 577
  German merchants xxix, 277, 401
  Hanseatic 463, 468
  in Libya 576
  Nazis 599, 600, 605–10, 611, 612
  seamen 454
  tourists 633, 636
  U-boats 582, 609
  World War I 582
  World War II 605, 606–10, 611, 612
  see also Germanic peoples; Germany
Germany
  and the 'kingdom of Italy' 275
  Nazi 605–10, 611, 612
  people of *see* Germans
  Rosicrucian enlightenment 481
Gezer 35, 56
Ġgantija 11
Ghaylan, Abdallah 492, 494
Ghent 347
ghettos 438–9, 442, 443, 458, 464, 559,
  599, 646
Ghibellines 351, 365
Giacometti, Alberto 123
Gibbon, Edward 226
Gibellet 305
Gibraltar 364, 394, 398, 490, 494–8, 509,
  605, 625–7
  Jews 497–8, 536
  Neanderthals 3–4
  Straits of 71, 78, 363–4, 366, 395, 398,
    492, 557

Gibraltar Woman 3
Giornata (trading company) 531
Giovanni Scriba ('John the Scribe') 278
Giraud, Henry 610
Giraud family 585
Giustiniani, Niccolò 415
goddesses
    earth-goddesses 57, 213
    Egyptian 199, 212–13
    Etruscan 111
    Great/Mother Goddess 11, 12, 18, 213
    Greek 31–2, 101, 171
    Minoan 26
    Mycenaean 32
    Phoenician 70, 101, 111, 130
Godfrey of Bouillon 290
gods
    Anatolian 104
    Canaanite 57, 644
    Carthaginian 171; see also Melqart
    Egyptian 154, 209
    Etruscan 644
    existence of pagan gods denied by Jews
        and Christians 213
    God of Israel 199
    Greek 31–2, 101, 105–6, 130, 138,
        150, 154, 165, 644
    Mycenaean 32
    Persian 135
    personification of 154
    Philistine 57
    Phoenician 73, 75, 101, 645
    posing as merchants 88
    Roman mixture of 209
    sea-gods 22, 73, 85, 165, 644
    storm-gods 104
    sun-gods 37
    see also specific gods
Goitein, Shlomo Dov 259, 266
Golan Heights 619
gold
    Alexandria and 156, 158
    Byzantine 242
    Castile and 411
    coins 236, 237, 247, 255, 263, 270,
        302, 308, 327, 358, 402
    dust 279, 298

Egyptian 37
    of Florentine businessmen 327
    Guinea trade 411
    Libyan 48
    Mycenaean 29, 32
    New World 468
    of the Sahara 263
    Tartessian 79
    Trojan 21, 22
Golden Horn 285, 294, 354, 578
Goliath 57
Gonzaga, Giulia 418
González de Córdoba, Fernando 409
Gortyna 236
Gothic Wars 235
Goths 229, 230, 232, 234, 235
Gozo 10, 11, 415, 428
Gracchus, Tiberius 200
Grado 252, 253
grain trade xxix, 28, 70, 144, 202–4, 642
    African 203
    Alexandria 157, 158–9
    Apulian grain 351, 357, 358
    Athens 139–40, 146, 147–8, 158,
        172–3
    Baltic grain 440, 466
    Black Sea traffic 140, 355, 368, 511
    and bubonic plague 368
    Byzantine 236
    Catalan 346, 347–8, 356
    Corinth 285
    and Crete 483
    and the Dutch 466
    Egyptian 157, 158, 164, 200, 203, 204,
        227, 242
    Florentine 356–7
    following the Black Death 373
    Genoese 347–8, 355–6, 392
    grain ships 202–3, 205
    in the Islamic world 263
    in the late sixteenth century 437–8
    Moroccan 298, 392
    and north European merchants 454
    Ostia 207–8
    Puteoli 207
    Rome 175, 195, 200–205, 207–8, 227;
        and pirates 196

Sicilian grain 144, 172–3, 179, 186, 263, 279, 319, 322–3, 346, 356, 392, 436, 468, 527–8
  between Sicily and Athens 172–3
  taxation 186
  Vandal control of 233
  Venice 285, 358
Granada
  Black Death 368
  conquest by Ferdinand and Isabella 408, 409
  Moriscos of 471–4
  Muslim kings of 363–4
  Nasrid 334, 347, 393, 395, 404
Grand Tours 562, 564, 632
Great Britain see Britain/the British
'Great Green' 38
Great/Mother Goddess 11, 12, 18, 213
Greece 53–55, 117
  and Austrian trade with the Turks 539
  the British and Greeks 564, 586–7
  civil war (1943) 611
  Communist insurgency 612, 613
  conflicts with Turks in the nineteenth century 538–9
  and Cyprus, enôsis 613, 623, 624
  Andrea Doria in 419
  early contact with Sicily 33
  economic collapse 639
  Etruscan trade 110–11
  Greco-Turkish wars 538, 586–8
  Greek art 89, 167, 562–3
  and Greek Cypriots 567–9, 623, 624–5
  Greek fleets 538, 588
  Greek nationalism 568–9, 623
  Greek pottery 75, 77, 108, 113; Attic 113, 126; Helladic 33, 35, 43, 53; in Massalia 124, 125; Mycenaean 34, 35, 43, 46, 51, 54, 56; in Sardinia 122
  Greeks in Alexandria 589–90, 591
  Greeks in Smyrna 584, 586–7
  Greeks of Salonika 570, 571–2
  Greeks servicing trade in the sixteenth century 459
  Hellas 95, 114–15, 132–3, 134, 137, 142, 171, 564
  migrations into southern Greece 54–55
  and NATO 620
  northern Greece and the second Punic War 186
  Persian invasion 132–7
  raids by Roger II 319
  romantic assumptions about 564
  under Slav rule 234
  trade network with Asia Minor 55
  Vandal raids on 233
  Venice and Greek corsairs 510–11
Greek civilizations/cultures
  Athenian see Athenians
  Dorian 53
  Euboian see Euboians
  first contact with Italian lands 89–94
  Greek Cypriots 567–9
  Hellenic identity 83, 132
  hellenization of Spain 126–30
  and Iberians 128–31
  Ionian see Ionians
  Minoan see Minoan civilization
  Mycenaean see Mycenaeans
  Phoenician relations 63, 64, 79, 90
  Phokaian see Phokaians
  political relations with Etruscans 113–16, 125
  in Sicily 282
  in southern Italy 123
  Spartan see Spartans
  the wanderers: heirs of Odysseus (800 BC–550 BC) 83–99
Greek Orthodox Church 354, 623
  in Crete 458, 485–6
  relationship with the papacy 282–3
Gregorios, governor of Sicily 250
Gregory of Tours 237
Gregory VII, Pope 344
Grimaldi family 360
Grivas, George 623
Grove, Alfred, and Rackham, Oliver xxix–xxx
Guelfs 351
Guglielmo Grasso 329
Guiscard, Robert 281–2, 283, 284, 294, 324
'Gulf of the Lion' xxviii
Gylippos 146

Ha-Levy, Judah 259
habiru 48, 58
Habsburgs 378, 410, 417, 420, 456, 494,
    495, 521, 557–8, 559
hadith 341
Hadrian, Roman emperor 208, 216, 382
Hadumar 250
Haganah 616, 617
Haifa 292, 598, 616–17
    Bay 605
Halfon ben Nethanel 264
Halikarnassos, Mausoleum 386
Hallstatt culture 125
Hamas 638
Hamet Bashaw 535
Hamilcar (Carthaginian commander in
    western Sicily) 173
Hamilcar (d. 480 BC) 167
Hamilcar Barca 184
Hamilton, Sir William 562
hamsin xxviii
Hannibal 184, 185, 186, 187
Hapag Lloyd 633
harems 248, 644
Harris, Sir James 509–10
Harun ar-Rashid 252
al-Hasan, emir of of Mahdia 319–20
al-Hasan ibn Muhammad al-Wazzan (Leo
    Africanus) 381
Hasday ibn Shaprut 266–7
Hasdrubal 172, 184, 185
Hatti 21, 22
Hazor 67
Hebrews 48, 58–59, 66–7, 70, 280
    see also Israel; Jews
Helladic pottery 33, 35, 43, 53
Hellas 95, 114–15, 132–3, 134, 137, 142,
    171, 564
    see also Greece
Hellenism, opposition to Judaism 153
Hellenistic culture 152, 162, 199, 211, 213
    and the modification of religious beliefs
    213
Hellenistic philosophy 162
Hellespont 135, 147
    see also Dardanelles
Henry, count of Malta 328, 330–31

Henry III, king of France 423
Henry IV, king of France 475
Henry, king of Portugal 453
Henry, prince of Castile 344
Henry the Navigator 393
Henry VI, German emperor and king of
    Sicily 327, 328
Herakles 74, 645
Heraklion *see* Candia
Herceg Novi 390, 438, 511
Hercegovina 390
    Bosnia-Hercegovina 440
Herculaneum 562
Hermapollo (Egyptian ship) 158
Hermes 165
Herod Agrippa I, ruler of Judaea 205
Herodotos 72, 79, 98, 101, 102–3, 106,
    111, 114, 123–4, 132, 133, 134
Herzl, Theodor 592
Herzliya Gymnasium, Tel Aviv 595
Hesiod 86, 87, 90, 126
Hesperides, Garden of 126
hides, animal 40, 437, 439, 532
    on ships 283, 284, 300
Hieron of Syracuse 114, 115, 178, 179,
    182–3, 186
Hillel 222
Himera 114, 167
    tyrant of 130
Himilco 170
Hippo 230, 231
Hiram, king of Tyre 66–7, 69
Hisarlık 19, 20, 42, 45
    see also Troy
Hitler, Adolf 605, 606, 609, 610
Hittites 41, 43–5, 46, 50, 51
Hohenstaufen 325, 327, 328, 331, 351
Holaies the Phokaian 106–7
Holland 461, 463
    Calvinist 493
    people of *see* Dutch
    see also Netherlands
Holocaust 599
Holy Grail 291
Holy Land 269, 293, 303, 348–9
    and the Crusades *see* Crusades
    Jewish pilgrims 304

pilgrimage to 379–80
see also Israel; Palestine
Holy Leagues 365, 419–20, 421, 447, 448,
    449, 450–51
Homer 20, 23, 32, 42, 43, 44, 52, 58, 63,
    68, 75, 88, 95, 645
    and Alexander the Great 150
    Iliad 19, 30, 86
    Odyssey 85–6, 87, 88–9, 93, 150
Homeric Hymns 90, 105
Hompesch, Ferdinand von 516, 517
honey 68, 114, 139, 157, 225, 401, 465,
    485
Hood, Samuel, 1st Viscount 513–14,
    515
Horace, poet 102, 199
Horden, Peregrine and Purcell, Nicholas
    xxiv–xxv, xxvii
Horns of Hattin 325
horse-breeding 117
Horthy, Miklós 581
Hospitallers *see* Knights Hospitallers
Hoxha, Enver 613–15, 636
human sacrifice 25, 28, 46, 75, 78
    child 66, 75, 76, 81–2
    Phoenician 81–2
Humbert of Silva Candida, Cardinal 283
Hunyadi, John, king of Hungary 383
Husayni, Amin al-, Grand Mufti of
    Jerusalem 604
Hussein I, king of Jordan 620
Hydra 538
Hyères 632
Hyksos dynasty 37, 38
hypogea 10–11

Iberians 78–9, 128–31, 167
    absorption into Syracusan forces 170
    alphabet and script 129
    art 129–30
    Celtiberians 184, 186
    Greek and Carthaginian interaction
        with 128–31
    and Hamilcar 184
    pottery 130
    Roman captives 192
    tombs 129, 130

Ibiza 78, 97, 339
    gay tourism 636
    salt 346
    see also Balearic islands
Ibn al- 'As, 'Amr 244
Ibn al-Athir 279
Ibn al-Hawas 281–2
Ibn ath-Thimnah 282
Ibn Hammud 302–3
Ibn Jubayr, Muhammad ibn Ahmad
    307–15
Ibn Khurdadbih, Abu'l Qasim 248
Ibrahim Pasha, Grand Vizier 418
ice caps 6
idols 18
Ilios 19, 44, 45
    see also Troy
Illustrious, HMS 607
Illyria 522
IMRO (Internal Macedonian
    Revolutionary Organisation) 571
India 515–16
    trade with Alexandria 158, 207
Indian Ocean 200, 296, 396, 446, 463,
    578
    trade routes to 155, 157, 262, 355,
        549–50, 561, 573
Indians 411–12
indigo 323, 326, 374, 466, 585
Innocent III, Pope 331
Inquisition 405–6, 442
    Aragonese 405–6
    banned from British territories 500
    and the Moriscos 470–71
    Portuguese 463–4
    treatment of Protestants 461
    Valencian 475
    Venetian 458
insurance, maritime 402, 439, 457, 465
Internal Macedonian Revolutionary
    Organisation (IMRO) 571
Intrepid (US ship) 534
Ionia 110, 123–4, 135, 137
    people of *see* Ionians
Ionian isles 233, 283, 313, 321, 460,
    518–19, 521, 525
Ionian Sea 13, 33, 98, 174, 439, 448

Ionians 80, 83, 96, 111
art 112
in Corsica 124
cult of the Delian Apollo 138
and the Lydians 134
at Massalia 123–4
and the Peloponnesian War 145
and the Persians 123–4, 134, 135, 137
relations with Etruscans 111, 114
see also Ionia
Iran 245
Iraq 69, 245, 619
oil pipeline from 605
iron 92, 94, 109, 300
and the Philistines 57
weapons 248
ironclads 555–6, 557–8
irrigation 474
Egypt 376
North Africa 204
Isaac II Angelos, Byzantine emperor 332
Isabella I, queen of Castile 398, 408
Isaiah 79
Ischia (Pithekoussai) 34, 89–90, 92–4, 95, 110, 268, 422
Isis, cult of 199, 213
Islam and the Muslim peoples 296
Almohad 296, 298, 299, 310, 322; see also Almohads
Arab capture of Carthage 246
bringing new unity across the Mediterranean 246
Byzantium and the conquests of 243–51
and Christendom: crossing the boundaries 258–70; Crusades see Crusades; mixture of Christian and Muslim soldiers in armies 344
and Christianity 244, 273, 340–41; Christian expansion into Muslim Mediterranean, late eleventh century 281–2; Pisa and the Muslims 279–81
converted Muslims, 'Moriscos' 408, 434, 447, 453, 470–76, 647
in Crete 485–6
and dhimmis 244–5
exiled Muslims struggling to retain knowledge of 408
expulsion of Muslims from Castilian lands 408
extinction of Muslim rule in Spain 408
Ferdinand II's war against 408, 409
Greek massacre of Muslims in Tripoli 538
Islamic ceramics 280
Islamization of North African Berbers 245–6
James I of Aragon and Muslims 339–41
view of Jesus (Isa) 244
jihad 366, 384
and Judaism 244, 340–41
modern migrants 630
Muslim aims in the time of Muhammad 243
Muslim merchants 257, 258, 261–2, 266, 296, 404, 453, 457, 465
Muslim naval power/piracy 249, 250–51, 268, 278–9, 364, 402, 414, 423–4
Muslim relations with Christians and Jews in Spain 340–41, 404–6
Muslim slaves 308, 346–7
Muslims in Salonika 598
Muslims of Valencia 339–40, 341
and Ottoman expansion 414, 423–4; see also Ottomans
and paganism 244
and the slave trade 246–7, 248
Sunni 298, 310, 334
trade networks 246–7
Ismail Pasha 545, 551–2, 553, 554–5
Isokrates 139–40
Israel 49, 52, 92
cult of the God of 199
Late Bronze Age 57–59
modern state of 616–17, 638; and Egypt 618–20; and the Mediterranean Union 639; tourism 632–3
and Tyre 66–7
see also Hebrews; Holy Land; Palestine
Issos, battle of 149

Istanbul 354
  see also Constantinople
Istria 252, 601
Italian culture 439
Italian language 439
Italian Social Republic 612
Italians
  Albania invasion 602–4
  and the British 607
  contraction of control in Mediterranean
    617–18, 621–2
  Fascist 601–4
  Gothic Wars 235
  and Libya 576
  merchants 164–5, 183, 264, 270, 285,
    291, 297–8, 324, 332, 338, 349,
    354, 441, 459, 646
  and North Africa 574–5
  and Rhodes 577
  spas 632
  trade routes 271, 288, 318, 404, 458;
    Etruria 95, 101, 110
  and Tunisia 576
  war fleets 558, 582, 609, 611
  war with Turkey 576
  World War I 581–2
  World War II 607, 608, 609, 611–12
  see also Italy
Italiote League 175–6
Italy
  Adriatic lagoons and marshlands
    251–4; and the emergence of Venice
    254–5
  Austrians in 601
  Charlemagne's defence of 250
  collapse of central authority in
    northern Italy 275–7
  divided under five powers in fifteenth
    century 383
  and the EEC 621
  Etruria *see* Etruria; Etruscans
  Exarchate of Ravenna 252, 253
  Fascist 601–4, 605, 611–12
  first Greek settlement in 89–94
  Greeks in southern Italy 123
  Jewish emigration to 598
  Justinian and the recovery of 235

  and Libya 603–4, 615; Libyan refugees
    629
  Lombards in 237
  Muslim slave-raiders in 246
  Mycenaean trade with 33, 34
  naval power 296, 558
  Normans in 283
  people of *see* Italians
  Prussia and the kingdom of 558
  Rome and the southern Greek cities in
    176–7
  threats to Sicily 54
  tourism 636
  Venice and the politics of Renaissance
    Italy 412–13
  see also specific cities
Ithaka 87
Ithobaal, king of Tyre 69
ivory 374
  brought to Egypt 37
  Cretan 23, 24, 26
  Indian 158
  Phoenician 69, 79, 80, 110
Izmir 477, 588
  see also Smyrna

Jacob the Pisan 332
Jacobins 513, 514
Jaffa xxxi, 290–91, 292, 593–6, 600, 616,
  617
James I 'the Conqueror', king of Aragon
  334, 335, 338–41, 345, 350
James II, king of Aragon 345, 361
James II, king of Majorca 339, 348, 353
James III, king of Majorca 362
James of Lusignan 392
Jamona 223, 224, 225
  see also Ciutadella
Janus, king of Cyprus 392
Japanese 607, 631, 638
  destroyers 582
  economy 638
  tuna imports 640
  tourists 638
Jefferson, Thomas 530, 532
Jennings, Asa 587–8
Jerba 86, 349, 352, 416, 428–9

Jeremiah 57
Jericho 8, 58
Jerusalem 59, 67, 304
 Amalfitans in 269, 270
 capture by Saladin 297, 310, 325
 destruction of 216
 and the First Crusade 270, 288, 289,
  290, 291–2
 Franks of the kingdom of 311
 Grand Mufti (Amin al-Husayni) 604
 Holy Sepulchre 252, 287, 290, 292
 hospice 269
 kingdom of 291, 292, 297, 298, 301,
  311, 328, 329, 332, 348–50
 rebuilt as Aelia Capitolina 216
 Temple 67, 153, 216; vessels 232–3
Jesolo 253
Jesus Christ 213
 Monophysite view of 244
 Muslim view of Isa 244
jewellery
 amber 34
 Egyptian 38
 Etruscan 109
 Phoenician 79
 'Treasure of Priam' 21, 565
Jews
 of Adrianople 482
 in Alexandria 153, 161, 162, 215, 218,
  224, 590–91
 Algerian 573–4, 622
 of Algiers 531
 and America 535–6
 in Ancona 442–3
 Ashkenazi 592, 593, 599
 attacks on 405
 'Babylonian' 259–60
 Bacri family 531, 535, 540
 banished under Ferdinand II 406
 in Barcelona 340
 and the Black Death 404–5
 Catalan 341
 in Dubrovnik 438–9
 early Hebrews 48, 58–59, 66–7, 70
 under the Edicts of Toleration 559
 encounter between Contardo and a
  rabbi 341

 Epikursin 305
 exiled from Spain 406–8, 442–3
 of Florence 464
 in France 598, 617
 Genizah Jews of Cairo 258–9, 262,
  263–4, 266, 279, 295–6, 646
 and Genoa 296, 406
 ghettoes 438–9, 442, 443, 458, 464,
  559, 599, 646
 on Gibraltar 497–8, 536
 Hellenization of 598
 impact of exiles on the Mediterranean
  world 406–7
 and James I of Aragon 340–41
 Jewish Berbers 245–6
 Jewish diaspora 215–16, 476–83
 Jewish rebellion (115–16) 208–9, 216
 Jewish relations with Christians and
  Muslims in Spain 340–41, 404–6
 Jewish revolt in Palestine (132–6) 216
 Karaite 260
 in Majorca 340, 646
 maritime 218–19
 mass conversions of 223–5, 405, 441
 Mediterranean fifteenth-century 404–8
 merchants 199, 248–9, 258–9, 262–4,
  266, 279, 295–6, 437, 438, 443,
  457, 531, 646, 647
 of Minorca 223–5, 500
 Nazism and the Holocaust 599, 617
 and Ottomans 407
 in Palestine 215, 216; in the twentieth
  century 592–600, 616–17, 620
 pilgrims 304
 Ponentine 437, 458, 464–5
 Portuguese 441, 443, 477–8
 Radhanites 248
 and the rise of the Italians 296
 Roman treatment of 213, 214–17
 in Rome 194, 199
 of Salonika 569–72
 in Salonika 598–9
 Sephardic 260, 407–8, 437, 438–9,
  443, 444, 458, 464, 467, 470,
  476–83, 486, 569–72, 599, 647
 and the slave trade 248–9
 of Smyrna 584–5

of Toledo 404
trade networks of the diaspora 443
of Trani 342
of Trieste 559–60
of Tripoli 538
of Tunis 531–2
Tunisian 260
in Turkey 482
in Valencia 404, 405, 408
and Venice 296, 458
Zionist 592, 596
see also Israel; Judaism
jihad 366, 384
Jijelli 417
Joanna II, quuen of Naples 382
John II Komnenos, Byzantine emperor 293, 294
John II, king of Aragon 399
John VI Kantakouzenos, Byzantine emperor 366
Jonah 79
Jordan 619, 620
Joseph I, Holy Roman Emperor 497
Joseph II, Holy Roman Emperor 559
Josephus 74, 203, 216
Jouktas, Mount 25, 28
Juan, Prince of Asturias 410
Judaism
  Almohad sect and 296
  Christianity and the assertiveness of 222–5
  Christianity's rift with 213–14, 217
  cult of the God of Israel brought to Rome 199
  Day of Atonement 598
  and Hellenism 153
  and Islam 244, 340–41
  Jewish relations with Christians and Muslims in Spain 340–41, 404–6
  Kabbalah 342, 407, 479, 482
  rabbinic 217, 218–19
  under Roman rule 214–17
  Sabbath travel 262
  and the synagogue of Ostia 212
Julian (the Apostate) 220–21
Julius II, Pope 416
Juno 206

Jupiter 206
Justin 125
Justinian I, Roman emperor 221, 235

Kabbalah 342, 407, 479, 482
Kadesh, battle of 41, 42, 48
Kahina, Queen 245–6
Kallimachos of Cyrene 160
Kaminia 106
Kane, Richard 499, 500
Karamanli, Yussuf 531
Karimis 296
Kastellórizo 384
Katsamba 25
Katzones, captain 510–11
Kemal Atatürk, Mustafa 583, 585, 586, 587
Kenamun tomb 35
Kenchreai 95
Kephalonia 284, 352, 409, 460, 611, 637
Kerkennah 352
Kerkyra (Corfu) 86, 87, 98, 99, 141–2, 174
Kesselring, Albert 607
Khan al-'Umdan 310
Khirokitia 8–9
kibbutz movement 592
Kimon 141
Kipling, Rudyard 545
Kition 70, 74, 91
Kittim see Kition
Kleon 144
Knights Hospitallers 269, 364, 365, 366, 386, 414, 415, 416, 431, 445
Knights of Malta 269, 415, 422, 428, 429, 432, 433, 434, 435, 436, 468, 517, 518, 519; and the Russians 512–13; Sovereign Military Order of Malta 269
Knights of Santo Stefano 452, 462
Knights Templars 300
Knossos 9, 23–6, 28, 29, 31, 38
  Evans and the 'palace of Minos' at 565, 566
  palace 24–6
Kolaios of Samos 79, 126
Komnene, Anna 283–4

Komnenos dynasty
    Alexios I Komnenos 283, 284–5, 293
    Andronikos I Komnenos 324
    John II Komnenos 293, 294
    Manuel I Komnenos 294, 300, 319,
       322, 324, 328, 329
Komnenos family, post-imperial 329
Korčula 448
    battle of 355
Kosmos 300
Kotor (Cattaro) 385, 438, 521, 581, 582,
    613
    Bay of Kotor 390, 457, 511, 521
Kotruljević, Benedetto 390
Kouass 97
Kourion 568
Kroisos (Croesus), king of Lydia 134
Küçük Kaynarca, Treaty of 508
Kurzolaris islands 450
Kyma (Cumae) 90, 110
    battle of 114–15, 116
Kypselos 96
Kythnos 17

La Tène culture 125
Lacco Ameno 92–3
Lachish 35
Ladino language 407, 570
Lambert, Frank 529
Lampedusa 250, 629
Languages, ancient
    Canaanite 36, 65
    Etruscan 104
    Luvian 27, 43
    Lydian 104
    Sard 119–20
Languedoc 125, 126, 332, 335, 358, 404
Laodicea 237
Las Navas de Tolosa 334
Lauria, Roger de 351, 352
Lausanne, Treaty of 588
Lawrence, D. H. 100, 112, 638
Lawrence, T. E. 592
le Paulin, French ambassador 423
Lear, Tobias 535
Lebanon 35–6, 293, 617, 619, 639
Lechaion 95, 96, 285

Lefkandi 91
Lelantine War 94–5
Lemnos 20, 106, 107, 135, 140, 143, 385
Leo Africanus 381
Leo IV, Pope 268
Leo X, Pope 268, 381
Leontini 145
Lepanto 426, 451, 452
Lepidus 197
Lesbos 83, 140, 143–4, 415, 420
Lesseps, Ferdinand, Vicomte de 546, 549,
    550, 551, 552–3, 554
Leukas 174
Levant Company 459–60, 477, 478
Levant trade xxix, 35, 311, 379, 397, 400,
    437, 440, 445, 459, 469
    England's 505
    and the French 499
    Levant Fairs 595
    Levantine merchants of Smyrna 585
    and Minorca 502
    spice trade *see* spice trade
    Turkey Company/Levant Company
       459–60, 477, 478
    Venice and 378, 457, 458
Levantine Jews 437, 458
Levanzo cave paintings 5–6, 7
Lewis, Bernard 244
Libya 576, 615–16, 622, 638
    Italy and 603–4, 615, 629
Libyans 48–50, 166–7
    refugees 629
    see also Libya
lighthouse of Alexandria, Pharos island
    154–5, 305, 309
Ligurian coast 249
Ligurians 124, 282
lingua franca 486–7
Lipari 7, 32, 33, 34, 63, 180
    islands 7, 12, 63, 115, 178, 179
    Neolithic 10, 12–13, 14
Liria 130
Lisbon 466
Lisle, Peter 531
Lissa 558
Litorius, Count 223
Littorio (Italian ship) 607

Livornine 464–5, 466
Livorno 462, 464–7, 531, 599
Livy 187, 199
Lixus 66
Lleida (Lerida) 346
llotjas (loggias) 341, 399–400, 402
Lloyd Austriaco 556
Lloyd George, David, 1st Earl 585, 586, 588
Llull, Ramon 342–4, 646–7
Lodi, Peace of 383
Lombardi 282
Lombards 237, 253, 255
London 347
Longobardia 281
Loria, Alessandro 589, 590
Louis I, king of Hungary 377
Louis IX, king of France 348
Louis the Pious, Frankish emperor 248, 250
Louis XII, king of France 409, 420
Louis XIV, king of France 491–2, 493, 494, 495
Louis XVI, king of France 510
Louis XVII, heir to French throne 513–14
Lucan 193
Lukka 49
Luli, King 70
Luni 237
Lusiads (Camões) 396
Lusignans 358, 359
Luther, Martin 423
Luvian language 27, 43
Luxardo family 601
Lycia 49
Lycians 41
Lydia 97, 98, 101
    Persian destruction of 134
    people of *see* Lydians
Lydians 101, 102
    language 104
    see also Lydia
Lysandros/Lysander 147

Maccabean revolt 153
Macedonians
    Alexander III (the Great) 149–52

IMRO 570–71
    Romans and 164, 186, 188
Madeira 393, 411
Madina Mayurqa (Ciutat de Mallorca) 338–9, 340
Madison, James 529, 536
Maghrib 298, 306, 344, 409–10, 417
    US envoy to 535–6
    see also Barbary states
Magon 76
Magona (Maó) 223, 225
    see also Mahón
Mahdia (al-Mahdiyyah) 263, 279–80, 319–20, 322, 428
Mahmudié (Austrian Lloyd ship) 556–7
Mahmudiyya canal 540
Mahón (Maó) 418, 498, 499, 506
    see also Magona
Maida, battle of 524
Maimon, son of William 332
Maimonides, Moses 259, 296
Mainake 127
Maiori 268
Mairano, Romano 299–301
Majorca 338–9, 340, 353, 358, 364
    attacks on Jews 405
    Black Death 368
    under Byzantine rule 242
    Fascist Italians in 604
    Jews 340, 646
    llotja 399–400
    merchants/shipowners 345, 348
    and Muslim pirates 414
    Neolithic 14
    shipping 347–8, 401–2
    social divisions 399
    tourism 631–2, 633, 634, 637
    trade in the fifteenth century 401–2
    and trade networks 362
    urban population drop (1329–43) 367
    see also Balearic islands
Makarios III 623–4
al-Makhzumi 297
Málaga 78, 124, 393
Malamocco 254
Mallia 24, 636
Mallone, Ansaldo 302

Malta xxxi, 202, 321, 352, 622
British 604, 605, 607–8, 610, 622
Catalan consuls 401
cotton 323
and the Hospitaller Order of St John of
Jerusalem 269, 415
as an immigrant entry point 629
importance to Christendom 429
Knights of 269, 415, 422, 428, 429,
432, 433, 434, 435, 436, 468,
517, 518, 519; and the Russians
512–13
and Napoleon 516–17, 520
Neolithic 10–12, 14
and the Russians 512, 518, 519,
520–21
sieges: of British Malta (World War II)
520, 608; Ottoman 428–34, 447,
451
slave market 435–6
Sovereign Military Order of 269
tourism 631
trade in the sixteenth century 436
and the Turks 269, 428–34
in World War II 607–8, 610
Mamertines 178–9
Mamluks 349, 355, 379, 392, 397, 537
in Syria 349, 414
Mandelli, Giovanni 380
Mantua 117, 406
Manuel I Komnenos, Byzantine emperor
294, 300, 319, 322, 324, 328, 329
Maó see Magona; Mahón
al-Maqrizi 368
marble 18, 19, 96, 138, 205, 222, 236,
238, 269, 275, 279
Marcionites 218, 220
Marcus Aurelius, Roman emperor 208
Maria Theresa, Empress 559
Marinids 334, 347, 363–4
maritime insurance 402, 439, 457, 465
maritime law 402–3
Mark the evangelist 255
Marmara, Sea of 439
Marmont, Auguste de 522
Marnas 221
Marneion temple 221–2

Marranos 442–3, 458, 463–4, 647
Marseilles 77, 110, 114, 126, 237, 247,
250, 358, 376, 622
bubonic plague 500
and Charles of Anjou 350
fall to the Allies 612
and James I of Aragon 338
merchant privileges 325
and Richard I of England 325
see also Massalia
Martell, Pere 338
Martial 129
Martin the Younger of Sicily 381
Martínez, Ferran 405
Martorell, Joannot 384
martyrs 214, 217–18, 223–4
Marzameni wreck 238
Masinissa 188
Massalia 123–5, 126
see also Marseilles
mastic 345, 358, 366, 374
Mataró 401
Mauretania 210
Mauretanians 208, 230
Mausoleum of Halikarnassos 386
Maxentius 219
Maximilian, Ferdinand 557, 558
Mazara 264, 279
Mazower, Mark 569
Mdina 429, 432
Medenine 610
Medes 136
Medici family 403, 462
Bank 376
dukes of Tuscany 452, 462, 466–7
Medina Sidonia, dukes of 398
Medinet Habu 50
Mediterranean economy see economy
Mediterranean features, physical xxvii–xxx
boundaries xxiii–xxiv
Mediterranean food 628–9
Mediterranean history literature xxiv–xxvii
Mediterranean language (lingua franca)
486–7
Mediterranean tourism see tourism
Mediterranean travel accounts (1160–85)
304–17, 462–3

Mediterranean's names xxiii
a 'faithful sea' xxxiii, 646–7
Megalé Idea 578
Mehmet Effendi 482
see also Zevi, Shabbetai
Mehmet II, the Conqueror, Ottoman sultan
383, 385, 386, 387, 388, 391, 415
Mehmet IV, Ottoman sultan 482
Meletius of Minorca 223
Melilla 409, 575
Melissa, wife of Periandros 98
Melkites 591
Meloria, battle of 334
Melos 5, 7, 9–10, 14, 24, 32
Melqart 74, 75, 78, 171, 645
Menander 152
Menasce, Félix de, Baron 590–91
Menasce family 591
Menelaos of Sparta 85
Menelaus of Caria 206
Mengebet 39, 40
Menton 632
mercenaries 36, 45, 47, 48, 49, 52
Merchant of Prato 373–5
merchants 644–6
Amalfi 294–5
of Barcelona 345
Catalan 344, 353, 359–60, 400
Genoese 277, 278, 298–9, 301–3, 341,
344, 358, 441
German xxix, 277, 401
gods posing as 88
and heroes of the First Mediterranean
29–41
Italian 164–5, 183, 264, 270, 285, 291,
297–8, 324, 332, 338, 349, 354,
441, 459, 646; *see also under*
specific cites
Jewish 199, 248–9, 258–9, 262–4, 266,
279, 295–6, 437, 438, 443, 457,
531, 646, 647
Levantine 585; *see also* Levant trade
mercenaries, missionaries and
merchants of the Third
Mediterranean 334–53
Muslim 257, 258, 261–2, 266, 296,
404, 453, 457, 465

north European merchants of grain 454
Phoenician 71, 88, 101, 111, 206, 644,
645
Pisan 297–8, 332
Puteolan 205
Roman 191, 194, 199–200
Savoyard 401
and shipowners of Majorca 345, 348
Venetian *see* Venetians: merchants
see also trade networks; trade routes
Merneptah, Pharaoh 48–50
Mers el-Kebir 606
Meryry, Libyan king 48, 49
Meshuda 533
Meshwesh 48, 50
Mesolithic 7
Messana 178, 179
Messina xxxi, 282, 295, 314, 462, 525
arsenal 424
bubonic plague 368
silk 468
Straits of 86, 115, 145, 179, 281, 282,
313–14, 526
in World War II 611
Metellus Balearicus, Quintus Caecilius 194
Methuen, John 496
Michael VII Doukas, Byzantine emperor
283
Michael VIII Palaiologos, Byzantine
emperor 330, 331, 350, 354, 364–5
migrations
Algerian 622
Asian migrants to the Mediterranean
629
and cuisines 628–9
Etruscan 101–5, 108, 117
Greek 83–99, 117
immigrants from beyond the
Mediterranean 629–30
Jewish migrants to Palestine 594–5,
617
Libyan 48–50
Neolithic 8
to the New World 573
from North Africa 622
out of Sicily and southern Italy 628
of Palestinians 616–17

migrations – *cont.*
  of the Sea Peoples 49, 55–59
  into southern Greece 54–55
  temporary migrations of mass tourism 631–8
Miguez, João (Joseph Nasi) 444–6
Milan 383, 404, 420
  Visconti lords 376, 382–3
Milan, Edict of 219
Milano Marittima 633
Milawanda *see* Miletos
Miletos 25, 33, 44, 45, 54, 55, 96
Military Orders of the Temple and Hospital of St John 326, 348
  see also Knights Hospitallers
Miltiades 134
Milvian Bridge, battle of 219
Mine (São Jorge da Mina) 411
Minerva 206
Minoan civilization 22–7, 28, 29–31
  art 36, 37
  Evans' view of Minoan Crete 566
  merging with Mycenaean 30–31
  pottery 22, 23, 24, 27
  trade routes 24
Minorca 339, 373, 418, 423, 495
  and the British 498–503, 514
  and the French 498, 501–3
  Jews 223–5
  Neolithic 14
  and the Russians 509–10
  and the Seven Years War 501–3
  see also Balearic islands
Minori 268
Minos, King 22
Mintoff, Dom 622
Misenum 208, 210
mistral xxviii
Modon 419, 538
Mogador 72
mommia 297
Monaco 360
Monemvasia 419–20
Mongols 342, 355
  and bubonic plague 367–8
Monophysites 220, 244
Monopoli 388

monotheism 153, 225
Montague, Edward, 2nd Earl of Manchester 489–90
Monte Carlo 632
Monte d'Accoddi 121
Montecassino, Benedictines of 269, 274
Montecatini 632
Montenegro 385, 440, 521, 581, 582
Montfort, Simon de 335
Montilla 78
Montpellier 305, 325, 333, 335, 338, 339, 358
Moors
  and Gibraltar 497
  pirates 208
  in Sardinia 233
  and Vandal shipping 232
Morea 488–9, 508, 537–8
  see also Peloponnese
Moriscos 408, 434, 447, 453, 470–76, 647
Moroccans 363–4
  Marinids 334, 347, 363–4
  pottery 280–81
  see also Morocco
Morocco 4, 258, 263, 296, 298, 355, 577, 617–18
  and America 532, 534
  defeat of Sebastian of Portugal in 453
  and the English 459
  grain 298, 392
  people of *see* Moroccans
  Tangier 396, 491–4, 577, 626
  tourism 633
Moscow 612, 638
Moses 58, 153
Mostar 439
Mother/Great Goddess 11, 12, 18, 213
Motya 76, 81, 166, 170
Mudros 579
Müezzinzâde Ali 449, 450
Muhammad Ali 537, 538, 539–40, 548, 565
Mujahid, Muslim warlord 273
mules 440
Murad II, Ottoman sultan 385
Murat, Joachim 524, 525–6
Murcia 398

Muret 335
Murlo 104
Murrow, Ed 609
Muscovy 504
    trade 459
Muscovy Company 460
Muslims see Islam and the Muslim peoples
Mussolini, Benito 574, 601, 604, 605, 606,
    608, 610, 611, 612
Mustafa, Lala 448–9
Mustafa Pasha 432, 433–4
Mycenae 29–30, 32, 46, 53, 87, 565
    high kings of 44
    Treasury of Atreus 563
Mycenaeans 29–35, 53, 54, 71, 565
    and the Anatolians 44–7
    pottery 34, 35, 43, 46, 51, 54, 56
    refugees in Cyprus 54
    tombs 32, 34–5, 54, 565
    trade 32, 33–4
    see also Mycenae
Mykale 137
Mylai 181
Myra 292
Myriokephalon 329
myrrh 158, 165
Mytilene 143–4

Nabataeans
    in Puteoli 206
    trade routes 165, 221
Nabis, king of Sparta 195
Nafplion (Nauplion) 419–20, 538
Nahmanides 341
Naples 179, 267, 390, 420
    Alfonso V of Aragon's capture of 383,
        401
    Aragonese 401, 409
    attack by Francis I 419
    banishment of Jews 406
    Bay of 75, 89, 194, 203, 205, 247
    bubonic plague 368
    Byzantine capture of 235
    Castelnuovo fortress 399
    Ferdinand II, king of Aragon in 410
    French and Aragonese claims to the
        throne 387–8

kings of 352, 354, 360, 365, 382, 387,
    388, 390
    pottery imports 236–7
Napoleon I 513, 514, 515–16, 517, 520,
    521, 523, 524, 526,
    546–7
Napoleon III (originally Charles Louis
    Napoleon Bonaparte) 547–8, 549,
    554
Napoleonic Wars 513, 522–3,
    524–6
Narbonne 358
Nasi, Gracia 441–2, 443, 444
Nasi, Joseph 444–6
Nasrid dynasty 334, 347, 393, 404
Nasser, Gamal Abdel 600, 618–19
Nathan of Gaza 480, 482
National Bank of Egypt 589
national identities/nationalism 568–72, 583
    Greek nationalism 568–9, 623
National Organisation of Cypriot Fighters
    623
NATO (North Atlantic Treaty
    Organization) 620, 621, 624
naturist resorts 636
Naukratis 96, 157
naval warfare 72
    see also warships/fleets/navies
Navarino, battle of 539
Navarre 335, 399
navicularii (guilds of shippers) 218, 227–8
navies see warships/fleets/navies
Naxians 138, 140, 444, 445–6
Naxos 134, 140, 444
Nazism/Nazis 599, 600, 605–10, 611, 612
Neanderthals 3–4
Negroponte 385
Nelson, Horatio, Viscount 463, 515–16,
    518, 519, 520
Neo-Platonism 220
Neolithic 8–14
    buildings 10–11
    Revolution 8
Neptune 644
Nero, Roman emperor 203, 204, 205, 217
Nerva, Marcus Cocceius, Roman emperor
    216

Neretva, river 456
Nestor's cup 92–3
Netherlands 427, 463, 471
    see also Dutch; Holland
Neve Tzedek 593, 595
New Carthage (Cartagena) 185, 187
New Zealanders, Gallipoli campaign 579
Nicaea, Council of 219
Nicaean creed 219, 231
Nice 422, 605, 610, 632
see also Nikaia (Nice)
Nicholas, St 292
Nicosia 446, 447, 623, 625
Nicotera 279
Niebla, count of 398
Niger, river 279
Nikaia (Asia Minor) 330, 349, 366
    see also Nicaea
Nikaia (Nice) 126
Nikomedeia 227
Nile Delta 14, 35, 38, 39, 51, 52, 53, 158,
    297, 376
Nile, river xxvii, xxix, 37, 38, 549–50
    floods xxix, 156, 158, 204
Nile Valley 28
Niqmadu, King 35
Noah, Mordecai 535–6
Nora 77
Nora stele 73
Normandy 612
Normans
    Bohemond I of Antioch and the First
        Crusade 288–90
    and Byzantium 281–4, 288–9, 319,
        322, 323–4
    collapse of kingdom of Sicily 327–8
    rule in Sicily 279–80, 281–4, 294, 318;
        and campaigns from Sicily 319–24
North Africa xxix, 14, 66, 74, 101, 174,
    227–30
    Aghlabid emirs 250
    agriculture 203–4
    Arab conquest 245–6
    Barbary see Barbary states
    Berbers see Berbers
    Carthage see Carthage
    Catalans in 345

Christian soldiers in Muslim armies
    344
coast xxvii, xxviii, 14, 71, 76, 171, 174
demotic culture 189
French emigration to 573–4
Genoese in 298–9
grain trade 203
Islamic Ifriqiya 246
Italian settlers 574–5
as Italy's 'fourth shore' 604
James I of Aragon and the Muslims of
    341
and Naples 236
Numidians 183, 187
pagan cults in 221
Pompey's actions against piracy 196
pottery 204, 236, 237
Roger II and 319–20
Roman province of Africa 203, 245–6
Spanish garrisons 409
trade with Catalonia 402
trade with Majorca 402
Tunisia see Tunisia
William II and 322
in World War II 607, 608, 609
    see also Maghrib
North Atlantic Treaty Organization
    (NATO) 620, 621, 624
North Sea 347, 436, 439, 488, 505, 520,
    579
Norwegians 528
Noto 282
Novi Pazar 439
Nubia 245
Numidians 183, 187, 188
nuns 422, 501, 595, 644
nuraghi 119, 121–2

Obadiah 408
obsidian 7, 8, 9–10, 12, 13, 15, 24, 32, 33,
    34
Octavian 197, 198–9, 208
    see also Augustus Caesar
Odessa 511
Odoacer 227, 233
Odysseus (Ulysses) 85, 86, 87, 380
oil, crude 578

Axis supplies 609
exploration 616
from Iraq 605
supplies via the Suez Canal
609
oil, olive 20, 34, 35, 56, 67, 73, 76, 79, 90,
285, 511
Corinthian trade in 97
and the Mediterranean diet
629
presses 57, 125
Ptolemies and oil industry 159
scarcity after World War II 628
Old Smyrna 55
olive oil *see* oil, olive
olive trees xxix, 159, 230, 234, 483
Oliverdar, Mateu 345
Olympia 113
Olympic Games 170, 178
Onomastikon of Amenope 55
Ophir 69
Oran 406, 409, 417, 475, 495, 540–41,
606
'massacre' of 622
Order of St John *see* Knights Hospitallers
Oristano 308
Ostia 175, 196, 203, 205, 207–8
naval battle off 268
religious buildings 212–13
Ostrogoths 233
Otho, Marcus Salvius, Roman emperor
208
Otranto 386–7, 388
Otto I, German emperor 275
Otto II, German emperor 272
Ottoman Bank 571
Ottomans 366, 384–8, 392–3
in the Balkans 440
and Hayrettin Barbarossa
417–18
battle for the White Sea 428–35,
445–51
battle of Navarino 539
and the British 525, 538–40, 568,
578–80, 585
Christian reaction to expansion in
sixteenth century 418–23

conflicts with Greeks in the nineteenth
century 538–9
and Corfu 419, 518
and Crete 448, 483–6, 565–6, 588
and Cyprus 446–51, 567–9
development of national identities in
Ottoman lands 568–72
and Dubrovnik 388–91
erosion of the Ottomam Empire 504,
521, 525, 538, 555, 568–9, 573–80;
and exit of the Ottomans 578–82,
583–92
expansion in the sixteenth century
414–15, 423–4
and the French 539, 546–8; Franco-
Turkish alliance 418–19, 420–23,
475
and Jews 407
and Malta 428–34
Mamluks *see* Mamluks
and the Moriscos 434–5, 471–6
and Muhammad Ali 537–40
Ottoman corsairs *see* Barbary corsairs
and Russians 505–8, 510–11, 518–19,
522
and Salonika 570–72
settlement with the Spaniards in the
sixteenth century 453
Sublime Porte 385–6, 390, 391, 417,
419, 423, 435, 438, 444, 452, 453,
472, 477, 483, 485, 518, 532, 552,
568
Suez Canal and reciprocal East–West
cultural relations 545, 548–55
Turkish-Russian war 505–8
and Venetians 385–6, 387, 388, 392,
419–20, 423, 446–7, 483–6, 489;
Cretan War (1645–1669) 484–5
warships 424–7, 447, 448, 449–50,
484, 506–7, 538, 539
western dress 545
Our Lady of the Conception (Hospitaller
galley) 416
Ovid 102

P & O (Peninsular and Oriental) 557
Pacifico, Don 564

package holidays 634–5
Paestum (Poseidonia), 112, 177
paganism 220–22
    and Islam 244
    see also fertility cults; goddesses; gods;
      religion
Palaeolithic era 4–7
Palaiologos family
    Andronikos II 354
    Demetrios 384
    Michael VIII 330, 331, 350, 354,
      364–5
Palermo 266, 279, 282, 295, 350, 351,
    353, 406, 527
    Allied occupation 611
    see also Panormos
Palestine 55, 57, 325, 445
    Arabs in 592, 594, 595, 616–17
    and the British 592, 616–17
    and the Crusades 292; see also
      Crusades
    and James II of Aragon 345
    Jews in 215, 216; conflicts with Arabs
      592, 594, 595, 616–17; influx of
      immigrants 594–5; Jewish revolt
      (132–6) 216; in the twentieth
      century 592–600, 616–17, 620
    kibbutz movement 592
    and the state of Israel 616–17, 618–20
    withdrawal of Turkish troops 580
    and Zionism 592
    see also Canaan; Holy Land; Israel
Palestinian Authority 639
Pallottino, Massimo 104
Palma, Majorca 338, 604, 621, 634
    see also Ciutat de Mallorca
Palma Nova 634
Palmerston, John Henry Temple, 3rd
    Viscount 550, 564
Panormos 166
    see also Palermo
Pantaleoni family 269
Pantelleria 10, 13, 611, 629
Paoli, Pasquale 514, 515
papacy 247, 274, 383
    papal fleets 429
    Papal Inquisition see Inquisition

    relationship with Greek Orthodox
      Church 282–3
    see also specific popes
Papyrella 14
papyrus 156–7, 161, 247
Paris 554, 586
Paros 18
Parthenon marbles 563
Patras 342
Patton, General George 611
Paul, St 202–3, 213–14, 643
Paul I, emperor of Russia 511–12, 513,
    518, 519–20
Paul IV, Pope 442–3
Pavia, battle of 420
pax romana 201, 209, 210, 231
Peace of Lodi 383
Pech Maho 110, 124
Pedro of Portugal 339
Peiraieus 639
Pelasgians 83, 106
Peleshet 50–51, 55
Peloponnese 488–9
    Peloponnesian War 96, 133, 141–8
    see also Morea
Peloponnesian League 140–41, 142, 143
Pelops 32
Peninsular Steam Navigation Company
    557
Peninsular War 524
pepper 247, 270, 279, 291, 296, 301, 374,
    560, 642
Pepys, Samuel 490, 492–3
Pera 354
Pergamon 161, 236
    altar 563
Periandros (Periander) 96, 97–8
Perikles 140
Periplus 127
Perpignan 353, 358, 399
Persia 378, 427, 440, 484, 578, 609
    people of see Persians
Persians 234, 446, 453
    Byzantium and 236
    defeat by Alexander III 149
    and the Delian League 139
    invasion of Greece 114, 132–7

invasion of Ionia 123–4
navy 134, 136–7, 141
and the Peloponnesian War 146–7
Persian empire 135
and the Phoenicians 134, 136–7
and the Scythians 135
wheat 158–9
see also Persia
Perugia 116
Peruzzi Bank 375
Pesaro 443
Pétain, Philippe 606
Peter, St 213
Peter I 'the Great', emperor of Russia 504, 512
Peter I, king of Cyprus 359
Peter II, king of Aragon 335
Peter III, king of Aragon 339, 348, 351, 353
Peter IV, the Ceremonious, king of Aragon 362
Petrarch 380
Petronius 206
Phaistos 9, 24, 25
Pharaohs 36–41, 48–50, 53, 63, 66
and Ptolemies 152
Pharisees 217
Pharos island 150, 152
lighthouse 154–5, 305, 309
Pharsalus 197
Philadelphia, USS 534
Philip II, king of Macedon 150, 174
Philip II, king of Spain 427, 432–3, 447, 451, 453, 471, 473
Philip III, king of Spain 476
Philip V, king of Macedon 186
Philip V, king of Spain, Philip de Bourbon/Philip of Anjou 494, 495, 496, 497, 498
Philippi, battle of 197
Philistines 55–57, 58–59, 644
Philo 152, 161, 162
Phocaea 347
see also Phokaia
Phoenicians 63–82, 90, 91–2, 104–5, 645
and Alexander the Great 149
alphabet 80, 644

at Cádiz 66, 72, 78, 126
Carthaginians see Carthaginians
Etruscan trade 111
merchants 71, 88, 101, 111, 206, 644, 645
and the Persians 134, 136–7
pirates 134
and the Ptolemies 156
in Puteoli 206
script 80, 644
and the Seleucids 156
shipyards 156
spread of culture 80–81, 128
trade routes/networks 63, 66, 67–79, 242
trading system 69–70, 80
warships 72, 134, 136–7
Phoibos Apollo 138
Phokaia 123–4, 347, 392
Phokaians 77, 106–7, 114, 123–4, 126, 134
Picenes 117
pilgrimage 379–80
crusaders and 280, 292; see also Crusades
female pilgrims 644
Jewish pilgrims 304
mixing of Muslim and Christian pilgrims 312–13
modern pilgrims 632
and piracy 446
sea journeys of pilgrims 308–15, 317
Pillars of Hercules 126
Pindar 95, 115, 160, 169
Piombino 383
Pionius 217–18
Pippin, king of Italy 254
pirates/piracy xxviii, xxx, 41, 49, 52, 54, 65, 194–6, 247, 360, 647
Aegean clearance of pirates by a 'Holy League' 365
Arab 249, 250–51, 278–9
Barbary see Barbary corsairs
based in Crete 163, 195
Christian 381, 414, 429, 435, 446, 449, 453
Cilician 165, 195

pirates/piracy – *cont.*
  Croatian 439, 440
  from end of the fifteenth century 413–14
  English 461
  Etruscan 63, 72, 105–6, 109
  Genoese 328–9, 331
  Greek 72
  Italian 275, 328–9
  by the Knights Hospitallers 414, 429, 435
  in the late sixteenth century 453–4
  Maltese 429, 435, 484
  Mauretanian 208
  Monegasque 360
  Moorish 208
  Muslim naval power based on 249, 250–51, 268, 278–9, 402, 414, 423–4
  Phoenician 134
  and pilgrim traffic 446
  Polykrates of Samos 134, 138, 147
  and the Romans 175, 194–6, 642
  Saracen 272–3
  ship technology 461
  and slavery 414, 417, 418
  small trading ships and the decline in piracy 201
  Turkish 428
  Tuscan 452
  'Tyrsenians' 54, 71, 83, 105, 106–7, 115, 195
  of the Uskoks 439
  and the Venetian *muda* protection 360, 642
  Volscian 175
Pirenne, Henri 247
Pisa xxxi, 109, 271–81, 286, 290, 301, 316, 326, 346, 358
  and Amalfi 294–5
  churches and cathedrals 275, 279, 280–81
  government of 276–7
  people of *see* Pisans
  tourists in 633
Pisans
  and Acre 310–11
  and Catalans 361

  commercial privileges 293
  commune 276–7
  and the Crusades 292
  and Genoese 273, 274, 275, 278–9, 305, 334
  in Majorca 338
  massacre in Constantinople (1182) 324, 329
  merchants 332; incident in Egypt 297–8
  navy 273, 294–5, 327
  and Sardinia 273, 274–5
  sheep 367
  and shipping 316–17
  see also Pisa
Pithekoussai (Ischia) 34, 89–90, 92–4, 95, 110, 268, 422
pithoi 34
Pius II, Pope 393
Piyale Pasha 429, 432, 433–4
Piyamaradu 44
plague 59, 399
  bubonic *see* Black Death/bubonic plague
Plataia, battle of 132, 137
Plato 169–70
Plautus, Titus Maccius 193–4, 199, 439
Pliny the Elder 180, 203
Plutarch 133, 146, 172, 195, 196
Po, river xxvii
Po Valley 117, 236, 255
Poland 599, 605
Poliochni, Lemnos 20–21
Polis 87
pollution 637, 640
Polo, Marco 355
Polybios 178, 179, 181, 647
Polykrates of Samos 134, 138, 147
Pomella 290
Pompeii 114, 206, 562
Pompeius Magnus Pius, Sextus 195, 200
Pompey the Great 196–7
Ponentine Jews 437, 458, 464–5
Ponza 268
Popular Front for the Liberation of Palestine 620
population 376
  and the Black Death 366–7, 368–9

Porphyry 221, 222
Port Said 551, 553
ports xxx–xxxi
    see also specific ports
Portugal 79, 398, 453, 465, 491, 580, 637
    exiled Jews from 441, 443
    people of *see* Portuguese
    and Philip II 453, 473
Portuguese 364, 393–6, 463–4
    in Ancona 442
    Inquisition 463–4
    Jews 441, 443, 477–8
    opening of route in 1497 to the East
        458
    war fleets 366, 393–5
    see also Portugal
Portus, Ostia 207–8
Poseidon 22, 73, 85, 165, 644
Poseidonia (Paestum) 112, 177
Potideia 143
Potnia, goddess 26
pottery/ceramics
    Aegean 20
    African 204, 236, 237
    Alexandrian 156
    amphorae 25, 67, 97, 201, 202, 206,
        232, 236, 237; of oil 92; of wine 73,
        92, 157, 164, 237
    Anatolian 20
    Athenian 55, 96, 101, 105–6
    Bronze Age Greek 26
    bucchero style 93, 109
    Carthaginian 96
    Corinthian 87, 95, 96, 101; in Sardinia
        122
    Cretan 236
    Cypriot 38
    Egyptian 280
    Etruscan 78, 110, 112–13; in Massalia
        124; in Sardinia 122; Villanovan
        109
    Euboian 87, 92
    Greek 75, 77, 108, 113, 126; Attic 113,
        126; in Massalia 124, 125; in
        Sardinia 122; *see also under specific
        Greek cultures*
    Helladic 33, 35, 43, 53

    Iberian 130
    Islamic 280
    Late Bronze Age 33
    Minoan/Cretan 22, 23, 24, 27
    Moroccan 280–81
    Mycenaean 34, 35, 43, 46, 51, 54, 56
    Neolithic 9, 12, 13
    from Philistine sites 55, 56
    Samian 237
    Scornavacche as a centre of ceramics
        industry 172
    Sub-Mycenaean 54
    and the sugar industry 393
    Syrian 38, 91
    of Troy 20, 43
    Valencian 403
Potyomkin, Grigory 509
Pozzuoli 205
    see also Puteoli
prehistoric society development 15
Preveza, battle of 420
prostitutes 74, 464, 644
Protestantism
    and confessional identity 488
    and the Inquisition 461
    Messianic ideas 481
    Philip II's wars with Protestants 453
Provence xxviii, 125, 126, 210, 250–51,
        346
Prussia 520, 554, 558
Pryor, John xxvii, xxviii
Ptolemies 152–64, 188
    grain trade 158
    navy 156
    and the olive oil industry 159
    Ptolemaic Alexander 152–4, 155–62;
        Alexandrian Library 159–61
    Ptolemy I Soter 152, 153, 154, 159–60
    Ptolemy II Philadelphos 153, 156, 161,
        549
    Ptolemy IV Philopater 156
    Ptolemy VIII 200
    Ptolemy XIII 197
    Ptolemy XV Caesar 197
    trade control 157
    see also Cleopatra
Ptolemy, Claudius 162

Punic Wars 177–90
  First War 177–8, 179–82
  origins of 178–9
  Second War 177, 178, 183–8
  Third War 177, 189
Punt 37
purple traders *see* Phoenicians
Puteoli 165, 203, 205–7, 210
Pylos 31, 32, 46, 52, 144
pyramids 37
Pyrgoi 111, 170, 175
Pyrrhos of Epeiros 174, 176, 177
Pytheas 127

Qayrawan 246, 263
Quintio 201

rabbis 217, 218, 219
Radhanites 248
Raeder, Admiral Erich Johann 609
Ragusa *see* Dubrovnik
Ragusans xxiii, 388–91, 437, 438, 439,
    442, 448, 478, 526–7, 532
  and Genoa 468
  and Ottomans 414
  and the Russians 521–2
  and trade from Alicante 465
  and Uskoks 457
Rahmi Bey 584, 585
railways 576, 582, 585, 594
  and tourism 632, 633, 634
Ramesses II, Pharaoh 41, 48
Ramesses III, Pharaoh 48, 50
Ramesses XI, Pharaoh 39
Ramesses, city of 37
Ramon Berenguer III 338
Ramon de Penyafort 341
Ravello 268, 295
Ravenna 208, 210–11, 235, 252, 253, 358,
    420
Real (Spanish flagship) 450
Red Sea 37, 38, 58, 158
  blockade of Israel 619
  Suez Canal *see* Suez Canal
  trade 69, 296, 355; routes 158, 248,
    296, 355

Reggio 203, 368
  see also Rhegion
Reis, Murad 531
Reis, Pirî 415
relics *see* religious relics
religion
  Baal worship 70, 81–2
  beliefs carried along trade routes 213,
    332, 481, 482–3
  Canaanite 57, 65–6
  changes of 426–7; mass conversions
    223–5, 405, 441
  Christian *see* Christianity
  Delian Apollo cult 138
  Demeter cult 171
  and the 'faithful sea' 646–7
  fertility cults 11, 18, 154
  in Gibraltar 496, 497
  and Hellenistic culture 213
  ideas spread by travel across the
    Mediterranean 213, 256, 266–7,
    332, 342, 481, 482–3
  Isis cult 199, 213
  Islamic *see* Islam
  Jewish *see* Judaism
  under Julian 220
  in Minorca 500
  and national identities 569–72
  Phoenician 81–2
  and the Romans 209, 213–22
  sacrifice *see* human sacrifice; sacrifices
  tolerance in 426
  in Trieste 559–60
  see also Bible; funerary rites; goddesses;
    gods; religious buildings; temples
religious buildings
  Anglican churches, Minorca 500
  at Ostia 212–13
  synagogues *see* synagogues
  temples *see* temples
religious relics 223, 224, 255, 329, 330,
    345, 368, 512
René of Anjou, king of Naples 382, 383,
    397
Renfrew, Colin 10, 17
Rethymnon 484

Revolutionary War, French 513–20
Rhegion 115, 178
   see also Reggio
Rheneia 138
Rhode (Roses) 124, 127, 352
Rhodes 25, 32, 53, 93, 414
   and Alexandria 157, 163–4
   Arab sea battle off 245
   besieged by Mamluks 392
   Catalans and 401
   Colossus of 155, 163
   earthquake 164
   and the Italians 577
   and the Knights Hospitallers 269, 364,
      386, 414, 415
   Mycenaean trade with 32, 33
   people of see Rhodians
   sieges of 163, 414–15
   and trade routes 53, 366
   and the Turks 269
   wine 164
Rhodians
   bankers 164
   coinage 164
   grain trade 158
   Sea Law 236
   see also Rhodes
Rhône delta 250
Rhône valley 125
Ricart Guillem 335–6
Riccione 633
rice 340, 374, 404, 465, 532, 560
Richard I, king of England 325
Richelieu, Armand de Vignerot du Plessis
   502, 503
Richelieu, Armand Jean, Cardinal 475–6
Rijeka (Fiume) 601–2
Rimini 358, 632, 633
   Ariminum 177
Robert, count of Flanders 290
Robert the Wise, king of Naples 360, 365
Roccaforte 360
Rodriguez, Marrano Daniel 440
Roger I, count of Sicily 279, 281–2, 283,
   294, 318
Roger II, king of Sicily 318–22

Roma 611
Romania 355
Romano, Ruggiero 465
Romans
   and the Aetolian League 188
   Christian persecution 214, 217–18
   Christianity legalized by 213, 219–20,
      227
   civil wars 196–7, 198–9
   coins 204, 220
   destruction of pagan temples 221–2
   development of 'Romanness' 191
   disintegration of the Roman Empire
      226–38
   and Egypt 197–200, 208–9
   and Etruscans 175
   garum sauce 76, 206, 641
   interference in Aegean trade networks
      164
   and Macedonians 164, 186, 188
   navy/fleets 175, 176, 177, 178, 179,
      180–82, 185, 186–7, 198, 208–9,
      210
   pax romana 201, 209, 210, 231
   and pirates 175, 194–6, 642
   pre-Punic War battles with
      Carthaginians 175
   and Ptolemies 188
   Punic Wars see Punic Wars
   and religion 209, 213–22
   and Rhodians 164
   Roman Republic 188
   and Seleucids 188
   slavery 191–3
   Tetrarchy 227
   treatment of Jews 213, 214–17
   treaty with Vandals 231
   and the Volscians 175
   see also Rome
Rome
   Amalfi and 268–9
   Arab attacks on 250, 268
   attack on Syracuse 186–7
   birth of Imperial Rome 199
   Carthaginian treaties with 127, 174–5,
      188

Rome – *cont.*
  Celtic attack on (390 BC) 118
  citizenship 191, 193
  as a cosmopolitan city 193–4, 199–200
  distinction between Senate and
    merchants 191
  Gallic invaders 175
  grain trade 175, 195, 200–205, 207–8,
    227; and pirates 196
  great fire 217
  Hannibal's attack on 185
  immigrant population 193–4
  Jews in 194, 199
  people of *see* Romans
  political and commercial relationship
    with the Mediterranean 174–7,
    183–4, 191–4, 196–211
  Punic wars *see* Punic Wars
  sacking by Alaric the Goth 223, 229–30
  salt supplies 109
  Samnite war 176
  and Sicily 175, 178–83, 186
  and southern Italy before the Punic
    Wars 176–7
  spoken languages in 193–4
  St Peter's Basilica 219, 268
  and Taras 175–6
  Vandal plundering of 232
  voting rights 191
Romegas 429, 435
Rommel, Erwin 608
Romulus Augustulus 227
Roses (Rhode) 124, 127, 352
Rosetta 548
Rosicrucian enlightenment 481
rostra 175
Rothschild, Jacob de 551
Rothschild bank 556
'Rough Cilicia' 195, 197
Roussillon 335, 339, 353, 501
Roussillon, count of 338
Royal Navy 514, 524–5, 564, 578, 579–80,
    588, 605, 606, 614, 622
Rozafa 385
Rufolo family of Ravello 295
Ruslan 594
Russian Orthodox Church 522

Russians 504–13, 514, 518–23, 568, 578
  and the British 504–6, 509–10, 515,
    522, 523, 612
  and Dubrovnik 521–2
  Gallipoli campaign 580
  and Malta 518
  and the Ottomans 505–8, 510–11,
    518–19, 522, 539
  Turkish-Russian war 505–8
  in World War I 578
  in World War II 609, 612
  see also Soviet Union

Sabbath travel 262
Sacramonte tablets 471
sacrifices 46, 184
  child 66, 75, 76, 81–2
  to deified emperors 213
  human *see* human sacrifice
  Jewish sacrificial cult 216, 220
Sadat, Anwar el- 620
Safavids 417, 446
Safed 407
saffron 27, 297, 327, 367
Sagrera, Guillem 399–400
Sagromoso, Michele 512
Saguntum 185
Said Pasha 550–51
St Elmo 430, 432, 433
Saint-Florent 515
St Petersburg 504
St Philip's fort, Minorca 498, 501, 502,
    503
St Sabas, War of 326
Saint-Simon, Claude Henri de Rouvroy,
    comte de 549
St-Tropez 636
Saladin 296, 297, 310, 325, 326
Salado, battle of 364
Salamis 114, 136–7
Salerno 301
  Gulf of 247
Salonika 407, 569–72, 595, 598–9
  see also Thessalonika; Thessaloniki
salt 76, 109, 252, 253, 285, 346, 358, 389,
    641
Samaria 69

Samaritans 260
Samnites 176
Samos 95, 137, 236, 237, 538
San Gimignano 326–7, 367
San Giovanni 428
San Mateu 373
San Roque 626
Sanctus Franciscus 345
Santa Maria della Grazia 461
Santa Trinità di Saccargia, abbey 275
Santo Stefano, Knights of 452, 462
Santorini 365
São Jorge da Mina (the Mine) 411
São Tomé 393
Sappho 160
Saracens 247, 271, 272–3, 346
Saragossa 335, 336
Sarapis 154, 209, 212
Sardinia 73, 119–23, 295, 362, 376
    Alfonso IV's invasion 361
    Arab invasion 250
    under Byzantine rule 235, 242, 249
    and Catalans 361, 381
    Gelimer and 232
    Jews sent to 215
    Mujahid in 273
    Mycenaeans in 34
    Neolithic 14
    nuraghi 119, 121–2
    people of *see* Sardinians/Sards
    Phoenician and Carthaginian settlement
        77
    Pisans and Genoese in 273, 274–5
    Pompey's actions against piracy 196
    salt 346
    and the Second Punic War 183–4
    silver 157, 361
    tombs 119, 120–21
    tourism 637
    and the Vandals 233
    in World War II 611
Sardinians/Sards 77, 122–3, 167
    and Carthaginians 122, 167
    and Catalans 361–2
    Etruscan trade 109
    Euboian contact 92
    and the Pisans and Genoese 274–5

Sard language 119–20, 274
    statuettes 123
    see also Sardinia
Sardis 102, 236
Sargon II 70
Sarkozy, Nicolas 639
Saronic Gulf 95
Saseno 603
Saul, King 59
Savona 316, 358
Savoy, duke of 462
Savoy, house of 558
Savoyard merchants 401
Scala 268
Scanderbeg, George Kastriota 384, 385,
        391
scarabs 27, 93, 108
Schechter, Solomon 259
Schliemann, Heinrich 18–19, 21, 87, 564–5
Sciaky, Leon 569–70
Scipio Aemilianus 189, 200
Scipio, Gnaeus 185
Scipio, Publius Cornelius 187
scirocco xxviii
Scoglio del Tonno 35, 87
Scornavacche 172
scurvy 463
Scutari (Shkodër) 385
Scythians 135, 158
sea level 6
Sea Peoples 42, 49–54, 55–59, 66, 644
sea warfare
    art of 424
    fleets *see* warships/fleets/navies
Sebastian of Portugal 453
Seeley, Sir John 139, 494
Segesta 145, 166, 167
Segorbe, bishop of 473–4
Seleucids 153, 156, 163, 188
Selim I, Ottoman sultan 418
Selim II 'the Sot', Ottoman sultan 444, 445
Selinous/Selinuntines 145, 166, 167
Seljuk Turks 289
Selwyn Lloyd, John Selwyn Brooke Lloyd,
        Baron 619
Sempronius 209
Seneca 102, 382

Senj 454–5, 456–7
Sephardic Jews 407–8, 438–9, 443, 444,
    464, 467, 470, 476–83, 486,
    569–72, 599, 647
  Levantine 437, 458
  Ponentine 437, 458, 464–5
Septuagint 161–2
Serapis *see* Sarapis
Serbia 329
Sestii 201
Seven Years War 501–3
Severus of Minorca 223, 224, 225
Severus, Publius Attius 206
Seville 405, 410, 412
Shalmanasar III, Assyrian king 69
Shardana 48, 49, 50, 51, 55
Shekelesh 49, 50–51, 52
shekels 70
shipbuilding
  in Barcelona 441
  Corinth as centre of 95
  Dutch 463
  Venetian 378–9
shipping
  accounts of crossing the Mediterranean
    (1160–85) 304–17, 462–3
  Adriatic 117
  Allied 610
  American 529–30
  from Barcelona 400–401
  boom in maritime traffic (168 BC–2nd
    century AD) 201
  British 498, 505, 524
  Bronze Age ships 18
  of Byzantine period 237–8
  Catalan 344–8, 359–60, 400
  close season 202
  Corinthian 136
  cruises 637
  between Egypt and Syria 38
  embargo imposed by William I 314
  English 396
  Etruscan 114, 115
  Florentine 404, 437
  French 397
  Genoese 315, 316–17, 347–8, 360, 378,
    404
grain ships 202–3, 205; *see also* grain
  trade
ironclads 555–6, 557–8
in the Islamic world 264, 265–6, 281
Levant trade xxix; *see also* Levant trade
Majorcan 347–8, 401–2
Minoan 25
and Muslim pirates/navies 249, 251
navicularii (guilds of shippers) 218,
  227–8
Neolithic boats 13–14
onboard conditions and food 462
Phoenician 71–3
and piracy *see* pirates/piracy
Pithekoussai and 93
Ragusan 390
Red Sea trade 69, 296
Rhodian 163–4
and the security of the seas 210, 440;
  see also pirates/piracy
Sicily and 264–5
steamshipping 555–8, 573
storms and 182, 403; *see also* storms
through the Suez Canal 553, 605
and Trieste 558–9, 560–61
Turkish 386, 422, 456–7, 484, 510, 511
types of vessel 315–16
Vandal 232
Venetian 255, 360, 378, 379, 440, 460
winds and xxviii, 71, 312, 313–14
in World War II 607, 610
shores xxviii
Sicilian Straits/Channel 13, 182, 233, 279,
  352, 429
Sicilian Vespers 350, 361
Sicily 119, 302–3, 353, 361, 424
  under Aragonese kings 351, 352, 381
  attacks on Jews 405
  and the British 525–6, 607
  Byzantine invasion and rule 235, 242,
    265
  Carthaginian invasion 137, 166–74
  Catalans in 381
  collapse of Norman kingdom of 327–8
  decline of Greek contact 54
  deforestation xxx
  destruction in thirteenth century BC 63

under Frederick II 349
and the Genizah trade network 264–5
and the Genoese 322–3, 328
grain 144, 172–3, 179, 186, 263, 279,
    319, 322–3, 346, 356, 392, 436,
    468, 527–8
Islamic 264–5
and the Knights Hospitallers 415
Latinization of 282
Mamertines in 178
Mesolithic 7
mixed population in the eleventh
    century 282
Muslim invasion 250, 264, 268
and Muslim pirates 414
Mycenaean trade with 33
navy/fleets 319–20, 321–2, 323–4, 349,
    429
Neolithic 12–13
under Norman rule 279–80, 281–4,
    294, 318; Sicilian campaigns
    319–24
Palaeolithic 5–7
and the Peloponnesian War 144–6
Phoenician settlement 76–7
Pompey's actions against piracy 196
Richard I on 325
Rome and 175, 178–83, 186
salt 346
Sicilian Vespers 350, 361
silk 264
Spain and xxxi
sugar mills 393
Syracuse see Syracusans; Syracuse
threats from Italian mainland 54
tyrants of 98–9, 130, 168–71, 173
and the Vandals 233
under viceroys in the fifteenth century
    381
in World War II 607, 611
Side 195
Sidi Barrani 607
Sidon 68, 69
Sidonians see Phoenicians
Sierra 408
Sikans 167
Sikels 167

silk 200, 255, 263–4, 355, 437, 440, 465,
    468, 474
silver
    Alexandrian 156
    American 441
    Balkan 98
    Byzantine 242
    coinage 97
    Egyptian 39, 40
    and the Knights of Malta 436
    Libyan 48
    mines 192
    Mycenaean 32
    New World 468
    Phoenician 69, 90
    and the Ragusans 389
    Sardinian 157, 361
    Spanish 78–9, 157, 192
    Tartessian 79
    Trojan 21
Sinai 38, 486, 549, 553, 619, 620
Six Day War 620
Skanderbeg see Scanderbeg
Skopje 391
slavery/slaves
    and the Atlantic 411
    of the Black Sea 349, 355, 373–4, 644
    Catalan trade in 346–7
    Celtic 117
    Christians and 249
    Cilician pirate slave auctions 195
    Corinthian 95
    Datini and the slave trade 373–4
    Delian 165, 205
    Eaton on 531
    female slaves 422, 644
    and freedmen 192–3, 199, 206
    galley slaves 425–7, 435
    Genoese 355
    in the Islamic world 246–7, 248
    Italic 117
    Jewish merchants and 248–9
    Jewish slaves 216
    from Kerkyra 98
    Knights Hospitallers and 445
    in Malta 435–6
    Muslim slaves 308, 346–7

slavery/slaves – *cont.*
of nuns of Antibes 422, 644
and piracy 414, 417, 418
Roman 191–3; carried off by Vandals 232
Sards 274
Slav *Saqaliba* 248
in Toulon 422
in the Tyrrhenian Sea 109
Slavs 234, 236, 241–2, 390, 521, 522
in Dalmatia 254
Macedonian 570–71
slaves 248
warfare with Germanic peoples 248
Slovenia 456, 640
Smendes 39
Smyrna 101, 218, 365, 440, 476–81, 500, 569
after the Great War 583, 584–5, 586–7
Levantine merchants of 585
Old 55, 599
World War II and the fall of 599
Sokollu, Mehmet 446–7, 448, 449
solar energy 640
Solomon, king of Israel 66–7, 69
Solomon ben Ammar 340
Solomon of Salerno 301–3, 316
soothsayers 113, 220
Sophokles 160
Sorrentine peninsula 268, 295
Sorrento 423
Sostratos 111
Sovereign Military Order of Malta 269
Soviet Union 607, 613, 615, 616, 620
disintegration of 638
and Egypt 618, 619
and Israel 620
and the US 620–21
see also Russians
Spain
Almohad sect 296
Armada 438
Carthaginian trade and settlement 126, 127–8
Catalonia *see* Catalonia
deforestation of Spanish coast xxx

disintegration into local kingdoms in thirteenth century 334
in the early twentieth century 575
extinction of Muslim rule in 408
Falangists 604
under Franco 604, 605, 621
Genoese alliance with 412, 468
and Gibraltar 625–7
Hamilcar Barca in 184–5
hellenization 126–30
Iberians *see* Iberians
Islamic (al-Andalus) 250, 258, 261, 263, 264, 306, 308, 476, 630
Jews: exiled from Spain 406–8, 442–3; relations with Christians and Muslims 340–41, 404–6
and the Moriscos 408, 434–5, 447, 470–76
naval power 424
pagan cults in 221
people of *see* Spaniards
silk 264
silver 78–9, 157, 192; American 441
southern: Byzantium and 235; silver 78–9, 192; and trade networks, eighth century BC 63; *see also* Tartessos
Spanish influence on Sardinia 119
Spanish lands and the second Punic War 184–5, 187
struggle against the Ottomans xxxi, 419
tin 123
tourism 634, 636
trade with Morocco 263
and the UN 626
Vandal and Alan invasion of 230
Visigothic invasion of 223, 233, 246
war fleets 424, 427, 429
War of the Spanish Succession 495
see also specific cities and regions
Spaniards 264, 382
after siege of Malta 434
alliances with English 488
and Barbary corsairs 417
conflicts with English 489–90
at Jerba 428–9

and Mahdia 428
in Muslim fleets 249
in the Netherlands 427
and Ottomans 416, 419, 421
in Rome 193
settlement with the Ottomans in the
sixteenth century 453
see also Spain
Spanish Succession, War of 495
Sparta 138
Corinthian wars 96
and the Peloponnesian League 141
people of see Spartans
Spartans 83, 90
Archidamian War 143
hoplites (soldiers) 138, 144
navy 144, 147
Peloponnesian War 133, 141–8
and the Persians 133, 136–7
sea power 136
see also Sparta
spas 632
spice trade 158, 165, 296, 297, 345, 355,
378, 397, 400, 437
and England 459
see also pepper
Spina 113, 117–18, 126
Split 439, 440
Spurinna family 115–16
Stadion, Johann Philipp 525
Stalin, Joseph 612, 613, 616, 620
Standard Oil Company of New Jersey 585
Stanhope, James 498–9
steamships 555–8, 573
Stentinello 12–13
Stephen, St 223–4
Sterghiades, Aristides 586
Stone Age
Middle (Mesolithic) 7
New (Neolithic) 8–14
Old and Middle (Palaeolithic) 4–7
storms xxviii, 182, 202, 283–4, 308, 312,
313, 393, 394, 403
Strabo 78, 155, 159, 195
Strasbourg (French ship) 606
Sturmy, Robert 396
Su Nuraxi 121–2

Suevi 223, 229
Suez Canal xxviii, 541, 618
blocking of 620
and Nasser 618, 619
nationalization 600
and oil supplies 609
and reciprocal East–West cultural
relations 545, 548–55
shipping through 553, 605
Suez Canal Company 550, 552, 554
sugar 323, 373, 374, 377, 392, 404, 411,
465, 585
production 393
Valencia 393, 474
Sulcis 77, 81
Süleyman the Magnificent, Ottoman sultan
414–15, 418, 419, 421, 423, 429,
433, 442–3, 444
Sulpicii 206
Sultana (Turkish ship) 429, 450
Sunnis/Sunni Islam 298, 310, 334
suntan 635–6
Sweden 520
Swedes 504, 528, 534
swimwear 635–6
Sybaris 116
Sybota 142
synagogues 153, 212, 217, 221, 222, 224,
258–60, 405, 465, 478–81, 569,
590
syncretism 113
Syracusans 114, 115, 137, 145, 166
and Carthaginians 168–73
see also Syracuse
Syracuse 98–9, 114, 115–16, 145, 168,
170–72, 173, 203, 525
Athenian attacks on 115, 146
Catalan consuls 401
and the Genoese 328
people of see Syracusans
Rome's attack on 186–7
tyrants of 98–9, 130, 168–71, 173, 178,
179, 182–3
Syria 8, 619, 638
and Egypt 35–6, 38, 39–41
Euboian ties 91
Islam in 244

Syria – *cont.*
　Jewish rebellion in 208–9, 216
　Mamluks in 349, 414
　and the Mediterranean Union 639
　Mycenaean trade with 32, 33, 35–6
　Ottomans in 414
　trade with Alexandria 157
Syrians, siege of Rhodes 163

Tacitus 102
Talamone 422
Talmud 219, 260, 341
Tamerlane (Timur) 365, 384
Tamin, emir 279
Tana 355
Tangier 396, 491–4, 577, 626
Tanis 39
Taranto 581–2, 607, 611
　Gulf of 175–6
　see also Taras
Taras 87, 90, 175–6, 179
　see also Taranto
Tarentines 176
Tarhun 104
Tarquin, king of Rome 98
Tarquinia (Tarquinii) 93, 94, 98, 104,
　107–10
　tombs 111–12
Tarragona 128, 304, 338
Tarshish 66, 68, 79
　see also Tartessos
Tartars 355
Tartessos 66, 78–9, 81, 90, 127
　see also Tarshish
Taruisa 45, 52
Tarxien 11
Taula de Canvi (bank) 400
Tawfik Pasha, Muhammad 555
taxation 157, 164, 294, 297
　in Alexandria 309, 310
　Busca and 399
　dhimmis 244, 310
　and the Genoese treaty with Sicily 322
　gesia 282
　on grain 186
　on Indians 411–12
　on Jews 216, 282

jizyah 244
　on Muslims 282, 309
　one-fifth tax (*khums*) 297
　under Selim II 445
　and the US 530
　Venetian privilege 285, 293, 294
tea 560
　Boston Tea Party 530
Tel Aviv 592–3, 594–6, 598, 600, 632–3
Tell Aytun 56
Tell el-Amarna 37
Templars 593
temples
　Canaanite 57
　Greek mythological decoration on 113
　Jerusalem Temple 67, 153, 216, 232–3
　of Melqart 75, 78
　Neolithic 10–11
　pagan temples reopened under Julian
　　220
　Phoenician 70, 73, 75, 78
　Puteoli temple 206
　Roman destruction of pagan temples
　　221–2
　to Sarapis 154, 212–13
Tenedos 376, 377
Tenenti, Alberto 462
Terence 199
Terra Amata 3
Tetuan 416, 575
Teucrians 52
textile trade 401
thalassocracies
　550 BC–400 BC 132–48
　Etruscan 116
　Roger II, king of Sicily 318–22
Thapsos 34–5
Tharros 77
Thebes 35, 342
Thefarie Velianas, king of Caere 111
Thera 26, 27–8
Thermi 20
Thermopylai 136
Thessalonika 324, 330, 384–5
　see also Salonika; Thessaloniki
Thessaloniki 572, 600
　see also Salonika; Thessalonika

Thessaly 53, 143
Thirty Years' War 484
Thomson Holidays 633, 634
Thourioi (Thurii) 176
Thrace 135, 140, 578
Thucydides 22, 94–5, 106, 138, 140, 141,
    142–3, 144, 145
Thutmose IV, Pharaoh 38
Tiber, river xxvii, 109, 205
Tiberius, Roman emperor 102, 207, 210,
    215, 444–5
Tibnin 310
Tiepolo family (Venice) 299, 331
Tilsit 523
timber 21, 67, 90, 180, 197, 301, 373, 401,
    436, 532, 642
    Egypt and 37, 39, 40, 263, 297, 537, 643
Timbuktu 279
Timoleon 171–3
Timur (Tamerlane) 365, 384
tin 17, 19, 33, 34, 37, 68, 123, 124, 125,
    127, 156, 465, 567
Tingitania 230, 231
Tirant lo Blanc (Martorell) 384
Tiryns 32, 46
Tito, Josip Broz 613, 614, 615
Titus 216
Tjaru (Tell Hebua) 38
Tjekker 39, 50–51, 52, 55, 65
Tlemcen 417, 475
tobacco 477, 576
Tobermory wreck 438
Toledo 340
    Cathedral 364
    Jews 404
Tolfa 393
tombs
    Egyptian 26, 35, 37, 39
    Etruscan 100, 101, 104, 108, 111–12,
      114, 117, 563
    hypogea 10–11
    Iberian 129, 130
    Maltese 10
    Mycenaean 32, 34–5, 54, 565
    Phoenician 77
    Sardinian 119, 120–21
    at Spina 117

tools
    copper and bronze 19
    Mesolithic 7
    Neolithic 8, 9, 10
    Upper Palaeolithic 5, 6
tophets 75, 81–2
Torcello 253
Torchitorio, Mariano 275
Tortosa 405
Toscanos 78
Tossa 401
Toulon 422, 495, 501, 502, 513–14, 523,
    524, 612
tourism 380–81
    gay 636
    Grand Tours 562, 564, 632
    mass tourism 631–8
    Mediterranean travel accounts
      (1160–85) 304–17, 462–3
Toussoun, Omar 591
Toya 129
trade networks 33–4, 63, 73, 91, 242, 296,
    302, 367, 401, 485
    Aegean 29, 35, 55, 164
    Alexandria and the Hellenistic network
      156–7
    Byzantine 236–8
    Catalan 344–8, 401, 410
    of a Catalan-Aragonese 'empire' 362
    and commercialization 367
    of Crete 485
    of the Crown of Aragon 400–401
    of the diaspora Jews 443
    to the East 262
    Euboian 92, 93–4
    focused on maritime trade of Genoa,
      Pisa and Venice 277
    fragmentation of: into Christian and
      Muslim sectors 296: in the mid-
      thirteenth century 348–9
    French 397
    Genizah network 262–4
    Genoese 271, 354
    Hellenistic 157, 165
    Islamic 246–7, 267
    Levantine 35
    Phoenician 63, 67–79, 242

trade networks – *cont.*
  Pisan 271–2
  Roman interference in Aegean
    networks 164
  under Roman rule 201–4
  and specialization 367
trade routes
  up the Adriatic 126, 385
  Aegean 17, 22, 44
  alphabet carried along 110, 644
  Athenian 116–17, 141
  belief systems and ideas carried along
    213, 266–7, 332, 481, 482–3
  Black Death's spread along 368
  to the Black Sea 227, 355, 508, 557
  Byzantion and 227
  Byzantium to Egypt 296
  Corinth and 95, 98–9
  Coron, Modon and 419
  Cyprus to Armenia 359
  through the Dardanelles 376
  Dodecanese islands and 577
  from Dyrrhachion to Constantinople
    269
  to the East, opened 1497 by the
    Portuguese 458
  between Egypt and the Tyrrhenian Sea
    93–4
  Epidamnos and 141
  to Etruria 95, 101, 110
  Euboian 92, 93–4
  Gaza and 221
  Iberians and 131
  to the Indian Ocean 155, 157, 262,
    355, 549–50, 561, 573
  to Islamic lands 300, 465
  Italian 271, 288, 318, 404, 458;
    Etruscan 95, 101, 110
  from Livorno 465
  Minoan 24
  Nabataean 165, 221
  New World 410
  to North Africa 465
  to northern Europe 125
  Ottoman 414
  up the Persian Gulf 263
  Persians and 134

  Phoenician 66, 73
  Radhanite 248
  down the Red Sea 158, 248, 296, 355
  reopened after Sicilian Vespers 361
  Rhodes and 53, 366
  trans-Asiatic 355
  Troy and 45
  Venetian control of Byzantium routes
    330
  Venetian nobility's domination of 360,
    365
trade shipping *see* shipping
Trafalgar, battle of 524
Trajan 208–9, 216, 382
Trani 342, 388
Trapani 76, 353, 401
travel industry *see* tourism
'Treasure of Priam' 21, 565
Treasury of Atreus 563
Trebinje 390, 439
Trebizond 329, 378
Treviso 377
Trieste 524, 558–61, 571, 600, 601
Tripoli 319, 409, 415, 428, 528
  American conflict with 529, 534–5
  American treaty with 529, 536
  bashaw of 534
  Italian rebuilding of 576
  massacre by the Greeks 538
  Mussolini in 604
Tripolitania 571
Trogus, Pompeius 125
Trojans
  identity of 42–3
  and the Sea Peoples 52
  Trojan War 19, 45, 87, 93
  see also Troy
Troubridge, Thomas 515
Troy 17, 18–22, 25, 32, 43–4, 53
  fall of 42, 47, 52, 84–5
  Hisarlık as Homer's 19, 20, 42, 45
  legends of 564
  Mycenaean trade with 32
  people of *see* Trojans
  and trade routes 45
  Troy I 19–20
  Troy II 20–21

Troy III 21
Troy IV 21–2
Troy V 22
Troy VI 27, 42, 45–6, 47
Troy VIIa 43, 47, 52
Truman, Harry S. 616
tuna-fishing 10, 19, 76, 640, 641
Tunis 170, 246, 263, 346, 531–2
   and America 535–6
   and the Barbary corsairs 416, 418,
     421
   bey of 528, 531
   Black Death 368
   Catalans in 345, 346
   and Charles V 418
   fall to the Allies 610
   grain 356
   Hafsid rulers 334, 416
   Llull in 343–4
Tunisia 13, 263, 334, 617–18
   and the Bedouins 279
   Capsian culture 7
   Carthage see Carthage
   economy 576
   and the French 574, 576, 621
   and the Italians 576
   Mahdia 263, 279–80, 319–20, 322,
     428
   Moriscos 476
   under Roman rule 203
   tuna fishermen 641
   Tunis see Tunis
   in World War II 610
Turgut 428, 430
Turkey 445, 459, 482, 499–500
   and the EU 638–9
   and Israel 638
   and the Mediterranean Union 639
   nationalism 583
   and NATO 620
   people of see Turks
   and the Turkish Republic of North
     Cyprus 625
   war with Italy 576
Turkey Company 459–60
Turkish Republic of North Cyprus 625
Turkish-Russian war 505–8

Turks 287, 289, 329, 364–5, 366
   and Alfonso V of Aragon 383–4
   Anatolian 625
   Austrian trade with 539
   Greco-Turkish wars 538, 586–8
   and the Hospitallers 386
   and Malta 269, 428–34
   Ottoman see Ottomans
   pirates 428
   and Rhodes 269
   and Russians 505–8, 510–11, 518–19,
     522
   in Smyrna 585, 586–7
   Turkish Cypriots 568–9, 623, 624–5
   Turkish shipping 386, 422, 456–7, 484,
     510, 511
   in World War I 577–8
   Young Turks 583
   see also Turkey
Turmeda, Anselmo ('Abdallah
    at-Tarjuman) 380–81
Tursha 49, 52
Tuscany 34, 81, 92, 104, 356–7
   dukes of 452, 462, 466–7
   Etruscans see Etruscans
   famines 367
   grain 466
   Livorno trade 464–7
   Medici duke's holy warriors 452
   tourism 633
   Tuscan pirates 452
   wool imports 373
Tutankhamun, Pharaoh 37
Tutugi 129, 130
Tyre 66–7, 68–9, 70, 79, 149, 325
   peoples of see Tyrians
   Venetians in 293
Tyrians 66–7, 70, 75, 77, 81, 82, 194, 206
   Carthaginians see Carthaginians
   Phoenicians see Phoenicians
   and Rome 194
   see also Tyre
Tyris (Valencia) 128
Tyrrhenia see Etruria
Tyrrhenian Sea 89–90, 92, 103, 109,
    114–15, 116, 125, 196, 272–3,
    295

Tyrrhenians
  Etruscans *see* Etruscans
  pirates 195; *see also* 'Tyrsenians'
  see also Etruria
'Tyrsenians' (pirates) 54, 71, 83, 105,
    106–7, 115, 195
  see also pirates/piracy
Tyrsenoi 52, 101–2, 106
  Etruscans *see* Etruscans
Tyrsenos 101

Ugarit 35–6, 46, 52, 58, 65, 80
  ships 72
Ukraine 355
Ulcinj 448
Ullastret 128
Uluburun wreck 33
Ulysses (Odysseus) 85, 86, 380
Umur Pasha 365
UNHCR 629
Uni (Etruscan goddess) 111
Union for the Mediterranean 639, 640
United Arab Republic 619
United Kingdom *see* Britain/the British
United Nations (UN) 600, 624, 626
United Provinces 463
United States of America
  American tourists 638
  Barbary Wars 529–36
  Boston Tea Party 530
  and the British 529–30, 535, 536
  and Israel 616, 620
  and Jews 535–6, 598
  and Libya 615–16
  Mediterranean trade 529–30
  migrations to 573
  neutrality in Greco-Turkish war
    587–8
  shipping 529–30
  and Smyrna 585, 586
  and the Soviet Union 613, 620–21
  War of Independence 529
  World War II 609, 612
Urban II 287
Ushakov, Fyodor Fyodorovich 518–19,
    520
Uskoks 439, 449, 454–7

Utica 66, 76
Utrecht, Treaty of 497, 498

Valencia 128, 339–40, 358, 364, 402–4
  ceramics 403
  Consulate of the Sea 402–3
  decline of city of 474
  Inquisition 475
  Jews 404, 405, 408
  llotja 399, 400, 402
  Moriscos and the kingdom of 473,
    474, 475
  sugar 393, 474
Valentinian III, Roman emperor 232
Valéry, Paul xxvi
Valette, Jean de 428, 432
Valletta 429, 516, 520, 607
Valona (Vlorë) 385
Van den Broecke, Bernard 467
Vandals 223, 230–33
  collapse of the Vandal kingdom 235
Veii 94, 109, 113, 175, 207
Velia 179
Velleius Paterculus, Marcus 66
Venetian Gulf 358
  see also Adriatic Sea
Venetians 250, 254–6
  in Acre 325–6
  and the Adriatic 385
  and Albania 385
  and Apulia 388
  and Catalans 376
  in Constantinople 458
  and Crete 331, 377, 483–5
  and the Crusades 292–4
  and Cyprus 446–7, 451, 458
  and Dutch 460, 461
  and Egypt 354
  and English 459, 460–61
  and the Fourth Crusade 329, 330
  and Genoese 325–6, 331, 355, 366,
    376–8
  grain trade 285, 358
  and Greek corsairs 510–11
  Inquisition 458
  and Mamluks 392
  and Manuel I Komnenos 294, 300, 319

merchants 299–301; and the Byzantine economy 285, 294; Golden Bull and privilege to trade free of tax 285, 293, 294, 319

muda protection system from pirates 360, 642

navy 322, 376, 448, 450, 461

nobility's domination of trade routes 360, 365

and Normans 284

and Ottomans 385–6, 387, 388, 392, 419–20, 423, 446–7, 483–6, 489; Cretan War (1645–1669) 484–5

and the Peloponnese 488–9

Serrata (closing to the noble ranks) 361

shipbuilding 378–9

shipping 255, 360, 378, 379, 440, 460

and Thessalonika 384–5

trans-Asia trade 355

and Trieste 559, 560

in Tyre 293

and the Uskoks 455, 456–7

Venetian carnival 637

see also Venice

Venice 237, 246, 301, 316, 330, 383

and Alexandria 255–6, 292

Arsenal 378–9, 445–6

Austrian control of 519, 557, 558

Beatrice de Luna in 442

Black Death 369

and Byzantium 278, 319

Catalan consuls 401

and Constantinople 256, 330

and Dalmatia 389

emergence of 254–5

garum sauce and the early prosperity of 641

and Germans 277

and the Habsburgs 456

and the Jews 296, 458

and Joseph Nasi 445–6

Milizia da Mar 425

Napoleon and 518, 519

people of *see* Venetians

political and economic reshaping in fifteenth and sixteenth centuries 457–9

and the politics of Renaissance Italy 412–13

and Ragusans 389

San Giorgio dei Greci church 458

Serenissima Repubblica 387, 413, 460, 489

St Mark's Basilica 255–6, 285, 330, 636

and the Turks 386, 387, 388, 419–20, 423, 446–7

and the Uskoks 455, 456–7

War of Chioggia 376–8

wool industry 458

Venizelos, Eleftherios 571–2, 578, 585, 586, 588, 598

Vespasian 208, 216

Vespers, War of the 350, 361

Vetulonia 109, 123

Via Egnatia 235, 252, 283, 350

Viareggio 633

Vichy France 606–7, 610

Victor III, Pope 280

Victor Emmanuel III, king of Italy 611

Victoria, British queen 554, 632

Victoria College, Alexandria 591

Villanovan culture 108–10, 113

Villefranche 462

Vincendon, Claude 591

vines/vineyards xxix, 125, 164, 234, 267–8, 295, 335, 483, 528, 629

Virgil (Publius Vergilius Maro) 74–5, 102, 189–90, 199

Visconti, Filippo Maria, duke of Milan 382–3

Visconti lords of Milan 376, 382–3

Visigoths 223, 233, 246

Vitellius, Aulus, Roman emperor 208

Vittoriosa (Birgu) 430, 432, 435

Vivara 34, 89

Vix 124

Volscians 175

Voltaire 505

della Voltas of Genoa 299, 315

Vukčić, Stjepan 390–91

wages 376

Waghorn, Thomas 550

Walsingham, Sir Francis 459
Ward, John 461, 462
Warrior Vase 51, 57
Warrior's Tomb 108
warships/fleets/navies
    Algerian 423
    American 529, 536
    Angevin 351–2
    Arab 249, 250
    Austrian 539, 558, 578, 580–82
    Barbary 427; see also Barbary
        corsairs
    bertoni 461, 462
    British 514, 524–5, 564, 578, 579–80,
        588, 605, 606, 614, 622
    Byzantine 233, 235, 249, 251, 324
    Caeretan 114
    Carthaginian 114, 167, 173, 178, 180,
        181, 186–7
    Castilian 364
    Catalan 347, 352, 359, 362–3, 366,
        434
    of Charles V 350, 351–2
    conditions on 425–7
    diets on 427, 463
    Dutch 463
    Egyptian 51, 156, 163, 293
    English 488
    Etruscan 114, 115
    French 423, 514, 523, 581, 606
    Genoese 273, 275
    German 578; U-boats 582, 609
    Greek 538, 588
    Holy Leagues of western navies 365,
        419–20, 449, 450–51
    Italian 558, 582, 609, 611
    Japanese 582
    light galleys 281, 315–16, 449–50
    Moroccan 364
    Muslim 249, 250–51, 268, 278–9, 364,
        402, 414, 423–4
    Neapolitan 363
    Ottoman 424–7, 447, 448, 449–50,
        452, 484, 506–7, 538, 539
    papal 429
    Persian 134
    Phoenician 72, 134, 136–7

    Phokaian 114
    Pisan 272, 273, 275
    Portuguese 366, 393–5
    Ragusan 438
    Rhodian 163
    Roman 175, 176, 177, 178, 179,
        180–82, 185, 186–7, 198, 208–9,
        210
    Russian 504–7, 512, 520, 523
    Sicilian 319–20, 321–2, 323–4, 429
    Spanish 424, 427, 429, 489; Armada
        438
    spiked ramming ships 72, 181
    Syrian 156
    Venetian 322, 376, 448, 450, 461, 557
Washington, George 529
water
    carried by ships xxx
    irrigation see irrigation
    and tourism 637
    transport 201; see also shipping
    Tyre and 68
    Valencian water tribunal 408
Waterhouse, J. W. 563
wax 68, 114, 349, 355, 440, 465, 485, 532
weapons
    bronze 12, 17, 20, 32, 109
    copper 20
    iron 248
    spiked rams 72, 181
weather systems xxviii
    see also storms; winds
weights 70
Weizmann, Chaim 591
Wenamun 39–41, 55, 70
Weshesh 50–51
West Bank 619, 638
Wheelus Field air bases 616, 621
Whitaker, Joseph 528
White Sea (Turkish name for
        Mediterranean) 386
    battle for 428–35, 445–51
Whittall family 585, 586
Wilhem II, Kaiser 577
William I, king of Sicily, 'the Bad' 305, 322
William II, king of Sicily, 'the Good' 314,
        323–4

William of Modica 321–2
William of Orange 495
Wilusa 44–5
Winckelmann, Johann Joachim 562, 563
winds xxiv–xxv, xxvi, xxvii, 71, 312,
  313–14
wine 20, 35, 56, 73, 76, 78, 90, 237, 367,
  511
  Alexandria and 157, 159
  amphorae 73, 92, 157, 164, 237
  Corinthian trade in 97, 285
  Etruscan 109
  expanding interest in Mediterranean
    wines 629
  Greek and Etruscan production
    technology 125
  Iberia and 129
  Malmsey 485
  Marsala 528
  Massalia and 124
  Joseph Nasi and 444
  poisoned 457
  Rhodian 164
Wisdom of Solomon 162
women 643–4
  display of the female body 635
  harems 248, 644
  nuns 422, 501, 595, 644
  prostitutes 74, 464, 644
wood see timber
Woodhouse, John 528
wool 272, 295, 347, 373, 511, 642
  Castilian 404
  Catalan cloth 401
  Crete 24
  English 326, 347
  Flemish cloth 277, 295, 323
  Italian cloth 323
  Ragusans and 389–90, 439, 465
  Spanish 444
  Troy 21
  Venetian wool industry 458
Woolley, Sir Leonard 91
World War I 577–82

Arab revolt 592
World War II 599, 605–12
Wren, Sir Christopher 493
writing
  Cretan 25, 27, 30–31
  disappearance after twelfth century
    BC 63
  early Greek 47, 64
  Iberian 129
  Mycenaean 30–31
  Phoenician 80, 644
  see also alphabet

xaloc xxviii
Xenophon 167
Xerxes, king of Persia 135, 137

Yom Kippur War 620
Young Turks 583
Ypres 347
Yugoslavia 611, 613–14, 615
  disintegration of 638
  tourism 636, 638
Yusuf Bashaw 535

Zaccaria, Benedetto 358
Zadar 448, 613
  see also Zara
Zakynthos 233
Zama, battle of 187
Zante 460
Zara 329, 601
  see also Zadar
Zekerbaal 39–41
Zeus 221
  Zeus Ammon 150
Zevi, Shabbetai 479–80, 481–2
Ziani, Pietro 301
Ziani, Sebastian 300
Ziani family 299
Zionism 592, 596
Zog I (Ahmet Zogu), king of Albania
  602–3
Zogheb family 591